ISBN: 9781313178259

Published by:
HardPress Publishing
8345 NW 66TH ST #2561
MIAMI FL 33166-2626

Email: info@hardpress.net
Web: http://www.hardpress.net

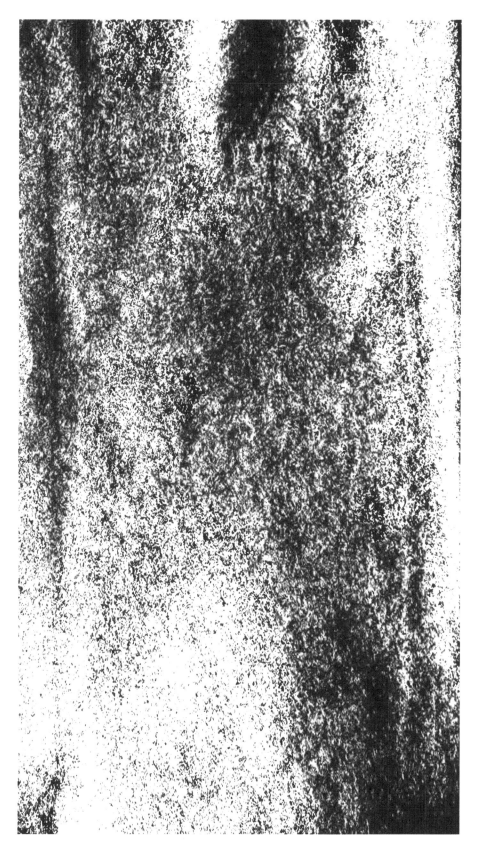

CHEMICAL PATHOLOGY

BEING A DISCUSSION OF GENERAL PATH-
OLOGY FROM THE STANDPOINT OF
THE CHEMICAL PROCESSES INVOLVED

BY

H. GIDEON WELLS, Ph.D., M.D.

PROFESSOR OF PATHOLOGY IN THE UNIVERSITY OF CHICAGO AND IN
RUSH MEDICAL COLLEGE, CHICAGO; DIRECTOR OF THE
OTHO S. A. SPRAGUE MEMORIAL INSTITUTE

FOURTH EDITION, REVISED AND RESET

PHILADELPHIA AND LONDON

W. B. SAUNDERS COMPANY

1920

PRINTED IN AMERICA

TO

Ludvig Hektoen

THIS BOOK IS RESPECTFULLY DEDICATED, AS A
SLIGHT TOKEN OF THE GRATITUDE AND
ESTEEM OF HIS PUPIL

PREFACE TO THE FOURTH EDITION

THE rapid growth of interest in the chemical problems of medical and biological science is shown by the great increase in the amount of material which must be included in each succeeding edition. Although this latest edition has been subjected to extensive revision and many minor alterations, yet the general plan has not been changed. The rapidly growing information concerning the nutritional factors that are essential to growth and repair, and without which serious "Deficiency Diseases" may arise, has necessitated the introduction of a new chapter to cover this subject, the importance of which has been accentuated by the war and its sequels. The growing bulk of material on the Reactions of Immunity required a rearrangement of this material, so that a separate chapter on Anaphylaxis and Allergy has been provided, for purposes of convenience. Numerous sections have been entirely rewritten, and few pages have not required revision or addition.

In order to prevent the increasing material that must be included from resulting in too cumbersome a volume, much more of the matter is printed in smaller type. It is hoped that this arrangement will achieve its aim without serious reduction in facility of use. The author recognizes fully that it would be easily possible to report the existing state of knowledge on the topics covered in "Chemical Pathology" in a much briefer space, if only completely established evidence were included. With the object of serving as a guide to investigators, and with the hope of stimulating further investigations, much more than this minimal amount of existing evidence is included. It is also recognized that the brief discussion of the elementary principles of physical chemistry and the fundamentals of the physics and chemistry of living cells, which constitutes the introductory chapter, may be out of place in a work on Pathology, and the elimination of this chapter has been seriously considered. Repeated assurances of the usefulness of such a presentation, however, have resulted in its retention, at least for the present.

As with all previous editions, my indebtedness must be acknowledged to numerous colleagues who have kindly read over the sections of this book which most closely concern their own fields, and especially to the members of my Department and of the Sprague Institute who have made many useful suggestions. The chapter on Diabetes is, as before, contributed by Dr. R. T. Woodyatt, Director of the Laboratory of Clinical Research of the Otho S. A. Sprague Memorial Institute.

H. G. W.

CHICAGO, ILL.,
July, 1920.

PREFACE TO THE FIRST EDITION

DURING the past score of years the subject of biological chemistry has attracted the attention and labors of a constantly increasing number of investigators, many of whom have, for one reason or another, been interested in pathological conditions. Sometimes the physiologist has sought for light on his problems in the evidence afforded by related pathological conditions. Frequently clinicians have studied the metabolic changes and the composition of the products of disease processes. Relatively seldom, unfortunately, has the pathologist attacked his problems by chemical methods. From the above and other sources have come scattered fragments of information concerning the chemical changes that occur in pathological phenomena. Only when bearing upon conditions such as gout and diabetes, which concern alike the physiologist, the clinician, and the pathologist, have the fragments been moulded together into a homogeneous whole. For the most part they still remain isolated, uncorrelated, frequently unconfirmed items of information, scattered through medical, chemical, physiological, and physical literature.

It has been the aim of the writer to collect these scattered fragments as completely as possible, and to use them as a basis for a consideration of General Pathology from the standpoint of the chemical processes which occur in pathological conditions. Owing to the diffusely scattered conditions of the literature on which this work is based, it cannot be claimed that all of the many contributions from which useful information might be obtained have been noticed; but it is hoped that a sufficiently thorough collection of material has been made to afford a fair basis for a consideration of "Chemical Pathology." The time seems ripe for an effort of this nature. Within the past few years great and encouraging advances have been made in biological chemistry, which in many instances seem to throw light upon pathological processes. In medicine, the use of chemical methods in the study of clinical manifestations has become more general, and has yielded valuable information. Pathologists have come to feel that the opportunities for the acquirement of knowledge by means of morphological studies have become reduced to a minimum, while the fields of pathological physiology and chemistry lie still almost unexplored. The development of research upon the subject of natural and acquired immunity has presented innumerable problems, all of which are essentially chemical. And perhaps most important of all is the general awakening of an appreciation of the importance of physiological chemistry to medical science, which has led to the introduction of laboratory courses on this subject in every medical school worthy of the name.

A book on Chemical Pathology should, therefore, seek to supply information to a varied group of readers. It should furnish collateral reading to the student who for the first time goes over the subject of General Pathology, which his text-books usually consider chiefly from the morphological standpoint. It should exploit to the graduate in medicine the advances that are being made along lines that are of fundamental importance to clinical medicine. It should serve for the investigator in biological chemistry or in pathology as a source of information concerning the ground upon which the two subjects overlap—the "Grenzgebiete" of Pathology and Physiological Chemistry. And, above all, it should afford a guide to the sources of our knowledge of these subjects, since nothing but direct familiarity with the original reports of the investigators themselves can give the student an impersonal view of the actual status of the questions under consideration. On account of this multiplicity of the objects in view, it has often been necessary to consider certain topics from more than one standpoint; which explains, perhaps, certain apparent irregularities in the style and manner of treatment.

It has been assumed that the reader has at least an elementary knowledge of organic and physiological chemistry. For the benefit of those whose studies in these subjects date back some years, it has seemed advisable to include in an introductory chapter an epitome of the more modern views concerning the chemistry of the protein molecule, the composition of the animal cell, and the principles of physical chemistry, in as far as they apply to biological problems. The general consideration of "Enzymes" in Chapter II is written with a similar object. In discussing these fundamental topics it has seemed advisable to omit detailed references to the numerous original sources,— these may be found quoted in the special text-books cited in the foot-notes; but in presenting the more distinctly pathological topics the attempt has been made to render all the important literature available to the reader and investigator. To economize space, a complete bibliography has not been inserted when this exists already collected in some readily accessible review or original article; hence the references cited in the foot-notes will generally be found to include only the more recent publications. These references have been so selected, however, that they will be found to furnish bibliographical matter sufficient to lead the investigator to all the important literature on the topics covered in this book. As to those subjects (such as gout, diabetes, and gastro-intestinal putrefaction) which, because of their great practical clinical interest, have already been discussed in available monographs at greater length than the scope of this work would permit, it has seemed appropriate merely to summarize the most recent views and advances, referring the reader to the special treatises for the general and historical discussions.

It is with the greatest pleasure that I acknowledge my indebtedness to many colleagues in the University of Chicago, who have kindly read the sections of my manuscript that touch upon their own special fields. and whose criticism and advice have been of the greatest assistance; their number alone prevents my thanking them by name. Most particularly, however, must I express my debt to my former instructor, Professor Lafayette B. Mendel, of Yale University, whose kindly criticism and suggestions have been of inestimable value. For constant assistance in the preparation of the manuscript, and for the revision of the bibliography, I am indebted to my wife.

H. G. W.

CONTENTS

CHAPTER I

CHAPTER XIV

CHAPTER XV

CHAPTER XVI

CHAPTER XVII

CHAPTER XXIII

CHAPTER XXIV

CHEMICAL PATHOLOGY

CHAPTER I

INTRODUCTION

THE CHEMISTRY AND PHYSICS OF THE CELL

SINCE Virchow founded modern pathology the unit of all anatomical considerations of disease has been the cell, and in physiology the same unit has been found equally useful. When either physiological or pathological processes are studied from a chemical standpoint, the cell is still found occupying nearly as fundamental a position, for we can seldom go back to molecules and atoms in investigating biological problems. Although we know that within each cell are many different chemical substances, and that numerous different enzymes and other agencies are exerting their influences upon them, yet we find that the reactions are all profoundly affected by the environment in which they occur, and it is the structure of the cell that determines the environment of its chemical constituents. All chemical reactions are modified by physical influences, and an enzyme may have quite a different effect upon a substance when it acts in a test-tube from what it will have when in a living cell, whose structure permits the diffusion of one substance while preventing that of another, and where countless other substances and enzymes may participate in the changes. The cell is the structural unit of the living organism, and as by its physical properties it modifies chemical processes, so it becomes practically the unit in physiological and pathological chemistry. All consideration of the chemistry of disease must thus refer back to the chemistry and physics of the normal cell, and on this account a brief résumé of these subjects may serve as a fitting introduction to the strictly pathological matters to follow.[1]

As applied to the animal tissues, the term "cell" is entirely a misnomer, for it describes accurately only such forms of "cells" as are

[1] Of necessity, only so much of the very extensive literature on cell structure and cell chemistry can be considered as will have direct bearing upon the subject matter to follow, referring the reader for more detailed information to such works as Wilson's "The Cell in Development and Inheritance;" Mathews' "Physiological Chemistry;" Hammarsten's "Physiological Chemistry;" Gurwitsch's "Morphologie und Biologie der Zelle;" Höber's "Physikalische Chemie der Zelle und der Gewebe;" Hamburger's "Osmotischer Druck und Ionenlehre;" Loeb's "Dynamics of Living Matter;" Oppenheimer's "Handbuch der Biochemie;" and Bottazzi, "Handbuch der vergl. Physiologie," Vol. I, for general discussion, and to the most important monographs for treatment of special points.

found in plants, in which the prominent feature is the limiting wall, forming a cell to enclose a fluid content. In most instances the "cell" answers better to the definition, "a mass of protoplasm;" but usage makes language, and no possible confusion can arise from the prevailing universal use of the original term, except, perhaps, that the term is prone to carry with it the thought of the walls of the cell being much more prominent than they really are. This is not so unfortunate a result, perhaps, for, as we shall see later, the limiting surfaces of the cell, even when too thin to be readily demonstrable, may play a much more important part in cell chemistry than their appearance indicates.

The morphological division of the cell into cell wall, cytoplasm, nucleus, and nucleolus can hardly be followed out chemically, for if we surmount to some extent the difficulties in the way of studying the different portions separately, we find that the differences between them are rather quantitative than qualitative. And, furthermore, however different the cells of one organ or tissue may appear from those of another organ or tissue under the microscope, when analyzed by the chemical methods at present at our disposal we find the differences very slight indeed. Certain substances are found in every living cell, and in quantities usually not greatly dissimilar; hence they are assumed to be the most important constituents of protoplasm, and are sometimes called the *primary* constituents of the cell. Many other *secondary* constituents may also be present, some of which are so nearly universal that we are not sure but that they really are primary cell components; such are fat and glycogen. Others are characteristics of certain cells, such as melanin and keratin, or specific products of cell metabolism, such as mucin and the specific enzymes. The great histological and chemical differences existing between different tissues depend often on these secondary products, as in fat tissue and squamous epithelium; or upon the intercellular substance, as with connective tissue, cartilage, bone, etc., which may be looked upon as products of cell activity.

Protoplasm, as the term is generally used, includes the various primary constituents with the fluids permeating or dissolving them, but does not include the more conspicuous secondary constituents, such as fat droplets, pigment granules, etc., nor the cell membrane when such exists. Evidently it is a very indefinite term, to be avoided as much as possible, particularly because of the confusion as to whether it includes the nucleus or not, different authors differing in this respect in their usage of the word.

CHEMISTRY OF THE ESSENTIAL CELL CONSTITUENTS

To enumerate the primary or essential constituents of the cell absolutely is not possible, for the rapid advances in chemistry may alter all classifications without warning, but practically they may be grouped under the headings of proteins, lipins, carbohydrates, salts, and water, and no attempt will be made to give here more than the most essential features concerning each.

PROTEINS [2]

In the last few years we have obtained something approaching a scientific understanding of the chemical nature of this great group of the most highly complex bodies known to chemistry. Our information has been obtained almost exclusively through studies of the products obtained by splitting up the protein molecule, for as yet relatively little has been accomplished through synthesis. Proteins can be decomposed by the action upon them of acids or alkalies in various concentrations, by superheated steam, by digestive ferments, and by bacteria. The products obtained in these different ways are not all the same, for some substances may be formed by oxidation, reduction, decomposition, combination, or condensation of the various products of simple cleavage, and it is necessary to distinguish between the primary cleavage products (those which exist as radicals within the molecule) and the secondary products (those not existing preformed in the molecule but formed by transformation of the primary products). This can usually be done, and it is found that so far as the primary products are concerned, it makes little difference which method of cleavage (or *hydrolysis*, since in the splitting, water is combined with the organic substances) is used.

At first the proteins split up into compounds still possessing many of the features of the typical protein molecule, such as albumoses and peptones, and these bodies are then further resolved into simpler substances, which are not aggregates of several smaller molecules as are the proteins, and which can be obtained in pure crystalline form. No matter which method is used we find the process going through these stages, and, as before mentioned, the primary crystalline products obtained are practically the same quantitatively as well as qualitatively. Some methods, *c. g.*, bacterial decomposition, however, lead in the end to more profound or different decomposition of the cleavage products into secondary substances. The similarity of the results obtained in these different ways indicates that there are definite lines of cleavage in the protein molecule along which separation takes place, independent of the nature of the agency at work, and that the substances obtained represent the "building stones" of the entire molecule.

These substances all have in common one important point: *each one is an acid, which has a NH_2 group substituted for a hydrogen atom on the carbon nearest the acid radical* (the α-position). It makes no difference what the rest of the radicals are, whether they are simple chains (leucine), or members of the cyclic or aromatic series (tyrosine), or sulphur-containing bodies (cystine), without exception this relation of a NH_2 group to an acid radical is constant, as in this formula:

$$NH_2$$
$$R\text{---}CH\text{---}COOH.$$

Through this arrangement every one of the constituents of the protein molecule is provided with a group with a strong basic character and a group with a strong acid character, and hence it is possible for them to unite with one another in indefinite numbers, and, because of the great variety of individuals, in practically an infinite number of combinations. It is believed that it is in just this way that the protein molecule is built up. By artificially uniting various cleavage products Emil Fischer succeeded in producing large molecules made up of several amino-acid radicals (called by him "polypeptids")[3] which show some of the characteristics of the peptones, and this is the nearest that investigators have yet come to synthesizing a protein molecule. The union is accomplished by the splitting off of water, corresponding to the addition of water that occurs when the protein

---

[2] For the complete literature of this subject see "The Chemical Constitution of the Proteins," Plimmer, London, 1917; "The General Character of the Proteins," Schryver, London, 1912; "The Vegetable Proteins," Osborne, London, 1910 (all in the series of "Monographs on Biochemistry"). Also "The Physical Chemistry of the Proteins," T. B. Robertson, New York, 1918.

[3] Reviewed by Fischer, in Ber. deut. Chem. Gesell., 1906 (39), 530.

molecule undergoes cleavage. It may be illustrated by showing the formation of the simplest polypeptid, *glycylglycine*.

$$\underset{\text{(glycine)}}{\overset{\text{NH}_2}{\overset{|}{\text{CH}_2}}-\overset{\text{O}}{\overset{\|}{\text{C}}}-|\text{OH}+\text{H}|\ \text{HN}-\text{CH}_2-\text{COOH}} = \underset{\text{(glycine)}}{} \underset{\text{(glycylglycine)}}{\overset{\text{NH}_2}{\overset{|}{\text{CH}_2}}-\overset{\text{O}}{\overset{\|}{\text{C}}}-\text{HN}-\text{CH}_2-\text{COOH} + \text{H}_2\text{O}.}$$

For these reasons it is believed that *the protein molecule consists of great numbers of amino-acid groups, combined with one another through their basic and acid radicals*, and that the various proteins are different from one another because they contain different numbers or varieties or orders of combination of amino-acids. For example, the *globin* of hemoglobin yields no glycine on hydrolysis, while gelatin yields 16.5 per cent. On the other hand, gelatin is free from tyrosine. Some of the *protamins* (proteins obtained chiefly from spermatozoa) yield as high as 58 to 84 per cent. of arginine, while the simpler amino-acids with but one N (mono-amino-acids) are scanty, and most varieties are lacking.

It will be noticed that when two amino-acids unite, as seen in the formation of glycylglycine, an acid radical and a basic radical are still left free. In this may be seen the explanation of the peculiar *amphoteric* nature of proteins. As long as these two groups are free the proteins can combine with either acids or bases, as they are well known to do, and hence they *react as either acids or bases under different conditions*.

It must not be imagined that the structure of the complete molecule is simply a long straight chain of amino-acids joined only in the same way as are the components of glycylglycine. The existence of the diamino-acids, of the benzene rings, of hydroxyl groups, (as in serine or tyrosine), of ring compounds, (as pyrrolidine carboxylic acid), of substances with two acid groups, (as glutaminic and aspartic acid), adds complications to the formation until it is impossible to estimate just how all the various building stones may be arranged. We must bear in mind the size of the protein molecule, which Hofmeister has estimated (for serum albumin) as having a molecular weight of 10,166, and for hemoglobin the molecular weight has been estimated at 16,669. Within such a "giant molecule" there is room for variety almost beyond computation.

The Proteins of the Cell.

By physiological chemists proteins are classified into *simple proteins*, of which egg and serum albumin are types; and *compound proteins*, which are characterized by having some special non-protein group which can be split off, leaving behind a characteristic protein residue, e. g., nucleo-proteins, glyco-proteins. As primary cell constituents the following varieties of proteins may be mentioned; albumin, globulin, nucleo-protein, nucleo-albumin or phospho-protein, and insoluble proteins. At one time it was thought that cytoplasm consisted chiefly of albumin, like white of egg, but we now know that this forms but a small part of the cell proteins, often occurring only as traces. It is held by some that true albumin occurs only as a building or intermediate cleavage product of the more complicated forms of cellular proteins, and is itself of relatively slight importance in cell life, not participating in chemical changes except as a food-stuff.

Albumins are characterized chiefly by their greater solubility in water, and in being less easily precipitated than most proteins. They seem to be a fundamental type of proteins. The three forms of albumin that have been described in animal tissues or products are egg-albumin, lactalbumin of milk, and serum albumin; probably cell albumin is most closely related to the last, and what has been described as cell albumin is perhaps in many cases but serum albumin that has been imperfectly removed.

Globulins also occur in all cells, but in small amounts in most animal cells except the muscles, whose chief proteins belong to this or a closely related group. The globulins are quite similar to the albumins, so that there is really no sharp line between the two groups. Their insolubility in water separates them from albumins, and their solubility in dilute neutral salt solutions from the more complex proteins. An important feature of the globulins is the low temperature at which they coagulate—some so low that Halliburton[1] believes it possible that they may be coagulated within the cells during high fevers.

Hammarsten has long maintained that simple proteins form a relatively insignificant part of the cytoplasm, in opposition to the once-prevalent view that the nucleo-proteins were limited to the nucleus, and that the cytoplasm was chiefly albumin and globulin. The general trend of opinion as influenced by the results of researches has been favorable to his contentions, and we shall probably not be far wrong in accepting his statement that—"The chief mass of the protein substances of the cells does not consist of proteins in the ordinary sense, but consists of more complex phosphorized bodies, and that the globulins and albumins are to be considered as nutritive materials for the cells or as destructive products in the chemical transformation of the protoplasm."[5]

Nucleo-proteins are considered to be the most important constituents of the cell, both in quantity and in relation to cell activity. In structure the nucleo-proteins are very complex, as indicated by the different products yielded on hydrolytic cleavage of the molecule. Furthermore, there are many varieties, depending both upon the nature and proportions of the component parts. They may be described as consisting of two primary constituents—(1) nucleic acid and (2) a protein body, in chemical combination with each other like a salt. The term *nucleic acid* covers a large group of substances, which are characterized, on the one hand, by their frequent occurrence bound with proteins, and, on the other hand, by their yielding phosphoric acid and purine bases, pyrimidines and pentoses or hexoses on cleavage. Diagrammatically the manner of cleavage of the nucleo-proteins may be indicated as follows:

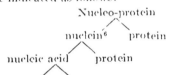

In the cell the nucleo-proteins probably exist partly as solid structures, *e. g.*, the chromatin framework of the nucleus, and partly dissolved in the plasma. An interesting phenomenon is the alteration in the chromatin nucleo-proteins during cell division, when they seem to lose part of the combined protein and approach more nearly pure nucleic acid—just as inorganic salts occur with the acids and bases saturating each other more or less incompletely, *e. g.*, mono-, di-, and tribasic phosphates. In this we have a chemical explanation of the intensity of the staining of dividing nuclei by basic dyes.[7]

Phosphoproteins resemble nucleo-proteins to the extent that they also yield phosphoric acid, and are somewhat similar in solubility and digestibility. They are essentially different, however, in that they *do not yield* nucleic acid or purine bases on cleavage. Probably members of this group are also constant components of cells.

Glycoproteins (or *gluco-proteins*) and *phospho-glycoproteins* are also believed to occur frequently or constantly in protoplasm. They are compounds of proteins with a sugar or sugar-like group, which probably usually contains nitrogen, thus differing from the ordinary hexoses and pentoses.

[4] Halliburton and Mott, Archives of Neurology, 1903 (2), 727; also see Halliburton's "Chemistry of Muscle and Nerve."

[5] See Kossel, Münch. med. Woch., 1911 (58), 65.

[6] Probably nuclein should be considered as merely one variety of nucleoprotein, with less protein than the other varieties.

[7] The chemistry of the nucleo-proteins is discussed in the chapter on Uric Acid Metabolism and Gout, Chap. xxiii.

Insoluble proteins, or bodies resembling the coagulated proteins in their lack of solubility in various fluids, are left behind after the other proteins have been extracted from the cells. Their significance is not known: whether to a large extent artificially produced or whether a normal structural element of the cell.

FATS AND LIPOIDS (LIPINS)[8]

Lipoids is a term in common use but of indefinite significance; most usually it comprehends the intracellular substances which are soluble in ordinary fat solvents, but which are not simple fats or fatty acids, lecithin and cholesterol being the most important of the lipoids.

For the entire group of fats and lipoids the term *lipins* has been proposed by Gies and Rosenbloom.[9] Lipoids and ordinary fats, that is, lipins, occur in all cells, but their demonstration is not always readily possible. The microscopic appearance of a cell, even when special stains for fat are used, gives no correct idea of the amount of lipins actually present. Thus normal kidneys contain 15 to 18 per cent. in their dry substance, but none of this can be detected readily with the microscope. A kidney which seems microscopically the site of marked fatty degeneration may show no more fat when examined chemically than a normal kidney, which in section appears to be quite free from fat. This is because some of the intracellular fat is so bound, chemically or physically, with the proteins that it cannot be seen, nor can it be stained by the dyes ordinarily used for that purpose; only when degenerative changes of certain kinds have liberated it from combination does it become visible and stainable by ordinary methods (Rosenfeld). By the special fixation method of Ciaccio the fatty compounds of even normal cells may be made stainable (Bell),[10] showing that the so-called masked fat is really in a not altogether invisible form. Whether the intracellular fat has any function other than that of serving as a food-stuff is not known, but there can be no question of the importance of the phosphorized fats, or phospholipins.

Phospholipins are primary cell-constituents and are probably important both in metabolism and physically. Hammarsten regards them as concerned in the building up of the nucleus. As will be shown later, many of the most essential physical properties of the living cell depend upon the presence in it of lipoids, of which phosphatids are apparently the chief. Of the ether-soluble substances in the heart, for example, 69 to 70 per cent. are phosphatids, 8 per cent. of the dry weight of the myocardium. Many different substances have been described as phosphatids, but the chemical identity of but few is sufficiently established. Of these the most important are *lecithin* and *cephalin*, which are most intimately associated.

There are several possible varieties of lecithin, depending upon the fatty

[8] Full discussion in "Lecithin and Allied Substances (The Lipins)," by Hugh MacLean, Monographs on Biochemistry, London, 1918.

[9] MacLean uses "lipin" to include "substances of a fat-like nature yielding on hydrolysis fatty acids or derivatives of fatty acids and containing in their molecule either N, or N and P." As there is need for a term covering the fats, phosphatids, cholesterols and related bodies, the suggestion of Gies and Rosenbloom is followed for the present in this book, and the word lipin used with the broader significance.

[10] Jour. Med. Res., 1911 (19), 539.

acid radical they contain. The assumed structural formula of one lecithin, stearyl-oleyl lecithin, is as follows:

$$CH_2—O—C_{18}—H_{35}O$$

$$CH—O—C_{18}—H_{33}O$$

$$CH_2—O—PO—OH$$

$$O—CH_2—CH_2—N \equiv (CH_3)_3.$$

$$OH$$

It differs from ordinary fats, therefore, in having two special groups, one the phosphoric acid, the other the choline radical, which last may be of some importance in pathological processes. In its physical properties it is quite similar to the ordinary fats, although it forms even finer emulsions in water, which are practically colloidal solutions (W. Koch).

Cephalin differs in having for the base amino-ethyl alcohol ($NH_2CH_2CH_2OH$) instead of choline, and is probably as widely spread in the tissues as lecithin.[11] It has been held by some that there are many phospholipins, which may be specific for different cells, tissues and species, but it seems more probable that these supposed specific lipoidal substances are merely mixtures of lecithin, cephalin and their derivatives in varying proportions (Levene).[12]

Cholesterol, which is another lipoid, is nearly as universally present as lecithin. It exists both free and in combination with fatty acids, for cholesterol is an alcohol and not at all similar to the fats chemically, although very similar physically. The empirical formula is $C_{27}H_{43}OH$ or $C_{27}H_{45}OH$, and it is related to the terpenes. It seems to be relatively inert chemically, and therefore is probably important only because of its effect on the physical properties of the cells. By some it is considered to be a decomposition or cleavage product of the proteins, which is in accordance with its abundance in masses of old necrotic tissue, *e. g.*, atheromatous masses, old infarcts, and old exudates.

Doubly Refractive Lipoids and Myelins.[13]—In practically all normal tissues there are present droplets of lipoid nature which are characterized by showing prominent crosses when examined with crossed Nicol prisms (anisotropic), the adrenal and corpus luteum containing them most abundantly. Chemically they seem to be mixtures of various lipoids in inconstant proportions, but probably the anisotropic character is most usually dependent upon the presence of cholesterol esters. The term myelin was first applied by Virchow to peculiar fatty substances found in various normal and pathological tissues, because they showed physical characters similar to those of the myelin substance of nerves, but as many of these substances are doubly refractive, or can be easily made so, some authors use the term myelin as if it were synonymous with doubly refractive lipoids. There are, however, myelins which are not always doubly refractive, and also doubly refractive lipoids which do not swell up in water to form myelin figures, etc., as is characteristic of true myelins. Chemically, however, the myelins and doubly refractive substances are probably related, consisting of mixtures of cholesterol, cholesterol esters, phospholipins and perhaps soaps, in varying proportion. They will be considered further in discussing Fatty Metamorphosis, Chap. XVI.

CARBOHYDRATES

The third great class of food-stuffs, the carbohydrates, is represented in the cell by *pentoses* and *hexoses* combined with proteins and with lipoids, and also by *glycogen*, which exists free. Glycogen is a difficult substance to isolate in minute quantities and, therefore, although it is not found in all cells by our present methods, yet it may well be that it is a constant constituent of the protoplasm. There is no evi-

[11] Koch and Woods, Jour. Biol. Chem., 1905 (1), 203.

[12] Jour. Biol. Chem., 1919 (39), 83.

[13] See Adami, Jour. Amer. Med. Assoc., 1907 (48), 463; Karwicka, Ziegler's Beitr., 1911 (50), 437; Schultze, Ergebnisse Pathol., 1909 (13, pt. 2), 253; Bang, Ergebnisse Physiol., 1907 (6), 131; 1909 (8), 463.

dence, however, that it is anything more than a source of heat and energy to the cell. Its properties and occurrence will be considered more fully in the discussion of glycogenic infiltration. Since glycogen is formed from dextrose and is constantly breaking down into dextrose, it is probable that the latter is also constantly present in the cells.

INORGANIC SUBSTANCES

Up to this point the substances of the cytoplasm that have been discussed have all been organic compounds which do not naturally exist independent from living or once living cells, yet the inorganic substances of the protoplasm are also of vital importance. As Mann says, "so-called pure ash-free proteins are chemically inert, and, in the true sense of the word, dead bodies. What puts life into them is the presence of electrolytes." The various salts of potassium, sodium, calcium, magnesium, and iron which all cells contain do not exist merely dissolved in the water of the cell, but in part they are combined with the organic constituents of the protoplasm. They are not combined as simple additions of the salts to the proteins; but *ions*, both anions and cations, are united in chemical combination to the large protein molecule (ion-proteins).[14] Possibly the proteins participate in vital chemical processes only as ion compounds with inorganic elements. It is extremely difficult, indeed almost impossible, to secure proteins entirely free from inorganic substances (ash-free proteins). The fact that inorganic substances are held in the cells chemically rather than by simple diffusion into them from the surrounding fluids is shown by the great difference in the proportions of various salts in the cells and in the extra-cellular fluids. Thus potassium is nearly always much more abundant in the cells than in the tissue fluids, while sodium is more abundant in the fluids. Phosphoric acid is also more abundant in the cells, and chlorin in the plasma. In cells iron seems to exist chiefly in combination with the nucleo-proteins.[15]

THE PHYSICAL CHEMISTRY OF THE CELL AND ITS CONSTITUENTS[16]

From the standpoint of physical chemistry the cell consists of a collection of colloids and crystalloids, electrolytes and non-electrolytes, dissolved in water, in lipoids, and in each other, surrounded by a semipermeable membrane, and perhaps subdivided by similar membranes or surfaces. Physical chemical processes, as we shall see later, play an all-important part in the life phenomena of the cell, and therefore some space may be occupied profitably in explaining the nature of these changes and of the substances that participate in them.

CRYSTALLOIDS AND THEIR PROPERTIES

Crystalloids, or substances that tend under favorable conditions to form crystals, and which diffuse readily through most diffusion membranes, form a relatively small part of the total mass of the cell, but they are fully as essential as the colloids. The chief representatives of this group that are found usually or constantly in the cell are the inorganic salts, sugar, and the innumerable decomposition products of the proteins, including particularly urea, creatine, purine bases, amino-acids, etc. Most of these are by no means so characteristic of living things as are the colloids, sometimes occurring quite inde-

[14] See J. Loeb, Science, 1919 (50), 439.
[15] See Macallum on Microchemistry, Ergebnisse Physiol., 1908 (7), 552.
[16] See Bayliss, "Principles of General Physiology," London, 1915, for a more extensive discussion of these topics.

pendently of a cellular origin, which the proteins never do. The inorganic salts in particular seem quite foreign to living processes, and as they enter and leave the body practically unchanged they are evidently not a source of energy through chemical change. Their importance to the cell lies almost entirely in their physical or physico-chemical properties. The organic crystalloids, although of nutritional value, also have physical properties in some respects similar to those of the inorganic crystalloids, and therefore to this extent they exert similar influences, but the essential difference between the organic and the inorganic crystalloids is that all the latter are electrolytes, while many of the organic crystalloids that occur in cells are non-electrolytes. The importance of this distinction lies not in the utility or non-utility of these substances as conductors of electrical currents in the ordinary sense, but rather on the existence of those properties which determine their conductive ability. Electrical conductivity is an index of ionization, and upon ionization depends the chief influence of the electrolytes upon vital activities. The importance of this process of dissociation or ionization lies in the fact that with most substances no chemical reaction can occur while the substance is in the non-ionized state. The chemical properties of ionizable substances are produced largely by the ions they liberate on dissociation. As a consequence, the physiological effects of electrolytes are due to their ionic condition, and through the ions that are present in the cell many of its various chemical processes are brought about. Not all substances ionize with the same readiness, which causes a great difference in their properties. The reason that acetic acid is a weaker acid than hydrochloric acid is that it does not ionize to such an extent, and so a corresponding quantity does not introduce as large a number of hydrogen ions into a solution. Larger molecules, as a rule, ionize less than smaller ones of similar nature, e. g., stearic acid ionizes less than acetic acid and therefore is a weaker acid. Likewise the properties of a substance which depend upon its ions will be less marked when it is in a solvent that produces little ionization. For example, bichloride of mercury owes its antiseptic properties to the Hg ions that it sets free when in solution. It is well known that solutions of mercury, and for that matter most other antiseptics, are much less actively germicidal in alcohol than when in water, because their ionization is less in alcohol; and the germicidal properties decrease as the proportion of alcohol increases, until the germicidal effect of the mixture is no greater than that of alcohol alone in the same strength.

If we had no electrolytes in the cell, electric charges could not be carried about in it, and hence chemical reactions could not occur. It is this fact that makes the inorganic salts of such vital importance to the cell life. To repeat Mann's words, it is the electrolytes that put life into the proteins. Water itself is almost absolutely non-dissociated, and proteins so little that for some time it was doubted if they really did ionize. Probably all soluble substances do dissociate to a certain minimal degree, but it is so slight for most of the constituents of the cell except the inorganic salts (the organic acids and alkalies, and a few dissociable organic products of protein metabolism, occur in such insignificant amounts as to be almost negligible) that without them there would be little chemical activity possible, and hence life would be absent or at a very low ebb indeed. As before mentioned, the inorganic salts probably exist in the cell not only as salts, but also, and perhaps chiefly, as ions and ionic compounds with the cell proteins.

Many applications of the facts and theories of ionization have been made in physiology and a few applications have also been made in pathology, especially the relation of ions to edema, to diuresis and glycosuria, and also to problems of immunity. No attempt will be made here to go further into the observations and theories concerning ionization or its rôle in physiology, but for more extensive information as well as for the complete bibliography the works mentioned below may be referred to.[17] The applications in pathology will be brought out as the subject under discussion in subsequent chapters necessitates and it is largely to facilitate the understanding of such reference that this brief summary of the subject of ionization has been introduced. In the same spirit we take up the subjects of diffusion and osmosis.

Diffusion and Osmosis.—Although the non-electrolytes do not ionize to any considerable extent, and therefore are relatively inactive chemically, the crystalloidal non-electrolytes, of which sugar and urea are the two chief examples among the cell constituents, possess in common with the electrolytes the important property of diffusion. By this process the exchange of chemical substances between the blood and the cell is brought about, by it the chemical composition of the different parts of the cell and between different cells is equalized, and without it chemical change would be practically impossible. Diffusion occurs most simply between two solutions of unlike nature, or between a solution of a substance and the solvent alone, when placed directly in contact with one another. If we place in the bottom of a cylindrical vessel a solution of copper sulphate and above it some water, carefully avoiding mixing, it will be found after some time that the fluid has become equally blue throughout. This is brought about by the movement of the dissolved particles which gradually carries them through the entire mass of fluid, and as their migration is against the force of gravity, they evidently accomplish

[17] "Physical Chemistry in the Service of Medicine," Wolfgang Pauli, translation by M. H. Fischer, New York, 1907. "Physikalische Chemie der Zelle und der Gewebe," Höber, Leipzig, 1915. "Osmotische Druck und Ionenlehre in den medicinischen Wissenschaften," Hamburger, Wiesbaden. "Studies in General Physiology," Loeb, University of Chicago Press, 1905. "Dynamics of Living Matter," Loeb, Columbia University Press, New York, 1906. Spiro and J. Loeb Oppenheimer's "Handbuch der Biochemie," 1908 (2), 1-141. "Physical Chemistry of Vital Phenomena," McClendon, Princeton Univ. Press, 1917.

work. This process is not dependent upon ionization, for a solution of cane-sugar or of urea will show the same diffusion. A solution of protein or other colloid does so much more slowly, however, indeed, quite imperceptibly.

If we were to introduce a piece of filter-paper between the water and the copper sulphate solution, the diffusion would go on the same, the pores of the paper permitting the passage of the molecules without hindrance. If, instead of filter-paper, there were introduced a sheet of some substance free from pores, the diffusion would be much more affected. If the septum was of such a nature that the substances in solution were insoluble in it (*e. g.*, glass), diffusion would of necessity stop; but if it were something in which the solvent or the solute was soluble, such as a gelatin plate, then these substances would dissolve in it, and diffusing through its substance escape into the fluid on the other side. The last example indicates the conditions afforded in the animal cell, and also in the usual laboratory diffusion experiments when the membrane is generally either an animal membrane or a parchment paper, both of which are composed of colloids. Crystalloids are generally soluble in colloids and hence pass through such diffusion membranes; colloids dissolve but slightly in colloids, and hence they do not pass through a diffusion membrane readily, and are, therefore, but very slightly diffusible.

The process of diffusion, if uninterrupted, always continues until the solution is of exactly the same composition throughout. If on one side of the diffusion membrane there is a substance that passes through the membrane rapidly, and on the other a substance that passes through slowly or not at all, there will soon be an unequal condition on the two sides of the membrane, for the diffusible substance would accumulate in equal amounts on each side, while the non-diffusible would remain where it was. On one side there would then be more material exerting osmotic pressure than on the other, and if the membrane were flexible, it would bulge toward the opposite side. The pressure is supposed to be due to the bombardment of the containing walls by molecules or ions of the substances in solution, and hence the more molecules and ions in solution, the more pressure. When equal numbers of particles are on each side of the partition, the pressure is equalized. It is quite possible to have membranes readily permeable to one substance and almost entirely impermeable to another; such membranes are called *semipermeable*. To produce osmotic pressure it is not necessary that the membrane be absolutely impermeable to any of the substances—it may only be relatively less permeable for the solute than for the solvent. If, for example, we fill a parchment bag with concentrated sugar solution, tie up the top tightly and throw it into water, it will swell up rapidly and eventually burst. But if the parchment is in the form of a tube, open at the top, and the lower end is placed in water, the amount of fluid inside the tube will increase at first, but eventually the sugar will diffuse out to such an extent that the solution is of the same concentration inside and outside of the tube, and the column of fluid will again become of equal height on both sides. These results indicate that the water passes through the membrane more rapidly than does the sugar, but that eventually the sugar can all pass through.

Exactly similar conditions exist in cells, particularly plant cells. The typical cell of plant tissue consists of a distinct wall, usually cellulose, lined internally by a layer of protoplasm which incloses a mass of aqueous solution, the cell sap, containing sugar and various other solutes. The outer wall is readily permeable by water and by most solutes, whereas the protoplasmic layer inside it behaves like a semipermeable membrane, which permits water to pass through readily but hinders greatly the passage of most solutes; that it is somewhat permeable is attested by the fact that the cell sap contains solutes derived from the external fluids. As a result of this arrangement there is a constant tendency for the cavity of the cell to be distended by water and for the solutes within it to exert their considerable pressure upon the cell wall. Because of the strength of the cellulose layer the cell can withstand great pressures that would tear apart the tender protoplasmic layer that really determines the osmotic pressure that causes the rigidity or *turgor* of plant cells, and explains the ability of a tender green shoot to hold itself upright or horizontal in the air; and it is the force that enables growing roots to lift great stones or tear apart rocks in whose clefts they grow. If certain plant cells are placed in distilled water, the pressure may rise to such an extent that the cells burst, and it was through studying this phenomenon that Pfeffer worked out the basis of our present knowledge of osmotic pressure. If the cell is placed in a solution of greater concentration than its cell sap, the pressure outside will be greater than that inside and the protoplasmic membrane will be forced away from the cellulose wall, while its central cavity shrinks and perhaps disappears entirely, the protoplasm forming a ball in the center. This is practically what occurs when a plant stem is cut and it "wilts"—the water is removed by evaporation, the osmotic pressure outside the cells becomes greater than that inside, and the water passes out. Likewise when a plant cell dies the turgor is lost because the membrane becomes permeable, and so pressure soon becomes the same on both sides of the cell wall.

In animal cells the wall is not so highly developed as in plants, nor is it backed up by a rigid material like cellulose; indeed for many animal cells there is no well-defined wall and the protoplasm appears to be naked. Nevertheless the behavior of the animal cells indicates that they do possess what resembles a cell wall, in that they behave when in solutions as if they were surrounded by a diffusion membrane. The degree to which phenomena of this nature are shown varies with different cells; with red corpuscles, for example, the osmotic pressure influences are very marked, as shown by the wrinkling or crenation of the corpuscles when they are placed in fluids of higher concentration than the blood plasma, and by their swelling and disintegration with escape of the hemoglobin (*hemolysis*) when they are put into distilled water or solutions of less concentration than the plasma. Other tissue cells seem to undergo more or less alteration from changes in the osmotic pressure in the fluids surrounding them. The diffusion membrane that surrounds the cell is generally not well defined, and for most cells seems to be but a surface condensation of the protoplasm, perhaps formed through the effects of surface tension. It seems probable that this surface diffusion membrane contains a large proportion of cell lipoids, *i.e.*, cholesterol and phospholipins (for the red corpuscles this is practically certain); hence substances soluble in lipoids penetrate the cell readily, while to many substances insoluble in lipoids the cell is nearly or quite impermeable (Overton). Probably the wall of the animal cell is not so nearly semipermeable as is that of the plant cell, for nowhere in the animal body do we get such turgor in the cells as we see in plant tissues. Lacking a cellulose wall, animal cells could not develop such an internal pressure without rupturing and such a process of rupturing (*plasmorrhexis, plasmoptysis*) does not seem to be a normal occurrence in animal tissues. We shall be most nearly correct, probably, if we look upon the animal cell as possessing a delicate diffusion membrane at its surface, through which water passes more readily than do most crystalloids, and through which colloids pass almost not at all, but the exclusion of each of these types of substances is merely relative and not absolute. Within the cell, also, the colloids probably exist as a more or less well-developed emulsion, so that we have here a practically limitless amount of surface formation all through the protoplasm; such a structure could permit the endless number of reactions of a living cell to go on side by side in the same cell. Studies by G. L. Kite[18] seem to show that all of the protoplasm has much the same relation to solutions as does the external layer or cell membrane, for he found that if drops of solutions which can penetrate a cell from outside be injected directly into a cell they diffuse through it, but substances which cannot penetrate from outside are also unable to diffuse through the cell after they have been injected into it.

Since osmotic pressure, exactly like gas pressure, is presumably produced by the bombarding of the walls of the container by particles in the solution, the amount of pressure will vary in proportion to the number of particles present. With non-electrolytes, such as sugar and urea, the moving particles seem to be molecules, and so a solution of sugar or urea will produce an osmotic

[18] Amer. Jour. Physiol., 1915 (37), 282.

pressure directly proportional to the number of molecules it contains. In the case of the electrolytes, however, the ions produce pressure as well as the molecules, and hence an electrolyte in solution will produce a relatively high osmotic pressure as compared with an equivalent solution of a non-electrolyte, since each molecule may yield two or more ions. Colloids, however, exert so slight an osmotic pressure that it is difficult of detection; this probably depends on the great size and slight motility of their molecules. In the many and important osmotic processes of the animal organism, therefore, the colloids take no part except in helping to form the diffusion membrane, and in preventing the diffusion of one another.[19]   It is interesting to consider also that colloids under ordinary conditions do not greatly modify the diffusion of crystalloids through a solution containing both classes of matter. The fact that a cell is full of dissolved colloids does not seriously affect the osmotic properties of the intracellular crystalloids, provided the colloids are not condensed in such a way as to form diffusion membranes. But as all the cleavage products of proteins after they have passed the peptone stage are crystalloids, by decomposition of the intracellular proteins the osmotic pressure may be greatly raised. As long as the cell is living there can be no constancy in composition, for metabolic processes, by producing from proteins that have no osmotic pressure crystalloidal substances that do have osmotic pressure, cause intracellular osmotic conditions to be continually varying. As a result, streams of diffusing particles are moving about in every direction, setting up new chemical reactions and consequent new osmotic currents. The greater the difference in osmotic pressure between a cell and its environment, and between the different parts of the same cell, the more powerful the osmotic effects, and as a result the greater the capacity for accomplishing work.

Indeed, *we may look upon cell life as a constant attempt at the establishment of equilibrium, both chemical and osmotic, which is never achieved* because the move towards one sort of equilibrium is always against the other. All the food-stuffs—fats, carbohydrates and proteins—are characterized by being colloids when intact and crystalloids when disintegrated, thus:

colloidal proteins $\rightleftarrows$ crystalloidal amino acids
colloidal glycogen $\rightleftarrows$ crystalloidal sugar
nondiffusible fats $\rightleftarrows$ diffusible soaps and glycerol.

In consequence of this, if the crystalloids diffuse from the blood into a cell there is at once an excess of this end of the equation, and, hastened by the intracellular enzymes, partial synthesis to the colloid soon

[19] Under experimental conditions it is found that the nature of the membrane greatly modifies the osmotic pressure; for if a given colloid is soluble in a certain membrane and a certain crystalloid is not, the colloid will diffuse through the membrane while the crystalloid is held back. (Kahlenberg, Jour. Physical Chem., 1906 (10), 141.)

occurs to establish chemical equilibrium. Chemical changes in the crystalloids, by oxidation, reduction or hydrolysis, upset this chemical equilibrium, and hence further diffusion, synthesis and hydrolysis continue, one upsetting the other continuously. If equilibrium were established we should have no further reactions, and the cells would be inactive. *The constant upsetting of the equilibrium is what constitutes cell life.*

The relation of osmotic pressure and osmosis to physiological problems is only beginning to be studied. It is apparent that they must be of essential importance in absorption from the alimentary canal, in absorption and excretion between the cells and the blood stream, and in secretion by glandular organs; but it is also certain that they are no less important in all the less obvious chemical and physical processes of the cell.[20] In pathological processes osmotic pressure may play an equally important rôle, and the facts discussed in the preceding paragraphs will be alluded to frequently in subsequent chapters.

COLLOIDS[21]

Since Graham in 1861 studied the differences between the substances that did or did not diffuse readily through animal or parchment membranes, soluble substances have been classified in the two main groups of *colloids* and *crystalloids*, which distinction Graham believed separated two entirely different classes of matter. Although at the present time the differences between the two classes do not seem so great, yet the same division is found useful in classification. By colloids Graham indicated those substances which were dissolved to the extent of showing no visible particles in suspension, but which either did not pass through diffusion membranes at all, or did so very slowly indeed, as compared to the crystalloid substances. Under certain conditions they tended to assume a sticky, glue-like nature, hence the name. (Many substances are now known which have the chief properties of the colloids and are therefore classified among them, but never are glue-like, *e. g.*, the colloidal metals, so that the name has lost some of its original significance.) The physical property which Graham particularly noted in the colloids, besides their non-diffusibility was the tendency to assume various states of solidity.

[20] For further consideration of the subject of osmotic pressure in these relations, see: Livingston, "The Rôle of Diffusion and Osmotic Pressure in Plants," University of Chicago Press, Chicago, 1903; Czapek, "Biochemie der Pflanzen," Jena. Also, Spiro, Pauli and Höber, all previously cited.
[21] For full discussions of the nature of colloids see: Höber, "Physikalische Chemie der Zelle," Leipzig, 1914; Pauli, Ergebnisse der Physiologie, 1907 (6), 105; Bechhold, "Colloids in Biology and Medicine," translated by J. G. M. Bullowa, 1919; Wo. Ostwald, "Grundriss der Kolloidchemie," and "Theoretical and Applied Colloid Chemistry," both translated by M. H. Fischer. A good brief discussion of colloids is given by Young in Zinsser's "Infection and Resistance."

Not only can they be in solution, when he called them "sols" (when the solvent was water, "hydrosols"), but they can become quite firm although containing much water (then called "gels" or "hydrogels"). The gels may assume a firm, coagulated condition, the so-called "pectous" state, which state is permanent in that the gel form cannot be reobtained from the pectous modification. Finally the colloid can be in a dry, solid state, quite free from water, and then not a gel at all.

Included in the great class of colloids are all forms of proteins, and also gums, starch, dextrin, glycogen, tannin, probably the enzymes, and also the greater number of organic dyes; also there are inorganic colloids, such as silicic acid, arsenic sulphide, hydrated oxide of iron, and many other similar compounds, besides the elements themselves, especially the noble metals, which may exist in colloidal form. It will be seen at once that the chief constituents of the cells, in fact nearly all the primary constituents except the inorganic salts, are organic colloids, and therefore *the properties of the cells are largely dependent upon the properties of the colloids.*

In considering the characteristics of the colloids we at once meet the question—What distinguishes the colloids from the crystalloids, on the one side, and from suspensions or emulsions on the other? The sum and substance of our present conception of the nature of colloidal solution may be briefly summarized as follows:

It is possible for solid substances to be so divided among the particles of a solvent that they remain permanently in this condition, neither aggregating into masses nor separating out through the action of gravity. With some substances, as sugar, for example, the solid seems to divide up into its molecular form, each molecule being free from all others of its kind except during occasional contacts. Some other substances, as salt, go still further, and the molecule divides into two or more parts, which have different electric charges (*ionization*). The first of these classes of substances forms a solution which contains no particles visible by any known means, does not contain particles large enough to reflect light impinging upon them, exerts a large osmotic pressure, but does not conduct electricity. The other, in which ionization has occurred, differs solely in its capacity to conduct electricity readily. Both are *true solutions* of crystalloids; the one which does not ionize is a *non-electrolyte;* the other, by virtue of its ionization, is an *electrolyte,* the ions carrying electric charges through the solution.

At the other end of the scale we have substances which are quite insoluble when in masses, but which, when very finely divided by mechanical means, can be suspended and uniformly distributed through a fluid without having any marked tendency to aggregate or settle out. Such *suspensions* or *emulsions* contain particles visible under the microscope, usually appear turbid, refract light, are non-diffusible, exert no osmotic pressure, and do not transmit electricity. Such mixtures are obviously very different from the true solutions above described. Between these two extremes stand the colloids, which vary in their properties so that they approach sometimes the suspensions (e. g., lecithin, or coagulated egg-albumin in colloidal suspension), and sometimes more nearly the true solutions (e. g., dextrin). No sharp boundaries can be drawn between any of the members of the series. Indeed, one substance may present all the different stages under different conditions, some agreeing with the properties of the typical suspensions, and some with the properties of the true solutions. The colloids stand in an intermediary position, differing quantitatively in one way or another from the true solutions, but yet approaching them closely and sometimes almost indistinguishably resembling them. For the most part, however, they show characteristics decided enough to entitle them to separate classification, and to make any confusion with the crystalloids impossible.

The Characteristics of Colloids.—The chief properties of the colloids are, then, as follows:

Amorphous Form.—This, like almost all other "colloidal properties," is not absolute, for in egg-albumin, hemoglobin, and various globulins we have proteins which in every respect are typical colloids, yet they form crystals readily and abundantly. Oxyhemoglobin, the molecular weight of which is calculated at about 14,000, exhibits Tyndall's phenomenon and will not pass through a very fine porcelain filter, and therefore resembles the colloids decidedly, yet it forms beautiful crystals. The very fact that crystals are formed, Spiro points out, is proof that when in solution the individual molecules must have been free and separate, for otherwise they could scarcely unite in the definite spatial relations necessary to produce crystalline forms. With these few exceptions, however, the colloids do not present any typical structure, and are not crystalline under any visible condition. But when they are made insoluble by chemical means they may, under certain conditions, produce rather characteristic non-crystalline structures, a matter that will be discussed in a subsequent paragraph.

Solubility.—Although we speak of "colloidal solutions," this term does not commit us to the theory of the identity of the solution of colloids with that of crystalloids. We have above stated what seems to be a fair view of the matter as shown by many methods of experimentation. Most colloids seem to be, in fact, suspensions of masses of molecules, or perhaps of very large single molecules, and a true solution is likewise a suspension of single molecules or of ions. When the aggregations of molecules are sufficiently large, we have an ordinary suspension; but a single protein molecule is as large as a very great number of molecules of such substances as sugar (crystalloid); or tannin, $C_{14}H_{10}O_9$ (colloid); or calcium carbonate (insoluble, suspension); and it would be strange if a true solution of a protein did not behave in many particulars like a suspension of molecular aggregates of dimensions similar to the dimensions of protein molecules. Nearly all colloidal solutions show Tyndall's phenomenon, which demonstrates the existence of particles in suspension large enough to reflect light from their surfaces.[22] Most of the colloids are held back by very fine filters to a greater or less degree; some are almost entirely retained by a hardened paper filter, while others pass through the finest-pored clay filters. Furthermore, the metallic colloids, such as those of platinum, gold, and silver, are unquestionably suspensions of finely divided particles of metal, yet they exhibit all the typical phenomena of colloids, passing through many sorts of filters, and even inducing the same hydrolytic changes as many enzymes.

[22] It is highly probable, however, that Tyndall's phenomenon when exhibited by true colloidal solutions (e. g., soluble proteins), depends on the presence of aggregates and not properly on the dissolved colloids. (See McClendon and Prendergast, Jour. Biol. Chem., 1919 (38), 549.)

3

It must also be mentioned that the solvent is probably an important factor in determining the colloidal or non-colloidal nature of a substance; *e. g.*, soaps form true solutions in alcohol and colloidal solutions in water; gelatin forms colloidal solutions in water but not in ether, whereas rubber forms colloidal solutions in ether but not in water.

Closely related to solubility is the phenomenon of *imbibition*, which may be defined as the taking up of a fluid by a solid body without chemical change. Not all colloids possess this property, but it is shown by most of the organic colloids, particularly the proteins. Fick distinguishes capillary, osmotic, and molecular imbibition, the latter of which is the form exhibited by colloids, and it occurs independent of the existence of pores or other preformed spaces in the imbibing body. The imbibition of water by colloids is more than a simple mechanical process, for it is accompanied by a contraction in the total volume of solid and water, and by the evolution of heat. The forces developed are far greater than those of osmotic pressure; *e. g.*, to prevent imbibition of water by starch requires a pressure of over 2500 atmospheres. On the other hand, the physical properties of an aqueous colloidal solution show that the colloid is not chemically combined in the form of a hydrate. To describe this peculiar relation Hofmeister and Oswald recommend the term "mechanical affinity." Hardy has shown that water held in a gelatin jelly cannot be removed by great pressures (400 pounds to the square inch), but after the nature of the jelly is so changed by formalin that it is no longer liquefiable by heat, the water can be easily expressed from the loose meshwork that is formed. It would seem from this that the imbibition and retention of water by colloids may be closely related to surface phenomena. Hofmeister has shown that organized animal tissues obey the same laws of imbibition as do simple gelatin plates, and probably this phenomenon of colloids is very important in physiological and pathological processes.

Non-diffusibility.—The lack of power to pass through animal and parchment membranes, which was Graham's starting-point in the study of colloids, is also only a relative condition. This is shown by the following figures, giving the relative time required by the same amount of different substances to pass through a certain diffusion membrane:

Sodium chloride	2.33
Sugar	7.00
Magnesium sulphate	7.00
Protein	49.00
Caramel	98.00

This difference of time is so great, however, as to permit of separation of salts from proteins, etc., by dialysis, a process in constant use. Primarily the ability to diffuse through a given membrane requires that the diffusing substance be soluble in the membrane. Diffusion membranes are always composed of colloids, *e. g.*, animal bladders, or parchment, which is a colloidal cellulose. Crystalloids are generally soluble in colloids, while colloids are little or not at all soluble in other colloids, and hence do not diffuse through one another readily and permeate diffusion membranes very slowly. For example, if a stick of agar jelly be placed in a solution of ammoniated copper sulphate (a crystalloid), and another be placed in a solution of Prussian blue (a colloid), it will be found that the copper solution penetrates the agar completely before the colloidal solution of Prussian blue has penetrated it at all. This property is of great importance, undoubtedly, in keeping the different colloidal constituents of the cell in given localities within its protoplasm, *e. g.*, the colloidal glycogen remains where it is formed in the cytoplasm, unable to escape from the cell, whereas the crystalloidal sugar from which it is formed and into which it is converted, diffuses rapidly into or out of the cell.

The **osmotic pressure** of the colloids is extremely small. The closely related phenomena of *diffusion, depression of freezing-point*, and *elevation of boiling-point*, are also exhibited by colloids to but an extremely slight degree. For example, in one experiment, the dissolving of from 14 per cent. to 44 per cent. of egg-albumin in water lowered the freezing-point but 0.02° to 0.06°; and some other colloids have even less effect. The results of the latest and best experiments seem to indicate that the trifling effects of colloids upon osmotic pressure and upon freezing- and boiling-points observed in colloidal solutions are due to the colloids themselves, rather than to included impurities, although it may possibly be that some of these effects are due to the high surface tension and cohesion affinity of the colloids. In all cellular processes accompanied by manifestations of osmotic pressure or diffusion, however, the crystalloids may be considered as almost entirely responsible.

Electrical Phenomena.—As colloids do not separate freely into ions when dissolved, they do not conduct electricity appreciably. However, when an electric current is passed through water containing colloids in solution, the colloidal particles tend to pass to one pole or the other. Most colloids move toward the anode. This phenomenon, *cataphoresis*, is also generally exhibited by suspensions, and hence in this particular the colloids resemble suspensions rather than solutions. Helmholtz has explained the movement of the suspended particles as due to the accumulation of electrical charges upon the surfaces of two heterogeneous media when in contact. The nature of the charge depends upon both the suspended substance and the fluid; e. g., sulphur or graphite particles suspended in water assume a negative charge and move toward the anode, but when suspended in oil of turpentine they become positively charged and move toward the cathode. Water has such a high *dielectric constant* that most substances suspended in water become negatively charged as compared with the water, and move toward the positive pole or anode.

Hardy has observed that colloidal solutions of coagulated proteins move toward the anode when in alkaline solution, and toward the cathode when in acid solution.[23] This peculiar property of proteins suggests that perhaps simple surface phenomena do not suffice to account for the electrification of all colloid particles. Knowing the peculiar amphoteric character of proteins, which is probably due to the presence of both NH_2 and $COOH$ groups in the molecule, we can readily understand that in an acid solution the NH_2 radicles are combined with the acid, leaving the $COOH$ radicles free. The molecule would then have acid properties, and could dissociate into an acid H ion and a basic or electrically positive colloid ion. The colloid ion would then go toward the negative pole slowly, because of its great size. When a suitable concentration of both ions is produced the proteins will move towards both poles, this concentration being, in the case of serum albumin, $H = 10^{-6}$ (Michaelis). Living protoplasm behaves in most instances, as if the proteins were acids bound to inorganic cations (Robertson), and is usually stimulated at the cathode on the "make" of the current. It is permeable to ions, and the vitality of a tissue is so dependent on the maintenance of normal permeability that the permeability may be employed as a sensitive and reliable indicator of its vitality (Osterhout[24]). This may be done by determining the electrical resistance of the cells, which is lowered by anything that lowers their vitality.

Surface tension,[25] which may be described as *the force with which a fluid is striving to reduce its free surface to a minimum*, is highly exhibited by colloids as compared with crystalloids. The formation of emulsions and the spreading out of oil upon the surface of water depend upon surface tension. Ameboid movement may be attributed to changes in surface tension, as also may phagocytosis. (The relation of surface tension to these processes will be considered under the subject of Inflammation.)

The effect of colloids upon chemical processes going on within their solutions or gels is surprisingly small. Salts in solution in a thick gel of agar or gelatin will diffuse almost as rapidly as in water; they will also ionize as rapidly as in watery solutions, and chemical reactions occur with nearly the same speed and completeness as if the colloids were absent. Furthermore it makes little difference whether these processes are measured in a colloidal solution that is liquid, or after it has set in the gel form. These facts merely indicate that the colloids do not greatly impede the movements of molecules or ions in

[23] According to Field and Teague (Jour. Exper. Med., 1907 (9), 222), *native proteins in serum* move towards the cathode, no matter what the reaction.

[24] Science, 1914 (40), 488.

[25] See article on "Surface Tension and Vital Phenomena," by Macallum, Ergebnisse d. Physiol., 1911 (11), 602.

solutions. On the other hand, as before mentioned, colloids diffuse very slowly into each other. Hence, in the cell the colloids are quite fixed in their positions, whereas the crystalloids may wander about freely, and this arrangement is certainly of great importance in biologic processes. Pauli suggests the probability that the fixation of the colloid causes the cell to have different properties in different parts, and so various reactions may occur independently in different areas of the cytoplasm. The possibility of the correctness of this view is increased when we consider that the enzymes are colloids, for there is much evidence to show that they are distributed in just such an uneven manner within the cells.

Although colloids permit the passage of dissolved crystalloids through them, they greatly interfere with the movement of larger particles. This property accounts for the ability of colloids to hold many insoluble substances in such extremely fine suspensions that they seem superficially to be in true solution. If, for example, sodium phosphate is added to a solution of casein in lime-water, the calcium phosphate formed does not precipitate. It is not in solution, however, but rather exists as a suspension of very finely divided particles of the salt which the colloid keeps from aggregating into particles large enough to be visible or to overcome the viscosity of the fluid and sink to the bottom. Probably in this way many substances, including calcium salts, are carried in the blood, held in permanent suspension by the proteins. Substances thus finely divided will have extremely large surface area for reactions, and, therefore, will undoubtedly undergo changes with considerable rapidity and facility, although not in solution.

Precipitation and Coagulation of Colloids.—Because of the slender margin by which the colloids are separated from the suspensions, their persistence in solution is generally in a precarious condition. Relatively slight changes suffice to throw the colloids out of solution, and when once precipitated, they are often incapable of again dissolving in the same solvent. Solutions of albumin may undergo spontaneous coagulation on standing for some time, and agitation rapidly produces the same effect in many protein solutions. Some inorganic colloids are as readily coagulated as the proteins. A comparatively small rise in temperature, less than to 50° C. with some proteins, renders the protein perfectly insoluble. Furthermore, we have coagulation of protein solutions by enzyme action. The inorganic "colloidal suspensions" may be precipitated by the addition of very small quantities of electrolytes. Colloidal solutions of the type of the proteins are not so readily precipitated by most electrolytes, but if to the solution large quantities of crystalloids are added, the protein molecules are practically crowded out of solution, as in the "salting-out" process used in separating proteins by ammonium sulphate and other salts. The effect of heat upon different colloids is peculiar, in that some varieties, as silicic acid, aluminium hydrate, and many proteins are rendered so insoluble that they cannot again be dissolved in any fluid without first being modified in some way; whereas colloids of the type of gelatin and agar are made more soluble by heat. The change of colloids into insoluble forms, the "*pectous*" condition of Graham, requires the presence of water, for the dry colloids may be heated to relatively high temperatures without losing their solubility. On the other hand, dehydration of colloids while in solution will result in their precipitation and coagulation, as occurs in protein solutions when alcohol is added.

If solutions of two oppositely charged colloids are brought together they may precipitate, but if either is present in excess the precipitation may be incomplete, or even completely absent. This inhibition of precipitation is of particular interest because it so closely resembles the phenomenon observed in the precipitin reaction, whereby an excess of the antigenic protein will prevent precipitation. Also certain colloids will prevent the precipitation of other colloids by electrolytes, which fact is the basis of the Lange reaction of spinal fluid with colloidal gold.

Colloids are precipitated by many electrolytes, apparently through the formation of true ion compounds, one or both of the ions of the electrolytes uniting with the colloid ion; although some writers, as Spiro, believe that the combination is merely an additive one between entire molecules. Mathews[26] has advanced the theory that the *solution tension* of the ions is an important factor in determining the precipitation of colloids by electrolytes. In general, precipitation of colloids results from the reduction of the surface in proportion to the mass, because of an aggregation of the particles; this may be brought about by changing the surface electrical conditions, by uniting the molecules chemically, or by reducing the amount of the solvent.

The Structure of Colloids and of Protoplasm.[27]—Two very different sorts of substances are usually included under the term colloid, because they show the essential features of colloids in most respects; but as in many other respects they are quite unlike each other, it may be well to distinguish between them in some way. As a type of one class we may take gelatin; of the other, such a substance as colloidal arsenious sulphide. Gelatin solutions form gels upon cooling or evaporation, and redissolve when heated or when more solvent is added. Arsenious sulphide does not form gels upon cooling, and when solidified in any way, does not redissolve. In addition, the gelatin type is very viscous, and is not coagulated by the presence of salts unless these are added in large amounts; while the other type does not render the fluid in which it is dissolved appreciably more viscid, and it forms a precipitate immediately if minute amounts of electrolytes are introduced.

[26] American Journal of Physiology, 1905 (14), 203.
[27] Review by Harper, Amer. Jour. Botany, 1919 (6), 273.

As the former type resembles in many details the true solutions, while the latter approaches more closely to the suspensions, it has been proposed to distinguish them by the terms "colloidal solution" and "colloidal suspension."[28]   Of the two types, the colloidal solutions are by far the more important in biological considerations, since the colloidal suspensions are usually prepared artificially and seldom occur in nature, *e. g.*, Bredig's colloidal suspensions of the noble metals.

The colloidal solutions of proteins are of two types—one, such as albumin, forms a coagulum when heated, which under ordinary conditions is not reversible; that is, it does not again go into solution. Gelatin, however, becomes more fluid when heated, and when cooled it forms a gel which is readily reversible to the soluble form under the influence of heat. Within the cell, as far as we know, occur only the first type, the proteins that form non-reversible coagula.

An extensive study of the physical structure of the colloids has been made by Hardy.[29]   As long as the colloid is in solution it is structureless, although, as before mentioned, the existence of free solid particles can be demonstrated by certain optical methods.   The solution is homogeneous, and although perhaps viscid, still it is a typical solution.   Such solutions can become solid, either by the effect of temperature, of certain chemical fixing agents, or physical means. It was found by Hardy that in undergoing this solidification there occurs a separation of the solid from the liquid, the solid particles adhering to form a framework holding the liquid within its interstices. Heat-reversible gels show no structure until they are made irreversible by hardening agents, etc.; *e. g.*, a jelly of gelatin appears structure'ess, but when treated with formalin or other fixing agent, the structural appearances described below appear.   The figures formed by the framework vary according to the nature and concentration of the colloid and of the solvent, and also with the fixing agent used, the temperature, and the presence or absence of extraneous substances. In general, however, the figures obtained in the solidification of protein solutions by fixing agents, such as bichloride of mercury or formalin, *bear a striking resemblance to the finer structures of protoplasm* as described by cytologists.   There is produced an open network structure with spherical masses at the nodal points, or minute vesicles hollowed out in a solid mass, or a honeycomb appearance, or, when the concentration of the colloid is very slight, perhaps there is only a precipitation of fine granules of protein such as we often see in histological preparations of edematous cells and tissues.   All these forms seem to depend chiefly upon the concentration of the colloid.   The important fact is that when the chemicals ordinarily used as fixatives of cells for histological purposes act upon solutions of colloids that are perfectly homogeneous, they produce very constant and charac-

[28] Noyes, American Chemical Journal, 1905 (27), 85.
[29] Journal of Physiology, 1899 (21), 158.

teristic formations which recall at once the structures found in the protoplasm of hardened cells. Moreover, the use of different fixing agents, such as osmic acid, formalin, and bichloride of mercury, produces just the same differences in the structure of colloidal solutions that they produce in the protoplasm of cells hardened by them. Neither are the appearances seen in unfixed specimens reliable indications of the true structure of the living protoplasm. Granules of secretion may disappear after or during the death of the cell (*e. g.*, glycogen) or they may swell up (*e. g.*, mucin granules), thus giving the appearance of a network or honeycomb which is then incorrectly ascribed to the protoplasm itself. Death of the cells, even when not produced by external influences, seems to be accompanied by coagulation of some parts of the cell constituents, and hence a cell examined in anything but its normal living condition, an extremely difficult matter, will not present a true idea of how it appears and is composed while in that condition. By microdissection with the Barber pipette method it is possible to study the properties of unaltered living cytoplasm, and Seifriz[30] concludes from his studies that protoplasm is a homogeneous structureless solution, probably an emulsion hydrosol, *i. e.*, a colloid in which both phases are liquid, one of them, the dispersion medium, being water. Normal cytoplasm is at all times nonmiscible in water, but readily degenerates into a condition in which it is miscible.

If, with these facts in mind, we consider the theories of morphologists as to the finer structure of the cell protoplasm based upon studies of cells fixed in various hardening agents, it becomes evident that the possibility that the "foam structure" advocated by Bütschli, or the "thread," "reticular," and "pseudo-alveolar" structures of Fromann, Arnold, Reinke, and others, are all simply the effect of fixatives upon colloid solutions, is very real. The objection always advanced to these theories of protoplasmic structure, namely, that the structures described were at least in part artificial productions, not present in the normal living cell, and variously described and interpreted by different investigators, because each worked with a different hardening fluid or different technic, is strongly supported by these observations upon colloids. This matter will receive further consideration in the next section.

THE STRUCTURE OF THE CELL IN RELATION TO ITS CHEMISTRY AND PHYSICS [31]

It is obviously impossible to separate nuclei, nucleoli, cytoplasm, and cell membranes from each other (except with sperm heads) and to isolate them in quantities sufficient for analysis, and therefore we

[30] Biol. Bull., 1918 (34), 307.
[31] Reviews of the significance of cell structure for pathology are given by Benda and Ernst in Zentrlbl. allg. Path., 1914, Bd. 25, Ergänzungsheft.

are still quite uncertain as to just the chemical differences that exist between them. That there are differences is certain, and by means of micro-chemical reactions, by comparing analyses of cells in which nucleus or cytoplasm predominate, and by studying their physico-chemical relations to one another, we have arrived at more or less tangible ideas on the question of the relation of the structural elements of the cell to its composition.

THE NUCLEUS [32]

Although the nucleus presents morphologically a sharp isolation from the cytoplasm, and displays equally sharp tinctorial differences, it is probable that chemically the differences between nucleus and cytoplasm are quantitative rather than qualitative. The characteristic affinity of certain elements of the nucleus for basic stains depends upon the presence in the nucleus of nucleoproteins in large proportion, and to a limited degree nucleoproteins are characteristic of nuclei. Their affinity for basic dyes depends upon the nucleic acid radical.[33] For example, the heads of spermatozoa contain nucleic acid bound to simple proteins in such a way that it readily forms a salt or salt-like combination with basic dyes, and so the sperm heads appear intensely stained by alum-hematoxylin, etc. Ordinary chromatin threads of nuclei appear to contain somewhat more firmly bound protein in their nucleoprotein molecules, and hence stain less intensely than do the spermatozoa heads, except when in karyokinesis, when the chromatin nucleoprotein seems to approach that of the spermatozoa in avidity for basic dyes. We also have nucleoproteins with the nucleic acid so thoroughly saturated by protein that they do not stain at all by basic dyes, and these seem to exist principally in the cytoplasm, and also to form the ground-substance of the nuclei, occupying the spaces between the chromatin particles (this achromatic substance of the nuclei is called *linin* or *plastin* by some cytologists). Besides the chromatin and the nucleoli, there is a peculiar chromatophile substance, suspended in the finer part of the nuclear structure in the same manner as the chromatin itself is in the coarser portions; this was called *lanthanin* by Heidenhain,[34] and is probably similar to the substances also described as *parachromatin* and *paralinin*. Undoubtedly the other forms of proteins found in the cell, such as globulin, albumin, and nucleoalbumin, exist both in the nucleoplasm and in the cytoplasm, the essential difference being that the proportion of nucleoprotein is much greater in the nucleus. As nucleoproteins are little affected by peptic digestion,

[32] Earlier literature by Albrecht, "Pathologie der Zelle," Lubarsch-Ostertag, Ergeb. der. allg. Pathol., 1899 (6), 1900; see also Kossel, Münch. med. Woch., 1911 (58), 65.

[33] Herwerden (Arch. Zellforsch., 1913 (19), 431) found that the basophilic granules are disintegrated specifically by nuclease, supporting the view that they are nucleic acid compounds.

[34] Festschr. f. Kölliker, 1892, p. 128.

it is possible to isolate nuclear elements, especially the chromatin, for analytic purposes, and it has been demonstrated by this means also that nuclein is the chief constituent of the staining elements. The distribution in the nucleus of the other primary constituents of the cytoplasm, such as lecithin, cholesterol, and inorganic salts has not yet been worked out, except that Macallum[35] found that nuclei contain no chloride, as indicated by their not staining with silver nitrate, and also no potassium,[36] but the chromatin contains firmly bound iron.

Nucleoli, which not all varieties of nuclei possess, differ from the other nuclear structures in having an affinity for acid rather than for basic dyes,[37] at least in fixed tissues. Their chemical composition has not been ascertained. Zacharias considers the nucleoli as composed of nuclein well saturated with protein, because of its staining reactions and its relative insolubility in alkalies, and classes it with plastin or linin, which forms the achromatic part of the nucleus and is also present in the cytoplasm. Macallum[38] found that they reacted for organic phosphorus microchemically, but less strongly than did chromatin fibers.

The nuclear membrane is an uncertain structure, at times dense and staining as if formed of a layer of chromatin, in other cells staining like the cytoplasm with which it seems to be continuous, in most cells disappearing during karyokinesis, and in some protozoa being entirely absent. Naturally the composition of the nuclear membrane is unknown, but it is probable that it acts as a diffusion membrane of partially semipermeable character, maintaining different conditions in nucleus and cytoplasm.

Functionally the nucleus is the essential element of the cell; an isolated nucleus with but a minimum of cytoplasm may be able to develop new cytoplasm, but isolated cytoplasm soon disintegrates, although it may manifest life for some time by movement and chemical activities. It has been frequently suggested that the nucleus controls oxidative processes, and there is some microchemical evidence for this.[39] Lynch[40] calls attention to the improbability that the part of the cell most removed from the oxygen should be the organ of oxidation, and finds evidence that the function of the nucleus is that of organic synthesis. An enucleated cell may move, respire, digest, respond to stimuli and exhibit any activity which is dependent solely upon catabolic or destructive processes of protoplasm. The group of phenomena which it never shows are those of growth, regeneration and division, *i. e.*, those depending on synthetic activities.

It should be mentioned that certain cells, such as bacteria and algæ, seem to have no true nuclei, but Macallum[41] found that the forms he examined gave reactions for phosphorus and iron in a similar way to the nucleoproteins of a nucleus, suggesting that in such cells the nuclear elements are diffused through the cell rather than differentiated. To quote Wilson: "The term 'nucleus' and 'cell body'

[35] Proceedings of the Royal Society, 1905 (76), 217.
[36] Jour. of Physiol., 1905 (32), 95.
[37] Nucleoli of nerve-cells are an exception, being basophilic.
[38] Proc. of the Royal Society, 1898 (63), 467.
[39] See Osterhaut, Science, 1917 (46), 367.
[40] Amer. Jour. Physiol., 1919 (48), 258.
[41] "Studies from the University of Toronto," 1900.

should probably be regarded as only topographical expressions, denoting two differentiated areas in a common structural basis."

Because of the relative acidity of the nuclei they are electrically negative to the cytoplasm, particularly when in karyokinesis, and the chromatic elements of the nucleus can be shown to carry a negative electric charge.[42] Sperm-heads in isotonic cane-sugar solution move rapidly—2000 microns a minute—toward the anode, when a current is passed through the solution; and leucocytes also go toward the anode under the same conditions, the rate depending upon the proportion of nucleoplasm and cytoplasm, large leucocytes sometimes even going slowly toward the cathode. The Sertoli cells of the testicle, which have a round mass of cytoplasm with a number of miniature spermatozoa heads at one side, orient themselves in the current so that the side or end containing the spermatozoa drags the mass of cytoplasm toward the positive pole.

THE CYTOPLASM

The cytoplasm, as before mentioned, contains all the primary cellular constituents, and also such secondary constituents as the particular cell possesses. Nucleoproteins are undoubtedly present in unknown proportions, but with the nucleic acid well saturated by proteins, and perhaps also to a large extent combined with carbohydrates to form the glyconucleoproteins. Sometimes the nucleoproteins of the cytoplasm may be partly of the unsaturated class, and show an affinity for basic stains, as in the case of the Nissl bodies of the nerve-cells, the basophilic granules of mast cells,[33] and perhaps also the cytoplasm of plasma cells. The great question concerning the cytoplasm is its structure—whether homogeneous, alveolar, areolar, fibrillar, foam-like, or granular. On a previous page have been mentioned the experiments of Hardy, which show that homogeneous solutions of protein, when fixed by the same reagents as are used in the customary fixation of histological materials, may show quite the same microscopical structures as are shown by the cytoplasm of cells. Network, foam, and alveolar structures are produced in albumin and gelatin solutions when they are hardened by bichloride of mercury, osmic acid, formalin, etc., and the same characteristic differences that are produced in cells by these different reagents are likewise produced in the hardened protein solution. Protein structures hardened under strain form radiating structures resembling centrosomes and the radiating threads seen in cells. If elder pith is saturated with protein solutions and then hardened, sectioned, and stained by the usual methods, appearances resembling closely the structure of a hardened cell may be found in the spaces of the

[42] Pentamalli, Arch. Entwick. u. Org., 1912 (34), 444; McClendon, Proc. Soc. Exp. Biol. and Med., 1910 (7), 111; Hardy, Jour. Physiol., 1913 (47), 108.

pith—even a central, nucleus-like mass may be suspended in a network of anastomosing threads. These and many other experiments indicate that much of the work done on cell structure by means of studies of hardened cells cannot be considered of value in deciding the structure of living cells; but, nevertheless, the fact remains that many cells that can be observed while alive and uninjured under the microscope are seen to have a definite structure in the cytoplasm, *e. g.*, sea-urchin eggs, which show a characteristic alveolar structure.

A compromise view of the structure of protoplasm (and cytoplasm in particular) which takes account of what appear to be facts brought out on both sides of the question, is that while in some cells definite structural arrangements of the cytoplasm exist, in most cells the proteins are chiefly in a homogeneous solution; most of the structures seen in fixed cells, except the mitochondria, chromatin threads, nuclear membrane, nucleoli, and centrosomes, are produced by the coagulation of the proteins, and are not present during life. When a framework does exist, it is a fair inference, by analogy with the cell membrane and the stroma of the red corpuscles, that the cell lipoids are largely responsible for its formation, and that they form a prominent part of its composition. This question of the presence or absence of structure in the cytoplasm is of more importance than as a mere morphological problem, for if the cytoplasm is subdivided into innumerable little chambers, each surrounded by a membrane, it is probable that processes of diffusion and conditions of osmotic pressure will be very different from what they would be if the cytoplasm were a simple homogeneous colloid solution, like a lump of semisolid gelatin or agar. In such colloidal masses diffusion and osmosis go on almost as if there were no colloids in the solvent at all, whereas most membrane structures that are found in living tissues seem to have a decidedly semipermeable character.

From what we know at the present time of intracellular physics and chemistry there is no necessity for assuming that semipermeable septa exist within the cell. All the intracellular processes with which we are familiar *could* go on without such structures. It is not necessary to assume a compartment structure to explain the possibility of different chemical reactions going on in different parts of the cell at the same time, for most of the cell reactions seem to depend on enzymes, which we know are not readily diffusible in solutions of colloids, and, therefore, might remain fixed without requiring any enclosing walls or retaining framework. Certainly, many cells are free from structural cytoplasm, for we see particles of solid matter moving about within them quite freely. In some cells the nuclei migrate about in the cell, as also do digestive and excretory vacuoles, which motion would seem to be rather destructive if the protoplasm had a structure at all permanent.

When a portion of the cytoplasm is cut free from the body of certain cells it at once forms a round drop, just as any insoluble fluid would do in another of different surface tension, and not at all as if it were bound into a fixed structure by a framework.   Other cells, however, retain their form under the same conditions.   The structure of even so evidently complicated a cytoplasm as that of striated muscle fibers is in doubt; a classical observation on this point is the passage of a minute worm through the substance of a muscle-cell, its progress being as unimpeded as if there were no such things as disks, bands, rods, and striæ in the cell.   Many features of ameboid movement also seem to indicate that the cytoplasm follows much the same laws as a drop of fluid in a heterogeneous medium, for we can make a drop of mercury or of chloroform in water, or of oil in weak alcohol, react to various stimuli in much the same way that an ameba would.   If we look upon the cytoplasm as a drop of emulsion colloid, the surfaces of the particles in the emulsion furnish of themselves adequate explanation of many of the phenomena of isolation of chemical reactions, etc., without lacking in harmony with the evidences of structural homogeneity.   This hypothesis fits all sides of the problem and has many supporters at the present time.[43]

The question of structure in the nucleus is quite a different matter, in so far as the chromatin threads and the nucleolus are concerned.   In ameboid movement the nucleus seems to play a passive rôle and to be dragged about by the cytoplasm, indicating quite a high degree of rigidity.   It is probable, however, that the achromatic portion between the chromatin threads and granules has much the same structure or lack of structure as the cytoplasm.

The various secretory granules, fat-droplets, pigment-granules, glycogen granules, keratin, etc., that may lie in the cytoplasm, are inconstant constituents, varying with different cells, and under varying conditions in the same cells, and lie beyond the scope of our discussion of the general composition of the cell.   According to Ruzicka[44] there is contained in all cells, both in nucleus and cytoplasm, an insoluble substance which corresponds structurally to the "plastin" of the cytologists, and chemically is related to the reticulins and other albuminoids; this he looks upon as the ground substance of the cells, corresponding to the albuminoid ground substance or stroma of organized tissues.

Certain of the granulations observed in the cytoplasm of cells seem to be definite, constant structures of the living protoplasm, and these are now called *mitochondria*, which term includes many forms of granules described under various names.[45]   Their solubility and staining reactions suggest that they contain phospholipins, perhaps associated with proteins.   Their functional importance is indicated by the fact that usually their number varies directly with the metabolic activity of the cells, and they may be related to histogenesis.

Other histological cellular structures also permit of more or less satisfactory identification by microchemical methods, and Unna[46] especially has contributed to this field.   By staining sections with dyes of varying reaction, after extracting the sections with various solvents, he has obtained evidence of the chemical nature

[43] An excellent discussion of this question is given by Alsberg, Science, 1911 (34), 97.
[44] Arch. f. Zellforsch., 1908 (1), 587.
[45] See review by Cowdry, Amer. Jour. Anat., 1916 (19), 423; Carnegie Inst. Publ., No. 25, 1918.
[46] See review by Gans, Deut. med.Woch., 1913 (39), 1944.

of some of the cell structures, although it is by no means certain that the conclusions drawn will all be verified. In the nucleolus he finds a substance resembling globulin, the granuloplasm of the cell body he regards as an albumose, the spongioplasm as histone, mast cell granules as mucin or mucoid substances. Nissl bodies he holds to be albumose, altho others have believed them to be nucleins.[47]

THE CELL-WALL[48]

The cell membrane in most animal cells is inconspicuous structurally, but in discussing osmosis it was shown that it is of the greatest biological importance. There is no direct chemical or microscopical evidence at hand showing the composition of the animal cell membrane, but by observations on its behavior when the cells are in solutions of different sorts, facts have been collected indicating that phospholipins and cholesterol, and probably allied fat-like bodies, are prominent constituents. The substances that diffuse through most cell walls are just the substances that are soluble in or dissolve these lipoids, e. g., alcohol, chloroform, ether, etc., and it is probable that the anesthetic effects of many of these substances depend in some way on their fat-dissolving power and the large proportion of lipoids in nerve-cells. These observations were made first by Overton[49] and Meyer,[50] and led to the now prominent but disputed hypothesis that the permeability of cells is determined by the lipoids. Of particular interest for our purpose are Overton's observations on the effects of dyes on living cells. The best known vital stains (i. e., stains that will enter the living cell without requiring or causing injury to it) are neutral red, methylene blue, toluidin blue, thionin, and safranin. If uninjured cells, e. g., frog eggs, are placed in watery solutions of these dyes they soon become filled with the coloring-matter, which seems to penetrate the cell menbrane quite uniformly at all points; if the dyed eggs are then placed in clear water, the stain diffuses out again, showing it to be simply absorbed, rather than chemically combined. In contrast to these stains the sulphonic acid dyes, such as indigo carmine and water-soluble indulin, nigrosin, and anilin blue, do not penetrate the living cell at all. Overton tested the solubility of dyes which are not vital stains and found them all insoluble in oils, fats, and fatty acids; but the dyes staining living cells were readily soluble in lecithin, cholesterol, "protagon," and cerebrin, the so-called cell lipoids. Furthermore, if crumbs of lecithin, "protagon," or cerebrin were placed in very dilute watery solutions of these dyes, they were found to absorb from the water the vital stains, but not the others, which indicates that stains that penetrate living cells are more soluble in lipoids than they are in water.

[47] See Unna, Berl. klin. Woch., 1914 (51), 444; Mühlmann, Arch. mikr. Anat., 1914 (85),361.
[48] See Zangger, "Ueber Membranen und Membranenfunktionen," Ergebnisse d. Physiol., 1908 (7), 99; also R. S. Lillie, "The Rôle of Membranes in Cell Processes," Popular ScienceMonthly, Feb., 1913.
[49] Jahrb. f. wissentschaftl. Botanik, 1900 (34), 669.
[50] Arch. f. exp. Path. u. Pharm., 1899 (42), 109.

Many exceptions to this rule of the fat-solubility of dyes which can penetrate living cells have been found, especially by Ruhland,[51] and the universal applicability of the Overton-Meyer hypothesis has been questioned. It is at once evident that the common foodstuffs which enter the cell, such as water, sugar, amino-acids, and salts are not lipoid-soluble, hence it has been suggested that the cell membranes must have a "mosaic" structure, some of the blocks being lipoids or lipoid compounds, and others proteins without lipoids. (Robertson[52] suggests that there is a superficial film of concentrated protein about the cells, underlaid by a discontinuous lipoid layer.) There is, furthermore, evidence that the entire cell substance has a profound effect upon diffusion within the cell, so that it is at present impossible to say whether the osmotic phenomena of cells depend upon a cell membrane or upon the entire cell substance.[53] It may be that there are membranes or surfaces within the cell, as postulated in the foam structure hypothesis of protoplasm, or that a homogeneous protoplasm develops surfaces where in contact with substances entering from the outside.

Many facts indicate that either the delicate external membrane of animal cells or the entire cytoplasm has the features of a semipermeable membrane, to the extent of permitting certain substances to diffuse through and not others. Had they the property of some of the artificial semipermeable membranes, of letting water pass through but holding back almost absolutely all crystalloids, the result would be the development of an enormous disproportion in the pressure between the inside and the outside of the cell. Furthermore, the exchange of nutritive material and excretion products between the blood and the cells would be impossible. But permitting some substances to pass into the cell results in their accumulation within the cell, until they are in sufficient concentration to neutralize the osmotic pressure exerted on the outside of the cell. As evidence of this elective permeability we have the fact that the proportion of certain salts within the cell is quite different from what it is in the fluids bathing them; e. g., animal cells generally contain more potassium and less sodium than the fluids surrounding them. The inorganic constituents of red cells are different from those of the plasma, the corpuscles not containing any calcium at all, while the magnesium seems to enter them freely; in other words, the red corpuscle seems to be impermeable to calcium and permeable to magnesium. If the salts in a corpuscle are in smaller proportions than in the surrounding fluid, it indicates that the cell membrane is not freely permeable for them; if in greater proportion, that some constituent of the cell is holding them in combination, possibly as ion-protein compounds. Probably

[51] Jahrb. f. Wissenschaft. Botanik, 1912 (51), 376.
[52] Jour. Biol. Chem., 1908 (4), 1.
[53] See Kite, Amer. Jour. Physiol., 1915 (37), 282; Chambers, *ibid.*, 1917 (43), 1.

inorganic salts are present in the cell by virtue of both physical and chemical influences, some simply diffusing in and out, others combining with the proteins and being held chemically.

Beehhold summarizes his conception of cell walls as follows:

"Every cell at its surface possesses a membrane which is dependent upon the composition of the interior of the cell. This membrane may be visible and may have been formed through the gelatinization of the cell protoplasm at the periphery. It may, on the other hand, be so thin as to be invisible, being formed by the concentration and spreading out of such albuminous and fatty colloids as diminish the surface tension of the cell content at the interface. The cell membranes, developing as a result of the gelatinization of cell protoplasm, are at first, in youth, expansile and elastic; with increasing age these membrane colloids, depending upon their environment and upon chemical influences, or as a result of mere colloid aging phenomena, become poor in water and lose their elasticity."

The intercellular substance varies greatly in different tissues. In the case of the supportive tissues it is the important element, and the cells seem to exist chiefly for the purpose of forming and keeping it in repair as it is worn out. In the epithelial and secreting tissues, however, the intercellular substance is reduced to a minimum, except in so far as a cement substance is required, and the cells generally lie in almost immediate apposition. It is probable that there is a greater or less amount of cement substance, even between the most closely applied cells, and this substance seems to be related to mucin. It can generally be brought out by staining with silver nitrate, and Macallum[54] points out that this reaction is merely a micro-chemical test for chlorides, and indicates that the cement substance contains them in larger proportion than does the cytoplasm.

[54] Proceedings of the Royal Society, 1905 (76), 217.

CHAPTER II

ENZYMES

EVERY cell is constantly accomplishing an enormous number of chemical reactions of varied natures, at one and the same time; how many we do not know, but the score or more that we do know to be constantly going on in the liver cell, for example, are probably but a part of the whole. Furthermore, reactions take place between substances that show no inclination to affect each other outside the body, and proceed in directions that we find it difficult to make them take in the laboratory. Proteins are being continually broken down into urea, carbon dioxide, and water; yet to split proteins even as far as the amino-acid stage requires prolonged action of concentrated acids or alkalies, or super-heated steam under great pressure. But all the time in the cell innumerable equally difficult changes are going on at once, within its tiny mass, always keeping the resulting heat within a fraction of a degree of constant, and the resulting products within narrow limits of concentration. We have already indicated the means used to keep the concentration of the cell products within safe limits; namely, the processes of diffusion and osmosis and their modification by the cell structure. The forces that bring about the chemical reactions reside, we say, in enzymes, although in so doing we only shift the attribute formerly conceded to the cell, to certain constituents of the cell whose nature and manner of action are equally unknown. When the only enzymes that were known were limited to those secreted from the cell, and found free in fluids, such as pepsin and trypsin, the chemical changes that went on in the cell were ascribed to its "vital activity." Buchner, by devising a method to crush yeast cells, and finding the expressed cell contents able to produce the same changes in carbohydrates that the cells themselves did, proved the existence within living cells of enzymes similar to those excreted by certain cells, and substantiated the belief of their existence that had become general before it was thus finally corroborated. Growing out from this and subsequent experiments has come a larger and larger amount of evidence that many of the chemical activities of the cells are due to the enzymes they contain, until now the point is reached where one may rightfully ask if cell life is not entirely a matter of enzyme activity. There are certain facts, however, which seem to indicate that there are some essential differences between cells and

48

enzymes. One of the most important of these is the difference in the susceptibility to poisons of enzymes and cells.[1] Strengths of certain antiseptics that will either destroy or inhibit the action of living cells, such as alcohol, ether, salicylic acid, thymol, chloroform and toluene, will harm free enzymes in solution little or not at all. This fact has been of great assistance in distinguishing between the action of enzymes and of possible contaminating bacteria in experimental work. Although this difference between enzymes and cells is characteristic, it does not finally decide that the cell actions are not enzyme actions, for it may well be that the poisons act chiefly by altering the physical conditions of the cell so that diffusion is interfered with, thus seriously interfering with the exchange of cleavage products between different parts of the cell, and checking intracellular enzyme action, which we shall see later requires free diffusion of the products for its continuance. At the very least, however, we may look upon the intracellular enzymes as the most important known agents of cell metabolism, and consequently of all life manifestations, and the changes they undergo or produce in pathological conditions must be fully as fundamentally important as is their relation to physiological processes. It therefore becomes necessary for us to consider carefully—

THE NATURE OF ENZYMES AND THEIR ACTIONS

Since up to the present time no ferment has been isolated in an absolutely pure condition we are entirely unfamiliar with their chemical characters, and consequently are obliged to recognize them solely by their action. As far as we know, true enzymes never occur except as the result of cell life—they are produced within the cell, and increased in amount by each new cell that is formed, and, furthermore, they are present in every living cell without exception. As the same facts are equally true of the proteins it is natural to associate the enzymes with proteins, and so explain the importance of the proteins for cell life.[3] If enzymes are obtained in any of the usual ways from animal cells or secretions they are always found to give the reactions for proteins, even if repurified many times. But it is well known that whenever proteins are precipitated the other substances in the solution tend to be dragged down by the colloids, and it is possible that the enzymes are merely associated with the proteins in this way. Furthermore, enzymes are known to become so closely attached to stringy protein masses, such as fibrin and silk, that they cannot be removed by washing. Some have claimed that they have secured active preparations of pepsin and invertase that did not give protein reactions and contained very little or no ash or carbohydrate; but it has so far been impossible to secure trypsin free from protein, and diastase seems to be certainly of protein nature. Davis and Merker[4] find that the more pepsin is purified the more

[1] See discussion by Vernon, Ergebnisse d. Physiol., 1910 (9), 234.

[2] It would not be profitable to discuss fully all the various theories and hypotheses that have been advanced, but the reader is referred to the following chief compilations of the entire subject: Oppenheimer, "Die Fermente und ihre Wirkungen," Leipzig; Bayliss, "The Nature of Enzyme Action," Monographs on Biochemistry, London; Stern, "Physico-chemical Basis of Ferment Action," in Oppenheimer's "Handbuch d. Biochemie," Vol. 4, pt. 2; Samueley, "Animal Ferments," ibid, Vol. I; A. E. Taylor, "On Fermentation," Univ. of California Publications; Euler, "General Chemistry of the Enzymes," translated by T. H. Pope, New York, 1912.

[3] Another important point is that the closest imitation of enzymes, Bredig's 'inorganic ferments," seem to owe their action to their colloidal nature.

[4] Jour. Amer. Chem. Soc., 1919 (41), 221.

it approaches the character of a protein, possibly a glycoprotein, with increasing proteolytic activity.[5] Analyses of enzymes purified as completely as possible do not have great worth, for the "purified" enzymes are probably far from pure; however, it is of some importance that they vary greatly in the proportions of carbon, hydrogen, and nitrogen which they contain, indicating that possibly different enzymes may be of very different nature. The enzymes have been found to possess definite electrical charges; in neutral solutions trypsin is negative or amphoteric, pepsin and invertase negative (Michaelis).[6] Macallum has shown microchemically that phosphorus is closely associated with the formation of zymogen granules in cells, which seem to be started in the nucleus; and there are many other observations suggesting that certain ferments are closely related to the nucleo-proteins. This is particularly true of the oxidases, which seem also to contain iron and manganese. A final point of importance in support of the protein nature of enzymes is that pepsin destroys trypsin and diastase, while trypsin destroys pepsin.[7]

So uncertain, however, is our information concerning the chemical nature of the enzymes, that it has become possible for an hypothesis to be developed urging that enzymes are immaterial, that the actions we consider as characterizing enzymes are the result of physical forces which may reside in many substances, and perhaps even free from visible matter, but the weight of evidence at present available is entirely in favor of the view that enzymes are specific colloidal substances, although perhaps of widely differing chemical nature. A valuable piece of evidence of the material existence of enzymes is their specific nature, lipase affecting only fats, and trypsin only proteins, indicating chemical individuality. They are true secretions, formed within the cell by recognizable steps; and, furthermore, when injected into the body of an animal, they give rise to the formation of specific immune bodies that antagonize their action. Emil Fischer's work with the sugar-splitting enzymes, moreover, indicates that they owe their action to their stereochemical configuration. He prepared two sets of sugar derivatives which differed from each other solely in the arrangement of their atoms in space (*i. e.*, isomers) and found that one specific enzyme would split members of only one of the varieties, while another enzyme would act only on the variety with the opposite isomeric form. These experiments make it very probable that there must be a certain relation of geometrical structure between an enzyme and the substances it acts upon, and leaves little question of its material nature.

Bredig has found that *colloidal solutions of metals* have many of the properties of true enzymes, accomplishing many of the decompositions produced by enzymes, being affected by temperatures of nearly the same degree, and even being "poisoned" by substances that destroy or check enzymes.[8] The only possible explanation of these observations seems to be that the enzyme effects are brought about by *surface phenomena.* A colloidal solution of platinum, as far as is known, differs from a piece of metallic platinum solely in the enormously great amount of surface it offers in proportion to its weight, and it is well known that surfaces may affect chemical action. Hence we have the possibility that some enzyme actions, at least, may depend upon the existence of a very large surface, and since by no means all colloids are enzymes, that this surface must bear a certain relation in form to the surface of the body that is to be acted upon.

The Principles of Enzyme Action

The effects produced by enzymes, which at one time were considered quite unique and remarkable, have now been made comparatively plain, chiefly through the observations of Ostwald on related

---

[5] Bokorny (Biochem. Zeit., 1919 (94), 69) finds that the amount of formaldehyde fixed by emulsin supports the hypothesis that this enzyme is a protein.

[6] Biochem. Zeit., 1909 (16), 81 and 486; (17), 231.

[7] Falk has obtained evidence that ester-splitting enzymes may be proteins owing their activity to the presence in the molecule of active groupings, perhaps of enol-lactim structure, $-C(OH) = N-$. By treating pure proteins with alkali, which favors the formation of enol-lactim groupings, the proteins were made to acquire esterase properties. (See Science, 1918 (47), 423.)

[8] See also Fischer and Hooker, J. Lab. Clin. Med., 1918 (3), 373.

chemical reactions; and by the investigations of Croft Hill, Kastle and Loevenhart, and others, on enzymes, which show that enzyme action is in no way different from chemical action observed independent of enzymes. The fundamental consideration is that chemical reactions are *reversible*, that is, that their tendency is to *establish an equilibrium*, and that the change may be from either side of the equation.[9] The action of enzymes is similar to that of all catalytic agents, that is, they *increase the speed of reaction*. In the case of such a reaction as that of NaOH and HCl, the reaction is so rapid that the effect of catalyzers could hardly be noticed; but with many other substances the reaction is very slow, and without the presence of catalyzers it would go on almost or quite imperceptibly. For example, ethyl butyrate saponifies on the addition of water according to the following equation:

$$C_2H_5 - O - OC - C_3H_7 + H_2O \leftrightarrows C_2H_5OH + HOOC - C_3H_7.$$

On the other hand, if ethyl alcohol and butyric acid, the products of this reaction, are placed together, they will combine to form ethyl butyrate; in other words, the reaction is reversible, as indicated by the arrows in the equation. In any event, however, the reaction is not complete, but continues only until there exists a certain definite proportion of ethyl alcohol, butyric acid, ethyl butyrate, and water, when the change will stop, *i. e., equilibrium is established.* The time that would be required for this reaction to occur at room temperature would be extremely long, the change being hardly noticeable, but in the presence of a catalytic agent the reaction goes on much more rapidly. Catalytic agents, therefore, merely hasten reactions which would go on without them, and they do not initiate or change the nature of chemical reactions at all. When equilibrium is established, the reaction stops and the enzyme has nothing more to do. Furthermore, enzymes will hasten synthesis just as well as they hasten catalysis. Croft Hill first showed that maltase would synthesize glucose into maltose; Kastle and Loevenhart soon after established the synthesis of ethyl butyrate under the influence of lipase. Taylor[10] first synthesized one of the normal body fats, triolein, by the action of lipase (from the castor-oil bean) upon oleic acid and glycerol. Successful synthesis of fats by pancreatic lipase is described by Lombroso.[11] It may seem improbable at first sight that the synthesis of proteins can be accomplished by enzymes, as is the relatively very simple synthesis of carbohydrates and fats, but the improbability disappears when we recall that the products of protein cleavage are reconverted into body proteins after absorption from the intestines. Proteins manifestly are synthesized and we have not a little reason to believe

[9] See Taylor, Arch. Int. Med., 1908 (2), 148.
[10] Univ. of California Publications (Pathology), 1904 (1), 33.
[11] Arch. di farmacol., 1912 (14), 429.

that this is accomplished by enzymes, presumably by a reversal of their action in the establishment of equilibrium. Abderhalden[12] has obtained some evidence of protein formation in mixtures of amino acids derived from autolyzing tissue when acted upon by ferment-containing extracts of the same tissue. Taylor[13] was able to synthesize protamin, one of the simplest proteins, by the action of trypsin upon its cleavage products, and it has been found that the addition of proteolytic enzymes to solutions of pure albumose leads to the formation of a jelly-like, insoluble protein substance, "plastein," which seems to be the effect of a reversed action on the part of the enzymes.[14] Another well known synthetic action that seems to be due to reversible ferment action is the formation of hippuric acid from benzoic acid and glycine in the kidney; the formation of glucose into glycogen and its reformation are also probably both accomplished by one and the same enzyme acting reversibly. Other reversible reactions less closely related to animal cells have also been described.

The reversible nature of enzyme action explains many problems of metabolism, and makes the whole field much clearer. The following consideration of the newer understanding of fat metabolism on this basis may explain the manner in which chemical changes are believed to occur in the cells and fluids of the body:[15]

In the intestines fat is split by lipase into a mixture of fat, fatty acid, and glycerol; but as the fatty acid and glycerol are diffusible, while the fat is not, they are separated from the fat by absorption into the wall of the intestine. Hence an equilibrium is not reached in the intestine, so the splitting continues until practically all the fat has been decomposed and the products absorbed. When this mixture of fatty acid and glycerol first enters the epithelial cells lining the intestines there is no equilibrium, for there is no fat absorbed with them as such. Therefore the lipase, which Kastle and Loevenhart showed was present in these cells, sets about to establish equilibrium by combining them. As a result we have in the cell a mixture of fat, fatty acid, and glycerol, which will attain equilibrium only when new additions of the two last substances cease to enter the cell. Now another factor also appears, for on the other side of the cell is the tissue fluid, containing relatively little fatty acid and glycerol. Into this the diffusible contents of the cell will tend to pass to establish an osmotic equilibrium, which is quite independent of the chemical equilibrium. This abstraction of part of the cell contents tends to again overthrow chemical equilibrium, there now being an excess of fat in the cell. Of course, the lipase will, under this condition, exhibit the reverse action and split the fat it has just built into fatty acid and glycerol. It is evident that these processes are all going on together, and that, as the composition of the contents of the intestines and of the blood-vessels varies, the direction of the enzyme action will also vary. In the blood-serum, and also in the lymphatic fluid, there is also lipase, which will unite part of the fatty acid and glycerol,

[12] Fermentforschung, 1914 (1), 47.
[13] Jour. Biol. Chem., 1909 (5), 381.
[14] See Micheli, Arch. ital. biol., 1906 (46), 185; Levene and Van Slyke, Biochem Zeit, 1908 (13), 458; Taylor, Jour. Biol Chem., 1909 (5), 399; Gay and Robertson, ibid. 1912 (12), 233; Abderhalden, Fermentforsch., 1914 (1), 47; v. Knafll-Lenz and Pick, Arch. exp. Path., 1913 (71), 296, 407.
[15] See Loevenhart, Amer. Jour. of Physiol., 1902 (6), 331; Wells, Journal Amer. Med. Assoc., 1902 (38), 220. The discrepancies between the action of lipase in the tissues and in vitro are well explained by Taylor, Jour. Biol. Chem., 1906 (2), 103.

and by removing them from the fluid about the cells favor osmotic diffusion from the intestinal epithelium, thus facilitating absorption.

Quite similar must be the process that takes place in the tissue cells throughout the body. In the blood-serum bathing the cells is a mixture of fat and its constituents, probably nearly in equilibrium, since lipase accompanies them. If the diffusible substances enter a cell containing lipase, *e. g.*, a liver cell, the process of building and splitting will be quite the same as in the intestinal epithelium. The only difference is that here the fatty acid may be removed from the cell by being utilized by oxidation or some other chemical transformation.[16]

To summarize, it may be stated that throughout the body there is constantly taking place both splitting and building of fat. Fat enters the cells, leaves them, and is utilized only in the form of its acid and alcohol, never as the fat itself. Fat constitutes a resting stage in its own metabolism.

If proteolytic enzymes also act reversibly, then the phenomena of protein metabolism are similarly explained, for there is no doubt that every cell and body fluid contains proteolytic enzymes.

All metabolism, then, may be considered as a *continuous attempt at establishment of equilibrium by enzymes, perpetuated by prevention of attainment of actual equilibrium through destruction of some of the participating substances by oxidation or other chemical processes, or by removal from the cell or entrance into it of materials which overbalance one side of the equation.*

In just what manner the enzymes accomplish their catalytic effect is yet unknown.[17] A favorite idea is that they form loose compounds with the substance to be split and with water; the resulting compound being unstable and breaking down, the water remains attached to the components of the substance.

Enzymes do not act catalytically on all substances by any means, but show a decidedly specific nature. They affect only organic substances, and the actions are limited to two processes—hydrolysis and oxidation, or the reverse processes of dehydration and reduction.[18] The most essential difference between the enzymes and the chemicals that can accomplish hydrolysis or oxidation is this: the ordinary chemical reagents produce their effects on many sorts of substances, whereas the enzymes are specific; thus hydrochloric acid will hydrolyze starch or protein with equal facility, but pepsin will not affect starch at all.

The very specific nature of the enzymes, their activation by other body products, the fact that they seem to be bound to the substance

[16] Bradley (Jour Biol. Chem., 1910 (8), 251; 1913 (13), 407–439) calls attention to the great concentration necessary for fat synthesis by lipase *in vitro*, and the lack of correspondence between the amount of fat and of lipase in various tissues, questioning the importance of lipase for fat synthesis in the living tissues as well as the significance of reversed enzyme reaction for biological processes in general.

[17] See Euler, "Chemical Dynamics of Enzyme Reactions," Ergebnisse d. Physiol. 1910 (9), 241.

[18] Alcoholic fermentation may be an exception, the change being $C_6H_{12}O_6 = 2C_2H_5OH + 2CO_2$, but it is very possibly an intramolecular oxidation.

upon which they act, that they are susceptible to heat, and that they produce immune bodies when injected into experimental animals, all suggest the probability of a *relationship between enzymes and toxins.* This matter will be discussed more fully in considering the chemistry of immunity against enzymes.

General Properties of Enzymes.—Other properties of enzymes may be briefly mentioned. The speed of reaction they produce increases with the amount of enzymes present. Very dilute acids favor the action of nearly all ferments, and alkalies are unfavorable for all but trypsin, ptyalin, and a few others. Weak salt solutions also are more favorable than distilled water. (These facts suggest strongly the possibility that *ions* play an important rôle in the process.) Water and dilute glycerol dissolve enzymes, which form always colloidal solutions that are very slightly dialyzable; and they may be precipitated from solution by alcohol, and redissolved again with but slight impairment of strength. Filtration through porcelain filters is not complete, from 10 to 25 per cent. of most enzymes being lost in each filtration and enzymes are subject to great absorption by surfaces, *e. g.*, charcoal, kaolin. [9] As before mentioned, many chemicals poisonous to bacteria have little influence on most enzymes, but nearly all substances when concentrated are injurious or destructive, and some enzymes are known that are more susceptible to antiseptics than are the cells that contain them. Formaldehyde is very destructive to most enzymes, even when dilute. The effect of protein-coagulating antiseptics upon enzymes is, of course, greatly modified by the amount of protein substances mingled with the enzymes; and the effects of heat and other injurious influences are greatly decreased by the presence of proteins and other impurities.

All enzymes are most active between 35° and 45° C., and it is interesting to note that Kobert found this equally true for enzymes derived from cold-blooded animals.[20] Although enzymes can stand temperatures of 100° C. or more when dry, in water they are generally destroyed somewhat below 70° C. Low temperature, even − 190° C. (liquid air), does not destroy them. The loss of power through heating occurs gradually, and there is no sharp line at which their action disappears. Sunlight is harmful to enzymes in solution, but only in the presence of oxygen; this effect is augmented by the presence of fluorescent substances. Nascent oxygen is destructive to enzymes.[21] Radium and *x*-rays seem to have a deleterious effect upon most enzymes, and retard their rate of action; but apparently, autolytic enzymes (Neuberg[22]) and tyrosinase (Willcock[23]) are not injured by these agencies.[24] Ultra violet rays are also injurious to enzymes,[25] and they can be destroyed by violent shaking (Shaklee and Meltzer.[26]). Labile as enzymes are, their persistence when dry is remarkable; Kobert found active trypsin in the bodies of spiders that had been in the Nuremberg Museum for 150 years, and Sehrt[27] found that the muscle tissue of mummies contained active glycolytic ferment.

All enzymes as ordinarily prepared have the property of decomposing hydrogen peroxide, a property possessed by substances of varied nature; this effect is prevented by CNH, which does not prevent other enzyme manifestations, indicating that this property is due to an associated enzyme, *catalase.*

The retardation of enzyme action by accumulation of the products of their

[19] See Hedin, Ergebnisse d. Physiol., 1910 (9), 433.

[20] However, Hosaka (Mitt. med. Gesell. Tokio, 1917 (31), 1) states that frog pancreatic diastase is most active between 5° and 37°, whereas for guinea pig pancreatic diastase the optimum temperature is 27°–55°. Activity begins to be inhibited at 45° and 65° respectively.

[21] See Burge, Amer. Jour. Physiol., 1914 (34), 140.

[22] Berl. klin. Woch., 1904 (41), 1081.

[23] Jour. of Physiol., 1906 (34), 207.

[24] Gudzent (Zeit. Strahlenther., 1914 (4), 666) denies that radium acts on enzymes.

[25] Agulhon, Ann. Inst. Pasteur, 1912 (26), 38; Burge *et al.*, Amer. Jour. Physiol., 1916 (40), 426.

[26] Amer. Jour. Physiol., 1909 (25), 81.

[27] Berl. klin. Woch., 1904 (41), 497.

action is simply explained as being due to establishment of equilibrium; in some instances, however, the substances produced are of themselves harmful to the enzymes, *e. g.*, alcohol and acetic acid. Changes in reaction, fixation of the enzyme by cleavage products, and other side reactions may also be at least partly responsible. There is a periodicity in enzyme action which makes quantitative results uncertain.[28]

Activation of Enzymes.—Within the cell, the enzymes—at least those that are excreted, such as trypsin and pepsin - exist with few exceptions in an inactive form, the *zymogen*. Their activation appears to take place normally only after they have been discharged from the cell, but after the death of an organ it may result from the decomposition products that are formed. Under physiological conditions this activation appears to be brought about by special activating substances. In the case of the pancreas it is the *enterokinase*, which is furnished by the epithelial cells of the intestine. Enterokinase appears to unite with trypsinogen to form an active enzyme, which reminds one of the way that complement and the intermediary body unite to form hemolytic and bacteriolytic substances.[29] *Kinases*, having the same action as enterokinase upon the trypsinogen, are found in various tissues and organs, but generally much less active than the enterokinase. It is very probable that it is through this mechanism that the rate of enzyme action is modified, and perhaps it is a means of defense of the body against its own enzymes; as the prozymes are more resistant to harmful agencies than the enzymes, it also may be a method of storage. The activity of various enzymes is greatly increased by certain more or less specific substances, referred to usually as "coenzymes;" thus bile-salts act as co-enzymes for lipase (Loevenhart).

THE TOXICITY OF ENZYMES

Although present normally in greater or less amounts in all the cells in the body, when artificially isolated and injected directly into animals nearly all enzymes seem to be extremely toxic. As foreign proteins, especially extracts of tissues, are generally more or less toxic, it is difficult to state how much of the toxicity of a given enzyme-containing solution depends on the enzyme and how much on the admixt proteins. *The following statements are taken at the face value placed on them by the several investigators quoted, and are subject to discount until the enzymes have been isolated and investigated in a pure condition, if such a thing shall ever become possible.*

The first thorough study of the toxicity of enzymes was made by Hildebrandt,[30] who found that pepsin, invertase, diastase, emulsin, myrosin, and rennin were all toxic. The symptoms produced in dogs were trembling, uneasiness, difficulty in walking, and finally coma. The anatomical changes observed were: numerous hemorrhages throughout the body, fatty degeneration of the liver and myocardium, renal congestion, and numerous thromboses. Considerable fever results, and Mayer considers this responsible for the relative harmlessness of rennin, the action of which is impaired above 40°. That these effects are due to the enzymes themselves rather than to contaminating

---

[28] Groll, Nederl. Tijdschr. v. Geneesk., 1918 (1), 1085.

[29] Bayliss and Starling (Jour. of Physiol., 1905 (32), 129), question the analogy of zymogen-kinase combinations to complement-amboceptor combination. Walker, however, finds evidence that many enzymes consist of a specific amboceptor and a non-specific complement or kinase (Jour. of Physiol., 1906 (33), p. xxi.)

[30] Virchow's Archiv, 1890 (121), 1.

bacteria is shown by Kionka and by Achalme[31] who obtained similar results with enzymes made sterile by filtration through porcelain. Wago[32] obtained also an amyloid-like degeneration widely spread in animals injected with filtered solutions of commercial trypsin, pancreatin and amylopsin. Achalme found that such sterile preparations of pancreatic juice injected subcutaneously into guinea-pigs produce a marked local pink gelatinous edema, followed by gangrene; if the animal dies, the blood is non-coagulable.

Apparently cells of nearly all types can be destroyed by trypsin, which may cause necrosis in one-fourth hour; however, spermatozoa and surface epithelium resist strong trypsin solutions. Intravenous injections cause death with lesions in the heart muscle and severe hemorrhages. After recovery from one injection of trypsin the animal is temporarily somewhat more resistant to another injection, and there are other resemblances to anaphylactic intoxication (Kirchheim[33]). Fiquet[34] also observed that trypsin and pepsin rendered the blood incoagulable, but after some time the coagulability of the blood is increased and thrombosis is frequent. Wells[35] found that pancreatic extracts containing very active trypsin and lipase, injected intraperitoneally, produced an acute inflammatory reaction, but no fat necrosis. Extracts containing active lipase and inactive trypsin were less toxic, but produced fat necrosis. Extracts of liver and blood serum, rich in lipase, were almost without effect on dogs and cats.

Papain was found to be much more toxic than any animal enzyme, causing violent local hemorrhagic inflammation. Schepilewsky[36] also found papain much more toxic than rennin and pancreatin; repeated injection of the two latter caused amyloidosis in rabbits. Active immunity does not follow repeated injections of papain.[37] Lombroso[38] found that inactive pancreatic juice was much less toxic than the activated, showing that it is the trypsin that is the important toxic agent. He also found that *succus entericus* in doses of 1 to 5 c.c. is toxic, but not lethal for dogs. Pancreatic lipase is hemolytic (Noguchi[39]) if activated by fats, which suggests that when this enzyme gets into the blood it may cause hemolysis. *Urease* has a definite toxicity because it decomposes the urea in the blood and tissues, fatal intoxication from NH_3 poisoning resulting.[40] Hildebrandt[41] observed that enzymes were positively chemotactic, but it is probable

[31] Ann. d. l'Inst. Pasteur, 1901 (15), 737.
[32] Arch. Int. Med., 1919 (23), 251.
[33] Arch. exp. Path. u. Pharm., 1911 (66), 352; 1914 (78), 99; 1913 (74), 374.
[34] Arch. d. Méd. Exper., 1899 (11), 145.
[35] Jour. Med. Research, 1903 (9), 92.
[36] Cent. f. Bakt., 1899 (25), 849.
[37] Stenitzer, Biochem. Zeit., 1908 (9), 382.
[38] Abstract in Biochem. Centralblatt, 1903 (1), 712.
[39] Biochem. Zeit., 1907 (6), 185.
[40] See Carnot and Gerard, Compt. Rend. Acad. Sci., 1919 (169), 88.
[41] Virchow's Arch., 1893 (131), 5.

that the products of their action on the tissues are the chief chemotactic agents.

The enzymes that are secreted into the gastro-intestinal tract seem to be chiefly destroyed, but part is eliminated in the feces, and part that is absorbed apparently reappears in the urine in very small quantities.[42] Pepsin, diastase, and rennin all have been found in normal urine; but trypsin is present chiefly as trypsinogen, especially abundant after a meat diet.[43] Pepsin and rennin enter the urine as the zymogens, in quantities in proportion to the amount in the stomach, and are absent in gastric carcinoma (Fuld and Hirayama[44]). During resolution of pneumonia, leucocytic protease may appear in the urine (Bittorf[45]). Ferments injected subcutaneously are said seldom to be eliminated in any considerable amounts in the urine, but Opie[46] has demonstrated the presence of lipase in the urine in pancreatitis with fat necrosis, and Wago[47] found that injected trypsin is excreted rapidly and abundantly. Hildebrandt was able to prove that emulsin remained active for at least six hours after it was injected into animals subcutaneously, by its splitting amygdalin which was then injected, the CNH liberated by the cleavage of the amygdalin causing death.

ANTI-ENZYMES

Injection of enzymes into animals leads to the appearance of substances in the serum of the animals that antagonize the action of the enzymes.[48] The principles involved are quite the same as in the immunization of animals against bacterial toxins or against foreign proteins. This seems to have been first observed by Hildebrandt, and it has been taken up extensively in recent years in the study of the problems of immunity. An interesting observation that was made rather early in these studies was that normal blood-serum possesses a marked resistance against the action of proteolytic enzymes, not being at all digested by dilutions of enzymes that will rapidly digest a serum that has been heated. This property seems to be shared by egg-white[49] and by the tissues and organs of the body (Levene and Stookey[50]). The anti-enzyme action is easily destroyed by heat of about 70°, by the action of dilute acids, and even by prolonged standing. It is

[42] Falk and Kolieb, Zeit. klin. Med., 1909 (68), 156.
[43] v. Schoenborn, Zeit. f. Biol., 1910 (53), 386.
[44] Berl. klin. Woch., 1910 (47), 1062.
[45] Deut. Arch. klin. Med., 1907 (91), 212.
[46] Johns Hopkins Hosp. Bull., 1902 (13), 117.
[47] Jour. Immunol., 1919 (4), 19.
[48] According to Porter (Quart. Jour. Exper. Physiol., 1910 (3), 375) enzymes in contact with various membranes are inactivated, and substances appear which are strongly inhibitive to the enzymes; it is possible that this effect depends largely on zymoids, which unite with the substrate and deviate the enzymes.
[49] Sugimoto, Arch. exp. Path., 1913 (74), 14.
[50] Jour. Medical Research, 1903 (10), 217.

exerted not only against the secreted proteolytic enzymes, pepsin and trypsin, but also against the intracellular enzymes of various organs. We therefore distinguish between normal and immune anti-enzymes.

It seems highly probable that the resistance of the body tissues to digestion by their own enzymes and by the enzymes of one another depends in some way upon the presence of anti-enzymes in the cells and tissue fluids, for self-digestion of tissues is greatly impeded by serum.[51] Weiland[52] has demonstrated that certain intestinal worms contain a strong antitrypsin, to which he attributes their ability to live bathed in pancreatic juice without being digested.[53] Similar properties have been ascribed by other observers to the cells of the mucosa of the stomach[54] and intestine, and to the mucus itself (de Klug),[55] but the work of Bensley and Harvey[56] indicates that the absence of free acid in the gland cells and lumen is perhaps the chief protection of the stomach from pepsin. Kirchheim[57] holds that the intestines are protected less by anti-enzymes than by rapid absorption and removal of the enzymes, which are really not present in any considerable excess in the intestinal contents. The anti-enzymes seem only to inhibit enzyme action, and not to destroy the enzyme itself.[58] Normal anti-enzymes do not seem to be at all specific, according to v. Eisler;[59] that is, human serum is no more resistant to human trypsin than is pig serum—indeed, it is less so.[60]

Cathcart[61] found that normal antitrypsin is connected with the "albumin fraction" of the serum, *i. e.*, the fraction precipitated between half and full saturation with ammonium sulphate. Globulins do not possess this action, but they are not easily digested. Antitrypsin is found in all varieties of serum, and is little or not at all specific. It is destroyed by 65–70°C.[62] for one-half hour, but retains its anti-enzymatic activity after drying, and is equally effective against all sorts of proteins. The normal anti-tryptic activity decreases during fasting and

[51] Wells, Jour. Med. Research, 1906 (10), 149.
[52] Zeit. f. Biol. 1903 (44), 45; see also Dastre and Stassano, Compt. Rend. Soc. Biol., 1903 (55), 130 and 254; and Hamill, Jour. of Physiol., 1906 (33), 479.
[53] Burge (Jour. Parasitol., 1915 (1), 179) suggests that the protection of parasites, and perhaps of the alimentary epithelium, depends on the active oxidative properties of these tissues destroying the enzymes.
[54] See Blum and Fuld, Zeit. klin. Med., 1906 (58), 505; Langenskiöld, Skand. Arch. Physiol., 1914 (31), 1.
[55] Arch. internat. d. physiol., 1907 (5), 297.
[56] Biological Bulletin, 1912 (23), 225.
[57] Arch. exp. Path. u. Pharm., 1912 (71), 1.
[58] Bayliss and Starling (Jour. of Physiol., 1905 (32), 129; and Meyer, Biochem. Zeit., 1909 (23), 68, oppose the view of Delezenne that the antitryptic action of the blood is due to an antikinase, and believe the antibody acts upon trypsin.
[59] Ber. d. Wien. Akad., 1905 (104), 119.
[60] This is contradicted by Glaessner, Hofmeister's Beiträge, 1903 (4), 79.
[61] Jour. of Physiol., 1904 (31), 497; also see Kämmerer and Aubry, Biochem. Zeit., 1913 (48), 217.
[62] Unless otherwise specified, all temperatures are given according to the Centigrade scale.

increases during digestion (Rosenthal[63]); it is increased during pregnancy[64] and the blood of the fetus shows less than that of the mother. Normal antitrypsin unites with trypsin according to the law of multiple proportions (Meyer) and the reaction is not reversible (Rondoni). It is found in the urine, and in inflammatory exudates, but not in normal serous fluids, and it resists putrefaction. Normal serum does not seem to inhibit the enzymes which act upon purines. Fuld and Spiro[65] found that the natural antirennin of normal horse serum is in the pseudoglobulin fraction. Since acids destroy the anti-enzyme property of the serum, it is not effective against pepsin-HCl mixtures. Against trypsin, however, it is very effective. Zunz[66] states that normal serum acts more upon enterokinase than upon trypsin, and believes that the inhibition depends upon colloids which modify surface tension and adhere to the proteins. Red corpuscles and living unicellular organisms, including bacteria, are likewise resistant to trypsin, and normal serum also seems to contain an antirennin.[67]

Oppenheimer and Aron[68] consider it probable that the resistance of normal serum to trypsin digestion depends upon the configuration of the protein molecules, which perhaps, when in fresh, uninjured condition, present no suitable surfaces for attack by the ferment. Hedin attributes antitryptic action to adsorption of the enzyme by some constituent of the serum, much as charcoal inhibits tryptic digestion.

Fresh and inactivated serum will prevent pepsin from digesting protein, but this is not due to a true antipepsin, according to Hamburger.[69]

Jobling[70] and his co-workers have advanced evidence that the normal antiprotease action of serum depends on the lipoids of the serum,[71] which vary in activity directly with the degree of unsaturation; therefore they were able to decrease the antiferment action of serum by extracting the lipoids with fat solvents (and to restore the activity by replacing the lipoids), or by saturating the double bonds of the fatty acids with halogens, or by modifying the degree of dispersion

[63] Folia Serologica, 1910 (6), 285; also Franz and Jarisch, Wien. klin. Woch., 1912 (25), 1441.
[64] See Franz, Arch. f. Gyn., 1914 (102), 579.
[65] Zeit. f. physiol. Chem., 1900 (31), 132.
[66] Mem. Acad. roy. med. Belgique, 1909 (20), fasc. 5.
[67] Czapek (Ber. Deut. botan. Gesell., 1903 (21), 229) states that anti-oxidases occur normally in certain plants, strongly specific against the oxidase of the same plant species.
[68] Hofmeister's Beiträge, 1903, (4), 279.
[69] Jour. Exper. Med., 1911 (14), 535; Arch. Int. Med., 1915 (16), 356. There seems to be no relation between the antipeptic and antitryptic powers of sera (Rubinstein, Ann. Inst. Pasteur., 1913 (27), 1074).
[70] Series of articles in Jour. Exper. Med.; also review in Jour. Lab. and Clin. Med., 1915 (1), 172. See also Zeit. Immunität., 1914 (23), 71.
[71] Yamakawa (Jour. Exp. Med., 1918 (27), 689), however, does not believe that the antienzyme which prevents autolysis of serum itself is of lipoidal nature.

of the lipoids. Soaps of saturated fatty acids do not inhibit serum protease.

Opie[72] has found that the serum of inflammatory exudates contains an anti-enzymatic substance, destroyed at 75° and by acids; it is not present in normal cerebrospinal fluid, but appears here as in other serous cavities during inflammation (Dochez).[73] Antitrypsin has also been found in pathological urines (v. Schoenborn).[74]

The power of the blood serum to inhibit the activity of trypsin and leucocytic protease has been found to vary greatly in disease, and, as having diagnostic possibilities, this property has been considerably investigated.[75] It is especially increased in conditions associated with cell destruction, such as pneumonia and cancer, which suggests that the increased antitryptic activity results from the formation of specific antibodies for the intracellular proteases liberated during the disease, but as yet this has not been satisfactorily established, so we do not know whether the "antitrypsin reaction" depends upon an antibody for trypsin or upon some entirely different factor. In cachexia the inhibiting effect of the serum is especially marked and it is therefore usually pronounced in cancer, but the increased inhibition is sometimes absent in cancer (10 per cent. of all cases) and often present in other conditions, so that the positive diagnostic value is slight. It may also be present without cachexia and often seems to parallel the number of leucocytes in the circulating blood. Sarcoma shows it less than carcinoma, while in exophthalmic goitre and tuberculosis an antitryptic increase is said to be quite constant (Waelli).[76] In pregnancy there is usually an increase demonstrable after the fourth to sixth months, continuing until two weeks after delivery, and highest in cases of pregnancy toxemias (Ecalle).[77] Severe traumatism may also cause an increase.[78]

As normal serum contains a tryptic enzyme as well as a substance inhibiting trypsin, the antitryptic activity is at most but a measure of the difference between these (Weil), and might depend on either lowered trypsin or increased antitrypsin content. Döblin[79] and many others believe with Jobling that the active agent is not a true immune antibody, but as yet general agreement has not been reached on this point (see Meyer). Kirchheim[80] has found that the union of trypsin and antitrypsin does not follow the physico-chemical laws to a true antigen-antibody reaction. Rosenthal has advanced evidence

[72] Jour. Exp. Med., 1905 (7), 316.
[73] Jour. Exper. Med., 1909 (11), 718.
[74] Zeit. f. Biol., 1910 (53), 386.
[75] For literature and review see Wiens, Ergebnisse Physiol., 1911 (15), 1; Weil, Arch. Int. Med., 1910 (5), 109; Meyer, Folia Serologica, 1911 (7), 471.
[76] Mitt. Grenz. Med. u. Chir., 1912 (25), 184.
[77] Arch. Mens. Obst. Gyn., 1917 (6), 97.
[78] Zunz and Govaerts, C. R. Soc. Biol., 1918 (81), 146.
[79] Zeit. f. Immunität, 1909 (4), 229
[80] Arch. exp. Path., 1913 (73), 139.

to support the hypothesis that the presence of products of protein cleavage in the serum is responsible for the antitryptic action, but this has not been confirmed. Attempts have been made to regulate suppurative processes by the introduction of either leucocytic proteases, or antiprotease in the form of active serum (see Wiens[75]). Whether antiprotease can be specifically developed by immunizing with leucoprotease is a matter of disagreement,[81] but no increase of antiprotease follows the enormous destruction of leucocytes caused by injecting thorium-X.[82]

The anti-enzymatic property obtained in the serum by injecting enzymes into animals differs from that normally present in the serum in many ways. It may be made much stronger than it ever is in normal serum, and against many varieties of enzymes for which an anti-enzyme does not naturally exist. Especially important is the fact that it is highly specific (v. Eisler); serum of an animal immunized against dog trypsin will show a much greater effect against dog trypsin than it does against trypsin from other animals. This fact permits us to distinguish between enzymes of apparently similar nature but of different origin, and proves that they have a structure at least in some respects different from one another, since they are combined by different antibodies. Apparently that element of the enzymes which determines their action on specific substances is involved in their antigenic properties, since antiproteases will not inhibit diastase or lipase. This specificity is limited, however, for the anti-enzymes for leucocytic and pancreatic proteases are said to be identical.[83] Artificial immune serum is said to have been obtained against trypsin, pepsin,[69] lipase, emulsin,[84] autolytic enzymes, laccase, amylase, invertin, diastase, tyrosinase, urease,[85] rennin, catalase, and fibrin ferment.[86] By immunization against bacteria an immunity against their proteolytic enzymes is also obtained,[87] which is independent of and different from antitrypsin, being especially in the globulin fraction, while the antibody for pancreatic trypsin is chiefly in the albumin (Kämmerer[88]). From the work of Kirchheim and Reinicke[89] it seems probable that the increased resistance following

[81] See Bradley, Jour. Hyg., 1910 (12), 209.

[82] G. Rosenow and Färber, Zeit. exp. Med., 1914 (3), 377.

[83] Jochmann and Kantorowicz, Münch. med. Woch.. 1908 (55), 728.

[84] Bayliss (Jour. of Physiol., 1912 (43), 455) was unable to obtain antiemulsin, and Pozerski (Ann. Inst. Pasteur, 1909 (23), 205) failed to obtain antipapain, but positive results are reported by v. Stenitzer (Biochem. Zeit.. 1908 (9), 382).

[85] Jacoby says that the disappearance of urease from the blood after repeated injection does not depend on the formation of an antienzyme (Biochem. Zeit., 1916 (74), 97).

[86] For a review of much of the earlier literature on this subject see Schütze, Deut. med. Woch., 1904 (30), 308.

[87] Dungern, Münch. med. Wochenschr., 1898 (45), 1040; Bertiau, Cent. f. Bact., 1914 (74), 374.

[88] Deut. Arch. klin. Med., 1911 (103), 341.

[89] Arch. exp. Path., 1914 (77), 412.

immunization with trypsin is simply an increase in nonspecific resistance, such as follows injection of peptone and many other poisonous substances. Wago[47] was able to demonstrate precipitins and complement fixing antibodies in antitryptic sera that were not strongly antienzymatic, and Young[90] was unable to produce antitryptic sera by immunizing with trypsin, in spite of the presence of active precipitins for the injected trypsin solutions. There is, indeed, a growing suspicion that much of the evidence of specific antibody formation for enzymes must be revised.

Resemblances of Enzymes and Toxins.—As can be seen from the above statements, the enzymes behave in many respects like the toxins, both in their manner of acting upon other substances and in the reaction they produce when introduced into the bodies of animals. As Oppenheimer says, "the bonds between enzymes and toxins are drawing closer and closer." According to some experiments, the enzymes behave much as if they possessed a haptophore and a toxophore group, the former of which combines with the substance that is to be acted upon; and immunity appears to be produced by the development of receptors that combine the haptophore groups, these receptors constituting the antiferments. There is abundant evidence of a toxin-like structure in enzymes, from the numerous observations on the formation of "zymoids" which can neutralize anti-enzymes or combine with the substrate, although no longer active as enzymes. The oxidizing enzymes especially, with their complex relationship of substrate, combining body (peroxides) and enzyme, present striking analogies to immune reactions (Moore[91]), and the proteolytic substances of the blood resemble the lysins in certain respects (Dick).[92] Enzymes and toxins also resemble one another in being readily absorbed by membranes, precipitates, and highly developed surfaces in general.[91] Finally, there is much reason to believe that the hemolytic toxin of cobra venom is a lipase, which acts by splitting lecithin into hemolytic substances (Coca).[91]

THE INTRACELLULAR ENZYMES [95]

Until a recent time our knowledge of enzymes in the animal body was limited to those present in the digestive secretions. With few exceptions these are without influence in pathological processes, since they seem to be but little absorbed, and rarely enter the blood or tissues in any other way. But with the more recently disclosed intracellular enzymes, many of which are present in every cell,[96] the relation to pathology is very intimate. These intracellular enzymes, as we now know them, and their chief properties, are as follows:

[90] Biochem. Jour., 1918 (12), 499.
[91] Biochem. Jour., 1909 (4), 165.
[92] Jour. Infectious Diseases, 1911 (9), 282.
[93] See Porter, Quart. Jour. Exp. Physiol., 1910 (3), 375.
[91] Jour. Infect. Dis., 1915 (17), 351.
[95] See Vernon, Ergebnisse d. Physiol., 1910 (9), 138; also his monograph, "Intracellular Enzymes," London, 1908.
[96] Herlitzka (Arch. ital. biol., 1907 (48), 119) and others have shown that the different enzymes appear one by one in the development of the ovum. Their activity is modified considerably by infections (Sieber, Biochem. Zeit., 1911 (32), 108) and other diseases (Grossmann, ibid., 1912 (41), 181).

OXIDIZING ENZYMES [97]

Although oxidation of organic compounds is the chief source of energy in the animal body, yet the way in which it is accomplished is very little understood. We only know that it is brought about within the cells, and that substances that outside the body are oxidized with difficulty, are completely oxidized to carbon dioxide and water within the cells, and that this is done with just such a degree of rapidity that the heat produced is in exactly the amount necessary for the wants of the body. There can be little question that this oxidation is accomplished through catalytic agents acting within the cells, and certain of them have been placed in a condition permitting of study. As yet their exact relations to intracellular oxidation are not clearly defined, but for the present they may be grouped provisionally as oxidizing enzymes. That some of them are highly specific is shown by those disorders, such as alkaptonuria and diabetes, in which the body loses the power to oxidize a certain chemical substance while retaining the normal power to oxidize innumerable other substances. According to Lillie[98] the oxidative processes in cells take place most actively in relation to the membrane surfaces (or phase boundaries) of the cells. Of the oxidizing enzymes as yet identified none can be considered as of importance in the energy-producing oxidations of the body (Battelli and Stern), all the enzymes of this class yet known being apparently concerned with less essential oxidizing processes; it is indeed possible that the essential oxidation of food-stuffs may not be dependent on enzymes (Engler and Herzog).[99] An agent accelerating the essential oxidizing activities of the tissues has been described by Battelli and Stern[1] under the name of *pnein,* and an *antipneumin* which holds it in check. Closely related to the oxidizing enzymes is—

Catalase.—It has long been known that most enzymes possess the power of decomposing hydrogen peroxide, with liberation of oxygen; but it was not until 1901 that it was finally demonstrated by Loew that this property was due to a separate enzyme and was independent of the specific properties of the various other enzymes. This ferment is very wide-spread, and so is generally obtained along with the other enzymes when attempts are made to isolate them from the cell. It was named *catalase* by Loew, and he described two forms, α-

[97] Complete bibliography and exhaustive discussion by Kastle, Bull. Hygienic Lab.,' No. 59; by Loele, Ergeb. allg. Path., 1912 (16, Pt. 2), 760; and by Battelli and Stern, Ergebnisse d. Physiol., 1912 (12), 96. Concerning the chemistry of vital oxidations see Dakin, "Oxidations and Reductions in the Animal Body," Monographs on Biochemistry, London, 1912. Good review by v. Fürth, "Chemistry of Metabolism," Chaps. 22 and 23; translated by A. J. Smith, Philadelphia, 1916.

[98] Jour. Biol. Chem., 1913 (15), 237.

[99] Zeit. physiol. Chem., 1909 (59), 327.

[1] Biochem. Zeit., 1911 (33), 315; 1911 (36), 114.

catalase, which was thought to be a nucleoprotein,[2] and *β-catalase*, which has the properties of an albumose. It has been demonstrated by Bach and Chodat that peroxides are contained in plant cells, and they also occur in animal cells. According to Golodetz and Unna[3] the catalases are held in the cytoplasm of the cells while the peroxidases are in the nucleus. Just what function the catalase performs is at present merely a matter of speculation, but that it serves an important purpose is indicated by the observation of Burge[4] that the amount of catalase in tissues varies directly with their activity. He also ascribes the specific dynamic action of proteins to their causing an increase in blood catalase. Becht,[5] however, questions the validity of the evidence so far brought forward in support of the hypothesis that catalase is essentilly responsible for tissue oxidation.[6]

Loew considers that it destroys peroxides formed in metabolism, which are very poisonous to cell life. Shaffer has found evidence that under the influence of catalase the oxygen liberated is in the molecular form, O_2, and therefore relatively inert; whereas when peroxides spontaneously decompose, they liberate atomic oxygen which is an active oxidizing agent. He found that uric acid is oxidized by peroxide of hydrogen, but when catalase is present, this oxidation is prevented. According to this the function of catalase is rather to prevent dangerous forms of oxidation than to help in normal oxidative processes. For the present, however, nothing can be said positively on this subject.

Occurrence of Catalase under Normal and Pathological Conditions.[7]—Battelli and Stern found that the catalytic power of the tissues endures many hours after death. Its abundance is different for different organs of the same animal, but remarkably constant for the same organ in the same species. In general the order in decreasing strength is: liver, kidney, blood, spleen, gastro-intestinal mucosa, salivary glands, lung, pancreas, testicle, heart, muscle. brain; but this order varies in different species. Catalase is abundant even in the early embryo (Mendel and Leavenworth) and in sea urchin eggs it increases rapidly after they are fertilized (Lyon).[8] Leucocytes contain little, most of that in the blood being in the stroma of the red blood-corpuscles. The body fluids contain little or none. Injected intravenously, catalase (of the liver) is destroyed rapidly, and does not appear in the urine; it does not cause any toxic effects, nor does it increase resistance to poisoning by venoms. The tissues also contain *anti-catalases*, and still further a substance which protects the catalase from the anti-catalase; this protective substance is called the *philocatalase* by Battelli and Stern.

The gas evolved by the action of pus on H_2O_2 was found by Marshall[9] to be pure oxygen, each c.c. of a certain sample of pus examined liberating 133.9 c.c. of gas. The active constituent of pus, he states, is contained in the serum and not in the

[2] Not corroborated by Waentig and Gierisch, Fermentforsch., 1914 (1), 165.
[3] Berl. klin. Woch., 1912 (49), 1134.
[4] Amer. Jour. Physiol., 1916 (41), 153; 1917 (42), 373; 1919 (48), 133. See also Alvarez and Starkweather, *ibid.*; 1918 (47), 60; Dutcher, Jour. Biol. Chem., 1918 (36), 63.
[5] Amer. Jour. Physiol., 1919 (48), 171.
[6] See also Stehle, Jour. Biol. Chem., 1919 (39), 403.
[7] Concerning the catalase of lower animals see Zieger, Biochem. Zeit., 1915 (69), 39.
[8] Amer. Jour. Physiol., 1909 (25), 199.
[9] Univ. of Penn. Med. Bull., 1902 (15), 366.

corpuscles. Catalase is abundant in the tissues of lower animal forms, *e. g.*, *Ascaris*.[10] Substances decomposing H_2O_2 have been found also in bacterial cultures, first by Gottstein, and later in the cell juices expressed from tubercle bacilli by Hahn. Loewenstein[11] found an enzyme agreeing with catalase in filtered bouillon cultures of diphtheria bacilli and staphylococci, but not from tetanus, typhoid, and colon bacilli or cholera vibrios; the catalase is quite distinct from the toxin. He also found that the addition of H_2O_2 to a diphtheria toxin-antitoxin mixture destroyed the toxin, leaving the antitoxin free. A similar destruction of tetanus toxin by peroxides, first demonstrated by Sieber, can occur without the catalase.

Winternitz[12] and his associates have made extensive studies of the catalase activity of the blood and tissues in disease. They found that all tissues have reduced catalase activity in chronic nephritis, in proportion to the severity of the condition, and experimental nephritis in animals has the same effect; the blood shows great reduction in catalase in uremia, and a less reduction with less severe nephritic manifestations. Eclampsia shows little or much reduction of catalase in the blood in proportion to the amount of renal involvement; normal pregnancy and labor have no effect. Anemia is associated with irregular decrease in catalase, including primary anemias and the secondary anemias of typhoid and pneumonia; cardiac disease has no effect if the kidneys are normal. Acute peritonitis causes a rise in blood catalase; diabetes, leukemia and jaundice were without effect. In hyperthyreosis the catalase tends to increase, in hypothyreosis to decrease; complete removal of the thyroid causes a decrease which disappears on feeding thyroid. Intravenous injection of salts, acids and alkalies decreases the catalytic activity of the blood. In shock, blood catalase is decreased.[13] Normal individuals show considerable variations in the catalase activity of the blood, but for each individual it is remarkably constant; age has very little influence. In the tissues *post mortem* change causes but slight reduction in catalase. Extirpation of large amounts of kidney or liver tissue has little effect, but removal of the spleen, ovaries or testicles causes a transient decrease in the catalase of the blood. In diabetes and starvation, tissue catalase is said to be decreased.[14] If the red corpuscles are prevented from laking, the catalase activity manifested by the blood *in vitro* is reduced (Strauss)[15] and iodides increase the catalase activity of the blood. Catalase and anticatalase have been found in pathological urine, in both acute and chronic nephritis (Primavera).[16] Kahn and Brim[17] also found traces of catalase in normal urine, greatly increased in urine containing blood, bile or acetone, normal in cancer, high in diabetic acidosis, Hodgkin's disease, septic infections and typhoid. Grossman[18] found that bacterial poisons generally increase the catalase content of the various viscera, and Rosenthal[19] observed a great decrease in the liver and blood of mice receiving intraperitoneal inoculations of cancer. The catalase activity of the non-cancerous organs of cancer patients is not affected, except slightly lowered by cachexia (Colwell);[20] however, the liver tissue between cancer nodules may show less catalase than normal liver.[21] In phosphorus poisoning the catalase content of the liver, heart and blood is decreased (Burge).[22]

But it is to be borne in mind that the questionable accuracy of our existing methods of determining quantitatively the amount or activity of catalase in tissues makes the foregoing statements of uncertain value.

True Oxidizing Enzymes.—While it is by no means certain that catalase is active in causing intracellular oxidations, there are other

[10] Magath, Jour. Biol. Chem. 1918 (33), 395.
[11] Wien. klin. Woch., 1903 (16), 1393.
[12] Review in Arch. Int. Med., 1911 (7), 624.
[13] Burge and Neill. Amer. Jour. Physiol., 1918 (45), 286.
[14] Burge, Science, 1918 (47), 347.
[15] Bull. Johns Hopkins Hosp., 1912 (23), 120.
[16] Riforma Med., 1906 (12), 1266.
[17] Amer. Jour. Obst., 1915 (71), 39.
[18] Biochem. Zeit., 1912 (41), 181.
[19] Deut. med. Woch., 1912 (38), 2270.
[20] Arch. Middlesex Hosp., 1910 (19), 64.
[21] Blumenthal and Brahn, Zeit. Krebsforsch., 1910 (8), 436.
[22] Amer. Jour. Physiol., 1917 (43), 545.

enzymes or enzyme-like substances that come more properly under the head of oxidases or oxidizing enzymes. Battelli and Stern contend that the only real oxidases which have yet been completely established are: 1. Polyphenoloxidases (oxidizing phenols and their amino compounds, but not tyrosine); 2. Tyrosinase; 3. Alcohol oxidase; 4. Xanthine oxidase; 5. Uricase. Chodat and Bach believe that the enzymes which are designated above as polyphenoloxidases have a complex structure, consisting of peroxidase and oxygenase.[23] Mathews[24] holds that "under the term oxidases there have been confused two classes of substances, one which activates the oxygen; the other the more important class, which activates, by dissociation, the reducing substances. The latter are specific, the former not." This view has received support by Bach.

Peroxidase.—This name is given to an enzyme that is believed to cause oxidation by activating peroxides, and is quite distinct from catalase and from the other oxidases. The peroxide on which it chiefly acts in the cell is supposed to be the so-called "oxygenase."

Oxygenase.—This can also act as an oxidizer independent of the peroxidase, in the presence of certain manganese compounds. Loevenhart and Kastle question the true enzyme nature of this and other "oxidases," which they look upon as organic peroxides, behaving like other peroxides rather than as catalyzers. Practically the existence of these bodies is demonstrated by their power to turn tincture of guaiac blue, and they are, therefore, present in pus.

Von Fürth[97] sums up the situation in these words: "In the tissues active catalytic agents, the peroxidases, are widely distributed; which seem, just like the coloring matter of the blood, to be capable of conveying the oxygen from peroxides to very readily oxidizable substances. We find too in the statements bearing upon the oxygenases, the aldehydases and indophenoloxidases, occasion for assuming that there are substances in the tissues charged with oxygen which are able to give this off to easily oxidizable matter; and these we may in a measure regard as peroxides. But that is all. We do not know whether the peroxidases are ferments or not."

By their conception of oxygenase and peroxidase Chodat and Bach would displace entirely the idea of enzymes oxidizing directly, the true "oxidases," which they consider mixtures of oxygenase and peroxidase. There have been, in any event, a number of ferments described that seem to possess distinct oxidative powers. As each is quite specific in its action, oxidizing but one substance, or one group of related substances, they are generally designated by the name of the substances upon which they act. Most studied of these are aldehydase and tyrosinase.

Aldehydase,[25] which is characterized by oxidizing aldehydes, particularly salicyl-aldehyde. According to Jacquet, this enzyme is so intimately bound with the cell that it cannot be obtained in extracts until after the cells are dead, but is present in expressed cell-juices. It can be isolated by the usual methods, is destroyed by boiling, acts best when no free oxygen is present, and its action is inhibited by CNH. It has been demonstrated in nearly all organs and tissues except pancreas, muscle, marrow, and mammary gland; it is present in the blood in small amounts, but not at all in the bile. It is most abundant in the liver[26] and spleen, and is present in pig embryos, 9 cm. long, but not in those 2-3 cm. long. Jacoby has obtained a body with the properties of aldehydase which did not give protein reactions. It is a true enzyme, since it oxidizes aldehydes without itself being

[23] See also Onslow, Biochem. Jour. 1919 (13), 1.
[24] Jour. Biol. Chem., 1909 (6), 1.
[25] Battelli and Stern do not include aldehydase among the oxidizing enzymes, on the ground that its action is not oxidative but hydrolytic.
[26] Battelli and Stern, Biochem. Zeit., 1910 (29), 130.

used up. Its range of action is limited, for Jacoby found it without effect upon acetic acid and stearic acid.

Tyrosinase.—This enzyme, which is found both in animal and plant tissues, is particularly interesting in relation to the formation of pigments. Bertrand found that the transformation of the juice of lac-yielding plants into the black lacquer was brought about by the action of an oxidizing ferment, *laccase*, upon an easily oxidized substance, *laccol*, which is a member of the aromatic series. He later found in a number of plants an enzyme acting on tyrosine, distinct from the laccase, which he named *tyrosinase*. Biederman later found tyrosinase in the intestinal fluid of meal worms. v. Fürth and Schneider found a similar enzyme in the hemolymph of insects and arthropods, which explains its darkening when exposed to air. This enzyme, as obtained from different sources, is not always specific for tyrosine, frequently oxidizing other substances. As yet the chemical processes and end results of the oxidation of tyrosine by tyrosinase are unknown. Bach[27] obtained evidence that tyrosinase is not a specific oxidizing enzyme, but consists of an aminoacidase, which disintegrates the tyrosine and makes it susceptible to the action of phenolase which is the oxidizing agent. v. Fürth and Schneider found the product of oxidation of tyrosine by animal tyrosinase related to certain of the *melanins* of animal tissues, and believe that tyrosinase is responsible for the production of many normal pigments.[28] In the ink-sacs of the squid, which eject an inky fluid containing melanin-like pigment, tyrosinase was also found, corroborating this hypothesis, and it is probable that tyrosinase in the skins of animals is responsible for their pigmentation.[29] Bacteria also contain tyrosinase,[30] and this or similar enzymes seem to be present in melano-sarcomas.[31]

Gonnermann[32] found that tyrosinase from beet-root produced *homogentisic acid* by acting on tyrosine, which is of interest in connection with the congenital hereditary disease, *alkaptonuria* (*q. v.*), in which the urine becomes dark upon exposure because of the presence of homogentisic acid. The action of tyrosinase upon the aromatic radicals of proteins is of importance in the study of both physiological and pathological pigment formation, and hence has received extensive study, which will be found fully described in the monograph by Kastle (*loc. cit.*)[97] and under the appropriate subjects in subsequent chapters.

Other Oxidizing Enzymes.—Of the great number of other less studied oxidizing enzymes little can be definitely stated. Some consider that they are largely different manifestations of the action of one oxidizing ferment, but against this view Jacoby mentions that they occur distributed unequally in different organs, can be separated from each other, and they cause different reactions. For the catalase and for laccase (which produces the Japanese lacquer by an oxidizing process) and perhaps for other oxidizing ferments, iron and manganese may be essential constituents. Of particular significance for pathology are the enzymes which accomplish the oxidation of purines to uric acid and the subsequent destruction of uric acid. These are discussed in Chapter xxiii. Also the enzymatic oxidation and reduction of β-oxybutyric acid and aceto-acetic acid in the liver, as studied by Dakin and Wakeman,[33] are of great importance in acidosis (*q. v.*).

Reducing enzymes have not yet been satisfactorily demonstrated.[34] It is possible that they do not exist, and that the intracellular reductions that are carried on within the cells are brought about by simple chemical reactions independent of catalysis. The best known intracellular reduction is that of methylene blue,[35] which can be readily studied experimentally because the blue color dis-

[27] Biochem. Zeit., 1914 (60), 221.
[28] Bloch (Zeit. physiol. Chem., 1917 (100), 226) describes under the name *dopaoxidase* an enzyme present in the protoplasm of the basal epidermal and hair follicle cells, which acts specifically on 3, 4—dihydroxyphenylalanine, causing oxidation and condensation with formation of a dark brown or black pigment.
[29] Meirowsky, Cent. f. Path., 1909 (20), 301.
[30] Lehmann and Sano, Arch. f. Hyg., 1908 (67), 99.
[31] Alsberg, Jour. Med. Res., 1907 (16), 117; Neuberg, Virchow's Archiv., 1908 (192), 514; Gessard, Compt. Rend. Soc. Biol., 1902 (54), 1305.
[32] Pflüger's Arch., 1900 (82), 289.
[33] Jour. Amer. Med. Assoc., 1910 (54), 1441.
[34] See Heffter, Arch. exp. Path. u. Pharm., 1908, Suppl., p. 253.
[35] See Thunberg, Skand. Arch. Physiol., 1917 (35), 163.

appears on reduction of the dye. It is open to question if this particular reduction is due to a reducing enzyme. According to Ricketts[36] the reduction depends upon two bodies, one thermostabile, the other thermolabile, recalling the reaction of complement and amboceptor. Strassner[37] found evidence that the SH groups of the tissues are responsible for the reduction of methylene blue; their activity is impaired by heating, but a thermostable element of tissues augments the reducing activity of SH compounds, thus corroborating and explaining the observations of Ricketts. Harris,[38] however, believes that the evidence for the existence of a true reducing enzyme is as good as for most other cellular enzymes. An enzyme has been found in the liver, muscle and kidney which transforms aceto-acetic acid into l-β-oxybutyric acid, and called *ketoreductase* (Friedmann and Maase).[39]

Oxidizing Enzymes in Pathological Processes.

—Although the oxidizing enzymes undoubtedly play an important part in pathological conditions, they have been but little investigated from this standpoint. Jacoby found that they did not disappear from the degenerated liver in phosphorus poisoning or in diabetes, or when the liver undergoes self-digestion, which speaks against Spitzer's contention that oxidase is a nucleoprotein.[40] Schlesinger[41] found that it is less in amount in livers of children dead from gastro-intestinal diseases than in normal livers, as also did Brüning.[42] I am inclined to believe that fatty metamorphosis, when brought about by poisons, is often due to inhibition of the oxidizing enzymes (v. fatty metamorphosis), although I found that livers the seat of the most profound fatty degeneration showed no evident impairment of their power to oxidize xanthine and uric acid.[43] Buxton[44] failed to find in *tumors* any enzyme giving the guaiac test alone, but found enzymes that did so in the presence of H_2O_2 (peroxidases). Catalase was present, but no very positive reactions for oxidizing enzymes were obtained by the indo-phenol reaction, the hydrochinon reaction, or with tyrosine for tyrosinase. v. Fürth and Jerusalem[45] have found evidence that the melanin of melanotic tumors of horses is produced by tyrosinase. Peroxidase has been demonstrated in the granules of pus cells (Fischel).[46]

Meyer[47] found that leucocytes, whether from pus or leukemic or pneumonic blood, contained a substance oxidizing guaiac directly, without the presence of H_2O_2, which is not liberated until the cells are destroyed. By microchemical reactions oxidases have been found present in the myelocytes and nucleated erythrocytes in leukemia, be-

[36] Jour. of Infectious Diseases, 1904 (1), 590.
[37] Biochem. Zeit., 1910 (29), 295.
[38] Biochem. Jour., 1910 (5), 143.
[39] Biochem. Zeit., 1912 (27), 474; 1913 (55), 458.
[40] Ducceschi and Almagia (Arch. ital. Biol., 1903 (39), 29) also found the aldehydase in livers of phosphorus poisoning usually no less abundant than in normal livers.
[41] Hofmeister's Beitr., 1903 (4), 87.
[42] Monat. f. Kinderheilk., 1903 (2), 129.
[43] Jour. Exper. Med., 1910 (12), 607
[44] Jour. Med. Research, 1903 (9), 356.
[45] Hofmeister's Beitr., 1907 (10), 131.
[46] Wien. klin. Woch., 1910 (23), 1557.
[47] Münch. med. Woch., 1903 (50), 1489.

ing absent from the polynuclear cells.[48] The observation of Natalie Sieber[49] that oxidases of the blood and of vegetable origin destroy diphtheria toxin rapidly, and also tetanus toxin and ricin, has been confirmed by Loewenstein as far as destruction by peroxide, with or without the presence of catalase, is concerned. Oxidation is undoubtedly an important process in defending the body against other forms of poisons, including the so-called "fatigue toxins," and Battelli and Stern consider that all the oxidizing enzymes so far definitely identified are concerned only in protective processes. Schmidt[50] has found that liver extracts render certain morphin derivatives nonpoisonous by oxidation. Oxalic acid and poisonous fatty acids are also oxidized into harmless substances; phosphorus and sulphur are oxidized into their acids, which are then neutralized. Indole and skatole are oxidized into less harmful substances.

The Indophenol Reaction.[51]—Alpha-naphthol and dimethyl-para-phenylendiamin, when brought together in alkaline solution, become oxidized in the presence of air and form an insoluble blue dye, indophenol. This reaction is greatly accelerated by oxidizing agents, and it has been found that certain tissues possess this property, hence the indophenol synthesis has been used for microchemical study of the presence and distribution of oxidizing enzymes in cells. As the intracellular agent which causes this reaction is, however, so resistant to heat and chemicals that it can be demonstrated in sections fixed in formalin and prepared by the ordinary paraffin imbedding method (Dunn), there is room for much doubt as to whether it represents a true enzyme, although it has been considered identical with phenolase.[52] In the presence of small amounts of peroxide the granules of leucocytes and myelocytes are stained with alphanaphthol alone, which Graham[53] interprets as oxidation by an enzyme of the peroxidase type. By using a d-naphthol and paraphenylenediamine and staining for long periods, Menten[54] has obtained positive reactions in all tissues, and has observed a similar effect with cholesterol esters. The evidence obtained indicates that the oxidation is not determined by enzymes but apparently is dependent on adsorption phenomena taking place on intracellular surfaces.

The indophenol reaction is observed best in the granules of neutrophile leucocytes of blood and in myeloid cells of bone marrow, leukemic blood and fetal organs; eosinophiles and basophile leucocytes also give reactions, but not lymphocytes, platelets, megakarocytes, plasma cells, mature erythrocytes, or most fixt tissue cells.[55] By using alkali-free, unfixt tissues Gierke found granules present in tissue cells generally, and Gräff states that they occur in proportion to the metabolic activity of the cells; they are abundant in carcinomas, scanty in sarcoma and connective tissue growths generally, are not destroyed in cloudy swelling or fatty changes, but disappear in infarcts and autolyzing tissues, and in tissues asphyxiated with illuminating gas.[56] Lung tissue is especially poor in this form of oxidative activity,[57] but giant cells of tubercles contain oxidase granules.[58]

[48] Fiessinger and Roudowska, Arch. de med. exper., 1912 (24), 585.
[49] Zeit. physiol. Chem., 1901 (32), 573.
[50] Dissertation, Heidelberg, 1901.
[51] Literature given by Schultze, Ziegler's Beitr., 1909 (45), 127; Dunn, Jour. Path. and Bact., 1910 (15), 20; Gräff, Frankfürter Zeit. f. Path., 1912 (12), 358; Rosenthal, Arch. Int. Med., 1917 (20), 185.
[52] Bach and Maryanovitsch, Biochem. Zeit., 1912 (42), 417.
[53] Jour. Med. Res., 1916 (35), 231.
[54] Jour. Med. Res., 1919 (40), 433.
[55] See Dunn, Quart. Jour. Med., 1913 (6), 293.
[56] See Klopfer, Zeit. exp. Pharm., 1912 (11), 467.
[57] Weiss, Wien. klin. Woch., 1912 (25), 697.
[58] Makino, Verh. Japan. Path. Gesell., 1915 (5), 71.

During experimental pneumococcus septicemia the indophenol oxidase reaction is decreased in the tissues.[59]

The nature of the granules that exhibit the stain is unknown, but as indophenol blue is a good fat stain it is probable that the stained granules are lipoidal, and it may well be that they are not the site of the oxidative action, but merely selectively stained lipoids in cells capable of forming the indophenol blue. These so-called "oxidase" granules have been divided into stable and labile, the former staining by the Winkler oxidase reaction, the latter by Gierke's reaction. The granules seem to pass from the leucocytes into their environment. When animals are exposed to x-rays the stable granules are destroyed sooner than the labile granules. The relation of the granules to other cell granules is undetermined, and their distribution is not identical with the granules that take the vital stains. Katsunuma[60] considers that they are probably not permanent specific structures, but transitional alterations produced in functional activity of the protoplasm.

Glycolytic Enzymes.[61]—The oxidation of sugar by the tissues, which is one of the chief sources of energy in the animal body, presumably takes place through several steps. Of these, it is believed by some that the first is the formation of glycuronic acid—

$$CH_2OH-(CHOH)_4\overset{O}{\overset{\|}{C}}-H + O_2 = COOH-(CHOH)_4\overset{O}{\overset{\|}{C}} - H + H_2O,$$
$$\text{(glucose)} \qquad\qquad\qquad\qquad \text{(glycuronic acid)}$$

but the subsequent changes which involve decomposition of the straight chain are not at present understood. Attempts to isolate from various organs an enzyme oxidizing glucose, particularly from the pancreas, muscle, and liver, have led to varying results and much dissension, but it is probable, because of these failures, that no such enzyme exists in quantities sufficient to account for the amount of sugar combustion that is normally accomplished. O. Cohnheim[62] attempted to explain the failures by his observation that the pancreas produces a substance that activates an inactive glycolytic enzyme in the muscles, liver, and probably in other organs. This work is not generally accepted, so we are still in the dark as to how the carbohydrate oxidations are accomplished. (See Chapter xxiv.)

LIPASE [63]

Lipase is probably present in greater or less amount in all cells. In the discussion of the reversible action of enzymes (see page 51) the modern conception of fat metabolism has been explained, which considers it to depend upon the existence of lipase in the cells and fluids throughout the body. On account of the technical difficulties in the way of using higher fats, such as triolein, in experimental work, the esters of lower fatty acids have generally been used, particularly ethyl butyrate, salicylic acid esters, and glycerol triacetate. Enzymes splitting ethyl butyrate, and other esters (*esterases*), have been demonstrated in practically all tissues examined, the names of Kastle and Loevenhart in this country, and Hanriot in France, being particularly connected with this work. What the relation of these esterases may be

[59] Medigreceanu, Jour. Exp. Med., 1914 (19), 303.
[60] Verh. Jap. Path. Ges., 1916 (6), 76.
[61] Also discussed under "Diabetes," chap. xxiv. As glycolysis by blood and tissues can occur without oxygen, Battelli and Stern exclude the glycolytic from the oxidizing enzymes.
[62] Zeit. physiol. Chem., 1903 (39), 336; also see Simpson, Biochem. Jour., 1910, (5), 126.
[63] For literature on lipase see Connstein, Ergebnisse Physiol., 1904 (3, Abt. 1), 194; concerning the behavior of lipase see Taylor, Jour. Biol. Chem., 1906 (2), 103; Falk, Proc. Natl. Acad., 1915 (1), 136; Science, 1918 (47), 423.

to the enzyme splitting fats, the true lipase, is not yet known. Much of the work so far reported on the occurrence of lipase in tissues is of questionable value, especially as to quantitative results, because of faulty methods. Saxl[64] points out and avoids some of these errors, and finds that during autolysis of tissues the splitting of the natural fats present in the cells is but slight; simple esters are attacked more, especially amyl-salicylate; muscle and blood are the least active tissues. Most authors agree that lymphoid cells are especially rich in lipolytic enzymes.[65] In the serum of normal individuals the esterase content seems to be quite constant,[66] and Quinan[67] found the tissue content also constant, the liver containing about twice as much as the kidney and over three times as much as the muscle. He states that different parts of the brain have characteristic lipase activity (butyrase).[68] Thiele[69] has found that blood, chyle, and various tissues also contain an enzyme which can hydrolyze lecithin, but except in the pancreas i' does not hydrolyze neutral fats. The brain contains enzymes hydrolyzing mono- and triacetin, lecithin and cephalin.[70]

Little is known about the part played by lipase in pathological conditions. According to Achard and Clerc,[71] the amount of splitting of ethyl butyrate by the blood-serum is lessened in most diseases, and increases and decreases with the health of the patient; according to Pribram[72] and Sagal[66] it is increased in the blood during fevers. Clerc[73] found that acute arsenic, phosphorus and diphtheria-toxin poisoning increased this property of the serum, while chronic poisoning and staphylococcus intoxication lowered it. Somewhat similar results were obtained by Grossmann,[74] but Saxl found no increased activity in phosphorus poisoning. Using the ethyl butyrate test, Winternitz and Meloy[75] found that the more nearly normal an organ is the more cleavage of the ester; lipolytic activity is low at birth, increases rapidly during the first few days of life, and does not decrease in old age. There is a decline in activity of tissues in diabetes, tuberculosis, and the toxemia of pregnancy, in the livers of passive congestion and fatty degeneration, in the pneumonic lung and the cirrhotic liver. After taking food there is a slight increase in esterase,

[64] Biochem. Zeit., 1908 (12), 343.
[65] The distribution of lipases in different species of animals and their various organs has been investigated by Porter, Münch. med. Woch., 1914 (61), 1774.
[66] Sagal, Jour. Med. Res., 1916 (34), 231.
[67] *Ibid.*, 1915 (32), 45.
[68] *Ibid.*, 1916 (35), 79.
[69] Biochem. Jour., 1913 (7), 275.
[70] English and MacArthur (Jour. Amer. Chem. Soc., 1915 (37), 653), who have also found in sheep brain, erepsin, amylase, catalase, enzymes decomposing arbutin and salol, probably pepsin and trypsin, but not peroxidase, oxidase, reductase, guanase, urease or rennin.
[71] Compt. Rend. Soc. Biol., 1902 (54), 1144.
[72] Cent. inn. Med., 1908 (29), 81.
[73] Compt. Rend. Soc. Biol., 1901 (53), 1131.
[74] Biochem. Zeit., 1912 (41), 181.
[75] Jour. Med. Res., 1910 (22), 107.

reaching a maximum in three hours.[76] Whipple[77] finds the blood lipase (butyrase) increased whenever there is injury to the liver, such as in chloroform anesthesia and puerperal eclampsia; it is lowered in cirrhosis. Poulain[78] found that the butyric-splitting power of lymph-glands draining infected areas was decreased. Fischer[79] observed, in a case of extreme lipemia in diabetes, that the lipolytic power of the blood was absent. The lipase of lipomas presents no demonstrable difference from that of ordinary fatty areolar tissues.[80]

Lipase has also been demonstrated in pus by a number of observers,[81] who agree that there is more in exudates than in transudates. Zeri[82] found lipase in the urine only when pus or blood was also present, but Pribram and Loewy[83] found it in nephritis, congestion, polyuria and other conditions. Lorenzini,[84] however, reports that in albuminuria the lipase content of the urine is reduced, in common with other enzymes, there being a simultaneous accumulation of enzymes in the blood.

Fiessinger and Marie[85] contend that the lymphocytes of exudates are the chief source of lipase, and suggest that this may be of effect in defense against the fatty tubercle bacilli. Toxins were found by Pesci[86] to increase the butyrase but not the other lipases of liver tissue. In syphilis the lipolytic activity of the serum is increased,[87] which may be related to Bergell's[88] observation on the origin of lipase in lymphocytes (corroborating Fiessinger and Marie). Jobling and Bull[89] state that a specific serum lipase increase occurs in animals immunized to red corpuscles, and that this lipase has to do with hemolysis; but Mendel[90] found no evidence that hemolysis by ricin is related to lipase. Abderhalden and Rona[91] found that excess feeding of fats leads to an increase in the lipase of the blood.

The part played by lipase in fatty degeneration must be of great importance, but as yet it has been little considered, except that Loevenhart, and Duccheschi and Almagia[92] found no appreciable difference

[76] Jobling et al., Jour. Exp. Med., 1915 (22), 129.
[77] Whipple et al., Bull. Johns Hopkins Hosp., 1913 (24), 207 and 357.
[78] Comp. Rend. Soc. Biol., 1901 (53), 786.
[79] Virchow's Arch., 1903 (172), 218.
[80] Wells, Arch. Int. Med., 1912 (10), 297.
[81] Achalme, Comp. Rend. Soc. Biol., 1899 (51), 568; Zeri, Il Policlinico, 1903 (10), 433; Memmi, Clin. Med. Ital., 1905 (44), 129.
[82] Il Policlinico, 1905 (12), 733.
[83] Zeit. physiol. Chem., 1912 (76), 489.
[84] Policlinico, 1915 (22), 358.
[85] Compt. Rend. Soc. Biol., 1909 (68), 177. See also Resch, Deut. Arch. klin. Med., 1915 (118), 179.
[86] Pathologica, 1912 (3), 207.
[87] Citron and Reicher, Berl. klin. Woch., 1908 (45), 1398.
[88] Münch. med. Woch., 1909 (56), 64.
[89] Jour. Exp. Med., 1912 (16), 483.
[90] Arch. Fisiol., 1909 (7), 168.
[91] Zeit. physiol. Chem., 1911 (75), 30.
[92] Arch. Ital. Biol., 1903 (39), 29.

in the lipase content of normal and phosphorus-poisoned livers, but in chloroform poisoning Quinan[93] found a decrease in the butyrase of the liver, although it was increased in the kidneys and muscles. This question will be considered more fully in discussing fatty metamorphosis.

An improved method of testing for lipase action has been devised by Rona and Michaelis, by measuring the change in surface tension caused by hydrolysis of a soluble ester, usually tributyrin. Using this, Bauer[94] found that every human serum contains fat-splitting enzymes, which are greatly decreased in carcinoma and advanced phthisis, somewhat decreased in syphilis and exophthalmic goitre, and increased in early pulmonary tuberculosis. Caro[95] found a decrease in all cases of cachexia, but there was no relation between the lipolytic enzyme and the blood picture. The blood contains no thermostable antilipase analogous to the antitrypsin. Red corpuscles are said to contain an enzyme splitting cholesterol esters, "*cholesterase.*"[96] In leucocytes a "*lipoidase*" has been found by Fiessinger and Clogne[97] that splits choline out of lecithin.

Fat necrosis, resulting from the escape of pancreatic juice into the peripancreatic tissues and abdominal cavity, undoubtedly is largely the result of lipase action. (See "Fat Necrosis," Chapter xv, for complete consideration.)

AMYLASE OR DIASTASE[97a]

Although under ordinary conditions starch is not supposed to enter the blood stream and tissues, yet all tissues and body fluids are capable of hydrolyzing starch. Apparently the amylase is derived from the pancreas and salivary glands, and possibly from many or all other tissues (King), but it is not quantitatively related to the amount of carbohydrate in the diet of a species or an individual (Carlson and Luckhardt). In the blood it occurs in the albumin fraction.[98] There is disagreement in the literature as to the variations in amount of amylase in the blood during disease, and little information concerning its distribution in the tissues. Normally the kidneys and liver seem to be most active and Winslow says that all glycogen-containing organs produce diastase. During acute infections the blood amylase is increased, presumably coming from the leucocytes (King). It is greatly increased when the pancreas is acutely inflamed or injured

[93] Jour. Med. Res., 1915 (32), 73.
[94] Wien. klin. Woch., 1912 (25), 1376 (bibliography).
[95] Zeit. klin. Med., 1913 (78), 286.
[96] See Cytronberg, Biochem. Zeit., 1912 (45), 281.
[97] Compt. Rend. Acad. Sci., 1917 (165), 730.
[97a] Literature given by Watanabe, Amer. Jour. Physiol., 1917 (45), 30; Geyelin, Arch. Int. Med., 1914 (13), 96; Stocks, Quart. Jour. Med., 1916 (9), 216; McClure and Pratt, Arch. Int. Med., 1917 (19), 568; Winslow, Hospitalstidende, 1918 (61) 832.
[98] Satta, Arch. Sci. Med., 1915 (39), 46.

(Stocks). In diabetes it is ordinarily increased, but not in syphilitic diabetes.[99] Intravenous or subcutaneous injection of starch is said to increase the blood amylase, presumably as a defensive reaction (Abderhalden), but the amylase ordinarily in the blood seems to be a waste substance on its way to excretion, rather than a functionating enzyme of the blood. There appears to be no normal antiamylase in the blood. Starch granules taken up by phagocytes show a glycogen reaction after some time, suggesting that these cells have intracellular diastases.[1]

Because of possible diagnostic significance, the amylolytic activity of the urine has been particularly studied, and found normally to be approximately constant for 24 hour specimens of the same individual.[2] Anything impairing the excretory capacity of the kidney decreases the urinary amylase, although sometimes when the urine contains blood, pus, or much albumen there may be an increased amylase excretion in spite of diminished functional activity. There may be an increase in the amylase in the blood when the urinary amylase is decreased, but with normal kidneys increase of the blood amylase causes an increase in the urine; hence, acute pancreatic diseases cause an increased urinary amylase (Stocks), but this is not constant (McClure and Pratt). In diabetic urine it is said to be usually decreased, but this is mostly accounted for by the dilution of the urine. Parenteral injection of starch causes a marked increase in the amount of diastase in the urine (King).[3]

[99] De Niord and Schreiner, Arch. Int. Med., 1919 (23), 484.
[1] Okazaki, Sei-I-Kwai Med. Jour., 1917 (36), 101.
[2] In infants the urine amylase is low (McClure and Chancellor, Zeit. Kinderheilk., 1914 (11), 483. Fetal blood contains much less than the maternal blood (Kito, Amer. Jour. Physiol., 1919 (48), 481).
[3] Proc. Soc. Exp. Biol., 1917 (15), 101.

CHAPTER III

ENYZMES (Continued)

INTRACELLULAR PROTEASES[1] (PROTEOLYTIC ENZYMES), INCLUDING
A CONSIDERATION OF AUTOLYSIS

To what extent synthesis of proteins goes on in the body is still a problem; still more uncertain is the part played by reversible action of proteases. There is evidence enough that somewhere in the body the amino-acids can be rebuilt into protein, for several investigators have succeeded in keeping animals in nitrogenous equilibrium by feeding them products of proteolysis that contained no proteins whatever, and as the proteins of the animal body are being broken down incessantly, it must be that they were replaced by synthesis of the non-protein material fed to the animals. In addition, it has long been questioned whether amino-acids absorbed from the intestines are not resynthesized into proteins while passing through the intestinal wall. Cohnheim found that in the intestinal epithelium there is an enzyme, *erepsin*, capable of splitting albumoses and peptones into the amino-acids, which enzyme presumably exists for the purpose of securing complete cleavage of all ingested proteins into their ultimate "building stones." This may be looked upon as a provision to reduce all varieties of proteins to their common elements, so that the body by quantitative selection can resynthesize them into its own types of protein, for, as is well known, foreign proteins (*e. g.* egg-albumin) introduced directly into the blood stream cannot be utilized, but are excreted unaltered in the urine.[2] As was shown for lipase, the assumption that such synthesis occurs as a normal physiological process by reverse enzyme action, requires that the proper enzymes be present in the cells throughout the body, and within recent years it has been abundantly demonstrated that such is the case.

For over half a century it has been known that amebæ digest solid proteins within their bodies, but it is only within a few years that proteolytic enzymes have been definitely isolated from them. It has been much the same with the intracellular proteases of the higher organisms. In 1871 Hoppe-Seyler referred to the liquefaction of

---

[1] As the possibility exists that ferments which digest proteins may be able to perform a certain amount of synthesis of proteins, the term "proteolytic enzyme" seems to be less suitable than the term "protease," which merely means an enzyme acting on proteins, and does not compel us to accept any particular view as to what the action is.

[2] According to Austin and Eisenbrey (Arch Int. Med., 1912 (10), 305), dogs on a nitrogen-free diet can utilize horse serum injected intravenously.

dead tissues within the body which occurred without putrefaction, and, as he noted, resembled the effects of the digestive ferments. It was nearly twenty years later that Salkowski[3] showed definitely that this softening of dead tissues was really brought about through a true digestion by intracellular enzymes, which produced the same splitting products that were at that time considered characteristic for tryptic digestion (leucine and tyrosine). The process he named "*autodigestion.*" This important observation remained almost unnoticed for ten years more, when Jacoby,[4] in 1900, took up the investigation of this matter of cellular self-digestion, and after this the importance of the principles involved became for the first time generally appreciated. Jacoby rechristened the process "*autolysis,*" by which name it is now commonly known.

AUTOLYSIS[5]

Autolysis is generally studied by the method used by Salkowski, which depends upon the difference in the susceptibility of bacteria and of enzymes to antiseptics. The organs are ground to a pulp, placed in flasks with or without the addition of water or dilute acids, and bacterial action is prevented by the addition of antiseptics that are not poisonous to enzymes—toluene and chloroform are most commonly used. It is possible also to secure organs in an aseptic condition and to permit them to undergo autolysis without the use of antiseptics, but the practical difficulties are such that this method is seldom used—it is sometimes designated as "*aseptic autolysis,*" in contradistinction to antiseptic autolysis by the Salkowski method. In a short time it can be seen that digestive changes have taken place, particularly if comparisons are made with control flasks in which the enzymes have been destroyed by boiling. To determine the rate of autolysis the amount of nitrogen that remains in the form of coagulable compounds, and that which is converted into soluble, non-coagulable compounds (albumoses, peptones, ammonia compounds, amino-acids, etc.), is compared. The method may be illustrated by a concrete example: A given specimen of emulsionized liver tissue was permitted to digest itself for twenty-two days. At the end of that time 39.4 per cent. of the nitrogen was still contained in the compounds that remained insoluble or became so after the autolysis was stopped by boiling; while 60.6 per cent. of the nitrogen was in a soluble form. A control specimen from the same liver was boiled while fresh to kill the enzymes, and then let stand under the same

[3] Zeit. f. klin. Med., 1890, supplement to Bd. 17, p. 77.
[4] Zeit. f. physiol. Chem., 1900 (30), 149.
[5] Résumé of literature by Salkowski, Deutsche Klinik, 1903 (11), 147; also see Schlesinger, Hofmeister's Beiträge, 1903 (4), 87; Oswald, Biochem. Centr., 1905 (3), 365; Levene, Jour. Amer. Med. Assoc., 1906 (46), 776; Nicolle, Ann. Inst. Pasteur, 1913 (27), 97; von Fürth, "Chemistry of Metabolism," Amer. Transl., 1916.

conditions. In this specimen 90.4 per cent. of the nitrogen was in an insoluble form, and 9.6 per cent. was soluble. Therefore, over half of all the protein of the liver had been changed into non-coagulable substances in the course of about three weeks (at 37° C.). Complete disintegration of the proteins with liberation of all the amino-acid complexes is probably never reached. Of 45.8 grams of amino-acids present in 100 grams of liver, in ten days' autolysis there had been set free but 1.85 gm., after 30 days 10.1 gm., and after 50 days but 29.1 gm. (Abderhalden and Prym.[6]) By determining the freezing point and conductivity of autolyzing mixtures, valuable evidence can be obtained as to the rate of change, which, in some cases, is much more significant than the usual estimation of soluble and insoluble nitrogen (Benson and Wells[7]). Titration of the free amino-acids by the formaldehyde method, together with the estimation of proteose and peptone nitrogen, also furnish valuable information, while the Van Slyke method of determining free amino-acids is especially useful for this purpose.

Since Jacoby's paper appeared, the field has been invaded by many workers, who have examined practically every tissue in the body, and found that all possess the power of self-digestion; or, in other words, *proteases are present in every cell in the body.*[8] The rate of digestion is very different in different organs, however, liver digesting rapidly while brain and muscle tissue digest much more slowly, and the autolytic activity varies under different conditions;[9] thus, fever causes a great increase in the proteolytic activity of the muscles.[10] The character of the antiseptic used modifies greatly the rate, salicylic and benzoic acids giving the most rapid autolysis, while of non-acid antiseptics toluene is perhaps the least inhibitory. One of the most important factors in modifying the rate of autolysis is the H-ion cencentration developing in the tissues.[11] Acidity acts, partly, at least, by so modifying the substrate that the enzymes can attack it, and a very small excess of acid will destroy the enzymes; Bradley[12] estimates this destructive acidity at about that concentration of H-ions which is indicated by methyl orange and Congo red, the maximum autolysis being obtained with an acidity at about $pH = 6.00$. A reaction approximating that of blood ($pH = 7.4 - 7.8$) reduces autolysis to a minimum. A latent period has been observed before autolysis *in*

[6] Zeit. physiol. Chem., 1907 (53), 320.

[7] Jour. Biol. Chem., 1910 (8), 61.

[8] Except, perhaps, the red corpuscles (Pincussohn and Roques, Biochem. Zeit., 1914 (64), 1).

[9] Concerning autolysis of skin, see Sexsmith and Petersen, Jour. Exp. Med. 1917 (27), 273.

[10] Aronsohn and Blumenthal, Zeit. klin. Med., 1908 (65), 1. Striated muscle autolyzes much less rapidly than cardiac and unstriated. (Bradley, Proc. Am. Soc. Biol. Chem., 1918 (33), xi).

[11] See Morse, Jour. Biol. Chem., 1916 (24), 163.

[12] Jour. Biol. Chem., 1915 (22), 113; 1916 (25), 261.

vitro seems to begin, part of which time may be occupied in the development of sufficient acidity to permit of autolysis, although Bradley's[13] results indicate that it can be accounted for largely by the time required for proteolysis to proceed far enough to be detected by chemical means. Dernby[14] finds that in several tissues studied, including leucocytes, there are two intracellular proteases, one resembling pepsin in carrying digestion only to the peptone stage and in requiring an acid medium, optimum $pH = 3.5$; the other resembling ereptase, splitting only peptones and peptids into amino-acids, with optimum reaction $pH = 7.8$, and inhibited by acid reaction. Autolysis of tissues proceeds furthest in a pH range between 5 and 6, presumably because in this condition both enzymes can act. From these facts it is evident that *quantitative studies of rates of autolysis are valueless if the H-ion concentration is not taken into consideration.*

The cleavage products resulting from tissue autolysis seem to contain a much larger proportion of the nitrogen in the form of ammonia and its compounds than is the case with simple tryptic digestion, because of the presence of deaminizing enzymes which split the NH_2 groups out of the amino-acids and purines. According to Bostock[15] the greater the acidity the less NH_3 is formed. It is quite probable that in tissue autolysis several intracellular enzymes are in action which may not be present in pancreatic or gastric juice; for example, in the liver is an enzyme, *arginase*, which splits the urea radical out of the arginine of the proteins (Kossel and Dakin[16]), and the enzymes which disintegrate purines are also absent from the digestive juices. On the whole, however, the products are quite similar to those obtained by tryptic digestion. To give a concrete example, Dakin[17] detected in the products of autolysis by the kidney in acid solution, the following substances: Ammonia, alanine, α-aminovalerianic acid, leucine, α-pyrollidine carboxylic acid, phenylalanine, tyrosine, lysine, histidine, cystine, hypoxanthine, and indole derivatives, including probably tryptophane.[18] The cleavage of simple *peptids* by different tissues shows characteristic differences, the distribution of the enzyme which splits glycyl-tryptophane having been most studied. During life the cells retain this enzyme, and hence it appears in the body fluids only when the tissues are being rapidly disintegrated (Mandelbaum).[19]

During autolysis the changes are by no means limited to the proteins. Glycogen is split into glucose very early, and the sugar undergoes further changes. Fats are also split by the lipase, fatty acids

[13] Jour. Biol. Chem., 1916 (25), 363.
[14] Jour. Biol. Chem., 1918 (35), 179.
[15] Biochem. Jour., 1912 (6), 388.
[16] Zeit. physiol. Chem., 1901 (42), 181.
[17] Jour. of Physiology, 1903 (30), 84.
[18] The results of autolysis by different tissues are said to be quite dissimilar. See Kashiwabara, Zeit. physiol. Chem., 1913 (85), 161.
[19] Münch. med. Woch., 1914 (61), 461.

being found in autolyzed organs. Reducing substances appear, and as before mentioned, numerous volatile fatty acids are said to be produced. Much doubt exists concerning the supposed formation of volatile fatty acids and gasses during autolysis since it was shown by Wolbach, Saiki and Jackson[20] that anaerobic bacteria are almost invariably present in aseptically removed dog livers, for control of autolysis by anaerobic cultures has seldom been carried out. However, there is much evidence that lactic acid is formed, and perhaps partially destroyed, in autolysis (Türkel,[21] Ssobolew[22]). Carefully controlled experiments by Lindemann[23] seem to show that even in the absence of bacteria, autolyzing liver and heart can produce volatile acids, CO_2 and hydrogen. The increase in fat described by some authors is probably only apparent, and due rather to the liberation of the fat from its combination with the proteins so that it is free and not "masked," as in normal organs.[24] Lecithin is decomposed, yielding choline, but cholesterol remains unchanged except for some hydrolysis of cholesterol esters.[25] Creatine is changed to creatinine in autolyzing muscle, and apparently both are formed in autolysis of blood and liver.[26]

The *nucleo-proteins* seem to be attacked by the autolytic enzymes, as the purine bases are prominent among the products of autolysis, and in quite different proportions from those obtaining in digestion of the same tissues by other means. Apparently autolytic enzymes, like trypsin, attack the protein group of the nucleoproteins, liberating the nucleic acids. These in turn are attacked by specific enzymes, *nucleases*,[27] which liberate the purine bases, which are further decomposed by specific enzymes, *guanase, adenase*, etc. (See Chap. xxiii).

It is improbable that the intracellular enzymes are merely pancreatic enzymes taken out of the blood by the cells, because of the differences previously cited; furthermore, Matthes[28] found that the liver retained its autolytic power after the pancreas had been extirpated (in dogs), and that the autolytic degeneration of cut peripheral nerves went on just the same, indicating that the autolytic enzymes do not owe their origin to the pancreas.

Whenever tissues are disintegrated in any considerable quantities, as after extensive burns, peptolytic enzymes become demonstrable in

[20] Jour. Med. Res., 1909 (21), 267.
[21] Biochem. Zeit., 1909 (20), 431.
[22] *Ibid.*, 1912 (47), 367. See also v. Stein and Salkowski, Biochem. Zeit., 1913 (40), 486.
[23] Zeit. f. Biol., 1910 (55), 36.
[24] See Krontowski and Poleff, Beitr. Path. Anat., 1914 (58), 407.
[25] Corper, Jour. Biol. Chem., 1912 (11), 37; Kondo, Biochem. Zeit., 1910 (27), 427.
[26] Myers and Fine, Jour. Biol. Chem., 1915 (21), 583; Hoagland and McBryde, Jour. Agric. Res., 1916 (6), 535.
[27] Sachs, Zeit. physiol. Chem., 1905 (46), 337; Jones, *ibid.*, 1903 (41), 101, and 1906 (48), 110.
[28] Arch. f. exp. Path. u. Pharm., 1901 (51), 442.

the blood and urine, and presumably these are related to the cell autolysis.[29]   They are noticeably increased in most infectious diseases in which the reaction between the body defenses and the infecting organism takes place in the blood stream (Falls).[30]   Also in the pre-mortal state a similar increase in peptolytic enzyme in the serum is associated with a high non-protein nitrogen figure for the serum.[31] The relation of the autolytic enzymes to the increased proteolytic power of serum in pregnancy, as evidenced in the Abderhalden reaction (q.v.) has not yet been determined,[32] but Falls finds evidence of their correlation.[30]   Blood proteases are also increased in pregnancy. They bear no constant relation to the leucocyte count.   Autodigestion of serum is normally prevented by the presence of a specific antienzyme, which latter can be inhibited by chloroform and various saturated monovalent ketones and alcohols (Yamakawa).[33]

Influence of Chemicals on Autolysis.—As a general rule the addition of anti-septics to tissues to prevent bacterial action reduces the rate of autolysis, but as most of the results of "aseptic" autolysis so far reported are open to question, there is a reasonable doubt as to just how much depression of autolysis there is. Yoshimoto[34] finds that of the antiseptics ordinarily used, salicylic acid, boric acid, and mustard oil (one-eighth saturated solution) permit the greatest auto-lysis; but it is probable that the acidity of the first two antiseptics plays an im-portant part, hence the value of the results obtained in autolysis with these acids is questionable.   However, sodium salicylate and benzoate are said to favor autolysis (Laqueur).[35]   Toluene seems to interfere much less with autolysis than chloroform or thymol (Benson and Wells[36]), and bromides are less harmful than toluene (Laqueur).   Toluene vapor, acting on solid aseptic tissues, seems to cause more depression of autolysis than is usually observed in autolysis in solution.[37]   Dorothy Court[38] found the only satisfactory antiseptics to be chloro-form, formaldehyde, benzoic and salicylic acids, and HNC; she emphasizes the fact that for different sorts of materials the different antiseptics give variable re-sults, so that the antiseptic used should be selected with reference to the material. Autolysis proceeds rapidly in weak ethyl alcohol, 5 per cent. being the minimum strength that will prevent putrefaction; for complete suppression of autolysis by alcohol the strength must be at least 90 per cent. net, after allowing for the water content of the tissues (Wells and Caldwell).[39]

Certain inorganic substances in proper concentrations have been reported as increasing the rate of autolysis [mercury[40] and silver,[41] (colloidal[42] or salts)],

[29] See Pfeiffer, Münch. med. Woch., 1914 (61), 1099, 1329.
[30] Jour. Infect. Dis., 1915 (16), 466; also Petersen and Short, Jour. Infect. Dis., 1918 (22), 147.
[31] See Schulz, Münch. med. Woch., 1913 (60), 2512; Mandelbaum, ibid., 1914 (61), 461.
[32] See Sloan, Amer. Jour. Physiol., 1915 (39), 9.
[33] Jour. Exp. Med., 1918 (27), 689.
[34] Zeit. physiol. Chem., 1908 (58), 341.
[35] Zeit. physiol. Chem., 1912 (79), 38 and 65.
[36] Jour. Biol. Chem., 1910 (8), 61.
[37] Cruickshank, Jour. Path. and Bact., 1911 (16), 167.
[38] Proc. Roy. Soc., Edinburgh, 1912 (32), 251.
[39] Jour. Biol. Chem., 1914 (19), 57.
[40] Truffi, Biochem. Zeit., 1910 (23), 270.
[41] Izar, ibid., 1909 (20), 249.
[42] The accelerating influence of colloidal metals is denied by Bradley, Proc. Amer. Soc. Biol. Chem., 1918 (33), xi.

yellow phosphorus,[43] iodides,[44] arsenic,[45] $CaCl_2$,[46] salts of Fe, Mg, and cobalt,[47] as well as salts of selenium, tellurium,[48] and manganese,[49] colloidal sulfur[50] but not colloidal carbon.[51] The favorable concentrations of these metals are very low; thus the optimum proportion of arsenic is 0.007 milligrams per 1 gm. tissue, while 0.04 mg. inhibits autolysis. CO_2 increases and oxygen decreases autolysis[52] *in vitro* (Laqueur). There is disagreement as to whether radium rays augment autolysis.[53] Injection of iodids into animals is said to increase the postmortem autolysis of their tissues (Stookey, Kepinow), as also do iron salts,[54] while large doses of salicylates decrease it (Laqueur). Morse[55] attributes the accelerating action of iodin and bromin to increased acidity from formation of halogen acids, and Bradley[12] finds evidence that most inorganic salts that stimulate autolysis act by increasing H-ion concentration. Addition of tuberculin to tissues at first delays and then increases the autolysis (Pesci[56]), and diphtheria toxin in small amounts increases autolysis (Barlocco,[57] Bertolini[58]), neutralization by anti-toxin not preventing this effect. Lipoids also accelerate autolysis (Satta and Fasiani[59]). According to Soula[60] narcotic poisons decrease, and convulsive poisons increase the rate of autolysis of nervous tissue. Glucose in one per cent. concentration decreases autolysis, and this may be related to the "protein-sparing action of carbohydrates." [61] Extracts of various ductless glands, or removal of these glands from animals, seem to have but slight effect on autolysis.[62]

In considering the foregoing statements allowance must be made for the fact that in most of the work cited there has been no proper consideration of H-ion concentration in the autolyzing mixtures.

RELATION OF AUTOLYSIS TO METABOLISM

It having been shown that proteases are present in all cells, the next question to be considered is, do they act only to destroy tissues after death, or are they of importance in metabolism? Since it is presumably necessary for proteins to be split into diffusible and easily oxidized forms in order that they may enter the cell, and be built up into the cell proteins, or be decomposed with the liberation of energy, the autolytic proteases may be assumed to be of prime importance in protein metabolism; but to prove it is another matter. Jacoby found

[43] Saxl, Hofmeister's Beitr.. 1907 (10). 447; Virchow's Arch., 1910 (202), 149.
[44] Kepinow, Biochem. Zeit., 1911 (37), 238. Kaschiwabara, Zeit. physiol. Chem., 1912 (82), 425. Not confirmed by Albrecht, Jour. Biol. Chem., 1919 (41), 111.
[45] Izar, Biochem. Zeit., 1909 (21), 46; Laqueur and Ettinger, Zeit. physiol. Chem., 1912 (79) 1.
[46] Brüll, Biochem. Zeit., 1910 (29), 408.
[47] Preti, Zeit. physiol. Chem., 1909 (60), 317; Pollini, Biochem. Zeit., 1912 (47), 396.
[48] Fasiani, Arch. sci. med., 1912 (36), 436.
[49] Bradley, Jour. Biol. Chem., 1915 (21), 209; 1915 (22), 113.
[50] Faginoli, Biochem. Zeit., 1913 (56), 291.
[51] Izar and Patane, *ibid.*, p. 307.
[52] M. Morse found oxygen without effect on autolysis. Biochem. Bullet., 1915 (5), 143.
[53] See Loewenthal and Edelstein, Biochem. Zeit., 1908 (14), 485; Brown, Arch. Int. Med., 1912 (10), 405.
[54] Kottmann, Zeit. exp. Path., 1912 (11), 355.
[55] Jour. Biol. Chem., 1915 (22), 125.
[56] Cent. f. Bakt., 1911 (59), 71 and 186.
[57] Cent. f. Bakt., 1911 (60), 43.
[58] Biochem. Zeit., 1913 (48), 448.
[59] Berl. klin. Woch, 1910 (47), 1500.
[60] Compt. Rend. Soc. Biol., 1913 (73), 297.
[61] Shaffer, Proc. Soc. Biol. Chem., 1915 (8), xlii.
[62] Izar and Fagiuoli, Sperimentale, 1916 (70), 265.

that if he ligated off a portion of the liver and let it remain *in situ* in the animal the necrotic tissues showed an accumulation of leucine, tyrosine, and other cleavage products of the proteins, which suggested that these same bodies are being formed in the liver constantly, but that they are as constantly removed from the normal organs by the circulating blood, or are undergoing further alterations which cease when the circulation is checked. The influence of various chemicals upon nitrogen elimination seems to correspond to their effect on autolysis (Izar,[63] Laqueur[64]). Also, the histologic changes of starvation are similar in many respects to those of autolysis (Casa-Bianchi[65]). Among other observations possibly bearing on the same question are those of Hildebrandt,[66] who found that autolysis in the functionating mammary gland is much more active than in the resting gland; and of Schlesinger,[67] who found that autolysis was at its maximum (in rabbits) in new-born animals, decreasing rapidly in the first few months of life, and that in conditions associated with emaciation the rate of autolysis varied directly with the degree of emaciation. Wells[68] sought for a possible influence on autolysis by thyroid extract, which increases protein metabolism, but could demonstrate none *in vitro;* Schryver,[69] however, reported that autolysis was more rapid in the liver of dogs fed thyroid extract for some days before death than it was in control animals. The results of the former observer, but not those of the latter, have been confirmed by Morse.[70]

DEFENSE OF THE CELLS AGAINST THEIR AUTOLYTIC ENZYMES

The question of why the autolytic ferments do not destroy the cells until after death is a revival of the old problem of "why the stomach does not digest itself," and the answer that satisfies some is that dead protoplasm is essentially different from living protoplasm. More specific replies are suggested by Wiener's studies on the relation of the reaction of the tissues to their autolysis. He found that autolysis does not begin in an organ until the original alkalinity is neutralized by the acids which are formed in all dead and dying cells.[71] If enough alkali is added to the material from time to time to neutralize the acidity as it develops, autolysis does not take place. Although

[63] Internat. Beitr. Ernährungstör., 1910 (1), 287.
[64] Zeit. physiol. Chem., 1912 (79), 1 *et seq.*
[65] Frankfurter Zeit. Pathol., 1909 (3), 723.
[66] Hofmeister's Beiträge, 1904 (5), 463; see also Grimmer, Biochem. Zeit., 1913 (53), 429.
[67] Hofmeister's Beitr., 1903 (4), 87.
[68] Amer. Jour. of Physiol., 1904 (11), 351; corroborated by Kottmann, Zeit. klin. Med., 1910 (71), 369.
[69] Jour. of Physiol., 1905 (32), 159.
[70] Jour. Biol. Chem., 1915 (22), 125.
[71] Opie (*loc cit.*) found, however, that autolysis of leucocytes was more rapid in an alkaline medium. Dochez (Jour. Exp. Med., 1910 (12), 666) states that liver also contains an enzyme active in an alkaline medium, but which exists as an inactive zymogen until activated by acids. See also Dernby.[14]

the spleen contains an enzyme digesting in alkaline solution,[72] and another which acts best in weak acids, the latter appears more prominently under ordinary conditions because the spleen and the blood contain antibodies which check the enzyme that acts in alkaline solutions, while acids destroy this antibody (Hedin).[73] Organic acids are formed in autolysis of the tissues, and the latent period between the time of the removal of an organ from the body and the appearance of autolysis may be explained partly by the time required for the neutralization or alkalinity. Bradley[12] has also obtained evidence that the acid renders the substrate susceptible to digestion by the proteases. Dernby's[14] demonstration of the existence of pepsin-like and erepsin-like enzymes suggests that there must be developed enough acidity to permit the peptase to form peptones before the ereptases can begin their further cleavage. Maximum autolysis is known to occur when tissues are first made acid and then neutralized or slightly alkalinized (Hedin). The old observation that rigor mortis disappears most rapidly in muscles that have been exhausted just before death is probably explained by the greater amount of acid in such muscles. If we imagine that autolysis is limited to periods when the cells have an acid reaction, however, we limit the range of usefulness in the living cell to a minimum, since during life the tissue fluids, and presumably the cell contents, are preponderatingly alkaline. The control of autolysis by maintenance of a low H-ion concentration is undoubtedly an important factor, for Bradley found that a reaction equal to that of blood almost completely inhibits autolysis, while the degree of increased H-ion concentration that may develop in local asphyxia, or after death, produces optimum conditions for autolysis.

Still another possible defense of the living cells may be found in the existence of *specific antienzymes*. Just as the serum contains antitrypsin, so it seems to contain substances antagonistic to the autolytic enzymes. Levene and Stookey found that tissue juices show a resistance to digestion, Yamakawa[33] found that serum autolysis is prevented by an antienzyme, and Opie found that the serum of inflammatory exudates retards the action of the autolytic enzymes that are contained within the leucocytes. Serum also inhibits autolysis of the tissues, so it is probable that continuance of the circulation may provide antibodies to the tissues to hold the intracellular enzymes in check, possibly without interfering with their action on other proteins than those of the cell structure.[74] (See Antienzymes.) It is

---

[72] Morse (Jour. Biol. Chem., 1917 (31), 303) considers this enzyme to be heterolytic, derived from the white cells.

[73] Festschrift f. Hammarsten, Upsala, 1906.

[74] According to Guggenheimer (Deut. Arch. klin. Med., 1913 (112), 248; Deut. med. Woch., 1914 (40), 63), the serum in various diseases has a characteristic stimulating or inhibiting effect on *in vitro* tissue autolysis, but the conditions of such experiments are so complex as to make their significance doubtful.

highly probable that serum checks autolysis at least in part by virtue of its "buffer" function, which interferes with the development of acidity. Lack of oxygen cannot be held solely responsible for autolysis, according to the studies of Morse,[75] who found that autolysis occurs in muscles with divided nerves but intact blood supply. Nevertheless, reduced blood supply results in increased H-ion concentration which greatly facilitates autolysis, and it cannot be denied that autolysis is observed chiefly if not solely in asphyxiated tissues.

There can be no question that the supply of food-stuff is of essential importance in determining autolytic changes, for it has been found by Conradi,[76] Rettger,[77] and Effront[78] that bacteria and yeasts begin to undergo autolysis when they are placed in distilled water or salt solution, which they do not do, to any such extent at least, when in nutrient media. (In this way it has been found possible to obtain the intracellular poisons of such bacteria as typhoid and cholera.) Autolysis is not marked so long as the bacteria are supplied with nourishment, but when nutrient material is lacking, autolytic decomposition is no longer repaired and the bacteria disintegrate. Presumably the changes are the same in tissue cells, and anemic necrosis may be explained in this way. Tissue enzymes are also capable of digesting bacteria (Turró[79]).

Another direction in which the key to the action of these enzymes may be sought has been indicated by Jacoby,[80] who found that to a certain degree the autolytic enzymes of each organ are specific for that organ. Liver extract will not split lung tissue, although it will split the proteoses that are formed in lung autolysis, possibly because these proteoses are less specific than the proteins from which they arise, or perhaps because of the erepsin the extract contains (Vernon). Leucocytic proteases, however, seem capable of splitting foreign proteins of all sorts. Richet[81] states that the protease of liver tissue does not attack either muscle tissue or liver tissue that has been coagulated. Another hypothesis has been advanced by Fermi,[82] who suggests that the protoplasm of living cells is not digested because its structural configuration is such that the enzymes cannot unite with it, an attractive but practically undemonstrable idea.

Lastly, it must be considered that at least to some extent the enzymes exist in the cells in their inactive zymogen form, and perhaps are changed into the active form as needed, and inhibited or changed back again when their work is temporarily finished. A

[75] Amer. Jour. Physiol., 1915 (36), 147.
[76] Deut. med. Woch., 1903 (29), 26.
[77] Jour. Med. Research, 1904 (13), 79.
[78] Bull. Soc. Chim., 1905 (33), 847.
[79] Cent. f. Bakt., 1902 (32), 105.
[80] Hofmeister's Beitr., 1903 (3), 446.
[81] Compt. Rend. Soc. Biol., 1903 (55), 656.
[82] Cent. f. Bakt., 1910 (56), 55.

rhythmical change of this nature might be imagined as occurring and accounting for interaction by the enzymes, particularly since rhythmical changes in metabolism are known to occur (e. g.,) rhythmical production of carbon dioxide (Lyon[83]), and enzyme action *in vitro* may show rhythmic variations (Groll).[84]

AUTOLYSIS IN PATHOLOGICAL PROCESSES

All absorption of dead or injured tissues, and of organic foreign bodies, seems to be accomplished by means of digestion by the enzymes of the cells and tissue fluids. We may distinguish between the digestion brought about by the enzymes of the digested tissue itself, or *autolysis*, and digestion by enzymes from other cells or tissue fluids, or *heterolysis* (Jacoby). Heterolysis is accomplished particularly by the leucocytes, which contain ferments capable of digesting not only leucocytic proteins but apparently every other sort,[85] from serum-albumin to catgut ligatures. The heterolysis may be intracellular when the material to be digested has first been taken up by the cells (phagocytosis); or extra-cellular, either by enzymes normally contained in the blood plasma and tissue fluids, or by enzymes liberated by the leucocytes and fixed tissue cells. On death and dissolution of a cell the intracellular enzymes are released,[86] but it is not known to what extent the enzymes may be secreted from intact living cells. As far as pathological processes show, the amount of liberation of enzymes from normal cells is very slight, if any, and the digestive enzymes of the blood plasma seem to be very feeble, but this is perhaps because they are largely held in check by the anti-enzymatic substances of the serum. Pathological autolysis and heterolysis, therefore, are brought about chiefly by enzymes liberated from dead or injured cells. Bacteria, however, can multiply upon a medium of coagulated protein, which suggests that they also secrete proteolytic substances. In pathological conditions digestion of degenerated tissues seems usually to be the result of both autolysis and heterolysis. An infarct softens because the intracellular enzymes digest the dead cells, exactly as

[83] Science, 1904 (19), 350.
[84] Nederl. Tijdschr. v. Geneesk., 1918 (1), 1085.
[85] Many authors suggest that the leucocytes merely carry enzymes from one organ, particularly the pancreas, to another, and that these enzymes are not formed by the leucocyte itself. Opie (Jour. Exp. Med., 1905 (7), 759) has shown, however, that the bone-marrow contains proteolytic enzymes which are like those of the leucocytes in that they act best in an alkaline medium, whereas the autolytic enzymes of the lymphatic glands and most other tissues act best in an acid medium. This leaves little room for doubt that the leucocytes are equipped with their characteristics enzymes when they leave the bone-marrow, and that they are not obtained later in the pancreas or elsewhere. More recently, however, van Calcar (Pflüger's Archiv., 1912 (148), 257) has revived the idea of the origin of leucocytic enzymes in the digestive glands.
[86] Peptolytic enzymes appear in the urine after severe superficial burning, presumably coming from the disintegrated cells. (Pfeiffer, Münch. med. Woch., 1914 (61), 1329.)

they do when the tissue is removed from the body, ground up, and put in the incubator under toluene. In addition leucocytes wander in, disintegrate, and their liberated enzymes help in the process, as also do, to a less degree, the enzymes of the blood plasma. It is because of the heterolysis by leucocytic enzymes that a septic infarct becomes softened so much more rapidly than does a sterile infarct, and by comparing the rate of softening in septic and aseptic infarcts we see that the cellular autolysis is a very slow process as compared to the heterolysis accomplished by the leucocytes. The explanation of this may lie in the fact that most intracellular proteases act best in an acid medium (Wiener), while leucocytic proteases act best in an alkaline medium (Opie), and the infarcts of small size are seeped through by alkaline blood fluids. When an infarct is large, we find it undergoing central softening while the periphery remains firm; this corroborates our hypothesis, for acids are developed during autolysis (Magnus-Levy), which at the periphery are neutralized by the blood plasma, so that only at the center is autolysis active. The inhibiting action of the serum also has a similar effect, limiting autolysis at the periphery. Necrotic areas of any kind are absorbed by similar processes.

Apparently all varieties of cells are subject to autolysis or heterolysis whenever they are killed or sufficiently injured. Involution of the uterus probably depends upon autolysis, which is much more active in the puerperal uterus (Ferroni[87]), and creatine is found in the urine when such autolysis occurs,[88] although A. Morse[87] considers this to be independent of the uterine autolysis. Atrophy may be looked upon as an autolysis in the normal course of catabolism, not met by a corresponding building up of the proteins, but M. Morse[89] could find no evidence that the atrophy and involution of the tadpole tail is accompanied by an accelerated autolysis. The solution of fibrin by tissues, *fibrinolysis*, is considered to be distinct from tissue autolysis by Fleisher and Loeb.[90] In atrophic cirrhosis the fibrinolytic activity of the blood is increased, which may explain the hemorrhagic tendency of this disease.[91] In the case of septic softening the action of the bacteria needs also to be taken into consideration, since they produce proteolytic ferments, but their effect seems to be relatively small as compared with leucocytic digestion.[92] Intracellular digestion of

[87] Ann. di Ostetrica e Ginecol., 1906 (2), 553; see also Slemons, Bull. Johns Hopkins Hosp., 1914 (25), 195; Arthur Morse, Jour. Amer. Med., Assoc., 1915 (65), 1613.
[88] Shaffer, Amer. Jour. Physiol. 1908 (23), 1.
[89] Max Morse, Am. Jour. Physiol., 1915 (36), 145.
[90] Jour. Biol. Chem., 1915 (21), 477.
[91] Goodpasture, Bull. Johns Hopkins Hosp., 1914 (25), 330.
[92] The enzymes of staphylococcus are much more strongly proteolytic than those of streptococcus (Knapp, Zeit. f. Heilk. (Chir.), 1902 (23), 236.) which may be one reason why the latter so much more frequently produces lesions without suppuration than does the former.

necrotic tissue by leucocytes seems also to be relatively unimportant. Suppuration, therefore, must be considered as the result of digestion of dead tissue by enzymes derived from the leucocytes, the plasma, the bacteria, and the destroyed cells themselves. A tubercle does not ordinarily suppurate, because the tubercle bacillus and the substances it produces are not strongly chemotactic, and hence not enough leucocytes enter the necrotic area to produce a digestive softening.

The products of autolysis may of themselves be toxic; albumoses and peptones certainly are, and the other cleavage products are probably not altogether innocuous. (See "Autointoxication.") Some of the symptoms of suppuration, particularly the fever and chills, have been ascribed to the autolytic products rather than to the bacterial poisons, particularly as aseptic suppuration is accompanied by fever. Jochmann[93] has found evidence that the protease of leucocytes can cause fever and also reduce the coagulability of the blood. The work of Vaughan and other recent students of the reaction to foreign proteins, shows that typical fevers can be produced by the enzymatic disintegration of proteins in the body.[94] Degenerative changes in nervous tissue are associated with autolytic decomposition of the lecithin (Noll[95]) and the liberated choline, or its more toxic derivatives, may be a source of intoxication.[96] In all conditions associated with autolysis, such as resolving pneumonic exudates, large abscesses, softening tumors, etc., albumoses (and peptones?) may appear in the urine. Autolytic products may also be hemolytic (Levaditi[97]), and they may prevent clotting of the blood (Conradi[98]). It is probable that among the products of autolysis are bactericidal substances,[99] although it is doubtful if the concentration is often sufficient for them to be of influence except in well walled areas.

There is also much evidence that after extensive traumatism, especially as observed in war, the products of the tissue autolysis may be responsible for serious intoxication, and possibly for conditions interpreted at times as *shock*.[1] The observations made in experimental anaphylaxis suggest that it is especially the slightly altered proteins, perhaps only changed in their colloidal properties, that are most likely to be responsible for these shock-like intoxications. However, it is also possible that amines derived from the aminoacids may be of

[93] Virchow's Arch., 1908 (194), 342.
[94] See Vaughan, "Protein Split Products," Philadelphia, 1913.
[95] Zeit. physiol. Chemie, 1899 (27), 380.
[96] See Halliburton, Ergebnisse der Physiol., 1904 (4), 24.
[97] Ann. d. l'Inst. Pasteur, 1903 (17), 187; also Fukuhara, Zeit. f. exp. Path. u. Pharm., 1907 (4), 658.
[98] Hofmeister's Beitr., 1901 (1), 136.
[99] See Bilancioni, Arch. farmacol., 1911 (11), 491.
[1] Delbet, Bull. Acad. Med., 1918 (80), 13; Cannon, Compt. Rend. Soc. Biol., 1918 (81), 850; Turck, Med. Record, June 1, 1918.

importance in producing shock whenever tissues are injured.[2]   Methyl guanidine may also be formed from disintegrating tissues and has considerable toxicity.

Work has been reported upon autolytic processes in a number of pathological conditions, which may be discussed briefly as follows:

Exudates.—The presence of leucine, tyrosine, proteoses, and peptones in pus has been known for many years, and the reason for their appearance is now clear.   Müller,[3] many years ago, observed that purulent sputum digested fibrin, but that non-purulent sputum did not have this property.   Achalme[4] found that pus would dissolve gelatin, fibrin, and egg-albumen.   Ascoli and Mareschi[5] detected autolysis in sterile exudates obtained experimentally.   Umber[6] found that ascitic fluid exhibited autolytic changes, which observation could not be confirmed by Schütz[7] in pleural exudates and ascitic fluids.   Zak[8] found that autolysis was inconstant in various exudates. The differences in these results are explained by Opie's[9] observation that in experimental inflammatory exudates the leucocytes are capable of marked autolysis, whereas the serum contains an antibody which holds this autolysis in check; if the antibody is destroyed by heat, then the serum proteins are also digested by the leucocytic enzymes.   This antibody seems to be contained normally in the albumin of the blood-serum.   In old exudates the antibodies are decreased, and autolysis then occurs, explaining the variable results of Umber, Schütz and Zak.   The intracellular proteases of the polynuclear leucocytes act best in an alkaline medium; those of the mononuclears in acid medium.   If the proportion of serum to leucocytes is high, then there is no autolysis, as in serous exudates; but if the leucocytes are abundant, then the antibody is overcome and we get autolysis, as in ordinary suppurative exudates.   Animals with but little protease in their leucocytes (*e. g.*, rabbits), do not ordinarily produce a liquid pus (Opie). Exudates produced by bacterial infection also seem to possess the properties above described.   Galdi[10] found autolysis greater in exudates than in transudates, but observed no constant relation between the number of leucocytes, or the amount of chlorides, and the rate of autolysis.   All exudates, according to Lenk and Pollak,[11] contain enzymes splitting glycyl-glycine (peptolytic enzymes); the most active

[2] See Abel and Kubota, Jour. Pharm. Exp. Ther., 1919 (13), 243.
[3] Kossel, Zeit. f. klin. Med., 1888 (13), 149.
[4] Compt. Rend. Soc. Biol., 1899 (51), 568.
[5] See Maly's Jahresbericht, 1902 (32), 568.
[6] Münch. med. Woch., 1902 (49), 1169.
[7] Cent. f. inn. Med., 1902 (23), 1161.
[8] Wien. klin. Woch., 1905 (18), 376.
[9] Jour. of Exper. Med., 1905 (7), 316 and 759; 1906 (8), 410 and 536; 1907 (9), 207, 391 and 414; also a full review in Arch. Int. Med., 1910 (5), 541.
[10] See Folia Hemat., 1905 (2), 529.
[11] Deut. Arch. klin. Med., 1913 (109), 350; See also Wiener, Biochem. Zeit., 1912 (41), 149; Mandelbaum, Münch. med. Woch., 1914 (61), 464.

exudates are those of cancer and tuberculosis, the least active are passive congestion fluids; pleural exudates contain more active enzymes than peritoneal exudates of similar character.

Knapp[92] holds that in pus the cocci and the enzymes they produce are responsible for much of the digestion. Pus cells alone do not undergo digestion so rapidly as when bacteria are present, and digestion is more rapid if the bacteria are alive than when inhibited or killed by antiseptics. Streptococcus is almost inactive, staphylococcus is quite active, and *B. coli* still more so. However, pus corpuscles free from bacteria are highly proteolytic, causing digestion in serum plates in dilutions of 1–700 (Jochmann). Knapp could find no relation between the autolytic power of the pus and the severity of the infection from which it resulted. A constant constituent of pus is d-lactic acid,[12] and it increases during autolysis; this may well modify the rate of autolysis of pus. (See also the discussion of the "Chemistry of Pus," Chap. xi.)

Proteolytic Enzymes of the Leucocytes.[13]—By the introduction of the plate method of testing the proteolytic activity of leucocytes, Müller and Jochmann brought the study of this particular vital activity into the range of clinical laboratories, and aroused much general interest in what had previously concerned only a few pathologists, especially E. L. Opie. The principle is that of permitting the leucocytes or other cells to act upon a blood serum plate at a temperature of 55°, which prevents bacterial action but permits the proteolytic enzymes of the cells to digest the coagulated serum, forming depressions in the surface ("Dellbildung"). This proteolytic activity is, of course, heterolysis rather than autolysis. Many modifications of this method have been introduced (such as using caseinagar), but the principle involved is the same, and they are fully explained and discussed in the article by Wiens. Normal blood does not contain enough leucocytes to cause observable digestion, but myelogenous leukemia blood causes distinct digestion while lymphatic leukemia does not, showing that it is the polynuclears and myelocytes that are responsible. Other observations fasten the proteolytic activity upon the neutrophile granules. Leucocytes of normal human blood will, if concentrated enough, cause digestion of serum plates, as also, of course, will pus. The leucocytes of rabbits, guinea pigs, and practically all animals except man, apes and monkeys, are devoid of proteolytic activity demonstrable by the plate method. Normal serum, both homologous and heterologous, exercises a strong inhibition on this digestion, so that it is necessary to have an excess of leucocytes present to obtain the reaction. The activity of leucocytic autolysis is indicated by the observation that in drawn cerebrospinal

[12] Ito, Jour. Biol. Chem., 1916 (26), 173.
[13] Full bibliography by Wiens, Ergebnisse Physiol., 1911 (15), 1; Jochmann, Kolle and Wassermann's Handbuch, 1912 (2), 1301.

fluid the leucocytes all disappear in from three to sixty-three days, and in 24 hours the count has been observed to drop from 392 to 6.[14]   The leucocytic enzymes seem to be very resistant against chemicals, especially against formaldehyde, so that museum specimens of leukemic tissues preserved in formalin for years are still proteolytic.   Liver tissue is but slightly proteolytic by this test, spleen more so, and leucocyte-containing fluids, such as saliva and colostrum, are quite active. Pancreas tissue, has, of course, strong proteolytic action, but it is shown to be distinct from the leucocytic protease by being inhibited by certain sera that do not inhibit the leucocytic protease.   In general, tissues do not cause much proteolysis of serum plates unless they are invaded by many leucocytes, which applies also to tumors, including multiple myelomas.

Besides proteases, leucocytes contain other enzymes.[15]   To quote the summary by Morris and Boggs[16] "it has been shown that the normal and pathological neutrophile leucocytes and myeloblasts contain an oxidase and probably a lipase and an amylase; myeloblasts contain an amylase.   In lymphoid tissues two proteases and a lipase have been shown to exist.   In leukemia leukoprotease has been demonstrated in the myeloid variety of the disease, while it has not been found in chronic lymphoid leukemia.   Lipase has been demonstrated in two cases of myeloid leukemia, and oxidase in all myeloid cases observed in which the neutrophilic cells were present in excess." Jobling and Strouse,[17] confirming Opie's observation of two distinct proteases in leucocytes, find also evidence of an creptic enzyme acting in either acid or alkaline fluids.[18]

Pneumonia.—In the stage of resolution lobar pneumonia presents a striking example of autolysis.   The often-remarked phenomenon that the lung tissue itself is not in the least affected, while the dense contents of the alveoli are rapidly dissolved and removed is explained by the invariable immunity of living cells to digestive enzymes.   Except for some slight possible assistance by the alveolar epithelium and the enzymes of the serum, the enormous and rapid digestion of pneumonic exudates is accomplished by the leucocytic enzymes.   The rapid rate of digestion may be accounted for by the absence of circulation within the alveolar contents, which permits the leucocytes to

[14] Bonaba, Anales de le Facultad de Med., 1919 (4), 111.
[15] According to Tschernoruzki (Zeit. physiol. Chem., 1911 (75), 216) amylase, diastase, catalase, peroxidase, and nuclease, but not lipase.   I also found uricase absent from dog leucocytes (Jour. Biol. Chem., 1909 (6), 321).   Fiessinger and Marie (Compt. Rend. Soc. Biol., 1909 (67), 177) state that the lymphocytes contain lipase, although myeloid cells do not.   (See also Resch, Deut. Arch. klin. Med., 1915 (118), 179).   Leucocytes are also said to contain a "lipoidase" splitting choline from lecithin (Fiessinger and Clogne, Compt. Rend. Acad. Sci., 1917 (165), 730.
[16] Arch. Int. Med., 1911 (8), 806.
[17] Jour. Exp. Med., 1912 (16), 269.
[18] Concerning enzymes of normal leucocytes see also Fiessinger and Clogne, Ann. de Méd., 1917 (4), 445; Parker and Franke, Jour. Med. Res., 1917 (37), 345.

act unimpeded by the anti-bodies of the blood plasma. Digestion of the exudate continues after death, accounting for the marked diffuse softening observed in pneumonic lungs in bodies kept some days before autopsy. As long ago as 1888, Kossel[19] mentioned that Fr. Müller had found that glycerol extracts of purulent sputum exhibited a digestive action upon fibrin and coagulated protein, whereas non-purulent sputum did not possess this property. In 1877 Filehne extracted ferments in the same way from the sputum in gangrene of the lung; Stolniknow, in 1878, found a similar ferment in pneumonic sputa, and Escherich in 1885 showed that the proteolytic action of tuberculous sputum was independent of putrefaction. Other early observations of similar nature are reviewed by Simon,[20] who demonstrated the presence of leucine and tyrosine in the autolyzed lungs. In a later work Müller reports finding three grams of leucine and tyrosine in a pneumonic lung, as well as lysine, histidine, and purine bases from the decomposed nucleoproteins. The appearance of free purines during autolysis of pneumonic lungs has been investigated by Mayeda,[21] Long and Wells.[22] Boehm[23] isolated histidine and arginine from the same material. Rietschel and Langstein[24] found 0.32 gm. leucine in the urine of a pneumonic child.

Flexner[25] noted that autolysis, while very rapid in the gray stage, is but slight in the red stage (because of paucity of leucocytes) and also in unresolved pneumonia, which he considers as due to some interference with autolysis. Silvestrini[26] found that in gray hepatization the reaction was strongly acid, in red faintly so; the gray hepatization showed more peptone, and leucine and lactic acid were both demonstrable. A fibrin-digesting enzyme was isolated, and milk was coagulated.

Weiss[27] has reported finding a toxic albumose in gray pneumonic lungs. Lord[28] has found in pneumonic lungs a proteolytic enzyme active at pH 7.3 to 6.7, but inactive at higher acidity; also an enzyme splitting peptone to amino acids and active at pH 8.0 to 4.8, but most active at 6.3 to 5.2. He, therefore, pictures resolution of pneumonic exudates as occurring in two stages: First, proteolysis while the reaction is nearly neutral, and later as the acidity increases the cleavage of the peptone increases. He also finds that the pneumococci cannot long survive a reaction more acid than pH 6.8, and their dissolution takes place at reaction from 6.0 to 5.0, which is of

[19] Zeit. f. klin. Med., 1888 (13), 149.
[20] Deut. Arch. klin. Med., 1901 (70), 604.
[21] Deut. Arch. klin. Med., 1910 (98), 587.
[22] Ibid., 1914 (115), 377.
[23] Ibid., 1910 (98), 583.
[24] Biochem. Zeit., 1906 (1), 75.
[25] Univ. of Penn. Med. Bull., 1903 (16), 185.
[26] Bull. del. Soc. Eustachiana, 1903, abst. in Biochem. Centralbl., 1903 (1), 713.
[27] Arch. Int. Med., 1919 (23), 395.
[28] Jour. Exp. Med., 1919 (30), 379.

significance in view of the observation that pneumonic lungs are more acid than normal organs, acidity as high as pH 6.0 to 5.4 having been found.[29]

Rzentkowski[30] found an increase of non-coagulable nitrogen in the blood of pneumonics, probably resulting from autolysis in the exudate. According to Dick[31] the blood serum after the crisis contains an enzyme which acts specifically on the pneumococcus proteins. Petersen and Short[32] found an increase of serum creptase in the blood preceding or accompanying crisis or lysis, and suggest that it may have a function in attacking the toxic protein fragments. In the liver during experimental pneumococcus septicemia, autolysis is said to be increased in rate.[33] Almagia[34] suggests that the bactericidal action of the products of fibrinolysis in pneumonia may be of importance in checking the disease.

Necrotic Areas.—Jacoby[35] found that if a portion of a dog's liver was ligated off and the animal kept alive for some time, the necrotic tissue contained the same products that he had obtained in experimental autolysis. The absorption of necrotic tissues generally is ascribable to either autolysis or heterolysis. Presumably there is no great difference in the self-digestion of an organ which is necrotic because its blood supply is cut off, and of a similar organ removed from the body aseptically and allowed to undergo aseptic autolysis in an incubator. At the periphery there might be some effects produced *in vivo* by the inhibitive action of the serum or the digestive action of the leucocytes, but beyond that no marked differences are to be expected. In both cases asphyxia is present, leading to increased acidity, without which little if any autolysis can occur. It has been found that in experimental infarction of the kidney there develops sufficient acidity to permit of autolysis, and the hydrolysis of the proteins increases with the development of acidity (Straus and Morse.[36])

A study of the relation of autolysis to the histological changes that occur in necrotic areas by Wells[37] gave evidence that there occurs early a decomposition of the nucleoproteins of the nuclei, which is probably brought about by the intracellular autolytic enzymes. The liberation of the nucleic acid and the reduction in the bulk of nuclear material through the digestion away of the protein is probably the cause of the *pycnosis* observed in necrotic areas. Later the nucleic acids are further decomposed through the special enzymes described by Jones, Sachs, and others, the "nucleases." This is presumably

[29] Jour. Amer. Med. Assoc., 1919 (72), 1364.
[30] Virchow's Arch., 1905 (179), 405.
[31] Jour. Infect Dis., 1912 (10), 383.
[32] Jour. Infect. Dis., 1918 (22), 147.
[33] Medigreccanu, Jour. Exp. Med., 1914 (19), 31.
[34] Festschr. for Celli, Torino, 1913, p. 459.
[35] Zeit. physiol. Chem., 1900 (30), 149.
[36] Proc. Soc. Exp. Biol. Med., 1917 (14), 171.
[37] Jour. Med. Research, 1906 (15), 149.

the cause of the loss of nuclear staining so characteristic of necrosis. That these changes are due to the intracellular enzymes was shown by implanting in animals pieces of sterile tissues, the enzymes of which had been destroyed by heating; these were found to undergo alterations only after several weeks, and then as the result of the action upon them of invading leucocytes. The slow rate of autolysis that occurs in infarcts and other aseptic areas is presumably due in part to the action of the antibodies of the serum, for it was found, experimentally, that the histological changes of autolysis when the tissues are placed in heated serum proceed about twice as rapidly as when they are placed in fresh serum. Chemotactic substances do not seem to be formed in aseptic dead tissues, but the slow absorption of such tissues is, however, finally accomplished by the leucocytes acting from the periphery, there being little actual autolysis of the dead cells by their own enzymes. The rapidity with which autolytic changes occur in different organs, as indicated by the disappearance of nuclear staining, seems to be about as follows: (1) Liver, kidney (epithelium of convoluted tubules); (2) spleen, pancreas; (3) kidney (collecting tubules, straight tubules, glomerules); (4) lung (alveolar and bronchial epithelium); (5) thyroid; (6) myocardium; (7) voluntary muscle; (8) skin (epithelium); (9) brain (cortical cells). Stroma cells seem to be attacked chiefly by enzymes from the parenchyma cells. Of all cellular elements, the endothelium of the vessels seems to have the greatest resistance to both autolysis and heterolysis.

The finer structural changes of aseptic autolysis of liver in salt solution, have been carefuly studied by Launoy,[38] who notes a period of relative latency (20 to 24 hours at 38°), followed by rapid changes in both cytoplasm and nucleus, associated with the appearance of myelin forms. Dyson[39] describes loss of the Altmann's granules in autolyzing cells. Cruickshank[40] states that when aseptic autolysis of tissues kept in a moist chamber is observed microscopically the changes are slower, and there is less solution of the cytoplasm, but in general the results are much the same. No fat could be found by special stains. Fetuses that have undergone aseptic autolysis in the uterus show complete loss of nuclei in 5 to 6 days, a stage corresponding to 8 to 15 days autolysis in the moist chamber. In experimental nephritis Simons[41] observed a decreased autolysis of the kidneys.

Degenerated *nervous tissue* also undergoes a slow autolysis which, according to Noll,[42] results in the splitting of "protagon" with liberation of lecithin. Mott, Halliburton,[43] Donath, and others have shown

[38] Ann. Inst. Pasteur, 1909 (23), 1.
[39] Jour. Path. and Bact., 1912 (17), 12; also Aschoff, Verh. deut. Path. Gesellsch, 1914 (17), 109.
[40] Jour. Path. and Bact., 1911 (16), 167.
[41] Biochem. Zeit., 1914 (67), 483.
[42] Zeit. physiol. Chem., 1899 (27), 390.
[43] General résumé in Ergebnisse der Physiol., 1904 (4), 24.

that in nerve destruction lecithin is split up with·liberation of choline (see "Choline"). Koch and Goodson[44] found that degenerated nervous tissue is characterized, chemically, by containing a relatively increased amount of nucleo-proteins, with an absolute decrease in solid constituents, while the lecithins are greatly altered.

In *caseation* autolysis is very slight, as is shown by the persistence of the caseous material for long periods of time without absorption. Presumably the toxin of tuberculosis destroys the autolytic ferments of the cells it kills,[45] and as there is little chemotactic influence, leucocytes do not enter the caseous area. Jobling and Petersen[46] find evidence that the soaps of unsaturated fatty acids present in tubercles are responsible for the inhibition of digestion. Spiethoff[47] found that pure caseous material is usually free from even traces of albumose and peptone, but the caseous material at the periphery mixed with tissue elements contains them in very small quantities, suggesting that at the periphery of caseous areas some slight autolysis does occur. The fact that *B. tuberculosis* is, itself, very poor in proteolytic enzymes as compared with most other bacteria may be another factor. When leucocytes are attracted into a tuberculous focus softening goes on rapidly, showing that there is no loss of digestibility of the caseous material, but merely a lack of enzymes. Pus from a cold tuberculous abscess will not digest fibrin, but if iodoform is injected, leucocytes enter in great numbers, softening is rapid, and the pus will then digest fibrin (Heile[48]). On serum plates tuberculous pus produces no digestion unless a secondary infection or other cause has resulted in a local accumulation of leucocytes.[13] Tuberculous material contains, like the lymphocytes, an enzyme which is proteolytic in acid media and which is inhibited by normal serum (Opie and Barker[49]).

Correlation of Histological and Chemical Changes.—A careful study of the relationship of the chemical changes produced by autolysis, to the histological changes of necrosis and autolysis, has been made by J. Corper,[50] and colored plates published together with analytical figures make it possible to correlate at a glance the structural and chemical changes of necrobiosis. Corper found that in the early stages, characterized by a high grade of pycnosis but no further nuclear changes, the nucleins are still intact; but with well developed karyorrhexis and beginning karyolysis, some ten per cent. of the nuclein nitrogen has become soluble in the form of purine bases. When karyolysis is completed so that no more nuclei remain in a stainable condition, only twenty-eight per cent. of the nucleo-proteins was found to have been decomposed to free purine bases,[51] the remaining seventy-two per cent. being intact although unstainable. This rather surprising observation indicates that the stainable chromatin represents but about one-fourth of the nucleins of the cell, which is in accord with the views of Hammarsten

[44] Amer. Jour. Physiol., 1906 (15), 272.
[45] However, Pesci (Pathologica, 1912 (3), 144) states that tuberculin increases autolysis *in vitro*.
[46] Jour. Exp. Med., 1914 (19), 383.
[47] Cent. f. inn. Med., 1901 (25), 481.
[48] Zeit. klin. Med., 1901 (55), 508.
[49] Jour. Exper. Med., 1909 (11), 686.
[50] Jour. Exper. Med., 1912 (15), 429.
[51] Marshall (Jour. Biol. Chem., 1913 (15), 81) has also found that much of the nucleic acid remains unaltered in autolysis of thymus.

and others. The lecithin disintegrates somewhat more completely, about one-half or two-thirds being disintegrated by the time nuclear destruction is complete, after which this and all other autolytic change is slow. The change from coagulable to non-coagulable forms of nitrogen was as follows: Normal spleen, non-coagulable nitrogen, 5.7 per cent. of the total: stage of marked pycnosis, without rhexis or lysis, 7.4 per cent.; stage of karyorrhexis and early karyolysis, 26.5 per cent.; stage of complete karyolysis, 30.3 per cent. That is, when nuclear structures in the spleen have lost their staining properties entirely through autolysis, about 72 per cent. of the nuclein nitrogen, 50 per cent. of the insoluble phosphorus compounds. 70 per cent. of the coagulable nitrogen, and about two-thirds of the lecithin are still intact.

Liver Degenerations.—The relation of the disintegration observed in *phosphorus-poisoning* and *acute yellow atrophy* to the experimental autolysis of the liver has been the object of much study. Salkowski originally pointed out that the same products were found in the blood, urine, and liver tissue in acute yellow atrophy as are produced in autolysis. Jacoby[52] found that the livers of dogs, taken just as the animals were dying of phosphorus-poisoning, contained free leucine and tyrosine; also, he found that the rate of autolysis of such livers after removal from the body was much greater than in normal livers. The oxidizing ferments (aldehydase) are not destroyed by the process. He found that addition of minute amounts of phosphorus to liver enzymes did not increase their proteolytic power; nevertheless, he seems inclined to assume that in phosphorus-poisoning alteration in the autolytic enzymes is an important factor in the liver degeneration. It would seem much more probable that phosphorus is a poison that kills cells and does not destroy their autolytic enzymes, hence favoring autolysis. The liver degeneration following chloroform poisoning may, perhaps, be explained in a similar way, the cells behaving exactly as bacteria would do under the same conditions. Taylor[53] has analyzed several livers in degenerative conditions for amino-acids and found them only in one liver, which showed necrosis probably due to chloroform poisoning, and which was from a case clinically resembling acute yellow atrophy. Here he obtained 4 gm. of leucine, 2.2 gm. of tyrosine, and 2.3 gm. of arginine nitrate. Waldvogel and Tintemann,[54] in phosphorus livers, found an increase in protagon, jecorin, fatty acids, cholesterol, and neutral fat, while lecithin was decreased. Wakeman[55] found arginine, histidine, and lysine decreased in phosphorus livers in proportion to the total nitrogen, indicating that the protein-splitting enzyme in this condition either picks out certain varieties of proteins first, or removes the nitrogen-rich constituents most rapidly.[56]

[52] Zeit. f. physiol. Chem., 1900 (30), 174.
[53] Univ. of Calif. Public. (pathol.), 1904 (1), 43.
[54] Cent. f. Path., 1904 (15), 97.
[55] Berl. klin. Woch., 1904 (41), 1067.
[56] Considerable quantities of amino-acids of various sorts have been isolated from the liver in acute yellow atrophy and chloroform necrosis by Wells (Jour. Exper. Med., 1907 (9), 627; Jour. Biol. Chem., 1908 (5), 129); but the value of these figures is questionable because it is possible that the alcohol in which the tissues were kept before analysis was not strong enough entirely to prevent autolysis (Wells and Caldwell, Jour. Biol. Chem., 1914 (19), 57).

It is probable that many poisons may injure the liver cells to such an extent that they cannot maintain their normal chemical equilibrium, but without destroying the autolytic enzymes. When this occurs, the liver undergoes autolysis, and we get marked degenerative changes with appearance of amino-acids in the blood and urine, reduction in coagulability of the blood and numerous hemorrhages, giving a picture both clinically and anatomically more or less like that of typical acute yellow atrophy. Chloroform is a poison that stops cell activities without destroying the proteolytic enzymes, hence the cells undergo autolysis, and, as a result, we have many cases of what appears to be acute yellow atrophy following chloroform anesthesia. The liberation of HCl in the liver cells during chloroform poisoning, as demonstrated by Evarts Graham,[57] may be largely responsible for the rapid disintegration of the liver in this condition.[58] (See "Acute Yellow Atrophy," Chap. xx.) Probably the liver changes in puerperal eclampsia, and in streptococcus and other septicemias are of a similar nature.[59] Autolysis of fatty livers in tuberculosis is said to yield more lactic acid than the livers from other conditions (Youssouf).[60]

Postmortem changes are undoubtedly due to two factors, bacterial action and autolysis. In tissues kept at a low enough temperature to exclude bacterial action, but not so low as absolutely to stop enzyme action,[61] there occurs a slow autolysis; this constitutes the "ripening" process of meat. Fish flesh may also ripen when made sterile in saturated salt solutions, as Schmidt-Nielsen[62] has shown occurs with salted herrings, oxy-acids and xanthine bases being prominent among the products. The softening of muscles in rigor mortis is probably also an autolytic manifestation, as muscles contain proteases acting best in acid medium, and the muscle is known to become increasingly acid after circulation ceases within it. The short duration of rigor mortis when the body is kept warm, and its early disappearance when death has been preceded by muscular exhaustion (which increases the acidity), agree with this view. The early postmortem softening of many organs in pathological conditions is also probably an autolytic manifestation. Flexner[25] has called attention to this in relation to the softening of the parenchymatous organs in acute infectious diseases, such as typhoid and septicemia. Schumm noted great autolytic activity in a swollen spleen from a case of perityphlitis.

[57] Jour. Exp. Med., 1915 (22), 48.
[58] Quinan (Jour. Med. Res. 1915 (32), 73) found no change in the rate of _in vitro_ autolysis of liver tissue from experimental chloroform poisoning. It was found increased by phlorhizin (Satta and Fasiani, Arch. di. Fisiol., 1913 (11), 391).
[59] Wells, Jour. Amer. Med. Assoc., 1906 (46), 341.
[60] Virchow's Arch., 1912 (207), 374.
[61] Some chemical change may take place at temperatures as low as -2 and -14 (Costantino, Arch. farm. sper., 1917 (24), 255).
[62] Hofmeister's Beiträge, 1903 (3), 267.

Histological changes are produced by autolysis in the organs after death that are, as might be expected, much like those seen in necrotic areas.[63] At first the changes resemble those of parenchymatous degeneration (cloudy swelling), and often there is an apparent increase in fat, which is probably due to liberation of masked fat through the destruction of the protein.[64] Nuclear staining is lost (karyolysis), and eventually even cell forms become indistinguishable. (See p. 94 on structural changes of postmortem autolysis.)

· Still-born children that have been carried for some time after death usually show considerable disintegration of the viscera, especially the liver. This is undoubtedly due to autolysis, which Schlesinger[65] has shown can begin before birth if the fetus dies *in utero*.

Autolysis in Relation to Infection.—According to Conradi[66] the substances produced in tissue autolysis have a decided inhibiting effect upon bacteria, which apparently depends upon the antiseptic properties of the aromatic derivatives that are split out of the protein molecule in autolysis. This action is manifested not only *in vitro*, but the autolytic products will also render harmless lethal doses of certain bacteria if they are injected simultaneously with the bacteria into an animal. One specific class of products of autolysis which is strongly bactericidal is the soaps.[67] It may well be questioned, however, whether enough of these substances ever accumulates in infected tissues during *intra vitam* autolysis to have much affect upon the infecting bacteria; yet this property may possibly explain the sterilization of old pus collections and similar infected localized accumulations within the body. The bacteria themselves also produce autolytic products that are powerfully bactericidal. (See "Bacteria," Chap. iv.)

Blum[68] says that the autolytic products of lymph-glands neutralize tetanus toxin, but are inactive against diphtheria toxin and cobra venom. Products from other autolyzed organs and from fresh lymph-glands were without influence on the tetanus toxin. The antitoxic principles of the autolytic product were destroyed by heating, weakened by acids and alkalies, and in other respects showed properties strikingly like those of true antitoxin. It is quite possible that bacterial toxins may be destroyed by autolytic enzymes, for Baldwin and Levene[69] have shown that trypsin, pepsin, and papain destroy tetanus and diphtheria toxin, while tuberculin is destroyed by trypsin, but not readily by pepsin, possibly because it is of a nucleoprotein

---

[63] More fully discussed by Wells, Jour. Med. Research, 1906 (15), 149.
[64] Siegert (Hofmeister's Beitr., 1901 (1), 114) found no actual increase in fats and fatty acids in autolysis even when an increase was apparent histologically, although ether-soluble materials of other nature than fat may be increased. See also Hess and Saxl, Virchow's Arch., 1910 (202), 149.
[65] Hofmeister's Beitr., 1903 (4), 87.
[66] Hofmeister's Beitr., 1901 (1), 193. See also Bilancioni[99] and Almagia.[34]
[67] See Lamar, Jour. Exp. Med., 1911 (13), 1.
[68] Hofmeister's Beitr., 1904 (5), 142.
[69] Jour. Med. Research, 1901 (6), 120.

7

nature. The leucocytic proteases, however, seem not to attack either toxins or living bacteria (Jochmann). Bertolini[70] states that autolyzing liver will destroy diphtheria toxin.

On the other hand, there are many pathogenic bacteria which do not secrete their toxic materials, but store them up within the cell body, e. g., typhoid, cholera, and, indeed, the majority of pathogenic forms. These *endotoxins* are probably liberated from the bacteria only through digestion of their cells, either by their own autolytic enzymes or by the enzymes of the infected tissues and leucocytes.

Leukemia.—The abundant elimination of uric acid and other purine bodies in the urine in leukemia testifies to the great amount of destruction of nucleoprotein that is going on during the disease, and these are probably derived from the autolysis of leucocytes, which perhaps depends on the relatively large proportion of leucocytes to serum. Schumm[71] has found that leukemic spleens and bone marrow autolyze rapidly and completely, and he isolated many of the cleavage products of protein digestion from such autolysates.

Leucocytes from myeloid leukemia liquefy alkaline gelatin vigorously, but those from lymphatic leukemia do not; the liquefaction is inhibited by normal serum (Stern and Eppenstein).[72] By the serum plate method this observation has been much extended, and the heterolytic action of the leucocytes has been found limited to the neutrophile granules. In neutral media evidence is obtained of the presence of protease in the lymphocytes of chronic lymphatic leukemia and the leucocytes of acute and chronic myeloid leukemia; maltase, lipase and amylase are found in both types of cells, and oxidase in the granular cells derived from the marrow (Morris and Boggs).[73] v. Jaksch,[74] Erben,[75] and others have noted the occurrence of peptones and albumoses in leukemic blood, particularly if removed postmortem. The improvement in leukemia that follows x-ray treatment is associated with an increased nitrogen elimination, probably due to autolysis of disintegrating cells,[76] although x-rays have no appreciable effect upon the leucocytic proteases *in vitro* (Müller and Jochmann). (See also "Leukemia," Chap. xiii.)

Tumors.—Probably because of the great amount of necrosis that is constantly going on in all malignant growths, with subsequent digestion of the dead cells, autolytic products are present in them in very considerable amounts. This was first demonstrated by Petry,[77]

[70] Biochem. Zeit., 1913 (48), 448.
[71] Hofmeister's Beitr., 1903 (3), 576; 1905 (7), 175.
[72] See discussion of leucocytic enzymes, p. 89. Longcope and Donhauser (Jour. Exper. Med., 1908 (10), 618) found proteases in the large lymphocytes in acute leukemia, which were most active in an alkaline medium.
[73] Arch. Int. Med., 1911 (8), 806.
[74] Zeit. f. physiol. Chem., 1892 (16), 243.
[75] Zeit. f. klin. Med., 1900 (40), 282; Zeit. f. Heilkunde, 1903 (24), 70; Hofmeister's Beitr., 1904 (5), 461.
[76] Musser and Edsall, Univ. Penn. Med. Bull., 1905 (18), 174.
[77] Zeit. f. physiol. Chem., 1899 (27), 398; Hofmeister's Beitr., 1902 (2), 94.

who found that carcinomas of the breast contained much of their nitrogen in compounds not coagulated by heat, while in the normal gland practically all is coagulable. He also demonstrated an autolytic property in tumor tissue, showing that tumor cells do not differ in this respect from normal cells. Beebe[78] found products of autolysis constantly present in several tumors; namely, a carcinoma of the broad ligament, a hypernephroma, an angiosarcoma, and a round-cell sarcoma.

Neuberg[79] found that while, according to other observers, most enzymes, as well as bacteria, are very susceptible to the action of radium rays, the autolytic enzymes of cancer cells are an exception, for cancer tissue exposed to radium undergoes autolysis much faster than cancer tissue not exposed to radium; x-rays are less active in this respect. He attributes the effects of radium on cancer to its deleterious effects on the oxidizing and other enzymes of the cells, destroying their activities, which results in destruction of the cells by the autolytic enzymes.[80] A cancer of the stomach was found to contain autolytic enzymes capable of digesting lung tissue (pepsin was excluded) and autolyzed cancers yielded much pentose. Blumenthal and Wolf[81] believe that tumor tissues have particularly active autolytic enzymes, since liver tissue added to tumor tissue underwent autolysis much more rapidly than normal; but tumors do not cause digestion of serum plates unless many leucocytes are present (Müller and Kolaczek).[82] Cancer extracts digest peptids in ways different from normal tissues, which seems to indicate some fundamental abnormality in their metabolism (Abderhalden,[83] Neuberg).[84] The almost constant presence in gastric juice of patients with carcinoma of the stomach, of ereptases hydrolyzing proteoses and peptids, is generally attributed to the disintegration of the cancer with liberation of these enzymes.[85] Tumors also contain nuclease[86] to disintegrate their nucleic acid, and the same outfit of purine-splitting enzymes as normal tissues,[87] so that in regard to the nucleoproteins of tumors, autolysis follows the same course as in normal tissues.

[78] Amer. Jour. Physiol., 1904 (11), 139.
[79] Zeit. f. Krebsforschung, 1904 (2), 171; Berl. klin. Woch., 1904 (41), 1081; *ibid.*, 1905 (42), 118; Arb. Path. Inst. Berlin, 1906, p. 593.
[80] Wohlgemuth, Berl. klin. Woch., 1904 (41), 704, found that autolysis in tuberculous lung tissue was three or four times more rapid when exposed to radium rays. Heile (Arch. klin. Chir., 1905 (77), 107) looks upon the favorable effects of x-rays as partly produced by their liberation of autolytic enzymes from the leucocytes.
[81] Med. Klinik., 1905 (1), No. 7.
[82] Müller and Kolaczek, Münch. med. Woch., 1907 (54), 354; Hess and Saxl, Wien. klin. Woch., 1908 (21), 1183; Kepinow, Zeit. f. Krebsforsch., 1909 (7), 517.
[83] Zeit. physiol. Chem., 1910 (66), 277.
[84] Biochem. Zeit., 1910 (26), 344.
[85] See Jacques and Woodyatt, Arch. Int. Med., 1912 (10), 560; Hamburger, Jour. Amer. Med. Assoc., 1912 (59), 847.
[86] Goodman, Jour. Exp. Med., 1912 (15), 477.
[87] Wells and Long, Zeit. Krebforsch., 1913 (12), 598.

The non-cancerous livers of cancerous patients were found by Youssouf[60] to produce more lactic acid during antiseptic autolysis than did livers in other conditions. Autolysis of organs of cancer patients is about as rapid as normal (Colwell[88]). Several observations have suggested that tumor tissues might contain proteolytic enzymes differing from those of normal tissues especially in their ability to digest heterologous normal tissues, but at present this work needs confirmation and amplification before it can carry the weight of speculation which has been heaped upon it.[89]

Micheli and Donati[90] attribute the hemolytic properties possessed by extracts of malignant tumors to the products of autolysis that are present, which Petry has also demonstrated to produce hemolysis. Emerson[91] attributes the disappearance of HCl from the gastric juice in carcinoma of the stomach to neutralization by basic products of autolysis, a hypothesis that may well be questioned. (See also "Tumors," Chap. xix.)

Various other intracellular enzymes have been described, which for the most part have as yet no significance in pathology. An exception is *fibrin ferment*, which will be considered fully in discussing thrombosis. Ferments coagulating milk seem to be widely spread in the tissues. The precipitation of plastein from proteose solution by organ extracts (Nürnberg) may be either the effect of a coagulating ferment or due to reverse action of the proteases. Ferments splitting specifically maltose, lactose, sucrose, glucosides, and nucleoproteins have been described, and the glycogenolytic ferment is probably nearly universally present. Other enzymes decomposing amino-acids into ammonium compounds may also exist. The enzymes acting specifically upon the nucleic acids and the purine bodies are discussed in Chapter xxiii.

[88] Arch. Middlesex Hosp., 1910 (19), 55.
[89] See, for example, Rulf, Zeit. Krebsforsch., 1906 (4), 417; Müller, Cent. inn. Med., 1909 (30), 89.
[90] Riforma med., 1903 (19), 1037.
[91] Deut. Arch. klin. Med., 1902 (72), 415.

CHAPTER IV

THE CHEMISTRY OF BACTERIA AND THEIR PRODUCTS

STRUCTURE AND PHYSICAL PROPERTIES[1]

In structure, as in nearly all other respects, bacterial cells stand intermediate between the cells of ordinary plant and animal tissues. Their cell wall seems to be generally more highly developed than that of animal cells, and less so than the wall of most plant cells. The much vexed question as to the existence or non-existence of a nucleus seems to be best answered by Zettnow, who considers that the portion of the bacterial cell usually made evident by ordinary staining methods consists of a mixture of nuclear substance (*chromatin*) with non-chromatic substance (*endoplasm*); the outer membrane, which requires special methods for its satisfactory demonstration, consists of a modified cytoplasm (*ectoplasm*). Some bacteria consist chiefly of chromatin (*e. g., vibrios*), but the proportion of the different elements varies greatly, not only in different varieties, but also in the same variety under different conditions. The fact that the chromatin is not aggregated into the usual nuclear form may be ascribed to the low stage of development reached by bacteria in the scale of evolution; or, as Vejdovosky has suggested, to the extremely rapid rate of cell division in the bacteria which prevents the chromatin from appearing in the resting stage which a nucleus constitutes. Finer structures within the bacterial cell have as yet been only imperfectly discerned.

The thickness of the ectoplasm varies greatly even in the same species, being generally greatest in older cultures. In some forms the ectoplasm may constitute one-half of the total mass of the cells. The capsule seems to arise through a swelling of the ectoplasm, and is probably present in at least a rudimentary stage in all bacteria (Migula).

Plasmolysis and Plasmoptysis.—Under conditions of altered osmotic pressure the bacterial cell behaves quite similarly to the plant cell.[2] If placed suddenly in a solution of higher osmotic pressure than

---

[1] In this chapter references will not generally be given that can be found by consulting Kolle and Wassermann's Handbuch. A general consideration of the Biology of the Bacteria, including references to the effects of light, heat, osmotic pressure, etc., is given by Müller. Ergb. der Physiol., 1904 (4), 138; concerning their chemistry see H. Fischer, Lafar's Handbuch der Technischen Mykologie, 1908 (1), 222.

[2] Literature, see Gotschlich, Kolle and Wassermann's Handbuch, vol. 1.

the one in which it has been, the cell contents shrink away from the cell wall (*plasmolysis*) indicating that there exists a semipermeable membrane through which water passes more rapidly than salts. If the change in osmotic pressure is gradual, the bacteria accomodate themselves to it by the slow diffusion of the salts through the cell membrane, indicating that it is not absolutely semipermeable. Different bacteria behave differently, some bacteria not being plasmolyzed by solutions that plasmolyze others. As a rule, old bacteria plasmolyze more rapidly than young, and in some varieties there seems to be a spontaneous plasmolysis, to which has been attributed the irregular staining of diphtheria and tubercle bacilli, the polar staining of plague bacilli, etc. Plasmolysis occurs only in living bacilli, but does not necessarily cause death. The Gram-staining bacteria cannot generally be plasmolyzed, and contain more water.[3]

When bacteria pass from solutions of higher osmotic concentration into solutions of lower concentration, the phenomenon of *plasmoptysis* is produced. The cell contents swell until the cell wall gives way at some point, and then exude as glistening drops, which may become detached from the wall and escape free into the fluid. Plasmoptysis is shown best by bacteria that have been grown on salt-rich media before being placed in the salt-free fluid. Not all varieties of bacteria can be made to undergo this change, depending probably upon the degree of permeability of their cell membranes for salts. The exposure of the naked cell contents to the hypotonic fluid outside the cells makes plasmoptysis more serious for bacterial life than plasmolysis, but how often, if ever, either process plays a part in the resistance of infected animals against bacteria is unknown. The resistance of bacteria to direct pressure is striking; spore bearers may not be killed under direct pressure of 12,000 atmospheres for 14 hours, and non-spored bacteria resist 3,000 but not 6,000 atmospheres.[4]

Chemotaxis.[5]—Just as with unicellular animal organisms, bacteria respond to chemotactic influences, in general being attracted by substances favorable for food, such as peptone, amino acids,[6] dilute potassium salts, etc., and being repelled by harmful substances, such as strong acids and alkalies. Attempts have been made to separate different organisms in mixed cultures by means of their response to chemotaxis, but without striking success. It is possible that chemotaxis may play a part in the localization of bacteria from the blood stream in favorable localities, just as leucocytes are attracted to points of injury, but this has not been demonstrated. (The chemotactic influence of bacteria upon leucocytes is discussed in Chapter xi.)

[3] Nicolle and Alilaire, Ann. Inst. Pasteur, 1909 (23), 517.
[4] Larson, Hartzell and Diehl, Jour. Infect. Dis., 1918 (22), 271.
[5] Concerning the adsorption of bacteria see Bechhold, Kolloid-Zeitschr., 1918 (23), 35.
[6] Pringsheim and Ernst, Zeit. physiol. Chem., 1916 (97), 176.

CHEMICAL COMPOSITION

This varies greatly, not only between different species, but even in the same species grown on different media;[7] in this respect bacteria are much more modified by their environment than are higher organisms. On the other hand, they can develop in solutions containing only a few of the simplest organic and inorganic compounds and synthesize the complex components of their cells, as well as enzymes, toxins, pigments.[8] They usually contain between 80 and 90 per cent. of water. Grown on a salt-rich medium they yield much ash; grown on a peptone-rich medium they contain much protein; grown on a fat-rich medium they contain much material soluble in ether. Cholera vibrios grown on a bouillon medium contained 69.25 per cent. of protein, and 25.87 per cent. of ash, whereas the same organism grown on Uschinsky's medium, which contains no proteins but only various simple chemical compounds, contained but 35.75 per cent. of protein and 13.7 per cent. of ash (Cramer). Even in the same medium two different strains of the same organism may show equally great differences: Two strains of cholera vibrios grown on the same medium showed respectively 65.63 per cent. and 34.37 per cent. of protein. It is evident, therefore, that quantitative analyses of bacteria show nothing as to their nature, and on account of the extreme limits of their variation are practically valueless. The specific gravity of bacteria, generally between 1.12 and 1.345, also varies with media and age.[9] In an electric field they move towards the anode.[10]

Qualitatively the variations are not so great—all bacteria contain proteins, lipoid substances, and salts, of which phosphates are most prominent in the ash. The character of the proteins and fats of bacteria grown on peptone bouillon is quite the same as when they are grown on protein-free media.[11] The older analyses of bacterial constituents are of little value. Recent studies prove that the chief constituent of the cell contents is a true nucleoprotein (Iwanoff[12]) containing some sulphur and iron; probably many of the "pyogenetic proteins," "bacterial toxalbumins," "bacterial caseins" of earlier investigators are true nucleoproteins.[13] The stainable substance of anthrax bacilli behaves as if it were a chromatin, while the spores resemble

---

[7] See Dawson, Jour. Bact., 1919 (4), 133.

[8] Concerning fundamentals of nutrition of bacilli see Koser and Rettger, Jour. Infect. Dis., 1919 (24), 301; Long, Amer. Rev. Tuberc., 1919 (3), 86.

[9] Stigell, Cent. f. Bakt., 1907 (43), 487.

[10] Buxton, Zeit. physikal. Chem., 1906 (57), 47; Girard and Audubert, Compt. Rend. Acad. Sci., 1918 (167), 301. Concerning the *electrical conductivity* of bacteria see Thornton, Proc. Royal Soc., London, Sec. B., 1913 (85), 331.

[11] Tamura, Zeit. physiol. Chem., 1913 (88), 190.

[12] Hofmeister's Beitr., 1902 (1), 524; bibliography by Lustig, Kolle and Wassermann's Handbuch, 1913 (11), 1362.

[13] The purity of many of the preparations worked with as bacterial nucleoproteins, is very doubtful. (See Wells, Zeit. Immunität., 1913 (19), 599.)

linin (Růžička).[14]   The predominance of nuclein compounds is shown by Ruppel's summary of the composition of dried tubercle bacilli, namely, in per cent., tuberculonucleic acid, 8.5; nucleo-protamine, 24.5; nucleo-protein, 26.5; fatty matter, 26.5; inorganic, 9.2; insoluble "proteinoid" residue, 8.3.   In a water bacillus Nishimura found xanthine, guanine, and adenine, indicating the presence of nucleo-protein; others have found that bacterial nucleoproteins split off pentoses, as do the nucleoproteins of higher cells.   If it is true that bacterial nucleo-proteins contain pentose it ranks them with the plant nucleo-proteins, for animal nucleic acids contain hexose.   On the other hand, Levene found in bacterial nucleic acid the pyrimidines, thymine and uracil, which are respectively characteristic of animal and vege-table nucleic acids.   Mary Leach[15] found evidence that the colon bacillus is largely made up of nuclein or glyco-nucleoproteins, but contains no cellulose.   Other proteins, namely, globulins and nucleo-albumins, have also been described as constituents of the bacterial plasma.

The complete amino-acid content of bacterial protein does not seem to have been worked out, although the workers in Vaughan's labora-tory have identified many of the usual amino-acids of proteins among the products of hydrolysis of bacteria.[16]   Analysis of B. mesentericus shows it to be deficient in diamino-acids, tyrosine, glycine, and to contain 16.6 per cent. of glutamic acid.[17]   Tamura[18] found phenyl-alanine and valine high in tubercle bacilli and very low in B. diph-theriæ, in which tyrosine is more abundant.   In an azobacterium, lysine has been found especially abundant.[19]   Cystine has been lacking in several analyses.   Tamura[20] also found that bacteria can synthesize from simple nonprotein media the purines, phosphatids and the typical proteins containing the aromatic amino-acids.   This syn-thetic activity of bacteria, in view of the large quantity of bacterial substances in feces, may possibly be of importance in metabolism studies, leading to erroneous conclusions as to utilization or synthesis of proteins by the subject.[21]   In common with other forms of cellular life, bacteria require certain specific substances, "vitamins," to permit of their growth;[22] also they produce substances with the value of vitamins.[23]

[14] Arch. Entwicklungsmk., 1906 (21), 306.
[15] Jour. Biol. Chem., 1906 (1), 463.   Full bibliography on Chemistry of Bac-teria.   See also Vaughan, "Protein Split Products in Relation to Immunity and Disease," Philadelphia, 1913.
[16] See Wheeler, Jour. Biol. Chem., 1909 (6), 509.
[17] Horowitz-Wlassowa, Arch. Sci. Biologique, 1910 (15), 40.
[18] Zeit. physiol. Chem., 1913 (87), 85; 1914 (89), 289.
[19] Omeliansky and Sieber, Zeit. physiol. Chem., 1913 (88), 445.
[20] Zeit. physiol. Chem., 1913 (88), 190.
[21] Osborne and Mendel, Jour. Biol. Chem., 1913 (18), 177.
[22] See Davis, Jour. Infect. Dis., 1917 (21), 392; Kligler, Jour. Exp. Med., 1919 (30), 31.
[23] Pacini and Russell, Jour. Biol. Chem., 1918 (34), 43.

The slimy material produced in cultures by some varieties of bacteria is, at least for certain forms, a body closely related to or identical with true mucin,[24] but in certain cases (*B. radicicola*) it is a gum related to the dextrans and free from nitrogen (Buchanan).[25] Tubercle bacilli grown for many years on artificial media may produce a true mucin (Weleminsky).[26] Heim[27] considers that anthrax bacilli also produce mucin. Some nonpathogenic bacteria contain granules of sulfur in their protoplasm, and others have noteworthy quantities of iron in the sheath.

Bacterial Carbohydrates.—The earlier descriptions of *cellulose* or *hemicellulose* in the cell membrane of bacteria have been contested.[28] Numerous investigators have reported that the insoluble bacterial cell wall consists chiefly of *chitin*, which on being split with acids yields 80 to 90 per cent. of the nitrogenous carbohydrate, *glucosamin*.[29] The distinction is a very important one, since cellulose is a typically vegetable product, while chitin is equally typically animal in origin, being found chiefly in the shells of lobsters and crabs, the wings and coverings of flies, beetles, etc. Chitin seems to be a polymeric form of glucose-amine,[30] an amino-carbohydrate, just as cellulose is a polymer of a simpler carbohydrate. Other carbohydrates seem to be scanty in the bacterial cell, but Tamura[31] does not accept the chitinous nature of bacterial carbohydrate, finding in tubercle and diphtheria bacilli a hemicellulose, apparently a pentosan yielding l-arabinose on hydrolysis. Wester[32] found no chitin in several varieties of bacteria, and cellulose only in *B. xylinum;* he therefore considers it probable that bacterial cell walls do not always consist of the same substance. Cramer could find no glucose in any variety, although there are some bacteria that contain material reacting like starch with iodin. Levene,[33] however, found in *B. tuberculosis* a substance with some of the properties of glycogen.

Bacterial Fats.—By staining methods, fats have been recognized in many species, and by extraction with fat solvents lecithin, cholesterol, simple fats, and specific bacterial fats have been isolated; this is particulary true of *B. tuberculosis*.[34] Numerous studies of these fats of

[24] Rettger, Jour. Med. Research, 1903 (10), 101.
[25] Cent. f. Bakt., II Abt., 1909 (22), 371.
[26] Berl. klin. Woch., 1912 (49), 1320.
[27] Münch. med. Woch., 1904 (51), 426.
[28] However, Dreyer (Zeit. ges. Brauw., 1913 (36), 201) states that the cell wall of yeasts contains a hemicellulose and a manno-dextran. See also Kozniewski, Zeit. physiol. Chem., 1914 (90), 208.
[29] See Viehofer, Ber. Deut. Chem. Ges., 1912 (30), 443.
[30] Morgulis states that chitin consists of two parts, one containing all the glucose and amino groups, the other being a stable nitrogenous compound yielding no glucose. (Science, 1916 (44), 866.)
[31] Zeit. physiol. Chem., 1914 (89), 304.
[32] Pharm. Weekblad, 1916 (53), 1183.
[33] Jour. Med. Research, 1901 (6), 135.
[34] See Camus and Pagniez, Compt. Rend. Soc. Biol., 1905 (59), 701.

B. tuberculosis have been made[35] and by using different extractives, from 20 to 40 per cent. of the entire weight of the bacilli has been found soluble in fat solvents. Kresling found that the substance soluble in chloroform had the following composition:

Free fatty acid	14.38 per cent.
Neutral fats and fatty acid esters	77.25 per cent.
Alcohols obtained from fatty acid esters	39.10 per cent.
Lecithin	0.16 per cent.
Substances soluble in water	0.73 per cent.

Bulloch and Macleod found that ethereal extracts did not contain the acid-fast substance which they consider to be a wax-like alcohol, soluble in hot, but insoluble in cold absolute alcohol or in ether. The simple fats seem to be formed by *oleic, isocetinic,* and *myristinic* acids, and there is some *lauric* acid in the form of a soap. Kozniewski[36] obtained what seemed to be a lauric acid ester of a dodecyl-alcohol, and Bürger[37] attributes the odor of tubercle bacilli to the presence of salicylic aldehyde. Cholesterol could not be found in tubercle, diphtheria and other bacteria examined by Tamura, although there probably are lipochromes giving the cultures their color.[38] There is still much disagreement as to whether the acid fastness of tubercle bacilli depends upon waxes, alcohols, fatty acids, or lipoid-protein compounds.[39] It must be admitted that a high content of fatty materials is regularly present in acid-fast bacilli; thus, in an acid-fast bacillus isolated from leprous lesions, 34.7 per cent. of fats, fatty acids and cholesterol, and 1.7 per cent. of lecithin were found by Gurd and Denis.[40] Miller[41] attributes the unstained, spore-like areas of tubercle bacilli to oleins, as bacilli grown on olive and sperm oil show a marked decrease in acid fast areas.

Tamura[42] states that the phosphatids of *B. tuberculosis* and a saphrophyte examined by him were not lecithin but a diaminophosphatid, although diphtheria bacilli seemed to contain lecithin.[43] He found in both a high molecular alcohol, "mykol," to which he ascribes acid- and Gram-fastness. In a Gram-negative bacillus[44] he found lecithin, but no cholesterol or mykol. Apparently the fats of tubercle bacilli resemble in character and complexity the "waxes" of plants (Bürger),[37] which are called "cerolipoids" by Czapek. By growing tubercle bacilli on suitable media they can be made to lose their acid-

[35] For literature see Bulloch and Macleod, Jour. of Hygiene, 1904 (4), 1.
[36] Anzeiger d. Akad. Wiss. Krakau, Math.-naturwiss Kl., 1912, p. 942.
[37] Biochem. Zeit., 1916 (78), 155.
[38] Panzer (Zeit. physiol. Chem., 1912 (78), 114) could not demonstrate cholesterol in tubercle bacilli but did find a small amount of some substance uniting with digitonin.
[39] See Camus and Pagniez, Presse Méd., 1907 (15), 65; Deyke, Münch. med. Woch., 1910 (57), 633.
[40] Jour. Exper. Med., 1911 (14), 606.
[41] Jour. Path. and Bact., 1916 (21), 41.
[42] Zeit. physiol. Chem., 1913 (87), 85.
[43] Ibid., 1911 (89), 289.
[44] Ibid., 1911 (90), 286.

fast property, although still Gram-positive (Wherry).[45] The observation of Miss Sherman,[46] that tubercle bacilli are almost absolutely impermeable to fat-soluble dyes which stain their isolated fats well, and her corroboration of Benians' demonstration that acid-fastness depends on the integrity of the bacillary envelope, make the rôle of the fatty substances uncertain. The high content in unsaturated fatty acids gives acid-fast bacteria a high antitryptic power, which may be concerned in the defense of the bacteria and also in the persistence of caseous material in tubercles (Jobling and Petersen).[47] The oily material obtained by extracting tubercle bacilli with cold ether is non-toxic, while the waxy material extracted with hot alcohol produces foreign body tubercles (Morse and Stott).[48]

By staining with Sudan III, Sata[49] demonstrated fats, not only in the acid-fast bacilli, but also in anthrax, *Staphylococcus aureus*, *B. mucosus*, and actinomyces; but not in diphtheria, pseudo-diphtheria, plague, cholera, and chicken cholera bacilli, or in members of the colon group.[50] Only a few bacteria form fat on agar free from glycerol, but potato is a favorable medium. Ritchie[51] obtained positive fat staining in *B. diphtheriæ* and *anthracis*, but not in *S. pyogenes aureus* or *M. tetragenus*, although these last forms contain chemically demonstrable lipins. Analyses of different bacteria show a relatively low content of lipins as compared with tubercle bacilli, varying from 1.7 per cent. in *B. subtilis* to 8.5 per cent. in staphylococci (Jobling and Petersen).[52] However, the degree of unsaturation of the fatty acids is less with tubercle bacilli than with other bacteria examined by these authors. Extensive studies of bacterial fat stains are reported by Eisenberg,[52a] but practically nothing is known of the character of the fatty or lipoid constituents of bacteria outside the acid-fast group.

Spores differ from their parent bacteria in containing a much greater proportion of the solid constituents and less water. In molds Drymont found that the spores contained over 60 per cent. of dry substance, and almost all the water was so held as to resist drying by temperatures below boiling; the dry substance is very rich in protein and poor in salts. As the spores may lose their chromatin content without loss of capacity to propagate, it would seem that this is not a nuclear chromatin but merely a reserve food supply.[53] The wall of the spore consists of a "cellulose-like" substance and a very hygroscopic extractive matter. The great resistance of spores to drying and to heat can be readily understood in view of these facts. They contain, and perhaps secrete, active enzymes (Effront).[54] Flagella also seem to be composed of a relatively condensed protein.

[45] Jour. Infect. Dis., 1913 (13), 144.
[46] Jour. Infect. Dis., 1913 (12), 249.
[47] Jour. Exp. Med., 1914 (19), 239.
[48] Jour. Lab. Clin. Med., 1916 (2), 159.
[49] Cent. f. allg. Path., 1900 (11), 97.
[50] Auclair (Arch. Méd. Exper., 1903 (15), 725) contends that the ether and chloroform extracts of many pathogenic bacteria contain important toxic substances. Holmes (Guy's Hosp. Reports, 1905 (59), 155) states that injection of fatty acids from tubercle bacilli into rabbits causes a lymphocytosis.
[51] Jour. Pathol. and Bact., 1905 (10), 334.
[52] Jour. Exp. Med., 1914 (20), 456.
[52a] Virchow's Archiv., 1910 (199), 502.
[53] Ruzicka, Cent. f. Bakt., 1914 (41), 641.
[54] Mon. sc. Quesneville, 1907, p. 81.

Staining Reactions.—The staining reactions of bacterial cells are much as if the bacteria consisted entirely of chromatin, so that at one time the theory prevailed that bacteria consisted merely of a nucleus and a cell wall, without any true cytoplasm. The demonstration of abundant nucleoprotein in the contents of bacterial cells explains their staining affinity for basic anilin dyes. Owing to some unknown differences in composition, not all bacteria are stained equally well by the same basic dyes.[55] Although the staining of bacteria depends upon a chemical reaction between the nucleoproteins and the basic dye, yet the combination is not usually a firm one, being readily broken by weak acids in most cases. That the decolorization of bacteria depends upon dissociation of the dye-protein compound is shown by the fact that absolutely water-free alcohol will not decolorize dry bacteria, nor do water-free alcoholic solutions of dyes stain dehydrated bacteria. There seems to be a marked difference in the accessibility of dead and living bacteria to stains; thus, only dead bacteria stain with $AgNO_3$.[56]

GRAM'S METHOD[57] of staining has been ascribed to the formation of an iodin-pararosanilin-protein compound which is not easily dissociated by water in the case of bacteria that stain by this method, and which is readily dissociated and dissolved out in the case of bacteria that do not retain the stain. Only pararosanilin dyes (gentian violet, methyl violet, victoria blue) form such combinations, the rosanilin dyes not being suitable.[58] It is probable, especially from the observations of Deussen, that the nucleoproteins are the essential cell constituents, and other cells than bacteria (e.g., sperm) may be Gram-positive.

The relation of bacterial protein to Gram staining is shown by the fact that trypsin will digest killed bacteria which are Gram-negative, but not Gram-positive forms; gastric juice attacks only a few Gram-positive bacteria.[59] They are also more resistant to alkalies, 1 per cent. KOH dissolving only the Gram-negative bacteria. Brundy[60] considers that they are more permeable to iodin, so that a more central iodin-dye precipitate occurs, and Eisenberg[61] suggests that lipoid-protein compounds in the surface are important, in support of which is the observation that ether extraction of staphylococci renders them negative to Gram's method, while colon bacilli treated with lecithin become positive.[62] Jobling and Petersen[52] have also found the lipoids of Gram-positive bacteria more resistant to extraction by fat solvents than lipoids of Gram-negative bacteria, and Tamura[63] found that the lipoid extract contains the bacterial element responsible for Gram staining. The first-named authors suggest a relation between the high content in unsaturated fatty acids, with the high affinity for iodin, and the positive Gram staining. On the other hand, Hottinger[64] attributes Gram staining solely to the degree of dispersion of the nucleo-proteins, which he believes to be higher in the

[55] The presence of serum interferes with staining, probably from protective colloid action (Fleisher, Jour. Med. Res., 1917 (36), 31.)
[56] Nyfeldt, Nordiskt Med. Arkiv, 1917 (50), 184.
[57] Full review by Deussen, Zeit. Hyg., 1918 (85), 235.
[58] Any metallic iodid may be substituted for KI (Leidy, Jour. Lab. Clin. Med., 1919 (4), 354).
[59] Burgers, Schermann and Schreiber, Zeit. f. Hyg., 1911 (70), 119; Weinkoff, Zeit. Immunitat., 1912 (11), 1.
[60] Cent. f. Bakt., II Abt., 1908 (21), 62.
[61] Cent. f. Bakt., 1910 (56), 193.
[62] Jour. Path. and Bact., 1911 (16), 146.
[63] Zeit. physiol. Chem., 1914 (89), 289.
[64] Cent. f. Bakt., 1916 (76), 367.

Gram-negative forms. Benians[65] has found that crushed Gram-positive bacteria are promptly decolorized, indicating that the dye and the cell contents do not form an insoluble compound, but that the bacterial cell wall is the chief factor in determining Gram positiveness; presumably the iodin renders the cell membrane impermeable to alcohol. This important contribution has been confirmed, as far as the staining of tubercle bacilli is concerned, by Hope Sherman,[66] who corroborates the finding of Benians that if the bacilli are not intact they are neither acid fast nor Gram positive. The same is true of yeast cells (Henrici),[67] but Deussen states that press juice from yeast (Buchner's zymase) contains Gram-positive granules.

BACTERIAL ENZYMES[68]

The metabolic processes of bacteria seem to be closely dependent upon enzyme action, just as with higher cells. Liquefaction of gelatin is a familiar example of the enzyme action of bacteria; and since the filtered cultures of liquefactive bacteria are also capable of digesting gelatin, the enzymes are evidently excreted from the cells. Dead bacteria, killed by thymol or by other antiseptics that do not destroy proteolytic enzymes, will also digest gelatin. Numerous investigations have established the wide-spread occurence of many soluble enzymes both in bacteria and in their secretions, indicating that bacterial cells are as dependent on enzymes for the production of their metabolic activities as are higher types of cells, and that these enzymes are not only present as intracellular constituents, but that they also escape from the cells. Even the spores contain active enzymes.[69] A striking property of bacteria is their reducing power, which has led to the introduction of selenium and tellurium salts, which are reduced to the metals, as an index of bacterial life and activity (Gosio).

The diffusion method of Wijsman, or, as it is more frequently called, *auxanographic* method of Beijerinck, offers a relatively simple means of detecting the presence of extracellular bacterial enzymes. Eijkman[70] in particular has used this method, which consists of mixing agar with milk, or starch, or whatever material is to serve as the indicator of the enzyme action; the agar is then inoculated with bacteria and plated (or else the bacteria are inoculated as a streak on the surface of the agar). About each colony there will appear a zone of clearing in the medium if it produces enzymes digesting the admixed substance. By this means Eijkman found that all bacteria that produce enzymes digesting gelatin also digest casein, and those that do not digest gelatin are equally without effect on casein; therefore, it is probably the same enzyme that digests both. As the hemolytic

[65] Jour. Path. and Bact., 1912 (17), 199.
[66] Jour. Infec. Dis., 1913 (12), 249.
[67] Jour. Med. Res., 1914 (30), 409.
[68] See Fuhrmann ("Vorlesungen über Bakterienenzyme," Jena, 1907) for complete bibliography to that date.
[69] Effront, Mon. sc. Quesneville, 1907, p. 81.
[70] Cent. f. Bakt., 1901 (29), 841.

action of bacteria is not constantly related to their gelatin-dissolving property, the hemolysis probably is produced by other means than the proteolytic enzymes.[71] A few pathogenic bacteria (anthrax, cholera and some strains of hemolytic streptococci[72]) digest starch[73] and *B. pyocyaneus*, *Staphylococcus pyogenes aureus*, and *B. prodigiosus* all produce fat-splitting enzymes demonstrable by this method.[74] *B. pyocyaneus*, Eijkman found, digested elastic tissue readily,[75] as also did a bacillus resembling *B. subtilis* obtained from the tissue of a gangrenous lung.

Rennin is produced by many bacteria, as is shown by their coagulating milk, independent of any acid reaction,[76] and protease from *pyocyaneus* causes "plastein" formation in albumose solutions (Zak).[77] Bacteria which give negative results by the plate method may contain active *lipase* demonstrable in killed bacteria by direct action upon fats and esters, these lipases behaving exactly like the lipase of animal tissues (Wells and Corper);[78] *staphylococcus* and *pyocyaneus* are more actively lipolytic than *B. coli*, *B. dysenteriœ* and *B. tuberculosis*. Urease seems to be widespread.[79] Tubercle bacilli contain enzymes resembling lipase, trypsin, erepsin, nuclease and urease, but not amylase; elastase or invertase.[80]

Schmailowitsch[81] stated that the amount and nature of enzymes produced by bacteria is modified by the amount and nature of their food, but Jordan found that gelatinase is produced by bacteria growing on non-protein media; he failed entirely to support the statement of Abbott and Gildersleeve[82] that bacteria grown on gelatin produce much more active gelatin-dissolving enzyme than do bacteria grown on bouillon.   Diehl[83] found that bacteria grown on media containing no organic nitrogen produce no proteolytic enzymes, and the enzyme content of bacteria is much modified by the composition of the media, depending on the character of the amino-acids present rather than the proteins themselves.   Jacoby[84] has made extensive studies on the

---

[71] See Jordan, Biol. Studies by the pupils of W. T. Sedgwick, 1906, p. 124.

[72] Tongs, Jour. Amer. Med. Assoc., 1919 (73), 1277.

[73] In relation to carbohydrate enzymes, the extensive studies of Kendall (Jour. Biol. Chem., 1912, vol. 12) should be consulted.   He emphasizes especially that as a rule bacteria ferment carbohydrates in preference to attacking proteins when both foodstuffs are available.

[74] See Buxton (American Med., 1903 (6), 137) concerning enzymes of numerous bacteria.

[75] Cent. f. Bakt., 1903 (35), 1.

[76] Contradicted by DeWaele, Cent. f. Bakt., 1905 (39), 353.

[77] Hofmeister's Beitr., 1907 (10), 287.

[78] Jour. Infect. Dis., 1912 (11), 388; literature on bacterial lipases.   See also Kendall.[73]

[79] See Jacoby, Biochem. Zeit., 1917 (80), 357.

[80] Corper and Sweany, Jour. Bact., 1918 (3), 129.

[81] Wratschebnaja Gazetta, 1902, p. 52.

[82] Jour. Med. Research, 1903 (10), 42.

[83] Jour. Infect. Dis., 1919 (24), 347.

[84] Biochem. Zeit., 1917 (83), 74.

requirements for the production of urease on Uschinski's medium, and finds that while bacteria will grow if the sodium asparaginate is present, no urease is formed unless leucine is also added. There does not seem to be any important relation between enzyme production and pathogenicity.[85]

In general, bacterial proteolytic enzymes resemble trypsin more closely than they do pepsin, acting best in an alkaline medium; but the enzymes extracted from bacterial cultures are very feeble as compared with pancreatic trypsin. It is probable that there are several distinct proteolytic enzymes in bacterial cells, gelatinase being a distinct protease (Jordan).[86] Abbott and Gildersleeve found that the gelatin-dissolving enzyme of bacteria resists a temperature of 100° C. for as long as fifteen to thirty minutes, but Jordan found that the reaction of the medium modifies greatly this heat resistance. Schmailo-witsch[87] states that some bacteria produce an enzyme acting in acid medium upon gelatin but not upon albumin, and this enzyme carries the digestion only as far as the gelatin-peptone stage, whereas the enzymes acting in an alkaline medium carry the splitting through to leucine, tyrosine, etc. Kendall and Walker[88] state that the proteolytic enzymes of *B. proteus* are not formed when the bacteria have enough carbo-hydrate supplied so that they need not depend on proteins for their energy requirements; deaminization is independent of proteolysis and represents intracellular enzyme action. Plenge[89] suggests that there is a special enzyme digesting nucleoproteins (nuclease). Bac-teria are able to split nucleic acids and to convert amino-purines into oxypurines, but they do not carry the oxidation to uric acid; putre-factive bacteria can slowly destroy uric acid (Schittenhelm),[90] and *B. coli* destroys purines.[91]

Cacace[92] investigated the cleavage products of gelatin and coagu-lated blood when digested by *B. anthracis, Staph. pyogenes aureus*, and *Sarcina aurantiaca*, and found that proteoses and peptone are produced, which disappear in the later stages of digestion. Rettger[93] found leucine, tyrosine, tryptophane, as well as phenols, skatole, indole, aromatic oxy-acids, and mercaptan, among the products of bac-terial decomposition of egg-albumen and meat: proteoses and pep-tones appear in the early stages, but later disappear, as also eventually do the leucine, tyrosine, etc. Choline has also been found in the

[85] Rosenthal and Patai, Cent. f. Bakt., 1914 (73), 406; (74), 369.
[86] Corroborated by Bertiau, Cent. f. Bakt., 1914 (74), 374.
[87] Abst. in Biochem. Centr., 1903 (1), 230; see also DeWaele, Cent. f. Bakt., 1905 (39), 353.
[88] Jour. Infect. Dis., 1915 (17), 442. See also Berman and Rettger, Jour. Bact., 1918 (3), 367.
[89] Zeit. f. physiol. Chem., 1903 (39), 190.
[90] Zeit. physiol. Chem., 1908 (57), 21.
[91] Siven, Zeit. physiol. Chem., 1914 (91), 336.
[92] Cent. f. Bakt., 1901 (30), 244.
[93] Amer. Jour. of Physiol., 1903 (8), 284

products of autolysis.[94]   Molliard[95] reports that *Isaria densa* produces
large masses of crystals of glycine, even when grown on proteins that
contain little or no glycine.

The digestive power of the filtrates of cultures and of killed bacteria
is far less than that of the living bacteria (Knapp).[96]   Streptococci
digest proteins of exudates feebly, staphylococci more rapidly, and
colon bacilli are still more active.   He could find no relation between
the proteolytic power of the bacteria and the severity of the infection
from which they came.   Staphylococci can cause coagulation of plasma
and then dissolve the coagulum, showing the presence of two enzymes,
staphylokinase and *fibrinolysin* (Kleinschmidt).[97]   Sperry and Rettger,[98]
however, found that even the most actively putrefactive bacteria are
unable to attack or grow upon carefully purified proteins, although
the presence of small amounts of amino acids or other available nutrient makes the proteins available to the bacteria; apparently they
must have some nutrient more available than intact protein molecules
to enable them to grow sufficiently to produce enough free enzymes to
attack the proteins.   By virtue of their proteolytic enzymes, filtrates
of bacteria that liquefy gelatin also can digest hardened liver, kidney
and other tissue elements *in vitro* the changes resembling those of
necrobiosis.[99]

Oxidizing Enzymes.—*Catalase* is demonstrable in bacteria, the anaerobic
forms showing the least activity (Rywosch),[1] but practically no species is entirely
inactive (Jorns);[2] it may exist as either endo- or ecto-enzyme.   *B. proteus* synthesizes catalase even when grown on a simple synthetic medium containing, besides
inorganic salts, sodium lactate and alanine or aspartic acid (Jacoby).[3]   Certain
bacteria and actinomyces exhibit oxidative effects, resembling *tyrosinase*, but such
an enzyme could not be extracted by Lehmann and Sano.[4]   Tsudji,[5] however,
not only observed oxidation of tyrosine, but states furthermore that proteus produces always a d-oxyacid product and subtilis a l-oxyacid type, regardless of
whether they have oxidized d-, l-, or dl-tyrosine.

Immunity against bacterial enzymes may be secured as it is against
other enzymes.   Abbott and Gildersleeve[32] found that by injections
into animals of proteolytic bacterial filtrates which were only slightly
toxic, the serum of the animals acquired a slight but specific increase
in resistance to the proteolytic enzymes of the filtrates.[6]   Normal
serum contains a certain amount of enzyme-resisting substance.

[94] Kutscher and Lohmann, Zeit. physiol. Chem., 1903 (39), 313.
[95] Compt. Rend. Acad. Sci., 1918 (167), 786.
[96] Zeit. f. Heilk. (Chir. Abt.), 1902 (23), 236.
[97] Zeit. Immunität., 1909 (3), 516.
[98] Jour. Biol. Chem., 1915 (20), 445; Jour. Bact., 1916 (1), 15.
[99] Bittrolff, Ziegler's Beitr., 1915 (60), 337.
[1] Cent. f. Bakt., 1907 (44), 295.
[2] Arch. f. Hyg., 1908 (67), 134.
[3] Biochem. Zeit., 1918 (88), 35 and (89), 350.
[4] Arch. f. Hyg., 1908 (67), 99.
[5] Acta Scholae Med. Univ. Kioto, 1918 (2), 115.
[6] Antigelatinase has also been obtained by Bertian, Cent. f. Bakt., 1914 (74)
374.

Other observers have found that immunization against living or dead bacteria leads to the production of substances antagonistic to their enzymes, but the degree of resistance acquired is never great. v. Dungern[7] found that the serum of animals infected with various bacteria prevented digestion of gelatin by the enzymes obtained from cultures of the same species of bacteria. He applied this fact to the diagnosis of infectious conditions, finding that the serum of a patient with osteomyelitis was over twenty times as strongly inhibitory to staphylococcus enzymes as was serum of normal persons. The reaction is specific, cholera vibrio enzymes not being inhibited to any corresponding degree.

Kantorowicz[8] and de Waele[9] state that bacteria contain an intracellular *anti-protease* which, with most bacteria, holds in check the proteolytic action; only with the liquefying bacteria are the proteases in excess. Bacteria grow well in strong solutions of enzymes, and without destroying the enzymes (Fermi).[10] After Gram-negative bacteria have been heated to 80° they are readily digested by trypsin, pepsin or leucocytic proteases; but Gram-positive bacteria are resistant even after heating. This is ascribed by Jobling and Petersen[11] to the unsaturated fatty acids, which are present in greater amounts in Gram-positive bacteria.

Autolysis of Bacteria.—Autolysis occurs also in bacteria, their proteolytic enzymes digesting the cell substance whenever the organisms are killed by agents (chloroform, toluene, etc.) that do not destroy these enzymes, and which, being fat solvents, may facilitate digestion by removing the inhibitory lipoids. Even the absence of food leads to autolysis, presumably because the normally existing autolytic processes are not counteracted by synthesis of new protein material; hence, autolysis occurs when bacteria are placed in salt solution or distilled water. Although it had been known for many years that yeast cells digest one another when there is nothing else for them to live upon, the first definite study of bacterial autolysis seems to have been made by Levy and Pfersdorff[12] and Conradi.[13] The former digested anthrax bacilli (in whose bodies are contained rennin, lipase and protease) under toluene for several weeks and obtained a slightly toxic product. Conradi permitted dysentery bacilli and typhoid bacilli to digest themselves in normal salt solution for twenty-four to forty-eight hours at 37° C., and obtained in this way the soluble, highly poisonous endotoxins of the bacteria, which are liberated by the destruction of the bacterial structure by the autolytic enzymes. Longer

[7] Münch. med. Woch., 1898 (45), 1040.
[8] Münch. med. Woch., 1909 (56), 897.
[9] Cent. f. Bakt., 1909 (50), 40.
[10] Arch. Farmacol., 1909 (8), 481.
[11] Jour. Exp. Med., 1914 (20), 321.
[12] Deut. med. Woch., 1902 (28), 879.
[13] *Ibid.*, 1903 (29), 26.

8

autolysis results in the destruction by the enzymes of the endotoxins themselves. Rettger[14] found among the autolytic products of bacteria, leucine, tyrosine, basic substances, and phosporic acid. Under favorable conditions complete autolysis can occur in two to ten days.

Brieger and Mayer[15] found that at room temperature (15° C.) practically no autolysis occurs with typhoid bacilli in distilled water, and the soluble products thus obtained are quite non-toxic, although if injected into animals they give rise to the production of agglutinins and bacteriolysins. Bertarelli[16] has used the products of autolysis of cholera vibrios successfully in the production of immunity, and states that the products of autolysis consist largely of nucleins.

It is probable that in every culture bacteria are constantly being destroyed, either by their own enzymes or by the proteolytic enzymes of the other bacteria. Some bacteria are much more rapidly autolyzed than others, cholera vibrios, colon, typhoid, and dysentery bacilli being rapidly digested, while streptococci, staphylococci and tubercle bacilli are very little and slowly autolyzed. In general, the Gram-positive organisms resist autolysis longest, but pneumococci autolyze readily.

Conradi,[17] who has shown that certain products of autolysis of tissues are bactericidal, believes that also in cultures powerfully bactericidal substances are produced through autolysis of the bacteria. This he thinks, accounts for the decrease in numbers of living bacteria that always sets in after a short period of growth on artificial media; but there is much doubt as to these substances being of any considerable importance in the body.[18] It has been found by Turró[19] that extracts from various tissues containing autolytic enzymes can digest bacterial cells.[20] It is very possible that the endotoxins contained within such pathogenic bacteria as typhoid and cholera are liberated through digestion of the bacteria, either by autolysis or by the enzymes of the leucocytes and tissues of the organism that they have infected. These, and a number of other bacteria, produce no soluble toxins that diffuse from the cells as do diphtheria and tetanus toxin, and it is difficult to explain the toxic effects these bacteria produce without assuming that their intracellular toxins are liberated in some such way. It is also quite probable that the enzymes found in filtrates from bacterial cultures are liberated from the bacterial cells

[14] Jour. Med. Research, 1904 (13), 79.
[15] Deut. med. Woch., 1904 (30), 980.
[16] Cent. f. Bakt., 1905 (38), 584.
[17] Münch. med. Wochenschr., 1905 (52), 1761.
[18] See Eijkman, Cent. f. Bakt., 1906 (41), 367; Passini, Wien. klin. Woch., 1906 (19), 627.
[19] Cent. f. Bakt., 1902 (32), 105.
[20] Sigwart (Arb. a. d. Path. Inst. Tübingen, 1902 (3), 277) found that trypsin and pepsin (without acid) do not injure living anthrax bacilli.

only when these have been autolyzed.[21] With the possible exception just mentioned, there is little evidence that the bacterial enzymes play any important rôle in infectious diseases. They may be a slight factor in the digestion of tissue and exudates in suppuration, but as compared with the leucocytic enzymes their influence is probably minute; beyond this they have no apparent influence upon their host, and are chiefly concerned in the metabolism of the bacteria. The proteoses and peptones produced by bacterial action and isolated from cultures do not seem to be any more toxic than those produced by pepsin and trypsin, but violent poisons may be liberated from bacteria during autolysis, as Rosenow[22] has shown for the pneumococcus and other bacteria; these poisons seem similar to or identical with the so-called *anaphylatoxin* which is supposedly formed by the digestion of bacteria with serum complement, and presumably they are proteoses or polypeptids, but their exact nature is not known. (See Anaphylatoxin, Chap. vii.)

POISONOUS BACTERIAL PRODUCTS

Almost without exception all the harm that bacteria do is brought about by means of the chemical substances produced in one way or another by their metabolic processes. Animal parasites may do harm mechanically, but with the possible exception of the effects of capillary emboli (especially with anthrax), bacteria produce all their effects through chemical means. The poisonous chemical substances produced by bacteria are commonly grouped into four classes:

I. Products of the decomposition of the media upon which the bacteria are growing; among these the best known are the *ptomaïns*.

II. Soluble poisons manufactured by the bacteria, and secreted from the cell into its surrounding media—the true *toxins*.

III. Poisons manufactured by the bacteria which do not escape from the normal cell but which are as specific in their poisonous properties as the true toxins; because of their intracellular situation they are called *endotoxins*.

IV. Poisonous protein constitutents of the bacterial cell which form part of the cell protoplasm, but which are not soluble, and the poisonous effects of which are not specific and not usually responsible for the disease; these are called *bacterial proteins*.

[21] Emmerich and Loew (Zeitschr. f. Hyg., 1899 (31), 1), having found that *pyocyanase* is capable of destroying and digesting other bacteria than pyocyaneus, suggested that it might be a potent factor in producing artificial immunity. Their rather remarkable hypotheses have been much contested, and are of questionable value. (See Petrie, Jour. of Pathol. and Bacteriol., 1903 (8), 200; also, Rettger, Jour. Infectious Diseases, 1905 (2), 562; Emmerich, Münch. med. Woch., 1907 (54), 2217).

[22] Jour. Infect. Dis., 1912 (10), 113; (11), 94, 235 and 480.

PTOMAÏNS

Ptomaïns, the soluble basic nitrogenous substances that are found in the medium in which bacteria have been growing, were the first bacterial products that were recognized, and for some time it was believed that it was through the production of such alkaloid-like substances that bacteria caused disease, just as poisonous plants owe their effects to poisonous alkaloids. It was soon found, however, that the ptomaïns that could be isolated from cultures of pathogenic bacteria were insufficient by themselves to cause the poisonous effects that such cultures produced when injected into animals. The isolated ptomaïns were not only far less poisonous than the original culture, but furthermore they did not produce the symptoms and anatomical changes characteristic of the diseases that the pathogenic organism caused. Moreover, the majority of ptomaïns are not very poisonous, and highly poisonous ptomaïns may be produced by non-pathogenic bacteria. As a result, the work on ptomaïns, which once occupied many laboratories and promised to reveal the entire chemistry of bacterial intoxication, has now been almost completely dropped. The interest in ptomaïns is by no means entirely historical, however, for it is possible that poisonous ptomaïns at times do enter the body and cause illness, perhaps even death. The close chemical resemblance to vegetable alkaloids of some of the ptomaïns that may arise in decomposing corpses, makes them of great importance to chemists searching for the cause of death in cases of supposed poisoning. Therefore the most essential features of the ptomaïns and their chief known relations to intoxications will be briefly discussed, referring the reader for a full consideration to Vaughan and Novy's "Cellular Toxins" and Barger's "The Simpler Natural Bases."

The ptomaïns owe their basic character to nitrogen-containing radicals, principally amino-groups, and hence are formed from nitrogenous substances, chiefly proteins, which contain their nitrogen in the amino form. Probably most ptomaïns arise from the decomposition of the protein medium upon which the bacteria grow, although undoubtedly part of the ptomaïns is also formed from the destruction of the bacterial cells themselves; how large a part of the ptomaïns is formed by intracellular bacterial processes and how much by cleavage of the proteins of the media by extracellular bacterial enzymes is unknown. The structure of the ptomaïns shows them to be very closely related to the amino-acids obtained by cleavage of the protein molecule by enzymes and other hydrolytic agencies; and the determination of the composition of the several amino-acids of the proteins has quite cleared up the problem of the origin of the ptomaïns. Presumably these secondary changes result from the action of special enzymes upon the amino-acids. Most of the ptomaïns are free from or poor in oxygen, hence reduction processes, or lack of sufficient oxygen for oxidation, are probably important in their production.

The poisonous ptomaïns, which are decidedly in the minority among the entire group, are themselves subject to decomposition, being most abundant in the cultures after a certain period of time, and then decreasing in amount. Very old cultures show almost none of the higher molecular forms of nitrogen, such as ptomaïns, these substances having been changed into ammonium and nitrate compounds. In sharp contradistinction to the toxins, *the ptomaïns are by no means specific.* No matter upon what medium diphtheria bacilli grow, the toxin produced has qualitatively the same properties, whereas the nature of the ptomaïns depends not only upon the nature of the bacteria producing them, but also even more upon the sort of soil upon which the bacteria are grown, the temperature, the duration of the process, and the quantity of oxygen furnished. The same organism may produce totally different ptomaïns when grown on different media or under different conditions. Another essential difference is that we cannot obtain an immune serum, antagonizing the action of ptomaïns, by injecting ptomaïns into animals.

If ptomaïns do cause intoxications presumably it is when they are taken in with food in which they have been produced by bacterial decomposition. Besides this food poisoning, it is also possible that ptomaïns may be formed by putrefaction within the gastrointestinal tract. Another possible source of ptomaïns is furnished by decomposing tissues in gangrene. It is doubtful if ptomaïns are produced in sufficient quantities by pathogenic bacteria infecting living tissue to be of any importance. Food poisoning is by no means uncommon, but we do not know how often it is due to ptomaïns; it may be the result of poisonous materials contained abnormally in the food, that are not ptomaïns, *e. g.*, botulism; or it may be due to an infection of the animal from which the meat came with pathogenic organisms, particularly the *B. enteritidis* of Gaertner and other bacteria related to the colon-typhoid group; or in other ways food ordinarily wholesome may become poisonous.[23] The commonest sources of ptomaïn poisoning are supposed to be imperfectly preserved canned meats, sausages, decomposing fish, cheese, ice-cream, and milk.[24]

Chemical Composition of Ptomaïns.—To indicate the composition and nature of ptomaïns a few of the more important ones will be described. As illustrative of the simpler forms may be mentioned:

Methyl amine,	$CH_3 - NH_2.$
Di-methyl amine,	$CH_3 - NH - CH_3.$
Tri-methyl amine,	$CH_3 - N - CH_3.$
	$\quad\quad\quad\;\; \mid$
	$\quad\quad\quad CH_3.$

These bodies, which are commonly found in decomposing proteins are but very slightly toxic, and of little pathological importance.

[23] See Jordan, "Food Poisoning," University of Chicago Press, 1917.
[24] All these matters are discussed at length by Vaughan and Novy, to whose book the reader is referred.

The source of the ptomaïns in the various amino-acids is usually easily traced through their chemical structure, and Ackermann and Kutscher[25] have classified them in this relation under the name "*aporrhegma*."

When we examine the structural formulæ of some of the larger ptomaïn molecules and compare them with the formulæ of the amino-acids that form the protein molecule, the relation is apparent, *c. g.*, compare iso-amylamine with leucine.

$$CH_3 \diagdown CH - CH_2 - CH_2 - NH_2 \qquad CH_3 \diagdown CH - CH_2 - CH - NH_2$$
$$CH_3 \diagup \qquad\qquad CH_3 \diagup \qquad\qquad \diagdown COOH.$$
$$\text{(iso-amylamine)} \qquad\qquad\qquad \text{(leucine)}$$

Putrescine, $C_4H_{12}N_2$, structural formula,
$$NH_2 - CH_2 - CH_2 - CH_2 - CH_2 - NH_2,$$
and *cadaverine*, $C_5H_{14}N_2$, structural formula,
$$NH_2 - CH_2 - CH_2 - CH_2 - CH_2 - CH_2 - NH_2,$$

are of interest because they have been found in the intestinal contents, arising from putrefaction of proteins, and also are sometimes present in the urine in *cystinuria*.[26] They are closely related to the diamino-acids, lysine and ornithine. They are but slightly toxic, although capable of causing local necrosis when injected subcutaneously. (See further discussion on these and the Pressor Bases in Chap. xxi.)

The Choline Group.—Another group of ptomaïns, including choline and closely related substances, is also of interest. These ptomaïns are:

Choline,	$CH_2OH - CH_2 - N(CH_3)_3 - OH$
Neurine,	$CH_2 = CH - N(CH_3)_3 - OH$
Muscarine,	$CH(OH)_2 - CH_2 - N(CH_3)_3 - OH$
Betaine,	$COOH - CH_2 - N(CH_3)_3 - OH$

The first point of importance is that choline is present in every cell normally, forming the nitrogenous portion of the lecithin molecule. Its source in putrefaction of tissues is, therefore, plain. It is possible that choline is liberated from nerve tissues when they break down in the body during life,[27] and there is a considerable literature on the supposed finding of choline in the blood and cerebrospinal fluid in diseases of the central nervous system and experimental lesions in nervous tissues. At present it seems probable that these observations depend upon faulty methods of analysis, and it is extremely doubtful if enough choline is ever set free at one time from even severe acute nervous lesions to be detected in the body fluids by chemical means.[28] Hunt[29] has devised a physiological test that permits of the detection of as little as 0.00001 mg., but he was unable to

[25] Zeit. physiol. Chem., 1910 (69), 265.

[26] Udránsky and Baumann, Zeit. physiol. Chem., 1889 (13), 562; 1889 (15) 77.

[27] Coriat (Amer. Jour. of Physiol., 1904 (12), 353) has studied the conditions under which choline may be produced from lecithin. Putrefaction of lecithin or lecithin-rich tissues liberates choline as also does autolysis of brain tissue; neither pepsin nor trypsin, however, splits it from the lecithin. In brain tissue, therefore, there seems to be an enzyme different from trypsin, which splits choline out of the lecithin molecule.

[28] See Webster, Biochem. Jour., 1909 (4), 123; Kajiura, Quart. Jour. Exper. Physiol., 1908 (1), 291; Handelsmann, Deut. Zeit. Nervenheilk., 1908 (35), 428; Dorée and Golla, Biochem. Jour., 1910 (5), 306.

[29] Jour. Pharmacol., 1915 (7), 301.

obtain evidence that choline is of any significance in either physiological or pathological processes. Normally the largest amounts by far are obtained from the adrenals, which also seem to contain choline derivatives of much greater physiological activity. Choline itself is somewhat toxic, but the closely related body, neurine, into which it may be transformed, is highly poisonous, which makes choline an important indirect source of intoxication. It is possible, for example, that lecithin taken in the food splits off choline in the gastro-intestinal tract, and this being converted into neurine gives rise to intoxication which may be ascribed to food intoxication. Likewise it has been suggested that the intoxication of fatigue may be due, at least in part, to choline and neurine produced from lecithin decomposed during the period of cellular activity. The close structural relation to choline and neurine, of the mushroom poison, muscarine, which produces physiological effects very similar to those of neurine, indicates the close relationship of the putrefactive ptomaïns and the vegetable alkaloids. Indeed a muscarine apparently identical with that of the mushroom has been found in decomposing flesh, and neurine, presumably derived from lecithin, may be found in human urine.[30] Betaine, the fourth member of the group, which has but slight toxicity, is particularly well known as a constituent of plant tissues.

Both neurine and muscarine are extremely poisonous and quite similar in their effects. Subcutaneous injection of but 1 to 3 mg. of muscarine in man produces salivation, rapid pulse, reddening of the face, weakness, depression, profuse sweating, vomiting, and diarrhœa. Neurine, likewise, causes salivation, lachrymation, vomiting, and diarrhœa. In fatal poisoning respiration ceases before the heart stops. Both poisons resemble physostigmine in their stimulation of secretion and are equally well counteracted by atropine. The toxicity of these substances is so great that not a large amount would need to be formed by oxidation of choline to produce severe symptoms, although it is not known that this actually occurs in the body. When introduced by mouth, the lethal dose of neurine is ten times as great as when injected subcutaneously, indicating that chemical changes in the gastro-intestinal tract or liver offer some protection against intoxication by these substances when taken in tainted food. Choline, although by no means so poisonous as neurine, has a similar action when administered in sufficiently large doses. According to Brieger, it is about one-tenth to one-twentieth as toxic as neurine.[31] Choline

[30] Kutscher and Lohmann, Zeit. physiol. Chem., 1906 (48), 1.
[31] Halliburton, "Chem. of Muscle and Nerve," 1904, p. 119, states that choline produces a fall in blood pressure by dilating the peripheral vessels, whereas neurine constricts the peripheral vessels; he uses this difference in physiological effect as a means of distinguishing the two substances. Injected into animals, choline causes a considerable but transient decrease in the number of leucocytes in the blood, followed later by an increase (Werner and Lichtenberg, Deut. med. Woch., 1906 (32), 22).

seems to be rapidly destroyed in the body, not appearing in the urine[32] but forming formic acid and perhaps glyoxylic acid. Donath[33] found that choline injected directly into the cortex or under the dura is extremely toxic, causing severe tonic and clonic convulsions, and believes that choline may be responsible for epileptic convulsions. This view has been opposed, and properly so, by Handelsmann[28] and others. The attempt to ascribe importance to choline as a cause of either toxic or therapeutic effect of x-rays seems also to be entitled to but slight consideration.[34] It is probably a factor in the lowering of blood pressure which results from injection of extracts of various tissues, in which it is commonly present in minute amounts,[35] for very minute amounts of choline will produce a decided fall in blood pressure.[36]

The Pressor Bases.—By decarboxylation of amino acids, amines are obtained, and some of them, notably those derived from leucine, tyrosine, phenylalanine and histidine, have a marked effect on non-striated muscle. These are discussed in Chapter xxi.

TOXINS

Certain bacteria produce soluble poisons by synthetic processes, which poisons are secreted into the surrounding medium and represent the chief poisonous products of the bacteria, being capable of causing most or all of the symptoms attributed to infection by the specific bacteria that have manufactured them. To this class of soluble poisons the term *toxin* has now become limited (for reasons that will be mentioned below), including not only toxins of bacterial origin, but also poisons of similar nature produced by animals (snake venoms, eel serum, etc.) and by plants (ricin, abrin, crotin). The chief bacteria secreting true toxins are B. diphtheriæ, B. tetani, B. pyocyaneus, and B. botulinus. Dysentery bacilli, the anaerobes of gas gangrene, and perhaps a few other pathogens also secrete a toxin. Pick considers the active constituent of tuberculin to be a true toxin, or closely related thereto. Also the hemolytic poisons produced by many bacteria seem to be true toxins. It will be seen that the term toxin has been greatly narrowed since the time when all ptomaïns and other poisonous bacterial products were called toxins, until now it has come to include the specific poisons of but a few of the great group of pathogenic bacteria.

Chemical Properties of Toxins.—The chemical nature of the toxins is entirely unknown. By various precipitation methods they

[32] v. Hoesslin, Hofmeister's Beitr., 1906 (8), 271.
[33] Zeit. f. physiol. Chem., 1903 (39), 526; also see Med. News, 1905 (86), 107, for literature and methods of analysis.
[34] See Schenk, Deut. med. Woch., 1910 (36), 1130.
[35] Schwarz and Lederer, Pflüger's Arch., 1908 (124), 353; Kinoshita, *ibid.*, 1910 (132), 607.
[36] Mendel et al., Jour. Pharm. and Exp. Ther., 1912 (3), 648; Hunt and Taveau, Bulletin 73, Hyg. Lab. U. S. P. H. Service.

may be carried down, but included with them are masses of impurities, chiefly proteins. They behave like electro-positive colloids,[37] but diffuse faster than proteins. It is not certain that toxins are not proteins, for although certain investigators report that by purification processes very active toxins have been obtained that did not give the protein reactions, yet the toxins are attacked by proteolytic enzymes, and, like proteins, are precipitated by nucleic acid (Kossel). Furthermore, accumulating experience with immunological processes adds increasing doubt as to the possibility of antibody formation being incited by anything but proteins. Oppenheimer says of the toxins, "we must be contented to assume that they are large molecular complexes, probably related to the proteins, corresponding to them in certain properties, but standing even nearer to the equally mysterious enzymes with whose properties they show the most extended analogies both in their reactions and in their activities." These similarities between toxins and enzymes are very striking, and in discussing the nature of the enzymes we have mentioned the reasons for considering them related to the toxins; we may now take up the other side of the question and consider the relation of the toxins to the enzymes.

Resemblance to Enzymes.—First of all we meet the same difficulty in isolating toxins that we do in isolating enzymes. "A pure toxin is as unknown as a pure enzyme" (Oppenheimer). At first both were believed to be proteins; now both are considered by many not to be proteins, but molecular complexes of nearly equally great dimensions. That toxins, like enzymes, are colloids, has been abundantly demonstrated.[38] Both pass through porcelain filters, but both lose much of their strength in the process, and they are almost entirely held back by dialyzing membranes. They behave similarly as regards adsorption by suspensions,[39] and have similar effects on the physical properties of their solutions (Zunz).[40] Neither will withstand boiling, and most forms are destroyed at 80° instantly or in a very short time; on the whole, however, toxins are more susceptible to heat, as well as to most other injurious agencies. Both stand dry heat over 100°, and extremely low temperature, without much injury. Left standing in solution for some time they gradually lose their specific properties, and in each case this seems to be due to an alteration in the portion of the molecule that produces the destructive effects (*toxophore* or *zymophore group*), while the portion of the molecule that unites with the substance that is to be attacked (*haptophore* group) remains uninjured, the toxin becoming a *toxoid*, the enzyme

[37] Field and Teague, Jour. Exper. Med., 1907 (9), 86.
[38] See Zangger, Cent. f. Bakt. (ref.), 1905 (36), 239.
[39] By flocculation of the colloids bearing adsorbed toxins it may be possible to secure them in comparatively pure condition (London, Compt. Rend. Soc. Biol., 1917 (80), 756.
[40] Arch. di Fisiol., 1909 (7), 137.

a *fermentoid*. Enzymes as well as toxins are poisonous when injected into animals, and the animals react to each by producing substances (*antibodies*) that render each inert, probably in the same way. On the other hand, enzymes and toxins seem to produce their effects according to different laws:—A small amount of enzyme can in course of time produce an almost indefinite amount of effect, whereas toxins act more nearly quantitatively. It seems as if the enzyme were bound to the body upon which it acts, as is the toxin, but that after it has destroyed this body it is set free in a still active form, ready to accomplish further work, whereas the toxin is either not set free, or it becomes inactive after it has once been combined.

Agencies Destroying or Modifying Toxins.—Toxins are very susceptible to light, direct sunlight soon destroying the power of toxin solutions. Fluorescent substances destroy toxins both *in vitro* and in the body.[41] They are generally destroyed by moist heat of 80°, but resist 100° when dry. Oxygen, even dilute as in air, is harmful; and all oxidizing agents, including oxidizing enzymes, destroy them quickly.[42] Like enzymes, they withstand such antiseptics as chloroform, toluene, etc., and are precipitated by the heavy metals. Some agencies seem to attack only the toxophore portion of the molecule, *e. g.*, iodin, carbon disulphid (Ehrlich). Certain toxins (diphtheria, dysentery) can be converted into non-toxic modifications by acids, the original toxicity being restored by bases (Doerr),[43] which fact, Pick maintains, is in support of the protein nature of toxins. Salts of monovalent metals have no effect on toxins, but bivalent and trivalent salts are injurious to them, tetanus toxin being more sensitive than diphtheria toxin. X-rays are said to weaken them.[44]

Introduced into the gastro-intestinal tract, most bacterial toxins are not absorbed (botulinus toxin excepted), cause no symptoms, and do not reappear in the feces; they are therefore destroyed by the contents of the tract, pepsin, pancreatic juice, and bile all being capable of destroying toxins.[45] They may, however, when injected subcutaneously, circulate unimpaired in the blood of non-susceptible animals, gradually disappearing, more through slow processes of destruction than by elimination. When injected into susceptible animals, they soon disappear from the blood, being fixed in the organs that they attack. Toxins are also bound by lipoids, fats and similar substances, which accounts, at least in part, for the affinity of tetanus

[41] Literature given by Noguchi, Jour. Exper. Med., 1906 (8), 263.
[42] According to Pitini (Biochem. Zeit., 1910 (25), 257) toxins cause their harmful effects by reducing the oxidizing capacity of the tissues.
[43] Wien. klin. Woch., 1907 (20), 5.
[44] Gerhartz, Berl. klin. Woch., 1909 (16), 1800.
[45] Baldwin and Levene (Jour. Med. Research, 1901 (6), 120) found that diphtheria and tetanus toxin are both destroyed, apparently through digestion, by pepsin, trypsin and papain acting for several days. Review of Literature by Last, Hofmeister's Beitr., 1904 (6), 132. See Vincent, Ann. Inst. Pasteur, 1908 (22), 341.

toxin for nervous tissues.[46] In common with other colloids they are adsorbed by surfaces, such as charcoal, kaolin, etc.; such adsorption is accompanied by little change in any of the physical properties of the solution, except an increase in surface tension (Zunz).

Differences from Ptomaïns.—While ptomaïns are formed by cleavage processes from the medium upon which the bacteria grow, and the same ptomaïns can be produced by several different kinds of bacteria, the *toxins are synthetic products of absolutely specific nature*. However, the toxins seem to be produced little if at all by growing the bacteria on Uschinsky's or similar media, which contain no proteins, carbohydrates, or fats, but merely simple organic and inorganic salts of known composition.[47] Nevertheless diphtheria toxin is essentially the same no matter on what sort of medium the bacteria are grown, whereas ptomaïns vary with the nature of the substance from which they are produced. Toxins are true secretions of bacterial cells, just as trypsin is of pancreatic cells, or thyroiodin of thyroid cells. Anti-bodies can be produced against toxins, but not against ptomaïns.

Ehrlich's Conception of the Nature of Toxins.

—Chemical studies of toxins being impossible, we have been obliged to study them through their physiological effects, just as we have obtained information concerning enzymes through their specific actions. In this way Ehrlich developed well-crystallized ideas concerning the structure of toxins, as well as the manner in which they act, which may be briefly summarized as follows: Each toxin molecule consists of a large number of organic complexes, grouped, as in other organic compounds, as side-chains about a central chain or radical. One or more of these complexes has a chemical affinity for certain chemical constituents of the tissues of susceptible animals, with which the toxin molecule unites; this binding group is called the *haptophore* (meaning "bearing a bond"). Another side-chain or group of side-chains exerts the injurious effects upon the tissue to which the molecule has been bound by the haptophore, and cannot produce these injurious effects unless it has been so bound. This injury-working group is called the *toxophore*. An animal is susceptible to a toxin only when its cells contain substances which possess a chemical affinity for the haptophore groups of the toxin, and also substances which can be harmfully influenced by the toxophore groups. Tetanus toxin, for example, owes its effects to the fact that nervous tissues contain chemical substances having a strong affinity for the haptophore group of tetanus toxin, and also substances that can be attacked with serious results by the toxophore group of the toxin. The nature of the changes brought about by the toxophore groups of toxins is not understood; there are many resemblances to the action of enzymes, but the analogy is by no means complete. We find perhaps the closest analogy to the enzymes in the toxic substances that destroy red corpuscles and bacteria (*hemolysins, bacteriolysins*), which will be considered in another place. The immunity against toxins and enzymes seems to be produced by

[46] Loewe, Biochem. Zeit., 1911 (33), 225, and (34), 495.
[47] See Rettger and Robinson, Jour. Med. Res., 1917 (38), 357.

identical processes, which consist in an overproduction of the cellular constituents (*receptors*) which bind the haptophore groups to the cells, these excessive receptors being secreted into the blood, where they combine with the toxin or enzyme so that it cannot enter into combination with the cells. This "side chain theory" of Ehrlich has been a useful working hypothesis, although it is becoming highly probable that it does not picture the exact method of toxin and antitoxin action.[48]

Immune substances cannot be produced against ptomaïns, or for that matter against the vegetable alkaloids, *or against any chemical bodies of known constitution.* Another difference between the action of toxins and simpler chemical poisons is, that while with the latter the effects are produced in a very short time after injection, there is a *latent period* of several hours before symptoms appear after injecting toxins. What occurs during this latent period is not fully known, but that there is a latent period suggests a resemblance to enzyme action. An alkaloidal or other chemical poison enters the cell, and its harm is done at once. A toxin combines with the cell, and then, if it produces its effects by an enzymatic alteration of the cellular structure, some time must elapse before the changes are great enough to cause the appearance of symptoms.

ENDOTOXINS [49]

By far the greater number of pathogenic bacteria do not secrete their poisons as toxins into the surrounding medium, although they manifestly cause disease by poisoning their host. Among them are such organisms as the typhoid bacillus, pneumococcus, the pus cocci, cholera vibrios, and many others. If cultures of these organisms are filtered, the filtrate will be found to be but slightly toxic (except for the hemolytic poisons), although the bodies of the bacteria after they have been killed by chloroform or other antiseptics are highly poisonous if injected into an animal. These bacteria, then, produce poisons which do not escape from the cells into the culture-medium, but are firmly held within them. By using various means these intracellular toxins, or *endotoxins*, can be obtained independent of the bacterial cells. One of these is to grind up the cells, which can be particularly well done if they are first made brittle by freezing at the temperature of liquid air (MacFadyen's method). By very great pressure in the Buchner press the cellular contents can be expressed. They may also be obtained by letting the bacteria autolyze themselves for a short time in non-nutrient fluids (Conradi,[50] *et al.*). Endotoxins obtained in this way are soluble and highly poisonous, and it is undoubtedly through their action that the characteristic diseases are produced by the bacteria that contain them. Presumably the endotoxins are liberated in the body either by autolysis, or by heterolysis by the enzymes of the body cells and fluids, and there is some question as to whether they are preformed specific constituents of the bacteria, or merely the poisonous product of enzymatic disintegration of the bacterial proteins, similar to the "anaphylatoxins."[51]

Endotoxins differ from the true toxins in one important respect: namely, *it is difficult or impossible to obtain an antitoxin for endotoxins by immunization of*

[48] See Coca, Jour. Infect. Dis., 1915 (17), 351.
[49] See general review by Pfeiffer, Jahresber. d. Immunitätsforsch., 1910 (6), 13.
[50] Deut. med. Woch., 1903 (29), 26.
[51] See Dold and Hanau, Zeit. Immunität., 1913 (19), 31; Zinsser, "Infection and Resistance," N. Y., 1914, Chap. xvii.

animals.[52] Animals immunized against endotoxins develop in their serum substances that are bactericidal and agglutinative to the bacteria from which the poisons are derived, but the serum will not neutralize the endotoxins. As a result, we are unable to perform experiments indicating whether endotoxins have the same structure as the true toxins, *i. e.*, a haptophore and a toxophore group, but presumably their nature is different in some essential particular. The chemical nature of the endotoxins is also unknown, for they are always obtained mixed with the other constituents of the bacteria.[53]

Tuberculin, once supposed to be an albumose, is produced even when the bacilli are grown on a protein-free medium, and in the active solution no albumose or other protein is then found. Hence it seems probable that tuberculin is of the nature of a polypeptid, which gives no biuret reaction but is destroyed by pepsin and trypsin, according to Loevenstein and Pick,[54] but not by erepsin (Pfeiffer).[55] Whether tuberculin should be considered an endotoxin liberated by the disintegration of the bacilli in the cultures is unknown; Pick looks upon it as a secretion of the bacilli, and closely related to the true toxins.

Since far more bacterial diseases are brought about by endotoxins than by true toxins, the failure to secure antitoxins for these substances has been a great check in the progress of serum therapy, and the problem of the endotoxins is one of the most important in the entire field of immunity.

POISONOUS BACTERIAL PROTEINS

If we filter a bouillon culture of diphtheria bacilli through porcelain, wash thoroughly with salt solution the bacteria remaining, and collect them thus freed from their secretion products, it will be found that extracts of the bacterial subtance or the bodies of the killed bacteria themselves are quite free from the typical toxin. This indicates that the toxin is eliminated from the bacteria as fast as it is formed, and no considerable quantity is retained within the cell. The bacterial substance, however, or proteins isolated from it, is found to produce severe local changes when injected into the bodies of animals, necrosis and a strong inflammatory reaction with pus-formation being the chief features. This local effect is not a specific property of the diphtheria bacillus, for other bacterial proteins, including proteins from non-pathogenic bacteria, will produce the same changes; indeed, many proteins that are derived from vegetable and animal sources have equally marked pyogenic properties. All foreign proteins when introduced into the circulation of animals are more or less toxic, and the toxic effects of the bacterial proteins are, for the most part, neither specific nor particularly striking. There are a few pathogenic organisms, however, which seem to produce neither true toxins nor endotoxins, notably the tubercle bacillus and the anthrax bacillus, and with these there may be a relation between their protein constituents and their specific effects.

Numerous protein substances have been extracted from bacterial cells, particularly nucleoproteins, but also proteins resembling albumins, nucleo-albumin, and globulins. In all probability the chief proteins of the bacterial cell are nuclein compounds, which is indicated both by their nuclear staining and by the analyses

[52] Positive results are claimed by Besredka (Ann. Inst. Pasteur, 1906 (20), 304), and some others; see Kraus, Wien. klin. Woch., 1906 (19), 655; Zeit. Immunität., 1909 (3), 646. It is suggested by Wassermann (Kolle and Wassermann's Handbuch, 1912 (2), 246) that this difficulty in obtaining antiendotoxins depends on the large size of the molecule,—the small diffusible toxin molecule is so altered in its physical condition through union with the antibody that its properties are much altered, whereas the large endotoxin molecule must be digested by complement before its toxicity is destroyed.

[53] The *Aggressins* of Bail, to which he ascribes the pathogenicity of bacteria, are too little established to permit of a discussion from the chemical standpoint. By many they are believed to be nothing more than endotoxins. (Literature given by Müller, Oppenheimer's Handb. d. Biochem., 1909 (II (1)), 681; Dudgeon, Lancet, 1912 (182), 1673). According to Ingravelle (Ann. d' ig. sperim., 1910 (20), 483), typhoid aggressins are found in the albumins.

[54] Biochem. Zeit., 1911 (31), 142.

[55] Wien. klin. Woch., 1911 (24), 1115; see also Lockmann, Zeit. physiol. Chem., 1911 (73), 389.

of Iwanoff;[56] and many of the nucleoproteins, both of bacterial and non-bacterial origin, cause considerable local inflammatory reaction when injected into animals. Tiberti[57] claims that vaccination with non-lethal doses of the nucleoproteins of anthrax bacilli will protect animals against inoculations of virulent anthrax bacilli. Some of the earlier observations on the toxicity of bacterial proteins were erroneous because impure proteins, containing toxins, endo-toxins, and ptomaïns were used. Schittenhelm and Weichardt[58] have found, however, that bacterial proteins are much more toxic than any ordinary proteins, as indicated by loss of nitrogen, temperature changes and alterations in the leucocytes of injected animals. Furthermore, there are few other proteins that produce so much inflammatory reaction as the bacterial proteins.

Vaughan and his students have been able to split off from the bodies of various pathogenic bacteria toxic materials which are stated to resemble in some respects the protamins,[59] a though they do not all give a satisfactory biuret test. These toxic materials are evidently quite different from either the true soluble toxins or the endotoxins, since they resist heating for ten minutes, at 110° in the autoclave with 1 per cent. sulphuric acid, this being a method used for securing the substance. Since the sarcinæ and B. prodigiosus also yield similar toxic products, they cannot be considered as the specific toxic substances of the pathogenic bacteria, but apparently are common to all proteins of whatever origin. With some bacteria the splitting process with sulphuric acid separates completely the toxic from the non-toxic insoluble bacterial substance,[60] e. g., B. co i communis; with others a toxic portion remains insoluble. The colon bacillus protein gives all the protein reactions, is synthesized on Uschinsky's medium, and does not yield a reducing carbohydrate. From B. typhosus about 10 per cent. by weight of protein can be split off by dilute acid, of which at least a part seems to be a phosphorized glycoprotein.[61] Poisonous substances have also been obtained from B. diphtheriæ, B. anthracis, B. tuberculosis[62] and B. pyocyaneus. They produce death without the usual latent period observed with toxins, and are very toxic, a few (10–20) milligrams of colon bacillus poison killing guinea-pigs in less than ten minutes.[63] A certain degree of immunity can be obtained against them.[64] Their relation to endotoxins and anaphylatoxins has yet to be determined.

BACTERIAL PIGMENTS[65]

The formation of pigment by bacteria seems to be, for the most part an adventitious, unessential property. There are a few bacteria which possess pigments of the nature of chlorophyll, or allied to it, and this pigment is undoubtedly of great importance in the life processes of these particular forms. Other varieties of pigment-forming bacteria, of which but very few are pathogenic (Bacillus pyocyaneus, B. proteus fluorescens, S. pyogenes aureus and citreus, M. cereus flavus), seem to produce pigment as a waste product which is excreted from the cell as fast as formed. Generally the pigments are produced in a colorless form (leuco-base) which is oxidized by the air into the pigment, e. g., in pyocyaneus infections the soiled dressings are most

[56] Hofmeister's Beitr., 1902 (1), 524.
[57] Cent. f. Bakt., 1906 (40), 742.
[58] Münch. med. Woch., 1911 (58), 811.
[59] A full review of this work is given in Vaughan's "Protein Split Products," Philadelphia, 1913; and in Jour. Lab. Clin. Med., 1916, Vols. 1 and 2.
[60] Wheeler, Jour. Amer. Med. Assoc., 1905 (44), 1271.
[61] Ibid., 1904 (42), 1000.
[62] See White and Avery, Jour. Med. Res., 1912 (26), 317.
[63] Jour. Amer. Med. Assoc., 1905 (44), 1310; American Medicine, 1905 (10), 145.
[64] Vaughan (Jr.), Jour. of Med. Research, 1905 (14), 67.
[65] For complete bibliography and résumé see Sullivan, Jour. Med. Research, 1905 (14), 109.

colored about the portions most exposed to air. Since pigment-forming bacteria produce pigments only under certain conditions, and can grow abundantly without producing any pigment, it is evident that the pigment formation is no very essential part of their metabolism. It is possible to modify pigment production almost at will, and even to develop races of bacteria that do not produce pigment at all from races that ordinarily are pigment-producers.

Of numerous classifications of pigment-forming bacteria, all faulty because of our slight knowledge of the chemistry of the process, that of Migula seems the best; it is based on the solubility of the pigments formed, as follows:

(1) **Pigments Soluble in Water.**—This includes the pigments of all fluorescent bacteria, as well as those giving a red or brown color to gelatin media. Most important among these is *Bacillus pyocyaneus*, whose pigments have been considerably studied. There seem to be two pigments, one, *pyocyanin*, characteristic for this organism; and a fluorescent pigment which numerous other organisms also produce. Pyocyanin has been analyzed by Ledderhose, who found it to be a ptomaïn-like body, a derivative of the aromatic series, probably related to the anthracenes. It can be reduced to a colorless leuco-base, in which form it is probably produced by the bacteria, and then is oxidized in the air into the pigment. Its composition is $C_{14}H_{14}N_2O$ (the sulphur-containing pyocyanin which has been described is probably impure).[66] The fluorescent pigment is insoluble in alcohol and chloroform, and can thus be separated from pyocyanin, which is soluble in chloroform. Although related to the ptomaïns, pyocyanin seems to be altogether non-poisonous to animals.

Jordan[67] and Sullivan[65] have studied the conditions under which pigments are formed, and found that pyocyanin can be produced in protein-free media, and without the presence of either phosphates or sulphates; but both sulphur and phosphorus must be present to produce the fluorescent pigment. As pigment can be produced on media containing only ammonium salts of succinic, lactic, or aspartic acid, or asparagin, they are evidently formed synthetically, and not by cleavage of the media.

(2) **Pigments Soluble in Alcohol and Insoluble in Water.**—The most important bacteria of this group are the *Staphylococcus pyogenes aureus and citreus*. Their pigment is of a fatty nature, a *lipochrome*, which lies among the bacteria in the form of dendritic crystals. Being a fat, it can be saponified, and when decomposed it gives the acrolein reactions and odor, from the breaking down of the glycerol of the fat molecule. Acted upon by strong sulphuric acid, the yellow pigment changes into blue granules and crystals (*lipocyanin* reaction). The lipochromes are soluble in the usual fat solvents, and form fat spots on paper.

(3) **Pigments Insoluble in Water and in Alcohol.**—The pigment of *Micrococcus cereus flavus* belongs to this class; its nature is quite unknown.

[66] Analysis of pyocyanin-HCl by Madinaveitia (Anales soc. espan. fis. quim., 1916 (14), 263) gave $C_{60}H_{69}N_{10}Cl_5O_3$, but the physical properties indicated a lower molecular weight.

[67] Jour. Exper. Med., 1899 (4), 627.

CHAPTER V

CHEMISTRY OF THE ANIMAL PARASITES[1]

THIS subject has received much less consideration than its importance deserves, and we are quite in the dark as to how much of the
effects produced by animal parasites are not merely mechanical, but
are due to soluble poisons that they may secrete or excrete. Some of
the parasites probably cause harm mechanically and in no other way,
but with most of them there is more or less evidence of the formation of poisonous substances. The composition of the bodies of the
animal parasites is an almost unexplored field, but we have no reason
to believe that the composition of the cells of invertebrates differs
essentially from that of the cells of higher organisms. Perhaps the
most characteristic constituent observed in many forms is *chitin*, which
forms a large part of the outer covering of the encysted forms, and
probably of many of the worms. *Glycogen* is usually abundant in
the invertebrates, and the animal parasites form no exception,[2] this
carbohydrate having been found in their bodies by many observers.

Eosinophilia.—One of the most characteristic features of the animal parasites
is that they exert a positive chemotaxis for eosinophile leucocytes.[3]
An increase in the number of these cells in the blood, as well as a local accumulation in the tissues nearest the parasite, has been observed in infection with practically all the animal parasites.[4] Of these, infection with *Trichinella spiralis*
causes the most pronounced eosinophilia, presumably because of the great number
of parasites present in the tissues at once. That the eosinophilia is due to the
action of the soluble products or constituents of the parasites has been shown by
experimental injection into animals of extracts from the bodies of the parasites.
Calamida has found that extracts of dog tapeworms also, when placed in the tissues
in a capillary tube, cause an accumulation of eosinophile cells in the tube.[5]
Experimental infection with excessive numbers of trichinella causes a rapid diminution in the number of eosinophile leucocytes, which also show evidences of disintegration in the bone-marrow and lymph-glands. Such large injections are fatal,
which suggests that the eosinophilia has a protective influence. In favor of this
view is the observation of Milian,[6] who found that sarcosporidia in beef are destroyed by a violent leucocytic reaction, the prevailing cell being the eosinophile.
As the eosinophile increase does not occur until several days after the infected
flesh is eaten, the chemotactic substance is not liberated from the encapsulated

---

[1] General references to this subject will be found in v. Fürth's "Vergleichende
chemische Physiologie der niederen Tiere," Jena, 1903; Faust's "Tierische Gifte,"
Braunschweig, 1906; Koch, Ergebnisse Pathol., 1910 (XIV(1)), 41.
[2] See Pflüger, Pflügers Arch., 1903 (96), 153.
[3] Literature by Opie, Amer. Jour. Med. Sci., 1901 (127), 477; Stäubli, Deut.
Arch. klin. Med., 1906 (85), 286; Hübner, *ibid.*, 1911 (101), 286; Schwarz, Ergeb.
allg. Pathol., 1914 (17₁), 138.
[4] Literature by Brauns, Liefmann and Mäckel, Münch. med. Woch., 1905 (52),
253; Vallillo, Arch. wiss. u. prakt. Tierhk., 1908 (34), 505.
[5] Negative results were obtained with extracts of *Sclerostoma equinum* by
Grosso (Folia Hematol., 1912 (11), 18).
[6] Bull. et Mem. Soc. Anat., 1901 (Ser. 6, T. 3), 323.

trichinellæ when their capsules are digested off in the gastric juice, but comes either from the free larvæ, or from the degenerated muscles in which they burrow. Coincident bacterial infection may reduce the number of eosinophiles. Herrick[7] finds that extracts of *Ascaris lumbricoides* cause a notable eosinophilia, but only when the animal has been sensitized previously with the same extract, the active agent of which is a protein; this suggests a relationship between parasitic and anaphylactic eosinophilia.[8] That the eosinophiles play a part in the immunity reactions observed in the hosts of animal parasites is indicated by the fact that hydatid fluid loses its antigenic properties when in contact with eosinophiles.[9]

PROTOZOA

These unicellular forms possess all the chemical characters of the cells of higher forms, even to the more specialized constituents. Thus it has been demonstrated that protozoa contain proteolytic enzymes,[10] and that they secrete an acid into their digestive vacuoles.[11] On the other hand, *Amœba coli* does not seem to digest the red corpuscles and the bacteria that it takes up.[12] Whether the *Amœba coli* produces any toxic materials, specific or non-specific, has not yet been determined, but the necrosis that it produces in liver abscesses, when bacterial coöperation can often be excluded by culture, strongly indicates the production of necrogenic substances. Apparently these substances are not chemotactic, in view of the absence of leucocytic accumulation in the lesions of amebic dysentery. There is also no evidence, clinical or experimental, that amebic infection causes the formation of anti-substances of any kind in the body of the host. The spontaneous recovery from amebic and other protozoan infections, however, may be considered as indicating the development of an *immunity* against these organisms.[13] Numerous observers have suggested the possibility of obtaining artificial immunity against protozoa, and Rössle[14] has obtained immune sera against infusoria.

The serum of rabbits immunized against amœbæ was found by Sellards[15] to be cytolytic for the same amœbæ, but no antibodies could be found in the blood of patients with amebic dysentery. The serum of persons infected with bilharzia is said to give specific complement fixation reactions (Fairley).[16] Novy[17] has obtained immunity against trypanosomes, but the serum of immune animals will not confer passive immunity. Braun and Teichmann,[18] however, claim

[7] Arch. Int. Méd., 1913 (11), 165.
[8] Supported by Paulian, Presse Med., 1915 (23), 403.
[9] Weinberg and Séguin, Ann. Inst. Pasteur, 1916 (30), 323.
[10] Mouton, Compt. Rend. Soc. Biol., 1901 (53), 801.
[11] Le Dantec, Ann. Inst. Pasteur, 1890 (4), 776; Greenwood and Saunders, Jour. of Physiol., 1894 (16), 441.
[12] Musgrave and Clegg, Bureau of Gov't. Laboratories, Manila, 1904, No. 18, p. 38.
[13] Concerning immunity to protozoan infections see Schilling, Kolle and Wassermann's Handbuch, 1913 (7), 566.
[14] Arch. f. Hyg., 1905 (54), 1; full review of this topic.
[15] Philippine Jour. Sci., 1911 (6), 281.
[16] Jour. Roy. Army Med. Corps, 1919 (32), 449.
[17] Jour. Infec. Dis., 1912 (11), 411.
[18] Zeit. Immunität., Ref., 1912 (6), 465.

9

positive results with immune serum from rabbits; they found no poisonous agent in trypanosome substance.[19] The fact that trypanosomes themselves readily become immune to various trypanocidal chemicals has been demonstrated and extensively studied in Ehrlich's laboratory. Gonder[20] has made the interesting observation that trypanosomes which can be stained by certain vital stains, become unstainable while alive if immune to arsenic compounds, suggesting that this immunity is associated with considerable structural or chemical changes.

Plasmodium malariæ undoubtedly produces toxic substances, which seem to be of such a nature that they do not diffuse from the red corpuscle, but are only liberated when the corpuscle breaks up on the maturation of the parasite. In this way the characteristic paroxysmal manifestations of the disease are produced. The nature of the poison or poisons is unknown, but we have evidence that it is hemolytic, since malarial serum may hemolyze normal corpuscles,[21] and extracts of the parasites are strongly hemolytic (Brem[22]); probably the malarial hemoglobinuria is caused by this hemolysis. Presumably malarial poisons are not extremely toxic for parenchymatous cells, since the parenchymatous lesions in malaria seem to be relatively slight as compared with the intensity and duration of the intoxication. Some authors state that the toxicity of the urine is increased after the paroxysm,[23] which, however, does not necessarily indicate that a poison formed by the parasites is excreted in the urine. Immunity seems to be seldom developed against the malarial poison or against the parasite itself, although some persons seem to be naturally immune, while some acquire immunity through previous infection.[24] The blood of persons with malaria seems to contain no antibodies for the parasite (Ferrannini),[25] although it seems to have some antihemolytic power (Brem). (Concerning the pigment present in the malarial parasites see "Pigmentation," (Chap. xviii).

Sarcosporidia of sheep yield aqueous and glycerol extracts that are highly toxic for rabbits (Pfeiffer), the poisonous constituent of which was called sarcocystin by Laveran and Mesnil.[26] This is so highly toxic that 0.0001 gm. is fatal to rabbits (per kilo), other animals being less susceptible. It loses its toxicity on heating at 85° for twenty minutes, and is impaired at 55–57° for two hours. It

[19] Hintze (Zeit. f. Hyg., 1915 (80), 377) obtained little immunity with T. brucei, but Schilling and Rondoni (Zeit. Immunität., 1913 (18), 651) obtained a poison from Nagana trypanosomes which produced active immunity in mice. When trypanosomes are killed by weak electric currents they may liberate an active poison (Uhlenhuth and Seyderhelm, Zeit. Immunität., 1914 (21), 366).
[20] Zeit. Immunität., 1913 (15), 257.
[21] See Regnault, Revue de Méd., 1903 (23), 729.
[22] Arch. Int. Med., 1912 (9), 129.
[23] Quoted from Blanchard, Arch. d. Parasitol., 1905 (10), 83; this article gives a résumé of the subject of the toxic substances produced by the animal parasites.
[24] See Celli, Cent. f. Bakt., 1900 (27), 107.
[25] Riforma Med., 1911 (27), 177.
[26] Compt. Rend. Soc. Biol., 1899 (51), 311.

produces pruritis and other anaphylactic symptoms, and although the
serum of sheep with this parasite does not confer passive anaphylaxis
to sarcosporidia, yet it does give positive complement fixation.[27] That
it is a true toxin is shown by Teichmann and Braun,[28] who produced
an effective antitoxin by immunizing rabbits; only rabbits seem to
be susceptible to the toxin. The sarcosporidia contain also a distinct
thermostable agglutinin. The lethal dose of dried substance of sarcosporidia is, for rabbits, but 0.0002 gm., and the poison seems to unite
with the lipoids of the nervous system (Teichmann).[29] It is probable
that the pathogenic protozoa, at least in some instances, have a semipermeable membrane about them, for Goebel[30] found that trypanosomes are very susceptible to changes in osmotic conditions.

[CESTODES]

Tænia echinococcus has been by far the most studied, its abundant
fluid content furnishing suitable material for investigation. That
this fluid is toxic has been repeatedly observed when, through rupture or puncture, the fluid has escaped into the body cavities; such
accidents are often followed by violent intoxication, sometimes by
death.[31] As long as the cyst is unopened no toxic manifestations are
observed. The most constant symptoms are local irritation and inflammation, accompanied by urticaria, which may also be produced
experimentally in man if the cyst contents are injected subcutaneously.

The symptoms are so strikingly similar to those of anaphylactic
intoxication, that it is now generally believed that they are the result
of such a reaction in a person sensitized by absorption of antigenic
substances from the cyst.[32] Carriers of echinococcus cysts have been
found to have in their blood antibodies giving precipitin[33] and
complement fixation[34] reactions with extracts of echinococcus, and
sometimes with other tænia.[35] The antigen of the echinococcus is believed by some to be a lipoid;[36] in the case of *Taenia saginata*, at least,
it seems to be associated with the lecithin (Meyer[35]). Graetz,[37]
however, states that the protein of the hydatid cyst is derived from
the host, and that it is therefore incapable of causing anaphylaxis in
that host, but it may undergo alterations in the cyst so that it is
toxic after the order of anaphylatoxins (*q. v.*). The complement fixa-

[27] McGowan, Jour. Path. and Bact., 1913 (18), 125.
[28] Arch. f. Protistenk., 1911 (22), 351.
[29] *Ibid.*, 1910 (20), 96; see also Knebel, Cent. f. Bakt., 1912 (66), 523.
[30] Ann. Soc. Méd. d. le Gand, 1906 (86), 11.
[31] See Achard, Arch. gén. de Méd., 1887 (22), 410 and 572.
[32] See Boidin and Laroche, Presse Méd., 1910 (18), 329; Ghedini and Zamorani,
Cent. f. Bakt., 1910 (55), 49.
[33] Welch, *et al.*, Lancet, 1909, Apr. 17.
[34] Kreuter, Münch. med. Woch., 1909 (56), 1828; Weinberg, Ann. Inst. Pasteur
1909 (23), 472.
[35] Meyer, Berl. klin. Woch., 1910 (47), 1316; Zeit. Immunität., 1910 (7), 732.
[36] Israel, Zeit. Hyg., 1910 (66), 487; Meyer, Zeit. Immunität., 1911 (9), 530.
[37] Zeit. Immunität., 1912 (15), 60; general review.

tion reaction with echinococcus fluid has been found quite reliable in
the clinic, 93 per cent. of positive reactions having been obtained in
500 cases collected by Zapelloni,[38] while controls were always negative.

The *fluid* of the echinococcus cysts has generally a specific gravity
of 1005–1015, and contains 1.4–2 per cent. of solids. Most abundant
are sodium chloride, about 0.8 per cent., and sugar, 0.25 per cent.,
the latter presumably coming from the glycogen contained in the
wall. Cholesterol is often abundant, while inosite, creatin, and succinic acid are often found. Clerc has found traces of lipase, but
other enzymes seem to be absent or in very small amounts. Proteins
are present only in traces, unless inflammation has occurred. Schilling[39] found the molecular concentration of the cyst fluid to be quite
the same as that of the patient's blood. The fluid is said not to be
toxic to laboratory animals.[40]

The *cyst wall* consists of a hyaline substance which seems to stand
between chitin and protein, and probably consists of a mixture of
both. Because of the chitin it yields about 50 per cent. of a reducing,
sugar-like body when boiled with acid. Glycogen is also usually
present, but it is limited to the germinating membrane.[41]

Other cestodes, when in the cystic form, contain fluids which are
more or less toxic. Thus Moursou and Schlagdenhauffen[42] found a
"leucomaïn" in the *Cysticercus tenuicollis*, the larva of *Taenia mar-
ginata*, which causes urticaria and other toxic symptoms when injected into animals (thus resembling histamine). The fluids of
Cysticercus pisiformis (the common cestode of rabbits) have been
found toxic for frogs, and Vaullegeard[43] has determined the presence
of an "alkaloid" and a "ferment toxin" in this fluid. The fluids of
the cysts of *Cœnurus cerebralis*, *Cœnurus serialis*, and *Echinococcus
polymorphus* have all been found toxic, and it is probable that this is a
general rule with the cestodes,[44] but human forms other than the echinococcus seem not to have been investigated;[45] according to Jammes
and Mandoul, extracts of taenia are bactericidal.[46]

Dibothriocephalus latus frequently causes anemia, which has been
attributed to a poison liberated by the parasite when it undergoes
disintegration, and possibly as a secretion of the living worm.[47] All
the intestinal cestodes are equipped with a well-developed excretory
apparatus, and it is easy to imagine that their excretory products
may be toxic to the animal into whose intestine they are excreted.

[38] Policlinico, Surg., 1915 (22), Nos. 6–11.
[39] Cent. inn. Med., 1904 (25), 833.
[40] Graetz, Cent. f. Bakt., 1910 (55), 231; Zeit. Immunität, 1912 (15), 60.
[41] Brault and Loeper, Jour. Phys. et. Path. gén., 1904 (6), 295.
[42] Compt. Rend. Soc. Biol., 1882 (95), 791.
[43] Bull. Soc. linnéenne de Normandie, 1904 (1), 81.
[44] Blanchard, *loc cit.*[23]
[45] Semaine méd., 1905 (25), 55.
[46] See also Joyeux, Arch. d. Parasitol., 1907 (11), 409.
[47] Literature by Blanchard, *loc cit.*[23]

Tallqvist[48] has made extensive studies of bothriocephalus, which show that the active hemolytic agent is contained in the lipoids of the parasites, presumably as a cholesterol ester of oleic acid.[49] The proglottides contain a proteolytic enzyme, which apparently digests the substance of dead segments, liberating the hemolytic lipoid, which constitutes about ten per cent. of the solids of the parasite. There is also a hemagglutinin, which, unlike the hemolytic substance, is thermolabile, and causes the appearance of an antibody in immunized animals. In common with other parasites, antitryptic and antipeptic effects are exhibited by extracts.

Rosenqvist[50] has studied the metabolism of twenty-one cases of bothriocephalus anemia, and found evidence in nearly all of a toxogenic destruction of protein, which ceases promptly when the worms are removed. He has found that these worms produce a poison which is globulicidal, and probably also generally cytotoxic, since in the anemias that they produce, the elimination of purine bodies of tissue origin (endogenous purine) is increased. The nitrogenous metabolism is quite the same in pernicious anemia and in bothriocephalus anemia. Isaac and v. d. Velden[51] state that the blood of patients infected with this parasite gives a *precipitin reaction* with autolytic fluid obtained from bothriocephalus, and that rabbits immunized with such autolytic fluids developed a precipitin. Complement fixation reactions may be demonstrated in human infections with bothriocephalus or other tænia (Jerlov).[51a]

Other Tænia.—There is much less evidence that other forms of tænia produce toxic substances which injure their host, although the clinical manifestations observed in persons harboring tænia are often of such a nature as to indicate strongly an intoxication. Jammes and Mandoul[52] found no toxic manifestations produced by extracts of *Tænia saginata*, which negative finding is supported by Cao,[53] Tallqvist and Boycott,[54] using various sorts of tænia. These results contradict the earlier positive findings of Messineo and Calamida,[55] who found extracts of tænia from dogs to be hemolytic, chemotactic (especially for eosinophiles), and to cause local fatty degeneration in the liver. Extracts of *T. perfoliata* and *plicata* (of the horse) were found highly toxic for guinea-pigs by Pomella,[56] the hematopoietic organs being greatly stimulated. Bedson[57] found that extracts of all sorts of helminths produced similar effects on guinea-pigs, the chief lesions being in the adrenals and thyroid. Possibly these differences in results are due to the fact that different parasites were studied by different investigators; furthermore, tests of toxicity of human parasites upon rabbits and guinea-pigs can hardly be considered conclusive. Le Dantec did not find a precipitin for *Tænia saginata* extracts in the blood of persons harboring this parasite, and negative results with

[48] Zeit. klin. Med., 1907 (61), 427.
[49] Faust and Tallqvist, Arch. exp. Path. u. Pharm., 1907 (57), 367.
[50] Zeit. klin. Med., 1903 (49), 193.
[51] Deut. med. Woch., 1904 (30), 982.
[51a] Zeit. Immunität., 1919 (28), 489.
[52] Compt. Rend. Acad. Sci., 1904 (138), 1734.
[53] Riforma med., 1901 (3), 795.
[54] Jour. Pathol. and Bacteriol., 1905 (10), 383.
[55] Cent. f. Bakt., 1901 (30), 346 and 374.
[56] Compt. Rend. Soc. Biol., 1912 (73), 445.
[57] Ann. Inst. Pasteur, 1913 (27), 682.

several other tænia were obtained by Langer,[58] but complement fixation reactions may be given.[59]

Picou and Ramond[60] state that tænia extracts undergo putrefaction very slowly, and attribute this to a bactericidal property, which was observed with several forms of tænia by Allesandrini. Weinland[61] has found that many intestinal parasites exhibit *antitryptic* properties,[62] but in a study of the histological changes of autolysis I observed a tænia in the intestine of a dog undergo more rapid karyolytic changes than did the intestinal epithelium. Dastre and Stessano[63] state that extracts of *Taenia serrata* act upon enterokinase rather than on trypsinogen.

NEMATODES

Ascaris.—The toxicity of members of this group has been a matter of dispute, although, as with the *Tænia*, there have been observed in patients symptoms that were more easily explained as due to chemical substances than as due to mechanical irritation. Miram, while studying *Ascaris megalocephala*, suffered from attacks of sneezing, lachrymation, itching, and swelling of the fingers. v. Linstow suffered from a severe attack of conjunctivitis with chemosis after touching his eye with a finger that had been in contact with one of these worms. Others have had similar experiences, and it has been found that the fluid from these worms is toxic to rabbits. In man it seems to affect especially those who have been sensitized by previous poisoning, some persons being entirely insusceptible.

An extensive investigation of ascaris from both the chemical and toxicological standpoint has been made by Flury,[64] which indicates the source and nature of these toxic substances. Because of the practically anaerobic conditions under which the worms live, Flury believes, the products of their metabolism are characterized by being incompletely oxidized, and resemble the products of anaerobic bacteria. Most important of these are volatile aldehydes and fatty acids, especially valerianic and butyric acids, in less quantities formic, acrylic and propionic acids. The toxicologic action of these volatile substances is of such a character as fully to explain the severe irritation of skin and mucous membranes observed in persons handling these parasites; aldehydes are notoriously inclined to produce conditions of hypersensitiveness, *e. g.*, formaldehyde. It is quite possible that the severe constitutional symptoms observed occasionally in persons infected with ascaris, are produced by these substances or by poisonous substances set free through disintegration of worms which have died and remained in the bowel. A capillary poison resembling sepsin, poisonous bases acting like atropine and coniine,

[58] Münch. med. Woch., 1905 (52), 1665.
[59] Meyer, Zeit. Immunität., 1910 (7), 732.
[60] Compt. Rend. Soc. Biol., 1899 (51), 176.
[61] Zeit. f. Biol., 1902 (44), 1 and 45.
[62] Corroborated for *Taenia saginata* by Fetterolf (Univ. of Pennsylvania Med. Bull., 1907 (20), 91).
[63] Compt. Rend. Soc. Biol., 1903 (55), 130.
[64] Arch. exp. Path. u. Pharm., 1912 (67), 275 (literature).

and hemolytic unsaturated fatty acids were also found, among other less toxic substances produced by ascaris, and the sum of their action is certainly adequate to account for anything ascribed to these parasites. Paulian,[65] however, would attribute the chief effect to anaphylaxis from absorbed proteins, while Brinda[66] believes that ascaris produces an active toxalbumin. This, he found, causes a tetany-like type of respiration, and a similar symptom is often noticed in children with ascarides. An actively toxic mixture of proteoses and peptones has been obtained from several species of ascaris, and designated as "askaron," by Shimamura and Fujii.[67] Horses can be immunized to withstand 400 lethal doses. Ether and alcohol extracts of ascaris are not poisonous in large doses, although they are hemolytic.

Analysis of a great quantity of ascaris from horse and hog gave as the chief results, the following:[64] They differ much in composition from the higher animals. About half the ash is water soluble; and of the dry substance about half is protein or related substances, from which the usual amino-acids and purines can be isolated. Uric acid and creatinin were lacking. The superficial layer does not consist of chitin, but of an albuminoid rich in sulphur and free from carbohydrates, resembling keratin. They have abundant and active enzymes of many kinds. Glycogen is the chief carbohydrate, but there are also glucoproteins and glucose. The ascaris differs from higher animals especially in the ether-soluble substances, which consist chiefly of free fatty acids, many of which are volatile. Also found were lecithin, aldehydes and neutral fats, but little glycerol, no cholesterol, and an "ascaryl alcohol" ($C_{42}H_{64}O_2$) which probably substitutes for both glycerol and cholesterol.

Trichinella Spiralis has been investigated from the chemical standpoint by Flury,[68] who found that the infected muscles of experimental animals differed from normal muscles in having more water because of edema, an increase in extractives, ammonia compounds, lactic acid and volatile acids, with fluctuating values in both creatine and purines. Glycogen is decreased not only in the infected muscle but also in the liver and kidneys. The parasites themselves are remarkably resistant to strong acids, perhaps because of the lipoid content of their surface covering, in which keratin could not be positively identified; cholesterol and glycogen were present. The blood of infected animals shows an excess of nuclein material, and may give albumose and diazo reactions; the red corpuscles have a lowered resistance to hemolysis by hypotonic solutions. Trichinous muscle contains substances that produce marked local tissue irritation, which may be purines; a curare-like poison was also found, which was believed to be a guanidine derivative, as well as a "fatigue poison" which probably consists of the lactic acid and other muscle extractives. The location of trichinella in muscle may be ascribable to their need for glycogen for nourish-

[65] Compt. Rend. Soc. Biol., 1915 (78), 73.
[66] Arch. de Méd., 1915 (17), 801.
[67] Japanese Jour. Bact. (Saikingaku Zassi), June 10, 1916.
[68] Arch. exp. Path. u. Pharm., 1913 (73), 164 and 214.

ment and the fact that their metabolism is carried out anaerobically may account for the character of the products (fatty acids, etc.).

The intoxication of trichinosis probably is the combined result of the products of the metabolism of the parasites, the products of muscle disintegration, and perhaps also of anaphylactic reaction to the proteins of the parasite and the altered muscle proteins. As evidence of the anaphylactic condition is the conspicuous eosinophilia, which we know is often the result of anaphylactic intoxication.[69] Metabolism studies show a preliminary nitrogen, creatinine and purine retention, followed by excessive loss of all three. There is also an intense diazo reaction, and increased excretion of lactic and organic acids. The hypothesis that bacterial invasion is responsible for the intoxication of trichinosis does not seem to be well supported (Herrick, Gruber).

The serum of infected animals is not toxic, and does not protect against infection with trichinella (Gruber[70]). Salzer,[71] however, found that the serum of recovered patients had a curative effect in persons acutely intoxicated with trichiniasis, and also a marked prophylactic effect in experimental animals;[72] it removed the eosinophilia both in men and animals. He also observed evidence of a reduction of the bilirubin of the feces by the trichinæ, so that the stools were clay colored without icterus. Positive complement fixation reactions are given by the serum of trichinella infected persons.[73]

Uncinaria duodenalis, which has for its chief effect the production of a severe anemia, seems to cause this anemia by producing repeated small hemorrhages rather than by any toxic action. The abundance of this loss of blood is explained by L. Loeb[74] as due to the presence, in the anterior portion of the parasite (they studied *Ankylostoma caninum*), of a substance that inhibits the coagulation of the blood.

However, Preti[75] would ascribe importance to a lipoidal or lipoid-like hemolytic constituent of the parasitic tissues of the European ankylostoma, but Whipple,[76] who has observed a weak hemolysin in the American hook worm, considers it too ineffective to be of practical importance. In *Sclerostoma equinum*, however, Bondonoy[77] found active hemolytic agents, ascribed by him to lipase; also a ptomaïn, an alkaloid and other substances. Corresponding to Flury's analyses of ascaris, he found that the cuticle is albuminoid and not chitinous.

[69] See Herrick, Jour. Amer. Med. Assoc., 1915 (65), 1870; Schwartz, Ergeb. allg. Pathol., 1914 (17), 136.
[70] Münch. med. Woch., 1914 (61), 645.
[71] Jour. Amer. Med. Assoc., 1916 (67), 579.
[72] Not corroborated by Schwartz, Jour. Amer. Med. Assoc., 1917 (69), 884; or Hall and Wigdor, Arch. Int. Med., 1918 (22), 601.
[73] Stroebel, Münch. med. Woch., 1911 (58), 672.
[74] Cent. f. Bakt., 1901 (37), 93; 1906 (40), 710; Loeb and Fleischer, Jour. Infec. Dis., 1910 (7), 625.
[75] Munch. med. Woch., 1908 (55), 136.
[76] Jour. Exp. Med., 1909 (11), 331.
[77] Arch. Parasitol., 1910 (14), 5; see also Asheroft, Compt. Rend. Soc. Biol., 1914 (77), 142.

and that the parasite produces much volatile fatty acids, especially butyric; both lecithin and cholesterol were absent. The dermatitis produced by uncinaria larvæ is ascribed by C. A. Smith[78] to an alcohol-soluble substance. Watery extracts of *Sclerostoma* were found by Grosso[79] to cause but slight chemotaxis without eosinophilia.

Filaria seem not to produce any appreciable amount of toxic material, if we may judge by the slight evidence of intoxication shown by infected individuals. An exception may be made in the case of the guinea-worm (*Dracunculus* or *F. medinensis*). This parasite causes chiefly mechanical injury unless its body is ruptured, which may happen in attempting to remove it forcibly; this accident is followed by violent local inflammation or gangrene, which indicates that some powerfully irritant substance is liberated from the torn body of the worm.[80]

[78] Jour. Amer. Med. Assoc., 1906 (47), 1693.
[79] Folia Hematol., 1912 (14), 18.
[80] Earthworms are said by Yagi (Arch. internat. pharmacodyn., 1911 (21), 105) to contain a hemolytic substance, "lumbricin," the properties of which he describes. Nukada and Tenaka (Mitt. med. Fakult., Tokio, 1915 (14), 1), found an antipyretic agent which seems to be derived from tyrosine.

CHAPTER VI

PHYTOTOXINS AND ZOOTOXINS

THE production of substances possessing the essential features of true toxins is by no means limited to the bacterial cell. In the plant kingdom such substances are formed, and called *phytotoxins*. Of these, the best known are ricin, abrin, crotin, and robin.[1] Among the toxins of animal origin, *zootoxins*, are the venoms of poisonous snakes, lizards, spiders and scorpions, and the serum of eels and snakes.

PHYTOTOXINS[2]

The chief phytotoxins are as follows:
Ricin, from the castor-oil bean (*Ricinus communis*).
Abrin, from the seeds of *Abrus precatorius*.
Crotin, from the seeds of *Croton tiglium*.
Robin, from the leaves and bark of the locust, *Robinia pseudoacacia*.
Curcin, from the seeds of *Jatropha curcus*.

In their general properties all these substances are very similar and may be considered together. They resemble proteins in many respects, for they can be salted out of solutions in definite fractions of the precipitate, are precipitated by alcohol, and are slowly destroyed by proteolytic enzymes. For some time they were referred to in the literature as toxalbumins, until Jacoby stated that, by combining the salting-out method with trypsin digestion, he was able to secure preparations of ricin and abrin that did not give the protein reactions. This seemed to place them in the same category with bacterial toxins and enzymes, *i. e.*, large molecular colloids, closely resembling the proteins with which they are associated, but still not giving the usual protein reactions. Because of their great similarity to bacterial toxins this seemed a very probable description, and it has been generally accepted. More recent work by Osborne, Mendel, and Harris,[3] however, does not support Jacoby's contention. They found the toxic properties of ricin associated inseparably with the coagulable albumin of the castor beans, and were able to isolate it in such purity that one one-thousandth of a milligram (0.000001 gram) was fatal *per kilo* of rabbit, and solutions of 0.001 per cent. would agglutinate red

[1] The poison in certain peas, especially *Lathyrus saturis*, which causes severe peripheral paralysis, (*lathyrism*) is believed to be an alkaloid. (Full discussion by Stockman, Edinb. Med. Jour., 1917 (19), 277).

[2] Résumé of literature by Ford, Cent. f. Bakt., 1913 (58), 129; Jacoby, Kolle and Wassermann's Handbuch, 1913 (2), 1153.

[3] Amer. Jour. of Physiol., 1905 (14), 259.

corpuscles. The toxicity was also impaired or destroyed by tryptic digestion. They consider that probably, because of its extremely great toxicity, Jacoby was able to get active preparations that contained too little active substance to give the protein reactions. As they remark: "If one-thousandth of a milligram of a compound giving on analysis every indication of being a relatively pure protein, is physiologically active in the degree characterized by our experiments, the toxicity of any impurity must be infinitely greater than that of any known toxins." Against the claim that the toxic principle is simply carried down with the protein is the fact that it does not come down in the first fraction that is precipitated, the globulin, which usually carries down all impurities. All the ricin comes down between the limits of one-fifth and one-third saturation with ammonium sulphate, exactly as does the albumin. During germination of the castor bean the ricin disappears with the albumin.[4] Field[5] has found evidence that the agglutinin and toxin of pure ricin are separable, but Reid believes them identical. Of 21 varieties of ricinus seeds examined by Agulhon,[6] all yielded hemagglutinins. Ricin agglutinates not only corpuscles, but tissue cells of all sorts, and causes precipitates in normal serum.[7] Curcin alone seems to have no hemagglutinative action.[8]

Immunity.—The phytotoxins have been very serviceable in the study of immunity, since they obey the same laws as bacterial toxins and can be handled in more definite quantities. By their use Ehrlich first determined that toxin and antitoxin act quantitatively. They seem to possess haptophore and toxophore groups, and immunity is readily obtained against them, not only by subcutaneous injection, but by dropping into the conjunctival sac, and also by feeding, showing their direct absorbability and their resistance to digestion. The antitoxin is present in the milk of the immunized mother and immunizes the suckling; but little is carried through the placenta into the fetal blood. The immunity is specific, ricin antitoxin, for example, not protecting against abrin (although it is said to protect against robin). Roemer found that in animals immunized by conjunctival application the eye so used became immune to the local action of the poison before the other eye did, indicating a local development of immune substance. In general immunization the immune substance appears first in the spleen and bone-marrow. Normal serum gives a precipitate with ricin, but immune serum gives a much heavier one. Antiricin, like other antitoxins, is inseparable from the proteins of the serum.

[4] Agulhon, Ann. Inst. Pasteur, 1915 (29), 237.
[5] Jour. Exper. Med., 1910 (12), 551; Reid, Landwirtsch. Versuchst., 1913 (82), 393.
[6] Ann. Inst. Pasteur, 1914 (28), 819.
[7] Michaelis and Steindorff, Biochem. Zeit., 1906 (2), 43.
[8] Felke, Landwirts. Versuchst., 1913 (82), 427.

Physiological Action.—Their poisonous action is manifold, most prominent being agglutination of the erythrocytes, local cellular destruction, and, to a less extent, hemolysis. Jacoby believes that in ricin there are several toxic substances differing in physiological properties, similar to Ehrlich's findings in diphtheria toxin (toxones, etc.). By long action of pepsin-HCl upon ricin, he secured a preparation with all the other properties of ricin except that it was inactive against erythrocytes; the same result could not be obtained with abrin. Heating to 65° or 70° does not destroy the toxicity of phytotoxins, but boiling does. There is a latent period of several hours after injection of the poison, the onset of symptoms being sudden; death rarely occurs in less than fifteen to eighteen hours (Osborne *et al.*).

Flexner[9] has studied particularly the histological changes produced by ricin and abrin poisoning in animals. Both act alike, affecting the tissues much as bacterial toxins do (diphtheria). Fever, albuminuria and convulsions are followed by exhaustion and lowered temperature. Punctiform hemorrhages are found beneath the serous surfaces, with fluid in the peritoneal cavity. At least in the case of ricin the hemorrhages are not due to blood changes, but to a special toxin destroying the endothelial cells.[10] There occur a general lymphatic enlargement and marked changes in the intestinal mucosa, with swelling of the Peyer's patches. The spleen is swollen and dark in color, as also is the liver, which shows much focal necrosis. The glycogen content of the liver is decreased in abrin poisoning.[11] Subcutaneous injection causes local edematous inflammation without suppuration. Histologically, in the most affected organs are found much cellular necrosis and disintegration, especially of lymphoid and epithelial cells. Changes in the capillary endothelium, fibrinous thrombi, and abundant hemorrhagic extravasations are widespread. Probably agglutinative thrombosis by red corpuscles plays an important part in these intoxications (Ehrlich), but Aschoff[12] ascribes the thrombosis to the fragments of disintegrated marrow and blood cells. The great amount of intestinal injury probably depends upon the fact that these poisons are largely eliminated through the intestinal mucosa. There are also severe changes in the bone marrow, accompanied by the appearance of nucleated erythrocytes in the blood.[13]

Mushroom Poisons.[14]—The poisons of the three chief poisonous mushrooms, *Amanita muscaria*, *Helvella esculenta*, and *Amanita phalloides*, differ from one another quite essentially. The poisonous principles of the first and second, muscarine and helvellic acid, are non-protein substances, of known chemical com-

[9] Jour. Exper. Med., 1897 (2), 197.
[10] Amer. Jour. Med. Sci., 1903 (126), 205.
[11] Doyon, Compt. Rend. Soc. Biol., 1909 (67), 30.
[12] Arch. Int. Med., 1913 (12), 503.
[13] Bunting, Jour. Exper. Med., 1906 (8), 625.
[14] Resume by Morner, Upsala Lakaref. Förh., 1919 (24), 1. Pathological anatomy described by Prym, Virchow's Archiv., 1919 (226), 229.

position, which are discussed elsewhere; but the *Amanita phalloides*, the most important of the three, owes its toxic properties to at least two poisonous constituents. One is powerfully hemolytic, is destroyed by heating thirty minutes at 65°, and acts directly upon red corpuscles without the presence of serum.[15]

The studies of Ford[16] and his associates have shown that this hemolysin is a glucoside, yielding on hydrolysis pentose and volatile bases, and yet capable of acting as an antigen, since actively antihemolytic sera can be produced by immunizing animals. This substance corresponds to the *phallin* of Kobert. Probably this hemolytic poison is not the important agent in poisoning by *Amanita*, as it is easily destroyed by heat and the digestive fluids. The thermostable poison, *Amanita-toxin*, gives no reactions for either glucosides or proteins,[17] and does not confer any considerable antitoxic property on the blood of immunized animals. The toxin kills acutely, the animals dying in 24—48 hours, and showing no changes beyond a fatty degeneration of the internal organs. The hemolysin kills slowly in 3—10 days, causing local edema and hemoglobinuria.

Amanita muscaria contains a heat-resistant agglutinin which also seems to be a glucoside, but it is not toxic nor antigenic.

An extensive study of many fungi by Ford[18] led him to classify the toxic action in three groups: (1) nerve poisons, *e. g.*, muscarine; (2) those causing structural changes in the viscera, *e. g.*, *A. phalloides*, causing fatty degeneration; (3) gastro-intestinal irritants, *e. g.*, *Lactarius torminosus*.

The poison of *Rhus toxicodendron* has also been found by Acree and Syme[19] to be a glucoside,[20] and the same is true of the poison oak, *Rhus diversiloba*, which has no antigenic properties.[21]

(The effects of the phytotoxins on the blood are discussed under "Hemolysis" in Chapter ix. Vegetable hemolytic poisons that do not resemble the toxins, *e. g.*, glucosides, etc., will also be found discussed under the same heading.)

ZOOTOXINS [22]

SNAKE VENOMS [23]

This important class of poisons, first thoroughly investigated by Weir Mitchell (1860), and Mitchell and Reichert (1883), has recently aroused great interest through its relations to bacterial toxins and the problems of immunity. The poisons of different species of snakes seem to have much in common with one another, whether derived from the *Elaperine* snakes (cobras and numerous other Indian and Australian snakes), or *Viperidæ* (including most poisonous American snakes), or *Hydrophinæ* (the poisonous sea-snakes), although very characteristic differences exist between each.

[15] The hemagglutinin of *Agaricus campestris* is precipitated at a H-ion concentration of 2.6 × 10⁻⁴ (Brossa, Arch. sci. med., 1915 (39), 241).

[16] See Jour. of Pharm., 1910 (2), 145; 1913 (4), 235, 241, and 321.

[17] Rabe (Zeit. exp. Path., 1911 (9), 352) considers it to be an alkaloid.

[18] Jour. of Pharm., 1911 (2), 285.

[19] Jour. Biol. Chem., 1907 (2), 547.

[20] Questioned by McNair, Jour. Amer. Chem. Soc., 1916 (38), 1417.

[21] Adelung, Arch. Int. Med., 1913 (11), 148.

[22] Full review and literature given by Faust, "Die tierischen Gifte," Braunschweig, 1906; also in Abderhalden's Handbuch, Vol. II, Sachs, Kolle and Wassermann's Handbuch, 1913 (2), 1407.

[23] Elaborate review and bibliography given by Noguchi, Carnegie Institution Publications, 1909 No. 111; also by Calmette, "Les vénins, les animaux vénimeux et la sérotherapie antivénimeuse," Paris, Masson, 1907; Calmette, Kolle and Wassermann's Handbuch, Vol. II, p. 1381; with reference to North American snakes, see Prentiss Wilson, Arch. Int. Med., 1908 (1), 516.

The essential anatomical differences between the different classes of snakes are as follows: *Colubridæ*, which include all the non-poisonous snakes, have no mechanism for injecting poisons into their victims. *Colubridæ venenosæ* are venomous snakes resembling in many particulars the harmless Colubrines, but having short poison fangs, firmly fastened to the maxilla in an erect position; in this class are included the cobra and the venomous snakes of Australia. *Viperidæ*, or vipers, are characterized by a highly specialized apparatus for injecting the poison; their poison fangs are very long, and the maxillary bone, to which they are fastened, is so articulated that it rotates about a quarter of a circle when the snake strikes, bringing the fangs into an erect position. The fangs are canalized and pointed at the end like a hypodermic needle, and the poison is forced through them under considerable pressure by a large muscle that contracts over the salivary gland. Accessory fangs in various stages of development are also present to replace any fang lost in action. All the poisonous snakes of North America, with one insignificant exception, belong to the vipers, and to a special class known as the "pit vipers," because of the presence of a deep pit of unknown function above the maxilla. The exception mentioned is the "coral snake" found on the coast of Florida, around the Gulf of Mexico and in the southeastern states; it is a member of the colubrine poisonous snakes, of small size, and seldom causes serious poisoning. The poisonous vipers are the rattlesnakes (*Crotalus*), of which there are some ten to twelve or more species, and *Sistrurus* of which there are two species; the copperhead adder (*Ancistrodon controtrix*) and the water mocassin (*Ancistrodon piscivorus*).

The classification used above is the one followed in most publications on poisonous snakes; a more modern classification divides the snakes (*Ophidia*) into several series, one of these including all poisonous snakes under the title of *Proteroglypha*, and dividing this series into the three families: (1) *Elapinæ*, including cobras, coral snakes, etc.; (2) *Hydrophinæ*, the poisonous sea-snakes; (3) *Viperidæ*, including all snakes with erectile fangs.[24]

The source of the venom is probably in part the blood, since snake blood has been found to contain poisons very similar to some of those in the venom; therefore these are presumably simply filtered out by the venom glands, and not manufactured by them.[25] Other poisonous constituents of venom are not found in snake serum, and therefore are probably manufactured by the venom gland. Apparently many of the harmless snakes produce a poisonous saliva, since extracts of their glands are said by Blanchard[26] to possess the properties of the venoms, and if so these snakes are harmless chiefly because they lack an apparatus for injecting the poison. As a rule, however, the venom glands are much more highly developed in the poisonous snakes, and are connected with a specialized injection apparatus; in structure they are compound racemose glands.

Properties of Venom.—As ejected, the venom is weakly acid or neutral in reaction, and free from bacteria, contrary to earlier ideas (Langmann). Its specific gravity is 1030 to 1077, and it contains a large amount of solids, generally 20 to 40 per cent. by weight. These are precipitated by alcohol, ether, tannin, and iodin, but do not ad-

---

[24] For a full discussion of the characteristics of the poisonous snakes of North America, see the monograph with that title by Stejneger, Report of U. S. National Museum, 1893, Washington. A good summary is also given by Langmann, Reference Handbook of Medical Sciences. Concerning poisonous sea-snakes, *Hydrophidia*, see Boulanger, Natural Science, 1892 (1), 44. The poisonous snakes of India are described by Fayrer, in "The Thanatophidia of India," London, 1874.

[25] Contradicted by Arthus, Arch. internat. physiol, 1912 (12), 162.

[26] Compt. Rend. Soc. Biol., 1894 (46), 35.

here to precipitates of phosphates as do enzymes and toxins (Calmette). They do not diffuse through dialyzing membranes. When dried, the venom can be kept almost indefinitely without losing its strength, specimens over twenty years old having been found unimpaired. Glycerol and alcohol also seem not to injure it, but oxidizing agents of all kinds are very destructive. Light impairs the power of venoms, as also does radium (Phisalix).[27] Eosin and erythrosin also reduce the power of venom through their photodynamic action, affecting the neurotoxic properties less than the hematotoxic components (Noguchi).[28] Cobra venom withstands even 100° for a short time, but crotaline venoms are destroyed at 80–85°.

Much work has been done upon the nature of the constituents of venom. As early as 1843 Prince Lucien Bonaparte found that there were proteins in the venom, which was corroborated by Mitchell in 1861. In 1883 Mitchell and Reichert described two poisonous protein constituents of venom, one of which was coagulable by heat and seemed to be a globulin; the other resembled the proteoses (they called it "peptone," according to the nomenclature of that time). To the globulin they ascribed the local, irritating properties of venom; to the albumose, the systemic intoxication. Corresponding to their action, venoms of different serpents were found to vary greatly in the proportions of these proteins. Cobra venom, which acts chiefly systemically, contains 98 per cent. of albumose and but 2 per cent. of globulin; rattlesnake venom, with its marked local effects, contains 25 per cent. of the irritating globulin; moccasin venom contains 8 per cent. of globulin. Several other observers soon corroborated the main facts of Mitchell and Reichert's report; but, as has been seen in connection with the consideration of the composition of enzymes, toxins, etc., the fact that a substance is carried down with a protein is no proof that it is itself a protein. What has been established is merely that the irritating component of venom can be destroyed by heat, and is removed with the globulin in fractional separation; while there remains a substance not destroyed by boiling, which comes down at least in part with the albumoses of the venom, and causes chiefly systemic manifestations.

Since venoms act as antigens and stimulate the formation of specific antibodies, it is to be presumed that the poisonous principles are proteins, or toxalbumins, although this conclusion does not necessarily follow. Faust[29] believes the poison of venoms not to be proteins, but glucosides, free from nitrogen, resembling very much quillajic acid, and therefore belonging to the saponin group of hemolytic agents. He has isolated such a substance from cobra venom, which he calls *ophiotoxin* ($C_{17}H_{26}O_{10}$), and from rattlesnake venom a sub-

---

[27] Compt. Rend. Soc. Biol., 1904 (56), 327.
[28] Jour. Exper. Med., 1906 (8), 252.
[29] Arch. exp. Path. u. Pharm., 1907 (56), 236; 1911 (64), 244.

stance which seems to be a polymer of the ophiotoxin, $(C_{34}H_{54}O_{21})$. Possibly these glucosides are bound to proteins, forming compound proteins which act as specific antigens. According to this work the snake venoms and the dermal poisons of toads and frogs are all closely related substances.

Enzymes in Venoms.—As venom causes rapid liquefaction of tissues into which it is injected, Flexner and Noguchi[30] tested crotalus and cobra venom for proteases, and found that they digested muscle rapidly, and also gelatin and unboiled fibrin; whereas boiled fibrin and boiled egg-albumen were undigested.[31] Kinases and nucleases are also present in venoms (Delezenne).[32] Wehrmann[33] found that venom digests fibrin and inverts saccharose, but does not digest starch. Martin[31] found fibrin ferments in various venoms, which are probably important agents in causing thrombosis. There are also active lipases in venoms, to which many of the effects, especially hemolysis and fatty degeneration of the tissues, may be at least partly due (Noguchi), and the hemolysin of cobra venom seems to be a lipase that splits lecithin into hemolytic substances (Coca).[35] Delezenne[32] found zinc always present in venom and attributes to it a relation to the enzyme activity.

Toxicity.—Calmette has determined the toxicity of several venoms, and gives the following figures:

1 gm. *cobra* or *aspis* kills.................... 4000 kgm. of rabbit.
1 gm. *hoplocephalus* kills.................... 3450 kgm. of rabbit.
1 gm. *fer de lance* or *pseudechis* kills.......... 800 kgm. of rabbit.
1 gm. *Crotalus horridus* kills................ 600 kgm. of rabbit.
1 gm. *Pelias berus* kills.................... 250 kgm. of rabbit.

The danger of the bite depends not only upon the difference in the strength of the venom of different varieties of serpents, but also upon the size of the snake, the time of year and condition of hunger or plenty, and particularly whether the entire discharge is injected successfully or not. The fatal dose of cobra venom for an adult man is variously estimated at from 0.01 to 0.03 gm., while the venom of Hydrophinæ is about ten times as toxic; for crotalus venom the lethal dose is probably 0.15 to 0.3 gm. (Noguchi). Probably in the majority of strikes, by no means all the fluid ejected by both fangs is injected beneath the skin of the victim. A large diamond rattler may eject as much as a half teaspoonful of venom at one discharge and such a dose would usually be fatal. Repeated ejections decrease the strength of the venom rapidly, until it may have almost no toxicity. In general, venom is most active in warm weather and immediately after the snake has fed; in winter its toxicity is slight.

The mortality in America from snake-bites is very hard to ascertain, various authors giving figures at wide variance. The extensive

[30] Univ. of Penn. Med. Bull., 1902 (15), 360.
[31] See also Houssay and Negrete, Revista de l'inst. bact. Buenos Aires, 1918 (1), 131.
[32] Ann. Inst. Pasteur, 1919 (33), 68.
[33] Ann. d. l'Inst. Pasteur, 1898 (12), 510.
[34] Jour. of Physiol., 1905 (32), 207.
[35] Jour. Infect. Dis., 1915 (17), 351.

studies of Willson[36] show about ten per cent. mortality from all venomous snake-bites in this country, the different species giving figures as follows: Coral snakes, twenty to fifty per cent.; water moccasins, seventeen per cent.; large rattlesnakes, eleven to twelve per cent.; copperheads and ground rattlers, no mortality except in children or in cases of complications. The mortality in children is at least double that in adults. Many deaths from snake-bites of all kinds are due to the treatment rather than to the bite. The poisonous snakes of Australia, although numerous, are not very virulent, and the mortality is given as about seven per cent. A full charge of venom from the cobra and many other Indian snakes is inevitably fatal (Fayrer). The crotaline snakes of the tropics are more venomous than those of the north, *Lacheris lanceolatus* of Central America and Mexico being nearly as dangerous as the cobra.

When venom is taken into the stomach in the intervals of digestion, enough may be absorbed to produce death, especially in the case of those venoms which contain a large proportion of the albumose, which is dialyzable; but during active digestion the venom undergoes alteration and is rendered harmless. It has been found experimentally in animals that cobra venom placed in the stomach causes ordinarily no harm whatever, but if a loop of the intestine is isolated, a fistula established and allowed to heal, venom introduced through this opening always produces death. It is probably not so much the pepsin and hydrochloric acid that destroys the venom, as the trypsin. If the bile-duct is ligated, the venom is destroyed just the same. Much of the venom seems to be eliminated into the stomach, no matter how it is introduced into the system, and apparently it is also partly excreted by the kidneys. Rattlesnake venom seems not to be absorbed through mucous membranes.

Physiological Action.—As indicated in the preceding paragraph, the effects of the bites of different classes of snakes are quite different. Langmann describes the symptoms as follows:

Cobra Poisoning.—"Within an hour, on an average, the first constitutional symptoms appear: a pronounced vertigo, quickly followed by weakness of the legs, which is increased to paraplegia, ptosis, falling of the jaw with paralysis of the tongue and epiglottis; at the same time there exists an inability to speak and swallow, with fully preserved sensorium. The symptoms thus resemble those of an acute bulbar paralysis. The pulse is of moderate strength until a few minutes after the cessation of respiration; the latter becomes slower, labored, and more and more superficial until it dies out almost imperceptibly. Death occurs at the latest within fifteen hours; in 32 per cent. of all cases in three hours. There are very few local changes." Cushny[37] finds that cobra venom produces paralysis of the motor nerve terminations of muscle, resembling the action of curare; the central nervous system is not directly involved. Death results from failure of the motor nerve ends in the respiratory muscles to transmit impulses to the muscles. Alkaloids that are antagonistic to curare (physostigmine, guanidine) are not effective in cobra poisoning, but are themselves rendered inactive.

[36] Arch. Int. Med., 1908 (1), 516.
[37] Trans. Roy. Soc., London (B), 1916 (208), 1.
10

Viper Poisoning.—"After the bite of a viper the local changes are most pronounced; there are violent pains in the bleeding wound, hemorrhagic discoloration of its surroundings, bloody exudations on all the mucous membranes, and hemoglobinuria. Usually somewhat later than in cobra poisoning constitutional symptoms develop; viz., great prostration with nausea and vomiting, blood pressure falls continuously, and respiration grows slow and stertorous. After a temporary increase in reflexes, paresis supervenes, with paraplegia of the lower extremities, extending in an upward direction and ending in a complete paralysis. It therefore resembles an acute ascending spinal paralysis. If the patient recovers from the paralysis, a septic fever may develop; not rarely there remain suppurating gangrenous wounds, which heal poorly."

It will be noticed that there is lacking the usual period of incubation that follows injection of bacterial toxins, and if it happens that the venom has been injected directly into one of the veins, death may occur within a few minutes. When recovery occurs, the disappearance of symptoms is remarkably abrupt, within a few hours a desperately sick person becoming almost entirely free from all evidences of the intoxication.

Pathological Anatomy.—*Postmortem examination* shows changes varying with the nature of the poisonous snake that has caused death. In the case of a cobra bite, according to Martin, the areolar tissue about the wound is infiltrated with pinkish fluid; the blood is often fluid; the veins of the pia are congested, and the ventricles often contain turbid fluid; the kidneys may show much congestion. When death occurs in a few minutes, enormous general intravascular clotting is found, which seems to be the cause of death. After death from a viper bite the site of the wound is the seat of intense edema and extravasation of blood; if in the muscles, these are much softened and disorganized. Hemorrhages are found in all organs and in the intestinal tract. If death occurs after several days it is generally because of sepsis, and shows the usual changes of this condition; in addition, as a rule, to marked gangrenous, ulcerative, and sloughing processes at the site of the bite.

Histologically there are found, in addition to innumerable hemorrhages in nearly all the organs, many vessels plugged with thrombi composed of more or less hemolyzed, agglutinated erythrocytes. The changes produced in the nervous tissue by the Australian tiger snake are described by Kilvington,[38] who found marked chromatolysis, the Nissl bodies breaking into dust-like particles, and eventually all stainable substance disappearing from the cytoplasm; the nucleus retains its central position, but often loses its outline and may disappear. The cells around the central canal of the cord are most affected. There are no inflammatory changes in the nervous system, and if death occurs very quickly there may be no microscopic alterations. Hunter[39] found similar changes in the Nissl bodies in both krait and cobra poisoning; in the medullated fibers he found the myelin sheath converted into ordinary fat. The venom of sea snakes (*Enhydrina valakadien*) has a severe action on the nervous tissues, while *Daboia* has none (Lamb and Hunter[40]). Nowak[41] studied experimental animals, and found much fatty change in the livers, even if death occurred one-half hour after poisoning; also focal necrosis in the liver, acute parenchymatous alterations in the kidney, and pneumonic patches in the lungs.

Effects on the Blood.—There has been much discussion concerning the part played by the abundant and prominent intravascular clotting in causing death after snake-bite. Lamb[42] states that when venoms are slowly absorbed the coagulability of the blood is decreased and it is found fluid after death, but when a fatal dose of venom (viper) is rapidly absorbed, clotting is increased and thrombosis is the chief cause of death. Martin has demonstrated very active fibrin

[38] Jour. of Physiol., 1902 (28), 426.
[39] Glasgow Med. Jour., 1903 (59), 98.
[40] Lancet, 1907 (ii), 1017.
[41] Ann. d. l'Inst. Pasteur, 1898 (12), 369.
[42] Indian Medical Gazette, Dec., 1901.

ferments in snake venom (*loc. cit.*). It is highly probable, however, that many of the thrombi of venom poisoning are not produced by coagulation of fibrin, but by agglutination of the red corpuscles, which Flexner[13] has shown can cause large clots in the heart and great vessels, as well as "hyalin" thrombi in the small vessels. Houssay[13a] states that most snake venoms destroy the cytozyme (which combines with serozyme and calcium to form thrombin), so that the blood becomes incoagulable. The Argentine crotalus and lachesis venoms, however, coagulate even citrated blood.

Nature of Venoms.—The varied effects produced by venoms have been found to be due to a number of poisonous elements which they contain, and which have been distinguished and separated from one another by Flexner and Noguchi.[44] These are *hemotoxins* (*hemolysins* and *hemagglutinins*), *leucocytolysins*, *neurotoxins*, and *endotheliotoxins* (*hemorrhagin*), but it must be taken into consideration that Faust[45] believes that the single glucosidal poison which he has found in rattlesnake venom is responsible for all the effects of the venom, except the hemagglutination. [In another place (see "Hemolysis") the nature of the hemolytic agent is discussed.] Venom agglutinin is quite independent of the hemolysin, for it is destroyed by heating to 75°–80°, whereas the hemolysin is destroyed only partly at 100°. Agglutinin acts in the absence of serum complement, and therefore is not an amboceptor; it is apparently more like the toxins in its nature. The agglutination of the corpuscles does not interfere with their subsequent hemolysis. Michel states that the agglutinin of cobra venom can be separated from the hemolysin and the toxin by means of ultrafiltration through collodion membranes, as the agglutinin exists in larger molecular aggregates.[46]

The leucocytotoxins were found by Flexner and Noguchi to be quite distinct from the hemolysins, for after saturating all the hemolysin with red corpuscles, the venom still shows its effects on the leucocytes, which effects consist in cessation of motility and disintegration, affecting particularly the granular cells. The leucocytotoxin, however, resembles the hemolysin in that it appears to be an amboceptor. Leucocytes are also agglutinated by venom, possibly by the same agglutinin that acts on the red corpuscles. Serum complement is inactivated *in vitro* by cobra venom through changes in the globulins brought about by the venoms.[47] By saturating venom with either red corpuscles or nerve-cells it was found by Flexner and Noguchi that the toxic principle for each is distinct and separate.[48] Other sorts of cells, however, are able to combine, or at least remove some parts of the toxic elements, but to a much less degree. The neurotoxin, like the hemolysin, resembles an amboceptor, and since

[43] Univ. of Penn. Med. Bull., 1902 (15), 324.
[43a] Prensa Med. Argentina, 1919 (6), 133.
[44] Jour. Exp. Med., 1903 (9), 257; Univ. Penn. Med. Bull., 1902 (15), 345.
[45] Arch. Exper. Path. u. Pharm., 1911 (64), 244.
[46] Compt. Rend. Soc. Biol., 1916 (77), 150.
[47] Hirschfeld and Klinger, Biochem. Zeit., 1915 (70), 398.

venom contains no complement, the neurotoxin has first to be supplied with complement by the victim's blood or tissues before it can harm the cells. The venoms are not only toxic for mammalian cells, but also for simple unicellular organisms, including bacteria; tadpoles are paralyzed in solutions containing one part of cobra venom per million.[48]

The pronounced hemorrhage-producing property of serums, particularly that of the rattlesnake, was also found to be due to a specific toxin acting on the endothelium of the capillaries and small veins, and not to the changes in the blood itself, as had formerly been thought. This endotheliotoxin, which Flexner and Noguchi call "hemorrhagin," is quite distinct from the other toxic substances, being destroyed at 75°, a temperature that leaves the neurotoxin and hemolysin uninjured. Its endotheliolytic action is show in the glomerular capillaries, where it causes hemorrhage and hematuria (Pearce).[49]

Variations in Venoms.—In distribution among the various poisonous reptiles these toxins seem also quite distinct from one another, which explains the difference in the effects of bites of snakes of various kinds. Cobra venom contains chiefly neurotoxin, hence the symptoms of cobra bite are largely of nervous origin, with but little local tissue change. Rattlesnake venom owes its effects chiefly to hemorrhagin, hence the marked local necrosis and extravasations of the blood, and the generalized hemorrhages; the nervous effects following viper bite are probably, in part, due to hemorrhages in the nervous tissue. Cobra venom produces great hemolysis and little agglutination. Rattlesnake venom has relatively little agglutinative or hemolytic power. Water moccasin and copperhead venoms are more agglutinative than either, and intermediate in hemolytic strength; they cause much local tissue destruction.

The exact action of cobra venom on various centers and organs has been studied by Elliot.[50] It raises blood pressure when in dilution of 1:10,000,000. by contracting vessels and stimulating the heart; low lethal doses kill by paralyzing the respiratory center.

Krait (*Bungarus cærulues*) venom acts similarly, but less powerfully, and cannot be neutralized by Calmette's antivenin.[51]

Sea-snake venoms are by far the most poisonous of all. For *Enhydrina valakadien* the lethal dose for rabbits is 0.00006 gram per kilo body weight. It acts by vagus stimulation and paralysis of respiratory centers and of motor nerve-endings.[52]

Russell's viper (*Daboia Russellii*) owes its effects chiefly to intravascular clotting, according to Lamb and Hanna,[53] and contains no neurotoxin. It is not neutralized by Calmette's antivenin. The clots are due to agglutination and contain no fibrin (Flexner).

[48] Bang and Overton, (Biochem. Zeit., 1911 (31), 213) state that corpuscles can take up the neurotoxin, which is soluble in fats and lipoids.
[49] Jour. Exper. Med., 1909 (11), 532.
[50] Lancet, 1904 (i), 715.
[51] Elliot, Sillar, and Carmichael, Lancet, 1904 (ii), 142.
[52] Fraser and Elliot, Lancet, 1904 (ii), 144; also Rogers, Jour. of Physiol., 1903 (30), iv. The above are also given completely in the Philosophical Transactions of the Royal Society, 1904-5, vol. 187.
[53] Jour. of Path. and Bact., 1902 (8), 1.

The "Gila Monster" (*Heloderma suspectum*) seldom causes serious poisoning in man, but may kill small animals, such as frogs.[54] Its poison is only slightly hemolytic, but produces degenerative changes in the nervous system (Langmann). The hemolysin is activated by lecithin (Cooke and Loeb). An elaborate series of studies by Leo Loeb and his associates give all the known facts concerning the Gila Monster.[55]

Loss of Bactericidal Powers.

—The frequency of marked and persistent sloughing and suppuration at the site of snake-bites, particularly from the vipers, and the common termination in sepsis, was attributed by Welch and Ewing[56] to a loss of bactericidal power of the blood, which they found followed experimental venom poisoning. This has been ascribed by Flexner and Noguchi to saturation of serum complement by the numerous amboceptors of the venoms, so that no complement is left for the serum to use against the bacteria. In serum whose complements do not combine with the venom amboceptors (e. g., *Necturus*) the normal bactericidal powers are not in the least impaired by the addition of venom. Morgenroth and Kaya ascribe the loss of complement to a destruction by some agent in the venom.

Snake Serum.—The *serum* of serpents is also toxic for other animals,[57] even when the serpent is not a venomous one; e. g., the harmless pine snake (*Pityophis cateniferis*). The toxicity of snake serum seems to depend chiefly upon its hemotoxic effects (hemagglutination and hemolysis), the toxic substances resembling amboceptors and similar to, but not altogether identical with, the amboceptor of the venoms. Crotalus tissues also produce poisoning in proportion to the blood they contain, but are without toxic effects of their own (Flexner and Noguchi).

Antivenin.

—Snake venom has the essential property of all true toxins of immunizing, with the appearance of an antitoxin in the blood. The first successful immunizations seem to have been made by Sewall,[58] but the practical production of antitoxic serum was first accomplished by Calmette[59] and by Fraser.[60] At first it was believed that cobra antivenin neutralizes the neurotoxins and hemolysins of venoms of *any* origin, and also of snake serums, and, therefore, should be quite effective against cobra and similar venoms which produce chiefly neurotoxic and hemolytic changes. This implies that these toxic substances are of identical nature in all snakes, no matter how dissimilar the snakes may be, but various investigators, especially Lamb, have found sufficient specificity exhibited by different venoms and antivenoms to indicate the necessity of employing the specific antiserum in each case of snake bite. A special antitoxin against rattlesnake venom and its hemorrhagic toxin has been successfully

[54] Thorough study by Van Denburgh and Wright, Amer. Jour. of Physiol., 1900 (4), 209.
[55] Carnegie Inst. Publication No. 177, 1913.
[56] Lancet, 1894 (1), 1236; Ewing, Med. Record, 1894 (45), 663.
[57] Questioned by Welker and Marshall, Jour. Pharmacol., 1915 (6), 563.
[58] Jour. of Physiol., 1887 (8), 203.
[59] Ann. d. l'Inst. Pasteur, 1894 (6), 275; also subsequent articles in 1897 (11), 214; 1898 (12), 343.
[60] British Med. Jour., 1895 (i), 1309.

prepared by Noguchi.[61]   This crotalus antivenin also neutralizes hemolysins of various venoms, and also of snake serums.

Presumably antivenin neutralizes venoms in exactly the same way that antitoxin neutralizes toxins; i. e., cell receptors are thrown off from the injured cells during immunization, which combine with venom amboceptors in the blood, and thus prevent their combining with the cells.   Antivenin also prevents the inhibiting action of venom on bactericidal serum, indicating that it prevents the venom amboceptors from binding the serum complement.   The reaction of venom and antivenin is certainly a chemical one, being likened by Kyes[62] to that of strong acids upon strong bases.

The serum of animals immunized to venoms contains precipitins for the proteins of these venoms, and, to some extent, for the serum proteins of the same species of snakes.   These precipitins are highly but not absolutely specific, and they bear no exact quantitative relation to the other antibodies present in the same sera.[63]

As is well known, snakes are nearly or quite insusceptible to snake venom.   Cunningham[64] found that serum of cobras was devoid of antitoxic property, so the immunity of snakes must be ascribed to an absence of cell receptors in their tissues, with which their venom amboceptor can combine.   The reputed immunity of the mongoose and hedgehog depends partly on a relatively low susceptibility, but probably more on the agility of the mongoose and the defensive spines of the hedgehog.

Platypus Venom.—The only mammal with a venomous secretion is that strange freak, the duck-billed platypus (*Ornithorhynchus paradoxus*).   The males have a hollow movable spur on each hind foot, communicating like a fang with the venom gland, which secretes a venom with properties resembling the venoms of the Australian snakes, but much weaker.

SCORPION POISON [65]

This poison is secreted by a pair of specialized glands in the posterior segment of the elongated abdomen, surrounded by a firm capsule with a sharp apex through which the poison is discharged.   Its effect on man is usually confined to local pain, swelling, and occasionally phlegmonous inflammation with constitutional symptoms after bites from the largest species.   In Africa a large scorpion (*Androctonus*) exists, that is reputed frequently to cause fatal poisoning, especially in children.   Manchurian scorpions (*Buthus martensi, Karchi*) seem to be less toxic than this or Mexican scorpions (*Centrurus*

[61] Univ. of Penn. Med. Bull., 1904 (17), 154; Jour. Exper. Med., 1906 (8), 614.

[62] Berl. klin. Woch., 1904 (41), 494.

[63] See Houssay and Negrete, Rev. inst. bact. Buenos Aires, 1918 (1), 15.

[64] Nature, 1896 (55), 139.

[65] A complete discussion of the literature on poisonous invertebrates, etc., is given by v. Furth, "Vergleichende chemische Physiologie der niederen Tiere," Jena, 1903; and by Faust, "Die tierischen Gifte," Braunschweig, 1906.   Concerning scorpions see Kubota, Jour. Pharmacol., 1918 (11), 417.

exticauda, Wood). In Korea, however, of 81 cases collected by Mori,[66] four were fatal. The majority of serious results following scorpion bites, as well as bites of poisonous insects to be considered later, are, however, due to infection of the wound, which occurs readily because of local necrosis and hemorrhages, and also because of the unfavorable conditions existing in tropical climates. Apparently these bites favor local infection much as do those of vipers.

When general symptoms do occur, they are described as resembling strychnine poisoning, with trismus, stiffness of the neck and eventually of the respiratory muscles, which seems to be the chief cause of death (Cavorez). Thompson,[67] however, observed only seldom severe symptoms, consisting of general paralysis that passed off in a few hours. Most experimenters with scorpion poison describe it as chiefly a nerve-tissue poison, and it also seems to act as a hemolysin and agglutinin (Bellesme and Sanarelli), but Todd[68] found it without action on corpuscles and not capable of combining with nervous tissues. Houssay[69] states that scorpion poison (*B. quinquestriatus*) is above all a muscular poison of the veratrine type, and a powerful peripheral excitant of the salivary and lachrymal secretions.

Calmette[70] gives the lethal dose for a guinea-pig as 0.5 milligram, while Phisalix and Varigny put it at 0.1 milligram and state that scorpion blood is also poisonous. Wilson[71] found the toxicity of the venom equal to 0.1 gram per million, that is, one gram of poison will kill 10,000,000 grams of guinea-pig,[72] hence it is much stronger than cobra venom. It is quite stable, and keeps many months in an ice chest; is not affected by heating to 100° for a brief period, but is destroyed after 12 or 13 minutes' heating. The active constituents are precipitated by saturating with ammonium sulphate, or by an excess of alcohol. They are destroyed by either pepsin or trypsin (Kubota).[65] The average amount of toxin in an Egyptian scorpion (*Buthus quinquestriatus*) is sufficient to kill about 35 kilos, which agrees with the fact that fatal poisoning by this scorpion is rare in adults, but reaches 60 per cent. in children. The venom is harmless when taken into the stomach, and is said to be made inactive by ammonia, calcium hypochlorite, and peroxide of hydrogen. Calmette claims that antivenin for cobra in part neutralizes scorpion poison, a statement which could not be corroborated by Todd, who succeeded, however, in preparing an efficient antiserum by immunizing horses with scorpion venom.[73]

[66] Korean Med. Soc. Jour. (Chosen Igakukai-Zasshi), 1917, p. 47.
[67] Proc. Acad. Nat. Sci. of Philadelphia, 1886, p. 299.
[68] Jour. of Hygiene, 1909 (9), 69.
[69] Jour. physiol. path. gén., 1919 (18), 305.
[70] Ann. Inst. Pasteur, 1895 (9), 232.
[71] Records of Egyptian Gov't., School of Med., 1904; abst. in Jour. of Physiol., 1904 (31), p. xlviii.
[72] Exactly the same toxicity is shown by Korean scorpions (Mori).[66]
[73] A successful serum has also been prepared in Brazil (see Brazil-Medico, 1918 (32), 161).

Houssay[69] also describes the antiscorpion serum as strictly specific. A large number of naturalists and raconteurs have furnished interesting tales of suicide by scorpions, which are more than improbable in the light of our present knowledge concerning natural immunity. Many animals seem to possess more or less immunity to scorpions (Wilson), especially such wild animals as are much exposed to them.

SPIDER POISON

The poison apparatus of the spiders consists of two long pouches lying in the thorax and extending into the jaws, at the apex of which the poison is discharged. Some of the larger members of the family are very poisonous, *e. g.*, the Malmignatte (*Latrodectes tredecim-guttatas*), of the vicinity of the lower Volga in southern Russia, is said to have destroyed 70,000 cattle in one year, the bite being fatal in 12 per cent. of all cases, although rarely killing man. Other members of this species in Chili, Madagascar, and other countries are not much less venomous. Kobert[74] has studied the poison of Malmignatte and found it distributed throughout the body of the spider, even in the eggs, and resembling in nature the snake venoms. It is destroyed by heating, and seems to be of protein nature; the chief effect is upon the nervous system and heart.[75]

A number of common spiders investigated by Kobert were apparently not poisonous for mammals, except the "cross spider" (*Epeira diadema*), which has since been thoroughly studied by him and by Sachs.[76] Walbum[77] states that the chief poison of these spiders is found in the ovaries, the salivary poison being much weaker, and the hemolysin is found chiefly in the albumin fraction. Epeiratoxin resembles the snake venoms strikingly, according to Sachs, for it contains a powerful hemolysin which he calls "arachnolysin," acting very differently with different sorts of blood, and destroyed by heating at 70°–72° for forty minutes, and it behaves with lecithin and cholesterol like cobra venom.[78] By immunizing a guinea-pig Sachs succeeded in securing an antitoxin of some strength. The agglutinin is quite distinct from the hemolysin.[79] Only such blood is hemolyzed as is able to bind the poison in the stroma of the red corpuscles. The discovery of this hemolysin explains Kobert's observation of hemoglobin, methemoglobin, etc., in the urine of persons bitten by spiders. Spider hemolysins have been studied extensively by Houssay,[80] who finds

[74] "Beiträge zur Kentnisse der Giftspinnen," Stuttgart, 1901.

[75] In western America and South America is found a spider (*Latrodectes mactans*) the bite of which is capable of causing severe spasm of the abdominal muscles, according to Atwood (Southern Californ. Pract., Vols. 10, 12 and 16). Kellogg and Coleman (Jour. of Parasitol., 1915 (1), 107), found extracts of the poison glands of this spider to be highly toxic.

[76] Hofmeister's Beitr., 1902 (2), 125.

[77] Zeit. Immunität., 1915 (23), 623.

[78] Pini, Il Policlinico (Sez. Med.), 1909 (16), 208.

[79] v. Szily, Zeit. Immunität., 1910 (5), 280.

[80] Comp. Rend. Soc. Biol., 1916 (79), 658.

that spiders without hemolysins poison flies exactly as those with hemolysins.

Von Fürth considers that the bite of the historically famous Italian tarantula is able to cause no more than local inflammation, and Kobert found that the entire extract of six Russian tarantulas (which are supposed to be more poisonous than the Italian) caused no symptoms when injected into a cat. An antitoxin is said to have been secured against the Russian tarantula.[80a]

In all probability the other poisonous spiders possess toxic substances allied to those of the venoms, with hemolytic, agglutinative, and neurotoxic products, Sachs' studies indicating the general similarity of all the zootoxins.

CENTIPEDES

Undoubtedly the severity of centipede poisoning has been greatly exaggerated, the results being usually limited to local inflammation, frequently spreading some distance in an erysipelas-like manner. An authentic case of fatal poisoning of a child four years old by a centipede (*Scolopendra heros*) has been reported from Texas by G. Linccicum,[81] death resulting five to six hours after the bite was received. Besides the local pain and inflammation, vomiting was marked, occurring also in five other non-fatal cases.

Centipedes secrete their poison in relatively large glands, which discharge at the apices of a pair of specialized claws that take the place of the first pair of legs. The nature of this poison seems not to have been investigated. Numerous chemical substances are described as secreted by other glands of these animals, including prussic acid and a camphor-like matter (see v. Fürth).

BEE POISON

Bee poison has been better studied than most insect poisons, beginning with the work of Paul Bert (1865). It is secreted by the glands into a small poison sac, and stored up until ejected. Cloez found that bee poison was precipitated by ammonia, tannin, and platinic chloride, and Langer proved it to be a non-volatile organic base. As excreted, it is acid, contains 30 per cent. of solids, and one honey-bee secretes 0.0003–0.0004 gm. It contains formic acid and much protein, but it has been stated that the poison is protein-free, and is not destroyed by heat (100°), weak acids, or alkalies. On the other hand, it is said to be destroyed by proteolytic enzymes, which would indicate that it is of protein nature. Arthus[82] believes the evidence indicates that the bee venom is a proteotoxin. However, there are many points of resemblance between the effects of insect stings and the local

[80a] Konstanzoff, Russky Wratsch., 1907, No. 17.
[81] Amer. Jour. Med. Sci., 1866 (52), 575.
[82] Jour. Pharm. Chim., 1919 (20), 41.

effects of histamine injection.[83]   Hemolysis is produced both *in vitro* and *in vivo* with all sorts of blood, but to very different degrees, thus resembling spider toxin.   The hemolytic action is greatly increased by the presence of lecithin, forming a toxolecithid like "cobra lecithid."[84] Locally bee poison causes necrosis, with marked hyperemia and edema. A 4500 gm. dog was killed by intravenous injection of 6 c.c. of a 1.5 per cent. solution of pure poison (Langer).[85]

Immunity is undoubtedly possible, for bee-keepers frequently show a great decrease in susceptibility.   On the other hand, abnormally great susceptibility is frequently seen, some cases of fatal poisoning having been observed.[86]   Dold[86a] was unable to secure experimental immunity to bee poison.

Wasps and Hornets presumably produce poisons similar to those of the bees. A study by Bertarelli and Tedeschi[87] establishes this for a species of wasp (*Vespa crabro L.*).

Ants also produce formic acid, a fact so well known that it has come to be considered that this is the source of their toxicity.[87a]   Von Fürth, however, suggests the probability that ant poison, like that of the bees, owes its chief effects to other more complex, unknown poisons.[88]

Lice.—Persons bitten by large numbers of lice may exhibit a distinct intoxication, accompanied by an eruption resembling measles.[89]   The nature of the poison is not known, but it does not produce a severe local urticaria like the sting of bees and wasps.

POISONS OF DERMAL GLANDS OF TOADS AND SALAMANDERS

It has been known for centuries that toads produce poisonous substances, Paré in 1575 having discoursed interestingly, if inaccurately, on this topic.   Numerous studies have been made of these poisons, which are secreted by the dermal glands and therefore cannot be used for poisoning either prey or enemies (except those that feed upon them); the most extensive study being that of Faust.[90]   He isolated two constituents, apparently the same in different species of toads; one, which he called *bufotalin*, is very active, resembling the digitalis group; the other, *bufonin*, is much less active.   Bufonin is neutral in reaction, soluble in warm alcohol, but slightly in cold.   Analysis in-

[83] See Eppinger, Wien. klin. Woch., 1913 (26), 1413; Sollmann and Pilcher, Jour. Pharm., 1917 (9), 309.

[84] Morgenroth and Carpi, Berl. klin. Woch., 1906 (43), 1424.

[85] Arch. exp. Path. u. Pharm., 1896 (38), 381; Arch. internat. Pharmac. et Ther., 1899 (6), 181.

[86] Hospitalstidende, 1905, No. 27.

[86a] Zeit. Immunität., 1917 (26), 284.

[87] Cent. f. Bakt., 1913 (68), 309.

[87a] The sting of nettles is said to be due to formic acid.   (See Dobbin, Natur Sept. 18, 1919.)

[88] An attempt by Barratt (Ann. Trop. Med. and Parasitol., 1910 (4), 177) to obtain a poison from culex mosquitos was unsuccessful.   The bodies of "black flies" contain an active poison that could not be identified by Stokes (Jour. Cut. Dis., 1911 (32), 830), beyond that it is insoluble in alcohol, which does not inactivate it, and that it is destroyed by trypsin.

[89] Hirschfelder and Moore, Arch. Int. Med., 1919 (23), 419.

[90] Arch. f. exp. Path. u. Pharm., 1902 (17), 279.   Complete bibliography and review.

dicates an empirical formula of $C_{34}H_{54}O_2$. It probably is the cause of the milky appearance of the dermal secretion. Bufotalin seems to be $C_{34}H_{46}O_{10}$, is acid in reaction, soluble in chloroform and alcohol, but not in petroleum ether. Subcutaneous injection of 2.6 mg. bufotalin killed a dog (weighing 4 kg.) in four to five hours; given by mouth it causes much vomiting and diarrhea, so that large doses are not fatal. It causes much local irritation when applied to mucous membranes, but produces no marked change at the site of injection. The effects on the circulation resemble in all respects those of the digitalis group; bufonin acting similarly but much weaker than bufotalin. Bufotalin seems to be derived from bufonin by oxidation, and the latter is quite similar to cholesterol, apparently having the following formula: $HO-H_{26}C_{17}-C_{17}H_{26}-OH$. An important consideration is that Faust has also isolated from the venom of cobra and crotalus, poisons which seem related to these toad poisons, the cobra poison being assigned an empirical formula of $C_{17}H_{26}O_{10}$, and the crotalus poison $C_{34}H_{54}O_{21}$. Fühner[91] considers bufotalin to be more closely related to the saponins.

Phisalix and Betrand[92] have found poison in the blood of toads similar to that of the glands. The hemolytic property observed by Pugliese[93] may be due to the acidity of the dermal secretion. The poisons of different species seem to be quite the same in all (Faust). From the dermal secretion of the large tropical toad, *Bufo agua*, Abel and Macht[94] have isolated two distinct active substances; one identical with epinephrine, which constitutes nearly seven per cent. of the crude venom; the other, which makes up 36 per cent., is called *bufagin*, has a composition indicated by the formula $C_{18}H_{24}O_2$, and therefore is presumably related to the rest of this group which arises from cholesterol. In physiological action bufagin resembles digitalis, and it is extremely active. The toad is relatively immune to bufagin, but not at all to the epinephrine. A Chinese drug derived from toad skins has been found to contain similar ingredients (Shimizu[95]), as well as a substance resembling picrotoxin in action.

Salamanders also produce poisonous secretions in their dermal glands, which have been studied especially by Faust,[96] and earlier by Zalesky,[97] who isolated an organic base which he named *samandarin*. Faust describes samandarin as first stimulating and then paralyzing the automatic centers in the medulla. The poison resembles the alkaloids, having the formula $C_{26}H_{40}N_2O$, and produces death in doses of 0.7–0.9 mg. per kilo (dogs) with respiratory failure. Immunization of rabbits was practically impossible. A second alkaloid, *samandaridin* ($C_{20}H_{31}NO$) is also present in even greater quantities than the samandarin, and differs only in being weaker.

Frogs also have similar poisons in their skins, extracts of *Rana esculenta* skin

[91] Arch. exp. Path. u. Pharm., 1910 (63), 374.
[92] Arch. d. physiol. norm. et path., 1893 (5), 511.
[93] Archivo di farm. e. terap., 1894 (2), 321; Arch. ital de Biol., 1895 (22), 79.
[94] Jour. Amer. Med. Assoc., 1911 (56), 1531; Jour. of Pharm., 1912 (3), 319.
[95] Jour. Pharmacol., 1916 (8), 347.
[96] Arch. exper. Path. u. Pharm. 1898 (41), 229 (literature); 1900 (43), 84.
[97] Hoppe-Seyler's Med. Chem. Untersuch., 1866, p. 85.

being highly toxic.[98] The dermal secretions of most of the amphibians are poisonous, not only for mammals, but also for reptiles, and in large doses for the animals producing them (Phisalix).[99] Bert[1] and also Dutartre[2] have described a digitalis-like poison in the secretion of the dermal glands of frogs.

It is evident that all these poisons are quite distinct from the venoms, and from the true toxins, apparently being simple chemical compounds not related to the proteins and not capable of causing immunization.

POISONOUS FISH [3]

There are numerous fish, especially in tropical waters, which defend themselves by injecting poisons into their enemies. This is accomplished by spines, to which are attached poison glands.[4] Dunbar-Brunton[5] has described two such fish (*Trachinis draco* and *Scorpæna scorpha*) of Mediterranean waters. Wounds by these spines cause in animals intense local irritation and edema and paralysis of the part, followed by gangrene about the site of the wound; in fatal poisoning death occurs in from one to sixteen hours, with general paralysis. The sufferings of persons so poisoned are said to be extreme, and death may occur either directly from the poison or later from sepsis following the local gangrene. Presumably this poison is not dissimilar to that of the snakes; it probably is not an alkaloid, as Dunbar-Brunton suggests. It affects chiefly the heart, according to Pohl,[6] and contains a hemolytic principle which behaves like the venom hemolysins in that it is activated by serum (Evan).[7]

Several other fish secrete poison in glands attached to long spines, one of the most poisonous being *Synanceia brachio*, which is known to have caused fatal intoxication in several instances. Only the *Murænidæ* seem capable of poisoning by biting; they have a well-developed poison apparatus on the gums, but nothing is known concerning the poisons they produce.

Many fish develop poisonous decomposition products remarkably soon after death, especially in tropical climates, so that a fish that is perfectly wholesome if eaten immediately after being caught may be very poisonous if kept but a few hours. There is a decided difference in fish of different varieties in this respect, so that some cannot be safely marketed. Some of the poisonous products of the decomposition of fish seem to be early products of protein cleavage, of high molecular

[98] Caspari and Loewy, Med. Klinik, 1911 (7), 1204.
[99] Jour. Phys. et Path. gen., 1910 (12), 325.
[1] Compt. Rend. Soc. Biol., 1885, p. 524.
[2] *Ibid.*, 1890, p. 199.
[3] Full discussion and literature given by Faust, "Tierische Gifte," p. 134.
[4] For a list of fish with poison glands see Pawlowsky, Zool. Jahrb., 1912 (31), 529.
[5] Lancet, 1896 (ii), 600.
[6] Prager med. Woch., 1893 (18), 31.
[7] British Med. Jour. 1907 (i), 73.

complexity, for they are digested by pepsin and trypsin, but not by erepsin.[8]

There are also other fish whose bodies, even when perfectly fresh, contain very powerful poisons. Savtschenko,[9] in his elaborate atlas of the poisonous fish describes a number of cases of poisoning by the famous "parrot fish" of Japan (*Tetrodon*), in which the poison seems to be developed and contained in the ovaries and eggs, and therefore the degree of toxicity varies with the season of the year in which the fish is taken.[10] Poisoning by these fish is very violent, the symptoms appearing quickly, and the cases are divided into two groups by Savtschenko, as the algid, or choleriform, and the gastro-intestinal type. The symptoms of the algid form appear almost immediately after eating the fish, and consist of pain in the stomach, with great fear and distress; soon diarrhea and vomiting set in, with cramps in the arms and legs; this terminates in collapse, coma, and death from either respiratory or cardiac paralysis. The entire course of the process may be but ten to twenty minutes, or it may be as many hours. On account of the localization of the poison in the eggs and ovaries not all persons who eat the fish are poisoned, and not all who are poisoned receive a fatal dose. In the gastro-intestinal form the symptoms appear later, consist chiefly of gastro-intestinal disturbances resembling more closely ptomaïn poisoning, and the prognosis is not so bad as in the algid form.

The pathological anatomy of this form of poisoning has not been carefully studied, but no characteristic or striking anatomical changes have been noted in the bodies examined. Tahara[11] has described a toxic body, *tetrodo-toxin*, isolated from the ovaries of *Tetrodon*.[12] The purest preparations had a minimum lethal dose of 0.0025 to 0.004 gm. per kilo, and a provisional formula of $C_{16}H_{31}NO_{16}$ was given to it. Tetrodotoxin is neither protein nor alkaloid, nor yet a protamin. It anesthetizes motor nerve endings and central nervous system, paralyzes both motor and sensory nerves, increases the excitability of muscle (Itakura)[13] and paralyzes sympathetic nerve endings (Ishihara).

In this connection may be mentioned the peculiar erysipelas-like lesions caused by bites of crabs, which indicates the formation of some toxic product by these crustaceans.[14] Gilchrist[15] obtained a history of bites or injuries by crabs in 323 of 329 cases of "erysipeloid."

[8] Konstanzoff and Manoiloff, Wien. klin. Woch., 1914 (27), 883.
[9] "Atlas des Poissons Veneneux," St. Petersburg, 1886 (literature).
[10] A Brazilian fish, *Spheroides testudineus*, has extremely toxic tissues, extract of 0.01–0.02 gm. of liver killing a guinea pig in a few minutes (Fonseca, Brazil-Medico, 1917 (31), 97). The ovaries of the American gar are also said to be toxic (Greene *et al.*, Amer. Jour. Phys., 1918 (45), 558).
[11] Biochem. Zeit., 1910 (30), 256.
[12] Arch. exp. Path. u. Pharm., 1890 (26), 401 and 453.
[13] Mitt. med. Fak. Univ. Tokio, 1917 (17), 455.
[14] The livers of the spiny lobster (genus *Penœus*) have been found to be very toxic (Nakano, Jap. Ztschr. Dermatol., 1917 (17), 1).
[15] Jour. Cutaneous Diseases, November, 1904.

Crabs, in turn, may be poisoned by cephalopods which secrete an active poison from their salivary glands.[16] Many coelenterates produce active poisons (most famous of these being the Portuguese-man-o'-war), which have especially a paralyzing and a local irritant effect.[17]

EEL SERUM

In 1888 Mosso[18] studied the toxic properties of eel serum, which he found was extremely poisonous for experimental animals, 0.1 to 0.3 c.c. per kilo being fatal for rabbits and dogs in a few minutes if intravenously injected; introduced into the stomach it is not toxic, but it produces a violent conjunctivitis when it enters the eye, the poisonous agent being contained in the albumin fraction.[19] The poisonous principle Mosso called *ichthyotoxin*. Death results from respiratory failure with large doses; small doses lead to cachexia and death after a few days. The coagulability of the blood is greatly reduced. Kossel[20] found histological changes in the central nervous system in such animals, that resembled the lesions of tetanus. He succeeded in securing an active antitoxin which neutralized the strongly hemolytic action of eel serum *in vitro*, and also prevented fatal effects in animals. Camus and Gley[21] have studied the physiological action of eel serum and found it strongly hemolytic, and also apparently neuro-toxic. The toxicity is destroyed by heating to 58° for fifteen minutes. By immunization an antitoxic serum can be obtained which neutralizes the eel toxin completely. Tchistovitch[22] secured antitoxic serum, which acted also as a precipitin for eel serum. De Lisle[23] found that eel serum does not act like an amboceptor, since after heating it cannot be reactivated with fresh mammalian serum, and it seems, therefore, to be different from snake serum in its structure.[24] Lamprey serum is likewise toxic,[25] as is also that of the Rays. Not only the serum, but also the palate glands of the Moray (*Murœna helena*) contain toxic antigenic substances resembling snake venoms (Kopaczewski).[26]

[16] Baglioni, Zeit. f. Biol., 1908 (52), 130.
[17] See von Fürth, Vergl. chem. Physiol.; also Lojacono, Jour. d. physiol., 1908 (10), 1001.
[18] Arch. Ital. de Biol., 1888 (10), 141; 1889 (12), 229.
[19] Pöllot and Rahlson, Graefe's Arch., 1911 (72), 183.
[20] Berl. klin. Woch., 1898 (35), 152.
[21] Arch. internat. d. Pharm., 1899 (5), 247.
[22] Ann. Inst. Pasteur, 1899 (13), 406.
[23] Jour. of Med. Research, 1902 (8), 396.
[24] Corroborated by Sato, Nippon Biseibutsugakkai Zassi, 1917 (5), No. 35.
[25] Gley, Compt. Rend. Soc. Biol., 1915 (78), 116; Camus and Gley, *ibid.*, p. 203.
[26] Compt. Rend. Acad. Sci., 1917 (165), 513; Ann. Inst. Pasteur, 1918 (32), 584.

CHAPTER VII

CHEMISTRY OF THE IMMUNITY REACTIONS—ANTIGENS, SPECIFICITY, ANTITOXINS, AGGLUTININS, PRECIPITINS, OPSONINS, AND RELATED SUBJECTS

ALTHOUGH immunity was first investigated in relation to bacterial infection, it was soon learned that the reactions by which the animal body defends itself against bacteria have not been developed as specific means of defense against bacteria alone, but are reactions against foreign substances of similar chemical nature, whether bacterial, animal, vegetable or artificially synthetic in origin. Furthermore, these reactions are chemical reactions, and the problems of immunity are chemical problems, although as yet most of the reacting substances are not accessible to chemical investigation. In this place, where our concern is with the chemical aspects of pathological processes, the subject of immunity will be discussed only from the standpoint of the chemistry of the processes and substances involved, leaving to other works the clinical and bacteriological aspects of the subject.[1]

The reactions of immunity are, we find, reactions to chemical substances entering the body from without, or abnormally developed within the body by invading organisms or by changes in the chemical processes of the body. Furthermore, there seems to be an essential difference between the reactions incited by simple chemical compounds to which the animal body can develop a certain degree of resistance (such as morphine, alcohol, and arsenic), and the reactions against more complex substances such as bacterial toxins, foreign proteins, venoms, etc. The complex substances of the latter group incite reactions which are to a greater or less degree specific, and usually very highly augment the defense of the body against the foreign substances; with the simple poisons the reactions are largely or altogether non-specific, and the resulting resistance is relatively slight. Substances of the first class we refer to as antigens.

[1] Especially to be recommended for a discussion of the scientific problems of immunology is Zinsser's "Infection and Resistance," Macmillan, New York, 1914; and for methods and applications see Kolmer's "Infection, Immunity and Specific Therapy," W. B. Saunders, Philadelphia, 1918. Also see Kolle and Wassermann, "Handbuch der path. Mikroorganismen;" Weichardt "Jahresbericht der Immunitätsforschung."

ANTIGENS[2]

This term includes those substances which, when introduced into the blood or tissues of an animal, in proper amounts and under suitable conditions, cause the generation and appearance in the blood of specific antibodies capable of reacting with the antigen.[3] Concerning the chemistry of antigens we can say that all antigens, so far as now known, are colloids. Furthermore, with one exception, every known soluble, complete protein may act at least to some degree as an antigen, and, as yet, it has not been finally established that any colloids other than proteins can act as antigens. The exception is the racemized protein of Dakin, which Ten Broeck[4] found to be entirely non-antigenic although soluble and possessed of all the amino-acids present in the egg albumin used in preparing it. Solubility is an essential character for antigenic action, for proteins that have been coagulated by heat lose their antigenic capacity, while proteins that are not coagulated (*e. g.*, casein, ovomucoid) retain their antigenic properties after boiling.[5] A typical incomplete protein, gelatin, is devoid of antigenic power (Starin).[6] The same is true of the protamines and histones.[7] Hemocyanin, however, is antigenic (Schmidt).[7a]

Of the cleavage products of proteins it is certain that none of the amino-acids and simple polypeptids can act as antigens, and even such large complexes as the proteoses are antigenic to but a slight degree if at all.[8] Whether the entire protein molecule, or only groups thereof, determine the characteristics of the antigen, is not known, there being evidence which can be interpreted in favor of either view, but Wells and Osborne[9] have submitted evidence which indicates that a single pure protein can act with and engender more than one antibody; this is supported by Klein's demonstration of the production of two distinct antibodies by immunizing with casein.[10] ·

There seems to be no very definite relation between the amount of antigen injected and the amount of antibody produced.[11] Nevertheless Herzfeld and Klinger[12] have advanced the hypothesis that the antibodies are really fragments of the antigen molecules which have

[2] See the Review on Antigens by E. P. Pick, Kolle and Wassermann's Handbuch d. path. Mikroorganismen, 1912 (1), 685.

[3] Attempts to influence the capacity to produce antibodies by modifying diet have not produced striking results. (See Zilva, Biochem. Jour., 1919 (13), 172.)

[4] Jour. Biol. Chem., 1914 (17), 369; also Schmidt, Proc. Soc. Exp. Biol. Med., 1917 (14), 104; Kahn and McNeil.[6]

[5] See Wells, Jour. Infect. Dis., 1908 (5), 449; Jour. Biol. Chem., 1916 (28), 11.

[6] Jour. Infect. Dis., 1918 (23), 139; corroborated by Kahn and McNeil, Jour. Immunol., 1918 (3), 277.

[7] Wells, Zeit. Immunität., 1913 (19), 599; Schmidt, Jour. Infect. Dis., 1919 (25), 207.

[7a] Proc. Soc. Biol. Chem., 1919 (14) lxix; Jour. Biol. Chem., 1920 (41).

[8] See Fink, Jour. Infect. Dis., 1919 (25), 97; full review on proteoses as antigens.

[9] Jour. Infec. Dis., 1913 (12), 341.

[10] Folia Microbiol., 1912 (1), 101.

[11] See Tsen, Jour. Med. Res., 1918 (37), 381.

[12] Biochem. Zeit., 1918 (85), 1.

been absorbed by the blood proteins, whereas Liebermann[13] suggests that they are altered, liquefied portions of the cells which the antigens have attacked.

It has been shown by Gay and Robertson[14] that if the non-antigenic cleavage products of casein are resynthesized by the reverse action of pepsin, into a protein resembling paranuclein, this synthetic protein is capable of acting as an antigen. Protamins and globin, they found, were not antigenic,[15] although globin when combined with casein forms a compound which engenders an antibody that gives complement fixation reactions with globin. Schmidt also found that protamin edestinate is antigenic for edestin and for itself, but not for protamins, whereas a compound protein, both elements of which were non-antigenic (globin-albumose), was not antigenic.[16]

NON-PROTEIN ANTIGENS

Among the many accounts of what the authors interpret as the successful production of specific antibodies as a reaction to non-protein antigens, are the following:

Ford[17] found that rabbits can be immunized to extracts of *Amanita phalloides*, and that the serum of such rabbits will neutralize five to eight times the lethal dose for guinea-pigs, and is anti-hemolytic for the hemolysin of amanita when diluted to 1-1000. As he and Abel[18] had found this hemolytic poison of Amanita to be a glucoside, this observation is to be interpreted as a successful production of an antibody for a non-protein poison, a glucoside. This work was further supported by successfully immunizing rabbits to extracts of *Rhus toxicodendron*, and finding that their serum in doses of 1 cc. will protect guinea-pigs from 5–6 lethal doses of the poison, which was found by Acree and Syme[19] to be a glucoside. Subsequent work by the same author confirms the main point, showing that an active hemolysin can be obtained free from demonstrable protein, and that immunization with this protein-free hemolysin will result in strongly active (1–1000) antihemolytic serum.[20] The antihemolysin unites with the hemolysin in simple multiple proportions.[21] Another, non-hemolytic poison from Amanita, which Ford designates as *Amanita toxin*, was found to contain neither protein nor glucoside, and no antitoxic serum or definite artificial immunity can be obtained for it.

Jacoby believed that he had obtained the phytotoxin ricin free from

[13] *Ibid.*, 1918 (91), 46.
[14] Jour. Biol. Chem., 1912 (12), 233.
[15] Jour. Exp. Med., 1912 (16), 479; 1913 17), 535.
[16] Univ. of Calif. Publ., Pathol., 1916 (2), 157. Review and bibliography on specificity.
[17] Jour. Infec. Dis., 1907 (4), 541.
[18] Jour. Biol. Chem., 1907 (2), 273.
[19] Jour. Biol. Chem., 1907 (2), 547.
[20] Jour. Pharmacol., 1910 (2), 145.
[21] Jour. Pharmacol., 1913 (4), 235.

protein, in which case the well-known and active antiricin must represent an antibody for a non-protein antigen.   However, the work of Osborne, Mendel and Harris[22] has shown that ricin is, in all probability, an albumin, and this, for the present at least, places ricin with the protein antigens.   Nucleic acid and nucleinates have been found to be non-antigenic (Wells,[23] Taylor).

The work of Ford is, in our estimation, the strongest evidence yet presented as to the possibility of non-protein antigens.   The newer developments in immunological research, moreover, make it seem entirely plausible that a complex glucoside, which can be hydrolyzed by enzymes, can act as an antigen.   If we consider the evidence that immunity consists in the development of a special power to hydrolyze foreign substances, when these substances are of such a nature as to stimulate the cells to activity, and that Abderhalden and others have found evidence that specific enzymatic properties appear in the blood of animals injected with carbohydrates and fats, it seems entirely reasonable that a toxic glucoside can have antigenic properties.   A similar line of reasoning will apply to the question of lipoid antigens.

Lipoids as Antigens.—The evident participation of lipoids[24] in immunity reactions, especially the complement-fixation and allied reactions, has naturally led to investigation of the possibility that lipoids may act as true antigens, a possibility made conspicuous by the fact that lipoids can be substituted for true antigens in the Wassermann reaction (*q. v.*).   Bang and Forssmann immunized with ethereal extracts of red corpuscles and obtained hemolysins, so that they concluded that the antigenic constituent of the corpuscles is a lipoid, probably a phosphatid. This work has caused much controversy and many workers have failed to confirm their results.[25]   It is a striking fact that when purified phosphatids, from sources favorable for obtaining pure materials, are used, the results are usually negative, while the positive results are generally reported with lipoids of more or less dubious purity.

"Nastin," the lipoid material from a streptothrix, has been used by Much and others, who state that sera are obtained which give complement fixation reactions with nastin used as the antigen.[26]   Similar results are described for the fatty materials from tubercle bacilli ("tuberculonastin").   Warden[27] reports securing positive precipitin and fixation reactions, not only with fatty complexes from bacteria and red cells, but also with artificial mixtures of soaps made up to resemble the cellular lipins; indeed, he states that the lipoidal antigens are more specific than proteins, and infers that the specificity of antibodies is in part or wholly due to the fats of the cells.

Meyers[28] has reported the production of specific complement fixation antibodies by immunizing rabbits with acetone-insoluble lipoidal material obtained from tape worms and echinococcus.   He has found the acetone-insoluble fraction of tubercle bacilli, presumably phosphatids, to serve as antigen in complement fixation reactions

[22] Amer. Jour. Physiol., 1905 (14), 259.

[23] Zeit. Immunität., 1913 (19), 599.   Lichtenstein (Arch.   Physiol., 1915, p. 189) claims to have produced agglutinins for spermatozoa and yeasts with sodium nucleinate from sperm and yeasts.

[24] Bibliography on Lipoids and Immunity given by Landsteiner, Kolle and Wassermann's Handbuch, 1913 (2), 1240; Jobling. Jour. Immunol., 1916 (1), 491.

[25] Review of literature by Landsteiner, Jahresb.   Immunitätsfrsch., 1910 (6), 209.   See also Hemolysis, Chap. ix.

[26] Literature in Beitr. Klinik d. Tuberk., 1911 (20), 341.

[27] Jour. Infect. Dis., 1918 (22), 133; (23), 501; 1919 (24), 285.

[28] Zeit. Immunität., 1910 (7), 732; 1911 (9), 530; 1912 (14),355.

with antibodies for tubercle bacilli,[29] and much more effectively than the protein residue of the bacilli, wherefore he concludes that the reactions obtained with the lipoids certainly cannot be ascribed to adherent traces of protein. Bergel[30] observed after lecithin injections in rabbits, not only an increase in the lipase content of the blood and tissues, but also the presence of complement-binding antibodies, and Jobling and Bull[31] have found an increase in serum lipase after immunizing with red corpuscles.[32]

The number of reputed positive results with lipoids makes it impossible at this time to state dogmatically that lipoids may not possess antigenic properties, but it must be taken into account that the successful use of lipoids as antigens in complement fixation reactions is not proof of their true antigenic nature, in view of our present lack of knowledge of the actual nature of this reaction itself. MacLean,[33] indeed, found evidence that even in the Wassermann reaction the active substance is not lecithin itself, but some other unknown substance which could be obtained practically lecithin-free. Furthermore, we have the testimony of Fitzgerald and Leathes[34] that a lipoidal material from liver, which was itself capable of serving as antigen in the Wassermann reaction, did not engender complement-fixing antibodies in rabbits immunized with this lipoid. Ritchie and Miller[35] could find no antigenic activity in the lipoids of serum or corpuscles. Also Kleinschmidt,[36] who accepts the antigenic nature of nastin, was unable to secure antibodies by immunizing rabbits with it. Thiele[37] says that as lipoids possess no specificity they cannot give rise to antibodies. Neufeld found that rabbits immunized with lecithin developed no opsonins for lecithin emulsions. A suggestive observation is that of Pick and Schwarz,[38] who found that the presence of lecithin increases the antigenic power of bacteria, which may help to explain the activity of possible traces of proteins in lipoid preparations used as antigens.

Simple Chemical Antigens.—Many drugs cause a hypersensitization, and in this respect seem to behave as antigens producing anaphylactic antibodies. It happens that most of these chemicals are of such a nature as to permit of their union with proteins, and it seems probable that such protein compounds behave as foreign proteins to the animal in which they are formed, for it has been found that guinea-pig serum treated with iodin can render guinea-pigs sensitive to the same iodized serum.[39] Hence, hypersensitiveness to iodin compounds would be a reaction to iodized proteins,[40] and not to the non-protein iodin compound; the same applies to anaphylactic reactions observed with salvarsan, atoxyl,[41] copper compounds,[42] and perhaps aspirin and antipyrin.[43] Zieler, however, has questioned the validity of many of the experiments on which these views are based. [44] It is possible that certain chemicals may react in such a way with the tissue or blood proteins as to make them sensitive to the animal's own complement, which then

[29] *Ibid.*, 1912 (14), 359; 1912 (15), 245.
[30] Deut. Arch. klin. Med., 1912 (106), 47.
[31] Jour. Exp. Med., 1912 (16), 483.
[32] Bogomolez suggests that the lipoids themselves may be produced in excess for defense against various poisons, which they serve to inhibit, especially the toxin of *B. botulinus*. (Zeit. Immunität., 1910 (8), 35).
[33] Lecithin and Allied Substances, Biochemical Monographs, 1918, p. 170.
[34] Univ. of Calif. Publ., 1912 (2), 39.
[35] Jour. Path. and Bact., 1913 (17), 429; but Wang. (*Ibid.*, 1919 (22), 224) obtained positive results with ether-chloroform extracts of corpuscles.
[36] Berl. klin. Woch., 1910 (47), 57.
[37] Zeit. Immunität., 1913 (16), 160.
[38] Biochem. Zeit., 1909 (15), 453.
[39] Friedberger and Ito, Zeit. Immunität., 1912 (12), 241.
[40] According to Block (Zeit. exp. Path., 1911 (9), 509) iodoform idiosyncrasy depends upon the CH₃ rather than on the iodin, and is a local cellular reaction rather than a humoral reaction, the protoplasm having an increased affinity for methyl radicals. (See Weil, Zeit. Chemotherapie, 1913 (1), 412.)
[41] Moro and Stheeman, Münch. med. Woch., 1909 (56), 1414.
[42] Hollande, Compt. Rend. Soc. Biol., 1918 (81), 58.
[43] Bruck, Berl. klin. Woch., 1910 (47), 1928; Klausner, Münch. med. Woch., 1911 (58), 138.
[44] Münch. med. Woch., 1912 (59), 401.

forms anaphylatoxin,[45] and thus causes reactions, but the whole anaphylatoxin question is in so uncertain a state at the time of writing that further speculation in this direction is not justifiable.

The attempts to produce antitoxin against cantharidin have not yielded convincing results,[46] nor against epinephrine.[47] De Angelis[48] claimed that he had produced specific precipitins for various natural and synthetic dyes, but this work has, as was to be expected, failed of confirmation.[49] Elschnig and Salus[50] state that melanin from the eye is antigenic, producing complement-fixing antibodies specific for melanin but not for the species. Woods[51] has corroborated this and also demonstrated anaphylactic sensitization. We know too little concerning the composition of melanin to interpret these observations.

In general terms, therefore, antigens are protein molecules, and the reactions of immunity are reactions against proteins foreign to the body of the host, and manifested by the presence in the blood of the reacting animal of substances which combine with and cause recognizable changes in the foreign protein.[52] These changes are recognized in many ways, such as precipitation, agglutination, complement-fixation, etc., and the question at once arises as to whether these different manifestations depend each upon a separate antibody, or if several or all of them are not caused by a single antibody, the action of which is indicated by the different reactions which are made manifest by different procedures in each case.[53] This question will be discussed further in later paragraphs.

Knowing that the antigens are merely foreign proteins which have been introduced into the body of an animal, there naturally occurs the thought that the animal body is continually receiving in its food foreign proteins, and against which it defends itself in the alimentary canal by enzymatic action, which disintegrates these proteins until they have lost their colloidal character.[54] Logically following this comes the idea that perhaps the reactions of immunity are simply the same or similar disintegrative enzymatic actions, carried on within the blood and tissues to protect the body in the same way against foreign proteins which the alimentary digestive apparatus has not had the opportunity to destroy. This conception of the nature of immune reactions to antigens has been especially advanced and in-

[45] See Manoilov, Wien. klin. Woch., 1912 (25), 1701.
[46] Champy, Compt. Rend. Soc. Biol., 1907 (62), 1128.
[47] Pollak, Zeit. physiol. Chem., 1910 (68), 69.
[48] Ann. di Ig. Sperim., 1909 (19), 33.
[49] Takemura, Zeit. Immunität., 1910 (5), 697.
[50] Graefe's Arch., 1911 (79), 428.
[51] Jour. Immunol., 1918 (3), 75.
[52] Drew has found no evidence of antibody formation by immunizing molluscs and echinoderms (Jour. of Hyg., 1911 (11), 188), from which he concludes that the reaction to foreign proteins is not a universal property of protoplasm; a sweeping generalization which requires more extensive investigation for its establishment.   Cantacuzene (Compt. Rend. Soc. Biol., 1913 (7 l), 111) obtained precipitins by immunizing *Phallusia mamillata* with mammalian blood, but no hemolysins with this or *Aphrodite aculeata* and *Eledone moschata*.
[53] See Dean, Lancet, Jan. 13, 1917.
[54] Carrel and Ingebrigsten (Jour. Exp. Med., 1912 (15), 287) have found that tissues growing *in vitro* with foreign blood produce hemolytic antibodies for that blood, indicating that isolated cells can react to antigens by antibody production.

vestigated by Victor C. Vaughan[55] and his co-workers, and by Emil
Abderhalden, who has demonstrated in various ways an increased
proteolytic power in the blood of animals which have received parenteral injections of foreign proteins.[56]   Thus, if the antiserum reacts on the specific proteins within a dialyzing sac, the products of
proteolysis diffuse into the surrounding medium where they can
be detected by simple chemical reactions.   Also, changes in the specific rotation of the protein or peptid solution can be observed by
the polariscopic reading before and after the action of the antiserum.
A particularly important corroboration of Vaughan's theory is furnished by the behavior of the racemized protein of Dakin. Although
soluble, this protein cannot be attacked by the digestive proteolytic
enzymes, presumably because of its altered configuration; and it is
non-antigenic, presumably because it cannot be attacked by the proteases of the blood and tissues. Likewise it cannot be metabolized,
whether fed or injected subcutaneously.[57]   Here we have good evidence of the fundamental identity of the three processes, digestion,
metabolism, antigenic activity.

As immunity reactions manifest themselves, however, there are
steps in the process besides simple hydrolysis of proteins, even if
this be the ultimate goal of them all.[57a]

SPECIFICITY OF IMMUNE REACTIONS

The many attempts to explain the various reactions of immunity
solely on the basis of known physico-chemical properties of colloids
all flatten out when the striking, characteristic, and often extreme
specificity of these reactions is considered. Chemical explanations
are but little more satisfactory.   In enzyme action we find many comparable examples of specificity,—but this does not help, as the enzymes
are as mysterious as the antibodies. But no proposed explanation of
any of the reactions incited by antigens can be of value if it fails to
take into account the specificity of the reactions. We lack the space
here to consider the many ideas and the items of evidence which have
been advanced concerning this all-important chemical problem, but
refer the reader to the excellent discussion by E. P. Pick.[58] The main
facts at present available are the following: Specificity was at first
supposed to depend solely upon biological relationships, for it was
found easy to distinguish the serum of animals of unlike nature by
means of the precipitin and other reactions, but the more closely related the animals the less sharply these reactions distinguish them,

[55] See Vaughan, "Protein Split Products," Philadelphia, 1913.
[56] Abderhalden, "Abwehrfermente des tierischen Organismus," Berlin, 1913.
[57] See Ten Broeck, Jour. Biol. Chem., 1914 (17), 369.
[57a] Tadokoro states that immune sera show spectroscopic differences from
normal sera (Jour. Infect. Dis., 1920 (26), 8).
[58] Kolle and Wassermann's Handbuch d. path. Mikroorganismen, 1912 (1),
685; full bibliography.

until, with such closely related animals as dog and fox, or man and apes, antisera for the blood of one react nearly as well with the blood of the other, the existing differences being only quantitative. The opinion therefore gained ground that the specificity depends upon some peculiar biological relationship of the antigens, and, as serum proteins which seem to be quite similar chemically but which are from unrelated species, are sharply differentiated by the biological reactions, that the specificity must depend upon something quite distinct from ordinary chemical differences. But even with closely related species, differences can often be brought out by means of the process of saturation (which consists in treating the antiserum with sufficient quantities of an antigen until it no longer reacts with additional quantities of this antigen, and then trying its reactive power with the other related antigen which one wishes to test).

As use began to be made of other materials than serum, and especially when more or less purified proteins were employed, it was found that within the tissues of a single animal or plant there might exist antigens which were quite distinct from one another—more so, indeed, than some of the chemically similar substances of different biological origins. Thus, in the hen's egg, by means of the anaphylaxis reaction, I have been able to distinguish five distinct antigens, and these correspond to as many different proteins which have been distinguished by chemical means.[59] Also, for another example, in the crystalline lens are found proteins which are specific for lens proteins, in that they produce antibodies reacting with lens proteins from varied species of animals, but not with the serum proteins of the species from which the antigenic lens substance was derived.[60] Here the chemical character of the protein is undoubtedly more significant than its biological relations. These and other observations leave little room for doubt that specificity does depend upon chemical composition, and that *the differences in species as exhibited by their biological reactions depend upon distinct differences in the chemistry of their proteins.*[61] Chemically distinct proteins (e. g. lens and serum proteins) of one animal may be immunologically distinct, and chemically related proteins of dissimilar species (e. g. casein from goat and cow milk) may show immunological relationship. Crystalline albumin from hen's eggs shows no immunological distinction from that of ducks' eggs, whereas each of the three proteins separable from horse serum— euglobulin, pseudoglobulin and albumin—can be distinguished from the other two by the anaphylaxis reaction.[62] Furthermore, it has been shown by Wells and Osborne[63] that a single pure protein may exhibit multiple antigenic properties, and react or fail to react with

[59] Jour. Infec. Dis., 1911 (9), 147.
[60] Krusius, Zeit. Immunität., 1910 (5), 699.
[61] See Wells and Osborne, Jour. Infect. Dis., 1916 (19), 183.
[62] Dale and Hartley, Biochem. Jour., 1916 (10), 408.
[63] Jour. Infect. Dis., 1913 (12), 341.

other pure proteins according to whether chemical differences can be demonstrated by recognized analytical methods.

A striking example of the existence of identical antigenic properties in materials of biologically unrelated origins, is furnished by the sheep corpuscle hemolysin discovered by Forssner,[64] who found that many different materials, when injected into rabbits, engender in the rabbits' serum active hemolytic amboceptors for sheep corpuscles. This antigenic property has been demonstrated in the organs of the guinea-pig, horse, cat, dog, mouse, chicken, turtle, and several species of fish,[65] although not exhibited by organs of many closely related species (e. g. pig, ox, rabbit, goose, frog, eel, man, pigeon, rat). It is not present in the red corpuscles of these animals, but is present in the corpuscles of the sheep, whose organs do not have this property. It has also been found in paratyphoid and Gärtner bacilli, mouse tumors and sheep spermatozoa. Not only does the serum of rabbits thus immunized show active hemolysis for sheep corpuscles, but if injected into the vein of an animal whose organs contain this antigen there results a prompt, severe anaphylactic intoxication, presumably through reaction between the antigen present in their tissues and the antibodies of the rabbit serum. Furthermore, the antibody can be specifically removed from the immune rabbit serum by contact with any of the antigen-containing tissues, but not by tissues that do not exhibit this antigenic property. The antigen seems to remain in the tissues when the fluids are forced out by pressure, and Doerr and Pick believe it to be associated with the nucleoproteins.

This series of observations, which seem to have been quite generally corroborated, indicates conclusively that the immunological specificity of an antigen is not necessarily related to the biological specificity of the living organism from which it is derived. The logical explanation is that there may exist proteins in different species which have chemical resemblances or identity, and this is scarcely to be doubted. We find identical lipoids, fats, nucleic acids, and carbohydrates in different species; many peculiar types of proteins show apparent chemical identity in different species (e. g. gelatin, keratin); some chemically similar, derived proteins also seem immunologically identical or closely related (e. g. lens protein, casein). Therefore, it is highly probable that many tissue proteins may be identical in different forms of animal cells, and even in animal and plant cells.

Another sort of manifestation of apparently non-specific immunity reactions has been observed especially in therapeutic immunization.[66] Beginning with the classical observation of Matthes that the tuberculin reaction could be produced with deutero-albumose, many similar non-specific reactions have been observed. Particularly the

[64] Review by Doerr and Pick, Biochem. Zeit., 1914 (60), 257.
[65] Tsunecka, Zeit. Immunität., 1914 (22), 567.
[66] See review by Jobling, Jour. Amer. Med. Assoc., 1916 (66), 1753.

sharp reaction that follows intravenous injections of killed typhoid bacilli into typhoid patients has been found to result equally well if colon bacilli are used, or deutero-albumose. One possible explanation of this type of reaction is that the injected substance acts as a common antigen, which causes the production of common antibodies that react also with the antigens of the cause of the disease. Another possibility is that the foreign protein stimulates the tissues that form antibodies, presumably the red marrow, so that they produce not only antibodies for this antigen, but also for the antigens of the specific etiologic factor of the disease that have been stimulating the bone marrow previously. Hektoen[67] has observed, for example, that if an animal that has previously produced precipitins for one foreign protein is reinjected with a different protein it will then produce precipitins for both these proteins, and possibly for other proteins with which it has not been injected.[68] Moreover, the febrile reaction, the leucocytosis, and other phenomena, such as the antiferment index of the serum (Jobling),[69] that injection of nonspecific protein produces, may be responsible for favorably affecting the disease, rather than actual antibody formation.

The opposite type of phenomenon, that is, non-specific interference with immunological reaction, is suggested by the observations of J. H. Lewis.[70] He found that small quantities of one protein injected into a guinea pig together with or shortly after large quantities of another protein (e. g., egg albumen in dog serum) would not sensitize the animal, although a similar amount injected alone would always sensitize. The suggested explanation is that the larger amount of foreign protein combines with so many of the available cell receptors that few of the small number of sensitizing protein molecules are able to be bound to the cells and to stimulate antibody formation; this explanation assumes a certain lack of specificity on the part of the cell receptors.

An interesting illustration of the fact that whatever stimulates the bone marrow may cause it to form, among other blood elements, specific antibodies, is furnished by the behavior of antitoxin-producing horses. If a horse that has been immunized to diphtheria toxin is bled as much as possible, it will be found to have regenerated the lost antitoxin within 48 hours,[71] even although the last immunizing dose of toxin was received long before. Also, it is stated that persons who have once had typhoid, but whose blood no longer contains much agglutinin, may show a high typhoid agglutinin content when infected by some other organism, or after any sharp febrile attack. It is highly possible that many therapeutic agents may similarly act by

[67] Jour. Infect. Dis., 1917 (21), 279.
[68] See also Herrmann, ibid., 1918 (23), 457.
[69] See review of this subject, Harvey Lectures, 1917 (12), 181; also Cowie and Calhoun, Arch. Int. Med., 1919 (23), 69.
[70] Jour. Infect. Dis., 1915 (17), 241.
[71] O'Brien, Jour. Path. and Bact., 1913 (18), 89.

stimulating the marrow to increased formation of specific antibodies, e. g., arsenic, mercury and other metals, heliotherapy, hemorrhage[71a] or phlebotomy, hot baths.

The other aspect of specificity, i. e., the presence of several antigens in a single organism, each entirely distinct from other antigens in the same organism, has been repeatedly demonstrated. Besides the identification of five distinct antigens in the hen's egg, mentioned previously, we have the repeatedly demonstrated individuality of serum proteins and milk casein of the same animal, and even the differentiation of casein from lactalbumin in the same milk, as contrasted with the common inter-reactions of caseins from different sources,[72] e. g., cow and goat. A certain but slight distinguishable specificity may be observed between proteins from different organs of the same animal, which differentiation is still sharper between the tissue proteins and serum proteins of the animal.[73] Sex cells especially seem to be rather distinct immunologically from the body cells.[74] Numerous instances of two separate proteins from the same plant seeds showing entirely distinct immunological specificities have been described.[75] Although hemoglobin itself seems not to be antigenic,[76] some of the most striking examples of absolute specificity are furnished by red corpuscles, which show readily demonstrable differences between closely related individuals. For example, take the remarkable observation of Todd,[77] who mixed together isolytic beef sera from over 60 animals, and then tested the mixture with the corpuscles of 110 different cattle, all of which were hemolyzed. When the mixture of sera was exhausted with the corpuscles of any one of the 110 cattle it would then hemolyze the corpuscles of all the other 109, but was absolutely without action on the corpucles of the individual with whose corpuscles it had been exhausted. This indicates that the red corpuscles of any individual possess characters which differentiate them from the corpuscles of any other individual even of the same species.

As satisfactory a conception of the nature of specificity as our present evidence warrants is that developed by Pick, largely on the basis of his own work. He properly accepts the influence of both the physico-chemical properties and the chemical composition of the colloids concerned in immunity reactions as determining specificity. Both these factors undoubtedly come into play in determining the possibility of interaction of antigen and antibody. The electric charges of the amphoteric colloidal antigen and antibody, and perhaps also their surface configuration and their surface forces, all

[71a] See Hahn and Langer, Zeit. Immunität., 1917 (26), 199.
[72] See Versell, Zeit. Immunität., 1915 (24), 267.
[73] See Salus, Biochem. Zeit., 1914 (60), 1.
[74] Graetz, Zeit. Immunität., 1914 (21), 150.
[75] Wells and Osborne, Jour. Infect. Dis., 1911 (8), 66 et seq., especially 1916 (19), 183.
[76] Schmidt and Bennett, Jour. Infect. Dis., 1919, (25), 207.
[77] Jour. of Genetics, 1913 (3), 123.

influence their reaction; these physico-chemical factors greatly complicate the possibility of reaction between two colloids, and to these influences are added the influence of the chemical structure in determining subsequent chemical reactions. It would seem possible that the existence of all these factors may account for specificity, it being necessary for each one of a long series of both physical and chemical adjustments to agree perfectly in order that reaction may take place —just as in a combination lock one lever after another is thrown by the proper manipulation of the dial, and only when all the long series of levers is in just the proper position does the bolt engage and the lock open.[78]

The studies of Pick and his colleagues, amplified somewhat by other investigations, have led to the following view of the chemistry of specificity: There exist two sorts of specificity in each protein molecule; one of these is easily altered by simple physical measures, e. g., heat, cold, partial coagulation, etc., without essentially changing the chemical composition of the protein. When so altered the antigenic properties of the protein are likewise altered, in that the antibody it engenders differs somewhat in the scope of its reactivity from the antibody engendered by the original unaltered protein; but the alteration does not affect the species characteristics of the antigen. Thus, a heated antigen may engender precipitins that will react with this heated antigen, but not with similar heated proteins from other species of animals, while the antibodies engendered by the same but unheated antigen will not react with the heated protein.

The other sort of specificity is not so easily affected, only marked chemical alterations of the antigen modifying it, and this concerns the species characteristics of the antigen. This fundamental species specificity seems to be closely related to the aromatic radicals of the protein antigen, for it is affected by introducing into the protein molecules substances which are known to combine with the benzene ring, e. g., iodin, diazo and nitro groups. Proteins thus chemically altered will act as proteins foreign to animals of the species from which they are derived, and the antigens they develop are devoid of species specificity, although quite specific for proteins like themselves; e. g., a nitroprotein made by treating rabbit serum protein with nitric acid, will, if injected into even the same rabbit, cause the formation of antibodies which will react with this same nitro-protein, and also with nitroproteins derived from entirely different species or even from plants,— but it reacts only with nitro-proteins. It is also possible to cause chemical modifications analogous to the physical modifications previously mentioned, which change only the scope of specificity of the

[78] The *"resonance theory"* of Traube assumes that the surface forces of reacting substances must harmonize, just as the vibration of one tuning fork starts vibrations in another fork only when the two are in harmony, or as electromagnetic waves incite resonance phenomena (see Zeit. f. Immunität., 1911 (9), 246 and 779).

antigen without altering its specificity for species. Appreciating that the number of different aromatic radicals in the protein molecule is not sufficient to account for the innumerable manifestations of specificity, Pick interprets the significance of these aromatic radicals as that of a central complex about which are the groupings which determine species specificity.[79] It is not merely the number and proportion of amino-acid radicals in the protein molecule which determine its specificity, but, more important because presenting greater possibilities for variations, the arrangement of these radicals in the molecule.

Landsteiner and Lampl[80] have also carried on an extensive study of the precipitin reactions of horse serum when combined with azo-compounds, with chlorine and bromine and with sulfonic and arsenic acids. Their results confirm the observations and conclusions of Obermayer and Pick and of Wells and Osborne, that specificity depends upon certain groups within the protein molecule. They made the interesting observation that if one derivative of a protein reacted with another sort of derivative, the position in the molecule of the substituted radicals was identical or closely related. That is, cross reactions depend on chemical relationships, as Wells and Osborne also found by means of the anaphylaxis reactions, and the specificity is determined by relatively small portions of the large antigen molecule. The observation that the location in the molecule of definite groups is indicated by their immunological reactions can best be explained as depending on spatial correspondence of antigen and antibody, just as Emil Fischer assumed for the specific action of ferments in his comparison to "lock and key." Here again we get evidence that both chemical composition and spatial relations are concerned in determining specificity. Presumably there are also innumerable isomeres that cannot be distinguished by our present methods, which correspond to the racial and individual differences which are so obvious and yet not to be detected by serum reactions.

Contemplating the possible number of variations in the arrangement of the amino-acids in a protein which the great number of these radicals provides, there is no difficulty in understanding the existence of an almost limitless number of specific distinctions between proteins. Abderhalden, indeed, calculates that the 20 amino-acids we find in proteins could form at least 2,432,902,008,176,640,000 different compounds, and this without including possible compounds varying in quantitative relations. A contribution to the chemical basis of specificity has been made by Kossel,[81] who finds certain relations in the

[79] Landsteiner and Prasek (Zeit, Immunität., 1913 (20), 211), however, state that alteration of proteins by simply treating them with acid alcohol also causes them to lose their species specificity, and this without any substitution in the aromatic radicals of the proteins. This observation throws doubt on the hypothesis of Pick that the aromatic radicals are the essential center of species specificity.
[80] Biochem. Zeit., 1918 (86), 343.
[81] Zeit. physiol. Chem., 1913 (88), 163.

proportions and groupings of the scanty number of amino-acids that make up the protamines and histones of sperm to be characteristic of the sperm of certain species and families.

In the subsequent discussion of the various reactions of immunity the subject of specificity will receive further consideration. Of these reactions, one of the simplest and most studied is that of

TOXINS AND ANTITOXINS

In the preceding chapter on the bacteria and their products the nature of the *true toxins* was defined, and attention was called to the fact that one of their most important characteristics is that immunization of animals against them leads to the accumulation in the blood of substances capable of neutralizing their poisonous action. Such true toxins are produced especially by the diphtheria bacillus and the tetanus bacillus; also, but less strikingly, by *B. pyocyaneus, B. botulinus,* pathogenic gas bacilli, dysentery bacilli, and possibly by a few others. In addition to these, numerous bacteria produce *hemolytic poisons* which seem to have properties similar to the toxins; and there are also toxins produced by plants (abrin, ricin, crotin, and mushroom poisons) and by animals (snake venom, scorpion and spider toxin, and eel serum). Against all of these, true antitoxins may be obtained by the immunization of animals.

Ehrlich's Conception of Toxins and Antitoxins.—According to Ehrlich's theory, the action of toxins upon cells is purely chemical. A toxin unites with a cell because some chemical group in the molecule of toxin has a chemical affinity for some particular group in the cell protoplasm. For convenience in description names have been given to these groups; the group of the toxin that combines with the cell has been called the *haptophorous* group, or haptophore, while the group in the protoplasm that combines with the toxin is known as the *receptor.*[82] It has been found that after being kept for some time, or when placed under certain unfavorable conditions, the toxin loses its poisonous properties without losing its power to combine with cells, as shown by the fact that immunization with such altered toxin gives rise to the formation of antitoxin. Therefore it is not the haptophore that causes the harm to the cell, but there must be some other groups with this particular function. To the group that produces the harm the name *toxophore* is given. If all the receptors of a cell are combined by toxin molecules that have lost their toxophore

[82] Ehrlich has used certain diagrams to illustrate these various groups and their relations to the cells and to one another, which are generally used in explaining his theory. From a teaching standpoint they have seemed to be undesirable, in that the student soon comes to ascribe physical properties and appearances to what should be considered as chemical combinations. The toxophore group becomes "the black fringed end of the toxin," etc. To one accustomed to thinking in chemical terms there is no difficulty in following the literature and understanding the reactions as chemical reactions, which they are.

group (*toxoid* is the name given to such altered toxins), the cell cannot then be injured by the corresponding active toxin, showing that the toxin must first become united to a cell receptor by its haptophore group before the toxophore group can cause an injury.

Animals that are naturally immune to toxins may owe their immunity to the fact that their vital tissues contain no substances with a chemical affinity for the toxin, and hence the toxin cannot unite with them to cause harm. (In Ehrlich's terminology, the cells contain no receptors for the toxin.) The toxin may not combine with any tissue element at all in such immune animals, and may circulate for some time harmlessly in the blood, or it may combine with some organ where it does little harm, e. g., tetanus toxin is said to combine chiefly in the liver of some animals, and therefore it does not harm their nervous system.

According to this theory, *the antitoxin consists of cell receptors that have been produced in excess and secreted by the cells into the blood.* In the blood they combine with any toxin that may have been introduced, and by saturating its affinities render it incapable of uniting with the cells. As the toxin harms cells only after it has been chemically united to them, it is rendered harmless when its affinities for the cell (the haptophore groups) are saturated by cell receptors in the blood stream. The process of immunization consists in injuring the body cells to such a degree that they are stimulated to regenerate the receptor groups with which the toxin combines; these receptor groups are produced in excess, and not only replace those combined by the toxins, but the excessive groups escape free into the blood. Hence the serum of an immunized animal is antitoxic *because it contains free cell receptors* that can unite with the toxin. An important point is that the receptors liberated by all animals which have been immunized with a given toxin seem to be the same—horse serum, or sheep serum, or goat serum will neutralize diphtheria toxin if the animals have been made immune to this toxin; and, furthermore, their serum when introduced into the body of an entirely different animal, e. g., a guinea-pig, will neutralize diphtheria toxin within its body. Equally important is the fact that the antitoxin for one toxin will not neutralize any other toxin; e. g., diphtheria antitoxin will not neutralize tetanus toxin, or conversely. This means that diphtheria toxin is attached to chemical groups of the body cells (receptors) which are quite different from the groups to which tetanus toxin unites, and hence different receptors are thrown out in immunizing against each. True toxins have been designated *monovalent antigens,* since animals immunized with a purified toxin produce only the one antibody, the antitoxin, whereas many protein antigens produce precipitins, lysins, agglutinins and other antibodies; presumably this is because of the relatively small size of the toxin molecule, which limits the number of its antigenic radicals (Pick). Or it may well be that the immune body for antitoxin is quite different from the antibody or antibodies resulting from immunization with non-toxic protein antigens, for there is some reason to believe that the several types of reactions that may be accomplished with the serum of animals immunized to foreign proteins or cells all depend on one single antibody, which accomplishes the destrution of the antigen by sensitizing it to the enzymes of the blood and tissues.

The neutralization of toxin by antitoxin is believed by many investigators to be a chemical process, which occurs as well in the test-tube as in the body. It seems to occur *according to the laws of definite proportion,* a given amount of antitoxin neutralizing a proportionate amount of toxin under equal conditions (hence the toxin is not destroyed by antitoxin through a ferment action, as was at first suggested). Neither the toxin nor the antitoxin is destroyed in the process of neutralization, as has been proved by suitable experiments, but they appear to be chemically united to each other, as any two large molecules may be. Pick and Schwarz believe that the union of toxin and antitoxin takes place in two steps—first, colloidal adsorption, and then the specific reaction.[83] There is some question as to whether the union with antitoxin completes the neutralization of the toxin, or whether there is then necessary a further destruction of the toxin in the body. But whether necessary or not, such further destruction does take place. Neutralization occurs more rapidly under the influence of warmth, and more slowly in the cold; and it is more rapid in concentrated than in dilute solutions, just as with ordinary chemical reactions. It is said that it requires two hours for tetanus toxin to be completely combined with the corresponding quantity of antitoxin at 37°. According to Arrhenius and Madsen, reaction of antitoxin upon toxin is accompanied by the liberation of much heat—6600 calories per gram molecule, or about half as much as is set free by the action of a strong acid upon a strong base.[84] Union of toxin and antitoxin causes no change in the surface tension of the fluid in which the reaction occurs (Zunz),[85] and the neutral toxin-antitoxin compound (diphtheria) is not absorbed by animal charcoal, which absorbs each of the constituents when free. The physico-chemical studies of the reaction between tetanolysin and its antibody gave results which led Arrhenius to conclude that in the reaction there are formed from one molecule of toxin and one molecule of antitoxin, two molecules of the reaction products (analogous to the reaction between alcohol and acid which yields one molecule of ester and one of water). In general, the union of toxin and antitoxin is

[83] Also von Krogh (Zeit. f. Hyg., 1911 (68), 251). Bordet, Biltz, and others look upon the neutralization of toxin as an adsorption process entirely.

[84] Literature of chemical and physical reactions of toxin and antitoxin given by Zangger, Cent. f. Bakt. (ref.), 1905 (36), 238; Arrhenius, "Immuno-chemistry," 1907 and "Quantitative Laws in Biological Chemistry," London, 1915; also review in Zeit. Chemother., Ref., 1914 (3), 157; Oppenheimer and Michaelis, Handbuch der Biochemie, Vol. II (1).

[85] Bull. Acad. Royal Med. Belg., 1911; also Bertolini, Biochem. Zeit., 1910 (28), 60.

dissociated by acids.[86] On dilution of a neutral toxin-antitoxin mixture, a certain amount of dissociation seems to occur, but there is opposition to the view that the law of mass action applies to the reaction between toxin and antitoxin. If toxin is added to antitoxin in several fractions, with some interval of time between each addition, the final mixture is much more toxic than if the same quantities of toxin and antitoxin were put together at one time. This phenomenon is commonly referred to as the Danysz effect, and indicates that the toxin-antitoxin union is physical rather than chemical, for it seems to be quite analogous to such a phenomenon as the taking up of more dye by several pieces of blotting paper added in series to a dye solution, than by the same amount of paper added in one piece.

There is no relation between antitoxins and enzymes. The antitoxin acts quantitatively, and produces no detectable alteration in the toxin, or in any other substance, as far as we know. It also has but one functioning group (haptophore), the one with which it combines with the toxin; whereas both toxins and enzymes seem to have two functionating groups, one which unites with the cell or substance that is to be attacked, the other which produces the chemical changes. But there is evidence that union with antitoxin or fixed receptors prepares the toxin for its disintegration, which, presumably, is then accomplished by enzymatic action as with other antigens.

CHEMICAL NATURE OF ANTITOXINS [87]

This is as entirely unknown as is the nature of the toxins. Investigation of antitoxic serum (principally diphtheria antitoxin) has shown that the antitoxic properties are closely related to the serum globulin, which, however, by no means proves that antitoxin is serum globulin or any other sort of protein. According to Ehrlich's theory, antitoxin consists of free cell receptors, and these receptors are presumably simple chemical groups which may be but a part of a larger molecule, or they may be entire protein molecules. In any event they behave as colloids; moving toward the cathode in an electrical field,[88] diffusing little or not at all, their reaction curve resembling more an absorption curve than the reaction curves of crystalloids, and being influenced by all conditions that influence colloids. Whether the receptor groups are secreted in a free condition in antitoxin formation, or combined in a large molecule, is unknown.

By saturating serum with magnesium sulphate, or half saturation with ammonium sulphate, three chief groups of proteins can be pre-

[86] Morgenroth and Ascher, Cent. f. Bakt., 1911 (59), 510.
[87] Review and bibliography given by Crawford and Foster, Amer. Jour. Pharmacy, 1918 (90), 765.
[88] According to Field and Teague (Jour. Exper. Med., 1907 (9), 86) both toxin and antitoxin move towards the cathode, which is opposed to the theory that this reaction is simply one of oppositely charged colloids. (See also Bechhold, Münch. med. Woch., 1907 (54), 1921.)

cipitated and isolated.[89]   These are *fibrinogen, euglobulin* (true globulin), and *pseudo-globulin* (soluble in water).   Pick[90] found that the precipitate obtained by 36 per cent. volume saturation with ammonium sulphate contained no antitoxin; the antitoxin came down in the precipitate obtained on raising the strength from above 38 per cent. to 46 per cent.[91]   According to Pick, in horse serum the antitoxin is associated with the pseudo-globulin,[92] and Gibson and Banzhaf found that the blood of horses immunized to either diphtheria or tetanus toxin shows a marked increase (40 to 114 per cent.) in serum globulin, varying somewhat according to the antitoxin content. the more soluble globulins being most increased.   At the same time the serum albumin and euglobulin content decreases in proportion, while the fibrinogen shows no characteristic alterations.[93]   Meyer[94] and his colleagues, however, find in their study of the blood proteins during immunization, that the proportion of globulins increases according to the severity of the intoxication, and not in any definite relation to the degree of immunity or antitoxin production.   The average antitoxic horse serum contains 12 per cent. albumin, 78 per cent. of soluble globulin containing antitoxin, 10 per cent. euglobulin.   By heating 12 hours at 57° a considerable part of the soluble globulin becomes insoluble, without a corresponding loss of antitoxin (Banzhaf).

The relation of antitoxins to proteins has also been investigated by permitting digestive enzymes to act on antitoxic serum.   Pick digested the antitoxin-containing globulin of horse serum for several days with trypsin; after five days, when part of the protein was still not digested, the antitoxin was but little impaired in strength; after nine days, when most of the protein was digested, the antitoxin had lost two-thirds of its strength.   This indicates a considerable resistance of antitoxin to trypsin, but also shows that it is affected in much the same way as the globulin (which is itself very resistant to trypsin) and therefore is presumably of similar nature.   Antitoxin seemed to be much more rapidly destroyed by pepsin-HCl digestion than by trypsin, in which respect it again resembles the serum globulin.[95]

[89] See résumé by Gibson, Jour. Biol. Chem., 1905 (1), 161; Gibson and Banzhaf, Jour. Exper. Med., 1910 (12), 411.

[90] Hofmeister's Beitr., 1901 (1), 351.

[91] Gibson and Collins (Jour. Biol. Chem., 1907 (3), 233) question the reliability of some of Pick's results, and repudiate the salt fractionation method of classifying proteins.

[92] Miss Homer found tetanus and diphtheria antitoxin associated with the pseudoglobulins, but the antibodies in antidysentery and antimeningococcus serum were chiefly in the euglobulin fraction (Jour. Physiol., 1918 (52), xxxiii).

[93] During immunization the *antitryptic* power of the horse serum increases with the antitoxin increase (Krause and Klug, Berl. klin. Woch., 1908 (45), 1454.)

[94] Jour. Exp. Med., 1916 (24), 515; 1917 (25), 231; Jour. Infect. Dis., 1918 (22), 1.

[95] Berg and Kelser (Jour. Agric. Res., 1918 (13), 471) found that trypsin and pepsin destroy the antitoxin and serum proteins at about the same rate, and their failure to observe "significant chemical changes" in the proteins of serum acted upon by weak acid or alkali that slowly inactivates antitoxin, does not seem to warrant their deduction that antitoxin is non-protein. See also Crawford and Andrus, Amer. Jour. Pharm., 1917 (89), 158.

In favor of the view that antitoxin is a definite protein body is also the fact that it is not carried down in indifferent precipitates, as are the enzymes, but comes down always in a certain fraction of the protein precipitates, *e. g.*, we can precipitate all the serum albumin from an antitoxic serum, and it does not carry down with it any of the antitoxin. Another important point has been brought out by Arrhenius and Madsen,[96] who determined approximately the molecular weight of toxin and antitoxin by means of their rate of diffusion, and found that the toxin (diphtheria toxin and tetanolysin) diffused ten or more times as rapidly as the corresponding antitoxin. Gelatin filters also hold back antitoxin and let toxin pass through, and toxins diffuse into cells which seem to be impermeable for the antitoxin. This indicates that the antitoxin molecules are much larger than the toxin molecules, agreeing with the idea that antitoxin is of protein nature and that toxin either is not protein or is smaller than most protein molecules.

Taken altogether, the evidence indicates a closer resemblance of antitoxins to proteins than has been shown for the toxins, and all attempts to separate antitoxins from proteins have so far failed.

Antitoxins are retained to greater or less extent by porcelain filters, do not pass through dialyzing membranes readily, and are in general easily destroyed by chemical and physical agencies, although much less so than are most toxins. Heating to 60°–70° injures, and boiling quickly destroys them, although like the enzymes and the proteins, they resist dry heat to 140°, and also extremely low temperature, without change. Putrefaction of the serum destroys the antitoxins (Brieger).[97] They can be preserved for a very long time when dried completely, but in the serum they gradually disappear, especially if exposed to light and air. Acids and alkalies destroy antitoxins, acids being the more harmful in low concentrations. Like the enzymes, antitoxins are destroyed by ultra-violet rays. They are destroyed in the alimentary tract, without appreciable absorption, except in the case of new-born animals sucking mothers whose blood and milk contain antitoxin.[98] When subcutaneously injected, antitoxin soon disappears from the blood; part may be bound to the tissues, part may be destroyed, since only traces appear in the urine. It resists autolysis.[99]

[96] Festskrift Statens Serum Institut, 1902.
[97] Behring states that tetanus antitoxin resists putrefaction.
[98] Römer and Much, Jahrb. f. Kinderheilk., 1906 (63), 684; McClintock and King (Jour. Infect. Dis., 1906 (3), 701) found appreciable absorption of antitoxin when digestion was impaired by drugs. Full review of literature on transmission of antibodies from mother to offspring given by Famulener, Jour. Infect. Dis., 1912 (10), 332; Heurlin, Arch. Mens. Obs. et Gyn., 1912 (1), 497.
[99] Wolff-Eisner and Rosenbaum, Berl. klin. Woch., 1906 (43), 945.

AGGLUTININS AND AGGLUTINATION[1]

The relation of agglutination of bacteria by the serum of immunized animals to their immunity is not known, for it is not established that agglutination helps in the defensive reaction.[2] Agglutinated bacteria seem not to be severely injured by the process, and can grow vigorously in agglutinative serum. Possibly agglutination favors phagocytosis and lessens dissemination of the infecting organisms, but it is not generally considered that the influence on the course of infection is great.[3] Agglutination, therefore, may be looked upon as an incident in the infection, rather than as a definite method of resistance, and it is equally well produced by immunizing with foreign cells or any foreign protein masses of suitable size which contain soluble antigens.

For the production of agglutination it is necessary that the cell contain an antigen (*agglutinogen*) which has an affinity for the specific constituent of the serum, *agglutinin*. Normal serum may contain agglutinin;[4] e. g., typhoid bacilli are sometimes agglutinated by normal serum, even when it is diluted thirty times, but by immunization this property can be greatly increased until agglutination may be obtained with dilutions as high as one to a million. Whether normal agglutinins are essentially different from immune agglutinins is not known.[5] Many protein solutions, especially extracts of plant tissues and leguminous seeds, cause marked non-specific hemagglutination.[6] Likewise, bacterial extracts may agglutinate red corpuscles.[7] In immunization the agglutinogen, which is probably an intracellular protein, acts as a stimulator to the formation of the specific agglutinin. Hence, when we inject either extracts of cells or entire cells, we secure agglutinins, for the agglutinogens are liberated from the cells upon their disintegration. In erythrocytes the agglutinogen seems to be in the stroma.[8]

We can obtain agglutinins against nearly all bacteria, including non-pathogenic forms, but in varying strengths. Agglutinins are found in the blood stream in the highest concentrations, but they are

[1] Bibliography given by Müller, Oppenheimer's Handbuch der Biochemie, 1909 (II (1), 592; Landsteiner, *ibid.*, p. 428; Paltauf, Kolle and Wassermann's Handbuch., 1913 (II), 483.

[2] Bull, however, would ascribe much importance to agglutination of bacteria for their removal from the circulation (Jour. Exp. Med., 1915 (22), 484). Fujimoto (Jour. Immunol., 1919 (4), 67) also attributes to agglutinins the power to impair the glucolytic action of *B. coli*, but there is no evidence in his experiments that it is agglutinin rather than some other serum component that is responsible. On the other hand Zironi (Atti accad. Lincei, 1917 (26), 19) found that agglutination does not modify reproductive or biochemical activities of bacteria.

[3] Blaizot (C. R. Soc. Biol., 1918 (81), 356) states that it is possible to modify typhoid bacilli by treating them with nitric acid, hydroquinone or by heat, so that they will produce immunity without producing agglutinins.

[4] Even cold blooded animals may have normal agglutinins for bacteria and mammalian corpuscles (see Takenouchi, Jour. Inf. Dis., 1918 (23), 393, 415).

[5] See Andrejew, Arb. kaiserl. Gesundhtsamt., 1910 (33), 84.

[6] Mendel, Arch. Fisiol., 1909 (7), 168.

[7] Fukuhara, Zeit. Immunitat., 1909 (2), 313.

[8] Chyosa, Arch. f. Hyg., 1910 (72), 191.

also present in the various organs, and to greater or less extent in the other body fluids, excepting usually the spinal fluid (Greer and Becht).[9] The place of their formation is unknown, but they can be formed by spleen tissue grown in artificial cultures.[10] Since bacteria contained within a collodion sac implanted in an animal give rise to the production of agglutinins, it is evident that the agglutinogens are diffusible to some extent, at least, through collodion. Old cultures of bacteria contain free agglutinogens, probably liberated from disintegrated cells, and filtrates of such cultures will neutralize agglutinins, showing both that the agglutinogens are filterable, and that the reaction of agglutination is a chemical one and not dependent upon the presence of cells. Agglutinogens are said to pass through dialyzing membranes, while agglutinins do not, so it is evident that the agglutinogen is of smaller molecular dimensions than the agglutinin, just as toxin molecules are smaller than antitoxin molecules. Agglutinogens are not destroyed by formalin, heat, or ultraviolet rays in concentrations sufficient to kill the bacteria containing them.[11]

Just what constituent of the bacteria acts as the stimulus to the production of the agglutinin is unknown. Apparently, there are at least two bacterial substances with this property, one of which seems not to be a protein, since it is soluble in alcohol, gives no biuret reaction and resists temperatures up to 165°. The other gives all protein reactions, and is destroyed by heating to 62°. We consider, therefore, that there are two agglutinogens in the bacterial cell, one, thermostable, the other, thermolabile. The difference in the function of these two agglutinogens is still a matter of dispute. Likewise, the question as to whether they occur in the membrane or within the bacterial cell is still open, but Craw found that the insoluble residue of crushed typhoid bacilli, after being washed free of all soluble constituents, was but slightly agglutinated by active serum; therefore, the agglutinogens are probably soluble intracellular substances. Stuber holds that bacterial agglutinogens are lipins.[12]

Properties of Agglutinins.—Like most of the other immune substances, agglutinins are precipitated out of the serum in the globulin fraction. All attempts to separate them from proteins have been unsuccessful. Stark[13] found that trypsin does not attack the agglutinins readily, corresponding to the resistance of the serum globulins to this enzyme; alkaline papayotin solution destroys them slowly, while pepsin acts more rapidly. Alkalies are destructive even when quite dilute, while acids are much less harmful. The temperature resistance of agglutinins seems to be variable, plague agglutinin being destroyed at 56°, while purified typhoid agglutinin may resist 80°–90°; most agglutinin serums lose their activity at 60°–65°. The rate of reaction of agglutinins increases with the temperature, as long as this is not high enough to injure the reacting substances.[14] They are not precipitated by specific precipitins, but are readily absorbed by charcoal.

[9] Jour. Infect. Dis., 1910 (7), 127.
[10] Pryzgode, Wien. klin. Woch., 1913 (26), 841.
[11] Stassano and Lematte, Compt. Rend. Acad. Sci., 1911 (152), 623.
[12] Biochem. Zeit., 1916 (77), 388; also Bauer, Biochem. Zeit., 1917 (83), 120.
[13] Inaug. Dissert., Würzburg, 1905.
[14] Madsen, et al., Jour. Exper. Med., 1906 (8), 337.

The observations of Bond[15] suggest that they may become physically bound to other colloids within the body.

The structure of the agglutinins (in the Ehrlich theory) is similar to that of the toxin; i. e., there is a haptophore group by which they combine with the agglutinogen, and a toxophore group by which they produce the changes that cause agglutination.   The agglutinogen is probably related to the antitoxins in structure, having a single haptophore to unite with the agglutinin.   By degeneration of the toxophorous group of the agglutinin, *agglutinoids* may be formed.   It is believed that agglutinins are cell receptors, which have a group with a chemical affinity for the agglutinogen of the bacterial protoplasm, and also another group which brings about the agglutination.   They are, therefore, more complex than the simple receptors that unite with toxins, and are called *receptors of the second order.* According to Ohno[16] the reaction of agglutinin and antigen is in constant proportions, and seems to be a chemical rather than a physical reaction.   Coplans[17] finds this reaction associated with an increase in conductivity in the solutions, but whether this depends upon the agglutinin reaction itself, or upon associated processes, is questionable.

Agglutinated bacteria can be again separated from one another by the action of organic and inorganic acids, alkalies, acid salts, and by heating to 70° or 75°. and after once being separated they cannot be reagglutinated by fresh serum.[18]

The Mechanism of Agglutination.—This has been a fruitful field of research, in which the application of physical chemistry has been very profitable.   At first it was believed that the clumping was brought about by loss of motility, until it was found that non-motile bacilli were equally affected.   Similarly, the hypothesis of adhesion of the flagellæ was disposed of.   Gruber[19] and others supposed that a sticky substance, *"glabrificin,"* was absorbed from the serum by the bacilli, which caused them to adhere on contact with one another; but this does not explain the flocking together of non-motile bacilli. Paltauf considered that the specific precipitin (see next section) produced by immunization carried the bacilli down in the precipitate formed, and there is reason to believe that this reaction is of importance, but it does not explain all the facts of agglutination, nor is the relation between agglutinating and precipitating power of immune serums a constant one.   In support of this hypothesis is the observation of Scheller[20] that mixtures of typhoid bacilli and agglutinating serum lose their agglutinability by vigorous shaking, which may be interpreted as the result of disintegration of the agglutinating precipitate.   Shaking of either bacteria or serum alone is without effect.   Neisser and Friedemann[21] found that if the bacterial cells were saturated with lead acetate, washed in water until all soluble lead was removed, and then treated with H_2S, they were promptly agglutinated and precipitated, supporting other observations that indicate that precipitation within the bacterial cells can lead to agglutination. This sort of agglutination is related to the process of formation of

[15] Brit. Med. Jour., June 14, 1919.
[16] Philippine Jour. Sci., 1908 (3), 47.
[17] Jour. Path. and Bact., 1912 (17), 130.
[18] Eisenberg and Volk, Zeit. f. Infektionskr., 1902 (40), 192.
[19] For complete bibliography, see Craw, Jour. of Hygiene, 1905 (5), 113.
[20] Cent. f. Bakt., 1910 (54), 150.
[21] Münch. med. Woch., 1904 (54), 465 and 827.

coarse flocculi in solutions, and probably depends upon alterations in surface tension.

Bordet[22] made the important observation that agglutination does not occur if both the bacterial suspension and the agglutinating serum are dialyzed free from salts before mixing; but if, to such mixtures, a small amount of NaCl is added, agglutination and precipitation of the bacteria occur at once. This observation brought the phenomenon of bacterial agglutination into close relation with the precipitation of colloids by electrolytes, Bordet comparing it to the precipitation of particles of inorganic matter suspended in the fresh water of rivers that occurs when the fresh water meets the salt water of the ocean. He found that the agglutinin combined with the bacteria in the absence of the salts, and the resulting compound was precipitated by the addition of minute amounts of electrolytes,[23] which alone did not precipitate or agglutinate the bacteria or the serum. This indicates that the agglutinins cause a change in the bacteria which brings them under the same physical laws as the inorganic colloidal suspensions, which are characterized by being precipitated by the addition of traces of electrolytes.[24] This precipitation is undoubtedly due to changes in solution tension and surface tension (see "Precipitation of Colloids," introductory chapter). Before the agglutinin combines with the bacteria they behave like the colloidal solutions of organic colloids, being precipitated only by the salts of heavy metals, alcohol, formalin, etc., or by great concentrations of neutral salts. Field and Teague[25] have found that agglutinins carry positive charges while bacteria are negative, and that by the electric current agglutinins can be separated from bacteria with which they have combined; this shows that the agglutinin is not destroyed in the reaction. Teague and Buxton[26] consider that neutralization of the electric charge of the bacteria is not, however, the only important factor in agglutination.

According to Bechhold[27] normal bacteria behave like inorganic suspensions that have each particle protected by an albumin-like membrane, which prevents them from being thrown out of suspension by solutions of alkali salts, etc. After being acted on by agglutinin they are so altered that they behave like the unprotected inorganic suspensions, and are precipitated by salts and other electrolytes. This suggests the possibility that the agglutinin makes the bacteria

[22] Ann. d. l'Inst. Pasteur, 1899 (13), 225.
[23] Corroborated for sensitized red corpuscles by Eisner and Friedemann, Zeit. Immunität., 1914 (21), 520.
[24] Arrhenius (Zeit. physikal. Chem., 1903 (46), 415) has attempted to show that the gas laws are applicable to the partition of agglutinin between the bacteria and the medium, which he compares to the partition of iodin between water and carbon disulphid. This idea is not accepted by Craw (*loc. cit.*), nor by Dreyer and Douglas, Proc. Royal Soc., 1910 (82), 185.
[25] Jour. Exper. Med., 1907 (9), 86.
[26] Zeit. physikal. Chem., 1907 (57), 76.
[27] Zeit. f. physikal. Chem., 1904 (48), 385.

permeable for these electrolytes. Buxton and Shaffer[28] also found that bacteria which have been acted upon by agglutinin behave as if their proteins had been so changed that they are more capable of absorbing or combining with salts than when in their normal condition. Strong salt solutions inhibit agglutination by preventing the binding of the agglutinin.[29] Tulloch[30] observed that in the presence of salts of mono- and di-valent cations, unsensitized bacteria do not readily precipitate or agglutinate, but sensitized bacteria, as Bordet showed, agglutinate with small quantities of salts. In this respect unsensitized bacteria behave like "non-rigid colloids," such as fresh egg white, while sensitized bacteria resemble "rigid colloids," such as denatured egg white. Hence he advances the hypothesis that the process of sensitization is akin to that of denaturation of proteins, the specificity perhaps depending on different degrees of denaturation. Mansfeld[31] would bring agglutination into line with other serological reactions as a protein digestion process, by his hypothesis that bacteria are held in suspension by protective colloids which are digested by an enzyme, the agglutinin. He finds in favor of this hypothesis that the temperature and reaction curves correspond to enzyme actions, that agglutinating serum contains an enzyme digesting protein extracted from bacteria, and that during agglutination the agglutinogen is destroyed.

Agglutination obeys the same laws as other similar physical phenomena; the rate of agglutination depends upon the concentration of the suspension and of the electrolytes, and varies with the valence of the cations. Although bacteria in an electric stream move toward the anode like all suspensions, after being acted on by agglutinin they are agglutinated by the current between the poles;[32] this indicates the importance of the electrical charges of the bacterial surfaces in their agglutination reactions.

In all respects the behavior of bacteria and agglutinin resembles the behavior of colloidal mixtures in suspension (Neisser and Friedemann)[33] which form an electrically amphoteric colloidal suspension, so that the ions of electrolytes or the electric currents, by discharging them unequally, cause precipitation. Physico-chemical researches, however, have yet failed to explain the specific character of the agglutinins for specific bacteria, but Michaelis[34] has developed an interesting analogy in the specific agglutination of bacteria by acids. This

[28] Zeit. physikal. Chem., 1907 (57), 47.
[29] Landsteiner and St. Welecki, Zeit. Immunität., 1910 (8), 397.
[30] Biochem. Jour., 1914 (8), 293.
[31] Zeit. Immunität., 1918 (27), 197.
[32] Bechhold; however, Buxton and Teague (Kolloid Zeitschr., 1908, II, Suppl. 2) state that agglutinin bacteria *do* move towards the anode, but slower than normal bacteria.
[33] Münch. med. Woch., 1904 (51), 465 and 827; see also Girard-Mangin and Henri, Compt. Rend. Soc. Biol., 1904, vol. 56; and Zangger, Cent. f. Bakt. (ref.), 1905 (36), 225.
[34] Folia Serologica, 1911 (7), 1040; also Beniasch, Zeit. Immunität., 1912 (12), 268.

is based on the fact that the optimum concentration of H-ions which precipitates proteins from solution is characteristic and constant for each protein, and the same is true for the agglutination of bacteria by acids, the agglutination by acids being even more sharply specific in some cases than the agglutination by immune sera; *e. g.*, typhoid and paratyphoid bacilli are readily distinguished because the former are agglutinated by a concentration of H-ions from 4 to 8×10^{-5}, while paratyphoids require 16 to 32×10^{-5}, and colon bacilli are not agglutinated at all by acids. The acid agglutination, however, does not always affect all strains in the same way, some strains which are not readily agglutinable by antisera also resisting acid agglutination.[35] According to Arkwright,[36] typhoid bacilli contain two extractable proteins that are agglutinated by acids, one at 3.6×10^{-5} and the other at 1.1×10^{-3}; the former seems to be related to, if not identical with, the substance that is precipitated by immune serum. Apparently acid agglutination of bacteria belongs to the same class of reactions as the coagulation by H-ions of amphoteric colloids of preponderatingly acid character. Bacteria which have been sensitized by serum are more sensitive to acid agglutination than are normal bacteria.[37]

Alterations in the agglutinability of bacteria are marked, *e. g.*, strains of typhoid bacilli freshly cultivated from human infections may be practically inagglutinable even by active serum, but after prolonged cultivation on media they may or may not develop agglutinability. This phenomenon has not yet been satisfactorily explained, but it may depend on an active immunity of the bacteria against the agglutinins. Such bacteria injected into rabbits produce antisera that will agglutinate ordinary agglutinable strains, but not themselves; hence they do not lack agglutinogens. They give normal complement fixation reactions, and hence do not lack receptors, and they agglutinate with acids and chemicals much the same as ordinary agglutinable strains.[38] Moreover, identical strains of bacteria grown on media of different composition may show considerable variations in agglutinability (Dawson).[39]

Conglutination.—Under this term Bordet and Gay described the observation that in ox serum there is a substance which combines with corpuscles (or bacteria) that have been acted upon by agglutinating sera, and augments the agglutination.[40] Dean finds that, in general, agglutination requires two agents, one being the specific antibody, and the other a precipitable substance, probably a globulin. When cells have combined with the antibody the precipitable substance is aggregated on their surfaces, and, presumably, determines the agglutination. *Co-agglutination*, described by Bordet and Gengou as the agglutination by an antigen and the homologous antibody, of the corpuscles of another animal, is probably closely related to these phenomena (Dean).

[35] See Kemper, Jour. Inf. Dis., 1916 (18), 209.
[36] Zeit. Immunität., 1914 (22), 396; Jour. Hyg., 1914 (14), 261.
[37] Krumwiede and Pratt, Zeit. Immunität., 1913 (16), 517.
[38] McIntosh and McQueen, Jour Hyg., 1914 (12), 409.
[39] Jour. Bact., 1919 (4), 133.
[40] Literature given by Dean, Proc. Royal Soc. (B), 1911 (84), 416; Hall, Univ. Calif. Publ., Pathol., 1913 (2), 111.

PRECIPITINS[41]

If to a solution containing proteins we add in proper proportions the serum of an animal immunized against the same protein, a precipitate will soon form. While not absolutely specific, the quantitative specificity of the precipitin reaction is sufficiently characteristic to be of great value in biological, bacteriological, and medicolegal work, and it is of importance to the physiological chemist, since it furnishes a means of distinguishing between closely related forms of proteins, more delicate by far than any known chemical reagent. The serum reactions also prove that there are sometimes essential differences between the proteins of different species of animals, even when by all other methods these proteins seem to be practically identical; *e. g.*, lactalbumin of cow's milk is in some respect different from lactalbumin of goat's milk since it produces a different precipitin. Medicolegally they offer an accurate method of determining the origin of blood and serum stains, no matter how old the stain may be; thus Hansemann[42] found that material obtained from a mummy 5000 years old gave the precipitin reaction.[43]

Production of Precipitins.—For the production of the precipitation reaction it is necessary to have in the substance used for immunization a certain group, the *precipitinogen*, which when injected gives rise to production of *precipitin* by the animal. Apparently almost any protein may act as a precipitinogen if injected into the proper animal, but it *must be a foreign protein;* rabbit serum will not produce precipitins if injected into a rabbit,[44] probably because it is normally present in the blood of the rabbit and therefore does not stimulate any reaction; but certain chemical alterations in the proteins of an animal, such as heating, iodizing, or partial digestion, may render them so different from the normal proteins of the same animal that they will act as an antigen when present in the blood of that animal, or another of the same species, from which they were derived. Of the natural proteins of serum the globulins are much more active precipitinogens than the albumins. In general the more foreign the protein, the greater the amount of precipitin; closely related animals, *e. g.*, rabbit and guinea-pig, produce little precipitin for one another's proteins. This indicates distinctly that difference in species depends upon or is associated with difference in chemical composition of the proteins. Different species of animals have very different capacity for producing precipitins, rabbits producing active sera, while guinea-pigs can

[41] For complete bibliography of the subject of "Precipitins" see the résumé by Michaelis, Oppenheimer's Handb. d. Biochemie, 1909, II (1), 552; Kraus, Kolle and Wassermann's Handb., 1913, II; Uhlenhuth and Steffenhagen, *ibid.*, III, 257; Zinsser, "Infection and Resistance."
[42] Münch. med. Woch., 1904 (30), 572.
[43] Not corroborated by Schmidt, Zeit. allg. Physiol., 1907 (7), 369.
[44] Rarely a slight reaction against homologous proteins has been obtained (*isoprecipitins*).

produce but feebly precipitating sera. Cantacuzene[45] believes that precipitins are formed chiefly in the lymphoid tissues and bone marrow, and that the mononuclear macrophages are most active in their formation.[46] This view is supported by the observations of Hektoen,[47] that any agent that injures the bone marrow and lymphoid tissues (*e. g.*, Roentgen rays), tends to interfere with antibody production.

Apparently only proteins can produce precipitins; when split to the peptone stage they lose this property, but the proteins of serum resist tryptic digestion a long time before losing their precipitinogenic property,[48] which is destroyed much more quickly by pepsin-HCl mixtures. The precipitate itself is very resistant to disintegrative agencies, including putrefaction (Friedberger),[49] but is soluble in dilute acids and alkalies. It has the power of binding complement (Gay)[50] and if the complement causes solution of the precipitate, poisonous substances are formed (Friedberger). Excess of antigen prevents the formation of precipitate, or redissolves it, but excess of antiserum has no effect. Since both reacting substances are colloids they follow the laws governing other mutually precipitating colloids, and precipitation occurs only when they are brought together in concentrations that lie within definite zones of relative proportions. It is, of course, perfectly possible to have a union of precipitin and antigen without any visible precipitate occurring, since the product of the reaction is not necessarily insoluble under all conditions; in this case the occurrence of a reaction must be demonstrated by some other method, *e. g.*, the complement fixation reaction. At present it is not established that precipitins can be secured against lipoids or other non-protein substances. Possibly precipitins can be produced for closely related substances with molecules approximating in size the protein molecule, *e. g.*, certain substances present in supposedly protein-free filtrates of bacterial cultures. As with the agglutinin reaction, electrolytes must be present or precipitation will not occur. Neither the precipitin nor the antigen seems to be altered appreciably by the reaction, since when either is separated from the precipitate it retains its original properties.

Since precipitation of colloids is accompanied by or dependent upon an aggregation of their particles, the precipitin reaction is closely related to the agglutination reaction. The amount of precipitation obtained is much modified by the amount of inorganic salts present, and, according to Friedemann,[51] there is a general resem-

[45] Ann. Inst. Pasteur, 1908 (22), 54.
[46] Spleen tissue cultivated artificially in the presence of horse serum produces specific precipitins for horse serum, and tissue from the spleen of a guinea pig that has received injections of horse serum also develops precipitins for horse serum when grown in cultures (Pryzgode, Wien. klin. Woch., 1914 (27), 201).
[47] Jour. Infect. Dis., 1915 (17), 415; 1918 (22), 28.
[48] Fleischmann, Zeit. klin. Med., 1906 (59), 515.
[49] Cent. f. Bakt., 1907 (43), 490.
[50] See Univ. of Calif. Publ. Pathol., 1911 (2), 1.
[51] Arch. f. Hyg., 1906 (55), 361.

blance between the precipitin reactions and the precipitations occurring when colloids precipitate one another; *i. e.*, when an amphoteric colloid reacts with either an acid or a basic colloid.[52]   So far, however, attempts to interpret the precipitin reaction, as Arrhenius has tried to do, on the basis of the laws of physical chemistry, have not met with much success (Michaelis).   We prefer the attitude of Krogh,[53] who states that the colloidal chemical part of immunological reactions is to be looked upon as only a preliminary step to the real chemical process that completes the reaction and gives it the specific characters. As mentioned in the preceding section, agglutination of bacteria is believed to be independent of the precipitins, although very probably influenced by them.   As with all the other substances of this class, the precipitins have a haptophore group by which they unite to the protein molecule, and another group by which they produce the change resulting in precipitation.   When the latter group is destroyed by heating to 72°, the precipitin is converted into a *precipitoid*, which possesses the property of preventing the precipitation of unheated precipitin by the specific antigen.[54]

The immune serum contains the *precipitin*, which is the passive reagent that is thrown down by a trace of the immunizing material (precipitinogen).   The resulting precipitate is the insoluble modification of the previously dissolved precipitin, and originates chiefly or entirely in the proteins of the immune serum,[55] according to the work of Welsh and Chapman, especially.   But as the precipitate is able to sensitize anaphylactically, both actively and passively, it would seem that it must contain both the antibody (which confers passive sensitization) and antigen, to cause active sensitization (Weil).[56]   The precipitate may, when of maximum amount, contain more nitrogen than corresponds to the entire euglobulin of the immune serum, and the euglobulin contains all the precipitin, so it seems probable that the precipitate consists of more than the precipitin alone; it may be added that the precipitate is always less in amount than the total globulin of the antiserum.[57]   It is always greater when the reaction is between homologous antiserum and antigen, than with even closely related but heterologous antigens,[58] so that the quantitative measurement of the amount of precipitate is of value in applying this reaction to determine the nature of protein solutions.   The dilution of the reacting solutions is of influence, however, for if in too dilute solutions weak

[52] See Friedemann and Friedenthal, Zeit. exp. Path. u. Ther., 1906 (3) 73; Iscovesco, Compt. Rend. Soc. Biol., 1906, Vol. 61, and subsequent volumes.
[53] Jour. Infect. Dis., 1916 (19), 452.
[54] Precipitinogens are relatively resistant to moderate heating, and heated extracts of bacteria are used for precipitin tests under the name *thermoprecipitins*. See review by A. Ascoli, Virchow's Arch., 1913 (213), 182.
[55] Moll, Zeit. exp. Path. u. Ther., 1906 (3), 325; Welsh and Chapman, Proc. Royal Soc., B., 1908 (80), 161; Zeit. Immunität., 1911 (9), 517.
[56] Jour. Immunol., 1916 (1), 35.
[57] Franceschelli, Arch. f. Hyg., 1907 (69), 207.
[58] Welsh and Chapman, Jour. Hygiene, 1910 (10), 177.

precipitins may fail to give reactions; with strong precipitins the influence of dilution is much less (Michaelis).

According to the source of the protein used we recognize *bacterial precipitins, phyto-precipitins* (for plant proteins),[59] and *zoöprecipitins* (for animal proteins). Although tissue extracts, body fluids, and exudates are generally used in immunizing, purified constituents of these protein mixtures will also excite precipitin formation, *e. g.*, we may immunize with caseinogen as well as with milk. Complete pepsin digestion of proteins deprives them both of their precipitability and their power to produce precipitins, the former property being lost first. Trypsin seems to produce the same effect more slowly.

Some of the fractions of protein cleavage may be slightly precipitinogenic (Fink).[60] Heating to coagulation—indeed, heating in the autoclave— does not destroy the precipitinogenous property of proteins, but modifies somewhat the reactions of the precipitin obtained,[61] and precipitinogen is destroyed by alkalies. The specificity of precipitinogens is so modified by heating that the precipitins engendered by a boiled antigen react with the boiled antigen and with similarly heated antigens from other species, but not with unheated antigens even from the homologous species.[62]

As proteins introduced into the stomach are normally destroyed before being absorbed, they do not enter the blood and cause precipitin formation. However, as is well known, eating of excessive amounts of egg-albumen or other easily absorbed proteins may result in their passing the barriers and entering the blood stream, and in this way precipitins have been experimentally produced. Presumably the precipitin reaction is a means of throwing such foreign proteins out of solution and rendering them harmless. According to Zinsser[63] and others, the function of the precipitin is to sensitize the unformed foreign proteins to the digestive complement, a view in harmony with the prevailing tendency to correlate the immunity reaction with defense through enzymatic hydrolysis.

Precipitin appears in the blood generally about six days after injection of the protein, but disappears after injection of each subsequent dose of protein, to reappear again after a somewhat shorter lapse of time. After injections are stopped, the precipitin disappears rather rapidly, but never appears in the urine, although it

---

[59] Literature on precipitins for vegetable proteins given by Wells and Osborne, Jour. Infect. Dis., 1911 (8), 66.

[60] Jour. Infect. Dis., 1919 (25), 97.

[61] See Obermayer and Pick, who consider in detail the effects of various modifications of proteins upon their power to incite precipitin formation (Wien. klin. Woch., 1906 (19), 327); also Landsteiner and Lampl, Biochem. Zeit., 1918 (86), 343. The precipitability of the serum, or its power to produce precipitins, is not affected by disease (Pribram, Zeit. exp. Path. u. Ther., 1906 (3), 28).

[62] Schmidt, Biochem. Zeit., 1908 (14), 294; 1910 (24), 45; Zeit. Immunität., 1912 (13), 173; also Zinsser, "Infection and Resistance," 1914, p. 260.

[63] Jour. Exper. Med., 1912 (15), 529; 1913 (18), 219.

may enter the fetal blood from the blood of pregnant female animals. The presence of precipitins in the blood does not seem to prevent the excretion of the foreign protein in the urine, nor are the animals less susceptible to the toxic action of the foreign protein; indeed, the reaction is even stronger in the immunized animals, and sometimes the ordinary dose becomes fatal. Precipitin and antigen may coexist ununited in the circulating blood under certain conditions.[64] Certain antibodies are carried down with the precipitates formed when the serum containing them reacts under proper conditions with an antiserum; e. g., diphtheria antitoxin is precipitated when added to the serum of a rabbit immunized to horse serum. This is not true of all antibodies, however.[65] As the precipitates formed in the precipitin reaction, when injected into a guinea-pig make it passively hypersensitive to the protein used as antigen in the precipitin reaction, it would seem that the precipitin and the anaphylactin are identical (Weil),[66] or at least closely associated.

Chemical Properties.—In its *chemical nature* precipitin resembles the "antibodies" generally, being precipitated in the euglobulin fraction of the serum,[67] and slowly destroyed by trypsin, rapidly by pepsin. It cannot be separated from the serum proteins. The precipitation by precipitins is not an enzyme action, for the precipitins are used up in the process. It apparently does not differ from precipitations of colloids by other colloids of opposite electrical charges, except in that the reaction is specific.

OPSONINS[68]

The correlation of phagocytic and serum immunity was accomplished when A. E. Wright showed that, before any considerable phagocytosis of bacteria can take place, the bacteria must first be acted upon by serum, which in some way prepares them to be ingested by the leucocytes. The hypothetical substances accomplishing this sensitization of the bacteria were called opsonins by Wright and they exist to a certain extent in normal serum, being increased by immunization. Not only bacteria, but cellular elements in general, including especially red corpuscles, and even unorganized particles (such as melanin),[69] are sensitized for phagocytosis by opsonins. Probably phagocytosis by endothelial[70] and other cells also requires sensitization of the bacteria by opsonins. Although there have been many expressions of the opinion that the opsonins are not distinct antibodies, but are identical with agglutinins, bacteriolytic amboceptors, or other antibodies, there is much evidence to the contrary.[71] However, the union of opsonin and bacteria seems to follow the same quantitative laws as other antigen-antibody reactions (Amato).[72]

There are two opsonizing elements in serum, one thermostable and one thermolabile, it being the former which is increased during immunization; the thermostable

[64] Bayne-Jones, Jour. Exp. Med., 1917 (25), 837.
[65] See Gay and Stone, Jour. Immunol., 1916 (1), 83.
[66] Jour. Immunol., 1916 (1), 1.
[67] Funck (Cent. f. Bakt. (Ref.), 1905 (36), 744) states that if the precipitin serum is very strong, part of the precipitin comes down in the pseudoglobulin.
[68] Bibliography given by Neufeld, Kolle and Wassermann's Handbuch, 1913 (2), 440.
[69] Shattock and Dudgeon, Proc. Royal Soc. (B), 1908 (80), 165.
[70] Briscoe, Jour. Path. and Bact., 1907 (12), 66. See also Manwaring and Coe, who found that the Kupffer cells can take up only opsonized pneumococci (Proc. Soc. Exp. Biol., 1916 (13), 171).
[71] See Hektoen, Jour. Infec. Dis., 1909 (6), 78; 1913 (12), 1.
[72] Sperimentale, 1918 (71), 459.

element unites firmly with the object which is to be opsonized, while the thermo-labile element seems to remain free in the fluid (Hektoen).[73]

It would seem that opsonization and phagocytosis constitute but one of a series of similar processes by which foreign proteins are removed from the blood and tissues; *i. e.*, by lysis by extracellular enzymes when this is possible, as it is with simple protein aggregates (albuminolysis)and with some of the more labile cells (hemolysis, bacteriolysis); but in the case of more resistant structures, notably Gram-positive cocci and acid-fast bacilli, extracellular lysis being unsuccessful, these protein structures are taken within the cells where a greater concentration of enzymes may destroy them. *Fundamentally serum bacteriolysis and phagocytosis seem to be the same—in each case specific antibody sensitization prepares the bacterium for lysis by enzymes, either inside or outside the cells that furnish the lytic enzyme.*

As yet nothing is known concerning the change brought about in the bacteria by the opsonin, although it has been established that it is the bacteria that are modified and not the leucocytes. The chemical nature of the opsonins is likewise unknown, except that they may combine with certain inorganic ions and are then inert (Hektoen and Ruediger),[74] since addition of $CaCl_2$, $BaCl_2$, $SrCl_2$, $MgCl_2$, K_2SO_4, $NaHCO_3$, sodium oxalate and potassium ferrocyanide, inhibit the opsonic effect of serum. On the contrary, calcium salts stimulate the phagocytic effect of leucocytes, salts of barium and strontium being inactive.[75] In common with other immune bodies, opsonins are thrown down in the soluble serum globulins.[76] They are very sensitive to acids and alkalies, being destroyed by a concentration of $n/_1$ and their maximum effect is at the neutral point.[77] However, treatment of either the bacteria or the leucocytes with very weak acids or alkalies, increases the rate and amount of phagocytosis (Oker-Blum).[78] Opsonins may be developed by immunizing against substances practically free from protein, *e. g.*, melanin granules.[79] Injection of nuclein preparations may increase the amount of opsonin present in the blood.[80] Cholesterol in excess diminishes phagocytosis, but apparently through its action on the leucocytes.[81] Both the sensitization of bacteria and their ingestion by leucocytes, either with or without sensitization, take place in accordance with the laws regulating an adsorption process (Ledingham,[82] Schütze[78]).

THE MEIOSTAGMIN REACTION

Reaction of antigens with their specific antibodies results in lowering the surface tension of the solution in which the reaction occurs, which may be demonstrated by counting the number of drops of the fluid per minute, under constant conditions. Ascoli and Izar[83] worked out methods for practical application of this phenomenon, giving it the name of "meiostagmin reaction," from the Greek, meaning "small drop." The number of drops from a stalagmometer is counted, and an increase of two or more per minute is considered a positive reaction, after two hours' incubation of the reacting mixture; the increase is seldom above eight drops. This reaction is said to be sharply specific and extremely delicate, detecting antigens diluted up to 1 in 100,000,000 or more. The antigens used are soluble

[73] Sawtchenko (Arch. Sci. Biol., 1910 (15), 145; 1911 (16), 161) holds that there are two steps in phagocytosis: (1) Fixation of the bacteria to the leucocyte because of modification of surface tension by the fixative substance (opsonin or amboceptor-complement complex); (2) Ameboid motion of the phagocyte; an entirely independent phenomenon. Neither phase of phagocytosis can occur in the absence of electrolytes.

[74] Jour. Infect. Dis., 1905 (2), 129.
[75] Hamburger, Biochem. Zeit., 1910 (24), 470; 1910 (26), 66.
[76] See Simon *et al.*, Jour. Exp. Med., 1906 (8), 651; Heinemann and Gatewood, Jour. Infec. Dis., 1912 (10), 416.
[77] Noguchi, Jour. Exp. Med., 1907 (9), 454.
[78] Zeit. Immunität., 1912 (14), 485; Schütze, Jour. Hyg., 1914 (14), 201.
[79] Ledingham, Zeit. Immunität., 1909 (3), 119.
[80] Bedson, Jour. Path. and Bact., 1914 (19), 191.
[81] Dewey and Nuzum, Jour. Infect. Dis., 1914 (15), 472.
[82] Jour. Hyg., 1912 (12), 320.
[83] Münch. med. Woch., 1910 (57), 62, 182 and 403.

in alcohol but their nature is unknown; the antibody involved in the reaction is referred to as the meiostagmin, but its relation to other antibodies is likewise unknown.

THE EPIPHANIN REACTION

Besides reduction in surface tension, other physico-chemical changes result from antigen-antibody reactions, including the rate of diffusion, the osmotic pressure, and, in consequence, according to Weichardt, the neutral point to phenol-phthalein of a mixture of barium hydroxide and sulphuric acid, is also changed towards the acid side by antigen-antibody reactions taking place in the mixture.[84] This phenomenon has been utilized by Weichardt, under the name of "epiphanin reaction," to determine the occurrence of such interaction of antigen and antibody. The reaction probably depends upon absorption phenomena, but the exact nature of the change is not yet understood. According to Rosenthal,[85] the epiphanin reaction is especially suitable for demonstrating cancer antibodies and antigens, but Burmeister[86] and others have not been successful with this procedure.

[84] See Weichardt, Berl. klin. Woch., 1911 (48), 1935; Rosenthal, Zeit. Immunität, 1912 (13), 383; Angerer and Stötter, Münch med. Woch., 1912 (59), 2035.

[85] Zeit. Chemotherapie, 1912 (1), 156.

[86] Jour. Infec. Dis., 1913 (12), 459.

CHAPTER VIII

CHEMISTRY OF THE IMMUNITY REACTIONS (Continued). ANAPHYLAXIS OR ALLERGY, ABDERHALDEN REACTION.

ANAPHYLAXIS OR ALLERGY

In many instances the injection of a foreign protein into an animal produces severe, perhaps fatal, intoxication. With some proteins this natural toxicity is very marked,—thus eel serum is fatal to rabbits and dogs in doses of 0.1 to 0.3 c.c. per kilo, and foreign sera are commonly toxic to other animals; e. g., fresh bovine and human serum are quite toxic to guinea-pigs. This so-called "primary" toxicity is reduced or destroyed in most cases by heating to 56° for 30 minutes.[1] Almost any non-toxic soluble protein, however, may be made toxic for animals by giving the animal a small dose of this same protein at least eight days previously. This preliminary dose, which may be extremely minute,[2] renders the animal hypersensitive to the same protein, so that a relatively small quantity (a few milligrams in the case of the guinea-pig) of an otherwise entirely harmless protein, such as egg white or milk, produces violent, often fatal, symptoms when introduced into the blood of the animal. We shall not discuss the general features of the reaction, its history and its relation to biology and pathology, which are fully covered in many easily accessible reviews,[3] but shall limit our consideration to the more definitely chemical aspects of the reaction.[4]

The Substances Involved (Anaphylactogens).—As far as now known, these are always proteins, and with the exception of gelatin[5]

[1] The nature of the toxic agent is unknown, but there is reason to believe that it is formed, at least in part, during the coagulation of the drawn blood.

[2] Julian Lewis has found that if a very small amount of protein is injected at the same time as a large dose of another foreign protein, no sensitization results to the former; presumably the available cell receptors are occupied by the protein given in larger amounts. (Jour. Infect. Dis., 1915 (17), 241.)

[3] Doerr, Kolle and Wassermann's Handbuch, 1913, Vol. II; and Zeit. f. Immunität., 1910; (2. ref.), 49; also v. Pirquet, Arch. Int. Med., 1911 (7), 259; Friedmann, Jahresber. Ergeb. Immunitätfrsch., 1911 (6), 31; Schittenhelm, ibid., p. 115; Hektoen, Jour. Amer. Med. Assoc., 1912 (58), 1081; Zinsser, Arch. Int. Med., 1915 (16), 223. Concerning anaphylaxis in man see Longcope, Amer. Jour. Med. Sci., 1916 (152), 625. Concerning cutaneous reactions see Kolmer, Bull. Johns Hopkins Hosp., 1917 (28), 163.

[4] Many of the chemical features of anaphylaxis I have covered in the following series of articles: Jour. Inf. Dis., 1908 (5), 449; 1909 (6), 506; 1911 (8), 66; 1911 (9), 147; 1913 (12), 341; 1914 (14), 364 and 377; 1915 (17), 259; 1916 (19), 183.

[5] Wells, Jour. Amer. Med. Assoc., 1908 (50), 527; Jour. Infect. Dis., 1908 (5), 459; Starin, Jour. Infect. Dis., 1918 (23), 139.

and a few others, practically any soluble protein will produce sensitization and intoxication of susceptible animals, i. e., almost any soluble protein may be an anaphylactogen. As with the other immunity reactions, observations have been made which are interpreted as indicating that non-protein substances can produce this reaction, but these interpretations are not generally accepted. (See Antigens, Chap. vii.) It is possible, however, for non-protein substances to combine with or alter the proteins of an animal so that they become as foreign proteins to that animal, and thus cause sensitization; in this way can be explained apparent anaphylactic reactions to iodin and arsenic compounds and other non-protein substances.[6] As far as my own experiments show, nothing less than an entire protein molecule will suffice, the products of protein cleavage all being inactive.[7] Zunz[8] and Fink,[9] however, report some positive results with proteoses. Presumably the inefficiency of gelatin as an anaphylactogen depends upon its deficiency in aromatic radicals, since these radicals have been shown (Vaughan, Obermeyer and Pick) to be particularly important in immunological reactions. It is not necessary for a protein to contain all the known amino-acids of proteins to be active, however, for certain vegetable proteins (zein, hordein, gliadin) which lack one or more of such amino-acids as glycine, tryptophane, or lysine, produce typical reactions. Some compound proteins are efficient anaphylactogens (mucin,[10] casein) but with alpha-nucleoproteins which have been thoroughly purified I have obtained only negative results;[11] as also with histon and nucleic acid, the isolated components of nucleins. Globin, from hemoglobin, is also non-antigenic. Bacterial substances, extracts of plant tissues, purified plant proteins, and proteins obtained from invertebrates and cold-blooded vertebrates, have all been found to be anaphylactogens, if they can be introduced by any means into the blood or tissues in a soluble unaltered condition.

If the proteins are rendered insoluble by coagulation they become inert, but proteins which cannot be made insoluble by heating (e. g., casein, ovomucoid) withstand boiling temperatures. Trypsin destroys anaphylactogens in just the same proportion as it splits the protein

[6] See Böttner (Deut. Arch. klin. Med., 1918 (125), 1), concerning collargol anaphylaxis.
[7] Abderhalden (Zeit. physiol. Chem., 1912 (81), 314) states that he has obtained a positive reaction with a synthetic polypeptid containing 14 amino-acid molecules, including only leucine and glycocoll. E. Zunz (Jour. physiol. path. gén., 1917 (17), 449) reports obtaining positive results with much simpler polypeptids (3–5 glycylglycine). These reactions consisted in changes in blood pressure and coagulability in rabbits, and we do not know whether typical shock can be obtained in guinea pigs with these peptids.
[8] Zunz (Zeit. Immunität., 1913 (60), 580).
[9] Jour. Infect. Dis., 1919 (25), 97.
[10] Elliott, Jour. Infect. Dis., 1914 (15), 501.
[11] See review in Zeit. Immunität., 1913 (19), 599, concerning alpha-nucleoproteins, which is the type usually designated as "nucleoproteins." I have found beta-nucleoproteins to be more effective antigens (Jour. Biol. Chem., 1916 (28), 11).

molecules; thus, globulins resist trypsin longer than albumins, both as regards coagulability and anaphylactic activity. Acids, alkalies and other chemical agents may modify the reactivity of proteins in proportion to the changes in solubility or constitution which they produce.[12]

The amounts of protein necessary to produce reactions in guinea-pigs are very small. With crystallized egg albumin sensitivity has been produced with one twenty-millionth of a gram (0.000,000,05 gm.) and fatal reactions are obtained after sensitization with one-millionth of a gram. No other animal seems to be so sensitive to this reaction as the guinea-pig, however, and rabbits and dogs require larger, and in many instances, repeated doses to render them anaphylactic. Within certain limits large doses are less effective in sensitizing guinea-pigs than small, e. g., one milligram of most proteins will usually be much more effective than one hundred milligrams. White and Avery[13] found that there is a certain relation between the minimum sensitizing and the minimum intoxicating dose; with extremely minute sensitizing doses a larger intoxicating dose is required to produce fatal reaction than when the sensitizing dose is larger. If too large intoxicating doses are used, however, the degree of reaction may be lowered.[14]

It is now generally assumed that both the sensitizing and intoxicating agent are (or are derived from) one and the same protein, but the minimum intoxicating dose is always larger than the minimum sensitizing dose; thus, with pure egg albumin the minimum lethal dose for sensitized pigs was one-twentieth to one-tenth milligram by intravascular injection, or about one hundred times more than the minimum fatal sensitizing dose. With less soluble proteins the disparity is even greater, for with such the sensitizing dose is not much changed, but the minimum intoxicating dose is relatively much increased. Apparently an animal may be killed by much less antigen than is required to saturate the antibodies present in its body (Weil). The exact fate of the injected antigens is unknown. Manwaring[15] observed no loss in antigen perfused through organs of sensitized animals, but others have found that antigen injected subcutaneously disappears more rapidly in sensitized or immunized than in normal animals.[16]

The proteins concerned must be foreign to the circulating blood of the injected animal, but they may be tissue proteins of the same animal (e. g., placenta elements, organ extracts, lens proteins) which are not normally present in its blood. Indeed it has been claimed that by injecting a guinea-pig with the dissolved lens of one eye it

[12] See Dold and Aoki, Cent. f. Bakt., Ref. Beilage 1912 (54), 246.
[13] Jour. Infect. Dis., 1913 (13), 103.
[14] Terry and Andrews, Proc. Soc. Exp. Biol. Med., 1915 (12), 176.
[15] Jour. Immunol., 1917 (2), 511.
[16] G. H. Smith and Cook, Jour. Immunol., 1917 (2), 269.

13

will become sensitized so that it will react to a subsequent injection of the lens from the other eye.[17]   In general, tissue proteins are less active antigens than the proteins of the blood, lymph, and secretions, but even keratins may produce anaphylaxis when dissolved[18] and positive results have been obtained with proteins from mummies.[19]

The Poisonous Agent (Anaphylatoxin).—The symptomatology of the intoxication which follows injection of the protein into an animal sensitized with the same protein, is such as to indicate that a poison is responsible, although as yet the poison has not been isolated.   As the symptom complex is practically the same no matter what sort of protein is being used, it would seem that the poison must always be the same or similar—no matter how varied the nature of the proteins capable of inciting anaphylactic intoxication.   Probably the poison is a product of cleavage of protein by tissue or blood enzymes, which act only in the presence of the specific antibodies which unite the protein to the enzyme (or complement).   Vaughan and his collaborators showed that proteins boiled with an alcoholic NaOH solution might be split into two fractions, one toxic and alcohol-soluble, the other non-toxic and insoluble in alcohol.   The toxic fraction gives all the protein reactions (except that of Molisch for carbohydrates) and in doses of 8 to 100 mg. kills guinea-pigs with symptoms practically identical with those of anaphylactic intoxication.   The uniformity of the toxic effects with preparations from different sorts of proteins suggests the existence in every protein molecule of some fundamental toxic group, common to all proteins, the specificity residing in other non-toxic attached groups. This and other observations led him to the hypothesis that specific enzymes are developed in response to the presence of foreign proteins in the blood stream, and that upon injection of a second dose of the same protein these enzymes at once disintegrate it, and some of the cleavage products being toxic the anaphylactic intoxication results.   Many of the later developments in this field, especially Abderhalden's studies on "protective ferments," have added support to this hypothesis, so that in its fundamental conceptions it is now the most generally favored explanation of the processes involved in anaphylaxis.[20]

Friedberger carried the matter a step farther by showing that if serum from a sensitized animal is incubated for a short time with the same protein, and in the presence of enough complement, a poison is developed which produces the typical symptoms of anaphylactic intoxication when injected into guinea-pigs.   This poison resists heating at 56°, but not at 65°, and is not a true toxin, for it will not produce

[17] Uhlenhuth and Haendel, Zeit. f. Immunität., 1910 (4), 761.
[18] Krusius, Arch. f. Augenheilk., Suppl., 1910 (47), 47; Clough, Arb. kais. Gesundhtsamte, 1911 (34), 431.
[19] Uhlenhuth, Zeit. f. Immunität., 1910 (4), 774.
[20] See Vaughan, Amer. Jour. Med. Sci., 1913 (145), 161; Zeit. Immunität., 1911 (9), 458.   Also a full review in his "Protein Split Products," Philadelphia, 1913.

an antitoxic immunity. In the absence of complement, or when the complement fixation is prevented by strong salt solution,[21] the poison (anaphylatoxin) does not develop, so that the anaphylactic reaction falls into the same class as the lytic reactions, in which the non-specific serum complement is united to a cell by the specific amboceptor, and then causes lysis of the cell; in anaphylaxis not an organized cell but a complex protein molecule is disintegrated by the complement, but in either case a poisonous substance may be liberated.

This agrees with Vaughan's hypothesis in ascribing the poisoning to products of protein disintegration formed by enzyme action, but differs in that specific intermediary substances or amboceptors are supposed to be developed by sensitization, rather than specific enzymes. Friedberger is of the opinion that many or all the different immunity reactions depend upon a single antibody, the different reactions merely being different methods of demonstrating the presence of the antibody in the serum. The precipitin reaction differs from the anaphylactic reaction, he contends, only in that in the latter the specific precipitate is dissolved by complement, yielding the anaphylatoxin. There are many objections[22] to accepting this idea in its entirety which we shall discuss later, but the formation of a poison resembling that of anaphylaxis, by a digestive action of complement fixed to the antigen by the antibody, seems to be well established, both as regards *in vitro* and *in vivo* reactions.

It would seem probable that proteins may yield a similar poison in whatever way their hydrolysis is brought about, provided the cleavage is not too deep-seated. For example, Rosenow[23] has found that pneumococci and other bacteria, permitted to autolyze for a proper length of time, produce poisonous substances with all the toxicologic characters of the anaphylatoxin. Too extensive autolysis again destroys the poison, which is also produced by digestion of pneumococci with serum from normal guinea-pigs, and more rapidly with serum from sensitized animals, which likewise causes a demonstrably more rapid proteolysis. The pneumococcus anaphylatoxic poison is soluble in ether and seems to be a base, containing amino-acids, but Friedberger did not find anaphylatoxin made from serum proteins to be soluble in ether or alcohol, nor was it precipitated with the globulins. The so-called "Abderhalden method" of sero-diagnosis of pregnancy, which depends on the presence of specific proteolytic properties in the blood, is an especially studied instance of these principles, and is discussed later.

Presumably anaphylactic intoxication is but an exaggeration of the normal process of defense of the body against foreign proteins (including

---

[21] Friedberger's explanation of the inhibiting effect of salt as interference with complement action, has been questioned. (See Zinsser, Arch. Int. Med., 1915 (16), 238.)

[22] See Besredka *et al.*, Zeit. Immunität., 1912 (16), 249.

[23] Jour. Infec. Dis., 1912 (11), 94 and 235.

bacteria) through digestion. Normally this is accomplished in the alimentary tract, and complete disintegration past the toxic stage is made certain by the presence of erepsin in the intestinal wall; but if intact foreign protein molecules reach the blood in any way, this same digestive destruction is performed by the enzymes of the blood or tissues. So abnormal is the "parenteral" introduction of foreign proteins that, once it has happened, the protective mechanism is stimulated to the production of large amounts of proteolytic substances, and on this account if another quantity of the same protein is again parenterally introduced the breaking down of the protein is extremely rapid. Certain of the disintegration products are toxic, but with the normal rate of disintegration the amount present at any one time is inadequate to cause poisoning; when the proteolysis is accelerated, as in the sensitized animal, a poisonous dose may be produced, with the resulting anaphylactic intoxication.[24] Whether this proteolysis takes place both in the blood and tissues is not known. It has been found that the specific proteolytic power of the blood is increased in sensitized animals, but on the other hand, there is evidence that without the intervention of the liver (at least in dogs) anaphylactic intoxication cannot take place (Manwaring and others).[25] During the reaction, in any event, products of protein hydrolysis appear in the blood (Abderhalden),[26] but there is no demonstrable destruction or binding of the injected foreign protein.[15]

Among possible cleavage products of proteins which may be the toxic agent in anaphylaxis, is β-imidazolylethylamine ("histamine"), which is derivable from histidine, and which produces effects resembling acute anaphylactic intoxication.[27] Not only does histamine cause marked fall in blood pressure, bronchial spasm in guinea-pigs and obstruction to the pulmonary circulation in rabbits, but also when applied locally it causes marked urticaria resembling closely that of anaphylaxis. Methylguanidine is said to produce somewhat similar but slighter symptoms,[28] and to protect sensitized animals from toxic doses of the antigenic protein.[29] Other amines possibly may be involved. (See Chapter iv, Ptomaïns; Chapter xxi, Pressor Bases.)

The relation of the normal toxicity of certain foreign sera to anaphylactic intoxication has not been determined, but there seem to be

[24] Heilner (Zeit. Biol., 1912 (58), 333) believes that the anaphylactic poisons are substances which normally are destroyed by proteolysis, but that in the sensitized animals there is a depressed catabolism which prevents their destruction.
[25] Falls found that a larger intoxicating dose must be injected into the portal system to produce the same effects than by peripheral injection. (Jour. Infect. Dis., 1918 (22), 83.)
[26] Zeit. physiol. Chem., 1912 (82), 109.
[27] See Barger, "The Simpler Natural Bases," London, 1914, p. 30.
[28] Heyde, Cent. f. Physiol., 1911 (25), 411; 1912 (26), 401.
[29] Burns, Jour. Physiol., 1918 (52), xxxix.

both definite similarities and differences,[30] which have been discussed by Loewit;[31] chief of these differences is the absence of the bronchial spasm with pulmonary emphysema which is characteristic of anaphylaxis in guinea-pigs.

The anaphylactic poison would seem to be after the order of the alkaloidal poisons, at least from the pharmacological standpoint, since it produces its effects quickly, and these effects, no matter how severe, are strictly transitory, passing off completely in a few hours, which indicates that (like morphine, strychnine, etc.) they do not produce any deep-seated structural alterations in the tissues. According to Schultz[32] the chief effects are directly on the smooth muscles. Such anatomical alterations as are produced, of which hemorrhages and waxy degeneration of the voluntary muscles of respiration[33] are most noticeable, are ascribable to the effect on respiration, which in the guinea-pig often amounts to total asphyxiation through spasm of the musculature of the bronchioles (Auer and Lewis)[34] with profound permanent emphysematous distension of the lungs. This effect is peripheral, and is inhibited by atropine.[35] Calcium salts also reduce anaphylactic reactions.[36] The poisonous fraction obtained from proteins by Vaughan's method resembles anaphylatoxin in that it causes a fall in blood pressure by paralyzing the vasomotor endings in the blood vessels (Edmunds[37]). It also produces local urticaria when rubbed into the skin and behaves much like histamine, with which, however, it is not identical. One gram of casein yields enough of Vaughan's poison to kill 800 guinea-pigs, and the poison seems to contain most of the aromatic radicals of the proteins. There is also

[30] It has been found that *organ extracts* are especially toxic to animals, but that this toxicity may be suppressed by a minute dose, for a few minutes later large doses can be injected with impunity, although the blood of the animal is highly toxic during the immune period, which is of brief duration. This condition is called *skepto-phylaxis*. (See Lambert, Ancel and Bouin, Compt. Rend. Acad. Sci., 1911 (154), 21.) Vaughan reports the finding in normal tissues of substances resembling his "protein poisons," which perhaps come from autolysis or tissue metabolism and may be related to the "primary toxicity" of organ extracts. N. R. Smith (Jour. Lab. Clin. Med., 1919 (4), 517, full review) would attribute this toxicity to the inorganic constituents of the extracts, especially the phosphorus compounds.

[31] Arch. exp. Path. u. Pharm., 1913 (73), 1. See also DeKruif and Eggerth. Jour. Infect. Dis., 1919 (24), 505.

[32] Bull. Hyg. Lab., U. S. P. H. and M. H. Service, 1912 (80), 1.

[33] See Cent. f. Pathol., 1912 (23), 945.

[34] In the rabbit the effects seem to be produced chiefly by spasm of the pulmonary arteries (Coca, Jour. Immunol., 1919 (4), 219) while the predominant hepatic and portal effects in dogs is attributed to the highly developed musculature of their hepatic veins by Simonds (Jour. Amer. Med. Assoc., 1919 (73), 1437).

[35] Jour. Exp. Med., 1910 (12), 151; Schultz, Jour. Pharm. and Exp. Ther., 1913 (3), 299.

[36] Kastle, Healy and Buckner, Jour. Infec. Dis., 1913 (12), 127.

[37] Zeit. Immunität., 1913 (17), 105. See also Underhill and Hendrix, Jour. Biol. Chem., 1915 (22), 465.

much other evidence of the importance of the aromatic radicals in anaphylaxis.[38]

Other effects of the anaphylactic toxin are leucopenia, local and general eosinophilia,[39] reduced coagulability of the blood,[40] and a severe fall of temperature unless the dose of antigen is very small when the temperature may rise.[41]   The antitrypsin content of the blood is not increased in the anaphylactic animal (Ando[42]).   Poisonous substances similar to anaphylatoxin appear in the urine during the anaphylactic intoxication (Pfeiffer).[43]   As with other poisons, anaphylatoxin produces different symptoms in different animals.[34]   In dogs the chief effects are a great fall in blood pressure,[44] loss of coagulability of the blood, hemorrhagic enteritis, but no bronchial spasm.   In rabbits the heart is severely affected, while in guinea-pigs there is a remarkable lack of interference with the heart, so that it beats long after respiration ceases.   A pressor substance has been found in the serum of intoxicated guinea-pigs, which is not present in the artificial anaphylatoxin and therefore presumably is produced in the body of the animal.[45]   In man the symptoms are most like those in the guinea-pig.   If the protein is injected into the skin of a sensitized animal there follows a severe local reaction—hyperemia, edema, even necrosis, —indicating that in this specific proteolysis, poisons are formed which have a profound local effect, especially on the blood vessels.   Repeated anaphylactic intoxication may result in structural changes in the kidneys, heart muscle and liver (Longcope[46]).   Metabolism studies may show an increased toxicogenic destruction of protein,[47] but the increase in amino-acids presumably resulting from proteolysis in the sensitized individual, is not large enough, if it does occur, to be significant.[48]   However, in anaphylaxis in guinea pigs, as well as after peptone poisoning, there is a considerable increase in noncoagulable and urea nitrogen in the blood, as well as a slight increase in amino nitrogen, but it is not known whether this comes from the tissues or from the antigen-antibody reaction in the blood.[48a]

[38] See Baehr and Pick, Arch. Exp. Path., 1913 (74), 73.

[39] Literature by Moschowitz, New York Med. Jour., Jan. 7, 1911; Schlecht and Schwenker, Arch. exp. Path. u. Pharm., 1912 (68), 163; Deut. Arch. klin. Med., 1912 (108), 405.

[40] See Bulger. Jour. Infect. Dis., 1918 (23), 522.

[41] See Vaughan, et al., Zeit. Immunität., 1911 (9), 458.

[42] Zeit. Immunität., 1913 (18), 1.

[43] Zeit. f. Immunität., 1911 (10), 550.

[44] Probably from influence upon the nerve endings of the vessels (Pearce and Eisenbrey, Jour. Infec. Dis., 1910 (7), 565).

[45] Hirschfeld, Zeit. Immunität., 1912 (14), 466.

[46] Jour. Exp. Med., 1913 (18), 678; 1915 (22), 793; also Boughton, Jour. Immunol., 1916 (1), 105; 1919 (4), 213.   Not confirmed by Bell and Hartzell, Jour. Infect. Dis., 1919 (24), 618.

[47] See Major, Deut. Arch. klin. Med., 1914 (116), 248.

[48] See Auer and Van Slyke, Jour. Exp. Med., 1913 (18), 210; Barger and Dale, Biochem. Jour., 1911 (8), 670.

[48a] See Hisanobu; Amer. Jour. Physiol., 1920 (50), 357.

There is, however, much doubt as to the identity of the process of anaphylatoxin formation (as it occurs when antigen, antibody and complement are incubated *in vitro*) and the process of anaphylactic intoxication. In the first place, a poisonous character, apparently identical with this "anaphylatoxin" may be given to serum without the use of any specific antibody whatever; merely agitating fresh serum with any finely divided foreign material that offers large total surfaces, such as kaolin, agar, or starch, is sufficient, as also is treatment with lipoid solvents, such as chloroform (Jobling). In fact, merely removing the fibrin from the plasma may make the resultant serum highly toxic, even for the very animal from which it came. Furthermore, if anaphylactic shock were the result of anaphylatoxin formation in the sensitized animal through the reaction of antigen with antibody and complement, the intoxication should occur if antibody and antigen are injected simultaneously into an animal; but as a matter of fact the animal receiving antibody in passive sensitization will not react unless the antigen is injected at least three hours after the sensitizing serum is injected.[49] This incubation period is supposed to be required for the anaphylactic antibody to be fixed in the cells where the reaction takes place (Otto), and perhaps, in modification of the antibody so that it has a greater affinity for the antigen than it has while free in the serum (Weil);[50] also in acquiring the capacity to affect the cells after union with the specific antigen. Finally, the isolated nonstriated muscle tissue (uterus) of a sensitized animal gives specific reactions when brought in contact with the specific antigen, no matter how thoroughly the animal's blood has been removed from the tissues; whereas, the uterine muscle of an animal injected with sensitizing immune serum only one hour before killing does not react when in contact with specific antigen. Weil disputes the toxic nature of anaphylaxis, even in the intracellular reaction, which he calls a "cellular discharge." He holds that in the guinea-pig the cellular reaction takes place chiefly in the nonstriated muscles, while in dogs the reaction is essentially hepatic, resulting in a profound congestion of the liver and consequent fall of blood pressure, decreased blood coagulability from hepatic action, and the increase in proteolytic products in the blood characteristic of all acute hepatic injuries.[51] Even in the guinea-pig, however, the liver is affected in anaphylactic shock, and Meinicke[52] adds to the evidence of cellular anaphylaxis by finding that the perfused liver of sensitized guinea-pigs reacts to antigen with a marked inhibition of its capacity to form urea from ammonium lactate.

Nevertheless, the formation of anaphylatoxin is an interesting phenomenon which may well be of importance in human intoxications,

[49] See Weil, Jour. Med. Res., 1914 (30), 87; Jour. Immunol., 1916 (1), 109.
[50] Jour. Med. Res., 1915 (32), 107.
[51] Jour. Immunol., 1917 (2), 525.
[52] Zeit. Immunität., 1918 (27), 489.

even if it is not the essential phenomenon of the anaphylactic intoxication. So readily is blood serum made toxic *in vitro* that it seems highly probable that a similar development of toxicity may take place in the body. Jobling[53] has found that intoxication from anaphylatoxin formation seems to occur when kaolin is injected intravenously into animals, and hence it is quite possible that the presence in the blood of abnormal, finely divided bodies, such as precipitated proteins, cellular fragments, even bacteria, may mechanically cause anaphylatoxin formation *in vivo* just as they do *in vitro*. It is necessary to distinguish, however, between the symptoms that result from capillary embolism and true anaphylaxis, failure to do this undoubtedly having caused many erroneous conclusions.[53a]

Recently it has been suggested that a process similar to anaphylactic intoxication is responsible for traumatic shock, disintegration of traumatized tissue proteins being the source of the toxic agent. (Quenu and Delbet, Cannon).[54]

The mechanism of anaphylatoxin formation is not yet understood but there is no lack of theories. The original explanation was that anaphylatoxin formation by specific antisera is the result of digestion of antigen *in vitro* by the action of complement united to the antigen by the immune antibody. For the formation of anaphylatoxin by inert finely divided particles the explanation advanced was that the highly developed surfaces of these particles either activated complement, or united it to the serum proteins so that it digested them. Jobling[55] has advanced the hypothesis that normal serum antiferments, which are believed by him to be lipoidal in nature, are bound by the particles or by specific precipitates, so that the complement is free to attack the serum proteins. In any case, it is now generally agreed that *the poisonous substance is derived chiefly, if not entirely from the serum of the intoxicated animal, and not from the antigen*, even in the case of anaphylatoxin formation by specific antigen-antibody-complement reactions.[56] This fact would seem to explain why the poison seems to be the same, as far as we can analyze it by pharmacological methods, no matter what protein is used as antigen, or whether produced by immune or by nonspecific reactions, or by chemical means, such as that of Vaughan.

Jobling, who holds to the importance of anaphylatoxin formation as the cause of anaphylactic intoxication, presents the following conception of anaphylaxis: During the course of sensitization there occurs the mobilization of a nonspecific protease, which is greatly increased during acute anaphylactic shock; at this time

[53] Jobling, Petersen and Eggstein, Jour. Exp. Med., 1915 (22), 590.
[53a] See Hanzlik and Karsner, Jour. Pharmacol., 1920 (14), 379.
[54] C. R. Soc. Biol., 1918 (71), 850; Rev. d. Chir., 1919 (38) 309.
[55] Zeit. Immunität., 1914 (23), 71; Jour. Exp. Med., 1915 (22), 401.
[56] That the antigen must be digestible, however, is suggested by the observation of Ten Broeck (Jour. Biol. Chem., 1914 (17), 369) that proteins racemized by Dakin's method, which cannot be digested by proteolytic enzymes, are unable to cause anaphylaxis.

there is also a decrease in antiferment which permits proteolysis of the animal's own proteins. As a result, there is to be found an increase in noncoagulable nitrogen and amino-acids of the blood, and a decrease in serum proteases. "The acute intoxication is brought about by the cleavage of serum proteins through the peptone stage by a non-specific protease. The specific elements lie in the rapid mobilization of this ferment and the colloidal serum changes which bring about the change in antiferment titer."

As a result of extensive studies, Novy and DeKruif have developed ideas concerning the nature of anaphylaxis quite different from those ordinarily held.[57] Following the observations of Bordet, and others, that incubation of fresh normal serum with agar renders it capable of producing symptoms resembling those of anaphylaxis, they have found reason to believe that the effects of bacteria may also depend on similar phenomena, rather than on hypothetical endotoxins. As little as 9 mg. of agar may produce fatal intoxication if injected in a suitable physical state intravenously into a guinea-pig. As perfectly dissolved Witte peptone or even distilled water also produce anaphylatoxin when mixed with serum, it seems improbable that the anaphylatoxin formation depends on surface phenomena. Apparently anaphylatoxin formation is closely associated with the coagulation of the blood, which becomes highly toxic in the early stages of clot formation. No evidence could be found of protein cleavage or enzyme action during the formation of anaphylatoxin. It is thought that in specific anaphylaxis the substance that induces the formation of anaphylatoxin is formed by the interaction of the antigen with the antibody. The process of anaphylatoxin formation parallels closely that of fibrin formation, to which it may be related. Anaphylatoxin is believed to be not a proteose but a larger molecular complex than serum albumin, possessing certain globulin characteristics. It is associated with the euglobulin fraction of the serum.[58]

These and many other observations in the literature support the idea that a change in the degree of dispersion of the blood colloids may be the fundamental matter in anaphylaxis.[59]

The Anaphylactic Antibody (Anaphylactin).—That anaphylaxis, like other immunity reactions, depends upon the presence of specific antibodies in the blood of the sensitized animal, is shown by the production of *passive anaphylaxis* in normal animals, by injecting into them a few cubic centimeters of blood or serum from a sensitized animal. Such animals become sensitive in a few hours to the specific antigen, no matter what species of animal furnishes the serum, showing that various anaphylactins can unite with the same complement, although strongly specific as to the antigen. In active sensitization the anaphylactin appears in the blood in appreciable quantities about eight days after the sensitizing injection, increases to a maximum between the 15th and 30th days, and then very slowly decreases. The reaction of antibody and antigen is strictly quantitative, as with all amboceptor reactions. The amount of antibody developed seems to be limited, for after a sensitized animal is given a sub-lethal intoxicating dose of protein it may be no longer sensitive to this protein, and this refractory or anti-anaphylactic condition persists for three weeks or more. It has been demonstrated especially conclusively by Weil and Coca,[60] that this refractory condition is, as Friedberger suggested, de-

[57] Jour. Infect. Dis., 1917 (20); recapitulation in Jour. Amer. Med. Assoc., 1917 (68), 1524.
[58] DeKruif and Eggerth, Jour. Infect. Dis., 1919 (24), 505. They state also that in primarily toxic sera the toxic element is associated with the pseudoglobulin.
[59] See Kritchewsky, Jour. Infect. Dis., 1918 (22), 101.
[60] Zeit. Immunität., 1913 (17), 141.

pendent upon saturation or exhaustion of all the anaphylactic antibodies, and hence the amount of these antibodies present free in the blood of a sensitized animal must be relatively small, for a few milligrams of the specific protein is sufficient to saturate them, *e. g.*, the amount of antibody present in 3 c.c. of serum from a guinea-pig sensitized with horse serum could be neutralized with from 0.0005 to 0.01 c.c. of horse serum.[61]   They are, however, very persistent, remaining in guinea-pigs through the entire life of an animal sensitized when young.   They also pass from the mother to the fetus, conferring a passive sensitization which, like passive sensitization from injection of serum from a sensitized animal, is of relatively brief duration, in contrast to the persistence of active sensitization.[62]   Anaphylactin, like amboceptor, resists heating at 56° for one hour, and is salted out from serum in the globulin fraction.[63]   It can be formed in animals made leukopenic with thorium-X.[64]   Friedberger contends that it is identical with the precipitin, a view yet under discussion,[64a] but strongly supported by Weil's observations.[65]

Weil[66] observed certain phenomena which led him to conclude that in anaphylaxis the specific antibody must be largely fixed in the cells, and that it is in the cells that the reaction occurs; apparently the antibodies present in the blood of the sensitized animal are insufficient to protect its cells from the foreign protein, hence the cellular intoxication.   In support of this idea is the observation of Dale[67] that the isolated smooth muscle of sensitized guinea-pigs is specifically sensitive to the foreign protein.   Weil states that "all the evidence proves conclusively that anaphylactic shock is induced by reaction between anchored antibody and antigen, and that circulating antibody plays absolutely no rôle in its production."

The anaphylactin shows quite the same characteristics of specificity as the other immune antibodies,[68] in that proteins of closely related species tend to interact, while proteins of very distinct biological or chemical nature are easily distinguished.   Thus, guinea-pigs sensitized with ape serum will react with human serum, but not with serum from dog or ox or fowl.   However, in the final analysis, the speci-

[61] Anderson and Frost, Jour. Med. Res., 1910 (23), 31.

[62] The brief duration of passive sensitization presumably depends on the formation of antibodies for the foreign sensitizing serum, constituting the condition of "antisensitization" as contrasted with the refractory period which results from the exhaustion of antibodies by antigen. (See Weil, Zeit. Immunität., 1913 (20), 199; 1914 (23), 1.)

[63] However, Schiff and Moore state that in immune sera the albumin fraction contains both the agent that confers passive sensitization and the constituent that causes the "primary toxicity" of foreign sera. (Zeit. Immunität., 1914 (22), 609.)

[64] Corper, Jour. Infect. Dis., 1919 (25), 248.

[64a] See Zinsser, Jour. Exp. Med., 1912 (15), 529.

[65] Jour. Immunol., 1916 (1), 1.

[66] Jour. Med. Research, 1913 (27), 497; 1914 (30), 299–364; 1915 (32), 107.

[67] Jour. Pharm., 1913 (4), 167.

[68] See review in Jour. Infect. Dis., 1911 (8), 73.

ficity depends upon the chemical composition of the antigenic protein, rather than its biological origin, for I have found it possible to distinguish in the hen's egg five distinctly different antigens, and these correspond to five proteins which have been distinguished by chemical measures.[69] Together with Dr. T. B. Osborne, working with purified vegetable proteins, I have found evidence that a single isolated protein (hordein or gliadin) may contain more than one antigenic radical.[70] As Osborne[71] has said, "chemically identical proteins apparently do not occur in animals and plants of different species, unless they are biologically very closely related." Whether the chemical differences that determine specificity are of quantitative nature, which can be disclosed by analytic means, or whether they are sometimes dependent upon spatial relationships of the amino-acid radicals, as Pick suggests, remains to be determined. My own experience indicates that usually, at least, proteins distinguishable by anaphylactic reactions also show readily distinguishable chemical differences.

HAY-FEVER

In 1902 Dunbar[72] demonstrated conclusively that typical hay-fever, in its several forms, is due to pollen of various sources; in all, twenty-five varieties of grass and seven varieties of plants of other sorts being found whose pollen, when placed upon the nasal or conjunctival mucous membranes of hay-fever patients, causes a typical attack of the disease. In Germany the disease seems to come chiefly from pollen of the grasses and grains (rye pollen being most active), whereas in America the most important pollen seems to come from members of the *Ambrosia* (ragweed)[73] and *Grammaceæ* (grasses). Dunbar also found that the toxic constituent could be dissolved from the pollen in salt solution, and seemed to be a protein.

The protein constituents of the pollen of rye have been studied further by Kammann,[74] who found three proteins, one of which, an albumin, was found to contain all the active matter. This constitutes about 5.5 per cent. of the entire weight of the pollen, is weakened but little by heating to $80°$, and is not destroyed by boiling; it is but partly destroyed by pepsin and trypsin, and resists acids but not alkalies. Analysis of pollen from *Ambrosia* by J. H. Koessler[75] showed that most of the nitrogen present was protein nitrogen, with 14.72 per cent. arginine, 14.05 per cent. histidine and 3.18 per cent. lysine. Heyl[76] obtained from *Ambrosia* pollen a mixture of albumose, peptone, albumin and glutelin, the latter being most abundant. A solution containing 0.008 mg. of pollen protein, which amount is contained in two or three pollen grains, produces a reaction in susceptible individuals, but large amounts have no effect on normal persons.

Dunbar manufactured an "antitoxic" serum by immunizing horses against the pollen, believing that he was dealing with a toxin, but its efficacy is more than

[69] The chief proteins obtained by fractionating serum give cross reactions with each other, but strongest with the homologous protein (Kato, Mitt. med. Fak. Univ. Tokio, 1917 (18), 195.

[70] Jour. Infec. Dis., 1913 (12), 341.

[71] Harvey Lectures, 1910–11.

[72] Full review of subject and literature given by Prausnitz, Kolle and Wassermann's Handbuch, 1913 (2), 1469; Koessler, Forchheimer's Therapeutics, 1914 (5), 671.

[73] See Cooke and Van der Veer, Jour. Immunol., 1916 (1), 201; Goodale, Boston Med. Surg. Jour., 1914 (171), 695.

[74] Hofmeister's Beitr., 1904 (5), 346; Biochem. Zeit., 1912 (46), 151.

[75] Jour. Biol. Chem., 1918 (35), 415.

[76] Jour. Amer. Chem. Soc., 1917 (39), 1470; 1919 (41), 670.

doubtful.   The processes involved in hay fever are characteristically of the nature of an anaphylactic reaction to a foreign protein, in which case we cannot speak of either a toxin or an antitoxic serum.   The hypersensitization seems sometimes to be established spontaneously through inheritance, but no antibodies can be demonstrated in the blood of sensitized persons, although the cells of the skin and mucous membranes are reactive,[77] so that the specific protein responsible for the trouble may be determined by skin or conjunctival tests.   Essentially, therefore, hay fever is one of the cases of hypersensitivity to foreign protein, of the same class as horse asthma, food urticarias, etc.

THE ABDERHALDEN REACTION

This reaction is based upon the hypothesis that the animal body reacts to the presence of foreign proteins by providing specific means of destroying them through proteolysis, and hence is fundamentally the same as the anaphylaxis reaction as conceived by Vaughan, Friedemann, Friedberger and others.   It differs from the other reactions of this class merely in that the methods used for determining the proteolysis are chemical rather than biological.   The occurrence of a reaction is indicated by the production of diffusible products of protein hydrolysis, which may be detected by any one of several methods, although most used is "ninhydrin" (triketohydrindene hydrate)[78] which reacts with any alpha-amino acid, the resulting condensation compound being a blue or violet color; or by observing the change in optical rotation that occurs in a solution of peptone under the hydrolytic action of the serum.

It has undergone much the same series of shifting explanations as the other reactions of this class.   At first, like the other proteolytic reactions, it was assumed that the antigen was digested; but, as with the precipitin and anaphylaxis reactions, evidence was found by numerous observers that not the antigen but the proteins of the immune serum are the chief or sole source of the cleavage products. For some reason, hard to explain, it has always been referred to as if it were the result of the formation of specific enzymes which attacked the antigen, in spite of the repeated demonstration that sera giving positive reactions can be inactivated by heat and reactivated by normal serum,[79] thus throwing it into the class of amboceptor-complement reactions, with which it agrees in principle.

Having been introduced first as a method for diagnosing pregnancy, on the principle that in pregnancy the chorionic cells of the placenta enter the maternal circulation and as foreign proteins cause the formation of specific "defensive ferments," it was at once taken up as a clinical procedure, and as a result an enormous literature on this reaction was rapidly produced.   Much of this represents highly uncritical work, largely from workers not trained or experienced in immunological principles, and hence it is not profitable to review it *in extenso* here.   Abderhalden's own views are given in full in his monographs[80] and there exist numerous critical reviews.[81]   The status of the reaction at this writing seems to be as follows:

Animals, or man, after having foreign proteins of any sort enter the blood stream, may, and commonly do show an altered condition of their serum, whereby when their serum is incubated with the antigen under suitable conditions very minute quantities of the products of protein cleavage may be set free, and recognized when dialyzed away from the digesting mixture; or, a measurable change in optical rotation of the digestion mixture occurs.   However, perfectly normal sera may at times cause a similar proteolysis, usually but not always less than with the immune serum.

The digestion seems to involve chiefly the serum proteins rather than the antigen, although under certain conditions there may be some digestion of the antigen.

[77] See Cooke, Flood and Coca, Jour. Immunol., 1917 (2), 217

[78] Concerning the mechanism of the ninhydrin reaction see Retinger, Jour. Amer. Chem. Soc., 1917 (39), 1059.

[79] See Stephan, Münch. med. Woch., 1914 (61), 891; Hauptman *ibid.*, p. 1167; Bettencourt and Menezes, Compt. Rend. Soc. Biol., 1916 (77), 162.

[80] Emil Abderhalden, "Schutzfermente des tierischen Organismus."

[81] See Wallis, Quart. Jour. Med., 1916 (9), 138; Bronfenbrenner, Jour. Lab. Clin. Med., 1915 (1), 79; 1916 (1), 573.   Hulton, Jour. Biol. Chem., 1916 (25), 163.

Bronfenbrenner holds that the enzymes exhibit no selectivity, digesting both the antigen and the serum impartially.[82]

Apparently the digestion is accomplished by serum complement, or at least normal serum enzymes, rather than by any new-formed specific enzyme, although enzymes set free from the tissues have been held responsible by some.

The mechanism of the reaction is not understood. Jobling and Petersen have suggested that the antigen-antibody combination may adsorb or bind the antiproteases of the serum, so that the normal protease digests the serum proteins. Or it may be that union of antigen and antibody activates the complement, or binds it to the antibody so that it digests either the antibody or other proteins of the serum. It also is suggested that enzymes are set free from the tissues injured by the specific protein, or by disease, which digest the foreign protein or the cellular proteins that may have escaped from the tissues into the blood stream.

The reaction possesses a certain specificity, but just the degree of this specificity has not been agreed upon. The claim of Abderhalden[83] and his followers, that it is by far the most specific of immunity reactions, whereby disintegration of small amounts of any given organ of an individual can be determined by specific reactions between his serum and that organ, with such refinement that even cerebral localization is possible,[84] is difficult to accept. There are so many possible sources of error in the original technic that even with great care the charge of incorrect results from incorrect technic cannot be escaped, and therefore, those who do not accept the doctrine of its specificity are always on the defensive. Nevertheless, so many careful and experienced investigators have found the original Abderhalden reaction to give at times absolutely non-specific and hopelessly paradoxical results, that its diagnostic value for either clinical or scientific purposes must be considered at present as unproved,[85] whatever the final decision as to its standing as a specific reaction may be.

Serum treated with various inert, finely divided particles, such as kaolin, starch, silicates, etc., may acquire the property of giving positive reactions. This is another point of resemblance to anaphylatoxin formation, and against the specificity of the reaction, indicating that the antigen merely acts as a non-specific adsorbent.

By far the most satisfactory results have been recorded in the diagnosis of pregnancy by means of placental antigen. This may be explained by the fact that the protease activity of the serum seems to be increased in pregnancy,[86] and hence the reaction with placenta is more marked than with the serum of non-pregnant individuals. But simply shaking normal serum with kaolin or other foreign substances may cause it to give strong reactions with placenta antigen (Wallis).

[82] Supported by Smith and Cook, Jour. Infect. Dis., 1916 (18), 14. De Waele states that it is the serum globulin that is digested (Compt. Rend. Soc. Biol., 1914 (76), 627).

[83] A reply to numerous criticisms is given by Abderhalden, Fermentforschung. 1916 (1), 351; this and other numbers of this journal also consist largely of articles on the Abderhalden reaction.

[84] See Retinger, Arch. Int. Med., 1918 (22), 234.

[85] O. J. Elsesser (Jour. Infect. Dis., 1916 (19), 655), working in my laboratory with the purified vegetable proteins of Osborne, found that at best the specificity of the reaction was less than that of the anaphylaxis reaction, and there were many absolutely non-specific and irrational reactions. As these pure proteins furnish a much more appropriate material for studying specificity than the tissues or sera commonly used, it would seem that the results thus obtained are excellent proof of the uncertainty and unreliability of the reaction. Careful quantitative studies of the setting free of amino-acids by serum incubated with placenta, by Van Slyke and his associates, also showed a complete lack of specific proteolysis by pregnancy serum (Arch. Int. Med., 1917 (19), 56; Jour. Biol. Chem., 1915 (23), 377; see also Hulton, *ibid.*, 1916 (25), 163).

[86] See Sloan, Amer. Jour. Physiol., 1915 (39), 9.

CHAPTER IX

CHEMISTRY OF THE IMMUNITY REACTIONS (Continued)— BACTERIOLYSIS, HEMOLYSIS, COMPLEMENT FIXATION, AND SERUM CYTOTOXINS

SERUM BACTERIOLYSIS[1]

THE bactericidal property of serum may be shown by its destruction of the life manifestations of bacteria without marked alteration in their structure, or it may be accompanied by dissolution of the bacterial cell (*bacteriolysis*). How much of the bacteriolytic process is performed by the serum itself, or how much by the autolytic enzymes of the bacterial cell, is unknown, but the latter is probably a factor. The bactericidal property of immune serum has been shown to be quite independent of the antitoxic properties and also to have quite a different mechanism. This last is shown in the following manner:

If we heat bactericidal serum made by immunizing an animal against bacteria, say the cholera vibrio, at 55° for fifteen minutes, it will be found to have lost its power of destroying these organisms.[2] Normal serum of non-immunized animals is equally without effect upon the vibrios. If however, we add to the inactivated heated serum an equal quantity of inactive normal serum, the mixture will be found to be as actively bactericidal as the original unheated immune serum. This phenomenon is interpreted to mean that, by immunization, some new substance has been developed which, although by itself incapable of destroying bacteria, is able, when united with some substance present in normal serum, to destroy bacteria readily. The substance present in normal serum is also incapable of affecting bacteria by itself, but needs the presence of the substance developed by immunizing to render it bactericidal. Hence *the bactericidal property in this case depends on two substances acting together:* one, developed during immunization and therefore called the *immune body*, is specific for the variety of bacteria used in immunization, and is not destroyed by heating at 55°. The other, present in normal serum, is not increased during immunization, is not (altogether) specific in character, and is destroyed by heating at 55°; as its action is com-

---

[1] Review and bibliography by Müller, Oppenheimer's Handb. d. Biochem., 1909 II (1), 629.

[2] Normal *human* serum often exhibits some power to destroy bacteria, even after heating to 55°. The nature of this thermostable bactericidal agent is unknown. (See Selter, Zeit. Hyg., 1918 (86), 313).

plementary to that of the specific immune body, it is called the *complement*.[3]

It is believed that the action of these substances is as follows: The immune body is, like antitoxin, a cell receptor which unites the bacteria to the cell. It differs from the antitoxin, however, in that it has two affinities, one for the complement and the other for the bacterial substance. On account of the existence of the two affinities it is called an *amboceptor*. Some serums contain such amboceptors for certain bacteria without previous immunization, hence the term *immune amboceptor* is reserved for amboceptors developed by immunization.

Amboceptor and Complement.[4]—The function of the amboceptor is to unite the bacterial protoplasm, to which it is attached by one affinity, to the complement which it holds by its other affinity, or, to put it in a more strictly chemical way, the addition of the amboceptors to the bacteria gives them a chemical affinity for complement. It is, therefore, an *intermediary body*, uniting the complement to the bacterial protoplasm. The complement[5] is the substance that actually destroys the bacteria, in which respect, as well as in its susceptibility to heat, it resembles the enzymes. Complement is present in normal serums, and, as it is not increased in amount during immunization it may not be sufficient to satisfy all the amboceptors, hence it may be impossible to secure marked bactericidal effects even when many amboceptors have been formed. If the complement in an immune serum has been destroyed by heating, it may be replaced by adding normal serum from another animal, even of some other species; indicating either that the complement is not absolutely specific in its nature, or that quite the same complement may be present in the blood of many different animals. The origin of the complement is unknown, but it has been urged that the leucocytes are an important source of this substance, if not its chief one;[6] there is evidence, however, that various organs and cells may also produce complement.[7] Its most important characteristics are its extreme susceptibility to heat, and the resemblance of its action to the action of enzymes.[8] Hektoen[9] found that it could be made to unite with Mg, Ca, Ba, Sr, and SO_4 ions, which rendered the complement (for typhoid bacilli and red corpuscles) inactive. Manwaring[10] found that these ions could be

[3] The polynuclear leucocytes also contain bacteriolytic agents, "endolysins." of a similar complex structure, but quite distinct from the serum bacteriolysins (See Kling, Zeit. Immunität., 1910 (7), 1).

[4] See also Hemolysis, Chapter X.

[5] Review and bibliography by Noguchi, Biochem. Zeit., 1907 (6), 327.

[6] Cholera antiserum will produce the Pfeiffer phenomenon of lysis of cholera vibrios in animals made leucocyte-free with thorium. (Lippmann, Zeit. Immunität., 1915 (24), 107.)

[7] See Dick, Jour. Infect. Dis., 1913 (12), 111; and Lippmann and Plesch, Zeit. Immunität., 1913 (17), 548.

[8] See Walker, Jour. of Physiol., 1906 (33), p. xxi.

[9] Trans. Chicago Path. Soc., 1903 (5), 303.

[10] Jour. Infectious Diseases, 1904 (1), 112.

separated again from the complement by simple chemical precipitation. Acids stronger than CO_2 and of the higher saturated or unsaturated fatty acid series, inactivate complement in strengths greater than $n/40$, and alkalies are equally inhibitive.[11] Ultraviolet rays destroy complement.[12] Sherwood[13] has made a study of various substances that may be present in the blood in excessive amounts during pathological conditions, such as CO_2, lactic acid, acetone, etc., and finds that they interfere seriously with the action of complement, which suggests that they may favor infection or interfere with recovery from infection.

Presumably the complement is a protein, for it has antigenic properties, so that immunization with sera containing either complement or complementoid causes anticomplement activity in the blood of the immune animal. Also, it is destroyed by trypsin free from lipase,[14] and, like other colloids, is readily adsorbed by surfaces; like enzymes, complement is destroyed by shaking,[15] and gradually disappears on standing. There are some striking resemblances between the behavior of complement and of certain compounds of protein with soaps and lipoids, as pointed out especially by Noguchi, but that these are identical with true complement is doubtful. (See Hemolysis.) Its colloid nature is attested by the large loss when complement is filtered through Berkefeld filters.[16]

A careful review of the evidence has led Liefmann[17] to the conclusion that the reaction of complement to sensitized corpuscles is more like that of ferment to substrate than of antigen to antibody. In its effect of dissolving bacteria (and also other cells against which animals may have been immunized) *complement resembles the enzymes*, and by many it is looked upon as related to them, but the changes it produces do not resemble those produced by proteolytic enzymes in all details.[18] In particular, complement seems to participate in reactions according to the law of definite proportions, unlike the enzymes.[19] In certain immune reactions, colloids (lecithin, silicic acid)[20] can play the rôle of complement and immune body, but these reactions are probably quite different from those of bacteriolysis by immune serum.

Structure of Complement.—According to the Ehrlich theory, complement, like toxins and enzymes, possesses at least two groups: one, the haptophore, by

[11] Noguchi, Biochem. Zeit., 1907 (6), 172.
[12] Courmont *et al.*, C. R. Soc. Biol., 1913 (74), 1152.
[13] Jour. Infect. Dis., 1917 (20), 185.
[14] Michaelis and Skwirsky, Zeit. Immunität,. 1910 (7), 497.
[15] Noguchi and Bronfenbrenner, Jour. Exp. Med., 1910 (13), 229; Ritz, Zeit. Immunität., 1912 (15), 145.
[16] See Schmidt, Arch. f. Hyg., 1912 (76), 284; Jour. Hyg., 1914 (14), 437.
[17] Zeit. Immunität., 1913 (16), 503.
[18] The curve of complement action resembles that of enzyme action. (Thiele and Embleton, Jour. Path. and Bact., 1915 (19), 372.)
[19] See Liebermann, Deut. med. Woch., 1906 (32), 249.
[20] Landsteiner and Jagic, Wien. klin. Woch., 1904 (17), 63; Münch. med. Woch., 1904 (51), 1185.

which it unites with the amboceptor; the other, the toxophore (or *zymophore*, because of its enzyme-like action), which attacks the bacterial protoplasm. It may degenerate and lose its toxophore group while retaining the power to combine by means of its haptophore group, thus forming a *complementoid*. Complement and amboceptor exist side by side in the serum, not uniting with one another until the amboceptor has become attached to the bacterial protoplasm.

It is generally stated that if serum containing complement be so treated as to separate the globulins from the albumin, it is found that the complement has been divided into two parts, one present in each of the protein fractions. The globulin fraction of the complement will unite to amboceptor which is fixed to cells, and hence is called the *mid-piece* of the complement, for it will unite also with the *end-piece* of the complement contained in the albumin fraction, and then cytolysis can take place. Without the intervention of the globulin mid-piece the albumin end-piece cannot unite with the amboceptor, while in the absence of end-piece the amboceptor mid-piece complex can cause no cytolysis. Both fractions of the complement are destroyed by heat, but if the mid-piece is bound to the amboceptor it resists heating. The mid-piece corresponds to Ehrlich's haptophore, the end-piece to the toxophore group, and this complex structure is common to both bacteriolytic and hemolytic complement. Bronfenbrenner and Noguchi,[21] however, contend that the supposed cleavage of complement is merely an inactivation by the agencies employed, all the complement being in the albumin fraction in a condition capable of reactivation, not only by globulin but by simple amphoteric substances, a view which has not been generally accepted.[22]

Amboceptors are formed, according to Wassermann, and Pfeiffer and Marx, in the spleen and hemopoietic organs, since in immunization they can be demonstrated in these organs before they appear in the circulating blood. The stability of the amboceptors is very considerable: serum prepared in 1895 by Pfeiffer against cholera vibrios was found to have lost almost none of its activity after eight years in an ice-box (Friedberger). Heating twenty hours at 60° scarcely injures them, but 70° for one hour destroys them almost completely, and heating the serum to 100° destroys all the immune bodies. They are quite resistant to putrefaction, and, like the antitoxins, do not dialyze. Strong salt solutions will prevent the union of complement and amboceptor *in vitro*, and probably to greater or less degree in the animal body, but the union of antigen and amboceptor is not prevented by salt.[23] Alkalies may prevent the union of amboceptor with the cells, or extract it from the cell to which it has united; and they may also inhibit the union of amboceptor and complement. Amboceptors are not inactivated by shaking, as is complement, but they are destroyed alike by ultraviolet rays, and both resist x-rays.[24]

According to Pfeiffer and Proskauer,[25] digestion of the globulin precipitate, in which amboceptors are carried down, does not destroy their activity completely even when all the proteins are thus removed. Removal of the nucleo-albumin or nuclein does not remove the amboceptors from the serum. Immune serum kept three months in alcohol yielded an extract with distilled water that was rich in immune bodies, but almost free from protein. Pick, Rhodain, and Fuhrmann found that immune bodies are precipitated entirely in the euglobulin fraction of the serum protein. From these experiments it has been thought by some that the bacteriolytic amboceptor is not itself a protein, although closely associated with the serum globulins.[26]

CYTOTOXINS

Just as precipitins can be obtained for proteins derived from other sources than bacterial cells, so also upon immunizing an animal

[21] Jour. Exp. Med., 1912 (5), 598; good review of literature.
[22] See Leschley, Zeit. Immunität., 1916 (25), 44.
[23] Angerer, Zeit. Immunität., 1909 (4), 243.
[24] Scaffidi, Biochem. Zeit., 1915 (69), 162.
[25] Cent. f. Bakt., 1896 (19), 191.
[26] Ascoli found that the active substance of anthracidal serum, which is not an amboceptor, is contained in the pseudo-globulin fraction of asses' serum, but in goat's serum part is in the euglobulin fraction. (Biochem. Centr., 1906 (5), 458.)
14

against various types of cells other than bacteria, substances appear in its serum that exercise a destructive effect upon the type of cells injected. In other words, the reactions of animals to infection are not specially devised for combating bacteria and their products, but can be equally exerted against non-bacterial cells and their products. In the case of soluble proteins, as before mentioned, the antibodies show their effects by precipitating them, with agglutination of the particles into flocculi and perhaps a subsequent digestion; in the case of cells, whether bacterial or tissue cells, the antibodies cause agglutination and loss or impairment of vitality. This injury may be manifested by loss of motion in the motile cells (bacteria, spermatozoa, ciliated epithelium) or by solution of their contents (bacteriolysis, erythrocytolysis, leucocytolysis, etc.), or by cell death without marked morphological alterations (B. typhosus, spermatozoa). If we inject red corpuscles, leucocytes, spermatozoa, renal epithelium, or any other foreign cell, the reaction is as specific as it is if we inject bacteria, and of exactly the same nature. Therefore, all that has been said previously concerning bactericidal substances and agglutinins can be transposed to apply to immunity against tissue cells. As a matter of fact, however, the transposition is generally made in the other direction, for red corpuscles are much easier cells to study than bacteria, because their laking gives prompt and readily recognized evidence that the toxic serum has brought about changes. Much of our knowledge of bactericidal serum has been obtained through studies of the mechanism of erythrocytolysis, the results of which have then been applied to the subject of bacteriolysis. Both on this account, therefore, and because solution of red corpuscles is of itself an important process in many intoxications and diseases, the subject is of great theoretical and practical importance.

HEMOLYSIS[27] OR ERYTHROCYTOLYSIS

In hemolysis the essential phenomenon consists in the escape of the hemoglobin from the stroma of the corpuscles into the surrounding fluid. As it is not exactly known in what way the stroma holds the hemoglobin normally, whether purely physically or in part chemically, or whether the stroma consists of a spongioplasm or of sac-like membranes, or both, the ultimate processes that permit the escape of the hemoglobin are not finally solved. However, the agents by which the escape is brought about are well known and extensively studied, and they are found to be of extremely various natures. They may be roughly classified as: (1) known physical and chemical agents; (2) unknown constituents of blood-serum; (3) bacterial products; (4) certain vegetable poisons; (5) snake venoms.

[27] Through usage this term has been limited to the solution of the red corpuscles, which is more accurately described by the term *erythrocytolysis*. For bibliography see Sachs, Ergebnisse der Pathol., 1902 (7), 714; 1906 (11), 515; Kolle and Wassermann's Handbuch, 1913 (II), 793; Landsteiner, Handbuch d. Biochem., 1909 (II (1)), 395.

HEMOLYSIS BY KNOWN CHEMICAL AND PHYSICAL AGENCIES

The Mechanism of Hemolysis.—If distilled water is added to corpuscles of any kind, osmotic changes are bound to occur, since within the cells are abundant salts, soluble in water, which will begin to diffuse outward in an attempt to establish osmotic equilibrium between the corpuscles and the surrounding fluid. Conversely, water enters the corpuscles at the same time, and accumulating there leads to swelling until such injury has been produced as permits the hemoglobin to escape and enter the surrounding fluid. Before this occurs the fluid is opaque because of the obstruction to light offered by the red cells, but on the completion of hemolysis the fluid becomes transparent. The stroma now settles to the bottom, while the hemoglobin diffuses into the fluid, making it red, but perfectly transparent. This process has long been known as the "laking" of blood, and is essentially the condition present in all forms of hemolysis. That the hemoglobin escapes only through injury of the stroma and not through simple osmotic diffusion, is shown by the fact that if salt solution of the same concentration as normal serum is used instead of distilled water, no such escape of hemoglobin occurs. As hemoglobin is perfectly soluble in salt solution, it should pass out if it diffused as do the salts. Since there is no escape of hemoglobin in such a salt solution, it is evident either that the stroma is not permeable to hemoglobin, or else the hemoglobin is in some way attached to or combined with the stroma. Again, if the corpuscles are placed in a solution of salt more concentrated than their own fluids, water escapes and the corpuscles shrink; as no hemoglobin escapes with the water, it is evident that the stroma is not permeable to hemoglobin when intact. Because of the resemblance of the process of hemolysis to the rupture of plant cells with escape of their contents when they are placed in distilled water, it might be assumed that hemolysis is largely a physical matter, but if a red corpuscle in an isotonic solution is cut into pieces, the hemoglobin does not escape, indicating that its structure is quite dissimilar to that of the simple vegetable cell and that there is some union of stroma and of hemoglobin, either physical or chemical.[28] Physico-chemical studies also indicate that there is no true covering membrane to red corpuscles, for the absorption of ions by hemoglobin is the same as the absorption by corpuscles.[29] M. H. Fischer[30] interprets hemolysis as a separation of lipoid-protein stroma and ad-

[28] Stewart (Jour. of Physiol., 1899 (24), 211) found that in hemolysis by physical means or under the influence of serums, there is no marked increase in the electrical conductivity, but hemolysis by saponin and by water causes an increase of conductivity, presumably because of the escape of electrolytes; corroborated by A. Woelfel, Biochem. Jour., 1908 (3), 146; see also Moore and Roaf, *ibid.*, p. 55.

[29] Rohonyi, Kolloid-chem. Beihefte, 1916 (8), 337, 391. Knaffel-Lenz (Arch. ges. Physiol., 1918 (171), 51) also finds evidence that there is no limiting lipoid membrane about red cells.

[30] Kolloid Zeit., 1909 (5), 146.

sorbed hemoglobin, which process can be duplicated experimentally with a combination consisting of a corresponding solid hydrophilic colloid, fibrin, and a hydrophobic colloid dye, carmine; this artificial combination behaves exactly like a corpuscle to simple hemolytic agents.[31]

Repeated alternate freezing and thawing is another physical means of bringing on hemolysis. Heating to 62°–64° C. causes hemolysis of mammalian corpuscles; in cold-blooded animals this seems to occur at a slightly lower temperature. Hypertonic solutions produce hemolysis, and it may be that freezing and desiccating cause hemolysis through the resulting hypertonicity.[32]

Some chemical agents are capable of liberating hemoglobin, even when the corpuscles are in isotonic solutions. The ordinary salts of serum, of course, do not have this property, but ammonium salts are strongly hemolytic. The chemical agents that dissolve red corpuscles seem to be those that have the power of penetrating the stroma. Ammonium salts and urea penetrate the corpuscles freely and cause hemolysis. Sugar and NaCl seem not to penetrate the corpuscles, and therefore do not produce hemolysis. Of the permeating substances, there seem to be two types: one, like urea, does not produce hemolysis when in a solution of NaCl isotonic with the serum; the other, like ammonium chloride, is not prevented from producing hemolysis by the presence of NaCl.[33]

All these agents seem to effect hemolysis *by acting on the stroma*, for when the stroma of corpuscles hardened in formalin has its lecithin and cholesterol removed with ether, *saponin*, a powerfully hemolytic substance, seems to have no effect. The action of saponin and of many other hemolytic agents can be prevented by the presence of *cholesterol* in excess, suggesting that it is this constituent of the stroma that is affected.[34] By studying hemolysis under dark field illumination Dietrich[35] found that in water hemolysis a diffusion of hemoglobin

[31] Concerning the influence of H-ion concentration on hemolysis see Walbum, Biochem. Zeit., 1914 (63), 221.

[32] Guthrie, Jour. Lab. Clin. Med., 1917 (3), 87.

[33] Hamburger, in his book, "Osmotischer Druck und Ionenlehre," reviews exhaustively the physical chemistry of hemolysis. The following is his summary of the permeability of red corpuscles by various substances:

Organic Substances.—(a) *Impermeable* for sugars; namely, cane-sugar, dextrose, lactose, also arabit and mannit. (b) *Permeable* for alcohols, in inverse proportion to the number of hydroxyl groups that they contain; also for aldehydes (except paraldehyde), ketones, ethers, esters, antipyrin, amides, urea, urethan, bile acids and their salts. (c) *Slightly permeable* for neutral amino-acids (glycocoll, asparagin, etc.).

Inorganic substances, not including the salts of the fixed alkalies. (a) *Completely impermeable* for the cations Ca, Sr, Ba, Mg. (b) *Permeable* for NH₄ ions, for free acids and alkalies.

[34] Ransom, Deut. med. Woch., 1901 (27), 194; Kobert, "Saponinsubstanzen" Stuttgart, 1901; Abderhalden and Le Count, Zeit. exp. Path. u. Ther., 1905 (2), 199. Noguchi (Univ. of Penn. Med. Bull., 1902 (15), 327) found lecithin without this property.

[35] Verh. Deut. Path. Gesell., 1908 (12), 202.

takes place through the corpuscular substance, which is not visibly altered; in serum hemolysis there is first a precipitate formed in the outer layer, which swells. There is no evidence that the erythrocytes contain proteolytic enzymes of their own that might disintegrate them.[36]

The fact that chloroform, ether, bile salts, soaps, and amyl alcohol will cause laking is probably intimately connected with the fact that lecithin and cholesterol, important constituents of the stroma, are both soluble in these substances.[37] In general it can be said that hemolytic agents dissolve lipoids or hydrolyze proteins or lipoids, thus destroying the power of the stroma to retain the hemoglobin.[38] Nearly all the non-specific hemolytic agents are inhibited to greater or less degree by the serum, in which inhibition both the proteins and cholesterol are concerned.[39] Cholesterol also influences many other immunity reactions, inhibiting some and stimulating others.[40] The resistance of the corpuscles to hemolysis by various agents differs greatly in disease, although fairly constant in normal blood, the differences being caused in some cases by changes in the permeability of the corpuscles, and sometimes by changes in the environment of the corpuscle or the presence of protective substances in either the corpuscles or the plasma.

Arseniuretted hydrogen, when inhaled, causes intravascular hemolysis, and there are many other drugs and chemicals with the same property, among which may be mentioned nitrobenzol, nitroglycerin and the nitrites, guaiacol, pyrogallol, acetanilid, and numerous aniline compounds. Probably the hemolysis produced by autolytic products belongs in this category.[41] Alcoholic extracts of tissues are commonly hemolytic; these extracts when added to serum take on properties which cause them to resemble closely hemolytic complement (Noguchi), and the soaps seem to be the active constituents of the extracts. AsH_3, although strongly hemolytic in the living body, does not hemolyze corpuscles in the test tube (Heffter), and this is true of some other poisons, which probably produce their effects through tissue changes.[42] The bile acids and their salts will also produce hemolysis, as seen in jaundice. Sodium bicarbonate solutions of one or two per cent. are hemolytic for some varieties of corpuscles, but 0.1 per cent. Na_2CO_3 and $NaHCO_3$ do not cause hemolysis. A study of the hemolytic properties of one class of lipolytic hemolytic agents,

[36] Von Roques, Biochem. Zeit., 1914 (64), 1.
[37] See Koeppe, Pflüger's Arch., 1903 (99), 33; Peskind, Amer. Jour. Phys., 1904 (12), 184; Moore, Brit. Med. Jour., 1909 (ii), 684.
[38] See Herzfeld and Klinger, Biochem. Zeit., 1918 (87), 36.
[39] See v. Eisler, Zeit. exp. Path., 1906 (3), 296.
[40] Walbum, Zeit. Immunität., 1910 (7), 544; Dewey and Nuzum, Jour. Infect. Dis., 1914 (15), 472.
[41] Concerning hemolysis by alcohols, ketones, etc., organic acids, and essences see Vandevelde, Bull. Soc. chim. de Belgique, 1905 (19), 288.
[42] Friedberger and Brossa, Zeit. Immunität., 1912 (15), 506.

the terpenes, shows that their hemolytic activity varies much according to their physical properties, generally decreasing directly with increase in the solubility in water (Ishizaka).[43]

Leucocytes are dissolved by some of these agents, particularly the bile salts although they are affected by no means so rapidly or so much as are the erythrocytes. There seems to be no relation between the erythrolytic and leucolytic powers of these substances. Water causes swelling, with solution of the granules in time, and the same is true of ammonium-chloride solutions.

Various chemicals cause morphological alterations in the leucocytes, and of bacterial products the toxins of pyocyaneus and diphtheria seem to be particularly leucocidal, causing a striking karyorrhexis (Schürmann).[44]

HEMOLYSIS BY SERUM

Normal blood-serum of many animals causes hemolysis to greater or less degree when mixed with red corpuscles of another species of animal, and this property can be greatly increased by immunizing the animal with red corpuscles in the usual way. This hemolysis occurs both in the test-tube and in the body, in the latter case causing severe anatomical changes or even death. In all respects *the mechanism of hemolysis by serum seems to be identical with that of bacteriolysis.* Two substances are concerned, one the *amboceptor*, which resists heat and which is increased by immunizing;[45] the other, *complement*, which is destroyed at 55° and which is present in normal serum. In this case the substances may be referred to as hemolytic amboceptors and hemolytic complements.

In spite of the availability of these particular cytolytic substances for study, very little has been learned of their exact nature and properties. It is known that amboceptor is combined with the red cells in a certain sense quantitatively, a definite amount being required to saturate a given amount of corpuscles so that they will all be hemolyzed when complement is added; and that this reaction is complete in less than fifteen minutes at 45°. What change this addition of amboceptor brings about in the corpuscles is unknown. It has also been shown that at 0° the affinity between the amboceptor and the corpuscle is greater than it is between amboceptor and complement, so that it is possible at this temperature to remove all the amboceptor from a serum by treating it with red corpuscles, and thus we can obtain complement free from amboceptor. This experiment also shows that the two bodies exist side by side in the serum without combining, and that combination occurs only after the amboceptor has become united to the erythrocyte. Moreover the hemolytic amboceptor can be separated from the antigen to which it has been

[43] Arch. exp. Path., 1914 (75), 195.
[44] Cent. f. Pathol., 1910 (21), 337.
[45] In an extensive study of the hemolytic antibody, Thiele and Embleton (Zeit. Immunität., 1913 (20), 1) describe its formation as in several steps, at first being thermolabile and uniting with the corpuscle only when warmed. They also find complement to have several components. This is not confirmed by Sherman, Jour. Infect. Dis., 1918 (22), 534.

combined.[46] Hemolysis by immune sera takes place best in a medium with a reaction corresponding to that of the blood, acids being more harmful than alkalies; with unfavorable reaction the complement does not unite with the amboceptor, although the latter unites with the corpuscle.[47]

The Amboceptor.—Amboceptor is, as a rule, destroyed by heating to 70° or higher.[48] Its place of origin is unknown. Metchnikoff holds that it is derived chiefly from the leucocytes, in support of which view is the fact that leucocytes dissolve red corpuscles after ingesting them; however, other phagocytic cells have the same power, particularly endothelial cells, and it is an open question whether the intracellular digestion of engulfed cells is the same process as extracellular hemolysis; probably it is not, for there seem to be more disintegrative changes in intracellular digestion than in hemolysis. Quinan[49] found that the diffusible constituents of hemolytic serum played no rôle beyond that of maintaining osmotic pressure. He was unable, however, to localize the immune body in any of the protein constituents, and Liebermann and Fenyvessy[50] believe that they obtained the amboceptor in a protein-free condition, in which it behaves like a weak acid. Amboceptors are insoluble in lipoids or lipoid solvents (Meyer),[51] and they move towards the cathode in an electric field, as do other antibodies.[52] The amboceptor complement reaction resembles a bimolecular reaction which is accelerated by its end products (v. Krogh).[53] Many of the effects of hemolytic amboceptors can be duplicated with silicic acid;[54] and a dye, brilliant green, may in minute quantities sensitize corpuscles so that they are hemolyzed by very small amounts of normal serum, or by lecithin.[55]

The amboceptors of normally hemolytic serum seem to be no different from those in immune serum, and amboceptors of one animal can combine with complement furnished by the serum of an entirely different animal. It is the amboceptor alone that gives the specific nature to the reaction, and, as is the case with all other immunizations, it is very difficult to secure antibodies by immunizing an animal with blood from another animal of its own species, *isohemolysins*. The place of origin of hemolysins is unknown, as with other antibodies, but that it is not in the blood seems to have been established conclusively by Hektoen and Carlson.[56] Immune hemolysins cannot pass from the mother to the fetus before birth[57] but they can be transmitted through the colostrum (Famulener).[58]

Although Ehrlich held that the union between cell and amboceptor is purely chemical and follows ordinary chemical laws, especially the law of multiple proportions, Bordet and other French observers have claimed that the union between amboceptor and corpuscle is physical and not chemical.[59] Probably the union is

[46] Kosakai, Jour. Immunol., 1918 (3), 109.
[47] Michaelis and Skwirsky, Zeit. Immunität., 1909 (4), 357.
[48] Ultraviolet light destroys immune hemolysin (Stines and Abelin, Zeit. Immunität., 1914 (20), 598).
[49] Hofmeister's Beitr., 1904 (5), 95.
[50] Jahresber. d. Immunität., 1911 (7), 2.
[51] *Ibid.*, 1909, Vol. 3.
[52] Teague and Buxton, Jour. Exper. Med., 1907 (9), 254.
[53] Biochem. Zeit., 1909 (22), 132.
[54] Landsteiner and Rock, Zeit. Immunität., 1912 (14), 14.
[55] Browning and Mackie, Zeit. Immunität., 1914 (21), 422.
[56] Jour. Infect. Dis., 1910 (7), 319.
[57] See Sherman concerning normal antibodies in the fetus. *Ibid.*, 1918 (22), 534.
[58] *Ibid.*, 1912 (10), 332.
[59] Bang and Forssmann (Hofmeister's Beitr., 1906 (8), 238) suggest that the amboceptor merely renders the corpuscle permeable for the complement, perhaps through action on the lipoid membrane; the complement then acts directly upon some constituent of the corpuscle, without the amboceptor acting as a combining substance in any way. They found that the substance in blood which stimulates the antibody formation in the case of hemolysin formation, is chemically separable from the substance in blood which unites with these antibodies; therefore, they conclude, the "receptors" of cells are *not* identical with the antibodies. (See controversy with Ehrlich in Münch. med. Woch., Vols. 56 and 57.)

with the stroma rather than with the hemoglobin, and the result of the union is to render the stroma permeable to the hemoglobin, or to separate the bonds that unite the hemoglobin to the stroma.[60] There are grounds for believing that the amboceptor not only binds the complement, but that it also produces changes in the corpuscles (Muir). Mathes[61] contends that red corpuscles cannot be dissolved by hemolytic serum or by pancreatic juice until after they have been killed; as heated serum does not kill them, this is presumably done by the complement. Corpuscles that have been killed can then be dissolved in their own serum. Levene[62] tried to produce hemolytic serums by immunizing with different constituents of corpuscles, using—(1) pure crystalline hemoglobin; (2) proteins of the stroma soluble in salt solutions; (3) an extract with alcohol-ether; and (4) an extract in 1.5 per cent. sodium bicarbonate. Only the last gave positive results, and the serum was almost devoid of agglutinative properties. Injection with corpuscles that had been digested with trypsin gave about the same results as alkaline extracts; corpuscles digested by pepsin gave a much weaker serum; in neither was agglutination obtained. According to Bang and Forssmann[63] and others ethereal extracts of red corpuscles give rise to production of hemolysins on immunization, and this "lysinogen" substance can be precipitated with acetone, is insoluble in alcohol, is not destroyed by boiling, and gives rise to no agglutinin. Numerous other observers, however, have failed to confirm these findings. Ford and Halsey[64] obtained serum with both lytic and agglutinative powers by injecting either the stroma or the laked blood free of stroma. Stewart[65] obtained similar results by immunizing with corpuscles laked by physical means, by serums, or by saponin. Pure hemoglobin itself is not antigenic.[66] According to Guerrini,[67] nucleoprotein obtained from dog's blood engenders specific hemolysins, and Beebe states that nucleoproteins from visceral organs do not have this effect. Levene's alkaline erythrocyte extracts probably also contained nucleoproteins. Vedder,[68] was unable to produce hemolysins when he used ether extracts of corpuscles as antigen, or with globulin from stroma, but the protein extract left after removing the globulin, presumably albumin, as well as lipoid-free stroma, produced hemolysin. The hemolysin itself seems to be a globulin. On the other hand, Bennett and Schmidt[69] obtained hemolysin by immunizing with the globulin precipitated from hemolyzed erythrocytes by CO_2.

Immunization with extracts of tissues and cells of various sorts, even when entirely free from blood (*e. g.*, spermatozoa), may produce hemolytic sera. The fact that various tissues from many different species of animals, when used as antigen, may give rise to hemolysin for sheep corpuscles, is an interesting but so far unexplained phenomenon, which is discussed under "Specificity" (Chapter vii).

The Complement.—Hemolytic complement possesses the same properties as bacteriolytic complement, resembling enzymes to the extent that it is susceptible to heat, causes a disintegration of cells, and is largely retained by Berkefeld filters.[70] The joint action of amboceptor and complement is strikingly like the activation of trypsinogen by kinase. On the other hand, hemolysis by serum is quite different from the effect of trypsin on corpuscles, as trypsin completely disorganizes the hemoglobin and destroys the stroma, while in hemolysis the stroma and hemoglobin seem to be merely separated from one another but not chemically altered. Again, *hemolysin acts quantitatively*, although that may be due to a

[60] Corpuscles treated with osmic acid will unite with hemolysins of diverse origin, but when used for immunizing they engender no hemolysins (Coca; also v. Szily, Zeit. Immunität., 1909 (3), 451). Heating corpuscle stroma alters greatly the reactivity (Landsteiner and Prasek, *ibid.*, 1912 (13), 403).

[61] Münch. med. Woch., 1902 (49), 8.

[62] Jour. Med. Research, 1904 (12), 191.

[63] Hofmeister's Beitr., 1906 (8) 238.

[64] Jour. Med. Research., 1904 (11), 403.

[65] Amer. Jour. of Physiol., 1904 (11), 250.

[66] Schmidt and Bennett, Jour. Infect. Dis., 1919 (25), 207.

[67] Riv. crit. di clin. med., 1903 (4), 561.

[68] Jour. Immunol., 1919 (4), 141.

[69] Jour. Immunol., 1919 (4), 29.

[70] Muir and Browning, Jour. Path. and Bact., 1909 (13), 232.

difference in the way the binding to the cell occurs, rather than in the method of action of the complement. Landsteiner and others have suggested that a lipoidal complement dissolves the corpuscle lipoids, liberating the hemoglobin, while Neuberg and others have supported the hypothesis that complement is virtually a lipase which splits the lipoids out of the corpuscles. Bordet believes that the hemolysin causes a lesion of the stroma which changes the resistance to osmotic influences. Complement is present in the plasma in about the same amounts as in the corresponding sera, so it is not a substance set free only by coagulation of the blood (Watanabe).[71] Dick[72] has found evidence that the complement is a ferment formed in the liver, and that it causes actual proteolytic changes. Jobling[73] associates the serum lipase with the hemolytic complement.[74] Ohta[75] observed no increase in non-coagulable nitrogen during hemolysis, but Dick found an increase in the free amino acids; therefore, as yet agreement has not been reached as to whether hemolysis depends in any way upon proteolysis or lipolysis in the corpuscle stroma.

Although the serum of one animal may complement the immune bodies in serum of several other varieties, and also produce lysis of many sorts of cells, it may be that not one complement does all the complementing; Ehrlich and others have asserted that one serum may contain several complements of slightly differing natures. Noguchi,[76] Liebermann and Fenyvessy, and others have pointed out the striking resemblance between hemolytic complement and certain compounds of soaps or lipoids with serum proteins, and it is possible that such compounds are of importance in serum hemolysis; but there seems also to be evidence of the existence of distinct protein complements, entirely different from these,[77] and it is possible that the protein complements are the important agents in specific hemolysis by immune sera.[78]

Antibodies can be obtained for both complement and hemolytic amboceptor by immunizing against serum containing them, and in many serums *antihemolysins* exist normally. Against certain vegetable hemolysins this antihemolytic action is very strong (Kobert). Antihemolysins are generally anticomplements, but in a number of instances anti-amboceptors have been obtained. The existence of immune bodies specific for hemolytic amboceptor and complement, supports the view that both of these agents are proteins.

In hemolysis as in bacteriolysis the complement exhibits two functions, corresponding to the "end-piece" and "mid-piece" fractions. Herzfeld and Klinger[78a] consider the mid-piece to be a globulin which renders the surface of the corpuscles more

[71] Jour. Immunol., 1919 (4), 77.

[72] Jour. Infect. Dis., 1913 (12), 111.

[73] Jobling and Bull, Jour. Exper. Med., 1913 (17), 61; also Bergel, Deut. Arch. klin. Med., 1912 (106), 47.

[74] Thiele and Embleton, however, state that hemolysin is not a lipase, and that the hemolytic power of serum has no relation to its lipolytic power (Jour. Path. and Bact., 1914 (19), 349).

[75] Biochem. Zeit., 1912 (46), 247; see also McNeil and Kahn, Jour. Immunol., 1918 (3), 295.

[76] Biochem. Zeit., 1907 (6), 172 and 327; Jour. Exper. Med., 1907 (9), 436.

[77] See Liefmann, *et al.*, Zeit. Immunität., 1912 (13), 150.

[78] Liebermann and Fenyvessy (*loc cit.*)[50] believe that serum hemolysis takes place as follows: First, the amboceptor acts on the corpuscle, injuring it so that it becomes less resistant; second, this combination acts upon the complement (a soap compound) and frees the soap so that it can unite with the amboceptor-corpuscle system; third, the soap causes hemolysis; fourth (as a separate step), the escape of the hemoglobin from the corpuscles. Tissot ascribes importance to the fatty acids of the plasma (Compt. Rend. Acad. Sci., 1919 (168), 1283). Bergel (Zeit Immunität., 1918 (27), 441) supports the hypothesis that immune hemolysis and agglutination depend on a solution of the lipoids of the cells. In this reaction the lipoids act as antigen, the new-formed amboceptor is formed by the lipoids of the lymphocytes as a zymogen which is activated by serum complement, and is specifically bound by the lipoid antigens of the corpuscles. That is, the lipoids are the haptophore groups of the antigen; they bind the receptor of the thermostabile lipase zymogen, which is activated by the non-specific complement.

[78a] Biochem. Zeit., 1918 (87), 36.

capable of taking up certain disintegration products contained in the serum (per-sensitization) which constitute the so-called end-piece, and which produce hemo-lysis by direct hydrolysis or solution of the stroma elements.

Hemagglutinin.—Agglutination of red corpuscles occurs under the influence of immune serum as well as under the influence of some normal serums.   In all respects the principles seem to be the same as those described for bacterial agglutination.   The hemagglutinating antibody behaves like the other antibodies and proteins under the in-fluence of chemical and physical agencies, but Landsteiner and Jagic have obtained strong agglutinating solutions containing very little protein.   Bergel[79] contends that hemagglutination is produced by lipase from the lymphocytes, which alters the lipoid membranes of the erythrocytes.   Agglutination occurs at much lower temperatures than hemolysis, and also is not checked by heating the serum to 55°; hence it is possible to observe hemagglutination independent of hemo-lysis.   Serums may contain hemagglutinins and not be hemolytic; the reverse is also true.   The *conglutinin* effect of beef serum (Bordet and Gay) is also observed with corpuscles as with bacteria.   As aggluti-nation occurs in corpuscles that have been fixed in formalin or sub-limate, it is probably not the proteins that are affected, but some other of the ingredients of the stroma, of which lecithin and cholesterol seem to be the chief.

Certain *vegetable poisons* produce agglutination of red corpuscles, especially ricin, abrin, and crotin, and the fact that ricin has little or no hemolytic action shows the independence of the processes.   Anti-sera for these vegetable poisons are also antiagglutinative, acting, as Ehrlich showed, on the poison and not on the corpuscles.   The seeds of many non-poisonous leguminous plants, and also of *Solanaceæ*, yield extracts that are strongly agglutinative for red corpuscles; in *Phaseolus multiflorus* the active substance is found in the proteose of the seed, and seems to be a part of the stored food (Schneider).[80] It is not present in other parts of the plant.   *Snake venoms* contain agglutinins, destroyed by heating to 75°; their agglutinating power being in inverse ratio to their hemolytic power.   Corpuscles aggluti-nated by venoms may be again separated by potassium permanganate solutions.[81]   Silicic acid and certain other *colloids* may act as agglu-tinins, their effects bearing a relation to the effects of electrical charges upon agglutination of bacteria or of colloids (*q. v.*).[82]   Corpuscles that have been sensitized by hemolytic amboceptors are much more readily agglutinated by salts of heavy metals, especially copper and zinc, presumably because of quantitative alterations in the electrical charge of the corpuscles induced by the antibody.[83]

[79] Zeit. Immunität., 1912 (14), 255; 1913 (17), 169.
[80] Jour. Biol. Chem., 1912 (11), 47; bibliography.
[81] See Flexner, Univ. of Penn. Med. Bull., 1902 (15), 324 and 361.
[82] See Landsteiner and Jagic, Münch. med. Woch., 1904 (51), 1185.
[83] Eisner and Friedemann, Zeit. Immunität., 1914 (21), 520.

Agglutination of the corpuscles during life may be of great pathological importance, for such masses of agglutinated corpuscles may readily produce capillary thrombi and emboli, which, if wide-spread, may create much disturbance. Sometimes the serum of one individual of a species agglutinates the corpuscles of another individual of the same species (*isoagglutination*),[83a] a fact which must be taken into account in performing transfusion of blood, lest dangerous agglutination take place. Agglutination of an individual's corpuscles by his own serum (*autoagglutination*), may also be observed under experimental, and perhaps under pathological conditions (Landsteiner),[84] this pathological autoagglutination probably occurring especially at temperatures below 37°. (See Paroxysmal Hemoglobinuria.) Many bacteria produce substances that are agglutinative for human red corpuscles, among them being *B. typhosus, pyocyaneus,* and staphylococcus. Flexner[85] has found in typhoid fever thrombi that seemed to be composed of agglutinated red corpuscles, almost free from fibrin and leucocytes. Probably many of the so-called "hyaline thrombi" found frequently in infectious diseases are really composed of agglutinated, partly hemolyzed red corpuscles (see "Thrombosis," Chap. xiii).

HEMOLYSIS BY BACTERIA[86]

Both pathogenic and non-pathogenic bacteria produce hemolytic substances that are excreted into the fluids in which they grow. During many infectious diseases marked hemolysis occurs, especially in those diseases accompanied by septicemia. After death the hemoglobin of the blood goes into solution, and the resulting staining of the walls of the blood-vessels, and later of the tissues everywhere, is generally familiar. In the *post-mortem hemolysis* probably the putrefactive organisms are chiefly concerned, although it is marked a very short time after death in many cases of septicemia, particularly when the infecting organism is the streptococcus, and here probably the pathogenic organism is the chief cause of the hemolysis. The hemolytic action of bacteria can be studied both *in vitro* and *in vivo*. Among the best known hemolytic bacterial toxins are *tetanolysin, pyocyanolysin, typholysin, staphylolysin,*[87] and *streptocolysin,* as they have been termed. Of these, the case of pyocyanolysin is question-

[83a] Review by Happ, Jour. Exp. Med., 1920 (31) 313.
[84] See also Clough and Richter, Bull. Johns Hop. Hosp., 1918 (29), 86; Rous and Robertson, Jour. Exp. Med., 1917 (27),509.
[85] Univ. of Penn. Med. Bull., 1902 (15), 324; Amer. Jour. Med. Sci., 1903 (126), 202.
[86] See Pribram, Kolle and Wassermann's Handbuch., 1913 (II), 1328.
[87] Analysis of staphylolysin by Burkhardt (Arch. exp. Path. und Pharm., 1910 (63), 107), showed it to be dialyzable, protein- and biuret-free, thermolabile and soluble in ether. From *B. putidum* he isolated a hemolytic substance which seems to be a derivative by oxidation of erucacic acid (oxydimethylthiolerucacic acid).

able, because it has been described as resisting heat above the boiling-point, and Jordan[88] seems to have proved that the hemolysis is ascribable to the alkalinity that this organism produces in culture-media. Other bacterial hemolysins are, however, destroyed by heat at 70° or less for two hours; but they are altogether different from ordinary immune hemolysins. Apparently streptocolysin is simply a toxin for red cells,[89] and unites directly to the cell receptors without the intervention of any intermediary body. As a similar structure has been shown for staphylolysin and tetanolysin, it is probable that the *bacterial hemolysins are all merely toxins with a particular affinity for red cells,* and against some of these bacterial hemotoxins antitoxic sera are obtainable, although there is usually some question as to how much of the antagonistic effect depends on true antitoxins and how much upon the cholesterol in the serum. However, a strong antiserum has been obtained against the hemotoxin of *B. Welchii*.[90] Of course bacteria may also form many non-specific hemolytic substances as products of their metabolism, such as acids and bases.

Secondary anemia occurring in the infectious diseases is probably to be explained largely by this hemolytic property of bacterial toxins. Hemoglobinuria may also be produced in the same way in some instances. Intravenous injections of filtrates of the saprophyte, *B. megatherium*, will produce hemoglobinuria in guinea-pigs, hence hemolysis is not an exclusive property of pathogenic bacteria, and with streptococci Lyall[91] found that the hemolysin titer did not afford a criterion of virulence. No immunity to streptococci is produced in animals immunized with streptococcus hemolysin.[92] Pneumococci produce an intracellular hemolytic toxin which is very labile and antigenic; living pneumococci convert hemoglobin into methemoglobin, but this the hemolytic extracts of pneumococci cannot do (Cole).[93] Streptococcus viridans has the same property,[94] which may play a part in the effects of infections with these organisms. von Hellens[95] states that streptocolysin is ether soluble and heat resistant.

HEMOLYSIS BY VEGETABLE POISONS

A number of plant poisons are strongly hemolytic, and some of them owe much of their toxicity to their effect on the erythrocytes. One group consists of the bodies often called "vegetable toxalbumins," because they seem to be proteins, and includes ricin, abrin, crotin, curcin and robin.[96] Of these, crotin and curcin are particu-

[88] Jour. Medical Research, 1903 (10), 31.
[89] Jour. Amer. Med. Assoc., 1903 (41), 962; Jour. Infect. Dis., 1907 (4), 277.
[90] Ford and Williams, Jour. Immunol., 1919 (4), 385.
[91] Jour. Med. Res., 1914 (30), 515.
[92] McLeod and McNee, Jour. Path. and Bact., 1913 (17), 524.
[93] Jour. Exper. Med., 1914 (20), 347, 363.
[94] Blake, Jour. Exper. Med., 1916 (24), 315.
[95] Cent. f. Bakt., 1913 (68), 602.
[96] The sap of *Cotyledon Scheideckeri* contains hemolytic substances of peculiar character. (See Kritchewski, Jour. Exp. Med., 1917 (26), 669.)

larly actively hemolytic, while ricin, abrin, and robin are more marked by their agglutinating action, hemolysis being produced only by relatively large doses. Their effects vary greatly, however, according to the species of animals whose blood is used. They resemble the bacterial toxins, in that immunity can be secured against them, and the immune serum will prevent their hemolytic action. Heating the toxalbumins to 65° or 70° does not destroy the hemolytic or agglutinating action except with phallin, but 100° does. The action of these substances is not like that of the enzymes, in that it is quantitative, a given amount acting on a given amount of corpuscles to which it is bound. Madsen and Walbum[97] observed that red corpuscles had the power of dissociating neutral mixtures of ricin and antiricin, the ricin entering the corpuscles from which it could be recovered.[98] Ford and Abel believe the hemolytic agent of amanita to be a glucoside. (The general nature and other properties of these substances are considered under the heading of "Phytotoxins," in Chap. vi.)

Saponin Group.—Another quite distinct group of vegetable hemolyzing agents consists of the "*saponin substances.*"[99] These are a closely related group of *glucosides*, found in at least 46 different families of plants, and they are strong protoplasmic as well as hemolytic poisons. They differ altogether from the true toxins, being heat resistant, having no resemblance to proteins, and not giving rise to antibodies on immunization of animals.[1] The degree of their toxicity is not directly proportional to their hemolytic activity; they seem to injure chiefly the nerve-cells. Apparently hemolysis is brought about by action upon the lipoids of the red corpuscles, for addition of cholesterol to saponin prevents its hemolytic effect;[2] lecithin does not have the same property.[3] Both cholesterol and lecithin combine with saponin, the cholesterol compound being quite inert, whereas the lecithin compound is both hemolytic and toxic. The compound formed between a typical saponin, digitonin, and cholesterol, is so insoluble that it has been found useful in the quantitative analysis of cholesterol.[4] Normal serum seems to contain

[97] Cent. f. Bakt., 1904 (36), 242.

[98] According to Pascucci (Hofmeister's Beitr., 1905 (7), 457), ricin combines directly with lecithin, the compound being strongly hemolytic.

[99] Complete literature on saponin given by Kobert, "Die Saponinsubstanzen," Stuttgart, 1904; also Kunkel, "Handbuch der Toxokologie," Jena.

[1] Saponins are characterized by their ready solubility in water and the foaming, soapy character possessed by the solution; hence their technical applications as soap bark, etc. Heated with dilute acids they split off sugar; also when acted on by glucoside-splitting enzymes (from spiders), according to Kobert. Saponin from *Quillaja* (soap-bark) has the formula $C_{19}H_{30}O_{10}$ (Stütz). Most are colloids, but some crystallize.

[2] Ransom, Deut. med. Woch., 1901 (27), 194; Madsen and Noguchi, Cent. f. Bakt., 1905 (37), 367; Pascucci, Hofmeister's Beitr., 1905 (6), 543.

[3] Noguchi, Univ. of Penn. Med. Bull., 1902 (15), 327; Meyer, Hofmeister's Beitr., 1908 (11), 357.

[4] Windaus, Chem. Berichte, 1909 (42), 238.

an antihemolysin for saponin, and therefore hemoglobinuria is not produced by all saponins on intravenous injection.   Careful immunization leads to a slight increase in this antihemolytic action of the serum, possibly due to an increased formation of cholesterol (Kobert).   The resistance of corpuscles to saponin hemolysis varies in disease, being especially low in jaundice (M'Neil).[5]

A study of the toxicity of the members of this group by Kobert[6] shows that in general they have similar properties, but that minor differences exist between them.   All cause hemolysis, some in dilution as great as 1:100,000.   Some produce hemoglobinuria when injected intravenously, others do not.   All paralyze the heart, but the injuries to the central nervous system are the chief cause of death. Marked local changes are produced at the site of injection, but the leucocytes are apparently not injured, although sterile suppuration is produced.   There is a period of latency after intravenous injection of small doses—twenty-four hours or more—before the appearance of symptoms.

SAPOTOXIN is one of the most actively toxic and hemolytic products of *quillaja*.

CYCLAMIN is also a member of this group (derived from *Cyclamen*), and is said to be the most active of all as a hemolytic agent (Tufanow).

SOLANIN[7] is obtained from all parts of the potato plant, combined with malic acid; it is found particularly in young sprouts, but not in any considerable amounts in normal potatoes.[8]   Its formula is unknown, but as it splits up into an alkaloid (*solanidin*) and sugar it is called a *glyco-alkaloid*.   In its action it resembles the saponins, being a powerful protoplasmic poison, killing bacteria, and hemolyzing blood in very great dilutions.[9]

A great number of hemolytic poisons are obtained from poisonous mushrooms. Best known of these is:

HELVELLIC ACID, from *Helvella esculenta*, which has the empiric formula $C_{12}H_{20}O_7$.[10]   Intravenously injected it produces hemoglobinuria and icterus, with hemoglobin infarcts in the kidneys (Bostroem).[11]

PHALLIN, or *Amanita hemolysin*, described by Kobert as a toxalbumin, has been found by Abel and Ford to be a glucoside, and thus belongs to the saponin group.   (See Chap. vi. for further discussion.)   In the leaves of the ivy, *Hedera helix*, a hemolytic glucoside has been found by Moore.[12]   It is of interest that Faust believes the poisonous agent of cobra venom to be a glucoside, closely resembling sapotoxin.

As will be seen, all these last-mentioned vegetable hemolytic agents are essentially different from either the bacterial or serum hemolysins, or from the abrin, ricin, crotin, or robin group, in that they are of relatively simple chemical composition, and quite unlike proteins, enzymes, or toxins.   The manner in which they cause hemolysis is unknown, but from their relation to saponin it is probable that, like

[5] Jour. Path. and Bact., 1910 (15), 56.
[6] Arch. exp. Path. u. Pharm., 1887 (23), 233.
[7] Literature, see Meyer and Schmiedeberg, Arch. f. exp. Path. u. Pharm., 1895 (36), 361; Perles, *ibid.*, 1890 (26), 88.
[8] See Kunkel, "Handbuch der Toxokologie," p. 873.
[9] Concerning human solanin poisoning see Rothe, Zeit. f. Hyg., 1919 (88), 1.
[10] Boehm and Külz, Arch. exp. Path. u. Pharm., 1885 (19), 403.
[11] Deut. Arch. klin. Med., 1883 (32), 209.
[12] Jour. Pharmacol., 1913 (4), 263.

it, they cause injury by combining with or dissolving the lipoids of the stroma of the corpuscles. Extracts of *Morchella esculenta* do not hemolyze corpuscles *in vitro*, although powerfully hemolytic when injected into animals, and causing severe hemoglobinuria; so that it is probable that they cause their hemolytic effects indirectly through the changes which they produce in the tissues of the poisoned animal.[13]

HEMOLYSIS BY VENOMS [14]

The laking of blood-corpuscles by venoms is of peculiar interest from the standpoint of immunity phenomena, since it was demonstrated by Flexner and Noguchi that the hemolytic principle of the venoms resembles an amboceptor, in that some substance behaving like complement has to be furnished by the blood. Kyes found that this complementing agent is lecithin,[15] and was able to produce what he considers to be compounds of the hemolysin with lecithin, called "lecithids." The hemolytic activity of these lecithids is very great, and they seem to be free from the neurotoxic principle of the venoms. Whether they represent true compounds of a hemolytic amboceptor with lecithin, or are simply actively hemolytic products of the cleavage of lecithin by an enzymatic activity of the venom, is at present unsettled;[16] it seems probable, however, that the hemolysin of cobra venom is a lipase that splits lecithin into two hemolytic components, oleic acid and "desoleolecithin" (Coca).[16] Noguchi suggests that not only lecithin, but also soaps, especially of unsaturated fatty acids, and probably protein compounds of soaps and lecithin, may act as the hemolytic "complement" which activates venoms. The hemolytic agents of venom seem to be secreted by the salivary glands of the reptiles from their blood, which contains almost identical amboceptors, differing chiefly in that they can be activated only by agents contained in snake blood, while the amboceptors of venom can be activated by nearly all sorts of blood. Venoms from cobra, rattlesnake, moccasin, and copperhead possess in each a variety of intermediary bodies (amboceptors) that seem to be at least partly identical in nature, although they may vary in quantity. In order of decreasing hemolytic power for mammalian corpuscles come venoms from cobra, water moccasin, copperhead, and rattlesnake. These venoms are also agglutinative for all corpuscles tried, and agglutination will occur at 0° C. Exposure for thirty minutes at 75°–80° C. destroys the agglutinating property. In general, the hemolytic power of the

[13] Friedberger and Brossa, Zeit. Immunität., 1912 (15), 506.
[14] General review of literature on the hemolytic properties of animal poisons given by Sachs, Biochem. Centralblatt. 1906 (5), 257; Noguchi, Jour. Exp. Med., 1907 (9), 436.
[15] Cruickshank also found that other lipoids than lecithin may activate cobra venom (Jour. Path. and Bact., 1913 (17), 619).
[16] See Kyes, Jour. Infect. Dis., 1910 (7), 181; v. Dungern and Coca, *ibid.*, 1912 (10), 57; Manwaring, Zeit. Immunität, 1910 (6), 513; Bang, *ibid.*, 1910 (8), 202; Coca, Jour. Infect. Dis., 1915 (17), 351.

venoms for different sorts of corpuscles varies in inverse proportion to their agglutinative power. The hemolytic intermediary bodies are resistant to heat, suffering but slight loss of power at 100° C. Red corpuscles of the frog are not hemolyzed by venom, and those of *necturus* (mud puppy) but slightly, agreeing with the known resistance of cold-blooded animals to snake-bites.

The erythrocytes of different individuals show considerable variations in their resistance to hemolytic agents, perhaps depending upon the amount or upon the manner of fixation of the lipoids in the corpuscles; thus the corpuscles of syphilitics show a heightened resistance to hemolysis by cobra venom (Weil)[17] except in the earliest stages, when they are hypersensitive. Also, the serum of persons suffering from various diseases, especially mental diseases, inhibits the hemolysis of human corpuscles by cobra venom.[18] After splenectomy there is an increased resistance to venom hemolysis.[19]

Eel serum is remarkably hemolytic, so much so that a quantity of 0.1 c.c. per kilogram of body weight will kill a rabbit or guinea-pig in three minutes when injected intravenously. Heating at 54° C. for fifteen minutes destroys the hemolytic action, and, unlike ordinary serum hemolysins the addition of complement does not restore its activity. Animals can be immunized against this serum. Introduced into the stomach in ordinary quantities eel serum is not toxic. It can be dried and redissolved without losing its activity, but acids and alkalies readily destroy it. Mosso, who first discovered the toxicity of eel serum, called the un known active principle *ichthyotoxin*. It is found chiefly in the albumin fraction of the eel serum.[20] Many other animals produce hemolytic poisons (e. g., spiders, bees) which are discussed under Zootoxins, Chapter vi.

HEMOLYSIS IN DISEASE

During health there is always going on a certain amount of destruction of red corpuscles that have outlived their usefulness; hence in disease we may have to deal with either an alteration in the normal processes of blood destruction or the introduction of entirely new processes. Although the place and manner of normal red corpuscle destruction is not completely known, yet it seems probable that there is relatively little hemolysis within the circulating blood. When a red corpuscle becomes damaged, it seems to become more susceptible to phagocytosis, and it is then picked out of the blood, chiefly by the endothelial cells of the sinuses of the liver, spleen, hemolymph glands, and bone-marrow. Within these cells it apparently undergoes hemolysis. Eventually, the resulting pigment is split up by the liver, the non-ferruginous portion forming the bile-pigments, while the iron seems to be mostly withheld to be worked over into new hemoglobin.[21]

[17] Jour. Infect. Dis., 1909 (6), 688; Stone and Schottstaedt, Arch. Int. Med., 1912 (10), 8.
[18] See articles on this subject in the Münch. med. Woch., 1909, Vol. 56.
[19] Kolmer, Jour. Exp. Med., 1917 (25), 195.
[20] Sato, Kyoto Jour. Med. Sci., 1917 (14), 36.
[21] Muir and Dunn (Jour. Path. and Bact., 1915 (20), 41), find that after acute hemolytic anemia in rabbits the excess iron stored in the organs has been nearly all absorbed by the time regeneration of the blood is complete.

(See "Pigmentation." Chap. xviii.) Whenever during disease red corpuscles are more rapidly injured than they are under normal conditions, these processes of normal hemolysis are exaggerated and we not only find the phagocytic cells of the spleen and glands packed with corpuscles, but endothelial cells elsewhere, and also leucocytes, take on the hemolytic function. At the same time there results an excessive production of bile-pigment from the destroyed red corpuscles, which has an etiological relation to the so-called "hemato-hepatogenous" jaundice. If hemolysis is very excessive, the blood pigment accumulates in other organs than the liver and spleen. According to Pearce[22] and his associates, when the blood contains at one time more than 0.06 gm. of free hemoglobin per kilo of body weight, it begins to be excreted by the kidneys; smaller amounts are cared for chiefly by the liver, and even when much larger amounts of hemoglobin are present in the blood the liver takes care of most of it, only a relatively small proportion, 17 to 36 per cent, being excreted in the urine. Hence it is possible to have hemolytic jaundice without hemoglobinuria. Part of the pigment is converted into urobilin, and the amount of this pigment in the stool is an index of the amount of hemolysis.[23] In persons with hemolytic hemoglobinemia, intravenous injection of hemoglobin will produce hemoglobinuria with smaller dosage than in normal persons, who require at least 17 c.c. of laked corpuscles to produce hemoglobinuria.[24]

It is possible that the globin, which is quite toxic when free,[25] may play a part in the symptomatology of hemolytic poisons. The stroma of the erythrocytes also seems to be toxic.[26]

The hemolysis of the *acute febrile diseases* is readily explained by the demonstrable hemolytic property of the products of the organisms that cause them, such as streptocolysin, staphylolysin, etc. Perhaps at the same time products of altered metabolism may also play a part, but it does not seem probable from experimental results that the thermic condition *per se* has much effect. In malaria, although the parasites enter and destroy the corpuscles in which they live, yet this alone does not account for all the blood destruction of the disease, for the amount of anemia is quite without relation to the number of parasites to be found. There is good reason to believe that the plasmodia produce hemolytic substances that are discharged into the serum.

In the *primary anemias* hemolysis seems to be the essential process, although the agents involved are at present unknown. Absorption of hemolytic products of intestinal putrefaction or infection has always come in for much suspicion, without ever becoming completely

[22] Jour. Exp. Med., 1912 (16), several articles.
[23] See Robertson, Arch. Int. Med., 1915 (15), 1072.
[24] Sellards and Minot, Jour. Med. Res., 1916 (34), 469.
[25] Schittenhelm and Weichardt, Münch. med. Woch., 1912 (59), 1089.
[26] Barratt and Yorke, Brit. Med. Jour., Jan. 31, 1914.

15

established.   Here also the hemolysis seems to take place in the endo-thelial cells rather than in the vessels.   In such a disease as pernicious anemia there is much reason to assume that defective or abnormal hematogenesis is an important factor.   Probably the anemia of nephritis is at least partly the result of hemolytic action of the retained products of metabolism, in which connection the hemolytic properties of ammonium compounds may be recalled.   In some diseases associated with anemia it has been found that the blood-serum of the patient is distinctly *isohemolytic,* although *isoagglutination* seems to be more frequent.   The fluids that can be obtained from cancers have been found to be hemolytic, while antihemolysin has been found in ascitic and pleural effusions.   Autolytic disintegration of liver, and presumably other tissues, may also cause the presence of hemolytic substances in the blood.[27]   Arseniuretted hydrogen may produce hemolysis in some such way, since it causes no hemolysis in the test tube (Heffter).   The very great hemolytic action of soaps and free fatty acids, which varies directly with the number of unsaturated carbon atoms they contain (Moore[28]), makes it possible that these substances play a part in the hemolysis of disease, especially since the fatty acids of the liver are characterized by their high content of free fatty acids.   Bile is strongly hemolytic, and in icterus this is an im-portant consideration.

In many forms of poisoning hemolysis is a prominent feature; in some it seems to be the chief effect of the poison, *e. g.,* potassium chlorate and arseniuretted hydrogen.   In severe extensive burns there may occur hemolysis, and hemoglobinuria may also result.   The hemo-globinuria of "blackwater fever" has been the cause of much discus-sion as to whether the malarial parasite or the quinine is the cause, with a divided opinion resulting, although, undoubtedly, cases do occur in malaria without administration of quinine.   The studies of Brem[29] indicate that the hemolysis is produced by a hemolysin coming from the plasmodium, and that the quinine influences the condition by preventing the action of an antihemolytic substance present in the blood.

After removal of the spleen, hemolysis by the hemolymph glands exceeds that of the primitive spleen, causing an excessive destruction of red corpuscles (Warthin[30]).   This suggests that the spleen may normally dispose of some hemolytic agent which acts either by stimu-

[27] Maidorn, Biochem. Zeit. ,1912 (45), 328.   Hemolytic lipoids are believed by some to be liberated from injured tissues (see Kirsche, Biochem. Zeit., 1913 (55), 169), but McPhedran (Jour. Exp. Med., 1913 (18), 527) could find no evidence that any particularly hemolytic fatty acid, more active than oleic acid, can be isolated from either normal or diseased tissues.
[28] Brit. Med. Jour., 1909 (ii), 684; see also Lamar, Jour. Exper. Med., 1911 (13), 380.
[29] Arch. Int. Med., 1912 (9), 129.
[30] Jour. Med. Research, 1902 (7), 435.

lating phagocytosis or by so altering the red cells that they are particularly susceptible to phagocytosis. This idea is not substantiated by the work of Pearce,[31] who found the anemia of splenectomy accompanied by an increased resistance of the corpuscles to hemolysis, and no hemolytic agent was present in the blood. There also occurs the group of anemias associated with great enlargement of the spleen, and in which removal of the spleen may result in a return to normal blood conditions; a fact suggesting, among other possibilities, that there may be poisons which stimulate directly the hemolytic action of the spleen independent of the natural stimulation of splenic hemolysis which comes from the presence in the splenic blood of injured red corpuscles.[32]

Resistance to hemolysis varies greatly in disease conditions[33] and often specifically,—*i.e.*, resistance may be increased to one agent, decreased for another, and normal with a third. Attempts have been made to use this resistance as a diagnostic or prognostic index, but not with great success in most cases. Apparently changes in the plasma lead to alterations in the permeability of the corpuscles, which determines their behavior with hemolytic agents; also changes in the proportion of lipoids and hemoglobin may modify hemolysis. As an example of this condition may be cited observations on hemolysis by cobra venom, the corpuscles having been found less resistant in dementia præcox, more resistant in carcinoma and syphilis. Butler[34] states that fragility of the corpuscles is abnormally high in exophthalmic goiter, cancer, syphilis, tabes, anemia and malaria. In obstructive jaundice the corpuscles show an increased resistance to hemolysis by hypotonic salt solution, but in congenital hemolytic jaundice the resistance is decreased.[35] Using saponin hemolysis, Bigland[36] found the resistance greatly decreased in icterus, although the serum had an increased protective action because of antagonism between the saponin and the bile salts; in all anemias resistance was found increased, except pernicious anemia, which showed normal or slightly subnormal resistance; high temperature decreases resistance. As will be seen from the few examples cited, the resistance to different hemolytic agents may vary with the same corpuscles.[37]

Paroxysmal Hemoglobinuria.[38]—This condition seems to depend upon the presence in the serum of a hemolytic amboceptor (an *autohemolysin*), which will combine with the corpuscles of the same individual and sensitize them for his own complement (Donath and Landsteiner, Eason). This au'ohemolysin can react with the corpuscles only at low temperature, such as may be furnished in the peripheral vessels by exposure to cold, and the complement unites when the temperature of these corpuscles again reaches 37° in other parts of the

[31] Pearce *et al.*, Jour. Exp. Med., 1912, Vol. 16. See also Roccavilla, Arch. Med. Exp., 1915 (26), 508.

[32] See Banti, Semain Méd., 1913 (33), 313.

[33] Review by Paltauf, Krehl and Marchand's Handb. allg. Pathol., 1912 (II (1),) 83.

[34] Quarterly Jour. Med., 1913 (6), 145.

[35] See Richards and Johnson, Jour. Amer. Med. Assoc., 1913 (51), 1586 Giffin and Sanford, Jour. Lab. Clin. Med., 1919 (4), 465.

[36] Quart. Jour. Med., 1914 (7), 370.

[37] Bibliography by Krasny, Folia Hematol., 1913 (16), 353.

[38] Landsteiner, Handbuch d. Biochem., Vol. 2 (1), p. 492; Meyer and Emmerich, Deut. Arch. klin. Med., 1909 (96), 287.

body. In susceptible persons attacks of hemoglobinuria may be brought on merely by holding the hands in cold water, and their blood serum will sensitize to hemolysis human corpuscles (even of normal individuals),[39] *in vitro* at low temperatures.[40] Certain infections, especially syphilis,[41] predispose to paroxysmal hemoglobinuria. Not only the hemolytic amboceptors, but also an auto-opsonin is present (Eason) and the resistance of the red corpuscles is decreased to various harmful agencies, including CO_2 and other weak acids.[42] The corpuscles of three cases studied by Moss[43] showed an increased resistance to hypotonic $NaCl$ solutions. Just before the rigor, hemolysins may be found in the blood, disappearing after the hemoglobinuria (Roberts).[44] In a case studied by Dennie and Robertson,[45] hematuria resulted from destruction of only 6.3 c.c. of the patient's blood, and 90 per cent. of the liberated hemoglobin was excreted within two hours. There also occur conditions in which *auto-agglutination* occurs without hemolysis when the blood is cooled.[46]

Pathological Anatomy in Hemolysis.—The lesions produced in the organs of animals poisoned with hemolytic agents are usually pronounced and quite characteristic. There is often a subcutaneous edema, which is usually blood-stained, and similar fluid may be present in the serous cavities. The fat is yellowish, and the muscles are darker in color than is normal. The spleen is usually much swollen, soft, friable, and very dark in color. The liver is usually swollen and mottled with red areas in a yellow background. The renal cortex is dark in color, even chocolate-colored, and the pyramids are comparatively light; hemoglobin is frequently present in the urine. In the lungs are often found hemorrhages or areas resembling small infarcts. The blood may be thin and even distinctly transparent. Microscopically the red corpuscles are found in all conditions of degeneration, and often fused together. In the liver, besides patches of congestion, fatty changes are present if the animal lives long enough. Large phagocytic cells packed with red corpuscles are abundant in the spleen and lymphglands, as well as diffuse accumulations of the blood-cells, which are often fused; and much pigment is also present, both free and in the cells. Pigment also accumulates in the renal epithelium, which often shows much disintegration; congestion is prominent, and hemorrhages into both interstitial tissue and glomerules are frequent. Some of the lesions are due to the hemolysis, and some to the associated agglutination of corpuscles, which form hyaline thrombi. Pearce[46a] has found that agglutinative serum when injected into dogs causes widespread necrosis in the liver, which is followed by proliferation of connective tissue and the production of changes resembling cirrhosis. There is a marked decrease in the glycogen content of the liver, and of its lipolytic activity (Andrea).[47]

[39] See Lorant, Deut. Arch. klin. Med., 1918 (126), 148.
[40] Widal looks upon paroxysmal hemoglobinuria as an autoanaphylaxis (Semain Méd., 1913 (33), 613).
[41] Matsuo, Arch. f. klin. Med., 1912 (107) 335.
[42] Berghausen, Arch. Int. Med., 1912 (9), 137.
[43] Folia Serologica, 1911 (7), 1117.
[44] Brit. Med. Jour., 1915 (2), 398.
[45] Arch. Int. Med., 1915 (16), 205.
[46] See Rous and Robertson, Jour. Exp. Med., 1918 (27), 563; Clough and Richter, Bull. Johns Hop. Hosp., 1918 (29), 86.
[46a] Jour. Exp. Med., 1906 (8), 64; Jour. Med. Research, 1906 (14), 511.
[47] Arch. internat. pharmacodyn., 1905 (14), 177.

COMPLEMENT FIXATION[48] AND WASSERMANN REACTIONS[49]

The original principle involved in these reactions was first demonstrated by Bordet and Gengou, and is essentially as follows: If a specific antigen and amboceptor unite in the presence of complement, the complement is then united to the amboceptor-antigen compound to complete the reaction. When sufficient amounts of amboceptor and antigen are present the entire quantity of available complement may be thus fixed, and, consequently, the mixture contains no more complement for further reactions. As complement does not ordinarily unite with amboceptors except when the amboceptors are united with their specific antigens the fact that in a given system of

$$\text{complement} + \text{amboceptor} + \text{antigen}$$

there is no free complement, is evidence of a reaction between amboceptor and antigen; in consequence of which this reaction can be used to determine the presence of a specific amboceptor in a serum, by using the corresponding antigen; or conversely, with a serum containing a known amboceptor we can detect the presence in a solution of the specific antigen. The indicator of the presence or absence of complement which is in universal use, is the ability of the mixture to hemolyze erythrocytes in the presence of the specific hemolytic amboceptor. Thus, if typhoid bacilli and a typhoid antiserum which contains both complement and specific amboceptor, are mixed in proper proportions and incubated for a short time, the complement will be bound to the bacilli. If we then add this mixture to sheep corpuscles which have been acted upon by an antisheep-corpuscle serum, from which the complement had been previously removed by heating, no hemolysis will occur, for we have added no *free* complement. But if our original mixture had contained dysentery bacilli instead of typhoid bacilli the complement would not have been fixed, and the addition of this mixture, containing free complement, to the sensitized sheep corpuscles would cause prompt hemolysis.

This reaction was at first used for the detection of antibodies in

[48] The reaction of "complement fixation" must not be confused with the entirely distinct reaction of *"complement deviation,"* a mistake very likely to happen because of the careless but erroneous use by some writers of the latter term in describing the first-named reaction. Complement deviation (or Neisser-Wechsberg phenomenon) is produced when an excess of amboceptors is present together with antigen and a limited amount of complement, which results in absence of complement activity. The mechanism of this reaction has not been satisfactorily explained. Thjötta (Norsk. Mag. Laegevid., 1919 (80), 1051) believes it to depend on some special substance, distinct from the known antibodies, which adsorbs complement.

[49] Literature given by Meier, Jahresber. d. Immunitätsforsch., 1909 (4), 58; Sachs and Altmann, Kolle and Wassermann's Handbuch, Ergänzungsbd., 2, 1909, p. 476; Noguchi, "Serum Diagnosis of Syphilis and Luetin Reaction," Philadelphia, 1912.

sera,[50] and for the identification of bacteria, and was found to be exquisitely delicate, detecting most minute amounts of antigens with the sharpest specificity limits of any of the immunity reactions. On account of the delicacy of this reaction it can be used to determine the presence in tissues of specific organisms which cannot be cultivated; thus, it has been possible to demonstrate the existence of a specific scarlatinal virus[51] in the tissues during this disease, although the actual organism cannot be isolated. This fact led Wassermann to use extracts of the livers of congenital syphilitic fetuses, which contain great quantities of spirochetes, as an antigen for complement fixation reactions, whereby it should be possible to determine in a given serum the presence of specific amboceptors for the virus of syphilis, such amboceptors being present in persons infected with syphilis as a result of the reaction to the infection. As originally introduced, then, the Wassermann reaction was supposed to be simply a specific reaction between syphilitic antigen, specific syphilitic amboceptors, and non-specific complement. It was soon learned, however, that the reaction as it occurred in syphilis was decidedly different from the original complement fixation reaction of Bordet and Gengou, for it was found possible to substitute in the reaction for extracts of tissues containing syphilitic virus (spirochetes), the most varied sorts of tissue extracts, coming from tissues certainly free from spirochetes (e. g., ox heart). Noguchi and Bronfenbrenner[52] summarize the present state of the matter in these words: "We know merely this: that complement in the presence of syphilitic antigen may be rendered inactive by one or more substances in the body fluids of a syphilitic or parasyphilitic patient."

Extended investigation of these non-specific antigens which give specific complement fixation with syphilitic sera, has shown them to be related to the lipoids, especially the lecithins, as indicated by the fact that the most efficient antigens contain the aceton-insoluble fraction of the tissue lipoids. The antigenic value of this fraction of different liver extracts varies nearly directly with its power to combine with iodin[53] (Noguchi and Bronfenbrenner), which indicates that the unsaturated fatty acids are important in the reaction.[54]

[50] According to Gay (Univ. of Calif. Publ., Pathol., 1911 (2), 1, full discussion) complement fixation is produced by an antigen-antibody complex distinct from precipitinogen-precipitin, but Dean (Zeit. f. Immunität., 1912 (13), 84) believes that they represent two phases or stages of the same reaction. Thiele and Embleton (Zeit. Immunität., 1913 (16), 430) consider that in syphilis it is not a specific antibody, but an anti-complementary substance which arises from the disintegrating tissues.

[51] Koessler and Koessler, Jour. Infec. Dis., 1912 (9), 366.

[52] Jour. Exp. Med., 1911 (13), 43.

[53] Not corroborated by Browning, Cruickshank and Gilmour.[55]

[54] An interesting observation made by Noguchi and Bronfenbrenner, is that extracts from fatty livers are almost devoid of antigenic properties; but So (Cent. f. Bakt., 1912 (63), 438) found that the extract from fatty hearts of guinea-pigs was more active than from normal hearts.

Crude lecithins from different sources vary in efficiency, heart lecithin being more active than liver lecithin, brain and egg yolk lecithin following. Pure lecithin is not effective, the activity of lipoid solutions depending upon some other substance which is difficult to separate from lecithin (MacLean).[55] Addition of cholesterol to the lipoid solutions increases greatly their activity.[56] An acetone-precipitated "antigen" of this class is not a true antigen, however, for fixation antibodies are not developed in animals injected with such a lipoid which has been shown to be entirely efficient in the Wassermann reaction.[57]

As for the substance in the syphilitic serum which participates in the Wassermann reaction, it would seem to be related to the globulins, which are decidedly increased in the blood and spinal fluid[58] of syphilitics,[59] especially the euglobulin.[60] P. Schmidt[61] ascribes the reaction to the physico-chemical properties of the globulins of the syphilitic serum, which, he believes, possess a greater affinity for the colloids of the antigen than normal globulins; this affinity is held in check in normal serum by the albumins of the serum, which are relatively or absolutely decreased. That physico-chemical factors do play a part is evidenced by the common observation that the turbidity of the antigen suspension is closely related to its efficiency, clear solutions being less active. Slight changes in H-ion concentration will change a reaction from negative to positive, or reverse; and neutral salts can change a negative to a positive reaction, but not the reverse (Cumming.)[62] The lipoids in syphilitic sera are said by Peritz[63] to be increased, but the lipoid content and the antibody titer do not show any constant relation (Bauer and Skutezky).[64] The cholesterol content of syphilitic blood shows no evidence of a quantitative relation to the Wassermann reaction.[65] Friedemann[66] believes that a globulin-soap compound is the active substance in syphilitic sera. McIntosh[67] says that the active component differs from typical antibodies in not

[55] Monographs on Biochemistry, "Lecithin and Allied Substances," London, 1918.
[56] Browning *et al.*, Zeit. Immunität., 1912 (14), 284; Jour. Pathol. and Bact., 1911 (16), 135 and 225. Klein and Fraenkel believe the "antigen" of ox heart extracts to be a combination of lecithin with cholesterol and small amounts of a soap-like substance similar to jecorin (Münch. med. Woch., 1914 (61), 651.)
[57] Fitzgerald and Leathes, Univ. of Calif. Publ., Path., 1912 (2), 39.
[58] Pfeiffer, Kober and Field, Proc. Soc. Exp. Biol., 1915 (12), 153.
[59] See Rowe, Arch. Int. Med., 1916 (18), 455.
[60] Müller and Hough, Wien., klin. Woch., 1911 (24), 167.
[61] Zeit. f. Hyg., 1911 (69), 513. See also Hirschfeld and Klinger, Zeit. Immunität., 1914 (21), 40.
[62] Jour. Infect. Dis., 1916 (18), 151.
[63] Zeit. exp. Path., 1910 (8), 255.
[64] Wien. klin. Woch., 1913 (26), 830.
[65] Weston, Jour. Med. Res., 1914 (30), 377; Stein, Zeit. exp. Med., 1914 (3), 309.
[66] Zeit. f. Hyg., 1910 (67), 279.
[67] Zeit. Immunität., 1910 (5), 76.

passing through collodion or porcelain filters, and there are many who hold that the reacting substance is a product of tissue disintegration. Wassermann[68] has found evidence that the antibody is derived from the lymphocytes, at least in the spinal fluid of syphilitics.

Whether true antibodies are concerned in the Wassermann reaction is a question. In favor of this view is the fact that the serum of rabbits immunized with congenital syphilis livers contains an antibody giving the Wassermann reaction, exactly like the serum of syphilitics.[69]   On the other hand, the actual substance of pure cultures of spirochetes does not ordinarily act as antigen with syphilitic sera in the Wassermann reaction (Noguchi). It is highly probable that when syphilitic liver extracts are used as antigen in the Wassermann reaction, we have a true Bordet-Gengou reaction of complement fixation with the syphilitic substance present in this extract, in addition to the reaction which is accomplished by the lipoids.

Whether the complement is destroyed by enzymes,[70] or is inhibited by anti-complement present in syphilitic serum, or is destroyed by some toxic substance in the serum[71] are matters still under discussion. A favorite interpretation of the Wassermann reaction, which seems to harmonize with the known facts, is that there is a precipitation of serum globulin by the lipoidal colloids of the antigen, and adsorption of the complement by this precipitate.

Apparently the globulins of the serum in syphilis are altered in some specific but as yet unknown way, whereby they acquire in greatly increased degree the capacity to form this adsorbent precipitate.[72] Alterations in the lipoids also seem to exist, for it is known that conditions that modify the serum lipoids also modify the reaction.   There seems little doubt that the reaction is not chemical but physical, and the union of complement to antibody follows essentially the laws of adsorption.   Also its intimate relation to the precipitin reaction seems to be established (Dean).[73]

The changes in character of the blood serum in syphilis are sufficient to give not only immunological but also frank chemical or physico-chemical manifestations.   For example, Bruck[74] states that the precipitate obtained when nitric acid is added to syphilitic serum is more abundant and of a characteristic gelatinous appearance.   Platinum cloride also produces a heavier precipitate in syphilitic sera (Brown and Iyengar).[75]   The globulin responsible for the Wassermann reaction is said to precipitate more readily by ammonium sulphate and other re-

[68] Wassermann and Lange, Berl. klin. Woch., 1914 (51), 527.
[69] Citron and Munk, Deut. med. Woch., 1910 (36), 1560; Eiken, Zeit. Immunität., 1915 (21), 188.
[70] Manwaring, Zeit. f. Immunität., 1909 (3), 309.
[71] Kiss, ibid., 1910 (1), 703.
[72] See Nathan, Zeit. Immunität., 1918 (27), 219; Walker, Jour. Path. Bact., 1917 (21), 181.
[73] Lancet, Jan. 13, 1917.
[74] Münch. med. Woch., 1917 (64), 25.   See also Smith and Solomon, Boston Med. Surg. Jour., 1917 (177), 321.
[75] Indian Jour. Med. Res., 1915 (3), 95.

agents.[76]   According to von Dungern[77] the heat coagulation of syphilitic serum is prevented by a smaller relative quantity of an alkaline solution of indigo than is the case with normal serum, a statement disputed by Flood and Fujimoto.[77]   Syphilitic serum also flocculates on addition of appropriate colloidal suspensions which will not coagulate normal serum (Vernes).[78]   Landau[79] states that syphilitic serum has a heightened power to decolorize and clear up an iodin precipitate produced in the serum.[80]

Among other reactions observed are the following:

Klausner's Serum Reaction.—When distilled water is added in certain proportions to fresh serum, a distinct flocculent precipitate separates out in a few hours, and this property is much more marked in syphilitic than in normal sera.   While not specific for syphilis, this reaction is almost invariably present in certain stages of syphilis.   This property is not due to the excess of globulin present in syphilitic sera, according to the later studies of Klausner,[81] who believes that the high lipoid content of syphilitic serum is responsible.

Porges-Hermann-Perutz Reaction.—If equal parts of a 2% solution of sodium glycocholate and an alcoholic cholesterol suspension (0.4%) are added to inactivated serum from syphilitic patients, a precipitate forms, while with normal serum there occurs no precipitate.[82]   Little is known concerning the nature of this reaction.

Coagulation Reaction.—This was described by Hirschfeld and Klinger,[83] and depends on the fact that tissue extracts digested with syphilitic serum lose their ability to coagulate blood.   The effect is believed to depend on adsorption of the lipoids of the tissue extract by serum constituents, and hence is fundamentally similar to the Wassermann reaction.

CYTOLYSIS IN GENERAL[84]

Not the same degree of success has been obtained in immunizing against other tissue elements as with the erythrocytes.   Immune serum can readily be obtained against cells that can be secured quite free from other cells, such as spermatozoa, ciliated epithelium, and leucocytes, but even then the immunity is not specific.   Much less is it specific when ground-up organs are used for immunizing, as is the case in the experimental production of *nephrolysins, hepatolysins*, etc., for at the same time antibodies are secured for not only the typical parenchyma cells, but also for endothelium, stroma cells, red and white corpuscles, and blood plasma.   As a consequence, the early expectations that by this process of immunization against specific cells great progress could be made in our knowledge of physiology, by

[76] See Heller, Biochem. Zeit., 1918 (90), 166; McDonagh., Proc. Royal Soc. Med., 1916 (9), 191, (Derm. Sect).
[77] Münch. med. Woch., 1915 (62), 1212. See also Flood, Jour. Immunol., 1916 (2), 69; Fujimoto, *ibid.*, 1918 (3), 11.
[78] Compt. Rend. Acad. Sci., 1918 (167), 383.
[79] Wien. klin. Woch., 1913 (26), 1702.
[80] Not corroborated by Stillians and Kolmer, Jour. Amer. Med. Assoc., 1915 (64), 1459.
[81] Biochem. Zeit., 1912 (47), 36.
[82] See Gammeltoft, Deut. med. Woch., 1912 (38), 1934; Ellermann, *ibid.*, 1913 (39), 219.
[83] Deut. med. Woch., 1914 (40), 1607. See also Kolmer and Toyama, Amer. Jour. Syphilis, 1918 (2), 505.
[84] Literature is given by Fleischmann and Davidsohn, Folia Serologica. 1908 (1), 173; Landsteiner, Handbuch d. Biochem., 1909 (II (1)). 542; Ritchie, Jour. Pathol. and Bact., 1908 (12), 140.

selectively throwing out of function an organ through the simple process of injecting an antiserum, have been disappointed. Equally little progress has been made in the treatment of malignant growths by the same method. The immune serums usually obtained do, to a certain extent, injure the specific organ, but they also usually injure other organs nearly as much or perhaps more; furthermore they generally contain hemolytic toxins, even if the tissues used in immunizing are free from blood, and, as we have seen, hemolytic poisons may cause serious tissue destruction.[85]

Beebe[86] claims to have secured serums by immunizing with tissue nucleoproteins, that were altogether specifically toxic for the type of cells from which the nucleoproteins were obtained; e. g., immunizing with liver nucleoproteins yielded serum destroying liver cells and no others. Other observers have failed to corroborate this work.[87] According to Zinsser[88] the cytolytic antibodies may be quite distinct from the proteolytic amboceptors which are developed against unformed protein antigens.

In view of the present uncertain state of the subject, and the very questionable value of much of the work so far done, the consideration of the various cytolysins or cytotoxins may be dismissed by briefly referring to a few of the most important results.

Leucocytolytic Serum.[89]—This may be obtained either by immunizing with leucocytes obtained from exudates or from the blood, or by using emulsions of lymph-glands. Specific leucocytolytic serum agglutinates leucocytes and produces observable morphologic changes, in the way of solution of the cytoplasm and cessation of ameboid movements; but it may also react with the fixed tissue cells of the same animal.[90] Of the leucocytes, the large granular cells seem most affected and the lymphocytes least. When injected into the peritoneal cavity such serum causes an apparent initial leucopenia, and later a decided leucocytosis in the peritoneal fluid. Corresponding with this, if bacteria are injected at the same time as the serum, resistance is found decreased, but later it is much increased. Such serum also contains anticomplement, according to Wassermann, indicating that the injected leucocytes contain complement. Leucocytotoxin obtained by immunizing against lymphatic tissue is very thermolabile, being destroyed by 55° C. for thirty minutes, and the serum can be only partially reactivated by the use of fresh serum. Bacterial filtrates may also contain "leucocidins" analogous to hemolysins. Normal foreign sera are more or less toxic to leucocytes, which can be shown by the reduced capacity of the leucocytes for phagocytosis.[91]

Antiplatelet Serum.—Several experimenters have produced antisera for platelets. Lee and Robertson[92] obtained a specific lytic and agglutinative action, requiring complement for its accomplishment. Injected into animals this antiplatelet serum caused a condition resembling exactly *purpura hemorrhagica* in man.

[85] See Sata, Ziegler's Beitr., 1906 (39), 1.

[86] Jour. Exp. Med., 1905 (7), 733.

[87] Pearce and Jackson, Jour. Infect. Dis., 1906 (3), 742. See also review by Wells, Zeit. f. Immunität., 1913 (19), 599.

[88] Biochem. Zeit., 1916 (77), 129.

[89] Literature, see Flexner, Univ. of Penn. Med. Bull., 1902 (15), 287; Ricketts, Trans. Chicago Path. Soc., 1902 (5), 178; Christian, Deut. Arch. klin. Med., 1904 (80), 333; Leschke, Zeit. Immunität., 1913 (16), 627; Reeser, Folia Mikrobiol., 1914, II. 3.

[90] Spät, Zeit. Immunität., 1914 (21), 565.

[91] Löhner, Arch. ges. Physiol., 1915 (162), 129.

[92] Jour. Med. Res., 1916 (33), 323.

Endotheliolytic Serum. - Every attempt at immunizing an animal with any sort of fixed tissue must of necessity involve the injection of endothelial cells as well as the cells specific to the tissue studied. Therefore, it is possible that cytotoxic serum so obtained will contain endothelial toxins, and so complicate any results of *intra vitam* experiments. There is every reason to believe that endotheliolytic substances are produced in this way. Ricketts [89] found that serum of animals immunized against lymph-glands was toxic to endothelial cells, which was indicated by hemorrhages at the point of injection, and marked desquamation of endothelium when the injection was made into a serous cavity. In snake-venom poisoning the extensive hemorrhages are also due to an endotheliolytic principle, called by Flexner *hemorrhagin.*

Lymphatolytic Serum.—This serum has been studied by Ricketts and by Flexner, who immunized animals with lymph-glands. As might be expected from the structure of the injected glands, the resulting serum contained endotheliotoxin, leucocytotoxin, hemolysin, hemagglutinin, leucocyto-agglutinin, and precipitins. When injected into animals, this serum has a marked effect upon the spleen and lymph-glands, producing great enlargement and congestion of these structures. The bone-marrow is also somewhat affected, and when marrow is used in immunizing, the *myelotoxic* serum produces marked proliferative changes in the lymph-glands as well as in the marrow.

Nephrolytic Serum.—It has been claimed that if a kidney is destroyed by ligating its vessels or ureter, the remaining kidney develops serious degenerative changes, which are not present if one kidney is entirely removed. This has been attributed to the development of nephrotoxic substances produced in reaction to the absorption of the injured renal tissue that has been left in the body. Other methods of renal injury have been thought to produce similar effects, and serum of animals with kidney disease was said to injure the kidneys of normal animals. Upon this basis it has been thought possible to explain the progressive nature of the chronic nephritides as the result of nephrotoxins produced through the absorption of the injured cells, which nephrotoxins injure still other renal cells.[93] Such a process, however, involves the production of cell toxins in an animal that are toxic for its own cells, that is, *autocytotoxins;* and as it has so far been extremely difficult to produce autolysins of other sorts, it is not altogether probable that the kidney is an exception. Furthermore, Pearce[94] was unable to produce isonephrotoxins, and could not corroborate the statements as to the changes said to have been found in the remaining kidney after ligating the vessels of its mate. He did obtain an active heteronephrolysin, but also found that immunization with liver produced nearly as actively nephrolytic serum as did immunization with kidney.

Neurolytic Serum.—Even as highly specialized cells as those of the nervous tissue seem to produce a reaction with the formation of immune bodies. Perhaps the most positive results are those of Ricketts and Rothstein,[95] who found that serum of rabbits immunized against the brains or cords of guinea-pigs was highly toxic when injected into the vessels of guinea-pigs, causing death with various symptoms only explainable on the assumption of nervous lesions. Microscopically, the ganglion cells showed marked changes in those animals that survived the injection long enough. All the results so far obtained have been with heterogeneous serum.[96] Venoms, particularly that of cobra, possess strong neurolytic substances that are the chief toxic agents in most of the venoms (rattlesnake venom excepted).

Thyrolytic Serum.—There are but few reports on this serum, but that of Portis[97] indicates that after removal of all hemolysis as a factor there do occur changes, in the nature of excessive absorption of colloid, and proliferation after the order of that seen in thyroid regeneration. However, the clinical picture of thryoidectomy was not produced in any case, and the anatomic changes were not great. By immunizing against nucleoproteins derived from thyroid tissue,

[93] See Kapsenberg, Zeit. Immunität., 1912 (12), 477.
[94] Univ. of Penn. Med. Bull., 1903 (16), 217.
[95] Trans. Chicago Path. Soc., 1903 (5), 207.
[96] An attempt to obtain a specific neurotoxin with corpus striatum was unsuccessful. (Lillian Moore, Jour. Immunol., 1916 (1), 525.)
[97] Jour. Infectious Diseases, 1904 (1), 127.

Beebe[98] has secured an antiserum to which he ascribes some effect upon diseased thyroids (exophthalmic goiter).   MacCallum[99] could not get a specific serum for parathyroid tissue.

Numerous reports may be found indicating attempts, with varying success, to obtain serum toxic for other tissues.   Among them may be mentioned *epitheliolysin*[1] (for ciliated epithelium), *spermatotoxin*,[2] *hepatolysin, cardiolysin, splenolysin*, and *syncytiolysin*.[3]   Special attention has been given to the production of specific lysins for cancer cells, without definite success. (See Chapter xix.)   In general it can be said that it has *not* been found possible in this way to throw out of function one particular organ, with or without involvement of other structures.[4]   The principles involved in all these experiments are the same, and the results are in no instance altogether satisfactory; therefore no further consideration of these special cytotoxic serums will be made here, the reader being referred to other sources for details.[5]   It may be said, however, that recent developments indicate that various tissues not only contain proteins which exhibit the species characteristics of the entire animal, but also other proteins or antigenic radicals which are more or less independent of these and characteristic to a certain degree for the tissue from which the antigen was obtained.   This being the case, we cannot consider the problem of specific cytotoxins a closed chapter; improved methods for separating our antigens may yet enable us to secure antibodies specific for a single tissue or organ. (See Specificity of Antigens, Chap. vii.)   However, by the useful method of studying the effect of cytotoxic serum on the growth of tissue cultures *in vitro*, Lambert[6] found no evidence whatever of specificity, although there is a non-specific inhibition of growth by the immune sera.

[98] Jour. Amer. Med. Assoc., 1906 (46), 484.   Not corroborated by Portis and Bach, *ibid.*, 1914 (62), 1884.
[99] Med. News, 1903 (83), 820.
[1] See Galli-Valerio, Zeit. Immunität, 1915 (24), 311.
[2] Taylor (Jour. Biol. Chem., 1908 (5), 311) made the interesting observation that no spermatolytic serum could be obtained by immunizing with isolated nucleic acid, protamines, or other extracts of sperm, although immunizing with whole sperm produced active sera.
[3] Lake, Jour. Infect. Dis., 1914 (14), 385.
[4] An attempt to produce a specific cytolytic serum for the islands of Langerhans by Kamimura was unsuccessful. (Mitt. med. Fak. Univ. Tokio, 1917 (17), 95). Ogata, however, reports the production of a specific *thymotoxic* serum (Rep. Univ. Kioto, 1917 (1), 449).
[5] Biochemisches Centralblatt, 1903 (1), 573, *et seq.;* also see Sata, Ziegler's Beitr., 1906 (39), 1; and literature cited previously.
[6] Jour. Exp. Med., 1914 (19), 277; also Walton, *ibid.*, 1915 (22), 194.

CHAPTER X

CHEMICAL MEANS OF DEFENSE AGAINST NON-ANTIGENIC POISONS[1]

ALTHOUGH the examples of acquired immunity against poisons of known chemical composition are few indeed, nevertheless the body possesses means of defense against many such poisons, which decrease to greater or less degree their harmful effects. It is to be noted, however, that the increased tolerance to such poisons is far less than the degree of tolerance characteristic of immunity to true toxins; thus, in arsenic eaters the maximum observed tolerance is but three or four times the minimum, and less than the certainly fatal dose (Hausmann): dogs can be made tolerant to only about three times the fatal dose of morphine (Faust). Furthermore, with many poisons of this class the tolerance is largely fictitious, since in spite of the absence of acute symptoms chronic poisoning is taking place; and, of course, with many poisons no distinct increase of tolerance can be produced. True immunity, associated with the production of neutralizing substances in the blood, has as yet been obtained only against substances of protein nature or substances very closely resembling the proteins. Ehrlich[2] believed that simple toxic chemicals are, like toxins, bound to the cells by special receptors, *chemoreceptors*, which, in view of their simpler function may be assumed to be simpler than the receptors for toxins. They seem to be more firmly fixed to the cells, and being, therefore, less easily discharged than bacterial receptors no free antibodies are produced by immunization. To be sure, there have been observations interpreted as evidence of immunity to large molecular complexes, especially such as lipoids and glucosides, but as yet the positive establishment of the formation of antibodies by reaction to non-protein antigens has not been accomplished. It must be taken into consideration, however, that various chemical substances introduced into the blood or tissues of an animal, may form compounds with the animal's proteins which behave like foreign proteins, to which the animal reacts by becoming hypersensitive; in this way are explained the instances of idiosyncrasy, with reactions of anaphylactic character, which are sometimes shown with iodoform, antipyrine, salvarsan, and other substances. (See Antigens, Chapter vii.)

Studies on bacterial immunity and allied topics have as yet shown nothing to explain the acquirement of tolerance to morphine, alcohol

[1] Bibliography by Hausmann, Ergebnisse Physiol., 1907 (6), 58.
[2] Beiträge z. exp. Path. u. Chem., Leipzig, 1909, p. 189.

arsenic, and other similar poisons.   A few observers have claimed that the serum of animals immunized to morphine will neutralize to some degree the toxic effects of morphine, but these results have not been generally substantiated.   Others have claimed that increased oxidative powers are developed under the stimulation of the poison, which permits of its more rapid destruction, especially in the liver, but the experimental support of this hypothesis is slight.   Still another idea is that, at least in the case of morphine, decomposition products are produced, and accumulate in the body, that neutralize physiologically to some extent the morphine itself; this hypothesis can scarcely be applied to arsenic and alcohol tolerance.[3]   It has been found that in animals habituated to morphine there is an increased power to destroy morphine, but, nevertheless, the blood of such animals still contains quantities of morphine toxic for normal animals, so there must be a certain refractoriness or cellular immunity in addition (Rübsamen).   Schweisheimer[4] has shown that when chronic alcoholics and total abstainers are given equal quantities of alcohol, the alcohol content of the blood reaches a higher level, and persists for a longer time at a high level, in the abstainers.   Apparently the alcohol-habituated organism can destroy alcohol more readily, presumably through more rapid oxidation.[5]   However, other factors are involved in alcohol tolerance, for with equal quantities of alcohol in the blood the abstainers show a more marked intoxication than the habitual drinker.   So, too, in morphine tolerance any general resistance through augmented oxidation seems inadequate in view of the specific increase in the tolerance of the respiratory center observed in this condition.[6] Also we find that tolerance to one drug may be accompanied by tolerance to other drugs exerting similar physiological action.[7]

It is possible, also, that the cell constituents with which the poisons ordinarily combine are produced in increased amounts under the

[3] Concerning immunity against morphine see DuMez, Jour. Amer. Med. Assoc., 1919 (72), 1069; full bibliography.   He summarizes the evidence as follows: "The only knowledge of a positive nature that we have at present concerning these problems is that the different organs and centers of the body acquire tolerance to morphine and heroine to a different degree and with varied degrees of readiness; that these drugs as such are excreted in the feces in diminishing amounts during the period of acquiring tolerance; and that there is evidently present in the blood serum of tolerant animals (dogs) during periods of abstinence a substance or substances which, when injected into normal animals of the same species, causes the appearance of symptoms identical with the so-called withdrawal phenomena. Whether or not the disappearance of these drugs from the feces is due to their increased destruction in the organism is still an unsettled question.   It has not been proved that the destruction of morphine in the organism, if it does take place to an increased degree, is a causative factor in the production of tolerance. It may be only a concomitant phenomenon."
[4] Deut. Arch. klin. Med., 1913 (109), 271.
[5] See also Völtz and Dietrich, Biochem. Zeit. 1915 (68), 118.   J. Hirsch, *ibid.*, 1916 (77), 129.
[6] Van Dongen, Arch. ges. Physiol., 1915 (162), 54.
[7] See Myers, Jour. Pharmacol., 1916 (8), 417.   However, Biberfeld finds morphine tolerance to be specific (Biochem. Zeit., 1916 (77), 283).

stimulus of the poison, just as they are in the case of immunization with toxins, with the difference that the combining substances are not thrown off into the blood. For example, it has been claimed that arsenic is ordinarily combined and held in the liver by a nucleoprotein, and the suggestion has been made that in arsenic habitués this nucleoprotein is increased in amount. Again, saponin seems to act upon the cholesterol of the red corpuscles, and Kobert observed increased resistance to the action of saponin exhibited by the serum of immunized animals, which he attributes to an increased amount of cholesterol, perhaps liberated by the corpuscles decomposed by the injected poison, or perhaps produced in excess by the tissues. Wohlgemuth[8] has also suggested that in the case of poisoning with large amounts of substances which combine with glycuronic acid (*e. g.*, lysol), excessive quantities of this substance are formed by the cells and excreted into the blood, where they neutralize the poisons in much the same manner as the antitoxins neutralize toxins.

But besides these scanty examples of tolerance to poisons, the body possesses a number of methods for opposing many other poisons with more or less success; and, poisons invariably acting chemically, the defenses are in turn largely chemical. We have elsewhere referred to the destructive action of the enzymes of the digestive tract upon bacterial and similar poisons; this means of defense cannot apply to non-protein chemical substances except possibly glucosides and toxic lipoids. But the acidity of the gastric juice, the alkalinity of the bile and pancreatic juice, and the precipitating effect of the hydrogen sulphide formed in intestinal putrefaction are all factors that help to neutralize or prevent the absorption of certain poisons, their total efficiency, however, being on the whole very slight. After absorption of a poison a large series of chemical reactions and physiological processes is brought into play, and there are few poisons indeed whose harmful influence is not more or less decreased by these means. Kobert[9] classifies these protective processes as follows:

1. **Rapid elimination**, either before absorption by means of diarrhea and vomiting, or by the same means after absorption in case the poisons are excreted into the digestive tract (*e. g.*, morphine, venoms, antimony, and many other metals). Many poisons are very rapidly eliminated by other routes (*e. g.*, anesthetics, curare), in some instances causing harm, particularly to the eliminating organ (*e. g.*, kidneys in phenol poisoning, intestines in ricin poisoning). The routes and conditions of elimination of poisons have been fully discussed by Lewin.[10]

2. **Deposition and Fixation in Single Organs or Tissues.**—In this respect the liver is especially important, probably because of its location and function as a filter for all the blood coming fresh from the alimentary tract.[11] The manner and

[8] Biochem. Zeitschr., 1906 (1), 134.

[9] "Lehrbuch der Intoxikationen," Stuttgart.

[10] Deut. med. Woch., 1906 (32), 169; see also Mendel *et al.*, Amer. Jour. Physiol., 1904 (11), 5; 1906 (16), 147 and 152.

[11] Concerning the detoxicating function of the liver see Woronzow, Dissertation, Dorpat, 1910; Rothberger and Winterberg, Arch. internat. Pharmacodyn., 1905 (15), 339.

means by which this fixation is brought about are unknown. It is possible that the power of the tissues to bind poisons may become increased by repeated doses, leading to "specific acquired tolerance."[12] According to Slowtzoff[13] arsenic is fixed by the nucleus in a very firm combination;[14] mercury by globulins in a less stable combination; copper by the nucleins, but less firmly than the arsenic. Other poisons, chiefly alkaloids, are probably combined with bile acids. Possibly some poisons combine with *glycogen*. These compounds are but slowly broken up, and thus the poison reaches the more susceptible and more important tissues in a relatively diluted condition. The bones seem to hold in harmless form poisonous fluorides, and to less extent arsenic, barium and tungsten, which persist in the bones for a great length of time. Leucocytes are possibly important binders of poisons, perhaps through combination with their nucleins,[15] but storage in these labile cells is necessarily of relatively brief duration.

3. **Combination** with substances formed or contained in the tissues; the resulting substance being less toxic than the poison alone. Under this heading may be included both chemical combination and physical absorption or solution, such as the deviation of the lipoid-soluble narcotics from the central nervous system by excessive tissue fats, or by fats therapeutically introduced.[16] Many poisons combine with the inorganic constituents of the tissues; e. g., barium and various aromatic substances with SO_4; silver with Cl, etc.

4. **Chemical alteration,** with or without subsequent combination with other substances, by such means as oxidation, reduction, hydrolysis, and neutralization.

5. **Impaired absorption** should also be considered as a means of defense against poisons. This may depend upon the injury to the gastro-intestinal tract produced either by the poison itself or by some independent pathological condition. Cloetta considers impaired absorption important in acquired immunity to arsenic (see below) and it may also modify the effects of other poisons.[17]

The chemical reactions employed in defense against simple chemical poisons have been particularly considered by E. Fromm,[18] whose outline is here partially followed, and to which the reader is referred for bibliography.

INORGANIC POISONS

Metallic poisons, such as lead, silver, mercury, and arsenic, are made insoluble, particularly by forming compounds with proteins in the alimentary tract, intestinal walls, blood, or internal organs; also by forming sulphides with the H_2S of the intestinal contents. According to Cloetta[19] immunization against arsenic depends entirely upon a reduction of absorption in the intestine, for the longer arsenic is taken, the less appears in the urine and the more appears in the feces.[20] At the same time the resistance to arsenic injected subcutaneously is not increased at all, and no increase in resistance can be obtained

[12] Santesson, Skand. Arch. Physiol., 1911 (25), 28.
[13] Hofmeister's Beitr., 1901 (1), 281; 1902 (2), 307.
[14] Denied by Heffter. (Arch. internat. de Pharmacodyn., 1905 (15), 399), who considers it more a physico-chemical process.
[15] Stessano, Compt. Rend. Acad. Sci., 1900 (131), 72.
[16] See Graham, Jour. Inf. Dis., 1911 (8), 147.
[17] v. Lhota, Arch. internat. pharmacodyn., 1912 (22), 61.
[18] "Die chemischen Schützmittel des Tierkörpers bei Vergiftungen," Strassburg, Karl Trübner, 1903. See also résumé by Ellinger, Deut. med. Woch., 1900 (26), 580.
[19] Arch. exp. Path. u. Pharm., 1906 (54), 196; Corresponbl. Schweizer Aerzte, 1911 (41), 737.
[20] Not accepted by Hausmann, Ergebnisse Physiol., 1907 (6), 58; or Joachimoglu, Arch. exp. Path., 1916 (79), 119.

by repeated subcutaneous injections of sublethal doses. There is, however, reason to question the authenticity of the reputed tolerance of habitués to arsenic (Joachimoglu).[20] Antimony does not produce tolerance in experimental animals (Cloetta).[21] The manner in which various inorganic ions antagonize the physiological action of one another (*e. g.*, sodium and potassium, calcium and magnesium) is still an important problem.[22]

Free acids and alkalies are partly neutralized by the alkaline and acid contents of the gastro-intestinal tract, partly by forming compounds with the proteins, and partly by the alkalies and carbonic acid of the blood stream. (See "Acid Intoxication," Chap. xx.) Phosphorus[23] and sulphides are oxidized after absorption into phosphoric and sulphuric acid, which are in turn neutralized by the alkalinity of the blood and tissues. Lillie[24] has called attention to the close, palisade arrangement of the nuclei of the epithelium lining the alimentary tract, which makes it necessary for all substances absorbed to pass through the zone of their active oxidative influence, a fact undoubtedly of great importance in the defense of the body.

Reduction of iodic acid, chloric acid, hypochlorous acid, and their salts occurs in the body, resulting in their conversion into the much less toxic iodides and chlorides. Tellurium compounds are also reduced and rendered insoluble. This reaction occurs to some extent in the intestines; how much in other organs is unknown.

Methylation, the addition of CH_3 groups, is observed in poisoning by tellurium, which is eliminated in the breath as methyl telluride, and also in the sweat and feces.[25] Selenium, pyridine, and some other substances also combine with methane. The source of the methane is possibly in the xanthine molecule.

Summary.—There are, therefore, three chief reactions used against inorganic poisons in the body, *oxidation, reduction,* and *splitting off of water;* neutralization of acids or alkalies and the formation of albuminates and sulphides being included under the last heading, since in these reactions the splitting off of water is an essential step.

ORGANIC POISONS

In the case of organic poisons an equally small number of primary reactions is employed in their detoxication, but in more complicated manners and combinations corresponding with the complexity of organic compounds.

[21] Arch. exp. Path. u. Pharm., 1911 (64), 352.
[22] See Osterhout, Proc. Phil. Soc., 1916 (55), 533.
[23] Increased tolerance to phosphorus may be obtained by repeated small doses, but it lasts only while the poison is being given continuously (Oppel, Ziegler's Beitr., 1910 (49), 543). Accompanying the tolerance are structural changes in the liver cells to which are ascribed some significance by Oppel.
[24] Amer. Jour. Physiol., 1902 (7), 412.
[25] See Mead and Gies, Amer. Jour. Physiol., 1901 (5), 105. Caffein may be demethylated in the liver, Kotake, Zeit., physiol. Chem., 1908 (57), 378.
16

Oxidation, which has already been mentioned as a means of destruction of bacterial toxins, is naturally one of the most effective agents in the destruction of simpler organic substances, since the ordinary decomposition of all organic food-stuffs is through oxidation. There are numbers of specific examples of the conversion of a poisonous into a less poisonous or non-poisonous substance by oxidation. All acids of the fatty acid series are oxidized vigorously in the body, eventually into CO_2 and H_2O; and pathologically produced acetic and lactic acids are destroyed in this way. The liver contains an oxidase destroying alcohol, which is not increased in the livers of animals made tolerant to alcohol (J. Hirsch).[26] Uric acid is oxidized vigorously by many organs (except in man), as are other members of the purine series, such as caffeine and theobromine. Presumably oxidation of organic poisons as well as of food-stuffs is brought about by the oxidizing enzymes of the cells, as shown by Ehrlich's *indophenol reaction*, which consists of the oxidation of paraphenylene diamine and α-naphthol, with a resulting synthesis. This reaction is said by Lillie[27] to occur principally in and about the cell nuclei or cell membranes.

Combination, with or without Preliminary Oxidation.—Oxidation is also an essential preliminary step to many of the protecting combinations, in which a cell constituent is united to an organic poison. The most important of these combining substances are:

1. **Sulphuric Acid.**—One of the earliest and most important observations on the protective action of sulphuric acid was made by Baumann and Herter,[22] who showed that phenol is eliminated as a potassium salt of the sulphuric acid derivative, as follows:

$$C_6H_5OH + HO-SO_3K = C_6H_5O-SO_3K + H_2O,$$

a reaction that has been put to practical use in treating phenol poisoning. As phenol and cresols are produced constantly in intestinal decomposition, this reaction is undoubtedly of great service, since the salt formed is relatively harmless. *Indole* and *skatole* are similarly detoxicated by being converted into corresponding salts, but only after a preliminary oxidation into *indoxyl* and *skatoxyl*, according to the following reaction:

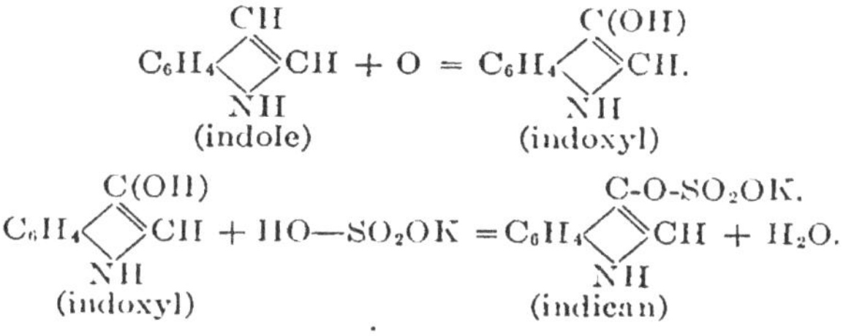

$$C_6H_4\!\!\begin{array}{c} CH \\ \diagdown \\ NH \end{array}\!\!CH + O = C_6H_4\!\!\begin{array}{c} C(OH) \\ \diagdown \\ NH \end{array}\!\!CH.$$

(indole)   (indoxyl)

$$C_6H_4\!\!\begin{array}{c} C(OH) \\ \diagdown \\ NH \end{array}\!\!CH + HO-SO_2OK = C_6H_4\!\!\begin{array}{c} C-O-SO_2OK. \\ \diagdown \\ NH \end{array}\!\!CH + H_2O.$$

(indoxyl)   (indican)

[26] Biochem. Zeit., 1916 (77), 129.
[27] Zeit. physiol. Chem., 1877 (I), 247.

A host of other aromatic organic substances are similarly combined with sulphuric acid,[28] with or without preliminary oxidation, including all substances resembling phenol or which through oxidation are changed into phenols, such as cresol, thymol, anilin, naphthalin, pyrogallol, and tannin. By this means a poisonous substance is converted into a relatively harmless one, which is readily soluble and rapidly eliminated.

2. **Glycuronic acid** occupies the same position as sulphuric acid, combining particularly with naphthol, thymol, camphor, chloral hydrate, and butyl chloral. Sometimes a substance may appear in the urine combined in part with sulphuric, in part with glycuronic acid, showing the similarity of their function. Apparently when there is not sufficient sulphuric acid in the body to combine with all the poison, the excess unites with glycuronic acid,[29] although combination between glycuronic acid and the aromatic substance begins to occur before all the sulphuric acid is exhausted.[30] Glycuronic acid represents merely a first step in the oxidation of glucose, as follows:

$$OHC\text{-}(CHOH)_4\text{-}CH_2OH + O_2 = OHC\text{-}(CHOH)_4\text{-}COOH + H_2O.$$
$$\text{(glucose)} \qquad\qquad\qquad \text{(glycuronic acid)}$$

This oxidation occurs after the aldehyde group of the glucose has been combined by some other substance; hence the aldehyde group escapes oxidation, although ordinarily more easily oxidized than the alcohol group.

Just as with the addition of sulphuric acid, oxidation may be a preliminary step to the addition of glycuronic acid; *e. g.*, naphthalin is oxidized into α-naphthol, before uniting to glycuronic acid, as follows:

(naphthalin)   (α-naphthol)

The same is the case with many camphors and terpenes. Reduction may be the preliminary step, as with chloral hydrate, which is first reduced to trichlor-ethyl-alcohol. In still other cases splitting off of water is the chief preliminary step.

3. **Glycine** is one of the longest known combining substances, the observation of the combination of glycine with benzoic acid to form *hippuric acid* being the first proof of synthesis in the animal body discovered by Wöhler (1824). The reaction is as follows:

$$C_6H_5COOH + H_2N\text{-}CH_2\text{-}COOH = C_6H_5CO - HN\text{-}CH_2\text{-}COOH + H_2O.$$
$$\text{(benzoic acid)} \quad \text{(glycine)} \qquad\qquad \text{(hippuric acid)}$$

[28] See Hammarsten's Text-book (fourth American ed.), p. 542.
[29] See Austin and Barron, Boston Med. and Surg. Jour., 1905 (152), 269. Wohlgemuth has observed a case in which all the sulphuric acid of the urine was in organic combination (Berl. klin. Woch., 1906 (43), 508).
[30] See Salkowski, Zeit. physiol. Chem., 1904 (42), 230.

A special enzyme has been found in kidney substance which can bring about this reaction outside the body. Normally this enzyme occurs chiefly in the kidney but may also occur in other organs. Many other aromatic compounds also combine with glycine before elimination, e. g., salicylic acid. Some are first altered to a suitable form by oxidation; e. g., toluene is oxidized to benzoic acid, xylene to toluic acid, nitro-benzaldehyde to nitro-benzoic acid. Many of the substances that can be made to combine with glycine in the body are of such a foreign nature that they never could need neutralization under any other than experimental conditions, but here, as with the sulphuric and glycuronic acid reactions, combination occurs whenever a suitable substance is present in the blood, glycine always being abundant as a cleavage product of the proteins.

4. **Urea** may also be a means of defense, forming salts with organic acids which are rapidly eliminated; e. g., amido-benzoic acid and nitro-hippuric acid.

5. **Methane.**—Methylation, which occurs also with tellurium, is observed on administration of pyridine, as shown by the following equation:

$$HC\overset{\overset{\text{H}}{C}-\overset{\text{H}}{C}}{\underset{\underset{\text{H}}{C}=\underset{\text{H}}{C}}{}}N + CH_4 + O = HC\overset{\overset{\text{H}}{C}-\overset{\text{H}}{C}}{\underset{\underset{\text{H}}{C}=\underset{\text{H}}{C}}{}}N\overset{CH_3}{\underset{OH}{}}$$
(pyridine)

This reaction is of special importance, because many alkaloids contain a pyridine group; and the resulting methyl compound may be less toxic than the original alkaloid —e. g., methyl morphine.

6. **Sulphur** split off from proteins may combine with CNH and CNK, converting them into the much less toxic sulphocyanides.[31]

7. **Bile Acids.**—All the above mentioned reactions are protective largely because the substances formed are soluble and rapidly eliminated, as well as being less toxic than the original poison. Compounds of many poisons are formed with bile acids which are insoluble, and therefore only slowly dissolve or decompose, thus protecting the body from overwhelming doses of the poison. Such compounds are formed, not only with inorganic poisons, but also with alkaloids, especially strychnine, brucine, and quinine. They are then deposited in the liver, to be slowly dissolved and eliminated.

(Occasionally *acetic acid* and *cysteine* have been observed to act as combining substances. *Calcium* may be considered a defensive agent against certain poisons [oxalic and citric acids] with which it forms insoluble compounds, although it is probable that the toxicity of oxalates depends largely upon their robbing the cells of calcium.[32])

[31] See Meurice, Arch. int. Pharmacodyn., 1900 (7), 11.
[32] See Robertson and Burnett, Jour. Pharmacol., 1912 (3), 635.

Neutralization of organic acids entering the body or formed in metabolism is accomplished by the sodium carbonate of the blood when in small amounts; if excessive in quantity (*e. g.*, diabetic coma), a portion is combined with ammonia and appears as an ammonium salt in the urine. Magnesium and calcium salts may also help in the neutralization, probably at the expense of the bone tissue.[33] (See "Acid Intoxication," Chap. xx).

Dehydration, which plays a prominent part in a number of the above-mentioned syntheses, is particularly important in the change of ammonium carbonate into urea:

$$\begin{matrix} NH_4 - O \\ NH_4 - O \end{matrix} \Big> CO = \begin{matrix} NH_2 \\ NH_2 \end{matrix} \Big> CO + 2H_2O$$

As ammonium salts of all sorts are very toxic, especially hemolytic, while urea is not, this process is probably one of the most important detoxicating reactions of the body because of the great amount of ammonium compounds that is constantly being formed in nitrogenous metabolism.

Summary.—As Fromm points out, the variety of reactions and the variety of defensive substances are both remarkably small in number. The reactions are: oxidation and reduction, hydration and dehydration, and perhaps simple addition (methylation). The chief known protective substances are the alkalies of the blood, proteins, hydrogen sulphide, sulphuric acid, glycine, urea, cysteine, bile acids, glycuronic acid, and acetic acid. *All these substances are normally present in the body, and none of them is specific against any one poison,* but each combines with several poisons. This last fact is interesting in comparison with the highly specific nature of the immune substances against bacteria and their products.

As far as we know, no particular increase in the neutralizing substances results from the administration of inorganic or organic poisons. The body does not appear to produce any excessive amounts of sulphuric acid in carbolic-acid poisoning, or of glycine when benzoic acid is administered. Both substances are present in the body normally, and as much as is available combines with the poison; if there is not enough, the remaining poison combines with something else, or goes uncombined. In other words, the neutralizing substances described above do not appear to be the result of any special adaptation to meet a pathological condition. They are present in the body as a result of normal metabolism; they have an affinity for various chemical substances, some of which happen to be poisons; if these poisons happen to enter the body, they may be combined and neutralized to some extent, but, as a rule, very incompletely. There appears

---

[33] In this connection it may be mentioned that the bactericidal power of the blood is increased if the blood is more alkaline, decreased if it is less alkaline, than usual.

to be no elaborate process of defense against the chemically simple poisons, such as seems to be called into action by bacterial infection, and hence a degree of resistance or immunity similar to that present after an attack of scarlet fever or smallpox does not exist for strychnine or phosphorus.

It is also of interest to consider that *unicellular organisms* may show a marked capacity to increase their resistance to poisons, as shown especially by Ehrlich's studies on trypanosomes, which readily become immune to various trypanocidal drugs, including arsenic compounds, and which transmit this acquired immunity through succeeding generations.   Yeasts and bacteria can also exhibit increased tolerance to antiseptics, and Effront found that yeasts owe their augmented tolerance to fluorides to an increased content of calcium, which precipitates the fluoride which enters the cells; this tolerance is also transmitted to new generations of yeasts.   The acquired tolerance is specific in all these cases, and may, indeed, be accompanied by a decreased resistance to other poisons; thus, protozoa acclimated to alcohol may be more susceptible to other chemicals.[34]   *Paramecia* made immune to antimony are not immune to arsenic, and this specific immunity is transmitted to succeeding generations (Neuhaus).[35]

[34] Daniel, Jour. Exper. Zool., 1909 (6), 571.
[35] Arch. Internat. Pharmacoydn., 1910 (20), 393.

CHAPTER XI

INFLAMMATION[1]

ALTHOUGH morphological alterations are prominent features of the reaction of the tissues to local injury and infection, yet at the bottom the processes of inflammation are brought about by and result in chemical alterations. The causes of inflammation are in nearly all cases chemically active substances, but for the most part their nature is too little known to permit of speculation as to what chemical characteristic or characteristics a substance must possess to exhibit the power of causing an inflammatory reaction. Even in the case of inflammation due to mechanical, thermal, and electrical injuries, it seems probable that most of the features of the inflammatory reaction are brought about by the action of chemical substances produced by alterations in the tissue constituents at the point of injury,[2] for tissue proteins that have been altered in necrosis are chemotactic,[3] as also are extracts of tissues.

The essential features of inflammation, namely, local hyperemia and related vascular disturbances, exudation of plasma, migration of leucocytes and their phagocytic action, all may be caused by the action of chemical substances upon the vessels and leucocytes. *Active hyperemia* in the case of inflammation is due to stimulation of the vasodilator nerves or paralysis of the vaso-constrictors, or direct paralysis of the muscular fibers of the arterioles; these may result from mechanical, thermal, or electrical stimuli, but in local infection the cause is usually chemical products of bacterial growth or of tissue disintegration. The *escape of blood plasma* (inflammatory edema) appears to depend upon a number of factors (discussed more fully under "Edema," Chap. xiv) of which the most important seem to be: (1) injury to the capillary walls, produced largely by the chemical

[1] For extensive reviews and bibliography see Adami, in Allbutt's System of Medicine; reprinted also as a monograph, "Inflammation," 1909; also Opie, Arch. Int. Med., 1910 (5), 541. Some interesting ideas are advanced by Klemensiewicz, "Die Entzündung," G. Fischer, Jena, 1908.

[2] Schlaepfer (Zeit. exp. Path., 1910 (8), 181) finds that the reduction of methylene blue is decreased in inflammatory areas, and advances the hypothesis that inflammatory stimulants are oxidation stimulants, inflammation occurring only when the amount of oxidation aroused by the stimulant is insufficient. In accord with this is the observation of Amberg (Zeit. exp. Med., 1913 (2), 19) that substances facilitating oxidation reduce inflammatory reactions. (See also Woolley, Jour. Amer. Med. Assoc., 1914 (63), 2279.) Another observation of similar significance is that phagocytosis is stimulated by H_2O_2, and that phagocytes react to HNC in the same way as the respiratory center (Hamburger, Internat. Zeit phys.-chem. Biol., 1915 (2), 245–264).

[3] Bürger and Dold, Zeit. Immunität., 1914 (21), 378.

causes or products of the inflammation; (2) increased osmotic pressure in the tissues, due to increased or abnormal formation of crystalloidal substances with high osmotic pressure from large molecular compounds, many of which are colloids (proteins) without appreciable osmotic pressure; (3) alterations in the hydration capacity of the colloids, whereby, through decrease in salts or increase in acidity, they come to possess a greater affinity for water (M. H. Fischer). By far the most characteristic feature of inflammation, however, is the *behavior of the leucocytes*—their increase in number in the blood, their migration from the vessels and accumulation about the point of injury, and their engulfing and destroying various solid particles, such as bacteria and degenerating tissue elements. These processes, which seem to indicate something approaching independent volition on the part of the leucocytes may, however, be well explained by application of known laws of chemistry and physics, without passing into the realms of the metaphysical. This will be attempted under the heading of:

AMEBOID MOTION AND PHAGOCYTOSIS

The accumulation of leucocytes at a given point in the body indicates that some means of communication must exist between this point and the leucocytes in the circulating blood. No direct communication by the nervous system or other structural method existing, the only possible explanation is that the communication is through the fluids of the body, and depends upon changes in their chemical composition or physical condition. As the latter generally depends upon the former, the communication is considered to be accomplished by chemical agencies, and called *chemotaxis*.

CHEMOTAXIS

Changes in the chemical composition of a fluid have been shown frequently to affect the motion of living organisms suspended in it. One of the earliest observations was that of Engelmann,[4] who noticed that *Bacterium termo* suspended in water tended to accumulate about a bubble of oxygen in the water. Pfeffer[5] discovered that the spermatozoids of certain ferns were attracted powerfully by very dilute solutions of malic acid, which is contained in the female sperm cell, indicating that the migration of the sperm cells in the proper direction depends on a chemical communication, and he proposed the term chemotaxis for this phenomenon. Strong solutions of malic acid, on the other hand, repelled spermatozoids. Cane-sugar was found to attract the spermatozoids of a certain foliaceous moss. In the case of the malic acid, it seems to be the anion that produces the effect, since salts of malic acid have exactly the same property.

[4] Botanische Zeitung, 1881 (39), 441.
[5] Untersuch. aus dem Bot. Institut in Tübingen, 1881–1888, Bd. 1 und 2.

Stahl's[6] experiment with a large jelly-like plasmodium (*Aethalium septicum*) growing on bark in wet places, has become classical. He found that if the plasmodium was placed on a moist surface, and nearby was placed a drop of an infusion of oak bark, the organism moved by the process of protoplasmic streaming toward and into the infusion. If a piece of oak bark was placed in the water, plasmodial arms were stretched out to it and the piece of bark was soon completely surrounded by the organism. These movements were found to occur in any direction, even exactly against the force of gravity. Other substances, as acids or strong solutions of salt or sugar, were found to cause the plasmodium to move away from them, although when sufficiently dilute they exerted an attraction. A plasmodium might, however, move into a strong sugar solution if kept with a scanty supply of moisture for some time, and after it had lived in such a strong solution (2 per cent.) for some time, a weaker solution or pure water was as injurious as the concentrated sugar solution previously had been.

Temperature was also found to exert a marked *thermotactic* effect. If a plasmodium was placed on a filter-paper, one end of which was in water at 7°, and the other in water at 30°, it would move toward the warmer end.

The Theory of Tropisms.—Ciliated protozoa, which can move about freely in water, show very distinct reactions to stimuli of all sorts. The first step in their change of direction of movement is considered by many observers to be an orientation of the organism until it is headed in the axis along which it is to move. This is ascribed by J. Loeb[7] to the existence of a certain degree of equality of irritability of symmetrical parts of the body. The stimulant, whether it be rays of light, or diffusing chemicals, or heat-waves, moves along definite lines, and the organism receives at first unequal stimuli on symmetrical parts of the body, unless the axis of the organism is parallel to the lines of motion of the stimulant. As long as the stimulant acts on symmetrical parts of the body unequally, these parts will react unequally until at length the body is swung into a position where the stimulation is equal, when it will stay in this position and move along a line parallel to the line taken by the stimulant. Not only protozoa, but much higher forms, including some vertebrates are believed to react in this way to stimuli—*e. g.*, the maintenance by fish of a position heading up stream. The above constitutes the so-called "*theory of tropisms,*" and we have such reactions to stimuli of all sorts, not only *chemotropism* and *thermotropism,* but also *heliotropism* (reaction to light); *geotropism* (to gravity), *electropism* (to electricity), *thigmotropism* (reaction to contact), etc.

The work done upon tropisms applies particularly to ciliated, freely motile organisms, and interests us less in connection with leucocytes than do the observations on such forms as *Amœba.*[8] In passing may be mentioned the *thigmotaxis* or *thigmotropism* (reaction to mechanical stimuli) shown by spermatozoa, which explains their apparently difficult feat of advancing in opposition to the cilia of the epithelial lining of the female generative tract. It may also be noted that the nature of reactions of organisms to various stimuli is not constant for even the same organism. Copepods (minute crustacea) may be negatively heliotropic in the day and go away from the bright surface of the water, whereas at night

[6] Botanische Zeitung, 1884 (42), 145 and 161.
[7] Comparative Physiology of the Brain, New York, 1900, p. 7.
[8] For full details see Jennings (Publication No. 16, Carnegie Institute, Washington, 1904; also J. Loeb, "Studies in General Physiology."

the same animals are positively heliotropic and swarm to the surface illuminated brightly by a lantern.   Variations in heliotropism may, in some cases, be explained as due to chemical changes that occur in the organism, which explanation is made more probable by J. Loeb's experiments, which show that change in composition in the fluid in which animals are suspended may cause a complete reversal in their reaction to a constant stimulus.   Motile bacteria seem to behave much like ciliated protozoa in their reaction to stimuli.

CHEMOTAXIS OF LEUCOCYTES[9]

That leucocytes come to the site of an infection because of chemical substances produced by bacteria at this point, that is to say, through chemotaxis, was first clearly pointed out by Leber[10] in 1879, who likened the attraction of such substances for leucocytes to the effect of malic acid upon spermatozoids as shown by Pfeffer.   He found that in keratitis, leucocytes invaded the avascular cornea from the distant vessels, not in an irregular manner, but all moved directly toward the point of infection, where they collected.   As dead cultures of staphylococci produced a similar, although less marked, accumulation of leucocytes, he sought the chemotactic substance in their bodies, and isolated a crystalline, heat-resisting substance, *phlogosin*, which attracted leucocytes in animal tissues.   He also observed that capillary tubes filled with phlogosin or with staphylococci were soon invaded by masses of leucocytes.

Since Leber's experiments, many other investigations have been made showing that chemical substances of many different origins other than bacterial exert a chemotactic influence on leucocytes.   Some substances are indifferent in effect, most are positive, while some are believed to repel leucocytes; *i. e.*, are negatively chemotactic.

Negative Chemotaxis.—Probably the substances that repel leucocytes are few in number; Kanthack, indeed, doubted the existence of really negative chemotactic action upon leucocytes.   Verigo[11] also considers that as yet no actual negative chemotaxis has been satisfactorily demonstrated; but, by analogy with the effects of chemicals on amebae, ciliata, and plasmodial forms, which all show a decided negative chemotaxis under certain influences, it would seem most probable that leucocytes also should be repelled as well as attracted by chemicals.[12]

Non-bacterial Chemotactic Substances.—One of the earliest significant studies of the effects of non-bacterial substances upon chemotaxis was made by Massart and Bordet,[13] who showed that products

[9] Review of literature on leucocytes by Helly, Ergeb. allg. Pathol., 1914(17(1)), 1.
[10] Fortschritte der Med., 1888 (6), 460.
[11] Arch. d. Méd. exper., 1901 (13), 585.
[12] Salomonsen's observation (Festskrift ved indvielsen af Statens Serum Institut, Kopenhagen, 1902, Art. XII), that ciliated infusoria when killed show a strong negative effect on other ciliates, is of much interest, particularly as it seems to be the opposite of the positively chemotactic effect of dead upon living leucocytes.   The negative reaction of different ciliata was specific for their own kind quantitatively, but not qualitatively.
[13] Ann. d. l'Inst. Pasteur, 1891 (5), 417.

of the disintegration of leucocytes and other cells had a strong positive chemotactic influence. They also corroborated the statement of Vaillard and Vincent that *lactic acid* is an actively repellant substance, for they found that tubes containing a pyocyaneus culture, which ordinarily became filled with leucocytes rapidly, did not become invaded at all if lactic acid was also added in a strength of 1:500, although leucocytes did enter when the dilution was 1:1000.

Gabritchevsky[14] studied the chemical influence of a large number of substances on leucocytes and divided them into three groups: I. Substances exerting "negative chemotaxis," including those that attracted only a few leucocytes.[15] II. Substances with "indifferent chemotaxis" which attracted moderate numbers of leucocytes. III. Substances with positive chemotaxis. If we correct the groupings made by Gabritchevsky we have the following classification:

I. Substances negatively chemotactic or indifferent:
   (a) Concentrated solutions of sodium and potassium salts; (b) Lactic acid in all concentrations; (c) quinine (0.5 per cent.); (d) alcohol (10 per cent.); (e) chloroform in watery solution; (f) jequirity (2 per cent., passed through Chamberland filter); (g) glycerol (10 per cent. to 1 per cent.); (h) bile; (i) B. cholerae gallinarium.
II. Substances with feeble chemotaxis:
   (a) Distilled water; (b) dilute solutions of sodium and potassium salts (1–0.1 per cent.); (c) phenol; (d) antipyrin; (e) phloridzin; (f) papayotin (in frog); (g) glycogen; (h) peptone; (i) bouillon; (j) blood and aqueous humor; (k) carmine.
III. Substances with strong positive chemotaxis:
   (a) Papayotin (in rabbits); (b) sterilized living cultures of bacteria, whether pathogenic or non-pathogenic.

These results can only be considered as suggestive and not as accurate findings, in view of other contradictory results. Buchner[16] obtained from the *pneumobacillus* of Friedlander, a protein which exerted a strong chemotactic influence, thus showing the chemical nature of the attraction of leucocytes by bacteria, and he isolated other similar proteins from other bacteria. He also obtained a "glutincasein" from grain which was related chemically to the bacterial proteins, and which was equally chemotactic. The metabolic products of bacteria, however, he found to be negatively chemotactic. Alkali albuminate and hemi-albumose were strongly positive, but peptone was not. Glycine and leucine were found to be chemotactic, but urea, ammonium urate, skatole, tyrosine, and trimethylamine were not. It was also observed that if the positively chemotactic substances were injected subcutaneously, they produced general as well as local leucocytosis. The products of the action of serum on bacteria, "anaphylatoxin," produce inflammatory reactions, and probably are

[14] Ann. d. l'Inst. Pasteur, 1890 (4), 346.
[15] Evidently these substances were not all negatively chemotactic, but were relatively slightly chemotactic or indifferent; yet in the literature generally these experiments have been cited as indicating a negative chemotactic influence of the substances studied.
[16] Berl. klin. Wochenschr., 1890 (27), 1084.

important factors in pathology; the products of tissue disintegration have similar effects.[17] Certain drugs (notably quinine, morphine and chloral) when injected subcutaneously seem to reduce the amount of leucocytic emigration at a point of local injury (Ikeda).[18] In gas gangrene negative chemotaxis is striking, possibly depending on the abundant organic acids produced by gas bacilli.[19]

v. Sicherer[20] found that chemotaxis of leucocytes may be observed outside the body. If a tube containing positively chemotactic substances (dead beer-yeast cells and dead staphylococci were the strongest) is placed with one end in a leucocyte-containing exudate, the leucocytes pass up into it against gravity.

Bloch[21] demonstrated that carbol-glycerol extracts made from each of the different viscera and tissues exerted a positive chemotaxis, discrediting the statements of Goldscheider and Jacob that only extracts of hematogenetic tissues showed positive chemotaxis. Egg-albumen, gelatine, albumen-peptone, and alkali albuminate were also positive, carbohydrates feebly so, and fat not at all. Metallic copper, iron, mercury, and their salts have also been found to be chemotactic substances, but it is very probable that they act in part through destroying the tissues in their vicinity, which give rise to decomposition-products having a positive effect. Adler,[22] however, found that bichloride of mercury as dilute as 1: 3000 caused more leucocytic invasion of a piece of saturated elder pith than did even cultures of pyogenic bacteria.[23]

Metchnikoff observed that leucocytes might, after a time, be attracted toward substances that at first seemed to repel them. If the blood is full of toxins, the subcutaneous introduction of bacteria does not lead to a local accumulation of leucocytes, presumably because the difference in chemotaxis between the blood and the tissue fluids is not great enough to cause emigration; in this connection should be mentioned Pfeffer's observation that *B. termo* in a peptone solution will not migrate toward another stronger peptone solution, unless the latter is at least five times as strong as the former. Leucocytes will migrate freely toward substances that kill them; of the bacterial products the toxins of pyocyaneus and diphtheria bacilli being especially destructive and causing typical karyorrhexis.[24] Substances soluble in lipoids are said by Hamburger[25] to increase phagocytic activity when in extreme dilutions, although stronger concentrations are highly

[17] See Dold, Arb. Path. Inst. Tübingen, 1914 (9), 30.
[18] Jour. Pharmacol., 1916 (8), 137.
[19] See Emrys-Roberts and Cowell, Jour. Path. Bact., 1917 (21), 473.
[20] Cent. f. Bakt., 1899 (26), 360.
[21] Cent. f. allg. Path., 1896 (7), 785.
[22] Festschr. for A. Jacobi, 1900, New York.
[23] Concerning the effects of iodin and iodides upon the leucocytes, see Heinz, Virchow's Arch., 1899 (155), 44.
[24] Schürmann, Cent. f. Pathol., 1910 (21), 337.
[25] Arch. Néerland., 1912 (III, B), 134; Brit. Med. Jour., 1916 (1), 37.

toxic for leucocytes. If an electric current is passed through two fingers there will be found more leucocytes in the tissues of the cathode finger than in the anode finger, presumably because the OH-ions increase ameboid movement.[26]

Many substances have been used to increase the number of leucocytes in the circulating blood in the hope of increasing resistance to infections, a result that does not seem to follow artificial leucocytosis with any recognizable uniformity. A compilation of the literature on this subject by Gehrig[27] shows such contradictory findings as to indicate that most of the recorded work is of little value. He was unable to corroborate the current statement that antipyretic drugs increase the number of leucocytes in the blood. Nucleinic acid and tissue extracts seem to increase circulating leucocytes with considerable regularity, while with thorium-X and benzol they can be reduced to almost complete extinction. The behavior of inflammatory processes in animals thus deprived of available leucocytes has considerable experimental interest.[28] If less than 1000 leucocytes per cubic mm. are present in the blood, no leucocytic exudate can be produced,[29] although the other features of inflammation occur as usual.

Relation of Cell Types to Migration.—Of the leucocytes, the most actively affected by chemotaxis is the polymorphonuclear variety, but not all substances affect each variety of leucocyte in the same way; for example, infections with most animal parasites result in both local and general increase in the eosinophilous forms, and similar effects have been obtained by the injection of extracts of animal parasites. *Lymphocytes* are much less active, presumably because they contain less of the mobile cytoplasm and consist chiefly of the structurally fixed nuclear substance. Undoubtedly many of the cells in so-called lymphocytic accumulations seen in certain conditions, such as tuberculosis, are not lymphocytes from the blood, but are newly divided cells of the tissue.[30] The experimental evidence concerning lymphocytic emigration is very contradictory. Fauconnet[31] has found that tuberculin injections cause in man general increase in leucocytes, but only of the polymorphonuclear form. Long-continued intoxication of animals, however, may result in lymphocytic increase, but local introduction of the toxin leads to accumulation of polymorphonuclear cells and not lymphocytes. Wolff[32] claims that tetanus and diphtheria toxins produce lymphocytosis in experimental animals. Wlassow and Sepp[33] state that lymphocytes are not capable of ameboid

[26] Schwyzer, Biochem. Zeit., 1914 (60), 454.
[27] Zeit. exp. Path., 1915 (17), 161.
[28] See G. Rosenow, Zeit. exp. Med., 1914 (3), 42.
[29] Camp and Baumgartner, Jour. Exp. Med., 1915 (22), 174.
[30] See résumé by Pappenheim, Folia Hematol., 1905 (2), 815; 1906 (3), 129.
[31] Deut. Arch. klin. Med., 1904 (82), 167.
[32] Berl. klin. Woch., 1901 (41), 1273.
[33] Virchow's Arch., 1901 (176), 185.

movement or phagocytosis in the body, although after heating to 44° they may become motile for a short time. Particularly significant is the experiment of Reckzeh[34] who found that in lymphatic leukemia with the lymphocytes greatly exceeding the polymorphonuclear forms in the blood, the pus from an acne pustule or from cantharides blisters contains practically no lymphocytes, but is composed of the usual polynuclear forms.

Experiments on the nature of the leucocytes attracted by different chemotactic agents have been made by Borissow[35] and Adler.[36] Both agree in stating that none of the substances tested shows any special affinity for any single type of leucocytes. Zieler[37] observed that in the skin of rabbits exposed to the Finsen light, active migration of lymphocytes takes a prominent part in the reaction. General lymphocytosis may be produced by certain substances (pilocarpine, muscarine, $BaCl_2$) which cause contraction of the smooth muscles and force these cells out of the spleen (Harvey),[38] but such a process has no relation to chemotaxis. It is notorious that infections with animal parasites cause both local and general increase in eosinophiles, and we may even have local mast-cell leucocytosis.[39]

Tissue cells were found by Alder to migrate far into blocks of elder pith, apparently rather later than the leucocytes. As they showed changes of form indicating ameboid motions he considers their migration to be an active process. The existence of the polymorphonuclear forms in the pith seems to be very transient.

The position taken by the young blood-vessels and cells in granulation tissue, at right angles to the surface, possibly also depends on chemotaxis determining the direction in which the new cells shall proliferate.

Thermotaxis of Leucocytes.—Heat seems to affect leucocytes much as it does amebæ, moderate temperatures being positively thermotactic. Mendelssohn[40] states that the thermotaxis is most pronounced at a temperature of 36°–39° C. (97°–102° F.), but is still marked as low as 20° C. Temperatures higher than 39° C. (102° F.) do not seem to attract them. Wlassow and Sepp[41] state that motility of leucocytes is increased by warming to 40° C., and that temperature of 42°–46° C. causes the movements to become very irregular, with feeble power of contraction. Lymphocytes are not motile at ordinary temperature, but at 44° they begin to move, and once motile, they continue their motion when cooled as low as 35°; this motility is considered to be entirely abnormal and only the result of degenerative changes. Murphy[42] and his colleagues have found that exposure of animals to suitable degrees of overheating, leads to marked lymphocytosis.

[34] Zeit. f. klin. Med., 1903 (50), 51.
[35] Ziegler's Beiträge, 1894 (16), 432.
[36] Festschrift f. A. Jacobi, New York, 1900.
[37] Cent. f. Pathol., 1907 (18), 289.
[38] Jour. of Physiol., 1906 (35), 115; see also Rous, Jour. Exper. Med., 1908 (10), 238.
[39] See Milchener, Zeit. klin. Med., 1899 (37), 194; Massaglia, Cent. f. Path. 1910 (21), 534.
[40] Roussky Vratch, 1903.
[41] Virchow's Archiv., 1901 (176), 185.
[42] Jour. Exp. Med., 1919 (29), 1.

If mixtures of leucocytes and bacteria sensitized with opsonins are kept at low temperature, the bacteria become attached to the surface of the leucocytes, not being ingested until the mixture is warmed.[43] This indicates that two separate processes are involved in phagocytosis.

Temperature probably plays but a minor part in attracting leucocytes in pathological processes, however. The local heat of an inflamed area is due chiefly to the accumulation of blood in the part, and would not influence the leucocytes to migrate from the still warmer blood into the tissues. Segale,[44] however, has demonstrated that there is some actual heat production through increased metabolism in inflamed tissues, which may have some slight effect. By increasing motility the temperature of fever may favor migration and phagocytosis, and local application of heat to inflamed areas may induce local leucocytic accumulation. In burns the duration of the period of excessive temperature is usually too brief to account for the attraction of leucocytes that results; this accumulation is undoubtedly due to the products of the resulting cell degenerations.

The influence of light, mechanical stimulation, and gravity upon leucocytes seems not to have been studied. The phagocytosis of insoluble non-nutritive particles has been ascribed to *tactile stimulation,* but the details of the operation of such stimuli are unknown, and the entire question of tactile stimulation is unsettled. In experiments with elder pith it has been observed that leucocytes penetrate to the center, even when the pith contains only physiological salt solution. As Adler remarks, it is difficult to explain such migration as due to tactile stimuli; but on the other hand, no other explanation has been offered.

PHAGOCYTOSIS [45]

The engulfing of bacteria, cells, tissue products, etc., by leucocytes seems to be but an extension of the phenomenon of chemotaxis. When the substance toward which the leucocyte is drawn is small enough, the leucocyte simply continues its motion until it has flowed entirely about the particle. Later the particle becomes, as a rule, more or less altered within the cell, unless it is a perfectly insoluble substance, such as a bit of coal-dust. This action upon the engulfed object is undoubtedly due to the action of intracellular enzymes.[46] Protozoa take their food into a specialized digesting vacuole which has been shown by Le Dantec[47] (in *Stentor, Paramœcium,* and some other varieties) to contain a strongly acid fluid. Miss Greenwood[48] has also demonstrated acid in several forms of protozoa, which is formed under stimulation of injected particles, whether nutritious or not. Mouton[49]

[43] Ledingham, Proc. Royal Soc., 1908 (80), 188; Sawtchenko, Arch. sci. biol. 1910 (15), 145.

[44] Jour. Exp. Med., 1919 (29), 235.

[45] See review by Metschnikoff, Kolle and Wassermann's Handb. d. Path. Mikroorganismen, 1913 (II), 655; also H. J. Hamburger. "Physikalisch-chemische Untersuchungen über Phagocyten," Bergmann, Wiesbaden, 1912, where is given a full account of the author's important researches on the principles of phagocytic behavior.

[46] See Opie, Jour. Exp. Med., 1906 (8), 410.

[47] Ann. d. l'Inst. Pasteur, 1890 (4), 776.

[48] Jour. of Physiol., 1894 (16), 441.

[49] C. R. Acad. des Sciences, 1901 (133), 244.

has been able to extract from the bodies of protozoa (rhizopods) a feebly proteolytic enzyme. This "*amibodiastase*," as he calls it, is active in alkaline, and faintly acid media, and digests colon bacilli that have been killed by heat, but not living bacilli. This last fact is highly suggestive in connection with the important question of whether leucocytes engulf and destroy virulent bacteria or only those that have been previously injured by the tissue fluid. It was impossible to secure either invertase or lipase in extracts of protozoa. Whether bacteria are digested in leucocytes by the same enzymes that digest the leucocytes themselves after they are killed (*i. e.*, the autolytic ferments), or by some specialized enzyme is not known. Metchnikoff, however, has noted the localized production of acid in the cytoplasm of leucocytes of the larva of *Triton taeniatus*. The eventual excretion of the remains of the bacteria or other foreign bodies by the phagocytes is ascribed by Rhumbler to changes in the composition of the particles through digestion, so that they have a greater surface affinity for the surrounding fluids than for the protoplasm of the cell. Calcium and magnesium salts increase phagocytosis and leucocytic migration,[50] while changes in osmotic pressure decrease these activities, as also does quinine even in dilutions of 0.001 per cent. Phagocytosis cannot take place in the absence of electrolytes, according to Sawtchenko.[51] Fat-soluble substances in general increase phagocytosis (Hamburger),[52] but cholesterol inhibits phagocytosis.[53] (its effects being suppressed by lecithin)[54] acting apparently by virtue of its OH group. Agents facilitating oxidation favor phagocytosis (Arkin).[55] Maximum phagocytosis occurs at the normal body temperature of the animal furnishing the leucocytes (Madsen and Wulf).[56]

Phagocytosis cannot be readily ascribed to chemotaxis, however, in the case of phagocytosis of perfectly insoluble, chemically inert particles, such as coal-dust. The leucocytes seem to take up foreign bodies without reference to their nutritive value, absorbing India-ink granules and bacteria impartially when they are injected together, and loading themselves so full of carmine granules that they cannot take up bacteria subsequently injected. It is possible that foreign bodies first become coated with a layer of altered protein which then leads to phagocytosis, but there is no sufficient evidence for this surmise. Kite and Wherry[57] state that leucocytes take up carbon parti-

[50] Hamburger, Biochem. Zeit., 1910 (26), 66; Eggers, Jour. Infect. Diseases, 1909 (6), 662. According to Radsma (Arch. neerl. physiol., 1918 (2), 301) calcium salts only favor phagocytosis in leucocytes that have previously had their calcium bound by citrate or oxalate in the process of isolation.
[51] Arch. sci. biol. St. Petersburg, 1911 (16), 161; 1912 (17), 128.
[52] Hamburger and de Haan, Arch. Anat. und Physiol., 1913, Phys. Abt., p. 77
[53] Dewey and Nuzum, Jour. Infect. Dis., 1911 (15), 72.
[54] Stuber, Biochem. Zeit., 1913 (51), 211; 1914 (53), 493.
[55] Jour. Infect. Dis., 1913 (13), 418.
[56] Over. Danske Vid. Selsk. Forh., 1916 (6), 339.
[57] Jour. Infect. Dis., 1915 (16), 109.

cles and similar substances because the leucocytes are "sticky," which presumably is correct, but what constitutes the "stickiness" and why it varies under the influence of serum is not indicated. Presumably it represents an altered viscosity, which is known to be increased by increased acid content such as might be produced by local asphyxia.[58] The nature of mechanical stimulation of cells is explained by Osterhout[59] as a chemical reaction to rupture of semipermeable cellular surfaces, and there is evidence from plant cells supporting this hypothesis, but its applicability to animal cells has not been investigated. The experiments of Schaeffer[60] seem to show that amebae exhibit positive chemotaxis towards such insoluble substances as carbon particles and glass fragments, even at a distance, although the mechanism is unexplained. Similar investigations have not been made with leucocytes.

Not only leucocytes but tissue cells are capable of moving and performing phagocytosis when properly stimulated, and apparently all or nearly all fixed cells may act as phagocytes under some conditions. Their power of independent movement is much less than their phagocytic power. Endothelial cells are particularly active in phagocytosis, as also are the new mesodermal cells produced in inflammation. Apparently they obey the same laws as the leucocytes, and not only take up bacteria, but also fragments of cells and tissues, red corpuscles, and even intact leucocytes and other cells. Brodie[61] considers that phagocytosis by endothelial cells in lymph-glands is the natural end of the leucocytes, and red corpuscles seem to have a similar fate.

Phagocytosis is usually accomplished solely by the cytoplasm of the cells, the nuclei maintaining a passive rôle; but, according to Detre and Selli,[62] the phagocytosis of particles of lecithin is accomplished by the nuclei, which seem to have a specific affinity for this substance.

Giant-cell formation may also be considered as the result of chemotaxis, the cells moving toward the attracting particle, and when the particle is larger than the cells they spread out upon its surface, their cytoplasm flowing together because of altered surface tension. The peripheral disposition of the nuclei probably depends on the fact that in ameboid motion the nucleus of the cell plays an entirely passive rôle, being dragged along by the cytoplasm, and hence it is located most remotely from the attracting particle. Digestion of materials taken into a giant-cell seems to go on as in the individual cells that compose it.[63]

[58] See Woolley, Jour. Amer. Med. Assoc., 1914 (63), 2279.
[59] Proc. Natl. Acad. Sci., 1916 (2), 237.
[60] Biol. Bull., 1916 (31), 303.
[61] Jour. of Anat. and Physiol., 1901 (35), 142.
[62] Berl. klin. Woch., 1905 (42), 940.
[63] See Faber., Jour. of Path. and Bact., 1893 (1), 349.

17

Influence of the Serum on Phagocytosis (Opsonins).—Phagocytosis of bacteria by leucocytes seems not to be merely a reaction between the leucocytes and the bacteria. Wright and Douglas have demonstrated that certain substances in the blood-serum are necessary to prepare the bacteria for phagocytosis, these substances being termed by them *"opsonins."* If leucocytes are washed free from serum with salt solution and let stand in a test-tube with such bacteria as *Streptococcus pyogenes, Staphylococcus pyogenes, B. typhosus, B. coli, B. tuberculosis,* and various other organisms, no phagocytosis occurs. If, however, some serum from a normal or an immunized animal is added to the mixture, active phagocytosis soon takes place. The action of opsonins is also involved in phagocytosis by endothelium.[64] The character and properties of the opsonins are further considered among the reactions of immunity (Chapter vii).

Results of Phagocytosis.—After phagocytosis has been accomplished, the fate of the engulfed object depends upon its nature. If digestible by the intracellular enzymes it is soon destroyed, but in the case of engulfed living cells, it seems probable that they must be first killed—they form no exception to the rule that living protoplasm cannot be digested. This brings forward the question of so much importance in the problems of immunity: Do living bacteria enter phagocytes, or are they first killed by extracellular agencies before they can be taken up? At the present time it seems to be positively established that leucocytes do take up bacteria which are still viable, and which may either grow inside the leucocytes or may be destroyed by intracellular processes.[65] On the other hand, leucocytes do not take up extremely virulent bacteria, and hence the question as to the relative importance played by the leucocytes and by the body fluids is still undetermined. It is probable that phagocytosis by fixed tissue-cells is of much less importance in checking bacterial growth than is phagocytosis by leucocytes. Thus Ruediger's experiments showed that emulsions of organs, with the exception of bone-marrow, do not destroy streptococci which are readily destroyed by leucocytes. However, the phagocytic activity of certain endothelial cells, especially in lymph sinuses and the Kupffer cells of the liver, is so great that these cells may equal or surpass the leucocytes in bactericidal power. Leucocytes do not seem to bind bacterial toxins.[66]

Indigestible substances may remain in cells, particularly in fixed tissue cells, for very long periods, if the substances are chemically inert. The leucocytes seem to transfer the indigestible particles which they have engulfed to other tissues, particularly to the lymph-glands; this is probably accomplished by phagocytosis of the laden leucocytes by the macrophages of the lymph sinuses, but how the insoluble particles are later transferred to the gland stroma or perilymphangial tissues, where they are chiefly found in such conditions as anthracosis, etc., is quite unknown.

[64] Briscoe, Jour. Path. and Bact., 1907 (12), 66.
[65] See Ruediger, Jour. Amer. Med. Assoc., 1905 (44), 198.
[66] Pettersson, Zeit. Immunität., 1911 (8), 498. Kobzarenko, however, states that horse leucocytes neutralize diphtheria but not tetanus toxin. (Ann. Inst. Pasteur, 1915 (29), 190.)

Leucocytes contain substances which are strongly bactericidal, independent of the action of the blood serum, and which have been called *endolysins*;[67] they are resistant to 65° or even higher, and seem to be bound rather firmly to the protoplasm of the leucocytes, for they resist extraction except by vigorous methods; they have a complex structure like the amboceptor-complement bacteriolysins of the serum, and are not specific (Weil).[68] They do not pass through porcelain filters readily, are precipitated by saturation with ammonium sulphate, and resemble the enzymes in many respects.[69] It is probable that the endolysins act upon bacteria that have been phagocyted, and perhaps also upon free bacteria when liberated in suppuration through disintegration of the leucocytes. Lymphocytes and macrophages seem to be devoid of this endolysin.[70]

Phagocytosis of living virulent bacteria may not always be an unmixed benefit. Besides the obvious possibility of transporting the bacteria and spreading infection, we have also evidence that living bacteria may be protected through phagocytosis, against the action of bactericidal substances in the blood and tissues (Rous and Jones).[71]

THEORIES OF CHEMOTAXIS AND PHAGOCYTOSIS

On the assumption that leucocytes obey the same laws in their motions as do the amebæ, studies of the latter and of other forms of protozoa have furnished most of the ideas, hypotheses, and theories of the forces involved in leucocytic activities. The structural relation of the leucocyte to the ameba is striking, although by no means complete; the relation of their activities is even closer. Each is a microscopic, independent, unicellular organism, moving freely in all directions by means of pseudopodia and protoplasmic streaming, taking other smaller bodies into its substance and digesting them, reacting similarly to like stimuli, and containing similarly a nucleus and many granules. The differentiation of the protoplasm of the ameba into a clear outer ectosarc and an inner granular endosarc is perhaps an important difference, but as far as the two forms of cells have been studied, the effect of this difference in structure does not seem to have been considered. That the unicellular protozoa, devoid of any central nervous system, and without any apparent co-ordinating mechanism, seem able to move about in a purposeful way, going toward food supplies and away from injurious agencies, toward or away from light, heat, and chemicals, has long attracted the interest of physiologists, particularly as in these single-celled organisms we may look for the simplest conditions of existence and the most elementary life processes. It seems absurd to imagine that a *paramœcium* goes toward

[67] For general review see Kling, Zeit. Immunität., 1910 (7), 1.
[68] Arch. f. Hyg., 1911 (74), 289.
[69] Manwaring, Jour. Exp. Med., 1912 (16), 250.
[70] See Schneider, Arch. f. Hyg., 1909 (70), 40.
[71] Jour. Exper. Med., 1916 (23), 601.

a dilute acid because it "likes it," that an ameba rejects a piece of glass because it "does not taste good," as we explain similar manifestations in higher forms; furthermore, it has been shown by Verworn that minute enucleated fragments of protozoan cells react to stimuli just as does the entire cell, and, therefore, it seems that the only possible explanation of movements in protozoa must be a direct reaction of the stimulated part to the stimulus. The nature of the stimulus and the nature of the stimulated substance must determine the nature of the resulting reaction, and most of the observations so far made suggest that these reactions can be explained according to the known laws of the physics of fluids. An ameba, or a leucocyte, may be looked upon as a drop of a colloidal solution, surrounded by a delicate surface layer which is more or less readily permeable to solvents and to substances in solution, and suspended in a fluid of quite different composition.

Surface Tension.—Such a drop of fluid suspended in another different fluid obeys well-known laws of physics. The particles of each fluid are all under the influence of a very considerable force, called the cohesion pressure, which tends to draw them together closely. Within the drop each particle is subjected to this force alike from all sides, so that the forces neutralize one another, and each particle is as free as if there were no cohesion pressure. But the particles on the surface are subjected to unequal pressure, for that of the fluid outside the drop is different from that inside, and so the pressure on the surface particles is equal to the difference of the cohesion pressure of the two fluids; this constitutes the surface tension. It is this tension that pulls in upon the surface continually, causing it to tend always to reduce the free surface to a minimum, which condition exists perfectly in the sphere. The amount of cohesion affinity is very different in different fluids, and therefore some have a high surface tension and some a low. When a substance dissolves in another the surface tension is a resultant of the surface tension of the two substances, and hence the surface tension of a liquid may be raised or lowered by dissolving various substances in it.

Artificial Imitations of Ameboid Movement

Imagine a drop of fluid suspended in water—let it be a drop of protoplasm, or oil, or mercury; the drop owes its tendency to assume a spherical shape to the surface tension, which is pulling the free surface toward the center and acting with the same force on all sides. The result is that the drop is surrounded by what amounts to an elastic, well-stretched membrane, similar to the condition of a thin rubber bag distended with fluid. If at any point in the surface the tension is lessened, while elsewhere it remains the same, of necessity the wall will bulge at this point, the contents will flow into the new space so offered, and the rest of the wall will contract; hence the drop moves toward the point of lowered surface tension. Conversely, if the tension is increased in one place, the wall at this point will contract with greater force than elsewhere, driving the contents toward the less resistant part of the surface, and the drop will move away from the point of increased tension. The resemblance of these changes of form and the type of motion produced, to ameboid movement, is apparent, and much experimenting has been done to determine how far the processes of motion as shown by amebæ and leucocytes can be reproduced by fluid drops under various conditions of experiment, and to ascertain if such ameboid movement of living cells can be entirely explained by the laws of surface tension.

Gad,[72] in 1878, pointed out the resemblance to ameboid motion of the changes in shape observed in drops of rancid oils in weak alkaline solution. These changes in shape are due to the formation of soaps which lower the surface tension of the drop in places, so that the fluid flows toward these places and produces pseudopodium-like projections.

G. Quincke[73] later ascribed the contractions and other movements of amebæ to alterations of the surface tension of the living substance in relation to that of the surrounding medium, believing the substances responsible for the alterations to be albuminous soaps.

Bütschli[74] found that drops of "foam structure" made by mixing rancid oil and potassium carbonate solution show "*protoplasmic streaming*" when placed in glycerol, and that they exhibit positive chemotaxis toward soap solution and other chemicals, the motion being accompanied by current formation in the drops. The "pseudopodia" formed by the drops also show currents rushing along their axes and returning by way of the surface. Heat leads to increased activity of motion. The motions were ascribed by Bütschli to the bursting of some of the superficial globules of the foam, which then spread over the surface of the drops, lowering its surface tension at the point of contact. He believed that ameboid motion, likewise, depended upon rupture of surface globules of protoplasm, for the "foam structure" of which he has been the leading advocate.

Bernstein,[75] basing his work on some observations of Paalzow, observed that a completely inorganic substance, a drop of quicksilver, could be made to imitate ameboid motion under the influence of chemical changes. If a crystal of potassium dichromate is placed near a drop of quicksilver in a nitric acid solution, as soon as the yellow color made by diffusion of the dichromate reaches the drop the quicksilver begins to show motion and advances toward the crystal. This movement is due to local oxidation of the surface mercury, which lowers the tension on that side of the drop, toward which the mercury then flows. If the crystal is removed, the drop follows, often flowing about it as if to take it in, but soon again withdrawing when the acid dissolves away the oxide formed on the surface, only to return again later. All these movements, which may be very life-like, are readily explained by changes in surface tension that take place under the influence of the bichromate and the acid, and are unquestionably referable to surface phenomena.

[72] DuBois Reymond's Arch. f. Physiol., 1878, p. 181.
[73] Wiedmann's Annalen, 1888 (35), 580.
[74] "Protoplasm," translation by Minchin, London, 1894.
[75] Pflüger's Arch., 1900 (80), 628.

Artificial Amebæ.—By far the most suggestive experiments on the simulation of ameboid activity by non-living substances are those of Rhumbler (1898) in his great work, "Physikalische Analyse von Lebenserscheinungen der Zelle."[76] On the assumption that the living protoplasm was but a more or less tenacious fluid, following the simple physical laws of fluids, especially in relation to its surface tension, he devised a number of experiments to determine the correctness of these views. An ameba may be regarded as such a mass of viscid fluid, in a medium in which it is nearly or quite insoluble; it is also constantly undergoing chemical changes within itself, and taking substances from or secreting them into the surrounding water. To reproduce partly these conditions a drop of clove oil is placed in a mixture of glycerol and alcohol; the alcohol and clove oil are miscible, the glycerol merely retarding the diffusion.[77] Such a drop of oil will move about, changing its form and sending out pseudopodia much as an ameba does. These movements are undoubtedly due to changes in the surface tension brought about by the irregular mixing of the alcohol and the clove oil. The effect of chemotaxis upon an ameba can likewise be imitated with such an "artificial ameba." If some stronger alcohol is carefully introduced into the fluid near the drop, the surface tension on that side will be lowered, and the drop will flow in that direction. The effect of chemical changes within the drop upon its motion may be demonstrated similarly by injecting a little alcohol into the substance of the drop near one edge—the drop will send out a pseudopodium on that side, and perhaps flow along in the direction of the pseudopodium. We can imagine that metabolic changes in the body of an ameba may account for many of its seemingly purposeless movements by altering surface tension in some part of its circumference. Thermotaxis, the effect of heat in modifying or impelling ameboid motion, may be equally well demonstrated in such an "artificial ameba," the drop being "positively thermotactic," and flowing rapidly toward a heated point in the solution, because heat lowers the surface tension.

Even as highly specialized a process as the taking of food may be closely simulated experimentally. Amebæ seem to possess the faculty of selecting substances that are suitable for their food, crawling over particles of sand, wood, etc., and rejecting them when they are pushed against or into the surface of the ameba, which, however, readily takes up bacteria, diatoms, algæ, etc., digests them, and later throws out the undigested particles. If there is any property of the ameba that suggests voluntary action, it seems to be exhibited in the choice of its food, although this is not so well developed a selective process as might be expected, for amebæ will take up many harmful objects, and they may be made to fill themselves so full of useless substances that they cannot take up food. However, a drop of chloroform in water, which makes a good artificial ameba, if "fed" with various substances, will refuse some and take in others in a surprisingly life-like manner. Pieces of glass or of wood placed in contact with the drop, exert no influence; if pushed into the substance of the drop, they carry the surface ahead, and on being released they are thrown out with some force. If a piece of shellac, paraffin, styrax, or Canada balsam be brought in contact with the surface of the drop, however, the drop flows around it immediately, and takes it within its substance, where it is soon dissolved. Even more strikingly like phagocytosis and intracellular digestion, however, is the result of a similar experiment with a piece of glass covered with shellac; the chloroform "ameba" takes it up as readily as it does the shellac alone, but after all the coating is dissolved away the piece of glass is then cast out of the drop. The resemblance to the engulfing, digestion, and excreting of indigestible particles of bacteria, etc., by amebæ, is so striking that it seems impossible that there can be any fundamental differences in the two processes. It will also be noticed that the drop takes in only what it can dissolve and rejects what it cannot.

One of the most remarkable actions of the amebæ, which seems almost certainly the result of voluntary action, is this: Oftentimes in feeding, an ameba gets hold of a suitable material which is in the form of a long thread, much too long for the ameba to surround. It then proceeds to coil up the thread within its body, by stretching a slight distance along the thread, bending over, and forming a bend in the thread, and by repeating the process it crowds the thread into a

[76] Arch. f. Entwicklungsmechanik, 1898 (7), 103.

[77] The details of these experiments are as given briefly by Jennings, Jour. of Applied Microscopy, 1902 (5), 1597.

neat coil within its body, where it can be digested. The process is done so systematically and with such evident adoption of the means at hand to the desired end, that it seems as if it must be an adaptation of the ameba to circumstances, the result of long experience or of heredity. That an artificial ameba can perform the same manouvers seems hardly credible, but it is readily done with almost no difference in detail. If the chloroform drop is given a long fine thread of shellac, it proceeds to bend the thread in the middle, and to send pseudopodia out along the thread to pull it into the drop, coiling it up inside as the chloroform softens the substance of the thread, until it is all contained within the drop, provided, of course, that it is not too long (a thread six times as long as the chloroform drop may be taken in completely). The bending and coiling of the thread in this experiment is entirely in accord with the known laws and phenomena of surface tension.

Fully as striking an ameboid action as the coiling up of a thread too long to be taken in, is the building, by some of the protozoa closely related to the ameba (*Difflugia*) of a shell which the animal seems to form by cementing together grains of sand, or diatom shells, or other suitable particles. The particles are united so closely and fitted together so well that they are almost perfectly free from crevices. Even this process is accurately imitated in Rhumbler's experiments. If a drop of oil is mixed with fine grains of quartz sand, and dropped into 70 per cent. alcohol, the grains are thrown out to the surface, where they adhere to the surface of the drop and to one another exactly as do the particles in a difflugia shell. So well fitted are the particles that the artificial shell may remain intact for months, and resemble the natural shell indistinguishably.

Furthermore, the phenomenon of cell division can be imitated to some extent by oil droplets. Bütschli considered that the cleavage furrow of dividing cells represented an area of greater surface tension, and McClendon imitated cell division as follows: He suspended a drop of rancid oil and chloroform between water and salt solution, and allowed sodium hydrate to flow from pipettes against two opposite points in the droplet, whereon the surface tension was lowered and the drop bulged at these points, the band of higher surface tension constricting the drop between these two points. Burrows states that the changes seen in cells dividing beneath the microscope correspond well to these experimental observations.[78]

RELATION OF THE ABOVE EXPERIMENTS TO THE PHENOMENA EXHIBITED BY LEUCOCYTES IN INFLAMMATION

The experiments cited indicate strongly, to say the least, that amebæ, and presumably leucocytes, react to stimuli of various kinds, chiefly through the effect of these stimuli upon surface tension. The stimuli may come from within the cell, being in this case the result of changes in composition brought about by metabolic processes; such chemical products alter the tension of the surface nearest their point of origin, causing what appears to be spontaneous motion. Stimuli acting from without may be chemical, thermal, electrical, or mechanical, but in any event they act as stimuli to motion through their effect upon surface tension; if they decrease the surface tension the cell goes toward them; if they increase the tension, the cell moves away.[79] The behavior of leucocytes in inflammation may be explained on these purely physical grounds very satisfactorily, as follows:

At the point of cell injury or of infection, substances are produced that exert positive chemotaxis, as can be shown by experiments both

[78] See Trans. Congress Amer. Phys., 1913 (9), 77.

[79] OH-ions decrease, H-ions increase the surface tension of leucocytes (Schwyzer, Biochem. Zeit., 1914 (60), 306, 447, 454), which may explain the fact that lactic and other acids exhibit negative chemotaxis.

outside and inside the body; these substances are chemotactic because they influence the surface tension of the leucocytes, and since with most if not all the products of cell disintegration the effect is to lower surface tension, the chemotactic effect is positive. As the chemotactic substances are produced, they diffuse through the tissues until they reach the walls of a capillary, through which they begin to pass, presumably most rapidly through the thinnest parts of the wall, the "stomata" and intercellular substance. The leucocytes passing along in the bore of the capillary will be touched by the chemotactic substances most on the side from which the substances diffuse; the surface tension will be lowered on this side, causing the formation of pseudopodia and motion in this direction. When the leucocytes come in contact with the wall, their surfaces, because saturated with the chemotactic substances, will have a tension much the same as that of the cells of the capillary wall, which are likewise saturated with the same substances, and the two surfaces will tend to cling to one another; explaining the phenomenon of adhesion of leucocytes to the capillary wall, when, according to the usual description, "the leucocytes behave as if either they or the capillary wall had become sticky."[80] Surface tension of the leucocytes will be least nearest the points where the most chemotactic substances are entering the capillary, namely, the stomata; hence the pseudopodia will form in this direction and flow through the openings, the rest of the cytoplasm flowing after and dragging the nucleus along in an apparently passive manner. Since it is the cytoplasm that seems to be chiefly affected in these processes, the nucleus appearing to be rendered inert by its relatively dense and fixed structure, the leucocytes with most cytoplasm are most active in migration, while those with the least, the lymphocytes, are affected relatively little or not at all.

Once through the vessel wall, the motion continues in the same manner, toward the side from which the chemotactic matter comes, just as the mercury drop flows toward the crystal of potassium dichromate, or the drop of oil flows toward the alcohol. If the leucocyte meets a substance that lowers its surface tension sufficiently, it will flow around the object and enclose it, just as the chloroform drop flows about the piece of shellac or balsam; this constitutes phagocytosis. The motion of the leucocyte will continue in a forward direction until one of several possible things happens: (*a*) The leucocyte may reach a point where the chemotactic substances are so thoroughly diffused that the effects on its surface are the same on all sides; there will then be no tendency to move in any direction. (*b*) It may reach a material that exerts a marked positive influence upon it, causing much lowering of the surface tension, but which is so large

[80] Kreibich (Arch. f. Dermatol., 1912 (114), 585) describes as chemical changes in the vessel walls during the early stages of inflammation, a diffuse sudanophile change throughout the endothelial cells, in the form of fine, dust-like particles. Probably this change depends simply on an aggregation of the intracellular lipoids.

that the cytoplasm flowing along its surface cannot surround it; other leucocytes will experience the same change, their cytoplasm will fuse together because of the equal lowering of their surface tension, and soon we get a mass of leucocytes with fused cytoplasm surrounding the object, forming a "foreign body giant-cell." (c) The leucocyte may reach a place where the concentration of the chemicals is so great that chemical changes are produced in its cytoplasm. If these changes are of a coagulative nature, the surface of the cell will be stiffened so that it cannot migrate further; if of a solvent nature, the leucocyte is destroyed. (d) It may reach the margin of an area where the preceding leucocytes have become coagulated or otherwise rendered immobile, so that they block its path, while it is held fixed by the attraction on this side. (c and d explain the formation of solid leucocytic walls about areas of inflammation, and the frequent absence of leucocytes within the central necrotic areas.) (e) The formation of chemotactic substances may cease because the substance causing the inflammation has been used up, or because the bacteria have been destroyed, or from any of the causes that terminate inflammation. Those leucocytes still advancing will reach a point where there is as much chemotactic substance behind as in front—they will then stop advancing.[81] As the fluids exuded in the central portion continue to dilute the chemotactic substances and wash them out, there will soon be less chemotactic substance in the center of the inflamed area than there is farther out, hence the leucocytes will move away from the center toward the periphery, following the chemotactic substances back into the blood-vessel and the lymph-stream. These are the conditions that exist at the close of the inflammatory process, which results in the dispersion of the leucocytes.

General leucocytosis can be explained equally well on the same grounds. Chemotactic substances from the area of inflammation enter the blood-stream, and so, in a very dilute form, pass through the bone-marrow. The chemotaxis in the blood will be greater than that of the marrow, and the leucocytes will move toward and into the blood. As long as the blood contains more chemotactic substances than the marrow, leucocytosis will increase, to stop when the amount in blood and marrow is alike or when there is less in the blood than in the marrow.

Behavior of Tissue=cells and Formation of Giant=cells. The free cells of the tissues involved in inflammation can, of course, obey the same influences as the leucocytes, and apparently do so in so far as they are not checked by structural impediments to flowing motion; *i .e.*, the more closely a cell is related to a single drop of fluid

[81] The phagocytic action of leucocytes *in vitro* is decreased by substances that lower the surface tension, e. g. chloroform (Hamburger, K. Akad. Wetensch., 1911 (XIII (2)), 892). Ether-soluble substances from bacteria have no effect on phagocytosis (Müller, Zeit. Immunität., 1908 (1), 61).

protoplasm, the more closely does it resemble in the simplicity of its reactions the "artificial ameba." An illustration of the chemotaxis of epithelial cells is furnished by B. Fischer,[82] who found that stained fats cause growth and migration of epithelial cells in the direction of the fat. Cells with much cytoplasm are best fitted to move freely, as a rule, and hence we see chiefly the large endothelial cells of the lymph sinuses and the serous cavities, and the large hyaline and granular cells of the blood acting as phagocytes, for phagocytosis is no different from ameboid motion which continues about a particle until it is surrounded; likewise we see the "epithelioid" and large endothelial cells with their abundant cytoplasm fusing together to form giant-cells. (Note that such giant-cells are formed particularly in conditions in which the epithelioid cell is more abundant than is the leucocyte, *e. g.*, tuberculosis and other chronic inflammations. The cells that fuse about an infected catgut ligature are the leucocytes, for they are most abundant in such a place.) A good illustration, also, is the giant-cell formed by fusing of leucocytes about blastomyces in minute abscesses in the epithelium in blastomycetic dermatitis; the epithelial cells cannot flow or coalesce well because of their abundance of stiff keratin and their specialized cell-wall, and hence do not participate; the leucocytes are individually too small to surround the fungus cells, and hence they flow about them in the abscess exactly as they will do experimentally in a test-tube or in a guinea-pig's abdomen (Hektoen). The method of growing tissues *in vitro* permits of observation of the process of giant-cell formation, and establishes that, for foreign body giant-cells at least, they are formed by fusion of wandering cells (Lambert).[83] The formation of giant-cells is, on this ground, but an amplification of ameboid movement and phagocytosis. The fusing of the individual cells is due to the lowering of their surface-tension by the materials diffusing from the body which is to be absorbed, until the surface of each cell becomes alike, when the surface tension at the point where each cell is in contact becomes zero and the cytoplasm runs together.

Objections to the above Hypothesis.—Physical explanations of ameboid movement seem to fit very perfectly the known facts concerning the actions of leucocytes. There arise but a few difficulties in applying these laws to leucocytic action; one is the phagocytosis of chemically inert bodies, such as coal particles, tattooing materials, stone dust, etc. We know that amebæ also may take up such inert materials, although they generally refuse them, and it is believed that the particles exert some local injury to the cell wall that leads to an alteration in its tension. Amebæ seem also sometimes to excrete a sticky substance over their surfaces or over the foreign matter that is to be engulfed, which excretion seems to be the result of surface stimulation. Possibly leucocytes do the same. We must bear in mind, however, that the protoplasmic cells have much greater possibilities for action than the "artificial ameba," since within the protoplasm countless chemical changes are going on which must cause continual alteration in surface tension; it is quite possible that mere mechanical action may alter chemical action at the

[82] Münch. med. Woch., 1906 (53), 2041.
[83] Anatomical Record, 1912 (6), 91.

point of contact, so that the injuring particle may become surrounded through local liquefaction of the protoplasm.

With the ameba, unfortunately, the explanation of all its activities by purely physical analogies is apparently not so successful. Although simple pseudopodia may be produced experimentally, and their formation explained readily on the surface tension basis, yet we find many forms of pseudopodia in the great family of amebæ. Some of them are branching, some are fixed in extension, some have a stiff elastic axis. It would also be difficult to explain cilia as produced by changes in surface tension, yet we find in some protozoa that pseudopodia may take on the persistence and action of cilia, and that cilia may seem to change into pseudopodia. Jennings has made a most extended study of the relations of the "Behavior of Lower Organisms"[84] to the physical theories of ameboid motion, and is unable to corroborate the claim that the processes that go on in "artificial amebæ" exactly reproduce those of living amebæ, or to accept the statement that living protoplasm behaves exactly as any similar drop of fluid would under the same conditions. He states that the currents set up in artificial amebæ by changes in surface tension are not the same as those in living amebæ, contrary to Rhumbler and to Bütschli. The movement of ameba, he maintains, is not due to the flowing of the contents of the cell in a central, axial current out into the pseudopodium and back on the sides, as occurs in the artificial ameba; but rather to a rolling forward of the upper surface over the anterior edge to the lower surface, where it becomes fixed to the surface on which the ameba is crawling. The part played by surface tension, he claims, is in the case of amebæ a very subordinate one, and it is not sufficient to explain the movements of the living cell.

However the discussion concerning the amebæ may turn, it must be appreciated that there are some important differences between even the ameba and the leucocyte. The latter has by far the simpler organization, and approaches in structure, and presumably, therefore also in response to stimuli, more closely to the simple drop of colloid matter. It has no pulsating vacuoles, no specialized pseudopodia, never forms shells or coverings, and does not conjugate as do the amebæ. The external surface of the leucocyte is much simpler, an important fact in connection with surface tension effects, for in the leucocyte the surface seems to be practically undifferentiated, naked protoplasm; whereas in amebæ it is formed of a well-differentiated "ectosarc," which has marked motile powers, being able to contract sufficiently to cut an injured ameba completely in two. At the very least *the surface tension explanation of leucocytic action agrees perfectly with most of the observed actions of leucocytes*, and it is the only reasonable theory offered. There seems to be no middle ground between such a physical theory and a metaphysical theory which would endow a single cell, without organs or nervous system, with the reasoning powers of highly developed animals, a position incompatible with the entire evidence of experience.

SUPPURATION[85]

For the formation of pus two conditions are necessary: (1) the accumulation of leucocytes, and (2) necrosis and liquefaction of cells

[84] Publication No. 16, Carnegie Institute, Washington, 1904; also see American Naturalist, 1904 (38), 625.

[85] Inflammatory Exudates, their formation and composition, are considered in Chapter xiv.

and tissue elements. Many leucocytes may be present in a tissue without suppuration; e. g., erysipelas. Necrosis of cells with their gradual liquefaction and absorption may also occur without suppuration; e. g., infarcts, aseptic liquefaction necrosis, etc. Hence for suppuration to occur there must be produced substances with positive chemotaxis, to cause accumulation of leucocytes, for if a necrotic area is devoid of leucocytes, it does not suppurate; e. g., caseous tubercles. Secondly, necrosis must occur, for digestion and liquefaction of *living* cells and tissues does not take place. Only substances meeting these requirements—i. e., causing positive chemotaxis and cell necrosis—will cause suppuration. Therefore, although bacterial infection is the usual cause of suppuration,[86] it may be produced by many other substances, among which the following are the best known: Bacterial proteins, even from non-pathogenic bacteria; oil of turpentine, mercury, croton oil, silver nitrate solutions (5 to 10 per cent.), and certain vegetable proteins (vegetable "caseins").

An excellent example of the importance of leucocytes for suppurative softening is the caseous tubercle, which is usually free from leucocytes and does not undergo suppuration. If for any cause leucocytes are attracted into the caseous area, softening and pus formation promptly occur. Hence Heile[87] found that while pus from a "cold" tuberculous abscess will not digest fibrin and does not give the biuret reaction, both reactions appear after a leucocytosis has been brought about by injection of iodoform. It was formerly considered that the softening was due to the digestive action of the enzymes of the infecting bacteria, many of which were known to produce digestive enzymes dissolving protein culture-media; e. g., *Staphylococcus pyogenes.* Although to some extent these enzymes may be a factor in causing the softening of the fixed tissues and of the killed leucocytes, their effect is probably insignificant as compared with the enzymes liberated by the leucocytes, as shown by the production of active experimental suppuration under aseptic conditions with turpentine, croton oil, etc.[88] Suppuration is, therefore, the result of three processes: (1) Necrosis of cells; (2) local accumulation of leucocytes; (3) digestion of the necrotic cells, fibrin, and tissue elements by enzymes which are derived from three sources, as follows: (a) the leucocytes; (b) the infecting bacteria (if such are present); (c) the fixed tissue-cells. Possibly small quantities of enzymes are also introduced in the blood plasma, but these are probably very inconsiderable.

[86] Buchner considers that bacteria will not produce suppuration unless they are broken down so that their *pyogenic* proteins are released; e. g., anthrax bacilli cause suppuration when acting locally, as in malignant pustule, but not when they are causing septicemia, because only in the former case are their pyogenic proteins liberated.

[87] Zeit. klin. Med., 1904 (55), 508.

[88] Apparently suppuration may occur in herpes zoster vesicles in the absence of bacteria, according to the findings of Kreibich (Wien. klin. Woch., 1901 (14) 583).

Normal serum, and probably also normal cells, contain antibodies for the proteolytic enzymes of the leucocytes, and hence neutralization or destruction of these antibodies must be an important factor in determining the rate and amount of suppuration.[89]

The influence of the antienzymes is well shown by the rabbit, with serum rich in antienzymes and leucocytes poor in protease, so that infections with pus cocci do not usually lead to the formation of liquid pus (Opie). In man we see a similar relation, in that exudates rich in serum do not suppurate because the enzymes are inhibited by the serum; but if the excess of serum is removed suppuration may then occur. With an excess of enzyme (*i. e.*, leucocytes) the inhibiting effect may also be overcome, and suppuration then begins. Variations in the proportion of leucoprotease and serum antiprotease determine, therefore, the occurrence of suppuration, and the inflammatory reaction is seen to be fundamentally the same as the humoral reactions of immunity, in that in each case the essential process is the provision of proteolytic enzymes to remove foreign or abnormal protein substances. In inflammation the proteolytic enzymes are brought in the leucocytes, in humoral reactions the enzymes are present free in the plasma. The antiproteases may be of the nature of lipoids, probably with unsaturated fatty acids (Jobling).

The proteolytic enzymes of the leucocytes and tissue-cells have been previously considered in connection with the subject of autolysis (Chap. iii), and it is necessary here only to call attention to the fact that these enzymes are of at least two varieties: (1) Proteolytic enzymes of the polymorphonuclear leucocytes, which act best in alkaline medium (Opie[90]); (2) autolytic enzymes of the tissue-cells, which act best in an acid medium or after a preliminary acidification (Hedin, *et al.*). The mononuclear leucocytes contain, like the tissue-cells, enzymes acting in an acid medium. The antienzymatic action of serum is favored by an alkaline reaction, but is altogether lost in an acid medium (Opie).

COMPOSITION OF PUS

Because of its method of production, pus consists of the following substances: (1) The constituents of the exuded blood plasma; (2) the constituents of the leucocytes (and tissue-cells) that exist free in the pus; (3) the products of digestion of the proteins of the leucocytes and necrosed tissues. All analyses of pus that are recorded in the literature are in harmony with the above statements. In general the analyses consider pus as composed of two chief portions, the pus corpuscles and the pus serum. As is to be expected, the composition of pus-corpuscles is simply that of a large mass of leucocytes, which

[89] See Opie, Jour. Exper. Med., 1905 (7), 316; 1907 (9), 207; Arch. Int. Med., 1910 (5), 541.
[90] Jour. Exper. Med., 1906 (8), 410.

contain minute quantities of substances taken up from the pus serum by absorption and phagocytosis.[91]   The old analyses of pus-corpuscles by Hoppe-Seyler[92] are given in the following table:

TABLE I.

Quantitative Composition of Pus-cells (in 1000 parts of the dried substance).

	I		II
Proteins	137.62		
Nuclein	342.57	685.85	673.69
Insoluble bodies	205.66		
Lecithin		143.83	75.64
Fat			75.00
Cholesterol	74.00	....	72.83
Cerebrin	51.99		
Extractive bodies	44.33	....	102.84

Mineral Substances in 1000 *Parts of the Dried Substance*

NaCl	4.35
$Ca_3(PO_4)_2$	2.05
$Mg_3(PO_4)_2$	1.13
$FePO_4$	1.06
PO_4	9.16
Na	0.68
K	trace

As abnormal constituents of the leucocytes contained in abscesses may be mentioned glycogen, fat (from phagocytosis and from "fatty degeneration" of the leucocytes), and "peptone" (Hofmeister).[93]

Pus serum differs from blood-serum chiefly in the substances added to it through the proteolytic changes that occur in the pus, and also in that it has lost its antiproteolytic property, containing instead free leucoprotease.   The fibrinogen that escapes from the vessels into suppurating areas becomes so altered that pus will not coagulate, even upon addition of fibrin ferment (defibrinated blood).   The reaction of the serum is usually slightly alkaline, becoming strongly alkaline if much ammonia is produced, which occurs especially if there is secondary infection with the organisms of putrefacton.   Sometimes, however, lipase derived either from bacteria or from the cells causes the splitting of sufficient amounts of fatty acids from the fats to make the reaction acid; lactic and other fatty acids are also sometimes formed.   Presumably the nature of the infecting organism will modify the reaction, for some (*e. g., staphylococcus*) cause an acid formation in media, while others (*e. g., pyocyaneus*) cause an alkaline reaction.   Pneumococcus pus is said to become markedly acid.[94] Hoppe-Seyler's analysis of pus serum gave the following results, which

[91] The *electrical conductivity* of whole pus is somewhat greater than that of blood, and pus plasma conducts much more than whole pus, because of the resistance of the leucocytes (Tangl and Bodon, Biochem. Zeit., 1917 (84), 183).

[92] Med.-Chem. Untersuchungen.

[93] Zeit. physiol. Chem., 1880 (4), 268.

[94] Netter, Bougault and Salanier, Compt. Rend. Soc. Biol., 1917 (80), 97.

show no considerable deviation from the composition of blood plasma, except in an increased proportion of fatty matter and extractive substances.

TABLE II

	Quantitative composition of pus serum		Plasma normal
	I	II	III
Water	913.7	905.65	908.4
Solids	86.3	94.35	91.6
Proteins	63.23	77.21	77.6
Lecithin	1.50	0.56	
Fat	0.26	0.29	1.2
Cholesterol	0.53	0.87	
Alcohol extractives	1.52	0.73	
Water extractives	11.53	6.92	4.0
Inorganic salts	7.73	7.77	8.1

Quantitatively the chief abnormal constituent of pus serum is the so-called *"pyin"* of the older writers, which is nucleoprotein derived from the decomposing leucocytes, and hence increasing in amount progressively with the age of the pus;[95] it is characterized by its insolubility in acetic acid. The same substance is found more abundantly in the entire pus, on account of the presence of the cells, and when treated with 10 per cent. NaCl solution it forms a stringy mass which was formerly called *"Rovida's hyalin substance."* Glucothionic acid, derived from the leucocytes, is also present in pus.[96] In the pus serum are found all the other constituents of the leucocytes, including particularly lecithin, cholesterol, fats (and soaps), cerebrin, "jecorin," and glycogen; and also the usual components of the blood-serum as well as some small quantities of pigment derived from decomposed red corpuscles.

The *products of autolysis* are of particular interest, and they are found in varying amount, but usually less abundantly than might be expected, probably because of their solubility and consequent rapid absorption. Albumoses and peptones seem to be constantly present (Shattock).[97] The common occurrence of albumosuria during suppuration presumably depends on the absorption of digestion products from the pus,[98] but true peptone has not been satisfactorily identified in the urine. Leucine and tyrosine have also frequently been found in pus,[99] but Taylor[1] could find no workable traces of either monoam-

[95] Strada, Biochem. Zeit., 1909 (16), 193.
[96] Mandel and Levene, Biochem. Zeit., 1907 (4), 78.
[97] Trans. London Path. Soc., 1892 (43), 225.
[98] Literature on albumosuria, see Yarrow, Amer. Med., 1903 (5), 452; Elmer, *ibid.*, 1906 (11), 169; Senator, International Clinics, 1905 (IV), series 14, p. 85. See also "Albumosuria," Chap. xxi.
[99] Müller (Cent. inn. Med., 1907 (28), 297) recommends the tyrosine reaction with Millon's reagent as a means of differentiating tuberculous from ordinary pus, the former not giving the reaction because of lack of leucocytic enzymes; but there is disagreement as to the constancy of this reaction in pus (Dold, Deut. med. Woch., 1908 (34), 869).
[1] Univ. of California Publications (Pathol.), 1904 (1), 46.

ino- or polyamino-acids in a liter of pus, which may depend on their
having been either absorbed or transformed into ammonium compounds.   Presumably this is in part the explanation of the large
urea excretion in persons with extensive suppuration, as observed by
Ameuille.[2]   From the nucleoproteins *purine bodies* are formed and
may be found in the pus.   The relation of the purine bases to local
leucocytosis is shown by Heile,[87] who found in cold tuberculous abscesses a proportion of purine bases equal to 0.5 per cent., in similar abscesses after injection of iodoform, 1.57, and in acute suppuration,
10.7.   *Spermin* crystals are also occasionally found in old pus collections.[3]   *Free fatty acids* and volatile fatty acids, such as butyric,
lactic,[4] valerianic, and formic, have been found.   Products of bacterial activity, such as bacterial proteins and pigments (*e. g.*, pyocyanin), may also be present.   It is probable that in many instances
these autolytic products are bactericidal, and thus help to terminate
the infection.   Direct tests have shown that the autolysate of fibrin is
bactericidal for staphylococci and streptococci.[5]   See also discussion
of "Autolysis of Exudates" (Chap. iii).

All the numerous *enzymes* of the blood plasma, the leucocytes and
the tissue-cells, are present in pus.   Thus Achalme[6] found evidence
of the presence of the following enzymes in pus: proteolytic enzymes,[7] lipase (splitting monobutyrin), diastase, rennin (coagulating
milk), gelatinase, catalase, and oxidase, the last being very abundant.
These seem to exist chiefly in the leucocytes, the pus serum being
quite free from them.   No evidence could be found of enzymes acting on amygdalin, saccharose, inulin, or lactose.   Fibrin ferment is
said to be absent from pus, which is quite surprising in view of the
fact that this enzyme is generally considered as being derived chiefly
from the leucocytes.   Presumably the bacteriolytic "endolysins" of
the leucocytes are also present in pus.

There is little difference in the effect on metabolism produced by a
sterile suppuration and one due to *localized* bacterial infection (Cooke
and Whipple),[8] one of the chemical features in each being a precipitous
and sustained rise in the urinary N excretion.   Presumably the reaction in both cases results from toxic products of protein cleavage,
rather than from bacterial secretions in the case of septic inflammation.
Probably only part of the excessive urinary N comes from the local
injury, the greater part being derived from toxicogenic destruction of
tissue proteins.

[2] Bull. Acad. Méd. Paris, 1917, (78), 8.
[3] See Williams, Boston Med. and Surg. Jour., 1901 (145), 355.
[4] d-lactic acid is a constant constituent of pus from the pleura (Ito, Jour.
Biol. Chem., 1916 (26), 173).
[5] Bilancioni, Arch. di Farmacol., 1911 (11), 491.
[6] Compt. Rend. Soc. Biol., 1899 (51), 568.
[7] Concerning proteolytic enzymes of pus see Opie, Jour. Exper. Med., 1906 (8),
410.
[8] Jour. Exp. Med., 1918, (28), 222.

SPUTUM[9]

The chemistry of sputum may be properly considered in this connection. In reaction, sputum is ordinarily alkaline, but in case of marked bacterial decomposition in cavities the reaction may become acid. Its specific gravity varies from 1.008 to 1.026, usually varying directly with the number of leucocytes; the average specific gravity is about 1.013 . The greenish color frequently observed depends generally upon blood-pigment (except in case of icterus), although in some instances the pigment is of bacterial origin. Renk[10] has studied the proteins of sputum with special reference to the loss of protein to the body and its relation to cachexia. In three patients (consumptives) studied, the daily amount of sputum of two averaged 145 grams for each; for the third it was 82 grams. This contained (average) 5 to 6 per cent. of solids; including mucin, 2–3 per cent.; protein, 0.1–0.5 per cent.: fat, 0.3–0.5 per cent.; ash, 0.8–0.9 per cent. The daily loss of nitrogen was 0.75 gram, which equals about 6 per cent. of the total daily nitrogen output of persons under condition of starvation.[11] Wanner[12] found characteristic variations in the amount of protein in sputum from different conditions, as follows: in bronchitis the amount of protein is very small; in bronchiectasis protein is present, but the amount of uncoagulable nitrogen (due to autolysis) is relatively large; in phthisis as well as in bronchiectasis the amount of protein does not exceed 1 per cent.; in pneumonia it may reach 3 per cent., but it is highest in pulmonary gangrene. Any protein content that causes more than a slight turbidity on boiling indicates an inflammation; e. g., in case of doubt between a diagnosis of pneumonia and infarct a high protein content speaks for the former. Rogers[13] stated that the sputum in every case of tuberculosis shows albumin,[14] but this has been questioned, especially as to chronic or quiescent cases.[15] Albumin, or better, coagulable protein is also present in the sputum of patients with pulmonary edema and pleurisy. According to Works[16] in active tuberculosis there is usually 0.2 per cent. or more of coagulable protein in the sputum. The mucin of sputum yields

[9] Complete bibliography given by Ott, "Chem. Pathol. der Tuberc.," Berlin, 1903; Falk, Ergebnisse Physiol., 1910 (9), 406; Plesch, Hanb. d. Biochem., 1908 (III (1), 7.
[10] Zeit. f. Biol., 1875 (11), 102.
[11] Plesch (Zeit. exp. Path. u. Ther., 1906, Bd. iii, July) found that 4.8 per cent. of all the absorbed calories were lost in the sputum in an advanced case of phthisis. Under similar conditions the amount of salts excreted by the sputum may equal or exceed that in the urine (Falk, *loc. cit.*).[9]
[12] Deut. Arch. klin. Med., 1903 (75), 347.
[13] Presse Méd., 1910 (18), 289; 1911 (19), 409; also Ganz and Hertz, *ibid.*, 1911 (19), 41; Kaufmann, Beitr. Klin. d. Tuberk, 1913 (26), 269; Hempel-Jörgensen, *ibid.*, p. 392.
[14] Review by Cocke, Amer. Jour. Med. Sci., 1914 (148), 724.
[15] Fischberg and Felberbaum, Medical Record, Oct. 21, 1911; Acs-Nagy, Wien. klin. Woch., 1912 (25), 1904.
[16] Jour. Amer. Med. Assoc., 1912 (59), 1537.

18

33.6 per cent. of *glucosamin* when split with HCl, which gives an index of the quantity of mucin; this is highest in chronic bronchitis and lowest in pneumonia and phthisis. Kossel found 0.1–0.33 gm. of nucleins in the sputum daily.

The following table by Bokay (taken from Ott) gives the proportion of the organic constituents of sputum in parts per thousand:

TABLE III

	Bronchitis in typhoid	Fibroid phthisis	Phthisis, early in apex	Phthisis, cavities	Phthisis, advanced	Phthisis, advanced
Fatty acids as fat....	0.224	0.845	0.462	2.468	3.468	9.725
Free fatty acids......	trace	0.184	0.521	0.370	0.307	0.902
Soaps................	traces	0.380	0.430	0.537	0.516	3.973
Cholesterol..........	traces	0.4	1.617	0.172	1.160	0.141
Lecithin.............	traces	traces	1.543		1.165	1.245
Nuclein.............	traces	0.102	......	.....	0.260	0.489
Protein.............	0.898	2.040	......	4.430	3.455	5.115

On account of the digestion of the exudates by the leucocytes, sputum contains proteoses, peptones, and amino-acids, generally in proportion to the richness of the exudate in leucocytes; they are, therefore, most abundant in pneumonia. Simon[17] found considerable albumose in phthisical sputum, but no nucleohiston or free histon. In febrile cases of tuberculosis the amount of albumose may exceed the coagulable albumen, which rarely exceeds one per cent. of the moist weight.[18] Staffregen, however, could find no true peptone in phthisical sputum, but Stadelmann[19] found that such sputum contained enzymes hydrolyzing fibrin, and attributed this largely to bacteria. Probably most of the enzymes present in sputum come from the leucocytes. In the early stage of pneumonia the sputum has no proteolytic action, presumably because inhibited by the large amount of serum present; but with resolution active proteolytic properties appear (Bittorf).[20] In tuberculosis sputum the tryptic and antitryptic properties fluctuate, and lipase is absent (Eiselt).[21] Pneumonic sputum before the crisis has but slight action on peptids, but acquires marked peptolytic activity thereafter.[22] Most sputa contain enzymes splitting casein and polypeptids.[23] Sputum may contain indole, derived either from the putrefying proteins or excreted from the blood.[24]

[17] Arch. exp. Path. u. Pharm., 1903 (49), 449.
[18] Prorok, Münch. med. Woch., 1909 (56), 2053.
[19] Zeit. klin. Med., 1889 (16), 128.
[20] Deut. Arch. klin. Med., 1907 (91), 212.
[21] Zeit. klin. Med., 1912 (75), 91.
[22] Abderhalden, Zeit. physiol. Chem., 1912 (78), 344.
[23] Maliwa, Deut. Arch. klin. Med., 1914 (115), 407.
[24] Binda and Cassarini, Gaz. Med. Ital., 1913 (64), 461.

The amount of *fats* seems to depend directly upon the number of pus-corpuscles and the age of the pus (*i. e.*, the amount of fatty degeneration). Jacobson found from 0.08 to 1.6 grams of fatty matter per day, containing on an average 14.76 per cent. of soaps, 15.79 per cent. of higher fatty acids, 0–10 per cent. of water-soluble fatty acids, 13.58 per cent. lecithin, and 10.49 per cent. cholesterol.

As to the *inorganic substances*, Bamberger found two types of sputum. catarrhal and inflammatory. In the inflammatory there is a deficiency in alkali phosphate, SO_3 constitutes more than 8 per cent. of the salts, and the ratio, $\dfrac{Na_2O}{K_2O}$ equals $\dfrac{15}{41}$. In catarrhal sputum the alkali phosphates constitute 10–14 per cent., $\dfrac{Na_2O}{K_2O} = \dfrac{31}{20}$, and the SO_3 is from 0.6–1.2 per cent. Chlorine is about the same in both forms. These differences are, however, not as constant as Bamberger believes, according to several later investigations. The results of his analyses are shown in the following table:

TABLE IV

	Chronic phthisis	Acute phthisis
Water	94.55	93.38
Organic matter	4.67	6.88
Inorganic salts	0.78	0.74
One hundred parts of the salts contain:		
Chlorine	35.78	33.40
SO_3	0.70	0.80
P_2O_5	13.05	14.15
K_2O	24.07	19.99
Na_2O	27.90	31.69
Calcium phosphate	1.63	4.32[25]
Iron phosphate	0.09	0.14
Magnesium phosphate	1.20	....
Ca and Mg carbonate and sulphate	1.74	0.22
Silicic acid	0.9	0.3

[25] Including magnesium.

CHAPTER XII

THE CHEMISTRY OF GROWTH AND REPAIR

PROLIFERATION AND REGENERATION

The factors that incite cells to proliferate, as well as those that cause the cessation of proliferation after it has once started, are too entirely unknown to permit of speculation as to their exact nature. It seems probable, however, that they are, as Ziegler says, "identical with the stimuli which excite or increase functional and nutritive activity," and these are certainly in many instances of chemical nature. Thus the application of various irritating substances in not too concentrated a form (e. g., painting the skin with iodin) may lead to proliferation without causing discernible degeneration of the cells. Mallory's[1] observations on the phenomena of proliferation and phagocytosis show that the same bacterial products which destroy the cells when concentrated, when sufficiently dilute cause proliferation of similar cells. Carnot and Lavlièvre[2] have obtained evidence that actively growing kidney tissue, whether fetal or adult regenerating kidney, contains something which is capable of stimulating growth of renal epithelium when injected into other animals. Numerous dyes are known to stimulate cell growth greatly, (e. g., the growth of epithelium into oils containing sudan III, etc.) and sometimes seem to lead by virtue of this fact to cancer growth (e. g., cancer of the bladder in dye workers). Chemical products from decomposition of vegetable matter have a particularly active stimulating effect, so that what seem to be true cancers have been experimentally produced by painting the ears of rabbits with tar (Yamagiwa). Many other instances of proliferation in response to chemical stimuli might be cited, but in nearly all cases it is extremely difficult to determine that the proliferation is not, after all, reparative in compensation for degenerative changes, and, therefore, possibly obeying some other biological law than that of a simple reaction to a chemical stimulus.

Perhaps the most striking example we have of growth stimulation by chemical agencies is furnished by the proliferation and hypertrophy which take place in the uterus[3] and mammary gland during pregnancy. The same phenomena can be produced by injecting the lipoid fraction of extract of placenta and corpus luteum (Frank).[4]

[1] Jour. Exp. Med., 1900 (5), 15.
[2] Arch. Méd. Exper., 1907 (19), 388.
[3] See Leo Loeb, Jour. Amer. Med. Assoc., 1908 (50), 1897; 1915 (64), 726.
[4] Jour. Amer. Med. Assoc., 1920 (74), 47.

Even transplanted bits of uterine tissue are stimulated to grow by these substances, thus excluding possible nervous control of growth.[5] Dried placenta fed to mothers also increases the rate of growth of the suckling infant (Hammett).[6] The nature of the growth-stimulating agency in placenta and corpus luteum is unknown but it strongly resists chemical agents. However, it may be pointed out that *tethelin*, described by Robertson[7] as the growth-promoting substance of the hypophysis, is soluble in lipoid solvents. Acromegaly and gigantism give evidence that even far more than normal growth may be produced, presumably through the agency of an internal secretion of the hypophesis, but whether tethelin actually is the substance responsible is at present unknown. This substance is obtained from the anterior lobe, about 10 mg. for each gland, and contains 1.4 per cent. of phosphorous. It is said to retard growth of animals before adolescence and to increase post-adolescent growth; also it has been reported that wound repair is stimulated by tethelin.[8] At this time, however, the status of tethelin is not fully determined. The influence of the other ductless glands on growth is discussed further in Chapter xxii.

The studies by Whipple and his colleagues on the repair of the liver after extensive chloroform necrosis indicate that a mixed diet rich in carbohydrate is more effective in facilitating this repair than meat or fat, and that thyroid extract does not stimulate repair.[9] Also the healing of wounds is more rapid in meat-fed than in fat-fed dogs. (Clark)[10] Attempts to find specific substances that will cause increased rate of wound healing have so far been unsuccessful.[11] Regeneration of blood protein after hemorrhage is said to be most rapid on a protein rich diet.[12] When an incomplete protein, gliadin, is the sole protein of the diet the hemoglobin is not regenerated.

Although proper nutrition is necessary for cell proliferation, yet it does not seem that excessive nourishment can lead to excessive cell multiplication, or by itself cause cell proliferation to take place.

Oxygen and certain inorganic salts are essential for cell division even in the lowest forms, and among such simple organisms as sea-urchins and certain other marine forms segmentation of the unfertilized ova may be incited by changes in osmotic concentration, leading eventually to formation of perfect larvæ (J. Loeb, et. al.).[13] In lower animals very dilute solutions of alkalies stimulate the rate of cell growth and somewhat higher concentrations cause extremely irregular cell division; in mammals the feeding of alkalies causes great wasting

[5] Frank, Surg. Gyn. Obst., 1917 (25), 329.
[6] Jour. Biol. Chem., 1918 (36), 569; Endocrinology, 1919 (3), 307.
[7] See Jour. Exp. Med., 1916 (23), 631.
[8] Review by Barney, Jour. Lab. Clin. Med., 1918 (3), 480.
[9] See Arch. Int. Med., 1919 (23), 689.
[10] Bull. Johns Hopkins Hosp., 1919 (30), 117.
[11] See DuNoüy, Amer. Jour. Physiol., 1919 (49), 121.
[12] Kerr *et al.*, Amer. Jour. Physiol., 1918 (47), 456.
[13] See J. Loeb, Studies in General Physiology, Chicago, 1905.

as if through cell stimulation.[14]   The products of nuclein hydrolysis are said to stimulate cell growth.[15] Potassium salts seem to be particularly important for proliferating cells, and Beebe and also Clowes and Frisbie[16] have found that actively growing malignant tumors are rich in potassium and poor in calcium, whereas in slow-growing tumors the reverse is the case.   Dennstedt and Rumpf[17] also found that in hypertrophy of the heart the amount of potassium is increased, while in chronic degeneration of the myocardium the calcium and magnesium are usually increased.   The proportion of nitrogen in the different parts of the heart is not changed during hypertrophy (Bence),[18] but the amount of NaCl is much increased in hypertrophy.[19]

Chemical studies of proliferation are lacking,[20] except in regard to the development of the embryo, etc.[21] New tissues differ from adult tissues in having a large proportion of water, and in having a larger proportion of the "primary" cell constituents and a smaller proportion of the various secondary constituents, since these last are largely products of the activity of the adult cell.   Of the primary constituents, the proportion of the nucleoproteins is particularly high, and a number of interesting facts concerning the nucleoproteins in cell division have been determined.   Most important, perhaps, is the classical observation of Miescher, who found that during the migration of salmon up stream to the spawning grounds, during which time no food is taken, the proteins of the muscular tissue become largely transformed into the protamin type of protein (characterized by containing large proportions of the polyamino-acids, such as arginine histidine, and lysine),[22] which unite with nucleic acids to form the abundant nucleoprotein of the spermatozoa and ova.[23] Whether such a transformation of proteins occurs in mammalian cells during cell multiplication cannot be stated, but certainly from some source an additional supply of nucleoprotein is derived.   Developing sea urchin

[14] Moore *et al.*, Biochem. Jour., 1906 (1), 294; 1912 (6), 162.
[15] Calkins *et al.*, Jour. Infect. Dis., 1912 (10), 421.
[16] See "Tumors," Chap. xix.
[17] Zeit. klin. Med., 1905 (58), 84.
[18] Zeit. klin. Med., 1908 (66), 441.
[19] Rzentkowski, *ibid.*, 1910 (70), 337.
[20] The composition of *granulation tissue* has been determined by Hirsch (Amer. Jour. Med. Sci., 1920 (159), 356, who analyzed the "castration granulomas" of swine.   These are large inflammatory tumors, probably resulting from subacute infection of the operation wound, and consist of dense fibrous tissue with few cells and a scanty blood supply, but sometimes more or less edematous.   His figures are as follows: Water 81.9 per cent.; solids, 18.1; lipins, 2.3; proteins, 14.4. The protein contained sulphur, 0.34 per cent; phosphorus, 0.32, purine N, 0.08. (Other details are given on p. 519.)
[21] Literature on the chemistry of growth given by Aron, Handbuch d. Biochem., Ergänzungsband, 1913.
[22] Concerning protamins, see résumé by Kossel, Biochem. Centr., 1906 (5), 1 and 33.
[23] See also Greene, Jour. Biol. Chem., 1919 (39), 435.

eggs synthesize great quantities of nucleoprotein,[24] even when in a solution free from phosphates, and here the only available source for the phosphoric acid of the nucleins would seem to be the phospholipins of the egg (J. Loeb). The nucleoproteins during karyokinesis undergo a chemical change in that they become of a more acid type (presumably through splitting off of part of the proteins from the nucleic acid), which results in the characteristic increase in affinity for basic dyes, and the increased negative charge which is easily demonstrated.[25] This suggests the participation of an enzyme in the process of karyokinesis, just as there seems to be in the production of pycnosis in degenerating cells, but there seems to be no conclusive evidence on this point. Gies[26] could find no enzyme in spermatozoa that incites cell division in the ova of sea-urchins (*Arbacia*). The fertilization of eggs makes them more permeable to ions,[27] which possibly determines many of the subsequent changes.

In *metaplasia* we have what may be interpreted as a chemical alteration due to mechanical stimuli, e. g., the formation of keratin by cells that ordinarily do not do so; the deposition of calcium salts and osteoid transformation of connective tissues in rider's bone, etc. That such is the case, however, cannot be positively stated from the evidence at hand.

CHEMICAL BASIS OF GROWTH AND REPAIR[28]

We do not know just what substances are necessary to maintain individual cells in normal condition, what are needed to stimulate them to multiplication, or what elements they require to permit them to multiply, but it has been learned that certain definite materials are required by the organism as a whole. It is not sufficient that a given number of calories with a certain quantity of proteins, carbohydrates, fats and salts be supplied; it is essential that certain specific constituents be provided among these foodstuffs. This fact was first clearly pointed out by Gowland Hopkins in 1906, although in 1897 Eijkman had discovered that beriberi and experimental neuritis might result from a one-sided diet of polished rice, and in 1902 Röhmann reported that purified food stuffs do not suffice to maintain and rear mice.

The proteins must not only provide a sufficient amount of nitrogen, but they must also provide certain specific amino-acids, as has been especially demonstrated by the investigations of Willcock and Hop-

[24] Not accepted by Masing, Zeit. physiol. Chem., 1910 (67), 161.
[25] See Gallardo, Arch. Entwickl. Organ., 1909 (28), 125; Pentimalli, *ibid.*, 1912 (34), 444.
[26] Amer. Jour. Physiol., 1901 (6), 54.
[27] See McClendon, Carnegie Inst. Publ., 1914. No. 183.
[28] See Mendel, "Nutrition and Growth," Harvey Society Lectures, 1914–15; Amer. Jour. Med. Sci., 1917 (153), 1; Lusk, "Science of Nutrition," Saunders, Phila., 1917.

kins[29] and Osborne and Mendel.[30]   Apparently the presence of some of the simple straight-chain amino-acids can be dispensed with (e. g., glycine), and the animal will grow and thrive if other nutritive supplies are adequate, but certain, at least, of the more complex cyclic amino-acids must be provided.   Furthermore, the requirements for growth (quantitatively speaking at least), seem to be something more than the requirements for mere preservation of health and equilibrium, for it was found that animals could live and preserve nitrogen equili-brium when the protein of the diet furnished at most small quantities of lysine, but young animals were unable to grow with such a restricted supply of this amino-acid.   If lysine was added to the defective pro-tein (gliadin from wheat) the animal would then be able to grow at a normal rate.   Of particular importance is the fact that animals can be kept in a stunted condition on such a deficient diet until they have reached an age at which normally all growth would have long since ceased, and then when supplied with sufficient lysine they will begin to grow and continue until full size is reached.[31]   This last observation proves that growth is not conditioned by age, and that we do not stop growing because a certain age is reached; the capacity for growth may remain latent and capable of exhibiting itself when proper conditions are furnished.   But no amount of any amino-acid will cause a fully grown animal to grow any more, so it would seem that the capacity for growth becomes extinguished when it has been utilized to a certain fixed extent, and remains potent until it has been completely utilized.

If the only protein furnished contains no tryptophane the animal cannot maintain itself and slowly loses weight until it dies, unless tryptophane is supplied.   If zein from corn, which yields neither ly-sine nor tryptophane, is the sole protein, then the animal cannot grow unless both lysine and tryptophane are added to the diet.   So too, pure casein is not adequate to maintain growth because of its low content in cystine, but if cystine is added the nutritive value is much increased.   That the pure isolated amino-acids can meet the deficiencies when added to the imperfect protein ration, demonstrates that proteins serve for food as amino-acids, and not as larger complexes.

VITAMINES OR FOOD HORMONES AND DEFICIENCY DISEASES[32]

Not only must the proteins present certain essential chemical compounds to the living and growing organism, but also an adequate

[29] Jour. Physiol., 1906 (35), 88.
[30] Series of papers in Jour. Biol. Chem., 1912, et seg.
[31] Jour. Biol. Chem., 1915 (23), 439.
[32] See "Report on the Present State of Knowledge Concerning Accessory Food Factors (Vitamines), Special Report No. 38 National Health Insurance Act, London, 1919; "The Newer Knowledge of Nutrition," E. V. McCollum, New York, 1919; Blunt and Wang, Jour. Home Economics, 1920 (12), 1; also Sympo-sium in Jour. Amer. Med. Assoc., 1918 (71), 937.

supply of the essential inorganic salts and certain other, as yet un-identified, substances are necessary to permit of maintenance, growth and repair. It has long been recognized clinically that certain diseases, notably scurvy, may result from the absence of some essential in the food supply. More recently other diseases have been proved to have a similar cause, and the study of one of these, beriberi, has led to a better appreciation of the nature of the food essentials concerned. This disease seems to result from the use of polished rice as the chief constituent of the diet, and can be checked by feeding unpolished rice, or rice polishings, or even extracts of rice polishings, as first demonstrated by Eijkman. A somewhat similar condition may be produced readily in birds by feeding them only polished rice, the chief feature being a severe neuritis, which is relieved with remarkable rapidity by supplying the food deficiency. This experimental neuritis of fowls (*polyneuritis gallinarum*) has served as a valuable means of study of diseases of this class, and led to the demonstration that not only extracts of rice polishings, but also many other food materials, contain the essential materials without which health cannot be maintained. One of the early investigators of this subject, Casimir Funk,[33] gave to "the hitherto unrecognized essential dietary factors" the name "vitamines," which, in spite of certain logical objections, has been widely adopted; but as Lusk states, the term "food hormones" would be preferable in our present state of knowledge. Although so essential for life the amount required is very small, for whole rice is said to contain not over 0.1 gm. per kilo, and perhaps much less, of the active substance.

McCollum[34] has summarized the evidence that two classes of substances are necessary for maintenance. These he designated, for convenience, "*fat soluble A*" and "*water soluble B.*" It is the former that is lacking in xerophthalmia, and the latter in polyneuritis. It now seems certain that other diseases are the result of deficiency in other specific substances,[35] particularly scurvy, which seems to result from lack of a "water-soluble C." It also is an open question whether under the water-soluble B are included two separate vitamines, one antineuritic, the other growth-promoting.[35a]

As yet the exact identity of the active agents in water or fat solutions has not been determined. The fat-soluble vitamines seem to be especially abundant in butter, egg yolk, and cod liver oil, which presumably accounts for the commonly accepted values of these particular fats. They cannot be replaced by any of the known components of fats, including phosphatids, lipochromes, cholesterol, etc.,[36] and

[33] See Ergeb. Physiol., 1913 (13), 125, for review of his work.
[34] Jour. Biol. Chem., 1916 (24), 491.
[35] See Jour. Biol. Chem. 1918 (33), 55.
[35a] See Mitchell, Jour. Biol. Chem., 1919 (40), 399.
[36] See Drummond, Biochem. Jour., 1919 (13), 81; Palmer, Science, 1919 (50). 501.

are scanty or absent in lard, olive oil, and most vegetable oils.   Funk believed the water-soluble antineuritic agents to be pyrimidine derivatives.   They are dialyzable (Drummond) and are adsorbed by Fuller's earth (Seidell).   Williams and Seidell[37] have found that hydroxypurines have marked anti-neuritic effects, and they suggested that an isomer of adenine is responsible for the anti-neuritic action of yeast extracts.   Later Williams[38] found an active hydroxypyridene, and suggested that the curative properties of yeast and rice polishings may be due to an isomeric form of nicotinic acid.   These observations await confirmation, and we still are in the dark concerning the character of antineuritic vitamines.[39]

The nature of the "fat-soluble A" is, if possible, even less known than that of "water soluble B."   Drummond's investigations[40] show that it is somewhat heat resistant, but it is destroyed at 100° for one hour, apparently not through oxidation or hydrolysis.   It cannot be extracted from oils by water or dilute acid, but is extracted to some extent by cold alcohol.   If the fats are hydrolyzed at room temperature the active factor disappears, and it cannot be identified with any of the recognized components of fats.   Because of its thermolability and other properties, Drummond is driven to the conclusion that "fat-soluble A" is not a clearly defined chemical substance, but rather it is a labile substance, perhaps possessing characteristics resembling those of an enzyme.[40a]

Vitamines, especially those that are water-soluble, also favor the growth of bacteria,[40b] and are essential for the growth of yeast, so that Williams[40c] has found it possible to determine the amount of this vitamine present in a food stuff by the rate of growth of yeasts thereon.   Typhoid bacilli are said to produce vitamines during their growth,[40d] and if it is true, as has been stated, that neither plants nor animals seem able to synthesize them, it would seem that they must be of bacterial origin.   Yeast is known to produce water-soluble vitamine in particular abundance, but not the fat-soluble vitamine.   Other sources of water-soluble vitamines are numerous, especially green vegetables and whole cereals, but they are not so abundant in meat or milk.[40e]

Why the vitamines are essential and how they act is unknown. It is suggestive that they are found especially in cells with an active metabolism, but whether as a result of this activity or because essential

[37] Jour. Biol. Chem., 1916 (26), 431.
[38] Jour. Biol. Chem., 1917 (29), 495.
[39] See review by Drummond, Biochem. Jour., 1917 (11), 255.
[40] Biochem. Jour., 1919 (13), 81.
[40a] See also Steenbock and Boutwell, Jour. Biol. Chem., 1920 (41), 163.
[40b] See D. J. Davis, Jour. Infect. Dis., 1917 (21), 392; Kligler, Jour. Exp. Med., 1919 (30), 31.
[40c] Jour. Biol. Chem., 1919 (38) 465; also Bachmann, ibid., (39), 235.
[40d] Pacini and Russell, Jour. Biol. Chem., 1918 (34), 43.
[40e] See Osborne and Mendel, Jour. Biol. Chem., 1919 (39), 29; 1920 (41), 515.

for cell growth is undetermined.[41] Vedder[42] has suggested that the anti-neuritic vitamine is essential for growth and repair of the nervous tissue, and in its absence normal wear cannot be made good.[43] There is evidence that substances rich in the anti-neuritic vitamine stimulate growth in infants.[44] Moore[45] suggests that deficiency diseases may be the result of lack of something needed to neutralize toxic substances produced in metabolism or derived from outside sources, just as in poisoning with tri-nitro toluene and similar compounds there is no intoxication so long as the body can furnish sufficient glycuronic acid to neutralize the poisons. Dutcher[45a] finds some relation between catalase and vitamine content in experimental polyneuritis, and suggests that the vitamines stimulate oxidative processes which remove toxic substances. It is probable that more than one vitamine is necessary for maintaining normal conditions, and deficiency of one causes beriberi, of another scurvy, for some dietaries lead to one disease and some to the other. Quite possibly minor, or less well-defined impairment in health may often result from quantitative deficiency in vitamine supplies. The main points concerning the most studied deficiency diseases may be summarized as follows:

Beriberi[46] occurs in two forms—the dry polyneuritic type and the edematous or wet beriberi, and mixed forms. The dry type resembles the experimental polyneuritis of birds, mentioned previously, for in the birds edema does not accompany the polyneuritis that can be produced experimentally by feeding polished rice. There now seems to be no doubt that human beriberi is the result of the absence of certain essential elements in the diet, observed especially when the diet is polished rice, but possibly occurring with other deficient diets, for the necessary vitamine is of course present in many other foods than rice. Not only has a condition closely resembling human beriberi been produced in animals, but also true beriberi has been experimentally produced in man by feeding on polished rice, as well as the repeated demonstration of both prevention and cure of the human disease by proper feeding or by administration of rice polishings or extracts

---

[41] See Voegtlin and Myers, Amer. Jour. Physiol., 1919 (48), 504.

[42] Jour. Amer. Med. Assoc., 1916 (67), 1494.

[43] McCarrison has observed hypertrophy of the adrenals in pigeons with experimental beriberi, although the other organs are atrophied. He considers a general nuclear starvation from lack of necessary nuclear nutritive materials to be the essential condition. (India Jour. Med. Res., 1919 (6), 275.) He found the sex glands particularly atrophied, and Houlbert (Paris Médicale, 1919 (9), 473, has found water-soluble vitamines essential for growth of sex glands. Emmett and Allen (Jour. Biol. Chem., Soc. Proc., 1920 (41), liii), obtained adrenal hypertrophy with thymus atrophy in rats fed diets deficient in water-soluble B, but not with diets deficient in A. Growth of tadpoles also seemed to be more accelerated by B than by A.

[44] Daniels *et al.*, Amer. Jour. Dis. Chil., 1919 (18), 546.

[45] British Publ. on Munitions, No. 11.

[45a] Jour. Biol. Chem., 1918 (36), 634.

[46] Full discussion and bibliography given by Vedder in his book "Beriberi," New York, 1913. See also Jour. Amer. Med. Assoc., 1916 (67), 1494.

thereof. From rice polishings has been obtained a crystalline substance, of which a dose of 20 to 30 milligrams will cure a polyneuritic bird. As stated above, the pure active substance has not been isolated and its exact nature is undetermined. Vedder believes that it is something that is needed for the repair of nervous tissue, so that in its absence the nervous tissues degenerate. The paralysis, he believes, depends more on central than peripheral· nerve changes, since the degeneration of the nerves precedes the paralysis and may persist long after the paralysis has disappeared. As rice polishings relieve the cardiac symptoms, which are important features of beri-beri, it is to be assumed that the vitamine is essential for the heart metabolism. Furthermore, heart muscle contains vitamine which will protect from polyneuritis birds fed on polished rice. This does not seem to be identical with the vitamine isolated by Funk, for while it relieves the cardiac symptoms and dispels the dropsy of wet beriberi, it does not cure the paralytic symptoms of dry beriberi, according to Vedder. This author "has a growing belief that dry and wet beriberi are separate and distinct diseases, which are, however, generally associated." Rice polishings, he says, clear up beri-beri dropsy quickly, but do not affect the paralysis unless the polishings have been hydrolyzed.

Walshe[47] calls attention to the fact that starved fowls live long enough to develop beriberi, yet nevertheless do not show it, so he thinks that there must not only be a deficiency factor, but also some positive factor, which may be the abundant carbohydrate of the rice diet. Possibly in the absence of the vitamine the carbohydrate metabolism is altered, with the production of toxic substances. Furthermore, in spite of the marked clinical results obtained with rice polishings, the disease is not always cleared up as readily as might be expected if only a lack of vitamines was concerned, and, therefore, there still remains the possibility that some infectious factor may play at least a subsidiary part in human beri-beri (see Mitchell[35a]).

Keratomalacia or Xerophthalmia,[48] a condition of opacity of the cornea, followed by ulceration and blindness, seems to be specifically due to lack of the fat-soluble vitamine which is present in egg yolk, butter fats, green leaves, etc., but not in lard or in many vegetable oils. This disease can be produced readily in experimental animals by feeding diets free from proper fats, and is relieved by administration of small quantities of these fats. I have had the opportunity to observe numerous instances of xerophthalmia among the famine sufferers in Roumania, and to observe its prompt relief under cod liver oil feeding. It should not be confused with simple

[47] Quart. Jour. Med., 1918 (11), 320.
[48] Bloch, Ugeskr. f. Laeger., 1918 (80), 815.

eye infections which are likely to occur in poorly nourished laboratory animals.[49]

Nutritional Dropsy. (**"War Dropsy" or Famine Edema**).[50] This condition, which was observed extensively during the war, especially among Russian prisoners in Germany, has been seen wherever famine occurs, and is undoubtedly caused by dietary deficiency. Apparently it is independent of scurvy. As it is often associated with xerophthalmia it has been thought to depend on absence of fat-soluble vitamines. It seems more probable, however, that it results from low caloric supply, although protein deficiency combined with excessive fluid and salt intake in the effort to maintain life with weak soups, are probably important factors.[51] Most of the adult subjects have been receiving 800 to 1200 calories per day, containing but 30 to 50 gms. of protein. It is much more likely to appear in undernourished persons who are compelled to work than in equally starved persons at rest, since work, and also cold, increase the caloric deficiency.

Numerous studies of metabolism and blood chemistry in persons exhibiting war dropsy have given concordant results, which show the extreme depletion of the body in all nutritive reserves.[52] The blood shows hypoglucemia, decrease in potassium, fatty acids, phospholipins and residual nitrogen, with an increase in NaCl, and of acetone bodies and ammonia from starvation acidosis. There is also a decrease in the amount of protein in the blood even to one-half the normal amount, with hydremia and a less marked decrease in both red and white cells. The lack of reserve nitrogenous material both in blood and tissues is shown by the fact that when patients with war edema are fasted a few days the N excretion may fall to 2 to 3 gms. per day, while in absolute starvation of previously normal persons the N output usually is 10–12 gms. (Falta). Schittenhelm and Schlecht suggest that the edema is merely the result of injury to the capillary endothelium, in common with all the other tissues, whereby their permeability becomes increased.

Famine edema seems to be closely related to the edema often observed in infants kept on a preponderatingly starchy diet, such as barley water, for long periods. Here most striking degrees of dropsy are observed, which seem in all respects similar to famine dropsy. There is probably also a close relation to the edema of pernicious anemia and cachexia. The relation of this form of edema to the

[49] See Bulley, Biochem. Jour., 1919 (13), 103.

[50] Full Review by Schittenhelm and Schlecht, Zeit. exp. Med., 1919 (9), 1; Mayer, Jour. Amer. Med. Assoc., 1920 (74), 934.

[51] See Guillermine and Guyot, Rev. Méd. Suisse Rom., 1919 (39), 115; Falta, Wien. klin. Woch., 1917 (30), 1637; Schittenhelm and Schlecht, Zeit. exp. Med., 1919 (9), 82.

[52] See Schittenhelm and Schlecht, *loc. cit.*: Feigl, Biochem. Zeit., 1918 (85), 365; Jansen, Münch. Med. Woch., 1918 (65), 925; Bürger, Zeit. exp. Med., 1919 (8), 309.

edema of wet beriberi has not been determined, but it is highly probable that their origin has something in common. Both are dropsies
due to diet deficiency, and it may well be that the deficiency is
the same in each case. In both these conditions, as well as in the
"Mehlnährschaden" of starch-fed babies, there is the common element of relatively excessive carbohydrate supply, which may have
something to do with the dropsy. The clinical evidence is against the
view that nutritional edema depends on a lack of specific vitamines.[52a]

Experimental work supports the clinical evidence as to the etiology
of nutritional edema. Miss Kohman[53] has found that rats fed diets
composed chiefly of carrots often develop a severe edema, which is
prevented by supplying protein, but not by butter fat or starch.
Evidently neither fat-soluble nor water-soluble vitamines are responsible. It was found that on a dry diet of equal caloric and protein deficiency the rats are not so likely to develop edema. Experiments
done in my laboratory by M. B. Maver[50] agree fully with those of Miss
Kohman. Apparently low protein and high fluid intake are the most
essential factors, although relatively high carbohydrate must also be
considered.

Scurvy would seem almost certainly to be a deficiency disease,
but there has been much disagreement as to this point, especially
among those who have studied experimental scurvy in animals. There
is room for doubt that the experimental disease in animals is identical
with human scurvy, at least there is reason to believe that more than
one condition has been described as scurvy in experimental animals.
Apparently guinea pigs, however, develop readily a disease which
resembles scurvy very closely both anatomically and in its relation to
dietary conditions. Hess, who has studied especially infantile scurvy,
finds that orange juice given intravenously will relieve scurvy, and
thus apparently disposes of all theories of gastrointestinal disorders as
the responsible factor. Artificial "orange juice," (containing sugar,
citric acid and inorganic salts in the proportions found in natural
orange juice) is ineffective, so that apparently scurvy is the result of
lack of some undetermined substance present in orange juice as well
as in other fresh vegetable foods. As yet we have no evidence as to
the character of this "vitamine," which has been designated as
"water-soluble C," but it is probably quite distinct from either water-
soluble B or fat-soluble A,[54] and Hess believes that our ordinary
dietary probably does not contain any great excess of the antiscorbutic
element, since scurvy so readily appears when the necessary vegetable
foods are reduced in amount. According to Chick and Hume this
vitamine is present in living vegetable and animal tissues, in largest

[52a] See Bürger, Zeit. Exp. Med., 1919 (8), 309.
[53] Denton and Kohman, Jour. Biol. Chem., 1918 (36), 249; Kohman, Amer.
Jour. Physiol., 1920 (51), 378.
[54] Cohen and Mendel, Jour. Biol. Chem., 1918 (35), 425.

amounts in fresh fruits and green vegetables, to a less extent in root vegetables and tubers. It is present in small amount in fresh meat and milk, and has not yet been detected in yeast, fats, cereals, pulses. The explorer, Stefansson,[55] has reported observations indicating the presence of antiscorbutic substances in raw meat, and their absence or deficiency in well-cooked meat and tinned foods. Evidently this antiscorbutic element is very unstable, since even drying vegetables at moderate temperatures, 65–70°, and cooking or salting meats, or heating with weak alkalies, destroys or greatly reduces their antiscorbutic value.[56] Pasteurization of milk also reduces the preventive value of this food[57] which, in its raw state, contains in abundance all necessary factors for nutrition, but apparently little more of the antiscorbutic substance than is barely sufficient to maintain health.

Pellagra[58] probably belongs among the deficiency diseases, despite numerous attempts to account for it as an infectious disease. The work of Goldberger[59] is especially valuable in affirmative evidence of the relation of dietary deficiency to pellagra. Here again we are entirely uninformed as to the nature of the deficiency. Goldberger[60] sums up his conclusions as follows: "The pellagra-producing dietary fault is the result of some one, or, more probably, of a combination of two or more of the following factors: (1) a physiologically defective protein supply; (2) a low or inadequate supply of fat-soluble vitamine; (3) a low or inadequate supply of water-soluble vitamine, and (4) a defective mineral supply. The somewhat lower plane of supply, both of energy and of protein, of the pellagrous households, though apparently not an essential factor, may, nevertheless, be contributory by favoring the occurrence of a deficiency in intake of some one or more of the essential dietary factors, particularly with diets having only a narrow margin of safety. The pellagra-producing dietary fault may be corrected and the disease prevented by including in the diet an adequate supply of the animal protein foods, particularly milk, including butter and lean meat."

McCollum calls attention to the fact that a diet is not adequate unless it contains active metabolizing protoplasm, as found in green leaves, eggs, meat and milk; and pellagra-producing diets are largely composed of seed foods and pork fat. To make cereal grains dietetically satisfactory there must be added inorganic elements, a protein, and substances containing "fat soluble A."[61]

[55] Jour. Amer. Med. Assoc., 1918 (71), 1715.
[56] Givens and Cohen, Jour. Biol. Chem., 1918 (36), 127; Amer. Jour. Dis. Chil., 1919 (18), 30.
[57] See Hess, Amer. Jour. Dis. Chil., 1919 (17), 221.
[58] Concerning metabolism in pellagra see Myers and Fine, Amer. Jour. Med. Sci., 1913 (145) 705. Chemical changes in the central nervous system described by Koch and Voegtlin, Hygienic Lab. Bull. 103, 1916.
[59] Public Health Rep., 1914 (29), 1683; 1915 (30), 3117, 3336.
[60] Jour. Amer. Med. Assoc., 1918 (71), 944.
[61] Jour. Biol. Chem., 1919 (38), 113.

Whatever the deficiency in diet may be, pellagra seems to develop most often in persons whose diet is preponderatingly maize seed products. Only in countries where maize is the chief dietary staple does pellagra occur with any great frequency, and in those countries where part of the population lives chiefly on maize, and other groups live on other foods, pellagra occurs chiefly or only in the former group. I have had the opportunity to observe much pellagra in Roumania during a period of protracted and serious food shortage, and this relation to maize was most striking and convincing. The peasants of this country have for their chief food a thick mush of boiled, coarsely ground corn meal, called *mamaliga*, supplemented by such other foods as they can secure. Dwellers in the towns rely on bread from wheat flour as their chief carbohydrate supply, and have a much more abundant and varied list of accessory foods. Pellagra is prevalent in Roumania, but restricted to the maize-eating peasants, and in very definite relation to their inability to secure accessory food stuffs. While Roumanian physicians seem generally inclined to accept the theory that spoiled maize is responsible, my own observations would indicate that the chief difficulty is lack of accessory foods. The relation of maize to pellagra becomes particularly striking if we compare Roumania with a country where maize is not a staple food, such as Korea. Here for centuries a large part of the population has existed on the verge of starvation, the chief food being rice. Although here beriberi is common enough, especially among those who can afford the luxury of polished rice, pellagra is not observed, despite a much greater deficiency in total food supply, both as regards calories and accessories, than prevails in Roumania.

Despite the abundant evidence of the relation of dietary deficiency there are those who interpret existing evidence as establishing or making probable that pellagra is nevertheless essentially an infectious disease.[62] The compromise view that pellagra is an infectious disease which can only manifest itself among those suffering from dietary deficiency has also been supported, especially by McCollum.[63]

Rickets.—Mellanby[64] holds that this disease results from a deficiency in fat-soluble vitamine, although admitting that the efficiency of malt extracts and lean meat in preventing experimental rickets is not in harmony with this hypothesis. As the total growth of rachitic puppies on a diet poor in fat-soluble A is about normal, he suggests that this agent is not necessary for growth, but merely for making growth normal. Without "A" the development of teeth is much interfered with. The recognized value of cod liver oil in rickets is in support of this view. Hess, McCollum and others do not accept the hypothesis that rickets is solely the result of lack of fat-soluble A.

[62] See Jobling and Peterson, Jour. Infect. Dis., 1916 (18), 501.
[63] Proc. Amer. Philos. Soc., 1919 (58), 41.
[64] Jour. Physiol., 1919 (52), liii; Lancet, 1919 (196), 407.

The former has observed children who have lived a long time in perfect health on a diet with a minimum of vitamine-containing fats.[65] McCollum finds that rats develop a condition apparently identical with true rickets when kept on a diet deficient in any two of the three essentials, viz., protein, calcium, fat-soluble A. A diet lacking only one essential seems to be well borne.

[66] Jour. Amer. Med. Assoc., 1920 (74), 217.

CHAPTER XIII

DISTURBANCES OF CIRCULATION AND DISEASES OF THE BLOOD

THE COMPOSITION OF THE BLOOD

The function of the blood being to maintain an equilibrium in the temperature, chemical composition and osmotic pressure between all parts of the body, it follows that it is never of exactly the same composition in any two places or at any two times. To the extent that every tissue is continually giving off something to the blood, we may consider that every organ is a factor in its formation, and as a result of this multiplex origin of the blood, the substances it may contain are beyond enumeration. There are probably but few chemical substances occurring in the tissue-cells that do not also occur in greater or less amount in the blood. In addition to these there are also the substances characteristic of the blood itself, besides a host of substances of unknown nature, apparently manufactured in response to the stimulation of substances entering the body from outside; for we find that the blood of every adult individual contains substances that make him immune to a multitude of diseases that he has had in childhood, as well as substances that in later life protect him to a greater or less degree from infection by such organisms as the colon bacilli of his intestine, the pneumococci and streptococci in his throat, etc. We have learned of these defensive substances within very recent times, and also of the "antienzymes" that possibly protect the blood from the digestive enzymes of the body cells. What other substances of importance we may yet find in the blood is an open question. There are no apparent limits to the possibilities of the study of the blood, for it represents a little of every organ, and much that is characteristic of itself.

In discussing briefly the substances that have been isolated from the normal blood, before considering the changes that occur in it during pathological conditions, we may roughly divide the blood into the formed elements and the plasma in which they are suspended.

THE FORMED ELEMENTS.—By weight, the red corpuscles constitute from 40 to 50 per cent. of the blood, the percentage varying under different conditions, while the total weight of the leucocytes and platelets is insignificant. The hemoglobin constitutes from 86 to 94 per cent. by weight of the solids of the red corpuscles, but the physical and chemical relations that it bears to the stroma of the corpuscles are as yet undetermined (see "Hemolysis"). Of the remaining constituents of the corpuscles, from 5 to 12 per cent. consist of proteins, probably chiefly *globulins* and *nucleoproteins;* 0.3 to 0.7 per cent. of *lecithin;* and about 0.2 to 0.3 per cent. of *cholesterol* (Hoppe-Seyler). The outer coat of the red corpuscles does not seem to be equally permeable for all substances, and therefore we find the composition of the fluid portion of the cell quite different from that of the plasma about it. The *salts* of the corpuscles consist largely of potassium phosphate, a little sodium chloride, some magnesium, but no calcium,[1] which is quite different from their proportion in the plasma. Probably many of the other constituents of the plasma, especially urea, penetrate the red corpuscles to a greater or less degree, but most of them, particularly the sugar, remain chiefly in the plasma.

Hemoglobin, the most characteristic constituent of all the heterogeneous components of the blood, is a compound protein, and probably exists combined with some other constituent of the corpuscle, most probably the lecithin. It splits up readily into a protein, *globin,* and an iron-containing substance, *hemochromogen,* which readily takes up oxygen to form *hematin.* Only about 4 to 5 per cent. of the hemoglobin is hemochromogen, and iron constitutes but about 0.4 per cent. Hematin may be further split up into other substances, which will be considered in the discussion of "Hemorrhage."

The **leucocytes** consist chiefly of nucleoproteins, with probably some globulin, and they also contain glycogen, phospholipins, and cholesterol. The *blood-platelets* are believed to be largely nucleoprotein, but little is known of their actual composition; microchemical examination shows no evidence of either fat or glycogen.[2]

BLOOD PLASMA differs from blood-serum in that the latter is formed from the former through the removal of the fibrinogen through its conversion into fibrin. Serum, therefore, contains no fibrinogen, but more fibrin ferment; otherwise it is practically the same as the plasma.[3] It is well for us to appreciate that the blood is fundamentally a tissue, with its more solid structural elements lying in a protoplasm, the plasma, somewhat more dilute than the protoplasm of other tissues but in other respects much the same.

Proteins.—*Fibrinogen* has the general properties of a globulin, with also a peculiar tendency to go into the insoluble form, *fibrin.* (This process will be discussed under "*Thrombosis.*") In the plasma are also other globulins,[4] one soluble in water (*pseudo-globulin*), the other insoluble in water (*euglobulin*). *Serum-albumin,* another protein of the plasma, probably consists of two or more varieties of albumin. There are also nucleoproteins (*prothrombin*) and noncoagulable proteins, which being poorly understood have been variously considered as glycoproteins, or mucoids, or albumoses. The serum proteins seem to be closely related to, or compounded with, the lipins of the plasma.

Other Constituents.—The *fat* of the plasma varies much according to the time which has elapsed after the taking of food; in fasting animals it amounts to from 0.1 to 0.7 per cent. The sugar fluctuates less, being normally about 0.1 per cent., while the urea has been estimated at 0.03 per cent. Most of the sugar is dextrose; but probably there is some levulose, possibly some pentose and other forms, and possibly also sugar combined with lecithin (*jecorin*) or other substances. Soaps, cholesterol, and phospholipins exist free in the plasma. There are also the numerous nonprotein nitrogenous substances that are excreted in the urine.

Plasma differs strikingly from the corpuscles in that its inorganic substances are chiefly sodium and chlorine, while potassium and phosphoric acid are almost entirely absent. Another important fact is that when the plasma is combusted, the acid radicals remaining do not suffice to balance the bases, indicating that much of the inorganic bases is joined with organic substances, probably as ion-

---

[1] The current statement that corpuscles are impermeable for calcium is refuted by Hamburger (Zeit. physikal. Chem., 1909 (69), 663).

[2] Aynaud, Ann. Inst. Pasteur, 1911 (25), 56.

[3] In the process of clotting certain changes occur, probably physical, that may make the plasma more or less toxic (see Anaphylaxis) and apparently alter its biological properties, since the reinjection of a person's own defibrinated serum may cause marked physiological and therapeutic effects (*e. g.,* autoserotherapy in psoriasis). Especially noteworthy is the vasoconstrictor effect of defibrinated blood (see Hirose, Arch. Int. Med., 1918 (21), 604).

[4] Literature given by Rowe, Arch. Int. Med., 1916 (18), 455.

protein compounds. The alkali joined to the protein is non-diffusible, and constitutes about five-sixths of the total alkali.

The concentration of the electrolytes of the blood has been determined by ascertaining the lowering of the freezing-point, which in human blood averages about 0.526°; this corresponds closely to the effect of a salt solution of 0.9 per cent. strength. About three-fourths of the dissolved molecules of the blood-serum are electrolytes, and about three-fourths of these are molecules of NaCl, most of which are in the dissociated state.[5] The calcium content is very constant, about 9 to 11 mg. per 100 cc. of plasma.

Enzymes.—A large number of enzymes exist in the blood, the following being among those that have been detected: *diastase, glucase, lipase, thrombin, rennin,* and *proteases.* The proteases and perhaps the other enzymes are held in check to a large extent by *"antiferments"* that are also present (see *"Enzymes"*). In relation to the antiferments are the innumerable antibodies that exist normally in the serum for foreign proteins, foreign cells, and for bacteria and their toxins, as well as those resulting from reaction, etc.

The proportions in which the constituents of the plasma normally occur have been determined by Hoppe-Seyler and by Hammarsten, as follows:[6]

TABLE I

	No. 1	No. 2
Water	908.4	917.6
Solids	91.6	82.4
Total proteins	77.6	69.5
Fibrin	10.1	6.5
Globulin		38.4
Seralbumin		24.6
Fat	1.2	
Extractive substances	4.0	
Soluble salts	6.4	12.9
Insoluble salts	1.7	

No. 1 is an analysis by Hoppe-Seyler.
No. 2 is the average of three analyses made by Hammarsten.

Reaction.—If we titrate the blood plasma with an acid, we liberate much of the alkali from the proteins, dissociate all the Na_2CO_3 present, as well as the $NaHCO_3$ and the sodium phosphate, and find in this way that the entire fresh blood contains *neutralizable alkali* corresponding to a solution of Na_2CO_3 of about 0.443 per cent. strength (Strauss). In other words the blood has a quantity of alkali in combination that can be drawn upon to neutralize acids to the extent indicated by the above figures. The *real alkalinity* of a fluid, however, is dependent upon the number of free OH ions in the solution; and Höber has determined by physico-chemical methods that the concentration of OH ions in blood is but little greater than in distilled water.[7] Michaelis[8] has found the H + concentration of the blood to be 0.45×10^{-7}, as contrasted with neutrality at 38° which is H + = 1.5×10^{-7}. The interchange between CO_2, phosphates and carbonates in the blood is such that it is impossible for any considerable quantities of free H or OH ions to exist, and the protoplasm is thus protected from an excess of either. The capacity of the blood to neutralize acids and alkalies is sometimes referred to as its "buffer value."[9] According to Henderson[10] not more than five parts of excess free H or OH ions can be present in ten billion parts of protoplasm. An alkalinity is impossible because this would cause an increased osmotic pressure which the kidneys would regulate; acidity is impossible because death would result

---

[5] Concerning relation of conductivity to freezing-point see Wilson, Amer. Jour. of Physiol., 1906 (16), 438.

[6] For complete analyses of the blood see Abderhalden, Zeit. physiol. Chem., 1898 (25), 106.

[7] For bibliography on Alkalinity of Blood, see Henderson, Ergebnisse Physiol., 1909 (8), 254.

[8] Deut. med. Woch., 1914 (40), 1170.

[9] See Levy and Rowntree, Arch. Int. Med., 1916 (17), 525.

[10] Amer. Jour. Physiol., 1907 (18). 250; 1908 (21), 427.

from the inability of the blood to carry CO_2. The blood and tissue proteins also can bind much of either H or OH ions,[11] so that the preservation of neutrality is elaborately guarded. In the tissues, because of the production of acids during metabolism, the H-ion concentration is slightly higher than that of the blood, being estimated by Michaelis at exact neutrality, 1.5×10^{-7}. Presumably one important purpose of the exact regulation of reaction is to provide proper conditions for enzyme action.

The alkali of the blood exists in part as alkaline salts, carbonate and phosphate (the *diffusible alkali*), and partly combined with protein (*non-diffusible alkali*). As the corpuscles are richer in diffusible alkali than the plasma or serum, the number of corpuscles modifies the alkalinity of the blood decidedly. Much importance is attached to the question of the alkalinity of the blood for two reasons: first, in certain conditions of disease the blood contains so much of organic acids that the alkali is partly saturated and the power of the blood to carry CO_2 is lessened, with serious results (see "Acid Intoxication," Chap. xx); and, second, the bactericidal power of the blood is found to vary according to its alkalinity. In fact, metabolic activity seems generally to be favored by certain degrees of alkalinity; for example, J. Loeb[12] found that sea-urchin eggs develop with much greater rapidity if a small amount of OH ions is free in the sea-water. Brandenburg[13] states that the non-diffusible alkali varies according to the amount of protein in the blood; in pneumonia and acute nephritis he found it low. In cancer the titrable alkalinity is distinctly increased, and Moore and Walker[14] hold that this is due to an increased alkalinity of the proteins of the blood. Auerbach[15] claims that in severe high fevers the bactericidal effect of the blood alkalinity is increased (see also "Passive Congestion" for further discussion concerning the relation of alkalinity to bactericidal power).

Viscosity of the Blood.[16]—Normal blood is about five times (4.5 times, Austrian) more viscous than water, chiefly because of the corpuscles and the dissolved proteins. This viscosity does not vary directly with the specific gravity or the hemoglobin, but is closely related to the number of red corpuscles (Burton-Opitz); laking the corpuscles increases the viscosity considerably. Most salts increase the viscosity, but some, especially iodides, are said to reduce it. Carbon dioxide increases viscosity greatly, even when in amounts possible in the circulating blood. Anemia decreases the viscosity, approximately in proportion to the number of corpuscles; polycythemia is accompanied by a corresponding increase; leukemia, because of anemia, shows a decrease; in nephritis there may either be an increase or a decrease in the viscosity, not corresponding in any way to the blood pressure. Cardiac disease with edema shows low viscosity because of the anemia and hydremia, but if there is polycythemia and no edema the viscosity may be high. Jaundice causes an increase, diabetes gives variable results. Typhoid causes no characteristic change beyond that resulting from anemia, and in pneumonia the cyanosis and salt retention usually cause an increase (Austrian). Gullbring[17] found the viscosity to vary directly with the per cent. of neutrophiles. As blood viscosity depends largely upon the corpuscles, it increases with reduction in the size of the lumen of the tube through which it passes, unlike a true solution; hence with narrow capillaries the viscosity is abnormally high until we reach the point where the corpuscles plug the capillary.

HEMORRHAGE

Hemorrhages result from an altered condition in the vessel-walls, which may be due either to trauma or to chemical injuries. Of the chemical agencies causing hemorrhages, bacterial products are the

[11] See Robertson, Jour. Biol. Chem., 1909 (6), 313; 1910 (7), 351.

[12] Arch. f. Entwicklungsmechanik, 1898 (7), 631.

[13] Deut. med. Woch., 1902 (28), 78; Zeit. f. klin. Med., 1902 (45), 157.

[14] Biochem. Jour., 1906 (1), 297; good discussion of blood reaction.

[15] Med. Obosrenije, 1903, p. 596.

[16] Review of literature by Determann, Zeit. klin. Med., 1910 (70), 185; also Austrian, Johns Hopkins Hosp. Bull., 1911 (22), 9. See also Traube, Internat. Zeit. physik-chem. Biol., 1914 (1), 389.

[17] Beitr. klin. Tuberk., 1914 (30), 1.

most important practically, but many poisons, such as phosphorus, formaldehyde, *phytotoxins* (ricin, abrin, and crotin), and *zoötoxins* (snake venoms) cause numerous and abundant hemorrhages. Formerly, the tendency was to ascribe hemorrhages from the above causes to mechanical injury of the vessels by thrombi, or by emboli of agglutinated corpuscles, but the work of Flexner[18] has shown that venoms cause hemorrhages by injuring the capillary walls, so that actual rents are produced by the intravascular pressure, and it seems highly probable that hemorrhages are produced by other chemical substances in a similar way. We may, therefore, refer such hemorrhages to an *endotheliotoxic* action of the poison, or to a solvent effect upon the intercellular cement substance. In the case of ordinary chemical poisons the endotheliotoxic action is not specific, but with some of the toxins it seems to be quite so; for example, rattlesnake venom contains an endotheliotoxic substance (*hemorrhagin*), which seems to be a specific poison for endothelium, and which is the most dangerous constituent of the venom. If we immunize animals against tissues containing much endothelium (*e. g.*, lymph-glands), their serum will be found to contain endotheliotoxins, so that when this serum is injected subcutaneously into a susceptible animal, large local hemorrhages result; if injected into the peritoneal cavity, there results marked desquamation of the endothelial cells, which soon undergo degenerative changes (Ricketts).[19] It is quite probable that the bacterial poisons that cause marked hemorrhagic manifestations likewise contain endotheliotoxins, although this matter does not seem to have been investigated.

Even *hemorrhage by diapedesis* seems to be due to, or at least associated with, chemical changes in the capillary walls, for Arnold[20] found that when capillaries from which diapedesis had occurred were stained by silver nitrate, dark areas were found between the endothelial cells. As silver nitrate is a stain for chlorides, and darkens intercellular substance because it is rich in sodium chloride (Macallum), it is probable that there is an increase in the amount or a difference in the method of combination of the chlorides of the cement substance between the endothelial cells at the places where red corpuscles escape. M. H. Fischer[21] suggests that diapedesis results from a change in the endothelial cells, which under the influence of acids or other agents of metabolic origin become excessively hydrophilic, swell up, and become so softened that corpuscles may pass directly through the cell, just as a drop of mercury can pass through a sufficiently soft jelly without leaving a hole in the jelly.

Hemorrhage in cachetic conditions is often ascribed to changes in the vessel-walls due to malnutrition, but it is difficult to imagine

[18] Univ. of Penn. Med. Bull., 1902 (15), 355.
[19] Trans. Chicago Path. Soc., 1902 (5), 181.
[20] Virchow's Arch., 1875 (62), 157.
[21] "Nephritis," New York, 1912, p. 78.

capillary walls suffering from lack of nourishment, even with the poorest of blood, and it seems more probable that the hemorrhages are due, even in cachexia, to chemical constituents of the blood that injure the endothelium. Hemorrhages that follow re-establishment of the circulation after complete occlusion, however, may be the result of asphyxial changes in the capillary walls, presumably colloidal swelling of the cells.

After severe hemorrhages the blood shows a decrease in specific gravity and viscosity, an increase in surface tension and electrical resistance, and either increase or decrease of the freezing-point depression, all these changes being transient if the individual is otherwise normal.[22] (See also Secondary Anemia.) There is a rapid absorption of fluid from the tissues and tissue spaces, resulting in a dilution of protein and formed elements, but not of salts. For the same reason the density of the blood decreases in direct relation to the proportion of the total blood that has been lost.[23] The alkali reserve of the blood is somewhat lowered by severe hemorrhage,[24] but there is not a marked acidosis. The total nitrogen of the blood of course falls, but there is a tendency for sugar, urea and non-protein N to increase, and there is increased elimination of creatine in the urine, presumably from destruction of muscle tissue to replace the lost blood proteins. There is said to be a decreased permeability of vessels, resulting in reduced exudative processes.[25] The proportion of the several blood proteins is variably altered after repeated hemorrhages; the sugar is little affected[26] but there may occur a marked rise in the content of immune bodies, especially specific agglutinins.[27] Rapid hemorrhages cause a decrease in the coagulation time because of a decrease in antithrombin and a slight increase in prothrombin, in spite of a decrease in fibrinogen.[28] If the blood is withdrawn repeatedly in large amounts, centrifuged, and the washed corpuscles reinjected suspended in isotonic salt solution (plasmaphaeresis), life can be maintained even after 4 to 5 times the total volume of blood has been removed and washed. This is possible because of rapid reformation of the plasma, and the blood shows the changes characteristic of secondary anemias.[29] Lipemia is often produced by severe or repeated hemorrhages, with a great increase in the phospholipins of the plasma and corpuscles.[29a]

Changes in the Extravasated Blood.—These begin soon after its escape. In most situations sufficient fibrin ferment is formed to

[22] Oliva, Folia clinica, 1912 (3), 213.
[23] Richet et al., Compt. Rend. Acad. Sci., 1918 (166), 587.
[24] Buell, Jour. Biol. Chem., 1919 (40), 29; Tatum, ibid., 1920 (41), 59.
[25] Luithlen, Med. Klin., 1913 (9), 1713.
[26] Taylor and Lewis, Jour. Biol. Chem., 1915 (22), 71.
[27] See Hahn and Langer, Zeit Immunität, 1917 (26), 199.
[28] Drinker, Amer. Jour. Physiol., 1915 (36), 305.
[29] Abel et al., Jour. Pharmacol., 1914 (5), 625; 1915 (7), 129.
[29a] Bloor and Farrington, Jour. Biol. Chem., 1920 (41) xlviii.

cause prompt clotting, but in the pleura and other serous cavities the blood may remain fluid for some time, possibly because of lack of cellular injury that might cause liberation of fibrin ferment.[30]   If the blood does not become infected, the rapidity of subsequent changes depends chiefly upon the location and amount of blood.   Small extravasations of blood into the tissues are subjected to the action of the tissue cells and of leucocytes emigrating freely from the capillaries; large masses of blood are but little affected by these agencies, the leucocytes within the mass soon die, and secondary changes go on very slowly.   In small subcutaneous hemorrhages (e. g., a bruise) enzymes from the invading leucocytes and tissue-cells soon dissolve the small quantities of fibrin present; even earlier the stroma of the red corpuscles is so altered that hemolysis occurs and the hemoglobin escapes and diffuses into the tissues.   This hemolysis may be brought about by the action of proteolytic enzymes on the corpuscles, or by the hemolytic action of the products of protein splitting.   Soon the hemoglobin disintegrates, forming the masses of pigment so characteristic of old hemorrhagic areas, and also giving rise to the discoloration observed beneath the skin in the later stages of resorption of hemorrhagic extravasations.   The first products of the splitting of hemoglobin are: (1) The protein, *globin*, which constitutes 94 per cent. of the hemoglobin; and (2) the iron-containing coloring-matter, *hematin* (in the absence of oxygen the pigment is *reduced hematin* or *hemochromogen*).   As hematin may be experimentally obtained by the action of proteases upon hemoglobin, the decomposition of the hemoglobin in the tissues is probably accomplished in a similar way by the proteases of the leucocytes, tissue-cells and blood plasma; the globin is thus digested away and the soluble products carried off, while the insoluble hematin remains.[31]   The hematin gradually undergoes further changes, forming an iron-free pigment (*hematoidin*) and an iron-containing pigment (*hemosiderin*).

Hematoidin is nearly or quite identical with the bile-pigment, *bilirubin*, and is absorbed from the hemorrhagic extravasation and eliminated as bilirubin in the bile.   Possibly some of the hematoidin undergoes transformation into *urobilin*, and is then eliminated in the urine.   *Hemosiderin* seems to be relatively insoluble and, therefore, is more slowly removed, so that it may be found at the site of a hemorrhage after the other evidences of blood extravasation have been removed.   It may be easily demonstrated by staining with potassium ferrocyanide, the Prussian blue that is formed being readily distinguished.   Unstained hemosiderin generally appears in the form

[30] Denny and Minot (Amer. Jour. Physiol., 1916 (39), 455) believe that the blood really does clot, and that it remains fluid when withdrawn because the fibrinogen has been removed by clotting.   Zahn and Walker (Biochem. Zeit., 1913 (58), 130), however, consider that the fibrinogen is altered by the pleural endothelium, so that it cannot clot.

[31] More fully discussed in the consideration of "Pigmentation," Chap. xviii.

of brown or yellowish-brown granules, never as crystals. After a time the hemosiderin is taken away, and probably is to a greater or less extent deposited in the liver and spleen, either as hemosiderin or as some other iron compound. Eventually it is probably utilized to make new hemoglobin; at any rate, the iron liberated by the breaking up of hematin within the body does not appear to be eliminated.[32]

The changes in the red corpuscles described above are not at all peculiar to extravasated blood, but are quite the same as the changes that are going on continuously and normally in the blood. Red corpuscles are short-lived, being but non-nucleated fragments of cells, and they are continually disintegrating with the production of iron-free pigments that are excreted as the coloring-matters of the bile and urine, while the iron is worked over again into new hemoglobin after a varying period of storage in the tissues, particularly in the spleen and liver. The destruction of red corpuscles under normal conditions seems to take place chiefly in the spleen, bone-marrow, and hemolymph glands, where injured or decrepit corpuscles are taken out of the blood by the phagocytic endothelial cells, and decomposed by intracellular enzymes. In hemorrhagic extravasations the changes are essentially the same; some corpuscles are destroyed by phagocytes, but more by extracellular enzymes. The products of decomposition also seem to be no different from those formed during normal katabolism of hemoglobin, and they meet the same fate in the end.

If the hemorrhages are very abundant, some hemoglobin may be absorbed as such and appear in the urine, but this probably seldom happens unless red corpuscles are also being destroyed in the circulating blood.[33] An increased amount of iron accumulates in the liver, but if much blood has been lost by hemorrhage on free surfaces, the iron content of the liver is decreased, as it is taken away to form new hemoglobin (Quincke).[34] Excretion of bile-pigments is increased by destruction of blood (Stadelmann), but not greatly in the case of internal hemorrhages, for the blood is decomposed and absorbed too slowly. Schurig[35] found that hemoglobin injected into the tissues is partly decomposed *in situ* with formation of iron compounds, but the greater part enters the circulation as hemoglobin, and is partly converted into bile-pigment by the liver-cells, the rest being converted into simpler iron compounds by the spleen, bone-marrow, and renal cortex.

If the hemorrhagic extravasation has been large in amount, the deeper portions of the mass are not soon, if ever, invaded by leucocytes

[32] See Morishima, Arch. f. exp. Path., 1898 (41), 291.

[33] In cerebral hemorrhage the blood serum may be greenish and somewhat fluorescent from absorbed pigment, according to Marie and Leri, Union Pharm., Aug. 15, 1914.

[34] Deut. Arch. klin. Med., 1880 (25), 567; 1880 (27), 193.

[35] Arch. exp. Path. u. Pharm., 1898 (41), 29.

or tissue-cells. Consequently the blood is acted upon very slowly by the enzymes liberated by the leucocytes it contains itself, and by the small amounts of proteases in the serum. Furthermore, the products of decomposition are not soon absorbed, but accumulate in considerable amounts, so that we often find crystalline deposits of hematoidin, sometimes even of hematin, hemoglobin, or *parahemoglobin* (Nencki)[36] or *methemoglobin*.

The least soluble constituent of the red corpuscle stroma, *cholesterol*, also accumulates in such extravasations as large, thin plates; after most of the other products of disintegration have been absorbed from such accumulations of blood, the most conspicuous part of the residue may be a mass of cholesterol crystals imbedded in proliferating connective tissue.

HEMOPHILIA[37]

There are several pathological conditions associated with increased tendency to bleeding, notably scurvy and the various forms of purpuras, but especially the remarkable hereditary condition, hemophilia. In the purpuric diseases various of the factors concerned in coagulation of the blood have been found altered,[38] notably the blood platelets,[39] but Howell found no change in either prothrombin or antithrombin in *purpura hemorrhagica* and other related conditions. Similar negative results were obtained in scurvy by Hess.[40] *Melena neonatorum* exhibits decreased prothrombin in the blood, while in leukemias and anemias there may be an excess of antithrombin,[41] leading to severe hemorrhage (see also Thrombosis).

Since hemophilia seems, superficially at least, to depend upon some alteration in a chemical property of the blood, namely, coagulability, it is frequently regarded as an example of hereditary transmission of a chemical abnormality. The exact cause of this peculiar tendency to prolonged bleeding from insignificant or perhaps imperceptible wounds has been sought vigorously by both histological and chemical means, but as yet without avail. Various observers have described abnormal thinness, or increased cellularity or fatty degeneration of the vessel-walls, but the findings have been far too inconstant to afford a satisfactory anatomical explanation of all the features of hemophilia. Likewise increased blood pressure can be ruled out, for

[36] Arch. exp. Path. u. Pharm., 1886 (20), 332.
[37] Literature and résumé given by Stempel, Cent. f. Grenzgeb. Med. u. Chir., 1900 (3), 753; Sahli, Zeit. f. klin. Med., 1905 (56), 291; Marchand, in Krehl and Marchand's Handb. allg. Pathol., 1912, II (1), 307. Also later references in this text.
[38] See Hurwitz and Lucas, Arch. Int. Med., 1916 (17), 543; Minot *et al.*, *ibid.*, 1916 (17), 101.
[39] See Lee and Robertson, Jour. Med. Res., 1916 (33), 323; Hess, Proc. Soc. Exp. Biol. Med., 1917 (14), 96.
[40] Amer. Jour. Dis. Children, 1914 (8), 386.
[41] Whipple, Arch. Int. Med., 1913 (12), 637.

although the left heart is frequently enlarged, there is usually no increased blood pressure demonstrable; furthermore, conditions of high blood pressure, such as nephritis, do not cause hemophilia. The theory of "hydremic plethora" is also without good foundation.

The most natural place to look for the fundamental fault is in the blood, but speaking strongly against this is the occasional occurrence of "local" hemophilia; e. g., in this type of hemophilia wounds of the skin may behave as in normal individuals, whereas any injury of the mucous surfaces is followed by pronounced hemophilic bleeding;[42] in other cases the hemophilic bleeding is limited to regions above the shoulders; in still another class the bleeding is always from one organ, e. g., the kidneys. Nevertheless, a great deal of investigation of the blood has been done, at first chiefly with negative results. There are no characteristic changes in the cellular elements of the blood, beyond the changes common to all secondary anemias, excepting possibly a decrease in the number of white corpuscles with a relative increase in the number of lymphocytes as observed by Sahli; the platelet count is normal. No constant alterations in the salts of the blood have been found, calcium usually being normal;[43] and the proportion of water, fibrinogen and the several other proteins, the alkalinity, and the osmotic pressure of the serum all seem to be normal. Metabolism is unchanged, except possibly for calcium loss in some cases.[44] Since bleeding is normally stopped principally by coagulation, a deficiency in fibrin or its antecedents might be expected, but most studies on this point have shown a normal amount of fibrinogen in the blood of hemophilics, the frequent formation of large tumors of clotted blood at the bleeding points supporting the experimental evidence that the blood contains an abundance of fibrinogen. The "bleeding time" following punctures in the skin is not excessive. As to the rate of clotting, Sahli,[37] who avoided a number of errors made in earlier investigations, found that in the intervals between the attacks of hemorrhage the rate of the coagulation of the blood is constantly much slower than normal. During an attack of bleeding the coagulation time approaches the normal; indeed, it may be faster than normal; apparently this is due to a reaction on the part of the organism to the loss of blood. If blood is collected directly from the site of bleeding the coagulation time is very rapid, because of the accumulation of fibrin ferment from the clot over which the escaping blood flows. Yet in spite of the normal coagulability of the blood and the rapid clotting after the blood escapes from the vessel, bleeding continues for long periods before it can be stopped. As he found no general change in the properties of the blood to account for the bleed-

[42] Abderhalden, Ziegler's Beitr., 1904 (35), 213.
[43] Klinger and Berg, Zeit. klin. Med., 1918 (85), 335, 406.
[44] Kahn, Amer. Jour. Dis. Children, 1916 (11), 103; Laws and Cowie, *ibid.* 1917 (13), 236; Hess, Bull. Johns Hopkins Hosp., 1916 (26), 372.

ing, and as local influences seem to be important in hemophilia, Sahli advanced the plausible hypothesis that the cause of hemophilia lies in hereditary deficiency of the fibrin-forming substances, thrombokinase or zymoplastic substance (see "Thrombosis"), in the vessel-walls, so that when the vessels are injured there is no local production of fibrin such as occurs normally. Local hemophilia may be explained readily as a local deficiency in fibrinoplastic material. In general hemophilia even the leucocytes may exhibit the same defect, in which case clotting of the blood is diminished even outside the tissues. This hypothesis seems to be in excellent agreement with many of the facts now known, but there yet remains to be demonstrated such a lack of fibrin-forming elements in the vessel-walls and other tissues of a hemophilic subject, and a single autopsy of a hemolytic subject gave, on the contrary, a very active thromboplastic extract from the vessels (Gressot).[45] The tissues of one case studied by Lowenburg and Rubenstone,[46] however, showed in the liver and thyroid a decreased capacity to accelerate coagulation.

With the improved methods of study of the factors in coagulation of blood introduced by Howell, it has been found by him and corroborated by others[47] that in hemophilia there is constantly a deficiency in prothrombin, the other factors being practically normal in amount, and as in other hemorrhagic conditions there is no equal alteration in the prothrombin, they look upon this change as an essential characteristic of hemophilia. Fonio, and Minot and Lee, however, find that the blood platelets of hemophilics are remarkably ineffective in causing coagulation of either normal or hemophilic plasma, although normal platelets cause normal coagulation of hemophilic plasma, and therefore conclude that there is some deficient activity on the part of the platelets in spite of their occurrence in normal numbers in hemophilia. The significance of the platelets is shown especially clearly by the observation of Ledingham and Bedson[48] that antiplatelet serum will produce a purpuric condition when injected into animals of the species furnishing the platelets, although no similar effect is produced by antileucocyte or antierythrocyte serum. Hess[49] states that there may be an hereditary purpura, sometimes occurring in the females of hemophilic families, differing from hemophilia in a deficiency in the number of platelets, hemorrhages following local congestions or puncture wounds and exhibiting an increase in the "bleeding time."

[45] Zeit. klin. Med., 1912 (76), 194.   Since corroborated by Minot and Lee.[47]
[46] Jour. Amer. Med. Assoc., 1918 (71), 1196.
[47] Howell, Arch. Int. Med.; 1914 (13), 76; Hurwitz and Lucas, ibid., 1916 (17), 543; Minot and Lee, ibid., 1916 (18), 474; Klinger, Zeit. klin. Med., 1918 (85) 335; Pettibone, Jour. Lab. Clin. Med., 1918 (3), 275; these papers review recent work on hemophilia.
[48] Lancet, Feb. 13, 1915.   Similar observations have been made by Watabiki (Kitasato's Arch. Exp. Med., 1917 (1), 195).
[49] Arch. Int. Med., 1916 (17), 203.

ANEMIA AND THE SPECIFIC ANEMIAS [50]

The customary although unsatisfactory and unscientific division of the anemias, is into— (a) *primary*, *i. e.*, those in which the anemia seems to depend upon some abnormality in the blood-forming organs or in the blood itself; and (b) *secondary*, embracing anemias the result of some obvious cause, such as hemorrhage, poisoning with blood-destroying poisons, cachexia, etc. In these various forms of anemia certain chemical differences prevail, but they are by no means so striking as are the histological differences in the formed elements of the blood. [51]

SECONDARY ANEMIAS

As the simplest variety, anemia following a single large hemorrhage may be considered first.

If loss of blood by hemorrhage is rapid, the effects are naturally much more serious than when the loss is slow. The total quantity of blood in the average adult is estimated at about $\frac{1}{13}$ to $\frac{1}{15}$ the total body weight (therefore about 10 to 12 pounds), although this proportion does not hold for extremely obese or extremely thin individuals; in infants the proportion is lower—about $\frac{1}{20}$. When one-third of the total amount of blood is lost rapidly, a marked fall of blood pressure occurs; loss of one-half of the total amount may be fatal, and loss of more than that at one time usually is fatal. The chief cause of death following large hemorrhages is the low blood pressure rather than the loss of any of the constituents of the blood; hence the successful results of the use of physiological salt solution after severe hemorrhage. The number of corpuscles may be greatly reduced after several small hemorrhages, even to as low as 11 per cent. of the normal number (Hayem), without fatal results, because in the intervals between the hemorrhages enough fluid has been taken up by the blood to maintain the blood pressure within safe limits. After a severe hemorrhage the composition of the blood changes rapidly, for the fluids contained within the tissues and lymph-spaces pass into the blood in large amounts. This helps to maintain blood pressure, but results in the blood containing a large proportion of water and salts and a smaller amount of protein and red corpuscles; the "total alkalinity" also falls, largely because of the scarcity of "fixed alkali," on account of the poverty in corpuscles and blood proteins. The proportion of water increases at first more rapidly than the proportion of salts, and as a consequence the size of the red corpuscles is increased because of imbibition of water; indeed, it is possible that this may even be sufficient to cause hemolysis, which will happen if the isotonic strength of the

[50] Metabolism in anemia reviewed by Mohr, Handbuch d. Biochem., 1910 (IV (2)), 372.
[51] Concerning local anemia, see "Infarcts."

blood becomes less than that of a 0.46 per cent. NaCl solution (Limbeck), while swelling may occur whenever the strength is below 0.8
per cent. The specific gravity of the erthrocytes is decreased;[52]
the depression of the freezing point increases,[53] while the viscosity
falls. The number of platelets is high.

Regeneration of the blood begins very soon, and for some time the
number of corpuscles exceeds the proportion of hemoglobin. During
this time the amount of iron in the liver and spleen is decreased, it
being taken up to be used in the formation of new hemoglobin. The
rate of regeneration is much increased by a meat diet, but not by
iron administration.[54] Red corpuscles do not regenerate in animals
kept on an incomplete protein diet (gliadin). If the hemorrhages
are numerous and the condition of anemia prolonged, secondary
changes in the viscera may occur, fatty metamorphosis being most
marked, supposedly because of decreased oxidation. Indeed, many
observers state that repeated bleedings greatly increase body weight
by causing increased fat deposition.

Metabolic Changes.—Gies[55] studied the *metabolism* of dogs after withdrawing
a total amount of blood equal to 11.5 per cent. of the body weight during four
bleedings, and found that a slight and temporary increase in nitrogenous elimination followed the bleedings, owing to an increased protein katabolism. Basal
metabolism may also be increased in anemia.[56] Sugar increases in the blood,
while albumin and lactic acid appear in the urine. After each successive hemorrhage the proportion of fibrin and the coagulability of the blood increase, while
the proportion of the ash obtained from both blood and serum remains practically
unchanged (Meyer and Gies). Baumann[57] states that in regeneration after hemorrhage the serum albumins increase more rapidly than the globulins, while others
have observed the opposite relation. The urine in secondary anemia shows the
effects of increased protein katabolism, its specific gravity, total solids, and total
nitrogen being raised; the total amount of urine is at first diminished because of
lowered blood pressure, but it soon rises above normal and later falls back to
normal. The view formerly held that oxidation is decreased in anemia has been
considerably modified by more recent investigations;[58] in fact, respiration studies
indicate heightened gas exchange in secondary anemia.[59]

Secondary anemia due to cachexia, or to malnutrition, is accompanied by a general decrease in all the elements of the blood, both
cellular and chemical. The proteins of the plasma, particularly, show
a decrease in starvation, being drawn on by the cells for food, and
the total quantity of blood as well as of each of its constituents is decreased (Panum),[60] but the proportion of blood to body weight remains about normal. With protracted starvation there is only a

[52] Bönninger, Zeit. exp. Path., 1912 (11), 1.
[53] Hoesslin, Hofmeister's Beitr., 1906 (8), 431.
[54] Hooper and Whipple, Amer. Jour. Physiol., 1918 (45), 573.
[55] American Med., 1904 (8), 155 (résumé of literature).
[56] Review by Tompkins *et al.*, Arch. Int. Med., 1919 (23), 441.
[57] Jour. Physiol., 1903 (29), 18.
[58] See Mohr, Zeit. exp. Path., 1906 (2), 435.
[59] Grafe, Deut. Arch. klin. Med., 1915 (118), 148.
[60] Virchow's Arch., 1864 (29), 241.

slight loss of hemoglobin and an increased coagulability, but practically no other changes.[61] In aplastic anemias the prothrombin and platelet content are likely to be low, with normal fibrinogen.[62]

Anemia due to hemolytic agencies presents quite different features, in that red corpuscles are almost solely attacked and the products of their disintegration are present in the plasma. As a result, the plasma or serum may contain free hemoglobin, and if the hemoglobin is in large amounts, it may escape into the urine. Thus *paroxysmal hemoglobinuria* is probably due to the presence in the blood of hemolytic substances, which can be demonstrated in the blood of the patients during the attack. (See Chapter ix.) The products of the decomposition of the hemoglobin set free by hemolysis are present not only in the blood, but also in the organs, particularly the liver and spleen, which become rich in iron. In acute anemia produced by hemolytic sera, with destruction of more than half the blood in three days, nearly all the iron from the destroyed hemoglobin can be found in the liver, spleen and kidneys, there being but little lost through the urine even in so severe an anemia as this (Muir and Dunn).[63] Excretion of bile-pigments increases, and *"hematogenous jaundice"* may result, the bile-pigments that are present in the blood being derived from the hematoidin of the hemoglobin molecule. Changes in metabolism occur which are quite similar to those observed in other forms of anemia, with fatty changes in all the parenchymatous organs, increased protein katabolism, and an excessive quantity of pigmentary substances, particularly urobilin, in the urine. The plasma chlorides are increased.[64]

¡CHLOROSIS

The characteristic feature of the blood in chlorosis is the relatively small amount of hemoglobin in proportion to the number of corpuscles. Apparently, therefore, the fault lies rather in the manufacture of hemoglobin than in either a destruction or a deficient formation of red corpuscles. Erben's[65] analyses of chlorotic blood showed that the total amount of protein is decreased, chiefly because of the deficiency of hemoglobin; the relation of serum globulins and serum albumin is unchanged, while the proportion of fibrinogen is increased. There is much more fatty substance than normal in both the serum and the erythrocytes, but the lecithin is decreased both in the serum

[61] Ash, Arch. Int. Med., 1914 (14), 8.

[62] Drinker and Hurwitz, Arch. Int. Med., 1915 (15), 733; Jour. Exp. Med., 1915 (21), 401.

[63] Jour. Path. and Bact., 1915 (19), 417. See also Dubin and Pearce, Jour. Exp. Med., 1918 (27), 479.

[64] Steinfield, Arch. Int. Med., 1919 (23), 511.

[65] Zeit. klin. Med., 1902 (47), 302. See also Frohmaier, Folia Hematol., 1915 (20), 115; Beumer and Bürger, Zeit. exp. Path., 1913 (13), 351.

and in the total blood, although somewhat increased in the red cells. Cholesterol is decreased in both serum and corpuscles. In the ash, phosphoric acid, potassium, and iron are decreased, while calcium and magnesium are both increased. An apparent increase in sodium chloride exists, but it is only apparent, being the result of the increase in the proportion of plasma in the blood. The total amount of plasma is greatly increased (polyplasmia).

The decrease in hemoglobin is demonstrable chemically as well as microscopically, Becquerel and Rodier[66] having found the amount of iron in the total blood decreased in direct proportion to the apparent decrease in hemoglobin, which frequently falls to 30–40 per cent., and may drop to 20 per cent., or possibly less. Alkalinity, as determined by titration, is diminished in some cases, but generally remains nearly normal. The corpuscles are said to contain a larger proportion of water than normal, independent of the proportion of water present in the serum. Limbeck found their *isotonicity* (*i. e.*, the strength of NaCl necessary to prevent hemolysis) very low—about 0.38–0.4 per cent. NaCl.

Very few changes seem to occur in the organs of the body; the usual tendency to lay on fat, and the occurrence of fatty degeneration observed commonly in anemias, may be exhibited, and are correlated with Erben's observation of an increased fat content in the blood; but these changes are often absent. The hypoplasia of the aorta, upon which Virchow laid so much stress, is now considered to be of little or no significance. Thrombosis is a not infrequent complication of chlorosis,[67] and is probably favored by the increased platelet and fibrin-content of the blood and the tendency to fatty changes in the vessel-walls.

Studies of *nitrogenous metabolism* by Vannini[68] showed practically no alterations except a slight retention of nitrogen.

Etiology.—As to the etiology of chlorosis, chemical findings indicate some possibilities and negative others, but decide nothing. That chlorosis does not depend upon a hemolytic poison is well established by the following facts: there is no free hemoglobin in the blood plasma, and even less iron in the serum ash than normal; lecithin and cholesterol, important products of disintegration of erythrocytes, are both decreased in the serum; hematogenous icterus does not occur, and the amount of pigments in the urine and feces is decreased.

Apparently, therefore, *hematogenesis* is at fault, particularly the formation of hemoglobin, since this is more deficient than is the total

---

[66] For literature see Krehl, "Basis of Symptoms," 1916, p. 106; Ewing, "Clinical Pathology of the Blood," 1901, p. 167; Kossler, Cent. f. inn. Med., 1897 (18), 657.

[67] See Schweitzer, Virchow's Arch., 1898 (152), 337, and Leichtenstern, Münch. med. Woch., 1899 (46), 1603.

[68] Virchow's Arch., 1901 (176), 375.

number of red corpuscles. The rapid improvement in the condition that follows the administration of iron would seem to indicate that a deficient supply of iron is the cause of chlorosis, but numerous objections exist to this hypothesis. Bunge advanced the idea that in chlorosis the iron taken with the ordinary food is precipitated in the intestines by sulphides or other products of intestinal putrefaction, and hence there results a deficiency in the amount of iron absorbed and available for the manufacture of hemoglobin. Many objections have been raised to this hypothesis, however, for competent observers have failed to find any abnormal putrefaction in chlorosis, and others have found that sulphide of iron itself gives good results in the treatment of chlorosis, while bismuth and other sulphur-binding substances are without effect. Furthermore, Bunge's contention that iron administered in medicinal form is not absorbed seems to have been completely disproved by several experiments.[69]

As a consequence of all these conflicting data we are at present completely in the dark as to the reason for that failure properly to manufacture hemoglobin which seems to be at the bottom of chlorosis. The hypothesis that iron and arsenic favor recovery by stimulating the hemogenetic tissues, which is urged by v. Noorden and others, is unsatisfactory in the extreme, and explains nothing. There is absolutely no question that administration of iron restores the composition of the blood to normal, usually quite rapidly, and this seems to leave as most probable the explanation that in some way an *iron starvation* is the fundamental cause of chlorosis. However, as Ewing says, any theory must be inadequate that fails to take into account the age of puberty, the female sex, and the function of menstruation.[70]

PERNICIOUS ANEMIA

In contrast to chlorosis many evidences of hematolysis may be found in pernicious anemia, particularly the increased amounts of iron in the liver, spleen, and kidneys; hemoglobinemia and hemoglobinuria, increase in urobilin, and not infrequently icterus.

Chemical Changes.[71]—Erben's[72] analysis of the blood in pernicious anemia gave the following results: The proteins are decreased, both in the serum[73] and in the blood as a whole; particularly in the latter, because of the great decrease in the number of corpuscles. The quantity of proteins in the individual corpuscles is increased, corresponding to their increased size. Fibrin is decreased in total amount, but is relatively normal as compared with the total proteins; albumin

[69] Full review with bibliography by E. Meyer, Ergebnisse Physiol., 1905 (5), 698; Meinertz, Cent. Physiol. u. Path. Stoffwech., 1907 (2), 652.

[70] von Jagic (Med. Klin., 1915 (11), 69) states that in chlorosis the Abderhalden test is positive with uterine and ovarian tissue.

[71] Review and bibliography by Squier, Jour. Lab. Clin. Med., 1917 (2), 552.

[72] Zeit. klin. Med., 1900 (40), 266. Beumer and Bürger, Zeit. exp. Path., 1913 (13), 343.

[73] See also Heudorfer, Zeit. klin. Med., 1913 (79), 103.
20

is normal; serum globulin much decreased. The proportion of water is much increased, both in the serum and in the corpuscles. Fat is present in normal amounts; cholesterol is decreased, although in relatively normal quantities in the corpuscles. Lecithin is decreased in the total blood, but increased proportionately in the corpuscles. The total ash is increased, owing chiefly to an excessively large proportion of NaCl and a slight increase in calcium and magnesium; potassium and phosphoric acid are decreased because of the small number of corpuscles; but the serum itself contains more P_2O_5 and potassium than normal. Although the total iron is, of course, much decreased, there is iron in the serum (indicating hemolysis) and the proportion of iron in the corpuscles is increased; but as the amount of iron in the corpuscles is even greater than corresponds to the hemoglobin increase, it would seem that either the hemoglobin in pernicious anemia is very rich in iron, or that the corpuscles contain iron bound in some form other than hemoglobin.

The analyses of Rumpf[74] agree quite closely with those of Erben, and, taken jointly with other analyses in the literature, show the large proportion of water in the blood, the small amount of solids, the large amount of NaCl, and the decrease in potassium and iron. Rumpf also examined the brain, liver, heart, and spleen in one case. Water was found increased in the heart, decreased in the other organs, the solids not being decreased in any of the organs. There was little fat in any of the organs or in the blood, but NaCl was generally increased. The liver contained four or five times as much iron as normal; the spleen three or four times. Rumpf is inclined to lay great stress on the general poverty of the body in potassium, and suggests its therapeutic application. By more modern methods Bloor[75] found the blood lipoids about normal unless the red corpuscles were below 50 per cent., when there appear high fat and low lecithin and cholesterol[76] in the plasma, but usually with normal corpuscular lipoid content. The proportion of cholesterol free and as ester is normal. Syllaba[77] found bilirubin and also free hemoglobin in the blood of seven patients. Fowell[78] found a considerable excess of iron in the blood over the amount combined with hemoglobin. Schumm[79] could find no proteoses or other evidences of protein decomposition in the blood in a case of pernicious anemia, but he did find free hematin.[80] The tendency to hemorrhage observed in this disease may depend on a slight decrease in the prothrombin and a reduction in the number of platelets.[81]

v. Jaksch and also v. Limbeck[82] have found some decrease in total alkalinity, which probably depends on the loss of proteins and their fixed alkali.[83] The red corpuscles are very susceptible to hemolysis by lowering of osmotic pressure ("high isotonicity," equal to 0.54 per cent. NaCl—v. Limbeck). The specific gravity of the whole blood is, of course, decreased, but the corpuscles themselves have practically normal specific gravity, while the decrease is chiefly in the serum.[84] Bile pigment is frequently found in the blood, but so bound that it does not escape into the urine and it does not always cause evident jaundice. Bile salts may be found in the blood, either with or without pigment (Blankenhorn).[85] There is a marked increase in the urobilin output, corresponding in degree to the amount of hemolysis.[86]

In six cases of pernicious anemia Stühlen[87] found abundant iron in the liver and spleen microscopically, and less constantly in the kidneys and bone-marrow.

---

[74] Berl. klin. Woch., 1901 (38), 477; See also Kahn and Barsky, Arch. Int. Med., 1919 (23), 334.

[75] Jour. Biol. Chem., 1917 (31), 79.

[76] Corroborated by Pacini, Amer. Med., 1918 (13), 92.

[77] Abst. in Folia Hematol., 1904 (1), 283 and 589.

[78] Quart. Jour. Med., 1913 (6), 179.

[79] Hofmeister's Beitr., 1903 (4), 453.

[80] Zeit. physiol. Chem., 1916 (97), 32.

[81] Drinker and Hurwitz, Arch. Int. Med., 1915 (15), 733.

[82] "Klin. Pathol. des Blutes," Jena, 1896, p. 311.

[83] See Brandenburg, Zeit. klin. Med., 1902 (45), 157.

[84] Bönninger, Zeit. exp. Path., 1912 (11), 1.

[85] Arch. Int. Med., 1917 (19), 344.

[86] See Hansmann and Howard, Jour. Amer. Med. Assoc., 1919 (73), 1262.

[87] Deut. Arch. klin. Med., 1895 (51), 248 (literature).

Hunter[88] gives the following results of analysis of the liver, kidney, and spleen for iron:

	Liver and kidney.	Spleen.
Pernicious anemia, seven cases average	0.360 per cent.	0.125 per cent.
Other conditions (with anemia), average	0 079 per cent.	0.362 per cent.
Healthy organs	0.084 per cent.	0 090 per cent.

Iron is also found in the hemolymph glands, sometimes more abundantly than in the spleen (Warthin).[89]

Extensive studies on the *protein metabolism* of pernicious anemia by Rosenquist[90] showed that there is a considerable destruction of tissue proteins, as indicated by nitrogen loss, but that at times nitrogen may be stored up for brief periods. At times there may also be an excessive elimination of purine nitrogen, indicating destruction of nuclear elements. Calorimetric studies show the metabolism to be slightly above normal.[91] In anemia due to *Bothriocephalus* quite similar changes were observed.

Hunter[92] describes the condition of the urine in pernicious anemia, particularly with reference to the elimination of much "pathological urobilin,"[93] which seems to be produced by intracellular destruction of hemoglobin. Iron may also appear in the urine in increased quantities.[94] There is an increased elimination of oxyproteic acid nitrogen, other urinary nitrogen constituents being normal (Kahn and Barsky).[74] No constant metabolic changes follow splenectomy in pernicious anemia.[95]

Summary.[96]—Putting together the above findings, we see that in pernicious anemia we have every evidence that excessive hemolysis is taking place, and the fact that continued poisoning by toluylendiamine[97] and other hemolytic poisons, such as that of *Bothriocephalus*,[98] may give rise to a condition resembling pernicious anemia very closely, indicates strongly that hemolytic poisons are the cause of pernicious anemia. Histological studies show the same thing, and, as Warthin[89] says: "The hemolysis of pernicious anemia does not differ in kind from that occurring normally or in certain diseased conditions; the difference is one of degree only." The hemolysis seems to go on chiefly inside of phagocytic cells instead of in the blood, probably because the phagocytes pick up the corpuscles as soon as they have been injured

[88] Lancet, 1903 (i), 283; similar results obtained by Ryffel, Jour. Path. and Bact., 1910 (14), 411.

[89] Amer. Jour. Med. Sci., 1902 (124), 674.

[90] Zeit. klin. Med., 1903 (49), 193 (literature). See also Minot, Bull. Johns Hopkins Hosp., 1914 (25), 338.

[91] Meyer and DuBois, Arch. Int. Med., 1916 (17), 965; Grafe. Deut. Arch. klin. Med., 1915 (118), 148. See also Tompkins *et al.*, Arch. Int. Med., 1919 (23), 441.

[92] British Med. Jour., 1890 (ii), 1 and 81.

[93] See also Mott, Lancet, 1890 (1), 287; and Syllaba, Abst. in Folia Hematol., 1904 (1), 283.

[94] Kennerknecht, Virchow's Arch., 1911 (205), 89. Not confirmed by Queckenstedt. Zeit. klin. Med., 1913 (79), 49; bibliography.

[95] Denis, Arch. Int. Med., 1917 (20), 79.

[96] Review on etiology of pernicious anemia given by Vogel, Jour. Amer. Med. Assoc., 1916 (66), 1012.

[97] Syllaba,[77] Hunter[88] (*loc. cit.*).

[98] In horses a condition resembling pernicious anemia seems to be produced by a toxic product of the larvae of a fly, *Oestrus equi*, which is found in the walls of the stomach of anemic horses (Seyderhelm, Arch. exp. Path. u. Pharm., 1914 (76), 149).

by the hemolytic poisons.   In some instances cholesterol administration improves the anemia, which suggests that the poison attacks the lipoids of the corpuscles,[99] as so many hemolytic agents do.   *Bothriocephalus* anemia, which so closely resembles the "pernicious" form, seems to be caused by a hemolytic lipoid,[1] presumably a cholesterol ester of oleic acid, and there is a growing tendency to associate hemolytic lipins with the etiology of pernicious anemia.[2]   However, although in hemolytic anemias there is an increased amount of unsaturated lipins in the blood[3] Medak[4] did not find the isolated lipoids to be particularly hemolytic.[5]   (See Hemolysis, Chapter ix.)   The origin and the nature of the specific hypothetical poisons have been sought in vain.   Some authors have referred them to infections of unknown nature, occurring perhaps in the mouth and gastrointestinal tract (Hunter),[88] or to hemolytic products of intestinal putrefaction,[6] or to faulty metabolism.   For example, Iwao[7] has found that tyramine (*p*-oxyphenyl-ethylamine) produces in guinea pigs a blood picture resembling pernicious anemia, and this amine may be produced either in the intestines or during metabolism.   Others, with perhaps the best of grounds, would ascribe pernicious anemia to a multiplicity of causes, which produce a protracted slight hemolysis that continues until the hematogenetic organs give out, their exhaustion being perhaps hastened by the influence of the toxic substances in the blood; hematogenesis then becomes insufficient to replace the lost corpuscles, and the picture of pernicious anemia is established.[8]   The relatively great proportion of the iron that is stored in the liver supports the view that the hemolysis takes place in portal territory, and many other facts point to the same conclusion, but it is not generally accepted that the spleen plays an essential rôle in causing pernicious anemia through excessive phagocytosis or production of hemolytic poisons.[9]

[99] See Reicher, Berl. klin. Woch., 1908 (45), 1838.
[1] Tallquist, Zeit. klin. Med., 1907 (61), 427; Arch. exp. Path. u. Pharm., 1907 (57), 367.
[2] See Lüdke and Fejes, Deut. Arch. klin. Med., 1913 (109), 433.
[3] See King, Arch. Int. Med., 1914 (14), 145; Csonka, Jour. Biol. Chem., 1918 (33), 401.
[4] Biochem. Zeit., 1914 (59), 419.
[5] See McPhedran, Jour. Exp. Med., 1914 (18), 527.
[6] See Külbs (Arch. exp. Path. u. Pharm., 1906 (55), 73), who found the intestinal contents of patients with chronic intestinal disorders to contain hemolytic substances of undetermined character.   Hemolytic lipoids in the intestinal contents have been described by Berger and Tsuchiga (Deut. Arch. klin. Med., 1909 (96), 252) and Lüdke and Fejes, *loc. cit.;* but this observation failed of confirmation by Ewald (Deut. med. Woch., 1913 (39), 1293).
    Herter (Jour. Biol. Chem., 1906 (2), 1) suggested a relation between intestinal infection with *B. aërogenes capsulatus,* which produces hemolytic substances, and pernicious anemia.
[7] Biochem. Zeit., 1914 (59), 436.
[8] See also Bunting, Johns Hopkins Hosp. Bull., 1905 (16), 222; Pappenheim, Folia Serologica, 1910 (10), 217.
[9] See Hirschfeld, Zeit. klin. Med., 1919 (87), 165.

LEUKEMIA

In leukemia the chemical changes in the red corpuscles take a less prominent position, resembling either those of a secondary anemia or chlorosis, while the enormous number of leucocytes is the prominent feature and causes marked alterations in the composition of the blood. Large quantities of nucleoproteins and also of the intracellular enzymes are introduced into the blood by the excessive leucocytes. As the leucocytes are constantly breaking down, more or less of the products of their decomposition are present in the blood and appear in the urine. Because of the relatively slight metabolic activity of the lymphocytes the various chemical alterations are all less marked in lymphatic than in myelogenous leukemia.[10] There is a notable reduction in antibody production in leukemia,[11] presumably because of the changes in the bone marrow; it is said that typhoid infection in leukemics may fail to result in agglutinin formation.

Chemistry of the Blood.—Considering the quantitative alterations in the constituents of the blood, we find the specific gravity lowered, but not so much as it would be in a simple anemia with equally low hemoglobin, for the loss of hemoglobin is partly compensated by the increase in leucocytes and their products. Fibrinogen is usually increased in myelogenous leukemia.[12] The serum shows but slight change in specific gravity, a slight decrease in proteins[13] being compensated by an increase in the NaCl. The freezing-point of the blood is lowered (Cohn[14]), which is probably due to the increase in crystalloidal products of cellular decomposition. Erben[15] found that in lymphatic leukemia the serum contains less cholesterol than normal, although the fat content may be rather high. Calcium is frequently found increased, probably because of destruction of the bone tissue. In the red corpuscles the proportion of iron, protein and potassium is decreased as is also that of the cholesterol, that of the lecithin and water being somewhat increased. The total amount of potassium and iron in the blood is decreased, but the P$_2$O$_5$ in the ash is increased because of the large amount of nucleoprotein in the blood. A number of the earlier writers describe a decreased alkalescence which probably is due to the deficiency in the fixed alkali of the proteins. There is an increased excretion of iron in the urine and feces.[16]

The poor coagulation of leukemic blood has long been known, but the reason for it has not yet been ascertained. Some investigators have reported a deficiency in fibrin, while others have found it increased. More recent reports, however, indicate that there is no marked change in either the amount of fibrinogen or of the fibrin-ferments. Erben[12] found a normal amount of fibrin in the blood in lymphatic leukemia; and in three cases of myelogenous and one of lymphatic leukemia, Pfeiffer[17] found the amount of fibrinogen nearly normal. This is quite remarkable in view of the fact that in ordinary forms of leucocytosis both the amount of fibrinogen and the rapidity of clotting are increased. It is, therefore, extremely difficult

[10] Stern and Eppenstein have observed that the striking proteolytic power of the leucocytes from the blood in myelogenous leukemia is not shown by the leucocytes in lymphatic leukemia (Sitz. d. Schles. Ges. f. vaterländ. Kultur, June 29, 1906).
[11] Rotky, Zent. inn. Med., 1914 (35), 953.
[12] Erben, Zeit. klin. Med., 1908 (66), 278; full details on composition of the blood in leukemia.
[13] Little change was found in the protein content of the serum by Hendorfer. Zeit. klin. Med., 1913 (79), 103.
[14] Mitteil. aus dem Grenzgeb. Med. u. Chir., 1906 (15), H. 1.
[15] Zeit. klin. Med., 1900 (40), 282.
[16] Kennerknecht, Virchow's Arch., 1911 (205), 89.
[17] Cent. f. inn. Med., 1904 (25), 809.

to understand the poor coagulability of leukemic blood, but study of the factors of coagulation by modern methods may clear this up, for in one case so studied Whipple[18] found an increase in antithrombin.

Decomposition Products.—Of particular interest is the finding in the blood of decomposition products of the leucocytes, which are probably produced by autolysis of the leucocytes. (See Leucocytic Enzymes, Chapter iii.)   Normal leucocytes are rich in autolytic enzymes, which under ordinary circumstances seem[1] to be held in check by the antienzymes of the blood.   In leukemia this antienzyme action seems to be insufficient to prevent leucocytic autolysis, for even in freshly drawn blood proteoses (or at least non-coagulable proteins) may be present.[19] According to Erben, this is true only of myelogenous leukemia, the fresh blood in lymphatic leukemia not only being free from non-coagulable protein, but furthermore this product of proteolysis does not soon develop when the blood is kept aseptically at incubator temperature.   This is, of course, what one would expect in view of the well-known enzyme-richness of the polymorphonuclear leucocytes neutrophile cells seem to be the chief source of proteoses, since their granules soon and the scarcity of proteolytic enzymes in lymphocytes.   Erben states that the disappear in blood that is undergoing autolysis, whereas the eosinophiles preserve their granules well, and true proteoses are not present in blood rich in mast cells (*i. e.*, myeloma).   The marrow, spleen and lymph glands are found strongly proteolytic (according to the plate method), in myelogenous leukemia, but in lymphatic leukemia and pseudoleukemia, only the marrow shows a slight activity.[20] Schumm[21] found in the blood in a case of myelogenous leukemia several varieties of proteoses, most abundant being the so-called deutero-albumose; in another he also found peptone, leucine, and tyrosine.   In addition he demonstrated the autolytic nature of the changes that occur in leukemic blood after death (see also "Autolysis in Leukemia," Chap. iii).   Most observers have failed to find *albumose* in the urine in leukemia.   Because of the involvement of the bone marrow, small amounts of Bence-Jones protein, as well as Mörner's body, may be found in the urine.[22]   Kolisch and Burián[23] not only found nucleoprotein constantly, and albumose frequently, but in one case of lymphatic leukemia they found histon in the urine, which undoubtedly came from nucleoprotein decomposition.

The oxidase reaction is conspicuous in certain of the cells of myeloid leukemia, especially the large, non-granular cells of acute leukemia,[24] but it is not known that these oxidases influence the chemistry of the disease.   In spite of the richness of leucocytes in lipases the serum shows no increased lipolytic activity.[25]

Protein Metabolism.—Stejskal and Erben[26] studied the metabolism of a case of myelogenous and of a case of lymphatic leukemia, and found the nitrogen loss much greater in the myelogenous form, although food-absorption was better than in the lymphatic; they consider that protein-destroying forces are at work in myelogenous leukemia, similar to those of cancer cachexia, so that nitrogenous equilibrium cannot be attained.

As the most characteristic products of decomposition of nucleoproteins are the purine bases, one would also expect to find them present in leukemia, and early writers mention the finding of purine bases and uric acid in the blood and spleen. The urinary findings in this respect have been very variable.   Ebstein[27] observed the complication of leukemia with gout which he considered a coincidence, and also noted uric-acid concretions in the urinary passages in four cases.   Numerous other authors have described increased uric-acid elimination, while some have observed increase in the purine bases, either with or without uric-acid increase. Magnus-Levy[28] observed a particularly large uric-acid output in acute leukemias,

[18] Arch. Int. Med., 1913 (12), 637.
[19] For literature see Erben, Zeit. f. Heilk. (Int. Med. Abt.), 1903 (24), 70.
[20] Jochmann and Ziegler, Münch. med. Woch., 1906 (53), 2093.
[21] Hofmeister's Beitr., 1903 (4), 442; Deut. med. Woch., 1905 (31), 183.
[22] Boggs and Guthrie, Bull. Johns Hopkins Hosp., 1913 (24), 368.
[23] Zeit. klin. Med., 1896 (29), 374 (literature on albuminuria in leukemia).
[24] Dunn, Quart. Jour. Med., 1913 (6), 293.
[25] Caro, Zeit. klin. Med., 1913 (78), 286.
[26] Zeit. f. klin. Med., 1900 (39), 151.
[27] For literature see résumé by Walz in Cent. f. Pathol., 1901 (12), 985.
[28] Virchow's Arch., 1898 (152), 107.

but also found that the relation be,ween the number of leucocytes and the uric acid is extremely variable. Sometimes the nitrogen loss is very great—even as much as 20 gm. per day—and, corresponding with the destruction of nucleoproteins and the resulting uric-acid formation, phosphoric-acid excretion is often greatly increased—even up to 15 gm. per day. On the other hand, the results obtained by many other writers have been in every respect extremely variable; some have found no increase in uric acid, some even report a decrease; likewise the P_2O_5 has been found even less than normal. For example, in a carefully studied case of lymphatic leukemia, Henderson and Edwards[29] found during six months no excessive excretion of uric acid or phosphoric acid. Zalesky and Erben found likewise no considerable increase in the uric acid in lymphatic leukemia, but in myelogenous leukemia the uric acid was much increased; on the other hand, the amount of elimination of purine bases was reversed in the two forms, and creatin was decreased in both. Lipstein[30] found no excessive elimination of amino-acids even in myelogenous leukemia. An increase in calcium is quite constantly observed, and attributed to the bone destruction[26] occurring in this disease.

Undoubtedly these variations in results depend upon the known fluctuations in the course of the pathological processes of leukemia; the number of leucocytes, the size of the lymphatic organs, and the general condition of the patient all vary greatly from time to time, often with remarkable rapidity, and the excretion of products of metabolic activity must vary likewise. It can hardly be questioned that the enormous increase in the amount of lymphoid tissue in the body and blood must give rise to a greatly increased nuclein catabolism, with consequent appearance of its products (uric acid, purine bases, and phosphoric acid) in the urine. This seems to be well demonstrated by the increased elimination of uric acid and purine bases, together with a general increase in the nitrogen output that has been frequently observed following the therapeutic use of x-rays in leukemia, which is attributed to the increased autolysis that x-rays are known to produce. Radium has a similar effect, increasing enormously the urinary total nitrogen, urea, ammonia, less markedly the uric acid, but especially the phosphates.[31]

According to Rosenstern[32] the x-rays affect chiefly the leucogenic tissues rather than the adult leucocytes. Lipstein also found an excessive elimination of amino-acids, in the urine of leukemic patients treated by x-rays.[33] According to Curschmann and Gaupp,[34] the blood of leukemic patients who have been exposed to x-rays contains a specific *leucocytotoxin*, which may be produced by a process of autoimmunization against the leucocytic substance set free by the disintegrated leucocytes. Capps and Smith[35] have obtained similar results. X-rays seem not to alter the total metabolism appreciably.[36]

Charcot's crystals (also called Charcot-Leyden and Charcot-Neumann crystals) represent a peculiar and striking product of nuclear destruction that has frequently been found associated with leukemia. These crystals were first observed by Robin[37](1853) in leukemic tissues, but have been named after Charcot, who, with Robin, described their properties. They were described by Charcot as colorless, refractile, elongated octahedra; insoluble in alcohol, ether, and glycerol; soluble in hot water, acids, and alkalies; size variable, from 0.016 by 0.005 mm. up. These crystals have been found not only in the tissues and blood of cadavers, but

[29] Amer. Jour. of Physiol., 1903 (9), 417.
[30] Hofmeister's Beitr., 1905 (7), 527.
[31] Knudson and Erdos, Boston Med. Surg. Jour., 1917 (176), 503.
[32] Münch. med. Woch., 1906 (53), 1063.
[33] Literature on effects of x-rays in leukemia, see Arneth, Berl. klin. Woch., 1905 (42), 1204; Musser and Edsall, Univ. of Penn. Med. Bull., 1905 (18), 174; Rosenberger, Münch. med. Woch., 1906 (53), 209; Williams, Biochem. Jour., 1906 (1), 249; Lossen and Morawitz, Deut. Arch. klin. Med., 1905 (83), 288; Königer, Deut. Arch. klin. Med., 1906 (87), 31.
[34] Münch. med. Woch., 1905 (52), 2409.
[35] Jour. Exp. Med., 1907 (9), 51; see also Klieneberger u. Zoeppritz, Münch. med. Woch., 1906 (53), No. 18; Milchner u. Wolff, Berl. klin. Woch., 1906 (43), No. 23.
[36] Arch. Int. Med., 1917 (19), 890.
[37] Literature given by v. Leyden, Festschrift für Salkowski, Berlin, 1904, p. 1.

also occasionally in the freshly drawn blood of leukemics. Poehl[38] believes them to be the same as Böttcher's *spermin crystals*, and derived from decomposed nucleins. Schreiner considers that these spermin crystals are phosphoric acid salts of spermin (C_2H_5N), or, as Majert and Schmidt give it, $C_4H_{10}N_2$, with the structure $HN <^{CH_2-CH_2}_{CH_2-CH_2}> NH$, thus being similar to, although not identical with, *piperazin*. The entire question of the composition of spermin is still unsettled,[39] however; and it is probable, furthermore, that the crystals found in leukemia are not identical with the crystals observed in semen.

Crystals that appear similar are also found in asthmatic sputum, empyema, and ascites fluid, bone-marrow, and tumors, and it has been suggested that they are derived from or related to the oxyphile granules of the eosinophiles.[40] This view implies an agreement with Gumprecht's opinion that the crystals seen in bone-marrow, asthmatic sputum, etc., are not spermin, but of protein nature. As can be seen, the nature and significance of Charcot's crystals are, at the present time, quite undetermined.

Summary.—The chemical changes observed in leukemia depend upon the excessive quantity of leucocytes and lymphoid tissue, which undergo processes of disintegration at irregular intervals, with the result that the products of nucleoprotein destruction (uric acid, purine bases, and phosphoric acid) appear in the urine in increased quantities. As the large neutrophiles contain abundant autolytic enzymes, the products of cell autolysis (proteoses, amino-acids, and products of nucleoprotein destruction) may appear at times in the urine and in the blood; because of the small amount of such enzymes in the lymphocytes, these changes are all much less marked in lymphatic leukemia. Charcot's crystals, which are perhaps derived from leucocytic nucleoproteins, may be found in the blood and tissues. The changes in the red cells are chiefly those of a secondary anemia, with occasionally some chlorotic features. The chemical findings of leukemia throw no light whatever upon the cause of the disease.

Pseudoleukemia and Hodgkin's disease show only the evidences of a secondary anemia, without the chemical changes of either leukemia or pernicious anemia. There seems to have been little study of the chemical processes of these diseases. Moraczewski[41] reports a study of metabolism in one case, designated by him as pseudoleukemia and so quoted in subsequent literature, although the only leucocyte count mentioned in the original article was 171,000. This case showed some retention of nitrogen and calcium, with little change in the phosphorus and purine bases in the urine.

HYPEREMIA

ACTIVE HYPEREMIA

This condition is associated with but few chemical changes. Certain chemicals may cause active hyperemia; some locally, as in the

[38] Deut. med. Woch., 1895 (21), 475.
[39] Literature, see Hammarsten, Amer. Transl., 1901, p. 420.
[40] Literature, see Floderer, Wien. klin. Woch., 1903 (16), 276; Predtetschensky, Zeit. klin. Med., 1906 (59), 29.
[41] Virchow's Arch., 1898 (151), 22.

case of irritants, such as alcohol, ether, ammonia, mustard, etc., which
act neither by producing a local vasodilator stimulus or by paralyzing
the vasoconstrictors. Other substances may produce active hyperemia in special vascular areas, e. g., cantharides causes active hyperemia
in the kidneys, probably because of its elimination through these
organs; pilocarpin causes active hyperemia in the salivary glands and
skin, which is associated with increased function. In general, functional activity is associated with active hyperemia, and Gaskell[42] has
suggested that this is due to atonicity of the vascular muscle, the result
of decreased alkalinity of the lymph flowing away from the active organ
along the vessel-walls, it having been found that alkalies cause a tonic
contraction and acids an atonic dilation of arterial muscle. [43]

Pathological active hyperemia is seldom of long enough duration
to lead to any alterations in the tissues in which it occurs. The blood
itself remains unchanged, except that the venous blood going from the
part contains much less CO_2 and more oxygen than usual, because
more oxygen is brought to the tissues than can be used.[44]

PASSIVE HYPEREMIA

Passive hyperemia is almost equally unassociated with chemical
changes, especially in its etiology, as it depends solely upon mechanical factors. Some chemical alterations result, however, from the
changes in the stagnating blood, which may, if the obstruction to outflow is severe, become of venous character in the capillaries of the congested area. Oxidation in the tissues is, therefore, impaired, and some
fatty changes may result, e. g., in the center of congested liver lobules.
Waste products accumulate, and possibly noxious products of metabolism are formed under lack of oxidation; either from these causes or
solely from pressure and lack of nutrition there is a tendency to atrophy
of the more specialized parenchymatous cells, and a proliferation of
connective tissues. The atrophy of parenchyma is seen particularly
in the liver, the increase of connective tissue in the spleen.[45] In the
kidney neither atrophy nor stroma proliferations are pronounced, but
the renal function is greatly impaired, since it depends upon the
amount and quality of the blood brought to the kidney.[46] Whether
connective-tissue proliferation in hyperemia depends upon overnutri-
tion or upon irritation by waste-products, or is compensatory to parenchymatous atrophy, may be looked upon as still an open question.

[42] Quoted by Lazarus-Barlow, "Manual of General Pathology," 1904, p.126.
[43] See discussion by Woolley, Jour. Amer. Med. Assoc., 1914 (63), 2279; and
by Adler, Jour. Pharm., 1916 (8), 297.
[44] Polycythemia (Vaquez-Osler disease) is accompanied by an increase in the
total nitrogen of the blood, in proportion to the number of erythrocytes; but the
nitrogen content of the individual erythrocyte is decreased. (v. Jaksch. Zent.
inn. Med., 1912 (33), 397).
[45] See Christian, Jour. Amer. Med. Assoc., 1905 (45), 1615.
[46] See Rowntree and Geraghty, Arch. Int. Med., 1913 (11), 121; Nonnenbruch,
Deut. Arch. klin. Med., 1913 (110), 162.

Probably only the first two factors apply to the connective-tissue growth observed in the congested spleen, the clubbing of the fingers in congenital heart disease, or the thickening of the subcutaneous tissues in passive congestion of the lower extremities.

Changes in the Blood.—Venous blood differs from arterial, not only in its increased load of CO_2 and other waste products, but also in other ways. Venous blood generally clots less readily than arterial blood.[47] It contains more diffusible alkali because the CO_2 combines with and tears away part of the bases that are held by the proteins, especially in the corpuscles, and so alkaline carbonates are formed and enter the plasma. Blood from the jugular vein on this account contains 20–25 per cent. more diffusible alkali than carotid blood (Hamburger).[48] Since the bactericidal power of the blood has been shown to increase directly with the alkalinity, this property may be of importance in pathology. For example, the relative infrequency of infections in the right side of the heart may not depend solely upon lessened liability to endocardial damage, as generally considered, but is possibly due in part to the greater bactericidal power of venous blood. The same property probably explains the favorable results obtained in the treatment of local infections by artificially produced passive congestion.[49] Too severe a stasis, with resultant edema, probably favors local infection.[50]

v. Fodor[51] found that animals surviving infections show an increased blood alkalinity, whereas in those that died, the alkalinity was decreased; also, he found the resistance increased by intravenous injections of alkalies. Other observers[52] have noted a decrease in resistance after injecting acids into the blood. According to Calabrese, the alkalinity of the blood increases in immunization of animals against toxins, while Cantani found the injection of toxin followed by a decrease in alkalinity. Hamburger has shown that the bactericidal power of the blood may be increased *in vitro* by shaking it with CO_2 as a result of the increased alkalinity, aided, perhaps, by some slight bactericidal power of the CO_2 itself; he also found the blood more strongly bactericidal in venous congestion than normally, and the lymph from a congested part was also found more strongly bactericidal than normal lymph. Hamburger[53] has also found, however, that chemotaxis is, if anything, slightly decreased under the influence of CO_2, as also is phagocytosis; large amounts of CO_2 may

[47] Vierordt (Arch. f. Heilk., 1878 (19), 193) found coagulation faster in the blood in passive congestion than in normal venous blood; but Hasebrock (Zeit. f. Biol., 1882 (18), 41) found that if the stasis is protracted, the coagulation becomes delayed because of the excess of CO_2.

[48] Virchow's Arch., 1899 (156), 329; also, "Osmotischer Druck und Ionenlehre."

[49] See Bier, "Hyperæmie als Heilmittel," Leipsic, 1903.

[50] Glasewald, Cent. Grenz. Med. Chir., 1915 (18), 507.

[51] Cent. f. Bakt., 1890 (7), 753.

[52] Literature, see Hamburger (loc. cit.[48]), p. 281

[53] Virchow's Arch., 1899 (156), 329.

reduce the phagocytic power for coal particles by 25–50 per cent. Hamburger's results as to the bactericidal power of human blood in venous stasis have been confirmed by Laqueur.[54] Schiller ascribes this not to increased alkalinity, but to disintegration of leucocytes with liberation of bactericidal substances.[55]

The blood in the veins and capillaries in passive congestion is generally richer in corpuscles than normal, perhaps because of some loss of water,[56] although this is not constant, applying particularly to more recent or more local processes; in long-continued stasis, as in congenital heart disease, the blood may be diluted.[57] In the concentrated blood of passive congestion the corpuscles may number six to eight millions per cubic millimeter, while the concentration of the solids of the serum may be at the same time reduced (Krehl). The viscosity of such blood is higher than that of normal blood.[58] In acute stasis the proportion of serum proteins, especially the albumin, increases with the duration of the stasis; no changes occur in the nonprotein constituents of the blood (Rowe).[59]

THROMBOSIS

The chemistry of thrombosis in most respects resolves itself into the chemistry of fibrin formation, a subject which is so extensively considered in most treatises on physiological chemistry and physiology that it does not seem desirable to give here anything more than the essential principles involved in the clotting of the blood, as now understood, as an introduction to the consideration of the same process as it occurs under pathological conditions. In spite of innumerable investigations, our knowledge of the actual participants and processes involved in the formation of fibrin is in a very unsatisfactory and fragmentary state. Some facts seem well established, however, and we have a general idea of the subject that may be applied with advantage to the consideration of thrombosis.

FIBRIN FORMATION[60]

Several different substances seem to be concerned in the formation of fibrin, of which the first of importance is its antecedent, *fibrinogen*. Fibrinogen is a simple protein, related to the globulins, and differing chiefly in its ready coagulability, not only by fibrin ferment, but also by heat, salts, and other coagulating agencies. By itself, however, it shows no tendency to coagulate spontaneously. According to Goodpasture,[61] fibrinogen is formed through the combined activity

[54] Zeit. exp. Path. u. Therap., 1905 (1), 670.
[55] Beitr. klin. Chir., 1913 (84), H. 1.
[56] Grawitz, Deut. Arch. f. klin. Med., 1895 (54), 588.
[57] See Krehl, "Pathologische Physiologie," 1901, p. 201.
[58] Determann, Zeit. klin. Med., 1906 (59), H. 2–4.
[59] Jour. Lab. Clin. Med., 1916 (1), 485.
[60] For literature and full discussion see Hammarsten's or Mathew's Physiological Chemistry; Morawitz, Ergebnisse der Physiol., Abt. 1, 1901 (4), 307, and Handbuch d. Biochem., 1908 II (2), 40; Leo Loeb, Biochem. Centr., 1907 (6), 829; Howell, Harvey Lectures, 1917.
[61] Amer. Jour. Physiol., 1914 (33), 70.

of the liver and intestines, although earlier writers have variously described its formation in the bone marrow, leucocytes, liver or intestines. The amount of fibrinogen present in the blood is actually quite small, the fibrin formed in normal clotting being but 0.1 to 0.4 per cent. of the weight of the blood. Acted upon by the fibrin-ferment, it yields the characteristic insoluble protein fibrin, in crystalline form under favorable conditions,[62] but we do not know definitely what changes the fibrinogen undergoes in this process. Fibrin resembles in its insolubility the proteins coagulated by heat, alcohol, etc., but when kept aseptically for some time, it becomes again dissolved; this process of *fibrinolysis* probably depends upon proteolytic enzymes, which fibrin, in common with other substances of similar physical nature, has the property of dragging out of solution and holding firmly. Undoubtedly entangled leucocytes are also an important factor in the fibrinolysis,[63] which is greatly increased in phosphorus poisoning and when the liver is excluded from the circulation, a fact suggesting that the liver may form inhibiting substances.

Theories of Fibrin Formation.—The great problem is the nature and the place and manner of origin of the fibrin-forming enzyme, generally called *fibrin-ferment* (also *plasmase*, *thrombin* and *coagulin*). The most fundamental theory of the origin and nature of fibrin-ferment is that of Alexander Schmidt, which may be briefly described as follows: The ferment, Schmidt believed, exists in the plasma in an inactive (*prozyme* or *zymogen*) form, which he called *prothrombin* Upon disintegration of the leucocytes there is set free a substance, which, acting upon the prothrombin, converts it into the active thrombin; this activating agent Schmidt designated as the *zymoplastic* substance. With various modifications this stands to the present day as a basic theory.

It having been shown that calcium facilitates the formation of fibrin, Pekelharing advanced the idea that the prothrombin does not exist in the plasma, but is liberated from the leucocytes, and, combining with the calcium of the plasma, forms the thrombin. Morawitz considers three substances necessary for the formation of thrombin. (1) the *prothrombin* or *thrombogen*, which he believes originates in the blood-plates; (2) the *zymoplastic substance* or *thrombokinase*, which is liberated from the leucocytes into the plasma; (3) calcium salts. Howell,[64] however, explains coagulation as follows: Circulating blood normally contains all the necessary factors for fibrin formation, *i. e.*, fibrinogen, prothrombin and calcium. But there is also present an inhibiting substance, *antithrombin*,[65] which prevents the calcium from activating the prothrombin into thrombin. In shed blood there appears a *thromboplastin*, derived from the platelets or the tissues, which neutralizes the antithrombin and thus permits thrombin to form. Rettger[66] holds that the coagulation of the blood is not a true enzyme action at all, while Bordet and Delange[67] consider that thrombin is formed by the interaction of *cytozyme* from the platelets or tissue cells, and *serozyme* of the plasma. Mathews follows Woolridge and considers the clotting of the blood as essentially the crystallization of a phospholipin-protein compound, blood plasma, the stability of which compound is easily upset in many ways. The fibrin threads are essentially liquid crystals coming out of a saturated solution, the blood plasma, which is practically a dilute protoplasm. It will not serve our purpose, however, to go further into the hypotheses and disputes over these questions, which are detailed more fully in the literature previously cited, but it may be stated that numerous American observers have found Howell's theory to fit well with both experimental and clinical observations on the variations in the coagulability of the blood.

The question has been raised as to whether the leucocytes or platelets secrete their fibrin-forming constituent (be it thrombokinase or prothrombin is a matter

[62] See Howell, Amer. Jour. Physiol., 1914 (35), 143; Hekma, Internat. Zeit. physik. chem. Biol., 1915 (2), 279.
[63] See Morawitz, *loc. cit.*; also Rulot, Arch. internat. d. Physiol., 1904 (1), 152.
[64] Amer. Jour. Physiol., 1911 (29), 187.
[65] The antithrombin is formed by the action of a phosphatid from the liver (*heparin*) upon a pro-antithrombin (Howell and Holt, Amer. Jour. Physiol., 1918 (47), 328).
[66] Amer. Jour. Physiol., 1909 (24), 406.
[67] Ann. Inst. Pasteur., 1912 (26), 657. See also Lee and Vincent, Arch. Int. Med., 1914 (13), 398.

of minor importance to the pathologist) or liberate it only after their disintegration. As far as pathological processes go, the latter seems to be the case, the disintegration apparently occurring whenever the leucocytes come in contact with a foreign body or with dead and injured tissues. The stroma of red corpuscles also contains thrombokinase.[68] Of the substances that may be isolated from tissues, *cephalin* is found especially active in producing thrombosis, and may be related to or identical with the thromboplastin.[69]

Tissue Coagulins.—Among the other points that are of importance in pathological conditions is the fact that not only the leucocytes, but also tissue-cells, can liberate fibrin-forming substances (*coagulins* is the non-committal term applied by Loeb). Howell considers that the effect of the tissue "coagulins" is merely to neutralize the antithrombin of the blood, if such coagulins actually exist; possibly there is thromboplastin in the tissues. These coagulating agents are present in tissue extracts and are liberated whenever the tissues are injured; muscle is rich in coagulin, as are also the liver and kidney, and, which is particularly important, the blood-vessel wall (L. Loeb). Pieces of these tissues placed in contact with fibrinogen solution will bring about prompt clotting. Another important fact is that the coagulins, whether derived from leucocytes or from the tissues, have a certain degree of specificity—that is, they act solely or most rapidly with fibrinogen of blood of the species from which they are obtained.[70] In some instances this specificity is absolute, but more generally (particularly in the mammalia) it is only relative. Loeb also found that the amount of tissue coagulin was not decreased in organs altered by phosphorus poisoning, although during experimental autolysis the coagulins disappear. When tissue coagulins and blood coagulins act together, the effect is greater than the sum of their independent actions, indicating the probability that they combine in some way to produce a particularly active coagulin. The blood coagulins are quite different from the tissue coagulins in many important respects, and the coagulins cannot be looked upon as a single substance of different origins.

Blood-platelets.—It is still undetermined just what part the platelets play in coagulation. The well-known observation that in thrombosis the fibrin is often first formed about masses of platelets clinging to the wall of the vessel indicates that they participate in the process, and Bizzozero and others have maintained that the platelets and not the leucocytes are the source of the prothrombin. Numerous studies on the relation of the platelets to disease conditions have indicated a certain parallelism between their number and the tendency to coagulation observed in the various diseases (Welch). Howell believes the platelets to be the chief source of thromboplastin, which neutralizes the antithrombin of the blood and thus causes clotting. Wright and Minot[71] find that a viscous metamorphosis of the platelets is intimately associated with the early stages of coagulation. Bordet and Delange consider the platelets of more importance than the leucocytes in producing participants of the coagulating mechanism. The histological evidence of the importance of the platelets in thrombus formation is conclusive (see Zurhelle, Derewenko), and Cramer and Pringle[72] state that coagulation cannot occur without platelets. However, the blood of fishes, birds and reptiles clots although no platelets are found in these animals. Human thoracic lymph also is devoid of platelets yet it clots; but it may contain products of platelet disintegration to explain this clotting (Jordan).[73] Kemp[71] concludes, from a thorough review of the subject, that the blood-platelets are usually normal or subnormal in number during acute infectious diseases, but increase rapidly if the disease terminates by crisis; in pernicious anemia the number is always greatly diminished, although in secondary anemias they may sometimes be increased; in *purpura hæmorrhagica* the number of plates is enormously diminished, which is

[68] Barratt, Jour. Path. and Bact., 1913 (17), 303.
[69] Howell, Amer. Jour. Physiol., 1912 (31), 1; MacLean, *ibid.*, 1916 (41), 250; 1917 (43), 586.
[70] Leo Loeb, Univ. of Penn. Med. Bull., 1901 (16), 382; Muraschew, Deut. Arch. klin. Med., 1904 (80), 187.
[71] Jour. Exp. Med., 1917 (26), 395.
[72] Quart. Jour. Exper. Physiol., 1913 (6), 1.
[73] Anat. Rec., 1918 (15), 37.
[74] Jour. Amer. Med. Assoc., 1906 (46), 1022.

perhaps related to the slowness of the clotting of the blood in this condition. Duke[75] states that when the platelet count falls below 10,000 per cubic mm. there is delayed coagulation and a tendency to purpura; with counts above 40,000 there is usually no hemorrhagic tendency.[75a] If the platelet count is reduced artificially (by benzene, diphtheria toxin) a similar purpuric tendency is observed. Poisons that in large doses reduce the platelet count, will increase it if in small doses.

Calcium Salts.—The exact significance of calcium in fibrin formation is still unsettled. Blood from which the calcium has been precipitated will not coagulate, and the addition of calcium salts will promptly cause it to do so. The various hypotheses advanced to explain the way in which calcium influences the clotting process are not in agreement. One hypothesis is that the calcium ions are necessary for the transformation of prothrombin into thrombin (Pekelharing, Hammarsten, Morawitz), the thrombin consisting of a compound of prothrombin, calcium salts, and thrombokinase. Howell considers that no kinase is necessary, the calcium activating the prothrombin whenever it is not inhibited by antithrombin.

Modification of Coagulability.—If blood is drawn into a glass vessel well coated with oil or vaseline, through a cannula similarly protected, no coagulation will take place; but if any unoiled foreign substance enters, even particles of dust, coagulation begins at once. The explanation is that the leucocytes do not liberate their coagulating substances until they have been injured by contact with some foreign body, and the experiment proves the importance of this action of the leucocytes, as well as explaining why the blood does not coagulate during life. The classical experiment of the ligation of a vein without injury to the endothelium, which permits the blood to remain stagnant for a long period without clotting, depends upon the same fact, namely, that normal endothelium neither liberates coagulin itself nor injures the leucocytes so that they disintegrate. Loeb recalls the observation of Overton that lipoids are important constituents of the cell membranes, and suggests a similarity between the vessel lining and the oiled cannula, but analyses of aortic endothelium have shown a rather low lipin content (8.41–9.25 per cent.), although peritoneal endothelium has much more (13 to 15 per cent.).[76] The suggestion that the vessel walls contain an *anti-coagulin* could not be confirmed by Loeb. Since leucocytes are constantly undergoing disintegration in the blood and tissues under normal conditions, it might be asked why they do not cause clotting then and there. In explanation Loeb advances his observation that the coagulins are destroyed during cell autolysis, and suggests that when leucocytes normally disintegrate, the coagulins are first destroyed by autolysis. It has also been shown that the cells and serum contain substances which inhibit or prevent coagulation, and it is possible that these play an important part under normal conditions in preventing coagulation by products of cell

[75] Jour. Exp. Med., 1911 (14), 265; Arch. Int. Med., 1912 (10), 445; Jour. Amer. Med. Assoc., 1915 (65), 1600.
[75a] Gram (Arch. Int. Med., 1920 (25), 325) states that platelet counts below 100,000 generally accompany a tendency to bleed. He gives the normal figure as 200,000 to 500,000, but usually over 300,000.
[76] Tait, Quart. Jour. Exp. Physiol., 1915 (8), 391.

disintegration, much as other antienzymes are supposed to act in preventing autodigestion of living cells.

Coagulation of drawn blood may be *retarded* experimentally by removal of the calcium by precipitation as oxalate, fluoride, etc.; also by diminishing the oxygen and increasing the CO_2, by addition of solutions of neutral salts in large amounts, by diluting greatly with water, or by keeping the blood cold. Bile salts retard coagulation markedly, by interfering with the conversion of fibrinogen into fibrin.[77] Coagulation may be hastened by moderate heat, by whipping, exposure to air, by contact with much foreign matter, and by the addition of watery extracts from many different tissues and organs. Poisons that destroy the platelets reduce the coagulation (Duke). Of particular interest pathologically is the retardation of coagulation that follows injections of proteoses (the so-called "peptone" solutions) and also various other protein-containing solutions, such as organ extracts, bacterial toxins, snake venoms, eel serum, extract of leeches or of *Uncinaria*, impure nucleo-protein solutions, or solutions of various colloids. Most of these substances *e. g.*, peptone, eel serum, cause reduction of coagulability when injected into animals, and are without effect on blood removed from the body. A few, however, prevent coagulation of drawn blood (snake venom, extract of leeches). When substances of the first class are injected in sufficient quantities, there occurs first a period of accelerated coagulation which may, particularly in the case of organ extracts, cause prompt death from intravascular clotting; if the animal survives, there follows a period of decrease or total inhibition of coagulability of the blood, both within the vessels and after removal from the body. The first period of increased coagulability undoubtedly depends upon the formation of a large amount of fibrin-ferment, but it has not yet been satisfactorily explained how the inhibition of coagulation is produced. Apparently the fibrin-ferment formed at first is rapidly destroyed, but it is thought by some that it is converted into a substance that neutralizes the fibrin-ferment that may be formed later, or that a true anticoagulin is formed. It is also among the possibilities that all the available prothrombin or thrombokinase is used up during the first stage of acceleration. As before mentioned, the blood and tissues contain substances that inhibit coagulation, and it may be that these are secreted in excessive amounts, a view which is receiving much support from recent observations. According to Davis[77a] injection of thrombin is followed quickly by an increase in the amount of antithrombin in the blood. It has been found that in animals deprived of the liver no coagulation-inhibiting substances are formed in the blood after injection of proteoses, hence Delezenne believes that the substances of this class act by causing a destruction of leucocytes, thus liberating a

[77] Haessler and Stebbins, Jour. Exp. Med., 1919 (29), 445.
[77a] Amer. Jour. Physiol., 1911 (29), 160.

substance which increases coagulation and also another substance retarding coagulation; the first of these is destroyed by the liver, leaving the retarding substance to act unopposed.[78] Leech extract (*hirudin*) prevents clotting by means of an antiferment action, combining with the thrombin.[79] Snake venom, however, acts upon the thrombokinase (Morawitz).

Coagulability of the Blood in Disease.—In disease the alterations in the coagulability of the blood depend upon much the same factors. In all conditions associated with suppuration and leucocytosis the amount of fibrinogen is increased. This is especially true of pneumonia.[80] The fluidity of the blood in septicemia is probably dependent upon the appearance of the coagulation-inhibiting phase that follows the action of the products of cell destruction, including among them proteoses. In this connection should be mentioned the observation of Conradi,[81] who found that among the products of autolysis is a coagulation-inhibiting substance which is not destroyed by heat, diffuses readily, and in general behaves unlike the proteins. This or similar substances may well play a part in affecting coagulation in infectious diseases, and Whipple[82] has found a decreased coagulability in septicemia because of the presence of an excess of antithrombin. It may also be mentioned that animals soon acquire an immunity against proteoses, so that their inhibiting influence is no longer shown. This corresponds to the observation of Kanthack[83] that immune serum against venom neutralizes very effectively the anticoagulating principle of venom; an amount of antiserum altogether insufficient to neutralize the toxic properties of venom will neutralize its property of preventing clotting. The bacterial products may also modify coagulation, and L. Loeb[84] has found that different organisms are unequally effective in this respect, *Staphylococcus aureus* being much more powerful in causing coagulation than any others tested;[85] typhoid, diphtheria, tubercle, and xerosis bacilli and streptococci being without any apparent effect, while pyocyaneus, prodigiosus, and colon bacilli occupy an intermediate position. Furthermore, after the organisms are killed by boiling, this effect is greatly reduced, showing that it does not depend merely upon the mechanical action of the bacteria, but probably upon bacterial products contained in the culture-media.

[78] The manner in which gelatin injections affect the blood coagulability is not yet understood (see Boggs, Deut. Arch. klin. Med., 1904 (79), 539); Moll (Wien. klin. Woch., 1903 (16), 1215) found an increase in fibrinogen.
[79] Hirudin may contain antikinase (Mellanby, Jour. of Physiol., 1909 (38), 441).
[80] Dochez, Jour. Exp. Med., 1912 (16), 693.
[81] Hofmeister's Beitr., 1901 (1), 137.
[82] Arch. Int. Med., 1912 (9), 365.
[83] Cited by Lazarus-Barlow, p. 141.
[84] Jour. Med. Research, 1903 (10), 407.
[85] Much (Biochem. Zeit., 1908 (14), 143) states that staphylococcus contains thrombokinase.

After phosphorus poisoning the blood may become non-coagulable, which Jacoby[86] ascribed to an absence of fibrinogen in the blood, because of a fibrinogen-destroying ferment in the liver. Doyon[87] has made a similar finding in chloroform necrosis of the liver, but he attributes especial importance to an excess of antithrombin liberated from the liver in these conditions. Whipple has also found a decrease in fibrinogen with chloroform necrosis and cirrhosis of the liver.[88] In other instances of decreased coagulability the fibrinogen is present, generally in normal amounts. After death the blood becomes incoagulable because the fibrinogen is destroyed through a process similar to that of fibrinolysis;[89] this fibrinolysis may be complete as early as ten hours after death. The other proteins of the blood do not seem to be correspondingly attacked. Thrombokinase is also scanty in cadaver blood, but there seem to be no coagulation-inhibiting substances present. In anaphylactic shock the coagulability is reduced or abolished, associated with which is a leucopenia.[90]

Whipple[91] states that the antithrombin-prothrombin balance in the blood is in delicate equilibrium, but preserved by strong factors of safety. The prothrombin factor is rarely involved, most notably in melena neonatorum and aplastic anemia, and such conditions may be relieved by injecting normal blood, through the added prothrombin. The antithrombin factor is often excessive in hemorrhagic conditions, especially with hepatic injury, or it may be lowered and lead to thrombosis from relatively slight injuries. Obviously the injection of normal blood will harm rather than help patients with hemorrhage due to excessive antithrombin. Antithrombin is often found increased in diseases of the blood-forming organs, e. g., leukemia, possibly as a reaction to the products of disintegration of corpuscles; and hence hemorrhagic tendencies are noted in these diseases. In icterus the notable tendency to hemorrhage seems to depend upon the binding of the calcium of the blood by the bile pigments,[92] and administration of calcium may bring the coagulation time back to normal with a corresponding decrease in the hemorrhagic tendency.

Pfeiffer[93] estimated the fibrin content of the blood in disease, and found it increased in diseases with leucocytosis (pneumonia, rheumatism, erysipelas, scarlet fever), except leukemia, where it was normal;

[86] Zeit. physiol. Chem., 1900 (30), 175; also Doyon *et al.*, Compt. Rend. Soc. Biol., 1905 (58), 493.
[87] Compt. Rend. Soc. Biol., 1905 (58), 704; Jour. phys. et path., 1912 (14), 229.
[88] Bull. Johns Hopkins Hosp., 1913 (24), 207.
[89] Morawitz, Hofmeister's Beitr., 1906 (8), 1.
[90] The incoagulability of menstrual blood is ascribed to a lack of fibrin ferment by Bell (Jour. Path. and Bact., 1914 (18), 462) and to an excess of antithrombin by Dienst (Münch. med. Woch., 1912 (51), 2799).
[91] Arch. Int. Med., 1913 (12), 637.
[92] Lee and Vincent, Arch. Int. Med., 1915 (16), 59.
[93] Zeit. klin. Med., 1897 (33), 214; Cent. f. inn. Med., 1898 (19), 1.

21

in diseases without leucocytosis (typhoid, malaria, nephritis), the fibrin was normal in amount. Stassano and Billon[94] have, furthermore, shown that the amount of fibrin-ferment varies directly with the number of leucocytes in the blood. Kollmann[95] found an increase in the fibrin of eclampsia, which Lewinski[96] could not substantiate. In experimental infections of animals Langstein and Mayer[97] found a specific increase in pneumococcus sepsis, which undoubtedly bears an important relation both to the characteristic fibrinous nature of the alveolar exudate in pneumonia, and the striking amount of fibrin found in pneumococcus pleuritis, peritonitis, etc. Mathews[98] found an increase in the fibrin with all experimental suppurations.

The **coagulation time** determined by different methods, in which different conditions for coagulation are presented, varies from 2 to 30 minutes; with most methods it is 5 to 8 minutes.[99] In general, coagulability is not constantly if at all altered by fever, cancer, diabetes, slight secondary anemias, or many other diseases, and in normal conditions it remains fairly constant. In infants the coagulation time is slightly shorter than in adults. The coagulation is hastened after considerable hemorrhages, in endocarditis, and perhaps in aneurism and thrombosis; and is commonly delayed in the acute exanthemata, in hemophilia, in *purpura neonatorum*, and occasionally in some other diseases.[1] There is entire lack of agreement concerning the reputed acceleration of coagulation by oral administration of calcium salts, and retardation by citrates; and the supposed thromboplastic influence of gelatin cannot be shown consistently by direct observations. In jaundice, calcium salts probably have an effect, since here the cause of the deficient coagulation seems to be the fixation or precipitation of the blood calcium by the bile pigments. The bile salts also prevent the conversion of fibrinogen into fibrin.[77] It seems probable that the measurement of the time required for coagulation to take place *in vitro* does not exactly represent the tendency of the same blood to coagulate in the body of the person from whom it is obtained; for example, the injection of foreign serum has a notable effect in stopping hemorrhages, but the coagulation time of the recipient's blood is not correspondingly altered. Whipple's observation that with a low fibrinogen content the blood may coagulate in normal time, and yet the clots be too delicate to stop hemorrhage, explains at least part of the discrepancy; and of similar signifiance is the fact that with a very

[94] Compt. Rend. Soc. Biol., 1903 (55), 511.
[95] Cent. f. Gynäk., 1897 (21), 341.
[96] Pflüger's Arch., 1903 (100), 611.
[97] Hofmeister's Beitr., 1903 (5), 69.
[98] Amer. Jour. Physiol., 1899 (3), 53.
[99] Full review and bibliography by Cohen, Arch. Int. Med., 1911 (8), 684 and 820.
[1] See Dochez (Jour. Exp. Med., 1912 (16), 693), who found some delay in coagulation in pneumonia. Corroborated by Minot and Lee, Jour. Amer. Med. Assoc., 1917 (68), 545.

low platelet count the blood may coagulate as rapidly as normal, but the clots do not shrink and become firm (Duke). Hence with a severe *purpura hemorrhagica* we may have a normal clotting time. In other conditions with normal coagulability, hemorrhages may result from excessive fibrinolysis which causes solution of the clot, especially in hepatic diseases. [2]

THE FORMATION OF THROMBI

If we apply the facts brought out in the preceding discussion relative to the factors in the coagulation of blood, to the manner and conditions under which thrombi are formed in the circulating blood, we find explanations for many of the features of thrombosis. Welch[3] describes the steps in the formation of a thrombus after injury to the vessel-wall, as follows: First, there is an accumulation of blood-platelets adhering to the wall at the point of injury. Leucocytes, which may be present in small numbers at the beginning, rapidly increase in number, collecting at the margins of the platelet masses and between them. Not until the leucocytes have accumulated does the fibrin appear. As Welch remarks, these findings afford no conclusive evidence as to whether fibrin-ferment is formed from the leucocytes or from the platelets, but since the fibrin does not appear until after the leucocytes have accumulated, and also since small thrombi may consist solely of platelets without fibrin, it seems probable that the leucocytes must be looked upon as the chief source of the ferment. If the blood is made incoagulable by injection of hirudin, injury to the vessel-walls causes the formation of thrombi composed entirely of platelets (Schwalbe). Sometimes small clots may form without the apparent participation of either platelets or leucocytes. These purely fibrinous thrombi seem to start from injured endothelial cells, particularly in inflammatory conditions, such as pneumonic lungs, and give the impression that the coagulin is derived from the endothelial cells. Zurhelle attributes by far the most important part to the platelets, an opinion shared by many, including Derewenko,[4] who holds that the coagulation of blood with entirely occluded vessels is quite distinct from true thrombosis because of the lack of platelets in stagnant blood.[5] Clots formed in the absence of platelets do not shrink like proper thrombi (Duke).

The process of clotting in the stoppage of hemorrhage offers some

[2] See Goodpasture, Bull. Johns Hopkins Hosp., 1914 (25), 330.
[3] Albutt's System, vol. 6, complete discussion of the general features of thrombosis; also see Küster, Ergeb. inn. Med., 1913 (12), 667; Zurhelle, Ziegler's Beiträge, 1910 (47), 539; Schwalbe, Ergebnisse Pathol., 1907 (XI (2)), 901; Lubarsch, Allg. Pathol., Vol. 1, Wiesbaden, 1905. See Aschoff, Ziegler's Beitr., 1912 (52), 205, and Arch. Int. Med., 1913 (12), 503, concerning the mechanics of thrombus formation.
[4] Ziegler's Beitr., 1910 (48), 123.
[5] Not accepted by Schwalbe, *loc. cit.*[3]

differences from intravascular clotting, in that the coagulins of the tissue-cells also come into play. It is rather difficult to determine how much of the coagulation depends on these, and how much on the coagulins of the leucocytes, for the same conditions that favor liberation of tissue coagulins, *i. e.*, much laceration and destruction of the tissue, also favor the disintegration of leucocytes by offering large areas of surface for contact. Loeb is of the opinion, however, that of the two, the latter factor is the more important. It may be re- called that the joint action of tissue and blood coagulins is greater than the sum of their individual actions, which also must be an im- portant factor in causing clotting in bleeding wounds.

As to the relative importance of stagnation and vessel injury in producing thrombosis, we know that total stasis in an uninjured vessel may not result in thrombosis, and, on the other hand, extensive in- jury or large calcified plaques in the intima of the aorta may also cause no thrombosis because of the rapidity of the blood flow; and, furthermore, clotting may occur even in intact vessels under the influ- ence of substances liberating fibrin-ferment in the blood; *e. g.*, snake venoms, nucleoprotein injections, and possibly in disease. As the red corpuscles contain thromboplastic substances we may have thrombi formed when hemolytic agents are present in relatively stagnant blood, even without injury to the vessel-walls.[6] Presumably the clot- ting does not occur when the stream is rapid, because any fibrin- ferment that may be liberated by injured leucocytes or endothelium is swept away before fibrin can become attached to the vessel-wall; or, according to Howell's hypothesis, because the current brings an excess of antithrombin to the point where the thromboplastin is being formed. Naturally, the combination of an injured vessel-wall, a slow current, and a high coagulability offer the most favorable conditions, and we owe to Welch the appreciation of the fact that in a large pro- portion of all thrombi, even those caused by apparently purely me- chanical agencies (*e. g.*, cardiac incompetence), bacteria are present and probably determine the injury to the vessel-walls and the libera- tion of fibrin-ferment.[7] We have previously referred to L. Loeb's observations on the effect of bacteria in causing coagulation of the blood.

Hyalin thrombi are frequently the cause of extensive degenerative lesions in the viscera, and although commonly formed of red corpuscles, they do not stain at all like normal corpuscles, presumably because a certain proportion of the hemoglobin has been altered or lost through hemolysis. Of particular interest is their reaction to Weigert's fibrin stain, by which they often, but not always, stain intensely, especially when hardened in Zenker's solution; a fact that has been the cause of much confusion in earlier studies. Flexner[8] first appreciated the nature of these thrombi as originating from agglutinated red corpuscles, although Klebs,

[6] Dietrich, Cent. f. Path. (Verhandl.), 1912 (23), 372.
[7] Welch, Venous Thrombosis in Cardiac Disease, Trans. Assoc. Amer. Phys., 1900, vol. 15.
[8] Jour. Med. Research, 1902 (S), 316.

Ziegler, and others had earlier suggested that hyalin thrombi were formed from red corpuscles. Boxmeyer[9] independently arrived at the same conclusion as Flexner, in studying hyalin thrombi as the cause of necrosis in the liver of animals infected with the hog-cholera bacillus. Flexner produced hyalin thrombi by injecting corpuscles agglutinated by ricin, or by injecting ricin itself, or hemolytic substances such as ether or foreign serum. As the thrombi become old, the corpuscles lose their form and color and produce the typical hyalin appearance. Pearce[10] proved conclusively the dependence of the thrombus formation upon agglutination, for he secured the same results, including the liver necrosis, by injecting specific agglutinating serums. He states that fibrin threads may occasionally be found at the periphery of the larger thrombi, but never in the smaller ones. It is extremely probable, from Flexner's observations, that in the thrombosis produced by injecting various toxic substances into the blood, the so-called *"fibrin ferment thrombosis,"* the thrombi are merely agglutinative thrombi, devoid of fibrin; this is undoubtedly true for many of the thrombi observed after poisoning with the powerfully agglutinative snake venoms (see Chap. vi). Bacterial hemagglutinins may also cause the formation of hyalin thrombi.[11] On the other hand, some, at least, of the hyalin capillary thrombi are undoubtedly composed of soft masses of fibrin which have not become fibrillar, although the successful staining by fibrin stain is not final proof of the fibrinous nature of a thrombus. The liver necrosis which follows ether injections in animals is caused by fibrinous thrombi which result from liberation of coagulins by the injured cells (L. Loeb).

Secondary Changes in Thrombi.—The changes that occur in thrombi after they have existed for some time are largely due either to ingrowth of new tissue or to calcification, the latter of which will be considered in a separate chapter. The only other change of interest from the chemical standpoint is the central softening which may occur in any large thrombus, but is particularly often observed in the large globular thrombi found in the heart. The center of the thrombus may be so completely softened that it resembles a sac of pus, the contents, according to Welch, consisting of necrotic fatty leucocytes, albuminous and fatty granules, blood-pigment and altered red corpuscles, and occasionally acicular crystals of fatty acids. Undoubtedly this softening is related to the process of fibrinolysis previously described, and depends upon digestion of the fibrin by leucocytic enzymes,[12] but the fact that the central portion alone undergoes softening is of interest, suggesting that the antibodies for leucocytic proteases, which Opie[13] found present in normal serum, prevent digestion at the surface of the clot. The same fact indicates that the tissue fibrinolysins[14] do not play an active part in softening clots.

EMBOLISM

Emboli offer little of chemical interest, because of the purely mechanical nature of their origin and of the effects they produce.[15] An exception exists in the case of *fat embolism,* for the manner in which the fat is removed from the blood has invited considerable speculation.[16] Part of the fat is eliminated in the urine,[17] but the problem of how it escapes from the glomerular capillaries is not satisfactorily explained; large emboli undoubtedly lead to rupture of the capillary

[9] Jour. Med. Research, 1903 (9), 146.
[10] Jour. Med. Research, 1904 (12), 329; *ibid.*, 1906 (14), 541.
[11] Pearce and Winne, Amer. Jour. Med. Sci., 1904 (128), 669.
[12] Barker, Jour. Exp. Med., 1908 (19), 343.
[13] Jour. Exper. Med., 1905 (7), 316.
[14] See Fleisher and Loeb, Jour. Biol. Chem., 1915 (21), 477.
[15] Fat embolism may follow poisoning with potassium chlorate (Winogradow, Virchow's Arch., 1907 (190), 92).
[16] Full discussion by Beneke, Ziegler's Beitr., 1897 (22), 343.
[17] Discussed by Sakaguchi, (Biochem. Zeit., 1913 (48), 1) who finds a little fat in the normal urine.

walls, and probably some fat also escapes through stomata or similar intercellular openings. Fat may also escape in the bile, and some is probably taken up by the tissue and endothelial cells by phagocytosis. Bencke found that the fat becomes partly emulsified by the mechanical action of the blood current, aided to a slight extent by saponification. The larger droplets after lodging in the capillaries are surrounded by leucocytes, to which Bencke ascribes an active part in the removal of the fat as fine droplets by phagocytic action. We may well believe, however, that the lipase of the plasma is an important agent in disintegrating the emboli, although its action is limited because of the relatively small surface which the large drops offer for attack. After fat droplets have been taken into the cells, they presumably are utilized in metabolism like normally acquired fat, as described previously.

The amount of fat free in the blood in fat embolism may be surprisingly large. Bissell[18] found from 2 to 6.5 per cent. in the venous blood of several typical cases, although sometimes figures within normal limits (0.2 to 0.6 per cent.) were found. The higher quantities represent such a great amount of free fat in the blood, even without considering the quantity held in the capillaries, that it is scarcely possible for it all to have come from the fractured bones.

Air embolism presents some features of interest from the chemical standpoint, especially in those cases following sudden decrease in atmospheric pressure in persons who have been exposed for some time to pressures considerably higher than that of the 'atmosphere (diver's palsy, caisson disease, etc.). This form of air embolism is due to the fact that fluids can dissolve much more gas at high pressures than at low pressures; consequently when the abnormally great pressure to which divers, caisson workers, etc., are subjected is too suddenly reduced to that of the atmosphere, the excessive gas that was absorbed during the period of high pressure by the blood and tissue fluids is released, and forms bubbles in the tissues and blood. The bubbles in the nervous tissues may cause paralyses of various sorts, or death; those in the blood may, if in sufficient amount, cause serious or fatal capillary obstruction. The bubbles consist chiefly of nitrogen, because the power of the blood to hold oxygen in combination is so great that not much of this gas becomes freed.[19] The body fluids of normal persons contain about 675 c.c. of nitrogen, all told, but at 22 pounds pressure this is increased to 1350 c.c., while but about 50 c.c. of free oxygen would be present (Langlois). Carbon dioxide is so readily combined in the blood that none is free even at high pressure, although McWhorter[20] reports that the gas collected from the right side of the heart in a fatal case contained 20 per cent. CO_2 and 80 per cent.

[18] Jour. Amer. Med. Assoc., 1916 (67), 1926.
[19] This subject is fully discussed by Leonard Hill in "Recent Advances in Physiology and Biochemistry," London, 1906.
[20] Amer. Jour. Med. Sci., 1910 (139), 373; Erdman, ibid., 1913 (145), 520.

nitrogen. Possibly some oxygen may also be released from solution during decompression.[21] At body temperature fats can dissolve five times as much nitrogen as serum or plasma,[22] which probably accounts for the severity of the changes in the nervous system with its rich lipoid content and delicate structure. Air embolism following obstetrical operations or surgical operations about the neck and chest presents chiefly mechanical features,[23] and large quantities of air must be present to cause dangerous obstruction to circulation.[24] Gas-bubbles may be produced in the blood soon after death by *B. aërogenes capsulatus*, but it is not probable that they are formed before death and cause air embolism.

INFARCTION

The changes that occur in infarcted areas are of much interest in connection with the study of autolysis, for the absorption of the necrotic tissue of aseptic infarcts is purely a matter of autolysis. Jacoby[25] found by ligating off a portion of a dog's liver, and keeping the dog alive for some time afterward, that in the infarcted tissues so produced leucine and tyrosine could be detected, just as they are found in liver tissue undergoing autolysis outside of the body. So, too, proteoses may appear in the urine when any considerable amount of tissue is cut off from its blood-supply. The processes of autolysis which occur in ordinary sterile infarcts are, however, extremely slow, and it is doubtful if enough of the products are ever in the blood or urine at any one time to be detected or to cause noticeable effects. For example, in an infarct of the kidney which was known to be almost exactly fourteen weeks old, there still remained a layer of necrotic cortex one millimeter thick, quite unabsorbed during this time. If we examine such aseptic infarcts in various stages, we get the impression that the digestion is accomplished by leucocytes acting on the periphery of the infarct, and not entering the dead area deeply, presumably because of a lack of chemotactic substances in the dead cells. On the other hand, it seems probable that the tissue enzymes themselves play an important part in the autolysis, for if we implant into animals pieces of tissue in which the enzymes have been destroyed by heating to boiling, it will be found that the cells and their nuclei remain unaffected for many weeks; whereas if sterile unheated pieces of tissue in which the enzymes are still active are implanted, they lose their nuclear stain and begin to disintegrate relatively soon, without apparent participation by the leucocytes.[26] Ribbert[27] found that in

[21] Hill and Greenwood, Proc. Royal Soc. (B), 1907 (79), 284.
[22] Vernon, *ibid.*, p. 366; Quincke, Arch. exp. Path. u. Pharm., 1910 (62), 464.
[23] Review of literature by Wolff, Virchow's Archiv., 1903 (174), 454.
[24] See Hare, Amer. Jour. Med. Sciences, 1902 (124), 843.
[25] Zeit. physiol. Chem., 1900 (30), 149.
[26] Wells, Jour. Med. Research, 1906 (15), 149.
[27] Virchow's Arch., 1899 (155), 201.

experimentally produced anemic infarcts in the kidneys of rabbits the nuclei retain their staining property well for nearly twenty-four hours, becoming then small and deeply stained, undergoing karyorrhexis, and in large part disappearing from the convoluted tubules inside of forty-eight hours, although some nuclei may persist in the glomerules for three or more days. In human infarcts, Ribbert believes, the process goes on faster, for he has osberved here a loss of nuclei within twenty-four hours. These nuclear changes undoubtedly depend upon autolysis, but it is probable that the enzymes concerned reside in the cytoplasm rather than in the nucleus, for I have observed that cells of lymphoid type, with practically no cytoplasm, generally retain their nuclear stain much longer than cells with more cytoplasm; this is particularly noticeable in splenic infarcts, where the Malpighian corpuscles retain their staining affinities much longer than the pulp elements. Whether the destruction of the nuclei is accomplished by the ordinary intracellular proteases, or by special nucleoprotein-splitting enzymes (nuclease,[28] etc.), remains to be determined. It is quite possible, however, that the first changes consist of a splitting of the nucleoproteins of the nucleus by the autolytic enzymes, liberating the nucleic acid, which gives the nuclei the characteristic intense staining with basic dyes (*pycnosis*) observed in areas of early anemic necrosis. The nucleic acid may then be further decomposed by the nuclease or similar enzymes. Taken all together, then, it would seem that the nuclear and cellular alterations that make up the characteristic picture of anemic necrosis are brought about by the intracellular enzymes—an autolytic process. The removal of the dead substance, however, seems to be accomplished rather by the invading leucocytes, through heterolysis. The relatively small part taken by the intracellular enzymes may possibly be due to the seeping through them of alkaline blood-plasma, for autolytic enzymes are not active in an alkaline medium; the leucocytic enzymes, however, act best in an alkaline medium.[29]

About the periphery of infarcts is usually observed more or less fat deposition (Fischler),[30] particularly in the endothelial cells (Ribbert). This is not peculiar to infarcts, however, for Sata[31] found a similar peripheral fatty metamorphosis common to all necrotic areas. The basis of this is possibly the persistence of the cell lipase, which synthesizes fatty acid and glycerol diffusing into the necrotic area with the plasma, unchecked by normal oxidative destruction of these substances. (See "Fatty Degeneration," Chap. xvi.)

Hemorrhagic infarcts offer in addition to the changes common to anemic infarcts, the alterations occurring in the blood-corpuscles.

[28] Sachs, Zeit physiol. Chem., 1905 (46), 337; Schittenhelm, *ibid.*, 354.
[29] More fully discussed by Wells,[26] *loc. cit.*, and under necrosis, Chap. xv.
[30] Cent. f. Path., 1902 (13), 417.
[31] Ziegler's Beitr., 1900 (28), 461.

Panski[32] found that after ligation of the splenic vein of dogs the red corpuscles begin to give up their hemoglobin in about three hours. After twelve hours fibrin formation begins in the tissues, the corpuscles continue to give up hemoglobin and become cloudy in appearance. Later, iron-containing pigment is formed in the cells beneath the capsule, but in the deeper tissue even the iron normally present in the spleen tissue seems to disappear;[33] this possibly depends upon the fact that pigment reacting for iron, hemosiderin, is formed only in living cells under the influence of oxygen, or it may be that acids formed during autolysis dissolve it. During autolysis *in vitro*, however, Corper[34] found no evidence of removal of iron from insoluble or coagulable compounds. The hemolysis is probably produced either by the action of autolytic products, which are notoriously hemolytic, or perhaps also by direct attack of tissue and blood proteases upon the corpuscles.

Other retrogressive changes that may occur in infarcts, such as septic softening and calcification, are not greatly different from the same processes occurring in other conditions, and will be considered with the discussion of these processes.

[32] "Untersuchungen über den Pigmentgehalt der Stauungsmilz," Dorpat, 1890.
[33] See also M. B. Schmidt, Cent. f. Path., 1908 (19), 416.
[34] Jour. Exper. Med., 1912 (15), 429.

CHAPTER XIV

EDEMA[1]

As the term edema indicates the excessive accumulation of lymph (which may be either normal or modified in composition) in the cells, intercellular spaces, or serous cavities of the body, the problems of edema are inseparably connected with the consideration of the processes of physiological formation and removal of lymph. For many years the study of these processes has been a favorite field of investigation by physiologists, and the great battle-place of the "vitalistic" and "mechanistic" schools; and to this day the forces that determine the formation of lymph and its subsequent absorption have not been completely understood. By the application of the principles of physical chemistry to the problem, however, great advances have recently been made, which seem to render our understanding of both lymph-formation and its pathological accumulation in the tissues much clearer and more nearly accurate than they were before. We shall first consider, therefore the physiological formation of lymph, before taking up the subject of edema.

Composition of Lymph.—Lymph consists of material derived from two chief sources. The greater part consists of fluid passing out of the capillaries into the tissue spaces; here it is modified by the addition of products of metabolism derived from the tissue-cells, and by the subtraction of materials that the cells utilize in their metabolism. It is, therefore, essentially a modified blood plasma, and the modifications the plasma undergoes are so slight, that, under ordinary conditions, lymph shows on analysis no considerable differences from blood plasma, except a relative poverty in proteins, due chifly to the impermeability of the capillary walls for colloids. Its quantitative composition varies greatly, depending upon the conditions under which it is collected, whether during activity or rest, etc. The following tables of analyses have been collected by Hammarsten:

	1	2	3	4
Water	939.9	934.8	957.6	955.4
Solids	60.1	65.2	42.4	44.6
Fibrin	0.5	0.6	0.4	2.2
Albumin	42.7	42.8	34.7	
Fat, Cholesterol, Lecithin	3.8	9.2		35.0
Extractive bodies	5.7	4.4		
Salts	7.3	8.2	7.2	7.5

1 and 2 are analyses of lymph from the thigh of a woman, 3 is from the contents of sac-like dilated vessels of the spermatic cord, 4 is lymph from the neck of a colt.

[1] A complete bibliography is given by Meltzer, American Medicine, 1901 (8), 19 et seq.; also by Klemensiewicz, in Krehl and Marchand's Handbuch d. allg. Path., 1912, II (1), 341; Magnus, Handbuch d. Biochem., 1908, II (2), 99; Gerhartz, ibid., p. 116.

Chyle differs from lymph chiefly in the presence of large quantities of fat; during starvation the lymph and the chyle are of practically the same composition.

Normal lymph contains much less fibrinogen than does the blood plasma, and hence coagulates slowly. Lipase and other enzymes have been found in the lymph, as in the plasma. The products of tissue metabolism added to the lymph by the cells may render it toxic (Asher and Barbera[2]). Under pathological conditions the lymph may be greatly altered, becoming poorer in solids under some conditions of edema, and becoming rich in proteins and blood-corpuscles under inflammatory conditions, until it partakes of the characteristics of an inflammatory exudate (see analyses of transudates and exudates).

An important fact to consider is, that *of the entire water of the body but about one-tenth is in the blood.* About two-thirds of the entire weight of the body is water, which is mostly in the cells and tissues, firmly bound by the colloids, only an unknown but smaller portion being as free movable fluid, and even here always associated with more or less colloid. A body weighing 60 kilos will, therefore, have 40 kilos of water, of which but about 4 kilos is blood.

FORMATION OF LYMPH[3]

Filtration Theory.—The simplest possible conception of lymph formation is that it is merely the result of filtration of the liquid constituents of the blood through the capillary walls under the influence of the blood pressure. This "filtration theory" was supported originally by Ludwig, and it was a prominent factor in the early applications of mechanical principles to biological processes. In support of this theory were advanced the results of numerous experiments in which it was shown that increasing the blood pressure by means of ligating the veins, or by causing arterial dilatation, resulted in an increase of the lymph flowing out of the lymph-vessels of the part. Also, when the blood pressure is raised by epinephrine or by other means, a large proportion of the fluid leaves the blood vessels; conversely, when the blood pressure is suddenly lowered by hemorrhage there is a rapid passage of fluid from the tissues into the blood. The experimental results were not always favorable to the theory, however, particularly in the experiments in which blood pressure was raised by arterial dilatation; often the flow of lymph was little increased, even when the arterial flow and pressure were greatly increased. Nevertheless, the filtration theory held for many years, not only as an explanation of lymph formation, but also as an explanation of urinary secretion and of the secretion by other organs. It was only within a comparatively short time that it became clear that filtration alone could not account for all the phenomena of secretion. For example, in many lower forms with undeveloped circulatory systems, and almost no blood pressure, secretion goes on vigorously; the pressure of glandular secretions may be much higher than the blood pressure within the capillaries; the activity of secretion is by no means

[2] Zeit. f. Biol., 1898 (36), 154.
[3] See review by Asher, Biochem. Centralblatt, 1905 (4), 1.

in proportion to blood pressure, etc. If in glandular secretion, therefore, fluids are removed from the blood and transferred into an excretory duct through the action of some force other than that of the blood pressure, it is probable that lymph formation is equally independent of blood pressure. On this basis Heidenhain advanced his—

Secretory theory of lymph formation, in which he suggested that lymph is the product of an active secretion by the endothelial cells of the capillaries, just as saliva is the product of the activity of the glandular cells. He showed that certain chemical substances may stimulate lymph flow, independent of blood pressure, just as pilocarpine and other drugs may stimulate the secretion of saliva. These lymph-stimulating substances, which he named *lymphagogues*, fall into two distinct classes. One which includes such substances as peptone, leech extract, strawberry juice, extracts of crayfish, mussel or oysters, and numerous other tissue extracts, are characterized by causing the secretion of a lymph which is rich in proteins, even richer in proteins than the blood plasma; and, furthermore, there is no simultaneous increase in urinary secretion. Heidenhain considered that these substances caused lymph secretion by stimulating the capillary endothelium in a specific manner; as they caused no appreciable rise in blood pressure the increased lymph secretion certainly could not be attributed to filtration. This independence of the lymph flow of blood pressure is most conclusively shown by *postmortem lymph secretion;* for example, Mendel and Hooker[4] observed lymph flow for four hours after death, in a dog that had received an injection of peptone eight minutes before being killed.[5]

The *second class* of lymphagogues includes crystalloidal substances, such as sugar, urea, and salts.[6] Lymph secreted under the influence of these substances is poorer in protein than ordinary lymph, and at the same time an increased urinary secretion is produced. With these crystalloidal lymphagogues the amount of effect is in inverse proportion to their molecular weight, which means that their effects depend upon the number of molecules in solution rather than upon their nature; in other words, the stimulation of lymph by crystalloids is dependent upon the osmotic pressure of the crystalloids. Heidenhain explained their action as follows: The crystalloids are secreted into the lymph-spaces by the action of the capillary endothelium, and there, owing to their raising osmotic pressure, cause a flowing of water out of the vessels. The difficulty here is to explain why the crystalloids while still in the vessels do not attract the fluids from

---

[4] Amer. Jour. of Physiol., 1902 (7), 380.

[5] A fact not sufficiently taken into account is that blisters filled with serum, *i. e.*, an inflammatory edema, may be produced in dead bodies by burns or scalds. (See Leers and Raysky, Virchow's, Arch., 1909 (197), 324).

[6] The action of many other substances has been investigated by Yanagawa, Jour. Pharmacol., 1916 (9), 75.

the lymph-spaces into the blood, and so cause rather a *lessened* lymph secretion.

While admitting that in pathological conditions (*e. g.*, passive congestion) pressure and filtration *may* play an important part, Heidenhain considered that an active secretion by the endothelial cells is the chief factor in the normal formation of lymph. The means by which the cells perform this function was unknown; it was considered as an example of "vital activity," Heidenhain meaning by this term such chemical and physical forces of living cells as are unknown or not understood at the present time, rather than any metaphysical conception of living matter, such as many vitalists assume.

Other observers, corroborating Heidenhain's results for the most part, have modified, or amplified his theory. Asher and his collaborators, for example, ascribe the work done in causing lymph formation to the cells of the various 'issues and organs, rather than to those of the capillary wall. The increased flow of lymph from the salivary gland that occurs during its activity they consider due to the work of the gland cells, and its function the removal of products of metabolism. The action of such a lymphagogue as peptone they ascribe to its stimulation of cellular activity, particularly in the liver, where it causes an increased formation of bile. Gies[7] and Asher also observed that after an injection of crystalloidal lymphagogues, such as sugar, a prolonged flow of lymph occurred after the death of the animal, proving completely that such lymphagogic action is independent of blood pressure.

Potocytosis.—In explanation of the process by which the cells, whether endothelial or tissue-cells, pass fluids through themselves from one place to another, Meltzer[1] has made an interesting suggestion, as follows: Considering the property of endothelial cells to act as phagocytes, MacCallum[8] has shown that solid granules (*e. g.*, coal pigment, carmin) are taken through the walls of the lymphatics by the phagocytic activity of their endothelial cells. Meltzer suggests that in a similar way the endothelial cells may transport through the vessel-walls not only solid particles, but also, by the same mechanism, substances in solution; and for this hypothetical process he suggests the name "*potocytosis.*" There can be little question that cells do take up substances in solution, and sometimes this is done in an apparently selective manner; *e. g.*, the taking up of bacterial toxins and vegetable poisons in the peritoneal cavity by the leucocytes. Presumably the mechanism of "potocytosis" is not different from that of phagocytosis, chemotactic forces determining the occurrence of the process. No experimental evidence has been advanced as yet for this very plausible hypothesis.

Permeability of Capillaries.—In explanation of the variability in the amount and composition of the lymph, Starling[9] has introduced the factor of altered permeability of the capillary walls, which presumably depends upon the number and size of the pores. He found that normally the lymph coming from the lower extremities contains

[7] Amer. Jour. Physiol., 1900 (3), p. xix; Zeit. f. Biol., 1900 (40), 207.
[8] Johns Hopkins Hosp. Bull., 1903 (14), 1.
[9] Lancet, 1896 (i), May 9, *et seq.*; Schäfer's Text-book of Physiology, vol. 1.

only 2 per cent. to 3 per cent. of proteins, while lymph from the intestines contains 4 per cent. to 6 per cent., and lymph from the liver contains 6 per cent. to 8 per cent. of proteins; hence he considers that the liver capillaries are the most permeable, *i. e.*, have the largest pores, so that more of the large colloid molecules can escape from them. The effect of lymphagogues of the first class (peptones, etc.) he attributes to their poisonous properties, and the consequent injury to, and alterations in, the capillary wall. The crystalloidal lymphagogues, he believes, act by first attracting fluids from the tissues into the blood with a resulting "hydremic plethora," which in turn leads to increased blood pressure and consequent filtration of a watery fluid out of the vessels. He considers, therefore, that the amount and quality of the lymph produced in any part are determined solely by two factors, the intracapillary blood pressure and the permeability of the capillary walls.

In connection with this question of the permeability of the capillary walls, Meltzer suggests that the contractility and irritability of the endothelium may be a potent factor in determining the size of the pores in the capillary walls. When in a tonic condition, the endothelium is firmly contracted about the pores, keeping their size small; when the endothelial cells become relaxed by any cause, such as poisons, high blood pressure, poor nourishment, etc., the pores are enlarged, and increased escape of fluid results.[9a] It must be borne in mind, however, that most histologists do not now admit that capillary walls contain pores.

M. H. Fischer holds that the endothelial cells undergo changes in consistency through changes in the affinity of the cell colloids for water; especially under the influence of acids the endothelium may become much more fluid and of greater permeability. Adolf Oswald[10] says that the normal capillary wall is somewhat permeable for the less viscous blood proteins (albumin and pseudoglobulin), and in inflammation this permeability becomes increased so that the more viscous euglobulin and fibrinogen can pass through.

Osmotic Pressure.—Still another possible factor in causing fluid to leave the vessels is osmotic pressure. Heidenhain refers to this cause the transudation produced by crystalloid lymphagogues, although in a rather unsatisfactory manner. As a result of the more recent studies of physical chemistry, and its application to biological processes, we have learned to appreciate the importance of osmotic pressure in cell activities (see Introductory Chapter), and in the question of lymph formation it occupies a particularly important place. We may consider it as follows: In the blood we have certain proportions of readily diffusible crystalloids and of non-diffusible

---

[9a] Evidence of the contractility of capillary walls is discussed by Krogh, Jour. Physiol., 1919 (52), 457.
[10] Zeit. f. exp. Path., 1910 (8), 226.

colloids. If no metabolic processes were going on in the tissues, we should have the diffusible substances leaving the vessel-walls (leaving out, for the present, any question of secretory activity on the part of the endothelium) until an osmotic equilibrium is established in the tissues and in the blood. As a matter of fact, however, the blood proteins are not absolutely non-diffusible, but small quantities do pass through the capillary walls, and so lymph under such a hypothetical condition would consist of a mixture of the same osmotic concentration as the blood plasma, with about the same proportion of crystalloids, but a smaller proportion of proteins; this, it will be noticed, is just about the composition of normal lymph. During life, however, the cells of the tissues are causing metabolic changes in these lymphatic constituents, and these changes consist chiefly in breaking down large molecules of proteins, carbohydrates, and fats into much smaller molecules. Now the osmotic pressure of a solution is dependent upon the *number* of molecules and ions it contains, hence by breaking down these few large molecules with very little osmotic pressure into many small molecules, the osmotic pressure in these cells and tissues becomes raised above that of the blood-vessels, and consequently water flows out of the vessels because of the increased pressure. We see here the probable explanation of the stimulating influence of metabolic products upon the formation of lymph, noted by Hamburger, Heidenhain, and others. For suggesting and urging the importance of osmotic pressure in the formation of lymph we are indebted particularly to Heidenhain, v. Korányi,[11] J. Loeb,[12] and Roth.[13] Loeb shows very clearly the relative greatness of the water-driving force of osmotic pressure as compared to that of blood-pressure, by his statement that the osmotic pressure of a physiological salt solution is about 4.9 atmospheres, which is *twenty times as great as the blood pressure* with which we have to do in ordinary physiological experiments. In varying osmotic conditions we may readily see an explanation for the increased lymph flow that occurs during tissue activity; namely, it is due to the increased formation of metabolic products. Many of the lymphagogues may act similarly by stimulating metabolic activity, with resulting increase in the formation of osmotic pressure-raising products of metabolism in the organs; e. g., the increased lymph flow from the thoracic duct that follows stimulation of hepatic activity by injection of peptone (Heidenhain) or ammonium tartrate (Asher and Busch).[14] As we shall see later in considering edema, osmotic pressure may play an important part in the pathological formation of lymph. It must be admitted, however, that there are many difficulties in the way of accepting unqualifiedly the original views as to the importance of

[11] Zeit. f. klin. Med., 1897 (33), 1; 1898 (34), 1.
[12] Pflüger's Arch., 1898 (71), 457.
[13] Englemann's Arch., 1899, p. 416.
[14] Zeit. f. Biol. 1900 (40), 333.

osmotic pressure in lymph formation.[15]   For example, the lymph
contains more chlorides and may have a much higher osmotic
pressure than the serum of the same animal (Hamburger, Carlson,
et al.).[16]

Variable Capacity of Colloids for Water.—Colloids of the type of the
tissue proteins, i. e., hydrophil colloids, imbibe water with great avidity, until a certain proportion of water is present, the proportion
varying under different conditions.   The importance of this force in
the production of edema and related processes was first pointed out
by Martin H. Fischer, and has been developed extensively by him.[17]
The amount of water which a given hydrophil colloid, such, for example, as gelatin, or fibrin, will take up, is greatly modified by the reaction of the solution and by its content of electrolytes.   Very small
concentrations of acids or alkalies will greatly increase the amount
of water absorbed, while salts reduce it, and the different acids and
salts vary in their effects; thus hydrochloric acid causes a greater
swelling of colloids than a corresponding strength of sulphuric acid,
and calcium chloride depresses the swelling more than potassium
chloride.   The effect of the salts is made up of their constituent ions.
Non-electrolytes have relatively little effect.   The forces developed
by this affinity of colloids for water are enormous; thus, to prevent
the taking up of water by starch requires a pressure of over 2500 atmospheres, dried gelatin will take up 25 times its weight of water,
and fibrin as much as forty times.   Different colloids differ greatly in
their affinity for water and in the way in which this affinity is modified by electrolytes, and change in a colloid may greatly alter its
capacity for swelling; thus, β-gelatin, which can be formed from ordinary gelatin by the action of proteolytic enzymes, has greater capacity
for swelling than the original gelatin.   Gies especially lays stress on
this factor, that is, the alterations of the hydrophilic tendencies of the
tissue colloids by enzymes.[18]   In the plant world we find striking
examples of this character; thus, the succulence of some plants results

[15] Gunzberg (Arch. néerland physiol., 1918 (2), 364) states that the passage of
water into the intercellular spaces is due to the electrical properties of the membrane separating the circulating fluid from the tissues.   The element potassium
and the ions H and OH play an important part in this electrical osmosis which is
able to drive the fluid in the opposite direction to osmotic pressure.   Thus, a
dialyzing sack containing Ringer solution minus K immersed in Ringer solution
loses weight.   Perfusion of frogs with Ringer solution minus K produces marked
edema.
    [16] Amer. Jour. Physiol., 1907 (19), 360; 1908 (22), 91.
    [17] See Fischer's Monograph, "Oedema and Nephritis," New York, 1915; also
numerous articles in the Zeit. f. Chem. u. Ind. d. Kolloide.   An especially thorough discussion of this theory is contained in the Biochemical Bulletin, Vol. I.,
giving a bibliography of Fischer's work, together with articles on Gies' observations on the modification of the hydrophilic tendency of proteins by enzyme
action.
    [18] A definite and clear-cut example of the swelling of a tissue under the in-
fluence of acid of metabolic origin is shown in the muscle cell in Zenker's waxy
degeneration (Wells, Jour. Exper. Med., 1909 (11), 1).

from the conversion of poly-saccharides with little hydration capacity into hydrophilic pentosans and mucilages.[19]

On the basis of the facts briefly summarized above, the proportion of water present in any cell or in any fluid of the body which contains colloids, is assumed to be determined by certain factors, namely (1) the character of the colloids themselves; (2) the proportion and nature of acids or alkalies present in the fluids in and about the colloids; (3) the proportion and nature of the salts. All these factors are changeable, and therefore the amount of water present in the cell or fluid varies accordingly. Thus, if a cell through its metabolism develops from such a non-electrolyte as sugar (which has no considerable effect on the water content of the protoplasm), an organic acid, such as lactic acid, which has a large effect in increasing the affinity of the colloids for water, the cell will, presumably, take on more water, perhaps to a degree to cause intracellular edema. The acids diffusing from the cell into the intercellular spaces or into the lymph will cause equally well an increased affinity for water in the colloids here present, leading to intercellular edema. Conversely, neutralization of acids present in a colloidal solution, by alkaline salts brought by the blood, will decrease the affinity of the colloids for water which will escape from the colloids as they shrink. ·

This theory, which introduces a hitherto unappreciated factor into the considerations of lymph formation and edema, is of the utmost importance. It practically eliminates osmotic pressure, also the cell membranes so essential for the efficiency of this force, and in view of the difficulties that have arisen in trying to fit the cell membrane hypothesis and osmotic pressure to many facts of normal and pathological biology, an alternative hypothesis is welcome. As pointed out above, the forces involved in the swelling of colloids are so large as to be of great significance, and the amounts of electrolytes necessary to cause considerable variations in colloidal swelling are not more than can be present under normal and pathological conditions; consequently the possible influence of colloidal swelling must be taken into account in all consideration of pathological processes. Whether or not it is capable of as universal application as Fischer maintains, remains to be demonstrated, and there are, indeed, some facts that do not seem to be in harmony with this theory.

Summary.—We see from the above discussion that numerous theories have been advanced to explain the normal formation of lymph, and as their basis exist several different possible factors. Filtration, active secretion by the capillary endothelium, attraction by the tissue-cells, osmosis in response to formation of crystalloids outside the vessels, and changes in the affinity of colloids for water; all have been shown to be possible causes of lymph formation. It is highly probable that in a certain way all are involved, particularly if we accept the

[19] MacDougal and Spoehr, Plant World, 1918 (21), 245.

22

view of the physical school that "secretion" and "attraction" by the cells are merely the outcome of physical forces; the causes of lymph formation then reduce themselves to absorption, filtration and diffusion. There has been, until recently, no question but that lymph does escape from the vessels through simple filtration, for the pressure inside the capillaries is presumably greater than outside, the capillary walls are not water-tight and they are not impermeable to the substances dissolved in the plasma.[20] Likewise osmotic exchanges surely go on between the vessels and the tissue-cells, and the conditions which determine the water content of our colloid solutions constantly vary. The question that remains is, do these few factors account for all of the lymph formation, and are they sufficient by themselves to explain the physiological regulation and the pathological variations in the lymph flow? They are purely physical or mechanical causes, and the "vitalist" school will claim that they are inadequate and that "vital activities" of the cells play the deciding rôle. But at present the evidence that is being accumulated seems to point more and more strongly to the conclusion that these "vital activities" are but the result of simple well-known physical forces acting under very complex conditions—complex because of the large number of different chemical compounds occurring together, and the varying influence of circulation, food supplies, cell structure, etc.

ABSORPTION OF LYMPH

By no means all the fluid that escapes from the vessels, nor all the products of cell metabolism, are carried away in the lymph—a considerable and perhaps the greater part of them is absorbed back into the capillaries directly. A classical proof of this is the experiment of Magendie, who observed that if poisons were injected into the leg of an animal, which had been separated from the body entirely except for the blood-vessels, that poisoning developed in the usual manner. In such experiments the lymph-vessels are severed and probably largely occluded; hence it does not solve the question as to whether substances are absorbed by the blood-vessels under normal conditions. Orlow found, however, that during absorption of fluid from the peritoneal cavity there is no perceptible increase in the lymph flow from the thoracic duct. Addition of sodium fluoride, a protoplasmic poison, was found to interfere with this absorption, for which and other reasons Heidenhain and Orlow considered that the absorption depended upon the "vital activity" of the cells. More nearly reproducing normal conditions were the experiments of Starling and Tubby, who found

---

[20] Hill ("Recent Advances in Physiology and Biochemistry," 1906, p. 618) disputes the possibility of such a thing as filtration pressure, on the ground that the structures within the capsule of an organ must all be under the influence of the blood pressure alike; but with the presence of an outlet for the fluid, as in glands with ducts, filtration pressure surely can apply.

that methylene-blue or indigo-carmine injected into the pleura or peritoneum appeared in the urine long before it colored the lymph in the thoracic duct.[21] Adler and Meltzer found evidence, however, that not all the absorption is accomplished by the blood-vessels, for obstruction of the thoracic duct retards absorption. That the absorption is not dependent solely upon the circulation and blood pressure is shown by the fact that absorption from the peritoneal cavity occurs in dead bodies (Hamburger, Adler and Meltzer).

The nature of the mechanism by which fluids are taken into the blood-vessels is still unknown. We can easily understand the entrance of injected poisons and coloring-matters from the tissues into the blood, because they are more concentrated at the point of injection than in the blood, hence they may diffuse directly through the capillary wall. Likewise we can understand the diffusion of water from a hypotonic solution into the blood, but how a solution of the same concentration as that of the blood can enter the blood is difficult to explain. Cohnstein and also Starling attribute this absorption to the proteins of the blood in the following manner: After a fluid is injected into the tissues or serous cavities there occurs a diffusion exchange between this fluid and the blood, until the concentration of the crystalloids in each is equal; but the proteins of the blood cannot diffuse, and as they exert a positive although very slight osmotic pressure, this difference in osmotic pressure in favor of the blood causes diffusion of the extravascular fluid into the blood. Roth has also applied this idea in a rather complicated manner to the absorption occurring in metabolic processes (see Meltzer), but it must be admitted that it is an unsatisfactory solution of the problem. Fischer would ascribe the passage of fluid to the relative affinity of the colloids of the blood and of the tissues for the fluid, and this would be towards the blood whenever the blood colloids had, from whatever possible cause, a greater affinity for the fluid than the tissue colloids.

Passage of the fluid from the tissues into the lymph stream was very easy to understand in the light of the older conception of the lymphatic circulation, namely, that the lymph-vessels were merely continuations of the interstitial spaces; we could then assume that as soon as the fluid left the blood-vessels it was practically within the lymphatic system, and was crowded along the lymphatic channels by the *vis a tergo*, aided by the valves of the lymph-vessels and the intrathoracic vacuum. But it now seems, particularly through the studies of MacCallum,[22] that the lymphatic vessels form a closed system, not in communication with the interstitial spaces. This being the case, we have to explain the passage of the lymph through the walls of the lymphatic vessels, and this is a problem which is not by any means a simple one, and which has yet to be investigated. It is significant

[21] See Mendel, Amer. Jour. Physiol., 1899 (2), 342.
[22] Johns Hopkins Hosp. Bull., 1903 (14), 105.

that the thoracic lymph has a higher osmotic pressure than the blood of the same animal (Luckhardt),[23] so that the lymph which enters the duct must do so against the osmotic pressure.

THE PATHOGENESIS OF EDEMA

With the facts and hypotheses mentioned in the preceding paragraphs in mind, we may consider their bearing on the production of abnormally large accumulations of lymph in the tissues, that is, edema. We can imagine any one of the following factors as causing or helping to cause such a pathological accumulation:

1. Obstruction to outflow through the lymph-vessels.
2. Increased blood pressure.
3. Decreased extravascular pressure.
4. Increased permeability of the capillary walls.
5. Increased filterability of the blood plasma.
6. Osmotic pressure changes—either an extravascular increase or an intravascular decrease.
7. Changes in the affinity of the colloids for water.

These may be taken up one by one, and considered in relation to their bearing upon the general problem of edema.

1. Obstruction to Outflow through the Lymph-vessels.—Because of the very abundant anastomosis of the lymphatic vessels it is extremely difficult or impossible to cause any appreciable obstruction to the lymphatic circulation by occlusion of lymphatic trunks in the limbs or organs of the body, and in pathological conditions this possible cause of edema is seldom actually observed. The chief instance of edema from lymphatic obstruction is observed after occlusion of the thoracic duct by tumors, tuberculous processes, animal parasites, or thrombosis; such occlusion is usually followed by rupture of the duct or its tributaries, with the production of *chylous ascites* or *chylothorax*, and *chyluria*. Filaria or their ova may occupy so many of the lymphatic channels of an extremity (leg) or part (scrotum) that the anastomotic channels are thoroughly blocked, with a resulting local edema that in course of time is followed by the production of inflammatory connective tissue and elephantiasis.[24] Chronic lymphangitis or plugging of the lymph vessels by cancer cells may also result in lymphatic obstruction to such an extent that chronic edema results. It would seem, from Opie's experiments,[25] that the acute edemas may at times depend upon lymphatic obstruction, for he found that experimental edema of the liver, produced by cantharidin, seems to be determined by inflammatory processes which occlude the sinuses of the lymph glands through which the hepatic lymph passes.

[23] Amer. Jour. Physiol., 1910 (25), 345.
[24] Manson, Allbutt's System, 1897 (ii), 1082.
[25] Jour. Exper. Med., 1912 (16), 831.

Another way in which edema may be caused or influenced by lymphatic obstruction is generally overlooked, but it is possibly of great importance; namely, from *pressure upon the lymph channels* by dilated vessels in hyperemia, or by cellular exudates and swollen tissues in inflammation. We see evidence of this in the rapid absorption of exudates that frequently follows the removal of but a part of the fluid in a chest cavity; apparently the decrease in pressure frees the paths of absorption and permits them to take up the remaining fluid. In inflammatory edema the lymphatic obstruction is probably not great, for Lassar found that the amount of lymph escaping from an edematous extremity is much greater than from a normal one; but in the case of strangulated hernias or other conditions in which edema results from circular constriction, obstruction of the lymphatic vessels may be a factor of no mean importance. In general stasis the increased pressure in the veins of the neck may interfere with the passage of the fluid out of the thoracic duct into the blood.

There is no difficulty in understanding edema from the above causes—it is simply a passive congestion of the lymphatic circulation, and no chemical factors are involved. The nature of the fluid found in such forms of edema will be discussed later.

2. **Increased Blood Pressure.**—This takes us back to the filtration theory of lymph formation, and as it is generally conceded that more or less fluid escapes from the vessels by this mechanical process,[26] the questions to be decided are: Can and does increased blood pressure, alone and without other aiding factors, cause edema? If not, does it play an auxiliary part in producing edema, and how important a part may this be? Many experiments have been performed with the object of answering these questions, with more or less conflicting results. Cohnheim demonstrated that vasodilation (active hyperemia) alone will never bring on an edema; and many observers state that ligation of the femoral or other large veins will not cause edema in animals. However, when the vein is occluded, and the arteries are dilated by cutting their vasoconstrictor nerves, then edema may result (Ranvier, Cohnheim); but whenever venous outflow is impeded, we have other factors than simply increased pressure to consider, for the nourishment of the parts is decidedly impaired, and, as we shall see later, this may be of much greater importance than is the associated rise in blood pressure. To produce edema in the lungs by mechanical forces it is necessary to ligate the aorta and its branches, or the pulmonary veins (Welch). As such high pressures do not occur in any pathological conditions, it is safe to assume that increased pressure alone is not capable of causing by itself the pulmonary edema so frequently observed clinically. Welch,[27] however, has supported the

---

[26] A rise of blood pressure leads to an increase in the hemoglobin of the blood, presumably because the fluid is forced out into the tissue spaces (Scott, Amer. Jour. Physiol., 1917 (44), 298).

[27] Virchow's Arch., 1878 (72), 375; see also Meltzer (*loc. cit.*).

hypothesis that a disproportion between the working power of the left ventricle and of the right ventricle may lead to pulmonary edema through pulmonary hyperemia. In the edema of passive congestion, increased blood pressure would seem to be an important factor, and there is no doubt that with an increased pressure of the degree observed in such conditions some increase in the lymph flow would result; but from the evidence at hand it is improbable that the amount of lymph so secreted would ever be more than the lymph-vessels could carry away. Even the added obstruction to lymphatic flow due to pressure upon the lymph capillaries by congested blood-vessels, and the resistance to the lymph escaping from the thoracic duct offered by the increased pressure in the subclavian vein, would not satisfactorily account for the edema of cardiac incompetence. Not to go into details here, it may be stated that the impression prevails that uncomplicated rise in blood pressure is not sufficient by itself to produce edema. Some of the reasons for belittling this factor will be brought out in the subsequent discussion.

3. **Decreased Extravascular Pressure.**—This factor is particularly prominent in the so-called "*edema ex vacuo*," which occurs after the absorption of an area of tissue so located that the surrounding tissues cannot contract or fall in to fill the gap, *e. g.*, brain softening, serous atrophy of fat. A still better example, however, is the edema that follows local decrease in atmospheric pressure in "cupping." In these instances the edema depends partly upon increased transudation, and partly on the retention of the fluid in the tissues, because it cannot well leave them against the atmospheric pressure. The idea advanced by Landerer that decreased elasticity of the tissues was a possible cause of edema has been attacked by Böninger.[28] During the early stages of edema the elasticity of the skin may be measurably decreased,[29] even when no edema is demonstrable by palpation, but this is not evidence that any loss of elasticity occupies a causative relation to the edema. The tissues can take up water until as much as six kilos has been added to the weight of the entire body before any edema can be detected by palpation (Widal). Edema *ex vacuo* is again an illustration of edema due to purely mechanical causes, but it is of little practical importance.

4. **Increased Permeability of the Capillary Walls.**—The importance of this factor in the production of edema was first demonstrated by Cohnheim and Lichtheim, who found that the production of an enormous increase in the amount of fluid in the blood (hydremic plethora) by injecting large quantities of salt solution, caused an edema of the viscera and serous cavities, but not any subcutaneous edema until the skin had been irritated by some means, such as hot water, iodin, etc. By this irritation the capillary walls are injured, and an

[28] Zeit. exp. Path. u. Ther., 1905 (1), 163.
[29] Schade, Zeit. exp. Path., 1912 (11), 369.

excessive escape of the blood fluids follows. Magnus also showed that poisoning with arsenic, which injured the vessels, favored the experimental production of edema by transfusion. Starling, as noted before, observed that the permeability of the capillaries varies normally in different organs and tissues, which determines quantitative and qualitative differences in the lymph normally flowing from various vascular areas. Heidenhain's "lymphagogues of the first class," which are all poisonous substances, probably act by increasing the permeability of the capillaries, and in this way they produce *local urticaria*, which is often observed as a result of poisoning by these same lymphagogues, *e. g.*, shellfish and strawberry poisoning. Just what changes are produced in the capillary walls that render them more permeable we do not know. Possibly in some instances it is a partial solution of the intercellular cement substances, possibly an enlargement of the stomata through loss of tonicity of the endothelium (Meltzer), sometimes it may be actual death of the endothelial cells, or, as Heidenhain and Cohnheim thought, it may be a stimulation of the endothelial cells to increased secretory activity. Fischer believes that a change in the hydrophilic tendency of the colloids, induced especially by acids formed in asphyxiated conditions of the cells, alter their structure and with that their permeability.

Under pathological conditions increased permeability of the capillary walls is probably one of the chief factors in the production of certain forms of edema. We see evidence of it particularly in inflammatory edema, with its protein-rich exudate. It cannot be doubted that in such conditions actual physical alterations take place in the capillaries, when we see that the slightly diffusible proteins escape from the vessels in the same proportions as they exist in the plasma; there can be here no question of heightened cell activity or increase in osmotic pressure, especially not when we note the indistinguishable transition of such an inflammatory exudate into one containing leucocytes and red corpuscles, which must pass through openings of some kind in the vessels. Edema due to inflammation and poisoning certainly depends to a large degree upon alterations in the vessel-walls. The question remaining is, do edemas that are not associated with distinct inflammatory or toxic influences depend also upon the vascular permeability?—does increased permeability ever lead to the formation of protein-poor transudates? Cohnheim was inclined to attribute nearly all edema to this cause, for in passive congestion, or nephritis, or any of the common causes of edema, it is easy to find reason for the belief that poisons may be present in the blood; and as there was good evidence that the blood pressure alone could not account for the edema, it was natural to ascribe all these forms of edema to the action of toxic substances upon the capillary walls, leading to increased permeability; or, what might amount to the same thing, increased secretory activity of the endothelium, as understood by Heidenhain. It is impossible at this time to eliminate as non-existent this secretory-activity doctrine, but, as we hope to show later, there exist other factors in all these non-inflammatory edemas that are sufficient to account for the edema without our having recourse to this hypothesis. For the present, therefore, we may consider altered capillary permeability as an essential factor in edemas characterized by protein-rich fluids (exudates), and state that the influence of altered permeability in the production of protein-poor fluids (transudates) is not proved, and is perhaps not of importance, although the evidence of recent studies on experimental nephritis seems to point more and more to the importance of vascular changes in acute nephritis, at least.[30]

5. **Increased Filterability of the Blood Plasma.**—This takes us back to Richard Bright's conception of renal dropsy. He imagined that through the great loss of albumin in the urine the blood became so thinned and watery that it could filter through the vessel-walls, while normal plasma, he thought, was too thick and viscid to do so. The same idea was applied to the edemas of cachexia in cancer, etc., chlorosis, and all forms of edema associated with a decrease in the corpuscular or protein elements of the blood. With our present knowledge of diffusion of crystalloids and colloids we can readily appreciate that a decrease in the blood colloids, such as might occur in these diseases, could not facilitate the filtration of fluids through the capillary walls to any considerable degree. On the other hand, the amount of colloids in the blood will greatly modify the amount of fluid held in the blood; e. g., acacia is used in intravenous injections because it holds in the blood vessels a large amount of fluid by virtue of its hydrophilic character.

Stewart and Bartels considered that in renal dropsy the increased filterability of the plasma was not due so much to the loss in albumin as to retention of water, which caused an hydremic plethora. But this factor was soon eliminated, for it was found that complete anuria, produced by ligating both ureters, does not cause edema; and also that to produce an edema by increasing the water of the blood it was necessary to increase it many times as much as it can ever be increased by disease. Simply increasing the proportion of water by removing part of the blood and injecting a corresponding amount of salt solution did not cause edema (Cohnheim and Lichtheim). We may, therefore, look upon the hypothesis of increased filterability of the blood as chiefly of historic interest, and not important in the causation of edema. In the presence of other factors for the production of edema, however, the amount of fluid in the vessels is important; thus Pearce[31] found that in experimental uranium nephritis hydremia exerted a marked influence on the production of edema.

[30] See Schmid and Schlayer, Deut. Arch. klin. Med., 1911 (101), 44.
[31] Arch. Int. Med., 1908 (3), 422.

6. Disparity of Osmotic Pressure in Favor of the Tissues and Lymph over the Blood.— On a preceding page we have already considered the means by which changes in osmotic pressure in the tissues are brought about, and how they may lead to an accumulation of fluid. The importance of osmotic pressure in causing pathological edema was suggested by J. Loeb[32] in his studies on the physiological action of ions. He stated that edema occurred when the osmotic pressure was higher in the tissues than it was in the blood and lymph, and the cause was to be sought in conditions that lowered the osmotic pressure of the blood and lymph or raised that of the tissues. This condition he found in the accumulation of metabolic products:—in the case of muscle, tetanization of a frog's muscle for ten minutes raised the osmotic pressure over one atmosphere; separating a muscle from its blood-supply led to such an increase in osmotic pressure that it took up water from a 4.9 per cent. NaCl solution, which has a pressure of *over thirty atmospheres*. When we consider that in his studies on lung edema Welch was able by ligation of the aorta to raise the blood pressure less than $\frac{1}{10}$ atmosphere, we begin to appreciate how much more powerful are the physico-chemical forces that are at work in the body than is the blood pressure, even of the aorta itself.

Loeb found that whenever oxidation is impaired in a tissue its osmotic pressure rises, which he ascribed to the accumulation of incompletely oxidized metabolic products, particularly acids, and as a result the muscle takes up water and becomes edematous. On this basis we might explain the edema of venous stagnation as due to accumulation of products of metabolism, partly because of impaired oxidation, partly, perhaps, because of their slow removal in the blood on account of the circulatory disturbance. The so-called "neurotic" edemas may possibly be explained by local increase in metabolic activity brought about by nervous stimuli, which causes increased formation of substances raising osmotic pressure in the stimulated tissues. In renal edema the retention of water also seems to depend rather on osmotic pressure than on circulatory disturbances or alterations in the vessel-walls, for it has been shown that retention of chlorides, which the diseased kidneys do not eliminate normally, is an important cause of the dropsy in some cases. The chlorides accumulating in the tissues lead to an increased osmotic pressure, which causes the abstraction of water from the blood and its retention in the tissues. (The details of this subject will be considered later.) Conversely, Meltzer and Salant found that salt solution is absorbed from the peritoneal cavity more rapidly in nephrectomized rabbits than in normal rabbits because metabolic products accumulate in the blood and raise its osmotic pressure above normal; and it was observed by Fleisher and L. Loeb[33] that the rate of absorption of fluid from the peritoneal cavity is increased when the osmotic pressure of the blood is raised.

[32] Pflüger's Arch., 1898 (71), 457.
[33] Jour. Exper. Med., 1910 (12), 510.

There are some difficulties, however, in applying the influence of osmotic pressure as an explanation of all edemas. For example, in edema of the lungs, as Meltzer points out, what is the force that drives the fluid into the empty air-cells? Equally difficult to explain as the result of osmotic disturbance is the distribution of fluid that is seen in cardiac dropsy. The fluid does not accumulate in the tissues where metabolism is greatest, or where the most oxygen is used; but rather in the inactive subcutaneous tissues and in the serous cavities. Possibly the original transudation does occur in the muscles and solid viscera, and the fluid is then mechanically forced out of them into the surrounding tissue-spaces, later settling according to the laws of gravity or according to the distensibility of the tissues. It is important to take into consideration the fact that demonstrable edema does not manifest itself until a very large quantity of fluid has been retained by the body—as much as six kilos, according to Widal.

Increased Hydration Capacity of the Tissue Colloids.—According to Fischer's theory this factor is of greater importance than any of the preceding, and of chief importance in increasing the amount of water present in the tissues are organic acids formed during metabolism. For example, the great power of asphyxiated muscle to take up water from a strong salt solution, which J. Loeb ascribed to the osmotic pressure of the acids formed in asphyxia, is attributed by Fischer to the influence of these acids upon the capacity of the colloids for water, and this explanation seems to be in better agreement with the facts, especially since Overton has shown that even if all the proteins, carbohydrates and fats in a muscle were split into the greatest possible number of simple molecules and ions, the resulting osmotic pressure would not be sufficient to account for the amount of water taken up. Furthermore, when cells with demonstrable semi-permeability die, they at once lose their semi-permeability, and in consequence their osmotic pressure falls—but dead cells and tissues often exhibit great power of taking up water and becoming edematous.[34] It is an indisputable fact that edema is especially associated with conditions of asphyxiation, and the attempt to explain this by the increased osmotic pressure of the products of incomplete oxidation seem to harmonize with the facts far less successfully than the application of the principle of colloidal swelling. A common error of the critics of this theory is that of assuming that *free* acid must be present to cause swelling. This is not at all true. An amount of acid far less than enough to saturate the acid-binding property of a protein or to be detected by indicators will greatly increase the amount of water which

[34] The secreted fluid of postmortem thoracic lymph flow differs from normal thoracic lymph in being more cloudy, often bloody, contains more solids, has a higher molecular concentration with decreased electrical conductivity (Jappelli and d'Errico, Zeit. f. Biol., 1907 (50) 1), all of which findings are in agreement with the hypothesis that postmortem lymph flow depends upon changes in the cells, caused by asphyxia and not dissimilar to the changes of acute nephritis.

this protein will combine. Presumably the colloidal carbohydrates and lipoids may also play a part in the water absorption of tissues.

Fischer's theory of edema, in his own words, is this: "A state of edema is induced whenever, in the presence of an adequate supply of water, the affinity of the colloids of the tissues for water is increased above that which we are pleased to call normal. The accumulation of acids within the tissues brought about either through their abnormal production, or through the inadequate removal of such as some consider normally produced in the tissues, is chiefly responsible for this increase in the affinity of the colloids for water, though the possibility of explaining at least some of the increased affinity for water through the production or accumulation of substances which affect the colloids in a way similar to acids, or through the conversion of colloids which have but little affinity for water into such as have a greater affinity, must also be borne in mind." In support of this theory he advances evidence which he interprets as indicating that: (1) "An abnormal production or accumulation of acids, or conditions predisposing thereto, exist in all states in which we encounter the development of an edema. (2) The development of an edema in tissues is antagonized by the same substances which decrease the affinity of the (hydrophilic) emulsion colloids for water (salts) and is unaffected by the presence of substances which do not do this (nonelectrolytes). (3) Any chemical means by which we render possible the abnormal production or accumulation of acids in the tissues is accompanied by an edema."

There are many features of lymph formation and edema with which this theory seems to harmonize well, and others with which it does not seem to agree so well, if at all, so that at this time it is a fair statement that the theory is under consideration, but the limitations of its applicability have not yet been agreed upon. It has met with much adverse criticism, some of which was poorly founded, but the fact cannot be disputed that the amount of water that colloids will hold varies greatly with changes in the colloids. We may not know absolutely, at present, whether the changes that take place in the colloids during life are great enough to alter their water content appreciably, but it is highly probable that they are. In many instances the principles of colloidal hydration offer the best explanation of observed conditions, and their application often elucidates matters more satisfactorily than any other working hypothesis. Certainly they cannot be disregarded in considering the factors that may come into play in producing edema.

Summary.—We find that a number of factors may be considered as responsible for edema, some of them being prominent in one instance, some in another, but *in few cases can we consider one factor alone as the sole cause.* In most of the forms of edema, such as those due to renal disease and cardiac disease, it now seems probable that either osmotic pressure changes or changes in the affinity of the tissue colloids for water, play the most important part; whereas in inflammatory edema there can be no question that alteration in the capillary walls is the most essential factor.   But the mechanical factor of blood pressure cannot be disregarded, although by itself seldom sufficient to cause edema; associated with other factors it is undoubtedly an important agency, for there are few edemas that are not associated with increased blood pressure.   Hydremia and hydremic plethora may almost be disregarded, except in so far as they may cause altered metabolism in the tissues, injury to vessel-walls, over-saturation of the blood colloids, and decreased osmotic pressure within the vessels.   Lymphatic obstruction is possibly a factor of some secondary importance if we consider that distended vessels and tense tissues may occlude the lymph capillaries.

Special Causes of Edema

We may now consider which of the above factors are at work in bringing about edema under the conditions in which it is usually observed.   Before taking up the detailed consideration of edematous conditions, however, it may be well to call attention to the fact that our knowledge of edema, and especially its clinical recognition and study, has been handicapped by the lack of a suitable objective method of detecting and measuring edema.   We are in the same position in respect to edema that we were to blood pressure when the only measure was the clinician's forefinger.   An attempt to remedy this defect has been made by Schade,[29] whose "elastometer" reveals and measures degrees of edema not discernible by the palpating finger.   A study of edema with this instrument in the hands of Schwartz[35] has revealed many interesting facts, but as yet the apparatus is too complicated for general clinical use.

"Cardiac" Edema.—Passive congestion introduces nearly all these aforementioned factors, for in addition to the increased blood pressure there is also an opportunity for changes in the capillary wall, either from stretching and thinning of the cells and cement substances, or from "loss of tone" in the endothelium surrounding the stomata (Meltzer), or from toxic injury by accumulated products of tissue metabolism.   When the stasis is nearly complete, or if it is complete for a time and then relieved, the endothelium may be injured through lack of nourishment.   As the edematous fluid in chronic passive congestion is usually of a watery type, poor in proteins, the edema is probably less dependent upon capillary permeability than upon other factors, except in the case of acute stasis, when the fluid partakes of the character of the exudates.   Presumably the accumulation of crystalloids within the tissues also plays a part in this form of edema, as the osmotic pressure is raised in tissues having deficient oxygen

[35] Arch. Int. Med., 1916 (17), 396 and 459.

supply. But Fischer holds that the reduction in oxidation acts chiefly by increased production of acids, which greatly increase the affinity of the tissue colloids for water and at the same time alter the colloidal state of the capillary endothelium so that the capillaries become more permeable. Finally, there is probably more or less obstruction to lymphatic outflow because of the increased pressure on the lymphatic channels, and perhaps, also, in the case of cardiac incompetence, obstruction to the discharge of lymph from the thoracic duct into the subclavian vein against the high intravenous pressure.

Renal Edema.—We must recognize under this heading two different types of edema. · In acute nephritis (e. g., in scarlatina) toxic materials appear to be the chief cause, and, as Senator contends, injure alike the capillaries of the renal glomerules and of the subcutaneous tissues; in each case there results an increased permeability which is manifested by albuminuria as a result of the injury to the renal capillaries, and by edema as a result of the injury to the tissue capillaries. This sort of edema is allied to that produced by peptone and similar lymphagogues, and we might well imagine that the mechanism consisted merely in an injury to the capillaries through which excessive fluid is driven by the blood pressure, were it not for such observations as those of Mendel and Hooker,[36] who found that postmortem flow is increased by these lymphagogues also. We can hardly account for the force exhibited in postmortem lymph flow on any other ground than that it is furnished by osmotic pressure or colloidal absorption unless we wish to fall back upon "vital activity" of the surviving cells. Hence it is probable that even in the edemas of toxic conditions, such as acute nephritis, physico-chemical factors play a part, the responsible substances probably being abnormal or excessive metabolic products of the cells affected by the poisons. An interesting observation made by Bence[37] is that nephrectomized rabbits develop an edema even when they are given no water at all; this would seem to indicate an increased affinity of the tissues for water when the renal functions are deficient. Hydremia is always a favoring factor, however, and probably important in nephritic edema,[38] while nearly all students of acute experimental nephritis find evidence that the resulting edema depends very much upon the changes in the vessel-walls.[39]

In the more common edema of chronic nephritis we have to consider, among other factors, the blood pressure. That this is not an essential or even important cause, however, is shown by the fact that edema is usually much less marked in interstitial nephritis with high blood pressure than it is in parenchymatous nephritis with a

[36] Amer. Jour. of Physiol., 1902 (7), 380.
[37] Zeit. f. klin. Med., 1909 (67), 69.
[38] Pearce, Arch. Int. Med., 1909 (3), 422.
[39] See Schmidt and Schlayer, Deut. Arch. klin. Med., 1911 (104), 44; Pollak Wien. klin. Woch., 1914 (27), 98.

much lower pressure. Toxic substances are, of course, also present in the blood, and may alter capillary permeability; these toxic substances may account for the localized edemas and erythemas sometimes observed in nephritis. But probably most important is the action of the crystalloids which the kidney does not excrete, and which seem to be stored up in the tissues, where they cause transudation of water under the influence of their osmotic pressure. For example, Rzentkowski[40] found that the average lowering of the freezing-point by the edematous fluid in nephritis was 0.583°, in cardiac dropsy it was 0.548°, and in tuberculous pleuritis 0.526°. This indicates that the osmotic concentration of the fluid is highest in renal dropsy, and supports the belief that here and in cardiac dropsy osmotic pressure plays a more important part than it does in inflammatory exudation.[41] Of the crystalloids that cause accumulation of fluid in the tissues, sodium chloride seems to be the most important.

Retention of Chlorides in Edema.[42]—From the investigations made by numerous clinicians, especially the French, it appears that—(1) in nephritis with edema a retention of sodium chloride frequently occurs; (2) that elimination of the chlorides is often increased during periods of improvement of the edema; (3) that a reduction of the amount of chlorides in the diet sometimes causes a great improvement in the edema, while administration of chlorides may make the edema much worse. There are, however, observations that also indicate that chloride retention does not account for many cases of renal dropsy, for commonly the above-mentioned conditions are not fulfilled.[43] Nevertheless, it cannot be denied that chloride retention is sometimes an important causative factor in the edema of parenchymatous nephritis.[44] If the retained chlorides obeyed the ordinary laws of diffusion, we should expect them to become distributed alike in the blood and tissues, so that they would merely cause an equal increase in the fluids of the blood and of the tissues; that is to say, there would be an hydremic plethora due to retention of water in the body by the accumulating chlorides. But, according to a number of observers, there is a specific retention in the tissues, which Strauss calls "*historetention*," and which explains the local edema. The way in which the historetention is produced is, however, not understood, and not all observers accept this hypothesis. If chlorides do bear a causative relation to edema, the predilection of the subcutaneous tissues for edematous accumulations may be explained by the observation that when salt is given to an animal an undue proportion (28-77 per cent.) accumulates in the skin.[45] In many conditions other than nephritis, there is also a chloride retention (e. g., pneumonia, cardiac incompetence, sepsis, typhoid), and the edemas observed in these diseases may possibly depend upon chloride retention, as many French authors

[40] Berl. klin. Woch., 1904 (41), 227.

[41] Epstein (Amer. Jour. Med. Sci., 1917 (154), 638) calls attention to the decrease of serum proteins (sometimes 60 to 70 per cent.) and ascribes the edema to lowered osmotic pressure of the blood from loss of colloids. Low protein content of the blood might more probably favor edema by reducing the amount of fluid which the blood can hold as a hydrophile colloid.

[42] Literature, résumé by Widal and Javal, Jour. Physiol. et Pathol., 1903 (5), 1107 and 1123; Rumpf, Münch. med. Woch., 1905 (52), 393. Review in Albu and Neuberg's "Mineralstoffwechsel," Berlin, 1906, pp. 171-178; Georgopulus, Zeit. klin. Med., 1906 (60), 411; Christian, Boston Med. and Surg. Jour., 1908 (158), 416; Palmer, Arch. Int. Med., 1915 (15), 329.

[43] See Blooker, Deut. Arch. klin. Med., 1909 (96), 80; Fischer, "Œdema and Nephritis."

[44] See Borchardt, Deut. med. Woch., 1912 (38), 1723.

[45] Schade, Zeit. exp. Path. u. Ther., 1913 (14), 1. Also gives an interesting discussion of the relation of the skin to edema.

suggest. Rumpf, indeed, often found more chlorides in edematous fluids of non-nephritic origin than in nephritic edema.[46] Fischer holds that the retention of chlorides in edema is secondary and not primary, for he found that tissues made to take up more water through acidification, also take up an increased amount of chlorides.

Inflammatory Edema.—Although here the alterations in the capillary walls play an essential rôle, as shown by the protein-rich nature of the exudates, yet most of the other factors are added. Increased blood pressure is prominent; lymph outflow is impeded by plugging of the lymphatic channels by clots and leucocytes, and by pressure on the outside; there is, undoubtedly, an excessive formation of metabolic products in the tissues, to cause exosmosis, and the asphyxial conditions in inflamed tissues favor acid formation which may cause in the colloids an increased affinity for water. According to Oswald[47] the permeability of the vessels for proteins becomes specifically altered in inflammation, so that not only the less viscous albumin and pseudoglobulin pass through their walls, but also the more viscous euglobulin and fibrinogen. To this class of edemas belong also the urticarias which follow the ingestion of various toxic substances, many of which can be shown experimentally to be lymphagogues. A good example is the urticaria which often follows the injection of antitoxic or other foreign serums, particularly their repeated injection; in experimental animals such a serum may cause death very quickly by acute pulmonary edema. All these poisons probably produce urticarial edema by injury to the capillary walls in the subcutaneous tissues, and possibly changes in the hydrophilic properties of the tissue colloids are also produced by the poisons. In the action of vesicants especially, it may well be questioned if changes in the capillary walls and active hyperemia are not supplemented by local metabolic alterations. The edema which follows the sting of insects, which are known to secrete into the wound such acids as formic, seems to be a particularly good illustration of the production of edema by the influence of acids on the tissues (Fischer).

Neuropathic Edema.—Until we understand better than we now do the manner in which nervous impulses modify metabolism, it will be difficult to estimate properly the importance of nervous impulses in the production of edema. That nervous control is a possible factor is well shown by many experiments; for example, simple ligation of the femoral vein in animals does not cause edema, but if the sciatic nerve is cut the vasoconstrictors are paralyzed, and edema may follow (Ranvier).[48] In this case the nervous influence is only indirect through its vasomotor effects. Similarly, stimulation of vasodilator

[46] Breitmann (Zentr. inn. Med., 1913 (34), 633) describes under the name of "soda dropsy" a form of edema which results from excessive administration of sodium bicarbonate to correct acidosis in diabetes.

[47] A. Oswald, Zeit. exp. Path., 1910 (8), 226.

[48] Similarly, pulmonary edema follows experimental hydremia only when the vagi are cut (F. Kraus, Zeit. exp. Path., 1913 (14), 402).

fibers may cause edema. It is furthermore possible that nervous stimulation may lead to excessive metabolic activity, with an accumulation of crystalloidal products and acids sufficient to cause edema when supplemented by active congestion and some resulting pressure upon the lymph-vessels. There are certainly many instances in which edema seems to depend upon nervous disturbance; for example, edema in the area of distribution of a neuralgic nerve; sudden joint effusions in tabetic arthropathy; and especially the typical "angioneurotic" edema.[49] The only explanation that seems open is the one given above, namely, a combination of local hyperemia and increased metabolic activity. Even the urticarias of apparently mechanical origin (*urticaria factitia*), show evidence of a toxic action, in that there occurs a severe nuclear fragmentation (Gilchrist).[50]

Hereditary Edema.—In a number of families there has been observed a peculiar inherited tendency to the occurrence of acute attacks of local edema, which not infrequently have proved fatal when involving the glottis.[51] There can be little question that these instances of hereditary edema depend upon a nervous affection of some kind, it being practically an angioneurotic edema; but how the edema is produced, and what the nature of the nervous alteration may be, are as mysterious as are most other so-called "nervous inheritances." There also are cases of *congenital edema*, which may occur repeatedly in the fetuses of the same mother and cause habitual miscarriage;[52] and still another class of cases in which the children are born apparently healthy, but develop fatal dropsy when a few weeks old.[53] Nothing is known as to the cause of this condition. Patein[54] has analyzed the fluid in a case of congenital ascites and found it somewhat more like an exudate than a transudate.

Nutritional Edema ("War Dropsy" or Famine Edema).—(Discussed under Deficiency Diseases, Chapter xii.)

COMPOSITION OF EDEMATOUS FLUIDS[55]

As is well known, the composition of edematous fluids varies greatly according to the cause of the edema and the place where it occurs. In general, non-inflammatory edemas (transudates) contain much less protein than do the inflammatory exudates, as is shown by the following table of analyses by Halliburton[56] and by Bernheim's[57] determinations of proteins in ascitic fluids.

[49] Metabolism in angioneurotic edema is discussed by Miller and Pepper, Arch. Int. Med., 1916 (18), 551.

[50] Johns Hopkins Hosp. Bull., 1908 (19), 49.

[51] Literature, see Fairbanks, Amer. Jour. Med. Sci., 1901 (127), 877; Hope and French, Quart. Jour. Med., 1908 (1), 312; Crowder, Arch. Int. Med., 1917 (20), 840.

[52] W. Fischer, Berl. klin. Woch., 1912 (49), 2103.

[53] Edgeworth, Lancet, 1911 (181), 216.

[54] Jour. Pharm. et Chim., 1910 (102), 209.

[55] Many data are given by Gerhartz, Handbuch der Biochemie, 1908, II (2), 137.

[56] Adami, Allbutt's System, 1896 (1), 97.

[57] Quoted by Hammarsten, "Physiological Chemistry."

TABLE I

	Sp. gr.	Parts per 100 of fluid			
		Total protein	Fibrin	Serum-globulin	Serum-albumin
Acute pleurisy..................	1.023	5.123	0 016	3.002	2.114
Acute pleurisy..................	1.020	3.4371	0.0171	1.2406	1.1895
Acute pleurisy..................	1.020	5.2018	0.1088	1.76	3.330
Hydrothorax } Aver. of 3 cases }	1.014	1.7748	0.0086	0.6137	1.1557

TABLE II

Ascitic fluid in	Parts of protein to 1000 c.c. fluid		
	Max.	Min.	Mean
Cirrhosis of the liver...................	34.5	5.6	9 69–21.06
Bright's disease......................	16.11	10.10	15.6–10.36
Tuberculous and idiopathic peritonitis....	55.8	18.72	30.7–37.95
Carcinomatous peritonitis..............	54.20	27.00	35.1–58.96

The specific gravity varies nearly in direct proportion to the amount of proteins, that of transudates usually being below 1.015, and exudates above 1.018, although there are many exceptions. Indeed, it is often very difficult to decide whether a given fluid is an exudate or a transudate.[58] According to Rzentkowski,[59] the transudates at the moment they pass out of the vessels are simply solutions of crystalloids in water and quite free from protein; the small amount of protein found in transudates he ascribes to protein pre-existing in the tissue-spaces. This idea is hardly acceptable in view of the known permeability of the vessel-walls for proteins in normal conditions; more probably in cardiac and renal dropsies the quantity of protein escaping from the vessels is not greatly different from normal, but the

[58] Rivalta (Rif. Med., 1903; Biochem. Centr., 1904 (2), 529) has suggested the following test to distinguish exudates and transudates: Into a beaker containing 200 c.c. of water with 4 drops of glacial acetic acid, let fall a few drops of the fluid to be tested. If an exudate, a bluish-white line is left transiently behind the sinking drops, due to precipitation of the euglobulin and fibrinogen. This test, and also certain modifications (see Rivalta, Policlinico, 1910 (17), 676), seem to give quite reliable results. (See Ujihard, Berl. klin. Woch., 1914 (51), 1112). With tuberculous effusions Rivalta's test is positive, but not Morelli's test, which consists in dropping the fluid into saturated HgCl$_2$ solution, a yellowish ring of albuminate forming with non-tuberculous exudates, and a granular precipitate with transudates. (See Zannini, Gaz. degli Osped., 1914 (4), 461). Memmi (Clin. Med. Ital., 1905, No. 3) suggests the larger content of lipase as a means of distinction of exudates. Tedeschi (Gaz. degli Osped., 1905 (26), 88) states that egg-albumen fed in large amounts appears in transudates and not in exudates, and can be detected by the biological precipitin test. Sugar is found more often in transudates (Sittig).
[59] Virchow's Arch., 1905 (179), 405.
23

excessive fluid escaping in these conditions carries with it no additional proteins, and to this extent transudates in *statu nascendi* are protein-free.

Transudates, even when produced by the same cause, vary in composition in different parts of the body, presumably because of variations in the permeability of the vessels in different vascular areas; just as pleural, pericardial, peritoneal, and meningeal fluids normally differ from one another. Thus C. S. Schmidt[60] found the composition of the transudates in different parts of the body of a patient who died of nephritis to have the following composition:

TABLE III

	Pleural	Peritoneal	Subarachnoid	Subcutaneous
Water	963.95	978.91	983.54	988.70
Solids	36.05	21.09	16.46	11.30
Organic matter	28.50	11.32	7.98	3.60
Inorganic matter	7.55	9.77	8.48	7.70

As in this case, the general rule is that while the proportion of salts remains nearly constant, the proportion of protein in edematous fluids in different localities varies in decreasing order as follows: (1) pleura; (2) peritoneum; (3) cerebrospinal; (4) subcutaneous.[61] In the last-named location the specific gravity of edematous fluids may be as low as 1.005, and the proteins even less than 0.1 per cent. (Hoffmann[62]). An increase in solids occurs after the effusion has existed for some time. presumably because of absorption of water and salts, leaving a slowly increasing proportion of proteins. Furthermore, the composition of the patient's blood has considerable influence on the composition of the effusion; this is particularly true in the case of ascites from portal obstruction, the contents of the blood coming from the intestine during digestion modifying the composition of the ascitic fluid.[63] Thus Müller,[64] in a case of portal vein thrombosis, found in the ascitic fluid of a patient on an ordinary mixed diet, 0.179 per cent. nitrogen; on a protein-rich diet, 0.2494 per cent. N; on a protein-poor diet, 0.1764 per cent. N. In cachectic conditions the proportion of proteins is less than in stronger individuals, and, as in the blood plasma, the albumin decreases more rapidly than the globulin as the cachexia advances (Umber).[65]

Physical Chemistry of Edema Fluids.—The differences between transudates and exudates depend almost solely on their protein contents, for the non-protein elements are almost identical with

[60] Hoppe-Seyler's Physiol. Chemie.
[61] Javal (Jour. phys. et path., 1911 (13), 508) places the fluids in this order: serum, peritoneal, pleural, subcutaneous, cerebrospinal.
[62] Deut. Arch. klin. Med., 1889 (44), 313.
[63] See Denis and Minot, Arch. Int. Med., 1917 (20), 879.
[64] Deut. Arch. klin. Med., 1903 (76), 563.
[65] Zeit. klin. Med., 1903 (48), 364.

the lymph and blood-serum, which naturally must be so since any original or temporary deviation in osmotic pressure must be rapidly equalized by diffusion. Thus Bodon[66] finds the concentration of the electrolytes nearly constant in spite of considerable differences in composition of various edema fluids, indicating that the serosa permits passage of inorganic salts always in the same concentration, while holding back the organic substances. Transudates contain an excess of NaCl over other electrolytes, while in exudates the proportion of electrolytes other than chlorides is increased over the findings in transudates.[67] The surface tension of exudates is lower than that of transudates,[68] depending chiefly upon the globulin content. Rzentkowski[69] found some slight differences in molecular concentration as indicated by the freezing-point; in tuberculous pleurisy the average lowering was 0.523°, that of the serum being $-0.56°$; in cardiac dropsy the subcutaneous fluid gave $-0.548°$, and in renal dropsy $-0.583°$; tuberculous peritonitis, $-0.523°$; cirrhosis $-0.536°$; carcinomatous edema $-0.547°$. Of these figures, the most significant is the comparatively high molecular concentration of the fluid in nephritis, supporting the contention that the cause of renal edema is retention of crystalloids.[70] Tieken[71] has found the results in transudates, exudates, and other body fluids shown in Table IV.

TABLE IV

Nature of fluid	Sp. gr.	Freezing-point of effusion, $-°$ C.	Freezing-point of blood, $-°$ C.	Disease
Pleuritic effusion	1,016	-0.55	-0.56	Pneumonia, lobar.
Pleuritic effusion	1,018	-0.55	-0.55	Pneumonia, lobar.
Pleuritic effusion	1,018	-0.54	-0.56	Tuberculosis.
Pleuritic effusion	1,020	-0.55	-0.56	Tuberculosis.
Pleuritic effusion	1,016	-0.55	-0.56	Tuberculosis.
Pleuritic effusion	1,018	-0.64	-0.56	Valvular heart disease.
Pleuritic effusion	1,030	-0.60	-0.58	Empyema: cyanosis.
Pericardial effusion	1,018	-0.55	-0.56	Pericarditis.
Pericardial effusion	1,016	-0.56	-0.56	Pericarditis.
Pericardial effusion	1,012	-0.56	-0.56	Hydropericardium.
Ascitic fluid	1,024	-0.60	-0.56	Cirrhosis of liver.
Ascitic fluid	1,020	-0.57	-0.56	Cirrhosis of liver.
Ascitic fluid	1,018	-0.58	-0.56	Tuberculous peritonitis.
Ascitic fluid	1,013	-0.62	-0.56	Organic heart disease.
Ascitic fluid	1,035	-0.65	-0.58	General peritonitis.
Hydrocele fluid	1,016	-0.56	-0.56	Tuberculosis.
Cerebrospinal fluid	1,018	-0.62	-0.58	Uremic coma.
Cerebrospinal fluid	1,016	-0.64	-0.68	Uremic coma.
Cerebrospinal fluid	1,020	-0.64	-0.64	Uremic coma.
Cerebrospinal fluid	1,014	-0.56	-0.56	Tuberculous meningitis.
Cerebrospinal fluid	1,017	-0.56	-0.56	Epidemic meningitis
Cerebrospinal fluid		-0.56	-0.56	Epidemic meningitis.

[66] Pflüger's Arch., 1904 (104), 519; also see Galeotti, Lo Sperimentale, 1901 (55), 425.

[67] Gruner, Biochem. Jour., 1907 (2), 383.

[68] Trevisan, Zeit. exp. Path., 1911 (10), 141.

[69] *Loc. cit.*,[59] and also Berl. klin. Woch., 1904 (41), 227.

[70] Purulent exudates may show a high molecular concentration ($-0.84°$ in one case), due to decomposition of the proteins into crystalloids (Rzentkowski).

[71] Amer. Medicine, 1905 (10), 822.

The very high figures for effusions in nephritis and cardiac incompetence indicate the concentration of crystalloids in these fluids, and support the belief that in the formation of both, osmotic pressure is an important factor.[72]

Edema fluids are usually alkaline except when bacterial changes lead to acid formation, but they are always able to neutralize less acid than the blood of the same individual (Opie). Bodon[66] found, however, that while they contain alkali that can be neutralized by titration against acids, yet they resemble the blood in being neutral as far as the presence of free OH ions is concerned.

Protein Contents.—As indicated in the tables given previously, these vary greatly in quantity in various fluids;[73] the quantitative relations of the different varieties of proteins have been less studied. Serum-albumins and globulins constitute by far the largest part of the proteins, fibrinogen being scanty except in some inflammatory exudates, so that coagulation very seldom occurs spontaneously; pneumococcus exudates seem particularly rich in fibrinogen, which coagulates rapidly and firmly. The differences in the proportion of different serum proteins in transudates is attributed by A. Oswald[74] to the relative viscosity of these proteins which determines their ability to pass through the capillary walls. The viscosity of serum proteins varies in the following increasing order: albumin, pseudoglobulin, euglobulin and fibrinogen; hence in transudates we may find only the first two, or perhaps only the albumin, while in exudates the two latter appear. Joachim[75] found in pleural transudates and exudates that the proportion of albumin, euglobulin, and pseudoglobulin is always lower in hydrothorax than in pleurisy. Of different forms of ascites, the largest proportion of globulin and the smallest of albumin occur in cirrhosis; while with carcinoma the proportions are reversed. In general the albumin is more abundant than the globulin,[76] but, as Umber[65] has found, the proportion of albumin sinks more rapidly in cachexia than does the globulin, corresponding to the similar changes in the blood proteins. The amount of protein lost in exudates is strikingly shown by one of Umber's cases of cancerous ascites; during one year the fluid removed by paracentesis contained not less than three kilos of pure protein, the patient weighing but 55.5 kilos.

Several authors have found in inflammatory ascitic exudates a protein having physical and chemical properties much resembling

---

[72] Meyer and His (Deut. Arch. klin. Med., 1905 (85), 149) claim that the lowering of the freezing-point is less than that of the blood in exudates while forming, the same as the blood while stationary, and greater during absorption, which they consider indicates a "vital process" on the part of the cells.

[73] See also v. Jaksch, Zeit. klin. Med., 1893 (23), 225; Rzentkowski (*loc. cit.*) [59]

[74] Zeit. exp Path., 1910 (8), 226.

[75] Pflüger's Arch., 1903 (93), 558.

[76] See Epstein, Jour. Exp. Med., 1914 (20), 334.

mucin; it has been especially studied by Umber,[77] who finds it quite similar to the synovial mucin isolated in arthritis by Salkowski, and calls it *scrosamucin*.

Non-Protein Organic Contents.—Proteoses,[78] leucine, and tyrosine may be present in small quantities in exudates, being produced by autolysis[79] (Umber); and also mucoid substances (Hammarsten). Nucleoproteins may be present from leucocytic disintegration in exudates, as well as the products of their further splitting, such as purines and phosphates. Galdi and Appiani[80] found uric acid constantly in amounts between 0.0055 g. and 0.0714 g., in all exudates, of which seven were tuberculous and two neoplastic. In three transudates amounts from 0.006 to 0.011 g. were found. Allantoin is said to have been found in exudates (Moscatelli),[81] but this is doubtful.

All the other innumerable components of plasma may be found in edematous fluids; thus sugar[82] and urea (Carriére)[86] are often present, as well as other extractives. The amount of urea varies quite as it does in the blood of the same individual,[83] and it seems probable that all the crystalloid substances present in the blood pass freely into and from inflammatory exudates, so that an equilibrium between blood and exudates is approximated.[84] Sugar is said sometimes to be greater in amount in transudates than in the blood, but in exudates it is usually, if not always, lower than 0.1 per cent.[85] Glycogen is not present (Carriére).[86] By using more accurate methods than have been employed by most of the observers quoted above, Denis and Minot[87] found urea, uric acid and creatinin to occur in exudates and transudates in the same concentrations as in the blood, but the sugar content of ascitic fluids is somewhat higher than that of the blood. Creatin, fats and cholesterol are much lower in transudates than in exudates in which they approach the concentration in the blood. In ascitic fluid the urea, uric acid and cholesterol are influenced by the diet.

Lipins.—Lecithin is always present, partly bound to globulin and partly free (Christen).[88] Cholesterol is present particularly in fluids that have been standing for a long time in the body, appearing often as visible crystals shining in the fluid; it probably originates from degenerating cells. Ruppert has described a case of pleural effusion with 1.129 per cent. of cholesterol when tapped the first time, 0.22 per cent. the second and 0.05 per cent. the third. Hedstrom reported finding in an old pleural effusion, 4.5 per cent. of cholesterol; one year later there was but 0.09 per cent. Zunz[89] has described a carefully studied case in which 14 aspirations were made; the cholesterol content was about 3 per cent. at first, but fell suddenly to 0.48 per cent. and then remained between 0.5 per cent. and 0.28 per cent. Lecithin varied from 0.1 to 0.04 per cent. As there did not seem to be enough cells present in the fluid to have yielded the obtained cholesterol through their disintegration, Zunz suggests that it may have been secreted by the walls

[77] Zeit. klin. Med., 1903 (48), 364; also Holst, Upsalalakar. Forhand., 1904, p. 304.

[78] Opie, Jour. Exp. Med., 1907 (9), 391.

[79] Histidine and arginine were found in a carcinomatous exudate by Wiener (Biochem. Zeit., 1912 (41), 149).

[80] Riforma Med., 1904, p. 1373; also Carriére, Compt. Rend. Soc. Biol., 1899 (51), 467.

[81] Zeit. physiol. Chem., 1899 (13), 202.

[82] Sugar was found in only 8 of 23 fluids by Sittig (Biochem. Zeit., 1909 (21), 14); but is present in pulmonary edema fluid in proportion equal to or even greater than the blood (Kleiner and Meltzer).

[83] Javal and Adler, Compt. Rend. Soc. Biol., 1906 (61), 235; Rosenberg, Berl. klin. Woch., 1916 (53), 1314.

[84] Wells and Hedenburg, Jour. Infect. Dis., 1912 (11), 349; Scheel, Nord. Med. Laeg., 1916 (77), 610.

[85] Hegler and Schumm, Med. Klinik, 1913 (9), 1810.

[86] Compt. Rend. Soc. Biol., 1899 (51), 467.

[87] Arch. Int. Med., 1917 (20), 879.

[88] Cent. f. inn. Med., 1905 (26), 329.

[89] Travaux Ambulance de L'Ocean, La Panne, 1918, Tome II, Fasc. 1.

of the cavity. Weems[90] has described a similar case, with 1.39 per cent. in the first fluid drawn, but smaller amounts in fluids withdrawn later; this patient had a marked hypercholesterolemia. Arnell[91] found 0.41 per cent. of cholesterol in a tuberculous pleurisy. In most of these cases some fats have been present, Weems finding 0.33 per cent. and Ruppert 0.36 per cent.

Toxicity.—Contrary to earlier ideas, transudates are not demonstrably toxic, even in nephritis (Baylac,[92] Boy-Teissier,[93] Lafforcade[94]), and therefore the toxic manifestations frequently observed after reduction of edema in nephritis, and ascribed to absorption of poisons in the transudates, are probably due to some other cause. In inflammatory exudates, of course, the causative agents as well as the products of cell destruction render the fluids poisonous.

Enzymes and Immune Bodies.—All the enzymes of the plasma may appear in edematous fluids, being in all cases probably more abundant in exudates than in transudates. According to Carrière,[95] oxidases are inconstant, even in exudates. Lipase is said to be much more abundant in exudates than in transudates.[96] (Concerning proteolytic enzymes see "Autolysis of Exudates," Chap. iii.) The various immune bodies, cytotoxins, hemolysins, bacteriolysins, agglutinins, etc., seem to pass freely into both transudates and exudates, and their presence is not characteristic of either,[97] but as a rule the proportion is much higher in exudates.[98] Peptid-splitting enzymes are usually found in such fluids,[99] especially tuberculous exudates,[1] and these enzymes seem to be different from both erepsin and trypsin. Probably this type of enzyme is more often present than trypsin. Antitryptic activity is usually high, unless exhausted by the presence of much trypsin from cell-rich exudates. Purulent fluids are usually poor in opsonins;[2] in non-purulent fluids the opsonin content varies with the amount of proteins.[3] Turpentine exudates may sometimes be more strongly bactericidal than the serum of the same animal.[4] Exudates usually contain about as much complement as the serum, but in suppuration the complement disappears; transudates contain little of either complement or hemolysins.[5]

Precipitin Reactions, etc.—Edematous fluids have been often used as a source of material in immunizing animals against human proteins. The precipitins thus formed are specific for human serum or for the proteins of the effusion, but can not be used to differentiate a transudate from an exudate, or a hydrothorax fluid from an ascites fluid (Quadrone).[6] Immune bodies, complement, agglutinins and antitoxins are present in effusions; e. g., the common use of blister fluid for the Widal test. Furthermore, according to Hamburger,[7] edema fluid is distinctly more bactericidal than normal lymph.

VARIETIES OF EDEMATOUS FLUIDS[8]

On the preceding pages have been mentioned the chief differences in the characters of the effusions in the usual sites,[9] with their varia-

[90] Amer. Jour. Med. Sci., 1918 (156), 20.
[91] Hygiea, 1917 (79), 737.
[92] Compt. Rend. Soc. Biol., 1901 (53), 519.
[93] Ibid., 1904 (56), 1119.
[94] Gaz. heb. Med. et Chir., Jan. 28, 1900.
[95] Compt. Rend. Soc. Biol., 1899 (51), 561.
[96] Zeri, Il Policlinico, 1903 (10), No. 11; Memmi, Clin. med. Ital., 1905, No. 3; Galletta, Clin. med. Ital., 1911 (50), 143.
[97] Granström, Inaug. Dissert., St. Petersburg, 1905.
[98] Not corroborated by Lüdke, Cent. f. Bakt., 1907 (44), 268. See also Delrez Bull. acad. Roy. Med. Belg., 1919 (29), 733.
[99] Hall and Williamson, Jour. Path. and Bact., 1911 (15), 351.
[1] See H. Koch, Zeit. Kinderheilk., 1914 (10), 1.
[2] Opie, Jour. Exper. Med., 1907 (9), 515.
[3] Böhme, Deut. Arch. klin. Med., 1909 (96), 195.
[4] Rastaedt, Zeit. Immunität., 1912 (13), 421.
[5] Aronstamm, Cent. f. Bakt., 1914 (74), 326.
[6] Cent. f. Bakt. (Ref.), 1905 (36), 270.
[7] Virchow's Arch., 1899 (156), 329.
[8] Chemistry of Pus and Sputum are discussed under Inflammation, Chapter xi.
[9] Literature and résumé on pleuritic exudates, see Ott, Chem. Pathol. der Tubere., 1903, p. 392.

tions in protein contents, which variation agrees with Starling's statement that the permeability of the capillary wall for proteins differs normally in different localities. Some of the other effusion fluids not mentioned previously have particular properties of some interest.

Subcutaneous Effusions.[10]—When of non-inflammatory origin these are very watery, having ordinarily a protein content of from 0.1 to 0.2 gm. per 100 c.c., there being more globulin in nephritic than in cardiac dropsy. The non-coagulable nitrogen and chloride content are not so high as in the blood of the same patients, but the ash is the same as that of the serum. The specific gravity may be as low as 1.005, but the solids increase with the duration of the edema.

Hydrocele and Spermatocele Fluids.—These have been studied particularly by Hammarsten, who found the average result of analyses of seventeen hydrocele fluids and four spermatocele fluids as follows:

TABLE V

	Hydrocele	Spermatocele
Water	938.85	986.83
Solids	61.15	13.17
Fibrin	0.59	
Globulin	13.25	0.59
Seralbumin	35.94	1.82
Ether-extractive bodies	4.02	
Soluble salts	8.60	10.76
Insoluble salts	0.66	

Marchetti[11] found in ten specimens of hydrocele fluid rather higher results for the solids than did Hammarsten. He found 57.8 to 104.2 p. m. of solids, containing organic substances 48.8 to 95.02, and inorganic substances 8.10 to 9.56; proteins, 33.5 to 90.19; ratio of globulin to albumin as 2.56 to 9.11. Among the proteins is found 1 to 4 p. m. that is not precipitated by heat. Corresponding with the analytic results, the specific gravity of hydrocele fluid is higher, 1.016 to 1.026 as against 1.006 to 1.010 for spermatocele fluid. Cholesterol is often abundant in hydrocele fluids, appearing to the naked eye as glistening scales. Patein[12] found sugar in most specimens of hydrocele. Apparently hydrocele fluid stands intermediate in properties between transudates and exudates.[13] Usually it contains but little of the immune bodies from the blood (Delrez).[98]

Meningeal Effusions.[14]—Normal meningeal fluid differs from all other serous fluids in being clear and watery, in its low specific gravity (1.004 to 1.007), in containing but a trace of protein which is chiefly globulin (with a trace of proteose (?)), and 0.05–0.13 per cent. of a reducing substance that is probably glucose,[15] which is decreased in

[10] See Epstein, Jour. Exper. Med., 1914 (20), 334.
[11] Lo Sperimentale, 1902 (56), 297.
[12] Jour. pharm. et chim., 1906 (23), 239; also Compt. Rend. Soc. Biol., 1906 (60), 303.
[13] Vecchi, Gaz. Med. Ital., 1912 (63), 211; Epstein, Jour. Exp. Med., 1914 (20), 344.
[14] Résumé by Blumenthal, Ergeb. der Physiol., 1902 (1), 285; Blatters and Lederer, Jour. Amer. Med. Assoc., 1913 (60), 811; Herrick and Dannenberg, *ibid.*, 1919 (73), 1321; Levinson, Amer. Jour. Dis. Child., 1919 (18), 568; Becht, Amer. Jour. Physiol., 1920 (51), 1.
[15] Schloss and Schroeder, Amer. Jour. Dis. Child., 1916 (11), 1; Hopkins, Amer. Jour. Med. Sci., 1915 (150), 847.

acute suppurative meningeal inflammation (Jacob).[16] There is normally in the adult from 60 to 150 cc., and Frazier estimates that from 360 to 720 cc. is secreted daily. Halliburton gives the following analyses of pathological accumulations of such fluids:

TABLE VI (Spina bifida)

	Case 1	Case 2	Case 3
Water	989.75	989.877	991.658
Solids	10.25	10.123	8.342
Proteins	0.842	1.602	0.199
Salts	9.626	{ 0.631	3.028
Extractives		{ 7.830	5.115

The percentage of solids in spina bifida is thus a little higher than in normal meningeal fluids. In hydrocephalus the percentage of solids is rather greater, as seen in Table VII.

TABLE VII (Hydrocephalus)

	Case 1	Case 2	Case 3
Water	986.78	984.59	980.77
Solids	13.22	15.41	19.23
Proteins and extractives	3.74	6.49	11.35
Salts	9.48	8.92	7.88

Normal cerebrospinal fluid seems to be hypertonic to the serum of the same animal[17] and slightly more alkaline than the blood.[18] In meningitis the alkalinity is often lowered.[19] The alkali reserve is nearly constant in systemic diseases, except diabetes (McClendon),[20] and is practically the same as that of the blood. By gas chain measurements Levinson[21] found the spinal fluid almost neutral (pH = 7.4–7.6); in epidemic meningitis it is 7.3–7.4. According to Fuchs and Rosenthal[22] the average freezing-point of the cerebrospinal fluid is lowered about the same in all diseases ($\triangle$ = −0.52° to 0.54°) except in tuberculous meningitis, where it is much less (average −0.43°). The amount of potassium is about the same as in the blood,[23] and not increased in degenerative diseases of the central nervous system;[24] after death the amount is much increased by post-mortem changes. Calcium is almost constant at 5 mg. per 100 c.c., or about one-half as much as in the plasma.[25] In diseases associated with destruction of brain tissue, such as general paralysis and epilepsy,[26] *choline* or some

[16] Brit. Med. Jour., 1912, Oct. 26.
[17] Ravaut, Presse méd., 1900 (8), 128; Zanier, Cent. f. Physiol., 1896 (10), 353.
[18] Hurwitz and Tranter, Arch. Int. Med., 1916 (17), 828.
[19] Levinson, Arch. Pediatrics, 1916 (33), 241.
[20] Jour. Amer. Med. Assoc., 1918 (70), 977.
[21] Jour. Infect. Dis., 1917 (21), 556.
[22] Wien. med. Presse, 1904 (45), 2081 and 2135.
[23] Myers, Jour. Biol. Chem., 1909 (6), 115, literature.
[24] Rosenbloom and Andrews, Arch. Int. Med., 1914 (14), 536.
[25] Halverson and Bergeim, Jour. Biol. Chem., 1917 (29), 337.
[26] Concerning spinal fluid in epilepsy see Larkin and Cornwall (Jour. Lab. Clin. Med., 1919 (1), 352.

other base[27] may be found in the spinal fluid.   (See "Choline," Chap.
iv.)

Under pathological conditions the amount of protein varies greatly
and to some extent characteristically.   Thus, in syphilis the euglobulin
is so greatly increased that it is readily identified by various precip-
tation methods,[28] while in more acute inflammations fibrinogen appears.[29]   According to Mott[30] the fluid is especially rich in nuclein
in progressive paralysis, and lipoids are increased in the fluid in degenerations of the central nervous system.   Pathological fluids show
also specific alterations in their colloidal property of preventing precipitation of colloidal suspensions by electrolytes (the "Goldzahl"
of Zsigmondy).[31]   The surface tension is higher than that of the
serum and is not characteristically altered in disease.[32]   The increased
organic matter of pathological fluids raises the permanganate reduction
index.[33]   In epidemic meningitis there is more positively charged
protein while in tuberculous meningitis there is more negatively
charged protein, which can be distinguished by suitable precipitants
(Tashiro and Levinson).[34]

Cholesterol can be found in all cases of mental disease. the amount
not bearing any relation to the type of psychosis (Weston);[35] ordinarily 0.2 to 0.7 mg. per 100 c.c. is found.   The changes in P_2O_5 content
in disease are doubtful,[36] while the amount of reducing substances is
said to be increased in disease.[37]   In general the inflammatory fluids
in the spinal canal resemble exudates elsewhere, but usually the concentration of the different components is relatively low, except the
chlorides.[38]   Normal cerebrospinal fluid contains no antiprotease (for
leucoprotease), as does the fluid in many cases of chronic inflammations; in acute inflammation proteases may appear (Dochez[39]).   Peptid-splitting enzymes are especially abundant in meningitis.[40]   Antibodies pass from the serum into the cerebrospinal fluid only in minimal
amounts or not at all, except when inflammatory exudation occurs,
and even then the antibody concentration is usually low,[41] and even

[27] Kaufmann, Zeit. physiol. Chem., 1910 (66), 343; Laignel-Lavastine and Lasusse, Compt. Rend. Soc. Biol., 1910 (68), 803.
[28] See Noguchi, Jour. Exp. Med., 1909 (11), 604.
[29] See Mestrezat, Rev. d. Méd., 1910, p. 189; Kaffka, Deut. med. Woch., 1913 (39), 1874.
[30] Lancet, July 9, 1910.
[31] Lange, Zeit. Chemother., 1912 (1), 44; Spät, Zeit. Immunität., 1915 (23),'426; Vogel, Arch. Int. Med., 1918 (22), 496.
[32] Kisch and Remertz, Münch. med. Woch., 1914 (20), 1097.
[33] See Hoffman and Schwartz, Arch. Int. Med., 1916 (17), 293.
[34] Jour. Infect. Dis., 1917 (21), 571.
[35] Jour. Med. Res., 1915 (33), 119.
[36] Apelt and Schumm, Arch. Psychiat. u. Nervenkr., 1908 (44), 845.
[37] Jacob, Brit. Med. Jour., Oct. 26, 1912.
[38] Javal, Jour. phys. et path. gén., 1911 (15), 508.
[39] Jour. Exp. Med., 1909 (11), 718.
[40] Major and Nobel, Arch. Int. Med., 1914 (14), 383.
[41] Lemaire and Debré, Jour. physiol. et path. gén., 1911 (13), 233.

simple chemicals enter the normal spinal fluid but very little,[42] except perhaps alcohol.[43] According to Rosenbloom[44] there is no creatin or creatinine. It contains normally from 2 to 4 mg. of amino-N per 100 c.c., or about half that in the blood, without definite changes in syphilis.[45] There is almost the same amount of urea as in the serum of the same person, *i. e.*, 20 to 42 mg. per 100 c.c.[46] In uremia the non-protein constituents of the spinal fluid increase with those of the blood, but to a less degree. Substances giving the ninhydrin test appear in meningitis,[47] but Rosenberg states that even with the highest indicanemia[48] no indican is found in the spinal fluid. Sugar is present in from 0.07 to 0.085 per cent. and is not modified significantly in mental diseases;[49] it is reduced in meningitis but increased in uremia.[50] There is only a very small amount of diastase, not bearing any constant relation to the cell count.[51]

Xanthochromia.—In cases of retention of spinal fluid, usually in a lumbar cul-de-sac, it may assume a yellow color although free from blood pigment, containing much globulin and coagulating spontaneously (Froin's syndrome). The color is apparently due to concentration of plasma held for some time in the spinal canal and may be from bilirubin.[52] Most usually this condition accompanies tumor of the spinal cord.[53]

Wound secretions obtained from large aseptic wounds, mostly amputation stumps, have been studied by Lieblein.[54] The reaction is generally alkaline, globulin and albumin abundant, but fibrinogen scanty, total nitrogen being less than that of the blood and decreasing from day to day; the proportion of albumin increases and globulin decreases as healing progresses. Occasionally albumoses were found, but only on the first day in aseptic wounds; if found later, they generally were antecedent to suppuration (concerning suppuration see "Inflammation," Chap. xi).

Blister fluid is generally rich in solids and proteins (40–65 p. m.). In a burn blister Mörner[55] found 50.31 p.m. proteins, among which were 11.59 p. m. globulin and but 0.11 p. m. fibrin; also a substance reducing copper oxide, but not pyrocatechin. By refractometric determinations the amount of protein in blister fluids is in direct proportion to the amount in the blood.[56] Antibodies of all

[42] See Rotky, Zeit. klin. Med., 1912 (75), 494.
[43] Schottmüller and Schumm, Neurol. Zbl., 1912 (31), 1020.
[44] Biochem. Bull., 1916 (5), 22.
[45] Ellis, *et al.*, Jour. Amer. Med. Assoc., 1915 (64), 126.
[46] Ellis and Cullen, Jour. Biol. Chem., 1915 (20) 511.
[47] Nobel, Münch. med. Woch., 1915 (62), 1355, 1786.
[48] Berl. kl. Woch., 1916 (53), 1314.
[49] Weston Jour. Med. Res., 1916 (35), 199; Kraus and Corneille, Jour. Lab. Clin. Med., 1916 (1), 685.
[50] Leopold and Bernhard, Amer. Jour. Dis. Chil., 1917 (13), 34. Discussion of chemistry of spinal fluid in children.
[51] Leschke and Pincussohn, Deut. med. Wochs., 1917 (43), 8; Katakura, Kyoto Jour. Med. Sci., 1916 (13), 1.
[52] Bauer and Spiegel, Deut. Arch. klin. Med., 1919 (129), 18.
[53] Review by Sprunt and Walker, Bull. Johns Hop. Hosp., 1917 (28), 80; Elsberg and Rochfort, Jour. Amer. Med. Assoc., 1917 (68), 1802.
[54] Beit. klin. Chir., 1902 (35), 43.
[55] Hammarsten, "Physiological Chemistry."
[56] Engel and Orszag, Zeit. klin. Med., 1909 (67), 175.

sorts seem to pass readily into blister fluids[57] although the complement-fixation reaction is not so strong as with the blood.[58]

Hydrops of Gall Bladder.—The watery fluid contains 99 per cent. water, a mucin-like substance, but no other proteins and no bile acids.[59]

Fetal Bronchiectasis. —The fluid resembles closely liquor amnii.[60]

Chylous Effusions.[61]—Fat may be present in effusions in sufficient quantity to cause a milky appearance, either from escape of chyle from a ruptured or obstructed thoracic duct, or through fatty degeneration of the cells in the effusion or the lining of the walls of the cavity. The former are designated as *chylous*, the others as *chyliform* or *adipose* fluids, but it is not always easy to distinguish between them. The composition of the fluids in true chylous exudates will vary according to the food taken and the amount of fat the food contains, and will resemble the composition of chyle, except to the extent that it is modified by the effusion or absorption going on in the cavity. They are characterized by strong bactericidal powers as evidenced by lack of putrefaction after long standing.

Analyses of human chyle are scanty. Panzer[62] found 90.29–94.53 per cent. water; 5.47–9.71 per cent. solids; 0.80–1.04 per cent. inorganic salts; 2.16 per cent. coagulable protein; 6.59 per cent. ether-soluble material; also diastatic enzyme, soaps, and occasionally traces of cholesterol, lecithin, and sugar. Carlier,[63] in a specimen from a child, obtained very similar results, except that the salts were much less abundant. The proteins and fats vary greatly with the diet; thus Sollmann[64] found variations in the proteins from 1.85 to 6.5 per cent.

Edwards[65] found that of 31 definitely established cases of chylous or chyliform ascites studied at autopsy, in 21 there was established the existence of a rupture in the thoracic duct or lacteals. Boston[66] in 1905 was able to collect 126 cases, including both chylous and chyliform ascites, and notes an associated *eosinophilia* in a case studied by him. Chylous ascites fluid often, but not always contains sugar,[67] but it may disappear after having once been present; the amount of fat is small, usually about 1 per cent., and the fluid is rich in solids. If due to a ruptured thoracic duct, it may be possible to detect special fats taken in the food, e. g., butter-fats (Straus).[68] The reaction is

---

[57] Eisenberg, Deut. med. Woch., 1909 (35), 613.
[58] Buschke and Zimmermann, Med. Klinik, 1913 (9), 1082.
[59] Sjöquist, Svenska Läk. Handl., 1916 (42), 1291.
[60] Koeckert, Amer. Jour. Dis. Chil., 1919 (17), 95.
[61] Literature by Gandin, Ergeb. inn. Med., 1913 (12), 218.
[62] Zeit. physiol. Chem., 1900 (30), 113.
[63] British Med. Jour., 1902 (ii), 175.
[64] Amer. Jour. Physiol., 1907 (17), 487; see also Hamill, Jour. Physiol., 1906 (35), 151.
[65] Medicine, 1895 (1), 257; also see "Chem. u. morph. Eigenschaften fetthaltige Exsudaten," St. Mutermilch, Warschau, 1903; Comey and McKibben, Boston Med. and Surg. Jour., 1903 (148), 109.
[66] Jour. Amer. Med. Assoc., 1905 (44), 513.
[67] For example, v. Tabora (Deut. med. Woch., 1904 (30), 1595) found as high as 0.864 per cent. of sugar in a typical case.
[68] Arch. Physiol. et Pathol., 1886 (Ser. 3, vol. 8), 367.

usually alkaline or neutral, and some specimens coagulate spontaneously. Specific gravity varies from 1.007 to 1.040, the average being about 1.017. Perhaps the most important characteristic is the variation produced by changes in diet.[69] Zdarek[70] found in a chyle-cyst 2.7 per cent. of fats, 7.2 per cent. of proteins, and 0.05 per cent. of sugar; feeding of fats increased their amount in the cyst and starvation decreased it. Schumm[71] found in the solids of such a cyst 35.76 per cent. of fat, some of which was in the form of calcium soap.

Chylothorax fluid is, of course, quite similar to that of chylous ascites. Thus, Buchtala[72] found 91.34 per cent. of water, 8.66 per cent. solid, 4.86 per cent. protein, 2.5 per cent. fat, 0.26 per cent. cholesterol, and 0.94 per cent. ash. Similar figures were obtained by Salkowski[73] and others.

Chyluria,[74] which seems to depend upon an abnormal communication between the lymphatics of the receptaculum chyli and the kidney,[75] shows no particular chemical features beyond those of an admixture of a considerable amount (100 to 1000 c.c. per day) of chyle with the urine. Carter[76] found the amount of fat in the urine to rise with increase of fat in the food. Pecker[77] observed a rise from a former average of 1.5 gm. fat per liter to 9.75 gm. after eating oils and milk. In some cases chyle escapes directly into the bladder or ureter from the lymphatics, in others the fat may be excreted directly from the blood, independent of lymphatic abnormality; in some cases the fluid entering the urine is true chyle and in others it is lymph.

Ascites adiposus is characterized by the absence of sugar and by a higher percentage of fat, the maximum observed being 6.4 per cent. It is ascribed to fatty metamorphosis of cells, particularly in carcinomatous and tuberculous exudates; Edwards was able to show experimentally that a transudate may change from serous to cellular, and later come to contain fat.

Pseudochylous effusions are also observed, not only in the abdominal and thoracic cavities, but even in the fluid of the edematous legs and scrotum; these resemble chylous fluids in being turbid or milky, but are said to contain little or no fat. The turbidity is ascribed chiefly to lecithin, which is largely combined with the pseudoglobulin of the fluid (Joachim).[78] Possibly in some cases the turbidity is partly or largely (Poljakoff)[79] due to poorly dissolved proteins. Strauss[80] has noted the occurrence of this form of ascites particularly in chronic parenchymatous nephritis, but believes the turbidity has a local origin. Hammarsten has observed turbidity due to mucoid substances, as also have Gouraud and Corset.[81] The pseudo-chylous effusions have a lower freezing point, a lower specific gravity,

---

[69] A sample of the composition of 1 liter of chylous ascitic fluid is shown by the analysis in the case studied by Comey and McKibben (*loc. cit*): Specific gravity, 1.010; solids, 21 gm.; protein, 9.75 gm.; urea, 1.28 gm.; fat, 1.45 gm.; inorganic matter, 8 gm.; peptone (?) and sugar, present; fibrinogen, mucin, nucleo-albumin, and uric acid absent.

[70] Zeit. f. Heilk., 1906 (27), 1.

[71] Zeit. physiol. Chem., 1906 (49), 266.

[72] Zeit. physiol. Chem., 1910 (67), 42.

[73] Virchow's Arch., 1909 (198), 189; also Tuley and Graves, Jour. Amer. Med Assoc., 1916 (66), 1844; Patein, Jour. pharm. Chim., 1915 (11), 265.

[74] Review of literature by Sanes and Kahn, Arch. Int. Med., 1916 (17), 181.

[75] See Magnus-Levy, Zeit. klin. Med., 1908 (66), 482.

[76] Arch. Int. Med., 1916 (18), 541.

[77] Jour. pharm. chim., 1917 (16), 139. See also Patein, ibid., 1917 (16), 230

[78] Münch. med. Woch., 1903 (50), 1915; also Christen, Cent. f. inn. Med., 1905 (26), 329; Wallis and Schölberg, Quart. Jour. Med., 1910 (3), 301; 1911 (4),153.

[79] Fortschr. d. Med., 1903 (21), 1081; also Haushalter, Compt. Rend. Soc. Biol., 1910 (68), 550.

[80] Note to Poljakoff's article;[79] also Biochem. Centr., 1903 (1), 437.

[81] Compt. Rend. Soc. Biol., 1906 (60), 23.

lower fat and greater lecithin content than typical chylous ascites. Gandin,[61] however, questions the possibility of always differentiating the three types of turbid fluids as above indicated. Collecting all the recorded analyses in the literature he finds wide discrepancies, as indicated in the following table: (The maximum and minimum percentage figures are given for each component determined quantitatively, with the average in parentheses.)

	Chylous	Adipose (Chyliform)	Pseudochylous
Ether extract	0.065–9.2 (1.65)	0.1–4.3 (1.15)	0.007–1.86 (0.25)
Cholesterol	+ in 7, − in 2	+ in 4	+ in 3, − in 2
Lecithin	+ in 4, − in 1	+ in 3	+ in 20, − in 2
Sugar	+ in 46, − in 28	+ in 1, − in 4	+ in 15, − in 14
Dry residue	3.1–10.6 (6.2)	1.6–11.7 (5.1)	1.2–7.6 (2.9)
Protein	0.9–7.7 (3.5)	0.6–6.8 (3.0)	0.1–4.2 (1.4)
"Pepton"	+ in 6, − in 4	+ in 1, − in 2	+ in 1, − in 5
Ash	0.1–1.0 (0.59)	0.45–1.03 (0.65)	0.49–0.90 (0.73)

It is quite evident that although the pseudochylous fluids usually contain little fat, they often contain more than the minimal content found in the other forms. Each type of fluid overlaps the others in one respect or another. Gandin states that to produce a turbid fluid but 0.01–0.1 per cent. of finely emulsionized fat is necessary, and he believes that milky fluids always mean admixture of chyle, rejecting the terms pseudochylous and chyliform as unwarranted. He admits that fluids may contain droplets of fats not emulsionized, and hence not milky, which may be properly called adipose fluids. There are no characteristic chemical differences in the fats extracted from the different types of fluids.

CHEMISTRY OF PNEUMOTHORAX

In connection with the subject of exudates the above topic may appropriately be considered. The composition of the gases found in the pleural cavity in pneumothorax will necessarily vary greatly according to the cause. If the pleural cavity is in free communication with the exterior, the gas will be simply slightly modified air; for example, Ewald[82] found the following proportions in the gases in such a pneumothorax: CO_2, 1.76 per cent.; O, 18.93 per cent.; and 79.31 per cent. N. Here the proportion of CO_2 is even a little less than in ordinary expired air, which contains 3.3–3.5 per cent. When air enters a closed pleural cavity and no effusion follows, it is slowly absorbed until a mixture of about 90 per cent. N, 4 per cent. O and 6 per cent. CO_2 results; but if there is a serous effusion the oxygen disappears nearly or quite completely (Tobiesen).[83] In a seropneumothorax Ewald found 8.13 per cent. of CO_2, 1.26 per cent. of O, and 90.61 per cent. of N, which is quite similar to the proportions of the gases in dry pneumothorax. Purulent pneumothorax generally shows more CO_2 than the serous form, the average in the former being 15–20 per cent., in the latter 7.5–11.5 per cent. The average of the analyses in six cases of pyopneumothorax is given by Ewald as 18.13 per cent. CO_2, 2.6 per cent. O, and 79.81 per cent. N. In open pyopneumothorax the gas approaches more closely the composition of air, but usually shows a slight excess of CO_2; it is thus possible by a determination of the carbon dioxide to determine quite accurately whether a given pneumothorax is in communication with the outside air. The transformation of a purulent into a putrid pneumothorax is accompanied by an increase of CO_2, even as high as 40 per cent. having been found. The products of decomposition by the putrefactive saprophytes also are present, one analysis having shown 4.3 per cent. of hydrogen, 6.25 per cent. of methane, and traces of hydrogen sulphide.

Infection of a pleural effusion by gas-producing organisms may also convert it into a pneumothorax, although this is not a common occurrence. The gases then

[82] Complete literature and résumé given by Clemens, in Ott's "Chem. Path der Tuberculose," Berlin, 1903, p. 406.

[83] Beitr., z. Klin. d. Tuberk., 1911 (19), 451; 1911 (21), 109; Deut. Arch. klin. Med., 1914 (115), 399.

present are the same as the organisms produce in similar culture-media, modified somewhat by absorption. The anaёrobic gas-producing organisms have been found as the cause of such gaseous accumulations; it is questionable if the ordinary pathogenic organisms can cause a pneumothorax, since they are for the most part not capable of producing gas. The colon bacillus produces gas in sugar-containing media, but the amount of sugar in the pathological exudates is too small to yield any considerable amount of gas; an exception is the pleural effusion in diabetes, and pneumothorax from infection of the pleural effusion in a diabetic by *B. coli* has been reported. Complete quantitative analyses of the gas in this form of pneumothorax seem not to have been made, but May found about 20 per cent. of CO_2. The combustibility of the gas has frequently been noted. and is probably due to hydrogen and methane.

CHAPTER XV

RETROGRESSIVE CHANGES (NECROSIS, GANGRENE, RIGOR MORTIS, PARENCHYMATOUS DEGENERATION)

NECROSIS

WE recognize that a cell is alive through its reproducing, functioning, and its taking on and utilizing nutritive substances; yet at the same time we appreciate that a cell may do none of these things and still be alive. For example, a bacterial spore is quite inert physically, and exhibits no chemical activity, yet it is by no means dead, since it still possesses the latent power to assume again an active existence under suitable conditions. In pathological conditions we are accustomed to recognize the fact that a cell is dead by certain alterations in its structural appearance, particularly disintegrative changes in the nucleus; but this is exactly equivalent to recognizing that an animal is dead by the appearance of postmortem decomposition, for most of the characteristic histological changes of necrosis are merely postmortem changes in the cell. A cell may be dead and show absolutely none of these microscopic disintegrative changes, either because it has not been dead long enough for them to have taken place, or because the changes have been prevented by some means, just as we can prevent the appearance of postmortem decomposition by embalming. For example, if we examine microscopically the mucous membrane of the stomach of a person who has died immediately after taking a large quantity of carbolic acid, although to the naked eye this mucous membrane is hard, white, and definitely necrotic, yet we find the histological picture presented by the cells almost absolutely unchanged from the normal. The cells are dead, but they have been so "fixed" that postmortem changes could not affect their structure. All cells examined by ordinary histological methods are, of course, dead—killed by the fixing agents outside of the body, in the same way that the carbolic acid fixes them within the body. It is evident, therefore, that it may be very difficult to determine always whether a cell is dead or not. Part of the difficulty, perhaps, lies in our failure to appreciate that not all parts of a cell die at the same time; i. e., the different chemical processes of the cell depend on its different intracellular enzymes, and these are not necessarily destroyed alike by the same agents. Even considerable respiratory activity may be exhibited by cells that have been killed.[1a]

We recognize that after an animal is dead as a whole the various cells of its body do not die for some time as shown by the following

---

[1a] See Haas, Bot. Gazette, 1919 (67), 347.

examples: (1) We can cause the heart to beat for a considerable period after its removal from the body; (2) if we perfuse a mixture of glycocoll and benzoic acid through the kidney of a recently killed animal, synthesis of these substances into hippuric acid will occur; and (3) the epithelium of the skin can be removed from the body of an animal long after death and transplanted successfully on another animal. So, too, in ordinary cell death (necrobiosis) not all the enzymes are destroyed together. When all are destroyed at once, as by strong chemicals or by heat, the customary disintegrative changes do not take place. If, however, not all the enzymes are thrown out of function, then the others may be able to act, producing the disintegrative changes by which histologists ordinarily recognize cell death. These disintegrative changes are, for the most part, apparently brought about by the intracellular proteases, that is, through autolysis. This may be shown as follows:[1] If we take two pieces of fresh normal tissues from an animal, and in one kill the enzymes by heating to 100° C., then implant both aseptically into the abdominal cavity of an animal of the same species, it will be found that the changes that follow in the two will be very unlike. In the unheated tissue nuclear changes soon occur, so that they lose their capacity for taking up basic stains, the cytoplasm becomes granular and fragmented, the tissue becomes friable so that it is difficult to secure good sections, and the changes are in general similar to those seen in areas of necrosis. The boiled tissue, on the other hand, retains its capacity for nuclear staining for months, except at the periphery, where it is slowly attacked by leucocytes and the enzymes of the blood plasma. Therefore it would seem that the characteristic changes of necrosis depend chiefly upon the intracellular enzymes, rather than upon the infiltrating plasma as Weigert[2] and other early writers imagined. In areas of anemic necrosis (see "Infarcts") we have another case, in which the oxidizing enzymes are thrown out of function through lack of oxygen, while the other enzymes are, presumably, at first unaffected. From studies of infarcts it would seem that the intracellular proteases bring about the subsequent nuclear and cytoplasmic alterations, but that the eventual digestion of the area is accomplished by the invading leucocytes working slowly inward from the periphery. Apparently when the supply of materials from outside ceases, and when the oxidation processes of the cells no longer accomplish necessary steps of synthetic reactions or destroy products of protein catabolism, the proteases continue to split proteins without the balancing by the above-mentioned factors, with a resulting disintegration of the cells.

Karyolysis and *karyorrhexis* are, then, the result of an autolytic process, which is perhaps due to intracellular proteases that act spe-

---

[1] Wells, Jour. Med. Research, 1906, (15), 149.
[2] Cent. f. Path., 1891 (2), 785.

cifically on nucleoproteins, and which may be designated as *nucleases*.[3]
Nuclear staining by the usual methods depends upon an affinity of the
acid nucleoproteins (in which the nucleic acid is not completely
saturated by proteins) for basic dyes. Presumably in karyolysis the
first step consists in a splitting of the nucleoprotein of the chromatin
into nucleic acid and protein; this can be accomplished, according
to Sachs, by the ordinary trypsin, and presumably, therefore, by the
trypsin-like enzymes of the cell. Corresponding with this change
we should expect the free nucleic acid to give an intense staining
with basic stains, and this has frequently been described by those
who have studied the cytological changes in anemic necrosis,[4] and
called *pycnosis*. As supporting this view still further may be quoted
Arnheim's[5] observation that in alkaline solutions the nucleus soon
stains diffusely and weakly, and not at all after twelve to eighteen
hours; this is to be explained by the fact that nucleic acid is both
dissolved and neutralized by alkaline solutions. Acids developed in
injured cells may, by combining with the basic elements of the nucleoproteins, render them still more acid and highly basophilic; thus,
in muscles showing waxy degeneration from accumulation of lactic
acid the muscle nuclei will be found pycnotic (see waxy degeneration). After the nucleic acid has been freed from the protein by
the autolytic enzymes, it is still further decomposed by the "nuclease" or similar intracellular enzymes that have the property of
splitting nucleic acid into the purine bases that compose it—corresponding with this change the hyperchromatic nucleus loses its
affinity for stains, and *karyolysis* is complete. When extensive necrosis occurs there will result, therefore, an increased elimination
of purines, as was found by Jackson and Pearce[6] in animals with
severe hepatic necrosis from hemotoxic serum.

A careful analytical study of the changes taking place in the autolyzing spleen,
for the purpose of correlating the chemical and microscopical changes, has been
made by Corper,[7] which corroborates the interpretation of necrosis advanced
above. He found that during the stage when pycnosis is the chief feature there
is no appreciable change in the nucleus; that is, the nucleic acid has not been
split into free purines and the rest of its components; at this stage but little
change has occurred in the lecithin, and a very slight amount of proteolysis is
demonstrable. During the stage of karyorrhexis and karyolysis the most active
disintegration is taking place, about one-fourth of the nucleic acid becoming disintegrated by the time all nuclear structures have disappeared; in the same
period nearly half the lecithin (phosphatids) is hydrolyzed, while about one-
fourth the coagulable protein has been hydrolyzed into non-coagulable compounds.
After this stage the changes are very slow. It is somewhat surprising to find
that when no vestige of nuclear substance remains in stainable form, there still
remains three-fourths of the nucleic acid in an intact condition. Corper publishes

[3] See Purine Metabolism, Chap. xxiii.
[4] Schmaus and Albrecht, Virchow's Arch., 1895 (138), supp., p. 1; Ergeb. allg.
Pathol., 1896 (3), 486 (literature).
[5] Virchow's Arch., 1890 (120), 367.
[6] Jour. Exper. Med., 1907 (9), 569.
[7] Jour. Exper. Med., 1912 (15), 429.
24

a series of plates, together with the chemical details, thus establishing a standard whereby the histological changes can be interpreted in terms of the chemical changes which cause them.

Autolysis of aseptically preserved tissues outside the body is much more rapid than is the autolysis of infarcts and similar aseptic necrotic areas within the body. This may be due to either or both of two factors:[8] First, autolysis is much slower in alkaline than in acid media; outside the body autolyzing tissues develop an acid reaction which favors their autolysis; within the body this is checked by the plasma. Second, the plasma contains inhibiting substances, which also may interfere with self-digestion in the body. In corroboration of the above may be recalled the fact that large necrotic areas show autolysis first in the center, where the alkaline, antagonistic body fluids presumably cause the least effect. Furthermore, it has been found by Wells[9] that the histological changes of autolysis proceed much faster in tissues placed in serum that has been heated to destroy the antibodies than in unheated serum. Leucocytes, as Opie has shown, contain autolytic enzymes acting best in an alkaline medium, hence they perform their digestive function readily at the periphery of necrotic areas, and coagulated tissue proteins, when acted upon by body fluids, produce chemotactic substances which attract leucocytes to dead areas.[10]

When a cell dies, certain *physical changes* occur that are probably of considerable importance. Bechhold says: "With the occurrence of death, protoplasm gelatinizes, Brownian movement of the smaller particles ceases, and the structure of the gel appears in the ultramicroscope as a conglomeration of many reflecting platelets. It makes a substantial difference whether the protoplasm slowly dies or is suddenly killed by a fixative (alcohol, formalin, etc.). In the first instance there is a precipitation (flocculation), whereas, in the latter there is a stiffening; this difference may be readily recognized under the ultramicroscope."

The permeability of the cell wall is almost immediately increased, so that all diffusible substances readily pass through, *i. e.*, its semipermeable character is lost. This we see particularly in plant cells, which lose their turgor with their semipermeability, and therefore the plant wilts. The cell structure is also disintegrated, and as a result coördination of the cell chemistry is at once destroyed.[11] Intracellular enzymes escape into the blood from areas of local death of cells,[12] or as an agonal manifestation in general death.[13] Various

[8] Literature and more complete discussion under "Autolysis."

[9] Jour. Med. Research, 1906 (15), 149.

[10] Bürger and Dold, Zeit. Immunität., 1914 (21), 378.

[11] See v. Prowazek, Biol. Centrbl., 1909 (29), 291. Pictet suggests that in dead proteins, aldehydes and amino radicals unite with one another to form cyclic compounds (Arch. sci. phys. nat., 1915 (40), 181).

[12] Mandelbaum, Münch. med. Woch., 1914 (61), 461.

[13] Schultz, Münch. med. Woch., 1913 (60), 2512.

dyes which cannot penetrate living cells may stain dead or dying cells.[14] These changes depend on alterations in permeability, and as permeability determines electrical resistance, Osterhout has used the resistance of plant cells as an indicator of vitality. He finds that normal cells have a rather constant resistance, which is reduced by anything that lowers the vitality of the cell, and in direct proportion to the degree of injury or loss of vitality.[15] The temperature coefficient is also considerably lower in dead than in living tissue.[16] When secondary disintegrative changes occur in the protoplasm, with the formation of many small molecules from the large molecules of the cell, both osmotic pressure and electrical conductivity increase rapidly. Changes in the permeability of cell protoplasm, however, may be of considerable degree without necessarily indicating serious injury of the cells (Osterhout).[17] Death is accompanied by changes of the character of a monomolecular reaction, which is continually going on and which is accelerated by the toxic agent.[18] Up to a certain point the reaction seems to be reversible.

A principle of colloid chemistry, the alteration of colloids with time, has an interesting bearing on the question of aging and natural death of tissues.[18a] It is characteristic of colloidal solutions (which, of course, is what cells are), that they continuously change in their properties, the change being generally in the direction of aggregation of the disperse colloidal particles, with a resulting tendency to precipitation or coagulation; the gels tend to decrease in elasticity and to become more turbid, associated with which are alterations in their permeability to crystalloids. A gelatin mass possesses its maximum elasticity three or four hours after it is first formed; and crystalloids penetrate fresh, quickly-formed gels at first more rapidly than later. As Bechhold says, we can imagine (1) a relation of such facts to the greater elasticity of young tissues; (2) to a presumably greater permeability for crystalloids and hence more rapid metabolism; (3) to the decreasing water of the tissue with age (94 per cent. of water in the fetus of three months, 69–66 per cent. at birth, and 58 per cent. in adults); (4) to the demonstrated greater permeability of young nerve tissues for vital stains, etc. "In general we can say that the tissue colloids decrease in their water affinity (*Quellbarkeit*) both in animal organisms, which become poorer in water with age, and in plants, as shown by the hardening of older plant tissues." The bearing of these principles on the problem of senility and degeneration of elastic tissue, regeneration and many other subjects is obvious.

CAUSES OF NECROSIS

Anemia.—After the cutting off of blood-supply, cells soon undergo morphological changes that we recognize as indicating their death, and after a time they also become incapable of returning to their normal condition when the blood-supply is re-established, probably because of these structural changes. In just what way lack of nourishment

[14] See Steckelmacher, Beitr. path. Anat., 1913 (57), 314.
[15] See Science, 1914 (40), 488.
[16] Galeotti's earlier observations with animal tissues (Zeit. f. Biol., 1903 (45), 65) do not harmonize with Osterhout's results, and Galeotti's idea that there is a special degree of ionization characteristic of living cells is not established.
[17] Botan. Gaz., 1915 (59), 242.
[18] Osterhout, Jour. Biol. Chem., 1917 (31), 585.
[18a] See H. Bechhold, "Die Kolloide in Biologie und Medizin," Dresden, 1912, p. 65.

causes death has not been determined, but, as has been before suggested, it seems probable that it is because catabolic processes are no longer balanced by anabolic processes, and with these latter oxidizing enzymes seem to be inseparab'y associated as far as our present knowledge shows us. That the loss of oxygen alone, with other materials presumably supplied to the cells in adequate amount, may cause necrosis, is shown by the presence of marked hepatic necrosis in animals kept a week in atmospheres extremely low in oxygen (5–9 per cent.).[19] The nature of the chemical changes taking place in a cell when oxygen is deficient must be very different from the normal changes, and hence abnormal toxic substances may accumulate, e. g., excessive amounts of organic acids. Were it not that the proteolytic enzymes continue in action after nutrition is shut off, the cells might remain in a completely unaltered condition for an indefinite period, and capable of resuming their function when nourishment is again supplied, which is decidedly contrary to the facts. (The general features of anemic necrosis have been already discussed in the preceding paragraphs, and also under the subject of infarction.)

Thermic Alterations.—These have been studied particularly in connection with the cells of the lower organisms.[20] While some unicellular organisms can survive a temperature of 69°, most of them are killed at from 40°–45°. For the great majority of metazoa the maximum temperature lies below 45°, and in the case of marine species below 40°.[21] The heating is accompanied by the appearance of granules in the cytoplasm, which become larger until the condition of "heat rigor" sets in. Kühne, in 1864, showed that in muscle cells, at least, there is contained a protein which becomes turbid through partial coagulation at 40°, and Halliburton[22] has found that in nearly all tissues are globulins coagulating at from 45°–50°; it is probable, therefore, that the granules formed in heated cells are produced through coagulation of these proteins. The importance of this coagulation in determining death is not yet fully established, but it would seem to be very great. Halliburton has observed that in both muscles and nerves to which heat is applied, contractions occur at various temperatures, corresponding exactly with the temperatures at which the several varieties of the proteins of the cells coagulate. Furthermore, Mott[23] has found that the temperature that is immediately fatal to mammals (47°) is exactly the same as the coagulating temperature of the lowest coagulating protein of

[19] Martin, Loevenhart and Bunting, Jour. Exp. Med., 1918 (27), 399.
[20] Literature, see Davenport, "Experimental Morphology," New York, 1897; Schmaus and Albrecht, Ergebnisse der Pathol., 1896 (3, Abt. 1), 470.
[21] The adaptation of animal cells to high temperatures is an interesting topic, especially in view of such results as those of Dallinger, who, by raising the temperature gradually during several years, caused flagellata, with a normal maximum of about 21° –23° to become capable of living at 76° (see Davenport).
[22] "Biochemistry of Muscle and Nerve," Phila., 1904.
[23] Quoted by Halliburton.

nerve-cells. This fact is undoubtedly of great practical importance in causing death from fever, for although 47° C. (117° F.) is probably never reached in man, yet application of much lower temperatures, even 42° (108° F.), for a few hours will cause coagulation of these proteins (all proteins coagulate at less than their ordinary coagulation point if the heating is continued for a long time). It would seem from the above observation that heat may cause cell death through coagulation of the proteins. Whether the cell death is in any way dependent upon destruction of the enzymes by heat has not been ascertained; but as most enzymes are not destroyed much below 60°–70°, it seems improbable that they are greatly injured at the temperatures at which cells are killed. It is possible, however, that under the conditions in which enzymes exist in the cell they may be more susceptible to heat than under other conditions. Just how coagulation of cell globulins can determine the death of a cell is difficult to understand, unless the physical conditions of the cell are greatly altered thereby. Ordinarily we have in the cell an equilibrium between colloids in solution and colloids in the solid or gel state; if the colloids are rendered insoluble by heat, or by any other cause, so that this equilibrium is destroyed, serious alterations in the mechanism of all metabolism must result (Mathews). Other chemical reactions will also have their point of equilibrium altered by changes in temperature, and such alterations might well have disastrous results.

Different tissues show unequal susceptibility to heat. Werhovsky[24] found the blood most affected by raising the temperature of living animals, next the liver, kidneys, and myocardium in order, the other tissues being little or not at all structurally injured. Animals exposed to heat show a fall in the leucocyte count, followed by a rise in lymphocytes which persists; there is an extensive degeneration of cells in the spleen and lymph glands, followed by marked mitotic proliferation in the germinal centers.[25]

Cold[25a] is well withstood by unicellular forms, and relatively poorly by more complex organisms, particularly by those with a highly developed circulatory system; this is because individual cells are not greatly affected by freezing, whereas the circulatory channels are readily blocked by this cause. Bacterial cells are not killed by exposure for long periods to the temperature of liquid air[26] (−190°). Reduction of the temperature of plant cells to −13° may result in a granular transformation of the cytoplasm, often with rather serious structural alterations. Cytoplasm seems to be more affected than the nucleus, for mitosis may occur slowly in plant cells at −8°,

[24] Ziegler's Beitr., 1895 (18), 72.
[25] Murphy and Sturm, Jour. Exp. Med., 1919 (29); 1.
[25a] Systemic effects of cold reviewed by Foord, Jour. Infect. Dis., 1918(23), 159.
[2] MacFadyen, Lan et, 1900 (i), 849.

and Uschinsky[27] noted that in animal tissues the nuclei were less affected by cold than the cytoplasm. Blood seems little affected by freezing temperature, for du Cornu found that dog's blood kept on ice for five to ten days could be employed for transfusion without causing hemoglobinuria. Grawitz saw motion persist in human ciliated epithelium kept for seven to nine days on ice. Ciliated epithelium from the mouth of the frog may survive cooling to $-90°$ and frog eggs are not killed by $-60°$. In many cells, however, the physical changes produced by freezing, and also by the subsequent thawing, are sufficient to render them incapable of further existence.[28] Cells devoid of or poor in water cannot be killed by freezing, hence it is probable that the currents set up about the crystals of ice in thawing, as well as the rapid contraction and expansion under the influence of the cold and the ice formation, are the cause of the effects of freezing, which, therefore, are not dependent upon chemical, but upon physical, alterations.

In the case of warm-blooded animals, the gangrene following freezing depends not so much upon the freezing of the cells themselves as upon the formation of hyalin thrombi in the injured vessels (v. Recklinghausen, Hodara).[29] Kriege[30] found that if the freezing is transitory, the thrombi may again disappear; if over two hours in duration, they are persistent. Rischpler,[31] however, considers that cell death is due primarily to the effect of the cold upon the cells, and Lake[32] found that for both isolated cells in culture and living tissues with intact blood supply, death occurred at $-6°$ C., this being the temperature at which protoplasm freezes. On the other hand, Steckelmacher[32a] found that freezing of liver tissue produced the same changes as ligation of the hepatic artery, *i. e.*, increased permeability of the cell wall followed by similar changes in the nucleus, suggesting that the changes produced by freezing depend on the vascular changes.

Light.[33]—Light may affect tissues seriously, apart from the effects of accompanying heat, although the experiments of Aron[34] indicate that *insolation* does not depend on the light rays, but solely on the heat. In the treatment of lupus by the Finsen method with concentrated light rays, the action is largely a stimulating one, but associated with or subsequent to a certain degree of cell injury. Ogneff[35]

[27] Ziegler's Beitr., 1893 (12), 115.
[28] In plant cells it is the freezing and not the thawing that causes the harm (Maximow, Berichte Deut. Bot. Gesell., 1912 (30), 504).
[29] Münch. med. Woch., 1896 (43), 341.
[30] Virchow's Arch., 1889 (116), 64.
[31] Ziegler's Beitr., 1900 (28), 541.
[32] Lancet, Oct. 13, 1917.
[32a] Beitr. path. Anat., 1913 (57), 314.
[33] Review by Bering, Ergeb. allg. Pathol., 1914, Abt. 1 (17), 790. See discussion of the principles of the action of light on tissues by Bovie, Amer. Jour. Tropical Dis., 1915 (2), 506.
[34] Philippine Jour. Sci., B, 1911 (6), 101.
[35] Pflüger's Arch., 1896 (63), 209.

found that moderate action of electric light, rich in violet and ultraviolet rays, causes mitotic cell division; if the action is stronger, the cells undergo amitotic division and then become necrotic. Blue rays have but slight cytotoxic action, and rays further towards the red end of the spectrum are without demonstrable effect. Light baths are said by Oerum[36] to increase greatly the quantity of corpuscles and hemoglobin, while residence in the dark reduces these elements. The destruction of bacteria by light is a well-known phenomenon,[37] but it has been suggested that their destruction depends rather upon the action of substances produced in the culture-medium under the influence of light than upon the effect of the light upon the bacterial cells themselves. In view of the fact that enzymes and antibodies in solution are quite readily weakened or destroyed by the action of light, it is possible that intracellular enzymes may be similarly destroyed by light, with resulting cell death. However, in the case of bacteria, at least, the effects of light seem to depend upon oxidation processes, for in the absence of oxygen, bacteria are not seriously injured by light, and D'Arcy and Hardy[38] found that "active oxygen" is formed by the same portion of the spectrum that is most active in destroying bacteria.[39] Light may also alter the solubility of cell proteins, especially in the presence of various organic and inorganic substances that act as sensitizers, such as silicates, sugar, lactic acid or urea.[40] In this may lie the cause of cataract, especially diabetic cataract.

The general effect of light acting on organic substances present in plant and animal cells, is to produce from carbonyl-containing materials aldehyde or ketone compounds, whose reactivity and availability for important synthetic changes are conspicuous (Neuberg).[41] Whether oxidative processes are the cause of death in animal cells is not known, but we are familiar with many chemical reactions of various sorts that are initiated or checked by the action of light.[42] Thus, bilirubin is oxidized into biliverdin, when acted upon by sunlight, even when not in contact with air; many vegetable oils are oxidized by sunlight, and it is probable that the oxidizing action of light upon organic compounds is of wide-spread occurrence. It is, therefore, quite possible that such oxidative changes may be the cause of necrosis produced by the action of light rays, especially as Bering[43] has found that chemically active light rays have a direct action on oxidizing enzymes.

[36] Pflüger's Arch., 1906 (114), 1.
[37] Literature given by Wiesner, Arch. f. Hyg., 1907 (61), 1.
[38] Jour. of Physiol., 1895 (17), 390.
[39] See also Agulhon, who found that ultraviolet rays may attack enzymes to some extent in the absence of oxygen (Ann. Inst. Pasteur., 1912 (26), 38).
[40] Schanz, Biochem. Zeit., 1915 (71), 406; Arch. Ophthal., 1918 (96), 172; Burge, Amer. Jour. Physiol., 1916 (39), 335; Neuberg and Schwarz, Berl. klin. Woch., 1917 (54), 84.
[41] Biochem. Jour., 1908 (13), 305.
[42] See Davenport, "Experimental Morphology," 1897, p. 162.
[43] Münch. med. Woch., 1912 (59), 2795.

It is very probable that not all of the effects of exposure to the sun depend upon the heat rays, for there is evidence that the light rays may also produce effects. This is definitely true in the case of individuals or animals with certain pigments in their blood, notably hematoporphyrin (*q. v.*). In them, not only may skin eruptions result from relatively small exposure to light, but mice may be so sensitized that a few moments of exposure to light is fatal.[44] Artificial fluorescent substances, such as eosin, also sensitize tissues and proteins to light.[45] Normal blood absorbs light rays in large amounts, as Finsen showed, and it is quite possible that changes in the chemistry of the blood result from the light rays. Exposure to the sun may cause a general leucocytosis with relative lymphocytosis.[46]

According to Hertel[47] the *ultraviolet* rays cause oxygen to split off the easily oxidizable compounds of protoplasm, and Bovie[48] found that they coagulate proteins; they also have a destructive effect on enzymes,[39] serum complement[49] and hormones.[50] However, Burge,[51] found that exposure of living cells to ultraviolet radiation of sufficient intensity to kill the cells does not decrease to any appreciable extent the activity of the intracellular enzymes; the cell death he attributes to coagulation of protoplasm. Harris and Hoyt[52] advance evidence that the susceptibility of protoplasm to ultraviolet light is conditioned by selective absorption of the toxic rays by the aromatic amino-acids of the proteins. Toxins are reduced in activity by ultraviolet rays.[53]

X=rays[54] stimulate cell growth when applied in small amounts,[55] but larger amounts produce necrosis, which is peculiar in that an interval of several days, or even weeks, may elapse after the exposure before the necrosis manifests itself. Ellis[56] considers that the amount of necrosis is out of proportion to the changes in the vessels, which some have believed to be the cause of x-ray gangrene, and therefore that the cells must be directly injured,[57] a view supported by Casemir's[58] experiments with plant cells. The extensive studies of the

[44] Hausmann, Biochem. Zeit., 1914 (67), 309.
[45] Full review on photodynamic action of light by Sellards, Jour. Med. Res. 1918 (38), 293.
[46] Aschenheim, Zeit. Kinderheilk., 1913 (9), 87; Taylor, Jour. Exp. Med., 1919 (29), 41.
[47] Zeit. Augenheilk., 1911 (26), 393.
[48] Science, 1913 (37), 24; see also Burge, Amer. Jour. Physiol., 1916 (39), 335.
[49] Brooks, Jour. Med. Res., 1918 (38), 345.
[50] Burge *et al.*, Amer. Jour. Physiol., 1916 (40), 426.
[51] Amer. Jour. Physiol., 1917 (43), 429.
[52] Science, 1917 (46), 318; Univ. Calif. Publ. (Pathol.), 1919 (2), 245.
[53] Hartoch *et al.*, Zeit. Immunität., 1914 (21), 643.
[54] Full review by Colwell and Russ, "Radium, X-Rays and the Living Cell," London, 1915. Also see Richards, Science, 1915 (42), 287.
[55] See Schwarz, Münch. med. Woch., 1913 (60), 2165.
[56] Amer. Jour. Med. Sci., 1903 (125), 85.
[57] Allen (Jour. Med. Research, 1903 (9), 462) states that protozoa and vinegar eels are killed by long exposure to x-rays, whereas plants are decidedly stimulated in their growth.
[58] Med.-Naturw. Arch., 1910 (2), 423; résumé on x-rays.

Hertwigs show that the chromatin is chiefly affected, which presumably explains the fact that immature cells, and cells in active division, are more sensitive to x-rays than adult cells, and that monstrosities develop from eggs exposed to radiant energy. As far as histological changes show, hard rays produce less but quite the same changes as soft rays. That x-rays have a marked effect on metabolism has been abundantly established.[59] According to Musser and Edsall,[60] the effect of x-rays upon metabolism is unequalled by any other therapeutic agent, and is manifested by excessive elimination of the products of protein destruction, which arise particularly from the lymphatic structures.[61] These changes have been studied, therefore, particularly in connection with the treatment of leukemia (*q. v.*). In consequence of the injury to the blood-forming tissues, resistance to bacteria is decreased (Läwen).[62] The renal epithelium seems also to suffer injury in some cases.[63]

Exposure of the entire body of animals, or large areas of hematopoietic tissue in man, leads to profound changes. Chief of these are destruction of lymphoid cells, pigmentation of the spleen, destruction of bone marrow cells, primary rise in polymorphonuclear cells followed by a fall to below normal, steady decline in lymphocyte count, and an increased resistance of the red cells to radiation.[64] So marked may be the effect of x-rays on the marrow and spleen that antibody formation is greatly depressed (Hektoen).[65] After heavy doses marked metabolic changes occur which indicate a profound intoxication, there being vomiting and diarrhœa, high non-protein N in the blood and a great increase in the urinary N (Hall and Whipple).[66] These authors also observed necrosis in the intestinal epithelium. Presumably these reactions are similar to those observed following superficial burns, and depend on disintegration of tissue proteins with production of toxic substances.

The long-continued action of x-rays upon the skin has, in many cases, led to the formation of cancer, apparently because the proliferation stimulated by the rays progresses until it exceeds normal

[59] See Harvey (Jour. Path. and Bact., 1908 (12), 548), concerning the effects of x-rays.

[60] Univ. Penn. Med. Bull., 1905 (18), 174; also Edsall and Pemberton, Amer. Jour. Med. Sci., 1907 (133), 426.

[61] A peculiar selective action for the generative cells is also shown by x-rays, which cause marked atrophy of the ovaries and testicles. In the latter it affects chiefly the germinative cells, sparing the cells of Leydig. (See Albers-Schönberg, Münch. med. Woch., 1903 (50), 1850; Frieben, *ibid.*, 1903 (50), 2295; Specht, Arch. f. Gyn., 1906 (78), 458; Thaler, Deut. Zeit. f. Chir., 1905 (79), 576; Reifferscheid, Zeit. f. Gyn., 1910 (34), 593.

[62] Mitt. Grenz. Med. u. Chir., 1908 (19), 141.

[63] See Schulz and Hoffman, Deut. Zeit. f. Chir., 1905 (79), 350; Warthin, Amer. Jour. Med. Sci., 1907 (133), 736.

[64] Résumé by Gudzent, Strahlentherapie, 1913 (2), 467. See also Taylor *et al*, Jour. Exp. Med., 1919 (29), 53.

[65] Jour. Infect. Dis., 1918 (22), 28.

[66] Amer. Jour. Med. Sci., 1919 (157), 453.

bounds.[67] Likewise leukemia has been observed several times in roentgenologists, presumably produced in the same way.[68]

As the metabolic changes produced by x-rays indicate an extremely high rate of autolysis, one may ascribe the effects either to a stimulating effect of x-rays upon autolytic enzymes, or as Neuberg[69] does, to an inhibitive action of x-rays and radium rays upon the other intracellular enzymes without a corresponding deleterious effect upon the autolytic enzymes.[70]   This hypothesis agrees with the facts at hand, but more details concerning the effects of these rays upon various enzymes are needed. The long latent period before the appearance of necrosis after exposure to x-rays is difficult to explain, and agrees rather with the hypothesis of slow proliferative and obstructive changes in the blood-vessels.

Radium, which shares with x-rays the power of causing tissue necrosis, does not have so marked an effect upon the blood,[71] nor do the ultra-violet rays (Linser and Helber).[72] In general, radium has much the same effect on tissues as x-rays,[73] but seems rather to stimulate the action of most enzymes;[74] autolysis, however, is not increased (Brown).[75] Radium partially destroys the growth-promoting "vitamines" of yeast, which may account for some of its effects on tumors (Sugiura and Benedict). Radium also causes severe skin lesions and a general lymphocytosis in those exposed to it for long periods.[76] Active deposit of radium emanation injected intravenously into animals is highly toxic, even small doses causing fatty degeneration in the liver associated with giant cell formation and hyperchromatic nuclei; larger doses cause multiple hemorrhages and death with severe enteritis. Lesions also occur in the kidneys, lungs, spleen and bone marrow.[76a] In proper amounts radium stimulates plant metabolism (Gager). Thorium-x also attacks specifically the leucocytes,[77] so that by proper dosage an animal may be made practically leucocyte-

[67] See review by Wyss. Beitr. z. klin. Chir., 1906 (49), 185; Porter and Wolbach, Jour. Med. Res., 1909 (21), 357.

[68] See Jagic and Schwarz, Berl. klin. Woch., 1911 (48), 1220.

[69] Zeit. f. Krebsforschung, 1904 (2), 171; also Meyer and Bering, Fortschr. Roentgenstrahlen, 1911 (17), 33; Richards, Amer. Jour. Physiol., 1914 (36), 400.

[70] Some authors have believed certain of the effects of x-rays to be produced by choline liberated through the decomposition of lecithin. (See Benjamin and Reuss, Münch. med. Woch., 1906 (53), 1860.)

[71] See Millet and Mueller, Jour. Cancer Res., 1918 (3), 127.

[72] Deut. Arch. klin. Med., 1905 (83), 479.

[73] Review by Guyot, Cent. allg. Path., 1909 (20), 243; also see Mills, Lancet 1910 (179), 462; Richards, Science, 1915 (42), 287. Full bibliography by Sugiura and Benedict, Jour. Biol. Chem., 1919 (39), 421.

[74] Loewenthal, Berl. klin. Woch., 1910 (47), 287; Kionka, Med. Klinik, 1911 (7), 685. Denied by Gudzent, Zeit. Strahlenther., 1914 (4), 666.

[75] T. R. Brown, Arch. Int. Med., 1912 (10), 405.

[76] See Ordway, Jour. Amer. Med. Assoc., 1916 (66), 1.

[76a] Bagg, Jour. Cancer Res., 1920 (5), 1.

[77] See Plesch et al., Zeit. exp. Path., 1912 (12), No. 1; Schweizer, Münch. med. Woch., 1916 (63), 341.

free,[78] which has been used for experimental studies on the functions of the leucocytes.

Electricity.—The effects of the electric current upon cells are described by Davenport as follows: A weak constant current causes a centripetal flowing of the protoplasm (in *Actinosphaerium*); if the current is increased or long continued, the cytoplasm of the pseudopodia becomes varicose, and droplets are formed which soon burst, causing a collapse of the protoplasmic framework. Finally, the protoplasm on the anode side begins to disintegrate, and the loose particles move toward the positive electrode; eventually the cell structure may be entirely destroyed. A similar disintegration of the anode side of ameba has been observed by McClendon,[79] which he attributes to anions which cannot pass through the cell wall, and therefore accumulate on that side of the organism. If an alternating current is used, both anode and cathode sides of the cell are affected. In moving organisms electric currents determine direction of motion, even certain vertebrates (tadpoles, fish) being made to orient themselves according to the current. The nucleus seems to be more susceptible to harm by electric currents than the cytoplasm (Pfeffer),[80] and there seems to be no oxidation-process involved in cell destruction by electricity (as is the case with light rays), for the effects are much the same in the absence of oxygen (Klemm). Schmaus and Albrecht state that the effect of electricity upon protoplasm depends upon a loosening of the cohesion and a solution of the constituents of the cell (vacuolization), which last is, perhaps, due to direct chemical alterations. It may be suggested that the electric current causes a migration of ions toward one or the other pole of the cell, in this way separating the movable inorganic ions of the ion-protein compounds of the cell from the immobile colloidal proteins, with consequent serious alterations in the chemistry of the cell. Zeit[81] found that continuous currents kill bacteria through the production of antiseptic substances in the culture-medium, but do not harm them directly.

Jellinek[32] has studied extensively the cause of death after severe electric shocks, and finds that there are produced intracerebral hemorrhages and degeneration of the nerve-cells, which are sufficient to explain the death of the individual without having recourse to the more indefinite idea of "shock." Cunningham[33] considers fibrillary contraction of the heart as the cause of death.[84] Spitzka and Ra-

[78] There is no increase in antitrypsin from this leucocyte destruction (Rosenow, Zeit. exp. Med., 1914 (3), 377).
[79] Pflüger's Arch., 1911 (140), 271.
[80] Literature given by Davenport, "Experimental Morphology."
[81] Jour. Amer. Med. Assoc., 1901 (37), 1432, literature.
[82] Virchow's Arch., 1902 (170), 56; Lancet, 1903 (i), 357.
[83] New York Med. Jour., 1899 (70), 581.
[84] Full discussion by Jelliffe in Peterson and Haines' "Legal Medicine and Toxicology," 1903 (1), 245.

dasch[85] find changes in the brains of electrocuted criminals, which indicate a sudden liberation of gas about the blood vessels, along which the current passes. The amperage seems to be far more important in determining the effect of a current than the voltage or wattage.[86]

Chemicals cause cell death whenever they are of such a nature as either to coagulate the cell proteins or to destroy its enzymes. The action of such substances as sulphuric acid, strong caustics, etc., hardly calls for explanation. Phenol (carbolic acid) may cause necrosis and gangrene even when in very dilute solution; this appears to be due more to the production of hyaline thrombi of agglutinated red corpuscles in the capillaries than to direct action upon the cells. In some unpublished experiments on the subject of "carbolic acid gangrene," I found this action of phenol very striking when dilute solutions were placed on the web of a frog's foot, under the microscope; as soon as the solution penetrated to a capillary, stasis with fusion of the corpuscles occurred in a very few seconds. Similar results have been obtained by Rosenberger.[87] Some poisons seem to cause necrosis without destroying the autolytic enzymes, in which case the cells are rapidly digested; at least, such an hypothesis seems to explain best the changes seen in the liver in chloroform poisoning, acute yellow atrophy, eclampsia, etc.[88] Not all poisons, by any means, cause cell death—tetanus toxin, morphine, and other alkaloids cause death of the individual as a whole without usually causing primary necrosis of any of the cells. Cell death does not necessarily depend upon destruction of *all* the cellular enzymes, as has been pointed out previously. Thus, bacteria may be killed by many chemicals which seem not to affect their autolytic enzymes seriously. Any considerable excess of either H or OH ions is incompatible with cell life, and it is possible that at times the production of acids within a cell may be sufficient to cause death;[89] *e. g.*, in the kidney in acute nephritis (M. H. Fischer), or in the muscle in waxy degeneration (Wells).[90] It is quite probable that many of the poisons act by interfering with the oxidative capacity of the cells; this seems almost certain in the case of chloroform necrosis, and even bacterial poisons (diphtheria and typhoid) were found by Pitini[91] to decrease the oxidizing power of the cells.

The term, "protoplasmic poison," has been variously used and defined. Kunkel says that a protoplasmic poison "is a poison which,

[85] Amer. Jour. Med. Sci., 1912 (144), 341.
[86] Jellinck, Wien. klin. Woch., 1913 (26), 1793.
[87] Verh. Phys. Med. Gesellsch. z. Würzburg, 1900, vol. 34.
[88] Wells, Jour. Amer. Med. Assoc., 1906 (46), 341.
[89] The partial protection afforded by a rich carbohydrate diet against the necrogenic action of chloroform, phosphorus and renal poisons, as observed by Opie and Alford (Jour. Exp. Med., 1915 (21), 1), may depend on the antiketogenic effect of carbohydrates.
[90] Jour. Exp. Med., 1909 (11), 1.
[91] Biochem. Zeit. 1910 (25), 257.

without producing directly evident alterations, harms or kills all living protoplasmic structures." HgCl₂ is such a poison, whereas H₂SO₄, bromine, and similar substances that destroy all life through their strong chemical action are not included in this category. The protoplasmic poisons presumably act by combining with one or more of the constituents of cell protoplasm; e. g., HgCl₂ probably combines with the proteins, chloroform with the cell lipoids (physically?). By means of his special technic Barber[92] is able to introduce minute quantities of poisons into living cells and observe their effect on the cytoplasm; HgCl₂ is thus found to be most toxic, while As₂O₃ is relatively inert. Mathews[93] has shown that the toxicity of ions depends on the ease with which they part with their electrical charges, and the toxicity of a salt is a function of the sum of the toxicity of the ions; hence the toxicity of a salt is in inverse proportion to its decomposition tension. Kunkel suggests that oxalic acid and fluorides are poisons because they combine the cell calcium, and barium salts may be poisonous because they precipitate the SO₄ ions. We can readily imagine that the combining of even one of the essential constituents of the cell may so upset the normal chemical processes that the cell no longer takes up substances to repair its waste, and hence necrosis ensues.[94]

Physical agents may cause necrosis, usually in ways too obvious to require explanation. With most cells, large portions of the cytoplasm can be destroyed without serious results, for so long as the nucleus is intact the cytoplasm can be reconstructed. The fact that necrosis frequently follows relatively slight injuries of the nucleus is perhaps best explained by considering that injury to the nuclear membrane modifies the permeability of the nucleus for substances in solution, which might readily affect its metabolic activities to a serious degree. It is possible, also, that solvents of lipoids, such as chloroform, etc., produce much of their deleterious effects by modifying the permeability of the cell, if the semipermeability of cell membranes depends largely upon the lipoids they contain.[95]

Physical injury of even slight degree may bring on severe alterations in cells, however, and indeed may cause severe chemical alterations. We know that many chemical reactions can be brought about by slight mechanical disturbances, e. g., the explosion of fulminate, nitrogen iodide, etc., and it is quite possible that mechanical disturbances can, likewise, cause chemical changes in the protoplasm. Mechanical injury of cells under the microscope results in an apparent increase

[92] Jour. Infect. Dis., 1911 (9), 117.

[93] Amer. Jour. Physiol., 1904 (10), 290; Nicholl, Jour. Biol. Chem., 1909 (5), 453.

[94] It is hardly profitable here to go further into the theories of the action of poisons, which are generally extensively considered in the treatises on toxicology and pharmacology (also by Davenport, loc. cit).

[95] See Pascucci, Hofmeister's Beiträge, 1905 (6), 552.

in the acid reaction of the part involved (Chambers)[96] and likewise traumatized nervous tissues develop an acid reaction (Moore).[97] Many lower animals devoid of a nervous system respond to mechanical stimuli by chemical activity; *e. g.*, the production of phosphorescence by marine organisms when agitated by an oar, etc. Possibly, the secretion of thrombokinase by the leucocytes, which occurs whenever they come in contact with a foreign body, is an example of a similar reaction to a mechanical stimulus. Even in *urticaria factitia* the simple mechanical irritation which suffices to produce the wheals is followed very quickly by extensive nuclear fragmentation,[98] but it may be that unknown poisons are present in the hypersensitive skin and cause the karyorrhexis, and not the trauma alone. We have no good evidence that mere contact with a chemically inert foreign body unaccompanied by cellular injury, can cause death of tissue-cells.[99] However, Chambers[99a] states that simple trauma, even mere compression, of the eggs of *asteria* may cause them to coagulate into a solid mass.

Extreme changes in osmotic pressure may lead to cell death, either by causing structural alteration in the cell (*e. g.*, the bursting of plant-cells in water), or concentration of the electrolytes may become so great that the colloids are thrown out of solution, as in the ordinary salting-out processes of the laboratory. It is doubtful, however, if osmotic changes *per se* ever become so abnormal within the animal body (except in experimental conditions) as of themselves to cause cell necrosis.

VARIETIES OF NECROSIS

Coagulation Necrosis.[1]—This name is applied to necrotic areas that are firm, dry, usually pale yellowish in color, and observed principally in areas of total anemia or tuberculosis. The question has been long disputed as to whether a true coagulation occurs in such tissues or not. Necrosis produced by heat, carbolic acid, corrosive sublimate, etc., is naturally a coagulation necrosis, the cells of the affected area having undergone true coagulation; *i. e.*, the conversion of their soluble colloids (*sols*) into the insoluble "*pectous*" modification. Whether the same change occurs in areas of anemic necrosis is not so well established. If the part contains a fair amount of plasma the liberation of the tissue coagulins from the dead cells will cause a conversion of the fibrinogen into fibrin—this can usually be demonstrated microscopically, but the presence of fibrin is not constant, and its quantity is usually insufficient to explain satisfactorily the condition

[96] Amer. Jour. Physiol., 1917 (43), 1.
[97] Proc. Soc. Exp. Biol. Med., 1917 (15), 18.
[98] Gilchrist, Bull. Johns Hopkins Hosp., 1908 (19), 49.
[99] Meltzer (Zeit. f. Biol., 1894 (30), 464) has shown that bacteria may be killed by violent agitation, which causes disintegration of the cells.
[99a] Trans. Roy. Soc. Canada, 1918, p. 41.
[1] Literature by Jores, Ergebnisse der Pathol., 1898 (5), 16.

of coagulation necrosis in infarcts, etc., as Weigert maintained.[2]
Schmaus and Albrecht believe that a true coagulation of the cell
proteins does occur in anemic infarcts, etc., for they found that the
cells of kidneys with ligated vessels contain at first granules soluble
in water and salt solution; after forty-eight hours the granules cannot
be dissolved in these solvents or in weak acetic acid, but are soluble
in 2 per cent. KOH; after five to six days the granules are insoluble
even in KOH. Beyond these experiments, we seem to have no proof
of the occurrence of intracellular coagulation within areas of coagulation necrosis due to anemia; exact chemical studies on this point are
much needed. Since tissue-cells contain coagulins for fibrinogen, it is
possible that they also contain coagulins for cell-proteins, but this
remains to be established. We do not know whether Chambers'
observations on the spontaneous coagulation of traumatized *asteria*
eggs[99a] are applicable to other cells. Bacteria produce substances
coagulating milk and fibrinogen. Bergey[3] calls attention to the
coagulation of serum by enzymes and acids produced by bacteria,
and Ruppel[4] found that the tubercle bacillus produces substances
precipitating proteins; hence coagulation necrosis in bacterial infections may be brought about in this way, and Schmoll[5] has shown
that the necrosis occurring in tubercles is associated with an almost
complete coagulation of the cell-proteins.

Necrosis associated with inflammatory exudation is, of course, accompanied by coagulation of the fibrinogen of the exudate (*e. g.*,
diphtheria); this type of coagulation necrosis is chemically a simple
fibrin-formation and readily understood. The peculiar hyaline degenerations of parenchymatous cells (*e. g.*, Zenker's degeneration
of muscles) are often included under this class, but it would seem
more probable that the processes consist rather of the fusion of the
structural elements of the cell into a homogeneous substance than a
true coagulation. When necrosis is produced by chemical means
more or less coagulation of some of the soluble proteins probably
takes place; even in plant cells this coagulation of dead protoplasm
is described.[6]

Liquefaction necrosis occurs particularly in the central nervous
system, where the cell substance seems not to undergo the coagulative

---

[2] Weigert believed that the dead area becomes permeated by plasma containing
fibrinogen, which is coagulated in and between the cells. He put much weight
on an increase in size of the necrotic area, which is by no means constant, as he
intimated; necrotic areas are inelastic, and when death occurs they do not shrink
with the fall of blood pressure as the surrounding tissues do, and hence they
may appear to project from the surface of the dead organ when they did not do
so during life. According to Moos (Virchow's Archiv., 1909 (195), 273) the plasma
does not permeate infarcted areas to the extent that Weigert assumed.

[3] Jour. Amer. Med. Assoc., 1907 (49), 680.
[4] Zeit. physiol. Chem., 1898 (26), 218.
[5] Deut. Arch. klin. Med., 1904 (81), 163.
[6] Gaidukov. Zeit. chem. Kolloide, 1910 (6), 260; Lepeschkin, Ber. Deut. Bot.
Gesell., 1912 (30), 528.

changes described in the preceding paragraphs. Whether this is due to a lack of tissue-coagulins or to a difference in cell composition cannot be said, but the large proportion of lipoids in brain tissue is probably an important factor. Probably "edema *ex vacuo*" is responsible for much of the accumulation of fluid, due to the anatomical conditions that prevent a shrinking or collapse of the tissues to fill in the gap, and the lack of connective-tissue formation. Aseptic softening in general may be safely ascribed to digestion of proteins by cellular enzymes, either from the dead cells or from the leucocytes. Suppuration is merely a form of liquefactive necrosis, in which such digestion is particularly rapid because of the large number of leucocytes that are present. Necrosis of the gastric mucosa or of the pancreas is also followed by rapid liquefaction, through the action of the digestive enzymes of these tissues. When necrosis is accompanied by edema (as in superficial burns), the fluid enters the cells in large amounts, and in this way another form of liquefaction necrosis may be produced. Bacterial enzymes may be a factor in producing liquefaction of dead tissues, but with most pathogenic forms there is little proteolytic activity.[7]

Caseation.—This term is applied to a form of coagulation necrosis in which the dead tissue has an appearance quite similar to that of cheese. If we bear in mind the fact that cheese is a mixture of coagulated protein and finely divided fat, and that in caseation we have a coagulation of tissue proteins associated with the deposition of considerable quantities of fat, the reason for the gross resemblance of the product of this form of necrosis to cheese is apparent. Schmoll[8] has analyzed caseous material, and found it almost entirely free from soluble proteins or proteoses. The protein material is almost solely coagulated protein, which in its elementary composition is related to the simple proteins or to fibrin, and not at all to the nucleoproteins. The extremely small amount of phosphorus present in the caseous material indicates that the products of disintegration of the cell nuclei must diffuse out early in the process. Caseation is, therefore, characterized by a coagulation of the proteins and a dissolving out of the nuclear components. Schmoll does not explain the cause of coagulation, however. It may be that it is the same as in the coagulation of anemic infarcts (since tuberculous areas are decidedly anemic), or possibly the tubercle bacillus produces substances coagulating proteins, as Ruppel states is the property of "tuberculosamin." Indeed, Auclair[9] claims that the fatty substance that can be extracted from tubercle bacilli by chloroform is the cause of the caseation. Dead tubercle bacilli do not produce true caseation, however, according to Kelber;[10] hence the substance causing the necrosis evidently does not

[7] See Bittrolff, Beitr. path. Anat., 1915 (60), 337.
[8] Deut. Arch. klin. Med., 1901 (81), 163.
[9] Arch. méd. exper., 1899, p. 363.
[10] Quoted by Dürck and Oberndorfer, Ergebnisse der Pathol., 1899 (6), 288.

diffuse readily from the bodies of the bacilli. Comparison of the chemical composition of bovine and human tuberculous lesions with the corresponding normal tissues by Caldwell[11] gave the following results:

The tubercle walls and the caseous material from lymph gland tubercles contain a lower percentage of water than does the normal tissue. In normal bovine liver tissue, the percentage of water present is less than that of the tubercle walls or of the caseous material from liver tubercles. The specimens of caseous material from lymph gland and liver tubercles approach each other closely in their water content, the average being about 75% for the bovine material.

The alcohol-ether-soluble substances from normal bovine lymph glands form about 24.4% of the dry weight, or about 4.4% of the moist weight. The walls of the lymph gland tubercles contain a distinctly larger amount of lipins than does the caseous material or the normal tissue. On the contrary, the walls of liver tubercles are poor in lipins as compared with the normal tissue, and they contain a smaller amount of fats than does the caseous material from these tubercles. When calculated on the basis of the dry weight, the caseous material from lymph gland tubercles contains a smaller percentage of lipins than does normal lymph gland tissue. When the ash is deducted, this difference disappears and the content of lipins becomes equal to or slightly greater than that of the normal tissue, but less than that of the tubercle walls. When calculated on an ash-free basis, the lipin content of the caseous material from liver tubercles is distinctly less than that of the normal tissue but greater than the lipin content of the tubercle walls.

Cholesterol forms about 6.5% of the lipins from normal bovine lymph glands, or about 1.5% of the dry weight. The lipins from the walls of lymph gland and liver tubercles contain, in every case, 2-3 times as much cholesterol as do the lipins from the normal tissues. This is an actual increase also when calculated on the basis of the dry weight. The caseous material contains even a larger percentage of cholesterol than do the tubercle walls. Phospholipins constitute about 32% of the lipin fraction of normal bovine lymph glands, or about 7.9% of the dry weight; the corresponding values for normal liver are 41.2% of the fats, or 14% of the dry weight. The phospholipin content of the fats from the tubercle walls is slightly less than that of the normal tissues, while there is a very marked reduction in the phospholipin content of the lipins from caseous material of bovine origin. In the specimen of caseous material from human lymph glands, phospholipins formed 30.9% of the total lipins. The iodin numbers obtained from the fats of the tuberculous specimens from lymph glands are higher than those from the normal tissues. This observation does not hold true for the liver specimens. In the latter, there is no difference noted between the iodin numbers obtained for the lipins from normal and tuberculous specimens, although the values are practically the same as those from the fats from the lymph gland tubercles.

In the residues of caseous material left after extraction with alcohol and ether the nitrogen content remains relatively high; in fact, the reduction in nitrogen content is only slight when the calculations are made on ash-free residues. The percentage of nitrogen does not differ much from that obtained from the normal proteins of these tissues. In specimens of caseous material in which there are no macroscopic evidences of calcification other than the presence of sandlike particles, calcium sometimes forms as much as 15% of the residue left after extraction of the fats. In such residues, the phosphorus content may reach 9%.

The amount of purine nitrogen in the walls of lymph gland tubercles is only slightly more than half that of normal lymph gland tissue, and the amount is apparently much less in the caseous material. In the residues from the walls of liver tubercles, purine nitrogen is present in only slightly higher percentage than in the normal liver. The results here obtained would seem to indicate that the purines are even more abundant in the caseous residues of liver tubercles. The amount of material which enters the water solution during extraction is distinctly less from caseous material than from the residues of normal tissues.

[11] Jour. Infect. Dis., 1919 (24), 81.   Full review on composition of tuberculous tissues.

25

The abundance of fat in caseous material on microscopic examination is very striking. In addition to the figures obtained by Caldwell,
Bossart[12] found from 13.7 per cent. to 19.4 per cent. of the dry substance of caseous material soluble in alcohol and ether.   In the scrap-
ings from tuberculous bovine glands I have found 22.7–23.9 per cent.
of the organic material soluble in alcohol and ether.[13]   Of this soluble
material, Bossart found 25 to 33 per cent. of cholesterol, and Leber[14]
found 38.31 per cent., which is a much higher phospholipin proportion than Bossart detected.   Caldwell found cholesterol higher
and phospholipins lower in caseous than in normal tissues.   The
total amount of lipins, however, constituted a smaller percentage of
the dry weight than in the normal tissues from which the caseous
material originated.   Presumably these fatty materials are derived
chiefly from the disintegrated cells; this is probably true of the phospholipin and cholesterol, but the fact that in histological preparations
most of the fat is found about the periphery of the caseous area,[15] supports the belief that it has wandered in from the outside.[16]   A certain
proportion of the fat is possibly derived from the bodies of the tubercle
bacilli, which usually contain about 40 per cent. of fatty matter; but
it has not been determined whether the fat from this origin forms an
appreciable part of the fatty matter of caseous material.

Caseous areas persist for extremely long periods of time without
undergoing absorption, which indicates that the autolytic enzymes
are destroyed early in the process, presumably by the toxins of the
tubercle bacillus; corresponding to this Schmoll found autolysis very
slight indeed in caseous areas, and even when the caseous material
breaks down to form a "cold abscess" the fluid differs from true pus
in containing less free amino-acids, *e. g.*, tyrosine is missing.[17]   Caldwell
also obtained lower figures for extractives in caseous than in normal
tissues.   Because of a lack of chemotactic substances no leucocytes
enter to remove the dead material, in consequence of which caseous
material gives no evidence of containing proteases, according to the
Müller-Jochmann plate method.   That the failure of absoprtion is not
due to a modification of the proteins into an indigestible form is
shown by the rapid softening of caseous areas when, through mixed
infection, chemotactic substances are once developed and leucocytes
enter.   Jobling and Petersen[18] suggest that in caseation the autolysis
is inhibited by the soaps of fatty acids, which are abundant in caseous
areas and have a marked antitryptic effect.

[12] Quoted by Schmoll, *loc. cit.*[8]
[13] Wells, Jour. Med. Research, 1906 (14), 491.
[14] Quoted by Schmoll.[8]
[15] Sata, Ziegler's Beitr., 1900 (28), 461.
[16] Fischler and Gross (Ziegler's Beitr., 1905 (7th suppl.), 344) could find no
fatty acids in caseous areas by histological methods.
[17] See Müller, Cent. inn. Med., 1907 (28), 297.
[18] Jour. Exp. Med., 1914 (19), 239; Zeit. Immunität., 1914 (23), 71.

FAT NECROSIS[19]

Through usage this term has come to indicate a specific form of necrosis of fat tissue, which is characterized by a focal, circumscribed arrangement, and by the splitting of the fat in the necrotic area into fatty acids and glycerol, the latter disappearing, the former combining with bases to form soaps.[20] In practically all cases fat necrosis is produced by the action of pancreatic juice upon fat tissue,[21] presumably through the action of the enzymes it contains, and the condition can be produced experimentally by any procedure that causes escape of the pancreatic juice from its natural channels.

Langerhans[22] made the first studies of the nature of the changes in fat necrosis and established the fact that the fat of the cells is split into its components, and that the fatty acids combine (at least in part) with calcium. Dettmer[23] found that, although fresh pancreatic juice caused fat necrosis, a commercial preparation of trypsin did not do so, and, therefore, he concluded that probably the lipase of the pancreatic juice was the active agent. Flexner[24] supported this contention by demonstrating the presence of a fat-splitting enzyme in foci of fat necrosis, which was corroborated by Opie.[25] The latter[26] was also able to demonstrate the presence of lipase in the urine of a patient with fat necrosis,[27] and the highest values for amylase in the blood and urine are found in pancreatitis (Stocks).[28]

In a study of the pathogenesis of fat necrosis, particularly with reference to the question whether the lipase or the trypsin of the pancreatic juice was responsible, Wells[29] found that typical fat necrosis could be produced by injecting extracts of fresh pancreas into

[19] General literature will be found in the articles cited in the text; also in Opie's "Diseases of the Pancreas;" and in Truhart's "Pankreas-Pathologie," Wiesbaden, 1902.

[20] The fatty acids form masses of crystals in the fat-cells, and they can also be demonstrated microchemically by Benda's method (Virchow's Arch., 1900 (161), 194), which consists of staining with a copper acetate mixture, blue-green copper salts of the fatty acids being formed.

[21] Wulff (Berl. klin. Woch., 1902 (39), 734), claims to have observed an exception to this rule, but his account is not by itself convincing. Fabyan (Johns Hopkins Hosp. Bull., 1907 (18), 349) reports a case of multiple subcutaneous fat necrosis without pancreatic lesions, in a 14 days' old baby, and gives a review of other similar cases. This case, however, may be one of scleroderma C. S. Smith, Jour. Cut. Dis., 1918 (36), 436).

[22] Virchow's Arch., 1890 (122), 252.

[23] Dissertation, Göttingen, 1895.

[24] Jour. Exper. Med., 1897 (2), 413.

[25] Contrib. of pupils of W. H. Welch, Baltimore, 1900, p. 859; Johns Hopkins Hosp. Rep., 1900 (9), 859.

[26] Opie, "Diseases of the Pancreas," Lippincott, 1903, p. 156; Johns Hopkins Hosp. Bull., 1902 (13), 117.

[27] It yet remains to be seen if this is a constant occurrence, and also if the lipase so excreted comes from the pancreas, for Zeri (Il Policlinico, 1905 (12), 733) has found lipase in the urine in hemorrhagic nephritis and inflammation of the urinary tract; also Pribram and Loewy, Zeit. physiol. Chem., 1912 (76), 489.

[28] Quart. Jour. Med., 1916 (9), 216.

[29] Jour. Med. Research, 1903 (9), 70.

animals, either of the same species as that from which the pancreas
was obtained, or into a foreign species. Commercial "pancreatins"
were also quite effective, whether in weak acetic acid or weak alkaline
solutions. The power of these materials to cause fat necrosis was
reduced by heating to or above 60° for five minutes, and completely
destroyed at 71°, indicating that the active agent is an enzyme. But,
as in the same material trypsin was injured by temperatures above 60°,
and destroyed at between 70° and 72°, and lipase was weakened above
50°, and destroyed above 70°, it was impossible to determine, by
heating pancreatic preparations, whether the lipase or the trypsin
was the essential factor. By permitting pancreatic extracts to digest
themselves it was found that the power to produce fat necrosis
decreased, *pari passu*, with the decrease in lipolytic strength. Preparations strongly tryptic, but very weak in lipase, produced no fat necrosis, and, on the other hand, extracts of pig's liver or of cat's serum,
both rich in lipase but devoid of trypsin, were equally ineffective.
Furthermore, mixtures of liver or serum lipase and trypsin were
incapable of causing fat necrosis. Fresh pancreatic extracts from
fasting dogs, containing lipase but almost no trypsin (which in fresh
extracts is still in the form of inactive trypsinogen), produced abundant fat necrosis, whereas after the trypsinogen in such extracts was
activated by enterokinase, no fat necrosis could be produced. It
therefore seems certain that trypsin alone cannot produce fat necrosis,
and that the decrease in strength of lipase in a pancreatic extract is
associated with a corresponding decrease in power to produce fat
necrosis. But, on the other hand, lipase of liver or blood-serum alone,
or when mixed with trypsin, will not produce fat necrosis. The possibility remains that pancreatic lipase is different from liver or serum
lipase, and can by itself cause fat necrosis; more probably, however,
the production of fat necrosis depends upon a double action, trypsin
causing the death of the cells, and lipase splitting the fats.[30] The
fatty acids alone will not cause necrosis of fat-cells, and it was shown
that the first steps in the process consist of a necrosis of the surface
endothelium extending into the connective and fat tissue; this may
occur in a few minutes, while evidence of fat-splitting can be obtained
only after about three hours, and the splitting occurs only in cells
that have already become necrotic; hence the fat-splitting is not the
cause of the necrosis, but occurs subsequent to the necrosis. After

[30] When fat tissue dies in the body from other causes, the lipase normally contained within the fat tissue does not cause the changes seen in fat necrosis. It is
possible, therefore, that the combining of newly split fatty acids by the alkali of
the pancreatic juice is responsible for the formation of the large amount of soaps
found in fat necrosis. Otherwise we might expect the lipase to produce only
an equilibrium, and that, in the case of fat, seems to exist when most of the substance is neutral fat. In support of this idea I found that strong alkalies injected
into fat tissue sometimes caused changes very closely resembling areas of fat
necrosis in the early stages.

about four hours a substance appears in the decomposed fat that stains with hematoxylin, which is probably calcium.

Fat necrosis may be produced by any means that will cause the escape of pancreatic juice from the natural channels within the gland. In human pathology it has followed trauma and acute infection of the gland, and the blocking of the ampulla of Vater by gallstones which permits the bile to back up into the pancreatic duct, where it produces an acute inflammation of the pancreas (Opie).[31] Flexner[32] has shown that it is the bile salts that cause the inflammation, and also that this effect is decreased or prevented by the presence of large amounts of colloids. Much emphasis is laid by some authors[33] upon the necessity of enterokinase passing up the ducts to activate the trypsinogen (an idea first advanced by Starling and Bayliss in 1902), but it should be remembered that there are kinases present in leucocytes, and that kinases can develop in the pancreas itself during autolysis, which can activate the trypsinogen; hence the presence of *entero*-kinase is not essential for sufficient activation of trypsinogen to account for pancreatitis and fat necrosis. Lattes[34] believes that fresh pancreatic juice, which digests tissues very slowly, can produce typical fat necrosis but not the characteristic intoxication; this results from the action of juice which has been activated by enterokinase, or by products of pancreatic autolysis which have a similar effect. The kinases of leucocytes he found unable to activate pancreatic trypsinogen sufficiently to make it highly toxic. These observations indicate that in pancreatic necrosis it is the kinase liberated from the autolyzing necrotic tissue which is responsible for the activation and resulting toxic effects of the trypsinogen. As a result of injury by bile salts, or any other agent that produces cell death, the dead and injured cells are digested by the pancreatic juice which is thus further activated and makes its escape into the surrounding fat tissue. Wells' experiments showed that the lesions of fat necrosis may be produced in three to five hours, large enough to be visible to the naked eye; their form and size depend solely upon the area of fat tissue exposed to the action of the pancreatic juice. The process progresses for but a few hours, the extension seeming to be limited by surrounding leucocytes. The lesions may appear at remote points in the thoracic and pericardial cavities or in the subcutaneous tissues, the causative agent probably being carried by the lymphatic vessels, possibly in the form of emboli of pancreas cells.[35] There may even be some splitting of the fats in the liver in these cases, with intrahepatic

[31] Bull. Johns Hopkins Hosp., 1901 (12), 182.
[32] Jour. Exp. Med., 1906 (8), 167.
[33] Pólya, Mitt. Grenz. Med. u. Chir., 1911 (24), 1; Rosenbach, Arch. klin. Chir., 1910 (93), 278.
[34] Virchow's Arch., 1913 (211), 1.
[35] Payr and Martina, Deut. Zeit. Chir., 1906 (83), 189.

necrosis.[36] Fat necrosis itself is not dangerous to the affected organism, the associated pancreatitis (and peritonitis) causing all the symptoms.[37] There is no evidence that sufficient quantities of soaps (which are toxic) are absorbed from the necrotic areas to cause appreciable intoxication. The soaps that are formed in the necrotic areas, indeed, are probably not much absorbed, but are precipitated as calcium soaps; in such areas at least as high as 85 per cent. of the soaps may be insoluble.[38] Healing follows rapidly in case of recovery; the foci may disappear as early as eleven days after their formation (in experimental animals).

In the urine of persons with pancreatitis is frequently found a substance forming an osazone, which has been the subject of much investigation because of its possible diagnostic value. Cammidge,[39] who first described a reaction based on this observation, considers that the substance is a pentose,[40] derived from the nucleoproteins of the pancreas; it bears no relation to the fat necrosis, but is commonly found with fat necrosis because of the associated pancreatitis. Presumably cell necrosis elsewhere than in the pancreas may at times cause the same reaction to appear.[41] In pancreatitis with fat necrosis, or whenever there is any injury to the pancreas, there may be found an increase in the amount of diastase in the blood and urine, sufficient to be of diagnostic value according to Y. Noguchi.[42] The peritoneal exudate in acute pancreatitis is not toxic, contains no free trypsin and is no more lipolytic than normal serum, presumably because of neutralization of the enzymes and poisons by the exuded plasma.[43]

[36] See Berner, Virchow's Arch., 1907 (187), 360.

[37] Guleke (Arch. klin. Chir., 1908 (85), 615) considers the intoxication of *acute pancreatitis* as an intoxication with trypsin, which can be checked by antitrypsin. Doberauer (Beitr. klin. Chir., 1906 (48), 456), Egdahl (Jour. Exp. Med., 1907 (9), 385), Petersen, Jobling, and Eggstein (*ibid.*, 1916 (23), 491), and Cooke and Whipple (*ibid.*, 1918 (28), 222), however, look upon the products of cellular disintegration as the source of the intoxication. v. Bergmann (Zeit. exp. Path. u. Ther., 1906 (3), 401), states that the toxicity is not due to either the enzymes or to albumoses; and that it is a true autointoxication which can be prevented by previous immunization with either pancreas extracts or commercial trypsin. (See also Fischler, Deut. Arch. klin. Med., 1911 (103), 156; and v. Bergmann and Guleke, Münch. med. Woch., 1910 (57), 1673.) The histones and protamines liberated from the digested tissue, and which are very toxic, have been suggested as a possible factor by Schittenhelm and Weichardt (Zeit. Immunität., 1913 (14), 609), while the beta-nucleo-proteins are included among the toxic elements by Goodpasture, Jour. Exp. Med., 1917 (25), 277.

[38] See Frugoni and Stradiotti, Arch. Sci. Med., Torino, 1910; also Berl. klin. Woch., 1910 (47), 386.

[39] Proc. Royal Soc. Med., 1910 (III, pt. 2), 163, bibliography; Lancet, 1914, Sept. 26.

[40] Weber believes that it is a hexose (Deut. med. Woch., 1912 (38), 166), and it may be urinary dextrin (Pekelharing and Van Hoogenhuyze, Zeit. physiol. Chem., 1914 (91), 151).

[41] See Whipple, *et al.*, Johns Hopkins Hosp. Bull., 1910 (21), 339; Karas, Zeit. klin. Med., 1913 (77), 125.

[42] Arch. klin. Chir., 1912 (98), II. 2.

[43] Whipple and Goodpasture, Surg., Gyn. and Obst., 1913 (17), 541.

Self-digestion of the pancreas occurs soon after death, and the pancreatic juice may in this way bring about a portmortem fat digestion that resembles somewhat the intravital fat necrosis in its gross appearances,[44] and Wells found that the same changes might be produced by injecting pancreatin into the bodies of dead animals, or by keeping fat tissue in pancreatin solutions. Wulff found that fatty acids were demonstrable by Benda's method in the pancreas of nearly all cadavers. The process differs from the *intra vitam* form in being less sharply circumscribed, and microscopically by the absence of cellular and vascular reaction. That the essential changes of fat necrosis can be produced postmortem is final proof that they are due to enzymes, rather than to circulatory or cellular action.

GANGRENE

This term indicates merely that certain marked secondary changes, either putrefaction or desiccation, have occurred in necrotic areas of some size. Hence we have the chemical changes of putrefaction added to those of necrosis in the case of moist gangrene, whereas in dry gangrene nearly all the chemical changes are brought to a standstill through the desiccation. In the latter it is only at the line of demarcation, where some moisture remains, that chemical changes still go on; these consist chiefly of autolysis of the dead tissues, and also of their digestion by leucocytes, which results eventually in the separation of the dead tissue from the living; this is best seen after surface burns, carbolic-acid gangrene, etc.

Moist gangrene is accompanied by the dual action of the cellular enzymes and of the putrefactive organisms that are growing in the dead tissue, and as a result such tissue contains all the innumerable products of the decomposition of proteins and fats. Thus Ziegler mentions as morphological elements that may be present in gangrenous tissue: Fat needles, the so-called "margarin" crystals (a mixture of stearic and palmitic acids), fine acicular crystals of tyrosine, globules of leucine, rhombic plates of triple phosphate, black and brown masses of pigment, and crystals of hematoidin. In solution we also have, beyond a doubt, all the substances formed in the decomposition of proteins, from proteoses and peptones down through the different amino-acids to such final products as ammonia and its salts, while CO_2 and H_2S are abundantly given off. In addition occur, undoubtedly, many of the ptomaïns which are formed by the action of the bacteria upon the amino-acids derived from the proteins.[45] In the sputum from pulmonary gangrene there is but little soluble protein, most of the nitrogen, of which there is much, is in the formed elements.[46] The fetid plugs which occur in the bronchioles in gangrene, the "Dittrich's plugs," were found by Traube to be composed chiefly of fatty

[44] Chiari, Zeit. f. Heilk.,'1896 (17), 69; Pförringer, Virchow's Arch., 1899 (158), 126; Liepmann, *ibid.*, 1902 (169), 532; Wulff, Berl. klin. Woch., 1902 (39), 734.
[45] An interesting observation concerning gangrene of the lung has been made by Eijkman (Cent. f. Bakt., Abt. 1, 1903 (35), 1), who found in this condition bacteria that secrete an enzyme dissolving elastic tissue.
[46] Orszag, Zeit. klin. Med., 1909 (67), 204.

acid crystals, and Schwartz and Kayser[47] ascribe their formation to the action of lipolytic staphylococci.

If the necrotic tissue is in contact with living tissue over a considerable area, enough of these products of autolysis and putrefaction may be absorbed to cause intoxication (*sapremia*). At the same time, the formation of such large quantities of crystalloids from the proteins of the dead tissue leads to a diffusion of water into this area, with consequent swelling, and often a lifting up of the skin in the form of blisters.

Emphysematous gangrene,[48] usually produced by gas-forming anaërobic bacteria, including *B. aërogenes capsulatus*, may also possibly be produced by *B. coli communis* in diabetic patients in whose blood and tissues there may occur sufficient sugar to permit of gas-formation. Hitschmann and Lindenthal found that the gas produced in cultures by an anaërobic organism which they isolated from a case of emphysematous gangrene, consisted of 67.55 per cent. hydrogen, 30.62 per cent. carbon dioxide, and traces of ammonia and nitrogen; this corresponds to the statement of Welch and Nuttall that the gas in the tissues of infected animals is inflammable. Dunham[49] found that the gas produced by *B. aërogenes capsulatus* in cultures has the following composition: Hydrogen, 64.3 per cent.; carbon dioxide, 27.6 per cent.; other gases, probably chiefly nitrogen, 8.1 per cent. Grown in a medium of muscle and water, Wolf[50] found 70–75 per cent of CO_2 produced by *B. sporogenes*, while *B. Welchii* produced 38 per cent. of CO_2, the rest being chiefly H. The former bacillus is very actively proteolytic, the latter less so. Organisms of this group produce much volatile organic acid which is probably an important factor in the local necrosis, especially in producing a negative chemotaxis; it may also contribute to the acidosis of the disease.[51]

RIGOR MORTIS

This topic may be appropriately considered in connection with cell death, since it is a characteristic change occurring after general death. All forms of muscle, striped, smooth, and cardiac, undergo this change, which is shown by a shortening and thickening of the muscle, which also becomes opaque and hard. Rigor mortis begins first in the heart muscle, according to Fuchs,[53] but it is generally observed first in the eyelids, then in the muscles of the jaw, from which point it proceeds downward, although the upper extremities

[47] Zeit. klin. Med., 1905 (56), 111.
[48] Complete literature by Weinberg and Séguin, "La Gangrène gazeuse," Paris, 1918.
[49] Johns Hopkins Hosp. Bull., 1897 (8), 68.
[50] Jour. Path. Bact., 1919 (22), 270.
[51] Wright and Fleming, Lancet, 1918 (i), 205.
[52] Literature, see v. Fürth, Handbuch d. Biochem., 1909 (II (2), 252; also Meltzer and Auer, Jour. Exp. Med., 1908 (10), 45).
[53] Zeit. f. Heilk., 1900 (21, Path. Abt.), 1.

may not become rigid before the lower. The time of onset is extremely variable, but the following general rules may be stated: All conditions that lead to excessive muscular metabolism, with its resulting increase in the acidity of the muscle fluids, will hasten the onset of rigor mortis; thus, people killed suddenly during violent activity may remain almost in the position in which they met death. Acute fevers, strychnine poisoning, tetanus, etc., cause likewise a rapid onset of rigor, which may, indeed, appear almost simultaneously with death or even before the heart has stopped beating. When a healthy individual meets death without previous exertion, rigor does not usually appear for four or six hours, but will be hastened by heat and retarded by cold. Death from hemorrhage or asphyxia is followed by a slow development of the rigor. Under ordinary conditions rigor usually begins between the first and second hour after death and is complete in one or two more hours.[54]

The duration of rigor mortis also is influenced by many factors. In general, it may be said that the duration is in inverse relation to the rapidity of onset, and directly to the musculature of the individual. Therefore, in an emaciated individual dying with fever, rigor may appear and disappear again within two or three hours, or, indeed, escape observation altogether. The body of a muscular man dying from accident or hemorrhage may, on the other hand, show rigor for two or three weeks if kept in a cold place. Once the rigor has been broken by force, it does not again return.

Rigor mortis may be produced even before death, through poisons (monobromacetic acid, quinine), and its occurrence, even postmortem, does not necessarily mean that the muscle is dead, for if the part is transfused with a salt solution the rigor may be removed, and the muscle will then be found to react to stimuli. This indicates that the chemical changes of rigor mortis are not very profound.[55]

The chemistry of the changes involved in rigor mortis has been a much-contested problem. Two chief doctrines have been supported: one that rigor was not essentially different from ordinary muscular contraction except in degree, and perhaps due to a loss of inhibition to contraction. The other looks upon it as a coagulation similar to the coagulation of the blood; and this idea, it may be said, has had the most general acceptance. Brücke in 1842 supported this view, and in 1859 Kühne extracted from muscle a plasma which coagulated like ordinary blood plasma. The protein which formed the clot is called *myosin*, and its coagulable antecedent, *myosinogen*.

This experiment has been since repeatedly verified and amplified, especially by v. Fürth and by Halliburton,[56] who have separated more

[54] Rigor mortis may develop in the dead fetus while in the womb, but it generally disappears within five or six hours. Literature by Wolff, Arch. f. Gyn., 1903 (68), 549; Das, Brit. Jour. of Obstet., 1903 (4), 545.

[55] See Mangold, Pflüger's Arch., 1903 (96), 498.

[56] "Chemistry of Muscle and Nerve," 1904.

definitely the proteins concerned in coagulation, and found them to be globulins. There seem to be two: one, coagulating at 47°, called *paramyosinogen* (Halliburton), constitutes but about one-fifth of the total clotting globulin, and passes readily into the insoluble clot, *myosin*; the other, which coagulates at 56°, constitutes the remaining four-fifths is called *myosinogen* (Halliburton), or *myogen* (v. Fürth), and before becoming changed into myosin it passes through a soluble stage called *soluble myogen-fibrin*, which is coagulated at the remarkably low temperature of 40°.

By analogy with fibrin-formation we should expect this clotting also to be brought about by an enzyme, but this has not been proved. Calcium is of influence, favoring coagulation greatly, but its presence is not absolutely essential (v. Fürth). Of particular importance is the acid reaction of the dead muscle. Normal muscle is amphoteric when at rest, but when active the reaction becomes more and more acid, as it also does when the circulation is shut off, and hence acidity increases greatly after death. The acidity is due chiefly to lactic acid (although the neutral phosphates may become converted into acid phosphates in the presence of the lactic acid, and thus seem to contribute to the acidity), and may increase in twenty-four hours after death by from 6.7 to 12.8 c.c. of $^n/_{10}$ acid for each 100 grams of muscle (v. Fürth[57]). The same author found that although the amount of acid might become in time sufficient to cause coagulation of the muscle proteins by itself, yet actually rigor mortis appears before the acidity has reached any such degree. Verzar[58] says that by vital stains it can be shown that in vital contraction no precipitation occurs, but it does take place in rigor mortis. Meigs[59] advanced the hypothesis that the rigor is due to the swelling of the muscle colloids under the influence of acids, a view which is accepted by von Fürth and Lenk.[60] When sufficient acid is formed in the muscle the swelling may be so great that the structure of the muscle cell is destroyed entirely, and it goes into the condition of "waxy degeneration."[61] This readily explains why the time of appearance of rigor is so modified by the amount of muscle metabolism before death. It is, indeed, possible to produce rigor in living animals by transfusing a limb with slightly acid salt solution,[62] and in strychnine-poisoning the muscular spasm may pass imperceptibly into rigor mortis.

[57] Hofmeister's Beitr., 1903 (3), 543; see also Fletcher and Hopkins, Jour. of Physiol., 1907 (35), 247; Wacker, Biochem. Zeit., 1916 (75), 101.
[58] Biochem. Zeit., 1918 (90), 63.
[59] Amer. Jour. Physiol., 1910 (26), 191.
[60] Biochem. Zeit., 1911 (33), 341; Wien. klin. Woch., 1911 (24), 1079.
[61] Wells, Jour. Exper. Med., 1909 (11), 1. Corroborated by Stemmler, Virchow's Arch., 1914 (216), 57.
[62] The hardness of a limb from which the blood-supply has been shut off by thrombosis or embolism, and also much of the cramp-like pain, is probably due to rigor mortis in the muscles caused by acid formation under conditions of suboxidation.

It has been suggested that the disappearance of rigor mortis depends upon beginning autolysis of the clot by the intracellular proteases of the muscle, which act best in an acid medium, but proteoses and peptones cannot be found in such muscle. It is improbable that the degree of acidity ever becomes so high that the myosin is redissolved through a conversion into acid albumin (syntonin), as was formerly supposed. v. Fürth holds that the re-solution of the rigor is caused by coagulation of the proteins, thus reducing this hydrophilic tendency, a view in harmony with recent developments in colloid chemistry.[63]

"Waxy" degeneration of muscles, although usually resulting from the action of toxic substances, is entirely different from cloudy swelling, in that the cytoplasm has become homogeneous and not granular. This is undoubtedly due to the increased accumulation of acid which takes place in muscles when they suffer from a defective oxygen supply, for I have found it possible to produce the typical appearance of Zenker's waxy degeneration by letting weak solutions of lactic or other acids act on muscle fibers. Even excessive stimulation of muscles was found to be sufficient to cause waxy degeneration, the acid being formed faster than it can be removed.[64]

Muscles showing the "reaction of degeneration" have been analyzed by Rumpf and Schumm,[65] who found a great increase in the fatty matter, which was about fifteen times the normal amount. The muscle, deducting the fat, showed a loss of solid matter and an increase of water; sodium and calcium were increased, potassium decreased. There is also a great relative increase in the proportion of phosphorus bound to protein in muscles which have atrophied after nerve section, because of the persistence of nuclear and loss of non-nuclear elements (Grund[66]), but there is little change in the proportion of mono- and di-amino nitrogen.[67] The creatine content decreases steadily after the reaction of degeneration is first well established.[68]

ATROPHY

The chemical changes of simple atrophy have not, so far as I can find, been definitely studied. It is to be presumed, in view of the structural changes, that analysis of atrophied tissues would show a relatively high nucleic acid and collagen content. It is known that in atrophy the cell lipoids are not much altered, while the simpler fats may be increased in parenchymatous organs. In fatty tissues, of course, the fat is greatly reduced, its place being partly taken by serum (serous atrophy of fat). In the heart muscle, especially, but

[63] Corroborated by Lentz, Zeit. angew. Chem., 1912 (25), 1513; and Schwarz, Biochem. Zeit., 1912 (37), 35.

[64] As this work antedates much of the recent work on the influence of acids of metabolic origin upon the swelling of cell structures, attention may be called to the fact that a preliminary report of these experiments was made in the first edition of this book, written in 1906.

[65] Deut. Zeit. f. Nervenheilk., 1901 (20), 445.

[66] Arch. exp. Path., 1912 (67), 393.

[67] Wakeman, Jour. Biol. Chem., 1908 (4), 137.

[68] Cathcart et al., Jour. Physiol., 1918 (52), 70.

also to a less extent in the liver and kidney, during atrophy there is an increased pigmentation (brown atrophy) apparently consisting of lipochromes or lipofuscins; but it is to be doubted that this represents so much an actual increase in pigment as a relative increase through loss of other cellular elements. Atrophied tissues also tend to undergo a marked compensatory invasion by fatty areolar tissue if located in contact with such tissue; e. g., atrophy of muscles after nerve section,[65] specific muscular dystrophies, and atrophy of the pancreas. In the muscle tissue of salmon migrating to the spawning grounds occurs one of the most marked examples of atrophy, and Greene[69] has found that at least 30 per cent. of the protein lost from the muscles may be considered as stored protein, since it can be lost without injury to the muscle.

Starvation, of course, produces typical atrophic changes in the tissues, and the general effects on metabolism have been especially fully worked out by Benedict.[70] The structural changes in parenchymatous cells are described[71] as of two types; first, granular changes and vacuolization of the cytoplasm, resembling the effects of osmotic pressure alterations; second and later, lysis of cytoplasm with also some involvement of the nuclei, after the order of autolytic changes. The cell walls may also become indistinct, so that the cells resemble a syncytium.[72] In the atrophied muscle after nerve section Wakeman[67] found a decrease in solids, and a lowered proportion of diamino acids.

Morse has studied, by experimental methods, the question of the mechanism involved in atrophy, using especially the involuting tail of the tadpole as his test object.[73] He believes that autolysis is the primary factor, probably induced by acidity that results from vascular occlusion. The involution of the puerperal uterus, whether it can properly be called atrophy or not, seems to be the result of heightened autolysis, the products of which are excreted quantitatively in the urine.[74] Bradley[75] calls attention to the fact that atrophy occurs commonly under conditions of reduced blood supply, which implies partial asphyxia and a resulting tendency to local excess of H-ions, which would favor autolysis. Conversely, hypertrophy is observed with abundant blood supply which tends to keep the reaction of the tissues so low in H-ions that autolysis is held at a minimum.

CLOUDY SWELLING[76]

The characteristic appearance of organs the seat of cloudy swelling, which is frequently likened to a "scalded" appearance, sug-

[69] Jour. Biol. Chem., 1919 (39), 435.
[70] Carnegie Inst. Publ., 1915, No. 203.
[71] Cesa-Bianchi, Frankf. Zeit. Path., 1909 (3), 723.
[72] Morgulis, Howe and Hawk, Biol. Bull., 1915 (28), 397.
[73] Biol. Bull., 1918 (34), 149.
[74] Slemons, Bull. Johns Hopkins Hosp., 1914 (25), 195.
[75] Jour. Biol. Chem., 1916 (25), 261.
[76] Review of general features by Landsteiner, Ziegler's Beitr., 1903 (33), 237.

gests that the change consists in a coagulation of the cell proteins, which idea is supported by the similarity of the microscopic changes observed in the cells and the earliest microscopic changes observed in cells after heating gently to about their maximum thermal point. On the other hand, the granules in cloudy swelling are generally described as being soluble in dilute acetic acid and dilute KOH, which indicates that they are not the result of ordinary heat coagulation. If we bear in mind, however, that cloudy swelling probably does not represent one single change, it may be possible to arrive at some understanding of the chemical changes that occur in the process. Albrecht[77] considers, with good reason, that we may have a granular appearance of cells which is simply an exaggeration of the normal granular structure, and, although it may be observed in tissues moderately affected by toxins, or in starvation, or in transitory anemia, the change is still to be looked upon as little more than physiological in response to stimuli and overwork. Such a "cloudy swelling" may also occur in cells in the beginning of autolysis, or simply under the influence of salt solution. If the injury is greater, however, as in profound sepsis, or extreme local anemia, the granules becomes coarser, less soluble in acetic acid and KOH, and droplets resembling "myelin" make their appearance. If the injury is still more severe, true coagulation of the granules occurs, and they become insoluble, the fatty droplets become more prominent, and the cell reaches a condition that may with propriety be termed necrosis or fatty degeneration, or both. There is no very sharp line separating necrosis and cloudy swelling, especially if we consider only the changes in the cytoplasm. In the earliest stages the granules are perhaps due, in some cases, to simple aggregation of the colloids, without the development of a true coagulation, and so the granules are still soluble. Possibly bacterial toxins may also cause soluble precipitates, but this does not appear to have been established. Halliburton has shown that temperatures that may be reached in high fevers can cause turbidity in solutions of cell proteins, and hence heat precipitation may be partly responsible for the turbidity of cells in cloudy swelling, but it is doubtful if the granules thus formed would be soluble in acetic acid. A careful discussion of the character and characteristics of this process is given by Bell,[78] who concludes that the term cloudy swelling is sound only as a gross description, since microscopically the cells may be found to show albuminous granules, or fatty metamorphosis or simple edema. When present, the granules are of unknown nature—they are not identical with Altmann's granules, although Aschoff and Ernst[79] both consider that many of them are derived from the mitochondria. An enormous number of granules may be present in the renal cells

[77] Verh. Deut. Path. Gesell., 1903 (6), 63.
[78] Jour. Amer. Med. Assoc., 1913 (61), 455.
[79] Verh. Deut. Path. Gesellsch., 1914 (17), 43 and 103.

without demonstrable impairment of function.[80]   They may disappear during acute infections, and they bear no constant relation to fatty changes.

We may speak with more assurance concerning the swelling of the cell, and attribute it to an edema of the cell contents, it having been shown that in cloudy swelling the water content of the organs is increased.[81]   This might be produced by a rise in osmotic pressure due to abnormally rapid splitting of proteins with incomplete oxidation of the substances formed, which results in formation of many crystalloid molecules with high total osmotic pressure, from a smaller number of colloid molecules with almost no osmotic pressure.   It has frequently been shown that the cell-walls do not lose their semipermeable character until the death of the cell occurs; hence in cloudy swelling water diffuses in much more rapidly than the crystalloids can diffuse out,[82] causing a hydropic swelling.   This hypothesis is supported by the observations of Cesaris Demel,[83] who found that by modifying the osmotic conditions of the cells, particularly epithelial cells, he could closely reproduce many of the characteristic features of parenchymatous degeneration.   It is possible, also, that too high concentration of crystalloids within the cells may be a factor in the precipitation of the cell colloids.   In view of the fact that in the earliest stages of autolysis, histologic and microscopic changes closely resembling those of cloudy swelling are pronounced, and that organs the seat of cloudy swelling notoriously undergo autolysis with extreme rapidity after death,[84] we may also consider that this process is possibly in part responsible for the change of ordinary *intra vitam* cloudy swelling.   The appearance of fine granules of lipoid substance[85] (myelin or "protagon") in cells during autolysis and during cloudy swelling is in support of this idea, and chemical analysis of organs showing cloudy swelling gives definite evidence of autolytic decomposition of the proteins and an increase in the water content.[86]   Presumably this increase in water is the cause of the lowered specific gravity of organs exhibiting parenchymatous degeneration.[87]   Landsteiner, through his studies of cloudy swelling in human material, also came to the conclusion that autolysis is an important element in its production.

Martin H. Fischer[88] applies the principles of colloidal chemistry to the problem and concludes that the changes of cloudy swelling

[80] Shannon, Jour. Lab. Clin. Med., 1916 (1), 541.
[81] Schwenkenbecher and Ingaki, Arch. exp. Path. u. Pharm., 1906 (55), 203.
[82] See introductory chapter concerning osmosis; also discussion of edema.
[83] Lo Sperimentale, 1905; Cent. f. Path., 1905 (16), 613.
[84] See Medigreceanu, Jour. Exp. Med., 1914 (19), 309.
[85] Orgler, Virchow's Arch., 1904 (176), 413; Hess and Saxl, *ibid.*, 1910 (202), 149.
[86] Verh. Deut. Path. Gesell., 1903 (6), 76.
[87] See Olsho, Arch. Int. Med., 1908 (2), 171.
[88] "Oedema and Nephritis," New York, 1915, p. 455; also Zeit. Chem. u. Indust. Colloide, 1911 (8), 159.

may be ascribed to acids developed in the cell. It is of significance that Chambers[59] has found that even slight mechanical injury of isolated cells under the microscope produces a demonstrable acidity in the protoplasm. Electro-negative proteins in the cell are precipitated by weak concentrations of acids, forming the granules in the cells, which can be dissolved again by a stronger concentration of acid as in the characteristic clearing of granular cells by acetic acid. The swelling is explainable by the increased affinity for water of other cell proteins under the influence of acids. This theory is supported by good experimental evidence and has much in its favor, the chief question being whether the blood cannot, under ordinary conditions of circulation, furnish sufficient neutralizing salts to prevent acidification in the cells to cause cloudy swelling.

[59] Amer. Jour. Physiol., 1917 (43), 1.

CHAPTER XVI

RETROGRESSIVE CHANGES (Continued)

Fatty, Amyloid, Hyaline, Colloid, and Glycogenic Infiltration and Degeneration

FATTY METAMORPHOSIS

In 1847, in the first number of his Archiv, Virchow divided the forms of fatty changes that may occur in pathological conditions into two groups—"infiltration" and "degeneration"—a division that has since become classical. By infiltration he indicated the excessive accumulation of fat in the cells in the form of large droplets, without destruction of the nucleus or irreparable damage to the cells, and by the use of the term infiltration he implied his belief that the fat entered the cell from without. When the fat remained in the form of fine droplets and the cell became much disintegrated, Virchow considered that the fat was derived from the breaking down of the cell proteins, and hence the process was considered to be a fatty degeneration of the protoplasm. Since that time scarcely any other subject in pathology has been more warmly discussed than that of the origin of the fat in fatty degeneration, and an appalling amount of literature has accumulated concerning the questions involved. · It will be impossible to give more than the essential facts that have been developed, referring the reader for the full details of the discussion and evidence to the numerous compilations of literature, particularly those of Rosenfeld,[1] and to the original articles cited in the text.

[1] "Fat Formation," Ergebnisse der Physiol., Abt. 1, 1902 (1), 651; *ibid.*, 1903 (2), 50. Also see discussion in the Verh. Deut. Path. Gesell., 1904 (6), 37–108, and the review by Leathes in his "Problems in Animal Metabolism," 1906, pp 71–121, and "The Fats," Monographs on Biochemistry, London, 1910; von Fürth, "Chemistry of Metabolism," Amer. Transl., New York, 1916. Concerning theories of rôle of lipase in fat metabolism see Chap. iii. Other reviews of literature on pathological fat formation by Christian, Johns Hopkins Hosp. Bull., 1905 (16), 1; Löhlein, Virchow's Arch., 1905 (180), 1; Pratt, Johns Hopkins Hosp. Bull., 1904 (15), 301 (particular reference to heart); Wohlgemuth, Handbuch d. Biochem., 1909, III (1), 150; Magnus-Levy and Meyer, *ibid.*, 1910, IV (1), 445; Dietrich, Ergebnisse der Pathol., 1909, XIII (2), 283. Concerning Obesity see v. Bergmann, Handbuch d. Biochem., 1910, IV (2), 208. Later references of importance cited in the text.

PHYSIOLOGICAL FORMATION OF FAT

Concerning the normal formation of fat we may summarize the evidence as follows:

(1) A large proportion of the fat of the body comes from the fat taken in the food, as also does the fat of the milk. This can be shown, as Rosenfeld particularly demonstrated, by starving an animal until it is as free from fat as possible, then feeding with a large amount of some fat that is of a type different from that normally found in the animal; the new fat that it then laid up in the fat depots of the animal will partake of the characters of the fat given in the food. In case the animal is lactating, the milk-fat will also resemble the fat of the food. As a matter of fact, the body fat is not of constant composition, even in the same individual; it varies greatly with age, having much less olein in infancy than in later years, varying somewhat in composition in the different fat depots in the same body, and apparently being more or less modified by diet.

(2) Fat may also be formed from carbohydrates. According to Rosenfeld, this fat differs from the fat formed on mixed diet in having less olein in proportion to the palmitin and stearin, and it is deposited particularly in the subcutaneous and mesenteric tissues rather than in the liver. Man does not seem to form fat readily from carbohydrates, but rather burns them to protect his proteins; on the other hand, swine and geese readily form fat from carbohydrates. As the fatty acid radicals of ordinary fat ($C_{18}H_{36}O_2$, $C_{16}H_{32}O_2$, $C_{18}H_{34}O_2$), are much larger than the carbohydrate radicals, a process of synthesis must be involved in the formation of fat from carbohydrates.[2]

(3) Proteins are a possible source of fat, but it has not been established that they are either a common or an important source of fat in either physiological or pathological conditions, or, indeed, that they really ever do form fat. Upon this statement rests our present tendency to refute the long-cherished conception of fatty degeneration as a true degeneration of cell proteins into fat, as suggested by Virchow. This view was supported by the earlier work of Voit and his school, who believed that they had demonstrated that animals could form fat from protein food, and their work was for a long time accepted as correct. Later Pflüger and his pupils pointed out what seem to have been essential errors in these investigations, and, after much discussion and experimentation, the majority of physiologists now support the view advanced in the sentence opening this paragraph. Since proteins contain carbohydrate groups, and since fats can be formed from carbohydrates, the possibility of the formation of fats from the proteins in this indirect way cannot be denied. It is also possible that the nitrogen-containing groups may be split out of the amino-acids of the protein molecule, and that the non-nitrogenous residues can then be built up into fatty acid molecules as large as the molecules of stearic, palmitic, and oleic acids; but we have no proof that either of these processes occurs in the normal cell or in the cell that is undergoing degeneration. Atkinson and Lusk[3] have obtained evidence of some fat formation from meat fed to a dog, but this was only slight and obtained with difficulty.

PATHOLOGICAL FAT ACCUMULATION

For a long time fatty degeneration was looked upon as one of the chief evidences that fat was formed directly from protein, for the cell protoplasm seemed, morphologically, to be changed directly into fat in this process. Additional support was also claimed from the supposed increase in fat in the ripening of cheese;[4] from the formation of abundant fat by maggots living in fat-poor blood or fibrin; and by the apparent conversion of proteins into fatty acids and soaps

[2] This, Magnus-Levy suggests, may be accomplished through lactic acid which is formed from sugar, and then, after reduction to an aldehyde, several of these molecules are combined into the higher fatty acid. See Leathes, *loc. cit.*, p. 82.

[3] Proc. Natl. Acad. Sci., 1919 (5), 246.

[4] Even the increase of fat in ripening cheese is doubtful (Nierenstein, Proc. Royal Soc., B., 1911 (83), 301; Kondo, Biochem. Zeit., 1914 (59), 113).

in the postmortem change, *adipocere*. But it has now been well established that there is no true conversion of protein into fat in the fatty degeneration produced experimentally by poisoning with phosphorus, etc.,[5] and the other supposed instances of fat-formation above cited have been discredited by various methods which it will not serve our purpose to discuss here, beyond mentioning that one of the chief sources of error lies in the fact that many fungi and bacteria[6] can form fat from protein.

It having been rendered probable that fat was not formed by disintegration of the protein of the degenerating cells, it remained to determine what the source of the fat observed in the cells under pathological conditions might be, and this part of the problem has been largely cleared up by Rosenfeld. This investigator proceeded as follows: Animals were starved until they were extremely poor in fat, then fed upon easily identified foreign fats, such as mutton tallow (which has a high melting-point and can combine with little iodin) or linseed oil (which has a low melting-point and can combine with much iodin). The animals under these conditions laid up in their fat depots, including the liver as well as the subcutaneous tissues, large quantities of these foreign fats. By starving again for a few days the foreign fat was removed from the liver, leaving still a large amount in the other storehouses, and the animals were then poisoned with phosphorus or other poisons that cause a typical fatty degeneration of the liver and other viscera. When the fat was extracted from the fatty liver of these animals, it was found that the new fat that had appeared in the liver during the process was not normal dog fat (which it should have been if formed by degeneration of the cell proteins), but was, in part, of the same type as the foreign fat which the animals had deposited in their subcutaneous tissues and other fat storehouses. Furthermore, it was found that animals starved to an extremely low fat content do not develop the typical fatty liver of phosphorus-poisoning, a fact which Lebedeff had already noted in a case of phosphorus-poisoning in an emaciated patient. Of similar significance is the fact that in fatty human livers the iodin number, normally high, falls as the amount of fat increases until it is approximately that of adipose connective tissue.[7] Therefore, it seems evident that *the fat accumulating in the liver during fatty degeneration is not derived, as Virchow thought, through a transformation of cell proteins into fat, but rather is an infiltrated fat brought in the blood from the fat deposits of the body to the disintegrating organ.* This work has since been corroborated and extended by many observers, and its correctness can now

[5] See Taylor, Jour. Exp. Med., 1899 (4), 399; Shibata, Biochem. Zeit., 1911 (37), 345.

[6] See Beebe and Buxton, Amer. Jour. of Physiol., 1905 (12), 466; Slosse, Arch. Internat. Physiol., 1904 (1), 348.

[7] Leathes, Lancet, Feb. 27, 1909; Hartley and Mavrogordato, Jour. Path. and Bact., 1908 (12), 371; Jackson and Pearce, Jour. Exp. Med., 1907 (9), 578.

hardly be questioned.[8] "Fatty degeneration," therefore, at least in some cases, differs from "fatty infiltration" chiefly in the fact that in the former the process is associated with serious injury to the cell, caused by the action of toxins or loss of nutrition, while in the latter the cell is not seriously injured and is capable of returning to its normal condition whenever the fat is removed.[9]

Fatty "Degeneration" without Infiltration.—By showing that new fat in fatty livers is infiltrated fat, Rosenfeld did not entirely clear up the subject, for, in the course of his analyses of organs that were micro- or macro-scopically the seat of fatty degeneration, he found that there is not always any correspondence between the amount of fat that seems to be present, as determined by microscopic methods, and the amount that chemical analysis shows to be present. This is particularly true of the kidney. Thus, the amount of fat and lipoids, or *lipins*, present in normal kidneys (dog) was found to vary between 18.5 per cent. and 29.12 per cent. of the dry weight, the average being 21.8 per cent.; whereas, after producing a typical "fatty degeneration" by means of phosphorus and other poisons, the lipin content was still found to be between 16.9 per cent. and 22.6 per cent.[10] In all instances the amount of lipins in kidneys showing typical fatty degeneration under the microscope was found equal to or less than the normal amount—it was never increased. The same conditions were found to obtain in human kidneys that showed fatty metamorphosis. Microscopic examination of specimens stained with the specific fat stains,[11] therefore, gives no indication of the amount of fat

[8] Schwalbe (Verh. der Deut. Path. Gesell., 1903 (6), 71) claims that in a similar way iodin compounds of fat can be demonstrated to be transported into the fatty organs. His analyses were merely qualitative and by quantitative determinations I was unable to corroborate his conclusions (Zeit. f. physiol. Chem., 1905 (45), 412).

[9] A striking proof of the lack of injury associated with fatty infiltration is shown by the fatty infiltration frequently seen in the liver, especially of alcoholics, in which it may be difficult to find, microscopically, any cell cytoplasm because of the fat, the tissue looking like fatty areolar tissue; and yet there may be no clinical evidence whatever that the liver function has been impaired by the process.

[10] Concerning the normal intracellular fats see introductory chapter.

[11] Fat-staining involves several principles of interest in this connection. (See reviews by Bullard, Jour. Med. Res., 1912 (27), 55 and Escher, Corrbl. Schweizer Aertze, 1919 (49), 1609.) Osmic acid (OsO_4), the longest used for this purpose, is reduced to OsO_2 by oleic acid, imparting a black or dark-brown color to the fat; but it does not stain staurated fatty acids, such as palmitic or stearic acid. Thus, Christian found in pneumonic exudates fat that stained by other methods but not by osmic acid, apparently because it contained no oleic acid (Jour. Med. Research, 1903 (10), 109). Sudan III and scarlet R (*fat ponccau*) are two synthetic dyes which stain fat in a purely physical way, entering and remaining in the fat-droplets because they are much more soluble in fat than they are in water or alcohol. (Fully discussed by Michaelis (who introduced scarlet R) in Virchow's Arch., 1901 (164), 263; and by Mann, "Physiological Histology," p. 306.) These stains have the advantage of staining all sorts of fats and not staining other substances that may reduce osmic acid. Fatty acids and soaps may be stained with copper acetate, which forms a green copper salt, and thus be distinguished from fats (Benda, Virchow's Arch., 1900 (161), 194). J. Lorrain Smith (Jour. Path. and Bact., 1907 (12), 1) has introduced as a fat dye, Nile blue sulphate, which forms a blue salt with free fatty acids, while neutral fats are stained red by the oxazone base.

contained in a degenerated kidney. A pathologic kidney containing
16 per cent. of lipins (18 per cent. is about the average amount in normal
human kidneys) may show extreme "fatty degeneration" under the
microscope, whereas another kidney may contain as much as 23 per
cent. of lipins, yet not show any fat whatever by staining methods.

The explanation of this remarkable discrepancy is as follows:
Every tissue and organ seems to contain a greater or less amount of
lipins, varying from 5 per cent. to 20 per cent. of the total dry weight
of the organ in the case of most of the important tissues, yet this is
usually held in such a form that it cannot be stained by any stains
available for the purpose. Thus in the kidneys, as before remarked,
we may have as much as 23 per cent. of lipins present and yet be unable
to stain any of it by ordinary methods. The greater part of this seems
to be essential to the cell, for it cannot be removed by the most extreme
starvation; e. g., the liver of the most emaciated dogs may contain
10 per cent. to 20 per cent. of fatty substances. Furthermore, the
same resistance is shown by part of the fat to extraction with ether.
A certain proportion of the fat can be extracted readily in twenty-
four hours or less by ether, but after this time no more can be made
to leave the tissues. Apparently the rest of the fat is held in a combination that is insoluble in ether, and a large proportion of this fixed
material is not simple fat, but lecithin, cholesterol, and compounds of
these lipoids. It has also been demonstrated that fatty acids can
combine with amino-acids to form compounds (lipo-peptids) very
similar in their properties to these "masked" fats.[12] By digesting
the tissue for a short time by pepsin, however, the fixed lipins become
freed, so that they can then be readily dissolved out in ether. We see,
therefore, that much of the fat of normal cells is so firmly combined
that it cannot be dissolved in ether, and under normal conditions all,
or nearly all, of it cannot be stained. (This applies particularly to
the parenchymatous organs; the fat of the areolar tissue is all readily
extracted—Taylor.) By the use of Ciaccio's method for microscopic
demonstration of intracellular lipoids, Bell[13] has been able to demonstrate in those cells that are fat-free by ordinary methods sufficient
lipoidal material to account for the normal "invisible fat," which is
probably identical with the "liposomes." But when pathological
changes in the cells result in decomposition of the cell protein through
autolysis, or produce physical changes in the colloids that hold the
lipins emulsionized, part of this normally invisible fat is set free, and,
becoming visible, "*phanerosis*,"[14] produces the so-called "fatty degeneration." This explains the observations of Rosenfeld, cited above,
that kidneys may show much fat to the naked eye and microscopically,
when they actually contain even less than normal amounts of fat. Tay-

[12] Bondi, Biochem. Zeit., 1909 (17), 543.
[13] Internat. Monats. Anat. u. Physiol., 1911 (28), 297; Jour. Med. Res., 1911
(24), 539.
[14] Klemperer, Deut. med. Woch., 1909 (35), 89.

lor[15] advanced this explanation, and supported it experimentally by showing that during fatty degeneration this protected fat actually is liberated, some two-thirds becoming ether-soluble in an experiment performed with phosphorus-poisoned frogs. Mansfeld[16] also found that in animals poisoned with phosphorus, the proportion of fat which is present in a form free from protein union in both blood and viscera, is increased, while the firmly bound fat is decreased. As further support may be mentioned the fact that organs undergoing experimental autolysis show microscopically an apparently typical fatty degeneration, although analyses show that no actual increase in fat occurs.[17]

Relation of Anatomical to Chemical Changes.—From the facts brought out in these various experiments we must consider that the anatomically established condition of "fatty degeneration" represents either or both of two conditions: (1) It may result from an increase in the normal quantity of fat in an organ undergoing parenchymatous degeneration, through an infiltration of fat from the outside; this is particularly true of the fatty degeneration of the liver, presumably because the liver normally receives the relatively saturated body fats to work them over into the more labile desaturated fats; (2) there may be no increase in the total amount of fat, but the invisible fat becomes visible through autolysis or hydration changes in the cell proteins. Thus, Bainbridge and Leathes[18] found that after ligation of the hepatic artery there is a marked fatty degeneration of the liver, without an increase in the amount of fat according to analysis. (3) Finally, of course, both factors may occur together. Of these various forms, in only the first would the chemist consider the organ "fatty," although from a morphological standpoint the second form is entitled to rank as a true "fatty degeneration," and the form that will occur seems not to depend upon the cause of the cell injury, but rather upon the organ under consideration. In a study of the relation of the morphological to the chemical changes Rosenfeld[19] arrived at the following results:

Normal human hearts contain, on an average, 15.4 per cent. of lipins; the hearts showing fatty degeneration contain 20.7 per cent. on an average.[20] The pancreas, which normally contains 15.8–17.4 per

[15] Jour. Med. Research, 1903 (9), 59.
[16] Pflüger's Arch., 1909 (129), 63.
[17] Dietrich, Arb. path. Inst. Tübingen, 1906 (5), H. 3; Hess and Saxl, Virchow's Arch., 1910 (202), 149; Ohta, Biochem. Zeit., 1910 (29), 1; Shibata, *ibid.*, 1911 (31), 321. The significance of the increase of lipins observed in perfused kidneys by Gross and Vorpahl is made doubtful by the article of Underhill and Hendrix, Jour. Biol. Chem., 1915 (22), 471.
[18] Biochem. Jour., 1906 (2), 25.
[19] Berl. klin. Woch., 1904 (41),587.
[20] The amount of phospho-lipins in the heart is usually nearly constant, but alimentary fat may accumulate in the myocardium under certain conditions. See Wegelin, Berl. klin. Woch., 1913 (50), 2125; Bullard, Amer. Jour. Anat., 1916 (19), 1.

cent., also contains an increased amount when showing fatty degeneration. The liver, however, takes on by far the greatest amount of fat after "steatogenetic" poisons,[21] and the microscopic picture usually gives a very good approximation of the amount of lipins it contains.[22] Apparently in these organs any excessive fat above the normal is observable microscopically, although the normal lipin content is not, and only in these three organs could Rosenfeld find an actual increase in fat after poisoning with phosphorus, etc. It would seem, on the other hand, that there is not often a real increase in the fat content of the "fatty" kidney.[23] Normal spleen contains 14.2 per cent. of lipins, and lung 17.3 per cent., but in both, "fatty degeneration" results in a lowering of this quantity. Degenerations in the nervous tissue, which Virchow considered the best evidence of the conversion of protoplasm into fat, also show a marked *decrease* in lipins, and voluntary muscle shows no increase in the normal quantity after poisoning. In general, these experiments support the contention of Taylor concerning the disclosure of the invisible fat through autolysis.[24] An explanation of many of the discrepancies lies in the newer studies on

The Relation of the Lipoids to Fatty Metamorphosis.[25]—Until within a few years the significance of the intracellular lipoids in fatty degeneration and related processes was not appreciated, beyond the

[21] In fatty livers in phosphorus-poisoning the amount of fat may reach 75 per cent. of the dry weight. Accompanying the fat increase are increase in water and a relative or absolute decrease in proteins, probably due to cell autolysis. In acute yellow atrophy a similar decrease in protein occurs, but without an increase in fat. (See v. Starck, Deut. Arch. klin. Med., 1884 (35), 481.)

[22] See Helly (Beitr. path. Anat., 1914 (60), 1) who examined 100 human livers which showed all variations in microscopic fat content, and chemically from 7.36 to 74.43 per cent. of lipins (dry weight). He found that there was usually a good correspondence between microscopic appearance and analytic results, altho some marked and unexplained discrepancies were observed. Generally the fat content was from 10 to 30 per cent. of the dry weight, with 19 to 21 per cent. the most common figures. When there is much fat present in the liver the fat content of the bile is increased (Le Count and Long, Jour. Exp. Med., 1914 (19), 234).

[23] This is contradicted by Landsteiner and Mucha (Cent. f. Path., 1904 (15), 752), and by Löhlein (Virchow's Arch., 1905 (180), 1) and Rosenthal (Deut. Arch. klin. Med., 1903 (78), 94), but is supported by Orgler (*ibid.*, 1904 (176), 413), and Dietrich, Verh. Deut. Path. Gesell., 1907 (11), 10. See also the later studies by Rosenfeld on the effects of various steatogenetic poisons on different organs, in Arch. f. Exp. Path. u. Pharm., 1906 (55), 179 and 344. It is probable that the truth lies between the opposing views, namely, the kidney may under some conditions take up fat from the blood, but it does so to a much less extent than the liver, and it may sometimes show marked fatty change anatomically without corresponding increase chemically.

[24] Pieces of tissue implanted into animals may show a peripheral fatty metamorphosis or infiltration, yet show upon analysis a decreased fat content (Dietrich, Verh. Deut. Path. Gesellsch., 1905 (9), 212).

[25] Literature by Leathes, "The Fats," London, 1910; Bang, Ergebnisse der Physiol., 1909 (8), 463, also, "Chemie u. Biochem. d. Lipoide," Bergmann, Wiesbaden, 1911; Kawamura, Virchow's Arch., 1912 (207), 469, also "Die Cholesterinesterverfettung," Fischer, Jena, 1911; Aschoff, Ziegler's Beitr., 1909 (47), 1, also Festschr. f. Unna, 1911 p. 23; Schultz, Ergebnisse d. Pathol., 1909 (XIII₂), 253; Hanes, Bull. Johns Hopkins Hosp., 1912 (23), 77; Anitschkow and Chalatow, Cent. f. Pathol., 1913 (24), 1.

fact that in most organs showing fatty changes the quantity of cholesterol and lecithin is not greatly changed. In 1902 Kaiserling and Orgler described under the non-committal name of "myelin" certain intracellular droplets that may be found in the cells of the normal adrenal cortex, and in amyloid kidneys, pneumonic exudates, tumor cells, retrogressive thymus tissue, corpus luteum, and bronchial secretions, and which differ from fat in being doubly refractile (anisotropic) when viewed through Nicoll prisms, and in staining but slightly gray with osmic acid, although taking up other fat stains well.

As explained in Chapter i, the myelins are probably mixtures of lipins, cholesterol-esters being prominent, and in many conditions in which fat-like vacuoles are prominent in cells, leading to the diagnosis of fatty degeneration, these substances are responsible, presumably having been liberated from combination with the cell proteins in some cases, in others actually being increased in the cell. This condition, which Aschoff refers to as a cholesterol-ester fatty metamorphosis, is especially seen in the parenchyma cells derived from the urogenital anlage—that is, the adrenal cortex, kidney, testicle and corpus luteum. Aschoff states that doubly refractile droplets can be formed by lecithin and phosphatids generally, oleates, cholesterol esters, cholesterol when dissolved in phosphatids or fats or fatty acids, as well as by cholesterol esters dissolved in fats. Of these the most important quantitatively is the cholesterol ester group,[26] and the analyses of Windaus have shown that in pathological processes the increase is much greater in the cholesterol esters than in the free cholesterol. Cholesterol compounds stain differently from neutral fats, being more yellow than red with sudan III, and grayish rather than black with osmic acid. Pathologically the anisotropic droplets are also found especially in the above-named tissues, but also in tissues the site of chronic inflammation, including the mucosa of the gall bladder where they may be of importance in the formation of cholesterol concretions. They are also found in the alveolar epithelium in pulmonary inflammation, in atheromatous patches in arteries, in many tumors, in most cells,[27] including even the adipose tissues themselves,[28] and occasionally in varied pathological tissues.[29] Perhaps the most conspicuous deposits are in the epithelium of the "large white kidneys," and in xanthomas. In Gaucher's disease there is also a remarkable lipoid accumulation in the foamy phagocytic cells.[30] According to Munk[31] true lipoid degeneration always means a serious injury to the cell, but there seem to be many exceptions to this. Indeed, according

[26] See also Verse, Ziegler's Beitr., 1911 (52), 1.
[27] Ciaccio, Cent. f. Path., 1913 (24), 50.
[28] Cramer, Jour. Physiol., 1917 (51), xi.
[29] Pathological decrease in lipoids may also be observed, especially in the adrenal cortex, usually under the influence of toxic agents; e. g., Hirsch found a marked decrease in delirium tremens (Jour. Amer. Med. Assoc., 1914 (63), 2186).
[30] See Wahl and Richardson, Arch. Int. Med., 1916 (17), 238.
[31] Virchow's Arch., 1908 (194), 527.

to Anitschkow and Chalatow (*loc. cit*). the feeding of foods rich in cholesterol may cause the appearance in the liver of great quantities of anisotropic droplets, lipoid deposits in the aorta, enlargement of the adrenal cortex, and the presence in practically all tissues of semifluid, doubly refracting crystalline structures (*cholesterol steatosis*).[32]

In cells undergoing autolysis the fat-like "myelin" droplets which appear, differ from the above in not being anisotropic, but are undoubtedly closely related to them in composition. These "myelin" droplets are also found in cells showing cloudy swelling, presumably representing cell lipoids set free through changes in the cell proteins. They are characterized by staining with osmic acid but not by sudan III, which shows them not to be simple fats nor yet lipoids, but they are undoubtedly precursors of true fatty degeneration;[33] they probably consist chiefly of lecithin, with more or less free fatty acids and relatively little cholesterol (Aschoff).

It is possible to distinguish the lipoids of cells, whether normal or pathological, from the neutral fats by means of Ciaccio's method.[34] This consists in a preliminary treatment with bichromate, which renders the lipoids insoluble; the tissues can then be hardened and imbedded by the usual methods which remove the unchromated fats, leaving the lipoids stainable by sudan III. By this method Bell[35] has been able to stain the lipoids in the normal kidney and other tissues, in sufficient amount to account for all the so-called "masked fat," which thus seems to be, as also indicated by chemical evidence, largely lipoidal.

Jastrowitz[36] has studied the relation of lipoids to fats in the fatty changes produced by various means, and finds that in severe fatty changes with much transported fats there may be little change in the lipoids; with blood poisons which cause little increase in total fats, the lipoid content of both blood and organs may be high; usually the phosphatid content is unchanged or slightly increased, but it may be decreased. The proportion of cholesterol to neutral fats is usually within normal limits in tissues showing fatty changes.[37] The mitochondria seem to be compounds of phospholipins with proteins, and these agglutinate and form fatlike droplets in phosphorus poisoning;[38] presumably they play an important rôle in fatty metamorphosis. Cells in tissue cultures, however, may take up fat droplets from the surrounding medium (*i. e.*, fatty infiltration), without any association with or changes in the mito-chondria.[39]

[32] See also Anitschkow, Deut. med. Woch., 1913 (39), 741; Wesselkin, Virchow's Arch., 1913 (212), 225; Rubinstein, Compt. Rend. Soc. Biol., 1917 (80), 191.
[33] Hess and Saxl, Virchow's Arch., 1910 (202), 149.
[34] Cent. f. Path., 1909 (20), 771; Arch. f. Zellf., 1910 (5), 235.
[35] Jour. Med. Res., 1911 (24), 539.
[36] Zeit. exp. Path. u. Ther., 1914 (15), 116.
[37] Czyhlarz and Fuchs, Biochem. Zeit., 1914 (63), 131.
[38] Scott, Amer. Jour. Anat., 1916 (20), 237.
[39] M. R. Lewis, Science, 1918 (48), 398.

Summary.—We must conclude, therefore, that fatty degeneration of an organ means, in the case of the liver, myocardium, and pancreas, an infiltration of neutral fat from outside into cells which have been degenerated by the action of poisons or other injurious influences, plus a certain amount of apparent increase in fat because of the setting free of previously invisible fats and lipoids normally present in the affected cells. In the kidney, spleen, and muscles an increase of fat seldom occurs from these causes, but the cells may show a marked fatty metamorphosis through the setting free of the invisible intracellular fat and lipoids by autolytic or physico-chemical changes. In the adrenal, kidney, and often in other tissues, the fatty material present in the cells is characterized by being doubly refractile, and then consists chiefly of cholesterol esters, together with greater or less quantities of phosphatids, fatty acids, soaps and neutral fats.

PATHOGENESIS OF FATTY METAMORPHOSIS

Nevertheless, the old anatomical distinction of infiltration and degeneration still remains, provided we do not hold to the original idea that the term degeneration implies that the cell protein has been converted into fat; for we must recognize that under some conditions the cells may take up great quantities of fat without suffering any appreciable degenerative changes, whereas in other instances the appearance of fat is associated with marked and complete disintegration of both nucleus and cytoplasm. Furthermore, we have yet to explain why, under some conditions, the fat is removed from the fat depots to be stored up in the liver or other organs. By applying the commonly accepted ideas concerning fat metabolism, a satisfactory explanation seems to be possible. Fat is always utilized and transported in the form of its two constituents, fatty acid (or soaps) and glycerol, which are diffusible and soluble. It enters and leaves the cells in this condition, being split or combined, as may be necessary to produce equilibrium, by the action of lipase, which is present within the cells and in the blood and lymph. Under normal conditions there is little free visible fat in the cells of the parenchymatous organs, because it is largely used up through oxidation of the glycerol and fatty acids by the action of the intracellular oxidases. Where there is abundant lipase and but little oxidative activity, as is the case in the areolar fat tissue, fat accumulates in large amounts. When, for any reason, the oxidative power of the parenchymatous organs is reduced, fat accumulates in them as it does in the fat depots normally, and we have an excess of fat in the parenchymatous cells; thus, in pulmonary tuberculosis, severe or protracted anemias, etc., a great accumulation of fat occurs, particularly in the liver, where normally active oxidative processes continually balance the action of the abundant lipase of the liver-cells. , The liver being normally concerned in the preparation of fat for metabolism, it is also perfectly possible to have an accumulation of fat in the normal liver merely as a result of increased function, and hence fatty changes may be purely physiological in this organ.[40]

If the fat accumulates in cells that are structurally normal or nearly so, the fat-droplets fuse together under the pressure of the cytoplasm, and we get the picture of a typical fatty infiltration; indeed, the only tissues in which we get this typical infiltration are the liver and the fatty areolar tissue, in both of which the process is presumably physiological in character even if not always physiological in degree. If the cells are much disintegrated through the action of the poison,—e. g., phosphorus, bacterial toxins, etc.,—the accumulating fat-droplets are not crowded into one large droplet, but lie free in the granular débris of the disintegrating cell, constituting the typical appearance of fatty degeneration. Fatty degeneration is usually brought about by poisons, while abnormal fatty infiltration depends usually upon decreased oxidation, due to lack of either oxygen or hemoglobin in the blood. If the anemia is extreme, however, the cells degenerate, and then we find a true fatty degeneration caused by lack of oxygen.[41] Thus, in an anemic infarct fat accumulates about the periphery of the dead area,[42] probably because fatty acids and glycerol diffuse in slowly from the surrounding parts where circulation still goes on, and are built up into fat by the cell lipase, for in anemic areas the intracellular oxidases cannot destroy these substances as they normally do, because of lack of oxygen. The accumulation of fat in dead areas depends, therefore, on the fact that the constituents of fat can diffuse into the dead tissue, whereas the oxygen, being held in the corpuscles, cannot enter the anemic area.[43] It is also possible that where fat is set free by autolysis of dead tissue, or when for any cause free fat or lipoid material is present in the vicinity of living cells, it may be phagocyted or in some way infiltrate the cells, causing a fatty metamorphosis by absorption (Dietrich).

It is to be supposed that poisons also cause fatty degeneration in a similar way—by interfering with oxidation. We have much evidence that in phosphorus, chloroform, and other poisoning associated with fatty degeneration of the liver, oxidation is impaired.[44] If we imagine for a moment, a cell in which oxidation is checked by any means, we shall have in this cell the lipase and the proteolytic enzymes not balanced, as they normally are by the action of the oxidases, and hence the processes of cell autolysis and of the accumula-

[40] See Coope and Mottram, Jour. of Physiol., 1914 (49), 23; Helly, Beitr. path. Anat., 1914 (60), 1.
[41] Mohr (Zeit. exp. Path., 1906 (2), 434), denies that oxidation is decreased in anemia; and in a man with but about half the normal lung area the metabolism was not found altered to any extent by Carpenter and Benedict, Amer. Jour. Physiol., 1909 (23), 412.
[42] Fischler, Cent. f. Path., 1902 (13), 417.
[43] See Griesser, Ziegler's Beitr., 1911 (51), 115.
[44] See Welsch, Arch. int. de pharm. et therap., 1905 (14), 211.

tion of fat by the lipase will go on uncontrolled. The result will be a disintegrated cell containing many fat-droplets, i. e., fatty degeneration.[45] In cloudy swelling there also appear droplets stained with osmic acid but not by sudan III, which Hess and Saxl[46] have shown to result from intravitam cell autolysis, and to be a precursor of true fatty degeneration.

Work with cells in tissue cultures indicates that fatty changes of all types may occur independently of the circulation. Lambert[47] states that the amount of fat in the culture cells is roughly proportional to the amount in the culture medium, and cells rich in fat may move actively and undergo normal mitosis. Lewis, however, observed fatty changes in cells growing in fat-free media, and made the especially interesting observation that cells grown in 2.5–3 per cent. alcohol will show a rich fat accumulation. Also, an accumulation of fats and lipoids in cells grown in the presence of such steatogenetic poisons as phosphorus and Oleum pulegii has been observed by others,[49] which indicates that free cells behave the same under the influence of such poisons as the cells of the fixed tissues.

The process of unmasking the masked fats is explained by M. H. Fischer[50] on a physical basis, as follows: The fats of the cells are distributed as an emulsion in a hydration compound of water with hydrophilic colloids, notably proteins and soaps. Such an emulsion breaks down whenever the hydrophilic colloid is either dehydrated or diluted beyond certain ranges. As the usual conditions that cause fatty degeneration, such as poisoning with phosphorus, arsenic, etc., or local circulatory disturbances with local acidosis, all tend to dehydrate some of the cell colloids and to dilute others, it would seem probable that the appearance of the fat droplets in the cells is the result of such changes in the colloids that previously held them in an emulsion too fine to exhibit readily visible fat particles. The relation of cloudy swelling to fatty degeneration is readily explained on this

[45] Interference with oxidation does not necessarily imply destruction of the oxidases. As yet we know practically nothing concerning the oxidases of the cells in disease, and the above hypothesis has yet to be demonstrated. Duccheschi and Almagia (Arch. Ital. Biol., 1903 (39), 29) found the normal amount of lipase in phosphorus-livers, but also observed no decrease in ability to oxidize salicylic aldehyde, which, however, does not prove a normal power to oxidize fats. Gierke's observation (Ziegler's Beitr., 1905 (37), 502) that glycogen and fat accumulate under identical conditions might be cited as indicating decreased oxidative power. Wells (Jour. Exper. Med., 1910 (12), 607) found that the power of liver tissue to oxidize purines was not decreased by the maximum degree of fatty degeneration, but Waldvogel (Deut. Arch. klin. Med., 1907 (89), 342) found that obese persons can burn fatty acids which arise in metabolism less readily than normal; and Quinan (Jour. Med. Res., 1915 (32), 73) found the ester-splitting lipolytic enzymes of the liver much reduced in the liver of chloroform necrosis, but the relation of these esterases to true lipases is not known.

[46] Virchow's Arch., 1910 (202), 149.

[47] Trans. Assoc. Amer. Phys., 1913 (9), 93; Jour. Exp. Med., 1914 (19), 398.

[49] Krontowski and Poteff, Beitr. path. Anat., 1914 (58), 407.

[50] Fischer and Hooker, Science, 1916 (43), 468; Fischer, Fats and Fatty Degeneration, Wiley, New York, 1917.

basis, as follows: When a local acid intoxication of a cell occurs, some of the proteins will swell and others will precipitate, resulting respectively in the swelling and cloudiness of the cells characteristic of cloudy swelling; but at the same time the emulsifying capacity of these proteins will be impaired, permitting the coalescence of the fat droplets and the resulting picture will be that of fatty degeneration.

Summary.—Fatty metamorphosis involves changes of two kinds. First, infiltration of fat, which occurs when the oxidative power of the cells is decreased, so that fat is not destroyed, but is accumulated from the blood under the influence of the lipase of the cells; if there is not any serious injury to the cells, the histological changes consist in the accumulation of one or a few large droplets of fat in each cell, constituting the condition known anatomically as "fatty infiltration." This occurs, pathologically, chiefly in the liver. If at the same time the cytoplasm is disintegrated through autolytic changes, the fat-droplets do not fuse, but remain as small, more or less discrete, fat granules among the granules of cell débris, constituting the microscopic picture of "fatty degeneration"; this condition occurs particularly in the heart and liver.

Second, each cell contains a large amount of fat and lipoids (5–25 per cent. of its dry weight), which is so combined that it cannot be detected microscopically; this may be liberated during the autolytic processes and colloidal changes of cell disintegration and become visible, constituting a macroscopical and microscopical degeneration, but without any actual increase in fat—this condition occurs particularly in the kidney and nervous system. Third, a combination of both of the above processes—infiltration of fat and liberation of masked intracellular fat—may occur simultaneously in an organ.[51] Fourth, in certain cells, especially in the kidney, adrenal, ovary and some tumors, there may be a great increase in the lipoids of the cell, "lipoidal degeneration," and especially of cholesterol esters and free cholesterol, part of which is infiltrated and part set free from combination in the cytoplasm.

PROCESSES RELATED TO FATTY METAMORPHOSIS
ADIPOCERE

This apparent transformation of the substance of dead bodies into a wax-like material was for a long time looked upon as evidence of a transformation of protein into fat, but in the light of more recent investigations this view can hardly be held. Adipocere is the product of a process that occurs particularly in bodies buried in very wet

---

[51] The above conception of the processes involved in fatty metamorphosis is more fully discussed by the writer in other publications (Jour. Amer. Med. Assoc., 1902 (38), 220; *ibid.*, 1906 (46), 341). Ribbert (Deut. med. Woch., 1903 (29), 793) has also advanced a similar explanation for the morphological differences between fatty "degeneration" and "infiltration," *i. e.*, that the degenerative changes are independent of fatty accumulation.

places or lying in water, and results in an apparent replacement of the muscles and other soft parts (but not the glandular organs) by a mass consisting of a mixture of fatty acids in crystalline and amorphous form, and soaps, particularly ammonium, magnesium, and calcium salts of palmitic and stearic acid (the oleic acid largely disappearing during the process). Analysis of samples of adipocere by Ruttan[52] gave the following figures:

COMPOSITION OF HUMAN AND PIG'S ADIPOCERE

	I Pigs (mature)	II Human hard	III Human soft
Ether soluble, per cent	94.1	82.9	75.8
Specific gravity at 100° C	0.8436	0.8397	0.8410
Refractive index 65° C	1.436	1.437	1.439
Melting point	60–63°	52–54°	50–51°
Acid value	201.7	207.3	203.8
Saponification value	207.0	211.0	212.2
Iodine value	6.04	9.65	12.52
Acetyl value	34.75	11.8	————
Mean molecular weight	271.0	266.0	264.0
Saturated fat acids, per cent	70.82	71.78	59.2
Unsaturated fat acids	5.24	8.87	11.6
Hydroxy fat acids	14.80	8.24	7.8
Stearin and palmitin	1.21	0.91	0.90
Olein	0.16	0.15	0.83
Unsaponified matter	0.87	0.69	0.75
Calcium soaps	4.41	6.76	12.3
Protein	0.665	1.93	4.14
Ammonia	0.035	....	0.054
Ash	0.574	1.99	2.25

Ammonium and other soluble soaps were absent. The hydroxy-stearic acids, which are so characteristic of adipocere, are formed from the oleic acid of the original triolein. Cholesterol has also been found in adipocere.[53]

The resulting material is absolutely resistant to putrefaction, and hence remains intact for many years. This replacement of the soft parts is, however, only apparent, for the total weight of a body in this condition is much lighter than that of the original body; indeed, one is always surprised at the light weight on lifting such a specimen. Adipocere occurs almost exclusively in fat bodies, and it seems probable that all the soaps and fatty acids found are *formed from the original fats of the corpse.*[54] These gradually flow into the places left by the disintegrating muscle, etc., a process that occurs readily in cadavers, according to Zillner;[55] or the infiltration may be accomplished through

[52] Jour. Biol. Chem., 1917 (29), 319; Trans. Roy. Soc. Can., 1916 (10), 169.
[53] Van Itallie and Steenhauer, Pharm. Weekblad, 1917 (54), 121.
[54] Fatty changes in the viscera may favor their transformation into adipocere (Müller, Vierteljahrs. gericht. Med., 1915 (50), 251).
[55] Vierteljahrsch. f. gericht. Med., 1885 (42), 1.

diffusion of the ammonium soaps formed during the decomposition. As the subcutaneous fat is hardened by the formation of soaps, and the bones remain to hold the parts in position, the general form of the body is preserved, creating the impression that its entire substance has been converted into adipocere, when the total mass may actually weigh but twenty pounds or so, and, according to Zillner's estimate, not more than one-tenth of the muscle substance is replaced by adipocere. This false impression is probably responsible for much of the mistaken idea concerning the conversion of tissue proteins into fatty acids. Thus, Schmidt[56] found that in early Egyptian mummies 60 per cent. of the weight of the lungs and 30 per cent. of the spleen consisted of fatty acids, and fell into the usual error of considering this conclusive evidence of transformation of proteins into fat.

Numerous attempts have been made to prove that muscle could be thus converted into fatty acids and soaps, but although success has been claimed by a few, the results are not entirely convincing.[57] Bacteria can convert proteins into fats, beyond a doubt, and they may do so to some slight extent in adipocere formation, but probably this factor is not important.

In the light of our present conception of fat metabolism it is probable that the process of adipocere formation occurs as follows: The fatty acids of the fat tissue are combined by the ammonia formed during putrefaction, removing these fatty acids from the normal balance of fat and fatty acids in the fat tissue; as a result, the lipase of the fat tissue continues to split the fat, and more fatty acids are produced, which likewise go to form soaps. This continues until practically all the neutral fat has been decomposed, the glycerol diffusing rapidly away. The soluble soaps, which the bacteria do not attack, diffuse into the softened muscle tissue, which they gradually replace in part. In the meantime, from the more soluble ammonium soaps, calcium and magnesium soaps are being slowly formed, according to the usual rule of double decomposition (that the least soluble salt will be formed under such conditions); or else, if an acid reaction develops, free fatty acids are precipitated. The oleic acid seems to be converted into the higher fatty acids (Salkowski).[58] It is also possible that the saponification is due to the gradual action of the alkaline fluids produced in decomposition of the tissues, or to the alkalinity of the water in which the body lies. Possibly bacteria may be responsible for this decomposition of the fats rather than the body lipase, for Eijkman[59] has observed that certain bacteria growing in fat-containing agar produce calcium, ammonium, and sodium soaps, simulating adipocere.[60]

[56] Zeit. allg. Physiol., 1907 (7), 369.
[57] See Rosenfeld, Ergeb. der. Physiol., Abt. 1, 1902 (1), 659.
[58] Festschr. f. Virchow, 1891, p. 23; corroborated by Schütze.
[59] Cent. f. Bakt., 1901 (29), 847.
[60] See also Cevidalli, Vierteljahrschr. gerichtl. Med., 1906 (32), 219; and Schütze, Arch. Hyg., 1912 (76), 116.

Zillner[55] gives the following scheme of the changes that take place in a cadaver undergoing adipocere formation: (1) Migration of fluid contents of the body (imbibition of blood and transudation)—one to four weeks. (2) Decomposition of superficial epidermis, then of corium—first two months. (3) Decomposition of muscle and gland parenchyma, until only the inorganic part of the bones and the connective and elastic tissues remain—three to twelve months. (4) Migration of neutral fat, crystallization and partial saponification of the higher fatty acids in the panniculus; transformation of the blood pigment into crystalline form—four to twelve or more months.[61]

LIPEMIA

Normally the blood contains a considerable amount of fats and lipoids, varying somewhat, but not greatly, with the diet. The older literature gave figures varying widely, but analyses by more modern methods[62] give figures for the ether-soluble constituents of the normal plasma (before breakfast) ranging ordinarily from 0.57 to 0.82 per cent., of which cholesterol and phosphatid[63] are about equal (0.2 to 0.3 per cent.) with very little neutral fat (0.1 to 0.2 per cent.). In various diseases, exclusive of diabetes, the total lipin content was found by Bloor to be about normal, but the proportion of the different lipins varied somewhat. After taking fat-rich food, however, there may be a considerable excess of the food fats in the serum, and it is, therefore, extremely difficult to say just when the amount of fat in the blood is large enough to be considered as a lipemia, especially since after every fatty meal there is enough fat in the blood to make it turbid.[63a] B. Fisher[64] states that we may speak of a pathological lipemia when we have a distinctly cloudy blood or serum, which is clarified by shaking with ether through the dissolving out of fat which can then be separated from the ether. We may, however, sometimes find turbid plasma with normal lipin content and clear plasma with hyperlipemia (Gray). Earlier writers described, incorrectly, lipemia in many conditions, but recent writers mention it chiefly as occurring in alcoholism[65] and diabetes. By far the greatest amounts of fat are observed in the latter condition, and diabetic lipemia is always accompanied by an acidosis, although acidosis often occurs without lipemia. Experi-

[61] *Sclerema neonatorum* is caused by hardening of the subcutaneous fat, perhaps because of a low proportion of oleic acid. (Beyer, Verh. Deut. Path. Gesell., 1908 (12), 305.) C. S. Smith, however, found normal oleic acid but a high figure for free fatty acids. Others have described high melting points for the fat, believing the condition to be merely an exaggeration of the normally high proportion of palmitic and stearic acids of infant fat tissues (Smith, Jour. Cut. Dis., 1918 (36), 436).
[62] Bloor, Jour. Biol. Chem., 1916 (25), 577.
[63] Concerning blood lecithin see Feigl, Biochem. Zeit., 1918 (90), 361.
[63a] Neisser and Brauning, Zeit. exp. Path. u. Ther., 1907 (4), 747.
[64] Virchow's Arch., 1903 (172), 30. Résumé and complete literature.
[65] Also occurs in experimental alcoholism (Feigl, Biochem. Zeit., 1918 (92), 282; Bang, *ibid.*, (90), 383).

mental pancreatic diabetes may be accompanied by lipemia.[66] Increases in the blood lipoids, not usually of sufficient magnitude to cause a distinct lipemia, may be found in nephritis (Bloor), cirrhosis, tabes and paralysis (Feigl).[67]

Neisser and Derlin[68] found 19.7 per cent. of fat in the blood of a patient with diabetic coma (after death 24.4 per cent. was found) whose urine contained 0.8 per cent. of fat, and through analysis of this and other material came to the conclusion that the fat comes directly from the chyle; i. e., that it is food fat, not body fat. Fischer found an average of 18.129 per cent. in his case, including at least 0.478 per cent. of cholesterol, with no lipuria and very small amounts of fatty acids; of the fat, about 67.5 per cent. was olein. Ringer[69] has found 14.4 per cent. of lipins, including 2.14 per cent. of cholesterol. As high as 27 per cent. of fat has been found in the blood.[70] In many cases the increase is chiefly in the lipoids, *lipoidemia*,[71] and in acidosis there is said to be an especial increase in cholesterol (Adler).[72]

Study of a large number of diabetic bloods by Gray[73] gave the following results: Normal lipin values are seldom found, the most marked increases being in the total glycerides, next the total fatty acids, then the cholesterol, and least the phospholipins. Increase of both cholesterol and glycerides seems to be pathognomonic of chronic diabetic lipemia, as in alimentary lipemia the increase is in the fatty acids. The greater the duration of the diabetes the lower the lipins, and high figures give a bad prognosis, being usually associated with acidosis. Hyperglycemia and hyperlipemia do not run parallel.[74] In general, the amount of blood lipins increases with the severity of the disease,[75] the averages in a large series of analyses being as follows: normal, 0.59 per cent.; mild diabetes, 0.83; moderate, 0.91; severe, 1.41. The changes concern chiefly the plasma. Coexistent nephritis does not modify the blood lipin figures. When the lipemia is accompanied by icterus the fats may clear up and a clear serum is present, despite a high fat content.[76]

It is an important question whether, with high quantities of fat in the blood, fat embolism may result, for it is possible that at least some of the cases of diabetic coma are due to such fat embolism in the cerebral vessels. Ebstein[77] considers this a possible, but not a common, occurrence, because the droplets are too small to cause oc-

[66] Seo, Arch. exp. Path. u. Pharm., 1909 (61), 1.
[67] Biochem. Zeit., 1918 (88), 53; (90), 1.
[68] Zeit. klin. Med., 1904 (51), 428.
[69] Proc. Soc. Exp. Biol. Med., 1917 (15), 40.
[70] Frugoni and Marchetti, Berl. klin. Woch., 1908 (45), 1844.
[71] See Weil, Münch. med. Woch., 1912 (59), 2096.
[72] Berl. klin. Woch., 1910 (47), 1323.
[73] Boston Med. Surg. Jour., 1917 (178), 16.
[74] Corroborated by Bang, Biochem. Zeit., 1919 (94), 359.
[75] See Jour. Amer. Med. Assoc., 1917 (69), 375.
[76] Feigl and Querner, Zeit. exp. Med., 1919 (9), 153.
[77] Virchow's Arch., 1899 (155), 571.

clusion of the vessels unless they combine to form large droplets. Fischer doubts if the droplets ever fuse together enough to cause embolism, supporting his contention both by experiments and clinical records, but cases have been reported as fat embolism from diabetic lipemia.[78]

The cause of lipemia has not yet been satisfactorily determined. In alcoholism it is commonly ascribed to a failure to burn fat, because of the presence of the more readily oxidized alcohol, and the common coexistence of diabetes and lipemia suggests for both a common cause; *i. e.*, lack of oxidation of fat and sugar. In corroboration may be cited the occurrence of lipemia in other conditions associated with defective oxidation; *i. e.*, pneumonia, anemia,[79] phosphorus-poisoning. As we are still unfamiliar with the essential factors and steps in the oxidation of fat, it would be mere speculation to attempt to explain further the reason for the failure of destruction of the fat. The origin of the fat in lipemia is likewise undetermined. Ebstein considers that it arises partly from the food, partly from fatty degeneration of the cells of the blood, the vessel-walls, and the viscera. Neisser and Derlin consider it as merely food fat coming from the chyle and accumulated in the blood. Fischer believes that it is largely derived from the fat depots, and that because of loss of the lipolytic power of the blood it cannot be rendered diffusible, and hence it cannot enter the tissues where it is normally consumed. Sakai[80] also found a low lipase content in the blood and suggests that fat entering the blood is unable to leave it because of defective lipolysis. Klemperer and Umber hold that it comes from disintegration of tissue cells, but are unable to determine the cells concerned. Ervin[81] attributes diabetic lipemia to the glycogen deficiency of the cells, assuming that glycogen acts as a protective colloid which holds the intracellular fats in emulsion.

Bloor's studies[82] support strongly the view that the fats come from the food, for he found lipemia only in diabetics receiving fat in their food, and under fasting an existing lipemia disappears. Cholesterol increases parallel with the fat, while lecithin is relatively little increased. Verse[83] says that a lasting lipemia can be produced by feeding rabbits mixed cholesterol and oil, but not with either of these alone. In severe diabetes without lipemia the lipins are all much increased in the plasma, but with the relative proportions about as in normal individuals, although with a tendency for the fats to accumulate in excess. The facts that fat oxidation depends upon carbohydrate oxidation, and also that in diabetics excessive fat feeding is

[78] Hedren, Svenska Läk. Handl., 1916 (42), 933.
[79] See Boggs and Morris (Jour. Exper. Med., 1909 (11), 553), who produced lipemia by repeatedly bleeding rabbits.
[80] Biochem. Zeit., 1914 (62), 387.
[81] Jour. Lab. Clin. Med., 1919 (5), 146.
[82] Jour. Biol. Chem., 1916 (26), 417; 1917 (31), 575.
[83] Münch med. Woch., 1916 (63), 1074.

27

usual, are probably significant in the causation of diabetic lipemia. (See also cholesterolemia.)

PATHOLOGICAL OCCURRENCE OF FATTY ACIDS

Fatty acids occasionally occur free in pathological processes. The best example of this is fat necrosis (*q. v.*)., where crystals of fatty acids appear in the necrotic fat-cells, arising through splitting of fat. and later becoming combined with calcium from the blood. Similar crystals, consisting of a mixture of palmitic and stearic acids, frequently called *margarin* or *margaric acid* crystals, may be found in decomposed pus, in sputum from bronchiectatic cavities and from gangrene of the lungs, in gangrenous tissue, and in atheromatous areas. According to Schwartz and Kayser[84] the free fatty acids, at least in pulmonary gangrene, arise from lipolysis by bacterial action rather than by the lipase of the tissues. Eichhorst found crystals of fatty acids in the neighborhood of acute patches of sclerosis in the central nervous system in *multiple sclerosis*, and McCarthy[85] found them in a spinal cord undergoing secondary degeneration from compression. Whipple[86] describes a case with deposits of fatty acids and neutral fat in the wall of the intestine and the mesenteric glands, while soaps and fatty acids are said to be present in excess in chronic appendicitis.[87] Soaps and fatty acids, especially oleic acid and oleates, are highly toxic, and their profound hemolytic power has been thought of importance in pathological conditions, especially bothriocephalus anemia.[88] (See Hemolysins, Chap. ix.) The fatal dose of sodium oleate for rabbits is 0.15 gm. per kilo (Leathes). The salts of higher fatty acids above capric are hemolytic, while those from caproic down are not, nonoic acid salts being the turning point (Shimazono).[89] The toxicity of soaps may be related to their marked power to inhibit proteolytic enzymes.[90]

The fatty acids may be stained green by copper acetate, according to Benda's method, and if then treated with hematoxylin, they turn black.[91] With Nile blue sulphate they stain blue, forming a blue salt, while the neutral fats are stained red by the oxazone base (J. L. Smith). Fischler and Gross[92] state that fatty acids are present in atheromatous areas and about the margin of anemic infarcts, but are not recognizable by this method in such fatty degenerations as pneumonic exudates, caseation, etc. Klotz[93] considers that calcium

[84] Zeit. klin. Med., 1905 (56), 111.
[85] Univ. of Penn. Med. Bull., 1903 (16), 141.
[86] Bull. Johns Hopkins Hosp., 1907 (18), 382.
[87] Anthony, Jour. Med. Res., 1911 (20), 359.
[88] Faust, Suppl. Bd., Schmiedeberg's Arch., 1908, p. 171.
[89] Z. Immunität., Ref., 1911 (4), 656.
[90] Jobling and Petersen, Jour. Exp. Med., 1911 (19), 251.
[91] Fischler, Cent. f. Path., 1904 (15), 913.
[92] Ziegler's Beitr., 1905 (7th suppl.), 343.
[93] Jour. Exp. Med., 1905 (7), 633.

soaps are formed as the first step in pathological calcification, according to microchemical evidence; but a chemical investigation of the same question did not give the writer positive results.[94] In fatty cells, especially in the liver, crystals are often found and interpreted as fatty acids, which are really crystals of neutral fats.[95]

PATHOLOGICAL OCCURRENCE OF CHOLESTEROL[96]

Cholesterol in crystals is found under somewhat the same conditions as the fatty acids, and although cholesterol is not a fat, but an alcohol, its physical properties are so similar that it may be considered in this place. (See "Gall-stones," Chap. xvii, for further discussion.) The characteristic large flat plates of cholesterol may be found in any tissue in which cells are undergoing slow destruction, and where absorption is poor. Therefore, they are found frequently in atheromatous patches in the blood-vessels, encapsulated caseous areas, old infarcts and hematomas, inspissated pus-collections, dermoid cysts, hydrocele fluids, etc.; especially large amounts occur in the cholesteatomatous tumors of the ear and cranial cavity.[97]

In degenerative conditions of the central nervous system[98] cholesterol may be present in the spinal fluid (Pighini[99]), and in an old pleural effusion as much as 3 to 4 per cent. of cholesterol has been found[1] (See Pleural Effusions, Chap. xiv.) Windaus[2] found that normal aortas contain about 0.15 per cent. cholesterol, while in two atheromatous aortas he found 1.8 per cent. and 1.4 per cent., the increase being more in the cholesterol esters than in the free cholesterol. Amyloid kidneys, however, show an increase only in the cholesterol esters, and not at all in the free cholesterol. (See Relation of Lipoids to Fatty Metamorphosis, p. 406.) Ameseder[3] found that 28.56 per cent. of the ether extract of atheromatous aortas was cholesterol. The claim of Chauffard that arcus senilis, xanthelasma, and other ocular conditions depend on cholesterol deposition is not substantiated by Mawas[4] but Verse[83] observed corneal opacity in rabbits fed cholesterol and oil. In liquids the crystals form glistening scales; in fresh tissues they may be recognized by their solubility in ether, cholorform, hot alcohol, etc., and by their color reactions. In histological specimens prepared by the usual methods the cholesterol is dissolved out, but the resulting clear-cut clefts are quite characteristic. In fresh specimens in which

[94] Wells, Jour. Med. Research, 1906 (14), 491.
[95] Smith and White, Jour. Path. and Bact., 1907 (12), 126.
[96] Concerning the chemistry of cholesterol see introductory chapter.
[97] See Bostroem, Cent. f. Path., 1897 (8), 1.
[98] Southard has described cholesterol concretions up to 2 cm. diameter in the brain and cord. (Jour. Amer. Med. Assoc., 1905 (45), 1731.)
[99] Riforma Med., 1909 (25), 67.
[1] Ruppert, Münch. med. Woch., 1908 (55), 510; Zunz, Hedstrom, and others (see Chap. XIV).
[2] Zeit. physiol. Chem., 1910 (67), 174.
[3] Zeit. physiol. Chem., 1911 (70), 458.
[4] Monatsbl. f. Augenheilk., 1912 (13), 604.

cholesterol crystals are present, on treatment with five parts concentrated sulphuric acid and one of water, the edges of the crystals become carmine red, then violet. Concentrated sulphuric acid plus a trace of iodin colors the crystals in sequence, violet, blue, green, and red. Hirschsohn[5] recommends a reaction with a 90 per cent. solution of trichloracetic acid in HCl, which gives red, then violet, then blue. The results of microchemical examination are said not to agree at all quantitatively with analytic results.[6]

Since all cells contain cholesterol,[7] it is perhaps accumulated as one of the least soluble products of their disintegration. The origin of the normal cell cholesterol is unknown, but that which is liberated by normal disintegration of cells seems to be retained and worked over.[8] It is not destroyed during autolysis.[9] Cholesterol is generally considered, but without convincing proof, to be a product of protein decomposition; if this is true, then the cholesterol found in disintegrating tissues may be formed from the cell proteins during their decomposition.[10] Apparently cholesterol crystals may be slowly removed, the chief factor probably being the giant-cells that are often found surrounding them,[11] and the large "foamy" endothelial cells that take up especially the uncrystallized cholesterol. In general they behave as inert foreign bodies. Xanthomatous masses of various kinds all seem to be composed of deposits of cholesterol esters which lead to proliferative and phagocytic reactions in the fixed tissues.[12]

Cholesterolemia.[13]—Normal blood contains 0.16 to 0.17 per cent. (Gorham and Myers) of cholesterol, of which about 55 per cent. is in the corpuscles, but in pathological conditions the amount in the plasma varies greatly (Bacmeister and Henes).[14] Cholesterol-rich diet causes a slight increase,[15] but a more marked increase is said to be obtained in pregnancy,[16] nephritis, early arteriosclerosis, obesity, diabetes, and obstructive but not in hemolytic jaundice.[17] According to some observations, in nephritis the amount of cholesterol bears no relation to the albuminuria, and in uremia it may be low; acute febrile diseases usually show a lowered cholesterol, which is unchanged in tuberculosis. Stapp[18] describes

[5] Pharm. Centralhalle, 1902 (43), 357.
[6] Thaysen, Cent. allg. Pathol., 1915 (26), 433.
[7] See Dorée, Biochem. Jour., 1909 (4), 72.
[8] Ellis and Gardner, Proc. Royal Soc., London, 1912 (84), 461.
[9] Corper, Jour. Biol. Chem., 1912 (11), 37; Shibata, Biochem. Zeit., 1911 (31), 321.
[10] Of historical interest is Austin Flint's idea that cholesterol in the blood is an important factor in intoxications, especially in icterus (Amer. Jour. Med. Sci., 1862 (44), 29). All recent evidence is to the effect that cholesterol is not toxic.
[11] See LeCount, Jour. Med. Research, 1902 (7), 166; Corper, Jour. Exp. Med., 1915 (21), 179; Stewart, Jour. Path. and Bact., 1915 (19), 305.
[12] Literature given by Rosenbloom, Arch. Int. Med., 1913 (12), 395.
[13] Bibliography by Dewey, Arch. Int. Med., 1916 (17), 757; Gorham and Myers, Arch. Int. Med., 1917 (20), 599; Pacini, Med. Record, 1919 (94), 441.
[14] Deut. med. Woch., 1913 (39), 544.
[15] See Luden, Jour. Biol. Chem., 1916 (27), 257.
[16] The blood of the fetus corresponds closely to that of the mother in respect to free cholesterol but contains no cholesterol esters. (Slemons and Curtis, Amer. Jour. Obst., 1917 (75), 569.)
[17] Rothschild and Felsen, Arch. Int. Med., 1919 (24), 520.
[18] Deut. Arch. klin. Med., 1918 (127), 439; corroborated by Epstein, Amer. Jour. Med. Sci., 1917 (154), 638.

marked cholesterolemia as accompanying severe parenchymatous nephritis, but not chronic interstitial types. Kollert and Finger[18a] state that hypercholesterolemia up to 0.28 per cent. may be found, but only when the kidney is excreting lipoids, and believe that the cholesterol is at least partly responsible for albuminuric retinitis. Bloor,[19] however, found no change in the blood cholesterol in nephritis. The blood content has been reported as low in febrile cutaneous diseases, but high in afebrile cutaneous diseases associated with eosinophilia.[20] However, Denis[21] states, after examination of a large number of cases, that hypercholesterolemia was found only in diabetes, and that low cholesterol values are found in cachexia or prostration, but are not characteristic of any particular disease. In Japan low values have been observed in beriberi, high in hemiplegia.[22] Numerous investigators have described hypercholesterolemia in patients with gall-stones (*q. v.*) and attribute a causal relation thereto. The importance of the cholesterol of the blood in hemolysis and protection therefrom has been discussed under that subject; in anemia there is usually hypocholesterolemia.

Experimental hypercholesterolemia in animals leads to a deposition of cholesterol in various organs, especially the aorta,[23] kidneys and liver, accompanied by degeneration in the parenchymatous structures, and excretion of cholesterol in the urine and bile; gall-stones may be formed (Dewey). Sometimes lipoid-filled endothelial cells become so abundant in the spleen as to resemble Gaucher's disease (Anichkov, McMeans[24]). Excessive cholesterol in the blood reduces phagocytic activity and antibody formation in experimental animals.[25] Robertson believes cholesterol to have an accelerative action on cancer growth, related to its hydroxyl radical,[26] but in cancer patients there seems to be no cholesterolemia (Denis).[26a]

The ratio of free cholesterol to cholesterol esters in normal human blood is nearly constant, the esters being about 33.5 per cent. in the blood and 58 per cent. in the plasma; in pregnancy and during fat absorption the proportion of cholesterol esters is high, in cancer and nephritis it is low.[27] The blood of the fetus contains free cholesterol but no cholesterol esters.

AMYLOID[28]

Virchow, in 1853, made the first study of the nature of the substance characteristic of "lardaceous" degeneration, and considered it to be a sort of animal cellulose, because it often became blue if treated with iodin followed by sulphuric acid. To this resemblance in staining reaction we owe the unfortunate, misleading, but generally used, name amyloid.[29] It was but a few years (1859) before Friedreich and

[18a] Münch. med. Woch., 1918 (65), 816.

[19] Jour. Biol. Chem., 1917 (31), 575; also Kahn, Arch. Int. Med., 1920 (25), 112.

[20] Fischl, Wien. klin. Woch., 1914 (27), 982.

[21] Jour. Biol. Chem., 1917 (29), 93.

[22] Bull. Naval Med. Assoc., Japan, Feb., 1919.

[23] See Adler, Trans. Assoc. Amer. Phys., 1917 (32), 255.

[24] Jour. Med. Res., 1916 (33), 481. The material in the cells in Gaucher's disease is perhaps a protein-phosphatid compound (Mandelbaum and Downey, Fol. Hematol., 1916 (20), 139.

[25] Dewey and Nuzum, Jour. Infect. Dis., 1914 (15), 472.

[26] Jour. Cancer Res., 1918 (3), 75.

[26a] Luden reports an increase (Jour. Lab. Clin. Med., 1916 (1), 662.

[27] Bloor and Knudson, Jour. Biol. Chem., 1917 (29), 7; 1917 (32), 337.

[28] General literature to 1893, see Wichmann, Ziegler's Beitr., 1893 (13), 487; also Lubarsch, Ergeb. allg. Path., 1897 (4), 449; discussion in the Verh. Deut. Path. Gesellsch., 1904 (7), 2-51; Davidsohn, Virchow's Arch., 1908 (192), 226, and Ergebnisse allg. Path., 1908 (12), 424.

[29] In view of the fact that this substance is chemically related to chondrin, and that it also closely resembles this substance physically, it has seemed to the writer that the name "chondroid" would be much more appropriate than any of the many more or less misleading and inappropriate titles that are at present in use. The very multiplicity of these terms, however, prohibits any attempt to introduce still another. A particularly unfortunate source of confusion exists in the use of the name amyloid for a vegetable substance, formed by the action of acids upon cellulose.

Kekulé showed that the substance in question was of protein nature; their methods were very crude, but the main fact was soon better substantiated by Kühne and Rudneff (1865). Krawkow,[30] however, in 1897 gave us the first good idea of the composition of amyloid substance through his amplification of Oddi's[31] observation that amyloid organs contain *chondroitin-sulphuric acid*, finding that amyloid is a compound of protein with this acid, similar to nucleoprotein, which is a compound of nucleic acid and protein. This work has received general acceptance, although a later paper by Hanssen[32] reports a study of amyloid material isolated in pure condition from sago spleens by mechanical means, which contained *no* chondroitin-sulphuric acid, although the amyloid organs taken *in toto* do contain an excess of sulphur as sulphate. This important contradiction to prevailing ideas has not, so far as I can find, been subjected to investigation by others, with the exception of a casual remark by Mayeda[33] that a preparation of amyloid which he had made did not yield sulphuric acid.

Chondroitin-sulphuric acid, which has been studied especially by Mörner and by Schmiedeberg,[34] has the formula $C_{18}H_{27}NSO_{17}$, according to the latter, and yields on cleavage *chondroitin* and sulphuric acid, as follows.

$$C_{18}H_{27}NSO_{17} + H_2O = C_{18}H_{27}NO_{14} + H_2SO_4$$

Kondo,[35] however, gives it an empirical formula of $C_{15}H_{27}NSO_{16}$, there being apparently two equivalents of the base for each SO_4 group. Levene and La Forge[34] have demonstrated that chondroitin-sulphuric acid consists of sulphuric acid, acetic acid, chondrosamine which is an isomer of glucosamine, and glucuronic acid. It unites with histones and forms a precipitate.[36] Chondroitin is a gummy substance which in turn may be split into acetic acid and a reducing substance, *chondrosin.* Chondroitin-sulphuric acid is the characteristic component of cartilage, but it is also found in the walls of the aorta and other elastic structures (Krawkow). It has also been found in a uterine fibroma and in bone tissue by Krawkow, but could not be found in the parenchymatous organs, normal and pathological, or in chitinous structures. Mörner has also found it in a chondroma.

Chemistry of Amyloid.—Krawkow separated amyloid from nucleoprotein, to which it is most closely related, by dissolving both substances from the minced amyloid organs with ammonia, precipitating with acid, and then taking up the amyloid with Ba (OH)₂ solution, in which the nucleoprotein does not dissolve. Amyloid thus isolated is a nearly white powder, which is easily soluble in alkalies, but slightly in acids, and is very resistant to pepsin digestion. The elementary composition was found by Krawkow to be approximately as follows: $C = 49-50\%$; $H = 6.65-7\%$; $N = 13.8-14\%$; $S = 2.65-2.9\%$; P in traces only.

[30] Arch. exp. Path. u. Pharm., 1897 (40), 196.
[31] *Ibid.,* 1894 (33), 377.
[32] Biochem. Zeit., 1908 (13), 185.
[33] Zeit. physiol. Chem., 1909 (58), 475.
[34] Mörner, Skand. Arch. Physiol., 1889 (1), 210; Zeit. physiol. Chem., 1895 (20), 357, and 1897 (23), 311; Schmiedeberg, Arch. exp. Path. u. Pharm., 1891 (28), 358. See also Levene and La Forge, Jour. Biol. Chem., 1913 (15), 69 and 155; 1914 (18), 123.
[35] Biochem. Zeit., 1910 (26), 116.
[36] Pons, Arch. internat. physiol., 1909 (8), 393.

Quite similar analytic results have been obtained by Neuberg,[37] who corroborated Krawkow's finding of a body of apparently similar composition in the normal aorta. Neuberg has studied especially the protein constituent of the amyloid compound, and found it characterized by a high proportion of diamino-nitrogen,[38] as compared with most proteins, as shown in the following table giving the percentage of the total N contained in each of the three forms, amid-nitrogen (ammonia), monamino-acids, and diamino-acids:

TABLE I

	Monamino-acid nitrogen	Diamino-acid nitrogen	Amid nitrogen
Liver amyloid	43.2	51.2	4.9
Spleen amyloid	30.6	57.0	11.2
Aorta "amyloid"	54.9	36.0	8.8
Gelatin	62.5	35.8	1.6
Casein	76.0	11.1	13.4

The variations in the composition of the different amyloids, as shown in the above table, indicate that the protein group may vary in different organs in different cases, and also indicate that the "amyloid-like" substance of normal vessels is not the same as the pathological substance. Corresponding variations were found in the apportionment of the sulphur between that which is in the form of oxidized sulphur and the unoxidized sulphur. The proportion of the different amino-acids in the protein constituent of amyloid is strikingly like that of thymus histon, and entirely dissimilar to the apparently closely related elastin, as shown by Table II.

TABLE II

	Cleavage products (in percentages)		
	Amyloid	Elastin	Thymus histon
Glycocoll	0.8	25.8	0.5
Leucine	22.2	45.0	11.8
Glutaminic acid	3.8	0.7	3.7
Tyrosine	4.0	0.3	5.2
a-Proline	3.1	1.7	1.5
Arginine	13.9	0.3	14.5
Lysine	11.6	....	7.7

[37] Verh. Deut. Path. Gesell., 1904 (7),19.
[38] Corroborated by Jackson and Pearce (Jour. Exp. Med., 1907 (9), 520), but not by Mayeda (Zeit. physiol., Chem., 1909 (58), 469), who found histidine, which Neuberg had missed, and a lower arginine and lysine content than histon requires.

This carries out the resemblance of amyloid to nucleoproteins, and, likewise, Neuberg found amyloid very slowly digested by pepsin, and much better by trypsin, although less rapidly than simple protein; it is also destroyed by autolytic enzymes, for amyloid tissues readily undergo autolysis.[39] Neuberg considers, from the above results, that amyloid is probably a transformation-product of the tissue protein, similar to the transformation of simple proteins into protamins that occurs in the testicle of spawning salmon as they go up the streams, as shown by Miescher's classical studies. Raubitschek[40] found that isolated amyloid, when used for immune reactions, behaved like a specific protein, different from the normal proteins of the animal from whence it came and apparently biologically the same in different species. (This observation awaits confirmation.)

Krawkow considers that amyloid differs from normal chondroitin-sulphuric acid compounds, such as cartilage, in that in the latter the acid radical is in a loose combination with the protein, while in amyloid the combination is a very firm one, perhaps in the nature of an ester. The occurrence of the typical amyloid reaction in what appears otherwise to be normal cartilage, occasionally observed in senile tissues, may be due to the transformation of loosely bound into firmly bound chondroitin-sulphuric acid. In any event, amyloid is not essentially a pathological product, but rather a slightly modified normal constituent of the body. However, in view of the contradictory results of Hanssen and Mayeda, as yet uncontroverted, the chemical nature of amyloid must be considered as undetermined. An important consideration is that amyloid deposition occurs under similar conditions in all sorts of animals, including birds; it is very often found in the livers of antitoxin horses, and mice are especially prone to a severe amyloidosis after relatively slight and brief infectious processes.[41]

Staining Properties.—The classical reaction for amyloid is its staining a reddish brown when treated with iodin (best as Lugol's solution) in the fresh state. Such stained specimens, if afterward treated with dilute sulphuric acid, usually become blue or greenish, but may merely turn a deeper brown. Occasionally old compact amyloid may stain bluish or green with iodin alone. The iodin reaction disappears in specimens that have been kept for some time in preserving fluids, or in tissues that have become alkaline, and is generally less persistent than the metachromatic staining by methyl-violet or methyl-green, which color the amyloid red. Occasionally an otherwise typical amyloid will fail to react to iodin, but will stain well with methyl-violet. All these variations may occur in different specimens from the same body, and the blue iodin-sulphuric acid reaction is usually given well only by splenic amyloid. These variations probably depend upon the age and stage of development of the amyloid, or upon secondary alterations, and are perhaps related to Neuberg's observations on the difference in composition of amyloid of different origins.

Krawkow studied these reactions with pure, isolated amyloid, and found evidence that the iodin reaction depends upon the physical properties of the

[39] Concerning the absorption of amyloid see Dantchokow, Virchow's Archiv., 1907 (187), 1.
[40] Verh. Deut. Path. Gesell., 1910 (14), 273.
[41] See Finzi, Lo Speriment., 1911 (65), 483; Davidsohn, Virchow's Arch., 1908 (192), 226.

amyloid, while the methyl-violet stain is a chemical reaction, and hence the iodin reaction is much the more readily altered or lost. As Dickinson[42] says, amyloid stains with iodin simply as if it absorbed the iodin more than does the surrounding tissue. Krawkow believed that the methyl-violet reaction is due to the dye forming a compound with the chondroitin-sulphuric acid, for he found that these substances unite with one another to form a rose-red precipitate. Hanssen, however, holds that the dyes react with the protein, the iodin with some other, unknown labile substance. Schmidt found that implanted pieces of amyloid lost their iodin reaction as they underwent digestion, while the methyl-violet reaction was still very distinct.[43] It is evident, therefore, that iodin is not by itself a specific stain for amyloid, especially as glycogen gives a similar reaction,[44] while true amyloid may not react.

Leupold[45] summarizes his investigations as follows: Amyloid is a complex of different substances which are differentiated by micro-chemical reactions. The protein ground substance of the amyloid is refractory to the typical amyloid reactions. The group which is responsible for the methyl-violet reaction is intimately combined with this protein substance and is separated from it only by the action of alkali. The groups which give respectively the iodin and the iodin-sulphuric acid reactions are closely related to each other. Nevertheless the iodin-sulphuric acid reaction is a completely independent one and is not a modification of the iodin reaction. The occurrence of different colors in the iodin-sulphuric acid reaction depends upon different degrees of oxidation. Amyloid is an emulsion colloid in the gel state. After oxidation with potassium permanganate it is soluble in ammonia, NaOH and Ba (OH)$_2$. Conjugated sulphuric acid plays an important part in the production of amyloid in the organism. The existence of large amounts of conjugated sulphuric acid produces amyloid which gives the iodin reaction. The methyl-violet reaction also depends on the presence of conjugated sulphuric acid; however, for its production there must probably occur a reduction in the amyloid protein. The group which gives the iodin-sulphuric acid reaction occurs through decomposition and perhaps does not depend upon the sulphuric acid.

THE ORIGIN OF AMYLOID

This question has not been at all cleared up as yet by the advances made in our knowledge of the chemistry of amyloid substance. The fact that chondroitin-sulphuric acid is a characteristic constituent suggests that this body may be liberated in considerable amount during the destructive processes to which amyloidosis is usually secondary; this idea is further supported by the fact that amyloidosis occurs particularly after chronic suppuration in bone and lungs, both of which tissues, according to Krawkow, contain chondroitin-sulphuric acid. This idea was not substantiated, however, by the experiments made by Oddi and by Kettner,[46] who fed and injected into animals large quantities of the sodium salt of chondroitin-sulphuric acid without producing amyloid changes. Unpublished experiments of the writer with the same material, as well as with ground-up cartilage and with mucin, were equally unsuccessful. Likewise mice injected by

[42] Allbutt's System, vol. 3, p. 225.
[43] Litten (Verh. Deut. Path. Gesell., 1904 (7), 47) states that thionin and kresyl-violet are the most specific stains for amyloid, which they color blue; whereas methyl-violet stains red not only amyloid but also mucin, mast cell granules, and the ground substance of cartilage. V. Gieson's stain usually colors amyloid pale yellow, and hyalin red.
[44] See Wichmann, Ziegler's Beitr., 1893 (13), 487.
[45] Beitr. path. Anat., 1918 (64), 347.
[46] Arch. exp. Path. u. Pharm., 1902 (47), 178.

Strada[47] with the nucleoprotein of pus, the so-called pyin, or with chrondroitin-sulphuric acid, did not develop amyloidosis. Oestreich[48] injected cancer patients with chondroitin-sulphuric acid for therapeutic purposes, but no amyloidosis resulted. As it is possible to cause amyloidosis experimentally in animals, especially chickens and rabbits, by causing protracted suppuration or chronic intoxication with bacterial filtrates, these negative results speak strongly against the idea of a transportation of chondroitin-sulphuric acid, but do not determine it finally. They may also, with propriety, be used in support of the statement of Hanssen that amyloid does not contain chondroitin-sulphuric acid. Leupold[45] advances the following hypothesis: In chronic suppuration a soluble protein circulates in the blood which stimulates the formation of "defensive ferments." This protein substance, under certain conditions, is deposited in organs where large amounts of sulphuric acid occur. For the development of amyloid there are necessary three factors: A preformed protein, an increased amount of conjugated sulphuric acid, and an inefficiency of the amyloid-filled organ to eliminate the increased amount of conjugated sulphuric acid.

There is usually much difficulty in producing amyloid experimentally, for in only a certain proportion of cases are the experiments positive (in but about one-third of Davidsohn's[49] 100 trials, and many other experimenters have been much less successful).[50] Davidsohn, failing always to get amyloid experimentally after the spleen had been removed, suggests that this organ (in which amyloid is usually earliest and most abundantly observed) produces an enzyme, which causes a precipitation of amyloid in the tissues from a soluble precursor brought in the blood from the site of cell destruction. Schmidt[51] considers it probable that some enzymatic action causes a precipitation or coagulation of the substance in the tissue-spaces or lymph-vessels. Amyloid is never deposited in the cells themselves,[52] and it seems to be now generally considered that the amyloid material is infiltrated in the form of a soluble modification or precursor and that it is not manufactured in the organ where it is found. It is an interesting fact that a practically identical substance is formed in all tissues and in al species of animals, even when the cause is quite different. Whether the precursors are brought to the organ in solution, or in leucocytes, is unknown—probably the former. Pollitzer[53] states that in various infections, especially coccus infections, chondroitinsulphuric acid is excreted in the urine; if this is correct it has an undoubted bearing on

[47] Biochem. Zeit., 1909 (16), 195.
[48] Zeit. Krebsforsch., 1911 (11), 44.
[49] Verh. Deut. Path. Gesell., 1904 (7), 39.
[50] See Tarchetti, Deut. Arch. klin. Med., 1903 (75), 526. Hirose, Bull. Johns Hop. Hosp., 1918 (29), 40.
[51] Verh. Deut. Path. Gesell., 1904 (7), 2.
[52] See Ebert, Virchow's Arch., 1914 (216), 77.
[53] Deut. med. Woch., 1912 (38), 1538.

the genesis of amyloidosis. The presence of glycothionic acid in pus[54] is of similar significance. The hypothesis that amyloid is formed from disintegrating red corpuscles is probably incorrect. Amyloidosis is produced by the most varied species of bacteria and by their toxins, although the staphylococcus is usually most effective in experimental work.[55] Neither is suppuration absolutely essential, for injection of toxins alone (*e. g.*, in preparing diphtheria antitoxin[56]), without suppuration, may produce amyloidosis, as also frequently does syphilis without suppuration and, less often, many other non-suppurative conditions (*e. g.*, tumors). Wago[57] reports finding a widespread "amyloid-like" degeneration in rabbits immunized with sterile pancreatic extracts.

Local amyloid accumulations are of some interest in considering the genesis of the usual generalized form. They occur particularly as small tumors in the larynx, bronchi, nasal septum, and eyelids; as all these tissues are normally rich in chondroitin-sulphuric acid, it seems probable that the amyloid arises from a local overproduction of chondroitin-sulphuric acid, which becomes bound with proteins *in situ*. This makes it seem more probable that, in spite of the lack of positive experimental evidence, general amyloidosis is due to liberation of excessive quantities of chondroitin-sulphuric acid in the sites of tissue destruction.

Another form of local amyloid is seen particularly in the regional lymph-glands of suppurating areas; *e. g.*, the lumbar glands in vertebral caries, the axillary glands in shoulder-joint suppuration. This local amyloidosis is undoubtedly due simply to the fact that these glands receive first, and in largest amounts, the cause, whatever it may be, of the amyloid production.[58] Less readily explained are cases of extensive amyloidosis limited to the heart.[59]

Corpora amylacea will be found discussed under "Concretions" (Chap. xvii).

HYALINE DEGENERATION[60]

Much confusion concerning this condition may be avoided if we appreciate that the term hyaline indicates a certain physical condition, which may be exhibited by many substances of widely different nature and origin. *There is no one chemical compound, "hyalin,"* which, accumulating in cells or tissues, produces a hyaline appearance. The limits of the application of the term "hyaline degeneration," even to histological findings, is not agreed upon, but in general it is used to apply to clear, homogeneous, pathological substances that possess a decided affinity for acid stains, such as eosin. Somewhat similar substances, usually of epithelial origin, which do not

[54] Mandel and Levene, Biochem. Zeit., 1907 (4), 78.

[55] In a series of experiments directed to ascertain, if possible, which constituent of pus might be the cause of amyloid formation, I was unable to secure amyloid by protracted intoxication of rabbits by Witte's "peptone," which consists chiefly of proteoses (Trans. Chicago Path. Soc., 1903 (5), 240).

[56] See Lewis, Jour. Med. Research, 1906 (15), 449.

[57] Arch. Int. Med., 1919 (23), 251.

[58] Quite unexplained is the cause of the rarely observed localization of amyloid in the wall of the urinary bladder. See Luecksch (Verh. Deut. path. Gesell., 1904 (7), 34). Concretions giving the amyloid reactions have been found in the pelvis of the kidney. (Schmidt, Cent. f. Pathol., 1912 (23), 865. Miyauchi, *ibid.*, 1915 (26), 289.)

[59] See Hecht. Virchow's Arch., 1910 (202), 168.

[60] General literature, see Lubarsch, Ergeb. allg. Path., 1897 (4), 449.

take either acid or basic stains strongly, are usually called "colloid." We may properly consider that pathological hyalin can be divided into two chief classes according to its origin: (1) connective-tissue hyalin; (2) epithelial hyalin.

Connective=tissue hyalin is characterized, like amyloid, by being deposited in or among the fibrillar substance of connective tissues, and not within the cells themselves, but there are undoubtedly several different sorts of chemical substances responsible for various forms of connective-tissue hyalin. One form is closely associated with amyloid, being found in organs showing amyloid degeneration, or in other tissues in the same body. In experimentally produced amyloidosis in animals it has been shown that such a hyaline substance may appear before the amyloid, which eventually replaces it; hence, it has been suggested that hyalin is a precursor of amyloid.[61] Such hyalin differs from true amyloid only in its failure to give the characteristic staining reaction of amyloid; in all other respects, e. g., cause, location, termination, it is the same. As it has been shown (see preceding section) that the staining properties of amyloid are very inconstant, it is probable that the above-described variety of hyalin is merely an *incompletely developed*, or occasionally a *retrogressively altered* amyloid. However, it is probably not necessary, as some authors have thought, that amyloid should always pass through this hyaline stage in its formation.

Quite different, without doubt, is the form of hyalin observed in *scar tissue*. This variety develops almost constantly in any scar-tissue after the blood-supply has been reduced to a minimum through contraction, and is seen characteristically in the corpora fibrosa of the ovary, fibroid glomerules in chronic nephritis, thickened pleural, pericardial, and episplenitis scars, etc. Such hyaline substance occurs independent of the usual causes of amyloid, affects only abnormal fibrous tissue, never changes into amyloid, and is prone to undergo calcification—it surely has no close chemical relation to the form of hyalin that does become amyloid. Presumably, it is similar in nature to the collagen of normal fibrous tissue intercellular substance, which has undergone physical rather than chemical changes into a homogeneous hyaline substance. For its physiological prototype it has the thick "collagenous" fibers of the subcutaneous connective tissue.

Probably of quite different origin is the hyalin that develops from elastic tissue, as seen best in the thick-walled, partly obliterated arteries of the senile spleen; and less characteristically in the early stages of arteriosclerosis, since here the preceding form of connective-tissue hyalin may also occur. Although arterial elastic tissue is related chemically to amyloid, these hyaline vessels do not develop the usual amyloid reaction, but retain more or less of the specific, elastic

---

[61] See Lubarsch, Cent. f. Pathol., 1910 (21), 97.

tissue stains. Presumably this form of hyalin is an increased and physically altered elastin.[62]

Epithelial hyalin occurs within the cells, and includes substances of presumably widely diverse chemical nature, from the keratin of squamous epithelium to the small intracellular hyaline granules of carcinoma and other degenerating cells (Russell's fuchsin bodies).[63] Fuchsin bodies are found also in plasma cells and, less often, in other cells, including granulation tissue; the fuchsin bodies of this class are believed by Brown[64] to be derived from red corpuscles, a view also held by Saltykow, but not accepted by all pathologists.[65] Extracellular substances of hyaline character, but of unknown composition, may also be produced by epithelium, e. g., hyaline casts in the renal tubules.

The composition of none of these forms of hyalin is known, except that by using microchemical methods Unna[66] has found evidence that keratohyalin consists of two elements, one of acid character, apparently derived from the chromatin, and a basic substance resembling the globulins.

Many other pathological materials of widely differing nature may, under certain conditions, assume a hyaline appearance; e. g., fibrinous exudates and thrombi, degenerated muscle-fibers (Zenker's or "waxy" degeneration), tumor-cells, (cylindroma), etc. In all of these the chemical nature of the parent substance or substances is probably much less altered than its physical appearance, but whether the change is related to the process of protein coagulation or not is unknown. Occasionally hyalin, both in epithelium and connective-tissue, takes on a crystalline structure (Freifeld).[67]

COLLOID DEGENERATION

This term, also, has a very indefinite meaning, and is applied to many different conditions by various authors. Thus, v. Recklinghausen includes under this name amyloid, epithelial hyaline, and mucoid degeneration. Marchand includes hyaline connective-tissue degeneration, and, also, as do most other writers, the mucoid degeneration of carcinoma. Ziegler rightly protests against the inclusion of mucin under this heading, but includes the corpora amylacea. On account of the discovery by Baumann of the specific chemical nature of thyroid colloid it becomes particularly unfortunate that the term "colloid" has such a wide and uncertain application. It would seem that the safest view to take is that *the word colloid is merely morpho-*

[62] See Schmidt, Verh. Deut. path. Gesell., 1904 (7), 2.

[63] Literature, see Hektoen, Progressive Med., 1899 (ii), 241.

[64] Jour. Exp. Med., 1910 (12), 533.

[65] See discussion, Verh. Deut. path. Gesell., 1908 (12), 265; Münter, Virchow's Arch., 1909 (198), 105.

[66] Berl. klin. Woch., 1914 (51), 598.

[67] Ziegler's Beitr., 1912 (55), 168; also Goodpasture, Jour. Med. Res., 1917 (35), 259.

logically and macroscopically descriptive of certain products of cell activity or disintegration, which have nothing in common except the fact that they form a thick, glue-like or gelatinous, often yellowish or brownish substance. *There is no one definite substance colloid*, according to the usual usage of the word in pathological literature, but many different protein substances may assume the appearance to which the name "colloid" is given. Looking at the matter in this way, we must recognize as the usual "colloid" substances, the following chemical bodies:

Thyroid colloid, the physiological prototype of the group. This consists of a compound of globulin with an iodin-containing substance, thyroiodin, the compound protein being called by Oswald iodothyreoglobulin. It occurs pathologically only in cystic and similar changes in the thyroid or accessory thyroids. Being a specific product of the thyroid with definite physiological properties, it manifestly has only a morphological relation to the other forms of colloid found in degenerating tumors, etc. In cysts of the thyroid, and less often in tumors, there is occasionally found a more dense "colloid" material of deeper color, the "caoutchouc colloid" of the Germans; this seems to result largely from transformation of red corpuscles in hemorrhagic cysts (Wiget).[68] (The nature of thyroid colloid is discussed more fully under "Diseases of the Thyroid," Chap. xxii.)

Mucin, when secreted in closed cavities, as in tumors, where it becomes thickened by partial absorption of the water, may take on a "colloid" appearance while retaining its chemical and tinctorial characteristics. This is particularly observed in the "colloid" carcinomas which arise especially from the mucous membrane of the alimentary tract. This substance is, of course, quite specific both in its chemical nature and its origin from specialized epithelial cells, and the process should properly be considered as a "mucoid degeneration."

Pseudomucin, which differs from mucin in not being precipitated by acetic acid, is a common component of ovarian cysts, and when somewhat concentrated by absorption of water, forms "typical colloid." Because it is alkaline, this form of colloid tends to stain rather with the acid dyes (eosin, acid fuchsin, etc.), while true mucin stains with basic dyes. Several varieties of pseudomucin have been described by Pfannenstiel, and their properties will be considered more fully in the section on "Ovarian Tumors" (Chap. xix). The clear, glassy, yellowish substance contained in small cavities of ovarian tumors, which is usually called "colloid," consists of nearly pure pseudo-mucin. All these substances yield a reducing substance on boiling with acids, which is a nitrogen-containing body, *glucosamin*.[69]

Simple proteins (e. g., serum-globulin, serum-albumin, nucleo-albumin, etc.) may, when in solution in closed cavities, become concentrated through absorption of water until they produce the physical appearance of "colloid." Probably the colloid contents of dilated renal tubules, cavities in various mesoblastic tumors, etc., are produced in this way.

MUCOID DEGENERATION

Mucin, in its typical form, is a compound protein, consisting of a protein radical and a conjugated sulphuric acid which contains a nitrogenous sugar. Hence, when boiled with acids, mucin yields a substance reducing Fehling's solution. Mucin is acid in reaction, probably because of the presence of the sulphuric acid and, therefore, is characterized microchemically by staining with basic dyes. It is readily dissolved in very weak alkaline solutions, is precipitated by

[68] Virchow's Arch., 1906 (185), 416; von Sinner, *ibid.*, 1915 (219), 279.
[69] Zängerle, Münch. med. Woch., 1900 (47), 414.

acetic acid, and its physical properties when in solution are quite characteristic. The term mucin, however, probably covers a number of related but distinct bodies. Some, such as the *pseudomucins*, are readily distinguished by not being precipitated by acetic acid, and by being alkaline in reaction; others yield reducing substances without previous decomposition with acids (paramucin); while even among the "true" mucins certain differences in solubility exist.[70] The studies of Levene[71] indicate that the non-protein radicals of mucins are of two sorts: One, chondroitin-sulphuric acid, contains the nitrogenous hexose, chondrosamine, and is found in cartilage, tendons, aorta and sclera; the other, mucoitin-sulphuric acid, has as its carbohydrate chitosamine, and is found in gastric and umbilical cord mucin, vitreous humor, cornea and ovarian cysts.

In the mammalian body we find mucin occurring in two chief localities: (1) as a product of secretion of epithelial cells; (2) in the interstices of connective tissue, especially of tendons.[72] (The resemblance of synovial fluid to mucin is more physical than chemical.) There is also evidence that mucin or a related body constitutes the cement substance between all the body-cells. Corresponding to these two chief sources of mucin we find mucoid degeneration occurring as distinct processes in mucous membranes (or tissues derived therefrom) and in connective tissue.

Epithelial Mucin.—As epithelial mucin represents a distinct product of specialized cells, it is questionable if the ordinary application of the term degeneration in the sense of the conversion of cell-protoplasm into mucin, is correct. Certainly the mucin formation of catarrhal inflammation is merely an excess of a normal secretion, and the degenerative changes that may be present in the epithelial cells are produced by the cause of the inflammation, and are not dependent upon mucin formation. Even in the extreme example of mucoid degeneration seen in carcinomas derived from mucous membranes (the so-called "colloid cancers"), the epithelial degeneration is not necessarily to be interpreted as a conversion of cell-cytoplasm into mucin, but is largely due to the pressure of secreted mucin upon the cells within the confined spaces of the tumor. The mucin in these forms of mucoid degeneration is chemically the same as the normal mucin coming from the same source, but mixed with larger or smaller quantities of other proteins derived from cell degeneration or from

[70] For special consideration see Cutter and Gies, Amer. Jour. Physiol., 1901 (6), 155.
[71] Jour. Biol. Chem., 1918 (36), 105.
[72] Schade (Zeit. exp. Path., 1913 (14), 23) says that the long controversy concerning the intercellular substance of mammalian connective tissue is settled by the work of Lier (Ledermarkt-Collegium, Frankfurt, 1909, p. 321), who found it to be a mucin similar to that of tendon or umbilical cord. Its behavior in edema supports this observation. That there are some chemical similarities in the protein moiety of epithelial and tendon mucin is indicated by their immunological inter-reactions (Elliott, Jour. Infect. Dis., 1914 (15), 501).

vascular exudates, and we do not yet know certainly the chemical character of the secretion of normal mucous membranes.[73] (The stringy, mucin-like substance seen in some purulent exudates is probably composed largely of nucleoproteins and nucleo-albumins derived from the degenerating leucocytes, and is not true mucin.)

Connective=tissue Mucin.—Excessive formation of connective-tissue mucin is observed most characteristically in myxedema (*q. v.*), but may also occur in connective tissues that are poorly nourished or otherwise slightly injured; it is seen particularly in the connective tissues surrounding the epithelial elements in adenomas and carcinomas. In the walls of large blood vessels there is a mucoid connective tissue, rich in mucin, which may be increased in arterio-sclerosis (Björling).[74] Connective-tissue tumors (myxosarcoma, myxofibroma, or myxoma) may also show a great quantity of mucinous intercellular substance, but many of the so-called myxomas are in reality merely edematous fibromas or polypoid tumors, in which the resemblance to true myxoma is largely structural rather than chemical. This form of mucoid degeneration seems to be merely a reversion to the fetal type of connective tissue, which is characterized, as in the umbilical cord, by an excessive accumulation of a mucin-containing fluid intercellular substance, and a paucity of collagenous fibrillar structure. Apparently, when connective tissue reverts to an embryonal type, either from intrinsic causes (tumor formation), or when the nourishment is insufficient, or possibly when the normal stimulus to cell growth is absent (myxedema), the mucoid characteristics of fetal tissue reappear.

The presence of mucin in the tissues seems to cause no reaction, and its absorption causes no harm. Rabbits that I injected with large quantities of pure tendon mucin almost daily for two to four months, showed absolutely no deleterious effects, either locally or constitutionally. Some of the French authors[75] claim that mucin possesses a slight bactericidal power. On the other hand, Rettger[76] and others have found an apparently typical mucin produced by certain varieties of bacteria.

GLYCOGEN IN PATHOLOGICAL PROCESSES[77]

It seems probable that all, or nearly all, cells contain larger or smaller quantities of glycogen, but it may be insufficient in amount to be detected either microscopically or chemically. Glycogen seems to be formed within the cells from the sugar of the blood, through a process of dehydration and polymerization, and to be reconverted whenever necessary into sugar, by a reverse process of hydrolysis. It

[73] See Lopez-Suarez, Biochem. Zeit., 1913 (56), 167.
[74] Virchow's Archiv., 1911 (205), 71.
[75] Arloing, Compt. Rend. Soc. Biol., 1902 (54), 306, and 1901 (53), 1117.
[76] Jour. Med. Research, 1903 (10), 101.
[77] Bibliography by Gierke, Ziegler's Beitr., 1905 (37), 502, and Ergebnisse Pathol., 1907, XI (2), 871; Klestadt, *ibid.*, 1911, XV(2), 349.

is quite possible that both of these processes represent merely the reversible action of an intracellular enzyme, but this has not been established. We do know, however, that soon after death the intracellular glycogen is rapidly converted into dextrose.[78]

Properties of Glycogen.—Glycogen is frequently called an "animal starch," having the same general composition as the starches $(C_6H_{10}O_5)x$, and apparently, like the starches, it represents a relatively insoluble resting stage of sugar in the course of metabolism. It is readily soluble in water, forming an opalescent, colloidal solution, and, therefore, has no effect on osmotic pressure, and it is not diffusible.[79] Because of its solubility and the rapidity with which postmortem change to dextrose occurs, specimens that are to be examined microscopically for glycogen must be hardened while very fresh in strong alcohol, in which glycogen is insoluble.[80] One of the most characteristic reactions is the port-wine color given by glycogen when treated with iodin; this reaction may be applied microscopically, solution of the glycogen being avoided by having the iodin dissolved in a solution of gum arabic or in glycerol. Salivary ptyalin rapidly converts glycogen into glucose, and this reaction may also be used microscopically to prove that suspected granules are glycogen. However, failure to find glycogen microchemically does not always mean its absence from a tissue.[81]

PHYSIOLOGICAL OCCURRENCE

According to Gierke, the normal glycogen of cells resembles fat in that part of it disappears during starvation, while the rest cannot be removed in this way and probably is something more than a reserve food-stuff. In distribution glycogen somewhat resembles fat, being abundant in the liver[82] and muscles, but Gierke considers that the microscopic evidence of the quantity of glycogen present in the cell agrees better with the results of actual chemical analysis than is the case with fat. Rusk,[83] however, finds only a general agreement, with marked exceptions. Neither iodin nor Best's carmin stain are absolutely specific for glycogen, but Gierke believes that we may safely consider a substance as glycogen when it is homogeneous, rather easily soluble in water and more so in saliva, gives the usual iodin reaction, and stains bright red with Best's carmin solution.[84] With these controls, the microscopic findings were found to agree closely with the results of direct chemical analysis, and glycogen was found microscopically visible in muscle, liver, lung, heart, uterus, and skin (but not in the brain,[85] where it may be demonstrated chemically in minute quantities).

Glycogen is commonly said to be especially abundant in fetal tissues, but it is not present in all fetal cells,[86] nor is it always most abundant in the most rapidly growing tissues. Although both fat and glycogen are quite abundant in fetal muscle and liver tissues, the liver of early embryos does not contain either.[87] Invertebrates and the lower vertebrates have more than the higher forms. In mammalian adults the liver and muscle contain the most glycogen, cartilage

[78] Literature concerning physiology of glycogen by Pflüger, Pflüger's Arch., 1903 (96), 398; and Cremer, Ergeb. der Physiol.. 1902 (1, Abt. 1), 803.

[79] See Gatin-Gruzewska, Pflüger's Arch., 1904 (103), 282.

[80] According to Helman (Cent. f. inn. Med., 1902 (23), 1017), glycogen may be found in specimens preserved in alcohol as long as fifteen years.

[81] Bleibtreu and Kato, Pflüger's Arch., 1909 (127), 118.

[82] In the livers of two executed criminals Garnier (Comp. Rend. Soc. Biol., 1906 (60), 125) found respectively 4 per cent. and 2.79 per cent. of glycogen.

[83] Univ. of California Publ., Pathol., 1912 (2), 83.

[84] Concerning staining methods see Klestadt, *loc. cit.*[77]

[85] May be present in fetal nervous tissues. (Gage, Jour. Comp. Neurol., 1917 (27), 451).

[86] See Glinke, Biol. Zeit., Moskau, 1911 (2), 1.

[87] Adamoff (Zeit. f. Biol., 1905 (46), 288) contests the idea that the amount of glycogen is in direct relation to growth energy; see also Mendel and Leavenworth (Amer. Jour. Physiol., 1907 (20), 117), who found no particular abundance in the tissues of the fetal pig.

28

standing next, and it is also present in squamous epithelium (particularly the middle layers), especially that of the vagina (Wiegmann), but not in slightly stratified (cornea), transitional, or cylindrical epithelium. Normal human kidneys do not seem to show glycogen, but it may be present in the kidneys of mice, rabbits, and cats. There is considerable in the heart muscle.[88] The amount in different skeletal muscles varies,[89] usually being especially abundant in the diaphragm. Glycogen is most abundant in the uterus at the time of child-birth, and is abundant in the placenta; but it is also present in the uterus and tubes independent of pregnancy.[90] After pancreas extirpation, Fichera[91] observed a disappearance of all visible glycogen, except a little in the cartilage and stratified epithelium; hence he considers the glycogen-content as a function of cell nourishment. Fat and glycogen often occur together, although one may be present without the other (Gierke). Presumably the failure to find glycogen in certain cells depends rather on a failure of technic than on a total absence of glycogen.

There has been some diversity of opinion as to whether glycogen occurs as granules in the living cell, or whether the granules are formed from a homogeneous substance by hardening fluids. In view of the clear-cut, definite spaces it may leave in cells when dissolved out, glycogen probably occurs as granules, especially when present in abnormally large quantities. Ervin[92] believes that glycogen, like fat, may exist within the cells so finely divided that it cannot be stained by glycogen stains. The studies of Arnold have shown that in many cells the glycogen takes on a definite structure in close relation to the plasmosomes. It has been suggested that the intra-epithelial hyaline bodies (Russell's fuchsin bodies) are glycogen, which idea is probably not correct. Habershon and others have suggested that eosinophile granules are either glycogen or related to it. The presence of glycogen in the cells seems to cause no injury to the cytoplasm, and if it again disappears, the cells become quite normal.[93] Even the nuclei may contain granules of glycogen without evident permanent injury.

PATHOLOGICAL OCCURRENCE

According to the results obtained by Fichera and Gierke, it seems probable that glycogen accumulation is produced under the same conditions as are fatty changes, *i. e.*, when oxidation is locally or generally impaired. Fat and glycogen are, therefore, often found together in the margins of infarcts and of tubercles, in passive congestion of the liver, and in heart muscle with fatty changes due to severe anemia. The glycogen, being more labile, seems to disappear early when the cells become necrotic, and hence glycogen is not present in older necrotic areas where the fat still persists. (This probably accounts for the frequently repeated statement that glycogen and fat do not occur together.) Ervin[92] believes that glycogen is important in holding intracellular fats emulsionized, and hence in its absence in diabetes the fats become visible as fatty degeneration—hence the inverse ratio of glycogen and fat. Whether the glycogen can be transformed into fat, perhaps forming an intermediary stage in a transformation of protein into fat, has not been determined, but there

[88] Berblinger, Ziegler's Beitr., 1912 (53), 155.
[89] Lipska–Mlodowski, Beitr. path. Anat., 1917 (64), 18.
[90] McAllister, Jour. Obs. Gyn. Brit. Emp., 1913 (34), 91.
[91] Ziegler's Beitr., 1904 (36), 273, literature.
[92] Jour. Lab. Clin. Med., 1919 (5), 146.
[93] Yet Teissier (Compt. Rend. Soc. Biol., 1900 (52), 790) believes the amount normally present in the liver is strongly bactericidal, and in a later publication (*ibid.*, 1902 (54), 1098) considers that it is toxic to liver-cells. Wendelstadt (Cent. f. Bact., Abt. 1, 1903 (34), 831) found that under certain conditions glycogen impedes hemolysis by normal serum.

seems to be little doubt that it is infiltrated from outside the cell, and not formed directly from degenerated protein. It seems to be deposited only in cells that are still living, although it can become split up in dead cells. All cells, but especially muscle-cells and leucocytes, seem able to lay up glycogen in visible amounts under certain conditions. In inflamed areas glycogen is found in both tissue-cells and leucocytes, but not in cells showing nuclear degeneration (Best, Gierke). In pneumonia the leucocytes of the exudate, and to a less extent the alveolar epithelium, contain glycogen as well as fat. In tubercles glycogen is found in the cells which contain bacilli, and it is generally present in the epithelioid cells, rarely in giant cells, not at all in lymphoid cells or in the necrotic elements (Devaux). Liver glycogen is altered most in poisoning, being reduced by phosphorus, arsenic, chloroform, $HgCl_2$, and many other poisons; the amount is reduced when death from any cause is slow, or when putrefaction has occurred, but it is increased in carbon monoxide poisoning (Massari).[94] In rabbits, at least, it is deposited in the liver first about the central vein, and in fasting animals it disappears first from the periphery.[95] It seems to have a marked protective effect in phosphorus poisoning.[96]

Glycogen in Tumors.—Glycogen has been observed frequently in tumors. Brault believed the quantity an index of rate of growth, on the principle that glycogen appears most abundantly in embryonal tissues, and therefore in tumors the amount of glycogen should agree with the degree to which the cells have gone back to the embryonic type. Lubarsch considered that only tissues normally containing glycogen give rise to glycogen-containing tumors. Gierke could corroborate neither of these ideas, and considers that glycogen appears in tumors under exactly the same conditions in which it appears in other tissues; *i. e.*, when cell nutrition and oxidation are impaired. Apparently, however, *both the embryonic origin and local retrogressive changes determine the deposition of glycogen in tumors.* Glycogen is particularly abundant in squamous epithelium of epitheliomas that have gone on to hornification;[96a] in testicular tumors, hypernephromas, parathyroid tumors (Langhans),[97] endotheliomas, chondromas, and myomas, and it also occurs in the connective tissues surrounding tumors. Of 1544 tumors of all sorts examined by Lubarsch,[98] 447 (or 29 per cent.) contained glycogen microscopically; fibromas, osteomas, gliomas, hemangiomas were always free from glycogen; and lipomas and lymphangiomas nearly always. Adenomas are almost

[94] Gaz. degli Ospedali, 1906 (27), 537.
[95] Ishimori, Biochem. Zeit., 1913 (48), 332.
[96] See Simonds, Arch. Int. Med., 1919 (23), 362.
[96a] In mouse tumors Haaland found glycogen only in squamous cell carcinoma, and in the connective tissue surrounding other tumors (Jour. Path. and Bact., 1908 (12), 439).
[97] Virchow's Arch., 1907 (189), 138.
[98] Virchow's Arch., 1906 (183), 188.

equally free from glycogen (two positive in 260 specimens), while it was constant in teratomas, rhabdomyomas, hypernephromas, and chorio-epitheliomas.   Fifty and seven-tenths per cent. of the sarcomas and 43.6 per cent. of the carcinomas showed glycogen, most abundant in squamous-cell epitheliomas; columnar-celled carcinomas contain glycogen much less often, and it is always absent in "colloid cancers."

Animal parasites, in common with other invertebrates, usually show abundant quantities of glycogen.[99]   It has been found in protozoa, as well as in all varieties of intestinal worms.   According to Barfurth, nematodes in glycogen-free animals may contain glycogen. The glycogen is found chiefly in the connective tissues of the intestinal parasites, but in some of the nematodes it occurs chiefly in the sexual organs and muscle-cells.   The walls of the hydatid cysts contain much glycogen, which is, perhaps, related to the usual presence of sugar in their contents.   If Habershon's contention is correct, that eosinophile granules are related to glycogen, we may have here an explanation of the occurrence of eosinophilia in infection with animal parasites. (See also "Animal Parasites," Chap. v.)

Glycogen in Leucocytes.—The occurrence of glycogen in the blood has aroused much interest, particularly in relation to its diagnostic value.   Many leucocytes contain granules that stain with iodin, and although it is possible that these are not all granules of glycogen, yet, for the most part, they probably represent this substance in excessive quantities.   The granules are observed chiefly in the polymorphonuclear neutrophiles, but seldom in large and small mononuclear cells and eosinophiles.[1]   Occasional granules are also found free (or perhaps contained in blood-platelets) in all blood, whether normal or pathological.[2]   Hirschberg[3] states that normal animals of all species have leucocytes giving an iodin reaction for glycogen if proper technic is used, but which is not obtained by the ordinary iodin-gum solution method unless the glycogen is rendered abnormally insoluble by toxic injury; this is an explanation for the relationship of iodophilia and infections.   According to Wolff-Eisner the leucocytes in myeloid leukemia contain no glycogen granules.   It does not seem to be settled whether the glycogen is taken on by the leucocytes at the place of pathological lesion, or in the bone-marrow under the influence of circulating poisons, or both.   Habershon states that from 1 to 16 per cent. of all leucocytes normally contain glycogen granules,

[99] Elaborate treatise on occurrence of glycogen in lower animals by Barfurth, Arch. mikros. Anat., 1885 (25), 269; also Busch, Arch. internat. physiol., 1905 (3), 49; Brault and Loeper, Jour. Phys. et Path. Gen., 1904 (6), 295 and 720.
[1] See Bond, Brit. Med. Jour., Feb. 3, 1917.
[2] Literature—Locke and Cabot, Jour. Med. Research, 1902 (7), 25; Locke, Boston Med. and Surg. Jour., 1902 (147), 289; Reich. Beitr. klin. Chir., 1904 (42), 277; Küttner, Arch. klin. Chir., 1904 (73), 438; Gulland, Brit. Med. Jour., 1904 (i), 880; Habershon, Jour. Path. and Bact., 1906 (11), 95; Wolff, Zeit. klin. Med. 1904 (51), 407.
[3] Virchow's Arch., 1908 (194), 367.

and Wolff believes that the glycogen seen in leucocytes represents normal glycogen made insoluble through injury. This may explain why the leucocytes in an infected area may give iodin reactions when the leucocytes in the circulating blood do not.

Locke gives the occurrence of this abnormal iodin staining of the leucocytes (termed *iodophilia*) as follows: "Septic conditions of all kinds, including septicemia, abscesses, and local sepsis (except in the earliest stages), appendicitis accompanied by abscess formation or peritonitis, general peritonitis, empyema, pneumonia, pyonephrosis, salpingitis with severe inflammation or abscess formation, tonsillitis, gonorrheal arthritis, and hernia or acute intestinal obstruction where the bowel has become gangrenous, have invariably given a positive iodophilia, and by its absence all these cases can be ruled out in diagnosis. In other words, no septic condition of any severity can be present without a positive reaction. Furthermore, the disappearance of the glycogen granules in the leucocytes in from twenty-four to forty-eight hours following crisis with frank resolution in pneumonia, and the thorough drainage of pus in septic cases, is of considerable importance." Clinical experience, however, seems not to have accorded any constant significance to iodophilia.[4]

In **exudates** glycogen is found in the leucocytes as long as they retain their vitality, but disappears soon after retrogressive changes begin; hence it is not usually present in old sterile pus. Loeper[5] made quantitative estimates of the glycogen in exudates, finding from 0.59–0.62 gram per liter in cellular pneumococcus pleural effusion, 0.25 gm. in cellular tuberculous effusion, but only traces in serous tuberculous effusion and in an old tuberculous pyothorax. A pneumonic lung contained 0.85 gm. of glycogen per kilo, and traces were found in pneumonic sputum and in the contents of tuberculous cavities. It is very abundant in tuberculous sputum, as much as 2 to 3 per cent. in advanced stages, but absent in bronchial catarrh; in pneumonia 0.05 per cent. was found, in putrid bronchitis 0.25 per cent. (Pozzilli). When glycogen solution (1 per cent.) is injected into the peritoneal cavity, the endothelial cells and invading leucocytes become loaded with glycogen granules.

Glycogenic Infiltration in Diabetes.— Although in diabetes the chief normal storehouses of glycogen, the liver and muscles, are either poor in or free from glycogen, yet in other tissues in diabetes the most marked accumulations of glycogen are found, the granules frequently fusing in the cells into droplets larger than the nucleus. When dissolved out in ordinary microscopic preparations, the clear round space left is exactly like the space left by a fat-droplet, except that the margins show a tendency to take the basic stain for some unknown reason. In even the most extreme cases, however, the nucleus

[4] See Bernicot, Jour. Path. and Bact., 1906 (11), 304.
[5] Arch. Méd. Exp., 1902 (14), 576.

is well preserved although it, too, may contain large masses of glycogen, in which case there is no glycogen in the cytoplasm.[6] Glycogen is found particularly in the epithelium of Henle's tubules,[7] in heart muscle, and in the leucocytes. Fütterer describes masses of glycogen in the cerebral capillaries, resembling an embolic process; it is also present in the tissues of the eye.[8] Experimental diabetes (pancreas extirpation, piqûre) produces a marked glycogenic infiltration.[9] We cannot yet change van Noorden's statement: "We lack the biological explanation as to why certain cells retain the capacity to store glycogen and even exert it more actively than before, whilst the proper organs for the storage of glycogen have lost it."

[6] Askanazy and Hübschmann, Cent. f. Path., 1907 (18), 641.
[7] See Fahr, Cent. f. Path., 1911 (22), 945.
[8] Shimagawora, Klin. Monatsbl. Augenheilk., 1911 (12), 682.
[9] Huber and MacLeod, Amer. Jour. Physiol., 1917 (42), 619.

CHAPTER XVII

CALCIFICATION, CONCRETIONS, AND INCRUSTATIONS

CALCIFICATION[1]

PATHOLOGICAL calcification occurs in two forms: one is a precipitation of calcium in secretions and excretions of the body; the other is the deposition of calcium salts in the tissues themselves. The former, which includes not only concretions in general, but probably also the deposition of calcium salts in the cells and tubules of the kidney,[2] both in disease and in experimental calcification after certain poisonings, is readily enough explained in most instances by recognizable alterations in the composition of the secretions, which lead to simple chemical precipitations. With this form we shall deal in the subsequent consideration of concretions, but, in referring to calcification, shall indicate only depositions from the blood directly into the tissues.[3]

Relation of Calcification to Ossification.—In normal ossification we have to deal with the accumulation of lime salts within the stroma or cells of a tissue that has usually undergone certain preparatory changes in the way of formation of a more or less homogeneous ground substance, but has not suffered a total loss of vitality, although vitality is possibly decreased. Pathological calcification is similar, in so far as we have to deal with deposition of quite the same salts in tissues that have suffered either total or partial loss of vitality, and which very frequently indeed are hyaline. What appear to be essential differences are these: (1) In calcification the lime salts always remain in clumps and masses, often fusing to greater or less degree, but never with the diffuse even permeation of tissue seen in ossification. (2) All the cells within a calcified area, if not dead at the beginning of the process, eventually disappear for the most part, and we have sooner or later a perfectly inert mass, practically a foreign body, instead of a specialized tissue as in ossification. (3) Ossification is accomplished only in varieties of connective tissue, but calcification may involve any sort of cell or tissue provided it is degenerated sufficiently. Furthermore, any area of calcification is likely to be replaced by bone, no matter what tissue may be involved; apparently the presence of calcium salt deposits in any part of the body can stimulate the connective tissues to form bone,[4] but in the absence of calcium salts even the cells which are normally osteogenic will not form bone.

[1] Literature and résumé: Pfaundler, Jahrb. f. Kinderheilk., 1904 (60), 123; Wells, Jour. Med. Research, 1906 (14), 491, and Arch. Int. Med., 1911 (7), 721; Hofmeister, Ergebnisse Physiol., 1910 (9), 429; Schultze, Ergebnisse Pathol., 1910, XIV (2), 706.

[2] See Wells, Holmes and Henry, Jour. Med. Research, 1911 (25), 373.

[3] Normally the calcium content of the blood is quite constant, about 9–11 mg. per 100 c.c. serum, and the quantity is not modified by most diseases, except nephritis in which the serum calcium is reduced; also in eclampsia, tetany and jaundice. (Halverson, Mohler and Bergeim, Jour. Biol. Chem., 1917 (32), 171.)

[4] See Nicholson (Jour. Path. Bact., 1917 (21), 287) concerning heterologous ossification.

Composition of the Deposits in Calcification.[5]—The composition of the inorganic salts in calcified areas in the body seems to be practically the same, if not identical, whether the salts are laid down under normal conditions (ossification) or under pathological conditions. With the blood continually passing between the bones and the calcified areas, the composition of the two must inevitably become similar or identical. This may be shown by a table giving the proportion of inorganic salts found by analysis of normal bone, and the proportion found in calcified materials.[6]

	$Mg_3(PO_4)_2$	$CaCO_3$	$Ca_3(PO_4)_2$
PATHOLOGICAL CALCIFICATION			
Bovine tuberculosis	0.84	12.8	85.9
Bovine tuberculosis	0.9	13.1	85.4
Bovine tuberculosis	1.2	11.7	86.4
Bovine tuberculosis (softened gland)	1.5	7.6	90.6
Human tuberculosis	1.2	10.1	87.8
Calcified nodule in thyroid	0.85	13.4	85.4
Thrombus, human	1.1	11.9	86.5
NORMAL OSSIFICATION			
Human bone (Zalesky)	1.04	±12.8	83.8
Human bone (Carnot)	1.57	10.1	87.4
Human bone (Carnot)	1.75	9.2	87.8
Ox bone (Zalesky)	1.02	....	86.1
Ox bone (Carnot)	1.53	11.9	85.7

Iron may be present in pathological calcification, and, according to Gierke,[7] in the fetus the entire skeleton contains iron as far as it has calcified, most at the points of active ossification. This statement has been questioned by Hück and others, who believe that most of the iron demonstrable in normal ossification is the result of an artifact, for calcium deposits seem to have a great affinity for iron. Because of this, pathological calcium deposits take up iron from old hemorrhages in the vicinity, and so in many areas where there have

[5] MacCordick (Lancet, Oct. 18, 1913) has advanced the interesting hypothesis that calcific deposits during life exist mostly as soft masses, like unset mortar. Only when sufficient accumulation of CO_2 occurs, as after death, or in the center of large areas of low vitality, such as fibroids, do the deposits become hardened; e.g., in a gangrenous leg the calcified vessels are stiff and brittle, while higher up in the living tissues they are soft and pliable. This would explain why we do not more often observe fractures of calcified arteries. As yet this hypothesis has not received the critical tests its importance deserves. If true it will explain the cases of extensive calcification of the pericardium in which the heart is so encased that function would seem impossible if the deposit were rigid during life. (See Trans. Chicago, Pathol. Society, 1911 (8), 109, for consideration of pericardial calcification.) However, Klotz (Jour. Med. Res., 1916 (34). 495) has questioned the correctness of MacCordick's views on the basis of the occasional occurrence of fractures of calcified arteries, but without experimental evidence contradicting MacCordick.

[6] Wells, loc. cit.

[7] Virchow's Arch., 1902 (167), 318.

been hemorrhages, especially in the vicinity of elastic tissue, there occur actual "calcium-iron" incrustations.[8]   S. Ehrlich[9] states that elastic fibers in the vicinity of hemorrhages take up the iron-containing derivative of the blood-pigment, and this acts as a mordant for subsequent calcium deposition.   Analysis of similar deposits in a syphilitic spleen by Gettler[10] showed the presence of large amounts of silicates as well as calcium and iron.   Potassium was much less than in normal spleen tissue.   The presence of iron in normal ossification is supported by Sumita[11] and Eliasscheff.[12]   In the so-called iron-lime lung Gigon[8] found but a trace of calcium and much sodium and potassium.

Structure of Calcified Areas.—As before mentioned, in calcification there is not the same uniform infiltration of the ground substance with lime salts that occurs in bone. yet the calcified area is possessed of a ground substance of organic material which does not dissolve in weak acids that remove the salts.   There is no definite ratio between the lime salts and this albuminoid matrix, however.   At first the salts occur in granules, which may become fused to a greater or less degree.   It has been thought by some that the deposition occurs in the form of "*calcospherites.*"

These are small calcareous bodies, usually of concentric structure, which were first described by Harting.   They appear to occur widely distributed in normal tissues, both animal and plant, and seem to be the result of the formation of insoluble calcium salts in the presence of colloidal substances, just as urinary and other concretions are formed about an organic nucleus.   If calcium chloride and soluble carbonates are allowed to combine very slowly to form calcium carbonate in a solution of egg-albumen, these or indistinguishable bodies are formed, which on being dissolved are found to possess an organic stroma that exhibits a marked affinity for any pigmentary substance that may be present.   Apparently, when the proper concentration exists, the salts in crystallizing hold between the crystals the albuminous substances by which they are surrounded.   Dastre and Morat believe that the substratum is lecithin, which others have found occupying a similar place in prostatic concretions.   Calcospherites have been found in tumors, in cystic cavities, and in bodies with beginning decomposition.   It may be mentioned in passing that Littlejohn[13] observed the abundant formation of calcium phosphate crystals in bodies that had been immersed for some time in sea water. Oliver has found calcospherites in the tissues of a cancer of the breast.   Pettit[14] found calcospherites in a sarcoma of the maxilla, presenting insensible transitions into the substance of the osseous tissue, and he suggests the possibility that the calcospherite formation may be related to the formation of bone.   It seems, however, that they are probably more closely related to the formation of the shells of invertebrates, which are largely composed of carbonates in crystalline structure with an organic ground substance between them, and very little phosphate indeed.

[8] See Gigon, Ziegler's Beitr., 1912 (55), 46; Sprunt, Jour. Exp. Med., 1911 (14), 59; Klotz, Johns Hop. Hosp. Bull.; 1916 (27), 363.
[9] Cent. f. Pathol., 1906 (17), 177.
[10] Symmers, Gettler, Johnson, Surg., Gyn. Obst., 1919, (28), 58.
[11] Virchow's Arch., 1910 (200), 220.
[12] Ziegler's Beitr., 1911 (50), 143.
[13] Edinburgh Med. Jour., 1903 (13), 127.
[14] Arch. d. Anat. Micros., 1897 (1), 107.

OCCURRENCE OF PATHOLOGICAL CALCIFICATION

As far as we know, calcification seldom occurs in normal tissue, except in the formation of bone. Often the infiltrated tissue is completely dead, as in infarcts, organic foreign bodies, caseous areas, and particularly in old inspissated collections of pus. It may be said that any area of dead tissue that is not infected, and that is so large or so situated that it cannot be absorbed, will probably become infiltrated with lime salts. Most frequently calcified, next to totally necrotic tissues, are masses of scar-tissue that have become hyaline subsequent to the shutting off of circulation in the scar by contraction of the tissue about the vessels. Elastic tissue also seems prone to an early calcification, and it is not uncommon to see the elastic laminæ of small arteries calcified in an apparently selective manner. A peculiar form of calcification is that frequently found in ganglion-cells of the brain which have become degenerated or necrotic, particularly in the vicinity of old hemorrhages; the cells become infiltrated with lime salts until a complete cast of the cell, with dendrites and axis-cylinder well impregnated, is formed. The calcification of renal epithelium obtained experimentally by temporary ligation of the renal vessels or by the administration of certain poisons, is more closely related to the formation of ordinary urinary concretions than to tissue calcification, the calcium being present as the phosphate only.[15] Calcification of epithelial cells does occur, however, and seems to be preceded by hyaline changes, in which hyaline substance the calcium is later deposited, as in epithelial pearls, for example.

Metastatic Calcification.—What is perhaps the only exception to the rule that some form of tissue degeneration is required before calcification occurs, is the *"metastatic calcification"* of Virchow.[16] In conditions with much destruction of bone, as osteomalacia, caries, osteosarcoma, etc., deposits of lime salts have been found distributed diffusely in various organs, particularly in the lungs and stomach. As much as 13.38 per cent. of the dry weight of the lung and 12.15 per cent. of the kidney have been found as CaO in such a case.[17] As there is no evidence that these organs have been the site of any diffuse tissue necrobiosis before the calcification occurred, it seems probable that the deposits have been made in practically or quite normal organs, because of oversaturation of the tissue fluids by calcium salts. The fact that the lung and stomach, and also to a less degree the kidney, are picked out, suggests that the calcification is related to the fact that in these same organs we have the excretion of acids into their cavities, which leaves the fluids in the substance of the organs correspondingly alkaline, and an increase in the alkalinity of the

[15] Jour. Med. Research, 1911 (25), 373.
[16] Virchow's Arch., 1855 (8), 103; review by Kockel, Deut. Arch. klin. Med., 1899 (64), 332. Bibliography and review by Wells, Arch. Int. Med., 1915 (15), 574.
[17] Virchow's Arch., 1909 (197), 112.

fluids makes the calcium salts decidedly less soluble. In the stomach the calcium deposits are limited to the interglandular tissue about the upper portion of the glands of the fundus, exactly corresponding to the parietal cells which are supposed to secrete the acid. Presumably, under normal conditions, the amount of calcium in the blood is too slight to be thrown down in this way, but when oversaturated because of the calcium absorption in the skeleton, precipitation occurs in the parts of the body where the alkalinity of the blood or tissue fluids is greatest, or the CO_2 concentration least. There also occurs a true metastatic calcification in the large arteries, pulmonary veins, and beneath the endocardium of the left side of the heart; that is, always in the places where the blood contains the least CO_2. This fact supports the hypothesis that the CO_2 is an important factor in the solution of calcium salts in the blood, and that when there is an oversaturation with calcium it is deposited where the CO_2 is least abundant. When the amount of calcium in the blood is increased by injecting or feeding calcium salts, depositions of calcium salts may take place in injured tissues,[18] or even in normal tissues, as in Tanaka's experiments.[19] Extensive calcification may take place in the lungs without any evident bone disintegration, nor yet nephritis which has been thought at times to lead to enough calcium retention to account for metastatic calcification (Harbitz).[20] A few cases of extensive subcutaneous calcification of unknown etiology have been described, but their relation to metastatic calcification is doubtful, as they seem to be localized deposits.[21]

Some have attempted to include the calcification of the vessels and other tissues in old age in the metastatic calcifications, ascribing the origin of the salts to the senile absorption of bone, but senile calcification is probably dependent rather upon the extensive hyaline degeneration of the connective tissues that occurs in the senile scleroses,[22] a change which seems to be more physical than chemical.[23]

CHEMISTRY OF THE PROCESS OF CALCIFICATION

In analyzing the etiological factors in the production of pathological calcification for the purpose of determining the chemical changes that occur in the process, we have the following facts upon which to base the consideration:

(1) The calcium salts must come from the blood, where they are

[18] See Thayer and Hazen, Jour. Exp. Med., 1907 (9), 1.
[19] Biochem. Zeit., 1911 (35), 113; (38), 285; see also Katase, Beitr. path. Anat., 1914 (57), 516.
[20] Norsk Mag. Laeg., 1917 (78), 1129.
[21] See Mosbacher, Deut. Arch. klin. Med., 1918 (128), 107.
[22] Under the name of "calcium gout," M. B. Schmidt has described a case with generalized deposition of calcium in other tissues than those usually affected in metastatic calcification (Deut. med. Woch., 1913 (39), 59).
[23] See analyses of elastin from calcified and normal aortas by Ameseder, Zeit. physiol. Chem., 1913 (85), 324.

held in solution or in suspension by the proteins, either as the carbonate and phosphate themselves, or as calcium-ion-protein compounds, or perhaps both. This suspension or solution is an unstable condition, possibly only because of the extremely small proportion of calcium in the plasma (about 1 : 10,000), and, therefore, capable of being overthrown by increased alkalinity of the blood, changes in the proteins or CO_2 content, or changes in the quantity or composition of the calcium salts. It is probable, from the work of Barillé, that the calcium of the blood exists as a soluble complex double salt, tribasic calcium-carbon-phosphate $(P_2O_8Ca_2H_2: 2CO_2(CO_3H)_2Ca)$, this compound being possible because of an excess of CO_2.

(2) Retrogressive changes in the tissues are a *sine qua non* except in metastatic calcification. Hyaline degeneration, the chemical nature of which is not understood, is a very favorable condition, as also is necrosis when absorption is deficient.

(3) In the areas that are to become calcified the circulation is very feeble, the blood plasma seeping through the tissue as through any dead foreign substance of similar structure, without the presence of red corpuscles to permit of oxidative changes.

We may, therefore, imagine that the deposition of calcium salts in such areas of tissue degeneration depends upon one or more of the following conditions:

(1) Increased alkalinity or decreased CO_2 in the degenerating tissues, causing precipitation of the inorganic salts in the fluids seeping slowly through them.

(2) Utilization of the protein of the fluids by the starved tissues so completely, because of its slow passage through them, that the calcium cannot be held longer in solution.

(3) The formation within the degenerated area of a substance or substances having a special affinity for calcium.

(4) Production of a physical condition favoring the local absorption of salts, the least soluble salts accumulating in excess.

The first of these conditions seems to come into play especially in metastatic calcification, already discussed. We have no evidence that in degenerating tissues, much less in normal ossification, there is an alkaline reaction developed; but rather the contrary, an acid reaction is more usual. But, as explained below, decrease in the CO_2 content in calcifying tissues, especially when combined with other changes, may be of importance.

Lichtwitz[24] especially has laid emphasis on the possible part played by changes in the proteins in inducing calcification. He advances the idea that precipitation of the colloids in the degenerated area, as in caseation, decreases the amount of crystalloids which can be held in solution, wherefore the least soluble salts, those of calcium, are precipitated; by laws of osmotic pressure more calcium in solu-

[24] Deut. med. Woch., 1910 (36), 704.

tion will then enter to establish equilibrium, be precipitated, and make way for more calcium, until the amount of deposit prevents further osmotic diffusion. Although suggestive in regard to pathological calcification, and probably of importance in the formation of concretions, this conception is difficult to apply to normal ossification; also in pathological calcification one would expect precipitation of calcium to occur in the outermost surface of the degenerated area, soon leading to a shell of inorganic material which would limit the deposition.

The possibility of the formation of calcium-binding substances within the degenerated area has always seemed the most attractive, and has received the most attention by investigators. Of the special substances that might be present in such areas that would have a high affinity for calcium, *phosphoric acid* usually receives first consideration, since it is as phosphate that most of the calcium is bound, and also since the possible sources of phosphoric acid in decomposed nucleoproteins and lecithin are so obvious. Less considered in the past, *fatty acids* offer another possibility, especially in view of the fatty degeneration that so frequently precedes calcification. Proteins might also be formed that would combine calcium, especially deutero-albumose, which Croftan[25] states has a high degree of affinity for calcium, and which would be present in areas undergoing autolysis.

Formation of Calcium Soaps.—In favor of the possibility that the calcium is first bound as soaps are the following facts: Calcification occurs chiefly in places where fatty degeneration has occurred, such as tubercles, atheromatous vessels, etc. In fat necrosis fatty acids are formed, which soon combine with calcium to form calcium soaps. Virchow observed calcification in the form of soaps in a lipoma, and Jaeckle[26] found that a calcifying lipoma contained 29.5 per cent. of its calcium in the form of calcium soaps. Klotz[27] obtained staining reactions in calcifying tissues that suggested the presence of soaps, which he also extracted by solvents, and he strongly urges, as the first step in the formation of pathological calcified masses, that the calcium is first laid down as soaps, afterward undergoing a transformation into the less soluble phosphate and carbonate. Fischler and Gross[28] also obtained microchemical reactions for soaps in the margins of infarcts and in atheromatous areas, but not in caseous areas; they therefore consider that calcium-soap formation is an important step in the process of pathological calcification, but that it is not essential. The value and the interpretation of the histological evidence of the participation of calcium soaps is, however, open to question.

[25] Jour. of Tuberculosis, 1903 (5), 220.
[26] Zeit. physiol. Chem., 1902 (36), 53.
[27] Jour. Exper. Med., 1905 (7), 663; 1906 (8), 322.
[28] Ziegler's Beitr., 1905 (7th suppl.), 339.

On the other hand, Wells,[29] studying large quantities of material chemically, found at most doubtful traces of calcium soaps in calcifying matter, even in the earliest stages, and also very small amounts of other soaps or fatty acids, and, therefore, questions the occurrence of calcium soaps as an essential step in calcification, although not doubting that under certain conditions (e. g., calcifying lipomas, fat necrosis) this may occur. In calcification at all stages the proportion of calcium carbonate and phosphate was found quite constant, and exactly the same as in normal bone; namely, in the proportion expressed by the formula $3(Ca_3(PO_4)_2:CaCO_3$, which Hoppe-Seyler advanced to express the composition of the salts of bone. Hence it seems probable that there are no essential differences between the processes of ossification and pathological calcification,[30] and there seems to be as yet no reason for assuming that in the former calcium soaps constitute an essential step in the process.

Phosphoric Acid in Calcification.—It has generally been assumed that in normal ossification the calcium is combined by phosphoric acid, which probably is derived from the cartilage cells, possibly through autolysis of the nucleoproteins or some similar process.[31] Grandis and Mainini,[32] by using microchemical methods, thought that they found evidence that the phosphorus of ossifying cartilage is converted from an organic combination into an inorganic form (P_2O_5), which then takes up calcium from the blood. The methods used have been questioned, and Pacchioni,[33] from his studies, was inclined to the opinion that the calcium entered the cartilage already combined as phosphate. Wells implanted into the abdominal cavity of rabbits various tissues that had been killed and sterilized by boiling, and found that tissues rich in nucleoproteins showed no tendency to take up calcium in greater amounts than did tissues poor in nucleoproteins, which result speaks against the idea that phosphoric acid derived from nucleic acid combines the calcium. On the other hand, implanted dead cartilage soon became thoroughly impregnated with calcium salts, which seemed to be deposited in the same proportion as to carbonate and phosphate as in bone.

Physical Absorption of Calcium Salts.—As there could be no question of "vital activity" on the part of this boiled cartilage, it seems most probable that there exists in cartilage a specific absorption affinity for calcium salts, similar to the absorption affinity that Hofmeister[34] observed exhibited by other organic colloids (gelatin

[29] See review in Arch. Int. Med., 1911 (7), 721.
[30] Dyes that stain the bones when fed to living animals (madder) also stain pathological calcific deposits (Macklin, Anat. Record, 1917 (11), 387).
[31] Hanes, who observed that the phosphatids disappear from the liver of the developing chick, suggests this as a source of the phosphoric acid required for ossification (Jour. Exper. Med., 1912 (16), 512).
[32] Arch. per la sci. Med. Torino, 1900 (24), 67.
[33] Jahrb. f. Kinderheilk., 1902 (56), 327.
[34] Arch. exper. Path. u. Pharm., 1891 (28), 210.

disks) toward various crystalline substances in solution. It is of significance that the substances in which calcium is deposited are, in most instances, of similar physical character, being homogeneous and often hyaline, although of the most varied chemical composition; in other words, they agree much more in physical than in chemical structure. Also we find that hyaline tissues with an affinity for calcium often exhibit a similar affinity for other substances, such as pigment and iron.[35] Hofmeister advances the hypothesis that when the cartilage or other matrix becomes saturated with calcium salts, any decrease in CO_2 content of the solution will lead to a precipitation of calcium salts, thus restoring to the cartilage its power of absorbing more calcium salts whenever the fluid comes to it with a higher degree of saturation with calcium salts and CO_2. This hypothesis is in harmony with Barillé's observation that when the CO_2 is reduced the complex carbon-phosphate of calcium precipitates a mixture of carbonate and phosphate in the same proportions as found in bones and calcific deposits generally. The fact that this ratio (10 to 15 per cent. $CaCO_3$ and 85 to 90 per cent. $Ca_2(PO_3)_4$), is found in all stages of calcification, is entirely in favor of the above hypothesis, and opposed to the idea that any special chemical precipitant formed in the calcifying area is responsible for the deposition of calcium. Taken all in all, the evidence seems in favor of the view that normal ossification and pathological calcification (except metastatic calcification and the calcification of fat necrosis and other areas of necrotic fat tissue) depend more upon physico-chemical factors and variations in CO_2 concentration than upon the presence of chemical precipitants in the tissues. This view is supported by the observation of Macklin[36] that calcifying and ossifying tissues become stained alike with madder fed during their formation, through the deposition of stained calcium salts from the blood.

OSTEOMALACIA[37]

In this condition the quantity of inorganic salts in the bone is greatly decreased, while, at the same time, their place is taken in part by new-formed osteoid tissue; as a result, the proportion of the weight of the bone formed by inorganic salts is reduced to as low as 20 to 40 per cent., instead of being from 56 to 60 per cent., as in normal bone. This has suggested that the cause of the disease may be a solution of the lime salts by some acid, but Levy[38] found that in osteomalacia the proportion of calcium carbonate and phosphate in the

[35] See Sprunt, Jour. Exp. Med., 1911 (14), 59.

[36] Jour. Med. Res., 1917 (36), 493.

[37] See also review in Albu and Neuberg's "Mineralstoffwechsel," Berlin, 1906, pp. 124–127; bibliography by Zesas, Cent. Grenz. Med. u. Chir., 1907 (10), 801; full discussion by McCrudden, Arch. Int. Med., 1910 (5), 596; 1912 (9), 273.

[38] Zeit. physiol. Chem., 1894 (19), 239.

bones remains constant, as also does the proportion of calcium and phosphoric acid; if the decalcification occurred through solution by lactic or other acids, he argued, the carbonate should be decomposed first,[39] whereas the lime salts seem to be taken out as molecules of calcium carbonate-phosphate; i. e., in the same proportion as they exist in the bone.   On the other hand, it has been found in Pawlow's laboratory that dogs kept for long periods after a pancreatic fistula has been established, develop a condition resembling osteomalacia,[40] which would seem most reasonably explained as due to the constant loss of alkali in the pancreatic juice.   Furthermore, investigation of Levy's objection to the acid solution theory has led to the observation that when mixtures of calcium carbonate and phosphate are *in colloids* they are dissolved at equal rates.[41]   Histologically, absorption seems to depend largely upon a direct eating out of bone tissue, both organic and inorganic substance, by osteoclasts (Cohnheim), followed by a formation of an uncalcified osteoid tissue.   (Senile osteoporosis differs chiefly in that no new osteoid tissue is formed.)   According to Dibbelt[42] when osteomalacia is experimentally induced in pregnant dogs and then recovery is allowed to take place, the decalcified bone substance present in the active stage does not become calcified, but is absorbed and replaced by new bone.

Studies of metabolism in osteomalacia have shown a loss of calcium by the body, especially in the urine, as shown by the following table given by Goldthwait *et al.*:[43]

	Limbeck	Neumann	Goldthwait
CaO in urine (gm.)	1.773	.....	3.859
CaO in feces	3.834	.....	1.800
Total excreted	5.607	11.65	5.66
Total in food	2.965	11.26	4.56
Loss of CaO	2.965	0.39	1.10

McCrudden also found a considerable retention of nitrogen and sulphur, which may be retained in the new-formed osteoid tissue; magnesium[44] is also retained, probably being substituted for calcium in the bones.   It is known that when magnesium and strontium are

[39] Goto reports that in experimental HCl acidosis the bones lost 20 per cent. of their $CaCO_3$ without appreciable loss of phosphate (Jour. Biol. Chem., 1918 (36), 355).
[40] Babkin, Zeit. Stoffwechsel, 1910 (11), 561; Looser, Verh. Deut. Path. Gesell., 1907 (11) 291.
[41] Kranz and Liesegang, Deut. Monat. Zahnheilk., 1914, p. 628.
[42] Arbeit. Path. Inst. Tübingen, 1911 (7), 559.
[43] Goldthwait, Painter, Osgood and McCrudden, Amer. Jour. Physiol., 1905 (14), 389.
[44] Corroborated by Cappezzuoli, Biochem. Zeit., 1909 (16), 355.

given to growing animals they will partially replace the calcium in the bones,[45] while it is said by Etienne[46] that excessive feeding of calcium itself leads in time to decalcification of the bones. Zuntz[47] found the respiratory metabolism in osteomalacia within normal limits, but tending to be low; protein metabolism shows nothing striking, but there is a high excretion of phosphoric acid through the feces.

Castration of women with osteomalacia has been frequently, but not always, followed by improvement or recovery,[48] and Neumann, and also Goldthwait, have found that in these cases the calcium loss is replaced by a marked calcium retention after the operation. What the relation of the ovaries to calcium metabolism or to osteomalacia may be has not yet been ascertained. Scharfe[49] and Bucura[50] both state that there are no characteristic or constant structural alterations in the ovaries in osteomalacia McCrudden[51] found that the improvement in calcium metabolism observed after castration may be but temporary, and therefore believes that the primary cause of the disease does not lie in the ovaries. He is of the opinion that repeated drains on the calcium of the bones, incited most often by pregnancy, occasionally by tumors, sometimes by unknown causes, result in an excessive reaction to the stimuli, so that eventually the losses become too great to be made up; that is, osteomalacia is an exaggeration of a normal process resulting either from excessive stimulation of that process, or a failure to recover when the stimulus ceases. The beneficial effects of castration are probably ascribable chiefly or solely to the prevention of pregnancy. Osteitis deformans seems to be a localized osteomalacia. The relation of the adrenals to osteomalacia advocated by Bossi,[52] is of questionable significance, and there is no definite evidence as to any relation of exophthalmic goiter[53] or the parathyroids,[54] although hyperplasia of the parathyroids has been described.[55]

RICKETS[56]

As with osteomalacia, chemical studies of the bones in rickets have thrown little light upon the etiology or pathogenesis of this condition.

[45] See Lehnerdt, Zeit. exp. Med., 1913 (1), 175.
[46] Jour. Physiol. et Path., 1912 (14), 108.
[47] Arch. f. Gyn., 1913 (99), 145.
[48] Bibliography by Schnell, Zeit. Geb. u. Gyn., 1913 (75), 178.
[49] Cent. f. Gyn., 1900 (24), 1216.
[50] Zeit. f. Heilk., 1907 (28), 209.
[51] Amer. Jour. of Physiol., 1906 (17), 211.
[52] Zent. f. Gyn., 1907 (31), 69 and 172.
[53] Tolot and Sarvonat, Rev. d. Méd., 1906 (26), 445.
[54] Erdheim, Cent. med. Wiss., 1908 (46), 163.
[55] Bauer, Frankfurter Zeit. Pathol., 1911 (7), 231.
[56] Complete literature and full discussion by Pfaundler, Jahr. f. Kinderheilk., 1904 (60), 123; also see Albu and Neuberg, "Mineralstoffwechsel," Berlin, 1906. pp. 119–124; symposium in the Verhandl. Deut. Path. Gesellsch., 1909 (13), 1. Metabolism studies by Meyer, Jahrb. Kinderheilk., 1913 (77), 28.

29

As the following table (taken from Vierordt[57]) shows, there is a marked deficiency in the proportion of inorganic salts in the bones in rickets. The proportion of the different salts seems to be quite the same as in normal bone.

	Normal bone of a two months old child			Rachitic bones			
	Tibia	Ulna	Femur	Tibia	Humerus	Ribs	Vertebræ
Inorganic matter	65.32	64.07	20.60	33.64	18.88	37.19	32.29
Organic substance	34.68	35.93	79.40	66.36	81.12	62.91	67.71
Calcium phosphate	57.54	56.35	14.78	26.94	15.60		
Magnesium phosphate	1.03	1.00	0.80	0.81			
Calcium carbonate	6.02	6.07	3.00	4.88	2.66		
Soluble salts	0.73	1.65	1.02	1.08	0.62		
Collagen (or ossein)	33.86	34.92	72.20	60.14	81.22		
Fat	0.82	1.01	7.20	6.22			

More modern analyses[58] show a relative increase in water and magnesium, with a persistence of the normal ratio of calcium phosphate and carbonate.[59]   Cattaneo[60] finds the increase in magnesium to vary in different parts of the skeleton, being greatest in the ribs.   Aschenheim states that the blood of children with rickets shows greater variations from the usual CaO content (8–10 mg. per 100 c.c.) than are found in normal children,[61] which is not corroborated by others.[65]

As an essential difference from osteomalacia is the fact that in rickets there is a failure on the part of the osteoid tissues to calcify, whereas in osteomalacia absorption of calcified tissue takes place with subsequent substitution by osteoid tissue.   Furthermore, in rickets the deficiency in calcium is said to be present only in the bones,[62] whereas in osteomalacia the soft tissues are also poor in lime salts.   According to Schmorl[63] the first structural abnormality in rickets is a failure to lay on calcium by small islands of cartilage in the zone of preparatory calcification.

None of the various hypotheses as yet advanced to explain this defective ossification has satisfactorily accounted for all the observed facts.   That a deficiency of calcium in the food is the cause of rickets is a most natural assumption, but it has not been proved that this is the case.   Young animals fed on calcium-poor foods show, naturally enough, defective development of the bone,[64] but this differs essentially from

[57] Nothnagel's System, vol. 7, part ii, p. 21.
[58] Gassmann, Zeit. physiol. Chem., 1910 (70), 161.
[59] The bones and muscles in Barlow's disease show quite the same deficiency in calcium as in rickets (Bahrdt and Edelstein, Zeit. Kinderheilk., 1913 (9), 415).
[60] La Pediatria, VII, 497.
[61] Jahrb. Kinderheilk., 1914 (79), 446.
[62] There is a decrease in the calcium of the muscles according to Aschenheim and Kaumheimer (Monatschr. f. Kinderheil., 1911 (10), 435)
[63] Verhandl. Deut. Path. Gesell., 1905 (9), 248.
[64] See Weiser, Biochem. Zeit., 1914 (66), 95.

rickets in that the bone formed is defective chiefly in amount rather than in quality (Stöltzner). Furthermore, such "pseudo-rachitic bone" possesses a marked affinity for calcium salts, and takes them up as soon as they are supplied (Pfaundler). As the blood in rickets contains nearly normal amounts of calcium[65] it seems quite certain that calcium starvation is not the fundamental trouble. In view of the fact that rickets is not solely a disease of bone tissue, but that all the various important viscera, as well as the muscles and tendons, show pathological changes, it seems most reasonable that rickets should be looked upon as a *constitutional* disease, in which the bone changes are prominent chiefly because the disease occurs at a time when the bone tissue is most actively forming and when the other organs are relatively quite completely developed. Stöltzner,[66] finding evidence that rickets does not depend upon either lack of calcium in the food or deficient absorption of calcium, and that the blood in rickets is of normal alkalinity, looks upon the failure of calcification as depending upon an abnormality in the calcified bone tissue itself.[67] He finds evidence of a preliminary alteration in normal osteoid tissue which prepares it to take the salts out of the blood, and Pfaundler[56] supports this view, suggesting that this preparatory change in the osteoid tissue may depend upon autolysis, which is perhaps deficient in rickets.[68]

On the other hand, after extensive experimental work, Dibbelt[69] comes to the conclusion that rickets results from excessive elimination of calcium into the intestine, presumably because of the presence of precipitating substances in the intestinal contents, such as P_2O_5 from casein. Agreeing with Dibbelt that the excessive elimination of calcium is chiefly through the feces, Schabad[70] after equally extensive investigations, believes that calcium starvation in children, from defective absorption, may cause at least a pseudo-rickets, indistinguishable clinically or chemically from true rickets. But the fact that children with rickets show nearly normal figures for blood calcium does not agree with these calcium starvation hypotheses.

As with osteomalacia, attempts have been made to associate with the etiology of rickets defects in the ductless glands, especially the adrenals,[71] thymus,[51] and parathyroids,[72] but as yet without convincing evidence.[73] There has also been an attempt to include rickets

[65] Howland and Marriott, Trans. Assoc. Amer. Phys., 1917 (32), 307.
[66] Jahrb. f. Kinderheilk., 1899 (50), 268.
[67] How metallic phosphorus causes growing bones to lay on increased calcium is an unsolved problem, but a striking fact. (See Phemister, Jour. Amer. Med. Assoc., 1918 (70), 1737.)
[68] See also Nathan, Med. News, 1904 (84), 391.
[69] Articles in the Arbeiten a. d. Path. Inst. Tübingen, Vols. 6 and 7; also Verh. Deut. Path. Gesell., 1910 (14), 294; Münch. med. Woch., 1910 (57), 2121.
[70] Arch. f. Kinderheilk., 1909 (52), 47; 1910 (53), 381; 1911 (54), 83; Fortschr. Med., 1910 (28), 1057.
[71] Stoeltzner, Verh. Deut. Path. Ges., 1909 (13), 20.
[72] Erdheim *et al.*, Frankfurter Zeit. Path., 1911 (7), 178.
[73] Concerning the chemical changes of *osteogenesis imperfecta* (congenital fragility of bones), see Schabad, Zeit. Kinderheilk., 1914 (11), 230.

among the diseases that depend upon specific deficiencies in the diet, especially the fat-soluble "vitamines" which cod-liver oil supplies abundantly. So far, however, this hypothesis is not positively established.[74] (See also Rickets, under "Deficiency Diseases" Chapter xii.),

CONCRETIONS

All pathological concretions appear to be laid down according to a definite law. There must first be a *nucleus* of some substance different from the substance that is to be deposited, and which is most frequently a mass of desquamated cells, but may consist of clumped bacteria, masses of mucus, precipitated proteins, or a foreign body of almost any sort. Upon this nucleus substances crystallize out of solution, much as cane-sugar crystallizes on a string to form rock candy, but with the important exception that among the crystals is usually deposited more or less mucin or other organic substance, which forms a framework in which the crystals lie, and which remains, if the crystals are dissolved out, as a more or less perfect skeleton of the concretion. In no case would the concretion form were it not that the solution is overcharged with some substance, but not infrequently it is the presence of the nucleus that leads to the precipitation of the substance; *i. e.*, the nucleus may play either a primary or a secondary rôle. With few exceptions, the dissolved substance is deposited in crystalline form, although the crystalline structure may in time partly disappear through condensation or through filling of the interstices with some other material. Even so structureless a substance as amyloid may, when forming concretions, appear in a crystalline form (Ophüls). The structure of a concretion depends upon two factors: The crystals tend to be deposited at right angles to the surface, and thus give a *radiating* structure; but the rate of deposition is usually irregular, and during the periods of quiescence the surface tends to become covered with mucin or other organic substances, hence we also get a *concentric, laminated* structure. Frequently both of these lines of formation are easily discerned, but either one or the other may become obscured.

Concretions consist, therefore, of mixtures of colloids and crystalloids deposited from solutions of the same character, and hence the application of the principles of colloidal chemistry throws much light on the conditions of their formation.[75] Colloidal solutions hold in solution greater quantities of crystalloids than simple solutions, for the reason that at the surface of each colloidal particle there is a zone in which the crystalloids are more concentrated than elsewhere, thus permitting more crystalloids to be dissolved in the solvent

[74] See Paton, Findlay and Watson, Brit. Med. Jour. Dec. 7, 1918; Mellanby, Lancet, 1919 (196), 407.

[75] See Schade, Münch. med. Woch., 1909 (56), 3; 1911 (58), 723; Zeit. exp. Path., 1910 (8), 92; also Lichtwitz, Ergeb. inn. Med., 1914 (13), 1; also his monograph "Ueber die Bildung der Harn- und Gallensteine," Springer, Berlin, 1914.

between the colloidal particles. On the other hand, the concentration of the crystalloids on the surface of the colloidal particles causes the colloids to serve as the starting point of precipitation whenever the crystalloids are in excess. When the crystalloid goes out of solution, therefore, it will form crystals or precipitates which are most intimately associated with the colloids, as we see when uric acid crystallizes out of urine, taking with it the colloidal pigments by which it is absorbed. Or, if the colloids are precipitated, the solvent power of the solution is reduced, and the crystalloids will deposit in intimate relation to the colloids. As Schade pointed out, if a colloid precipitates in an irreversible form (*e. g.*, fibrin), the concretion will be permanent, as with ordinary concretions, but if the colloid precipitate is reversible the mass may be dissolved again, as with the precipitate of urates in the tubules of the infant's kidney.

BILIARY CALCULI[76]

As may be judged from the above statements, concretions are never composed of one substance in a pure form, but usually consist of a mixture of the constituents of the fluid in which they are developed. This is particularly true of gall-stones, which contain in greater or less quantities several or all of the constituents of the bile. While cholesterol forms the greater part of nearly all biliary concretions, and is present in greater or less amounts in all, calcium salts of the bile-pigments are always present; usually inorganic salts of calcium (carbonate and phosphate) are also present, as well as small amounts of fats, soaps, lecithin, mucus, and other products,[77] and occasionally traces of copper,[78] iron, and manganese.[79] The quantity of bile salts, the chief constituent of the bile, is usually extremely minute, apparently only so much as may percolate into the crevices of the concretion. However many stones there may be in a gall-bladder, they usually are all of approximately the same composition and structure.

In gall-stones from the domestic animals the proportion of inorganic salts is usually much higher than it is in man.

Naunyn has classified gall-stones according to their composition, as follows:

1. **"Pure" Cholesterol Stones.**—The purity is only relative, since even the purest always contain some pigment as well as a stroma and a nucleus; but the amount of cholesterol may reach 98 per cent., and is usually over 90 per cent. Crystalline structure is usually well marked, while stratification is slight. The color varies from nearly pure white to yellow, or even brown on the surface.

2. **Laminated Cholesterol Stones.**—These consist of about 75–90 per cent. of cholesterol, and differ from the preceding form in containing more pigment, which

[76] Bibliography by Baemeister, Ergeb. inn. Med., 1913 (11), 1.

[77] Fischer and Rose found about 0.1 gm. *carotin* in 1280 gms. gall stones from cattle. (Zeit. physiol. Chem., 1913 (88), 331.)

[78] See Mizokuchi, Cent. f. Pathol., 1912 (23), 337.

[79] Gall-stones have been found enclosing droplets of mercury. (Naunyn, Frerichs.)

is deposited in layers alternating with the white layers of cholesterol. The pigment here, as in all other gall-stones, consists always of the calcium salts of the pigments—not of pure bilirubin and biliverdin themselves. Considerable calcium carbonate is also usually present, particularly in the green layers of biliverdin-calcium.

3. **Common Gall-bladder Stones.**—The composition of this form is but little different from the above, the chief difference being in the structure. They present externally a firmer crust, usually distinctly laminated; in the center is a softer pigmented nucleus which frequently shows a central cavity containing fluid. Such calculi are not distinctly crystalline in structure, and are small, seldom larger than a cherry.

4. **Mixed Bilirubin-calcium Calculi.**—These generally occur singly, but sometimes in groups of three or four, and are of large size. Although the chief constituent is bilirubin-calcium, there is always much cholesterol, often over 25 per cent. Copper and traces of iron may also be present. Their structure is laminated, with sometimes a crystalline cholesterol nucleus.

5. **"Pure" Bilirubin-calcium Calculi.**—In addition to the chief constituent, *bilverdin-calcium, bilifuscin* and *bilihumin*[80] are practically always present. *Bilihumin* is at times the chief ingredient, and may form over half of the substance; *bilicyanin* is rarely present. There is always some cholesterol, but sometimes only traces. These calculi are small, from the size of a grain of sand to that of a pea, and they occur in two distinct forms. One form is of wax-like consistence; the other is harder, steel-gray or black in color, with a metallic luster. Pure bilirubin and biliverdin, not combined with calcium, are practically never present in concretions.

6. **Rarer Forms.**—(a) *Amorphous and incompletely crystalline cholesterol gravel.* Cholesterol externally giving a pearly luster; pigment in the center.

(b) *Calcareous Stones.*—Consist chiefly of a mixture of calcium carbonate and bilirubin-calcium. Calcium carbonate may occur either as a superficial crust, or as small masses within an ordinary calculus; calcium sulphate and phosphate occur rarely in traces. Stones consisting mainly of calcium carbonate are extremely rare in man, but more frequent in cattle and other herbivora, in which all forms of concretions contain much calcium, either combined with pigment or as carbonate and phosphate. A calcium oxalate gall-stone has also been described.[81]

(c) *Concretions with included bodies, and conglomerate stones.*

(d) *Casts of Bile-ducts.*—Occur particularly in cattle, and consist chiefly of bilirubin-calcium. Rarely and imperfectly formed in man.

Aschoff and Bacmeister differ somewhat from Naunyn as to the composition of gall-stones, which they classify as follows:

1. Pure cholesterol stones.

2. Stratified cholesterol-calcium stones.

3. Cholesterol-pigment-calcium stones.

4. Composite stones, composed of cholesterol and a mantle of cholesterol and calcium.

5. Bilirubin-calcium stones, usually found in the bile passages of the liver.

6. The very rare calcium carbonate stones.

Formation of Gall=stones.—Until quite recently our views concerning the chemistry and pathology of the formation of gall-stones

[80] *Biliverdin* differs from *bilirubin* in containing one more atom of oxygen in the molecule, and it is easily formed from bilirubin—even exposure to air will slowly bring about the oxidation. *Bilifuscin* is a still more oxidized derivative—so much so that it does not give Gmelin's reaction (with $HNO_3 + HNO_2$) for bile-pigments. *Bilihumin* represents the most oxidized of these products, is brown in color, and is the chief constituent of the residue left after treating gall-stones with ether, alcohol, and chloroform to dissolve out the cholesterol.

[81] Montlaur, Bull. sci. pharmacol., Vol. 18, p. 19.

were dominated by the observations and conclusions of Naunyn[82] and his pupils. Former observers, having learned that bile normally contains cholesterol (Hammarsten found from 0.06–0.16 per cent. in human bile), sought the cause of gall-stones in either an increased elimination of cholesterol by the liver, or a decrease in the power of the bile to hold the cholesterol in solution. Thus Frerichs, finding that the presence of large amounts of bile salts and an alkaline reaction favored the solution of cholesterol, imagined that a diminution of either bile salts or alkalinity led to the precipitation of the cholesterol. Naunyn and his pupils, however, not finding that the amount of cholesterol present in the bile depends upon the amount taken in the food or the amount present in the blood, and that it did not vary in disease, except when gall-stones were present, concluded that the cholesterol of the bile is neither a product of general metabolism nor a specific secretion-product of the liver. Finding that pus and the secretions from inflamed mucous membranes (bronchitis) contained as much cholesterol as did normal bile, and often more, they concluded that the chief source of cholesterol in gall-stone formation was from the degenerating and desquamated epithelial cells of the gall-bladder and bile tracts. This idea was supported by the large amount of cholesterol found in the contents of gall-bladders shut off from the common duct, and by the formaton of gall-stones in such isolated gall-bladders. Some further evidence has since been brought forward in favor of this same view,[83] but others, finding no abundance of cholesterol in the wall of the gall-bladder have not accepted this origin.[84]

On the basis of Naunyn's hypothesis the ordinary steps in the formation of a cholesterol concretion are as follows: Some injury to the mucous membrane of the bile tracts is the starting-point; this injury is usually produced by infection, the colon and typhoid bacilli being the most common organisms in this process.[85] Through the degeneration of the epithelial cells an excess of cholesterol is formed, while at

[82] An English translation of this classic work, by A. E. Garrod, has been published by the Sydenham Society, 1896, vol. 15S.

[83] Thus Wakeman (quoted by Herter, Trans. Congress Amer. Physicians, 1903 (6), 158) was able to cause an increase in the cholesterol of the bile in the gall-bladder of dogs by injecting into it $HgCl_2$, phenol, or ricin. At first the cholesterol seems to be contained largely in the degenerating desquamated cells. Also the interesting case of a cholesterol calculus in a pyosalpinx, described by Thies (Arb. Path. Inst. Tübingen, 1908 (6), 422), shows the possibility of an inflammatory origin for such concretions, and independent of bile.

[84] Aschoff, Münch. med. Woch., 1906 (53), 1847 and 1913 (60), 1753; Aschoff and Bacmeister, "Cholelithiasis," Gustav Fischer, Jena, 1909; Laroche and Flandin, Compt. Rend. Soc. Biol., 1912 (72), 660.

[85] See Cushing (Johns Hopkins Hosp. Bull., 1899 (10), 166), who produced gall-stones experimentally by injecting typhoid bacilli into the circulation after injuring the gall-bladder. Literature on the relation of bacteria to gall-stones given by Funke, Proc. Path. Soc., Philadelphia, 1908 (11), 17; also see Rosenow who finds that streptococci are often responsible (Jour. Infect. Dis., 1916 (19), 527). Grieg notes the frequent occurrence of gall-stones in rabbits immunized with cholera vibrios (India Jour. Med. Res., 1916 (3), 397).

the same time the desquamated cells and clumped bacteria offer suitable nuclei upon which the cholesterol begins to crystallize out. Apparently after the calculi have reached a certain size they cause sufficient mechanical injury to keep up the cell degeneration and cholesterol formation, even after the infection has subsided.   A certain amount of infection and inflammation is a favoring condition, however, for Harley and Barratt[86] found that fragments of cholesterol calculi introduced aseptically into the gall-bladders of dogs were slowly dissolved and disappeared, but this was prevented by infecting the gall-bladder with B. coli.   According to Naunyn's investigations, it is not an alteration in the composition of the bile, as formed in the liver, which causes the precipitation of cholesterol, but rather the presence of the nidus, and the production of large quantities of cholesterol in immediate proximity to this nidus, that determines the formation of a concretion.   In case the bile stagnates in the gall-bladder, the cholesterol that is being constantly formed by the normal disintegration of surface epithelium accumulates, until, even without infection, there forms a sediment of soft yellowish and brownish masses, consisting chiefly of cholesterol and bilirubin-calcium.   From this material calculi may eventually form, and by their irritation lead to further formation of cholesterol and increased growth.[87]   But bacteriological studies indicate that generally an infectious influence is present in cholelithiasis, and bacilli may be found alive in gall-stones for remarkably long periods.

Recent applications of colloidal chemistry add much to our understanding of gall-stone formation.   Thus, Lichtwitz points out that the colloids of normal bile, all of which are electro-negative, may be precipitated by positive serum colloids coming from the blood when the gall-bladder is inflamed; hence we get a precipitate of cholesterol, bilirubin and proteins.   When the colloids are thus thrown down the solvent power of the bile for the alkali earths it contains is decreased, and so calcium or magnesium are added to the mixture.   Cholesterol is in solution in the bile as an emulsion colloid, and when stagnation of the bile leads to absorption or disintegration of the cholates and fats which keep it in solution, the droplets become confluent, and then crystallization takes place (Schade) with formation of spheroliths, and eventually a crystalline cholesterol calculus.   If even the slightest pressure is brought to bear on the myelin-like masses before they crystallize, however, they will be pressed into scales, and the common laminated structure results; hence crystalline calculi are single, while multiple gall-stones are laminated, with perhaps partial crystallization between the lamellæ.   Also when the gall-stones result from inflammation, and there is much serum colloid present, the stones are lamellated

[86] Jour. of Physiol., 1903 (29), 341; see also Hansemann, Virch. Arch., 1913 (212), 139.
[87] Concerning the structure of gall-stones see Ribbert, Virchow's Arch., 1915 (220), 20.

because these colloids deposit in that form (*e. g.*, corpora amylacea and other protein concretions). These considerations explain the formation of gall-stones in the gall-bladder from either inflammation, or stagnation without inflammation.

Aschoff and Bacmeister,[88] however, hold that the usual series of events in the formation of gall-stones is first the formation of a pure cholesterol stone without inflammatory cause, because of actual increased excretion of cholesterol by the liver, because of cholesterolemia; or because of resorption of solvent substances from stagnating bile: these primary cholesterol stones then cause inflammation and occlusion, leading to the formation of the common mixed stones. Bacmeister ascribes more importance to calcium than do most other investigators, in which he is supported by Rosenbloom,[89] while Kuru[90] states that fibrin is usually present. Rosenbloom reports a small series in which concretions composed chiefly of calcium were found in all cases with a history of infection, while in cases without infection the stones were cholesterol.

More recent studies of the cholesterol content of the blood and bile also have reacted against the concept that all the cholesterol of gall-stones comes from the wall of the bile tract through inflammatory changes. It has been found that patients with gall-stones often show a hypercholesterolemia;[91] that pregnancy, which seems to be a predisposing cause of cholelithiasis, is accompanied by hypercholesterolemia; that in races subject to cholelithiasis there is more cholesterol in the diet and in the blood than in those races that seldom have gall-stones (DeLangen); that with hypercholesterolemia there is an increased output of cholesterol in the bile, and that experimental hypercholesterolemia may lead to the formation of gall-stones without evident infection of the bile tracts (Dewey[92]).

As far as the existing evidence permits one to draw conclusions, it would seem probable that *both local and systemic conditions are of importance in gall-stone formation.* Apparently, gall-stones may form from cholesterol derived from the inflamed bile tract walls, independent of the amount of cholesterol present in the bile; but presumably they may derive part if not all the cholesterol from the bile in some cases. In either event, a hypercholesterolemia will favor their formation, and hence any given condition of injury to the gall bladder will more often give rise to concretions in persons with a high cholesterol content in the blood.[93] Changes in the bile itself may be produced by disease

[88] Ziegler's Beitr., 1908 (44), 528.

[89] Jour. Amer. Med. Assoc., 1917 (69), 1765.

[90] Virchow's Arch., 1912 (210), 433.

[91] Henes, Surg., Gyn. and Obst., 1916 (23), 91.

[92] Arch. Int. Med., 1916 (17), 757; see also Aoyama, Deut. Zeit. Chir., 1914 (132), 234.

[93] This relation of hypercholesterolemia and infection to cholelithiasis is supported by the extensive observations of Rothschild and Wilensky (Amer. Jour. Med. Sci., 1918 (156), 239, 404, 564; Arch. Int. Med., 1919 (24), 520), who find some types of cases accompanied by cholesterol increase, which is missing in many cases of inflammatory cholelithiasis. (See also Reimann and Magown, Surg., Gynec. and Obst., 1918 (26), 282; Fasiani, Arch. Sci. Med., 1918 (41), 144.

of the liver that will alter bile compositon in such a way that its capacity to sustain cholesterol in solution or suspension will be lowered,[94] and this factor also cannot be dismissed as without importance; transient thickening of the bile, such as may occur in any febrile disease, may also very possibly initiate precipitation and stone formation. More and more this last factor is receiving consideration, together with hypercholesterolemia, as of importance in producing cholelithiasis. Rovsing,[95] quoting Boysen's analysis of 200 autopsy cases of cholelithiasis, which showed that all recent deposits and the centers of older concretions consisted of calcium-pigment, especially emphasizes this transitory concentration of bile.

It was formerly supposed that the calcium-pigment concretions were produced by the presence of excessive calcium in the bile, derived particularly from lime-laden drinking-water, but it has been demonstrated that increase of calcium in the food does not cause an increase in the amount in the bile. Furthermore, on concentrating bile, which contains both bilirubin and calcium, the free bilirubin separates out and not the calcium compound of bilirubin; and also, Naunyn found that the bile salts prevent precipitation of calcium-bilirubin, even when calcium salts are added in considerable amounts. Apparently it is the presence of positively charged protein substances that leads to the precipitation of this electro-negative substance from bile, and hence the formation of pigment calculi is also favored or initiated by inflammation of the bile tracts, particularly as most of the calcium salts seem to come from the mucous membrane;[96] later, as we have seen, these pigment concretions often become covered with cholesterol derived from the injured epithelium, and the common mixed calculi are then formed. In view of the fact that much of the pigment in these calculi is composed of the oxidation products of bilirubin, especially *bilihumin*, it is possible that oxidation processes in the stagnating bile are important causes of the precipitation; Naunyn suggests that bacteria may be the cause of the oxidation. Pigment calculi are particularly important as the starting-point of the larger mixed calculi. Aufrecht,[97] indeed, holds that gall-stone formation usually begins with particles of pigment that are expelled from the liver cells as such, and ordinarily are discharged into the intestine; if they make their way back into the gall-bladder they form the nuclei of concretions. It is possible, Naunyn believes, for the pigment to be later gradually replaced by cholesterol.

[94] See D'Amato, Biochem. Zeit., 1915 (69), 353.
[95] Hospitalstidende, 1915 (58), 249.
[96] This commonly-held view is denied by Lichtwitz and Bock (Deut. med. Woch., 1915 (41), 1215), who found the calcium content of bile from fistulas to be from 65-84 mg. per liter, and in bladder bile to vary from 85 to 325 mg., but not according to the presence or absence of inflammation.
[97] Deut. Arch. klin. Med., 1919 (128), 242.

URINARY CALCULI[98]

These differ from the bile concretions in two important respects: First, there is no evidence that any considerable part of their constituents may come from the walls of the cavities that contain them; they are usually deposited on account of an over-saturation of the urine, or on account of a change in composition of the urine, which renders them insoluble. Second, the composition of urinary calculi is usually less mixed than that of biliary calculi, although seldom, if ever, is it pure. Thus, Finsterer found but six concretions composed of only one substance, in a collection of 114 calculi. As with the bile, the chief constituent of the urine (urea) is so soluble that it never forms concretions, but only the less soluble minor constituents are thrown down. For the formation of calculi, however, it is not sufficient to have merely an excess of a substance in the urine, for we may have deposition of urates, phosphates, or uric acid in simple crystalline form without the formation of calculi. A *nucleus* of some sort is present as well as a *binding substance*,[99] which is often mucus derived from the walls of the passages, although the center of the concretion most often consists of uric acid or urates.

Although the amount of colloidal material in urine is relatively small, yet it undoubtedly plays an important part in maintaining in solution the less soluble crystalloids, which are especially the urates and calcium oxalate. Normal urine contains no colloids which form irreversible gels, and hence ordinary deposits can be readily dissolved, but in inflammatory conditions there appears fibrinogen which readily forms the irreversible fibrin, and conditions thus become favorable for the formation of concretions of any crystalloid with which the urine may be saturated or over-saturated at the time (Schade). Possibly other colloids may play a similar rôle. Aschoff and Kleinschmidt[1] hold that most urinary calculi begin as primary calculi, formed independent of inflammation from excess of the main constituent (uric acid, oxalates, xanthine, but chiefly ammonium urate); this calculus forms the crystalline nucleus of the laminated secondary deposits of other substances, chiefly uric acid, oxalates and phosphates, all being deposited without inflammation. The inflammatory formations consist chiefly of ammonio-magnesium phosphate and ammonium urate, usually deposited on a foreign body or a primary calculus. The extensive study of the microscopic structure of urinary calculi by Shattock,[2] shows also that a nucleus of cells or other organic material is, at least in uric acid calculi, extremely rare, the center being almost always a primary crystalline deposit from a supersaturated solution.

[98] General Bibliography given by Finsterer, Deut. Zeit. klin. Chir., 1906 (80), 414; and Lichtwitz.[75]
[99] Hippocrates appreciated the existence and importance of the mucoid binding substance in urinary concretions (Schepelmann, Berl. klin. Woch., 1911 (48), 525).
[1] "Die Harnsteine," Berlin, Julius Springer, 1911.
[2] Proc. Roy. Soc. Med., Path. Sec., 1911 (4), 110.

Calculi formed because of changes in the urinary composition independent of evident infection are often called "primary," in contradistinction to those arising from changes in composition brought about by infection and ammoniacal decomposition. Because of the injury produced by a primary calculus, infection frequently results, and then the primary calculus may become the nucleus of a secondary calculus; indeed, on account of the change of reaction, the crystalloids of the primary calculus may be dissolved out, and their place taken by the secondary deposit (*metamorphosed calculi*). In structure urinary calculi usually show both radiating and concentric lines of formation, and when the chief constituents are dissolved away, an organic framework remains. They are generally classified according to their prominent component, as follows:

Uric=Acid Calculi.—Uric acid is but slightly soluble, only one part dissolving in 39,480 of pure water at 18°, and it is even less soluble in the presence of acids.[3] The presence of sodium diphosphate in the solution makes it much more soluble, and various organic bodies also favor its solution, among them being the urinary pigments. As can be seen, the maintenance of uric acid in solution is by a small margin, even in normal conditions; hence the mere cooling of the urine frequently suffices to cause an abundant deposition of uric acid combined with pigment, as the familiar "brick-dust" deposit. The formation of uric-acid calculi is, therefore, not only a question of the amount of uric acid in the urine, but depends even more upon the amount of the substances that hold it in solution, and as both these factors are subject to wide variations under both physiological and pathological conditions, uric acid and urates are common in urinary concretions.

The older literature indicates that the most common calculus is of this nature, but a number of recent analyses indicate that the importance of uric acid and urates has been overestimated. On the contrary, this material rarely forms a considerable part of the calculi, but is usually present in greater or less amount in most or all urinary calculi (Kahn).[4] It is probable, however, that uric acid is important as furnishing the primary nucleus of calculi of preponderatingly calcareous or mixed composition. Apparently there are marked differences in the prevailing composition of calculi in different countries; in China, for example, Pfister[5] found eleven of twelve calculi composed of uric acid.

Uric acid is eliminated combined chiefly with sodium, potassium, and ammonium; according to some authors, as a biurate, according to others, as a quadriurate. If the urine is excessively acid, it con-

---

[3] Concerning solubility of uric acid in urine see Haskins, Jour. Biol. Chem., 1916 (26), 205.

[4] Arch. Int. Med., 1913 (11), 92; review of literature. Rosenbloom, (Jour. Amer. Med. Assoc., 1915 (65), 161) found but two uric acid stones of twenty-six analyzed.

[5] Zeit. Urol., 1913 (7), 915.

tains much acid phosphates, which withdraw part of the bases from the uric acid, and this, when free, crystallizes out if in excess. Hence the formation of uric-acid concretions is favored by high acidity of the urine, by concentration of the urine, or by an increased elimination of the uric acid. The last may result from excessive nuclein-rich food, or from excessive catabolism of the tissue nucleoproteins (*e. g.*, leucocytosis from inflammatory diseases or leukemia), which conditions are also usually associated with an increased urinary acidity. The chemistry of uric acid is discussed more fully in the chapter on Gout, Chap. xxiii.)

Uric-acid calculi are formed chiefly in the pelvis of the kidney, but many pass into the bladder. They are quite hard, and yellow or reddish-yellow in color, because of the presence of *urochrome* and *urobilin*, the former of which seems to be chemically combined and the latter but physically, since it can be washed out with water. *Urærythrin* or *uromelanin* (a decomposition product of urochrome) may also be present. Not infrequently calcium oxalate is present, .sometimes in considerable quantities. Other urinary constituents may be present in small amounts. In case the calculus enters the urinary bladder it may set up irritation leading to infection; the urine then becoming alkaline, calcium and ammonio-magnesium phosphate will be deposited upon the surface, and the uric acid will be more or less dissolved out and replaced by the phosphates (metamorphosis).

Urate calculi occur chiefly in new-born or young infants, and rarely in adults. In the young they are related to, and may originate in, the deposits of urates in the pyramids of the kidney (the so-called urate or uric-acid "infarcts"), which have been supposed to result from the decomposition of the nucleoproteins of the nucleated fetal red corpuscles. (See Uric Acid, Chap. xxiii.) The concretions are composed chiefly of either ammonium or sodium urate, but potassium and even calcium and magnesium urate may be admixed. Their genesis in the young probably depends upon injury to epithelium by the excessive urates of the "infarcts," which affords a suitable nucleus for their start; their growth depends chiefly upon the concentration of the infant's urine. In adults they may arise secondary to an ammoniacal decomposition of the urine. Urate concretions are not common; they are generally rather soft, and often much colored by pigments.

Calcium oxalate calculi are, according to recent observers,[4] the most common urinary concretions.[6] Often they show admixtures of urates or uric acid, which latter frequently constitutes the nucleus, and when urinary infection occurs they may in turn serve as the nucleus to phosphatic deposits. On account of the hardness and roughness of these stones they frequently cause bleeding, which may result in their

[6] Concerning their structure see Fowler, Johns Hopkins Hospital Reports, 1905 (13), 507.

being very dark in color and containing blood-pigment. They are usually first formed in the pelvis of the kidney, and arise chiefly in persons excreting excessive quantities of oxalic acid. Normally but about 0.02–0.05 gram of oxalic acid is eliminated daily in the urine, apparently all as calcium oxalate, which is kept in solution by the acid phosphates. The amount may be increased by certain foods rich in oxalates, particularly rhubarb, grapes, spinach, etc.; also probably by gastric fermentation.[7] Oxalic acid may possibly be formed from uric acid, and perhaps also from the carbohydrate group of proteins,[8] and it is possible that abnormally large amounts arise from these sources under pathological conditions. During bacterial decomposition of the urine oxalic acid may be formed from uric acid (Austin).[9]

Phosphate calculi are formed as a result of decomposition of the urine, with formation of ammonia from the urea.[10] In the ammoniacal solution thus formed the magnesium is precipitated as NH_4MgPO_4, the calcium as $Ca_3(PO_4)_2$, and calcium oxalate and ammonium urate are also thrown down, so that the concretions consist of a mixture of these substances, the magnesium salt being the most abundant. In none does one substance occur in a pure state. Pigments of various kinds, and more or less mucus or other organic constituents of the framework are also present. Phosphate calculi are the typical "secondary" concretions, and they are formed usually in the bladder as a consequence of cystitis, but may be formed in the renal pelvis or in the urethra. In some cases the salts are precipitated in such large quantities that they form great masses of a sediment which does not aggregate into concretions. Occasionally stones consisting principally of $Ca_3(PO_4)_2$ or $CaHPO_4$ are formed, but these are rarities. As the calcium taken in the food is chiefly eliminated in the feces, the amount in the urine does not vary directly with the amount in the food, and the formation of phosphatic concretions is always a matter or urinary reaction and not of diet.[11] As these stones fuse to a black, enamel-like mass under the blow-pipe, they have been called "fusible calculi."

Calcium carbonate calculi are formed frequently in herbivora, but they are very rare in the urinary passages of man, although occurring elsewhere in the body

[7] Baldwin, Jour. Exp. Med., 1900 (5), 27.

[8] See Austin, Boston Med. and Surg. Journal, 1901 (145), 181. Contradicted by Węgrzynowski, Zeit. physiol. Chem., 1913 (83), 112.

[9] Jour. Med. Research, 1906 (15), 314.

[10] Under the name "struvit stone," Pommer (Verh. deut. Path. Gesell., 1905 (9), 28) describes a urinary calculus composed of very pure ammonio-magnesium phosphate, forming the hard, rhombic crystals known to mineralogists as "struvit." This is an example of a phosphate stone formed independent of ammoniacal decomposition, a rare occurrence.

[11] Osborne (Jour. Amer. Med. Assoc., 1917 (69), 32) has observed numerous cases of formation of phosphate calculi in the urinary bladder of rats kept on diets deficient in fat soluble vitamines. The reason for this association of diet and concretions is not known; possibly the dietary deficiency causes lessened resistance to urinary infection.

not infrequently. Occasionally these are soft and chalky, but if well crystallized, they are the hardest of concretions.

Cystine calculi[12] are rare but very interesting formations. Cystine

$$S-CH(NH_2)-COOH$$
$$|$$
$$S-CH(NH_2)-COOH$$

is important as the sulphur-containing portion of the protein molecule. Under normal conditions all the cystine taken in food is completely oxidized and none (or uncertain traces) appears in the urine. In certain individuals the urine contains considerable quantities of cystine constantly (*cystinuria*, see Chap xxi), and occasionally in these cases soft concretions of nearly pure cystine are formed in the urinary passages. Cystine calculi may reach the size of a hen's egg, are crystalline in structure, and in the urine of such patients the characteristic hexagonal crystals may usually be found. The cystine of calculi is identical with that from proteins and may be associated with tyrosine.[13]

Xanthine Calculi—Xanthine is the most abundant of the purine bases normally present in urine, but the total amount is extremely small. Like uric acid, it fluctuates in amount according to the amount of destruction of nucleoproteins, either of the food or of the tissues. Concretions consisting chiefly of xanthine, which is often mixed with uric acid, are extremely rare, but a few isolated specimens having been described. Rosenbloom could collect but six cases in the literature, adding one himself.[14]

Indigo calculi, derived from the indican of the urine through oxidation, have also been described a few times.

Urostealith calculi, composed of fatty matter, have been occasionally observed. Although some of the concretions described under this head have really represented foreign bodies introduced through the urethra (e. g., Kruckenberg's concretion of paraffin from a bougie), yet true fat concretions do occur. The origin of the fat in these stealiths is unknown; possibly it comes from degenerated epithelium. Horbaczewski[15] analyzed such a specimen which had the following percentage composition:

Water	2.5
Inorganic matter	0.8
Organic matter (chiefly protein)	11.7
Fatty acids	51.5
Neutral fat	33.5
Cholesterol	traces

The fatty acids consisted of stearic, palmitic, and probably myristic acid.

Cholesterol calculi have been found in the urinary bladder in a few instances, the cause being unknown. Horbaczewski[15] describes one weighing 25.4 grams, found in a patient who had previously had cystine calculi; it contained 95.87 per cent. of cholesterol and but 0.55 per cent. of inorganic material. Gall-stones have been known to enter the urinary bladder through a fistula between the gall-bladder and urinary bladder.[16]

Fibrin "calculi," formed from blood-clots, often more or less impregnated with urinary salts, have occasionally been observed. Other proteins may also form similar calculi.[17]

General Properties of Urinary Concretions.[18]—The hardness depends partly upon the chemical composition of the calculus, but more upon the rate and condition of formation (Rowlands, Kahn).

[12] Literature concerning cystine, see Friedmann, Ergeb. der Physiol., 1902 (i), 15; Marriott and Wolf, Am. Jour. Med. Sci., 1906 (131), 197.

[13] Abderhalden, Zeit. physiol. Chem., 1907 (51), 391; 1919 (104), 129.

[14] N. Y. Med. Jour., Jan. 16, 1915.

[15] Zeit. physiol. Chem., 1894 (18), 335.

[16] See Finsterer, Deut. Zeit. klin. Chir., 1906 (80), 426.

[17] See Morawitz and Adrian, Mitt. Grenz. Med. u. Chir., 1907 (17), 579.

[18] Systems for procedure in determining the nature of urinary calculi are given by Hammarsten (Text-book of Physiol. Chem.) and by Smith (Reference Hand-book of Med. Sci.).

Under comparable conditions it is said that those composed of amorphous phosphates are the softest; next come those with some admixture of crystalline phosphates. Urate concretions are harder than these, but are still softer than uric acid and crystalline phosphate calculi. Oxalates are usually the hardest, except for the rare crystallized calcium carbonate stones. Cystine and amorphous concretions can be scratched with the finger-nail, while even the hardest varieties of calculi can be scratched with a wire nail. Genersich[19] gives the following degrees of hardness for different calculi: Cholesterol, 1.5–1.6; ammonium urate, 2.5; soft phosphate (Mg), 2.6; hard phosphate (Ca), 2.75; uric-acid stones (also salivary and prostatic calculi, atheromatous patches, and phleboliths), 2.9; calcium oxalate (also rhinoliths and lung stones), 3.3–3.5; calcium carbonate stones of herbivora, 4.5. But the hardness or gross appearance of a urinary calculus give little or no indication of its chemical composition.

The rate of growth also varies according to composition, but is, of course, much modified by other factors. Oxalate and urate stones grow most slowly, phosphate stones most rapidly. A urate stone has been known to increase by about two ounces during seven and one half years, while a catheter fragment or other foreign body may become covered with a crust several millimeters thick in a few weeks.[20]

Spontaneous disintegration of urinary concretions is limited almost solely to calculi composed entirely or largely of uric acid. Out of 121 cases collected by Englisch,[21] in all but 7 this was the case, these being composed of calcium and magnesium phosphate (5), or calcium phosphate or carbonate (1 each). The disintegration is brought about through solution of the binding substance and mechanical shattering of the stone into fragments. This occurs but rarely, Bastos[22] estimating that perhaps one calculus in ten thousand undergoes disintegration.

CORPORA AMYLACEA[23]

In the case of these widely-spread concentric bodies we find the name misleading, for the bodies are not a form of animal starch, as was suggested by their laminated structure and iodin reaction, nor are they so closely related to amyloid material as the name implies. Different authors disagree decidedly concerning the staining reactions of these bodies, but it may be said that the reactions are extremely inconstant. Sometimes the corpora are stained bluish or green with iodin, sometimes brown, often little at all; occasionally they react partly with methyl-violet, but more often they do not; sometimes portions of one body react one way, while the remainder behaves differently. Seldom if ever do the ordinary concretions of the prostate

[19] Virchow's Arch., 1893 (131), 185.
[20] Zuckerkandl, Nothnagel's System, vol. 19, pt. 2, p. 229.
[21] Arch. klin. Chir., 1905 (76), 961 (elaborate review).
[22] Folia Urol., 1913 (8), 81.
[23] General literature, Posner, Zeit. klin. Med., 1889 (16), 144; Lubarsch, Ergeb. allg. Pathol., 1894 (1₂) 180; Ophüls, Jour. Exp. Med., 1900 (5), 111; Nunokawa, Virchow's Arch., 1909 (196), 221; Brutt, ibid., 1912 (207), 412.

give all the amyloid reactions characteristically, but the corpora amylacea of the lungs are much more likely to do so (Stumpf).[24] It seems improbable that these bodies, which occur in the prostate of every adult, can be the same as the amyloid, which is seldom observed except as the result of serious processes of tissue destruction. According to their structure they obey the usual laws of the formation of concretions, having a central nucleus and a structural framework of different composition from the chief substance. It seems most probable that they should be interpreted as simple concretions of protein nature, which form under certain conditions when a nucleus of some sort (usually pigment, degenerated cells, or inorganic crystals) exists in a stagnating, protein-rich fluid. At times the resulting concretion may be of such a physical nature that it absorbs iodin readily (just as they often show a marked absorption-affinity for pigments), and occasionally it may react metachromatically with methyl-violet, possibly because of the presence of chondroitin-sulphuric acid derived from the mucin of the cavities where the concretions form, but perhaps for some other unknown reasons. Occasionally pure amyloid may form in the tissues typically concentric (or even crystalline) bodies, as in Ophül's case, but this is the exception. It seems probable that corpora amylacea are usually protein concretions,[25] and neither amyloid nor animal starch. Those formed in the central nervous system may be of myelin or neuroglia origin.[26]

The small amount of material available prevents an accurate analysis of the corpora amylacea; it is known that they are very insoluble in water, acids, alkalies, etc., behaving like coagulated protein in this respect. Even hot concentrated nitric acid will not dissolve them, according to Posner. This author considers lecithin and cholesterol to be important constituents, and by Ciaccio's staining method lipoids can be found in prostatic corpora amylacea.[27] However, it is said by Björling[28] that the ordinary hyaline and granular corpora do not contain fats or lipoids, but that a certain class of "lipoid" prostatic concretions contain many granules of this nature. The corpora amylacea of the lateral ventricles seem to consist chiefly of calcium salts deposited in a concentric arrangement through the medium of an organic basis. Posner considers that the presence of lecithin in prostatic corpora prevents their calcification, although this change occasionally does occur.

OTHER LESS COMMON CONCRETIONS

Pancreatic Calculi.[29]—The cause of the formation of stones in the pancreatic duct is not definitely known, but apparently infection is the most important factor,

[24] Virchow's Arch., 1910 (202), 134.
[25] Ramsden's observations (Proc. Royal Soc., 1903 (72), 156) on the precipitation of proteins by the action of surface contact may have some bearing on the formation of such protein concretions.
[26] See Lafora, Virchow's Arch., 1911 (205), 295.
[27] Posner, Zeit. f. Urologie, 1911 (5), 722.
[28] *Ibid.*, 1912 (6), 30.
[29] Literature by Scheunert and Bergholz, Zeit. physiol. Chem., 1907 (52), 338.

30

since simple experimental stasis will not cause their formation.[30]   The calculi consist usually of a mixture of calcium phosphate and carbonate, associated with more or less organic matter, including frequently cholesterol, but all the usual products of proteolysis may be present because of the presence of trypsin.   Occasionally the calculi consist chiefly of calcium carbonate, which may be almost pure.[31]   Shattock[32] has observed a pancreatic concretion composed of calcium oxalate.   Sodium phosphate and chloride, magnesium phosphate, and proteins have also been found in these concretions.   Taylor[33] describes a pancreatic concretion containing, according to the analyst, chiefly silicate (!), a finding difficult to understand or accept.

Baldoni[34] found, on analysis of a stone weighing 3.1 grams, the following percentage composition:

Water	3.44
Ash	12.67
Proteins	3.49
Free fatty acids	13.39
Neutral fatty acids	12.40
Cholesterol	7.69
Pigments and soap	40.91
Undetermined	6.01

Usually, however, pancreas stones consist chiefly of inorganic substances. Johnson and Wollaston report analyses of two stones, one containing 72.30 per cent. calcium phosphate and but 8.80 per cent. organic matter; the other 91.65 per cent. calcium carbonate, 4.15 per cent. magnesium carbonate, and but 3 per cent. organic matter.   Legrand[35] found only 0.7 per cent. organic matter in another concretion which contained   93.1 per cent. calcium carbonate.   Pancreatic juice being strongly alkaline, can hold but a small quantity of calcium salts in solution (normally but 0.22 part per thousand—C. Schmidt); presumably the little normally present is held in the form of a colloidal suspension by the proteins.   Possibly when stasis occurs, digestion of the proteins leads to the precipitation of the calcium salts, or, more probably, the excessive calcium is largely derived from the exudate from the inflamed ducts, as seems to be the case with the calcium of biliary calculi.

Salivary Calculi.[36]—These have a similar composition, in the main, to the concretions of the pancreatic duct, except that they generally contain more organic matter, resembling in this respect the "tartar" of the teeth.[37]   Bessanez found in one 81.3 per cent. of calcium carbonate and 4.1 per cent. of calcium phosphate, whereas in another the carbonate was but 2 per cent. and the phosphate 75 per cent.   Potties has described a calculus with a central portion composed chiefly of uric acid and a peripheral portion containing 69 per cent. of calcium phosphate and 20.1 per cent. of calcium carbonate.   Harlay[38] found in one specimen 15.9 per cent. organic matter, 75.3 per cent. calcium phosphate, 6.1 per cent. calcium carbonate.   Roberg believes that bacteria alone do not usually cause salivary calculi to form, but that a foreign body entering the duct is the chief factor.   Increased alkalinity may also favor precipitation of calcium from the saliva.   In Roberg's case of sialolithiasis the saliva was of normal composition.

Intestinal Concretions.—These always have a nucleus of some indigestible foreign substance, most often hair, but sometimes cellulose structures or solid indigestible particles, including gall-stones, fruit-stones, bone, etc.   The bulk of the concretions is usually made up chiefly of ammonio-magnesium phosphate, with some calcium phosphate, carbonate, and sulphate, protein matter, and occasionally

[30] See Lazarus, Zeit. klin. Med., 1904 (51), 530.   Literature.
[31] Rosenthal, Arch. f. Verdauungskr., 1914 (20), 619.
[32] Brit. Med. Jour., 1896 (i), 1034.
[33] Lancet, Dec. 18, 1909.
[34] Schmidt's Jahrb., 1900 (268), 210.
[35] Jour. Pharm. et Chim., 1901 (14), 21.
[36] Literature, see Roberg, Annals of Surgery, 1904 (39), 669.
[37] Particles of gold have been found in a salivary calculus by Maurin (Report pharm., 1919 (30), 257), presumably derived from fillings.
[38] Jour. Pharm. et Chim., 1903 (18), 11.

calcium and magnesium soaps. Two intestinal concretions analyzed by Schuberg[39] had the following percentage composition when dried:

Ammonio-magnesium phosphate.	57 1	63 9
Calcium phosphate	15 7	23 8
Calcium carbonate		4 6
Calcium sulphate	3.0	0.7
Alcohol-ether extract	1.9	0 8
Other organic substances	21.5	6.0

In countries where oatmeal is largely eaten, intestinal concretions are not infrequent; they contain calcium and magnesium phosphate, about 70 per cent.; oatmeal bran, 15–18 per cent.; soaps and fats, about 10 per cent. (Hammarsten). Occasionally concretions consisting largely of fats and soaps are found, and after taking large doses of olive oil masses of solidified oil may be passed that are readily mistaken for softened gall-stones, for the removal of which the oil is usually given. The "fecal stones" found in appendices often show the structure of calculi, and, unlike other enteroliths, consist less of ammonio-magnesium phosphate than of calcium salts;[40] soaps may be important constituents.[41]

Bezoar stones are intestinal concretions probably coming from *Capra aegagrus* and *Antelope dorcas*. One variety consists chiefly of *lithofellic acid*, $C_{20}H_{36}O_4$, which is related to cholalic acid, and gives an aromatic odor when heated. The other variety ("false bezoars") does not give the aromatic odor, and consists chiefly of *ellagic acid*, $C_{14}H_6O_8$, a derivative of gallic acid, and, therefore, probably derived from the tannin of the food of the antelopes.

Intestinal "sand" occurs as (1) "false sand," consisting of particles of indigestible food, such as the sclerenchymatous particles in the flesh of pears and bananas;[42] and (2) true sand, consisting largely of inorganic material, and formed, according to Duckworth and Garrod,[43] in the upper part of the large intestine. Analyses of specimens by Garrod showed the following composition:

Water	12.4	calcium oxide	54.98
Organic material	26.29	phosphorus pentoxide	42.35
Inorganic material	61 31 containing	carbon dioxide	2.20
		traces of Mg, Fe, etc.	0 47

Analyses by other observers have given similar results, the absence of the large proportion of magnesium found in larger concretions being striking. The color is usually brown, due chiefly to urobilin, unaltered bile-pigments being scanty.

Preputial concretions sometimes form beneath a prepuce that cannot be retracted, through deposition of urinary salts on and in the accumulated smegma.[44] The composition is, therefore, very mixed, and consists of an organic base containing much cholesterol, fats, and soaps, incrusted with inorganic substances, of which ammonio-magnesium phosphate and calcium phosphate are usually the most abundant.

Prostatic concretions originate in the corpora amylacea through growth accretion of inorganic salts, until they may reach considerable size. Stern[45] gives the following results of analysis of such a prostatic stone:

Water	8.0
Organic matter	15 8
Lime	37.64
Magnesia	2.38
Soda	1.76
Potash	0.5
Phosphoric acid	33.77
Iron	trace

[39] Virchow's Arch., 1882 (90), 73.
[40] Harlay, Jour. pharm. et chim., 1910 (2), 433.
[41] Williams, Biochem. Jour., 1907 (2), 395.
[42] Myer and Cook, Amer. Jour. Med. Sci., 1909 (137), 383.
[43] Lancet, 1902 (i), 653. Full résumé and literature.
[44] See Zeller, Arch. klin. Chir., 1890 (41), 240.
[45] Amer. Jour. Med. Sci., 1903 (126), 281.

Lung stones.[46]—These may be formed in the bronchi, through accretion about an inorganic nucleus, similar to the formation of calculi in other epithelial-lined passages; or they may consist of calcified areas of lung tissue or peribronchial glands, which have been sequestrated through suppuration and have entered the bronchi. In the latter case, the calculi present the usual composition of pathological calcified areas. That the expectorated stones frequently represent calcified tubercles is shown by Stern[46] and by Bürgi,[46] who demonstrated tubercle bacilli in decalcified lung stones. The following percentage figures are taken from Ott:[47]

Calcium phosphate	52.0	72.8
Magnesium phosphate		1.0
Magnesium carbonate	2.0	
Calcium carbonate	13 0	6.0
Fat and cholesterol	24.0	7.0
Other organic substances	4.0	10.0

Rhinoliths[48] are formed about nasal secretions, blood-clots, and most frequently about foreign bodies. They therefore contain much organic substance in addition to the inorganic salts deposited upon them Berlioz[49] gives the following table from the analysis of four specimens;

Weight of specimens, grams	1 3.75	2 1.34	3 0.63	4 0.95
Water	5.80	5.10	4.00	6.90
Organic matter	16.60	18.20	16.00	18.10
Calcium phosphate	62.02	60.61	61.40	47.63
Magnesium phosphate	5.08	6.28	3.93	6.68
Calcium carbonate	10.50	9.81	14.67	20.69
Traces of iron	Doubtful.	Distinct.	Doubtful.	Distinct.

Tonsillar concretions consist chiefly of carbonate and phosphate of calcium deposited upon the inspissated secretions and desquamated cells of the tonsillar crypts.[50] According to some authors, leptothrix threads frequently form the nucleus of the concretions.

Cutaneous concretions are occasionally observed, located chiefly in the subcutaneous tissue, often occurring multiple. The origin is possibly in dilated sebaceous glands with retained secretions. Unna considers that calcium soaps are formed as a first step, but an analysis of such material by Harley[51] showed 87.2 per cent. of ash, 12.8 per cent. organic matter, 0.9 per cent. of fat; calcium phosphate constituted 65.2 per cent., and calcium carbonate 16.4 per cent. Gascard[52] found in similar material 23.4 per cent. organic matter, and of the inorganic matter, 91.1 per cent. was calcium phosphate, and 8.9 per cent. calcium carbonate.

Gouty deposits observed in the subcutaneous tissues, as well as along the tendons, articular cartilages, etc., consist usually of nearly pure biurate of sodium and potassium. Ebstein and Sprague[53] found the composition of such material to be as follows:

Uric acid	59.70
Tissue organic matter	27.88
Sodium oxide	9.30
Potassium oxide	2.95
Calcium oxide	0.17
MgO, Fe, P_2O_5, S	traces

[46] Literature. Poulalion, Thesis, Paris, 1891; Stern, Deut. med. Woch., 1904, (30), 1414; Bürgi, Deut. med. Woch., 1906 (32), 798; Gerhartz and Strigel, Beitr. z. klin. Tub rc., 1908 (10), 33.
[47] "Chem. Path. der Tuberc.," 1903, p. 92.
[48] Literature, Scheppegrell, Jour. Amer. Med. Assoc., 1896 (26), 874; Gerber, Deut. med Woch., 1892 (18), 1165.
[49] Jour. Pharm. et Chim., 1891 (23), 447.
[50] McCarthy, Brit. Med. Jour., Oct. 28, 1911.
[51] Jour. Pharm. et Chim., 1903 (18), 9.
[52] Ibid., 1900 (12), 262.
[53] Virchow's Arch., 1891 (125), 207.

After a time, however, calcium salts may be deposited, and Dunin[54] has observed deposits resembling gouty tophi that were merely calcium salts.

PNEUMONOKONIOSIS

In a number of cases of the different forms of this condition quantitative analyses have been made, which may be briefly discussed as follows: Not only does the lung of every adult contain considerable amounts of coal-pigment stored up in the connective tissues (and also in the peribronchial glands), but also, which is perhaps less generally appreciated, considerable quantities of silicates are also present (chalicosis) from inhaled dust. Woskressensky[55] found silicates in all of 54 lungs examined, except two from infants. The lungs of individuals whose occupations do not expose them especially to dust inhalation contain increasing amounts of silicates in direct proportion to age; the silicates constitute then from 3.5 to 10 per cent. of the total ash of the lungs. There is always a larger proportion of silicates in the peribronchial glands than in the lungs, constituting from 6 to 36 per cent. of the ash, corresponding with Arnold's observation that in gold-beaters the glands contain more metal than the lungs. In stone-workers Schmidt found a higher proportion of SiO_2 in the lungs than in the glands. In normal adults the amount of coal-pigment is greater than the amount of silicates; in children the reverse is the case.

Thorel[56] reports that the lungs of a worker in soapstone contained 3.25 per cent. of ash, including 2.43 per cent. of soapstone.

In *siderosis* iron has been found in the lungs in proportions varying from 0.5 per cent. to 7.9 per cent. of the dry weight, the last amount having been found by Langguth[57] in the lungs of an iron miner, which contained also 11.92 per cent. of SiO_2.

An analysis of a lung from a knife-grinder is reported by Hodenpyl,[58] which gave the following results: Total weight of dried and powdered lung, 48.1009 grams; total solids, 44.7986; ether-soluble substance, 14.6017. Composition of the ether-soluble substance: free fatty acids, 7.498; neutral fats, 4.044; cholesterol, 3.037. Proteins, 15.4759; charcoal (total carbon less protein carbon), 7.198; ash, 4.2903. The composition of the ash (in grams) was as follows: K_2O, 0.2167; Na_2O, 0.3523; CaO, 0.0965; Fe_2O_3, 0.0879; Al_2O_3, 1.4628; SO_3, 0.0704; P_2O_5, 0.9565; SiO_2, 1.2043. The amount of emery, represented by the oxides of aluminum and silicon made up more than one-half of the ash, and the iron constituted about one-fourth. The man had worked at the trade of knife-grinder for about fifteen years.

[54] Mitt. Grenzgeb. Med. u. Chir., 1905 (14), 451; also Kahn, Arch. Int. Med., 1913 (11), 92, and M. B. Schmidt, Deut. med. Woch., 1913 (39), 59.
[55] Cant. f. Path., 1898 (9), 296.
[56] Ziegler's Beitr., 1896 (20), 85.
[57] Deut. Arch. klin. Med., 1895 (55), 255.
[58] Medical Record, 1899 (56), 942.

McCrae[59] has analyzed the lungs of six gold mine workers, in South Africa, finding from 9 to 21.7 grams of ash per lung, of which 29 to 48 per cent. was silica; aluminum was also high, and an increased P_2O_5 content was ascribed to the accompanying fibrosis. Klotz[60] found from 1.2 to 5.3 grams of free carbon in each lung, of dwellers of Pittsburg, as contrasted with 0.145 and 0.405 grams found in the lungs of residents of Ann Arbor. Hirsch[61] analyzed four average Chicago lungs, finding in grams per lung:

	I	II	III	IV
Carbon	2.72	0.71	1.20	0.19
Silica	0.18	0.28	0.69	0.04
Calcium Oxide	0.45	0.12	0.02	0.05

[59] "The Ash of Silicotic Lungs," John McCrae, Johannesburg, 1914.
[60] Amer. Jour. Publ. Health, 1914 (4), 887.   General review on anthracosis.
[61] Jour. Amer. Med. Assoc., 1916 (66), 950

CHAPTER XVIII

PATHOLOGICAL PIGMENTATION[1]

MELANIN[2]

MELANIN occurs normally as the coloring-matter of hair, of the choroid of the eye, of the skin, in the pigment matter of many lower animals, and most strikingly as a defensive substance in the "ink" ejected by squids to render themselves invisible in the water. Pathologically melanin occurs chiefly as the result of an excessive production of this pigment by cells normally forming it, as in freckles, melanotic tumors, and Addison's disease (probably). Cells that do not normally form melanin probably do not acquire this power in pathological conditions. Pathological failure to form melanin is also observed, as in skin formed in the healing of wounds and after syphilitic lesions; or in *albinism*, in which the failure to form melanin may be attributed to hereditary influences.[3] Occasionally in domestic animals, especially in calves, a congenital melanosis is observed involving many parts of the body.[4] A melanin or some similar pigment may be found in nerve cells (*e. g.*, *substantia nigra*), and Dolley[5] believes it to be a result of nuclear metabolism under conditions of depression. The function of melanin is evidently that of protection from light rays, and Young[6] has found that isolated melanin from human skin absorbs violet and ultra-violet rays. Probably this protection is responsible, at least in part, for the relative infrequency of skin cancers in the colored races.[7]

Melanin seems always to be produced through metabolic activity of specialized cells. The idea, which was formerly advanced, that it is derived from hemoglobin as a product of disintegration, seems to have failed entirely of substantiation. In malaria we frequently find a diffuse pigmentation of the skin of such a nature as to suggest

[1] Literature by Oberndorfer, Ergebnisse Pathol., 1908 (12), 460, and Hueck, Ziegler's Beitr., 1912 (54), 68.

[2] Literature and résumé given by v. Fürth, Cent. f. Pathol., 1904 (15), 617; Handb. d. Biochem., 1, 742.

[3] Gortner holds that dominant whites are due to the presence of antioxidase, while regressive whites have neither the power to form pigments nor to inhibit their formation (Amer. Naturalist, 1910 (44), 497).

[4] See Caspar, Ergebnisse allg. Path., 1896 (III₂), 772.

[5] Science, 1919 (50), 190.

[6] Biochem. Jour., 1914 (8), 460.

[7] However, Hanawa found white areas in skin less affected by chemical irritants and infections than dark areas. (Dermatol. Zeit., 1913 (20), 761.) This is not in agreement with most observers who have found pigmented skin more resistant. (See Hanzlik and Tarr, Jour. Pharm., 1919 (14), 221.)

strongly a melanin formation, and this has been cited as an example of the production of melanin from hemoglobin. Carbone has proved, however, that this malarial pigment is derived from hematin. The amount of iron contained in melanin has been much investigated, as bearing upon the question as to whether the melanin is derived from hemoglobin or not, and the results obtained by the best methods indicate that the amount of iron present is usually extremely small, and often it is entirely absent; furthermore, the presence of iron is no proof that the pigment is derived from hemoglobin, since other iron-protein compounds undoubtedly exist,—especially nucleoproteins, and chemical examination shows that melanin does not contain hemopyrrole groups.[8]

Composition of Melanin.—The elementary composition of different specimens of melanin examined by various observers has been found to vary greatly. This probably depends on three factors: First, it is extremely difficult to obtain melanin in a pure condition; second, the process of purification requires the action of strong acids and alkalies, which undoubtedly modify the composition of the melanin; thirdly, melanin is probably not a single substance of definite composition, but includes several related but different bodies. The values found vary for carbon from 48.95 to 60.02 per cent.; for hydrogen from 3.05 to 7.57 per cent.; for nitrogen, 8.1 to 13.77 per cent. Hofmeister gives, as a characteristic of melanins, that their elementary molecular composition is always nearly in the proportions $N : H : C = 1 : 5 : 5$.

Gortner's[9] studies have led him to accept the general principle that melanin is formed through the action of an oxidase on an oxidizable chromogen, but that in keratinous structures there exist at least two types of melanins, one, a "melanoprotein," soluble in dilute acids and existing dissolved in the keratins; the other, insoluble in dilute acids, exists as pigment granules and is of unknown nature. Piettre[10] believes that melanin from sarcoma of the horse consists of a protein united to a pigment. Those whose studies of melanin formation have been made with the microscope, state that the nucleus is active in the process,[11] and some find the melanin so closely related to the lipoids that they consider it a lipochrome.[12]

A particularly prominent constituent of some melanins is sulphur, which has been found in as high proportions as 10 per cent. in melanin from sarcomas, and even 12 per cent. in sepia from the squid; in melanin from hair the sulphur is usually about 2-4 per cent.; but in choroid melanin, and in some other forms, sulphur seems to be absent. The proportions of sulphur obtained from the same specimen purified by different methods show wide variations, and hence v. Fürth considers that neither the sulphur nor the iron are indispensable constituents of the melanin. Probably the melanin molecule contains atom-complexes that have a tendency to bind certain sulphur and iron compounds (*e. g.*, cystine or hematin derivatives).

There is much reason to believe that the melanin is derived from certain groups of the protein molecule that seem readily to form colored compounds. The aromatic compounds of the protein molecule, such as tyrosine, phenylalanine, and tryptophane, readily condense with elimination of water and absorption of oxygen, to produce dark-colored substances. When proteins are heated in strong hydrochloric acid, we obtain a dark-brown material, which closely resembles the melanins both in elementary composition and in general properties, so that it is referred to

[8] Spiegler, Hofmeister's Beitr., 1907 (10), 253.
[9] Biochem. Bulletin, 1911 (1), 207; résumé.
[10] Compt. Rend. Acad. Sci., 1911 (153), 782; also see Reprint from 1st Internat. Cong. Compar. Pathol., Paris, 1912.
[11] Staffel, Verh. Deut. Path. Ges., 1907 (11), 136; Schultz, Jour. Med. Res., 1912 (26), 65.
[12] Dyson, Jour. Path. and Bact., 1911 (15), 298; Kreibich, Wien. klin. Woch., 1911 (24), 117.

as "artificial melanin" or "melanoid substance." These substances, like the natural melanins, when decomposed by fusing with caustic potash, yield skatole, indole, and pyrrole derivatives, which are undoubtedly derived from the tyrosine and tryptophane of the protein molecule. Therefore, it seems probable that both the melanoid substances and the true melanins are formed from the chromogen groups of the protein molecule through processes of condensation, elimination of water, and the taking up of oxygen.[13]

In the sepia sacs of the cuttle-fish, in meal-worms which form a melanin-like pigment, and in plants that produce the black Japanese lacquer, have been found *oxidizing enzymes* that have the property of producing black pigment by their action upon tyrosine and other aromatic compounds. Neuberg[14] found that extracts of a melanosarcoma of the adrenal could produce pigment from epinephrine and β-oxyphenylethylamine, but not from tyrosine. The ink sacs of the squid contain an enzyme forming a pigment from epinephrine, apparently through oxidation and condensation. These enzymes may, therefore, possibly be responsible for the production of melanin in animal tissues, by causing oxidative changes in the chromogen groups of the protein molecule that are liberated by autolysis (see "Tyrosinase"). v. Fürth urges strongly the view that both normal and pathological melanin formation depend upon the action of the tyrosinase or allied enzymes in conjunction with autolytic enzymes; the latter split free the chromogen groups of the protein molecule, which are then oxidized by the tyrosinase, undergo condensation, and take up sulphur- and iron-holding groups and also other organic compounds, the entire complex forming the melanin.

Bruno Bloch[15] has found that the occurrence of melanin in the skin corresponds to the location of cells with the capacity of oxidizing 3.4-dioxyphenylalanine, which is closely related in structure to epinephrine, and which he believes may be the usual antecedent of melanin. He has found this oxidizing property exhibited by the dark patches in variegated animals, but not by the white areas; the pigmented ocular structures do not oxidize this substance.

Properties of Melanin.—When isolated in a pure condition, melanin is a dark-brown substance of amorphous structure, no matter how black the material from which it is derived may be.[16] It is quite insoluble in all ordinary reagents except alkalies, in which some melanins dissolve easily, and some with difficulty. Strong boiling hydrochloric acid scarcely affects non-protein melanins. By the action of sunlight or oxidizing agents on melanin-containing sections the pigment can be bleached out. The chief decomposition-products formed on fusing with alkalies are indole, skatole, and "melanic acid"; no cystine, leucine, tyrosine, or other amino-acids can be isolated. Most authors, therefore, consider the melanins as heterocyclic compounds standing in some relation to the indole nucleus.

If melanin is injected subcutaneously into animals (rabbits and guinea-pigs), there appears in the urine a substance which turns dark brown after the urine has stood for some time (Kobert, Helman). The pigment is apparently reduced, particularly by the liver, to a colorless melanogen, which is eliminated in the urine. The same process occurs when melanin is produced in excess and enters the

[13] See Herzmark and von Fürth, Biochem. Zeit., 1913 (49), 130.
[14] Zeit. f. Krebsforsch., 1909 (8), 195.
[15] Bloch and Ryhiner, Zeit. exp. Med., 1917 (5), 179; Zeit. physiol. Chem., 1917 (100), 226.
[16] Spiegler (Hofmeister's Beitr., 1903 (4), 40) claims to have isolated from white wool a white chromogen, closely related to melanin chemically, but Gortner (Amer. Naturalist, 1910 (44), 497) believes this to be a decomposition product of keratin, unrelated to melanin.

blood, as in the case of melanosarcoma, a colorless melanogen being formed which is excreted in the urine, constituting "melanuria." Occasionally the urine is dark when first passed, because of the presence of melanin, but usually it must be subjected to oxidizing agencies (bromine water, nitric acid, hypochlorites, etc.), or exposed to air to bring out the brown color. Helman[17] says that true melanogen may be considered to be present in urine: (1) If the careful addition of ferric chloride causes the development of a black precipitate. (2) If this precipitate dissolves in sodium carbonate, forming a black solution. (3) If from this solution mineral acids precipitate a black or brownish-black powder. All three reactions must be obtained, for substances other than melanin may give the first two. Especially to be distinguished are alkaptonuria, chronic intoxication with phenols, and some cases of extreme indicanuria.[18] In support of the view that tryptophane is the mother substance of melanin is the fact that feeding tryptophane to melanurics increases the melanin excretion (Eppinger).

The coloring power of melanin is very great, for urine containing but 0.1 per cent. of melanin has the color of dark beer (Hensen and Nölke), and the entire skin of a negro contains only about 1 gram of melanin (Abel and Davis).[19] Excessive quantities of melanin may be in part deposited in the lymph-glands and skin, causing diffuse pigmentation; it may be deposited in the endothelium lining the blood-vessels. Kobert injected melanin into albino rabbits, but did not succeed in getting any deposition in the choroid or skin. Helman found some evidence of toxicity when large doses of melanin dissolved in sodium carbonate are injected into animals, but this is possibly due to the alkali rather than to the melanin.

Melanotic Tumors.[20]—Tumor melanin does not differ from melanin produced by normal cells in any essential respect. Usually it contains much sulphur, even as much as 10 per cent., yet Helman in eight specimens found but four that contained both sulphur and iron, in three only sulphur, in one only iron and no sulphur; therefore, tumor melanins show the same variations in composition as do normal melanins. Iron is frequently found microscopically in the pigment in melanosarcoma, but this is chiefly due to admixture of blood-pigment coming from extravasations of blood. The peculiar fact that melanosarcoma is very common in white or gray horses, but very seldom

[17] Cent. f. inn. Med., 1902 (23), 1017; Arch. internat. Pharmakodynam., 1903 (12), 271.
[18] Melanuria fully discussed by Feigl and Querner, Deut. Arch. klin. Med., 1917 (123), 107.
[19] Jour. Exp. Med., 1896 (1), 361.
[20] Under the title *Acanthosis Nigricans* (see Pollitzer, Jour. Amer. Med. Assoc., 1909 (53), 1369) is included a group of cases of widespread cutaneous pigmentation with papillary hypertrophy, commonly associated with cancer, most often abdominal. While ascribed to action of the sympathetic nervous system injured by the cancer, this explanation is far from satisfactory, and the possibility of metabolic pigmentary disturbance must be considered.

occurs in dark-coated horses, has not been explained. The frequent occurrence of melanuria and melanemia in patients with melanosarcoma is not due to any peculiar property of sarcoma melanin, but to the enormous quantity of melanin that is produced by the tumor and set free in the degenerating portions. Thus, while Abel and Davis[19] estimate that there is only about 1 gram of melanin in the entire skin of a negro, Nencki and Berdez have obtained from a sarcomatous liver 300 grams of melanin, and estimate that the entire body contained 500 grams. Helman[17] states that the melanin may constitute 7.3 per cent. by weight of the fresh substance of some melanosarcomas. According to Lubarsch and to Helman, melanotic tumors rarely contain glycogen.

As mentioned above, Neuberg found that a melanotic sarcoma of the adrenal produced pigment from epinephrin and from β-oxyphenylethylamine, but he failed to get positive results with melanosarcomas of the eye and from the horse, but Alsberg[21] succeeded in finding in melanosarcoma from the liver an enzyme oxidizing pyrocatechin and Jager[22] found that horse melanosarcoma extracts will oxidize epinephrin to a pigment. The "dopa reaction" of Bloch,[15] which depends on the presence of specific oxidizing enzymes in the cells, may be exhibited by the connective tissues quite generally throughout the body in some cases of melanosarcoma.[22a]

Eppinger[23] found that the urine of a patient with melanosarcoma gave intense reactions for indole and tryptophane, and that when tryptophane was fed to a patient there was a great increase in the melanuria. He therefore concludes that the power of the body to destroy the pyrrole ring is reduced, and instead it undergoes reduction, methylation and union with sulphuric acid, to form an ethereal sulphate of methylpyrrolidine-hydroxy-carbonic acid (CH_3-$C_5H_9N_2O_4$). Abderhalden[24] also found a relation to tryptophane, for in the urine of a melanuric was present a substance rich in tryptophane; and Primavera[25] found the urine in a case of melanosarcoma containing free tyrosine, fluctuating in amount with the pigment.

Addison's disease is associated with the deposition of a pigment in the skin that is generally considered to be a melanin, differing from that produced normally in the skin only in quantity and not in origin or composition.[26] No satisfactory explanation of the relation of the adrenal to this pigmentation seems yet to have been made, although it is natural to assume that when the function of the adrenal is destroyed, substances accumulate in the blood that have a stimu-

[21] Jour. Med. Res., 1907 (16), 117.
[22] Virchow's Arch., 1909 (198), 62.
[22a] Matsunaga, Frankf. Zeit. Path., 1919 (22), 69.
[23] Biochem. Zeit., 1910 (28), 181.
[24] Zeit. physiol. Chem., 1912 (78), 159.
[25] Giorn. Int. Scienze Med., 1908 (29), 978.
[26] Concerning histogenesis of the pigment see Pförringer, Cent. f. Path., 1900 (11), 1.

lating effect on the pigment-forming cells. Abnormal protein catabolism, with excessive accumulation of the chromogenic constituents of the protein molecule, has been suggested, as also have alterations in the influence of the sympathetic nervous system upon the chromophore cells, for nerve lesions (*e. g.*, neurofibroma) often are accompanied by pathological pigmentation of the skin.[27]

It is significant that the active constituent of the adrenal medulla, the epinephrin, is an aromatic derivative closely related to tyrosine, since the production of pigment by the action of oxidizing enzymes upon such substances is well known. Furthermore, Neuberg has described a melanotic adrenal tumor which produced pigment by oxidizing epinephrine. On this basis the pigmentation of Addison's disease would seem to be the result of an abnormal accumulation or distribution of aromatic compounds, because of their failure to be converted into epinephrine. In support of this hypothesis is the observation of Meirowsky that the human skin contains an enzyme capable of oxidizing epinephrine to a pigment, and that pieces of skin kept warm will develop a postmortem pigmentation, and this is supported by Königstein[28] who found that the pigmentation was greater in animals deprived of their adrenals or given injections of epinephrine. Bloch[15] believes that the pigmentation results from the precursor of epinephrine, 3.4-dioxyphenylalanine, which is oxidized in the epidermal cells to melanin.

As exact chemical studies of the pigment in Addison's disease have not been made, however, we have no positive proof that it is a melanin, hence any speculation as to the cause of its formation is premature. Carbone[29] claims to have isolated from the urine in Addison's disease a pigment that contains much sulphur, and which he considers similar to or identical with the melanogen of melanuria. A similar observation is reported by Eiselt.[30] v. Kahlden,[31] however, has observed crystals resembling hematoidin in the pigmented tissues.

Ochronosis[32] is a condition characterized by a black pigmentation of the cartilages, first described by Virchow in 1866. In 1904 Osler[33] reported two cases, and found but seven others in the literature to that time. Virchow suspected that the condition was due to a permeation of cartilage by hematin derivatives, but Hausemann, finding a case associated with melanuria, considered that the pigment is probably of metabolic origin. Hecker and Wolf studied the urine of a similar case, and concluded that the pigment must be melanin. Albrecht,[34]

---

[27] See résumé by Schmidt, Ergeb. der Pathol., 1896 (Bd. 3, Abt. 1), 551.
[28] Wien. klin. Woch., 1910 (23), 616.
[29] Giorno R. Acad. med. di Torino, 1896.
[30] Zeit. klin. Med., 1910 (69), 393; full discussion on the pigment of Addison's disease.
[31] Virchow's Arch., 1888 (114), 65.
[32] See Adler, Zeit. f. Krebsforsch., 1911 (11), 1; Poulsen, Ziegler's Beitr., 1910 (48), 346.
[33] Lancet, 1904 (i), 10 (literature).
[34] Zeit. f. Heilk., Path. Abt., 1902 (23), 366.

however, suggested a relation of ochronosis to *alkaptonuria*, having found homogentisic acid in the urine of a case reported by him (see "Alkaptonuria"). Osler's two patients were brothers with alkaptonuria, the evidence of ochronosis consisting of discoloration of the cartilages of the ears. Langstein[35] has examined a specimen of urine preserved from Hansemann's case, and found no evidence of alkaptonuria.[36]

Pick[37] summarizes the results of his study of his case and of the literature, as follows: Ochronosis is a definite form of melanotic pigmentation, the pigment of ochronosis being in most of the cases very closely related to melanin. The pigment, or its chromogen, circulating freely in the blood, is imbibed not only by cartilage, but also by loose connective tissue, voluntary and involuntary muscle-cells, and epithelial cells, without any decrease in vitality of these cells being observable; however, degenerated tissues show the greatest amount of pigmentation. The diffuse pigment can become granular after a time; it is iron-free, but under certain circumstances may contain fat. *This melanin arises from the aromatic nucleus of the protein molecule* (tyrosine, phenylalanine), and the related hydroxylized products, *under the influence of tyrosinase.* In some cases the constant absorption of minute quantities of phenol from surgical dressings seems to have been the cause of the condition. Besides this formation of pigment from such "exogenous" aromatic substances, however, it is probable that in alkaptonuria the "endogenous" aromatic substance (homogentisic acid) present may be converted into pigment by the tyrosinase. In many of the cases of ochronosis the pigment or a precursor may be excreted in the urine, which then undergoes spontaneous darkening when exposed to the air. The kidneys may also become pigmented and granular masses of pigment may be present in the renal tubules.

Poulsen[38] states that of the 32 known cases of ochronosis (in 1911) in 17 there was alkaptonuria, in 8 carbolic acid dressings had been used for long periods, and in the remaining 7 cases the cause was not determined. These facts are conclusive evidence of the origin of ochronotic pigment from aromatic radicals, whether these radicals are converted into true melanin or not. The localization of the pigment is explained by the demonstration by Gross and Allard,[39] that cartilage has a greater affinity than other tissues for homogentisic acid. Ochronosis can be produced experimentally with homogentisic acid, and often is associated with an arthritis.[40] There are, however, numerous cases of alkaptonuria without ochronosis. The ochronosis described in lower animals is not the same as human ochronosis, affect-

[35] Hofmeister's Beitr., 1903, (4)145.
[36] Also see Langstein, Berl. klin. Woch., 1906 (43), 597.
[37] Berl. klin. Wochenschr., 1906 (43), 478.
[38] Münch. med. Woch., 1912 (59), 364.
[39] Arch. exp. Path. u. Pharm., 1908 (59), 384.
[40] Gross, Deut. Arch. klin. Med., 1919 (128), 249.

ing the bones rather than the cartilages (Poulsen),[41] and being more properly designated by the name *osteohemachromatosis* (Schmey).[42]

Malarial pigmentation, according to Ewing,[43] may have any one of the following origins:
(1) Pigment elaborated by the intracellular parasite. (2) Hematoidin derived from the remnants of infected red cells. (3) Hematoidin or altered hemoglobin deposited in granular or crystalline form from red cells dissolved in the plasma. (4) Bilirubin or urobilin granules or crystals.
Of these, the pigment formed by the parasites has been considered by many as a true melanin, but this cannot be considered as established, especially as Ewing finds it to have the same relation to solvents as do the blood-pigments. Carbone and Brown[44] consider the malarial pigment to originate from hematin, with which it agrees in solubility, spectroscopic properties, and in containing iron.

Pigmentation of the Colon.[45]—Sometimes the mucosa of the entire colon is found deeply pigmented, with a material of unknown character, but resembling in many respects a melanin. The cause of the condition is unknown. Abderhalden[46] has found pigments that seemed to be derived from tryptophane, while Niklas[47] attributes the coloration to tyrosinase activity.

Pigmentation of the oral mucosa, with a pigment resembling melanin, has been described especially in pernicious anemia. It does not seem to be related to the adrenal.[48]

LIPOCHROMES

In normal plant and animal tissues occur pigments that are either fats or compounds of fat, or substances highly soluble in fats. In animals they occur normally in the corpus luteum, in the epithelium of the seminal vesicles, testicles, and epididymis; in ganglion-cells, especially in the sympathetic nervous tissue; in the Kupffer cells of the liver and in fat tissue. Pathologically, such pigments are found particularly in the muscle-cells in brown atrophy of the heart, and less abundantly in the epithelium of atrophied livers and kidneys (Lubarsch[49] and Sehrt[50]). All are characterized by staining by such fat stains as sudan III and scarlet R, and usually, but not constantly, by osmic acid; they are dissolved by the usual fat solvents. It is questionable if all pigments that stain for fat should be considered as true lipochromes, however, for their other reactions are variable; and Borst would distinguish these pathological pigments from the true lipochromes by calling them *lipofuscins*, including under this term the brown "waste pigments," which Hueck believes to be formed from disintegrated lipoids or fatty acids. Many pigmentary substances

[41] See Ingier, Ziegler's Beitr., 1911 (51), 199.
[42] Frankfurter Zeit. Pathol., 1913 (12), 218; also Teutschlaender, Virchow's Arch., 1914 (217), 393.
[43] Jour. Exp. Med., 1902 (6), 119.
[44] Jour. Exper. Med., 1911 (13), 290.
[45] Full review by McFarland, Jour. Amer. Med. Assoc., 1917 (69), 1946.
[46] Zeit. physiol. Chem., 1913 (85), 92.
[47] Münch. med. Woch., 1914 (61), 1332. See also Hattori, Mitt. med. Gesellsch., Tokio, 1916 (30), No. 6.
[48] See Weber, Quart. Jour. Med., 1919 (12), 404.
[49] Cent. f. Pathol., 1902 (13), 881.
[50] Virchow's Arch., 1904 (177), 248. See also Mayer *et al.*, Jour. physiol. et path. gén., 1914 (16), 581.

are probably soluble in fats, and in this way the lipofuscins are formed.[51] In the renal epithelium is found a pigment resembling the lipofuscins, increasing with age and not related to the urinary pigments.[52]

Typical plant lipochromes, as also the pigments of *Staphylococcus pyogenes aureus* and *citreus*, are colored blue by concentrated sulphuric acid with formation of small blue crystals of *lipocyanin*. With iodin-potassium-iodide solution they are colored green. Lipochrome of frog-fat stains blue with this solution (Neumann);[53] lipochrome of the corpus luteum (called lutein) occasionally gives a faint blue with sulphuric acid or Lugol's solution (Sehrt); but the fat-holding pigments of the other tissues mentioned above do not give either of these reactions. Possibly these last are not true lipochromes, therefore, but rather pigments chemically or physically combined with fat. Cotte[54] believes that the true lipochromes of plants and animals have a cholesterol base, but the presence of glycerol in plant and bacterial lipochromes can be demonstrated by the acrolein test—possibly, therefore, both cholesterol and neutral fats are present. Melanins and pigments derived from hemoglobin do not stain with sudan III and are not soluble in ether, etc., and hence can be readily distinguished from the fatty pigments.

It has been shown by Escher[55] that the pigment of the corpus luteum is identical with the *carotin* of carrots. Apparently carotin and xanthophyll (a crystalline pigment from green plants)[56] are the chief pigments of milk fats, egg yolk, and probably of body fats.[57] In the body lipins these pigments accumulate throughout life because of their great solubility in lipins, which explains the high color of the fats of old persons. Carotin seems to be almost or quite devoid of toxicity,[58] and in persons eating carrots in large quantities there may be enough pigment present in the blood (*carotinemia*) to produce skin pigmentation resembling jaundice.[59]

The work of Palmer indicates that carotin and xanthophyll are much more widely distributed than was formerly appreciated. Animals with colored fats owe the color to these plant pigments, which are also present in the blood of these same animals, but not in the blood of animals with colorless fats (swine, rabbits, dogs, sheep, goats), and the so-called lipofuscin of the ganglion cells has been shown to be

---

[51] Ciaccio (Biochem. Zeit., 1915 (69), 313) agrees with Hueck, and finds it possible to distinguish between pigments from phosphatids, which stain poorly with sudan III, and those from free fatty acids which stain deeply with this dye.

[52] Schreyer, Frankf. Zeit. Pathol., 1914 (15), 333.

[53] Virchow's Arch., 1902 (170), 363.

[54] Compt. Rend. Soc. Biol., 1903 (55), 812.

[55] Zeit. physiol. Chem., 1913 (83), 198.

[56] Concerning plant pigments see review by West and Horowitz, Biochem. Bullet., 1915 (4), 151 and 161.

[57] See articles by Palmer and Eckles, Jour. Biol. Chem., 1914, Vol. 17 *et seg.*

[58] Wells and Hedenburg, Jour. Biol. Chem., 1916 (27), 213.

[59] Hess and Myers, Jour. Amer. Med. Assoc., 1919 (73), 1743; see also *ibid.*, 1920 (74), 32.

carotin.[60] Palmer found that carotin is the pigment of milk fat, body fat and corpus luteum of the cow, while xanthophyll with some carotin colors the egg yolk, body fat and blood serum of the fowl. Chickens deprived of these pigments from the time of hatching have no pigment in their fats or egg yolks although the fowls are healthy and their colorless eggs are fertile.[61] This work makes doubtful the existence of other fat-soluble intracellular pigments in man, such as lipofuscin, and Dolley states that even the typical lipofuscin of brown atrophy of the heart is sometimes insoluble in all reagents that dissolve fats.

Xanthosis diabetica[62] also seems to depend on an excess of lipochromes in the blood, probably partly endogenous from mobilization of tissue fats and chiefly exogenous from the abundance of green vegetables in the diet. Accompanying hypercholesterolemia is usually present.

Chloroma.[63]—The pigment that causes the peculiar green color characteristic of these malignant growths, was considered by Chiari, Huber and others as a fatty substance related to or identical with the lipochromes. It commonly fades on exposure to air, and also when in the usual preservative fluids, to which it does not impart its color. The color may be brought back after formaldehyde preservation by H_2O_2 or by weak alkalies (Burgess).[63] Ottenberg[64] has suggested that the green color may be due to eosinophiles which abound in chloromas, since in fresh preparations eosinophile granules have a faint greenish tinge. It contains no iron, is soluble in absolute alcohol and in ether, and is usually, but not always (v. Recklinghausen), stained black with osmic acid.[65] Treadgold states that as the green color is not present from the beginning it would seem that cellular degeneration must play a part. Possibly a degeneration of the granules of the myelocytes and myeloblasts, aided by the products of hemoglobin disintegration, is responsible.[66]

Chromophile cells may be considered in this connection. Kohn[67] has described certain cells with a decided affinity for chromic ocid and its salts, found abundantly in the sympathetic nervous system, in the carotid gland, and in the medulla of the adrenal. They are also present in tumors derived from these organs. Extracts from such organs have a marked effect in raising blood pressure, and, according to Wiesel,[68] they are greatly involved in Addison's disease. The nature of the chromophile substance is unknown, but it can be fixed only by chromic acid or chromates; cells hardened by other means show merely spaces in the places occupied by this substance. It is generally believed to be the same as the epinephrine, but it does not always seem to parallel in amount the quantity of epinephrine as determined chemically. Ogata[69] states that the chrome reaction depends on the reduction of chromic acid to chromium dioxide by epinephrine.

[60] Dolley and Guthrie, Jour. Med. Res., 1919 (40), 295. Marinesco, however, says that the pigment of nerve cells resembles that produced during autolysis in ganglia (C. R. Soc. Biol., 1913 (72), S3S).

[61] Jour. Biol. Chem., 1919 (39), 299.

[62] Bürger and Reinhart, Ziet. exp. Med., 1918 (7), 119.

[63] Literature by Dock, Amer. Jour. Med. Sci., 1893 (106), 152; and Dock and Warthin, Med. News, 1904 (85), 971; Burgess, Jour. Med. Res., 1912 (27), 133.

[64] Amer. Jour. Med. Sci., 1909 (138), 565.

[65] The pigment of *xanthelasma multiplex* seems to be a fatty substance (Poensgen). Virchow's Arch., 1883 (91), 354.

[66] Quart. Jour. Med., 1908 (1), 239; Weber, Proc. Roy. Soc. Med., Clin. Med. Sec., 1916 (9), 7.

[67] Prag. med. Woch., 1902 (27), 325.

[68] Zeit. f. Heilk., Path. Abt., 1903 (24), 257.

[69] Jour. Exp. Med., 1917 (25), 807.

BLOOD PIGMENTS[70]

Red corpuscles behave much as do other non-nucleated fragments of cells, undergoing disintegration rapidly and constantly when under normal conditions, as well as when subjected to various harmful influences (see "Hemolysis"), or when outside of the vessels in extravasations of blood. The processes and products of their disintegration are, therefore, much the same whether occurring under normal or pathological conditions. The hemoglobin molecule is large and complex, and from it are derived many substances of the nature of pigments; indeed, hemoglobin itself may appear free as a pigment.

Hemoglobin is a compound protein, consisting of a protein group (*globin*) and a coloring-matter (*hematin* or *hemochromogen*).[71] The protein globin is of a basic nature, and seems allied to the histons; the hematin is, therefore, presumably acid. Hemoglobin ordinarily does not crystallize readily, especially the hemoglobin of man, and it is doubtful if it ever does so in the living tissues, although possibly this may occur in the center of large hematomas. In bodies that have undergone postmortem decomposition, and occasionally in specimens kept for microscopic purposes, irregular orange-yellow crystalline masses of hemoglobin may be found. This occurs particularly if the blood has been acted upon by hemolytic agents or has undergone putrefactive changes, and then is hardened in alcohol. The crystals are either oxyhemoglobin, or more often an isomeric or polymeric modification, *parahemoglobin* (Nencki). Hemoglobin also enters cells unchanged, imparting a diffuse yellowish color, and apparently it is non-toxic.[72] If present in the blood in large enough amounts it is excreted unchanged in the urine, but at least one-sixtieth of the total number of red corpuscles must be in solution at one time to produce hemoglobinuria; in man at least 17 c.c. of laked corpuscles must be injected to accomplish this.[73]

Addis[74] has developed the following conception of the metabolism of hemoglobin. Free hemoglobin, liberated especially by the phagocytes of the spleen, is taken up by the other phagocytes, notably the Kupffer cells of the liver, which pass it on to the liver cells. The pigment moiety, *hematin* is separated from the globin, and converted through removal of its iron into *bilirubin*. The bilirubin excreted into the intestine is there reduced to *urobilinogen*, which is in part reabsorbed and polymerized into *urobilin*, which in turn is possibly polymerized into a larger complex. In the liver this urobilin complex has restored to its pyrrol nuclei the original side chains, and then is used

[70] Literature by Schmidt, Ergebnisse der Pathol., 1894 (1₂), 101; and 1896 (III₁), 542; Schulz, Ergebnisse der Physiol., 1902 (I₁), 505.
[71] Halliburton and Rosenheim recommend that the name "hemochromogen" be dropped in favor of "reduced hematin". (Biochem. Jour., 1919 (13), 195).
[72] Barratt and Yorke, Brit. Med. Jour., Jan. 31, 1914.
[73] Sellards and Minot, Jour. Med. Res., 1916 (34), 469.
[74] Arch. int. Med., 1915 (15), 412.

31

to form new hemoglobin molecules. This hypothesis is merely tentative, but it affords a useful "working hypothesis" for the consideration of many phases of pigment metabolism.

In the decomposition of hemoglobin the first step is the splitting of the globin (which does not form pigments) from the hematin, from which many pigments may be derived.

Hematin.—The formula given for this substance by Nencki is $C_{32}H_{32}N_4FeO_4$ while Hoppe-Seyler proposed the formula $C_{34}H_{34}N_4FeO_5$, although it is not certain that the hematin of all animals is the same. It is found frequently as an amorphous, dark-brown or bluish-black substance, in large, old extravasations of blood, but seldom in small hemorrhages. As a pathological pigment hematin is by no means so frequently found as its derivatives. Schumm[75] observed a patient with chromium poisoning who showed for several days abundant hematin free in the blood. He has also found it in malaria, pernicious anemia, congenital hematoporphyria, and generally with acute toxic hemolysis, including patients infected with *B. emphysematosus*, when the hematin may be accompanied by methemoglobin without a corresponding urinary excretion of these pigments. Feigl found hematinemia in many cases of poisoning with the war gases.[76] Brown[77] found that solutions of hematin cause chills and fever, and suggests that his pigment may be at least partially responsible for the symptoms of malaria.[78] Hematin has been believed to split up gradually into an iron-free pigment (*hematoidin*) and an iron-containing pigment (*hemosiderin*). This change may be represented by the following equation, according to Nencki and Sieber:[79]

$$C_{32}H_{32}N_4O_4Fe + 2H_2O = 2C_{16}H_{18}N_2O_3 + Fe.$$
$$\text{(hematin)} \qquad\qquad \text{(hematoidin)}$$

However, finding that the pigment in the malarial spleen is hematin, Brown[80] suggests that hematin cannot well be an intermediary product in hemoglobin disintegration, since this malarial pigment persists a very long time in the tissues without change. He has made other observations that led him to conclude that hematin is not an intermediary substance between hemoglobin and hemosiderin, but that when once formed it is destroyed very slowly, by oxidation rather than hydrolysis. Injected into rabbits it produces vascular lesions in the kidneys[81] and in large doses causes a marked fall in blood pressure.[82]

Hematoidin may be found in old, large extravasations, as orange-

[75] Zeit. physiol. Chem., 1912 (80), 1; 1913 (87), 171; 1916 (97), 32.
[76] Biochem. Zeit., 1919 (93), 119.
[77] Jour. Exper. Med., 1912 (15), 580; 1913 (18), 96.
[78] Disputed by Butterfield and Benedict, Proc. Soc. Exp. Biol., 1914 (11), 80.
[79] Arch. exp. Path. u. Pharm., 1888 (24), 440; Brugsch and Yoshimoto, Zeit. exp. Path., 1911 (8), 639.
[80] Jour. Exper. Med., 1911 (13), 290; 1911 (14), 612.
[81] Arch. Int. Med., 1913 (12), 315.
[82] Brown and Loevenhart, Jour. Exp. Med., 1913 (18), 107.

colored or red rhombic plates, first described by Virchow. Sometimes, however, hematoidin occurs in the form of yellowish granular masses, and it may be associated with lipoids; it is also found in crystalline form in icterus (Dunzelt).[83] It seems to be nearly or quite identical with the bile-pigment, bilirubin, and it is probably the source of this substance under normal conditions. When formed in excessive amounts, either through increased destruction of corpuscles in the vessels or in extravasations, the amount of bile-pigment is increased (see "Icterus"). Possibly some of the hematoidin becomes transformed directly into urobilin, and is then eliminated in the urine.

Hemosiderin[84] is relatively insoluble, and, therefore, is more slowly removed when formed in hemorrhages, and more abundantly deposited in the tissues when formed after excessive hemolysis. In acute hemolytic anemia a third of the total iron of the blood may be deposited in the liver, spleen and kidneys within 24 hours.[55] In infarcts hemosiderin soon disappears (Schmidt),[86] presumably because dissolved by the acids formed during autolysis. According to Neumann, hemosiderin is produced only under the influence of living cells and in the presence of oxygen, while hematoidin arises independent of cellular activity;[87] but Brown[88] has found that hemosiderin can be formed during autolysis of the liver, especially when air is present, and therefore probably by an oxidizing enzyme. He suggests that in hemosiderin the pigment is still hematoidin, and that the formation of hemosiderin takes place in the nuclei, the hemosiderin being made directly from hemoglobin without the intervention of hematin. It may also be formed from the iron-containing protein of the cells during autolysis, independent of hemoglobin.[89] Milner[90] considers that, under similar conditions, an iron-containing pigment is also formed, which differs from hemosiderin in having the iron so combined that it cannot react with the usual reagents; this pigment may later change into hemosiderin. Up to the present time we do not know the chemical nature of hemosiderin, nor its exact fate in the body, but it is probably utilized in the manufacture of new hemoglobin, for it is known that the iron liberated when hematin is broken up in the body under experimental conditions is deposited and not eliminated (Morishima).[91]

Unstained hemosiderin generally appears in the form of brown

[83] Cent. f. Path., 1909 (20), 966.
[84] See Neumann, Virchow's Arch., 1888 (111), 25; 1900 (161), 422; 1904 (177), 401; also Arnold, *ibid.*, 1900 (161), 284; Leupold, Beitr. path. Anat., 1914 (59), 501.
[85] Muir and Dunn, Jour. Path. and Bact., 1915 (19), 417.
[86] Verh. Deut. Path. Gesell., 1908 (12), 271.
[87] The accumulation of iron in the liver which follows poisoning with hemolytic agents, is not prevented or diminished by preliminary removal of the spleen (Meinertz, Zeit. exp. Path. u. Ther., 1906 (2), 602).
[88] Jour. Exper. Med., 1910 (12), 623.
[89] Sprunt *et al.*, Jour. Exp. Med., 1912 (16), 607.
[90] Virchow's Arch., 1903 (174), 475.
[91] Arch. exp. Path. u. Pharm., 1898 (41), 291.

or yellowish-brown granules, and not as crystals. After a time it is taken up and deposited to a large extent in the liver, spleen, bone-marrow, and kidney, either as hemosiderin or possibly as some other iron compound of similar nature. From these sites it seems to be later taken up to be utilized in the manufacture of new red corpuscles. Whenever there is hemosiderin deposition in the kidney, granules of the pigment may be found in the urine, free or in cells (Rous).[92]

All told the average human body contains about 3.2 grams of iron, of which 2.4 to 2.7 grams is in the blood. According to Meyer[93] iron is present in the body in three forms: 1. Not demonstrable by reagents because so firmly bound (hemoglobin). 2. Loosely bound iron, colored by $(NH_4)_2S$ acting for a long time (ferratin). 3. Salt-like compounds with proteins, and inorganic compounds, reacting at once with reagents. *Ferratin* is the iron compound in the liver, containing 6 per cent. iron. He believes that probably *hemosiderin* is not a definite substance, but merely indicates compounds of the third class. Iron pigments may be transformed from one class to another, *e. g.*, in corpus luteum scars, whose age can be estimated, class three may be replaced by class two. We may have in the sputum and lungs "Herzfehlerzellen" that either do or do not stain with ferrocyanide. In *morbus maculosus*, Kunkel found the pigment of the internal organs to be pure iron oxide. Hueck also holds that hemosiderin is an inorganic iron compound, loosely bound to proteins and fats, and that it never forms an iron-free pigment, as has been stated. He believes that there is very little iron in the tissues in a firm union like hemoglobin, and that by proper technic some iron can be stained in every organ which contains iron chemically demonstrable. Ischida[94] believes that an iron-containing pigment may be formed in striated muscles from the iron normally there, without requiring a hematogenous origin.

Hematoporphyrin.[95]—There are several closely related pigments derived from hematin that are appropriately grouped under the designation of *porphyrins*, for they are not all identical with the pigments prepared artificially from hematin by Nencki and called by him *hematoporphyrin* and *mesoporphyrin*, the former apparently representing a reduction, the latter an oxidation product.[96] The porphyrins found in the urine and feces are different from each other and from those prepared by Nencki.[97] Physiologically, these pigments are of great interest, because of the close chemical relation they have been found

[92] Jour. Exp.Med., 1918 (28), 645.
[93] Ergeb. der Physiol., 1905 (5), 698; literature.
[94] Virchow's Arch., 1912 (210), 67.
[95] Literature and full review by Günther, Deut. Arch. klin. Med., 1912 (105), 89; and by Jesionek, Ergeb. inn. Med., 1913 (11), 525.
[96] Fischer and Meyer-Betz, Zeit. physiol. Chem., 1912 (82), 96.
[97] H. Fischer, Münch. med. Woch., 1916 (63), 377; Zeit. physiol. Chem., 1916 (97), 109 and 148; Schumm, *ibid.*, 1915 (96), 183.

to bear to *chlorophyll*,[98] with which hemoglobin is so closely related functionally. It is also interesting to consider that whereas carnivora obtain much hemoglobin in their food, herbivora obtain much chlorophyll. Pathologically, porphyrin is of interest as a urinary pigment, being found normally in the urine in traces, but present in considerable quantities in many diseases,[99] such as rheumatism, tuberculosis, various liver diseases, and, most strikingly, after the administration of sulphonal, veronal or trional. A congenital form of hematoporphyria occurs, in which the blood contains free hematin and a porphyrin (Schumm),[1] about 0.3–0.4 gm. being usually excreted daily in the urine; in the blood it is accompanied by hematin and bilirubin. When in abundance it may color the urine a rich Burgundy red, and it is sometimes accompanied by a precursor, *uro-fuscin*. It is present in the bones of animals showing hemochromatosis and in the bones of persons[2] exhibiting the congenital form of "hematoporphyria," described by Günther, which is accompanied by severe skin lesions that are ascribed to the action of light upon the skin sensitized by the hematoporphyrin. Hausmann[3] and others have studied extensively the photosensitizing action exhibited by hematoporphyrin and other porphyrins, and find evidence suggesting a relationship between hematoporphyria and "hydroa aestiva," and other conditions in which the skin is abnormally sensitive to light. An acute form of porphyrinuria has been described, usually in women, and sometimes associated with ascending motor paralysis.[3a]

After injection of 0.2 gm. hematoporphyrin into his own veins Meyer-Betz[4] found himself so sensitized to light that exposure to the sun caused severe skin reactions during a period of weeks, and exposure to the Finsen light produced severe ulceration; but little hematoporphyrin escaped in the urine. Many other products of blood destruction tested on animals were without sensitizing effects. Methylation of the pyrrol groups only partially removes the activity of hematoporphyrin. Porphyrin obtained from urine and feces by Fischer also sensitized mice to light. Sufficient doses of hematoporphyrin may sensitize mice so that they become narcotized and die in a few minutes after exposure to intense light, a true "light stroke."

Pseudomelanosis.—When loosely bound iron is present in the tissues, and in the same tissues sulphides are produced through bacterial action, a discoloration with sulphide of iron will result, which is called *pseudomelanosis*, because the pigment resembles true melanin in its blackness. This is most frequently observed as a postmortem

[98] For literature see Abderhalden, "Lehrbuch der physiol. Chemie," 1906.
[99] See Garrod, Jour. of Physiol., 1892 (13), 598.
[1] Zeit. physiol. Chem., 1916 (98), 123; 1919 (105), 158.
[2] Hegler *et al.*, Deut. med. Woch., 1913 (39), 842.
[3] Biochem. Zeit., 1910 (30), 276; 1914 (67), 309.
[3a] Löffler, Corr.-bl. f. Schweizer Aerzte, 1919 (49), 1871.
[4] Deut. Arch. klin. Med., 1913 (112), 476.

phenomenon in and about the abdominal cavity, and in the ordinary postmortem discoloration both the liberation of the iron from its firm organic combination, and the production of hydrogen sulphide, are the work of bacteria.   Pseudomelanosis may occur *intra vitam*, particularly in the margins of infected areas, and it may also be observed in the intestines, liver and spleen, and about the peritoneum, in bodies examined immediately after death, before any evident postmortem decomposition has set in.   This seems to depend upon the previous *intra vitam* formation of hemosiderin, which is then combined by sulphur liberated from tissue proteins through bacterial action.[5]

Methemoglobin.—If hydrogen sulphide acts upon hemoglobin that has not been decomposed, a greenish compound of *sulphur-methemoglobin* is formed (Harnack[6]), which is the cause of the greenish color seen in the abdominal walls and along the vessels of cadavers. This union of hemoglobin and hydrogen sulphide occurs only when oxygen is present (oxyhemoglobin).   The sulphur-hemoglobin compound is readily decomposed by weak acids, even by CO_2, with the formation of *methemoglobin*, which in turn readily becomes decomposed to form hematin.   During life *sulphemoglobin* may form in the circulating blood, the sulphur presumably coming from intestinal putrefaction, and hence the condition is called "enterogenous cyanosis," which term also covers *methemoglobinemia* produced by nitrites formed in the intestines.[7]   The latter condition is also present in poisoning by phenacetin,[8] aniline and acetanilid, and related pigments appear in the blood in poisoning with chlorates and nitrobenzol.   Pneumococci and *Streptococcus viridans*, as well as some other bacteria, may produce methemoglobin.[9]   In infections with *B. emphysematosus*, Schumm found this pigment free in the blood.   Van den Bergh[10] has found sulphemoglobinemia in puerperal sepsis, and probably these pigments could be found in other conditions if sought.

Hemofuscin is the name given by von Recklinghausen to the brownish pigment found in involuntary muscle-fibers, particularly in the wall of the intestine.   It does not react for iron, and is insoluble in alcohol, ether, chloroform, or acids; therefore it is not a lipochrome. It is bleached by H_2O_2, and is often found associated with hemosiderin which is not bleached.   Von Recklinghausen, and also Goebel,[11] ascribe this pigment to an alteration of hemoglobin which enters the cells in dissolved form, but Rosenfeld,[12] who has submitted the mater-

[5] Ernst, Virchow's Arch., 1898 (152), 418. Literature.

[6] Zeit. physiol. Chem., 1899 (26), 558.

[7] West and Clarke, Lancet, Feb. 2, 1907; Davis, *ibid.*, Oct. 26, 1912; Gibson Quart. Jour. Med., 1907 (1), 29; Long and Spriggs, *ibid.*, 1918 (11), 102; Jamieson, *ibid.*, 1919 (12), 81.

[8] See Heubner, Arch. exp. Path., 1913 (72), 241.

[9] Cole, Jour. Exp. Med., 1914 (20), 363; Blake *ibid.*, 1916 (24), 315; Schumm, Zeit. physiol. Chem., 1913 (87), 171.

[10] Nederl. Tijd. Geneesk., 1918 (1), 1774.

[11] Virchow's Arch., 1894 (136), 482.

[12] Arch. exp. Path. u. Pharm., 1900 (45), 46.

ial to analysis after isolation, found 3.70 per cent. of sulphur, from which he considers that it is related to the melanins or melanoid substances. The substance is readily dissolved by alkalies, and contains no iron. According to Taranoukhine,[13] the pigment in the myocardium in *brown atrophy of the heart* is also derived from proteins, and is neither a lipochrome nor a hemoglobin derivative. Other observers, however, consider this pigment a lipochrome or a lipofuscin. It is probable that the name hemofuscin has been given to several different pigments, which resemble one another only in that they do not contain iron. Sträter[14] says that the name hemofuscin cannot be used for the pigment of the involuntary muscles, as he finds evidence that it does not arise from hemoglobin and is probably a waste pigment; but hemofuscin is found in epithelial and connective tissue cells.

Hemochromatosis.[15]—This name was given by von Recklinghausen to a condition in which the organs and tissues throughout the body are abundantly infiltrated with two pigments; one, iron-containing, identical with hemosiderin; the other seems to be the same as the hemofuscin described above. It is usually distinguished from general hemosiderosis in which only the iron pigment is deposited,[16] although there are numerous observers who believe that all the pigment in hemochromatosis contains iron, but in some of the pigment the iron is firmly bound and difficult of demonstration. The hemosiderin is found chiefly in the parenchyma cells of the glandular organs, especially the liver and pancreas, which organs usually show marked interstitial proliferation. The hemofuscin is found in the smooth muscle fibers of the gastro-intestinal tract, blood vessels, and genito-urinary tract. Under the heading of local hemochromatosis, von Recklinghausen grouped such conditions as brown atrophy of the heart and pigmentation of the intestinal wall, which probably are quite distinct from the generalized hemochromatosis, since the local form occurs as a physiological process in old age. Hess and Zurhelle found 38.7 gm. of iron in the liver in one case (the normal amount is 0.3 gm.), and Bernouille[17] found 18.3 gm. or 2.95 per cent. of the dry weight in the liver, 2.65 per cent. in the pancreas, and the same in the spleen. Anschütz found 14.69 per cent. in the lymph glands, 7.62 per cent. in the liver, and 5 per cent. in the pancreas of a case. Muir and Dunn[18] obtained the following percentage figures: Liver, 6.43; pancreas, 2.49; spleen, 0.825; retroperitoneal glands, 11.64; kidneys, 0.406;

[13] Roussky Arch. Patol., 1900 (10), 441.
[14] Virchow's Arch., 1914 (218), 1.
[15] Literature given by Sprunt, Arch. Int. Med., 1911 (8), 75; Potter and Milne, Amer. Jour. Med. Sci., 1911 (143), 46; Roth, Deut. Arch. klin. Med., 1915 (117), 224; McCreery, Canada Med. Assoc. Jour., 1917 (7), 481; Howard and Stevens, Arch. Int. Med., 1917 (20), 896.
[16] In lower animals occurs a form of hemochromatosis affecting especially the bones, and sometimes mistaken for ochronosis. (See Teutschlaender, Virchow's Arch., 1914 (217), 393.)
[17] Corr.-Bl. Schweiz. Aertze, 1911 (40), 610.
[18] Jour. Path. and Bact., 1914 (19), 226.

adrenals, 0.121; heart, 0.714; skin, 0.188; small intestine, 0.14.   (Other analytical results are given by Howard and Stevens.)

Opie's conclusions concerning this disease are as follows: (1) There is a distinct morbid entity, hemochromatosis, characterized by widespread deposition of an iron-containing pigment in certain cells, and an associated formation of iron-free pigments in a variety of localities in which pigment is found in moderate amount under physiological conditions.   (2) With the pigment accumulation there occur degeneration and death of the containing cells and consequent interstitial inflammation, notably of the liver and pancreas, which become the seat of inflammatory changes accompanied by hypertrophy of the organ.   (3) When chronic interstitial pancreatitis has reached a   certain grade of intensity, diabetes ensues and is the terminal event in the disease.

Diabetes occurs in the majority of the cases of generalized hemochromatosis (50 of 63 collected by Sprunt) and was called by Hanot, "bronzed diabetes," because of the coloration of the skin. It has been suggested that the pigmentation is due to decomposition of the blood-corpuscles in the diabetic blood, but the pigmentation and sclerotic changes precede the diabetes, which is secondary to the atrophic and sclerotic changes in the pancreas.   It seems probable that both the pigment formation and the tissue changes depend upon some intoxication, the origin and nature of the toxic agent being entirely unknown.   In many cases it has seemed possible that alcohol might have been the inciting cause.   There is no evidence of abnormal boold destruction which might account for the pigmentation, and Meltzer and Parker have suggested that the difficulty lies in the inability of the tissues to get rid of the iron set free in normal catabolism.   Metabolism studies have indicated that there is some retention of food iron which may be interpreted as supporting but not proving this hypothesis.[19]   Rous and Oliver,[20] finding that protracted hemolysis of foreign corpuscles in rabbits produces a typical mild hemochromatosis, suggest that the liver cirrhosis is primary and renders this organ unable to deal adequately with the blood pigments, which therefore accumulate in the organs and cause diffuse fibrosis.

ICTERUS[21]

Pigmentation of the tissues of the body in jaundice depends upon the presence in them of bile-pigments, which usually have been formed in the liver and reabsorbed either into the lymph or blood (or both). However, a pigment that seems to be chemically identical with bilirubin (*hematoidin*) may be formed from hemoglobin liberated on the

[19] See Howard and Stevens (*loc. cit.*) and McClure, Arch. Int. Med., 1918 (22), 610.

[20] Trans. Assoc. Amer. Phys., 1918 (33), 132.

[21] Literature by Stadelmann, "Der Icterus," Stuttgart, 1891; Minkowski, Ergebnisse der Pathol., 1895 (2), 679.

breaking up of red corpuscles, and possibly this may be produced in sufficient amounts outside of the liver to give rise to general icterus. Certainly the local greenish-yellow pigmentation occurring in the vicinity of extravasations of blood, due to hematoidin formation, may be looked upon as a "local jaundice," and in icterus hematoidin[22] crystals may be found in the tissues.[23]

Bile-pigments.—*Bilirubin* is of a reddish-yellow color, and it is the chief pigment of human bile. Its formula is $C_{34}H_{38}N_4O_6$ or $C_{33}H_{36}N_4O_6$, and its relation to hematin, from which it is formed, is shown by the following formula, which expresses the manner in which blood pigment may be converted into bilirubin by the liver under normal conditions, and into hematoidin (its isomer) in the tissues and fluids of the body in pathological conditions:

$$C_{34}H_{34}N_4O_5Fe + 2H_2O = C_{34}H_{38}N_4O_6 + FeO.$$
$$\text{(hematin)} \qquad\qquad \text{(hematoidin or bilirubin)}$$

Bilirubin is not soluble in water, but dissolves in the alkaline body fluids as a soluble compound, "bilirubin alkali." It is very slightly soluble in ether, benzene, carbon disulphide, amyl-alcohol, fatty oils, and glycerol, but is more soluble in alcohol and in chloroform.

Biliverdin, $C_{34}H_{38}N_4O_8$, as its formula indicates, is an oxidation product of bilirubin. Bilirubin in alkaline solutions will oxidize into biliverdin merely on exposure to the air, and the change from yellow to green of icteric specimens when placed in oxidizing solutions (*e. g.*, dichromate hardening fluids) is due to the formation of the green biliverdin. Biliverdin is the chief pigment of the bile of carnivora, but it is also present in varying amounts in human bile.

The various other biliary pigments, namely, *bilifuscin, biliprasin, choleprasin,*[24] *bilihumin,* and *bilicyanin,* are probably not normal constituents of bile, but are oxidation products of bilirubin, and are found chiefly in gall-stones (*q. v.*). A pigment similar to urobilin may be present in normal bile. The total amount of pigments present in bile is probably not far from one gram per liter; rather under than above this amount.

Etiology of Icterus.

—Although hematoidin, which is isomeric if not identical with bilirubin, may be formed outside of the liver when red corpuscles are broken up in hemorrhagic extravasations, and possibly also when they are broken up within the vessels by hemolytic agents, yet it was formerly held that a true general icterus does not occur without the liver being implicated. This view rested on evidence of various sorts. First, the classical experiments of Minkowski and Naunyn,[25] which demonstrated that in geese the production of hemolysis by means of arseniuretted hydrogen leads to icterus, but if the livers of the geese have been previously removed, no icterus follows the poisoning. Second, the repeated demonstration that in icterus produced by septic conditions, poisoning, etc., which was formerly looked upon as a "hematogenous" icterus, the urine contains bile salts as well as pigment, indicating an absorption of bile from the liver. Third, the finding of histological evidence that in so-called hematogen-

[22] See Guillain and Troisier, Semaine Méd., 1909 (29), 133; Widal and Joltrain, Arch. méd. expér., 1909 (21), 641.
[23] Dunzelt, Cent. f. Path., 1909 (20), 966.
[24] See Küster, Zeit. physiol. Chem., 1906 (47), 294.
[25] Arch. f. exp. Pathol. u. Pharm., 1886 (21), 1.

ous icterus there occur occlusions or lesions of some sort in the bile capillaries, which can account for the reabsorption of the bile into the general circulation.[26] Therefore, it was believed that the pigments that produce the general discoloration of icterus are, at least for the most part, manufactured by the liver, whatever the cause of the re-absorption of the bile from the liver into the blood may be. That hemolytic agents cause icterus was explained by the fact that on account of the large amounts of free hemoglobin brought to the liver, excessive amounts of bile-pigments are formed, which render the bile so viscid that it blocks up the fine bile capillaries; on account of the low pressure at which bile is secreted, a slight obstruction of this kind is sufficient to stop entirely the outflow of bile, which then enters the capillaries of the liver and also, to a less extent, the lymphatics.[27] It is also possible that the hemolytic poisons injure the liver-cells so much that the minute intra- and intercellular bile capillaries become disorganized, and permit of escape of bile into the lymph-spaces and its absorption into the blood-vessels.[28] Swelling of the degenerated liver-cells may also be an important factor in the occlusion of the bile capillaries; swelling of the lining cells of the bile capillaries may also coëxist, and fibrin may occlude them in toxic or infectious icterus.

However, Whipple and Hooper[29] have obtained experimental evi-dence that after intravenous injection of hemoglobin into dogs with the liver excluded from the circulation, bile pigments appear in the urine and icterus is manifested in the fat tissues, from which observa-tions it is concluded that the liver may not be the only place in which bile pigment can be formed from hemoglobin.[30] Several authors have found bilirubin produced in hemorrhagic effusions located where the liver could have had no influence.[31] We also recognize types of hemo-lytic icterus in which the liver does not seem to be concerned, and with bile pigments present in the blood and urine unaccompanied by bile salts (dissociated icterus), so that the old dictum of the essential implication of the liver in icterus seems to be incorrect.[32] Joanno-vics[33] gives, as a result of a comparative study of icterus from bile obstruction and icterus from hemolysis, the following chief differ-

---

[26] See Eppinger, Ziegler's Beitr., 1903 (33), 123; Gerhardt, Münch. med. Woch., 1905 (52), 889. Lang (Zeit. exp. Path. u. Ther., July, 1906 (3), 473) has demon-strated the presence of fibrinogen in the bile in phosphorus-poisoning, which perhaps accounts for the "bile thrombi" observed by Eppinger in toxic icterus.

[27] See Mendel and Underhill, Amer. Jour. Physiol., 1905 (14), 252; Whipple and King, Jour. Exp. Med., 1911 (13), 115.

[28] Sterling, Arch. exp. Path., 1911 (64), 468; Fiessinger, Jour. Physiol., et Pathol., 1910 (12), 958. Oertel (Arch. Int. Med., 1918 (21), 73) suggests that intracellular precipitation of bile pigment within liver cells altered by poisons may prevent its excretion into the bile canaliculi.

[29] Jour. Exper. Med., 1913 (17), 593 and 612.

[30] Attempts to produce bile pigments from hemoglobin by bacterial action have been unsuccessful. (Quadri, Fol. Clin. Chim., 1914, No. 10.)

[31] Hooper and Whipple, Jour. Exp. Med., 1916 (23), 137.

[32] See Lepehne, Beitr. path. Anat., 1917 (64), 55.

[33] Zeit. f. Heilk., Path. Abt., 1904 (25), 25.

ences: Icterus due to hemolysis appears sooner than icterus from bile-duct occlusion, and reaches a much higher degree; the obstruction in hemolytic icterus, when present, is intra-acinous; in stasis it is chiefly inter-acinous; in hemolytic icterus there is a large splenic tumor due to accumulation of degenerated red cells in the spleen, where they become disintegrated preliminary to the formation of bile-pigment. If the spleen is removed, hemolytic agents may not cause icterus, because the corpuscles are not then prepared for pigment formation.[34] In obstructive icterus from gall stones there is a cholesterolemia in proportion to the amount of icterus, which is not usually true of icterus from other causes.[35]

Toxicity of Bile.—In any event, we must appreciate that in icterus not only are abnormally large quantities of bile-pigment present in the blood, but also usually the other less conspicuous constituents of the bile. Whole bile of rabbits is fatal to rabbits in doses of 0.25 to 0.5 cc. per kilo, by intraperitoneal injection, and about half as much intravenously (Bunting and Brown[36]). Death is the result of changes in the myocardium, where necrosis is produced; and severe degenerative changes are also found in the kidneys and liver; when the bile is injected into the peritoneum, pancreatitis and fat necrosis result. The relative toxicity of the bile-pigments and the bile salts is not as yet uniformly agreed upon.

Bile-pigments.—Bouchard[37] and others have claimed that the bile-pigments are far more toxic than the bile salts, which is contradicted by Rywosch and others. Bilirubin is normally present in the blood, and is probably responsible for the yellow color of the plasma.[38] It is always present in excess in icterus of whatever degree.[39] A series of analyses by Gilbert[40] and others gave the following results: Normal blood-serum contains 0.027–0.08 gram bilirubin per liter; in obstructive icterus they found 0.7 to 1.0 gram of bilirubin per liter, in biliary cirrhosis 0.33 gram per liter, in icterus neonatorum 0.2 to 0.5 gram; in pneumonia 0.068 gram was found. These figures, however, are far in excess of those described by later investigators. Bauer and Spiegel[41] give figures of about 1 part in 100,000 to 200,000, or 0.01 to 0.005 gm. per liter. In icterus the highest figure given by these authors was 0.07 gm. There is a marked variation between different normal individuals, but for the same person the figures are nearly constant. The threshhold value for the blood seems to be about 1 part in 50,000;

[34] The etiology of *icterus neonatorum* (when not obstructive) has not been ascertained, but a natural tendency towards icterus is said to exist in the newborn, their blood containing much more bile pigment then than later. (Hirsch, Zeit. Kinderheilk., 1913 (9), 196; Ylppö, Münch. med. Woch., 1913 (39), 2161.)
[35] Rothschild and Felsen, Arch. Int. Med., 1919 (24), 520.
[36] Jour. Exper. Med., 1911 (14), 445.
[37] Literature and discussion by Stadelmann, Zeit. f. Biol., 1896 (34), 57.
[38] Blankenhorn, Arch. Int. Med., 1917 (19), 344; 1918 (21), 282.
[39] Feigl and Querner, Zeit. exp. Med., 1919 (9), 153.
[40] Compt. Rend. Soc. Biol., 1905 and 1906.
[41] Deut. Arch. klin. Med., 1919 (129), 17.

when this proportion is exceeded the pigment begins to be deposited in the skin and excreted by the kidneys (v. d. Bergh). However, Blankenhorn believes that at times the bilirubin in the plasma is so bound that the kidneys do not excrete it, and yet it may be able to diffuse into the skin.[42] With reduced renal function the amount of pigment in the blood may be increased without hepatic disease.

King and Stewart[43] state that the amount of pigment in a lethal dose of whole bile will cause death, but the bile salts present in the same quantity of bile will not cause recognizable effects; uncombined pigment is more toxic than its calcium or magnesium salts. Bile from which the pigment is removed has very little toxicity. They suggest that calcium is increased in the blood in icterus as a protection against the toxic effects of the pigments. The combining of the calcium with bile pigment, however, renders it unavailable for fibrin formation, and this seems to be an important factor in the hemophilic tendency of icterus,[44] and Pettibone records a marked decrease in blood calcium in protracted jaundice.[45] The decrease in available calcium may also be responsible for the bradycardia and some of the mental and nervous symptoms.

Bile salts are said to be toxic, generally producing depression of the central nervous system, with resulting coma and paralysis; they are also decidedly toxic to cells of all sorts, causing hemolysis and marked destruction of tissue-cells. Small quantities of bile salts stimulate the central end of the vagus, and large amounts influence the heart itself; hence in icterus we observe a slowing, and often an irregularity, of the pulse, and the blood pressure is lowered. Although there has been much dispute as to whether the chief effects of icterus upon the heart depend upon action of the bile salts upon the vagus, or upon the intracardiac ganglia, or upon the muscle itself,[46] yet Weintraud demonstrated that in some cases of icterus administration of atropin, which paralyzes the vagus, stops the bradycardia, indicating the importance of the effects of the bile salts upon the vagus in causing this feature of cholemia. According to Meltzer and Salant,[47] bile also contains a tetanic element which disappears from stagnating bile; the bile salts contain this tetanizing agent in less amount than does the whole bile. But King[48] and others ascribe most of the effects of bile on the heart to the bile pigments, perhaps through abstraction of the calcium. Taurin given in 10 gm. and even larger

---

[42] Corroborated by Meulengracht (Ugesk. f. Laeger., 1919 (81), 1785) who states that when bilirubin reaches a certain concentration it passes into the tissues, but not into the urine until a higher concentration is reached.

[43] Jour. Exper. Med., 1909 (11), 673.

[44] See Lee and Vincent, Arch. Int. Med., 1915 (16), 59.

[45] Jour. Lab. Clin. Med., 1918 (3), 275.

[46] See Minkowski, Ergeb. der Pathol., 1895 (2), 709.

[47] Jour. Exp. Med., 1906 (8), 128; review and literature concerning toxicity of bile.

[48] See King, Bigelow and Pearce, Jour. Exper. Med., 1912 (14), 159.

doses by mouth, subcutaneously and intravenously to man produced no noticeable effects (Schmidt).[49]

Since the bile salts cause hemolysis, and since in even "hematogenous" jaundice they may enter the blood, it can readily be seen that in this way an increased formation of bile-pigment may be incited which leads to further obstruction to the outflow of bile from the liver, and a "vicious circle" may thus be established. The necroses observed in the liver in icterus, *"icteric necrosis,"* are generally ascribed to the cytotoxic effects of the bile salts, although it is difficult always to exclude infection extending along the bile-ducts to the liver tissue. Possibly the power of bile salts to dissolve lipoids may be responsible for the cytotoxic effects[50] as well as for the hemolysis. The itching and irritation of the skin in icterus may be due to the effect of the bile-salts deposited in it, for pruritus is said to be absent in the pigmentary jaundice of congenital hemolytic icterus. There is also an increase in the cholesterol in the blood, which may be related to the "xanthomas" that form in chronic icterus.[51] Unfortunately we have no accurate method for quantitative determination of the amount of bile salts in the blood.

A remarkable tendency to spontaneous hemorrhages, frequently observed in icterus, probably depends upon injury to the capillary endothelium by the bile salts,[52] while the protracted, often uncontrollable, hemorrhage that may occur from operation wounds in icteric patients, is related to the slowed coagulation of the blood observed in icterus. The bile salts themselves may delay coagulation by interfering with the conversion of fibrinogen into fibrin.[53] The cytotoxic effect of the bile salts is also shown by the albuminuria of icteric persons, which frequently results from the renal lesions the bile produces. Although bile itself is toxic to many bacteria, especially the pneumococcus,[54] yet in icterus the bactericidal power of the blood is lowered, and infections are prone to develop and to be severe; moreover, the growth of several species of bacteria is favored by bile.[55]

Croftan[56] summarizes the physiological effects of bile acids as follows: (1) A powerful cytolytic action, affecting both blood-corpuscles and tissue-cells. (2) A distinct cholagogue action. (3) In small doses (1–500) they aid coagulation. (4) In large doses (1–250 and over) they retard coagulation. (5) Slow the heart action.[57] (6) In small doses they act as vasodilators; in large doses, as vaso con-

[49] Schmidt *et al.*, Jour. Biol. Chem., 1918 (33), 501.
[50] Neufeld and Händel, Arb. kaiserl. Ges.-Amte, 1908 (28), 572.
[51] Chauffard, Presse Méd., 1913 (21), 81; Chvostek, Zeit. klin. Med., 1911 (73), 479; Pinkus and Pick, Deut. med. Woch., 1908 (34), 1427.
[52] See Morawitz, Arch. exp. Path., 1907 (56), 115.
[53] Haessler and Stebbins, Jour. Exp. Med., 1919 (29), 445.
[54] See Neufeld and Haendel, *loc. cit.*
[55] See Meyerstein, Cent. f. Bakt., 1907 (44), 434.
[56] New York Med. Jour., 1906 (83), 810; see also Faust, "Die tierische Gifte," Braunschweig, 1906, p. 29.
[57] See Berti, Gaz. degli Osped., 1916 (37), 1233.

strictors. (7) Reduce motor and sensory irritability. (8) Act on the higher cerebral centers, causing coma, stupor, and death. Sellards[58] found that injection of bile salts into guinea pigs causes ulceration and hemorrhage in the stomach.

It is difficult to decide how much of the profound intoxication that is sometimes present in icterus ("cholemia" and "icterus gravis") to ascribe to the reabsorbed bile, for frequently there is an accompanying infection, and even if there is no infection the impairment of liver function by the obstruction of bile outflow must also be reckoned with. The liver is not only the great destroyer of toxic substances absorbed from the alimentary canal, but it is also an important seat of nitrogenous metabolism, interference with which may lead to accumulation of many toxic nitrogenous substances in the blood.[59] The long duration of severe icterus in some cases of occlusion of the bileducts, with relatively slight evidences of intoxication, would seem to indicate, however, that on the whole the bile is not so much responsible for the intoxication observed in icterus as are the associated conditions. On the other hand, in not a few instances it has been observed that escape of large quantities of bile into the peritoneal cavity may be followed by symptoms similar to those of icterus gravis; in these cases only the bile can be held responsible for the intoxication.[60]

Dissociated Jaundice[61] is the existence of either bile salts or bile pigment separately in the blood. This may be produced either by the bile salts being excreted by the kidney, leaving only the less diffusible pigment in the blood, or by separate escape of bile salts from the liver into the blood. Also in true hemolytic icterus we may have bile pigments present in the blood without bile salts.

Congenital Hemolytic Icterus.[62]—This term describes a condition characterized by a chronic, non-obstructive jaundice, without evident intoxication. A similar condition is also observed developing in adults, without familial tendencies. The congenital form usually shows familial character, but isolated congenital cases do occur. It is the result of active hemolysis, apparently taking place chiefly in the spleen, and leading to an icterus without evident participation of the liver. The cause of the hemolysis is entirely unknown, although there is a marked fragility of the erythrocytes evidenced by reduction of their resistance to hypotonic solutions, and it results in a moderate anemia, with excretion of much urobilin in both stools and urine; the blood contains bilirubin which is not excreted in the urine. The jaundice is usually unaccompanied by evidence of cholemia, icteric pruritus or hemophilia. The spleen is greatly enlarged and improvement has generally followed splenectomy but the exact relation of the spleen to the disease is not known.[63] The frequent occurrence of gall stones in this condition may be the result of hypercholesterolemia from hemolysis.

The metabolism of a case[64] showed loss of nitrogen, calcium, magnesium and iron, and a much increased uric acid excretion. These conditions may improve after operation.[65]

[58] Arch. Int. Med., 1909 (4), 502.

[59] See Bickel, Exper. Untersuch. über der Pathol. der Cholaemie, Wiesbaden 1900.

[60] See Ehrhardt, Arch. klin. Chir., 1901 (64), 314.

[61] Hoover and Blankenhorn, Arch. Int. Med., 1916 (18), 289.

[62] See Richards and Johnson, Jour. Amer. Med. Assoc., 1913 (61), 1586.

[63] See series of articles by Pearce et al., in Jour. Exp. Med., on Relation of Spleen to Blood Destruction.

[64] McKelvy and Rosenbloom, Arch. Int. Med., 1915 (15), 227.

[65] Goldschmidt, Pepper and Pearce, Arch. Int. Med., 1915 (16), 437.

The Pigmentation in Icterus.—Living tissues have but a slight tendency to take up bile-pigments, much of the tissue-staining observed at autopsy being due to postmortem imbibition from the blood and lymph. Quincke[66] found that after subcutaneous injection of bilirubin only the connective tissue, both cells and intercellular fibrils, becomes diffusely colored; later, it fades out of the cells, leaving only the fibrils stained. Muscle-cells, fat-cells, and vessel-walls take up the pigment only after their death. If the jaundice continues for a long time, the subcutaneous deposits of bilirubin may undergo a slow oxidation, the color changing to an olive or to a dirty grayish green. The pigment in the connective tissues is at first in solution, but may be deposited in a granular form after a considerable amount has accumulated. Bile pigments and bile salts may both be present in considerable amounts in the blood and not pass through the kidneys, and also they may fail to pass into the tissues; hence we may have cholemia without icterus or choluria, because of the firmness with which the pigments are bound in the plasma (Hoover[61]).

The question whether in icterus the skin may be colored by other pigments than bilirubin, especially by its reduction product, urobilin, seems to have been decided negatively. Bile-pigment is probably not absorbed as such from the intestine in sufficient quantity to cause icterus. Such bile-pigment as enters the blood from the liver is excreted through the kidneys chiefly, but also in the sweat. Ordinarily, other secretions (milk, tears, saliva, sputum) are not colored in jaundice, but if the secretions are mixed with inflammatory exudations, they may then be colored (e. g., pneumonic sputum). When the bile-pigment is resorbed from the skin, it may be in part transformed into urobilin, which appears in the urine in increased amounts during the period of recovery from jaundice. Part of the bile-pigment is probably eliminated by the liver after the cause of obstruction has been removed from the bile-passages.

UROBILIN[67]

This pigment is probably formed chiefly, if not solely, from bile pigments by the action of reducing bacteria in the intestine. It is excreted in the urine only as its chromogen, urobilinogen, but in the feces both urobilin and urobilinogen may be found; when exposed to air the chromogen oxidizes quickly to urobilin. Addis[68] states that bilirubin is reduced to urobilinogen in the bowel and is then largely absorbed, to be at once oxidized and polymerized into urobilin, two molecules of urobilinogen uniting under the influence of oxygen to form one of urobilin. In the liver the urobilin is largely worked over

[66] Vichow's Arch., 1884 (95), 125.
[67] Bibliography and review by Meyer-Betz, Ergeb. inn. Med., 1913 (12), 734; Wilbur and Addis, Arch. Int. Med., 1914 (13), 235.
[68] Arch. Int. Med., 1915 (15), 412.

to form new hemoglobin, and hence the functional capacity of the liver is indicated by the completeness with which it utilizes the urobilin, except in cases of excessive formation of urobilinogen as a result of hemolysis. The amount of urobilinogen in the urine will be found increased, therefore, in hemolytic icterus, and decreased in obstructive icterus. Exceptionally, urobilinogen may be formed from blood disintegrated in bloody effusions without evident participation of the liver, e. g., urobilinogenuria with hemorrhagic ascites, hemolytic poisons, etc. With a normal liver urobilinogenuria is found only when there is excessive hemolysis, otherwise urobilinogenuria occurs only with an injury to the liver parenchyma (Hildebrant). In general, the amount in the urine is an index of the amount of blood destruction.[69] There seems to be little if any retention by imperfectly functioning kidneys (Blankenhorn) and it can often be found in the urine when not demonstrable in the blood. Occlusion of the bile ducts stops an existing urobilinogenuria by preventing the formation of urobilinogen in the intestine. Normally there is a very small amount of urobilinogen and related substances in the urine, which disappears when there is no bile in the intestine. Fromholdt[70] considers that increased bacterial reduction in the intestines may by itself account for urobilinogenuria. The amount of urobilin and urobilinogen excreted in the feces, seems to vary directly with the amount of hemolysis,[71] and the same is true for the duodenal contents.[72] The evidence of abnormal hemolysis is said to occur first in the stools, then in the duodenal contents, and lastly in the urine; the presence of even small amounts of urobilinogen in the urine being evidence of a probable pernicious anemia in the absence of signs of biliary and hepatic disease.[72a]

Digestive Disturbances in Obstructive Icterus.[73]—In case the icterus depends upon the occlusion of the main bile-passages by stones, tumors, etc., the situation is complicated by the effects of the absence of this natural secretion in the intestinal canal. Carbohydrate and protein digestion seem to be but little affected, especially the former, but the proportion of the ingested fat that appears in the feces increases from the normal 7–11 per cent. to 60–80 per cent. The products of bacterial decomposition of the undigested fat may lead to injury of the intestinal wall and disturbance of its function. Failure of absorption of fat also favors intestinal putrefaction by enveloping the protein substances so that they are not readily digested and absorbed. The relation of bile to intestinal putrefaction is still not exactly determined. Frequently, but by no means always, there is an increased intestinal putrefaction which may result in diarrhea and the appearance of excessive quantities of indican and phenol in the urine. The idea once held that the bile salts acted as intestinal antiseptics has not been established by experimental investigations; however, it is possible that through their function as natural cathartics, by stimulation of peristalsis, they prevent stagnation and putrefaction of proteins.

[69] Dubin, Jour. Exp. Med., 1918 (28), 313.
[70] Zeit. exp. Path., 1911 (9), 268.
[71] Robertson, Arch. Int. Med., 1915 (15), 1072; McCrudden, Bost. Med. Surg. Jour., 1917 (177), 907.
[72] Giffin, Sanford and Szlapka, Amer. Jour. Med. Sci., 1918 (155), 562.
[72a] Hausmann and Howard, Jour. Amer. Med. Assoc., 1919 (73), 1262.
[73] Concerning metabolism in icterus see Vannini, Zeit. klin. Med., 1912 (75), 136.

CHAPTER XIX

THE CHEMISTRY OF TUMORS[1]

CHEMICAL investigations of tumors have been relatively few in number, but, so far as they have yet been made, there has been detected little that indicates any important deviation of the chemical processes of tumors from those of normal cells of similar origin. Likewise, the chemical composition of tumor tissue resembles closely, on the whole, the composition of related normal tissues. It is hardly to be imagined that the course of chemical changes is greatly different in tumor cells from that in normal cells, in view of the abundant evidence that the metabolic products of tumor cells are identical with those of the cells from which they arose. Thus, metastatic growths of thyroid tissue will produce thyroiodin in any part of the body, liver carcinoma metastases produce bile, tumors from the choroid or from pigmented moles produce melanin, etc.[2] The capacity of tumor cells to produce complicated products of metabolic action specific for the parent cells from which they arose, as illustrated above, indicates beyond question that the course of their chemical activities is very much like that of normal cells. So, too, the composition of the cells is found to be similar indeed to that of the parent cells, both in regard to primary and secondary constituents. Thus, Bang found that sarcomas derived from lymph-glands contain the particular nucleo-proteins that are found normally only in lymph-glands, hyperne-phromas contain much fat, lecithin, and cholesterol; squamous cell carcinomas develop great amounts of kerato-hyalin; carcinomas of mucous membranes may contain much mucin, etc.

Many have sought in cancer tissues a poison that might account for the cachexia characteristic of new-growths. Extracts have been obtained that were destructive to red corpuscles (hemolytic), and that were sometimes slightly toxic to animals, but the results have not seemed sufficiently striking to account for the appearance of cachexia. Because of the interference with circulation, brought about in tumors by pressure of the growing tissues upon their blood-vessels, areas of necrosis frequently develop, and these, undergoing autolysis, yield substances that are hemolytic and toxic. Whether these are the cause of cancer cachexia, however, may be questioned; but they are sufficient to account for most of the experimental results as yet obtained. No

[1] Earlier literature given by Neuberg, Zeit. Krebsforsch., 1910 (10), 55; and Blumenthal, Ergebnisse Physiol., 1910 (10), 363.
[2] See Wells and Long, Zeit. Krebsforsch., 1913 (12), 598.

substance has yet been isolated from or detected in malignant growths that is peculiar to them and not found in normal cells, and still less has any substance been detected that accounts in any way either for the occurrence of tumors or for the effects that they produce.

Tumor cells seem to depend upon much the same conditions as normal body cells for their growth, since anything that leads to wasting, malnutrition, or atrophy in the tissues of the host usually tends to impede the rate of growth of the tumor cells, in marked contrast to infectious diseases. Specific attempts to modify tumor growths by diets (Mendel-Osborne diet) which stunt the animals because lacking certain amino-acids necessary for growth, have been successful,[3] but it is difficult to be sure that this effect depends on the specific absence of a definite substance rather than on general malnutrition.[4] Tumor cells made incapable of utilizing carbohydrate through complete phlorizin diabetes[5] may be unable to grow, and even retrogress completely. Furthermore, the constituents of the hypophysis that stimulate somatic tissue growth are also said to stimulate growth of tumor tissues.[6]

The discovery by B. Fischer[7] that fat stained with scarlet-R and injected beneath the skin causes epithelial proliferation resembling but not terminating in cancer, has led to much speculation as to the nature of substances which might cause cells to proliferate lawlessly and malignantly.[8] The great frequency of cancer in workers in products of destructive distillation of wood (tar, soot, paraffin[9]) has also indicated the possibility of chemical stimuli causing cancers. A striking instance of chemical stimulation causing cancer formation is furnished by the cases of carcinoma of the urinary bladder, which is a common cause of death in men who work in aniline dyes, both dyers and dye makers being subject to this condition. The dyes that seem to be responsible belong to the group of aromatic amido-hydroxyls, including safranin, congo-red, benzopurpurin, fuchsin, eosin and others.[10] Nassauer,[10a] however, believes that the aniline itself is the active agent. H. C. Ross[11] has made extensive studies of the relation to cancer of substances which cause leucocytes to multiply,

[3] See Sweet, *et al.*, Jour. Biol. Chem., 1915 (21), 309.
[4] Rous, Jour. Exp. Med., 1914 (20), 433.
[5] Benedict and Lewis, Proc. Soc. Exp. Biol., 1914 (11), 134.
[6] Robertson and Burnett, Jour. Exp. Med., 1916 (23), 631.
[7] Verh. Deut. Path. Gesell., 1906 (10), 20; see also Haga, Zeit. Krebsforsch., 1913 (12), 525; Sachs, Wien. klin. Woch., 1911 (24), 1551; Stoeber, Münch. med. Woch., 1910 (57), 739 and 947.
[8] Stoeber has considered substances related to scarlet-R that might have this stimulating effect, and found naphthylaminol most active. In general, fat-soluble organic basic substances only were found to have this property, among them being indole, skatole and pyridine. (Münch. med. Woch., 1909 (56), 129; 1910 (57), 947).
[9] See Bayon, Lancet, 1912 (ii), 1579.
[10] See Leuenberger, Beitr. klin. Chir., 1912 (80), 208.
[10a] Zeit. angew. Chem., 1919 (32), 333.
[11] "Researches into Induced Cell Reproduction and Cancer," London.

designating them as "auxetics." These seem to be present in the anthracene fractions of tar,[12] which may explain the frequency of cancer in workers in tar, soot and paraffin. Japanese investigators report that protracted irritation of rabbits' ears with tar leads to strikingly infiltrative proliferation of the epithelium, with metastasis.[13] The influence of various salts on cell growth has also been applied to cancer pathology, and while we have abundant evidence that chemical substances may either stimulate or check cell growth, as well as regulate it, our biological chemistry has not yet given us any very substantial facts on these problems.[14]

Nevertheless, numerous observations have been made concerning the chemistry of tumors, which, although they do not as yet throw any important light on the fundamental problems of tumor pathology, are of much interest. These may be briefly summarized as follows:

A. CHEMISTRY OF TUMORS IN GENERAL

(1) **Proteins.**—Earlier studies showed that tumor growths contain the same sorts of proteins as do normal tissues, apparently in about the same proportions, and in spite of certain contradictory reports this statement seems to be correct.

In all probability the nucleoproteins of tumors share the specific characteristics of the nucleoproteins of the tissues from which they arise—at least this is the case with the nucleoproteins of lymphosarcoma, according to Bang.[15] This seems to have been confirmed by Beebe,[16] who found nucleo-histon only in lymph-gland tissue, but the distinction between thymus and lymph-gland nucleohiston is probably not so easily made as Bang intimates. Because of their richly cellular structure cancers may contain more nucleoprotein than the tissues from which they arise.[16a] However, Wells and Long[17] found the proportion of purine nitrogen in tumors of several classes to be much lower than might be expected from the nuclear content as shown by the microscope; also, Satta[18] found unexpectedly low phosphorus figures and Yoshimoto[19] found no parallelism between the number of nuclei and the nuclein content. The purines present in tumor tissues are quite the same in nature and proportion as in normal tissues (Wells and Long), as also are the nucleoproteins.

Bergell and Dörpinghaus[20] have studied the nature of the proteins

[12] Norris, Biochem. Jour., 1914 (8), 253.
[13] Yamagiwa, Mitt. Med. Gesellsch., Tokio, 1916 (30), 1.
[14] A theory of cell division in cancer as a result of electric forces is given by Jessup *et al.*, Biochem. Jour., 1909 (4), 191.
[15] Hofmeister's Beitr., 1903 (4), 368.
[16] Amer. Jour. Physiol., 1905 (13), 341.
[16a] Petrey, Zeit. physiol. Chem., 1899 (27), 398.
[17] Zeit. f. Krebsfrsch., 1913 (12), 598.
[18] Arch. Ital. Biol., 1908 (49), 380.
[19] Biochem. Zeit., 1909 (22), 299.
[20] Deut. med. Woch., 1905 (31), 1426.

in tumors by determining the proportion of the various amino-acids that compose them. Because of the amount of material necessary for the ester method, they were obliged to use a mixture of various primary and secondary cancers and one sarcoma. The protein of this tumor-mixture was characterized by the very high proportion of alanine, glutaminic acid, phenylalanine and aspartic acid, there being from 5 to 10 per cent. of each. Leucine was very low, 5–10 per cent., as against 20 per cent., or higher, found in most normal tissues. Glycine and tyrosine were present in small quantities, and serine was probably also present. Neuberg[21] found in cancer protein 1.3 per cent. of tyrosine, 17 per cent. of leucine, scarcely 1 per cent. of glutaminic acid, and 4.92 per cent. of glycine. In five human tumors of different sorts, Kocher[22] found high figures for diamino-nitrogen; his averages were: arginine, 12.42; histidine, 4.86; lysine, 11.23; total, 28.47 per cent. of the protein nitrogen. Drummond's[23] careful studies in this field have shown that the diamino-acid content of tumors is generally slightly higher than in corresponding normal tissues, probably varying directly with the amount of nuclear material, there being nothing found to indicate that the hexone bases are in any way responsible for increased growth. Strange, and as yet unexplained, variations in tryptophane content in various tumors were found by Fasal,[24] some having a very high tryptophane figure, while in others none could be found. Centanni[25] found that tryptophane and tyrosine inhibit, while skatole and indole stimulate carcinoma growth.

Certain authors have believed that the cancer cell has a specific chemistry,[26] but most of these analyses, including that of Abderhalden and Medigreceanu,[27] seem to indicate that cancer proteins have much the same composition as normal proteins. Cramer and Pringle[28] find that there is less nitrogen in mouse cancers than in equal amounts of other mouse tissue, the decrease being in the coagulable nitrogen, incoagulable nitrogen being relatively increased; a given amount of nitrogen produces more cancerous than normal tissue. The water content of rapidly growing tissues, whether normal or cancerous, was found to be high. This corresponds with the analysis of Robin,[29] who found the water content high and nitrogen low in carcinomas of the liver, sulphur being especially low, and Chisholm[30] has found the proportion of nitrogen in several human tumors lower than in the soma-

[21] Arb. a. d. Path. Inst. zu Berlin, 1906, p. 593.
[22] Jour. Biol. Chem., 1915 (22), 295.
[23] Biochem. Jour., 1916 (10), 473.
[24] Biochem. Zeit., 1913 (55), 88.
[25] Tumori, 1913 (2), 466.
[26] Blumenthal, Zeit. Krebsforsch., 1907 (5), 183.
[27] Zeit. physiol. Chem., 1910 (69), 66.
[28] Proc. Royal Soc., B., 1910 (82), 315; Jour. Physiol., 1916 (50), 322.
[29] Cent. Phys. Path. Stoffwechs., 1911 (6), 577. Bull. Acad. Méd., 1919 (81), 799; Compt. Rend. Acad. Sci., 1919 (168), 1071.
[30] Jour. Pathol. and Bact., 1913 (17), 606.

tic tissue. However, the lack of any marked specific individuality of cancer proteins when tested by immunological reactions, indicates a very close chemical agreement with normal tissue proteins.

On account of the amount of autolysis going on in tumors the products of protein splitting are usually present. Beebe[31] found in a number of tumors leucine, tyrosine, tryptophane, proteoses (biuret reaction), and in one glycine. Drummond[32] has found leucine, tyrosine and creatinine commonly present in water extracts of malignant tumors. Because of the deficient circulation in the tumors, the amino-acids accumulate in the cancer tissues in sufficient amounts to be detected, and may be found even when no macroscopic evidences of degeneration are present. Possibly on account of this poor absorption no proteoses, peptones, or amino-acids could be found in the urine of cancer patients by Wolff;[33] but Ury and Lilienthal[34] found a positive reaction for albumose in the urine in about two-thirds of all carcinoma cases examined by them; however, it may be absent even in advanced stages. Lactic acid is also present in tumors, according to Fulci[35] and Saiki,[36] the latter finding 0.48 gm. of lactic acid per 100 gms. cancer of the stomach. According to Clowes[37] cancer tissues are much more permeable to ions than are normal tissues.

(2) **Other Organic Constituents.**—These, in general, resemble the organic constituents of the tissue from which the tumor arises, for a structural resemblance to the parent tissue always exists, and as structural features depend largely on the proportion of the chemical components, a structural similarity fairly implies a chemical similarity. For example, adrenal and renal tissue contain much lecithin and cholesterol, and hypernephromas show a similar composition; the fat of a lipoma is, in its qualitative features, almost identical with the normal fat of the same individual; tumor melanin shows no characteristic chemical distinction from normal melanin, etc.

Glycogen has been particularly studied in tumors, especially because of the erroneous idea advanced by Brault that the quantity of glycogen is in direct proportion to the malignancy. From a summary of all the evidence, it seems that two chief factors determine the presence and amount of glycogen in tumors. One is the embryonic origin of the tumors; thus tumors of cartilage, striated muscle, or of squamous epithelium, which tissues normally contain much glycogen, are likewise provided with an abundance of this material. Second, the occurrence of areas of impaired cell-nutrition favors the accumulation of glycogen in the degenerating tumor-cells just as it leads to

---

[31] Amer. Jour. Physiol., 1904 (11), 139.
[32] Biochem. Jour., 1917 (11), 246.
[33] Zeit. f. Krebsforschung, 1905 (3), 95.
[34] Arch. f. Verdauungskr., 1905 (11), 72.
[35] Gaz. internaz. di med., 1910, No. 24.
[36] Arch. méd. expér., 1911 (23), 376.
[37] Proc. Soc. Exp. Biol. Med., 1918 (15), 107.

a similar accumulation in all other tissues (Gierke).[37a] The most extensive consideration of this topic is reported by Lubarsch,[38] who found glycogen microscopically in 447 (or 29 per cent.) of 1544 tumors examined. It was present in but 3 out of 184 fibromas, osteomas, gliomas, hemangiomas, lipomas, and lymphangiomas, and in but 2 out of 260 adenomas from various parts of the body. It occurred in all teratomas, rhabdomyomas, hypernephromas, and syncytiomas. In 138 sarcomas glycogen was present in 70 (50.7 per cent.); of 415 carcinomas it was found in 181 (43.6 per cent.). In the squamous epithelial cancers 70 per cent. contained glycogen, while the mucoid or colloid cancers were always free from glycogen. The glycogen undoubtedly enters the cells from without, probably entering as sugar, and being converted into glycogen by intracellular enzymes. We have no reliable studies of the actual quantity of glycogen in various tumors, although Meillère[39] states that the microscopic and chemical examination of tumors give corresponding comparative results, which Gierke states is generally true with glycogen estimations.

Pentoses.—Neuberg[40] reports finding, as a product of autolysis of a carcinoma of the liver, a pentose which was not produced by autolysis of either normal liver tissue or the primary growth in the stomach. Beebe[41] found that in carcinoma of the mammary gland the percentage of pentose (*xylose*) is somewhat higher than the amount in normal mammary glands (about 0.23 per cent.). Carcinoma in the liver did not show any constant excess of pentose above that of normal liver tissue (about 0.38 per cent.). A primary carcinoma of the liver showed quite the same pentose and phosphorus content as normal liver tissue. In general, no constant relation of pentose to origin, malignancy, or degeneration of tumors was observed.

Purines and Purine Enzymes.—The purines of both benign and malignant tumors have been studied by Wells and Long,[42] who found them the same as those in normal tissues, and in much the same relative proportions. The proportion of the total nitrogen of tumors which is constituted by the purine nitrogen is less than would be expected from the histological evidence of the amount of nuclear material contained in the tumors. Tumors also seem to contain much the same purine enzymes as the normal tissues. Thus, guanase seems universally present in tumors derived from human tissues, and adenase is missing, although autolyzing tumors can disintegrate their nucleic acid (nuclease) and change the adenine radicals of the nucleic acid into hypoxanthine, presumably by way of adenosine and inosine (Amberg and Jones). Secondary tumors growing in the human liver do

[37a] Ziegler's Beitr., 1905 (37), 502.
[38] Virchow's Arch., 1906 (183), 188.
[39] Compt. Rend. Soc. Biol., 1900 (52), 324.
[40] Berl. klin. Woch., 1904 (41), 1081; 1905 (42), 118.
[41] Amer. Jour. Physiol., 1905 (14), 231.
[42] Zeit. f. Krebsforsch., 1913 (12), 598.

not acquire the enzyme, xanthine-oxidase, which is a characteristic enzyme of this organ. The liver tissue between the cancer nodules seems to oxidize purines less actively then normal liver tissue. Long[43] has also found similar conditions in tumors from sheep, pigs and cattle, observing that primary carcinoma of the liver does not contain xanthine oxidase, a point of interest in view of the fact that in the development of mammals the xanthine oxidase does not appear until late. Water extracts from various tumors have been found to contain small amounts of free purines, chiefly adenine, guanine and hypoxanthine (Drummond).[32]

Lipins.—Tumor cells seem to contain much the same fats and lipoids as normal cells, and, as far as known, in much the same proportions as characterize the cells from which the tumors arose. Thus Wells[44] found that hypernephromas show the same high proportions of lecithin and cholesterol as he found in normal adrenal, and as are found in the renal cortex. Other malignant tumors have much less lipoids and fats(see Hypernephromas). A secondary carcinoma of liver cells, metastatic in the skull, was found by Prym[45] to show the same sort of fatty infiltration that is characteristic of fatty liver cells. On account of the poor blood supply of many tumors, fatty changes are usual, occurring under the same conditions and showing the same microscopic features as fatty degeneration in other tissues,[46] being more common in malignant than in benign tumors; especially abundant in squamous cell carcinomas, and scanty in sarcomas. Crystals of cholesterol or cholesterol compounds are described in tumors by White.[47] Dewey[48] found the chief lipoid in jaw tumors to be cholesterol, with more or less free fatty acids and soaps, according to microchemical determinations. Even lipoma fat shows no difference from normal fat,[49] and the depot fat of tumor patients is quite the same as in patients with other diseases associated with equal wasting,[50] in whom some increase in unsaponifiable material (cholesterol) is usual. Murray[51] says that the lipoids of degenerating uterine fibroids are strongly hemolytic, which may account for the so-called "red degeneration" of these tumors. Freund and Kaminer[52] suggest that the fatty acids of tissues are of importance in determining whether a tissue is a suitable soil for secondary growth, these substances being deficient in tissues where growths develop. Mitochondria, which seem to be closely related to the intracellular lipins, show no constant differences

[43] Jour. Exper. Med., 1913 (18), 512.
[44] Jour. Med. Res., 1908 (17), 461.
[45] Frankf. Zeit. Path., 1912 (10), 170.
[46] See Haga, Berl. klin. Woch., 1912 (49), 342; Joannovics, Wien. klin. Woch. 1912 (25), 37.
[47] Jour. Path. and Bact., 1908 (13), 3.
[48] Jour. Cancer Res., 1919 (4), 263.
[49] See Wells, Arch. Int. Med., 1912 (10), 297.
[50] Wacker, Zeit. physiol. Chem., 1912 (78), 349; 1912 (80), 383.
[51] Jour. Obst. Gyn. Brit. Emp., 1910 (17), 534.
[52] Wien. klin. Woch., 1912 (25), 1698.

in cancer, benign tumors and normal cells, except that sometimes in cancer they fix stains less firmly (Goodpasture).[53]

There has been some effort to correlate the cholesterol and lecithin contents of blood and tissues with the rate of cancer growth; apparently lecithin inhibits growth and cholesterol stimulates.[54] However, Bullock and Cramer[55] found much more cholesterol in a slowly growing mouse carcinoma than in a rapidly growing one, somewhat more phosphatid in the latter, much more phosphatid in a sarcoma than in the carcinoma, and cerebrosides only in the latter; in necrotic portions of tumors they found an increase in simple fats. These figures are based on too few observations to be interpreted as yet.

(3) **Inorganic Constituents.**—These have been studied by Clowes and Frisbie[56] under exceptionably favorable conditions, in that the age of the tumor could be accurately estimated, in the inoculable carcinoma of mice. They found that rapidly growing tumors contain a high percentage of potassium and little or no calcium, whereas in old, slowly growing, relatively necrobiotic tumors the relation is reversed, the potassium decreasing greatly while the calcium increases. Magnesium is present only in traces, while the proportion of sodium fluctuates much less, but is usually greater than either the potassium or calcium, although in very old tumors the latter may become excessive. The most rapid growth, however, seems to occur in tumors in which both calcium and potassium are present in the ratio of

$$\frac{K}{Ca} = \frac{2}{1} \text{ or } \frac{3}{2}$$

Beebe[57] analyzed a number of human tumors with the following results: Phosphorus was found in proportion to the amount of nuclear material, varying from 0.139 per cent. (uterine fibroid) to 1.06 per cent. (sarcoma). Iron varied from 0.013 per cent. to 0.064 per cent., probably depending on the amount of blood and nucleoproteins. Calcium is most abundant in old degenerated tumors, and potassium in rapidly growing tumors. These results, supported by Clowes and Frisbie's findings, indicate the importance of potassium for cell growth. Injection of potassium salts into mice increases their susceptibility to inoculation (Clowes),[58] while calcium decreases cancer growth (Goldzieher).[59] Exposure of isolated cancer cells to calcium salts reduces their growth capacity when inoculated, apparently through reducing their water content; both effects are counteracted by sodium

[53] Jour. Med. Res., 1918 (38), 213.
[54] See Robertson and Burnett, Jour. Exp. Med., 1913 (17), 344; 1916 (23), 631; Sweet et al., Jour. Biol. Chem., 1915 (21,, 309; Luden, Jour. Lab. Clin. Med., vols. 3 and 4.
[55] Proc. Royal Soc. London (B), 1914 (87), 236.
[56] Amer. Jour. Physiol., 1905 (14), 173.
[57] Amer. Jour. Physiol., 1904 (12), 167.
[58] British Med. Jour., Dec. 1, 1906.
[59] Verhandl. Deut. Path. Gesellsch., 1912 (15), 283.

(Cramer).[60] A greater proportion of potassium was found in primary than in secondary growths by Mottram;[61] sodium was the same in each; there is more potassium in squamous cell carcinoma than in round cell sarcoma. Robin[62] states that in cancerous livers the cancer tissues contains more inorganic matter than the normal liver tissue about it. Cattley[63] found the microchemic distribution of potassium the same in cancer as in normal cells, and the same seems to be true of manganese.[64]

Schwalbe[65] found that cancer-cells contain iron in a condition demonstrable by the Berlin-blue reaction, and occurring independent of hemorrhages. Tracy[66] found that tumors reacted microscopically for iron, either free or in the form of an albuminate, only in areas where hemorrhages had occurred. Nuclear or organic iron could be detected in the nuclei, occurring in a network arrangement. In other words, iron occurs in tumors, both quantitatively and qualitatively, exactly as in normal cells of the same type. The same writer[67] found in tumors by microchemical reactions, that phosphorus in the form of nucleoproteins likewise shows no essential differences from its distribution in normal tissues.

In this connection may be mentioned the observations of Hemmeter,[68] who found that the cells of carcinoma of the mammary gland will shrink when placed in physiological salt solution or in the serum of the patient, whereas normal cells swell when placed in cancer-juice. This suggests that the osmotic pressure, and, by inference, the amount of inorganic constituents, is lower than in normal tissues. Crystalloids, such as KI, diffuse readily into cancer tissue.[69]

(4) **Enzymes.**—The rapid and extensive autolysis that occurs in tumors, as shown both morphologically and by the presence of the products of protein cleavage in them, indicates that tumor cells resemble all other cells in possessing intracellular proteolytic enzymes. Because of autolysis, puncture fluids in cancer of serous surfaces show an increased amount of incoagulable nitrogen (Morris),[70] and they may show free amino-acids (Wiener),[71] while there is a slight increase in the incoagulable nitrogen of the blood (Takemura).[72]

There is considerable but not undisputed evidence that cancer tis-

[60] Biochem. Jour. 1918 (12), 210.
[61] Arch. Middlesex Hospital, 1910 (19), 40.
[62] Compt. Rend. Acad. Sci., 1913 (156), 334.
[63] Lancet, 1907 (172), 13.
[64] Medigreceanu, Proc. Royal Soc., B, 1912 (86), 174.
[65] Cent. f. Path., 1901 (12), 874.
[66] Jour. Med. Research, 1905 (14), 1.
[67] Martha Tracy, Jour. Med. Research, 1906 (14), 447.
[68] Amer. Jour. Med. Sci., 1903 (125), 680.
[69] Van den Velden, Biochem. Zeit., 1908 (9), 54; see also Wells and Hedenburg, Jour. Infect. Dis., 1912 (11), 349.
[70] Arch. Int. Med., 1911 (8), 457.
[71] Biochem. Zeit., 1912 (41), 149.
[72] *Ibid.*, 1910 (25), 505.

sue autolyzes somewhat more rapidly than corresponding normal tissues,[73] and, according to Neuberg, Blumenthal and others,[74] that cancer extracts digest other tissues than themselves (heterolysis), a property not exhibited by extracts of normal tissues. Müller and others would ascribe this heterolysis to the leucocytes present in the tumors. Nucleases have been found in tumors as in other tissues,[75] and in general the enzymes which deamidize adenine and guanine (adenase and guanase) are usually present if the original tissue possessed these enzymes but no instance of the presence of xanthine oxidase or uricolytic enzyme has been obtained (Wells and Long, *loc cit.*[42]).

Hamburger finds that the enzymes of cancer tissue upon which the glycyl-tryptophane and other enzyme tests for cancer are based, are ereptases, resembling in all their properties the ereptases of normal tissues, and not present in particularly large amount. However, Abderhalden[76] has found evidence that certain peptids may be split in a different way by cancer than by normal tissues, supporting those who hold that cancer enzymes are different from normal tissue enzymes. Autolysis of tumors is said to be augmented by x-ray, and especially by radium (Neuberg), and tumor tissue is readily digested by trypsin.

The presence of ereptases in carcinomatous gastric juice has been especially studied because of its diagnostic possibilities, and the careful investigation of Jacques and Woodyatt[77] seems to show conclusively that such an enzyme is rarely present in gastric juice except when derived from a cancer present in the wall of the stomach, provided peptolytic bacteria are excluded by filtration. Deaminizing enzymes may also be found in gastric cancer secretions.[78] In the blood of cancer patients there is usually an increased antitryptic activity, ascribable to the reaction against enzymes absorbed from the cancer; it is less pronounced with sarcoma.[79] The body tissues of patients dying with cancer show a low ereptic activity, but the same occurs in persons dying from other wasting diseases (Colwell).[80] This is also true of other tissue enzymes;—at least purine oxidizing enzymes are deficient in the liver tissue between secondary cancers (Wells and Long[42]) and the catalase is also reduced in liver tumors (Blumenthal and Brahn)[81] and in the blood of tumor mice (Rosenthal);[82] in human blood the catalase may vary either side of normal.[83] Brahn[84] reports

[73] See Yoshimoto, Biochem. Zeit., 1909 (22), 299; Daels and Delenzé, Bull. Acad. Med. Belg., 1913 (26), 833.
[74] Bibliography by Hamburger, Jour. Amer. Med. Assoc., 1912 (59), 847.
[75] Goodman, Jour. Exp. Med., 1912 (15), 477.
[76] Zeit. Krebsforsch., 1910 (9), 266.
[77] Arch. Int. Med., 1912 (10), 560.
[78] Halpern, Mitt. Grenz. Med. Chir., 1915 (28), 709.
[79] Citronblatt, Med. Klin., 1912 (8), 138.
[80] Arch. Middlesex Hosp., 1909 (15), 96.
[81] Zeit. f. Krebsforsch., 1910 (8), 436. See also Weidenfeld, Wien. klin. Woch., 1918 (31), 324.
[82] Deut. med. Woch., 1912 (38), 2270.
[83] Rohdenburg, N. Y. Med. Jour., 1913 (97), 824.
[84] Zeit. Krebsforsch., 1917 (16), 112.

that the liver tissue between secondary cancer nodules, and also the liver in cases of cancer in the portal area, shows diminished catalase, lipase and lecithinase function, with increased autolysis, but these changes are not observed in the livers when the cancer is in other parts of the body. However, choline has been found in necrotic sarcomas of rats,[85] which would seem to indicate the presence of enzymes disintegrating lecithin. As mentioned elsewhere (See Melanin), melanotic tumors may contain enzymes oxidizing tyrosine, epinephrine, pyrocatechin, or other related aromatic substances, with the formation of pigmentary substances. (See also, Autolysis in Tumors, chap. iii.)

Other enzymes are also present in tumor cells. Buxton[86] examined a large number of tumors for their enzymes by the plate (*auxanographic*) method, and found considerable variations in different growths. All contained amylase (splitting starch) and lipase (splitting butyrin). Most, but not all, tumors coagulated milk and liquefied casein, and also liquefied gelatin (rennin, proteases). Peroxidase was nearly always, and catalase always, present. Digestion of fibrin, coagulated serum, and coagulated egg albumen could not be observed. Practically all tumors split glycogen. Tyrosinase could not be demonstrated. The fact that early embryonic tissues were found poor in enzymes[87] speaks against the common assumption that tumors represent strictly an embryonic formation, but Long[88] found that xanthineoxidase, which in normal development does not appear until late in fetal life, was absent from primary carcinomas of sheep livers, although normal adult sheep liver tissue is rich in this enzyme.

MacFadyen and Harden[89] studied the juices obtained by grinding up tumor cells made brittle by liquid air, and found by direct methods (chiefly in breast cancers) invertase, maltase, amylase, proteases acting in both acid and alkaline solutions, catalase, oxidase, with perhaps traces of lipase and peroxidase, but no lactase.

Tumors arising from the gastric mucosa, according to Waring,[90] contain both pepsin and rennin; those from the pancreas, both primary and secondary growths, contain trypsin, steapsin, amylase, and rennin.

(5) **Internal Secretion.**—If tumors are derived from an organ with an important internal secretion, the tumor cells in many cases produce the same internal secretion, which seems to have the same functional properties as the normally produced secretion. Thus a metastatic growth from a thyroid tumor has been said to functionate in place of the resected gland; Gierke[91] found in about 20 grams of

[85] Ellinger, Münch. med. Woch., 1914 (61), 2336.
[86] Jour. Med. Research, 1903 (9), 356.
[87] *Ibid.*, 1905 (13), 543.
[88] Jour. Exper. Med., 1913 (18), 512.
[89] Lancet, 1903 (ii), 224.
[90] Jour. Anat. and Physiol., 1894 (28), 142.
[91] Hofmeister's Beitr., 1902 (3), 286.

material from metastatic thyroid tissue in the vertebral column about 5 mg. of iodin, which was a trifle larger proportion than was present in the thyroid itself.   Carlson and Woelfel[92] found much iodin in the metastases of a thyroid carcinoma of a dog, while in another dog whose cancerous thyroid contained no iodin the secondary tumors were also devoid of this element.   I have also analyzed metastases from a carcinoma of the thyroid which contained no demonstrable iodin, despite the presence of colloid.   Marine and Johnson[93] found that in two cases of cancer of the thyroid in man, and one in the dog, the cancer tissue showed no ability to retain iodin given by mouth, in contrast to normal thyroid and simple adenomas.   Meyer-Hürlimann and Oswald[94] have described a remarkable case of cystic carcinoma of the thyroid, from which in six weeks 2840 c.c. of secretion was obtained by puncture.   It contained 0.077 mg. iodin per 10 c.c. (the patient having previously been given KI) as compared with normal thyroid which contains 0.4 to 4 mg. per 10 gm.   It contained both globulin and albumin, the former corresponding to true thyroglobulin, even to increasing vagus irritability experimentally.   The "adenomatous" nodules of the thyroid often show evidence of active secretion, Goetsch[95] having found their cells rich in mitochondria, while Graham[96] found that they take up iodin and metabolize it so that the adenomatous tissue produces the typical thyroid effect on the development of tadpoles.   Adrenal cancers do not usually cause Addison's disease, perhaps because they functionate in the place of the destroyed gland (Lubarsch).

In the characteristic production of cachexia, often apparently out of all proportion to the amount of tumor tissue, there would seem to be evidence that a peculiar and abnormal product of metabolism is formed by cancer-cells, and extracts from cancers have been found toxic for protozoa.[97]   As yet, however, it has been impossible to demonstrate any characteristic toxic substance in cancers.[98]   Girard-Mangin[99] claims that malignant tumors contain colloidal poisonous substances in proportion to their softness, extracts causing paralysis and fall of blood pressure; but others have failed to substantiate this.[1]   Because of the constant disintegration of the tumor tissues, products of autolysis are formed, and undoubtedly enter the circulation in small quantities; possibly they are a factor in the systemic manifestations of malignant growths, analogous to the action of cleavage

[92] Amer. Jour. Physiol., 1910 (26), 32.
[93] Arch. Int. Med., 1913 (11), 288.
[94] Korr.-Bl. Schweizer Aerzte, 1913 (43), 1468.
[95] Bull. Johns Hopkins Hosp., 1916 (27), 129.
[96] Jour. Exp. Med., 1916 (24), 345.
[97] Woodruff and Underhill, Jour. Biol. Chem., 1913 (15), 401; Calkins, Jour. Cancer Res., 1916 (1), 205 and 399.
[98] See Blumenthal, Festschr. f. Salkowski, Berlin, 1904; Hansemann, Zeit. Krebsforsch., 1906 (4), 565.
[99] Presse Méd., 1906, p. 1739; Compt. Rend. Soc. Biol., 1909 (67), 117.
[1] See Bruschettini and Barlocco, Cent. f. Bakt., 1907 (43), 664.

products of foreign proteins which may produce "protein fever" and other toxic effects. It has often been observed that when extensive necrosis is produced in experimental tumors in rats and mice the animals may show profound toxemia, presumably because of absorption of autolytic products.

Since all normal tissue-cells produce substances through their metabolism that enter the circulation, it is quite certain that tumor-cells do likewise, and it is highly probable that the presence of abnormal quantities of such products, even if they are of quite normal composition, may cause disturbances in the body. As yet, however, no such substances, either normal or abnormal, have been isolated, nor has their presence been demonstrated. Numerous isolated observations of ptomaïns or similar substances in the urine of cancer patients may be found in the literature,[2] but their importance is extremely questionable. A large proportion of cases of malignant tumors exhibit renal injury (Kast and Killian)[3] but whether from products of the tumor or from bacterial infection has not been determined.

Hemolytic Substances.—A number of observers have described the finding of hemolytic substances in cancer extracts. Bard[4] observed that in hemorrhagic carcinomatous exudates in serous cavities the blood is rapidly hemolyzed, which is not the case in exudates from other causes, but this was not corroborated by Weil.[5] Kullmann[2] found that extracts of carcinomas contain hemolytic substances acting energetically both in the body and *in vitro*; these are soluble in alcohol and in water, are not complex in composition, are not specific for human corpuscles, but are toxic for all varieties of corpuscles. Micheli and Donati[6] likewise found hemolytic substances in 8 of 15 tumors, of which 5 acted on all varieties of corpuscles, and 3 acted on only certain varieties; they regard the hemolytic substances as the products of autolysis in the tumors. Weil[7] also found the hemolytic property of tumor extracts to vary with the amount of necrosis, and to depend on dialyzable hemolytic substances distinct from the hemolysins of normal tissues. It is well known that among the products of autolysis of normal tissues are hemolytic substances. Whether the severe anemia frequently present in carcinoma is due, either largely or in part, to these products of autolysis is unknown, but it is very probable that they have some effect.

Hemolysis in Cancer.—The blood serum of cancer patients has often a hemolytic action on the corpuscles of normal persons (Crile), but this property is quite inconstant, being present in 67 per cent. of a series of 472 cancer cases collected by Krida, while 15 per cent. of

[2] See Kullmann, Zeit. klin. Med., 1904 (53), 293.
[3] Proc. Soc. Exp. Biol. Med., 1919 (16), 141.
[4] La Semaine Méd., 1901 (21), 201.
[5] Jour. Med. Res., 1910 (23), 86.
[6] Riforma Med., 1903 (19), 1037.
[7] Jour. Med. Res., 1907 (16), 287.

cases of other diseases and 2.6 per cent. of normal persons showed hemolytic activity of the serum.[8] Elsberg found that normal corpuscles injected subcutaneously into cancer patients are hemolyzed, but Gorham and Lisser found this reaction positive in but 60 per cent. of their cases, the subcutaneous hemolysis not corresponding at all to the hemolytic activity of the patient's serum in the test tube. The stomach contents in cancer of the stomach, when ulcerated, are hemolytic (Grafe and Röhmer).[9] The red corpuscles of cancer patients are said to have usually a greater resistance to hemolysis by cobra venom than normal corpuscles, but this is not characteristic, there being similar alterations in other diseases.[10] The reputed power of the serum in cancer to protect corpuscles from hemolysis by oleic and lactic acid could not be demonstrated by Sweek and Fleisher.[11]

An extensive review of the literature and methods led Cohnreich[12] to the conclusion that resistance of erythrocytes to hypotonic solutions and to poisons vary independently of one another. He has devised an improved method for testing resistance to hypotonic solutions, which seems to vary directly with the amount of stroma and PO_4 content, and finds that determinations of maximum and minimum resistance are of little value, as these concern only a small part of the corpuscles; he therefore determines the "plurimum" resistance, involving most of the corpuscles. The most significant results were obtained in cancer of the alimentary tract, in which an increased resistance was always demonstrable. Farmachidis[13] finds the cobra venom resistance more specific for cancer than do most other investigators.

(6) **Metabolism in Cancer.**—There are numerous observations indicating that cancer cachexia is in no way different from the cachexia of other conditions. The behavior of the nitrogen metabolism seems to be quite the same as in tuberculosis and other wasting diseases. There is the same excessive elimination of aromatic substances (phenol,[14] indican) and oxyacids (Lewin,[15] Blumenthal[16]), which Lewin considers to arise from the abnormal metabolism of proteins, and not from putrefactive decomposition in the tumor or in the intestines. In rats with sarcoma, increased excretion of uric acid and creatin has been observed.[17] There is also the same excessive elimination of mineral salts that is observed in pulmonary tuberculosis, and termed "demin-

---

[8] Literature by Gorham and Lisser, Amer. Jour. Med. Sci., 1912 (144), 103.
[9] Deut. Arch. klin. Med., 1908 (94), 239.
[10] Kraus, Ranzi and H. Ehrlich, Sitz. Ber. Akad. Wien., 1910 (119), 3; see also Grünbaum, Jour. Path. and Bact., 1912 (17), 82.
[11] Jour. Med. Res., 1913 (27), 383.
[12] Folia Hematol., 1913 (16), 307, full bibliography.
[13] Gaz. degli Osped., 1915 (36), 689.
[14] Somewhat higher than average figures for phenol in the blood were found in sarcoma cases by Theis and Benedict (Jour. Biol. Chem., 1918 (36), 99).
[15] Deut. med. Woch., 1905 (31), 218.
[16] Festschr. f. Salkowski, Berlin, 1904.
[17] Ordway, Jour. Med. Res., 1913 (23), 301.

eralization" by Robin,[18] but no alteration in the excretion of chlorides.[19] As in other cachexias, the creatin content of the muscles is decreased.[20] Fraenkel[21] finds evidence that there may be some difficulty in tryptophane metabolism in tumors and in tumor patients, especially marked with melanotic tumors. Extensive respiratory studies by Wallersteiner[22] showed enormous variations in the amount of heat production in different cases, in about 10 per cent. of which figures as high as those of severe fevers or exophthalmic goiter were obtained repeatedly; most of the cases showed high normal figures. Nitrogen loss did not ordinarily occur if the calorimetric findings were considered in the calculations; nitrogen equilibrium was maintained if sufficient nourishment was obtained and utilized. In general, metabolism in cancer resembles that of fever, and warrants the assumption of a toxic stimulation of tissue destruction. It is entirely possible that the products of cancer protein destruction are responsible for this toxicogenic metabolic abnormality, since Vaughan has demonstrated that the effects of bacteria and foreign proteins are quite the same in their pyretic and toxic action.

Salkowski demonstrated that the amount of colloidal nitrogenous material, precipitated from the urine by strong alcohol, is increased in cancer. Numerous observers have corroborated this, but find that a similar condition obtains in other cachectic diseases, although in cancer the amount of colloidal nitrogen seldom is as low as normal unless the tumor is removed.[23] Much of this colloidal nitrogen seems to be in the form of "oxy-proteic acid" (Salomen and Saxl),[24] which is a mixture of incompletely oxidized polypeptids, containing much unoxidized sulphur.[25] The proportion of neutral sulphur in the total sulphur in the urine seems to be increased in cancer (Weiss), but not so constantly or characteristically as to be of great diagnostic value.[26] Much clinical investigation has been made of these urinary changes, which has generally substantiated the fact that there usually is more increase in colloidal nitrogen and ethereal sulphate in the urine of cancer than in other diseases, but that in no sense are these changes specific for cancer, and the fundamental metabolic disturbances responsible have

[18] Quoted by Lewin, *loc. cit.*[15] Clowes *et al.* (5th Ann. Rep., N. Y. State Dept. of Health, 1903–4) report observing a slight chloride retention in cancer patients, and review the literature of metabolism in cancer.

[19] Robin, Compt. Rend. Acad. Sci., 1913 (156), 1262.

[20] Chisholm, Biochem. Jour., 1912 (6), 243.

[21] Wien. klin. Woch., 1912 (25), 1041.

[22] Deut. Arch. klin. Med., 1914 (116), 145.

[23] See Mancini, Deut. Arch. klin. Med., 1911 (103), 288; Semenow, Folia Urol., 1912 (7), 215; de Bloeme *et al.*, Biochem. Zeit., 1914 (65), 345.

[24] Wien. klin. Woch., 1911 (24), 449.

[25] Killian reports finding in the blood two to three times the normal amount of nonprotein sulphur while the total sulphates remain normal. ("Cancer: Its Nature, Causes, Diagnosis and Treatment." By R. H. Greene, New York, 1918.)

[26] Stadtmüller and Rosenbloom, Arch. Int. Med., 1913 (12), 276; Interstate Med. Jour., 1916 (23), No. 2; bibliography. Kahn, Jour. Cancer Res., 1917 (2), 379.

not been ascertained.[27]   They seem more indicative of the excessive catabolism of cachexia than of cancer tissue itself.   Saxl[28] has ascribed part of the increased sulphur elimination to abnormal excretion of sulphocyanid, and as small doses of sulphocyanides lead to increased oxyproteic acid in the urine he suggests that in cancer there is a specific disturbance in sulphocyanid metabolism, an hypothesis that awaits confirmation.   Of similar status is the excessive excretion of glycuronic acid described by Roger.[29]

Israel, and also Engelmann, have reported the occurrence of a marked increase in the lowering of the freezing-point of the blood in carcinoma (as low as −0.60° to −0.63°, the normal being −0.56°), which they attributed to the presence of excessive products of protein decomposition in the blood.   Engel,[30] however, found no such increased lowering of the freezing-point in his cases, and questions the significance of the results of Israel and Engelmann.   There may be a dietary increase in the blood sugar in cancer,[31] which rises more rapidly and remains high longer than normal.[32]   The total protein of the blood is low, with some increase in the proportion of globulin as is usual in cachexia.[33]   According to Moore and Wilson[34] the acid-neutralizing power of the blood ("alkalinity") is increased in cancer; this is probably related to if not the cause of the decreased HCl content of the gastric juice, which occurs whether the cancer is in the stomach or not. As this alkalinity is not associated with an increase in the inorganic bases of the blood, it may be that the proteins have an increased basicity.   Although numerous other observers describe a decreased alkalinity as in other cachectic conditions,[35] Menten,[36] making direct H-ion measurements, found an increase in alkalinity in the serum of nearly all cases of carcinoma and sarcoma.   The blood in cancer contains less calcium than normal which results in a tendency to osteoporosis[37] and to deposition of calcium in the kidney epithelium;[38] there is an increase in the potassium of both the blood and tissues.[39] Blood analyses in 189 cases of cancer, by Theis and Stone,[40] gave usually low figures for non-protein and urea nitrogen, but with amino-N

[27] See Goodridge and Kahn, Biochem. Bull., 1915 (4), 118; Damask, Wien. klin. Woch., 1915 (28), 499; Sassa, Biochem. Zeit., 1914 (64), 195.

[28] Biochem. Zeit., 1913 (55), 224.

[29] Bull. Soc. Med. Hôp., Paris, 1915 (31), 499.

[30] Berl. klin. Woch., 1904 (41), 828.

[31] Williams and Humphreys, Arch. Int. Med., 1919 (23), 537.

[32] Rohdenburg, Bernard and Krehbiel, Jour. Amer. Med. Assoc., 1919 (72), 1528.

[33] Loebner, Deut. Arch. klin. Med., 1918 (127), 397.

[34] Biochem. Jour., 1906 (1), 297; Watson, Jour. Path. and Bact., 1909 (13), 429; Sturrock, Brit. Med. Jour., 1913 (2), 780.

[35] See Traube, Int. Zeit. Physik.-Chem. Biol., 1914 (1), 389.

[36] Jour. Cancer Res., 1917 (2), 179.

[37] Goldzieher, Verh. Deut. Path. Ges., 1912 (15), 283.

[38] M. B. Schmidt., Verh. Deut. Path. Ges., 1913 (16), 329.

[39] Mottram, Arch. Middlesex Hosp., 1910 (19), 40.

[40] Jour. Cancer Res., 1919 (4), 349.

slightly above normal; uric acid and sugar were within normal limits. Cholesterol, fatty acids and total fats are generally increased in the blood in malignancy.[40a]

(7) **Diet and Tumor Growth.**—In general, any condition that decreases the nutrition of the body as a whole, or of the tissue in which a tumor is located, decreases the rate of growth of the tumor, in which respect neoplasms exhibit quite the opposite behavior to infectious processes. Thus, the older the individual the more slowly the tumor usually grows; ligation of the lingual artery retards the growth of cancer of the tongue; repeated pregnancy and lactation delay the progress of cancer in mice,[41] suggesting that tumor cells have a greater avidity for nutritive elements in the blood than have ordinary somatic cells, but less than the cells of the fetus or of the active mammary gland. Numerous attempts have been made to determine the relation of tumor growth to specific dietary deficiencies. Sweet, Corson-White and Saxon[42] found that rats kept upon a diet deficient in specific amino-acids (lysine), so that body growth did not occur although nutrition was maintained, show a slower growth of implanted tumors than animals on an adequate diet. Rous[43] obtained similar results with some transplanted tumors, but not with all, nor with spontaneous tumors. Van Alstyne and Beebe[44] found that rats living on casein and lard showed much less growth of inoculated tumors than when lactose was added to the diet. Robertson and Burnett[45] observed that the addition of cholesterol to the diet increases the rate of growth and the development of metastases in inoculated rat tumors, which has been corroborated by others. This accelerative action depends on the hydroxyl radical, although other hydroxy-benzol derivatives do not have this effect.[46] The growth-promoting principle of the hypophysis, tethelin, is also said to stimulate cancer growth. Funk[47] found greater growth of inoculated sarcoma in fowls given normal diets than in those fed polished rice. Benedict and Rahe[48] supplied vitamines by adding to an otherwise inadequate diet, just enough yeast to keep the rats in fair condition, and found that inoculated tumors grew, although extremely slowly, even when the animal itself could not grow. Evidently tumor cells cannot manufacture substances essential for growth *i. e.* vitamines. Corson-White[49] states that, generally, vitamine-rich diets favor tumor growth, especially if there is also an abundance of cholesterol. Fraenkel,[50] however, observed no stimulating effect from rice polishings or yeast extracts.

[40a] De Niord *et al.*, Arch. Int. Med., 1920 (25), 32.
[41] See Maud Slye, Jour. Cancer Res., 1919 (4), 25.
[42] Jour. Biol. Chem., 1913 (15), 181; 1915 (21), 311.
[43] Jour. Exp. Med., 1914 (20), 433.
[44] Jour. Med. Res., 1913 (24), 217.
[45] Jour. Exp. Med., 1913 (17), 344.
[46] Jour. Cancer Res., 1918 (3), 75.
[47] Zeit. physiol. Chem., 1913 (88), 352.
[48] Jour. Cancer Res., 1917 (2), 159.
[49] Penn. Med. Jour., 1919 (22), 348.
[50] Wien. klin. Woch., 1916 (29), 483.

(8) **Immunity Reactions in Cancer.**—The fact that a certain degree of specific immunity can be developed against normal tissue cells (see Cytotoxins, Chap. x), has encouraged study of the possibility of securing immune antibodies which might be specific for cancer, and has led to much research on this subject,[51] with results as yet of little value. There is no doubt that the body has distinct powers to inhibit to a greater or less degree the growth of tumors, and to destroy many of the cells which escape from cancers into the lymph and blood,[52] while in experimental animals inoculated tumors are in most instances unable to grow, and they may, after growth has once begun, recede or even disappear. Furthermore, animals may be made immune to tumors to which they would otherwise be susceptible. Many schemes of immunization of patients by injection of extracts or autolysates made from their own tumors, or similar tumors of others, have been tried,[53] but in the hands of competent and critical observers the results seem to have been practically negative.[54] It is not always kept in mind that inoculated cancers in rats and mice represent an artificial condition behaving very differently from spontaneous tumors.

There is no lack of evidence that cancers do produce, in greater or less amounts, various antibodies of some degree of specificity for cancer, which must be interpreted as evidence that cancer proteins are in some respects different from the normal proteins of the host; however, the amount and specificity of these antibodies seem to be low,[55] and, in many observations, they have failed to be demonstrated. Indeed, Coca in his review states unqualifiedly, "The usual biological tests of complement deviation and specific precipitation fail to show the hypothetical antibodies, though a distinct cytotoxic influence can be demonstrated in the plasma of animals of foreign species that have been actively immunized against a tumor." His own experiments failed to demonstrate specific complement-fixation antibodies in patients injected with extracts of their own tumors. Lewin[56] also fails to find conclusive evidence of the demonstration of specific antibodies in cancer, yet accepts the immunity which is produced by injections of virulent cancer material as an active immunity dependent upon cancer antibodies. It may, however, depend on a stimulation of the local cellular reactions that inhibits cancer growth.[57] Pfeiffer[58] claims to find specific anaphylactic antibodies in the blood of cancer patients, but this has not been confirmed by several other observers.[59]

[51] Literature by Coca, Zeit. Immunität., 1912 (13), 525; Kraus *et al.*, Wien klin. Woch., 1911 (24), 1003.
[52] Reviewed by Wells, Jour. Amer. Med. Assoc., 1909 (52), 1731.
[53] Review by Fichera, Jour. Cancer Res., 1918 (3), 303.
[54] See Blumenthal, Zeit. Krebsforsch., 1914 (14), 491; Bauer, Latzel and Wessely, Zeit. klin. Med., 1915 (81), 420.
[55] See Morgenroth and Bieling, Biochem. Zeit., 1915 (68), 85.
[56] Folia Serologica, 1911 (7), 1013; literature.
[57] Tyzzer, Jour. Cancer. Res., 1916 (1), 125.
[58] Wien klin. Woch., 1909 (22), 989; Zeit. Immunität., 1910 (4), 455.
[59] See Weil, Jour. Exp. Med., Oct., 1913, (18), 390.

v. Dungern[60] has described positive complement fixation reactions, partially specific for cancer and benign tumors, by using alcoholic extracts of the tumors or acetone extracts of human erythrocytes as antigen, but he interprets these reactions as not due to specific antibodies, but to abnormal products of metabolism.[61] The complement content of the blood is said to be slightly increased in cancer (Engel),[62] but there is nothing characteristic about this. Ascoli and Izar[63] have applied the meiostagmin test (*q. v.*) and state that this gives very positive results in determining the existence of cancer, their work having been corroborated by many but not by all of those who have repeated it.[64] Burmeister[65] could obtain no reliable results with the epiphanin reaction.

Freund and Kaminer[66] have found that the serum of cancer patients is unable to dissolve cancer cells, as normal serum does, and even protects them against the lytic power of normal serum. The lysis is ascribed to a non-nitrogenous fatty acid, while the protective agent of cancer serum is said to be a "nucleo-globulin" which is increased in the serum in cancer. They also find that cancer extracts give a specific turbidity or precipitation with cancer serum, which is attributed to a carbohydrate content of the extract. According to Kraus and v. Graff[67] the serum of full term, pregnant women, and normal umbilical cord serum, behave like serum from cancer patients. In support of Freund and Kaminer's observation is the experiment of Neuberg[68] who found that cancer cells plus normal serum underwent digestion more rapidly than cancer cells plus cancer serum, as measured by the incoagulable nitrogen. A critical test of many recommended methods of serum diagnosis of cancer by Halpern[69] gave disappointing results. With the von Dungern technic he obtained 80 per cent. of positive results, with the meiostagmin reaction 85 per cent., but with the Abderhalden method but 30 per cent. The other methods he finds of little value. The testimony concerning the specificity of the Abderhalden reaction (*q. v.*) in cancer is so conflicting that it seems unprofitable to discuss it, the results varying from such

[60] Münch. med. Woch., 1912 (59), 65,1093 and 2854; also Rosenberg, Deut. med. Woch., 1912 (38), 1225.
[61] Farmachidis (Riforma med., 1918 (34), 382) states that only with malignant disease occurs the activation by cobra venom of the hemolytic action of the serum in the complement fixation reaction.
[62] Deut. med. Woch., 1910 (36), 986. Not corroborated by Ordway and Kellert, Jour. Med. Research, 1913 (28), 287.
[63] Münch. med. Woch., 1910 (57), 2129; Biochem. Zeit., 1910 (29), 13.
[64] See Rosenberg, Deut. med. Woch., 1913 (39), 926; Wissung, Berl. klin. Woch., 1915 (52), 998. Roffo, Revista Inst. Bact., Buenos Aires, 1917 (1), 53.
[65] See Burmeister, Jour. Inf. Dis., 1913 (12), 459; Bruggemann, Mitt. Grenz. Med. u. Chir., 1913 (25), 877.
[66] Biochem. Zeit., 1912 (46), 470; Wien. klin. Woch., 1911 (24), 1759; 1913 (26), 2108.
[67] Wien. klin. Woch., 1911 (24), 191.
[68] Biochem. Zeit., 1910 (26), 344.
[69] Mitt. Grenz. Med. Chir., 1913 (27), 370. See also Mioni, Tumóri, 1914 (3), 697.

as those cited by Halpern above, to 100 per cent. correct reactions described by others.[70] Coca[71] obtained entirely unsatisfactory results with both the von Dungern complement fixation test and the Freund-Kaminer reaction.

Many observations have been made on the antitryptic activity of the blood in cancer (see Chap. iii) which has usually shown an increase (in all but about 10 per cent. of the cases); but many other conditions, especially cachexia, may cause positive reactions. Cancer serum is said to have a lessened power to activate pancreatic lipase[72] when the disease is progressive, but on improvement or recovery this effect is increased.

B. CHEMISTRY OF CERTAIN SPECIFIC TUMORS

In the literature are to be found a few studies of chemical features of some forms of tumors, which may be briefly discussed to advantage.

(1) BENIGN TUMORS

(a) **Fibromas and Myomas.**—The few specimens studied show but a small amount of nucleoprotein, as might be expected from the small amount of their nuclear material. Because of the tendency of fibromas to undergo retrogressive changes, the amount of calcium is likely to be large. No studies as to the special features of their collagen, as compared with normal connective-tissue collagen, seem to have been made. Lubarsch[73] found no glycogen (microscopically) in any of 66 fibromas he examined. Wells and Long[74] found that in uterine fibro-myomas but one per cent. of the total nitrogen is purine nitrogen, distributed as guanine, 44 per cent.; adenine, 31 per cent.; hypoxanthine, 25 per cent. The relatively large proportion of preformed hypoxanthine corresponds with the abundance of this purine free in normal unstriated muscle. Fibromyomas are able to deamidize their guanine and adenine to xanthine and hypoxanthine, and contain guanase but not adenase. Extracts from uterine fibromyomas show practically the same composition as extracts of normal uterus.[75]

A uterine fibroid analyzed by Beebe[76] contained 14.56 per cent. of nitrogen, 0.981 per cent. of sulphur, 0.139 per cent. of phosphorus, 0.013 per cent. of iron, 0.12 per cent. of calcium oxide, 0.44 per cent. of potassium, and 1.115 per cent. of sodium. The proportions of nitrogen and sulphur are high as compared with most tumors; the phosphorus, iron, and potassium are low, corresponding to the small amount of nucleoprotein and the slow rate of growth. If degeneration

[70] See de Crinis and Mahnert, Fermentfrsch., 1918 (2), 103.
[71] Jour. Cancer Research, 1917 (2), 61.
[72] Shaw-Mackenzie, Lancet, Nov. 8, 1919.
[73] Virchow's Arch., 1906 (183), 188.
[74] Zeit. Krebsforsch., 1913 (12), 598.
[75] Winiwarter, Arch. f. Gynäk., 1913 (100), 530.
[76] Amer. Jour. Physiol., 1904 (12), 167.

is marked, the amount of calcium is greatly increased. Krawkow[77] found a trace of chondroitin-sulphuric acid in a uterine fibroid. Lubarsch found glycogen occasionally in richly cellular uterine leiomyomas, and in the vicinity of degenerating areas; however, 76 out of 85 showed no glycogen. Pfannenstiel[78] analyzed the alkaline fluid of a cystic fibromyoma, which coagulated spontaneously; it contained sugar, but no mucin or pseudomucin. The cysts were dilated lymphspaces, and the fluid corresponded to lymph in composition. A similar result was obtained by Oerum,[79] who found in the fluid serum-albumin, serum-globulin, and 0.358 per cent. of fibrin; the total proteins constituted 6.3056 per cent. Sollmann[80] found in the "colloid" of a cystic degenerated fibromyoma both pseudomucin and paramucin (see "Ovarian Cysts"), which differed somewhat from the same substances found in ovarian tumors.

The common occurrence of marked *cardiac weakness* in patients with uterine fibroids has led to the suggestion that in the fibroids some toxic product is formed which acts on the heart, or that both the fibroid and the heart defect might result from a common cause. The experimental evidence concerning the relationship is not convincing, and there is much ground for the belief that the heart suffers solely from the anemia common in these cases.[81] There is said to be a hemolytic poison, a lipoid according to Murray,[82] formed in the degenerating fibroids which causes local hemolysis and "red degeneration," and there are cases of acute aseptic degeneration of fibromyomas which seem to have caused systemic intoxication.

(b) **Myxomas.**—From a myxoma of the back Oswald[83] obtained a mucin with the following elementary composition: C, 50.82; H, 7.27; N, 12.24; S, 1.19; P, 0.25 per cent. This differs from other mammalian mucins in the presence of phosphorus, but Oswald does not consider this a contamination. It also contained 12 per cent. of carbohydrate, apparently glucosamine.

(c) **Chondromas,** like normal cartilage, always contain much glycogen (Lubarsch). Mörner[84] found chondroitin-sulphuric acid in several chondromas that he examined, although Schmiedeberg had failed to do so.

[77] Arch. exp. Path. u. Pharm., 1898 (40), 195.
[78] Arch. f. Gyn., 1890 (38), 468.
[79] Maly's Jahresber., 1884 (14), 462.
[80] Amer. Gynecol., 1903 (2), 232.
[81] See Jaschke, Mitt. Grenz. Med. u. Chir., 1912 (15), 249; McGlinn, Surg. Gyn., Obst., 1914 (18), 180.
[82] Jour. Obs. and Gyn., 1910 (17), 534.
[83] Zeit. physiol. Chem., 1914 (92), 144.
[84] Zeit. physiol. Chem., 1895 (20), 357.

(*d*) **Lipomas**[85] have been studied by Schulz[86] and by Jaeckle.[87] The former found in a retroperitoneal lipoma 75.75 per cent. of fat, 2.25 per cent. of connective tissue, and 22 per cent. of water. Of the fat, 7.31 per cent. was in the form of the free fatty acids and 92.7 per cent. as neutral fats. The fatty acids of the fat consisted of 65.57 per cent. oleic acid; 29.84 per cent. stearic acid; 4.59 per cent. palmitic acid. Cholesterol was only qualitatively demonstrable. In the connective tissue was found chondroitin-sulphuric acid. Lubarsch found glycogen in lipomas only when they were degenerated. Jaeckle observed the formation of calcium soaps in a calcifying lipoma, the calcium being distributed as follows: calcium soaps, 29.5 per cent.; calcium carbonate, 28.61 per cent.; calcium phosphate, 41.89 per cent. The fats of lipomas he found practically identical with those of the subcutaneous tissues, except sometimes for a deficiency in lecithin, as shown by the following figures:

COMPOSITION OF FATS IN—

	Subcutaneous tissue	Lipoma I	Lipoma II	Lipoma III
Refraction, at 40°..........	50.6	50.1	50.9	50.5
Saponification number.......	197.3	197.7	197.7	195.9
Reichert-Meisser number....	0.25	0.33	0.35	0.35
Iodin number..............	63.7	59.0	64.0	64.1
Olein.....................	74.1	68.6	74.4	74.5
Oleic acid.................	70.9	65.7	71.2	71.3
Acid number..............	0.39	0.31	0.48	0.67
Free acid.................	0.196	0.155	0.24	0.34
Palmitic acid..............	18.5	24.9	.....	18.5
Stearic acid...............	6.2	5.1	.....	5.9
Lecithin..................	0.084	.....	.....	0.015
Cholesterol...............	0.32	.....	0.34	

Lipomas are able to hydrolyze fats and esters, their lipase behaving in all respects like the lipase of normal areolar tissue.[88] Lipoma fat is hydrolyzed by lipase as readily as is normal human fat. No reason for the reputed unavailability of lipoma fat for the metabolism of the host could be found. It is doubtful if the fat of benign lipomas

[85] In *xanthoma tuberosum multiplex*, which shows local deposits composed largely of cholesterol esters and contains also pigment with the properties of a lipochrome, the presence of hyper-cholesterolemia is disputed. (Rosenbloom, Arch. Int. Med., 1913 (12), 395; Schmidt, Dermatol. Zeit., 1914 (21), 137).
Edsall found the composition of the fat in the fatty tumors of *adiposis dolorosa* (*Dercum's disease*) but little different from that of normal fat. (Quoted by Dercum and McCarthy, Amer. Jour. Med. Sci., 1902 (124), 994). Martelli (Tumori, 1918 (6), 1) on histological grounds states that in 2–3 per cent. of the cells the fats are mixed with fatty acids, while cholesterol, phospholipins and chromolipins are very scanty; he attributes the condition to disturbed lipogenesis from endocrin-sympathetic disfunction.
[86] Pflüger's Arch., 1893 (55), 231.
[87] Zeit. physiol. Chem., 1902 (36), 53.
[88] Wells, Arch. Int. Med., 1912 (10), 297; full review.

is entirely unavailable for metabolism, at least in all cases, but in malignant fatty tumors this seems to be true. Hirsch[89] and Wells have studied such a tumor in which, despite most complete exhaustion of the fat from the normal fat depots, about two pounds of fat and four and one-half pounds of protein were stored up in the growing tumor. This tumor was an edematous *retroperitoneal lipo-sarcoma*, weighing 69 pounds (the heaviest solid tumor on record) and its chemical composition is given below as compared with the composition of granulation tissue (castration granuloma of swine).

	Fibro lipo sarcoma, per cent.	Granuloma, per cent.
Alcohol ether residue	6.53	15.84
Alcohol ether extract	2.94	2.28
Total solids	9.47	18.12
Water	90.53	81.88
	Alcohol ether residue (per cent. of solids)	
Total protein	66.91	91.16
Protein sulphur	0.65	0.33
Protein phosphorus	0.44	0.31
Total Purine Nitrogen	0.13	0.07
	Lipins contained, per cent.	
Total nitrogen	0.17	0.09
Total sulphur	0.13	0.05
Total phosphorus	0.19	0.09

(e) **Ovarian cyst contents** have been studied more than almost any other tumor products, because in their gelatinous or slimy substance are contained numerous interesting forms of proteins, many of which are combined with carbohydrates and related to the true mucins. These substances are frequently referred to under the names of *pseudomucin, paralbumin, metalbumin,* and *ovarian "colloid,"* and belong to the class of *"mucoids."*[90] In view of the fact that the fluids in the Graafian follicles of the ovary do not contain these particular forms of protein, their presence in cysts derived from adventitious structures (Pflüger's epithelial tubes) suggests a specific form of metabolism on the part of the epithelium of these structures.

Serous cysts, formed by dilation of Graafian follicles, usually are small in size, and the contents resemble those of the normal follicles (Oerum),[91] consisting of a serous fluid with a specific gravity usually from 1.005 to 1.014 (occasionally 1.020 or more), and containing 1.0–4.0 per cent. of solids. Occasionally in these cysts the contents become solidified through absorption of the water, and a gelatinous or glue-like "colloid" content results. Mucoids are never present (Pfannenstiel).[92]

[89] Amer. Jour. Med. Sci., 1920 (159), 356.
[90] Concerning mucoids see Mann's "Chemistry of the Proteins," 1906, pp. 541–551.
[91] See Maly's Jahresbericht, 1884 (14), 459.
[92] Arch. f. Gynæk., 1890 (38), 407 (literature).

Proliferating cystomas contain the peculiar characteristic mucoid proteins mentioned above. Usually the contents are fluid, but of a peculiar slimy, stringy character, due to the mucoid substance, and often opalescent or slightly turbid. The specific gravity is generally high—1.015–1.030. The reaction is usually slightly alkaline to litmus, and neutral or slightly acid to phenolphthalein. If hemorrhage has occurred into them, the fluid is discolored, and may contain blood-pigments in crystalline and amorphous forms. Small cysts often show a condensation of the proteins into a semisolid "colloid" material, but sometimes their contents resemble those of a serous cyst. Often masses of proteins fall out of solution, forming yellowish flocculi or large deposits half filling the cysts. As with all stagnant fluids of this type, cholesterol crystals are frequently found. The characteristic proteins are members of the class of pseudomucins, which are constantly present (Oerum).

Intraligamentary papillary cysts contain a yellow, yellowish-green, or brownish-green liquid, which contains little or no pseudomucin; the specific gravity is usually high (1.032–1.036) and the fluid contains 9 to 10 per cent. of solids. The principal constituents are the simple proteins of blood serum (Hammarsten).

According to the same author, the rare *tubo-ovarian cysts* contain a watery serous fluid with no pseudomucin.

Chemistry of the Mucoids of Ovarian Cysts.—Pseudomucin has the following elementary composition: C, 49.75; H, 6.98; N, 10.28; S, 1.25; O, 31.74 per cent. (Hammarsten). In common with the true mucins it yields a sugar-like reducing body, which has been investigated by numerous chemists (Müller, Panzer, Zangerle, Leathes, Neuberg, and Heymann[93]). Panzer considers that this reducing substance is in the form of a sulphuric-acid compound, similar to, but not identical with, chondroitin-sulphuric acid. Hammarsten, however, did not find this substance constantly present. Leathes determined for the carbohydrate group the composition $C_{12}H_{23}NO_{10}$, named it *"paramucosin,"* and considers it a reduced *chondrosin* (which is the carbohydrate group of chondroitin-sulphuric acid). Neuberg and Heymann established, however, that the reducing body must come from *chitosamin* ($C_6H_{13}NO_5$), and do not consider paramucosin a constant constituent of ovarian mucoids. The amount of reducing substance varies greatly in the mucoids found in different cysts; in some the mucoid yields but about 3 to 5 per cent., in others as much as 30 to 35 per cent., of reducing substance.

Pseudomucin dissolves readily in weak alkalies, and differs from true mucin in that it is not precipitated by acetic acid, and from the simple proteins in that its solutions are not coagulated by boiling. With water a slimy, stringy, semi-solution is formed, resembling in appearance the material found in ovarian cysts. Leathes distinguishes two forms of ovarian mucoids: One, *paramucin*, occurs as a firm, jelly-like substance, which is converted by peptic digestion into easily soluble pseudomucin. Ovarian *"colloid"* probably consists of a thickened pseudomucin, often mixed with other proteins. Pfannenstiel[92] considers the *"colloid"* material as representing a modified pseudomucin, strongly alkaline and relatively insoluble, which he calls *"pseudo-mucin β."* He also describes a very soluble mucoid found only in certain ovarian cysts, naming it *"pseudo-mucin γ."*

The reason why these variations in the pseudomucins exist is not understood; they cannot be explained as due to variations in the cell type in the cyst wall, although pseudomucin is probably the result of true secretion. The smallest cavities of ovarian cystadenomas contain nearly pure pseudomucin, which presents

[93] Hofmeister's Beitr., 1902 (2), 201 (literature)

a clear, glassy structure; the larger the cysts become, and the more turbid and thinner the fluid is, the more simple are the proteins it contains. True mucin is never present in ovarian cysts. Pseudomucin occurs only in the glandular proliferating cystomas and the papillary proliferating cystadenomas, in the former appearing constantly and abundantly, in the latter not constantly and never abundantly (Pfannenstiel). *Paralbumin* (Scherer) is a mixture of pseudomucin with variable amounts of simple proteins. *Metalbumin* (Scherer) is the same body that is called pseudomucin by Hammarsten. *Paramucin* (Mitjukoff)[94] is a mucoid differing from mucin and pseudomucin in reducing Fehling's solution directly, without having the carbohydrate group first split off by boiling with an acid. Hydrolysis of paramucin by Pregl[95] showed an absence of glycine, but traces of diamino-acids, and the presence of leucine, alanine, proline, aspartic and glutamic acids, tryptophane and tyrosine.

Substances similar to pseudomucin have been occasionally found in cancerous ascitic fluid and in cystic fibromyomas (Sollmann); and they are abundant as constituents of the contents of the peritoneum in the condition known as "*pseudo-myxoma peritonei*,"[96] when the material is in reality the product of cells implanted on the peritoneal surface through the bursting of an ovarian cyst (or a cyst of the vermiform appendix (Fränkel)).[97] The physically similar substance found in pathological synovial membranes by Hammarsten differs in yielding no reducing substance. Parovarian cysts arising from the Wolffian body present an entirely different content, which is a clear, watery fluid, with specific gravity usually under 1.010; the solids amount to but 1 or 2 per cent., and consist chiefly of salts (the ash being often over 80 per cent.), mostly sulphates and chlorides. They are usually (or always) free from pseudomucin, mucin, or other sugar-containing substances, and other proteins occur only in small amounts, unless the cyst is inflamed. Apparently mucoids do not form in cysts lined by ciliated epithelium (Pfannenstiel).

Santi[98] has studied the physical chemistry of ovarian cysts, and finds the freezing point very near that of blood, having no relation to density, viscosity or nitrogen content; the specific electrical conductivity is higher than that of blood serum. The physicochemical properties are less dependent upon chlorides, and more on other substances (Gruner).[99]

(*f*) **Dermoid cysts** of the ovary contain, as their chief and most characteristic constituent, a yellow fat, which melts at 34°–39° and solidifies at 20°–25°. Ludwig and Zeynek[1] have examined over sixty such tumors, and found that the fatty material constantly contains two chief constituents: one, crystallizing out readily, they believed to be *cetyl alcohol*,

$$(CH_3 - (CH_2)_{14} - CH_2OH);$$

the other, remaining as an oily fluid, seems to be closely related to cholesterol, although not consisting of one substance alone. Small quantities of *arachidic acid* ($C_{20}, H_{40}O_2$), as well as *stearic, palmitic* and *myristic acid* ($C_{14}H_{28}O_2$), existing as glycerides, are also present. Ameseder,[2] however, found evidence that the supposed cetyl alcohol is really eikosyl alcohol ($C_{20}H_{42}O$). These substances are secreted by the glands of the cutaneous structures of the cyst, and re-

---

[94] Arch. f. Gynæk., 1895 (49), 278.
[95] Zeit. physiol. Chem., 1908 (58), 229.
[96] Literature by Peters, Monatschr. f. Geb. u. Gyn., 1899 (10), 749; Weber, St. Petersb. med. Woch., 1901 (26), 331.
[97] Münch. med. Woch., 1901 (48), 965.
[98] Folia clin. chimica et microscop., 1910 (2), 73.
[99] Biochem. Jour., 1907 (2), 383.
[1] Zeit. physiol. Chem., 1897 (23), 40.
[2] *Ibid.*, 1907 (52), 121.

semble in composition sebaceous material, which is characterized by containing a large proportion of cholesterol partly combined with fatty acids. Dermoids sometimes contain masses of fatty concretions which seem not to depend on chemical changes but on the presence of formative nuclei and framework of desquamated epithelium; they consist of a mixture of neutral fats and cholesterol esters, with some free cholesterol.[3] *Cholesteatomas*, in addition to their abundant cholesterol content, contain keratin.[4]

(g) **"Butter" Cysts.**[5]—In the mammary gland retention cysts form, filled with products of alteration of the milk, including butyric acid and lactose (Klotz),[6] and these are called "butter cysts" or milk cysts. Analysis of the contents of such a cyst by Smita[7] gave the following results, as compared with human milk:

	Cyst contents	Human milk
Fat	72.97	3.90
Casein	4.37	0.63
Albumin	1.91	1.31
Milk-sugar	0.88	6.04
Ash	0.36	0.49
Water	20.81	87.09

Fats consisted of—

	Cyst	Cows' milk
Stearin and palmitin	37.0	50.0
Olein	53.0	42.2
Butyrin	9.0	7.8

Occurring independent of lactation usually, but not always, are the "*soap cysts*," which contain chiefly calcium and magnesium soaps, but also neutral fats, free fatty acids, and traces of cholesterol (Freund).[8]

(2) MALIGNANT TUMORS

The chief general features of the composition of these growths have been considered in the discussion of the chemistry of tumors in general. A malignant tumor differs from a similar benign tumor chiefly in having usually a larger proportion of the primary cell constituents, and a smaller proportion of the secondary constituents and intercellular substances, since these are largely the product of the functional activity of the cells, which, in malignant tumors, do not often develop sufficiently to functionate extensively. Hence malignant tumors usually show a rather high proportion of the characteristic constituents of nucleoproteins; i. e., phosphorus and iron. If rapidly

[3] Lippert, Frankf. Zeit. Path., 1913 (14), 477.
[4] Risel, Verh. Deut. Path. Gesell., 1909 (13), 322.
[5] An "oil cyst" behind the ear has been fully analyzed by Kreis (Schweiz. Apoth. Ztg., 1918 (56), 81) and found to contain, in addition to much neutral fat and cholesterol, considerable amounts of high unsaturated hydrocarbons.
[6] Arch. klin. Chir., 1880 (25), 49.
[7] Wien. klin. Woch., 1890 (3), 551; see also Zdarek, Zeit. physiol. Chem., 1908 (57), 461.
[8] Virchow's Arch., 1899 (156), 151.

growing, they contain much potassium; if undergoing much retrogression, little potassium and a larger amount of calcium (Beebe, Clowes and Frisbie). On account of the extensive disintegration, the products of autolysis are usually much more abundant than in benign tumors. The composition varies greatly with the origin, although to a less extent than with the benign tumors. In Fraenkel's laboratory[9] it was found that cancers are often defective in tryptophane, and from a squamous cell carcinoma of the skin little or none of this amino-acid could be obtained, although normal squamous epithelium is rich in tryptophane. Fasal,[10] however, found usually a high tryptophane figure in cutaneous epithelioma, but very irregular results in other tumors. As Bang and Beebe have shown, the tumors arising from lymphatic tissues show the chemical characteristics of these structures, and contain histon nucleinate. Tumors from squamous epithelium develop keratin in direct proportion to the amount of maturity the cells reach. Even the most complex and specific products of metabolic activity may be developed by malignant tumors (e. g., thyroiodin, epinephrine, bile), and in a form and condition capable of performing function. As Buxton and others have shown, malignant tumors produce a great variety of intracellular enzymes. The idea that glycogen is present in tumors in proportion to their malignancy has been disproved by Lubarsch, Gierke, and others; among the malignant tumors glycogen is found particularly in choriocpitheliomas, hypernephromas, and squamous cell carcinomas. Of particular importance is the observation of Beebe, that the composition of metastatic growths is modified by the organ in which they are growing, so that they tend to resemble the organ serving as their host; which, however, does not hold for certain of their enzymes (Wells and Long). In a case of primary carcinoma of the liver, Wolter[11] found the tumor tissue richer in nuclein phosphorus and poorer in phosphatids than the adjacent liver tissue; cholesterol was 0.25 per cent. of the fresh weight, fatty acids 1.67 per cent. and water 82.33 per cent., the water of the normal tissue being 79.34 per cent.

As to the special varieties of malignant growths, there is little as yet determined concerning their chemistry beyond what has been stated previously. The variations in compositon of tumors are largely the direct result either of their resemblance to some normal tissue or of degenerative changes that they have undergone.

"**Colloid**" **carcinoma** may be mentioned specially, in view of the confusion caused by the lax use of the term "colloid" (*q. v.*). The fluid contents of colloid cancers of the gastro-intestinal tract are usually chiefly epithelial mucus, containing mucin mixed with a greater or less quantity of proteins from degenerated cells and serous effusion. This mucin is acid in reaction, is precipitated by acetic acid,

[9] Wien. klin. Woch., 1912 (25), 1041.
[10] Biochem. Zeit., 1913 (55), 88.
[11] Biochem. Zeit., 1913 (55), 260.

and has an affinity for basic dyes.[12]   The colloid cancers of the mammary gland, in which the "colloid degeneration" involves the stroma, probably contain a connective-tissue mucin analogous to that of the umbilical cord, as also do the myxosarcomas, if we may judge by their origin and staining reactions, but no exact chemical study of these substances can be found.   Colloid cancers of the ovary, arising usually from the same structures as the ovarian cysts, contain pseudomucin or allied bodies (see "Ovarian Cysts").   Colloid tumors of thyroid tissue often contain the typical colloid of normal thyroid tissue, even when metastatic in other organs; in the tumor-colloid may be a relatively normal proportion of iodin (Gierke[13]).

Hypernephromas possess several interesting chemical features. For example Gatti[14] brought forward the fact that such a tumor analyzed by him contained 3.4735 per cent. of lecithin, which agreed very well with the amount of lecithin in normal adrenals.   Beebe[15] found in the watery extract of a hypernephroma the following substances: tryptophane, proteoses, glycogen, leucine, and tyrosine, indicating the occurrence of autolysis.   About 29 per cent. of fat was present, which was all extractable without pepsin digestion, and the fat contained about 18 per cent. of its weight as cholesterol.   Lecithin was also present, but not quantitatively determined.   A study of the fats and lipoids of hypernephromas and other tumors gave the results shown in the following table:[16]

	Normal adrenal	Hypernephromas				Carcinoma of gall bladder	Carcinoma of breast	Sarcoma, secondary, in liver
		1	2	3	4			
Ether-soluble material	36.3	28.0	33.0	38.4	85.0	8.6	21.4	14.5
Cholesterol, per cent. total dry weight	7.6	4.6	6.7	8.7	0.5	2.2	0.9	1.6
Cholesterol, per cent. dry, fat-free substance	11.9	6.4	10.0	14.0	3.3	2.4	1.2	1.9
Cholesterol, per cent. ether-soluble substance	20.6	16.9	20.4	22.9	0.7	26.1	4.3	11.0
Lecithin, per cent. total dry weight	11.8	6.0	9.0	8.3	2.0	1.7	0.7	6.2
Lecithin, per cent. dry, fat-free substance	18.4	8.3	13.4	13.4	13.3	1.9	0.9	7.3
Lecithin, per cent. ether-soluble substance	33.0	22.7	27.5	21.4	2.4	20.0	3.0	39.8

Hypernephroma No. 1.—Typical specimen, with the usual amount of hemorrhage and necrosis cells much vacuolated.

Hypernephroma No. 2.—Similar to No. 1.

Hypernephroma No. 3.—Primary growth resembled more a papilloma than an ordinary hypernephroma in most places; no vacuolization of cells, little necrosis, and no hemorrhage.

Hypernephroma No. 4.—Tumor resembling a lipoma, with a stroma in places resembling a fibrosarcoma in structure.   In only a few areas were cells present resembling adrenal tissue most of the tissue resembling fatty areolar tissue.

[12] The fluid of a colloid cancer of the peritoneum examined by Hawk contained a protein resembling serosa mucin, containing 11.5 per cent. of N and 0.8 per cent. of S.   (McCrae and Coplin, Amer. Jour. Med. Sci., 1916 (151), 475.)

[13] Hofmeister's Beitr., 1902 (3), 286.

[14] Virchow's Arch., 1897 (150), 417.

[15] Amer. Jour. Physiol., 1904 (11), 139.

[16] Wells, Jour. Med. Res., 1908 (12), 461; see also Steinke, Frankfurt. Zeit Path., 1910 (5), 167.

It will be at once observed that the two typical hypernephromas, Nos. 1 and 2, show a marked resemblance to the normal adrenal in the proportion of fat and lipoids. (The lower figure for lecithin in No. 1 probably is due to the fact that this specimen had been preserved longer than the others.) This was what was to be expected from the microscopic resemblance of these tumors to adrenal tissue, and corroborates the results of Gatti's and Beebe's observations on isolated cases. More surprising is the fact that equally comparable results were obtained in the hypernephroma (No. 3), which contained only cells free from vacuolization and not at all resembling adrenal cells. From this it may be concluded that in these tumors of adrenal origin the amount of fats and lipoids present cannot be estimated from the degree of cytoplasmic vacuolization of the cells, or the extent of necrosis; *the fatty materials are an integral part of the cells, present in them as an essential constituent and not as the result of degeneration.*

The results of analysis of two carcinomas and a sarcoma indicate that the hypernephromas are peculiar in their close resemblance to adrenal tissue in respect to fat and to lipoid content. The amount of all these constituents in these three tumors is far below that found in the hypernephromas, although in the carcinoma of the breast the amount of simple fats is relatively large, as might be expected in view of the function of the cells from which it arose. It is interesting to note that a carcinoma of the gall-bladder shows a rather high proportion of its fatty material as cholesterol, for this observation may bear a relation to the well-known tendency of the epithelium of the gall-bladder to form cholesterol. The large proportion of lecithin in the sarcoma of the liver may possibly be due to the influence of the soil upon which the tumor was growing, but we need more information concerning the lipoid content of other malignant tumors arising in different sites.

Renal hypernephromas reproducing the adrenal cortex in structure do not contain epinephrine,[17] but tumors of the adrenal arising in the medulla may do so.[18] Microscopically, hypernephromas contain much glycogen. The special tests for hypernephroma tissue recommended by Croftan seem not to be specific.[19]

Melanotic tumors produce melanin, which seems not to differ at all from the melanin found in normal pigmented structures. Helman[20] found as high as 7.3 per cent. by weight of melanin in melanosarcomas. (See also Melanin, p. 474, and Enzymes in Tumors, p. 505. Concerning Chloromas[21] see p. 480.)

MULTIPLE MYELOMAS AND MYELOPATHIC "ALBUMOSURIA"

Multiple myelomas are of particular chemical interest, because of the appearance in the urine in such cases of the peculiar protein first described as an *albumose* by Bence-Jones,[22] and now, because of lack of grounds for its definite classification, generally known as the "*Bence-Jones body*" or "*Bence-Jones protein.*" Because of the extensive bone destruction there is also an excessive excretion of calcium,[23] and sometimes metastatic calcification may occur.[24] This

[17] Greer and Wells, Arch. Int. Med., 1909 (4), 291; Brooks, Jour. Exp. Med., 1911 (14), 550; Ciaccio, Deut. Zeit. f. Chir., 1910 (104), 277.
[18] Wegelin, Verh. Deut. Path. Ges., 1911 (15), 255.
[19] Koerber, Virch. Arch., 1908 (192), 356.
[20] Arch. internat. Pharmacodyn., 1903 (12), 271.
[21] Metabolism in chloroma does not differ from leukemia (Sakaguchi, Mitt. Med. Fak., Tokio, 1914 (13), 198).
[22] For literature, see Rosenbloom, Biochem. Bulletin, 1911 (1), 161; Vance, Amer. Jour. Med. Sci., 1916 (152), 693.
[23] Blatherwick, Amer. Jour. Med. Sci., 1916 (151), 432.
[24] Tschistowitsch and Kolessnikoff, Virchow's Archiv., 1909 (197), 112.

variety of tumor differs from the standard types of malignant tumors in that it involves the marrow of many bones simultaneously, in a very diffuse manner, without usually giving evidence of a true metastasis. In many respects it resembles the leukemias, pseudoleukemia, and chloroma, and it is extremely uncertain as to where in the classification of tumors and of the diseases of the blood-forming organs this disease should be placed.   Histologically, the tumors show evidence of being derived from the specific cells of the marrow, either from the plasma cells (Wright) or from the neutrophile myelocytes[25] or their predecessors (Muir).   Cases of myeloma without the proteinuria have been described, and also a few instances of the presence of apparently typical Bence-Jones protein in the urine without myelomas, but with bone carcinomas, leukemia or chloroma.[26]

Properties of the "Bence=Jones Protein."—Not to go into details, which are given in the literature cited, the important facts concerning the "*Bence-Jones protein*," and its appearance in the urine ("*myelopathic albumosuria*," Bradshaw), are as follows:

It is a protein, the exact nature of which has not been determined; at first considered an albumose because of its peculiar reactions to heat, its nature has since been contested, but the weight of evidence seems to be in favor of the contention of Simon that it is most closely related to the water-soluble globulin of the blood.   In certain cases it partly precipitates spontaneously from the urine,[27] and it may crystallize in the renal tubules.[28]   Its most characteristic properties are the following:

The coagulation temperature is low, varying from 49°–60° in various cases, and being considerably modified by the amount of salts and urea present in the solution.   Probably the protein forms a molecular compound with the salts which is more stable at 100° than at lower temperatures (Hopkins and Savory).

In many cases the coagulum is redissolved on heating, and reappears on cooling, but this characteristic feature is not always present, and often disappears in cases where at first it is present.

A precipitate is formed by strong (25 per cent.) nitric acid, which disappears on heating and reappears on cooling.   Strong hydrochloric acid causes a dense precipitate, which is quite typical (Bradshaw).

No precipitate is produced by acetic acid, even in excess, and the addition of acetic acid to a hot coagulated specimen causes prompt solution of the coagulum.

Unlike albumoses, this substance does not dialyze; the salt-free solution left in the dialyzing bag does not precipitate.

A purplish-violet color is usually given with the biuret reaction, but it may be more reddish in color, especially if little copper is present.

[25] Forman and Warren (Jour. Cancer Res., 1917 (2), 79) found the cells to contain granules giving the indol-phenol blue reaction and hence belonging to the myeloid group.

[26] Glynn has described a glycoprotein resembling Mörner's body, in the urine during myeloma (Liverpool Med. Chir. Jour., 1914, p. 82).   A crystallizable protein, resembling the Bence-Jones body, has been found in the urine of a woman with gastric cancer without any bone involvement (Schumm and Kimmerle, Zeit. physiol. Chem., 1914 (92), 1).

[27] Rosenbloom, Arch. Int. Med., 1912 (9), 255.

[28] Loehlein, Cent. allg. Path., 1913 (24), 953.

Sulphur is readily split off by alkalies, reacting with lead acetate to produce lead sulphide (Boston).

After standing in alcohol, by which the protein is precipitated, it loses its solubility (differing in this respect from albumose).

As to the exact nature of this protein, little can be said at the present time. Since protoproteoses, deuteroproteoses, and peptone are split off on digestion with pepsin, the molecule is evidently larger than that of any of the albumoses. The well-purified substance is free from phosphorus, and hence contains no nucleins; but it contains considerable sulphur (between 1 and 2 per cent.), which is readily split off. Like casein, it contains no hetero-group (lack of heteroproteoses on digestion), but differs in containing a carbohydrate group (in small amount) and in the absence of phosphorus. On hydrolysis Magnus-Levy[29] obtained glutaminic acid, tyrosine, and leucine, but no glycine. He found the nitrogen distributed as follows: amid-nitrogen, 9.9 per cent.; humin-nitrogen, 9.8 per cent.; diamino-nitrogen, 6.4 per cent.—which last was composed of : histidine, 0.9 per cent.; arginine, 2.4 per cent.; lysine 3.0 per cent. The extensive analytic studies of Hopkins and Savory[30] show that the amino-acid grouping is that of a typical protein, with a high proportion of aromatic radicals, similar proteins not being found in the tumors or muscles of a typical case. In fact, the amino-acid content, as given below, indicates that Bence-Jones protein is as distinct from other proteins in chemical composition as in its physico-chemical properties. The amino-acids, in round numbers, were isolated in the following percentage proportions of the entire protein: Valine-leucine fraction, 14; glutamic acid, 8; aspartic acid, 2; proline, 2.7; phenylalanine, 4.8; tyrosine, 4.2; tryptophane, 0.8; cystine, 0.6; arginine, 6; histidine, 0.8; lysine, 3.7; sulphur, 1.2. An important point in this work is the agreement in composition of the proteins from two different cases, being identical within the limits of the analytic methods, showing that the protein is of constant and characteristic properties.

Occurrence of "Myelopathic Albumosuria."—Not all cases of multiple myeloma show the presence of Bence-Jones protein in the urine, however, and it is present occasionally in other conditions. Multiple bone involvement by other tumors does not often cause "albumosuria."[31] There is no evidence that it occurs in the normal body, even in the bone-marrow, or that it is produced as a step in the splitting of any form of proteins. A few cases of supposed osteomalacia have been reported, with the Bence-Jones body in the urine, but on more careful investigation these seem to have been unrecognized mye-

[29] Zeit. physiol. Chem., 1900 (30), 200.

[30] Jour. of Physiol., 1911 (42), 189.

[31] A case of this kind has, however, been described by Oerum (Ugeskrift f. Lager., 1904, No. 24), in which the bone tumors were multiple metastases of a gastric carcinoma. See also Boggs and Guthrie, Amer. Jour. Med. Sci., 1912 (144), 803.

lomas (*e. g.*, the cases of Bence-Jones and of Jochmann and Schumm). Similarly the case reported by Askanazy as leukemia with Bence-Jones protein in the urine, on reëxamination was found to be multiple myeloma.   However, at least eight cases of true chronic leukemia with Bence-Jones proteinuria have been reported.[32]   Coriat[33] describes a substance found in a pleuritic fluid which gave the reactions of the Bence-Jones body, and he believes that it may have been formed from serum globulin through the digestive action of the leucocytes or bacteria.   Zuelzer reports finding the same body in the urine of a dog poisoned with pyridin.[34]   It is a striking fact that the kidneys eliminate such great quantities of this protein without being permeable to the very similar normal blood proteins, and usually without showing evidence of structural changes.   Also that when injected into animals it does not escape freely in the urine as it does in man. It may be found in the blood and exudates of patients with myeloma,[35] as much as 7.8 per cent. having been found in the blood by Jacobson.[36] Miller and Baetjer[37] report finding a protein corresponding closely to Bence-Jones protein in the urine of three apparently normal persons and in two cases of hypertensive nephritis without evidence of bone disease, thus opening the question as to whether, after all, this protein is invariably associated with bone disease.   Simon[38] has observed that the protein may be accompanied by dialyzable substances giving the ninhydrin reaction, probably amino-acids or peptids.

Origin of the Protein.—As to the place of formation of this peculiar protein, there is much diversity of opinion. Magnus-Levy advanced against the idea that it is formed by the tumor cells, the following arguments: In the urine of myeloma patients are excreted great quantities of the protein,—as much as 30 to 70 grams per day, —whereas the total amount of protein in all the tumor tissue in the body seldom exceeds, or, indeed, equals this quantity.   It seems improbable that so little tumor tissue can form so much urinary protein, and Magnus-Levy suggests that it must come from the food proteins as a result of altered protein metabolism. Against this view, however, are the following facts: (1) The Bence-Jones body has been found (but not constantly) in the myeloma tissue, but not in other organs or tissues; (2) the quantity in the urine is not dependent upon diet; (3) it is associated almost exclusively with this form of tumor.   Simon considers it probable that the protein is formed from serum-globulin, perhaps by an enzymatic action of the tumor cells, and once formed, it is rapidly eliminated by the kidneys, as are all foreign proteins.

[32] Boggs and Guthrie, Bull. Johns Hopkins Hosp., 1913 (24), 368.
[33] Amer. Jour. Med. Sci., 1903 (126), 631.
[34] Wolgemuth (Arb. a. d. Path. Inst. zu Berlin, Festschrift, 1906, p. 627) states that normal human bone marrow may contain true albumoses.
[35] Taylor *et al.*, Jour. Biol. Chem., 1917 (29), 425.
[36] Jour. Urol., 1917 (1), 167.
[37] Jour. Amer. Med. Assoc., 1918 (70), 137.
[38] Jour. Amer. Med. Assoc., 1918 (70), 224.

Normal bone marrow does not contain this protein (Nerking[39]). Rosenbloom[40] has found evidence that Bence-Jones protein may possibly be derived from the osseo-albumoid of the bones. Weber and Ledingham[41] have suggested that it comes from the cytoplasmic residue of karyolyzed plasma cells. The observation that under benzol treatment the amount of Bence-Jones protein in the urine of leukemic patients is reduced (Boggs and Guthrie[32]) is also good evidence of its myelogenous nature. The fact that Abderhalden and Rostoski[42] found that the serum of rabbits immunized with Bence-Jones protein gives the precipitin reaction with human serum, is evidence that the protein is a human tissue protein and not merely an absorbed and excreted food protein. This has been corroborated by Hopkins and Savory,[43] who also found that the amount of protein in the urine, which contained about one-third the total nitrogen excreted, varied with the general metabolism and was not controlled by the diet. Massini[44] reports securing positive complement fixation tests with immune sera, differentiating the Bence-Jones protein from normal serum proteins; positive sensitization tests were not obtained by cutaneous injections of the protein by Boggs and Guthrie. Injected into the blood it is non-toxic and does not lower coagulability as a proteose would. It is capable of acting as an antigen in anaphylaxis reactions, which also indicates that it is a complete protein and not a cleavage product.[45] When injected into dogs it is partly utilized, although nephritic animals excrete it partly hydrolyzed into proteose.[35]

[39] Biochem. Zeit., 1908 (10), 167; corroborated by Hopkins and Savory, Jour. Physiol., 1911 (42), 189.
[40] Arch. Int. Med., 1912 (9), 236.
[41] Folia Hematol., 1909 (8), 14.
[42] Zeit. physiol. Chem., 1905 (46), 125.
[43] Corroborated also by Boggs and Guthrie, Amer. Jour. Med. Sci., 1912 (144), 803; Folin and Denis, Jour. Biol. Chem., 1914 (18), 277.
[44] Deut. Arch. klin. Med., 1911 (104), 29.
[45] Taylor and Miller, Jour. Biol. Chem., 1916 (25), 281; 1917 (29), 425.

CHAPTER XX

PATHOLOGICAL CONDITIONS DUE TO, OR ASSOCIATED WITH, ABNORMALITIES IN METABOLISM, INCLUDING AUTOINTOXICATION

DURING the course of metabolism innumerable organic compounds are formed, some of which are of a more or less poisonous nature. As long as the body is in a normal condition, these injurious substances are kept from accumulating in sufficient quantities to do harm; this is accomplished in one of the following ways: (1) elimination from the body in the urine, feces, etc.; (2) combination with other substances into harmless, or relatively harmless, compounds; (3) chemical alteration into compounds that are non-toxic or relatively innocuous. Therefore a harmful accumulation of metabolic products may be the result of any one of the following conditions:

(1) Failure of elimination because of abnormal conditions in the eliminating organs; e. g., uremia.

(2) Failure of neutralization by chemical combination, presumably due to abnormalities in the organs or tissues through whose activities the neutralization is normally accomplished; e. g., diseases of the liver.

(3) Failure in the chemical transformation of the metabolic products; this may result either from abnormalities in the functionating tissues, or through a checking of the normal steps of metabolism by the failure of elimination of the end-products.

(4) Excessive formation of certain normal products of metabolism; e. g., hyperactivity of the thyroid.

(5) Production of abnormal toxic chemical substances; e. g., the intoxication following superficial burns.

Numerous classifications of autointoxication have been proposed by various authors, some excluding from the causes of autointoxication all but the products of metabolism within the blood and tissues of the body, as has been done in the preceding consideration; many including intoxications caused by the products of gastro-intestinal fermentation and putrefaction; and still others (v. Jaksch) including even the intoxications produced by bacterial invasion of the body.[1] It is extremely difficult to draw the line as to just what should be

[1] See résumé by Weintraud, Ergeb. der Path., 1897 (4), 1.

included under the term autointoxication, and particularly difficult to decide the proper placing of the intoxication resulting from fecal retention and from processes of decomposition in the alimentary canal. For example, the poisoning following the eating of partially decomposed canned food could not be looked upon as an autointoxi- cation, and yet there is no fundamental difference whether the decom- position occurs, as in this case, before the food enters the body, or whether it occurs in the intestinal tract because of abnormal bacterio- logical or anatomical conditions. On the other hand, since many of the obnoxious products of metabolism are eliminated through the bowels, failure of elimination through this channel may lead to a true autointoxication as much as may deficient renal elimination. On the whole, it seems best to restrict the term autointoxication, as far as possible, to the disturbances produced by products of metabolism that have been formed within the tissues of the body (*intermediary metabolism*), considering as a distinct but related subject gastro-in- testinal autointoxication.

In the discussion of autointoxication from the standpoint of chemi- cal pathology, we are interested particularly in the chemical nature of the substances that cause the intoxication, and in the chemical processes by which their action is kept at a minimum, rather than in the clinical features or anatomical results that may be produced. Unfortunately, in but a few instances have the exact chemical sub- stances causing these intoxications been accurately determined, prob- ably because in most cases not one but a number of poisonous substances are present; and, furthermore, we do not always know ex- actly when a certain disease is to be ascribed to autointoxication, nor can we always determine that the cause of a certain intoxication lies in an abnormality in metabolism and not in an infection of hidden nature. It is, therefore, quite impossible, with the uncertain informa- tion available at this time, to consider autointoxication in a systematic way, and we must limit ourselves to a consideration of certain patho- logical conditions in which there appears to be an element of abnormal metabolism with resulting intoxication. In some cases this intoxica- tion is a prominent feature of the disorder, in others it is subordinate to other manifestations of the disease; and, finally, we may have marked alterations in metabolism without evidences of disturbance of health (*e. g.*, cystinuria, alkaptonuria).

Of the autointoxications due to the retention of poisonous products of metabolism that should be excreted from the body, first in order of importance stand uremia and cholemia (the latter has already been considered in connection with the discussion of Icterus, Chap. xviii). Of apparently less significance are autointoxications due to failure of elimination of gaseous metabolic products by the lungs, and failure of the excretory function of the skin.

UREMIA[2]

The cause or causes of the severe, often fatal, intoxication that may occur when the outflow of urine is completely checked, or when it is qualitatively and quantitatively altered for long periods of time, have not yet been definitely determined. As the kidney seems to be the chief organ for the removal of the products of nitrogenous metabolism, it is naturally assumed that uremia is the result of a retention of these products, but as yet it has not been ascertained which of the many products is responsible, and, indeed, there are very good reasons for questioning if the substances present in normal urine do or can cause uremia when their elimination by the kidney is defective. There is no question but that the urine contains toxic substances. Among them are the salts of potassium, which, however, cannot alone explain all the urinary toxicity, for the symptoms produced by the injection of urine are different from those produced by potassium salts, and it has been found that the inorganic constituents (ash) of urine are less poisonous than the entire urine. Furthermore, toxic mixtures of organic, ash-free substances have been obtained from normal urine.[3] Of the known normal constituents of the urine there are few, however, that are toxic to any considerable degree, and these occur in but very small quantities. Urea is generally considered as almost absolutely non-toxic, the animal body withstanding injection of large quantities without appreciable injury. Uric acid, the purine bases, hippuric acid, creatinine, and the urinary pigments are all possessed of very slight toxicity, and their effects do not explain uremia. Injections of urine into animals may cause more or less disturbance, but it is different, on the whole, from the manifestations of uremia. (The experiments of Bouchard and his school present such serious errors of technique and interpretation that they are now largely disregarded.)

For these and other reasons, it has been generally considered that the intoxication of uremia is not due solely or chiefly to the substances that are normally eliminated in the urine, but rather to more toxic antecedents of the nitrogenous constituents of the urine. Urea represents but the final product of a long series of reactions by which the huge protein molecule is broken up into its "building-stones," the various amino-acids, and these in turn are decomposed in such a way that their NH_2 groups are combined with carbonic acid[4] and eliminated as the diamido-compound of carbonic acid, namely urea, $O = C\begin{smallmatrix}NH_2\\NH_2\end{smallmatrix}$.

We know that the liver is able to accomplish the conversion of amino-acids to urea, for it has been experimentally shown that if leucine and

---

[2] General résumé with earlier literature by: Honigmann, Ergeb. der Pathol., 1894 (Bd. 1, Abt. 2), 639; 1902 (8), 549; Ascoli, Vorlesungen über Urämie, Jena, 1903.

[3] See Dresbach, Jour. Exp. Med., 1900 (5), 315.

[4] Arginine alone of all the amino-acids splits off urea directly from its molecule.

glycine are passed through the vessels of the isolated liver they disappear in part, while an increased amount of urea escapes from the hepatic veins. It is probable that the liver is the chief site of urea formation, but it is also probable that urea can be formed in other organs. We do not know, however, the intermediate steps by which the aminoacids of the protein molecule are converted into urea. It has been repeatedly shown that urea can be formed from ammonium salts of organic acids (including ammonium carbonate), and ammonia is a constant product of autolysis, being characteristically more abundant as a product of autolytic proteolysis than as a product of tryptic proteolysis; therefore, one of the antecedents of urea is probably ammonia, which is somewhat toxic and especially hemolytic.[5] Another antecedent of urea is ammonium carbamate, which stands in structure intermediate between urea and ammonium carbonate, as shown by the following graphic formulæ:

$$O = C \diagup \substack{OH \\ \diagdown OH} \qquad O = C \diagup \substack{O-NH_4 \\ \diagdown O-NH_4} \qquad O = C \diagup \substack{NH_2 \\ \diagdown O-NH_4} \qquad O = C \diagup \substack{NH_2 \\ \diagdown NH_2}$$

(carbonic acid)   (ammonium carbonate)   (ammonium carbamate)   (urea)

That ammonium carbamate is possibly an important precursor of urea has been shown particularly through the results of studies of dogs with Eck's fistula,[6] which consists of a fistula between the portal vein and the inferior vena cava, the blood from the portal system then passing directly into the general circulation without first passing through the liver. In such animals the urine becomes poor in urea and relatively rich in ammonium carbamate. At the same time, the dogs show severe symptoms of intoxication from which they die, and which are similar to the symptoms that follow intravenous injection of ammonium carbamate. Ammonium carbamate, being a substance of considerable toxicity[7] when free in the blood, it has, therefore, been quite widely considered that it may be an important factor in the production of uremic symptoms. On the other hand, it seems most probable that the condition of uremia does not depend upon one but upon many various and varying substances, especially as Hawk[8] found that sodium carbamate did not produce uremic symptoms in his Eck fistula dogs, while Liebig's extract did.[9] Clinically, the symptoms of uremia in different cases are widely different; thus if uremia is due to complete suppression of urine through mechanical

---

[5] Concerning the toxicity of ammonium salts see Rachford and Crane, Medical News, 1902 (81), 778.
[6] See Hahn, Massen, Nencki, and Pawlow, Arch. f. exp. Path. u. Pharm., 1893 (32), 161.
[7] See Bickel, "Exp. Untersuch. über Cholaemie," Wiesbaden, 1900.
[8] Amer. Jour. Physiol., 1908 (21), 260.
[9] Fischler believes the intoxication which occurs after feeding meat to Eck fistula dogs to be an alkalosis, probably from NH₃ salts (Deut. Arch. klin. Med., 1911 (104), 300).

obstruction, the symptoms are quite different from those observed in the uremia following a chronic nephritis; drowsiness, weakness of heart action, and syncope being the chief manifestations of obstructive uremia, the convulsions and other manifestations of nervous irritation characteristic of uremia in chronic nephritis being absent.[10]

Chemical Changes in Uremia.—The attempts to isolate from the blood and organs of uremic patients or animals toxic substances that explain the manifestations of uremia have thus far failed. That there is an actual retention of organic substances in the blood in uremia is shown conclusively, however, by the studies of the physico-chemical properties of the blood. It has been repeatedly found that in uremia the *freezing-point* of the blood is reduced markedly below the normal;[11] instead of the normal depression of 0.55°–0.57° the freezing-point is usually reduced more than −0.60°, and sometimes as much as −0.75°, which shows that the number of molecules in the blood is increased.[12] At the same time, the *electrical conductivity* may not be at all increased (Bickel),[13] but may even be reduced; and as the electrical conductivity of the blood depends upon the number of dissociable molecules, chiefly inorganic salts, these are evidently not increased.[14] Therefore, the increased number of molecules must represent an excess of organic molecules that dissociate but little if at all, and hence are not conductors of electricity. Some authors, indeed, have ascribed uremia to the increased osmotic pressure of the blood from the retained molecules, but this is improbable, according to Strauss,[15] who found that a marked increase in molecular concentration may occur without uremia, and that we may have a severe uremia without increased osmotic pressure.

Careful metabolic studies have shown that nephritics (chronic interstitial) are not able to convert proteins into urea as rapidly or as completely as normal persons.[16] Erben[17] has studied the variations in the normal components of the blood during nephritis, and found the albumin generally decreased in proportion to the globulin, especially in cases of parenchymatous nephritis; lecithin and calcium are also decreased. Rowe[18] found the serum proteins greatly lowered in chronic nephritis with uremia, an increased proportion of globulin being present; with uremia the total protein content is normal or slightly higher, with usually increased globulin, while nephritis with-

---

[10] Chiari, however, observed true uremia, both clinical and anatomical, in a man with ureteral obstruction (Verh. Deut. Path. Gesell., 1912 (15), 207).

[11] See Tiecken, Amer. Med., 1905 (10), pp. 393, 567, and 822; Butterfield et al Amer. Jour. Med Sci., 1916 (151), 63.

[12] See table of freezing points of blood and effusions on page 355.

[13] Deut. med. Woch., 1902 (28), 501.

[14] See Bienenstock and Csaki, Biochem. Zeit., 1917 (84), 210.

[15] Die chronischen Nierenentzündungen, etc., Berlin, 1902.

[16] Levene et al., Jour. Exper. Med., 1909 (11), 825.

[17] Zeit. klin. Med., 1903 (50), 441; 1905 (57), 39.

[18] Arch. Int. Med., 1917 (19), 354.

out edema or uremia produces a marked increase in the globulin. The decrease in red corpuscles and hemoglobin in nephritis is a well-known feature. Bloor[19] found in the blood high fat content in both corpuscles and plasma, high lecithin in the corpuscles, and normal cholesterol, these changes probably depending on the lowered alkali reserve.

Measurements of the partial pressure of CO_2 in the alveolar air in uremia indicate a certain degree of acidosis.[20] This seems to occur to a sufficient degree to be responsible for definite clinical symptoms of acidosis only in advanced nephritis, but earlier in nephritis an acidosis may be demonstrable by the alkali tolerance test when it is not sufficient to affect the alveolar air.[21] The maximum degrees of acidosis found in uremia are about equal to those of diabetic coma, and may be an important feature of uremia, although usually the convulsive features of uremic coma are quite different from the air hunger of diabetic coma.

The development of this terminal acidity, together with the finding of albumose in the blood of a nephritic by Schumm,[22] suggests the probability of active autolytic processes occurring in uremia. Neuberg and Strauss[23] have also found glycine in considerable quantities (1.5 per mille) in the blood-serum of a uremic patient and in the blood of nephrectomized rabbits. The amount of colloidal material present in the urine is decreased in nephritis, according to Pribram,[24] who suggests that retention of this material, which is rich in aromatic radicals, may be of importance in the toxicity of uremia. Rumpf found that the organs of nephritics contain an excess of potassium, and Blumenfeldt[25] attributes this to a defective elimination of potassium salts which he observed in nephritis. Basal metabolism is somewhat lowered.[26]

Numerous attempts have been made by both chemical and immunological methods to determine whether the proteins in the urine in nephritis come from the food, the blood, or from the renal cells themselves. In alimentary albuminuria the urinary proteins seem not to be those of the food, but human proteins.[27] In nephritis differentiation between serum proteins and kidney proteins has not yet been satisfactorily accomplished.[28]

The development of improved methods of analysis of small quan-

[19] Jour. Biol. Chem., 1917 (31), 575.
[20] Straub and Schlayer, Münch. med. Woch., 1912 (59), 569; Whitney, Arch. Int. Med., 1917 (20), 931.
[21] Peabody, Arch. Int. Med., 1915 (16), 955.
[22] Hofmeister's Beitr., 1903 (4), 453.
[23] Berl. klin. Woch., 1905 (43), 258.
[24] Fortschr. d. Med., 1911 (29), 951.
[25] Zeit. exper. Pathol., 1913 (12), 523.
[26] Aub and DuBois, Arch. Int. Med., 1917 (19), 865.
[27] Wells, Jour. Amer. Med. Assoc., 1909 (53), 863.
[28] Cameron and Wells, Arch. Int. Med., 1915 (15), 746.

tities of blood, and other fluids, especially by Folin and Denis, Marshall, and Van Slyke, has enabled us to obtain exact knowledge of many of the chemical changes of nephritis and uremia.[29] It has been found that the normal blood contains from 25 to 40 mg. of nitrogen in non-coagulable form in each 100 c.c., there being usually about 5 mg. increase after meals, and ordinarily about one-half of this nitrogen is in the form of urea.[30] In all conditions that impair renal function, whether renal changes or circulatory deficiency, there is a rise in this noncoagulable nitrogen, and when there is excessive tissue destruction there may also be a slight rise independent of renal injury. As a general rule, but with some exceptions, the amount increases with increased renal impairment, the highest figures being seen in uremia, in which figures as high as 460 mg. have been obtained. In 130 nephritics, Foster found the average to be 84 mg. of nitrogen.

Analyses of the blood in 600 cases of nephritis by Gettler and St. George[31] have given the following figures in mg. per 100 c.c. of blood:

	Normal	Nephritis
Nonprotein nitrogen	25 to 40	40 to 460
Urea nitrogen	10 to 18	20 to 375
Creatinin	0.1 to 0.8	2 to 42
Uric acid	0.5 to 3.0	3 to 17
Sugar	60 to 110	75 to 160
Alkali reserve—per cent	53 to 80	40 to 75

From their observations these authors conclude: All the waste nitrogen products, nonprotein nitrogen, urea, creatinin and uric acid, are present in increased amounts in cases of true nephritis, and generally, but not invariably, present in greater concentration in the blood of those cases which are primarily considered as chronic interstitial nephritis (retention nephritis). The degree of retention (when taking into account the functional efficiency of the cardiac muscle) is a direct criterion of the severity of the lesion. The sugar content in the blood is similarly increased in nephritis, and more marked in the patients suffering with the chronic parenchymatous form of the disease. The alkali reserve is a valuable index of the degree of acidosis present. There is no definite lesion of nephritis referable to a certain clinical picture.

There is no constant relationship between the blood pressure and the nitrogen figure, but functional tests usually show a correspondence between the excretory power of the kidney and the retention of metabolites in the blood. The symptoms of asthenic uremia are rarely well defined when the concentration of urea in the blood is less than

[29] Good reviews and bibliographies are given by Tileston and Comfort, Arch. Int. Med., 1914 (14), 620; Schwartz and McGill, *ibid.*, 1916 (17), 42; Woods. *ibid.*, 1915 (16), 577; Karsner, Jour. Lab. Clin. Med., 1916 (1), 910; Feigl, Biochem Zeit., 1919 (94), 84.
[30] See Kast and Wardell, Arch. Int. Med., 1918 (22), 581.
[31] Jour. Amer. Med. Asso., 1918 (71), 2033.

100 mg. per 100 c.c., and they are rarely absent when the concentration exceeds 200 mg.[32] With these high blood nitrogen figures there is also an increase in nonprotein nitrogen in the tissues (Foster)[33] and metabolism studies show nitrogen retention of considerable degree, sometimes over 1 gram retention when the intake is but 10 grams per day.

Along with the other nitrogenous constituents the uric acid is increased from a normal 2 to 3 mg. up to 7 to 10 mg., and even higher. Creatinin rises from 1 to 2 mg. up to 5 to 20 mg.[34] On the other hand the amino-acid nitrogen may be normal in the blood even with extremely high nonprotein nitrogen figures,[35] although sometimes it is much increased, as high as 30 mg. amino acid N having been found by Bock[36] in uremia (the normal figure being 7 mg.). Feigl[29] reports finding as high as 125 mg. amino-N, with frequently 60 to 85 mg. The retention of various substances varies directly with the solubility and diffusibility of the substances, so that with renal disease we first get retention of uric acid, then urea, and last of creatinin (Myers).[34] Ammonia nitrogen may show a slight increase, rising in half of Foster's cases from the normal 0.5 mg. to from 0.7 mg. to 2.2 mg. per 100 c.c. *Indicanemia* may also be present but it is not a toxic factor (Dorner).[37] The blood normally contains about 0.05 mg. per 100 c.c.; in uremia it may rise to 0.2 mg., and as much as 2.2 mg. has been found in one case.[38]

The Pathogenesis of Uremia.—The fact that the highest figures for non-protein nitrogen are usually found in uremia might be accepted as proving that uremia is caused by poisoning with these metabolites, were it not for certain contradictory observations.

(1) Occasionally quite typical attacks of uremia are observed without high nonprotein nitrogen figures for the blood, even as low as 28 mg. having been recorded in a fatal case.[39]

(2) Extremely high nonprotein nitrogen content may be observed without uremia. Thus, Tileston and Comfort found 169 and 150 mg. in two cases of acute intestinal obstruction without uremic symptoms, and similar results have been obtained in bichloride of mercury poisoning,[40] and mechanical anuria. The occurrence of albuminuric retinitis also seems to bear no relation to the nitrogen retention (Woods).

[32] Hewlett, Gilbert and Wickett, Arch. Int. Med., 1916 (18), 636.
[33] Arch. Int. Med., 1919 (24), 242.
[34] See Myers and Fine, Arch. Int. Med. 1915 (16), 536; 1916 (17), 570.
[35] Foster, Arch. Int. Med., 1915 (15), 356.
[36] Jour. Biol. Chem., 1917 (29), 191.
[37] Deut. Arch. klin. Med., 1914 (113), 342; Rosenberg, Arch. exp. Path., 1916 (79), 260; Tscherkoff, Deut. med. Woch., 1914 (40), 1713; Rev. Méd. Suisse Romande, 1918 (38), 15.
[38] Hass, Deut. Arch. klin. Med., 1916 (119), 177.
[39] There are few who would go to the extreme of Strauss (Berl. klin. Woch., 1915 (52), 368) and limit the term uremia to cases showing a high non-protein nitrogen in the blood, no matter what the symptomatology and pathology may be. A totally different viewpoint is expressed by Reiss, Zeit. klin. Med., 1914 (80), 97, 424, 452.
[40] See Foster, Arch. Int. Med., 1915 (15), 754.

(3) None of the known nitrogenous constituents of the urine can be held responsible for all the manifestations of typical uremic poisoning. The highest purine, uric acid and creatinine concentration in a given case may occur entirely independent of uremic conditions,[41] the amino-nitrogen is not increased in uremia, urea is not supposed to be toxic in this degree and uremia may occur without high urea concentration or be absent when there is much urea in the blood. To be sure, an unknown toxic substance may be responsible, but in some cases of uremia the total non-protein nitrogen can be accounted for by the known nitrogenous components found in the blood (Foster).

We may consider one of the following alternatives:

(1) The nerve cells may be made hypersensitive to some one of the known constituents by the excessive amounts of the other metabolites. This is a purely speculative hypothesis, without any actual evidence in its support.

(2) The portion of unidentified nitrogen usually present in the blood may contain a specific, highly efficient poison.

In support of this hypothesis is the finding in a series of cases that the proportion of noncoagulable blood nitrogen that could not be accounted for by the known nitrogenous metabolites seemed to vary directly with the severity of the symptoms (Woods).[42]

Hartman[43] has suggested that the substance which causes the characteristic odor of the urine may be responsible for at least some of the intoxication of uremia. This substance, which he has isolated and described under the name "urinod," he believes to be a cyclic ketone with the empirical formula C_6H_8O; it is highly toxic, and causes mental symptoms. This important observation awaits confirmation.

Foster[44] has described the finding of a toxic base in the blood of uremics, absent from the blood in other conditions, which causes death of guinea pigs with symptoms suggestive of the eclamptic type of uremia. Further development of this work is also awaited.

(3) Uremia may not depend on intoxication of the nerve cells, but upon the mechanical effects of edema involving these cells.

One of the striking features of autopsies of uremics is often the "wet brain" and the excessive amount of cerebrospinal fluid which, during life, may be found to be under a heightened pressure. We know that not only general but localized edemas occur in nephritis, and that localized edema in the brain may be associated with and apparently responsible for paralyses, convulsions, hyperirritability and mania. The wet brain of nephritis is similar to the wet brain of acute alcoholism and delirium tremens. Oftentimes the nervous symptoms of uremia are distinctly focal, and a complete hemiplegia from hemorrhage may be exactly simulated; convulsive seizures identical with those of brain tumor may be seen. It is extremely difficult to explain these localizations by the action of a soluble poison, and simple if we assume a local edema. It is, of course, as difficult to explain the localization of the edema, but we know that in nephritis localized edemas do occur, so we have a basis for the assumption of localized cerebral edemas. A general acidosis (q. v.) is usual in nephritis and marked in uremia[45] but we have no means of knowing whether local acidosis occurs in the nervous system that may be responsible for local edemas according to Fischer's hypothesis. Or, osmotic effects may be responsible, in view of the demonstrated high

[41] Myers and Fine, Jour. Biol. Chem., 1915 (20), 391.
[42] Arch. Int. Med., 1915 (16), 577.
[43] *Ibid.*, 1915 (16), 98.
[44] Trans. Assoc. Amer. Phys., 1915 (30), 305.
[45] Henderson, Bull. Johns Hopkins Hosp., 1914 (25), 141; Peabody, Arch. Int. Med., 1915 (16), 955; Sellards, "Principles of Acidosis," Harvard Press, 1917.

osmotic pressure of the blood in uremia, and the fact that the life of nephrecto-mized rabbits is prolonged by giving them water.[46] In any event, the existing evidence on the pathogenesis of uremia does not explain it on a toxicologic basis, and hence the alternative explanation of cerebral edema must be taken into con-sideration. Ervin[47] proposes the hypothesis that convulsions occur when the blood pressure becomes lower than the intracranial pressure so that the blood sup-ply of the brain is reduced; the convulsion raises the blood pressure. He comments on the difficulty in explaining the transient character of uremic convulsions if caused by concentration of chemical poisons.

On the other hand the pathologist recognizes evidence of systemic intoxication in uremia. The uremic pericarditis and endocarditis, which have often failed by ordinary methods to yield bacteria, are apparently toxic processes. The diphtheritic colitis indicates vicari-ous excretion of poisonous substances. Structural changes are found in cells that suggest poisoning; chromatolysis of the cortical ganglion cells has been repeatedly observed in uremia, and in nephrectomized rabbits Lewis[47a] found acute parenchymatous and fatty degeneration of the myocardium and endothelial cells of the liver. The localized edemas of nephritis often show a fluid of the character of an exudate rather than a transudate.

It would seem, despite the prevailing opinion to the contrary, that it is entirely possible that the manifestations of uremia may be caused by the known nitrogenous substances that the kidneys have failed to excrete, and that the only difficult thing to explain is the failure of investigators to consider the time element in experimental intoxica-tions. The presence of 200 mg., and upwards, of nonprotein nitrogen per 100 c.c. of blood, which is often found in uremia, indicates that the blood plasma that is bathing the tissue cells contains somewhere between 0.5 and 1.0% of soluble organic substances, a strength of solution that certainly does not require any very high degree of toxicity when *continuously maintained* at this concentration, as it is in nephritis. The reported experimentally determined toxicities with these substances have only represented transitory conditions which are entirely dissimilar to the actual conditions in the body. They corre-spond to the cases of high nonprotein nitrogen in the blood in in-testinal obstruction, bichloride poisoning, etc., in which absence of the uremic symptom complex has been noted and remarked upon. To study the relation of uremia to retained metabolites we need observa-tions on their effects when maintained in the organism for long periods at the concentrations occurring in uremics and this can be done readily by such methods as have been devised by Woodyatt.[48] A start in this direction is furnished by Hewlett, Gilbert and Wickett,[32] who found that when large doses (100 to 125 gm.) of urea were given to normal men there occurred symptoms comparable to those of asthenic uremia,

[46] Couvee, Zeit. klin. Med., 1904 (54), 311.
[47] Jour. Amer. Med. Assoc., 1918 (70), 1208.
[47a] Jour. Med. Res., 1907 (17), 291.
[48] Jour. Amer. Med. Assoc., 1915 (65); 2067; Jour. Biol. Chem., 1917 (29), 355.

which appeared only when the urea concentration of the blood had reached levels of 160 to 245 mg. of urea per 100 c.c. *i. e.*, just the concentrations that are usually seen in well developed uremia. If in these experiments of brief duration such marked symptoms were produced by urea, what striking effects must be expected when these same urea concentrations are continued in the blood for days and weeks at a time.[49] We must find out what results not only from urea, but from creatinine and uric acid kept in the blood at the concentration found in uremia for long periods, as well as any other substance that may be increased in the blood in uremia. An experiment of a few minutes' or hours' duration cannot be expected to duplicate or elucidate a condition of weeks duration. In chronic diseases our experimental investigations must be of some reasonably comparable duration, and this principle of investigation is now made possible by Woodyatt's methods.

And finally, in view of the extremely varied symptomatology of renal incompetence, we must recognize that it is highly probable that in different cases these symptoms vary because of different conditions. In one case, urea may be the chief factor, in another the action of urea may be complicated by the effects of acidosis or high blood pressure per se, while in others cerebral edema may be the chief influence. Some continental writers hold that there is a true uremic picture due solely to cerebral edema from salt and water retention, occurring especially in the young, to be distinguished from the uremia of nitrogenous retention, and from a pseudouremia resulting from the circulatory disturbances of arteriosclerosis.[50] Howland and Marriott call attention to the reduced calcium in the blood in uremic acidosis, and as nervous irritability is increased by reduction of calcium this may also be a factor in the nervous manifestations of uremia. All possible shades of coöperating influences may be expected to occur when the kidneys fail, and to explain the confused, variable, changing picture of the uremic state.[51]

TOXEMIAS OF PREGNANCY[52]

Under this heading are included eclampsia, as characterized by convulsions and certain anatomical changes, together with those instances of intoxication with similar anatomical changes and no con-

---

[49] However, in *Salachians* the normal urea content in the blood is over two per cent. and ammonium salts exceed $\frac{n}{10}$ NH_3, (See A. B. Macallum, Amer. Jour. Med. Sci., 1918 (156), 1), but it may well be that in such species the tissues are adapted to their environment.

[50] See Haim and Tchertkoff, Rev. Méd. Suisse Romande, 1918 (38), 15.

[51] The influence of a hypothetical internal secretion of the kidney (Brown-Séquard)), or of the products of nephrolysis (Ascoli), as a cause of uremia, may now be considered as of historical interest only. (See Pearce, Arch. Int. Med., 1908 (2), 77; 1910 (5), 133.) The same is true of the attempt to explain the high blood pressure as the result of adrenal hypertrophy. (Pearce, Jour. Exp. Med., 1908 (10), 735; 1910 (12), 128.)

[52] Review and bibliography by Ewing, Amer. Jour. Med. Sci., 1910 (139), 829.

vulsions, and the related pernicious vomiting of pregnancy. Acute yellow atrophy of the liver belongs in the same category, although often occurring independent of pregnancy.

ECLAMPSIA[53]

In many respects eclampsia resembles uremia; so much so, indeed, that Frerichs and others have referred to eclampsia as "puerperal uremia." Considering it as a simple uremia occurring in pregnancy, uremia and eclampsia have in common the constant occurrence of renal disturbance with albuminuria and decreased elimination of urea, and also violent convulsions and profound coma terminating in death. On the other hand, eclampsia differs greatly from uremia in the anatomical changes observed in the organs of the body other than the kidneys; these are of such a nature that in some cases it becomes difficult to distinguish eclampsia from acute yellow atrophy of the liver.[54] while in other cases the picture resembles that of a profound bacterial intoxication, so that numerous authors have urged that eclampsia is the result of a bacterial infection. At the present time the cause of puerperal eclampsia is quite unknown, but there is a decided tendency to assume that poisonous substances are developed in the placenta or fetus, or are formed in the body as a reaction of the maternal organism to the foreign fetal elements. These theories will be discussed after considering the known facts concerning the chemical changes of the disease that have been reported by various observers.

Chemical Changes in Eclampsia.—*Urinary changes* are practically invariably present, and usually they are profound, although there are no known characteristic qualitative or quantitative differences from the urinary changes of puerperal albuminuria without eclampsia. Proteins are abundant, including a large proportion of globulin, decreasing rapidly after delivery as a rule. The urea is usually very low, but generally increases with great rapidity after delivery, until two or three times the normal amount is passed per day; as urea and ammonia do not seem to be greatly increased in the blood, this has been interpreted as indicating that during eclampsia there is an accumulation of the precursors of urea in the system (Sikes). However, the involution of the uterus itself results in an increased nitrogen excretion which probably accounts for much if not all of these findings (Slemons).[55] There is an excessive elimination of nitrogen in the form of ammonia, which is said to be due to the formation of abnormal quantities of sarcolactic and other organic acids in the body, which are combined with ammonia in the blood and

[53] Literature is given by Sikes in The Practitioner, 1905 (74), pp. 478 and 642; L. Zuntz, Handb. d. Biochem., 1909, III (I), 366; Seitz, Arch. f. Gyn., 1909 (87), 79.

[54] Concerning the liver changes see Konstantinowitsch, Ziegler's Beitr., 1907 (40), 483.

[55] Bull. Johns Hopkins Hosp., 1914 (25), 195.

eliminated in the urine.[56]   This fact has led many to look with favor upon the idea that eclampsia is due to an acid intoxication.   Other nitrogenous urinary constituents may also be increased, so that the relative proportion of nitrogen eliminated as urea is often greatly reduced.   It is said that the toxicity of the urine, which is high in normal pregnancy, is increased if the kidneys are not impaired, but decreased if their permeability is impaired by nephritis, the character of the toxicity being such as to indicate that it is from substances derived by disintegration of proteins (Franz).   The proportion of sulphur eliminated in an unoxidized form, as compared with that eliminated as SO_4, is much greater than normal.   These findings all indicate that oxidation within the body is impaired.   There is more or less retention of chlorides, but there is nothing characteristic in this.[57] In spite of the hepatic lesions of eclampsia the tolerance for levulose was not found impaired by Alsberg.[58]

The nonprotein nitrogen of the blood is but little increased in eclampsia, and not to the extent usually seen in uremia, and it bears no definite relation to the severity of the symptoms (Farr and Williams).[59]   They found from 25 to 72 mg. per 100 c.c. in seven cases. These figures can be reasonably explained as the result of tissue disintegration rather than renal retention and indicate that the renal changes are the result rather than the cause of the intoxication. Losee and Van Slyke could find no increase of amino-acids or other intermediates of protein destruction in either blood or urine in pregnancy toxemias,[60] their total nonprotein blood nitrogen figures ranging from 25 to 46 mg.   Similar results are reported by Slemons,[61] who also found normal amounts of fat, with increased cholesterol and decreased lecithin, and after the convulsions some increase in blood sugar.   The uric acid content of the blood is high (5–9 mg.).[62]   With the observed low blood urea of eclampsia it is difficult to account for Hammett's[63] finding of a high urea content in eclamptic placentas. Macallum describes a high proportion of potassium in the blood in eclampsia.[64]

The decrease in the alkalinity of the blood observed by Zangmeister and others has been ascribed to the formation of sarcolactic acid by Zweifel,[65] who failed, however, to find an excess of CO_2, or to detect oxybutyric acid or oxalic acid in the blood.   As to the blood pro-

[56] See Zweifel and Lockmann, Münch. med. Woch., 1906 (53), 297; Cent. f. Gyn., 1909 (33), 847.
[57] Zinsser, Zeit. f. Geb., 1912 (70), 200.
[58] Cent. f. Gyn., 1910 (34), 6.
[59] Amer. Jour. Med. Sci., 1914 (147), 556.
[60] Amer. Jour. Med. Sci., 1917 (153), 94, corroborated by Morse, Bull. Johns Hopkins Hosp., 1917 (28), 199.
[61] Amer. Jour. Obst., 1918 (77), 717.
[62] Slemons and Bogert, Jour. Biol. Chem., 1917 (32), 63.
[63] Jour. Biol. Chem., 1918 (34), 515.
[64] Amer. Jour. Med. Sci., 1918 (156), 1.
[65] Arch. f. Gyn., 1905 (76), 537.

teins, fibrin ferment has been found increased by Dienst,[66] while Schmidt found a relative increase in the globulin. Sikes concludes that the statements to be found in the literature concerning the toxicity of the blood in eclampsia leave nothing proved concerning this point, but more recent studies by Graf and Landsteiner[67] affirm an increase of toxicity of the blood, not due to any special poison but to an increase in the amount of the toxic substances ordinarily present; however, any studies of toxicity of the blood are of doubtful value because of the reactions produced by injections of even normal blood. More attention may be given to the observation of Hüssey[68] that while the serum of pregnant women has a slight vasodilator effect, in eclampsia and other pregnancy toxicoses there is a marked vasoconstrictor effect. The antitryptic titer of the blood may be much increased.[69] Zangmeister[70] ascribes importance to edema of the brain. Ballerini[71] found that the physico-chemical changes in the blood are quite the same as in corresponding conditions of nephritis. An increase in the sugar content of the blood has been observed[72] but no other abnormality of carbohydrate metabolism is usually present. Blood lipase is much increased because of the hepatic injury (Whipple).[73]

Theories as to Etiology.—The anatomical changes of eclampsia are such as to leave little or no room for doubt that there is a severe intoxication with poisons that have a markedly toxic effect upon all the organs of the body, thus differing from the toxic materials at work in uremia, which seem to affect chiefly the central nervous system and to produce no marked tissue changes. Repeated bacteriological and histological studies have failed to demonstrate that infection with either vegetable or animal parasites is the cause, and clinical observations do not support such an hypothesis. The association of the condition with pregnancy, and particularly the rapid improvement that often follows the removal of the contents of the uterus, almost compels us to admit that the causative agent is produced by the fetus or the placenta. Some investigators (Politi, Liepmann) believe that they have found a greater degree of toxicity in extracts from the placentas from eclamptic than from normal women. We have no exact ideas as to the nature of the supposed toxic substances, except that recent developments in the study of immunity reactions point to their origin from proteolysis of tissue proteins, presumably from the placenta. The hypothesis of

[66] Arch. f. Gyn., 1912 (96), 43; Zeit. Geb. u. Gyn., 1919 (82), 102.
[67] Cent. f. Gyn., 1900 (33), 142.
[68] Corrbl. Schw. Aerzte, 1918 (48), 691.
[69] Franz, Arch. f. Gyn., 1914 (102), 579; Ecolle, Arch. Mens. Obst. Gyn., 1917 (6), 97.
[70] Deut. med. Woch., 1911 (37), 1879.
[71] Annali Ostet. e. Gin., 1910 (32), 273.
[72] Benthin, Monats. Geb. u. Gyn., 1913 (37), 305; Ryser, Deut. Arch. klin. Med., 1916 (118), 408; Slemons, *loc. cit.*[61]
[73] Jour. Med. Res., 1913 (24), 357.

Zweifel that lactic acid is responsible seems untenable, and the degree of acidosis present is not sufficient to account for the intoxication (Losee and Van Slyke).

The Placenta as a Source of Intoxication.—Histologists having frequently observed placental cells in the blood and vessels of eclamptic patients, it was once suggested that multiple *capillary emboli of placental cells*, detached from chorionic villi and forced into the placental circulation, cause the manifestations of the disease; this theory is entirely inadequate, however, to explain all the features of eclampsia. Related to this hypothesis is the idea that the placental tissues, being foreign to the maternal organism in so far as they are derived from the ovum, give rise to the production of antibodies (*syncytiolysins*) by the mother, which are toxic for pregnant animals (Ascoli), and which may have to do with eclampsia in some unknown way. Rosenau and Anderson found that guinea pigs could be made anaphylactic to guinea-pig placenta, showing conclusively that the placenta contains proteins foreign to the mother. Attempts to establish the anaphylactic nature of eclampsia have, like so many other theories, foundered on the fact of the characteristic anatomy of this disease, which is never seen in anaphylaxis.[74] The studies of Abderhalden have shown that the blood of every pregnant female animal contains enzymes which have a specific proteolytic action, and so the possibility exists that abnormal or excessive products of such proteolysis, or a lack of adequate defensive digestive action, may be responsible for the toxemias of pregnancy. Esch[75] and Franz[76] have, indeed, found evidence of the presence in the serum and urine of eclamptics, of substances resembling anaphylactic poisons in their action, and presumably derived from proteolysis somewhere in the body. Franz found that if the poison injures the kidneys seriously it is retained in the body, the urine ceasing to be toxic, which has, presumably a relation to the toxicosis of eclampsia.[77]

Liepmann[78] and others have reported the finding of a considerable degree of toxicity in eclamptic placentas, but this is probably related to the increased autolysis observed in eclamptic placentas by Dryfuss.[79] Obata[80] found no great difference in the toxicity of eclamptic

---

[74] See Felländer, Zeit. Geb. u. Gyn., 1911 (68), 26; Mosbacher, Deut. med. Woch., 1911 (37), 1021. Vertes (Monat. Geb. u. Gyn., 1914 (40), 361, 466) states that animals dying from anaphylaxis may show typical eclamptic tissue changes, which is not in accordance with the observations of many others.

[75] Münch. med. Woch., 1912 (59), 461.

[76] *Ibid.*, page 1702.

[77] Hull and Rhodenburg (Amer. Jour. Obst., 1914 (70), 919) ascribe importance to leucine derived from proteolysis of the placental elements, while Kiutsi (Zeit. Geb. u. Gyn., 1912 (72), 576) considers the nucleins of the placenta the toxic agents, both statements being unconfirmed and improbable.

[78] Münch. med. Woch., 1905 (52), 687 and 2484; Boos, Boston Med. and Surg. Jour., 1908 (158), 612.

[79] Biochem. Zeit., 1908 (7), 493.

[80] Jour. Immunol., 1919 (4), 111; bibliography on etiology of eclampsia.

and normal placentas, but believes that in eclampsia there is a reduced capacity of the maternal blood to neutralize this poison. According to Mohr and Heimann,[81] the eclamptic placenta shows a great decrease in lecithin, which they ascribe to the increased autolysis, and to the hydrolyzed lecithin they attribute the hemotoxic effects. On the other hand Murray and Bienenfeld[82] report the finding of an increased amount of lipoids in eclamptic placenta.[83]

The Fetus as a Source of Intoxication. —A reasonable view of the cause of eclampsia is that it is initiated by the excessive or abnormal products of metabolism thrown into the blood of the mother, both from the fetus and from her own overactive tissues; these cause injury to the kidneys, leading to a further retention, or injure the liver so that the normal metabolic processes of that organ (particularly oxidation) cannot be carried on; or, perhaps more often, both liver and kidney as well as other organs are injured. In this way a vicious circle might be established and rapidly lead to an overwhelming of the maternal system with toxic products derived from both her own and the fetal tissues. It must be admitted, however, that the rapid improvement that so often follows removal of the products of conception indicates strongly that the poisonous substances arise chiefly, if not exclusively, in the fetus or the placenta. But, as Liepmann points out, the child shows relatively little evidence of intoxication, while, on the other hand, eclampsia may develop *after* delivery of the fetus, which facts speak in favor of the place of the origin of the poison being the placenta and not the fetus, and death of the fetus seems to have no effect on the eclampsia.[84] Especially important in this connection is the observation of cases of eclampsia in patients with a hydatid mole and no fetus.[85]

The Ductless Glands in Eclampsia.—In view of the mystery surrounding the cause and effect of the enlargement of the thyroid during pregnancy, it is not strange that the suggestion has been made that the enlargement is for the purpose of neutralizing the excessive amounts of toxic materials in the maternal blood, and that failure of this enlargement is responsible for eclampsia. In support of this idea Lange[86] states that absence of the normal thyroid enlargement is usual in eclampsia, and Fruhinsholz and Jeandelize[87] note the frequency of eclampsia in myxedematous women. The notable influence of calcium upon convulsions, and the possible deficiency in calcium during pregnancy, has led to the suggestion that this may be responsible for eclampsia,[88] and, since the parathyroids are re-

[81] *Ibid.*, 1912 (46), 367.
[82] Jour. Obst. and Gyn. Brit. Empire, 1910 (18), 225; Biochem. Zeit., 1912 (43), 245.
[83] The hypothesis of Mohr and Freund that oleic acid from the eclamptic placenta is a hemolytic factor, is not corroborated by Polano (Zeit. Geb. u. Gyn., 1910 (65), 581).
[84] See Lichtenstein, Zeit. f. Gyn., 1912 (36), 1419.
[85] Hitschmann, Cent. f. Gyn., 1904 (28), 1089. See also Gross (Prager med. Woch., 1909 (34), (365) who found records of seven cases of eclampsia with hydatid mole, with or without a fetus.
[86] Zeit. f. Geb. u. Gyn., 1899 (40), 34.
[87] Presse Méd., 1902 (10), 1023.
[88] See Silvestri, Gaz. degli Osped., 1910 (31), 689; Mitchell, Med. Record, 1910 (78), 906.

35

lated to calcium metabolism, that they are concerned;[89] but such theories fail to explain the many changes other than the convulsions, and have not been accorded much importance.   Kastle and Healy[90] consider that parturient paresis of cattle, which bears some resemblance to human eclampsia, is caused by absorption of toxic substances produced in the formation of the colostrum; it is cured by dilating the lacteal ducts by oxygen or other means.   This observation lends support to the theory advanced by Sellheim[91] that human eclampsia is of mammary gland origin.

Pernicious Vomiting of Pregnancy.—This condition is inseparably associated with eclampsia and non-convulsive toxemias of pregnancy, there being transitional and border-line cases of all sorts.   ·In fatal cases of pernicious vomiting anatomical changes resembling those of eclampsia have been found, and albuminuria and icterus are often observed.[92]   The chief chemical interest in these cases lies in the urinary findings, there being commonly observed a relatively high proportion of ammonia and undetermined nitrogen with decreased urea, which findings have been considered indicative of defective oxidation or deaminization (Ewing and Wolf) and of prognostic and diagnostic significance (Williams).   There is also excretion of acetone bodies and other evidence of more or less acidosis.[93]   Underhill and Rand[94] hold that the urinary changes are entirely compatible with those which can be produced by starvation which is present, of course, in pernicious vomiting; but Ewing[95] contends that there are other underlying factors beyond those of starvation.

Summary.—Most of the facts at hand speak against the idea that one definite chemical substance is responsible for the anatomical changes and symptomatic manifestations of eclampsia.   More probably there are present not only the poisonous substances that initiate the tissue changes, and which probably originate in the placenta itself or from digestion of placenta proteins in the maternal blood or organs, but also toxic substances that accumulate because of the disorganization of the liver and kidney cells, and which are possibly similar to the toxic substances most prominent in uremia and in acute yellow atrophy, for eclampsia seems to stand intermediate between these two diseases, encroaching upon the characteristics of each. Acid intoxication, which undoubtedly exists to a greater or less degree in some cases of eclampsia, is not an important cause of the clinical manifestations of the disease.   The finding of minute quantities of lactic acid in the blood, urine, and in the cerebrospinal fluid (Füth and Lockemann) is not of great significance, for, as Wolf[96] rightly

[89] Massaglia and Sparapani, Arch. ital. Biol., 1907 (48), 109.
[90] Jour. Infec. Dis., 1912 (10), 226.
[91] Zent. f. Gyn., 1909 (34), 1609.
[92] See Ewing and Wolf, Amer. Jour. Obstr., 1907 (55), 289.
[93] See Gilliatt and Kennaway, Quart. Jour. Med., 1919 (12), 61; Losee and Van Slyke, Amer. Jour. Med. Sci., 1917 (153), 94; Duncan and Harding, Canad. Med. Assoc. Jour., 1918 (8), 1057.
[94] Arch. Int. Med., 1910 (5), 61.
[95] Amer. Jour. Med. Sci., 1910 (139), 828.
[96] New York Med. Jour., 1906 (83), 813.

insists, similar amounts may be found in other conditions associated with convulsions and partial asphyxia, or in partial starvation, such as results from the vomiting of pregnancy. The excretion of these organic acids, as well as the large proportion of unoxidized sulphur in the urine, indicates that incomplete oxidation is an important feature of eclampsia, and under such conditions a large number of imperfectly known toxic substances may accumulate in the blood and tissues. The defective oxidation indicated by the urinary findings are probably the result of the injury to the liver-cells, which have such a prominent oxidizing function. The hypotheses which ascribe the intoxication to products of specific proteolysis of the foreign proteins of the placenta which have entered the maternal organism, are suggestive, but as yet are not sufficiently developed to permit of any definite conclusions as to the extent to which they apply.

ACUTE YELLOW ATROPHY OF THE LIVER

In this condition there is presented a striking picture of autolysis, in that a large parenchymatous organ undergoes a rapid reduction of size because of a solution of its structural elements, while at the same time products of protein digestion (leucine, tyrosine, etc.) appear free in the liver, the blood, and the urine. Because of these prominent features and their relation to the questions of metabolism in general, and the function of the liver in particular, acute yellow atrophy of the liver has been the object of much greater interest and investigation than its clinical importance would warrant, for it is not a common disease.[97]

The etiology of the disease is quite unknown, but it is very probably not a specific one for we find that numerous forms of intoxication may lead to a condition closely resembling acute yellow atrophy,[98] particularly puerperal eclampsia, and some cases of septicemia (especially with the streptococcus),[99] and poisoning with phosphorus, arsenic, nitrophenols and mushrooms.[1] It seems probable that any poison which does not directly cause death, but which causes a severe injury to the liver-cells without at the same time destroying the autolytic enzymes, so that the cells die and undergo rapid autolysis, may produce a condition identical with or similar to acute yellow atrophy (Wells and Bassoe).[2] In the typical cases of the disease, of "idiopathic" origin, the poisonous agent possibly comes from the alimentary canal, as indicated by a preliminary period of gastro-intestinal disturbance

[97] Up to 1903 there had been reported about 500 cases (Best, Thesis, University of Chicago, 1903).
[98] It is to be borne in mind that the color is yellow only during the earlier stages, "red atrophy" occurring later, but the name acute "yellow atrophy" has come through usage to apply to the disease as a whole.
[99] Babes, Ann. Inst. Path. Bucarest, vol. 6.
[1] Frey, Zeit. klin. Med., 1912 (75), 455; Prym, Virchow's Arch., 1919 (226), 229.
[2] Jour. Amer. Med. Assoc., 1904 (44), 685.

that usually precedes the onset of the disease, and secondly by the fact that the liver seems to receive the chief effect of the poison. Whether these hypothetical poisons are produced by abnormal fermentation and putrefaction in the alimentary tract, or by a specific organism elaborating its poison in this location, is quite unknown. Bacteriological studies of the disease have so far given inconstant and non-instructive results. In the countries where phosphorus poisoning is common (especially Austria) there has been found much difficulty in distinguishing in many cases the results of phosphorus poisoning from acute yellow atrophy of the liver, and many have contended that there is no real difference; i. e., that phosphorus, as well as unknown poisons, may cause acute yellow atrophy. The present trend of opinion, however, seems to favor the view that there is a primary liver atrophy which is different from that caused by phosphorus or other known poisons in several essential respects.[3]

Phosphorus Poisoning.—*Between phosphorus poisoning and "primary" hepatic atrophy the following chief differences may be discerned:* Phosphorus produces a general injurious effect upon all the organs of the body, the liver merely showing the most marked anatomical changes, which at first consist of a fatty metamorphosis of the liver, due to migration of the body fat from the fat deposits into the injured cells (Roseneld, Taylor); subsequently the liver cells disintegrate, the cytoplasm being affected before the nucleus, and the liver may become smaller than normal, although it is usually enlarged because of the fat deposition. Typical acute yellow atrophy is characterized by an early necrosis of a large proportion of the liver-cells, the nucleus becoming unstainable while the cytoplasm is still little altered in appearance, and fatty changes play a subordinate rôle or are absent. As Anschütz says, the poison seems to strike at the life of the cell, its nucleus, while phosphorus attacks the cytoplasm. Furthermore, the poison of yellow atrophy seems to be very specific, for it attacks the other organs of the body almost not at all, and within the liver it affects only the hepatic cells proper, while the bile-duct epithelium and the stroma cells are so little injured that they are able to proliferate greatly, this proliferation being a prominent feature. There are also clinical and chemical differences that will be discussed later, but yet, on the whole, the resemblances of yellow atrophy and phosphorus poisoning are so great that we have obtained much information concerning the former by means of experimental studies of phoshorus poisoning.

Delayed Chloroform Poisoning.—After *chloroform narcosis*, and rarely after ether, there occasionally develops a severe intoxication, with clinical and anatomical findings very similar to acute yellow atrophy and phosphorus poisoning;[1] in point of the fatty changes the cases usually stand intermediate between acute yellow atrophy and phosphorus poisoning. This action of chloroform would seem, from the studies of Evarts Graham,[5] to be produced by the hydrochloric acid formed from it in the liver. Some cases of puerperal eclampsia also present such profound

[3] See Anschütz, Arb. a. d. Path. Inst. Tübingen, 1902 (3), 230; Paltauf, Verh. Deut. Path. Gesell., 1903 (5), 91; Riess, Berl. klin. Woch., 1905 (42), No. 44a, p. 51.

[1] Complete review and literature by Bevan and Favill, Jour. Amer. Med. Assoc., 1905 (45), 691; Muskens, Mitt. Grenz. Med. u. Chir., 1911 (22), 568. Full discussion of chemistry of chloroform necrosis by Wells, Jour. Biol. Chem., 1908 (5), 129. Experimental necrosis—see Whipple and Sperry, Johns Hopkins Hosp. Bull., 1909 (20), 278; Graham, Jour. Exper. Med., 1912 (15), 307; Simonds, Arch. Int. Med., 1919 (23), 362; Davis and Whipple, *ibid.*, p. 612.

[5] Jour. Exp. Med., 1915 (22), 48. This hypothesis receives support from the conclusion reached by many investigators that dichlorethylsulphide ("mustard gas") also injures tissues through intracellular dissociation liberating HCl. (See Lillie *et al.*, Jour. Pharm., 1919 (14), 75.)

liver changes that they are distinguished as eclampsia chiefly on the basis of the convulsive manifestations, rather than on the ground of anatomical changes. So, too, the hepatic changes in certain septicemias and acute syphilis may resemble those of acute yellow atrophy to a greater or less degree.

Summary of Views on Etiology.—From a review of the literature and the study of a few cases, the writer has reached the following understanding of the condition described as acute yellow atrophy of the liver: The "atrophy" is due entirely to autolysis of necrotic liver-cells by their own enzymes. In the most typical cases of "primary" or "idiopathic" yellow atrophy we have to do with a poison having a very specific effect on the liver-cells, which destroys their "life" (*i. e.*, stops synthetic activities) without injuring their intracellular proteolytic enzymes,[6] and consequently autolysis occurs; as the poison affects other organs but little, the necrosis and autolysis continue until there is so much loss of liver function that systemic poisoning results from the hepatic insufficiency and from the resulting accumulation of poisonous products of incomplete metabolism. That the intoxication comes in large measure from the changes in the liver, even in phosphorus poisoning, is shown by the greater resistance to phosphorus of dogs with Eck's fistulas.[7] The patient dies from this poisoning,[8] and the liver is found at autopsy to have decreased by from one-third to one-half or more in its volume. This great change would not be possible if the poisons affected the heart, kidneys, or brain as much as they do the liver structure, which is probably the reason that phosphorus, bacterial poisons, snake poisons, and other poisons that affect many sorts of cells do not ordinarily produce the typical picture of liver atrophy. When these poisons affect the liver more and the other tissues less, we approach the condition of acute yellow atrophy; *e. g.*, if the dose of phosphorus is not so great as to kill the patient through injury of other more vital organs, after a few days the necrosed liver-cells undergo autolysis, and if enough liver-cells have been destroyed, hepatic insufficiency may cause death, with the finding of an anatomical condition in the liver that can be properly designated as acute atrophy. Hence it is possible for many poisons to cause this condition under certain circumstances, and there seem to be certain unknown poisons (possibly of intestinal origin[9]) that are of such a nature that they cause specifically acute hepatic atrophy. The above hypothesis seems to explain all the known facts concerning this disease. That phosphorus, chloroform, and some other poisons lead particularly to fatty changes may, perhaps, be due

[6] According to some investigators phosphorus augments autolysis even *in vitro* (see Krontowski, Zeit. f. Biol., 1910 (54), 479).

[7] Fischler and Bardach, Zeit. physiol. Chem., 1912 (78), 435.

[8] The mortality of cases sufficiently typical to be diagnosed antemortem is estimated by Rondaky (Roussky Vratch. Oct. 28, 1900) at 97 to 98 per cent. Concerning the regenerative changes in the cases which recover, see Yamasaki (Zeit. f. Heilk., Path. Abt., 1903 (24), 248).

[9] See Carbone, Riforma Med., 1902 (1), 687 and 698.

to their acting especially upon the oxidizing enzymes,[10] leaving the autolytic enzymes and the lipase free to digest the cell and to form fat.[11]   That it is particularly the oxidizing enzymes that are attacked is well shown by the chemical findings, and also by Loewy's[12] observation that in poisoning with CNH, which acts by impairing oxidation, the alterations in protein metabolism are very similar to those of phosphorus poisoning.[13]   To be sure, Lusk[14] found no deficiency in general oxidation in phosphorus poisoning, but this does not signify that the local changes do not depend upon *local* defective oxidative processes.   Furthermore, the marked power of sugar to protect the liver from such poisons as phosphorus and chloroform seems to depend on its furnishing easily oxidizable material to cells with reduced oxidative capacity (Simonds).[15]

Not only phosphorus but many metals, especially mercury, seem able to cause the anatomical changes of acute yellow atrophy, for the condition has been observed very frequently in persons receiving mercurial and arsenical treatment for syphilis.[16]   Here the syphilis has been held responsible by some, but the fact that in many of the cases the syphilis was quiescent or chronic at the time, and that mercury and arsenic are known to kill cells and stimulate autolysis, seems to incriminate the metals,[17] at least in some cases.   On the other hand, Stewart,[17a] calls attention to the fact that acute yellow atrophy occurs especially often after poisoning with picric acid, trinitro-toluene, dinitrobenzene and aromatic arsenicals; as in all these substances the only common component is the benzene radical, its responsibility is strongly suggested.

CHEMICAL CHANGES OF ACUTE YELLOW ATROPHY

The Urine.—Most striking, and long regarded as pathognomonic, is the presence of *leucine* and *tyrosine* in the urine, first described by

[10] See Verworn, Deut. med. Woch., 1909 (35), 1593; Joannovics and Pick, Arch. ges. Physiol., 1911 (140), 327.
[11] Wells, Jour. Amer. Med. Assoc., 1906 (46), 341.
[12] Cent. f. Physiol., 1906 (19), 23.
[13] The hypothesis suggested by Quincke (Nothnagel's Handbook, 1899, vol. 18, p. 307) that possibly regurgitation of pancreatic juice up the bile ducts might be responsible for the degenerative changes in the liver, is contradicted by the fact that the bile pressure is greater than the pancreatic juice pressure, and that the bile-ducts and peripheral portions of the lobules are least affected.   Nor could Best[97] prove that trypsin injected into the liver by way of the bile-ducts is able to cause such changes.   (See Wells and Bassoe.[2])
[14] Science of Nutrition, Philadelphia, 1909.
[15] Arch. Int. Med., 1919 (23), 362.   Ervin, however, ascribes the protective effect of carbohydrate feeding to the glycogen, which protects the protein-fat emulsion of the liver cell cytoplasm from the action of acids.   (Jour. Lab. Clin Med., 1919 (5), 146).
[16] Severin, Zeit. klin. Med., 1912 (76), 138.   Bendig, Münch. med. Woch., 1915 (62), 1144.
[17] Tileston (Boston Med. and Surg. Jour., 1908 (158), 510) has described a case of acute yellow atrophy from mercurialism without syphilis.
[17a] Stewart, Vining and Bibby, Jour. Path. Bact., 1919 (23), Proc. Path. Soc., p. 120.

Frerichs. While we now know that these and other amino-acids may occur in the urine in any conditions in which there is a great breaking down of tissue within the body, yet it is true that in no other condition are they found so abundantly as in acute hepatic atrophy (as high as 1.5 gm. of tyrosine per diem has been found).[18] They are nearly constantly present (in thirteen out of fourteen cases studied by Riess),[19] tyrosine being usually the more abundant. *Deutero-proteose* is also frequently (but not constantly) found, as further evidence of abnormal protein splitting.[20] Uric acid and other purines are often somewhat, but not characteristically, increased, probably resulting from the nuclear destruction in the liver. There is often an increase in ethereal sulphates (Salkowski),[21] and in phosphorus poisoning various bases have been found in the urine,[22] which presumably might also be found in acute yellow atrophy if sought for. The total elimination of nitrogen is increased[23] (particularly if the scanty intake is considered), and the proportion that appears as urea is decreased, largely because of the presence of much ammonia,[24] part of which, at least, is eliminated combined with organic acids. Chief of these acids is *sarcolactic* acid, but of particular interest is the supposed appearance of *oxymandelic acid*,

$$HO\langle\;\rangle CHOH—COOH,$$

which might be derived from tyrosine (Schultzen and Riess),

$$HO\langle\;\rangle CH_2—CH(NH_2)—COOH,$$

by the splitting out of the NH_2 group, the benzene nucleus failing to be completely oxidized as it normally is. The researches of Ellinger and Kotake,[25] however, make it probable that the supposed oxymandelic acid is something else, most likely *p-oxyphenyl-lactic acid*,

$$HO\langle\;\rangle CH_2—CHOH—COOH$$

[18] An interesting exception has been reported by W. G. Smith (Practitioner, 1903 (70), 155) who found great quantities of leucine in the urine of a young woman who was apparently not at all ill. Rosenbloom has found tyrosine crystals in the urine of a healthy pregnant woman, and cites other cases of tyrosinuria without hepatic atrophy (N. Y. Med. Jour., Sept. 19, 1914).

[19] Berl. klin. Woch., 1905 (42), No. 44 a., p. 54.

[20] Salkowski (Berl. klin. Woch., 1905 (42), 1581) found in the urine of a case of acute yellow atrophy a large quantity of nitrogen in a colloidal but non-protein form, apparently of carbohydrate nature. Mancini (Arch. di farm. sperim., 1906, Bd. v) also observed an increase in the colloidal nitrogen of the urine in liver diseases.

[21] Virchow's Arch., 1909 (198), 188.

[22] Takeda, Pflüger's Arch., 1910 (133), 365.

[23] See Welsch, Arch. int. pharm. et thér., 1905 (14), 211.

[24] See Voegtlin, Johns Hopkins Hosp. Bull., 1908 (19), 50; White, Boston Med. and Surg. Jour., 1908 (158), 729.

[25] Zeit. physiol. Chem., 1910 (65), 397 and 402; also Fromherz, *ibid.*, 1911 (70), 351.

which can be demonstrated in the urine of dogs poisoned with phosphorus, and which represents a simple deaminization of tyrosine without further oxidation. It is evident from the urinary findings, therefore, that oxidation is decreased, which is presumably because of the destruction of liver tissue with its important oxidizing functions. The reduction of oxidation can also be shown experimentally by studying the respiratory exchange, Welsch having found the oxidation decreased by from $\frac{1}{9}$ to $\frac{1}{5}$ in phosphorus poisoning. Carbamates do not seem to be present in recognizable amounts, and sugar is also absent.

In phosphorus poisoning the urinary findings are similar, but with marked quantitative differences. Tyrosine cannot usually be detected, at least by ordinary methods, being found by Riess in but 7 of 36 cases of (human) phosphorus poisoning, and in but 4 of these was it abundant. Leucine is even less frequently found. With experimental animals glycine and other amino-acids have been found[26] in the urine, and they could probably be found in acute hepatic atrophy if the same delicate methods were employed. Wohlgemuth[27] has indeed found glycine, alanine, and arginine in human urine after phosphorus poisoning. The small quantity of amino-acids in phosphorous poisoning is probably due to the relative slowness of the autolytic changes. On the other hand, the deficiency of oxidation in phosphorus poisoning is shown by the abundant elimination of organic acids, Riess having obtained as high as 4 to 6 grams of the zinc salt of *paralactic* acid from the urine (per liter) in human cases, and its presence seems to be constant.

The Liver.[28]—In the liver may be found an abundance of the free amino-acids that have not yet escaped by diffusion, their presence having been first detected by Frerichs microscopically. Taylor[29] was able to isolate from a liver weighing 900 grams, 0.35 gm. of leucine and 0.612 gm. aspartic acid, which probably represent much less than the total amount present. Deuteroalbumose was also found, but no peptone, arginine, histidine, or lysine, and glycogen was also absent. In another case that appeared to be the result of chloroform intoxication, Taylor[30] obtained 4 grams of leucine, 2.2 grams of tyrosine, and 2.3 grams of arginine nitrate. Wells found several amino-acids free in sufficient quantity to identify in the liver in cases of acute yellow atrophy and chloroform necrosis, an increase in gelatigenous substance in the former, and of organic non-lipoidal phosphorus in both, sulphur being unchanged. The increase in tissue phosphorus is striking, and agrees with Slowtzoff's and Wohlgemuth's[31] finding that the tissue phosphorus persists in experimental phosphorus poisoning. Wakeman[32] found that in phosphorus poisoning of dogs the liver shows a diminution of the hexone bases as a whole, the arginine being espe-

[26] Abderhalden and Barker, Zeit. physiol. Chem., 1904 (42), 524; Abderhalden and Bergell, *ibid.*, 1903 (39), 464.
[27] Zeit. physiol. Chem., 1905 (44), 74.
[28] Full analyses and discussion of the chemistry of the liver in acute yellow atrophy and choloroform necrosis given by Wells, Jour. Exper. Med., 1907 (9), 627; Arch. Int. Med., 1908 (1), 589; Jour. Biol. Chem., 1908 (5), 129.
[29] Zeit. physiol. Chem., 1902 (34), 580; Jour. Med. Research, 1902 (8), 424.
[30] Univ. of Calif. Publications (Pathol.), 1904 (1), 43.
[31] Biochem. Zeit., 1911 (32), 172.
[32] Jour. Exper. Med., 1905 (7), 292; Jour. Biol. Chem., 1908 (4), 119.

cially reduced; but no such change was found by him in acute yellow atrophy, nor by Wells in chloroform necrosis. Jackson and Pearce[33] found an increase in the diamino nitrogen with extensive necrosis of the liver in dogs and horses. Wohlgemuth[34] found arginine in the urine in phosphorus poisoning. The lecithin of the liver is also decreased (Heffter[35] and Wells), and the increase in P_2O_5 observed in the urine presumably comes partly from this source; cholesterol is unchanged. Beebe[36] found the pentose of the liver not greatly altered from the normal relations. The typical idiopathic atrophied liver shows *little or no increase in fat*, either chemically or microscopically, whereas there is considerable replacement of the lost liver substance by water, as shown in the following table:

	Water	Fat	Fat-free Dried Substance
Normal liver (Quincke)	76.1	3.0	20.9
Normal liver (Wells)	77.6	5.0	17.4
Acute atrophy (Perls)	81.6	8.7	9.7
Acute atrophy (Perls)	76.9	7.6	15.5
Acute atrophy (v. Starck)	80.5	4.2	15.5
Acute atrophy (Taylor)	85.8	2.0	12.2
Acute atrophy (Wakeman)	79.3	...	....
Acute atrophy (Wells)	83.8	2.5	13.7
Acute atrophy (Voegtlin)	78.0	6.6	15.4
Phosphorus poisoning (v. Starck)	60.0	29.8	10.0
Fatty degeneration (v. Starck)	64.0	25.0	11.0
Chloroform necrosis (Wells)	72.4	8.8	18.8

Similar results have been obtained frequently by other observers, Taylor estimating that in his case about three-fourths of the liver parenchyma had disappeared. The yellow color of the liver tissue characteristic of this condition seems to be due to bilirubin rather than to fat, because as soon as the tissues are put into oxidizing agents (e. g., dichromate hardening fluids) they turn grass-green from the oxidation of the bilirubin into biliverdin. There seems to be a marked increase in free fatty acids, probably the unsaturated higher fatty acids, which are strongly hemolytic.[37] Glycogen is greatly reduced in phosphorous and chloroform poisoning, and presumably in acute yellow atrophy.

Jacoby[38] found that the livers from phosphorus-poisoned dogs underwent autolysis with greater rapidity than normal livers, which was attributed to increased activity or amount of the autolytic enzymes, although addition of phosphorus to a solution containing liver ferments was not found to increase their activity. The aldehydase was not found decreased, and tyrosinase could not be demonstrated,

[33] Jour. Exper. Med., 1907 (9), 520.
[34] Zeit. physiol. Chem., 1905 (44), 74.
[35] Arch. exp. Path. u. Pharm., 1891 (28), 97.
[36] Amer. Jour. of Physiol., 1905 (14), 237.
[37] Joannovics and Pick, Berl. klin. Woch., 1910 (47), 928.
[38] Zeit. physiol. Chem., 1900 (30), 174; see also Porges and Pribram, Arch. exp. Path. u. Pharm., 1908 (59), 20.

but Slowtzoff[39] found both peroxidase and protease decreased, and attributed the increased autolysis to a greater acidity of the liver. Burge[40] describes decrease in the catalase of liver and blood in experimental phosphorus poisoning, and Simonds[41] found hepatic ereptase also decreased, but not in chloroform poisoning; esterase was not altered.

The Blood.—In the blood marked changes are found, one of the most prominent, besides the icterus, being the *decreased coagulability* of the blood. This seems due to a loss of fibrinogen,[42] which, with the globulin, is greatly decreased, the albumin remaining less altered.[43] The fibrin-ferment also seems to be decreased. These changes may be due to direct autolysis of the blood constituents (Jacoby having found that thrombi become rapidly dissolved in phosphorus-poisoning) or to the changes in the liver. The icterus depends apparently upon lesions of the finest bile capillaries,[44] although there is also some increase in hemolysis, and a decrease in the total blood and all its elements (Welsch);[45] and both bile salts and pigments appear in the urine. In all these diseases with marked liver changes there is an increase in the lipase of the blood.[46] Neuberg and Richter[47] have analyzed the blood drawn during life from a patient with acute hepatic atrophy, and isolated from 355 c.c. of blood 0.787 gm. tyrosine, 1.102 gm. leucine, and 0.240 gm. of lysine; they estimated the amount of free amino-acids in the entire blood to be about 30 grams.[48] This amount is so large that they question the possibility of it all arising from the degenerated liver tissue. In dogs suffering from chloroform necrosis of the liver or phosphorus poisoning the amount of free amino acids in the blood and urine is usually very small.[49]

By the use of Van Slyke's method it has been found that acute yellow atrophy is accompanied by the highest amino-N figures in the blood recorded in any disease, Feigl and Luce[50] having reported

[39] Biochem. Zeit., 1911 (31), 227.
[40] Amer. Jour. Physiol., 1917 (43), 545.
[41] Jour. Exp. Med., 1918 (28), 673.
[42] Whipple and Hurwitz (Jour. Exper. Med., 1911 (13), 136) find a great decrease in fibrinogen during experimental choloroform necrosis of the liver.
[43] Jacoby, *loc. cit.*;[52] see also Doyon, Compt. Rend. Soc. Biol., 1905 (58), 493; and 1909, Vol. 66.
[44] Lang (Zeit. exp. Path., 1906 (3), 473) found fibrinogen in the bile of a dog poisoned with phosphorus, which may account for the occlusion of the bile vessels and the resulting jaundice.
[45] Arch. int. Pharm. et Thér., 1905 (14), 197.
[46] Whipple et al., Bull. Johns Hopkins Hosp., 1913 (24), 207 and 357. Quinan found the lipase content of liver tissue much reduced in chloroform necrosis (Jour. Med. Res., 1915 (32), 73). A review of work published on blood changes and liver function in phosphorus and chloroform poisoning is given by Marshall and Rowntree, Jour. Exp. Med., 1915 (22), 333.
[47] Deut. med. Woch., 1904 (30), 499.
[48] v. Bergmann (Hofmeister's Beit., 1904 (6), 40) was able to isolate 2.3 grams of amino-acids combined with the chloride of naphthalene sulphonic acid, from 270 c.c. of blood in a case of acute yellow atrophy.
[49] See Van Slyke, Arch. Int. Med., 1917 (19), 77.
[50] Biochem. Zeit., 1917 (79), 162.

200 mg. per 100 c.c., or over 1 per cent. of amino acids. The urea content is usually below 50 mg. The lipin content of the blood is also greatly increased,[51] with cholesterolemia but a decrease in phospholipins, the total ether extract being as high as 1.9 per cent. Sugar is at first increased and later decreased; acetone bodies are but slightly increased.

Origin of the Amino=acids.—The earliest conception of the source of the leucine and tyrosine found in the urine was that it came from the products of tryptic digestion absorbed from the intestinal tract, which the liver could not convert into urea because of its damaged condition. On the demonstration by Jacoby[52] that these same bodies were present in the livers of phosphorus-poisoned animals because of autolysis, it became probable that the leucine and tyrosine found in the urine were formed from the degenerated liver-cells rather than in the intestine, which view has become generally accepted. It seems most probable, however, that the urinary amino-acids are derived partly (and perhaps chiefly) from the autolysis of the liver, and partly from amino-acids produced both in the intestine and within the body during tissue metabolism, and which the liver cannot transform into urea as it normally does, for several observers have reported that even relatively slight disturbances in hepatic function are accompanied by a considerable rise in the amino-acids in the urine.[53]

ACID INTOXICATION AND ACETONURIA[54]

If a rabbit is given in repeated small doses by mouth considerable quantities of inorganic acids, such as hydrochloric or phosphoric acids, which it cannot destroy by oxidation, it soon becomes extremely ill. The manifestations are characteristic—unsteadiness of motion and stupor being followed by coma, in which the striking feature is the excessively active respiration, as if the animal were being asphyxiated (the so-called "air hunger"), while at the same time there is no cyanosis and the blood is bright red, containing much less CO_2 than normal, while the amount of oxygen remains quite normal. The current explanation of this interesting condition is as follows: Normally the blood carries the CO_2 away from the tissues to the lungs in combination with the inorganic alkalies of the blood, of which sodium is by far the most abundant. This combination is the bicarbonate of sodium (or other base), which in the lungs is decomposed into the carbonate, the CO_2 escaping into the alveolar air, according to this equation:

$$2NaHCO_3 \rightleftarrows Na_2CO_3 + H_2O + CO_2$$

[51] *Ibid.*, 1918 (86), 1.
[52] Zeit. physiol. Chem., 1900 (30), 174.
[53] See Masuda, Zeit. exp. Path., 1911 (8), 629; Labbé and Bith, Compt. Rend. Soc. Biol., 1912 (73), 210.
[54] General liturature to 1908, given by Ewing, Arch. Int. Med., 1908 (2), 330; also see Magnus-Levy, Ergebnisse inn. Med., 1908 (1), 374; Lusk, Arch. Int. Med., 1909 (3), 1. More recent literature given by Hurtley, Quart. Jour. Med., 1916 (9), 301, and see also monograph by Sellards, "Principles of Acidosis," Harvard Univ. Press, 1917; Whitney, Bost. Med. Surg. Jour., 1917 (176), 225.

The carbonate thus formed goes back to the tissues to combine again with more CO_2 and form bicarbonate. If acids are introduced into the blood they combine with the alkalies there, forming neutral salts which are eliminated in the urine, and in this way the amount of alkali in the blood is reduced, with a consequent reduction in the capacity of the blood to carry CO_2 away from the tissues; the amount of CO_2 in the blood sinking to as low as 2.5 and 3 per cent. (Walter). Consequently, in acid poisoning the CO_2 produced in metabolism accumulates in the tissues where it is formed, and blocks the processes of oxidation, so that the animal suffers from asphyxia exactly as if it were deprived of air. In other words, the lack of alkalies in the blood in acid intoxication checks the "internal respiration," as intracellular gas exchange is called, by preventing the removal of CO_2 from the cells. The acids stimulate the respiratory center, which is extremely sensitive to them, and the increased respiration tends to reduce the acidity by getting rid of the CO_2, but under the conditions of the experiment this is not sufficient to prevent asphyxia.

If the urine of such an animal is analyzed, it is found to contain increased quantities of the four chief inorganic bases, Na, K, Ca, and Mg (the last two apparently being derived from the bones);[55] but in addition to these it is found that the amount of ammonia in the urine is decidedly increased. If instead of a rabbit a carnivorous animal, such as a dog, is given acids, it will be found relatively insusceptible, so that much larger quantities can be given without causing acid intoxication. Examination of the urine of such a dog will show that the elimination of ammonia is increased much more than it is in the herbivora, while the inorganic alkalies are increased but little. From this it is deduced that in acid intoxication part of the nitrogen that normally goes to form urea becomes, while in the antecedent form of ammonia, combined with part of the acid that has entered the blood. In this way much of the neutralization of the acids is accomplished by ammonia, and the inorganic alkalies of the blood are spared. As in carnivora the amount of protein metabolism is much greater and more rapid than in herbivora, the ammonia available for neutralization of acids is much greater than in the latter, and hence the relative lack of susceptibility of carnivora to acid poisoning.[56] The proteins of the blood also combine some of the acid, perhaps one-fifth of the neutralizing capacity of the blood being attributable to them. Another factor is the possible accumulation of acids within the cells, which must modify greatly any conclusions based upon studies of the blood and urine. It is within the cells that the effects of acids must be manifested, and it is perfectly possible, and indeed almost certain,

[55] See Coto, Jour. Biol. Chem., 1918 (36), 355.

[56] This has been nicely shown by Eppinger (Wien. klin. Woch., 1906 (19), 111), who found that administration of considerable quantities of amino-acids (glycine alanine, aspartic acid) to rabbits greatly increased their resistance to acid intoxication, presumably by yielding ammonia through normal steps of protein metabolism.

that we may have degrees of acidity and alkalinity in the cells which are quite different from those in the blood.

As pointed out especially by Henderson,[57] the normal reaction of the body is kept practically constant chiefly by: 1. The salts of CO_2 and H_3PO_4, existing in such proportions of carbonate, bicarbonate and carbonic acid, or disodium- and monosodium-hydrogen-phosphate, as to produce an almost neutral solution. These being salts of weak acids with strong bases it follows that when a stronger acid, such as lactic or butyric, combines with the bases there is only the weak acid liberated and hence the influence of the strong acid on the blood reaction is greatly reduced. (2) The acid most abundantly formed in metabolism, CO_2, is volatile and hence is rapidly excreted by the lungs without withdrawing bases from the blood. (3) The kidneys can eliminate the other buffer acid, PO_4, with but a minimum of base attached in the form of NaH_2PO_4; and they also remove the basic product of metabolism, ammonia. By the combined influence of these factors the acids formed in metabolism are passed out with a maximum rapidity and with a minimum alteration in the reaction of the fluids by which they are carried through the body. In addition to these we have, as mentioned before, the capacity of the proteins to combine with both acids and alkalies, the reserve neutralizing capacity of ammonia formed in metabolism, and also the enormous reserve supply of bases in the bone salts. So effective is this mechanism that accurate determination of the H-ion concentration of the blood shows that very rarely is there more than the slightest deviation from the normal proportion of free H and OH ions, which is slightly on the alkaline side of exact neutrality. This neutrality is one of the most fixed of all the constants of the body.

Acidosis, therefore, is a condition in which the essential feature is not an actual acidity of the blood, but the impoverishment of the body in available bases, whereby there results a decreased capacity of the tissues to get rid of CO_2 and other acids formed in their metabolism. This reduction in bases may be, and most usually is, the result of excessive production of acids, in excreting which the bases are eliminated in excess, but it may also result from deficient capacity of the kidneys to excrete acids, since the kidneys play an important rôle in regulating acidity. Macleod[58] summarizes the conditions that might give rise to changes in the hydrogen ion concentration in the blood (C_H) as follows:

Increase of C_H.

Addition or accumulation of acid	Accumulation of CO_2 (asphyxial conditions). Incomplete oxidation of carbohydrate (lactic acid in muscular exercise).
	Defective oxidation of fat (ketosis).
	Renal insufficiency (nephritis).
	Decomposition of protein (as in acidosis of fever).
	Intestinal fermentation.
	Administration of acid (experimental).

[57] See Harvey Society Lectures, 1914-5.
[58] See reviews by Frothingham, Arch. Int. Med. 1916 (18) 717; Macleod, Jour. Lab. Clin. Med., 1919 (4), 315.

<table>
<tr><td></td><td>Increase of C_H.</td></tr>
</table>

	Increase of C_H.
Decrease of base	Diarrhea and hemorrhage, respectively (may explain acidosis in cholera and in certain forms of shock).[59]
	Decrease in C_H.
Addition or accumulation of base	Ammonia (faulty metabolism of urea). Intestinal putrefaction (infantile conditions). Administration of alkalies (experimental).
Removal of acids	Excretion of CO_2 (excessive pulmonary ventilation, as in faulty ether administration). Excretion of acid urine.

Practically, acidosis results either from defective oxidation of organic acids formed in metabolism or from defective elimination of mineral acids (acid phosphate) because of impaired renal function. The chief example of the former is the acidosis of diabetes, of the latter the acidosis of nephritis, and mixed forms may occur.

The degree of acidosis may be estimated in several ways; as follows:[58]

1. By determining the CO_2 content of the blood, which must decrease as other acids increase, or as the bases decrease.

2. Direct estimation of the H-ion concentration of the blood.

3. By determining the amount of acid or alkali necessary to change the reaction of the blood to different indicators.

4. Determination of the CO_2 tension of the alveolar air, this varying directly with the CO_2 tension of the arterial blood.

5. The "alkali tolerance test" of Sellards, which consists in ascertaining the amount of sodium bicarbonate that must be taken by mouth in order to produce an alkaline urine.

6. Estimation of the amount of organic acids, H-ion concentration, and ammonia content of the urine; a method which is fundamentally defective since it indicates merely the acids and bases that have been removed from the body and not those that remain to modify its reactivity.

7. Determination of the capacity of the blood serum to bind CO_2. Normal serum binds about 55 to 75 per cent. of its volume of CO_2, whereas in acidosis it may bind but 20 per cent. (Van Slyke)

DIABETIC COMA[54]

In man, poisoning with inorganic acids, as in the experiments cited above, is a rare occurrence, but not infrequently acid intoxication results from the presence of undue quantities of organic acids produced in metabolism. The most striking example of this is the coma of diabetes, in which the asphyxia without cyanosis, dependent upon failure of the blood to carry CO_2, is sometimes strikingly similar to that observed in experimental animals poisoned with acids. In diabetic coma the acid intoxication is due chiefly to the accumulation in the blood or tissues of large quantities of *β-oxybutyric acid*. Associated with it, in smaller quantities, are usually found *diacetic (acetoacetic) acid* and *acetone*, which are chemically so closely related that it has been

[59] To this may be added loss of base from biliary or pancreatic fistulæ.

generally considered that they are derived from the oxybutyric acid, as follows:

β-oxybutyric acid is—

$$CH_3—CHOH—CH_2—COOH,$$

and by oxidation this readily forms—

$$CH_3—CO—CH_2—COOH,$$

which is diacetic acid (being two molecules of acetic acid united to each other, as follows):

$$CH_3—CO—|OH—H_|—H_2C—COOH.$$

Diacetic acid is, in turn, readily deprived of its carbon dioxide, forming acetone,

$$CH_3—CO—CH_3.$$

All these reactions are easily accomplished in the laboratory, and there seemed to be reason for believing that they may normally occur in the same way in the animal body. Wakeman and Dakin,[59a] and others, however, found evidence that the liver cells may also *reduce* diacetic to β-oxybutyric acid, and it seems probable that this is the usual direction of the reaction, which they have found to be produced by a specific enzyme. Hurtley[54] concludes that the reduction of aceto-acetic acid to oxybutyric acid is accomplished by the body under ordinary conditions far more readily than the oxidation of oxybutyric to aceto-acetic acid. Marriot[60] gives the following scheme as indicating the normal path of fatty acid catabolism:

Fatty acid——→Butyric acid(?)——→Aceto-acetic acid——→ d-oxybutyric acid (readily burned) / l-oxybutyric acid (difficultly burned)

The study of the utilization of the acidosis substances when injected intravenously at accurately measured rates for considerable periods by Wilder,[61] furnishes conclusive evidence of the origin of β-oxybutyric acid from acetoacetic acid. He found that normal dogs excrete β-oxybutyric acid when it is injected at the rate of 0.4 gm. (0.0032 gm. molecule) of the sodium salt per kilo of body weight per hour, but not with lower rates. Sodium acetoacetate was excreted when injected in rates of 0.2 gm. (0.0016 gm. molecule) per kilo per hour, and when injected at the 0.4 gm. rate it was excreted accompanied by β-oxybutyric acid. Evidently, then, the acetoacetic acid must be converted almost quantitatively into β-oxybutyric acid. On the other hand, acetoacetic acid did not appear in the urine when larger quantities of β-oxybutryic acid were injected, and hence it is

[59a] Jour. Biol. Chem., 1909 (6), 373; 1910 (8), 105.
[60] Jour. Biol. Chem., 1914 (18), 241.
[61] Jour. Biol. Chem., 1917 (31), 59.

apparent that not much if any urinary acetoacetic acid is derived from this source.

As long as a normal individual is burning at least one molecule of carbohydrate to three of higher fatty acids the urine is free from more than traces of these three "acetone bodies,"[62] but when for any reason daily oxidation of carbohydrates falls below this minimum the two the acids appear, combined largely with ammonia, but partly with mineral bases. Fats burn in the fire of the carbohydrates, and, as Woodyatt[63] puts it, when the proportion of fat is too great for the fire it "smokes" with unburnt fats and acetone bodies. Normally but 2 to 5 per cent. of the nitrogen of the urine is in the form of ammonia, but in diabetic *acidosis* the proportion may reach from 10 to 25 per cent., the proportion of urea being correspondingly reduced.[64]

The presence of large quantities of these acids in the urine presages coma, during which the amount of oxybutyric acid often reaches 15–20 grams per day, and has been known to reach 150 grams (Külz claimed to have found 226 grams). Diacetic acid appears in relatively small amounts, rarely exceeding 10 per cent. of the total organic acids of the urine;[65] as a rule, when any one of the three acetone bodies is present in large amounts, there is an abundance of each of the others. Kenneway[66] confirms Neubauer's statement that oxybutyric acid is rather constantly from 60 to 80 per cent. of the total acetone bodies excreted in the urine. In the internal organs the acetone bodies may also be detected, especially in the liver.[67] In normal blood Marriott found less than 4 mg. of oxybutyric acid, and 1.5 mg. of acetone and aceto-acetic acid together, per 100 c.c.; but in diabetic coma the figures rose as high as 45 mg. and 28 mg. respectively for each fraction, the amount in the blood not corresponding to the urinary excretion,[68] or to the bicarbonate content of the blood.[69] Associated with acidosis is usually an increase in the blood lipins.[70]

Relation of Acidosis to Diabetic Coma.—There seems to be little room for doubt that the typical diabetic coma with "air hunger"

[62] Veeder and Johnson (Amer. Jour. Dis. Chil., 1916 (11), 291) give as the normal daily average excretion 32 mg. of ketones (diacetic acid and acetone) and 38 mg. oxybutyric acid. The old statement that acetone appears in advance of the two acids is incorrect, the error being due to faulty methods (See Howland and Marriott, Amer. Jour. Dis. Chil., 1916 (12), 459). Concerning normal occurrence of acetone in blood and tissues, see Halpern and Landau, Zeit. exp. Path. u. Ther., 1906 (3), 466.

[63] Jour. Amer. Med. Assoc., 1916 (66), 1910.

[64] According to Edie and Whitley (Biochemical Jour., 1906 (1), 11), administration of excessive amounts of alkali causes, conversely, elimination of increased amounts of organic acids.

[65] Folin says that perfectly fresh diabetic urine does not contain any acetone, that which is commonly found being derived from diacetic acid which rapidly decomposes into acetone.

[66] Biochem. Jour., 1913 (8), 355.

[67] Sassa, Biochem. Zeit., 1914 (59), 362.

[68] Marriott, Jour. Biol. Chem., 1914 (18), 507.

[69] Fitz, Trans. Assoc. Amer. Phys., 1917 (32), 155.

[70] Gray, Bost. Med. Surg. Jour., 1917 (178), 16–156.

depends upon an excess of these substances in the blood—*i. e.*, is an acid intoxication—for the following reasons: (1) The coma usually appears when the amount of organic acids in the urine is highest, and is absent when there is little or none of them in the urine. (2) Because of the resemblance of the symptoms to those of experimental acid intoxication. (3) Because of the repeated demonstration of a reduced amount of alkali in the blood, as determined by titration, and a great reduction of the amount of CO_2 carried in the venous blood. The capacity of the serum to absorb CO_2 *in vitro* is also greatly reduced, from a normal 55 to 75 per cent. to as low as 20 per cent. (Van Slyke). By means of gas-chain measurements Rolly[71] found that by far the lowest OH values ever observed in the blood are in diabetic coma;[72] and Sellards[73] showed that in diabetes the tolerance for alkalies may be increased. He states[54] that a deficit of 20 to 30 grams of sodium bicarbonate produces a degree of acidosis demonstrable by blood examination only, 40 to 50 grams deficit usually causes only dyspnoea on exertion, 75 to 100 grams deficit may produce persistent dyspnoea, 150 grams deficit may accompany coma, while the maximum deficits reported have been about 200 grams. (4) The marked improvement that sometimes results from the administration of alkalies (usually sodium bicarbonate). Associated with this improvement is an elimination of greatly increased amounts of organic acids, indicating their previous retention in the body because of lack of alkali with which they could combine.

But there are cases of diabetic coma without typical air hunger, and it is the exception rather than the rule for alkali therapy to produce a marked improvement in the fully developed coma of diabetes. Furthermore, coma may occur in diabetics who are producing no such quantity of organic acids as would seem theoretically to be necessary to cause enough acid intoxication to result in acidosis, and coma develops in diabetics who are being supplied with sufficient bases for all requirements. Hence it must be concluded that only a part of the symptomatology of diabetic coma depends on acids as such, but as yet we do not know what other agents are acting.[74]

β-oxybutyric and diacetic acid, according to many authorities, seem to have no specific poisonous effects, but act simply as acids in the blood. Acetone does not have this effect, not being an acid, and seems not to be toxic to any considerable degree; doses of 4 grams per kilo cause effects similar to ethyl alcohol in dogs, 8 grams per kilo being fatal, which corresponds to a dose of 500 grams for an adult

[71] Münch. med. Woch., 1912 (59), 1201.
[72] Menten, however, reports that in diabetes before acidosis the OH concentration is usually somewhat above normal (Jour. Cancer Res., 1917 (2), 179).
[73] Johns Hopkins Hosp. Bull., 1912 (23), 289.
[74] Pribram and Loewy (Zeit. klin. Med., 1913 (77), 384) suggest that abnormal products of protein cleavage are responsible, and Rosenbloom (N. Y. Med. Jour., Aug. 7, 1915) reports cases of typical diabetic coma without acetone bodies in the urine.

man.   According to Rhamy[75] acetone is more toxic (for guinea-pigs) than methyl alcohol, while for rabbits Desgrez and Saggio[76] found acetone the least toxic of the acetone bodies, diacetic acid next, and β-oxybutyric acid most.   Ehrmann[77] also claims that he has produced typical coma with the sodium salts of butyric and of β-oxybutyric acid, but as high as 40 grams of·β-oxybutyric acid have been found in the day's urine of a non-diabetic without any evidence of intoxication.   Ewing suggests that the acetone bodies may cause renal injury, which is usually evident in acidosis, and M. H. Fischer's views on the relation of acids to nephritis accord with this fact.   The withdrawal of the inorganic bases, especially Ca and Mg, may also be responsible for symptoms, as it is well established that a proper balancing of these ions is necessary for normal cell activity, especially in the nervous system.[78]

Hurtley[54] sums up the evidence on the toxicity of the acetone bodies by saying that aceto-acetic acid seems to be highly toxic only in depancreatized animals, while oxybutyric acid is practically non-toxic.   He favors the view that aceto-acetic acid poisoning is responsible for diabetic coma, for it increases in the urine on the approach of coma, and the ratio of aceto-acetic to butyric acid in the urine increases with the severity of the intoxication.   The increased proportion of aceto-acetic acid presumably means that it is being produced in such quantities throughout the body that the liver cannot reduce as large a proportion to oxybutyric acid as it normally does.   In considering the possibility that the acetone bodies may be responsible for at least part of the intoxication of diabetic coma we must bear in mind that the evidence of their low toxicity is based on short time experimental intoxications, and that they may be found to be much more toxic than is generally assumed when they are allowed to act for many days and weeks on the nervous tissues, as they do in diabetes.   That is, the experimental evidence concerning the toxicity of the acetone bodies has not been obtained under conditions comparable to those of diabetic acidosis.

Origin of the Acetone Bodies.—The chemical nature of the acetone bodies is such that they might readily be produced from any or all of the three classes of foodstuffs.

They might be derived from *carbohydrates*, as is the closely related lactic acid, but we know that this it not the usual source.   On the contrary, administration of a proper amount of carbohydrates under certain conditions may cause the acids to disappear from the urine, and acetone bodies may be eliminated in large quantities while the patient is on a diet almost free from carbohydrates.   Carbohydrates are, indeed, the most active agents in preventing the formation of these ketone bodies, i. e., they are *antiketogenic.*[79]

[75] Jour. Amer. Med. Assoc., 1912 (58), 628.
[76] Compt. Rend. Soc. Biol., 1907 (63), 288.
[77] Berl. klin. Woch., 1913 (50), 11.
[78] See Cammidge, Amer. Med., 1916 (11), 363.
[79] Concerning antiketogenesis see Woodyatt, Jour. Amer. Med. Assoc., 1910 55), 2109.

They might readily be formed from *proteins* through splitting out of the NH_2 group from the amino-acids; indeed the amino-acids are generally considered as a source of the acetone bodies,[80] particularly because, whenever there is considerable pathological breaking-down of proteins, these bodies, especially acetone, may appear in the urine; *e. g.*, during absorption of exudates, in carcinoma, and in starvation or other conditions with great wasting of the tissues. Dakin[91] has shown that only leucine, histidine, phenylalanine and tyrosine yield diacetic acid when perfused through the liver, while most of the other amino-acids are able to yield sugar in diabetic animals, and hence are antiketogenic.

On the other hand, the amount of acids sometimes found in the urine seems to be greater than can be explained by the protein destruction that occurs (Magnus-Levy),[82] and in diabetes it is often observed that feeding of fats and fatty acids increases the output of acetone bodies, and hence it is evident that acetone bodies may be derived from the *fats*. β-oxybutyric acid can be produced readily from fatty acids, especially, of course, from butyric acid, and we usually observe an increase in the acetone excretion in a diabetic given large quantities of butter. Other higher fatty acids are also found to cause increased acetone excretion.

The studies of Knoop,[83] and his associates have indicated that in the catabolism of fatty acids, the chains are broken down by oxidation of the carbon atom third from the end, that is, the β-position, and the two end carbon atoms are then split off. Therefore, two carbon atoms are always split off at a time, and hence there can be oxidized into oxybutyric acid only those fatty acids which contain an *even* number of carbon atoms, which includes the ordinary fatty acids (oleic, palmitic and stearic) of fat tissue, which have each an even number of carbon atoms (16 or 18), and also butyric, caproic and similar acids. Normal fatty acids which contain an odd number of carbon atoms cannot yield oxybutyric acid. However, according to A. Loeb,[84] aceto-acetic acid may be built up from acetic acid in the liver, and the urine in diabetes may contain acetic acid. "The formation of oxybutyric acid and of diacetic acid in all these cases may be said to be due to the fact that the diabetic organism is not able quite to finish the attack on the beta-carbon atom of butyric acid" (Folin).

From the results of these studies it seems that the acetone bodies *can*, theoretically be formed from any of the three classes of food-stuffs, but that ordinarily they come chiefly from the fats, and in severe diabetes also to a considerable extent from fatty acids formed by deaminization of amino-acids. Although it is probable that the acetone bodies are formed in many if not all tissues, yet there is abundant evidence that the liver plays an important part in ketogenesis, as shown by the decrease in acetone bodies in Eck fistula dogs, and their great increase when the blood supply of the liver is augmented.[85]

ACIDOSIS AND ACETONURIA IN CONDITIONS OTHER THAN DIABETES[85a]

When our chief method of recognition of acidosis consisted of determining the presence of acetone bodies in the urine, the term acetonuria was used as synonymous with acidosis, but we now know that we may have varying degrees of acetonuria without significant

[80] Embden and his associates have (Hofmeister's Beitr., 1906 (8), 121; 1908 (11), H. 7–9) demonstrated that the liver can form acetone from many substances perfused through it in the blood, including not only amino-acids of the fatty acid series, but also the aromatic radicals of the protein molecule.

[81] Jour. Biol. Chem., 1913 (14), 328.

[82] Arch. exp. Path. u. Pharm., 1899 (42), 149; Ergeb. inn. Med., 1908 (1), 374.

[83] Full bibliography and discussion by Porges, Ergebnisse Physiol., 1910 (10), 6. See also Ringer, Jour. Biol. Chem., 1913, Vol. 14.

[84] Biochem. Zeit., 1912 (47), 118.

[85] Fischer and Kossow, Deut. Arch. klin. Med., 1913 (101), 479.

[85a] See Sellards "Principles of Acidosis, Harvard Press, 1917; also Frothingham, Arch. Int. Med., 1916 (18), 717.

acidosis as determined by examination of the blood, and severe acidosis may occur with little or no acetonuria.

Furthermore, we may have high urinary ammonia not only because of excretion of diacetic and oxybutyric acids as in diabetic acidosis, but also from excretion of excessive quantities of lactic acid, as in puerperal eclampsia, pernicious vomiting of pregnancy, acute yellow atrophy, and other conditions associated with severe injury to the liver. As high ammonia excretion is characteristic of diabetic acidosis, the presence either of acetone bodies or high urinary ammonia was formerly considered to indicate the existence of acidosis, but it is now recognized that as a general rule there is not a severe acidosis in these hepatic diseases, the intoxication being dependent on neither lactic acid nor acidosis, but upon poisons of unknown character. This group of diseases has been considered in previous pages. Because of its significance as one of the chief organic acids formed in metabolism, rather than as a cause of serious acidosis, we may in this chapter briefly consider lactic acid and its relation to disease.

Sarcolactic Acid often is found in the urine, but in origin and significance it is entirely different from the acetone bodies, and it probably is never present in sufficient amounts to cause an acid intoxication by abstraction of alkalies from the blood. *In vitro*, we obtain sarcolactic acid whenever sugar is placed in an alkaline solution, *provided the supply of oxygen to the solution is deficient*; but if the oxygen supply is adequate, sugar will not yield lactic acid with alkalies (Nef). Similarly, an isolated surviving muscle, when asphyxiated by any means, shows a rapid accumulation of lactic acid, which fails to occur when sufficient oxygen is supplied. This lactic acid comes chiefly from sugar, but about 25 to 30 per cent. of it can have its origin in protein (or fat?) (Woodyatt). If an organism as a whole is insufficiently supplied with oxygen, lactic acid accumulates in the tissues and appears in the urine, disappearing when the oxygen supply is restored. Lactic acid often appears after poisoning with a large number of drugs, which Loewy has classified as drugs whose action in the body resembles that of lack of oxygen (arsenic, phosphorus, hydrazine, chloroform, etc.). These poisons are all characterized by causing impoverishment of glycogen, fatty liver, and acute degenerative changes especially in the liver cells and the endothelium. Therefore the assumption seems justified that the poisons and conditions which lead to lactic acid excretion depend ultimately upon impairment of the interchange of oxygen in the cells. Woodyatt states that, as far as known, lactic acid has never been demonstrated in any tissue in which deficient oxygenation can be excluded, and regards lactic acid as the metabolite of asphyxia or its equivalent. Over against this view is that of Embden and his associates, which is shared by others, that lactic acid is a normal intermediary in the breakdown of the sugars in the body, its direct antecedent being a triose, but perusal of their work only emphasizes that in all the conditions in which their data were obtained asphyxial conditions were present; furthermore, this conception of lactic acid as a chief intermediate in normal sugar catabolism is not in harmony with the best ideas of carbohydrate chemistry (Woodyatt). This author has furthermore found, by direct observation of the utilization of lactic acid when injected intravenously, that it cannot well be an important intermediate in carbohydrate catabolism.[86] (See also discussion of lactic acid under Diabetes, Chapter xxiv).

It is possible that the presence of lactic acid in the urine may also result from defective transformation of ammonia into urea by a diseased liver, the acid neutralizing, and being excreted with, the ammonia; in this case no defective oxidation need be assumed. However, administration of phlorhizin to phosphorus

[86] Harvey Society Lectures, 1916.

poisoned dogs causes both ammonia and lactic acid to disappear from the urine, indicating that the ammonia is the protective substance which neutralizes the lactic acid, and not the reverse. Likewise, lactic acid acts as a defensive mechanism when excess, of alkali is administered, appearing in the urine in slightly increased amounts.[87]

Sarcolactic acid, which is dextrorotary, must be distinguished from its optical isomer, the inactive lactic acid that is produced by fermentation. When this fermentation lactic acid is formed in the stomach and enters the blood, it ordinarily, like other ingested organic acids, is combined by the blood alkalies and oxidized to carbonates. It is doubtful if it ever enters the urine.[88]

As a general rule sarcolactic acid is not found abundant in the urine together with the acetone bodies, but is, indeed, antiketogenic. Its appearance in the urine indicates that glycogen is not completely burned, and this condition is usually accompanied with fatty changes in the liver, which also depend on lack of oxidation. Throughout the clinical forms of acidosis, lactic acid and fatty degeneration are always associated (Ewing). To assume, as has been generally done, that the lactic acid appears in the urine when hepatic alterations are marked, because of the loss of the liver tissue which should destroy it, is probably not warranted. Rather, the liver conditions and the formation of lactic acid depend upon the same cause, which is a defective oxygen supply or interchange, either general or local.[89]

Acidosis in Nephritis.—This presents a very different urinary chemistry from diabetic acidosis, in that there is no excessive excretion of organic acids or ammonia, and indeed no other striking urinary change to account for the acidosis which may be severe, undoubtedly often terminating life.[90] There is a definite increase in the inorganic phosphate content of the blood (Marriott and Howland[91]) in nephritis with acidosis, and often the urinary acidity is decreased, so the acidosis is attributed to reduced capacity of the kidney to excrete acid phosphates which is one of the most important normal mechanisms for maintaining the neutrality of the blood. The most marked acidosis is observed in those types of nephritis that are associated with uremia, i. e., advanced chronic glomerulo-nephritis and acute nephritis, but not in the chronic parenchymatous types. The nocturnal hyperpnœa of nephritis probably is the result of acidosis (Whitney). Acidosis generally parallels in degree the impairment in excretory capacity of the kidney, and, in contrast to diabetes, it does not reach a high grade so long as the excretion of acid by the kidney is comparatively efficient (Sellards). While administration of sodium bicarbonate corrects the acidosis it has little effect on the course of the disease, or on the amount of phosphate in the blood. With this high phosphatemia there is a reduction in the blood calcium, which may have an unfavorable influence on the irritability of the nervous tissues. Whitney believes that in nephritis with acidosis there is probably some excessive production of acid, as a kidney with greatly impaired excre-

[87] Macleod and Knapp, Amer. Jour. Physiol., 1918 (47), 189.
[88] The theory of Boix that cirrhosis of the liver may be produced by butyric acid formed in gastric fermentation could not be corroborated by Joannovics, Arch. int. Pharmacodyn., 1905 (15), 241.
[89] See Macleod and Wedd (Jour. Biol. Chem., 1914 (18), 446) who found that reducing the oxygen supply to the liver caused a marked rise in the lactic acid content of the hepatic blood.
[90] See Whitney, Arch. Int. Med., 1917 (20), 931.
[91] Arch. Int. Med., 1916 (18), 708.

tory capacity may be able to maintain a normal acid threshhold Begun and Münzer[91a] attribute part of the acidosis to a decreased formation of NH_3 in metabolism.

Other Diseases with Acidosis.—While a slight degree of acidosis undoubtedly may occur in many conditions, there are few conditions in which it is of importance. Chief of these are the following:

Asiatic Cholera exhibits often a severe acidosis, presumably because of the frequency of severe renal lesions (Sellards[54]). Loss of bases in the evacuations may also be a factor. The acidosis differs from that of nephritis in the excretion of large amounts of ammonia, but usually without acetone bodies. Other infectious diseases do not commonly exhibit any significant degree of acidosis, rheumatic fever alone excepted.

Acidosis in infancy.—Both true acidosis and acetonuria, with or without acidosis, occur frequently and easily in the young. Normally the urine of infants and children contains about 3 mg. of acetone per kilo of body weight, and may be increased to ten times that amount by fasting.[92] Also the amount of acetone bodies in the blood is greater and more readily increased by fasting than in adults.[93] Presumably the infantile organism has a lower oxidative capacity, since it excretes unoxidized organic acids from relatively slight causes, in corroboration of which is the observation of Pfaundler[94] that the proportion of nitrogen in the urine of infants in forms other than urea is higher than in adults. However, according to Howland and Marriott[95] serious acidosis in infancy and childhood, although frequent, is usually not due to the acetone bodies. It is especially important in severe choleriform diarrhea, possibly because of excretion of bases in the discharges, and in burns and severe nephritis, acidosis is of significance. In ileocolitis true acetonemic acidosis has been observed.

Terminal Acidosis.—In many dying persons the final symptomatology is strikingly like that of death from acidosis, and Whitney has found that the final figures for alkali reserve in the blood of animals killed by acid intoxication are of the same order as those that may sometimes be obtained from dying patients with many different diseases. Of forty cases studied by him, in all but three there was marked acidosis, and in many there was a degree of acidosis sufficient of itself to cause death. Sellards notes typical acidosis in advanced *atrophic cirrhosis*, but this has not yet been sufficiently studied to permit of proper interpretation. Whenever the blood pressure becomes greatly lowered, as in *shock*, there may occur an actual acidosis.

Severe anemia, both primary and secondary, may exhibit a moderated degree of acidosis, but in only about one fifth of all cases examined by Sellards.

ALKALOSIS

The occurrence of an increase in OH ions of the blood, or of an abnormally high alkali reserve and increased capacity to carry CO_2, seems to occur infrequently, presumably since the trend of metabolic processes is to produce acid substances. The chief example is furnished in tetany, whether the result of parathyroid insufficiency or pyloric obstruction;[96] in the latter case excretion of acid which does not enter the intestine to be neutralized might account for an excess

[91a] Zeit. exp. Path., 1919 (20), 78.

[92] Veeder and Johnstone, Amer. Jour. Dis. Child., 1917 (13), 89.

[93] See Moore, *ibid.*, 1916 (12), 244. The statement that there is usually a relative acidosis in newborn infants could not be corroborated by Scham, *ibid.* 1919 (18), 42.

[94] Jahrb. f. Kinderheilk., 1901 (54), 247.

[95] Amer. Jour. Dis. Child., 1916 (12), 459.

[96] See Wilson *et al.*, Jour. Biol. Chem., 1915 (21), 169; 1915 (23), 89; McCann, *ibid.*, 1918 (35), 553.

of bases in the blood. Tetany is improved by giving acids, and presumably the convulsions of the disease have a similar effect through increased acid production. Menten[97] has found an increased OH-ion concentration in the blood to be characteristic of cancer, whether involving the stomach or not, although sometimes observed in other conditions, especially diabetes before the stage of acidosis. A slight degree of alkalosis may be produced by feeding large amounts of alkali, in which case some of the alkali is removed in the urine combined with lactic acid.[98]

ACETONURIA WITHOUT MARKED ACIDOSIS

Not infrequently acetone bodies are found in the urine of patients suffering from the most diverse diseases. It is customary to refer to this condition as *"acetonemia"* or *"acetonuria,"* and to ascribe many of the observed symptoms to "acid intoxication." The presence of these substances in the urine, however, is by no means evidence of acidosis, for excretion of considerable amounts of acetone bodies may occur without reduced CO_2-carrying capacity of the blood and they may be absent with marked acidosis. In addition, it must be kept in mind that acidosis may result from other causes than overproduction of organic acids; e. g., acid phosphate retention in nephritis, or loss of bases from biliary or pancreatic fistula. In no other conditions do the amounts of organic acids in the urine approximate the amounts found in diabetic coma. Therefore, the intoxication in these cases is probably not due to the acids, but, on the contrary, the presence of the acetone bodies is due more often to the effects of toxic substances of diverse origins and natures.

Anesthesia.—As shown first by Greven (1895), and especially by Brewer and Helen Baldwin[99] acetone is nearly always present in the urine during the first twenty-four hours after administration of chloroform or ether, and occasionally diacetic acid appears on the second or third day after; but ordinarily there is no increase in organic acids in the urine. There is usually little or no demonstrable acidosis.[1] The starvation preceding and following the operation is also a factor of considerable importance. It does not seem probable that the symptoms observed in typical cases of delayed chloroform-poisoning (*q. v.*) are due chiefly, if at all, to acid intoxication *per se*, but rather are the result of extensive injury to the parenchymatous organs, particularly the liver, by the chloroform, which causes a condition resembling acute yellow atrophy or phosphorus-poisoning.

Cachectic Acetonuria.—Acetone and diacetic acid, but less abundantly the oxybutyric acid are found in the urine in many *conditions associated with wasting*, among which may be especially mentioned:

Starvation.—Acetone, which is normally excreted through the lungs for the most part (80-90 per cent. of that produced) appears in excess in the urine very soon after fasting begins, there being more produced than can be exhaled. It is associated with diacetic acid and oxybutyric acid, which may reach 10 to 20 grams per day in starvation, and even higher figures are recorded. The urinary ammonia nitrogen runs parallel to the acid excretion. The use of a carbohydrate free

[97] Jour. Cancer Res., 1917 (2) 179.
[98] Macleod and Knapp, Amer. Jour. Physiol., 1918 (47), 189.
[99] Jour. of Biol. Chem., 1906 (1), 239.
[1] See Caldwell and Cleveland, Surg. Gyn. Obst., 1917 (25), 22.

diet is also accompanied by a marked acetonuria,[2] no matter how much fat is supplied, and may reach a point where several grams of oxybutyric acid are being excreted per day without symptoms of serious intoxication. A relatively small amount of carbohydrate (80 grams) is sufficient to prevent this acidosis. If the meat-fat diet is continued for some time, however, there seems to be some sort of adaptation so that the acetonuria diminishes until practically normal figures may be reached.

Pregnancy.—During pregnancy the urine usually contains acetone bodies in slight excess, and occasionally in large excess in women who are suffering from the toxemias of pregnancy. Here there is a rise in ammonia far beyond the proportion of acetone bodies, partly because of the large amounts of lactic acid which are excreted, and partly from abnormal protein metabolism and tissue destruction, but the proportion of the urinary nitrogen which is constituted by ammonia is too inconstant to serve as a prognostic and operative guide. Ewing has observed a case of pernicious vomiting with 75 per cent. of the total nitrogen as ammonia, and no urea,—while there may occur fatal cases without large excess of ammonia. Higher ammonia figures are usually reached in pernicious vomiting of pregnancy than in eclampsia; in neither is the acidosis present sufficient to account for the intoxication. (See discussion of "Eclampsia.") Even normal pregnant women seem to show a reduced ability to tolerate a deficiency in the carbohydrates of the diet.[3]

Cyclic Vomiting.—Here the urine usually shows acetone bodies, lactic acid, indican in excess, and a rise in the proportion of neutral to oxidized sulphur (Howland and Richards). As these findings may persist in spite of absorption of carbohydrates, they are not entirely due to starvation, and there are severe fatty changes in the liver and kidneys, indicating a toxemic origin associated with defective oxidation. Mellanby[4] found a considerable creatine elimination in a typical case. There is, however, usually no acidosis, although it may develop.

Inanition and Cachexia.—Under this heading may be grouped the acetonuria observed in intestinal disturbances in children,[5] hysterical vomiting, psychoses, and cancer. In each of these conditions coma of the type of diabetic coma has sometimes been observed, and in all of them acetonuria is common, the reasons being obvious after the above discussion. A relative acidosis may also result from deficiency of bases in the diet of growing infants. In many cases of acidosis of infants there is not sufficient increase in the acetone bodies of the blood to account for the acidosis;[6] on the other hand, most of the children excreting acetone bodies in the urine do not have acidosis.

Retention of placenta or fetus, acetonuria being considered of diagnostic value in determining the death of the fetus *in utero*,[7] but not in extrauterine pregnancy (Wechsberg).[8]

In uremia, as previously mentioned, organic acids may appear in the urine, but apparently as a result, and not as the cause, of the uremia (Orlowski). There is usually some acidosis in advanced nephritis, but marked only in uremia as discussed above.

Other Conditions.—Acetonuria is observed inconstantly in fever, especially in children;[3a] also after poisoning by many drugs, including, besides the heavy metals, morphine, atropine, antipyrine, and phlorhizin. Pneumonia is accompanied by acidosis,[9] often of serious degree, subsiding rapidly after the crisis. Acidosis seems to be an important feature in gas gangrene.[10] At high altitudes there is always an acidosis, which stimulates the respiratory center to increased activity. In asphyx-

[2] See Higgins, Peabody and Fitz. Jour. Med. Res., 1916 (34), 263.
[3] Porges and Novak, Berl. klin. Woch., 1911 (48), 1757.
[4] Lancet, July 1, 1911.
[5] See Howland and Marriott, Amer. Jour. Dis. Child., 1916 (11), 309; (12), 459.
[6] Moore, Amer. Jour. Dis. Child., 1916 (12), 244.
[7] See Frommer, Berl. klin. Woch., 1905 (12), 1008.
[8] Wien. klin. Woch., 1906 (19), 953.
[8a] See Garland, Arch. Pediat., 1919 (36), 468; Veeder and Johnston, Amer. Jour. Dis. Chil., 1920 (19), 141.
[9] Lewis and Barcroft, Quart. Jour. Med., 1915 (8), 108.
[10] Wright and Fleming, Lancet, Feb. 9, 1918.

ial conditions of all sorts more or less acidosis is present, *e. g.*, uncompensated cardiac defects, severe anemia, gas poisoning, surgical or traumatic shock.

FATIGUE[11]

The symptoms of fatigue, whether general or local, seem to be due to an intoxication with the products of the excessive metabolic activity, and part of the symptoms, at least, seem to be due to acid intoxication. Among the metabolic products of muscular activity are known to be creatin, creatinin, sarcolactic acid, and carbon dioxide. The amount of acid developed in an active muscle is quite considerable, and when the activity is violent or prolonged the sarcolactic acid accumulates, being formed faster than it can be removed. Part of the acidity of the muscle is due, however, not to the sarcolactic acid itself, but to monopotassium phosphate (KH_2PO_4), which is formed by the action of the sarcolactic acid upon the dipotassium phosphate present in the blood and muscle. The effect of these various substances upon muscular fatigue has been studied experimentally, and while the creatin seems not to be a "fatigue substance," sarcolactic acid, monopotassium phosphate, hydroxybutyric acid, and carbon dioxide all cause muscle tissue to react to stimuli in the same way that a fatigued muscle does (Lee[12]). Presumably these substances act chiefly by virtue of their carrying hydrogen ions, although there is some evidence that the negative ions of lactic and oxybutyric acids and some positive ions, especially potassium, are capable of producing certain fatigue phenomena (Scott). Indole, skatole and phenol may also produce fatigue conditions.

It is quite probable that the muscular weakness of diabetics, and the exhaustion associated with many conditions in which organic acids appear in the urine in abnormal quantities, depend, at least in part, upon the effect of these acids upon the muscle tissue, for Lee found that β-oxybutyric acid causes the same fatigue reaction in muscles as does sarcolactic acid. Furthermore, sarcolactic acid itself often appears in the urine in these conditions. It may be added that in fatigued animals the alkalinity of the blood (by titration) has been found decreased (Geppert and Zuntz), and the proportion of the urinary nitrogen that appears in other combinations than urea is increased (Poehl).[13] Fatigue in man causes an increased urinary acidity.[13a]

The "Toxins" of Fatigue.—In extreme exhaustion the evidences of a general intoxication often become severe, so that the condition may resemble an acute febrile disease and last for several days. It

[11] Full bibliography by Spaeth, Jour. Indust. Hyg., 1919 (1), 22.
[12] Jour. Amer. Med. Assoc., 1906 (46), 1491; where is given a complete review of the subject of fatigue, with the literature. Also see Scott, Public Health Reports, 1918 (33), 605.
[13] Deut. med. Woch., 1901 (27), 796.
[13a] Hastings, Public Health Rep., 1919 (34), 1682; Barach, Amer. Jour. Med. Sci.; 1920 (159), 398.

seems very probable that substances more toxic than the above-mentioned acids are involved. Weichardt[14] claimed that he had demonstrated a toxic substance, produced by muscular fatigue, which in structure resembles the bacterial toxins, called by him *kenotoxin*,[15] and against which an antitoxin may be obtained. This toxic material is, he believes, formed from the protein molecule in the first stages of its decomposition, as a side product which is normally protected against by a formation of an antitoxin, rather than by being split up further, as is the case with the rest of the protein molecule. The study of anaphylaxis has led to so many evidences of the remarkable toxicity of the products of protein cleavage, that the possibility that some of these may be responsible for fatigue cannot be entirely disregarded at present,[16] although Lee and Aronovitch[17] could not demonstrate toxic substances in fatigued muscles, and no one has been able to confirm Weichardt's specific findings. The following observation of Mosso indicates that the blood of fatigued animals contains toxic substances: If blood is transfused from an exhausted dog to a normal dog, from which an equivalent amount of blood has been withdrawn, this second dog will show the usual manifestations of fatigue. Mendenhall[18] has found that the heart is also affected by the products of muscular fatigue. Recent studies in shock (Bayliss, Cannon) attribute the manifestations of shock, at least in part, to toxic cleavage products of injured tissues, and many of these manifestations are allied to fatigue.

Mental Fatigue.—The chemical changes of mental fatigue are not known, but the ganglion-cells show marked structural alterations as a result of fatigue, chromatolysis often being very striking. Since lecithin forms so important a part of the nervous system, it is tempting to imagine that in fatigue excessive quantities of its toxic decomposition-product, *choline*, and the still more toxic derivative of choline, *neurine*, are formed in considerable amounts and cause part, at least, of the intoxication.

That choline or neurine actually are the cause of any of the symptoms of fatigue, however, has not been established; but Donath[19] considers choline an important factor in the production of *epileptic convulsions*.[20] Animals kept for a long time from sleeping are said to show the presence in their blood, cerebro-spinal fluid and brain tissues, of a poisonous property causing somnolence in other animals (Legendre

[14] " Ueber Ermüdungsstoffe, " Enke, Stuttgart, 1912; Kolle and Wassermann's Handbuch, 1913 (2), 1499.
[15] See Weichardt and Schwenk, Zeit. physiol. Chem., 1913 (83), 381.
[16] The failure of various investigators to corroborate Weichardt is discussed by Konrich, Zeit. f. Hyg., 1914 (78), 1; Korff-Petersen, *ibid.*, p. 37.
[17] Proc. Soc. Exp. Biol. Med., 1917 (14), 153.
[18] Amer. Jour. Physiol., 1919 (48), 13.
[19] Zeit. physiol. Chem., 1903 (39), 526.
[20] Concerning the theories and literature of the subject of epilepsy in relation to its pathological chemistry and to autointoxication, see the review of Masoin. Arch. internat. de Pharmacodynamie, 1904 (13), 387.

and Piéron).[21] This cannot well be choline or any similar substance, for it does not filter, is insoluble in alcohol, and is destroyed by heating at 65°.

THE POISONS PRODUCED IN SUPERFICIAL BURNS[22]

In a certain proportion of cases of extensive but superficial burns, death follows after an interval of from six hours to a few days, apparently because of a profound intoxication. As evidence of intoxication we have not only clinical manifestations, such as delirium, hemoglobinuria, and albuminuria, vomiting, bloody diarrhea, etc., but, more convincingly, the anatomical findings at autopsy, which are strikingly similar to those resulting from acute intoxication with bacterial products. Bardeen found quite constantly cloudy swelling and focal and parenchymatous degeneration in the liver and kidneys; softening and enlargement of the spleen with focal degeneration in the Malpighian bodies; and particularly degenerative changes in the lymph-glands and intestinal follicles resembling those observed in diphtheria, which McCrae[23] considers due to proliferation and phagocytosis by the endothelial cells of the lymphatic structures. The severe degenerative changes seen in the adrenals and myocardium especially recall diphtheria intoxication (Weiskotten).[24] Marked changes are usually present in the blood, consisting of fragmentation and distortion of the red corpuscles, hemoglobinemia, loss of water with a relative increase in the number of corpuscles by from one to four millions per cubic millimeter, an increase in the blood platelets, and a rise in the number of leucocytes as high as 30,000 to 50,000.[25] Hemoglobinuria is also frequently present, and almost constantly gastrointestinal irritation occurs, with anatomical evidences of acute enteritis, acute gastritis, and occasionally gastric or duodenal ulcers. According to Korolenko,[26] the sympathetic nervous system is seriously involved.

It therefore seems probable that poisons are formed as a result of superficial burns, which have the effect of causing hemolysis, and which are also cytotoxic for parenchymatous cells. These hypothetical poisons seem to be eliminated by the intestines and kidneys, which are injured by the poisons in their passage through these organs. The attempts to explain all the observed effects of burns as due to thrombosis or to embolism by altered corpuscles seem to have failed, for the peculiar location of the lesions (*e. g.*, duodenal ulcers, necrosis in the

[21] Zeit. allg. Physiol., 1912 (14), 235.
[22] Literature given by Bardeen, Johns Hopkins Hosp. Reports, 1898 (7), 137; Eyff, Cent. Grenzgeb. Med. u. Chir., 1901 (4), 428; Pfeiffer, Virchow's Arch., 1905 (180), 367. Full discussion of theories by Vogt, Zeit. exp. Path. u. Pharm., 1912 (11), 191.
[23] Amer. Med., 1901 (2), 735.
[24] Jour. Amer. Med. Assoc., 1917 (69), 776; 1919 (72), 259; also Nakata, Corr Bl. Schw. Aerzte, 1918 (48), 1283.
[25] Locke, Boston Med. and Surg. Jour., 1902 (147), 180.
[26] Cent. f. Path., 1903 (10), 663.

Malpighian bodies of the spleen, etc.) does not agree with this hypothesis, and there are too many evidences of the presence of some decidedly toxic substance in the blood. There can be no question that the poisonous substance or substances are formed in the burned area, and not in the internal organs as a result of hyperpyrexia, as shown by numerous observations. Thus, if the burned area is removed immediately (in narcotized experimental animals), death will be prevented, whereas if the burned tissue is permitted to remain for a few hours, death will occur. If the burned skin is transplanted to a normal animal, this animal will develop symptoms of intoxication, while the burned animal may be saved by the transplantation (Vogt). The poison appears to be absorbed from the burned area into the blood, for if the circulation is shut off from the burned area, no intoxication results; this probably explains in part why deep destructive burns of small areas, which are associated with local thrombosis, are much less serious than a superficial slight scalding over a large area. Apparently the poison is produced chiefly or solely in the skin, for burning of muscle is not followed by intoxication (Eijkman and Hoogenhuyze).[27] When one of a pair of animals united to another by operative procedure (parabiosis) is burned, the other animal may become intoxicated, while the intoxication of the burned animal is less than it would be if it were alone (Vogt).

Numerous investigators have reported finding poisonous substances in the blood, tissues, or urine of burned men and animals, but the reports disagree widely in details.[28] Thus Dietrichs states that the blood of burned animals contains hemolysins and hemagglutinins, which could not be corroborated by Burkhardt[29] or by Pfeiffer.[30] The latter, however, finds that the urine, serum, and organs of burned animals contain substances poisonous for the same and for different species, which is in accord with the results of numerous earlier investigators. The poisons, according to Pfeiffer, are neurotoxic and necrogenic in their properties, and act without a period of incubation; they are rapidly weakened on standing in solution and by the action of sunlight, are absorbed from the gastro-intestinal tract, are soluble in water, alcohol, and glycerol, but not in chloroform or ether, are precipitated by $HgCl_2$ in acid solution, and by phosphotungstic acid, and they are not volatile. Apparently, according to Pfeiffer, they are not ptomains, nor yet pyridine derivatives, as many investigators have contended, but resemble more closely the labile poisons of snake venom, and have effects similar to the unknown poisons that are concerned in uremia. The neurotoxic substance is more thermostable

[27] Virchow's Arch., 1906 (183), 377.
[28] Ravenna and Minassian (Ref. in Biochem. Centr., 1903 (1), 348) state that blood heated outside the body to 55°–60° is toxic, and causes the same anatomical changes as does death from burning, which finding is corroborated by Helsted. Arch. klin. Chir., 1906 (79), 414.
[29] Arch. klin. Chir., 1905 (75), 845.
[30] Virchow's Arch., 1905 (180), 367; Zeit. f. Hyg., 1906 (54), 419.

than the necrogenic substance, which is very easily destroyed by heat. Pfeiffer believes it probable that the poisons are derived from the cleavage of proteins altered in composition by burning, and he finds an enzyme splitting glycyltryptophane in the blood and urine of burned animals.[31] The hemolysis he attributes to direct injury of the blood in its passage through the heated area, and not to the action of poisons; this is very possible, since red corpuscles fragment after being heated to 52°, and may be seriously impaired functionally at 45°. There are many authors, indeed, who consider the blood changes the chief cause of death, but the weight of evidence is in favor of the theory of the development of toxic substances in the burned skin.

Kutscher and Heyde[32] believe methyl guanidine to be the toxic substance eliminated in the urine, stating that it produces effects similar to that caused by injections of the toxic urine from burn cases. These symptoms are quite similar to those characteristic of anaphylaxis, and Heyde states that small burned areas sensitize an animal to later injections of extracts of burned tissue. He, as well as Vogt, are therefore inclined to believe that some cases, especially those dying unexpectedly 12 or 13 days after the burning, may be the result of anaphylactic reaction to proteins made of foreign character by the heat.[33] The newer observations concerning the presence of toxic substances in the urine during anaphylactic intoxication are in harmony with the findings in burn cases,[34] although the identity of methyl guanidine with the toxic agent is questionable.

Burn Blisters.—The contents of burn blisters resemble the fluid of inflammatory edemas generally. K. Mörner[35] found 5.031 per cent. of proteins, which included 1.359 per cent. of globulin and 0.011 per cent. of fibrin; there was also present a substance reducing copper oxide, but no pyrocatechin.

[31] Zeit. Immunität., 1915 (23), 473.
[32] Cent. f. Physiol., 1911 (25), 441.
[33] Heyde, Med. Klinik, 1912 (8), 263.
[34] See Pfeiffer, Zeit. Immunität., 1913 (18), 75.
[35] Skand. Arch. Physiol., 1895 (5), 272.

CHAPTER XXI

GASTRO-INTESTINAL "AUTOINTOXICATION" AND RELATED METABOLIC DISTURBANCES

UNDER this heading are commonly included all intoxications that can be ascribed to the absorption from the gastro-intestinal tract of toxic substances that have been formed within its contents, either by the action of the digestive ferments or of putrefactive bacteria. The propriety of considering such conditions as examples of auto-intoxication is properly questioned, since it is often difficult to determine whether the putrefaction occurred within the body, or had already taken place in the food before it was eaten. But even those who would limit the use of the term autointoxication to intoxication with the products of cellular metabolism, must admit the possibility of products of metabolism reëntering the blood from the contents of the bowels through the intestinal wall, since the bile, and perhaps also the intestinal juice, contain excrementitious substances which may, in case of defective fecal elimination, be reabsorbed into the blood. Therefore, in gastro-intestinal disturbances we have the possibility of both true autointoxication and intoxication by putrefactive products occurring together in an inseparable way, and the usual inclusion of gastro-intestinal intoxication in the discussion of auto-intoxication would seem to be justifiable as well as expedient.

The possible sources of poisonous substances arising in the gastro-intestinal tract are numerous. They may be formed either from the food-stuffs, or from the secretions and excretions of the body that enter the alimentary canal; and they may be formed either by the digestive ferments or by the bacteria of the intestinal contents. Hence the number of these products is enormous, and we are by no means sure that those that have yet been identified include the most important or most toxic; furthermore, at the present time we are far from sure that any of these materials, known or unknown, are important factors in human pathology. To classify the poisonous substances that are known to be formed in the alimentary canal, and which might, under certain conditions, cause an intoxication, is extremely difficult, because of the uncertainty of our information; but, using as a basis the sources of the substances, they may be classified as follows:[1]

[1] Modified from Weintraud, Ergeb. allg. Pathol., 1897 (4), 1, who gives exhaustive discussion and bibliography to that date.

I. The constituents of the digestive secretions, including the bile salts and pigments, pepsin, and trypsin.

II. Products of normal digestion:
  (a) From proteins—proteoses, peptones, amino-acids.
  (b) From fats—fatty acids and glycerol.

III. Products of putrefaction and fermentation:
  (a) From proteins:
    (1) From the aromatic radicals (tyrosine, phenylalanine, tryptophane)—indole, skatole, skatole-carbonic (or indole-acetic) acid, phenol, cresol, dioxyphenols, and the pressor bases.
    (2) From the fatty acid radicals—fatty acids (especially butyric and acetic), acetone, ammonia, amino-acids, carbon dioxide, hydrogen, marsh-gas. Also ptomains; cadaverine, putrescine, ethylidendiamine, isoamylamine.
    (3) From the sulphur-containing radicals—H_2S, methyl mercaptan, ethyl mercaptan, ethyl sulphid.
  (b) From carbohydrates:
    Fatty acids, the following having been detected—formic, acetic, propionic, butyric, valerianic, lactic, oxybutyric, and succinic; also acetone, CO_2, CH_4, H_2.
  (c) From fats:
    Higher fatty acids, as well as butyric acid; also glycerol. From lecithin—choline, neurine, and muscarine-like bodies.

IV. Synthetic products of bacterial activity (*e. g.*, botulismus) which cannot properly be considered as causing "autointoxication."

I. THE CONSTITUENTS OF THE DIGESTIVE FLUIDS

These call for but brief consideration, for, although many of them are known to be toxic, yet there is no evidence that they cause autointoxication, either in health or disease. Both pepsin and trypsin, especially the latter, are decidedly toxic when injected experimentally into the blood (see Enzymes), but they do not appear ever to pass through the intestinal wall in sufficient quantity to cause harm, although minute traces may appear in the urine; this harmlessness probably depends largely on the known inhibiting action of the blood upon enzymes.

The bile salts are also toxic, especially hemolytic, but those that are reabsorbed from the intestines are taken back into the liver and re-excreted. This protective arrangement seems to be sufficient for all emergencies. The bile-pigments become converted into *urobilinogen* through reduction, and this is largely absorbed and eliminated as *urobilin*. Icterus and cholemia do not seem ever to be produced by absorption of bile-pigments and bile salts from the intestines.

II. PRODUCTS OF NORMAL DIGESTION

Proteoses and Peptones.—Under normal conditions, these are broken up in the intestinal wall into the amino-acids, through the agency of erepsin, and do not appear in the blood in appreciable quantities. To be sure, certain authors claim to have found *albumose* in normal blood, but if present the amounts are extremely minute. In conditions in which ulceration or other lesions are present in the gastro-intestinal tract it is possible to find small amounts of proteoses in the urine, probably absorbed through the abnormal areas, but not in quantities sufficient to account for any appreciable intoxication, although proteoses are distinctly toxic. This last statement has been much contested, because the difficulty of purifying proteoses obtained from ordinary sources has left open the possibility that such toxic effects as have been observed are due to contaminating substances, such as histamine, and not to the proteoses themselves. More recent work, however, particularly that of Underhill,[2] Gibson[3] and Zunz,[4] seems to have established affirmatively the toxicity of proteoses, whether from animal or vegetable proteins. Besides the classical effect of inhibiting the coagulation of the blood, the proteoses have a lymphagogue effect (Heidenhain),[5] cause a marked febrile reaction,[6] and in doses of some size are fatal to experimental animals (rabbits being much less susceptible than dogs and many other animals). Locally they cause a mild inflammatory reaction, which is followed by the appearance of much connective-tissue formation.[7] Long continued injection of proteoses does not produce visceral lesions.[8] The careful studies of Zunz show that intravenous injection of hetero-albumose, thio-albumose, deutero-albumose and proto-albumose cause a rise in blood pressure, but large doses may cause a fall in pressure; the abiuret products of tryptic digestion are much more actively depressor than the albumoses. As a general rule, however, it has been observed that the first products of protein hydrolysis are the most toxic, and with further cleavage the toxicity lessens and finally disappears, as shown especially in the studies on anaphylaxis and anaphylatoxin formation.[9]   Thus Wolf[10] found that the amino-

---

[2] Amer. Jour. Physiol., 1903 (9), 345; Jour. Biol. Chem., 1915 (22), 443 (literature). See also Hanke and Koessler on the relation of histamine to peptone shock, Jour. Biol. Chem., 1920.

[3] Philippine Jour. Sci., 1914 (9), 499.

[4] Arch. internat. physiol., 1911 (73), 110.

[5] See also Nolf, Arch. internat de Physiol., 1906 (3), 343.

[6] Gibson finds that carefully purified proteoses have but a slight pyrogenic effect. (Philippine Jour. Sci., 1913 (8), 475.)

[7] In a paper appearing in the Transactions of the Chicago Pathological Society, 1903 (5), 240, I published the observation that repeated injections of Witte's "peptone" (which consists chiefly of proteoses) into rabbits led to the production of marked cirrhosis of the liver, and suggested the possibility that proteoses escaping through a diseased gastric or intestinal wall into the blood might be a factor in the production of cirrhosis in man. Subsequent observations, however, have shown that repeated injection of almost any foreign protein material (e. g., emulsions of organs, foreign blood, etc., used in immunization experiments) will cause a similar cirrhosis in rabbits, which animals, indeed, often spontaneously show this condition when apparently otherwise normal. "Peptone" injections in dogs and guinea-pigs have failed to cause a similar cirrhosis, and hence the value of these and all other rabbit experiments on cirrhosis of the liver is very questionable; however, the possibility of the correctness of the original conclusions still remains open.

[8] Woolley et al., Jour. Exp. Med., 1915 (22), 114. Boughton describes acute degenerative changes from Witte's peptone. (Jour. Immunol., 1919 (4), 381.)

[9] The statement of v. Knafll-Lenz (Arch. exp. Path. u. Pharm., 1913 (73), 292) that the toxicity of the cleavage products varies directly with their tryptophane content could not be corroborated by Underhill and Hendrix, Jour. Biol. Chem., 1915 (22), 443.

[10] Jour. of Physiol., 1905 (32), 171.

acids do not cause a fall of blood pressure, nor do polypeptids.[11] Proteoses have little if any power to stimulate antibody formation (see Antigens, Chap. vii). Whipple[12] has described the isolation of highly toxic proteoses from the contents of closed intestinal loops, and injection of these proteoses causes a marked increase in nitrogen elimination, presumably from toxicogenic destruction of tissue proteins. With this is a great increase in the non-protein nitrogen of the blood, partly due to renal injury. He also observed an increased resistance of the animals to these proteoses after repeated injections.

"**Albumosuria.**"[13]—If proteoses enter the blood stream they appear in large part in the urine, indicating that the tissues do not readily utilize them in this form.[14] Consequently, when proteoses are produced in considerable amounts by autolysis of pathological tissues they appear in the urine, and their presence is considered to be of diagnostic value.[15] True peptone seems rarely, and according to many observers never, to appear in the urine; but in view of the observations that polypeptids often appear in the urine,[16] it is probable that true peptones also do. Albumoses, therefore, may be found in the urine whenever any considerable amount of tissue or exudate is being autolyzed and absorbed, and it has been found in the following conditions: Suppuration of all kinds; resolution of pneumonia; involution of the puerperal uterus; carcinoma (two-thirds of all cases—Ury and Lilienthal), and other malignant growths; febrile conditions with tissue destruction (37.5 per cent. of all cases, Morawitz and Dietschy);[17] acute yellow atrophy, phosphorus poisoning, and eclampsia; leukemia, especially under x-ray treatment; absorption of simple and inflammatory exudates; ulcerating pulmonary tuberculosis,[18] and after tuberculin reactions (Deist).[19] Albumosuria is present in smallpox and may serve in differential diagnosis.[20] In ulcerative conditions of the alimentary canal albumoses may be absorbed unchanged and cause alimentary albumosuria. The normal kidney seems to be impermeable to the small amounts of proteose that may be present normally in the blood, or even after large oral ingestion of proteoses, but in parenchymatous nephritis it may escape in the urine (Henderson,[21] Pollak).[13]

[11] Haliburton, *ibid.*, 1905 (32), 174.
[12] Jour. Exp. Med., 1917 (25), 461; 1918 (28), 213; 1918 (29) 397.
[13] Critical review given by Pollak, Zeit. exp. Med., 1914 (2), 314.
[14] They may be partly hydrolyzed into smaller complexes, however, primary proteoses being partly changed to deutero-proteoses, and the latter partly to peptones (Chittenden, Mendel, and Henderson, Amer. Jour. Physiol., 1899 (2), 142).
[15] See Yarrow, Amer. Med., 1903 (5), 452; Ury and Lilienthal, Arch. f. Verdauungskr., 1905 (11), 72; Senator, International Clinics, 1905 (4, series 14), 85.
[16] Chodat and Kummer, Biochem. Zeit., 1914 (65), 392.
[17] Arch. f. exp. Path. u. Pharm., 1905 (54), 88.
[18] See Parkinson, Practitioner, 1906 (76), 219.
[19] Beitr. z. klin. Tuberk., 1912 (23), 547.
[20] Primavera, Gaz. Int. Med. e Chir., 1913, No. 10.
[21] Lancet, Mar. 6, 1909.

37

It is possible that some of the symptoms of these conditions are due to intoxication with proteoses, for 0.07 to 0.1 gram deutero-albumose will cause a febrile reaction in a healthy man,[22] but probably their amount is usually too small to cause appreciable effects.[23] It is well known, however, that the characteristic rise of temperature following the injection of tuberculin into tuberculous individuals is also produced if minute quantities of proteose solutions are injected in place of tuberculin; therefore, proteoses arising from autolysis in tuberculosis may be of importance in causing fever and other symptoms.[24] Tuberculous animals are said to succumb to a much smaller dose of deutero-albumose than normal animals.[25]

The so-called "Bence-Jones albumose" that appears in the urine of patients with multiple bone-marrow tumors is not a true albumose, but is more closely related to the simple proteins, and is discussed under the head of "Chemistry of Tumors."

III. PRODUCTS OF PUTREFACTION AND FERMENTATION[26]

We may perhaps gain some appreciation of the enormous amount of bacterial action that goes on in the normal intestinal digestive processes by considering the fact that as much as one-third of the total weight of the solids of normal feces may consist of bacteria (Strasburger), their proportion being increased in diarrheal disorders and decreased in constipation. They attack all food-stuffs, and among the decomposition-products formed through their activity are undoubtedly many of considerable toxicity. Most of the products of intestinal putrefaction that have as yet been isolated are, however, not extremely poisonous; but many of them are toxic to some degree, and their long-continued absorption may possibly lead to serious disturbances. Considering them first according to their origin and chemical nature, we take up first the products of:

A. PROTEIN PUTREFACTION

(1) SUBSTANCES DERIVED FROM THE AROMATIC RADICALS OF THE PROTEIN MOLECULE

In the protein molecule are contained the following amino-acids with an aromatic nucleus:

$$NH_2$$

Tyrosine, $HO\langle \rangle CH_2-CH-COOH$

[22] See Matthes. Arch. exper. Path. u. Pharm., 1895 (36), 437.

[23] In a series of unpublished experiments I was unable to cause amyloid degeneration in rabbits by protracted intoxication with proteose solutions.

[24] Simon, Arch. exp. Med., 1903 (19), 449. Concerning relation of tuberculin to proteoses see review by Jolles in Ott's "Chemische Pathol. der Tuberculose."

[25] Kirchheim and Tuczek, Arch. exp. Path. u. Pharm., 1914 (77), 387.

[26] Complete bibliography given in the résumé on "Intestinal Putrefaction" by Gerhardt, Ergebnisse der Physiol., 1901 (III, Abt. 1), 107.   Chemistry of Putrefaction is reviewed by Ellinger, ibid., 1907 (6), 29.

Phenylalanine,

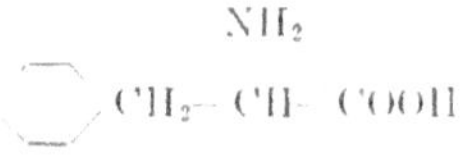

$$\underset{\underset{NH_2}{|}}{\text{CH}_2-\text{CH}-\text{COOH}}$$

Tryptophane,

$$-\text{C}-\text{CH}_2-\overset{\overset{NH_2}{|}}{\text{CH}}-\text{COOH}$$

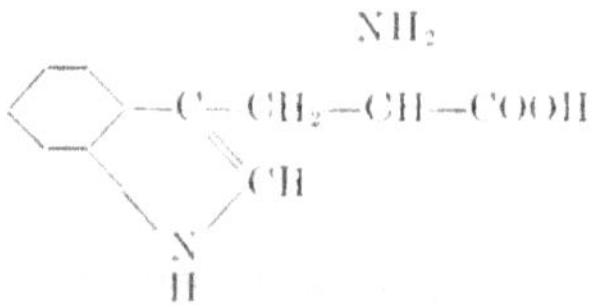

In the intestinal contents have been found a number of substances that are undoubtedly derived from these aromatic radicals. They are (1) *phenol*,

$$\text{OH}$$

which is formed in small quantities, presumably from tyrosine, as also is the closely related (2) *paracresol*,

$$\text{HO}-\text{CH}_3$$

and also (3) *para-oxyphenyl acetic acid*,

$$\text{HO}-\text{CH}_2-\text{COOH}$$

and (4) *para-oxyphenyl-propionic acid*,

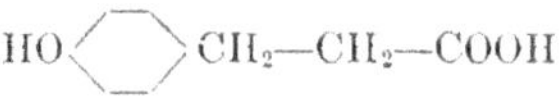

$$\text{HO}-\text{CH}_2-\text{CH}_2-\text{COOH}$$

From the tryptophane are formed numerous important substances, as follows:

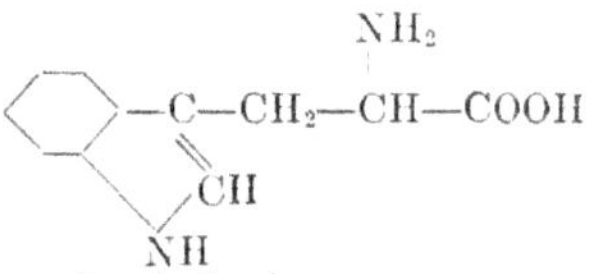

$$-\text{C}-\text{CH}_2-\overset{\overset{NH_2}{|}}{\text{CH}}-\text{COOH}$$
$$\text{CH}$$
$$\text{NH}$$
(tryptophane)

readily yields, through splitting off the NH_2 group and addition of H, *indole propionic acid* (formerly incorrectly called *skatole acetic acid*), which is

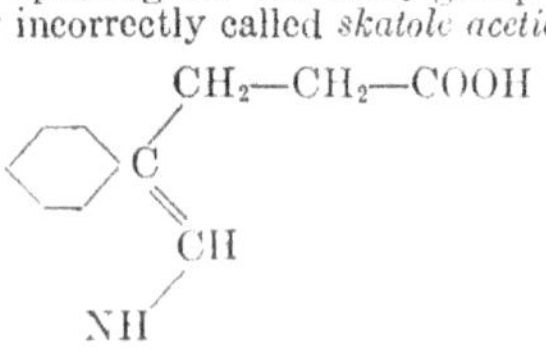

$$\text{CH}_2-\text{CH}_2-\text{COOH}$$
$$\text{C}$$
$$\text{CH}$$
$$\text{NH}$$

and from which in turn may readily be formed *indole acetic acid* (erroneously called *skatole carboxylic acid*), which is

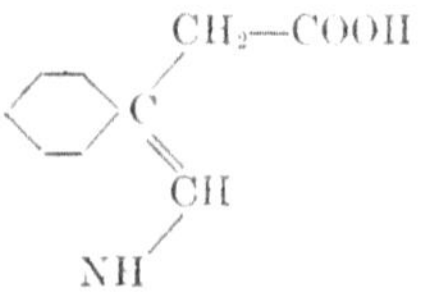

$$\text{CH}_2-\text{COOH}$$
$$\text{C}$$
$$\text{CH}$$
$$\text{NH}$$

Both of these substances have been found in the intestinal contents.   From them are formed the better known *skatole*,

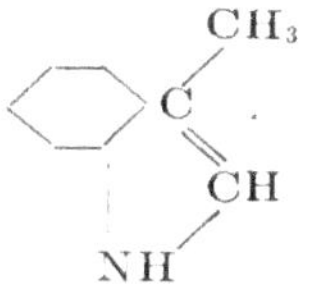

$$CH_3$$

and *indole*,

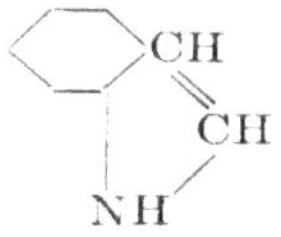

In dogs, but not in man, *kynurenic acid*.

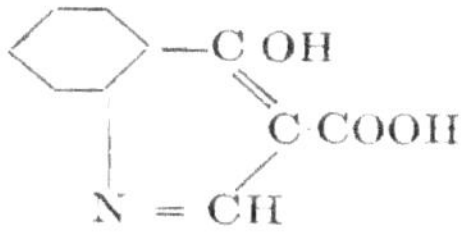

$$-C\ OH$$
$$C\ COOH$$
$$N = CH$$

is also formed from tryptophane.[27]

The greatest interest concerning these bodies arises from the fact that after they are absorbed from the intestine they become combined with sulphuric or glycuronic acid, and are excreted in the urine as salts of these acids; consequently the amount of sulphuric acid appearing in the urine in such organic combination ("ethereal sulphuric acid") is considered as an index of the amount of intestinal putrefaction.   In the case of indole and skatole, which have no hydroxyl group, a preliminary oxidation occurs, whereby indole is converted into *indoxyl*,

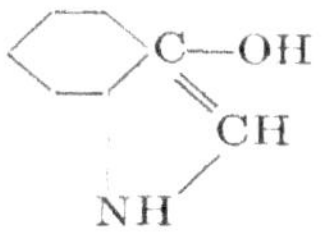

$$C{-}OH$$
$$CH$$
$$NH$$

and skatole into *skatoxyl*,

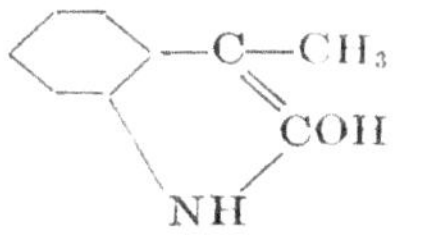

$$-C{-}CH_3$$
$$COH$$
$$NH$$

and they are then combined with sulphuric or glycuronic acid, as follows:

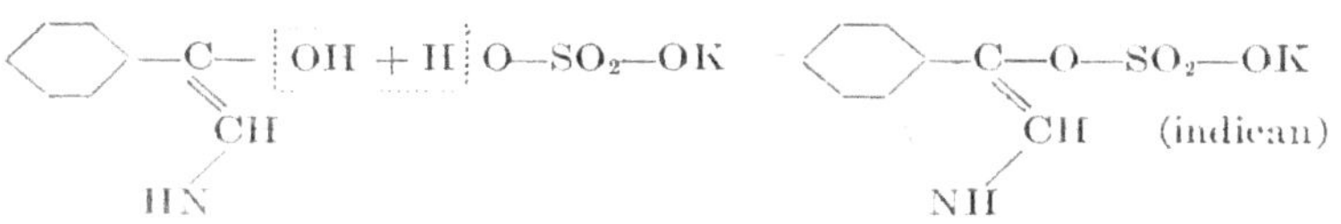

$$-C-\ OH + H\ O{-}SO_2{-}OK$$
$$CH$$
$$HN$$

$$-C{-}O{-}SO_2{-}OK$$
$$CH \quad \text{(indican)}$$
$$NH$$

By far the greater part of these aromatic substances, when excreted in the urine, is combined with sulphuric acid, and but a small part with glycuronic acid;[28] but in case the amount of sulphuric acid avail-

[27] See Ellinger, Zeit. physiol. Chem., 1904 (43), 325.
[28] Sherwin (Jour. Biol. Chem., 1917 (31), 307) states that phenylacetic acid is excreted by monkeys combined with glycine, but by man it is excreted combined with glutamine.

able is too small to combine with all the aromatic radicals entering the blood, a large amount of the glycuronic acid compound appears in the urine (e. g., after therapeutic administration of phenol, cresol, thymol, camphor, etc.). Both the preliminary oxidation and the combining with acids seem to occur chiefly in the liver, this process constituting one of the most important of the many protective offices of that organ, since the resulting compounds are much less toxic than are the original substances.[29] Herter and Wakeman[30] have shown that living cells have the power of acting upon indole and phenol (and presumably upon the rest of this group) in such a way that they cannot be recovered by distillation. Most active in this respect is the liver, then in order come kidney, muscle, blood, and brain. The change seems to be a loose chemical combination with the protoplasm of the cells, and the power of the tissues to bring about this combination is not greatly decreased by serious pathological changes in the organs (e. g., ricin poisoning).[31]

Indole.—This is probably the most important member of this group of substances, the striking color of its derivatives making its detection in the urine easy, so that it is generally used as the most available index of the amount of putrefaction that is occurring in the intestines.[32] The greatest quantities are found when intestinal putrefaction is marked, especially in intestinal obstruction involving the small intestine; obstruction of the large intestine, as Jaffe first demonstrated, does not cause marked indicanuria unless the stagnation involves the ileum, as it may in the later stages of obstruction. With marked impairment of renal function indican may accumulate in the blood (see Uremia). There can be no question that the indican of the urine is derived, at least in part, from the indole formed in the intestine, for administration of indole by mouth to either animals or man causes a considerable increase in the indican present in the urine; however, but 40 to 60 per cent. can be recovered in this way, the rest apparently being oxidized to other compounds, part of which may also appear in the urine.[33] Whether part of the urinary indican is derived from tryptophane liberated during intracellular protein metabolism, and not from intestinal putrefaction, has long been a disputed point among physiological chemists.[34] The demonstration by Ellinger and Gentzen[35] that tryptophane, when fed or injected subcutaneously, causes no increase in urinary indican, whereas its injection into the cecum causes much indicanuria, would indicate that indole is formed

[29] Metchnikoff insisted that these sulfo-compounds still retain considerable toxicity. (Ann. Inst. Pasteur, 1914 (27), 893).
[30] Jour. Exper. Med., 1899 (4), 307.
[31] For further discussion of this topic, see "Chemical Defences against Poisons of Known Composition," Chapter x.
[32] See Houghton, Amer. Jour. Med. Sci., 1908 (135), 567.
[33] If gelatin is substituted for proteins in the dietary, indican is not excreted, because gelatin does not contain tryptophane (Underhill, Amer. Jour. Physiol., 1904 (12), 176).
[34] Literature by Gerhardt, Ergeb. der Physiol., 1904 (III, Abt. I), 131.
[35] Hofmeister's Beitr., 1903 (4), 171.

from tryptophane only through putrefaction, and not in cellular metabolism. Other experiments support the same view.[36] However, it is possible that part of the indican present in the urine during conditions associated with gangrene, putrid cancers, putrid placentas, or putrid purulent exudates, may be derived from these decomposing materials. The statement that indicanuria is of significance in insanity could not be substantiated by Borden,[37] who used quantitative methods and careful controls. A large proportion of the data and conclusions in the literature concerning indicanuria are valueless because of improper or inadequate methods.

Probably the chief agent in the formation of indole in the intestines and in putrid tissues is the colon bacillus, which, as is well known, produces indole in ordinary culture-media.[38]

Toxicity of Indole.—Although the toxicity of indole seems to be relatively slight, and this toxicity is further reduced by the conversion of indole into indoxyl and indican, yet Herter[39] found that administration to healthy men of indole in quantities of 0.025 to 2 grams per day caused frontal headache, irritability, insomnia, and confusion; the continued absorption of enough indole to cause a constant strong reaction for indican in the urine is sufficient to cause neurasthenic symptoms. Long-continued injection of indole leads to hypertrophy of the adrenal medulla and slight interstitial changes in the kidneys,[40] but the reputed responsibility of indole for arteriosclerosis is most doubtful.[41] Lee[42] has also demonstrated that indole, skatole, and methyl mercaptan cause muscles to react to stimuli like fatigued muscles. Normal urine contains but about 12 milligrams of indican per day, which amount is so insignificant in proportion to the above-mentioned doses that were found necessary to produce symptoms, that we may well doubt the occurrence of noticeable intoxication from this substance under ordinary conditions. Nesbitt[43] states that twenty times as much indole or skatole as are excreted daily by an adult man may be injected into the jugular vein of a dog of four kilos without causing appreciable effects. Richards and Howland, however, have demonstrated the possibility, that defective oxidation of substances of this group may permit of intoxication.[44] When subcutaneously injected, dissolved in oil, indole and skatole have the property of greatly stimulating epithelial proliferation, similar to the

---

[36] See Scholz, Zeit. physiol. Chem., 1903 (38), 513; Underhill, loc. cit. Sherwin and Hawk found an absence of indican in the urine in the latter part of a long fast (Biochem. Bull., 1914 (3), 416).
[37] Jour. Biol. Chem., 1907 (2), 575.
[38] See Distaso and Sugden, Biochem. Jour., 1919 (13), 153.
[39] New York Med. Jour., 1898 (68), 89.
[40] Woolley and Newburgh, Jour. Amer. Med. Assoc., 1911 (56), 1796.
[41] See Steenhuis, Folia Mikrobiol., 1915 (3), 76.
[42] Jour. Amer. Med. Assoc., 1906 (46), 1499.
[43] Jour. Exper. Med., 1899 (4), 5.
[44] See note in Science, 1906 (24), 979.

action of scarlet R and other fat stains (Stoeber),[15] but we have no direct evidence that these substances cause similar effects in the human body.

Other Aromatic Compounds.—Skatole seems to accompany indole in small amounts, but apparently in no constant quantitative relation. Herter[46] states that skatole is formed under entirely different conditions from indole, and that *B. coli* does not produce skatole. It is not always present in the contents of the large intestines of healthy persons, and seems to be formed later than indole.

Indole-acetic acid appears in the normal urine in extremely minute quantities, and is increased in the same conditions as skatole. It is the mother substance of *uroroscin*, and can be found in the intestines of patients who show this substance in the urine (Herter).[47] Ross[48] found indole-acetic acid in the urine in 21 per cent. of normal persons, and in 48 per cent. of dementia precox cases, and obtained evidence in favor of an endogenous origin in two cases studied especially to determine this point.

Phenylacetic acid[49] is formed from phenylalanine on putrefaction, as also are phenylpropionic and benzoic acids. Benzoic acid combines with glycine and is excreted as hippuric acid, and the phenylpropionic acid is excreted as *p*-hydroxyhippuric acid. Phenylacetic acid combines with glutamine and is excreted as phenylacetylglutamine. It is but slightly toxic, 5 gm. doses in man causing slight symptoms resembling alcoholic intoxication; 16 gms. not producing serious results.

Phenol[50] appears in the urine normally in very minute quantities—from 0.005 to 0.07 grams per day, according to various observers. These figures are undoubtedly too low, for Folin and Denis[51] found the total excretion of phenols to be from 0.2 to 0.4 gm. per day, the amount varying with the protein intake.[52] They seem to come chiefly, if not entirely, from tyrosine.[53] Much more is undoubtedly formed in the intestines, for but a small fraction of phenol given by mouth (2 to 3 per cent., according to Munk) appears in the urine as a sulphuric-acid compound; part of the rest is oxidized to hydrochinon and pyrocatechin, $C_6H_4(OH)_2$, and eliminated as ethereal sulphates. These sulphates, although distinctly toxic are much less so than the phenol itself (Metchnikoff).[54] Contrary to prevailing ideas, Folin and Denis found the greater part of the phenols to be excreted uncombined. The largest quantities are found in the same conditions as indican except, of course, in "carbolic-acid" poisoning, when the amounts may be so great that practically all the sulphuric acid in the urine is in this organic combination, much of the phenol under these conditions being also combined with glycuronic acid.[55] This pairing is accomplished chiefly in the liver (Dubin). A small amount of urinary phenol may be of endogenous origin.[52] Rhein[56] ascribes the phenol of intestinal origin to the action of a specific sort of colon bacilli, *B. coli phenologenes*, which does not produce indole but produces phenol from tyrosine, and also from *p*-hydroxybenzoic acid which therefore may be an intermediary in tyrosine cleavage.

Blood contains small amounts of free phenols, about one-third being polyphenols, none being conjugated. In a series of pathological cases Theis and Benedict[57] found from 1.87 to 7.96 mg. per 100 cc. blood, somewhat higher figures being found in sarcoma and hernia cases than in other diseases.

Cresol (chiefly paracresol), *para-oxyphenyl acetic acid*, and *para-oxyphenyl pro-*

[45] Münch. med. Woch.. 1910 (57), 947.
[46] Jour. Biol. Chem., 1908 (4), 101; general discussion.
[47] Jour. Biol. Chem., 1908 (4), 253.
[48] Arch. Int. Med., 1913 (12), 112 and 231.
[49] See Sherwin and Kennard, Jour. Biol. Chem., 1919 (40), 259.
[50] Literature given by Dubin. Jour. Biol. Chem., 1916 (26), 69.
[51] Jour. Biol. Chem., 1915 (22), 309.
[52] Moore, Amer. Jour. Dis. Child., 1917 (13), 15.
[53] Tsudji, Jour. Biol. Chem., 1919 (38), 13.
[54] Ann. Inst. Pasteur, 1910 (24), 755.
[55] See the observations of Wohlgemuth and of Blumenthal (Biochem. Zeitschrift, 1906 (1), 134), on the detoxication of lysol and similar poisons.
[56] Biochem. Zeit., 1917 (84), 246.
[57] Jour. Biol. Chem., 1918 (36), 99.

pionic acid appear under similar conditions, except that the two oxy-acids are possibly also formed within the body through cellular metabolism, as they have been found present in the urine independent of intestinal putrefaction. Para-cresol is quantitatively the most important of the urinary phenols, and long con-tinued feeding produces no noticeable effects in rabbits.[58] Probably part of the benzoic acid that appears in the urine combined with glycine, as hippuric acid, is derived from intestinal putrefaction.[59]

THE PRESSOR BASES[60]

Among the products of protein putrefaction are several amines that have marked power to stimulate the sympathetic nervous system and thus to raise the blood pressure, hence resembling epinephrine physiologically as well as chemically. There are also bases derived from amino-acids which stimulate non-striated muscle without raising general blood pressure. The most important of these bases are:

Phenyl-ethylamine $C_6H_5.CH_2.CH_2.NH_2,$
derived from *phenylalanine* $C_6H_5.CH_2CHNH_2.COOH.$

Para-hydroxy-phenyl-ethylamine (tyramine) $OH.C_6H_4.CH_2.CH_2.NH_2$
derived from *tyrosine.* $OH.C_6H_4.CH_2.CHNH_2.COOH.$
Its relation to *epinephrine* is seen on comparing with the structural formula of
the latter $(OH)_2C_6H_3.CHOH.CH_2NH.CH_3$

Beta-iminazolyl-ethylamine (histamine) $CH \underset{N\underline{\quad\quad}C-CH_2:CH_2.NH_2}{\overset{NH-CH}{\diagdown}}$

derived from *histidine* $CH \underset{N\underline{\quad\quad}C-CH_2.CHNH_2.COOH}{\overset{NH-CH}{\diagdown}}$

It will be observed that these are all amines derived from the cyclic amino-acids of proteins by the process of *decarboxylization* (loss of CO_2). The straight chain amines are much less active physiologically. The lowest amine having any considerable pressor action is *isobutylamine*, but *paraphenylamine* is at least five times as active as any aliphatic amine (Barger). Tyramine injected subcutan-eously or intravenously increases blood pressure and slows the pulse rate,[61] resembling epinephrine, but it is only one-twentieth as active. Histamine causes ordinarily a fall of blood pressure, although it does constrict many peripheral vessels. Capillaries are dilated by his-tamine and Dale and Laidlaw compare it to a capillary poison.[61a] Its most striking effect is in causing profound contraction of the uterine and bronchial muscle. The relative effects of epinephrine, tryamine and histamine are given by Barbour, as follows:

[58] Denny and Frothingham, Jour. Med. Res., 1914 (31), 277.
[59] See Prager, Med. News, 1905 (86), 1025; Magnus-Levy, Münch med. Woch., 1905 (52), 2168.
[60] Full bibliography given by Barger, "The Simpler Natural Bases," Mono-graphs on Biochemistry, London, 1914.
[61] See Hewlett, Proc. Soc. Exp. Biol. Med., 1917 (15), 12.
[61a] See also Dale and Richards, Jour. Physiol., 1918 (52), 110.

	Blood pressure	Peripheral vessels	Coronary vessels (Ox)	Non-pregnant uterus
Epinephrine	+	+	−	−
Tyramine (ρ-hydroxyphenyl-ethylamine)	+	+	+	−
Histamine (β-iminazolyl-ethylamine)	−	+	+	+

+ means rise of blood pressure or constriction, — the opposite; the last-named amine may have a pressor effect in some animals.

Another difference is the production of severe urticarial reactions by histamine introduced into the skin, while tyramine and epinephrine both cause local blanching (Sollman and Pilcher).[62]

These substances have all been found in putrid protein materials produced by the action of anaerobic bacteria, and possibly they are formed in the intestines, as colon bacilli are able to form histamine from histidine.[63] Para-hydroxy-phenyl-ethylamine is also one of the active constituents of ergot, and has been found in the salivary gland of cephalopods, where it functions as a venom in paralyzing the prey. Beta-iminazolyl-ethylamine is said to be the most important constituent of ergot. It has been found regularly present in the intestinal mucosa, presumably formed by intestinal bacteria. According to Abel[64] histamine is widely distributed in all animal tissues, organ extracts, Witte's peptone, etc., or at least some substance that has similar physiological effects. He believes it to be especially abundant in the hypophysis and to form its chief active constituent, but histamine exhibits distinct differences from pituitrin. Hanke and Koessler[64a] however, have shown, by using purely chemical methods, that the perfectly fresh hypophysis contains no histamine. They could further demonstrate that peptone prepared from fibrin under aseptic conditions is free from histamine yet capable of producing typical peptone shock.

All these amines are detoxicated by the liver, and hence have little effect when given by mouth.[65] It is probable that no inconsiderable amounts are taken in our food and formed in the intestines every day (Abel). Their detoxication is accomplished by deaminization and oxidation, the resulting carboxylic acids being excreted or burned. Therefore it is not certain whether pressor bases formed in the intestines ever have any pathological effect, but it is quite possible that outside the portal territory various infections may give rise to pressor

[62] Jour. Pharm., 1917 (9), 391.
[63] Koessler and Hanke, Jour. Biol. Chem., 1919 (39), 539.
[64] Jour. Pharmacol., 1919 (13), 243.
[64a] Jour. Biol. Chem., 1920.
[65] See Guggenheim and Loeffler, Biochem. Zeit., 1916 (72), 325.

bases which enter the general circulation directly and escape the defensive mechanism of the liver. They may also cause local effects in the tissues where they are formed, e. g., the bronchi.[65a]

In some respects their effects resemble those of anaphylactic intoxication, and as the latter apparently results from toxic products of protein cleavage the possibility that here too pressor bases are concerned at once presents itself, but as yet the relation is undetermined (see Anaphylaxis, Chap. viii). The resemblance is especially seen in the profound effect on the bronchial musculature, which can be thrown into strong contraction, especially by beta-iminazolylethylamine which in 0.5 mg. doses kills guinea pigs from asphyxia, with distended lungs as in fatal anaphylaxis; also it causes a similar fall in temperature. Another point of similarity is the severe local urticaria when weak solutions (1–1000) of histamine are placed on a scarified area of skin,[66] recalling vividly the fact that urticarial eruptions are conspicuous in some types of anaphylactic reactions. Furthermore, in guinea pigs histamine kills by bronchial spasm, in rabbits by obstruction to the pulmonary circulation (Dale and Laidlaw),[67] which difference is also characteristic of anaphylaxis in these animals. On the other hand, histamine does not produce the profound alteration in the coagulability of the blood that is characteristic of anaphylaxis and of peptone shock, but it may be that in each of these cases some other poison is responsible for the effect on the blood, in addition to histamine or a similar substance. In doses of 1 mg. and upward in cats, histamine causes a condition resembling traumatic shock, there being oligæmia from passage of plasma out of the vessels and retardation of blood in the periphery because of loss of tone by the capillaries. Possibly in traumatic shock histamine is liberated in the injured tissues.

ALKAPTONURIA[68]

Alkaptonuria may be appropriately considered in this connection, since it depends on an abnormal metabolism of the aromatic groups, tyrosine and phenylalanine, which are, partly at least, split out of the protein molecule in the intestine. This condition is characterized by the tendency of the urine to turn dark on exposure to air, due to the presence in it of homogentisic acid.[69] Homogentisic acid has been.

[65a] Compare K. K. Koessler, "The pathogenesis of bronchial asthma," Arch Int. Med., 1920. In this article asthma is considered as an aminosis (amine intoxication).

[66] Eppinger and Guttmann, Zeit. klin. Med., 1913 (78), 399.

[67] Jour. Physiol., 1919 (52), 355.

[68] Résumé and literature by Falta, Biochem. Centralblatt, 1904 (3), 174, and Deut. Arch. klin. Med., 1904 (81), 231; Garrod, "Inborn Errors of Metabolism," Oxford Med. Publications, 1909; also Lancet, July, 1908; Frommherz, Biochem. Centr., 1908 (8), 1.

[69] It should be mentioned that *hydrochinon*, when present in the urine (usually after ingestion of large quantities of phenol), may also turn dark on exposure to air; and *melanin* may be excreted as a chromogen which turns dark on exposure, by patients with melanotic tumors or ochronosis (*q. v.*).

found in the blood but not in the feces of alkaptonurics, and the urine shows no other deviations from the normal except a slight increase in ammonia, with which the acid is combined. It is of rare occurrence, persists throughout life with but little apparent effect upon the health of the individual, and is often hereditary, being grouped by Garrod along with cystinuria, pentosuria and albinism as a "chemical malformation" of hereditary origin.[70] The relation of these aromatic bodies to the aromatic constituents of the proteins is best shown by comparing their structural formulæ:

Phenylalanine, ⬡ CH₂—CHNH₂—COOH.

Tyrosine, HO— ⬡ CH₂—CHNH₂—COOH.

Uroleucic acid,[71] OH ⬡ CH₂—CHOH—COOH. HO

Homogentisic acid, OH ⬡ CH₂—COOH. HO

Apparently the condition depends upon an abnormality in the intermediary metabolism, and not upon an abnormal formation of homogentisic acid through intestinal putrefaction, as was at first believed. Alkaptonuria is never observed in slight degrees; if there is any homogentisic acid in the urine at all it is there in large amounts (4–5 grams per day), depending on the diet, for when the error in metabolism is present at all it is complete. On a mixed diet the ratio of homogentisic acid to nitrogen in the urine is 40–50 to 100. The prevailing idea has been that the abnormality consists not in the excessive formation of homogentisic acid, but in a lack of ability on the part of the alkaptonuric individual to split open the benzene ring. It is generally stated that tyrosine and phenylalanine first suffer a splitting out of the nitrogen radical from the alanine side-chain, and then are oxidized into homogentisic acid, following which changes comes a disintegration of the benzene ring, with subsequent complete oxidation. On this basis the alkaptonuric accomplishes the conversion into the oxy-acid but the process stops there. Wakeman and Dakin,[72] however, have obtained evidence that in the normal oxidation of tyrosine

[70] Alkaptonurics may give a positive Wassermann reaction without other evidence of syphilis, and in one case this reaction disappeared when the patient was given large amounts of tyrosine (Söderbergh, Nord. Med. Arkiv., 1915 (48 , 1).

[71] The older writers stated that uroleucic acid commonly accompanied homogentisic acid in the urine of alkaptonuria, but later observations do not confirm this. (Oswald, Zeit. physiol. Chem., 1914 (93), 307).

[72] Jour. Biol. Chem., 1911 (9), 139 and 151.

and phenylalanine, homogentisic acid is not an intermediary product, and Dakin states that the alkaptonuric can destroy simple derivatives of phenylalanine and tyrosine, provided their structure is such that the formation of substances of the type of homogentisic acid is precluded He believes that in alkaptonuria there is abnormal formation of homogentisic acid as well as a failure to destroy it when formed. On the other hand, Abderhalden[73] has been able to cause the appearance in the urine of homogentisic acid in a normal individual by feeding large amounts of tyrosine, which is in favor of the view that it is a normal intermediary in tyrosine catabolism.[74] In any case the administration of tyrosine or phenylalanine, or of tyrosine-rich foods—i. e., proteins—causes a marked increase in the amount of homogentisic acid eliminated in the urine; indeed, this increase is almost quantitative. Normal individuals when given these substances in moderate amounts, or homogentisic acid itself, destroy them completely, so that the latter does not appear at all in the urine.[75] If alkaptonurics are kept without protein food for some time, the elimination of alkaptonuric acid goes on, although in diminished amounts, indicating that the aromatic amino-acids formed in tissue catabolism also fail to be destroyed and, therefore, appear in the urine as these derivatives.

Since *gentisic acid*,

$$\underset{HO}{\overset{OH}{\langle\quad\rangle}}-COOH,$$

when given by mouth, is also eliminated unchanged by alkaptonurics, although completely destroyed by normal individuals, it seems evident that the difficulty in metabolism affects the benzene ring itself and does not depend upon the character of the side-chain. Normal organisms seem to be capable of destroying such aromatic compounds as pass through a stage of homogentisic acid in being oxidized, which indicates that the benzene ring can be broken up only when oxidized in this particular manner (the 2, 5 position); the alkaptonuric differs in being unable to break up even this form (Falta). According to Garrod[76] the conversion of tyrosine and phenylalanine into homogentisic acid is so complete that the ratio of homogentisic acid to nitrogen is constant and the same in all cases. Frommherz and Hermanns[77] advance the suggestion that normal oxidation of the aromatic radicals may take place by two routes, one by way of homogentisic acid, the other by way of the 3–4 dioxy-derivatives (i. e., pyrocatechin), since such derivatives can be readily oxidized in the metabolism

[73] Zeit. physiol. Chem., 1912 (77), 454.
[74] Katsch (Deut. Arch. klin. Med., 1918 (127), 210) believes that homogentisic acid is converted into acetone.
[75] Gross states that normal serum destroys homogentisic acid, which property is lacking in the serum of alkaptonurics (Biochem. Zeit., 1914 (61), 165).
[76] Garrod and Clarke, Biochem. Zeit., 1907 (2), 217.
[77] Zeit. physiol. Chem., 1914 (91), 194.

of alkaptonurics who cannot destroy homogentisic acid. That is, their deficiency involves only one of two possible methods of oxidizing aromatic compounds, leaving them considerable capacity for this important metabolic function. The tissues of the alkaptonuric are probably not chemically affected in this condition, for Abderhalden[78] found that the hair and nails of an alkaptonuric contained normal proportions of tyrosine. There is often an arthritis, from deposition of pigment in the joints, designated by Gross[79] as "arthritis alkaptonurica."

In some cases of alkaptonuria a pigmentation of the cartilages also occurs, *ochronosis*, but the association is not constant; ochronosis may occur without alkaptonuria, and conversely. (See "Ochronosis.")

(2) Substances Arising from the Fatty Acid Radicals (Amino Acids) of Proteins

As stated in the introductory chapter, the protein molecule consists of a combination of a great number of organic acids, of various sorts, all of which have as a common characteristic the presence of a NH_2 group attached to the carbon atom nearest the acid radical, the α position; thus, $R - CHNH_2 - COOH$. A few of the amino acids contain an aromatic group, and the relation of these to intestinal decomposition has been considered above. The greater number have a simple fatty acid radical (the simplest amino-acid being glycine, $CH_2NH_2 - COOH$), and from them are derived by intestinal putrefaction substances that are, for the most part, chemically simple and, as far as known, pathologically unimportant. From leucine alone is derived a substance of known considerable toxicity, the pressor base *isoamylamine.* $\begin{matrix} CH_2 \\ \diagdown \\ CH_3 \end{matrix} CH - CH_2 - CH_2 - NH_2$ which is less powerful than the cyclic pressor bases described previously. Bain[79a] found it the most abundant pressor base of the urine.

Fatty acids may readily be formed from them by splitting out the NH_2 group; thus acetic acid may be formed from glycine, propionic acid from alanine, etc. Apparently butyric and acetic acid are the acids most commonly formed in this way. Gaseous derivatives, such as hydrogen, ammonia, carbon dioxide, and marsh-gas, are also produced. *Acetone* is perhaps formed from these fatty acids; it is often present in the intestinal contents, but may come from other sources.

Certain conditions of cyanosis have been designated as *enterogenous cyanosis.* (See Methemoglobin, Chap. xviii) because of the belief that the methemoglobin responsible for the cyanosis is caused by nitrites derived from intestinal putrefaction and demonstrable in the blood.[80] Presumably the nitrites come from the NH_2 groups of the protein molecule, the colon bacillus being an active former of nitrites. Under the same term are included the cases of *sulph-hemoglobinemia.* This condition is ascribed by Wallis[81] to bacteria which produce from the proteins a hydroxylamine derivative, capable of reducing oxyhemoglobin, and which he finds present in the blood of patients with sulph-hemoglobinemia.

Diamines.—Of much interest are the substances that are formed from the amino-acids by bacterial action, which still retain their nitrogen radicals—the *ptomaïns* (See Chap. IV). Two of these, the diamines *putrescine,* $NH_2 (CH_2)_4 NH_2$, and *cadaverine,* $NH_2(CH_2)_5 NH_2$ are of particular interest,[82] because they have been

[78] Zeit. physiol. Chem., 1907 (52), 435.

[79] Deut. Arch. klin. Med., 1919 (128) 249.

[79a] Quart. Jour. Exp. Physiol., 1914 (8). 229.

[80] See Gibson, Quart. Jour. Med., 1907 (1), 29; West and Clarke, Lancet, Feb. 2, 1907; Davis, Lancet, Oct. 26, 1912.

[81] Quart. Jour. Med., Oct., 1913.

[82] For discussion of formation and properties of these two ptomaïns, see Vaughan and Novy's "Cellular Toxins."

observed in the feces and urine of persons with *cystinuria*. The stools in cholera also seem to contain these ptomaïns frequently. Their etiological relation to the cystinuria is no longer accepted, however, and their toxicity is slight. They are probably derived from the diamino-acids of the protein molecule, putrescine being closely related to *ornithine*,[83] and is probably formed from it as follows:

$$NH_2 \qquad NH_2 \qquad NH_2 \qquad NH_2$$
$$CH_2-CH_2-CH_2-CH-COOH = CH_2-CH_2-CH_2-CH_2 + CO_2$$
$$\text{(ornithine)} \qquad\qquad \text{(putrescine)}$$

while cadaverine is probably formed from, *lysine*,

$$NH_2 \qquad NH_2 \qquad NH_2 \qquad NH_2$$
$$CH_2-(CH_2)_3-CH-COOH = CH_2-(CH_2)_3-CH_2 + CO_2$$
$$\text{(lysine)} \qquad\qquad \text{(cadaverine)}$$

Ethylidendiamine, $CH_3—CH\diagup^{NH_2}_{\diagdown NH_2}$ which is somewhat toxic, has also been detected in the contents of the gastro-intestinal tract.

Apparently these substances are absent from normal feces, but this does not exclude the possibility of their normal formation, absorption and destruction. There is no evidence that they ever cause symptoms or pathological alterations.

(3) SUBSTANCES ARISING FROM THE SULPHUR-CONTAINING RADICAL OF PROTEINS

Most if not all of the sulphur in the protein molecule seems to be contained in the amino-acid, *cystine*, which has the following composition:

$$S-CH_2-CHNH_2-COOH$$
$$S-CH_2-CHNH_2-COOH.$$

From this is formed the *hydrogen sulphide* of the intestinal gases, of which about 0.058–0.066 gram is present in each one hundred grams of normal colon contents. Although Senator has described a case in which an intoxication with H_2S of intestinal origin occurred, this gas seems not to be a frequent cause of intoxication, and Senator's case stands almost alone. Under normal conditions H_2S does not appear in the urine, any that may be absorbed probably being oxidized to SO_4. If enough H_2S should enter the blood so that it was not completely destroyed, it might well cause harm, for it is decidedly toxic, particularly affecting the nervous system; but we have no evidence that this often happens. Van der Bergh[84] has observed cases of intestinal obstruction in which the presence of *sulphemoglobin* in the patient's blood was demonstrated.

Methyl mercaptan, CH_3SH, has also been found in the feces, although it seems not to be abundantly or constantly present, according to Herter,[85] who found also that mixed bacteria from normal feces rarely produce mercaptan in cultures. However, bacteria from the feces of persons suffering with various diseases often produce mercaptan. *Ethyl mercaptan*, C_2H_5SH, and *ethyl sulphide*, C_2H_5-S-C_2H_5, have also been described as fecal constituents. It is not known that the mercaptans are a cause of intoxication.

CYSTINE AND CYSTINURIA[86]

Cystine has been observed in the urine in a number of cases, and when present at all it is usually found in considerable quantities.

[83] Ornithine forms part of the arginine molecule, which is the most universally present (in proteins) of all the amino-acids, ornithine being formed when urea is split from arginine.

[84] Deut. Arch. klin. Med., 1905 (83), 86.

[85] Jour. Biol. Chem., 1906 (1), 421.

[86] Literature concerning cystine given by Friedmann, Ergebnisse der Physiol., 1902 (1. Abt. 1), 15; and by Mann, "Chemistry of the Proteins," pp. 56–64. Cystinuria reviewed by Bödtker, Zeit. physiol. Chem., 1905 (45), 393; Garrod, "Inborn Errors of Metabolism," and Lancet, July, 1908; Kretschmer, Urol. and Cut. Rev., 1916 (20), No. 1.

Because of its slight solubility it appears as a deposit of hexagonal crystals, and frequently forms *cystine concretions (q. v.)* in the urinary bladder.[87] According to Garrod it is more common than alkaptonuria, and, like the rest of the "Inborn Errors of Metabolism," occurs much more often in males than in females. Hofmann[88] was able to collect from the literature to 1907 a total of 175 cases, of which 85 were males and 45 females. Baumann and others observed that in cystinuria the urine often contains, besides the cystine, the diamines *cadaverine* and *putrescine*, which are formed from lysine and ornithine respectively in the intestines through putrefaction, and they naturally suspected that cystine arose in the same way. Another view was that the diamines interfered with the oxidation of sulphur in the body, so that it was eliminated in the unoxidized form of cystine. But it has been demonstrated that neither of these hypotheses is correct, for (1) cystine could not be found in the feces; (2) if given by mouth, it is completely oxidized, and causes only the appearance of excessive amounts of sulphates in the urine; (3) cystinuria has been observed to occur independent of the presence of the diamines, and not to be modified or caused by their administration or pathological formation. The view now prevalent is that the cystine that escapes in the urine in cystinuria is not derived from intestinal putrefaction, but is formed in the tissues from the protein molecule, and fails to be further decomposed because of some anomaly of metabolism. This view is supported by the fact that cystinuria often appears to be an hereditary disease, occurring in families for several generations, it is independent of the diet, cystine appearing even if proteins are withheld, and also independent of intestinal putrefaction.[89] It having been found that *leucine* and *tyrosine* may also occur in the urine in cystinuria,[90] it seems probable that this condition depends upon a general abnormality of protein metabolism. The relation of the diamines to the condition is, however, very uncertain. Cystine does not seem to exert any toxic effect, and patients with cystinuria do not usually appear to suffer greatly from the abnormal metabolism, the chief trouble observed being due to the formation of the concretions in the bladder.[91] Sometimes in children, however, emaciation and early death without other apparent cause, have been observed, and may be due to the metabolic anomaly.

The metabolic error in cystinuria is not complete, for only a portion of the total cystine of the catabolized proteins is excreted as

[87] Abderhalden (Zeit. physiol. Chem., 1903 (38), 557) has described a case in a child in which the organs were infiltrated with masses of the cystine crystals.
[88] Cent. Grenz. Med. u. Chir., 1907 (10), 721.
[89] An isolated case of transient cystinuria in a patient with Raynaud's disease is described by Githens (Penn. Med. Jour., 1910 (1), 507).
[90] See Abderhalden. Zeit. physiol. Chem., 1919 (104), 129.
[91] This may be avoided by decreasing the cystine by means of a low protein diet, and increasing its solubility by keeping the reaction of the urine alkaline (Smillie, Arch. Int. Med., 1915 (16), 503).

such (Garrod). This would amount to some five grams per day, whereas the average excretion is only about 0.3–0.5 gram, and sulphates and other neutral sulphur compounds are always present in the urine. In no condition other than cystinuria have putrescine and cadaverine been found in quantities which could be detected by ordinary methods in 24-hour specimens; they may also be found in the feces of cystinurics, where cystine is never found. In the urine their presence is inconstant, and the amounts are at best very small. Leucine and tyrosine are found much less often than the diamines; lysine, has been found in one case,[92] which supports the view that cadaverine and putrescine come from the diamino-acids of the protein molecule by metabolism rather than by putrefaction.

B. Products of Fermentation of Carbohydrates

These include practically all the members of the fatty acid series, from *formic acid* to *valerianic acid;* and the oxy-acids, *lactic, succinic,* and *oxybutyric;* also, *oxalic acid, acetone, ethyl alcohol,* and the following gases: CO_2, CH_4, H_2. For the most part, the various organic acids are absorbed through the intestinal walls, and are oxidized completely in the tissues without causing any harm whatever. The possibility that acid intoxication may be produced in this way has been suggested, but it is generally believed that this does not occur, except possibly in infants. *Lactic* and *butyric*[93] acids are formed particularly in gastric fermentations in persons with deficient hydrochloric acid, motor insufficiency, or organic obstruction. Most of the disturbances observed in these conditions seem to be due to distention of the stomach with gas, chiefly CO_2, which is formed during the fermentation. It is possible, however, that the organic acids exercise some irritant effects on the mucous membrane; and they may also cause diarrhea, lactic and acetic acid often being present in diarrheal discharges due to excessive feeding with carbohydrates (Herter).

These acids or their salts do not appear in the urine, unless possibly as minute traces, except the *oxalic acid.* Minute quantities (0.02 gm. per day) of this substance are present in normal urine, but larger quantities (*oxaluria*) seem to depend either upon the taking of food containing much oxalic acid (rhubarb, spinach, etc.) or upon excessive gastric fermentation of carbohydrates (Baldwin),[94] and perhaps upon excessive destruction of purines, from which oxalic acid may be derived. Of the amino-acids it is presumably the diatomic acids, glutamic and aspartic, which yield oxalic acid (Jastrowitz).[95] Others, however, do not admit that any appreciable amount of oxalic acid is derived from proteins.[96] Probably the small quantities of oxalic acid thus formed do not cause toxic effects, and are important chiefly as causing urinary concretions of calcium oxalate, although there is evidence that long-continued excretion of oxalic acid may cause renal lesions. (See also consideration of oxalate calculi, Chap. xvii.)

C. Products of the Decomposition of Fats

These differ but little in nature from the products of carbohydrate fermentation, the large fatty acid molecules being broken down to smaller ones. In infants these fatty acids have been believed to be a cause of acid intoxication and acetonuria,[97] but probably they are seldom, if ever, of pathological importance. It is

[92] Ackermann and Kutscher, Zeit. f. Biol., 1911 (57), 355.
[93] Coleman (Ann. Inst. Pasteur, 1915 (29), 139) attempts to incriminate butyric acid in the production of arteriosclerosis, while Oswald Loeb believed lactic acid to be important, a view which could not be altogether supported by Denny and Frothingham, Jour. Med. Res., 1914 (31), 277.
[94] Jour. Exp. Med., 1900 (5), 27.
[95] Biochem. Zeit., 1910 (28), 34.
[96] Wegrzynowski, Zeit. physiol. Chem., 1913 (83), 112.
[97] Meyer and Langstein, Jahrb. f. Kinderheilk., 1906 (63), 30.

possible, however, that a serious reduction in the bases of the blood may result from the formation of excessive amounts of fatty acids in the intestines, the bases being combined to unite with the fatty acids, and then excreted in the feces.

It is quite otherwise with the products of decomposition of *lecithin*.[98] From its molecule is split off the ptomain, *choline*,

$$(CH_3)_3 \equiv N - CH_2 - CH_2OH$$
$$\mid$$
$$OH$$

which is easily oxidized into a highly poisonous compound, isomeric with *muscarine*, or by losing a molecule of water it forms *neurine*,

$$(CH_3)_3 \equiv N - CH = CH_2$$

$$OH$$

which is also very poisonous (discussed under "Ptomaïns," Chap. iv.). It has been demonstrated by Nesbitt[99] that in the contents of obstructed intestines of dogs that have been fed lecithin-rich food (eggs) both choline and neurine may be found free, and Kutscher and Lohmann[1] have found neurine in human urine. It seems possible that some of the toxic effects observed after eating excessively of such food as calves' brains, or eggs, may depend upon intoxication with the products of lecithin decomposition. Also, the normal presence of trimethylamine in the blood and cerebrospinal fluid (Dorée and Golla)[2] may be from this source. Hunt,[3] who has done extensive work with choline, states that at present we have no grounds for believing that choline has any significance in physiological or pathological processes. There is no evidence that the highly active acetyl-choline[4] is produced from choline in the body, but in view of the enormous toxicity of this choline derivative there must always be considered the possibility that such toxic choline compounds may at times develop in amounts too small to be detected but large enough to cause effects.

RESULTS OF GASTRO-INTESTIONAL INTOXICATION

As we have seen from the above, but few of the known products of gastro-intestinal putrefaction are toxic to any considerable degree, and these are probably produced in too small quantities to cause any appreciable effect, especially in view of the detoxicating and eliminatory powers of the liver, kidney, and other organs. And yet we have abundant clinical evidence that excessive intestinal putrefaction or retention of the intestinal contents causes marked disturbance in health. The slight malaise, headache, and lassitude observed as the result of simple constipation may possibly be adequately accounted for by intoxication with indole and similar substances, although we have no conclusive proof that such is the case. Two explanations may be suggested: One is that the intestinal flora becomes altered because of the changed conditions, and bacteria thrive that produce specific soluble toxic substances, analogous to those formed by *B. botulinus*, or similar to the *tyrotoxicon* (Vaughan) that may be formed in milk and milk products. Thus Clairmont and Ranzi[5] found heat-resistant

[98] Literature given by Halliburton, Ergebnisse der Physiol., 1904 (4), 24.
[99] Jour. Exp. Med., 1899 (4), 1; see also Hoesslin, Hofmeister's Beitr., 1906 (8), 27.
[1] Zeit. physiol. Chem., 1906 (48), 1.
[2] Biochem. Jour., 1910 (5), 306.
[3] Jour. Pharmacol., 1915 (7), 301.
[4] See Dale, Jour. Pharmacol., 1914 (6), 147.
[5] Arch. klin. Chir., 1904 (73), 696.

38

toxic substances in the intestinal contents in ileus (experimental), and similar substances could also be obtained by growing cultures of the intestinal contents on bouillon. Another explanation is that many unidentified poisonous substances are produced in the alimentary canal which ordinarily are destroyed, but under certain conditions may be reabsorbed. That unrecognized toxic substances are formed in the intestines is almost certain, for it has been repeatedly shown that extracts of the contents of the alimentary canal are very poisonous. Although the technic of many of these experiments has been questionable, the results have been obtained so often as to render it probable that the main contention is correct.[6] Thus Magnus-Alsleben[7] has found in the upper part of the small intestine of dogs (except when on milk diet) a very poisonous substance which killed rabbits by respiratory paralysis, but which is inert when injected into the portal vein. Extracts of the wall of the large intestine are also toxic, and lose their toxicity at 60°, by passing through porcelain filters and by treatment with alcohol; extracts of fetal intestines are not toxic (Distaso).[8] There is reason to believe that histamine is responsible for much of the toxic effects obtained with intestinal materials.

In any case, correctly or incorrectly, a great number of disease conditions have been attributed to poisons of gastro-intestinal origin, including not only such minor conditions as headache, malaise, lassitude, etc., but also sciatica, tetany, epilepsy, eclampsia, many forms of dermatitis, various forms of nervous diseases, myxedema and cretinism, chlorosis and pernicious anemia, cirrhosis, nephritis, and arteriosclerosis.[9] While in many cases the severity of these various conditions is apparently augmented by intestinal disturbances, the etiologic relation is not so clear. That long-continued intoxication of intestinal origin may cause serious injury to the tissues is, however, extremely probable. There is much reason for believing that many cases of non-alcoholic cirrhosis are due to this cause; not improbably chronic nephritis, myocarditis, and arteriosclerosis may occasionally be the result of long-continued intoxication from the same source. Arteriosclerosis especially has been attributed to indole and related substances by Metchnikoff and his associates, who have produced arteriosclerosis in rabbits by injecting indole, but not with skatole. As is well known, Metchnikoff believed that most of the manifestations of senility come from putrefaction in the large bowel,[10] and a number of observers have described as products of intestinal putrefaction certain pressor substances of high potency which, presumably, might cause serious arterial and cardiac injury.[11] An elaborate study of

[6] For example, see Roger and Garnier, Compt. Rend. Soc. Biol., 1905 (59), 388 and 674; 1906 (60), 666.
[7] Hofmeister's Beitr., 1905 (6), 503.
[8] Zeit. Immunität., 1913 (16), 466.
[9] The supposed relation of gastro-intestinal intoxication to these various diseases is reviewed by Weintraud, Ergeb. allg. Pathol., 1897 (4), 17.
[10] See Ann. Inst. Pasteur, 1910 (24), 755.
[11] See Granger, Arch. Int. Med., 1912 (10), 202.

a certain type of cases of defective development led Herter[12] to the conclusion that intestinal intoxication is responsible, and hence he designated this condition "intestinal infantilism."

Tetany associated with gastric dilatation offers perhaps the strongest case, numerous observers having reported finding a marked toxicity of the stomach contents.[13] Pincles[14] considers that all forms of tetany, whether of gastric origin or following thyroidectomy, are due to one and the same "tetany poison," but recent studies indicate that alkalosis is an important factor in tetany. There is also considerable evidence that the tetany, when present, is associated with a deficiency in calcium in the blood and nervous tissue, and that this is further related to the functional activity of the parathyroids (*q. v.*).

Although there are usually evidences of intoxication in *acute dilatation of the stomach*, yet there is no good evidence as to its nature. It is suggested by Woodyatt and Graham[15] that the dilatation is produced by CO_2 secreted into the stomach from its walls.

The relation of intestinal intoxication to the various anemias, particularly chlorosis and pernicious anemia, has been repeatedly indicated and discussed. Clinical evidence strongly indicates that such a relation exists, and there is no doubt that hemolytic substances may be formed in the alimentary tract,[16] but that chlorosis and pernicious anemia do depend upon intestinal putrefaction or infection is far from established (see "Anemia," Chap. xiii).

As yet, however, *we cannot say positively that any human disease is caused by the products of intestinal putrefaction*, and with growing knowledge the importance ascribed to this source of disease is becoming steadily less.[17] The fact must not be overlooked that many persons habitually eat putrefied proteins, from the "high" game of the epicure to the carrion masses that delight many primitive people, without the slightest evidence of intoxication therefrom.

It seems highly probable that gastro-intestinal "autointoxication" would be a much more serious matter were it not for the mechanisms of defence possessed by the body, especially in the liver.[18] For example, Richards and Howland have indicated the increased toxicity of indole when the oxidizing power of the liver is reduced, and Herter and Wakeman have shown the power of the liver to combine indole and thus remove it from circulation. This topic has been discussed more fully elsewhere (Chap. x).

[12] See McCrudden, Jour. Exper. Med., 1912 (15), 107.
[13] Bibliography by Halliburton and McKendrick, Brit. Med. Jour., 1901 (i), 1607.
[14] Deut. Arch. klin. Med., 1906 (85), 491.
[15] Trans. Chicago Path. Soc., 1912 (8), 354.
[16] See Külbs, Arch. exper. Path., 1906 (55), 73; also Herter, Jour. Biol. Chem., 1906 (2), 1.
[17] See Alvarez, Jour. Amer. Med. Assoc., 1919 (72), 8; E. O. Jordan, "Food Poisoning," Univ. Chicago Press, 1917.
[18] For discussion and literature see Lust, Hofmeister's Beitr., 1905 (6), 132.

ACUTE INTESTINAL OBSTRUCTION

The violent effects that follow complete occlusion of the intestine, especially in the upper portion, must be due to some highly toxic substance or substances. The clinical features of obstructive ileus, namely, vomiting, collapse, complete muscular relaxation, and subnormal temperature, are associated with the excretion of large quantities of indican and other substances combined with sulphuric acid, proving that intestinal putrefaction is active. Undoubtedly in ileus we have a profound and rapidly fatal intoxication with substances formed in the obstructed intestines.

Whipple[19] has demonstrated that closed duodenal loops in dogs come to contain a highly toxic substance of unknown nature, apparently formed in the epithelium of the gut rather than in its contents, which causes severe splanchnic congestion, vomiting and diarrhœa when injected into normal dogs. The toxic agent is not destroyed by autolysis, filtration or heating at 60°, yet dogs can be made somewhat refractory or immune. From the contents of such loops, and from the bowel above obstructions, he has isolated a very toxic proteose,[20] which he believes may be responsible for the intoxication. Whether this proteose, or whatever the active poison may be, comes from bacterial infection, autolysis, duodenal secretion, or what, is not yet agreed by the numerous investigators in this field.[21] There is much evidence in favor of the essential importance of bacteria, and it is held by some that toxic amines may be produced by bacterial action in the closed loops,[22] and that injury to the mucosa facilitates absorption of the poisons. Apparently the liver does not have much detoxicating effect, for dogs with Eck fistula behave much the same when the intestine is obstructed as dogs with normal circulation. A similar material cannot be obtained by hydrolysis or autolysis of normal duodenal mucosa, the obstruction being an essential feature. The normal intestinal secretions do not have any considerable toxicity.[23] Obstruction of lower portions of the intestine has much less effect[24] and it has been suggested that the poison formed in the duodenum is neutralized or destroyed farther down in the intestine.[25] A striking feature of intestinal obstruction is the high non-protein nitrogen content of the blood, figures similar to those of fatal uremic coma being common,[26] which may be the result of absorption of cleavage products from the intestine, or toxicogenic destruction of tissue proteins, or both. There is also probably an element of renal injury and reduced excretion.[27]

[19] Whipple, Stone and Bernheim, Jour. Exp. Med., 1913 (17), 286.
[20] Jour. Amer. Med. Assoc., 1915 (65), 476; 1916 (67), 15; Jour. Exp. Med., 1916 (23), 123; 1917 (25), 231 and 461.
[21] Review by South and Hardt, Arch. Int. Med., 1918 (21), 292.
[22] Dragstedt et al., Jour. Exp. Med., 1919 (30), 109.
[23] Davis and Stone, Jour. Exp. Med., 1917 (26), 686.
[24] See Bunting, Jour. Exp. Med., 1913 (17), 192.
[25] Maury, Amer. Jour. Med. Sci., 1909 (137), 725.
[26] Cooke, Rodenbaugh and Whipple, Jour. Exp. Med., 1916 (23), 123.
[27] McQuarrie and Whipple, Jour. Exp. Med., 1919 (29), 397.

CHAPTER XXII

CHEMICAL PATHOLOGY OF THE DUCTLESS GLANDS[1]

DISEASES OF THE THYROID[2]

As we have much evidence that the thyroid has a marked influence upon metabolism, and also that it may be of importance in preventing and in producing autointoxication, the chemistry of diseases of the thyroid may be appropriately considered in connection with the auto-intoxications.

THE FUNCTIONS OF THE THYROID

Metabolic Function.—That the thyroid has an important relation to metabolism, especially of proteins, is shown by the following facts:

(1) Administration of the gland substance, or active preparations made from it, to healthy men or animals, causes a greatly increased elimination of nitrogen in the form of urea.[3] This nitrogen comes not only from the food, but also from increased tissue-destruction, as is shown by the loss of weight and strength, and by the increased excretion of sulphur and phosphorus. An increased destruction of the body fat also occurs, so that thyroid therapy has been found efficient in the treatment of obesity, but often dangerous because of the relatively great amount of tissue-destruction. Basal metabolism is most markedly raised in hyperthyroidism, and is lower in cretinism and myxedema than in any other disease.[4]

(2) Loss of thyroid tissue, either through operation or disease, greatly reduces both nitrogenous metabolism and oxidative processes. Administration of thyroid preparations under these conditions will bring the nitrogen elimination and the gas exchange back to normal.

(3) Deficient thyroid secretion in young animals prevents their developing normally, the amount of deficiency varying from nearly total lack of development in extreme cretinism to slight grades of defective development (infantilism) or delayed maturity. In adult animals, besides decreased metabolism there occur also various trophic changes in the skin and its appendages, an increased amount of mucin-like material in the tissues, and greatly decreased nervous and mental activity. All these conditions are relieved to greater or less degree by administration of thyroid tissue or its preparations.[5] Evidently, therefore, the thyroid exerts an influence upon growth and tissue changes; whether this depends upon its influence upon metabolism, or is an independent and specific function, cannot be determined.[6]

[1] Thorough reviews of the entire subject of the ductless glands are given by Biedl, "Innere Sekretion," Urban and Schwarzenberg, Berlin, 1913; and Vincent, Ergebnisse Physiol., 1910 (9), 451; 1911 (10), 218.

[2] Concerning the thyroid see besides Beidl and Vincent, the review by Bircher, Ergebnisse Pathol., 1911, XV (1), 82; Crotti, "Thyroid and Thymus," Phila., 1918.

[3] See Rohde and Stockholm, Jour. Biol. Chem., 1919 (37), 305.

[4] Du Bois, Arch. Int. Med., 1916 (17), 915.

[5] Concerning the influence of thyroid on skeletal growth see Holmgren, Nordiskt Med. Arkiv, 1910 (43), No. 2. Literature given by Basinger, Arch. Int. Med., 1916 (17), 260.

[6] See the interesting experiments of Gudernatsch (Arch. Entwickl., 1912 (35), 457; Amer. Jour. Anat., 1914 (15), 431; Anat. Record, 1917 (11), 357), who found that feeding thyroid to tadpoles hastens their differentiation but checks growth; also removal of the thyroid from tadpoles increases growth but delays or entirely prevents metamorphosis (Hoskins, Jour. Exp. Zool., 1919 (29), 1).

How the thyroid or its secretion modifies metabolism is not yet understood. One is reminded of the effects of kinases upon enzymes and their antecedents, and it may be imagined that the thyroid secretion activates both proteolytic and oxidative enzymes within the cells. Shryver,[7] indeed, did find that administration of thyroid to dogs for some time before killing them causes their liver tissue to undergo autolysis more rapidly than normal, although Wells[8] had been unable to observe any increased amount of autolysis when thyroid extracts acted upon liver tissue *in vitro*. Experimental observations show that carbohydrate metabolism is much influenced by the thyroid, so that thyroidectomized animals may fail to show glycosuria from various procedures that usually produce it (King),[9] and they are incapable of utilizing sugar injected parenterally as well as normal animals;[10] they also exhibit an excessive creatine output. Protracted feeding of thyroid to growing animals reduces the weight attained and causes marked enlargement of suprarenals, heart, liver, spleen, testes, ovaries and pancreas; the pituitary and uterus are reduced in size.[11]

Detoxicatory Function.—The evidence that the thyroid has for its function the *destruction or neutralization of poisonous substances* formed in metabolism or through intestinal putrefaction is as follows:

(1) After total removal of the thyroid from many species of animals acute symptoms develop that suggest strongly an intoxication.

(2) After removal of the thyroid, marked changes occur in the blood, there being a severe anemia (as low as 2,000,000 red corpuscles), with some leucocytosis, and there occur structural changes in the blood-vessel walls (Kishi).[12] Cytoplasmic degeneration of the liver, kidneys, and myocardium may also result (Bensen).[13] These effects suggest strongly the presence of poisonous substances in the blood of persons or animals lacking sufficient thyroid tissue.

(3) All the effects of thyroidectomy are more marked in carnivorous animals than in herbivora; indeed, the latter may be able to live in fair condition for several years without a thyroid.[14] Administration of meat to thyroidectomized herbivora or omnivora causes a great increase in the symptoms, while thyroidectomized carnivora do much better if kept without meat. Thus, Blum[15] found that thyroidectomized dogs, which were doing well on a milk diet, developed symptoms of athyreosis immediately they were given meat. This fact has been interpreted as indicating that toxic materials are formed from meat in the intestinal tract, which under normal conditions are neutralized by the thyroid. On the other hand, one may well imagine that the so-called autointoxication in athyreosis is not from intestinal putrefaction, but is due to the products of incomplete metabolism of proteins within the tissues, which are destroyed when protein metabolism is normal, but not when the metabolism-favoring influence of the thyroid is wanting. It should also be added that the presence of specific poisonous substances in the blood or urine of thyroidectomized animals has not been conclusively established.[16]

[7] Jour. of Physiol., 1905 (32), 159.

[8] Amer. Jour. Physiol., 1904 (11), 351; corroborated by Morse, Jour. Biol. Chem., 1915 (22), 125.

[9] Jour. Exper. Med., 1909 (11), 665.

[10] Underhill and Saiki, Jour. Biol. Chem., 1908 (5), 225.

[11] Herring, Quart. Jour. Exp. Physiol., 1917 (11), 231; Kojima, *ibid.*, p. 255.

[12] Virchow's Arch., 1904 (176), 260.

[13] Virchow's Arch., 1902 (170), 229.

[14] Part of these results may be due to the fact that in some herbivora the parathyroids are so far separated from the thyroid that they are not ordinarily removed in thyroidectomy, whereas in many carnivora complete removal of parathyroids with the thyroids is more likely to be accomplished.

[15] Virchow's Arch., 1900 (162), 375.

[16] Remedi (Lo Sperimentale, 1902; abst. in Cent. f. Path., 1903 (14), 695) claims that tetanus toxin and other bacterial poisons, when injected into the thyroid gland, are harmless, which he attributes to a neutralization by the colloid. This observation is discredited by the work of Basinger, Jour. Infect. Dis., 1917 (20), 131.

(4) Reid Hunt[17] found that mice fed thyroid preparations have a greatly increased resistance to poisoning by aceto-nitrile; however, this is not necessarily nor even probably a direct detoxication, but more likely it results from alterations in metabolism.[18] Rats and guinea pigs behave just the opposite, showing a decreased resistance to acetonitrile after being fed thyroid, and according to some authors morphine is more toxic for such animals.[19]

Whether the thyroid exercises its detoxicating effect, assuming that it has one, by a direct neutralizing action of its secretion upon the toxic substances in the blood or in diverse tissues, or indirectly by stimulation of the function of other tissues which perform the detoxication, or in part locally within the gland itself, is an unsettled problem. In relation to the last-named hypothesis is the extreme vascularity of the thyroid, which, according to Burton-Opitz[20] has passed through it much more blood in proportion to its weight than any other gland. Against the idea of a *local* detoxication is the fact that after extirpation of the thyroid all abnormal conditions may be prevented by proper administration of thyroid substance.

Biedl summarizes his views as to the function of the thyroid, in the following statement: "The thyroid is a secretory organ which discharges its secretion eventually into the blood, in the form of an iodin-containing protein. This secretion acts as a hormone, in that it modifies the activities of remote tissues. As far as we now know the thyroid secretion plays the rôle of a 'disassimilatory' hormone, in that it causes an increased disassimilation and increase of normal activity in many tissues. This effect is exemplified by the augmented metabolism, the activity of the heart and many parts of the sympathetic nervous system, and of a series of internal secretory organs (adrenals, hypophysis). · In other tissues are found evidence of the action of an inhibiting and assimilatory hormone, as shown in the increase in growth of bone, development of the sex glands, and decreased internal secretion of the pancreas."

CHEMISTRY OF THE THYROID[21]

Whether the function of the thyroid is the neutralization of toxic substances, or a complementary action upon intracellular metabolism, there can be little question that it owes its action to constituents of its specific secretion, the colloid.[22] Furthermore, the chief, if not the sole, active ingredient of the colloid is the iodin-containing substance

[17] Jour. Amer. Med. Assoc., 1907 (49), 240; Hygienic Lab. Bull., 1909, No. 47; Jour. Pharmacol., 1910 (2), 15.
[18] Koopman (Endocrinology, 1919 (3), 318) states that administration of thyroid increases antibody formation in immunized animals.
[19] See Olds, Amer. Jour. Physiol., 1910 (26), 354.
[20] Quart. Jour. Physiol., 1910 (3), 297.
[21] Reviews are given by Rahel Hirsch, Handb. d. Biochem., 1909, III (1), 271; and A. Kocher, Virchow's Arch., 1912 (208), 86.
[22] Beyond the characteristic colloid secretion product, the thyroid presents no chemical features of interest; it differs from the other endocrine glands in being poor in lipoids (Fenger, Jour. Biol. Chem., 1916 (27), 303). .

first discovered by Baumann in 1896, and called by him *thyroiodin* (or *iodothyrein*).[23]

The chemical nature of thyroid *colloid* has been studied particularly by A. Oswald.[24] He found that all the iodin of the thyroid is dissolved out in physiological salt solution, and that none of it is present in an inorganic form. In the salt solution extract are two protein bodies; one, precipitated by half saturation with ammonium sulphate, contains all the iodin, and seems to be a globulin; it resembles myosin in being precipitated by weak acids, and it contains an easily separated carbohydrate group. The other, precipitated by saturation with ammonium sulphate (exact limits of precipitation are between 6.4 and 8.2 tenths saturation), is a nucleoprotein, containing 0.16 per cent. phosphorus, but no iodin; it is without marked physiological activity as also is the protein-free watery extract of the thyroid.[25] The colloid seems to contain practically all the iodin present in the gland (Tatum).[26]

The iodin-containing protein, called *thyreoglobulin*, constitutes one-fourth to one-half the dry weight of the gland, and seems to contain the sole active constituent of the colloid; at least, its administration to animals has the same physiological effects as does the entire colloid (great increase in the urea elimination and decrease in blood pressure in animals, curative effect on myxedematous patients, increased tonus of both sympathetic and peripheral nervous systems.)[27] Analysis of the thyreoglobulin from various animals has shown it to be of quite constant quantitative composition except for the iodin, which may vary greatly in amount. Normal human thyreoglobulin (from persons living in non-goitrous districts) has the following percentage composition:

$$C = 51.85, H = 6.88, N = 15.49, I = 0.34, S = 1.86.$$

Thyreoglobulin from goitrous districts contains much less iodin (0.18–0.19 per cent.), and from calves born with goiters a thyreoglobulin was obtained that agreed in all respects with normal thryreoglobulin, except that it contained no iodin at all. On the other hand, administration of iodides to patients causes the thyreoglobulin to become rich in organically bound iodin.[28] From these facts Oswald

[23] Iodin is present in the thyroid of all species, most in marine forms (Cameron, Jour. Biol. Chem., 1914 (16), 465; Biochem. Jour., 1914 (7), 466).

[24] His work is reviewed in his dissertation, "Die chem. Beschaffenheit und die Function der Schilddruse," Strassburg, 1900; also see Virchow's Arch., 1902 (169), 444.

[25] A. Oswald, Arch. ges. Physiol., 1916 (166), 169. Kocher and his collaborators, however, ascribe to the thyreonucleoprotein some slight metabolic effects antagonistic to the thyreoglobulin (See Mitt. Grenz. Med. Chir., 1916, vol. 29).

[26] Proc. Soc. Exp. Biol. Med., 1919 (17), 28.

[27] A. Oswald, Arch. ges. Physiol., 1916 (164), 506.

[28] Nagel and Roos (Arch. f. Anat. u. Physiol., 1902, p. 297) found that administration of bromides had no effect upon the amount of iodin in the thyroid, and no storage of bromin takes place. Administration of pilocarpine does not increase the amount of iodin in the thyroid.

believes that the thyreoglobulin, as first secreted by the glandular epithelium, is free from iodin, and that it combines later with iodin from the circulating blood. Thyreoglobulin is not, however, simply an *iodized protein*, for the iodized proteins that can be artificially prepared do not possess the physiological activity of the thyreoglobulin, nor do other naturally occuring iodin-containing proteins (gorgonin, spongin). F. C. Koch[29] finds that the full activity of the gland is contained in the thyreoglobulin, and also in the metaprotein fraction of this globulin, while simpler cleavage products show less and less activity per unit of iodin content. He could find no thyroid activity in iodin compounds of histidine, and di-iodotyrosine was found inactive by Strouse and Voegtlin.[30]

The remarkable influence of the thyroid on the development of tadpoles (Gudernatsch[6]) is exhibited by the thyreoglobulin but also by iodized blood proteins.[31] Swingle[32] states that inorganic iodin itself, even in thyroidless tadpoles, will bring about metamorphosis that would not take place in the absence of iodine. Bromine will not substitute for iodin in causing metamorphosis. The division rate of even unicellular organisms (*Paramecium*) is increased by thyroid extract.[33] Lenhart[34] considers the effect of thyroid on tadpoles to be merely an expression of the general stimulation of metabolism, rather than a specific effect on differentiation.[35]

By decomposing thyreoglobulin by boiling with 10 per cent. sulphuric acid, a body is obtained containing as high as 14.5 per cent. of iodin; this is the *thyroiodin* of Baumann, which gives no biuret reaction, yet is physiologically active. The stability of this active constituent of the thyreoglobulin explains the successful administration of thyroid preparations by mouth. It appears to be absorbed unchanged and, unless enormous doses are given, none appears in the urine (Oswald).[36] Long-continued digestion with trypsin, or autolysis of thyroid glands, causes a complete splitting out of the iodin. One part of the iodin seems to be more firmly bound than the rest. A small amount of the iodin may exist as inorganic and lipoid compounds.[37]

Thyroxin.—Kendall[38] has isolated from the thyroid, after alkaline hydrolysis, a crystalline compound containing 65 per cent. of iodin which seems to be an indole derivative, designated as "thyroxin"

[29] Jour. Biol. Chem., 1913 (14), 101.
[30] Jour. Pharm. and Exp. Ther., 1910 (1), 123.
[31] Rogoff and Marine, Jour. Pharm., 1917 (10), 321.
[32] Jour. Gen. Physiol., 1919 (1), 593; Jour. Exp. Zool., 1919 (27), 397.
[33] Shumway, Jour. Exp. Zool., 1917 (22), 529.
[34] Jour. Exp. Med., 1915 (22), 739.
[35] See also Kahn, Arch. ges. physiol., 1916 (163), 384.
[36] Arch. exp. Path. u. Pharm., 1910 (63), 263.
[37] Blum and Grützner, Zeit. physiol. Chem., 1914 (91), 400.
[38] Jour. Amer. Med. Assoc., 1918 (71), 871; Trans. Assoc. Amer. Phys., 1918 (33), 324; Endocrinology, 1919 (3), 156; Jour. Biol. Chem., 1919 (39), 125; 1919 (40), 265.

(thyro-oxy-indole) with the following structural formula which has been confirmed by its synthetic production:

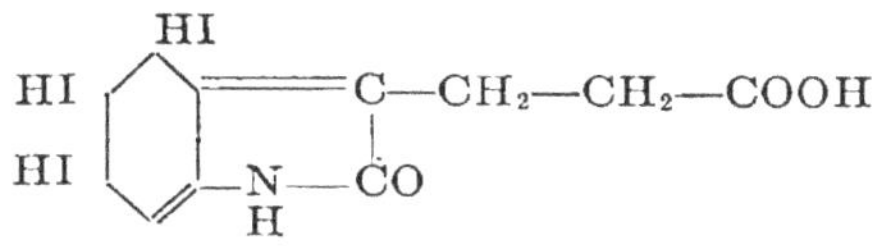

$$\text{HI}$$
$$\text{HI} \diagup\!\!\!\diagdown \!\!== C\!-\!CH_2\!-\!CH_2\!-\!COOH$$
$$\text{HI} \diagdown\!\!\!\diagup \!-N\!-\!CO$$
$$\qquad\qquad H$$

The activity of this substance is referable to the CO-NH groups, since acetylating the imino group removes the physiological effect. In the body the indole ring seems to exist in the open form shown below, corresponding to the open and closed structure of creatine and creatinine.

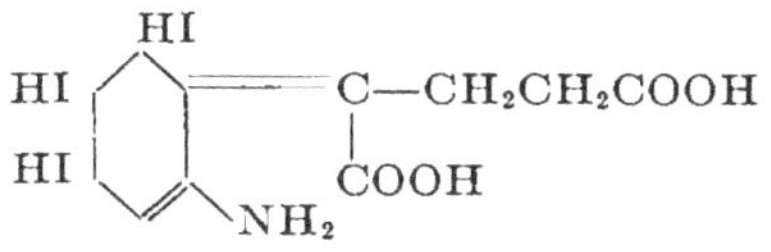

$$\text{HI}$$
$$\text{HI} \diagup\!\!\!\diagdown \!\!== C\!-\!CH_2CH_2COOH$$
$$\text{HI} \diagdown\!\!\!\diagup \qquad\; COOH$$
$$\qquad\quad NH_2$$

This substance is highly active, causing rapid pulse, nervous irritability, and increased metabolism.

Through its action on the metabolism of all the cells of the body thyroxin relieves all the manifestations of myxedema and cretinism. It is estimated that one-third milligram increases the basal metabolism of an adult by 1 per cent., on which basis it may be calculated that from 23 to 50 mg. are functioning in the entire body. It acts like a true catalyst in carrying on action for two or three weeks after being administered. It contains only one-fourth of the iodin of the thyroid but the nature of the other iodin compounds is unknown, beyond the observation that they have no appreciable effects on normal persons but greatly improve the condition of cretins, presumably they represent intermediate stages in the formation of thyroxin. When fed to tadpoles, Kendall's active principle produces the characteristic thyroid effect.[39]

Persons with complete atrophy of the thyroid have a basal metabolism 60 per cent. of normal, which can be brought to normal by thyroxin, but what carries the 60 per cent. metabolism when the thyroid is functionless is unknown. Presumably thyroxin merely increases the rate of metabolism that goes on at a lower level without it, in which case the function of the thyroid seems to be merely to permit a greater range of flexibility in energy output. A single large injection has little effect while repeated small doses cause death, indicating that thyroxin of itself is not toxic, but only through its effect on metabolism. The limit of tolerance is 2 mg. daily.

Iodin Content of Thyroid.—The physiological activity of thyroid preparations, according to nearly all investigators, is in direct propor-

[39] Rogoff and Marine, Jour. Pharmacol., 1916 (9), 57.

tion to the iodin content,[40] which is the best of evidence that the formation of this compound is one of the chief functions of the gland, and that the iodin in the thyroid is not merely stored there as an undesirable foreign substance like copper in the liver. The selective deposition of iodin in the thyroid is remarkable, and when iodin is fed to animals it is stored very rapidly but it seems to require several hours before the active growth-modifying hormone is formed.[41] Marine and Lenhart[42] find that the normal human gland contains an average of 0.4 mg. of iodin per gram of fresh weight (2.17 mg. per gram of dry weight), being less than that of domestic animals in the same part of the country. These figures agree closely with those obtained in thyroids from various parts of America by Wells[43] (2.10 mg. per gram dry weight). They found, as Oswald and Kocher also have, that the amount of iodin varies directly with the amount of colloid, being decreased when cellular hyperplasia is present, in direct proportion to the amount of hyperplasia, and administration of iodin causes a reduction in the hyperplasia and a return to the colloid type of gland, while the iodin is deposited in the gland. Kocher, however, disputes the regularity of the variation of iodin and colloid content, stating that it is especially the *concentrated* follicle contents which hold the iodin. Seidell and Fenger[44] have found a marked seasonal variation in the thyroid iodin of animals, there being about three times as much between June and November as between December and May.[45] In man it has been found that before birth the thyroid of the fetus contains little or no iodin, but in domestic animals the fetal glands contain not a little iodin (Fenger).[46] The cells of the gland contain very little iodin (A. Kocher). Extracts of the thyroid have little effect on the blood pressure, except for an alcohol-soluble fraction, poor in iodin, which is a depressor.[47] On the other hand, thyroid secretion increases the sensitiveness of the sympathetic nervous system to epinephrine.[48]

Wasting diseases are associated with a considerable decrease in the size of the thyroid and the amount of colloid, and with this a decrease

[40] Fonio, Mitt. Grenz. Med. u. Chir., 1911 (24), 123; Frey, *ibid.*, 1914 (28), 349; Hunt, Jour. Amer. Med. Assoc., 1907 (49), 1323; and Jour. Pharm. and exp. Therap., 1910 (2), 15.

[41] Marine and Rogoff, Jour. Pharm., 1916 (9), 1.

[42] Arch. Int. Med., 1909 (4), 440.

[43] Jour. Amer. Med. Assoc., 1897 (29), 897.

[44] Jour. Biol. Chem., 1913 (13), 517.

[45] Valuable figures on the iodin content of foods are given by Forbes *et al.*, Bullet. Ohio Agric. Expt. Station, June, 1916 No. 299.

[46] Jour. Biol. Chem., 1912 (11), 489; 1912 (12), 55; 1913 (14), 397.

[47] Fawcett *et al.*, Amer. Jour. Physiol., 1915 (36), 113.

[48] The thyroid is very rich in lipase, catalase and peroxidase; extirpation is followed by a decrease in these enzymes in the blood, while thyroid feeding increases them as well as the antitrypsin (Juschtschenko, Biochem. Zeit., 1910 (25), 49; Zeit. physiol. Chem., 1911 (75), 141.).

in the iodin; especially is this true of tuberculosis.[49]   Patients or animals to whom iodin compounds are administered deposit it in the thyroid in large amounts, especially if the gland is previously defective in iodin, and at times there results even an acute thyroiditis from the iodin administration.[50]   Iodides are said to increase the amount of thyreoglobulin itself (Wiener).[51]   The variation in iodin content under various conditions is given in the following table from Jolin,[52] his figures for normal glands being somewhat lower than found in America.

Number and condition of glands	Dry wt. gms.	Mg. iodin per gm.	Total iodin
152 glands from persons over 10 yrs. old (44 not normal)	7.04	1.63	11.20
28 glands from children (1 mon. to 10 yrs.)	0.54	0.28	0.145
108 normal glands from adults only (both sexes)	5.38	1.56	8.05
67 normal glands from adults (males)	5.07	1.56	7.83
41 normal glands from adults (females)	5.90	1.55	8.40
38 glands from chronic diseases	4.29	1.90	7.81
29 glands from acute diseases	5.54	1.47	8.11
21 glands from sudden death	6.88	1.29	8.45
10 glands showing marked goiter	23.09	1.09	26.49
25 colloid-rich glands	8.25	2.24	18.20
34 glands from persons receiving iodin	5.79	2.56	15.06

CHEMISTRY OF GOITER

In connection with his earliest studies of thyroiodin Baumann observed a great difference in the amount of iodin in the thyroid glands of normal individuals living in goitrous districts, as compared with those living in non-goitrous districts.   Thus in Freiburg, a goitrous district, the average weight of the dried thyroid was 8.2 grams, each gram containing 0.33 mg. of iodin, a total of 2.5 mg. of iodin to each gland.   Glands from Hamburg averaged 4.6 gm. in weight, containing 0.83 mg. of iodin per gram, a total of 3.83 mg. per gland.   Berlin glands weighed 7.4 grams, and contained 0.9 mg. of iodin per gram, or a total of 6.6 mg. of iodin per gland.   Both of the last-named cities are in districts where goiter is not endemic.   The thyroids of young children show the same relative paucity of iodin in goitrous districts, as compared with non-goitrous districts.   Wells[53] found that the thyroids throughout the United States contain even larger amounts of iodin than the Berlin glands, averaging 10 to 12 mg. per gland, agreeing with the fact that goiter is comparatively rare in this country.[54]

[19] See Vitrey and Giraud, Compt. Rend. Soc. Biol., 1908 (65), 405.   Aeschbacher, Mitt. Grenz. Med. Chir., 1905 (15), 269; Pellagrini, Arch. sci. Med., 1915 (39), 276.
[20] See Mendel, Med. Klinik, 1906 (2), 833.
[51] Arch. exp. Path. u. Pharm., 1909 (61), 297.
[52] Festschr. f. O. Hammarsten, Upsala Lakareförën. Förh., 1906, XI, Suppl.
[53] Jour. Amer. Med. Assoc., 1897 (29), 897.
[54] It is probable, in view of the higher results obtained by later analyses, that the results of Baumann and of Monery are somewhat too low.

Monery[55] has found for France, as Baumann did for Germany, that the amount of iodin contained in the glands of normal individuals is in inverse proportion to the frequency of goiter in districts in which they live. Oswald, and also Aeschbacher,[56] however, state that normal thyroids in goitrous districts contain more iodin than thyroids from goiter-free districts.

Chemical analyses of goiters have given extremely variable results, which are found to depend upon the histological type of the goiter. Baumann found that in a series of twelve cases of goiter, in which the average dry weight was 32 grams, the amount of iodin in each gram was but 0.09 mg., but the total amount, 2.6 mg., was about the same as in normal glands of the same goitrous district. However, in two goiters large amounts of iodin were found, namely, 17.5 mg. and 31.5 mg. Wells found that the amount of iodin depended upon the structure, for two hyperplastic goiters contained respectively 8.23 and 8.3 mg. of iodin, or about the amount normal for thyroids in this country, whereas two colloid goiters contained 53.16 and 24.59 mg. of iodin. This is corroborated by the more extensive studies of Marine and his co-workers, who have found the proportion of iodin low in all glands showing epithelial hyperplasia, but high in colloid goiters.[57] Administration of iodin causes a reversion of the hyperplastic to the colloid type of gland, while deprivation of iodin causes hyperplasia. Presumably, therefore, during the active growth of a goiter the iodin is low, but in the quiescent colloid state it is high. The physiological activity of colloid or other preparations from goiters is found to be quite the same as that from normal glands, varying in direct proportion to the iodin content.[58] In an adenomatous goiter, in the new growth, Wells found 1.98 mg. of iodin per gram, while the rest of the gland contained but 0.8 mg.; the total amount of iodin was 9.26 mg., or the same quantity as found in normal glands. In nine fetal adenomas Marine and Lenhart found iodin in eight in amounts averaging 0.174 mg. per gram of dry weight. However, when iodin is given to persons with thyroid adenomas the tumor tissue does not take up the iodin to the same extent that the normal gland tissue does. The presence of great numbers of mitochondria in the cells of adenomas indicates their high functional activity.[59]

Oswald found that colloid goiters contain a thyreoglobulin that is relatively very poor in iodin; in goiterous calves the thyreoglobulin contained no iodin; in human goiters it contained but 0.07 to 0.19 per cent. of iodin, as against a normal proportion of 0.34 per cent. Administration of iodides to a goiterous patient caused a rise in the proportion of iodin in the colloid to 0.51 per cent., showing that in

[55] Jour. Pharm. et Chim., 1904 (95), 288.
[56] Mitt. a. d. Grenzgeb. Med. u. Chir., 1905 (15), 269.
[57] Arch. Int. Med., 1908 (1), 349; 1909 (3), 66; 1909 (4), 440.
[58] See Fonio, Mitt. Grenz. Med. u. Chir., 1911 (24), 123.
[59] Goetsch, N. Y. State Jour. Med., July, 1918.

colloid goiters in goitrous districts the thyreoglobulin is probably poor in iodin because of a lack of iodin for it to unite with, and not because it is of an abnormal nature that prevents its chemical combination with iodin.[60]   Possibly this explains the greater iodin content observed in colloid goiters in the United States as compared with colloid goiters observed in goitrous districts.   In general, Oswald[61] found the amount of iodin to vary with the amount of colloid in the goiters, although occasionally goiters with exceptionally large amounts of iodin were found, and the proportion of iodin is not usually so great when the amount of colloid is very large.   Simple hyperplastic goiters he found poor in iodin, or free from it if they contained no colloid; however, they were found to contain a thyreoglobulin typical in all respects except an absence of iodin.   Presumably in such goiters the little thyroiodin present is contained in the parenchymatous cells.   The physiological activity of thyreoglobulin obtained from goiters was found to be the same as that from normal glands, except that it was weaker in direct proportion to the amount of iodin it contained, and, therefore, when iodin-free it was without effect.[62]   In colloid goiters the greater part of the weight of the gland, three-fourths or more, is made up of this colloid-poor thyreoglobulin.   The fluid contents of cystic goiters may be free from iodin, but if they contain much colloid, iodin will be found, and Rositzky[63] found 0.193 mg. of iodin in 20 c.c. of the jelly-like contents of a thyroid cyst.

It has been frequently suggested that the cause of endemic goiter is a deficiency in the iodin in the food, or in the drinking-water, or in the air of the goitrous district.   This is supported by the relative infrequency of endemic goiter in districts on the sea-coasts, where the iodin-containing sea-water is sprayed through the air, and where the inhabitants eat largely of sea-foods.   Also administration of minute amounts of iodin, even in the air, seems to reduce existing goiter and to prevent its occurrence in inhabitants of goitrous districts.[64]   However, there are many exceptions, and it cannot be said that this hypothesis of the etiology of all goiter rests on satisfactory evidence, particularly in view of the abundant iodin content of colloid goiters.   Epidemics of goiter presumably are the results of an infection with some unknown organism, and possibly the endemic form has a similar cause.[65]   .There is much evidence, in any event, that whatever the cause of goiter may be, it often is related to the drinking water,[66] but numerous well-controlled experiments fail to support this hypothesis.[67]   Very probably

[60] See Kocher, Mitt. a. d. Grenzgeb. Med. u. Chir., 1905, vol. 14.

[61] Virchow's Arch., 1902 (169), 444.

[62] See Oswald, Arch. ges. Physiol., 1916 (164), 506.

[63] Wein. klin. Woch., 1897 (10), 823.

[64] See Hunziker, Corr. Bl. Schw. Aerzte, 1918 (48), 220.

[65] See McCarrison, "The Thyroid Gland," New York, 1917.

[66] See de Quervain, Mitt. a. d. Grenzgeb. Med. u. Chir., 1905 (15), 297; Bircher, Zeit. exp. Path. u. Ther., 1911 (9), 1.

[67] See Münch. med. Woch., 1913 (60), 393 and 1813; Sitzber. Wien. Akad., 1914 (123), 35.

the causes of colloid goiter and parenchymatous goiter will be found to be different from the causes of cystic and adenomatous goiters.

MYXEDEMA AND CRETINISM

These conditions depend upon a deficiency of thyroid secretion, whether from operative procedure or from pathological alterations in the organ. Consequently we find evidences of a decreased protein metabolism, the urine containing a diminished quantity of nitrogen, especially in the form of urea, while ammonia and other forms of nitrogen are relatively excessive. A retention of nitrogen and phosphorus has been found, but not of calcium and chlorine.[68] The temperature is usually subnormal, and the energy metabolism is low.[69] Basal metabolism is lower than in any other known condition (Du Bois).[70] Fat and carbohydrate metabolism seem not to be proportionately affected,[71] and hence the elimination of CO_2 is relatively high as compared to the nitrogen elimination. Gastro-intestinal disturbances are common, with resulting increase in the amount of indican and ethereal sulphates in the urine. Whether from this cause or from deep-seated metabolic anomalies, there is a decided anemia, and the ability of the corpuscles to combine with oxygen seems to be decreased, so that the arterial blood may contain less oxygen than normal venous blood. It is impossible to say whether the failure of growth and development of the young (cretinism), and the mental and physical torpidity of the adult, are due to an autointoxication from products of intermediary metabolism which accumulate because of the failure of the thyroid to furnish the "stimulus" necessary for their complete destruction, or to a lack of some essential action of the thyroid secretion upon the nervous tissues and the growing cells themselves. Administration of thyroid extract to cretinoid children causes retention of nitrogen and phosphorus, but more strikingly of calcium,[72] and obese cretins lose weight, chiefly from the non-nitrogenous elements (Scholz). The amount of iodin in human cretin thyroids seems not to have been estimated, but in five cretin dogs Marine and Lenhart could find no thyroid iodin at all.[73]

The myxedematous change in the connective tissues is in the nature of a reversion to the fetal type of tissue, and suggests that the thyroid

[68] Benjamin and Reuss, Jahrb. f. Kinderheilk., 1908 (67), 261. In a cretin Greenwald found little deviation from normal. (Arch. Int. Med., 1914 (14), 374.)

[69] Talbot, Amer. Jour. Dis. Chil., 1916 (12), 145.

[70] Arch. Int. Med., 1916 (17), 915; Means and Aub., *ibid.*, 1919 (24), 404.

[71] Rarely myxedema and diabetes have been observed conjointly (see Strasser, Jour. Amer. Med. Assoc., 1906 (44), 765).

[72] See Hougardy and Langstein, Zeit. f. Kinderheilk., 1905 (61), 633. Full figures are given by Scholz, Zeit. exp. Path. u. Ther., 1906 (2), 270.

[73] Related to cretinism is the "hairless pig malady," in which hairless pigs are born dead or die soon after birth, the mothers and offspring often having goiter; administration of KI checks the appearance of the disease (See Hart and Steenbock, Jour. Biol. Chem., 1918 (33), 313).

secretion is necessary for proper cell growth. This effect might be either specific, or depend simply on the effect on protein metabolism. Horsley[74] describes the appearance of the tissues of animals dying after thyroidectomy as follows: "The subcutaneous connective tissue is swollen, jelly-like, bright and shining, and excessively sticky. The same thing is observed in the loose tissue of the mediastinum, about the heart, and in the omentum. The submaxillary and parotid glands are greatly enlarged, and have a semi-translucent, swollen appearance; from the cut surface a sticky, glairy fluid exudes. Apparently the parotid becomes transformed into a mucous gland; likewise the mucous membrane of the alimentary tract is swollen and transparent." Fetal tissues contain normally more mucin than those of adults (0.76 per cent. as against 0.37 per cent. in the subcutaneous tissues, according to Halliburton), and in the early stages of the formation of excessive subcutaneous tissue in myxedema such an increase of mucin may be present. But, under ordinary conditions, the term myxedema seems to be entirely a misnomer, for Halliburton's analyses showed that the skin of myxedematous patients contains quite the same amount of mucin as is present in normal skin.[75] When the condition is of long standing, the amount of mucin may even be much reduced, because of the development of a fibroid character in the connective tissue. However, in monkeys upon which thyroidectomy had been performed, Halliburton[76] found a decided increase in the mucin in the tissues throughout the body, especially in the salivary glands, but also in the skin, subcutaneous tissues, and tendons; and mucin was found in the blood, as shown by the following table:

	Skin and sub- aneous tissue	Tendon	Muscle	Parotid	Sub- max- illary	Blood
Normal monkey..............	0.89	0.39	0	....	....	0
Normal monkey.............	0.9	0.5	0	0	0.1	0
After thyroidectomy—						
55 days......................	3.12	2.55	0	0.72	6.0	0.35
33 days......................	....	....	...	....	....	trace
49 days......................	2.3	2.4	trace	1.7	3.3	0.8
7 days......................	0.45	0.904	0	trace	0.16	trace

It has been suggested that the thyroid produces an enzyme which destroys mucin, but that such is the case has never been demon-

---

[74] Brit. Med. Jour., 1885 (i), 211.
[75] Jour. of Pathol. and Bact., 1893 (1), 90.
[76] Quoted by Horsley, *loc. cit.* Later experimenters, however, have had difficulty in producing experimental myxedema as described by Horsley, or have failed entirely.

strated.[77] Levin[78] states that mucin is toxic for thyroidectomized rabbits, but this is not substantiated by Néfédieff.[79]

That the thyroid is connected with general growth is shown not only by the thyroid abnormalities present in cretinism, but also by the frequent observation of thyroid defects in conditions of delayed growth and development of less extreme degree (*infantilism*), and the favorable effects of thyroid feeding in many such cases. Also in certain types of short-limbed dwarfs (*chondrodystrophia foetalis*) some thyroid anomaly may have an etiologic bearing, for in such a case, in which the thyroid was histologically greatly altered and quite free from colloid, I could find no trace of iodin.[80] On the other hand, the thyroid of a giant which I have analyzed contained 62.9 mg. of iodin, or six times the amount present in normal glands.[81]

EXOPHTHALMIC GOITER

It has by no means been conclusively determined that exophthalmic goiter is due to an intoxication with excessive amounts of thyroid secretion, either normal or abnormal, but there is abundant evidence in favor of this view. Most important is the similarity of exophthalmic goiter to the effects of "hyperthyroidism" or "thyroidismus," produced either experimentally or through overuse of thyroid extract for therapeutic purposes. In thyroidismus there are observed a rapid, weak pulse; greatly increased metabolism, especially of proteins;[82] a striking increase in basal metabolism, paralleling the degree of intoxication; marked mineral loss, especially of Ca and P from the bones;[83] increased secretion, especially of perspiration; marked nervousness and irritability, often with mental confusion and delusions; gastro-intestinal disturbances, especially diarrhea; sweating, flushing, tremors, palpitation of the heart, loss of weight, and slightly increased temperature are also often observed, and not rarely typical exophthalmos may appear.[84] These manifestations, which are common to both thyroidism and to exophthalmic goiter, are quite the opposite of the characteristic changes of myxedema, with its general lowering of all metabolic and nervous processes. Alike in experimental hyperthyroidism and exophthalmic goiter there is a greatly increased sensitiveness of the sympathetic nervous system to epinephrine.[85] Reid Hunt's

[77] See Parhon, Compt. Rend. Soc. Biol., 1916 (79), 504.
[78] Med. Record, 1900 (57), 184.
[79] Vratch, 1901 (22), Oct. 27.
[80] Reported by Hektoen, Amer. Jour. Med. Sci., 1903 (125), 751.
[81] Reported by Bassoe, Trans. Chicago Path. Soc., 1903 (5), 231.
[82] Metabolism in exophthalmic goiter, see Du Bois, Arch. Int. Med., 1916 (17), 915; Halverson, Bergeim and Hawk, *ibid.*, 1916 (18), 800; Means and Aub, Arch. Int. Med., 1919 (24), 645.
[83] Kummer, Rev. Méd. Suisse Rom., 1917 (55), 442.
[84] Sugar utilization is decreased, as shown by study of the utilization of sugar given intravenously (Wilder and Sansum, Arch. Int. Med., 1917 (19), 311): also a dietary hyperglucemia is readily induced (Denis, Aub and Minot. Arch. Int. Med., 1917 (20), 964; McCasky, Jour. Amer. Med. Assoc., 1919 (73), 243).
[85] See Goettsch, N. Y. State Jour. Med., July, 1918.

acetonitrile test for thyroid secretion has been found positive in the blood from patients with exophthalmic goiter,[86] which presumably means the presence of an excess of thyroid secretion circulating in the blood in this disease. Furthermore, the histological changes observed in the thyroid may resemble those of compensatory hypertrophy, suggesting strongly that the goitrous change of this disease is due to a true hypertrophy, with increased production of the specific secretions. There is a marked increase in the mitochondria of the thyroid epithelium in exophthalmic goiter, which also is evidence of heightened activity.[87] Kocher[88] says that when iodin is given to patients with cancer of the thyroid they may develop symptoms of exophthalmic goiter, as if an excess of thyroiodin were formed. Also speaking strongly in favor of the view that exophthalmic goiter is the result of overactivity of the thyroid, is the frequent cure of the disease through removal of a large part of the diseased gland. Although at times the colloid type of gland is found in exophthalmic goiter, Marine contends that it has been preceded by a hyperplastic stage.[89]

Oswald[90] found that the thyroid in exophthalmic goiter contains generally a smaller proportion of iodin than normal glands, but with the total amount approximately normal. However, the findings are very inconstant, corresponding with the fact that in some cases of exophthalmic goiter the amount of colloid is abundant (in which case the amount of iodin may be large), while usually the amount of colloid is small, and its highly vacuolated condition in hardened sections suggests that it is of unusually fluid consistency. A. Kocher[91] found that either the amount of iodin is small, which is usual, or else very high, but it is seldom the same as in normal thyroids; the more dense the colloid in the follicles the higher iodin content he observed; the phosphorus content is both relatively and absolutely increased. Marine has found that in exophthalmic goiter as well as in other conditions the amount of iodin is in direct proportion to the colloid and inverse to the hyperplasia. E. V. Smith[92] obtained in simple hyperplastic glands an average of 0.54 mg. of iodin per gram dry weight, as compared with 1.52 mg. in hyperplastic glands showing retrogressive changes with more densely staining colloid. Fonio found that, as with normal thyroids, the physiological effect of exophthalmic goiter glands varies directly with the proportion of iodin, and such glands take up iodin administered therapeutically just as a normal thyroid does (Kocher,[93] Marine and Lenhart).[94] These results, therefore, indicate

[86] See Ghedini, Wien. klin. Woch., 1911 (24), 736; Hunt and Seidell, Jour. Pharm. and Exp. Ther., 1910 (2), 15.
[87] Goetsch, Bull. Johns Hopkins Hosp., 1916 (27), 129.
[88] Deut. Zeit. Chir., 1908 (91), 302.
[89] See also Wilson, Amer. Jour. Med. Sci., 1908 (136), 851.
[90] Virchow's Arch., 1902 (169), 475.
[91] Virchow's Arch., 1912 (208), 86.
[92] Jour. Amer. Med. Assoc., 1914 (62), 113.
[93] Arch. klin. Chir., 1910 (92), 442; 1911 (96), 403.
[94] Arch. Int. Med., 1911 (8), 265.

nothing either for or against the hypothesis that exophthalmic goiter is due to autointoxication with the secretion of the thyroid, but Wilson and Kendall[95] find that in the toxic type of goiters there is but $\frac{1}{20}-\frac{1}{15}$ as much of the active iodin compound of Kendall as in normal glands, and hence they suggest that in thyroid intoxication this toxic material has been discharged from the thyroid into the circulation.

On the other hand, it is impossible to produce a symptom-complex completely resembling exophthalmic goiter[96] in animals by excessive feeding of thyroid,[97] either normal or from exophthalmic goiter; and after extensive study of the subject Marine and Lenhart have come to the conclusion that "the essential physiological disturbance of the thyroid in exophthalmic goiter is insufficiency, its reaction compensatory and its significance symptomatic." This view, however, certainly fails to agree with the excellent results which come from partial extirpation of the thyroid in exophthalmic goiter. Oswald,[98] also an experienced investigator in this field, invokes an abnormally irritable nervous system, which stimulates the thyroid and in turn is stimulated by the thyroid secretion, constituting a vicious circle. Other observers are of the opinion that not an excessive, but a perverted, secretion is at fault,[99] a view not confirmed by tests of the effects of thyroid extracts on animals.[1] However, it is stated by Blackford and Sanford,[2] that extracts of the thyroid in this disease, as well as the blood of patients in the acute toxic stages, exhibit a marked depressor effect on blood pressure, which is distinct from that of choline, and which they believe to be specific for exophthalmic goiter.

There can be no doubt that the thyroid secretion is capable of causing serious intoxication, for patients who have overused thyroid preparations in the treatment of obesity, skin diseases, etc., have often suffered severely from the symptoms mentioned previously, and, in at least one such case, a diagnosis of exophthalmic goiter was made before the cause of the disturbance was detected. Not infrequently evidences of acute intoxication have followed immediately after operations upon the thyroid, and these have been considered as due to intoxication with the large quantities of thyroid secretion that have escaped from the gland during the operative manipulation. The fact that *amblyopia*, resembling that produced by tobacco, etc., may follow overuse of thyroid preparations[3] is indicative of their toxicity, as also is the *glycosuria* that may result from thyroid administration.[4]

[95] Amer. Jour. Med. Sci., 1916 (151), 79.

[96] The pathogenesis of the exophthalmos is unknown. See Troell, Arch. Int. Med., 1916 (17), 382.

[97] See Carlson *et al.*, Amer. Jour. Physiol., 1912 (30), 129; Marine, Jour. Amer. Med. Assoc., 1912 (59), 325.

[98] Correspondenzblatt Schweizer Aerzte, 1912 (42), 1130.

[99] Klose *et al.*, Beitr. z. klin. Chir., 1912 (77), 601.

[1] See Schönborn, Arch. exp. Path. u. Pharm., 1909 (60), 390.

[2] Jour. Amer. Med. Assoc., 1914 (62), 117.

[3] Birch-Hirschfeld and Inouye, Graefe's Arch., 1905 (61), 499.

[4] See Geyelin, Arch. Int. Med., 1915 (16), 975.

Even if the hypothesis that exophthalmic goiter is due to intoxication with thyroid secretion is correct, we have no satisfactory explanation of the cause of the hyperactivity of the thyroid.   In some cases degenerative changes have been observed in the superior cervical sympathetic ganglia, and cure or improvement of exophthalmic goiter is said to have followed resection of these ganglia; however, this relation has not been observed at all constantly.   In other cases there has been evidence that suggested a primary intoxication with the products of intestinal putrefaction, leading to a secondary hyperplasia of the thyroid, but this also seems to be an exceptional observation.[5] All things considered, it seems most probable that the hyperactivity of the thyroid is due to some exciting condition, and is not of itself primary, although the resulting hypersecretion of the thyroid may cause the dominant features of the disease.   The frequent association of exophthalmic goiter with puberty and pregnancy suggests that some abnormality in the function of the generative organs may be a frequent starting-point of the thyroid derangement.[6]   In not a few cases diabetes or pancreatitis have been associated,[7] and some observers state that the pressor substance (presumably epinephrine) in the blood is much increased in exophthalmic goiter.[8]   Although the *thymus* is often found enlarged, sometimes greatly so, in 70 to 80 per cent. of cases of exophthalmic goiter, its relation to the disease is as yet entirely unknown.[9]

[5] *Antithyroid Serum.*—Based on the theory that the normal function of the thyroid is the detoxication of metabolic products, is the serum treatment advocated first by Ballet and Enriquez, and later by Lanz, and Burghart and Blumenthal. (Deut. med. Woch., 1899 (25), 627.   Also Möbius, Münch. med. Woch., 1901 (48), 1853; v. Leyden, Med. Klinik, 1904 (1), 1; Eulenberg, Berl. klin. Woch., 1905 (42), 3.)   On the principle that after thyroidectomy the blood should contain an accumulation of those substances, which the thyroid normally neutralizes, they injected the serum of thyroidectomized goats into patients with exophthalmic goiter, in the hope that these accumulated substances might in turn neutralize any excessive thyroid secretion.   Favorable results were obtained, and it was subsequently found that the milk of thyroidectomized goats possesses the same qualities, and may be administered by mouth; this has led to quite extensive clinical use of this method of treatment, which has failed to show any regular beneficial effects in the hands of most careful observers.   (See Sonne, Zeit. klin. Med., 1914 (80), 229.)   Of similar significance are the favorable effects obtained by Beebe (Jour. Amer. Med. Assoc., 1905 (46), 484; 1906 (47), 655) and Rogers (*Ibid.*, 1906 (46), 487; 1906 (47), 661) with a serum made by immunization of animals with the nucleoproteins of the thyroid, which have not been corroborated by others.

[6] The serum of patients with exophthalmic goiter shows by Abderhalden's method a constant power to digest thyroid tissue, and sometimes ovary or testicle (Lampé and Fuchs, Münch. med. Woch., 1913 (60), No. 39).

[7] Thompson, Amer. Jour. Med. Sci., 1906 (132), 835; Cohn and Peiser, Deut. med. Woch., 1912 (38), 60.

[8] Bröking and Trendelenburg, Deut. Arch. klin. Med., 1911 (103), 168.

[9] Review by Eddy, Canad. Med. Assoc. Jour., March, 1919.

THE PARATHYROIDS[10]

The parathyroids were originally considered as but a form of undeveloped accessory thyroids, but they are now generally believed to be independent organs of fully as great importance as the thyroid. Their independence is conclusively shown by the cases of cretinoid children in whom the thyroid proper has failed to develop, while the parathyroids are found to be normal,[11] thus proving their distinct origin, the inability of parathyroid tissue to change into thyroid tissue,[12] and their inability to prevent the changes of cretinism.[13] Parathyroids contain no appreciable amounts of iodin (Estes and Cecil),[14] although 14 per cent. of parathyroids obtained at autopsy contain a colloid material (Thompson and Harris).[15] Glycogen is demonstrable in the epithelium. To their removal are ascribed by many investigators the acute manifestations of athyreosis, while the more chronic changes of myxedema are attributed to the loss of the thyroid. MacCallum's studies support this view, for he found the results of parathyroidectomy in dogs very different from the results of thyroidectomy. The most prominent symptoms are muscular twitchings, gradually passing into tetanic spasms, and due to nervous impulse rather than to muscular changes, since they did not appear in muscles from which the nerve-supply has been cut off. Trismus, protrusion of the eyes, and rapid respiration without cyanosis (*i. e.*, air hunger) were also observed, and death usually resulted from exhaustion. Apparently these symptoms are due to some toxic substance which accumulates on account of the absence of the parathyroids, for it was found that simply diluting the dog's blood by withdrawing part of it, and injecting a corresponding amount of salt solution, caused a temporary cessation of the tetanic symptoms; and injections of emulsions of parathyroid checked the symptoms for some time, presumably through neutralizing the hypothetical poisons. Degenerative changes that were observed in the cerebral ganglion-cells also favor the view that some unneutralized toxin is responsible for the symptoms following parathyroidectomy. On the other hand, profound mental symptoms and insomnia have resulted from feeding parathyroid to man.[16] Recent studies make it seem probable that tetany parathyreopriva and idiopathic tetany are either identical or very closely related.[17]

The *metabolism after parathyroidectomy* may show the following changes:[18] There is a reduction in the assimilation limit for carbohydrates (Hirsch, Underhill[19] and others). There is a disagreement concerning inorganic metabolism, for while MacCallum and Voegtlin[20] found an increased elimination of calcium and a loss of the same element from the blood and brain (which they would make responsible for the increased nervous irritability), Cooke found no such loss of calcium,[21] but she did find an increased urinary excretion of magnesium. According to most observers, nitrogenous metabolism is altered as shown by the increased excretion of nitrogen, and especially of ammonia. Greenwald[22] found increased ammonia less conspicuous than increased undetermined nitrogen and sulphur, and decreased phosphorus excretion. There may occur an increase in the bases of the blood (alkalosis, *q. v.*) which disappears under the acidosis that results from tetany.[23]

In view of the conflicting facts, the theory that the increased irritability and

[10] A review of this subject is given by Thompson in "The Surgery and Pathology of the Thyroid and Parathyroid Glands," by A. J. Ochsner and R. L. Thompson, St. Louis, 1910. See also MacCallum. Ergeb. inn. Med., 1913 (11), 569.

[11] Roussy and Clunet, Compt. Rend. Soc. Biol., 1910 (68), 818.

[12] See Edmunds, Jour. Path. and Bact., 1910 (14), 288.

[13] See MacCallum, Johns Hopkins Hosp. Bull., 1907 (18), 341.

[14] *Ibid.*, 1907 (18), 331; also Cameron, Jour. Biol. Chem., 1914 (16), 465.

[15] Amer. Jour. Med. Sci., 1908 (19), 135.

[16] Morris, Jour. Lab. Clin. Med., 1915 (1), 26.

[17] See Paton and Findlay, Quart. Jour. Exp. Physiol., 1917 (10), 203.

[18] See review by Cooke, Amer. Jour. Med. Sci., 1910 (140), 404.

[19] Jour. Biol. Chem., 1914 (18), 87.

[20] Jour. Exp. Med., 1909 (11), 118; 1913 (18), 618.

[21] See also Bergeim, Stewart and Hawk, Jour. Exp. Med., 1914 (20), 225.

[22] Amer. Jour. Physiol. 1911 (28), 103; Jour. Biol. Chem., 1913 (14), 363.

[23] Wilson, Stearns and Thurlow, Jour. Biol. Chem., 1915 (23), 89, 123. McCann, *ibid.*, 1918 (35), 553; Togawa, Jour. Lab. Clin. Med., 1920 (5), 299.

spasm of tetany result from hypocalcification of the nerve tissue is at present unproved. Calcium does diminish nervous irritability, as shown by J. Loeb, and hence when administered it may favorably influence the symptoms of tetany parathyreopriva, but this does not establish the theory. That numerous experimenters have been able to stop these symptoms, both in man and animals, by feeding of parathyroid,[24] or parathyroid nucleoprotein, establishes the relationship of this gland to the tetany, but not the calcium deprivation hypothesis. A critique of this hypothesis by Berkeley and Beebe[25] brings out the following points: Strontium, magnesium and barium have the same effect in tetany as calcium, whereas severe calcium loss in diabetic acidosis does not cause tetany. The fact that bleeding reduces the symptoms is against the calcium deprivation theory and supports the intoxication theory. Wiener[26] even states that it is possible to secure an antitoxin for the poison of tetany thyreopriva by immunizing with the serum of animals in tetany. On the other hand, the marked changes in dentition and bone repair observed in parathyroidectomized animals by Erdheim[27] indicate an abnormality in calcium metabolism, which, however, might be secondary to an intoxication. Also, in osteomalacia and osteoporosis the parathyroids are said to show hyperplasia,[28] and Howland and Marriott have found a definite decrease in the calcium of the blood in human tetany and in parathyroidectomized dogs.[29] Injection of phosphates reduces blood calcium, and when the reduction has reached 6 mg. per 100 c.c., symptoms of tetany appear.[30]

MacCallum[31] has found evidence that in parathyroidectomized dogs the blood contains something which greatly increases the irritability of the nerves, possibly by abstracting calcium from the tissues. Removal of calcium from the blood by dialysis results in nerve hyperexcitability resembling that seen in tetany. W. F. Koch[32] found guanidine and methyl guanidine in the urine of dogs deprived of parathyroids. Burns and Sharpe[33] corroborated this, and also found the same bases in the urine of children with idiopathic tetany. Salts of guanidine produce typical symptoms of tetany, including the hypoglucemia, calcium loss and acidosis observed in this disease.[34] After parathyroidectomy there is a fall in the guanidine content of the muscle (Henderson).[35] Apparently the parathyroids control the metabolism of guanidine in the body by preventing its development in undue amounts, in this way exercising a regulative action on the tone of the skeletal muscles (Paton and Findlay). Administration of guanidine to dogs produces much the same symptoms as removal of the parathyroids (Burns).

Cooke states that the metabolic changes precede, and presumably incite the tetany. Implantation of parathyroid tissue in persons with tetany parathyreopriva has been successful in removing symptoms in a few cases.[36] The relation of the parathyroids to tetany of infants is not so well established,[37] although several observers have found hemorrhages in the parathyroids in these cases. Some cases of "gastric tetany" have improved under parathyroid feeding, which is also said to be beneficial in *paralysis agitans*,[38] although there seems to be no anatomic basis for assuming a parathyroid deficiency in this disease.

The Relation of the Parathyroids to Exophthalmic Goiter.—This has not yet been definitely established. As nervous manifestations are prominent after parathyroidectomy, it has seemed probable that these organs may be more closely associated with exophthalmic goiter than is the thyroid itself.[39] Against the hypo-

[24] See Halsted, Amer. Jour. Med. Sci., 1907 (134), 1.
[25] Jour. Med. Res., 1909 (20), 149.
[26] Pflüger's Arch., 1910 (136), 107.
[27] Frankfurter Zeit. Pathol., 1911 (7), 175.
[28] Todyo, Frankf. Zeit. Pathol., 1912 (10), 219.
[29] Trans. Amer. Ped. Soc., Vol. 28, p. 202.
[30] Binger, Jour. Pharmacol., 1917 (10), 105.
[31] Verh. Deut. Path. Ges., 1912 (15), 266; Jour. Exp. Med., 1914 (20), 149.
[32] Jour. Biol. Chem., 1913 (15), 43; Jour. Lab. Clin Med., 1916 (1), 299.
[33] Quart. Jour. Exp. Physiol., 1916 (10), 345.
[34] See Watanabe, Jour. Biol. Chem., 1918 (33), 253; 1918 (36), 531.
[35] Jour. Physiol., 1918 (51), 1.
[36] Danielsen, Beit. klin. Chir., 1910 (66), 85.
[37] See Haberfeld, Virchow's Arch., 1911 (203), 282.
[38] Berkeley, Med. Record, 1916 (90), 105.
[39] This subject is thoroughly reviewed by MacCallum, Med. News, 1903 (83), 820; Iversen, Arch. Internat. de Chir., 1914 (6), 255.

thesis that exophthalmic goiter is due to parathyroid insufficiency, however, stand the following facts:

(1) Removal of one lobe of the thyroid often causes improvement or recovery in this disease, yet with the lobe of the thyroid is generally removed the adjacent parathyroid, which would decrease the amount of parathyroid tissue, and make worse any existing parathyroid insufficiency. (2) Therapeutic administration of parathyroid tissue or extract has had no significant effect on the disease. (3) No considerable or characteristic anatomical changes occur in the parathyroids in exophthalmic goiter,[10] while the great majority of all cases show changes in the thyroid. (4) The parathyroids seem to have but slight influence on metabolism (MacCallum), while metabolic abnormalities are very marked in exophthalmic goiter.[41]

THE ADRENALS AND ADDISON'S DISEASE[42]

Like the hypophysis, the adrenals are essentially double organs, containing nervous and glandular tissues. The medulla is of sympathetic nervous system origin, a part of the chromaffin[43] system, which in most animals is enclosed in a layer of entirely different nature and origin, the cortex being an epithelial structure, derived from the urogenital anlage, and resembling most closely in structure (and perhaps in function) the corpus luteum of the ovary. In some marine animals, indeed (eels, sharks, etc.), the sympathetic tissue portion and the cortical tissue exist as separate organs.

The adrenal cortex seems to be related especially to the generative system,[44] as shown by the following facts:

1. The embryologic origin in the urogenital anlage, and the histologic structure which is similar to the corpus luteum.

2. In many animals there occurs hypertrophy of the cortex during the breeding season, and there are histological differences in the glands of males and females (Kolmer).

3. Many cases of sexual precocity have been observed in association with tumors or hypertrophy of the adrenal cortex; and defective sexual development has been found associated with atrophy of this tissue.[45]

4. The medulla increases relatively little in size after birth, while the cortex increases with the development of the individual.

Whether the cortex has other functions or not is not yet known.[46] Biedl has found evidence that cortical substance is essential for life.[47] Animals with accessory adrenals, which contain only cortical substance, withstand ablation of the adrenals proper, presumably because the

[40] MacCallum, Johns Hopkins Hosp. Bull., 1905 (16), 287.

[41] The calcium excretion in exophthalmic goiter parallels the nitrogen (Towles, Amer. Jour. Med. Sci., 1910 (140), 100).

[42] Literature given by Bayer, Ergebnisse Pathol., 1910 (XIV₂), 1.

[43] The chrome reaction (observed in the adrenal medulla, carotid and coccygeal glands and the sympathetic ganglia), as well as other reactions for these tissues, is based on reduction of chromic acid to chromium dioxide by epinephrine (Ogata, Jour. Exp. Med., 1917 (25), 807).

[44] See Kolmer, Pflüger's Arch., 1912 (144), 361; Vincent, Surg., Gyn., Obst., 1917 (25), 299.

[45] See Glynn, Quart. Jour. Med., 1912 (5), 157; Jump et al., Amer. Jour. Med. Sci., 1914 (147), 568.

[46] It does not have a marked effect on the development of tadpoles, hence differing from thyroid and thymus (Gudernatsch).

[47] See also Crowe and Wislocki, Bull. Johns Hopkins Hosp., 1914 (25), 287; and Wheeler and Vincent, Trans. Roy. Soc. Canada, 1917 (11), 125.

rest of the chromaffin substance remains to compensate.[48]   Chemically the cortex is characterized by not containing the specific vaso-constrictor principle, the epinephrine, and by containing a very large proportion of lipoids.   Thus, in water-free human adrenals (cortex and medulla both included) there was found 36.3 per cent. of ether-soluble material, of which 20.6 per cent. was cholesterol and 33 per cent. was phospholipins.[49]   The proportion of fats and lipoids varies greatly during changes of age, disease, and perhaps of function, and there are those who believe the adrenal cortex to be a chief source of the lipoids of the blood, to which much important function is ascribed in the reactions of immunity.   (See Lipoids, under Fatty Metamorphosis.)   When cholesterol is fed in large amounts some is deposited in the adrenal cortex,[50] while in many diseases, notably delirium tremens (Hirsch,)[51] the lipoid content of the adrenals is greatly decreased.   In renal and arterial disease the adrenal lipoids have been found increased.[52]   The lipins of the adrenal cortex are said to contain little or no neutral fat,[53] but free fatty acids which may be increased when the cholesterol decreases.   Loss of body fats is not accompanied by a loss of adrenal lipoids ordinarily, although they decrease in acute infections, especially pneumonia.[54]   A vaso-depressor effect is produced by extracts of adrenal cortex, perhaps caused by choline which has been found in such extracts, or possibly by histamine.

The medulla is characterized, besides, by its pigmentary content, by the remarkably active internal secretion, epinephrine,[55] which it always contains in greater or less amount.   Presumably epinephrine, of which the formula is

$$HO\left\langle\right\rangle HOH-CH_2(NH)-CH_3$$
$$HO$$

is derived from the aromatic radical of the proteins, its close relationship to tyrosine being seen when the formula of the latter is compared

$$HO\left\langle\right\rangle CH_2-CH(NH_2)-COOH$$

That epinephrine is formed from tyrosine directly, is, however, not yet demonstrated.   There are also other amines and aromatic

[48] See Fulk and MacLoed (Amer. Jour. Physiol., 1916 (40), 21) who found that the active principle of other chromaffin tissues has the same physiological effect as that of the adrenal medulla.
[49] Wells, Jour. Med. Res. 1908 (17), 461.
[50] Krylov, Beitr. path. Anat., 1914 (58), 434.
[51] Jour. Amer. Med. Assoc., 1914 (63), 2186.
[52] Chauffard, Compt. Rend. Soc. Biol., 1914 (76), 529.
[53] Borberg, Skand. Arch. Physiol., 1915 (32), 287.
[54] Elliott, Quart. Jour. Med., 1914 (8), 47; Laignel-Lavastine, Compt. Rend. Soc. Biol., 1918 (81), 324.
[55] This name, given by Abel and Crawford, is to be preferred to the others in common use, especially the most-used term "adrenalin," which has been copyrighted by a manufacturing establishment so that this name means specifically their product, and not the active principle of the adrenal from whatever source.

compounds which might be formed in the body, that have a pressor effect, and which perhaps are formed, although not yet identified.[56] It is to be borne in mind that the formation of epinephrine is not limited to the adrenals, but that other islands of chromaffin sympathetic tissue can do the same,[57] which explains the observed discrepancies between the anatomic changes in the adrenals and the clinical manifestations of a deficiency in epinephrine.

According to Goldzieher[58] the normal human adrenals contain together about 4 mg. epinephrine, which may be increased in conditions with high blood pressure, such as arteriosclerosis and nephritis, in which he found an average of 5.8 mg.; and in septic conditions with low pressure he found it reduced to an average of 1.5 mg.[59] Lucksch[60] gives a normal figure of 4 mg. for each gland, also finding the amount lowered in infectious diseases and increased in nephritis. The human adrenal contains no epinephrine before birth,[61] but Fenger[62] found it present in the adrenal of unborn domestic animals. Autolysis of the adrenal decreases the amount,[63] but not all of the epinephrine is destroyed even several days after death, as shown by Ingier and Schmorl,[64] who, using both morphological and chemical methods, also found a gradual increase in the epinephrine content of normal glands from birth to the ninth year, after which it remains practically constant at about 4.5 mg. (males 4.4, females 4.71 mg.). They also found a slight increase in arteriosclerosis, more in acute and chronic nephritis and a decrease in diabetes and narcosis, there being practically no epinephrine in the adrenal of Addison's disease. In most of the infectious diseases they found no changes, and in amyloid infiltration the amount was about normal. The amount of chromaffin substance and epinephrine do not always run parallel, although Borberg[65] found a close parallelism; this author also failed to observe any marked decrease of chromaffin substance in narcosis. Elliott[54] found a low epinephrine content in acute infectious diseases, and especially low in acute cardiac failure associated with great mental distress; he did not find any increase in the epinephrine in nephritis or in any other disease.

The function of the epinephrine is manifestly to modify the tone of the non-striated muscle fibers which are under control of the sympathetic nervous system, acting upon some receptive substance present

[56] See Barger and Dale, Jour. Physiol., 1910 (41), 19.
[57] See Vincent, Proc. Roy. Soc., B, 1908 (82), 502.
[58] Wien. klin. Woch., 1910 (23), 809.
[59] See also Reich and Beresnegowski, Beitr. klin. Chir., 1914 (91), 403. Ohno (Verh. Japan. Path. Gesell., 1916 (6), 15) found the normal content to be about 5.6 mg. averaging 8.32 mg. in chronic nephritis.
[60] Virch. Arch., 1917 (223), 290.
[61] Moore and Purinton, Amer. Jour. Physiol., 1900 (4), 51; Julian Lewis, Jour. Biol. Chem., 1916 (24), 249.
[62] Jour. Biol. Chem., 1912 (11), 489.
[63] Commessatti, Arch. exp. Path. u. Pharm., 1910 (62), 190.
[64] Deut. Arch. klin. Med., 1911 (104), 125.
[65] Skand. Arch. Physiol., 1912 (27), 341; 1913 (28), 91.

in the muscle, perhaps at the nerve endings.   But it is a fact of much practical importance that administration of epinephrine will not compensate successfully for the loss of the adrenals, whether because the gland secretes other things, or because the intermittent artificial administration of the epinephrine will not compensate for the regulated secretion of the gland under normal conditions, or both.   It would seem that the adrenal has an effect on other glands, for injections of epinephrine cause glycosuria in animals, as also does manipulation of the adrenals, or painting the epinephrine on the pancreas.   There is much disagreement as to the effects of extirpation of the adrenals on carbohydrate metabolism, and the nature and cause of the effects observed.   Biedl sums up the evidence with the statement that the internal secretion of the chromaffin system is of importance in the mobilization of the sugar of the blood, and the formation of the glycogen in the tissues.   That the adrenal is at all implicated in human diabetes has not been demonstrated.   There seems to be a relationship of mutual stimulation between thyroid and adrenal, for thyroid secretion sensitizes the sympathetic nerve endings to epinephrine, and both liberate carbohydrates from the sugar depots.[66]

Acute insufficiency of the adrenals, caused most often by hemorrhagic infarction, but sometimes by other lesions, may cause sudden collapse, asthenia or death.[67]   The extent to which the cortex and medulla respectively are responsible is undetermined.   The French authors especially lay great weight on adrenal insufficiency as a cause of pathological states.[68]   Surgical shock has also been attributed, at least in some cases, to exhaustion of the adrenals, which takes place under the influence of the anesthetic and the stimulation to the nervous system by the operative manipulation, perhaps augmented by concurrent infections.[69]

It is possible that in some cases of trauma to the adrenal, acute hemorrhage or infection, intoxication from an excess of epinephrine might occur, but it is improbable that fatal results could be produced in this way, for the lethal dose for dogs and rabbits is about 0.1 to 0.25 mg. per kilo, and the two adrenals in man contain in all but about 4 to 5 mg. epinephrine.   Moderna, however, states that there is so much epinephrine set free after hemorrhage into the adrenal, that it can be demonstrated microchemically in the liver, and that the symptoms and autopsy findings are identical with those of acute epinephrine intoxication.   In animals, repeated doses of epinephrine produce decreasing effects, not only on blood pressure but on the glycosuria and other symptoms, indicating an acquirement of tolerance, but, because

[66] See Endocrinology, 1917 (1), 404.
[67] Literature by Lavenson, Arch. Int. Med., 1908 (2), 62; Materna, Ziegler's Beitr., 1910 (48), 236.
[68] See Sergent, Presse Méd., 1909 (17), 489; Cowie and Beaven, Arch. Int. Med., 1919 (24), 78.
[69] See Hornowski, Arch. méd. expér., 1909 (21), 702; Virchow's Archiv., 1909 (198), 93.

of its nonprotein nature, epinephrine does not cause the production of antibodies.[70]

Many studies have been directed to determine the relation of the adrenal to hypertrophy of the heart and to interstitial nephritis with high blood pressure. Some have found more or less increase in size in the adrenals under these conditions, chiefly involving the cortex, and a slight increase in the epinephrine content has been reported, but it is very doubtful if these observations are of significance.[71] It has been reported by several investigators that the blood in such conditions contains sufficient epinephrine to permit of its detection and measurement by its physiological effects (dilatation of the frog's iris, contraction of the rabbit uterus or blood vessels, inhibition of contraction of the intestine). The critique of this work by Stewart,[72] however, makes it necessary to discount most of the published results, as being inadequately controlled. He found no epinephrine even in blood coming direct from the adrenal veins, unless the gland had been stimulated or manipulated, and none could be detected in the serum from several patients with high pressure from various causes, as well as in mental disturbances and exophthalmic goiter. Vaso-constrictor substances may be present in serum, both normal and pathological, which are not epinephrine. His negative results are corroborated by Janeway and Park.[73] Bröking and Trendelenburg,[74] using a perfusion method which they believe to be reliable, found a normal pressor effect from the blood of persons with arteriosclerosis and high blood pressure, a decrease in nephritis with high pressure, a great increase in exophthalmic goiter, and no changes in pregnancy, chlorosis and diabetes.

Arterial Degeneration from Epinephrine.[75]—An interesting result of repeated injections of epineprhine into animals is the appearance of a marked atheromatous degeneration of the aorta, with calcification. This was first observed by Josué, and since confirmed by Erb, Fischer, Gouget, Loeb and Githens, and many others. These lesions are quite different from those of human aortic arteriosclerosis, the chief change being degeneration of the muscle-cells of the media, without any considerable inflammatory reaction. There is, however, more resemblance to the atheromatous changes seen in the arteries of the extremities. They do not seem to be due to the heightened blood pressure, since simultaneous administration of substances that keep the blood pressure down does not prevent the atheroma from developing (Braun), while other substances that raise blood pressure, such as nicotine (Josué) or pyrocatechin (Loeb and Githens), do not cause atheroma. Presumably, therefore, epinephrine causes the arterial changes by a direct toxic action, but the influence of increased blood pressure cannot be entirely excluded. However, slow injection of epinephrine, so regulated that there is an increase in the blood content without significant rise of pressure, fails to produce arteriosclerosis.[76] Myocardial degeneration is also observed in experimental animals,

[70] See Elliott and Durham, Jour. of Physiol., 1906 (34), 430.
[71] See Pearce, Jour. Exper. Med., 1908 (10), 735; Thomas, Ziegler's Beitr., 1910 (49), 228.
[72] Jour. Exp. Med., 1911 (14), 377; 1912 (15), 547; also Rogoff, Jour. Lab. Clin. Med., 1918 (3), 209.
[73] Jour. Exp. Med., 1912 (16), 541.
[74] Deut. Arch. klin. Med., 1911 (103), 168.
[75] Literature given by Saltykow, Cent. f. Path., 1908 (19), 369.
[76] van Leersum and Rassers, Zeit. exp. path., 1914 (16), 230.

and later may lead to an interstitial myocarditis (Pearce). These experiments suggest the possibility that oversecretion of epinephrine may be a cause of arteriosclerosis, but there is no evidence that this actually occurs in man.

ADDISON'S DISEASE[77]

As pointed out before, the profound deficiency in the pressor principles evident in the manifestations of Addison's disease implies loss of function, not only of the adrenal medulla, but also of the rest of the chromaffin tissues which produce this same sort of material. Therefore it is possible to have any amount of destruction of the adrenals without Addison's disease, if there is sufficient compensation by the other chromaffin structures, or, conversely, Addison's disease may occur when the adrenals seem morphologically little altered, which occurs in about 10 per cent. of all cases. In typical cases, however the adrenals have been found entirely devoid of epinephrine,[78] and usually the structural alterations are conspicuous. While some have held that the destruction of the adrenal cortex is of importance in Addison's disease, this does not seem to have been conclusively demonstrated.

The pigmentation of the skin[79] has not yet been explained, but in view of the fact that oxidizing enzymes readily convert epinephrine, tyrosine, and related aromatic substances into pigments, and that in Addison's disease we have a deficiency in a tissue which is known to be concerned in the metabolism of aromatic compounds, it seems probable that the pigmentation is the result of this defective metabolism of the chromogenic aromatic compounds. In support of this view is the observation of Bittorf[80] that the skin of persons with Addison's disease has an augmented power of oxidizing epinephrine and tyrosine to pigmented substances. Bloch[81] believes the pigmentation to result from the presence of excessive quantities of 3.4-dioxyphenylalanine, which may be a precursor of epinephrine, and which is oxidized to a melanin

$$HO \diagdown \diagup CH_2.CHNH_2—COOH$$
(with H and O above the ring)

by special oxidizing enzymes ("dopaoxidase") present in the skin. Until the pigment of Addison's disease has been isolated and analyzed, however, these hypotheses will probably remain unproved. (See pigmentation, Chap. xviii.) Addison's disease can occur without pigmentation.

That there is a deficiency in the formation of epinephrine is at-

[77] Literature on Chemistry, by Eiselt, Zeit. klin. Med., 1910 (69), 393.
[78] Ingier and Schmorl, Deut. Arch. klin. Med., 1911 (104), 125.
[79] According to Straub (Deut. Arch. klin. Med., 1909 (97), 67) pigmentation may occur within 17 days after thrombosis of the adrenal vein.
[80] Arch. exp. Path., 1914 (75), 143.
[81] Zeit. exp. Med., 1917 (5), 179; Arch. f. Dermatol., 1917 (124), h. 2.

tested by the low blood pressure and general low tone of the unstriated muscle tissue. Carbohydrate metabolism is also altered, Porges[82] having found hypoglucemia in Addison's disease, and an increased sugar tolerance having been observed by others. Whether the adrenals exert a detoxicating effect, and the symptoms of the disease are partly the result of an autointoxication of some sort, is at present unknown, although this idea has often been advanced. The general metabolism of Addison's disease shows no very striking or characteristic changes, over and above those associated with the emaciation. Wolf and Thacher[83] found a decrease in endogenous creatine and purine excretion, and some evidences of acidosis towards the end of the disease; deaminizing power and oxidation of cystine sulphur to SO_4 were not impaired. Eiselt believes that there is a toxicogenic loss of tissue.

Administration of adrenal tissue and extracts, or epinephrine, whether by mouth or subcutaneously, is not effective in ameliorating the course of Addison's disease, at least in most cases. Thus, in 97 cases collected by Adams,[84] adrenal treatment caused some improvement in 31, 43 were not benefited, 7 were made worse, while 16 were described as permanently improved. The most favorably affected is usually the muscular and gastro-intestinal asthenia, while the pigmentation is not usually altered. There is little effect on metabolism.[85]

THE HYPOPHYSIS AND ACROMEGALY[86]

Although the hypophysis contains in its anterior lobe and in the pars intermedia, a certain number of spaces filled with colloid and resembling the alveoli of the thyroid in appearance,[87] there is no evidence that an appreciable amount of iodin is present here except when therapeutically administered.[88] The posterior lobe contains an active diuretic and pressor substance,[89] the exact nature of which is not yet known, although in many respects its action resembles that of epinephrine. It seems less active in producing arteriosclerosis than is epinephrine, and its pressor effects are of longer duration. It seems to stimulate smooth muscle without respect to innervation (thus differing

[82] Zeit. klin. Med., 1909 (69), 341; also Bernstein, Berl. klin. Woch., 1911 (48), 1794. Normal blood sugar was found by Brockmeyer, Deut. med. Woch., 1914 (40), 1562.
[83] Arch. Int. Med., 1909 (3), 438.
[84] Practitioner, 1903 (71), 472.
[85] Beutenmüller and Stoltzenberger, Biochem. Zeit., 1910 (28), 138.
[86] Full bibliography in the monograph by Harvey Cushing, "The Pituitary Body and its Disorders," Philadelphia, 1912; also Aschner, Pflüger's Arch., 1912 (146), 1.
[87] Composition of hypophysis given by MacArthur, Jour. Amer. Chem. Soc., 1919 (41), 1225.
[88] Wells, Jour. Biol. Chem., 1910 (7), 259.
[89] Lewis, Miller and Matthews, Arch. Int. Med., 1911 (7), 785; Herring, Quart. Jour. Exp. Physiol., 1914 (8), 245 and 267.

from epinephrine), but with a special potency in stimulating contractions of the uterus; and hence it has a wide clinical use under the name *pituitrin*. The chemical nature of pituitrin is not yet determined, but it seems to be closely related to β-iminazolylethylamine, the base derived from histidine,[90] and which also stimulates uterine contractions, but which differs in causing bronchial spasm and urticarial reactions. Abel believes that histamine is the chief constituent of pituitrin, presumably associated with a pressor base of some sort. Hanke and Koessler,[90a] however, seem to have demonstrated the absence of significant quantities of histamine in fresh hypophysis. Injection of the posterior lobe extract lowers the assimilation limit for carbohydrates and causes glycogenolysis (Cushing),[91] and is a powerful galactagogue (Ott).

Removal of the anterior lobe of the gland in young animals is followed by marked metabolic and developmental changes, notable being adiposity, nutritional changes in the skin and its appendages, sexual inactivity and underdevelopment, subnormal body temperature and increased carbohydrate tolerance.[92] These manifestations correspond to those observed in certain human conditions (Froehlich's syndrome)[93] associated with defects in the hypophysis. Removal of the posterior lobe does not produce any characteristic and constant effects, although marked polyuria and erotism have resulted. The anterior lobe fed to young rats has a stimulating effect on growth, and especially on sexual development and activity, while posterior lobe feeding has a retarding influence (Goetsch[94]). Robertson describes a modification of growth in mice fed anterior lobe substance, which he attributes to a specific substance, *tethelin*, containing phosphorus and probably an iminazolyl group, and hence related to the active constituent of the posterior lobe, although it has no pressor effect.[95]

Puncture of the hypophysis produces the same effect as puncture of Bernard's diabetic center in the fourth ventricle,[96] and stimulation of the gland has a similar effect, presumably because of the secretion of a glycogenolytic agent. A diminution of posterior lobe secretion occurring in certain conditions of hypopituitarism leads to an acquired high tolerance for sugars, with the resultant accumulation of fat. In hibernating animals, also, the adiposity and lowered temperature are associated with hypoplasia of the anterior lobe of the hypophysis. There also seems to be some relation between the hypophysis and

[90] See Abel and Kubota, Jour. Pharm. Exp. Ther., 1919 (13), 243.
[90a] Jour. Biol. Chem., 1920.
[91] See also Bull. Johns Hopkins' Hosp., 1913 (24), 40.
[92] Concerning metabolism after hypophysectomy see Benedict and Homans, Jour. Med. Res., 1912 (25), 409.
[93] Metabolism in Froehlich's syndrome has been studied by Rosenbloom (InterstateMed. Jour., 1917 (24), 475) who found a slight loss of sulphur and phosphorus.
[94] Johns Hopkins Hospital Bulletin, 1916 (27), 29; Growth of tadpoles is also stimulated (P. E. Smith, Univ. Calif. Publ. (Physiol.), 1918 (5), 11.
[95] Jour. Biol. Chem., 1916 (24), 409.
[96] Amer. Jour. Physiol., 1913 (31), xiii.

urinary secretion, for extracts of the posterior lobe cause marked polyuria, and in some instances of "diabetes insipidus," lesions have been found in the hypophysis. Simmonds[97] holds that the pars intermedia is responsible. Like the thyroid, the hypophysis enlarges during pregnancy.[98] Feeding of hypophysis is said to increase both gaseous and nitrogenous metabolism, and in a case of hypopituitarism the urine has been found to contain a high proportion of undetermined nitrogen and of neutral sulphur.[99] Varying results have been obtained in studies on the basal metabolism of hypopituitarism.[1]

Acromegaly.—The accumulating evidence seems to have practically proved that acromegaly depends upon a hyperfunctionating of the anterior lobe tissue of the hypophysis, one of the most important facts being the improvement which has followed removal of the hyperplastic tissues in several cases successfully operated. Although there are many cases of tumor of the hypophysis without acromegaly, this is of no significance since it is not to be expected that all tumors will carry on the functions of the tissue in which they arise. Acromegaly without hypophyseal changes is rare, especially if we consider the finer cytological evidence of cellular activity.[2] So far, little of chemical interest has been learned concerning this disease. The metabolism studies generally indicate a retention of nitrogen, phosphorus and calcium, because of the overgrowth of bone and soft tissues.[3] According to some observers this retention is decreased, or changed to an excess elimination, by administration of hypophyseal substance.[4] The elimination of endogenous uric acid is said to be greatly increased in acromegaly, and decreased in cases with hypofunction of the gland.[5] A considerable excretion of creatine was observed by Ellis.[6]

Glycosuria and actual diabetes is frequently present in acromegaly (40 per cent. of the cases collected by Borchardt),[7] presumably from interference with the regulating function of the hypophysis, but this assumption has been questioned because of the fact that lesions in this location might also produce glycosuria by affecting the "diabetic center." However, since puncture of the hypophysis causes glycosuria, while injection of posterior lobe extract produces glycosuria dependent upon hyperglycemia (Cushing), and in view of the fact brought out by Borchardt that in cases of tumor of the hypophysis without acromegaly, glycosuria has never been observed, there is

[97] Münch. med. Woch., 1913 (60), 127.
[98] See Erdheim and Stumme, Ziegler's Beitr., 1909 (46), 1.
[99] Stetten and Rosenbloom, Proc. Soc. exp. Biol. and Med., 1913 (10). 100.
[1] Means, Jour. Med. Res., 1915 (32), 121.
[2] See Lewis, Bull. Johns Hopkins' Hosp., 1905 (16), 157.
[3] See Bergeim, Stewart and Hawk. Jour. Exp. Med., 1914 (20), 218.
[4] See Rubinraut, Dissert., Zurich. Gebr. Leeman, 1912; Medigreceanu and Kristeller, Jour. Biol. Chem., 1911 (9), 109.
[5] Falta and Nowaczynski, Berl. klin. Woch., 1912 (49), 1781.
[6] Jour. Amer. Med. Assoc., 1911 (56), 1870.
[7] Zeit. klin. Med., 1908 (66), 332.

much probability that in many if not all of the cases of glycosuria with acromegaly, it is the hypophysis itself that is concerned, and that both the acromegaly and the glycosuria are caused by hyperactivity of the gland.

In later stages of acromegaly there may develop a hypoactivity because of pressure upon the posterior lobe or infundibular stalk, whereupon the sugar disappears and is replaced by an increased tolerance for sugar.[8]

THYMUS[9] AND OTHER DUCTLESS GLANDS

From the chemical standpoint little of interest is known concerning this organ. It is frequently used as a source of nucleic acids, in which it is rich, but there is no study of its chemical changes that is of interest in pathology. Numerous reports have indicated that removal of the thymus causes marked changes in ossification and development, but the more recent studies do not indicate that the thymus is essential for life or growth (Park and McClure[9]). Gudernatsch[10] found that feeding thymus to tadpoles causes a great increase in the rate of growth, and decreases or suppresses the developmental changes, having exactly the opposite effect from thyroid feeding, and Abderhalden[11] has found that this property persists after digestion of the thymus tissue. The failure of metamorphosis on thymus diet presumably depends on a lack of some substance rather than on the presence of a specific agent inhibiting metamorphosis.[12]   As yet no substance has been isolated which can be considered as a specific internal secretion of the thymus, although the frequent concurrence of abnormal conditions in the thyroid and thymus, in the adrenals and thymus, in the hypophysis and thymus, together with the frequency of polyglandular conditions, leaves no question that the thymus is to be considered with the other members of this system, however different its histological structure may be.[13]   Thymus administration by mouth is said to counteract the effect of thyroid feeding in stimulating metabolism.[14]   The enlargement of the thymus that occurs in most cases of exophthalmic goiter is accompanied at times by symptoms that suggest an intoxication from this source.[15]   Uhlenhuth[16] considers the thymus to be antagonistic to the parathyroids and responsible for tetany parathyreopriva.

The chemistry of the PINEAL GLAND can be dismissed practically without consideration, since no positive facts have been brought to light.[17]   Extracts from the organ show no distinct physiological effects.[18]   Tumors of the pineal gland have been found associated with adiposity and with precocious sexual development, but whether from the action of the gland itself or from the pressure on the brain, cannot be said.[19]   Extirpation of the pineal seems to have no noticeable effects of

[8] Full discussion in Johns Hopkins Hosp. Bull., 1911 (22), 165; 1913 (24), 40.
[9] In addition to Biedl's "Innere Sekretion," see Wiesel, Ergebnisse Physiol., 1911 (XV (1)), 416; Park and McClure, Amer. Jour. Dis. Chil., 1919 (18), 317.
[10] Arch. Entwicklgs., 1912 (35), 457; Amer. Jour. Anat., 1914 (15), 431.
[11] Arch. ges. Physiol., 1915 (162), 99.
[12] Uhlenhuth, Endocrinology, 1919 (3), 284.
[13] Literature given by Basch, Zeit. exp. Path., 1913 (12), 180.
[14] Halverson et al., Arch. Int. Med., 1916 (18), 800.
[15] See review by Halsted, Bull. Johns Hopkins Hosp., 1914 (25), 223; Eddy, Canad. Med. Assoc. Jour. March, 1919.
[16] Jour. Gen. Physiol., 1918 (1), 23; Endocrinology, 1919 (3), 285.
[17] Bibliography by McCord, Trans. Amer. Gyn. Soc., 1917 (43), 109; Gordon, Endocrinology, 1919 (3), 437.
[18] Jordan and Eyster, Amer. Jour. Physiol., 1911 (29), 115; Dixon and Halliburton, Quart. Jour. Exper. Physiol., 1909 (2), 283.   Dana and Berkeley, Med. Record, 1913 (83), No. 19.
[19] See Pappenheimer, Virchow's Arch., 1910 (200), 122.

any sort (Dandy[20]) although McCord[21] reports increased growth and early sexual maturity in animals fed pineal substance.[22]

The CAROTID GLAND is more directly related to the adrenal medulla, in that it contains chromaffin tissue. It should, presumably, contain a pressor principle, as Moulon found, but Gomez[23] obtained only lowering of blood pressure from extracts of this gland, and bilateral removal causes no characteristic effects.[24]

[20] Jour Exp. Med., 1915 (22), 237.

[21] Jour. Amer. Med. Assoc., 1914 (63), 232 and 517.

[22] Concerning the composition of the pineal gland see Fenger, Jour. Amer. Med. Assoc. 1916 (67), 1836.

[23] Amer. Jour. Med. Sci., July, 1908.

[24] Massaglia, Frankf. Zeit. Path., 1916 (18), 333.

40

CHAPTER XXIII

URIC-ACID METABOLISM AND GOUT[1]

These subjects have been the object of such a prodigious amount of research that it is far beyond the scope of this work to review the history and the details of the investigations. Such a review is also particularly unnecessary, since it can be found in the works on physiological chemistry and various treatises on metabolism. Consequently the attempt will be made in this chapter merely to give, as briefly as possible, the views now most generally accepted concerning the nature and metabolism of uric acid, and its relation to pathological processes. For the historical discussion, indicating by what devious steps we have reached our present understanding concerning this long-disputed subject, the reader is referred to the articles mentioned below, upon which I have drawn freely. A particularly clear summary of the subject is given by Walter Jones in his monograph on nucleic acids.[1]

THE CHEMISTRY OF URIC ACID

It is the very great service of Emil Fischer to have shown us the structure of the uric-acid molecule, the empirical formula of which, $C_5H_4N_4O_3$, had long been known. He demonstrated that it is a member of a group of substances, which are all characterized by being built up about a certain nucleus, C_5N_4. As the simplest member of the group is a synthetically formed body, *purine*, the nucleus is called the *"purine nucleus."* The structural relations of the better-known *"purine bodies"* to this purine nucleus and to each other are clearly shown by their structural formulæ, as given below:

The atoms in the "purine nucleus" are arranged as follows:

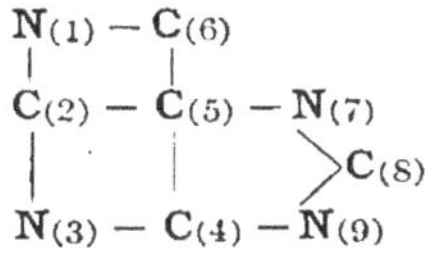

$$
\begin{array}{l}
N_{(1)} - C_{(6)} \\
\;\;|\qquad\;\; | \\
C_{(2)} - C_{(5)} - N_{(7)} \\
\;\;|\qquad\;\; |\qquad\;\; \rangle C_{(8)} \\
N_{(3)} - C_{(4)} - N_{(9)}
\end{array}
$$

To each atom has been given a number, as shown, for the purpose of facilitating reference to the location of various atoms and groups

---

[1] Complete reviews are given by F. H. McCrudden, "Uric Acid," New York, 1906; Wiener, Ergebnisse der Physiol., 1902 (1), 555; *ibid.*, 1903 (2), 377; Burian and Schur, Pflüger's Arch., 1900 (80), 241; 1901 (87), 239; Schittenhelm, Handb. d. Biochem., 1910, IV (1), 489; Brugsch and Schittenhelm, "Die Nukleinstoffwechsel und seine Störungen," Jena, 1910; Walter Jones, "Nucleic Acids," Monographs on Biochemistry, 1914. An excellent summary of recent work is given by Benedict, Jour. Lab. Clin. Med., 1916 (2), 1.

that are attached to this nucleus. The structure of purine itself is
as shown below :[2]

$$\textbf{N} = \textbf{CH}$$

$$\textbf{HC} \quad \textbf{C} - \textbf{NH}$$
$$| \qquad \qquad \rangle\textbf{CH}$$
$$\textbf{N} - \textbf{C} - \textbf{N}$$
$$\text{Purine}$$

The derivatives of purine are described by stating to which atom
of the purine nucleus the combining groups are attached. Thus,
adenine is referred to as 6-amino-purine, and therefore has the following formula:

$$\textbf{N} = \textbf{C} - \textbf{NH}_2$$
$$|$$
$$\textbf{HC} \quad \textbf{C} - \textbf{NH}$$
$$\rangle\textbf{CH}$$
$$\textbf{N} - \textbf{C} - \textbf{N}$$
$$\text{Adenine (6-amino-purine)}$$

Other important members of this group of "purine bodies," (also
called *xanthine* bodies, *alloxuric* bodies, and *nuclein* bodies) are built
up about the purine nucleus as shown below:

$$\textbf{HN} - \textbf{C} = \textbf{O}$$

$$\textbf{H}_2\textbf{N} - \textbf{C} \quad \textbf{C} - \textbf{NH}$$
$$\rangle\textbf{CH}$$
$$\textbf{N} - \textbf{C} - \textbf{N}$$
$$\text{Guanine}$$
$$\text{(2-amino-6-oxypurine)}$$

$$\textbf{HN} - \textbf{C} = \textbf{O}$$

$$\textbf{HC} \quad \textbf{C} - \textbf{NH}$$
$$\| \quad \rangle\textbf{CH}$$
$$\textbf{N} - \textbf{C} - \textbf{N}$$
$$\text{Hypoxanthine}$$
$$\text{(6-oxypurine)}$$

$$\textbf{H}_3\textbf{C} - \textbf{N} - \textbf{C} = \textbf{O}$$

$$\textbf{O} = \textbf{C} \quad \textbf{C} - \textbf{N} \diagdown \textbf{CH}_3$$
$$| \qquad \rangle\textbf{CH}$$
$$\textbf{H}_3\textbf{C} - \textbf{N} - \textbf{C} - \textbf{N}$$
$$\text{Caffeine}$$
$$\text{(1-3-7 trimethyl-2-6 dioxypurine)}$$

$$\textbf{HN} - \textbf{C} = \textbf{O}$$

$$\textbf{O} = \textbf{C} \quad \textbf{C} - \textbf{NH}$$
$$\rangle\textbf{CH}$$
$$\textbf{HN} - \textbf{C} - \textbf{N}$$
$$\text{Xanthine}$$
$$\text{(2, 6-dioxypurine)}$$

$$\textbf{HN} - \textbf{C} = \textbf{O}$$

$$\textbf{O} = \textbf{C} \quad \textbf{C} - \textbf{NH}$$
$$\diagdown \textbf{C} = \textbf{O}$$
$$\textbf{HN} - \textbf{C} - \textbf{NH}$$
$$\text{Uric acid}$$
$$\text{(2-6-8-trioxypurine)}$$

$$\textbf{HN} - \textbf{C} = \textbf{O} \quad \textbf{CH}_3$$

$$\textbf{O} = \textbf{C} \quad \textbf{C} - \textbf{N}$$
$$\diagdown \textbf{CH}$$
$$\textbf{H C} - \textbf{N} - \textbf{C} - \textbf{N}$$
$$\text{Theobromine}$$
$$\text{(3-7-dimethyl, 2-6 dioxypurine)}$$

As shown by their structural formulæ, the *pyrimidines* present in
the nucleic acids are also closely related to the purines, viz:

$$\textbf{N} - \textbf{CH}$$
$$\| \quad |$$
$$\textbf{HC} \quad \textbf{CH}$$
$$| \quad |$$
$$\textbf{N} = \textbf{CH}$$
$$\text{Pyrimidine}$$

$$\textbf{N} - \textbf{C} - \textbf{NH}_2$$
$$\textbf{O} = \textbf{C} \quad \textbf{CH}$$
$$\textbf{HN} - \textbf{CH}$$
$$\text{Cytosine}$$
$$\text{(2-oxy, 6-amino-pyrimidine)}$$

$$\textbf{HN} - \textbf{C} = \textbf{O}$$
$$\textbf{O} = \textbf{C} \quad \textbf{CH}$$
$$\textbf{HN} - \textbf{CH}$$
$$\text{Uracil}$$
$$\text{(2-6-dioxy-pyrimidine)}$$

$$\textbf{HN} - \textbf{C} = \textbf{O}$$
$$\textbf{O} = \textbf{C} \quad \textbf{C} - \textbf{CH}_3$$
$$\textbf{HN} - \textbf{CH}$$
$$\text{Thymine}$$
$$\text{(5-methyl, 2-6-dioxy-pyrimidine)}$$

[2] In these formulæ the symbols of the atoms forming the purine nucleus are
in heavy type.

Properties of Uric Acid.—Uric acid, when pure, is white, and crystallizes in rhombic tablets. Its solubility is very slight; at room temperature (18°) it dissolves but about one part to 40,000 of water, so that a saturated solution contains but 0.0253 gram to the liter. It is much more soluble in blood-serum, dissolving in 1000 parts,[3] probably held in some complex combination. His and Paul have shown that in a saturated solution only 9.5 per cent. of the molecules are dissociated, the dissociation occurring in two steps; the first and chief dissociation is into H and $C_5H_3N_4O_3$, which then undergoes further dissociation into H and $C_5H_2N_4O_3$, the latter dissociation being very slight. If any other acid is present in the solution, its dissociation and liberation of free hydrogen ions interferes with the dissociation of the uric acid, and as the undissociated uric acid is extremely insoluble, the amount dissolved in an acid solution is much less than in a neutral solution.[4]

Gudzent[5] found that saturated solutions of urates gradually precipitate out the salts because of a transformation of part of the uric acid into what he believes to be a *lactim* form. (The lactim form is shown in the following formula, as compared with the isomeric lactam form shown above, in which uric acid is supposed to exist ordinarily.)

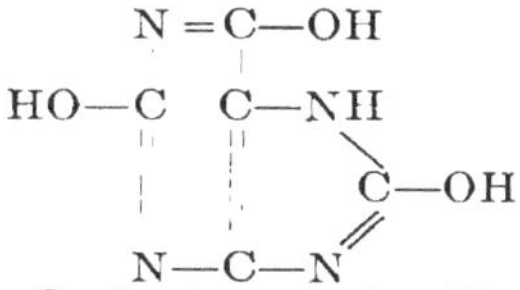

$$N=C-OH$$
$$HO-C \quad C-NH$$
$$C-OH$$
$$N-C-N$$

(Lactim form of uric acid)

With alkalies uric acid yields two series of salts, corresponding to these two steps in dissociation: one, in which one atom of the base enters, is called the *biurate* or *monobasic* urate; the other is the so-called "neutral" or *bibasic* urate.[6] Of the two, the latter is much the more soluble. The monosodium urate forms colloidal solutions in water, from which the crystalline salt gradually falls out. The quadriurate, of which much was said in the earlier literature, probably does not exist (Kohler).[7]

In the urine the uric acid and the urates are kept in solution by the phosphates, the disodium phosphate preventing the decomposition of the urates into uric acid by the acid salts of the urine. Possibly other constituents of the urine, especially the pigments and NaCl, also aid in its solution. Urine may form quite stable supersaturated solutions and Kohler states that the urine is a truly supersaturated solution of sodium urate. How the uric acid is kept in solution in the blood is not exactly understood, but Gudzent believes that uric acid can exist in the blood only as the monosodium urate, and in the less soluble but more stable lactim form, which is soluble only to the extent of 8.3 mg. per 100 c.c. serum (the lactam form being soluble up to 18 mg.). However, amounts over 20 mg. per 100 c.c. have been detected in the blood of nephritics; here solution may have been aided by the other retained metabolites. Bechhold[8] and others have maintained that urates may be present in the blood in a colloidal state which cannot pass out through the kidneys.

FORMATION OF URIC ACID[9]

The origin of uric acid is chiefly, although not exclusively, from the nucleoproteins, and it is customary to refer to uric acid formed from the nucleoproteins of the foods as "*exogenous*" uric acid, in contrast

[3] Taylor, Jour. Biol. Chem., 1906 (1), 177.

[4] Concerning the solubility of uric acid in urine see Haskins, Jour. Biol. Chem., 1916 (26), 205.

[5] Zeit. physiol. Chem., 1909 (60), 38.

[6] As a matter of fact, both salts give a slightly alkaline reaction when dissolved in water (Taylor).

[7] Zeit. physiol. Chem., 1911 (72), 169; 1913 (78), 205; Zeit. klin. Med., 1919 (87), 338.

[8] Biochem. Zeit., 1914 (61), 471.

[9] See review in International Clinics, 1910, XX (1), 76.

to the *"endogenous"* uric acid that is formed from the nucleo-proteins of the body cells during their catabolism. This may be readily explained by a brief consideration of the composition of the nucleo-proteins. The nucleoproteins may be looked upon as salts formed through combination of proteins with nucleic acid. Nucleic acid in turn is a compound of phosphoric acid with purine bases, pyrimidine bases, and carbohydrate radicals, constituting a complex sort of glucoside.

A long series of careful analytical studies has at last shown us that nucleic acids, are, whatever the source, quite similar in composition, consisting always of a complex containing phosphoric acid, the two amino purines (adenine and guanine), two pyrimidines (either cytosine and uracil or cytosine and thymine); and a carbohydrate, which may be either a pentose or a hexose. Apparently there are two sorts of nucleic acids, one from plants, which contains always uracil and pentose, and one from animal tissues, containing instead thymine and a hexose. So constant are the findings in regard to these compounds that it has seemed feasible to consider their manner of union in the intact nucleic acid molecule, and Levene and Jacobs have proposed as the structure of thymus nucleic acid the following arrangement:

$$H \quad PO_3—C_6H_{10}O_4—C_5H_6N_5O$$
$$|$$
$$O \qquad \text{(guanine group)}$$

$$H_2PO_4—C_6H_8O_2—C_5H_5N_2O_2$$
$$|$$
$$O \qquad \text{(thymine group)}$$

$$H_2PO_4—C_6H_8O_2—C_4H_4N_3O$$
$$|$$
$$O \qquad \text{(cytosine group)}$$

$$H \quad PO_3—C_6H_{10}O_4—C_5H_4N_5$$
$$\text{(adenine group)}$$

It will be seen that this proposed formula postulates in the nucleic acid molecule, one radical of each of the two purines and pyrimidines, each of these being united by a carbohydrate radical to a phosphoric acid radical. Recognizing that this must be looked upon as a provisional formula,[10] it will serve as a base of departure from which to consider the metabolism of nucleic acid.

The grouping of hexose + purine or hexose + pyrimidine is referred to as a "nucleoside," analogous in terminology to "glucoside." The same groupings plus the phosphoric acid radical constitute the "nucleotids," nucleic acid thus being made up of four nucleotids. Emil Fischer has reported[11] the synthetic production of a nucleotid, composed of phosphoric acid united to a glucoside of theophyllin, this

[10] Jones and Read (Jour. Biol. Chem., 1917 (29), 111) have advanced evidence to indicate that the linkage between the nucleotids is between the carbohydrate radicals rather than between the phosphoric acid groups. See also Thannhauser and Dorfmüller, Zeit. physiol. Chem., 1917 (100), 121.

[11] Sitzungsber. k. Akad. Wissensch., Berlin, 1914 (33), 905.

really constituting the long-sought synthesis of a nucleic acid, even though the artificial product is not the same as any known to occur in nature. With these facts before us we may consider the manner in which nucleic acids are disintegrated in the animal body.

So large a molecule can conceivably be disintegrated in many different ways; that is, the lines of cleavage might pass through several different points and in many different orders, but there is evidence available which causes us to believe that the process is quite constant in animal metabolism. Jones considers it probable that the first step is a decomposition of the tetranucleotid into dinucleotids, and that these are in turn split into mononucleotids. Little is known about the subsequent career of the two pyrimidine nucleotids, but we have an abundance of information concerning the nucleotids containing the purines, and it is in these our present interest lies. Each nucleotid has two points at which it might be split, and we have reason to believe that there exist in animal tissues enzymes which may specifically attack each bond. One enzyme separates the phosphoric acid radical from the nucleoside, thus:

$$H_2PO_4 - C_5H_8O_3 - C_5H_4N_5O + H_2O \xrightarrow{\text{phospho-nuclease}} H_3PO_4 + C_5H_9O_4 - C_5H_4N_5O$$
$$\text{guanylic acid} \qquad\qquad\qquad\qquad\qquad\qquad\qquad \text{guanosine}$$

and this enzyme is therefore designated as *phospho-nuclease*.

Another enzyme, *purine nuclease*, splits off, instead, the purine radical, thus:

$$H_2PO_4 - C_5H_8O_3 - C_5H_4N_5O + H_2O \xrightarrow{\text{purine-nuclease}} H_2PO_4 - C_5H_9O_4 + C_5H_5N_5O$$
$$\text{guanylic acid} \qquad\qquad\qquad\qquad\qquad\qquad\qquad \text{guanine}$$

Following either of these cleavages, the enzymes which deaminize purines begin to act, and we have formed as a result either the free oxypurines or the oxypurines still bound in the glucoside-like combination with sugar. If the purines are free the reaction will be:

$$C_5H_5N_5O + H_2O \xrightarrow{\text{guanase}} C_5H_4N_4O_2 + NH_3$$
$$\text{guanine} \qquad\qquad\qquad \text{xanthine}$$

or, in case the guanine glucoside is present:

$$C_5H_9O_4 - C_5H_4N_5O + H_2O \xrightarrow{\text{guanosine-deaminase}} C_5H_9O_4 - C_5H_3N_4O_2 + NH$$
$$\text{guanosine} \qquad\qquad\qquad\qquad\qquad\qquad\qquad \text{xanthosine}$$

In the latter case a hydrolytic enzyme, xanthosine-hydrolase, then splits off the xanthine, so that by either route the end result is the same. By a similar series of changes the adenine radical is converted into hypoxanthine, either directly by adenase:

$$C_5H_5N_5 + H_2O \xrightarrow{\text{adenase}} C_5H_4N_4O + NH_3$$
$$\text{adenine} \qquad\qquad\qquad \text{hypoxanthine}$$

or by adenosine-deaminase the hypoxanthine-glucoside (inosine) is formed, and later the hypoxanthine is split off.

We now have hypoxanthine and xanthine, which, in the presence of oxygen, are oxidized to form uric acid, thus:

$$C_5H_4N_4O + O \xrightarrow[\text{hypoxanthine-oxidase}]{} C_5H_4N_4O_2$$
hypoxanthine   xanthine

$$C_5H_4N_4O_2 + O \xrightarrow[\text{xanthine-oxidase}]{} C_5H_4N_4O_3.$$
xanthine   uric acid

Further oxidation of the uric acid causes its conversion into the much more soluble allantoin, thus:

$$C_5H_4N_4O_3 + O + H_2O \xrightarrow[\text{uricase}]{} C_4H_6N_4O_3 + CO_2$$
uric acid   allantoin

It is thus evident that the steps of the disintegration of nucleic acid are numerous, but that each separate process is a simple one; and also, that it has been possible to follow out and distinguish the several steps and to establish the fact that each step depends on a distinct and specific enzyme. Not every tissue possesses all the enzymes of purine destruction, and in different species of animals the distribution of the enzymes is different. For example, the enzyme xanthine-oxidase, which oxidizes xanthine into uric acid, is found in man only in the liver, and also in other animals it is of limited distribution, being found usually only in the liver or in the liver and kidney, but in the dog it seems to be present in several tissues. The deaminizing enzymes, adenase and guanase, are much more widely distributed, but by no means universally. Adenase, for example, is not present in the tissues of the rat, and not in the tissues of adult human beings.[12] Guanase is absent from the spleen and liver of the pig and from human spleen, although present in most other tissues. Uricase, the enzyme which destroys uric acid, also has peculiarities of distribution, being seldom found in any other tissue than the liver or kidney, and being absent entirely from the tissues of man, and from the birds and reptiles so far examined. The significance of this distribution of uricase will be discussed at greater length a little later.

The following graphic expression of the series of steps leading to the formation of uric acid has been presented by Amberg and Jones;[13]

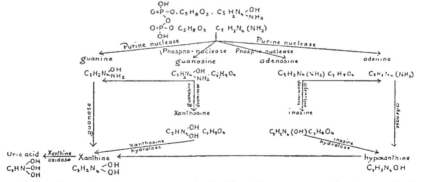

[12] There have been some reports indicating the presence of adenase in fetal human tissues (Long, Jour. Biol. Chem., 1913 (15), 449).

[13] Zeit. physiol. Chem., 1911 (73), 407.

Another possible source of uric acid is through synthesis. In birds, which eliminate most of their nitrogen in the form of uric acid, synthesis of uric acid undoubtedly occurs. It must also be considered that young mammals can synthesize the purines necessary for their growth from foods which contain no purines.[14] It would seem possible, therefore, for synthesis of uric acid to occur in adult mammals, but as yet satisfactory experimental evidence is lacking that such synthesis does occur, although an apparently reversed reaction, whereby uric acid destroyed by liver tissue can be resynthesized by the same tissue acting upon it in the absence of oxygen, has been described by Ascoli and Izar.[15] Their work has not been repeated successfully by others. I have failed in several attempts to secure resynthesis of uric acid by dog livers, and Spiers,[16] who made a more extensive investigation, was unable to corroborate their findings.

It should also be mentioned that not all of the purine bases of the body is bound in the form of nucleic acid. A considerable amount is present in a free condition, or at least not bound in nucleic acid, especially in muscle tissue. Uric acid can be formed as well from the free purine bases as from purine bases liberated from nucleic acid—indeed, evidence has been brought forward indicating that a large proportion of the uric acid arising during metabolism (endogenous) comes from the free hypoxanthine of the muscles.

As to the place where uric acid is formed, it seems probable that in different animals different organs are chiefly concerned, for it has been found that the distribution of the enzymes mentioned above varies greatly in the various organs and tissues of different species.[17] In most animals the xanthine oxidase, which forms uric acid from xanthine, is localized chiefly or solely in the liver, and this is the case in man; therefore it is presumable that uric acid is formed chiefly in the liver from purines by the steps described above. That there may be other methods of forming uric acid is possible.

DESTRUCTION OF URIC ACID[18]

With most mammals but little of the total amount of purine bases taken as food or set free in the tissues, appears in the urine as uric acid, most of it being converted into allantoin, which seems to be excreted with little or no loss.[19] Thus, when dogs, pigs or rabbits are fed nucleic acid, about 93 to 95 per cent. can be recovered as allantoin, 3 to 6 per cent. as uric acid, and 1 to 2 per cent. as purine bases (Schittenhelm). It would seem that practically all the purines can be found

[11] McCollum, Amer. Jour. Physiol., 1909 (25), 120.
[15] See Zeit. physiol. Chem., 1910 (65), 78.
[16] Biochem. Jour., 1915 (9), 337.
[17] A compilation of this distribution is given by Wells, Jour. Biol. Chem., 1910 (7), 171.
[18] See discussion by Wells, Jour. Lab. Clin. Med., 1915 (1), 164.
[19] Allantoin may be found in the blood of other mammals but not in man (Hunter, Jour. Biol. Chem., 1917 (28), 369).

in these three forms combined, the proportions varying in different species. In man alone, except for the chimpanzee[20] and orang-utan, does a considerable proportion escape as uric acid, a fact in complete harmony with repeated observation that the tissues of man have no power whatever to destroy uric acid *in vitro;* the earlier reports of positive uricolysis undoubtedly being erroneous. Even the monkey has active uricolytic enzymes in its liver, and therefore excretes its purines chiefly as allantoin. With mammals as a whole, therefore, uric acid is destroyed to the extent of being converted into allantoin,[21] the close relationship of which to uric acid is shown by the structural formula:

$$NH - CH - NH$$
$$O = C \qquad C = O$$
$$NH_2 \quad CO - NH$$
(allantoin)

With most mammals the oxidation of uric acid takes place chiefly in the liver, but in some of the herbivora the kidneys are more active, as far as experiments *in vitro* can show.

Whether man can destroy uric acid at all has been a matter of dispute. It has been shown by Wiechowski and others that uric acid injected subcutaneously is excreted almost quantitatively and unchanged in the urine. To be sure, human urine does contain a very little allantoin, 7 to 14 mg. per day, but this amount is too small to be of much significance, for it is possibly all derived from the food, as the human organism cannot destroy allantoin.[22] On the other hand, it has been found repeatedly that nucleic acid or purines given by mouth are by no means quantitatively excreted in the urine, even when uric acid, allantoin and purine bases are added together. Apparently a considerable proportion of the purine nitrogen fed, about half in most experiments, is excreted as urea.[23] As allantoin seems not to be at all disintegrated in the human body it would seem probable that if purines are destroyed, as these experiments indicate, they pass through some other route than allantoin, and possibly that part of the purines which is destroyed does not pass through the stage of uric acid. Experiments show that outside the body uric acid can be destroyed by other routes than through allantoin; thus, it can be disintegrated into glycine, ammonia and CO_2; or by another method of destruction it yields first alloxan ($C_4H_2N_2O_4$), then parabanic acid ($C_3H_2N_2O_3$) which in turn yields oxalic acid and urea. There is no

[20] Wiechowski, Prager med. Woch., 1912 (37), 275; Wells and Caldwell, Jour. Biol. Chem., 1914 (18), 157.
[21] See Hunter and Givens, Jour. Biol. Chem., 1914 (18), 403.
[22] See Ackroyd, Biochem. Jour., 1911 (5), 217, 400, 442.
[23] See Taylor, Jour. Biol. Chem., 1913 (14), 419; Givens and Hunter, *ibid.*, 1915 (23), 299. About one-tenth as much uric acid is excreted in the sweat as in the urine, sweat containing 0.1 mg. per c.c. (Adler, Deut. Arch. klin. Med., 1916 (119), 548).

evidence, however, that any of these alternative routes is ever followed in the animal body. It is possible that the failure to find all the purines of the food as uric acid in the urine depends on their partial destruction in the intestine by bacteria.[24] It is highly probable, in view of all available evidence, that in man most of the purine absorbed from the food, and practically all the purine from cell metabolism, is converted into uric acid and excreted as such.

THE OCCURRENCE OF URIC ACID IN THE BLOOD, TISSUES, AND URINE

As can be seen from the foregoing discussion, the amount of uric acid that appears in the urine depends upon a number of factors, which may be enumerated as follows:[25] (1) The amount of purine bodies taken in the food, upon which, chiefly, depends the amount of exogenous uric acid. (2) The amount of destruction of tissue nucleoproteins. (3) The amount of purine bases formed in the muscle tissue. (4) The amount of conversion of purine bases into the uric acid. (5) The amount of destruction of uric acid, if any, occurring in the body. (6) Possibly upon the capacity of the tissues to synthesize uric acid; and in case such power to synthesize uric acid exists, upon the presence of the precursors of uric acid in the body. (7) The retention of uric acid in the blood and tissues. (8) The power of the kidneys to excrete uric acid.

If we also take into account the fact that the solubility of uric acid in the urine depends chiefly upon the amount of neutral phosphates present in the urine, and also upon the temperature, reaction, and concentration of the urine, it becomes apparent how totally devoid of significance is the presence of crystals of uric acid and urates in the urine, and how fallacious is any theorization based upon the excretion of considerable quantities of uric acid when all the above-mentioned factors, especially the diet, are not controlled and taken into consideration. Yet on just such an inadequate basis was once constructed an enormous amount of theorization as to "uric-acid diathesis," "uric-acid intoxication," "lithemia," etc., until it came to be popularly believed that a large share of the minor ailments of humanity, and in particular all non-infectious diseases of the joints and muscles, are dependent upon the presence of excessive quantities of uric acid or urates in the blood. But it may safely be stated that at the present time there exists no good evidence which makes it probable that uric acid is responsible for any pathological conditions whatever, except uric-acid calculi, "uric-acid infarcts" in the kidneys, and certain manifestations of gout. Uric acid is possessed of but a very slight degree of toxicity, and the body is able to get rid of it in such large

[24] See Siven, Arch. ges. Physiol., 1914 (157), 582; Thannhauser and Dorfmüller, Zeit. physiol. Chem., 1918 (102), 148.
[25] Review on uric acid metabolism and many data given by Höst, Nord. Mag. Laev., 1917 (78 Suppl.). See also Jour. Biol. Chem., 1919 (38), 17.

measure that an actual intoxication with uric acid probably never occurs.

The amount present in the urine may be very considerably increased by eating food rich in purines, of which sweet-breads, liver, and kidney are the best examples; and also coffee with its caffeine (trimethyl purine), may give rise to a little uric acid, although the methylated purines seem to be destroyed in large part, or eliminated as something else than uric acid. Large quantities of meat will also increase the uric acid, because of the free purines contained in muscle; and even a diet rich in proteins free from purine will also increase the uric acid excretion over that of a low protein diet.[26] On a purine-free diet the excretion of endogenous uric acid is increased by increasing even the non-protein calories (Höst).[25] However, the amount of uric acid in the blood is not correspondingly raised by purine-rich diets,[27] this being regulated by the binding function of the tissues and by excretion through the kidneys.[28] According to Folin and Denis[29] human blood normally contains 1.5–2.5 mgs. uric acid in 100 c.c., and the amount bears no fixed relation to the amount of urea and total non-protein nitrogen of the blood.[30] All the uric acid in human blood seems to exist free as monosodium urate, and not in a colloidal state (Gudzent).[31] Any difficulty in renal elimination is usually accompanied by an increase in the amount of uric acid in the blood, in uremia as much as 15 to 20 mg. being sometimes found per 100 c.c.[32] In early interstitial nephritis there may be 4 to 8 mg. of uric acid per 100 c.c. blood without a corresponding increase in urea and creatinine, which suggests that uric acid may be less easily excreted by the diseased kidney than the other chief nitrogenous constituents of the urine.

In normal individuals there seems to be little uric acid present in the tissues. By using Folin's method, Fine[33] found that various tissues contain quantities comparable to that in the blood of the same person, whether this is normal or increased in amount. Ordinarily these quantities are not sufficient to permit readily of isolation of the uric acid in a pure state, but in the tissues of a young woman who died after complete suppression of urine for nine days following poisoning with $HgCl_2$, I found considerable amounts.[34] Whenever much de-

[26] Taylor and Rose, Jour. Biol. Chem., 1914 (18), 519; Lewis and Doisy, *ibid.*, 1918 (36), 1.

[27] See Denis, Jour. Biol. Chem., 1915 (23), 147.

[28] Stocker found uric acid in saliva, increased in all conditions associated with uricemia (Inaug. Dissert., Zurich, 1913).

[29] Jour. Biol. Chem., 1913 (14), 29; Arch. Int. Med., 1915 (16), 33.

[30] In infants the amount is slightly lower, about 1.3 to 1.7 mg. Liefmann, Zeit. Kinderheilk., 1915 (12), 227.

[31] Zeit. klin. Med., 1916 (82), 409.

[32] See Folin and Denis, Arch. Int. Med., 1915 (16), 33; Meyers and Fine, *ibid.*, 1916 (17), 570; Baumann *et al.*, *ibid.*, 1919 (24), 70.

[33] Jour. Biol. Chem., 1915 (23), 473.

[34] Jour. Biol. Chem., 1916 (26), 319.

struction of the nucleoproteins of the tissues is occurring in the body, the elimination of endogenous uric acid becomes abnormally raised, the best examples being the resolution of pneumonic exudates, and leukemia, especially leukemia under x-ray treatment (*q. v.*). In neither of these conditions, however, do any symptoms or tissue changes arise that can be referred to the excessive uric acid.

GOUT

Introducing this subject, one cannot do better than to quote v. Noorden's statement that "It is not to-day very alluring to write any thing regarding the theory of gout, especially in a book which is essentially devoted to the presentation of facts. All the theories advanced up to the present time have fared badly. The positive material is much too insufficient and much too ambiguous." After adjusting the many contradictory statements of earlier investigators, the present status of our conception of uric-acid metabolism in gout may be briefly summarized as follows: The excretion of uric acid in patients with *chronic gout*, when kept upon a definite diet, does not differ greatly from the excretion of normal individuals on the same diet. Normally the elimination of uric acid varies within rather wide limits, even on a constant diet, but the excretion in chronic gout tends to fall at or slightly below the lower normal limits. As a rule, gouty patients on a purine-free diet excrete less endogenous uric acid than normal persons, and when given purines in the food the rate of excretion of these exogenous purines is slower than normal.[35] There seems to be no particular relation between the amount of uric acid in the blood and the occurrence or severity of attacks.[36] This uric acid is, according to the best evidence, in a free state, and not combined, as was at one time urged by several students of gout.

Analyses of the blood in 120 cases of gout by Gettler and St. George[37] gave the following figures, in mg. per 100 c.c. of blood:

	Normal	Gout
Nonprotein nitrogen	25 to 40	30 to 55
Urea nitrogen	10 to 18	15 to 35
Creatinine	0.1 to 0.8	1 to 2.8
Uric acid	0.5 to 3.0	1.5 to 8.5
Sugar	60 to 110	85 to 140
Alkali reserve—percentage	53 to 80	50 to 80

[35] According to Gudzent's studies (Zeit. physiol. Chem., 1909 (63), 455) in nearly all cases of gout the blood contains as much or more mono-sodium urate than it can hold in solution (8.3 mg. per 100 c.c.), so that it is often actually a supersaturated solution of the relatively insoluble lactim form of urate. Even on a purine-free diet the blood of the gouty usually contains an excess of uric acid (4 to 9 mg. per 100 c.c.). These figures, however, are much higher than those obtained by more modern methods.
[36] Pratt, Amer. Jour. Med. Sci., 1916 (151), 92; Bass and Herzberg, Deut. Arch. klin. Med., 1916 (119), 482.
[37] Jour. Amer. Med. Assoc., 1918 (71), 2033.

Their deductions are as follows: Cases of gout as a general rule show some increase in the uric acid content of the blood, though some of the chronic cases were within normal limits from this standpoint. The increase is more marked in the acute type of the disease. The uric acid content of the blood in cases of gout is abnormally high without a corresponding increase in the nonprotein nitrogen products of the blood; but the majority of cases show a slight but constant increase in the nonprotein nitrogen and creatinin. An increase of uric acid in the blood, with the patient on a purin-free diet, may be a symptom, but is not diagnostic, of gout.

McClure and Pratt[38] found more than 3 mg. per 100 c.c. in their cases when on purin-free diet, and also recognize that this uricaemia is not diagnostic of gout. The former reports that in gout there is evidence of impaired renal function.[39] If abundant purines are fed to gouty patients they may be found to have less than normal capacity to excrete the excess,[40] also explainable on the ground of renal inefficiency.

In the intervals between the attacks of *acute gout* the elimination of uric acid is said to remain within the normal limits; however, for a period of one to three days before each acute attack the amount of uric acid is usually decreased considerably. With the onset of the attack the amount of uric acid excreted becomes increased, and for a few days remains above the average, then subsides to about the normal. Of these two features, the increased output of uric acid during the attack seems to be more constant than the reduced output preceding it, but cases occur in which the uric acid excretion shows no variation from that of normal persons. In certain cases of rheumatoid arthritis the behavior of the purine metabolism resembles that of gout.[41]

As yet we have no definite information either as to the cause of this behavior of the uric acid during the paroxyms of acute gout, or as to its part in causing the paroxysm. However, in view of the fact that monosodium urate is found in the joints during the attacks, it seems most probable that for some as yet unknown reason there occurs a precipitation or anchoring of the urates in the tissues, which is associated with the attacks of pain and swelling. We do not know, however, that it is the deposition of urates that causes the attacks. Indeed, the fact that uric-acid retention precedes the attack, rather than accompanies it, seems to suggest that it is the absorption of the urate rather than its deposition in the joints that is responsible for the local disturbances. It is also possible that during the period of retention the uric acid is held in the blood in some form that cannot be eliminated by the kidney, and that its deposition in the joints in

[38] Arch. Int. Med., 1917 (20), 481—bibliography.
[39] *Ibid.*, 1917 (20), 641.
[40] Rosenbloom, Jour. Amer. Med. Assoc., 1918 (70) 285.
[41] W. J. Mallory, Jour. Path. and Bact., 1910 (15), 207; Ljungdahl. Zeit. klin. Med., 1914 (49), 177.

an absorbable form occurs simultaneously with the attack. The failure of recent studies on the enzymatic transformation of purines to locate anywhere in the human body an enzyme destroying uric acid, makes hazardous the attempt to explain gouty metabolism as a result of enzymatic abnormalities. However, there can be little doubt that the fundamental reason for the existence of uric acid gout in man lies in the inability of the human organism to destroy uric acid. Because man cannot destroy uric acid rapidly by oxidation, as can all other mammals, he is always a potential victim of uric acid retention and deposition.

It should be mentioned in addition that it is not the uric-acid metabolism alone that is altered in gout. Irregular periods of nitrogen retention and nitrogen loss are quite constant features. The cause of this variability, and the form in which the nitrogen is retained, are quite unknown, although there is some evidence that the retained nitrogen is in the form of purine bodies (Vogt). Most of the excessive loss occurs during the acute attacks,[42] and the retention of nitrogen between attacks may be partly to repair the loss; against this, however, is the fact that there is not sufficient gain in weight to account for all of the nitrogen retention. Associated with the delayed excretion of ingested purines is also a delayed excretion of the other nitrogenous products of protein food.[43] The proportion of purine bases to uric acid, is not altered in gouty urine.[44] The statements in regard to phosphoric acid elimination, which depends largely on decomposition of nucleins, are contradictory, but it seems probable that it shows no characteristic alterations in gout. Amino acids, especially glycine, are said to be excreted in excess.[45] There is no significant change in the basal metabolism.[46]

It may be seen from the foregoing discussion that we neither understand fully the intricacies of metabolism in gout, nor know whether uric acid is responsible for either the acute painful attacks or for the anatomical alterations in the kidneys, heart, and blood vessels. Indeed, Daniels, and McCrudden[47] have shown that it is possible for gouty patients to have a persistently low content of uric acid in the blood, below the average normal quantity, and to have typical acute' attacks without change in either the uric acid content of the blood or its excretion; attacks were even observed to occur when the blood uric acid was at a subnormal figure from administration of atophan, which increases its elimination. Furthermore, Bass and Herzberg[48] found that uric acid can be injected into the blood of gouty subjects until the blood contains as much as 10 mg. per 100 c.c. without causing any joint symptoms.

[42] Brugsch, Zeit. exp. Path. u. Ther., 1906 (2), 619.
[43] Levene and Kristeller, Jour. Exp. Med., 1912 (16), 303.
[44] Heffter, Deut. Arch. klin. Med., 1913 (109), 322.
[45] Bürger and Schweriner, Arch. exp. Path., 1913 (74), 353.
[46] Wentworth and McClure, Arch. Int. Med., 1918 (21), 84.
[47] Arch. Int. Med., 1915 (15), 1046.
[48] Deut. Arch. klin. Med., 1916 (119), 482.

It is very possible that some entirely different product of metabolism than uric acid is responsible for most of the changes and symptoms of gout[49]—indeed, this would seem to be the case were it not for the great frequency of the deposition of monosodium urate in the joints and cartilages, both during the acute attacks and in chronic gout. This indicates that there is surely something abnormal in the conditions of uric-acid solution and circulation. Why the urate is precipitated in these definite places is another of the many unsolved problems of gout. The local nature of the deposition indicates that it must depend upon local changes; but the hypothesis that there occur first degenerative changes in the tissues which determine the precipitation of the urate, seems to have been disproved by the demonstration that the deposition of the urates precedes the necrosis. The fact that the presence of other sodium salts in a solution decreases the solubility of urates in that solution, and the fact that cartilage and tendons are richer in sodium salts than the blood, may possibly have something to do with the fact that the urates are precipitated in these particular tissues. On the other hand is the fact that in leukemia and nephritis we may have a higher concentration of uric acid in the blood than in gout, and this uricæmia may be protracted, without gouty deposits or joint symptoms. Bass and Herzberg[4] found that the uric acid content of the joint fluid was approximately the same as that of the blood in patients without gout, although in two gouty uremics they found 18.5 and 20.8 mg. in the joint fluid with only 10 and 8.2 mg. in the blood. They also found that intravenous uric acid injection caused less uricæmia in the gouty, in spite of reduced renal excretion, and hence they conclude that in gout the tissues have an increased capacity for taking up uric acid.

The histology of urate deposits, both experimental and gouty, has been carefully studied by Freudweiler,[50] His,[51] Krause,[52] and Rosenbach.[53] Their results all indicate that uric acid and urates excite some slight inflammatory reaction, cause a slight local necrosis, and seem to act as a weak tissue poison (His). However, they may be deposited without causing necrosis (Rosenbach). Possibly part of the material observed in areas of urate deposition, and generally considered as necrotic tissue, merely represents the framework of the crystalline deposit (Krause). When experimentally injected, the urates are absorbed slowly by phagocytic leucocytes and giant-cells. Why the gouty tophi can be deposited in the chronic process and cause no pain or inflammation, while in acute gout deposition of urates seems to cause such marked symptoms, is also an unanswered question, unless we accept the explanation that the slower rate of deposition and the lack of dissolved urates account for the absence of symptoms with the tophi.[54] Magnus-Levy holds with Pfeiffer, that the local inflammatory processes must be ascribed to dissolved urates, since they often extend for some distance about the joints, and hence the attack is ascribable to the solution rather than the forma-

[49] In swine a "guanine gout" occurs; see Schittenhelm and Bendix, Zeit. physiol. Chem., 1906 (48), 140.
[50] Deut. Arch. klin. Med., 1899 (63), 266.
[51] *Ibid.*, 1900 (67), 81.
[52] Zeit. klin. Med., 1903 (50), 136.
[53] Virchow's Arch., 1905 (179), 359.
[54] Almagia (Hofmeister's Beitr., 1905 (7), 466) has found that joint cartilage placed in urate solutions becomes filled with crystals, which infiltration does not occur with cartilage of any other origin, or with tendons.

tion of the deposits, a fact in harmony with the known increased elimination of uric acid during the attack.

That urates may cause necrosis of the tissues has been definitely established, and this may lead to connective-tissue formation and contraction.[55] But the actual increase of uric acid in the blood and tissues in gout is so slight that we are not warranted in saying that the usual tendency to sclerosis in all the organs in gout is due to the action of uric acid, rather than to some other unknown agent or agents. Excess of uric acid in the blood is by no means pathognomonic of gout, for we may have relatively great excesses of uric acid in the blood in leukemia, in some cases of nephritis, and after eating large amounts of nucleoproteins, without a symptom of gout. Furthermore, it is quite possible that the precursors of uric acid, the purine bases, are responsible for more harm than the uric acid itself. Thus, administration of adenine to dogs and rabbits will produce degenerative changes in the kidneys, associated with the deposition of substances resembling uric acid and urates in the renal tissue; and Mandel[56] states that purine bases may cause fever, independent of infection.

Many have looked upon renal alterations, leading to failure of excretion of uric acid, as the primary cause of gout; but the evidence in favor of this is faulty, because frequently renal changes are slight or entirely absent in gout, whereas marked nephritis of all forms may exist without the coexistence of gout, and, as mentioned above, the kidney in gout may show no lack of ability to excrete uric acid injected into the tissues. Magnus-Levy, however, seems to believe that a renal retention of uric acid is of importance, and that it may occur without morphological changes in the kidneys. The newer methods of blood analysis (Folin) have given support to this view, and, as pointed out in preceding pages, Fine[57] and numerous others have called attention to the fact that in early interstitial nephritis the blood shows a greater increase in uric acid than in urea or creatinine, as if the diseased kidney found more difficulty in excreting uric acid than the other substances.[58] As a result the blood in early nephritis may show quite the same figures for uric acid, urea and creatinine as are found characteristically in gout. Although in some cases one finds normal amounts of uric acid in the blood in gout, this seems to be exceptional. Hence we are still confronted with the question whether gout is anything more than a form of nephritis in which chiefly uric acid excretion is impaired or whether there does exist a special disease, gout, which causes uric-acidemia more or less independently of renal abnormalities.[59]

URIC-ACID INFARCTS[60]

Uric-acid infarcts, as the deposits of urates and uric acid observed in the kidneys of at least half of all children dying within the first two weeks of life are called, give evidence of the slightness of the toxic effects of these substances upon the tissues. Usually little or no change occurs in the renal tubules as a result of

[55] Because the gouty tophi do not suppurate, even when ulcerated through the skin, it has been suggested that the urates have antiseptic properties. Bendix (Zeit. klin. Med., 1902 (44), 165), however, could not demonstrate such antiseptic properties experimentally. Not always do the tophi consist solely or even largely of urates, but these may be replaced by calcium salts (Kahn, Arch. Int. Med., 1913 (11), 92).

[56] Amer. Jour. Physiol., 1904 (10), 452; 1907 (20), 439.

[57] Jour. Amer. Med. Assoc., 1916 (66), 2051.

[58] See also Denis, Jour. Biol. Chem., 1915 (23), 147.

[59] See McClure, Arch. Int. Med., 1917 (20), 641.

[60] See discussion by Wells and Corper, Jour. Biol. Chem., 1909 (6), 321.

these depositions, except such as can be attributed to their mechanical effect,[61] but they may serve as the starting point of calculi. The reason for the formation of these infarcts is not at all understood. Spiegelberg[62] found it possible to cause them experimentally in young dogs, in which they do not occur naturally, by injection of 0.25 gram of uric acid per kilo. He was unable to explain why this deposition should occur in young animals but not in old, for he could not find evidence of lessened oxidative power on the part of young animals, and the solvent power of infants' urine was found equal to or greater than that of adults. Other authors, however, have found a lower oxidative power in young animals, and Mendel and Mitchell[63] have found that in the embryo pig uricolytic enzymes do not appear until just at or just after the time of birth. As human tissues have no demonstrable power to oxidize uric acid, however, these animal experiments cannot be applied to the uric acid infarcts in human infants. Possibly the uric-acid infarcts of infants are the result of the great destruction of nucleoproteins that results from the change of the nucleated fetal red corpuscles to the non-nucleated adult form, or from a destruction of leucocytes which is said to take place at the time of birth. Flensberg believes that a hyaline substance is secreted in the urine of new-born infants which acts as a matrix for urate deposition. McCrudden considers the high concentration of infants' urine an important factor. Minkowski[64] observed that administration of adenine to dogs led to a deposition of uric acid or some similar substance in the kidneys.[64a] Schittenhelm[65] found the same deposits in the kidneys of rabbits fed adenine, but not when they were fed guanine. According to Nicolaier,[66] the crystals thus deposited are not uric acid or urates, but 6-amino-2-8-dioxypurine, derived from the adenine (6-amino-purine) by direct but incomplete oxidation. He could not find this substance in either human urine or in a uric-acid calculus. Eckert[67] obtained urate deposits by intravenous injection into rabbits of at least 0.08 gm. per kilo, but subcutaneous injections were ineffective; injury to the renal epithelium by whatever cause interferes with this deposition of urates. These experimental infarctions are undoubtedly related to the human form, and indicate that the latter depend upon the presence of an excessive amount of uric acid in the infants' urine, in which a ratio of uric acid to urea of 7.9 to 74.9, as against the adult ratio of about 2 to 85, was found by Sjoquist. According to Niemann,[68] in the first few days of life the infant excretes from 80 to 100 mg. of uric acid daily, while after the fifth day the amount falls to 30 to 40 mg. daily. Similar figures were obtained by Schloss and Crawford,[69] who also found a corresponding increase in the phosphoric acid, showing that the uric acid must originate from nucleoproteins. The blood of fetus and mother have the same uric acid content,[70] but after birth the infant's blood has more during the first three or four days, paralleling the high excretion.[71]

Adult kidneys may also show uric acid deposits in the tubules of the papillæ, independent of gout. They occur as a result of cell decomposition, according to M. B. Schmidt,[72] who found them especially in pneumonia, leukemia and sarcoma, but not in carcinoma.

[61] I have observed a case of fatal *hematuria neonatorum*, associated with most extensive hemorrhagic infarction of both kidneys. In the bloody urine *B. coli* was found in large numbers. From the anatomical findings and history it seemed quite possible that the injury of the kidneys by uric-acid infarcts might have determined the localization of the bacteria in these organs, with resulting hemorrhages. (Trans. Chicago Path. Soc., 1909 (7), 242.)

[62] Arch. exp. Path. u. Pharm., 1898 (41), 428.

[63] Amer. Jour. Physiol., 1907 (20), 97.

[64] Arch. exp. Path. u. Pharm., 1898 (41), 375.

[64a] Abderhalden and Kankeleit (Zeit. exp. Med., 1916 (5), 172), have produced renal deposits by feeding large amounts of tyrosine, glycine and leucineimid to rabbits. These deposits consisted of the amino acid as fed, and caused suppression of urine by blocking up the tubules. They also caused necrosis and inflammatory reactions.

[65] *Ibid.*, 1902 (47), 432.

[66] Zeit. klin. Med., 1902 (45), 359.

[67] Arch. exp. Path., u. Pharm., 1913 (74), 244.

[68] Jahrb. f. Kinderheilk., 1910 (71), 286.

[69] Amer. Jour. Dis. Children, 1911 (1), 203.

[70] Slemons and Bogert, Jour. Biol. Chem., 1917 (32), 63.

[71] Kingsbury and Sedgwick, *ibid.*, 1917 (31), 261.

[72] Verh. deut. Path. Ges., 1913 (16), 329.

CHAPTER XXIV .

DIABETES

By R. T. Woodyatt

Introduction.—As with gout and the problems of purine metabolism, so with diabetes a vast amount of study has been expended because of the integral connection of this disease with broader problems of physiology, and in particular with the metabolism of the carbohydrates and the fats, the nature of internal secretions, and the function of the kidneys. It is impossible in this place to review the entire literature and history of the subject, a key to which will be found in the works of the writers cited below.[1] This chapter will be devoted only to an outline of the chief established facts, with an indication of the main lines along which the thought of leading students has been directed. It will involve a brief discussion of the problems of carbohydrate physiology, but only in so far as they are contingent upon the main topic—while for a discussion of that anomaly of the metabolism

[1] *Older Literature:*
Bouchardat—De la glycosurie ou diabète sucré, Paris, 1875.
Külz—Beiträge zur Path. und Ther. der Diabetes Melitus, Marburg, 1874–5.
Bernard—Leçons sur le Diabète et la Glycogenèse Animale, Paris, 1877; Vorlesungen über Diabetes, Berlin, 1878.
Cantani—Diabetes Melitus (German translation by Kahn), Berlin, 1880.
Frerichs—Ueber den Diabetes, Berlin, 1884.
Larger Works:
Naunyn—Der Diabetes Melitus, Berlin, 1906. Diabetes Melitus; in Nothnagel's Handbuch (2nd), Vienna, 1906.
Lépine—Le diabète sucré, Paris, 1909.
von Noorden—(a) Die Zuckerkrankheit (6th), Berlin, 1912. (b) New Aspects of Diabetes, New York, 1913.
Pavy—Carbohydrate Metabolism and Diabetes, London, 1906.
McLeod—Diabetes (Longmans, Green), 1913.
Cammidge—Glycosuria and Allied Conditions. (Longmans, Green), 1913.
Allen—Glycosuria and Diabetes, Boston, 1913.
Foster—Diabetes Melitus, Philadelphia, 1915.
Joslin—Treatment of Diabetes Melitus, New York, 3rd. Ed., 1919.
Monographs, etc.:
Magnus-Levy—Diabetes Melitus; in Kraus and Brugsch, Spezielle Path. u. Ther. innerer Krankheiten, Berlin, 1913.
Gigon—Neuere Diabetes Forschungen, Ergebnisse der inneren Medizin, 1912, IX, p. 206.
von Mering—Behandlung der Diabetes melitus; in Penzoldt and Stinzing's Handbuch der Spezielle Therapie (2nd), 1912.
Lusk—Elements of the Science of Nutrition (3rd), New York, 1917.
Benedict and Joslin—Metabolism in Diabetes Melitus, Carnegie Institution, Washington, 1910.
Benedict and Joslin—A Study of Metabolism in Severe Diabetes, *ibid.*, 1912.
Allen, Stillman and Fitz—Total Dietary Regulation in the Treatment of Diabetes. Monograph of the Rockefeller Institute for Medical Research, New York, 1919.

which leads to the excretion of acetone, aceto-acetic acid and β-hydroxybutyric acid in the urine, the reader is referred to the section on acidosis. (Chapter xx).

Whereas the normal urine at all times contains reducing substances and substances which are optically active, which yield crystalline compounds with the hydrazines and respond to other so-called sugar tests, these substances are not all sugars, nor are all the sugars glucose. The quantity of fermentable reducing substance in normal urine averages about 4 parts in 10,000 (0.04 per cent.) acording to Lavesson.[2] If the total quantity of urine were 1500 c.c. this would imply a daily excretion of about 0.6 gm. Bang and Bohmannson[3] estimated the total reducing substance in the urine of normal adults as between 0.21 and 0.24 per cent., of which about 18 per cent. was fermentable (0.038 to 0.043 per cent. of fermentable reducing substances in the urine). This is doutbless subject to change depending on the diet and other factors. Benedict, Osterberg and Neuwirth[4] found an excretion of fermentable reducing substance ranging between 0.903 and 1.161 gm. in twenty-four hours in the case of a normal adult on an ordinary mixed diet. During a fast it fell to zero, according to these writers, and on a diet low in carbohydrate it averaged 0.75 gm. while with a high carbohydrate diet it rose to 1.5 gm.

When an abnormal amount of sugar occurs in the urine, regardless of the kind, the condition may be called, in accordance with Naunyn's suggestion, *melituria*. When the sugar is glucose (dextrose), the term *glycosuria* is applied; when levulose, *levulosuria*, and so on. Other known forms of melituria are lactosuria, galactosuria, fructosuria, pentosuria, etc. All these are but symptoms, many of them being caused by a variety of mechanisms, which will be discussed presently.

The term diabetes is often loosely used to cover any variety of melituria, but is is preferably limited to certain forms; namely, to the *glycosurias* (or the mixed meliturias in which d-glucose is the predominating sugar), and further than this, to those particular *glycosurias which continue* even after the glycogen reserves of the body have become depleted and when the diet is free of carbohydrate; or, to those transient glycosurias whose nature by one means or another can be proved to be identical with the continuous forms (latent or mild diabetes). Over against these are the *meliturias in which other sugars than glucose play the chief rôle, and glycosurias which are essentially transient* because they depend solely on the ingestion or administration of excessive quantities of glucose or the sudden liberation into the blood of glucose derived from preformed glycogen or other fixed compound of sugar.

[2] Biochem. Zeit., 1907 (4), 40.
[3] Zeit. physiol. Chem., 1909 (63), 443.
[4] Jour. Biol. Chem., 1918 (34), 217.

Thus, the glycosuria which follows puncture of the floor of the fourth ventricle (Claude Bernard's piqûre) does not occur in animals which contain little glycogen. The same applies to the adrenal, thyroid and hypophysis glycosurias. But after complete pancreas extirpation (pancreas diabetes) and in the spontaneous human disease (diabetes melitus) or its counterpart in animals, and during the continuous administration of phlorhizin, the glycogen may be nearly or quite exhausted and the diet consist solely of meat and fat and still the glycosuria will continue. On the other hand a partial pancreas extirpation, a mild diabetes melitus, or an interrupted phlorhiziniza-tion may give rise to transient glycosuria, the diagnosis of which may be difficult. In general, experience teaches that all persistent glycosurias prove to be diabetic and that, except in phlorhizin poisoning, every genuine diabetes implies a disturbed function of the pancreas. In forming a judgment of the value of any experimental work on diabetes (histological, chemical or clinical), the student will do well to examine critically the records of quantitative food and urinary analyses offered by the investigator, to show what type and what grade of diabetes is under consideration.

CARBOHYDRATE PHYSIOLOGY

Certain facts concerning the physiology of the carbohydrates may be briefly recalled before entering into the discussion of the individual meliturias.

The appearance of sugar in the urine implies a source or sources of sugar and the existence of a kidney membrane of such a physical character that molecules of sugar may migrate through it with a certain degree of facility. The factors which may influence the purely physical penetrability of the kidney membrane to sugar molecules are those involved in a discussion of kidney function and secretion in general and need not be elaborated here.

Assuming that the physical penetrability of the kidney membrane to sugar molecules is normal and that it varies only within constant limits, there are then two basic moments which determine how much sugar will pass into the urine. These are: 1. The rate at which sugar molecules enter the cells constituting the kidney membrane. 2. The rate at which these molecules of sugar undergo chemical change into something else within the membrane.

These same factors of supply and utilization determine the elimina-tion of sugar from any cell or tissue or the organism as a whole, but in the case of internally situated cells the elimination is directly or indirectly into the blood, whereas, in the case of the kidney cells sugar may pass into the urine as well as into the blood and thus leave the body permanently.

Sugar may pass out of a cell unchanged when the rate at which it enters the cell (from internal and external sources) exceeds the rate at which it undergoes change into something else within the cell, the same holding in the case of the cells forming the kidney membrane. *Thus sugar passes from the kidney membrane into the urine when the rate at which sugar molecules enter the kidney membrane exceeds the rate at which they are denatured or utilized within it.* In order to understand the various ways in which melituria may be produced it is necessary to analyze further these factors of *supply* and *utilization.*

The Sugar Supply to the Kidneys is chiefly via the blood, although some may be liberated within the kidney cells themselves from glycogen deposits or from the transformation of protein during metabolism. The factors which influence the rate at which sugar molecules enter the kidney membrane from the blood, are *immediate* and *remote.*

The more *remote factors* are those which determine the quantity of sugar in general circulation, and the distribution of blood to the kidneys. The relative quantity of sugar circulating in the blood will depend on the combined rates at which sugar enters the blood from the outside and from all the organs, and on the rate at which sugar passes out of the blood into the cells. The absolute value of these factors, supply and depletion, and their ratio, will determine fluctuations of the total blood sugar. The supply to the kidneys is accordingly influenced by the balance of supply and depletion elsewhere.

The *immediate factors* which determine the rate at which sugar is brought to the kidney membrane will include all of those which may influence the state of the blood as to viscosity etc., and the rate at which sugar actually enters the kidney membrane will be influenced by changes in the state of that membrane, but apart from those things there are two factors of major importance in determining the supply of sugar to the kidney membrane at any instant, namely, the *concentration of sugar in the blood plasma of the kidney capillaries* and the *extent of the surface of contact between the blood plasma and the kidney membrane.* In accordance with a method followed by M. H. Fischer it is convenient to think of the kidney membrane simply as including all that lies between the blood plasma on the one hand and the urine on the other. So considered, the surface of contact between the blood plasma and the kidney membrane is the internal surface of all the capillaries of the cortex, in so far as these are filled with circulating blood. The kidney membrane might be conceived otherwise and be made to include only the layer of epithelial cells, in which case the surface of contact might be considered as the surface of those cells in so far as they are bathed in plasma; or the matter might be carried within the cells, in which case the problem of surface would become one of surfaces between phases of an heterogeneous system in the chemical sense, and so on.

For present purposes it is convenient to mass all such intermediate factors and deal with the sum of their effects, *i. e.,* to think of this surface as the internal surface of the active capillaries. The surface of contact between the blood plasma and kidney membrane, so considered, is clearly subject to variations, for as more or less blood is forced into the capillaries of the cortex there must be changes in the diameter, length or number of capillaries containing circulatory blood, or in all three. Any or all of these changes imply changes of capillary surface. It therefore becomes apparent that other factors remaining the same, changing volumes of blood in the cortical capillaries would imply changing rates of sugar diffusion from the blood into the kidney cells, even though the concentration of sugar in the blood should remain unchanged. And it is also apparent that if the blood should be diluted with water in such a way as to double its volume and halve the blood sugar percentage this would not of necessity change the rate at which sugar was passing from the blood into the kidney membrane, provided the extra volume of blood developed for itself a proportional amount of extra capillary surface.[4a] Thus it has been shown by Epstein[5] that the rate at which sugar is

[4a] This raises the question of the geometrical form of capillaries and the mechanism by which an organ or a tissue accommodates varying volumes of blood. It is interesting to note that in capillary systems, notably that into which the efferent artery from the glomerulus breaks up, the capillary strands may vary in calibre, which would lead one to expect that a pressure just sufficient to force blood through

excreted in diabetes is not always proportional to the concentration of sugar in the blood, but is more nearly proportional to the product obtained by multiplying the blood sugar percentage by a number representing the approximate blood volume and other experiments to be described later point in the same direction.

The Utilization of Sugar may be considered for present purposes as the sum of the processes by which a sugar such as glucose is converted into something else within the cells. In the case of glucose it includes *oxidation* to yield finally CO_2 and water; *polymerization* to yield a series of substances, chief of which is glycogen; *reduction* to fat; *transformation*, as to lactic acid; *combination*, etc. The rate of utilization[6] by all of these methods taken collectively is influenced in the first place by the rate at which glucose molecules enter the cells and secondly by the reaction conditions encountered within it. The utilization rises with an increasing supply of glucose. As to the factors which enter into what we have called the reaction conditions found within the cell there is little definite knowledge. With a constant glucose supply the rate of utilization may fall as the result of a deficiency of that hypothetical substance derived from the pancreas. It is well known that acid may retard glycogen formation and hasten glycogen hydrolysis. It would appear from the work of Murlin and Kramer[7] that alkali may increase glucose utilization. The rate of actual oxidation is influenced by the supply of oxygen, etc. The following may serve to suggest other factors.

It might be conceived that the cell contained molecules of a glucolytic catalyst or enzyme similar in its effects to metallic hydroxides, that glucose molecules as fast as they entered the cells would come into collision with catalyst molecules, perhaps combining with them, and that as a result of the encounter the glucose molecules would be dissociated into unsaturated fragments or ions. From the moment of union or dissociation they would cease to behave as glucose molecules. The unsaturated fragments might subsequently suffer various fates, depending upon the character and quantities of various substances in the cell. Thus, some might combine with oxygen to yield, finally, carbon dioxide and water. Others might combine with each other to form polymers like glycogen, others again undergo reduction to fat or molecular rearrangement to give lactic acid. The relative quantities undergoing those several changes, would depend upon the

the larger tubes would not suffice to inject the smaller, while a rising pressure should throw into action erstwhile empty collaterals and vice versa. A system of collateral spillways would limit the distension of already filled capillaries and make the accommodations of varying blood volume largely a matter of throwing in and cutting out capillary cylinders. Such a method if followed exclusively would make the surface rise faster than the volume, since the new channels would be of somewhat smaller diameter. On the other hand, if a capillary were cylindrical, increasing its volume by increasing its diameter would lessen the ratio of surface to volume. Increasing the volume of a cylinder by increasing its length would increase lateral surface in proportion to volume. Possibly in health, and within certain limits, variation of the blood volume may cause proportional changes of capillary surface.

[5] Jour. Biol. Chem., 1914 (18), 21; Proc. Soc. Exp. Biol., 1916 (13), 67; also "Studies in Hyperglycemia in Relation to Glycosuria," Albert A. Epstein, N. Y., 1916.

[6] It might not seem desirable to include such processes as temporary storage in the form of glycogen under the heading of utilization. The term is used for convenience.

[7] Jour. Biol. Chem., 1916 (27), 499.

relative quantities of H and OH ions, of available oxygen, salts, etc., found in the various phases of the cell. This conception is based on that used by Nef to explain the behavior of sugars in alkaline solutions. For a concrete conception of the dynamics of a reaction between an organic substrate and catalyst the reader is referred to Van Slyke's study of the enzyme urease.[8]

The general principles outlined above may be illustrated by experiments with timed intravenous injections of glucose. It has long been known that if a comparatively large dose of glucose is injected rapidly into a peripheral vein a marked glycosuria usually results. Pavy, however, emphasized the fact that a material fraction of a dose so given fails to be excreted and appears to be utilized. Doyon and Du Fourt demonstrated that with a standard dose of glucose the percentages excreted and utilized respectively are influenced by the time consumed in injection, the slower rates of injection causing lower percentage excretions and vice versa. Blumenthal chose a standard injection time of about 10 seconds and varied the weight of sugar given in that time. He found that a certain dose of glucose might be injected into the ear vein of a rabbit without causing any glycosuria at all. However, the maximum dose which could be so injected once could not be repeated 15 minutes later without causing glycosuria. He assumed from this that the first dose "saturated" the tissues and that fifteen minutes later the utilization of sugar had only resulted in a partial desaturation. He, therefore, determined the dose of glucose which might be injected repeatedly at 15 minute intervals for as long as 3 hours without ever causing glycosuria. His figures varied between 0.6 and 1.3 gm. per kg. of body weight per hour. This he termed the "utilization limit," whereas the largest dose which could be given within 10 seconds *once* without causing glycosuria he called the "saturation limit." The latter he placed at 0.8 gm. per kg. but R. M. Wilder has been unable to confirm this latter observation. Woodyatt, Sansum and Wilder[9] made continued intravenous injections of glucose at uniform rates by means of a motor driven pump for 2 to 17 hours with the following findings:

If chemically pure glucose in aqueous solution is injected continuously into the peripheral venous blood of a normal resting man, dog or rabbit at the rate of 0.8 gm. per kg. of body weight per hour, or at any slower rate, the injection may be sustained in most cases, hour after hour for 7 hours and probably longer without producing any glycosuria in the usual sense of the word. If the rate is advanced to 0.9 gm. of glucose per kg. of body weight per hour, while all other conditions remain the same, the injection may be sustained for a short time without causing glycosuria, but in nearly all cases abnormal quantities of glucose begin to appear in the urine after 5 to 30 minutes

[8] Jour. Biol. Chem., 1914 (19), 141.
[9] Jour. Amer. Med. Assoc., 1915 (65), 2067 (preliminary report); Woodyatt, Harvey Society Lectures, 1916; Wilder and Sansum, Arch. Int. Med., 1917 (19), 311; Woodyatt and Sansum, Jour. Biol. Chem., 1917 (30), 155.

of injection. Once established, the glycosuria then tends to proceed at a uniform rate as long as the rate of injection and other conditions remain fixed. However, if the injection rate is again reduced to 0.8 gm. per kg., glycosuria promptly ceases. Thus during the continuance of an injection at the latter (0.8 gm.) rate there can be no continued accumulation of unchanged glucose in the body, but the rate of injection is equalled by the rate of utilization if we leave out of consideration the trace of sugar which can be detected in the urine by refined methods. It is important to note that it makes no appreciable difference whether one uses an 18 or a 72 per cent. glucose solution for injection. The tolerance limit for glucose may be demonstrated at the same point regardless of wide variation in the quantity of water administered with the glucose, even though the blood volume and the blood sugar percentages may be influenced by variation of the water supply. Also, if glucose is injected continuously and uniformly at a rate productive of some glycosuria, the glucose excretion may proceed at a constant rate in spite of marked variation in the water supply during successive hours. A certain dog receiving by vein 20 gm. of glucose per 10 kg. per hour for 8 hours, excreted every hour close to 0.42 gm. of sugar per 10 kg. of body weight. Yet during the experiment water was injected at varying rates into the same vein with the glucose, so that the hourly volume of urine varied between 6 c.c. and 128 c.c. and the percentages of sugar in the urine varied between 0.35 and 4.9. This emphasizes the fundamental importance of the *rate* at which sugar is supplied to the organism in determining the occurrence or non-occurrence of glycosuria and in fixing the rate of excretion when the latter occurs.

In view of the above generalities several specific mechanisms suggest themselves by which glycosuria might be produced:

(1) An increased supply of preformed glucose to the whole organism from without (alimentary glycosuria).

(2) A decreased utilization in the organism as a whole (pancreatic diabetes).

(3) An increased supply to the kidneys resulting from the liberation into the blood of sugar previously stored or combined in other organs. Thus, the rapid hydrolysis of glycogen following puncture of the floor of the fourth ventricle and analogous nerve stimulations, and occurring in the acid, asphyxial, narcotic, thyroid, epinephrine, and hypophysis glycosurias. In an analogous manner lactose may enter the circulating blood from the mammary gland, and pentose from unknown sources.

(4) An increased supply to the kidneys due to decreased utilization in other organs. The breaking down of glycogen mentioned in (3) might be so interpreted and one might think of the possibility that in various diseases the ability of a part to utilize sugar may be altered.

(5) Decreased utilization in the kidney itself.

(6) Increased physical penetrability of the kidney membrane to glucose.

Both (5) and (6) are hypothetical conditions, the latter having been proposed as the basis of so called kidney diabetes, a state in which glycosuria occurs with a normal or subnormal *percentage* of sugar in the blood, in which the rate of sugar excretion is, in comparison with other forms of glycosuria, little influenced by the diet,[9a] and in which the glycosuria tends to grow progressively worse.

THE BLOOD SUGAR

The normal blood sugar concentration is found to average 0.10 per cent., but, as statistics show, it may vary at least between 0.06 and 0.11 per cent. The literature contains numerous references to that blood sugar concentration which if exceeded leads to glycosuria ("threshhold" value). In accordance with the general principles above discussed we should expect this value to vary. It has been placed at 0.147 to 0.164 per cent. by Foster, between 0.17 and 0.18 per cent. by Haman and Hirschman, at about 0.20 per cent. by Pavy, and other writers have reported greater variations, due in part doubtless to differences in the analytical methods used. How widely the threshhold blood sugar percentage may be varied by extreme variations of the blood volume and other factors has not been settled. Following the ingestion of free glucose the blood sugar percentage ordinarily rises, and in a similar way, but more slowly, after feeding of starch. Fisher and Wishart gave 50 gm. of glucose in 150 c.c. of water by stomach to dogs weighing 8 to 9 kg. and found in the first hour blood sugar percentages of 0.16 and 0.13. In succeeding hours there was little variation from 0.11 per cent. In harmony with the previous work of Gilbert and Baudoin and the more recent studies of others on man, these experiments showed that the blood sugar percentage rises during the first hour, then falls and thereafter remains normal. There was no increase of the blood volume during the first hour, the hemoglobin percentage remaining unchanged, probably because the large quantity of glucose in the bowel held water there. But in the second hour the blood volume became large and the hemoglobin showed the effects of dilution. In this same hour the sugar percentage returned to normal. But the absorption of glucose was only completed in the fourth hour and calorimetric observations by Lusk showed that the metabolism also ran at a uniform rate 20 per cent. above the basal level into the fourth hour. Accordingly the observed blood sugar percentages first rose as the rate of sugar supply was increased, but fell again *during the maintenance of the increased supply and while the metabolism was constant,* owing to the shifting of water.

When concentrated (54 to 72 per cent.) glucose solutions are in-

[9a] Cf. Epstein;[5] Strouse, Jour. Amer. Med. Assoc., 1914 (62), 1301; Lewis and Mosenthal, Johns Hopkins Hosp. Bull., 1916 (27), 133.

jected continuously into the blood at rates of 0.4 to 0.8 gm. per kg. per hour, there is at first a steep rise of the blood sugar percentage, followed by a fall coincident with an increased hydremia, after which a new equilibrium is established and the blood sugar percentage may become constant at a "normal" level exactly as in the above. By injecting glucose at the same rates in sufficiently dilute solutions this initial rise may be very much reduced and the blood sugar percentage established in later hours may even be lower than that observed before injection began. On the other hand, if glucose is injected at rates above 0.9 gm. per kg. per hour, glycosuria begins, and if the rate of injection is rapid enough may be made intense. As glucose passes through the kidney membrane, water tends to accumulate with the glucose on the urinary side of the membrane (increased diuresis, polyuria). In the same way that glucose in the bowel lumen may tend to withhold water from the blood, so a sufficient quantity of glucose in the urinary tubules may manifest the same tendency in this locality. Whether the glucose in the urinary tubules will have the effect of concentrating the blood or vice versa will depend on the quantitative distribution of free sugar between these two fluids, and the quantity of water available for distribution between the blood sugar and the urinary sugar. During continuous intravenous injections of glucose at rates from 2.7 gm. per kg. per hour upward, 30 to 40 per cent. of the glucose injected may be excreted and there is a strong tendency toward dehydration of the whole body. This may be neutralized by supplying water with the sugar as fast as it flows away in the urine, provided the rate of injection is not so great that the necessary traffic in water overtaxes the cardio-renal mechanism. By employing these high rates of injections and maintaining the water balance at as low levels as compatible with life and recovery, it is possible to produce and maintain for hours blood sugar concentrations as high as 2.38 per cent. Joslin observed 1.49 per cent. of sugar in the blood of a fatal case of diabetes with nephritis. The blood sugar of diabetics passing sugar in the urine is as a rule higher than normal, but not necessarily so, much depending on the water balance. Joslin's statistics show a range of 0.07 to 0.43 per cent.

THE STATE OF THE SUGAR IN THE BLOOD

It has long been believed that the sugar circulating in the blood exists in two physical states, a diffusible and a non-diffusible, *i. e.,* as (*a*) Free glucose in a state comparable to that of glucose dissolved in water, *sucré actuelle* of Lépine. (*b*) Sugar in a colloid state, *sucré virtuelle*, Lépine. By the former term a very specific idea is conveyed. One might think for instance of single molecules or clusters of two or three, each holding in its sphere of influence a certain number of water molecules like suns in solar systems. Such small masses move at high velocities, "diffuse" readily and create high "osmotic pressures."

By the latter term is meant sugar in the blood which does not behave physically like glucose in aqueous solution nor respond to the ordinary chemical tests for sugar, but from which free glucose may be reliberated by such simple procedures as boiling with dilute acids. Such sugar is supposed to exist as a component of particles having the larger dimensions which characterize colloids (non-diffusoids). But as to the actual chemical nature of these a great variety of proposals have been made. Thus Pavy proposed glucose molecules held entire to the colloids of the blood in a state of simple adsorption (comparable to the state of molecules of a dye electrically bound to particles of a colloid clearing agent). He also proposed glucose chemically incorporated in the structure of the protein molecule, and between these extremes by the same author a score of suppositions have been made by others, among which Drechsel's jecorin, a lecithin-sugar compound, is a notable example. Another worthy of serious consideration is that of glucose built up into polymers intermediate between disaccharides and glycogen. The basis for assuming the existence of combined sugar in the blood lies chiefly in the observation that following glucose administrations the increase in the reducing power of the blood which results from heating the blood with dilute acid is greater than the increase resulting from the same process before sugar administration (see Pavy, Lépine, Loewi). Also, if glucose is added to fresh blood and the mixture placed in the incubator, the reducing power falls but may be in part rehabilitated by boiling with dilute acid.[10]

As to the sugar which is determined by the ordinary methods of blood analysis, it would appear that we are dealing almost exclusively with free glucose. As yet no one has succeeded in proving the existence in blood of a combined sugar capable of spontaneous conversion into free sugar. Michaelis and Rona dialyzed separate portions of the same blood against isotonic salt solutions containing graduated quantities of sugar. A sugar solution which neither lost nor gained sugar during the dialysis they regarded as having an amount of free sugar equal to that in the blood. Titration of the blood sugar and of the sugar in such a solution gave almost identical figures. They accordingly concluded that all of the reducing sugar in this blood must have been as free to diffuse as was that in the simple salt solution. But this ingenious experiment of Michaelis and Rona does not show conclusively that in circulating blood there is no sugar in a state of colloidal adsorption, because drawn blood rapidly undergoes survival changes (e. g., lactic acid formation) which might influence the affinity of its colloids for sugar. However, McGuigan and Hess[11] led the blood of living animals through collodion tubes enclosed in jackets filled with isotonic salt solutions and found that when equilibrium was established

[10] A critical review of the literature to 1912 will be found in the books by McLeod and Allen. Compare also the article by Levene and the recent studies of Lombroso favoring the polymerization idea.
[11] Jour. Pharm. and Exp. Ther., (1914) (6), 45.

the concentration of reducing sugar in the salt solution and in the plasma was the same, proving that even in life all of the titrable plasma sugar is in a state of subdivision which lets it migrate through the interstices of a collodion membrane. This would make the adsorption idea seem untenable.

Closely related to the question of the state of the sugar in the blood is that of its state in the cells. Palmer[12] has studied the percentages of sugar found in the various tissues in relationship to the plasma sugar concentration. The titrable sugar of the tissues was found below that of the blood in all organs except the liver. Of course, owing to the large quantities of glycogen which occur in that organ and the rapidity with which it breaks down into glucose, liver tissue would naturally analyze high for sugar. In the muscles the titrable sugar was found at 0.04 and 0.041 per cent. with blood sugar at 0.10 and 0.105 per cent. On the other hand the tissues generally when boiled with dilute acid show a higher content of "combined" sugar than the blood. This is most striking in the case of the liver and due by common consent to the polymers of glucose in that organ.

It serves a useful purpose to consider the body as a whole as an heterogeneous system made up of phases, and to assume that glucose on entering the body distributes itself between these phases as acetic acid may distribute itself between the fat droplets and the aqueous part of milk; that glucose in a certain type of phase behaves as though in water and in another type of phase rapidly undergoes chemical changes. The blood is a tissue in which the dominant phase is in the nature of a physical solvent for glucose, like water. In the cells the dominant phases are of such a character that glucose on entering them rapidly undergoes chemical change. But both types of phase are present in both blood and cells although in different proportions. The blood is therefore the phase par excellence in which to study the "sucré actuelle" and the tissues the place to study the "sucré virtuelle." According to this conception "sucré virtuelle" would be glucose in process of utilization or storage and not beyond recall, hence chiefly glucose polymers.

DIOSE[13]

Diose, glycollic aldehyde, $CH_2OH-COH$, the simplest sugar, of which there is but one possible form, is highly sensitive to oxidative influences and, *in vitro*, readily condenses with alkali to yield a complex mixture of higher sugars and saccharinic acids in a manner analogous to that manifested by the trioses. Notwithstanding its instability and sensitiveness to oxidative changes in the test tube, it would appear that glycollic aldehyde is insusceptible of direct oxidation in the body but that it may be converted into glucose, like other sugars, and then utilized. When given intravenously at the rate of only 0.1 gm. per kg. per hour,

[12] Jour. Biol. Chem., 1917 (30), 79.
[13] Literature on diose: Mayer, P., Zeit. f. physiol. Chem., 1903 (38), 135; Woodyatt, R. T., Jour. Amer. Med. Assoc., 1910 (55), 2109; Parnas and Baer, Biochem. Zeit., 1912 (41), 386; Smedley, Ida, Jour. Physiol., 1912 (44), 203; Sansum, W. D. and Woodyatt, R. T., Jour. Biol. Chem., 1914 (17), 521.

unchanged diose appears in the urine after the first few minutes of injection (author). P. Mayer reported glycosuria and death following administration of impure glycollic aldehyde to rabbits. Parnas and Baer saw an increase of glycogen in tortoise livers perfused with glycollic aldehyde. This is confired by Barrenscheen. Smedley noted the rapid disappearance of diose added to liver emulsions. Sansum and Woodyatt, and also Greenwald observed slight increases of the glycosuria following parenteral administrations of diose in phlorhizinized but not completely deglycogenized dogs. The extra sugar could have come from glycogen in these experiments. A final proof of the conversion of diose into glucose in the living body has not been brought. The relationship of this substance to glycine, CH_2NH_2-COOH; glycollic acid, $CH_2OH-COOH$; and ethyl alcohol, CH_3-CH_2OH; is close. Lusk states that glycine is capable of conversion into glucose in the body. However, glycollic acid and alcohol are apparently not sugar formers.

TRIOSES[14]

There are three possible trioses, d- and l-glyceric aldehyde and the ketotriose dihydroxyacetone. The optically inactive d, l-glyceric aldehyde has been prepared and recently the d- and l-forms. The preparation is still tedious and expensive. Dihydroxy-acetone is somewhat easier to prepare. Both trioses are unstable, easily oxidized and very prone to undergo rearrangements and condensation with even traces of alkali. Under the influence of alkali they yield complex mixtures of hexoses, chiefly 3-ketohexoses, formerly known as α and β-acrose from which Schmitz[15] has recently isolated d,l-fructose and d,l-sorbose. If oxygen is available as well as alkali, they burn. If the alkali is strong and oxygen lacking, much lactic acid is formed together with certain rearranged tetrose, pentose and hexose molecules, known as saccharinic acids (or "saccharines," of Kiliani). The same phenomena occur when the alkali is dilute, but more slowly. The structural formulæ of the trioses and their relationship to glycerol, glyceric acid and lactic acids (the latter of which might be regarded as a 3-carbon saccharinic acid) may be seen from the following chart:

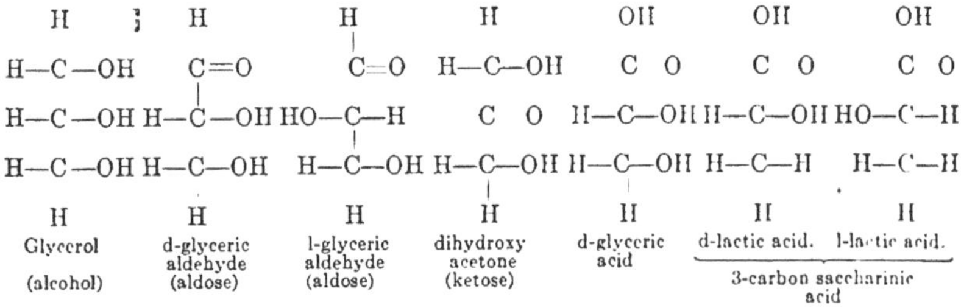

```
  H     ;  H          H          H        OII      OII        OH

H—C—OH    C=O       C=O      H—C—OII    C  O     C  O      C  O

H—C—OH H—C—OII   HO—C—H      C  O    II—C—OII II—C—OII  HO—C—II

H—C—OH H—C—OH   H—C—OH    H—C—OII  II—C—OII  H—C—II    H—C—II

  H       H         H          H         II       II         II
Glycerol d-glyceric l-glyceric dihydroxy d-glyceric d-lactic acid.  l-lactic acid.
          aldehyde   aldehyde  acetone     acid    ────────────────────────────
(alcohol) (aldose)   (aldose)  (ketose)             3-carbon saccharinic
                                                            acid
```

Neuberg fed animals and men considerable doses of impure d.l-glyceric aldehyde (glycerose) and saw its apparently complete utilization. Parnas demonstrated increased glycogen in tortoise livers perfused with d,l-glyceric aldehyde. Smedley noted the rapid disappearance of glyceric aldehyde added to liver emulsions. Sansum and Woodyatt fed pure crystalline d,l-glyceric aldehyde to rabbits and guinea pigs in doses as high as 2.8 gm. per kg. with no apparent ill effects. A dose of 5 gm. per kg. in a rabbit caused diarrhea with

[14] Literature on Trioses: The chemical literature is reviewed and an improved method of preparing glyceric aldehyde described by Witzemann, E. J., Jour. Am. Chem. Soc., 1914 (36), 1908, and *ibid.*, p. 2223. The biological literature is reviewed by Sansum, W. D. and Woodyatt, R. T., Jour. Biol. Chem., 1916 (24), 327.

[15] Ber. Deut. Chem. Ges., 1914 (46), 2327.

unchanged triose in the passages. There was marked diminution of
urine with albuminuria, which then persisted for 10 days. A dose
of 6.8 gm. per kg. killed in 4 hours. In no case was there an alimentary
triosuria. The average lethal dose by the subcutaneous route was
2.2 gm. per kg. as compared with 18 gm. of glucose per kg. in the
same set of animals. Suppression of urine is a regular manifestation,
but the visceral changes at autopsy are slight. When d,l-glyceric
aldehyde is injected intravenously at the rate of only 0.15 gm. per kg.
per hour, and possibly at slower rates, unchanged glyceric aldehyde
appears in the urine, but no glucose. (It will be recalled that glucose
may be injected continuously at the rate of 0.8 gm. to 0.9 gm. per kg.
per hour without causing glycosuria.) When administered to diabetic
individuals d,l-glyceric aldehyde may increase glycosuria. When
given to completely phlorhizinized and glycogen-free dogs it is possible to demonstrate a quantitative conversion of the triose into glucose,
the increase in glycosuria corresponding exactly with the weight of
glyceric aldehyde given. However, owing to the toxic effects of glyceric aldehyde on the kidneys there may be an incomplete excretion
of all the sugar formed. The suppression of urine has in the past
been mistaken for a beneficial effect, since it may lead to diminished
excretions of sugar, acetone, aceto-acetic and β-hydroxybutyric acids.

Embden and his coworkers demonstrated the formation of lactic
acid from glyceric aldehyde added to washed blood corpuscles. The
keto-triose, dihydroxyacetone, was observed to produce less lactic acid,
but otherwise it is not improbable that the behavior of the ketotriose
is analogous to that of the aldo forms. Thus Mostowski found dihydroxyacetone to be a glycogen former, and Ringer[16] reported its complete transformation into glucose in the fully phlorhizinized dog.

The complete conversion of d,l-glyceric aldehyde into glucose in
phlorhizinized dogs—its transformation into glycogen in the perfused
liver, its disappearance as such when added to liver emulsions, all
indicate that glyceric aldehyde (like diose and other sugars in general)
is converted into glucose in the body as a preliminary step in utilization. The fact that large doses may be given by the alimentary
route without causing melituria or death, whereas much smaller doses
given subcutaneously may prove lethal, together with the very low
rate at which glyceric aldehyde has to be given by vein in order not to
produce melituria, all point to the liver (and bowel wall) as the chief
sites of its conversion. Glyceric aldehyde has figured prominently
in theories of the normal catabolism of glucose, and on the basis of his
observations concerning the formation of lactic acid from this triose
by blood corpuscles Embden regards it as a chief normal intermediate
substance in the oxidation of glucose in the cells. Now glucose may
be oxidized in the body at the rate of 0.6 gm. per kg. per hour under
suitable circumstances, and if every molecule of glucose oxidized were

[16] Ringer and Frankel, Jour. Biol. Chem., 1914 (18), 233.

first split to give two molecules of glyceric aldehyde, as the Embden hypothesis would demand, then glyceric aldehyde would be formed in the body at the rate of 0.6 gm. per kg. per hour, and the place of formation would be within the cells of the body at large, the muscles representing the most important sites of oxidation. However, if glyceric aldehyde is introduced into the systemic blood at only one-fourth of this rate, unchanged triose appears in the urine and may be demonstrated in the blood. But glyceric aldehyde has never been found in the blood, urine or tissues under any other circumstances. Glyceric aldehyde may of course enter the body via the portal route at faster rates without causing triosuria, but then, as stated, it would appear not to be oxidized directly but first assimilated, *i. e.*, transformed into glucose. Recently, for other reasons, von Fürth[17] has also questioned the tenability of Embden's hypothesis.

Lactic acid from triose: When alkali acts on glucose (or hexoses in general) in the absence of oxygen, lactic acid is formed in amounts as high as 40 to 60 per cent. of the weight of the sugar used, provided the conditions are properly controlled. But in the presence of sufficient oxygen no lactic acid is formed. Still, preformed lactic acid will not be destroyed if it is added to this latter mixture. So it is clear that lactic acid is not an intermediate in the oxidative breakdown of sugars in the alkaline solution. Meisenheimer accordingly suggested the obvious probability that there was some labile precursor of lactic acid which burned in the presence of oxygen; in the absence of oxygen, rearranged to give lactic acid. He proposed glyceric aldehyde as such a body. Nef, however, holds that the immediate precursor of lactic acid is methyl glyoxal (CH_3— CO— COH), which forms lactic acid by undergoing what is known to chemists as a "benzilic acid rearrangement." These phenomena are remarkably similar to those that occur in the body.

One other important point should be emphasized in this place. The trioses condense in the presence of alkali to yield among other things certain hexoses, and, as described under *hexoses*—any sugar of that type will in the presence of alkali enter into a complex equilibrium with several other hexoses. Any of these may again split into 3-carbon compounds such as the trioses and then again condense, and so on, as long as they do not become converted into lactic acid or the saccharinic acids—substances which are not reconvertible into sugar. Nef formulated the view that—were it not for the occurrence of these irreversible reactions —*any sugar in the presence of alkali would come finally to represent an equilibrium of every possible sugar of 2 to 6 carbon atoms (i. e., 56)* together with all of the myriad intermediate forms. In the body, however, lactic acid can be converted into sugar. So this bar to the great equilibrium is there nonexistent, and it is conceivable that in the body there actually exists an equilibrium of this sort.

In all of Embden's experiments there was perhaps a lack of oxygen, so that the phenomena *in vivo* and in alkaline solution *in vitro* are strikingly parallel. Embden, on the basis of these experiments, regards sarcolactic acid (*i. e.* d-lactic) as a *chief normal* breakdown product of glucose in the body over the glyceric aldehyde route. But it is hard to see why this assumption is more rational than it would be to say that lactic acid is an intermediate in the oxidative breakdown of sugars in the alkaline solution outside the body, which it certainly is not. Although lactic acid will disappear from a surviving asphyxiated muscle if oxygen be resupplied to it (Fletcher)[17a] and although this disappear-

[17] Biochem. Zeit., 1916 (69), 199.
[17a] Jour. of Physiol., 1907 (35), 247.

ance will not occur in a simple alkaline peroxide solution it may nevertheless be effected by the addition of a second catalyst, and still we know that the lactic acid was not an intermediate in the original solution until the oxygen supply became deficient. Lactic acid is probably an intermediate in the sugar catabolism only during relative asphyxia.

All the substances whose formulæ are given above have been shown to be capable of conversion into glucose in the body. The details of the steps involved have not been established, but, in conformity with the chemical theories developed by Nef and discussed under hexoses, the transformation of these substances into glucose, as well as their occurrence in the course of its breakdown, are best explained on the basis that all of them participate in the same great chemical equilibrium with the sugars, and that this participation depends upon their dissociation into unsaturated residues. These residues are in dynamic chemical equilibrium with the molecules from which they are derived and with those derived from sugars. When there is a rapid loss of glucose from the body these substances tend to become glucose, in accordance with the laws of chemical equilibrium.

TETROSES

There are six possible tetroses (4 aldo- and 2 keto-). The entire subject of their physiology, which has undoubtedly considerable biologic importance, has been little studied. They have never been found in the urine, since there are at present no established methods for their detection, and efforts have been lacking.

PENTOSES

Chemical theory demands the existence of fourteen pentoses, *i. e.*, six aldo-pentoses, four 2-keto-pentoses and four 3-keto-pentoses. Only those better known to chemists have received biological study, *e. g.*, arabinose and xylose.[18] Of these the optically inactive or d- l-arabinose, the l-arabinose and l-xylose are the best known. When even small quantities of pentose gain access to the circulating blood, pentose is excreted in the urine. Ebstein[19] reports the appearance of traces in the urine of a man (in which none had been previously demonstrated), after the administration of so little as 0.25 gram of l-arabinose by mouth. Bergell[20] found reactions for pentose in the urine seven to ten minutes after ingestion of the same sugar, and when given subcutaneously. Fr. Voit[21] saw about 50 per cent. excreted. Neuberg and Wohlgemuth[22] gave a normal man 15 grams of d-l-arabinose and recovered 4.5 grams of d-, and only 1.04 grams of l-arabinose in the urine. On the other hand l-arabinose becomes converted in part into the dextro-form, since both forms appear in the urine when only one is given. Xylose has been found to behave in general like arabinose.[23]

Since all writers agree that 10 to 50 per cent. of administered pentoses are excreted in the urine even when given per os in very small quantities, and since pentoses occur in many foods (plums, cherries, apples, etc.) or result from the

[18] Rhamnose is a methyl pentose, representing a class of substances closely related to the pentoses.
[19] Virchow's Archiv., 1892 (129), 401.
[20] Festschr. f. E. v. Leyden, 1902 (2), 401.
[21] Deut. Arch. f. klin. Med., 1897 (58), 523.
[22] Zeit. f. physiol. Chem., 1902 (35), 41.
[23] For literature, see Neuberg, "Der Harn sowie die übrigen Ausscheidungen, etc." (Springer, Berlin, 1911), 1, p. 370.

bacterial decomposition of other carbohydrates, it is inevitable that *alimentary pentosurias* should occasionally occur in nearly every normal individual, and, as a matter of fact, most normal urines give reactions which indicate the presence of some pentose (Cremer, Funaro, Cominotti). Vice versa, one may conclude that very little pentose normally occurs in the blood, since otherwise more of it would appear in the normal urine than does; and finally, that pentoses must play but a minor rôle in the general metabolism of the carbohydrates. Therefore it is highly improbable that during the breakdown or synthesis of glucose in the body the hexoses split to any extent into a pentose and formaldehyde. The same holds good for the behavior of hexoses in the presence of alkali. They split almost exclusively into chains of 2, 3 and 4 carbon atoms (Nef).

CHRONIC PENTOSURIA[24]

The literature contains reports of some 30 cases in which considerable quantities of pentose have been excreted steadily in the urine regardless of the character or quantity of the food. Even during a fast the quantity excreted has remained virtually constant in some cases. Outputs as high as 36 grams per day have been recorded. Such quantities of pentose could not be introduced into the body from without by any known means without causing pentosuria of marked degree. Accordingly, in some cases there is either an overproduction of endogenous pentose, or an abnormal entry into the blood stream of pentose which is normally bound in the tissues. The process would then be analogous to that in which lactose from the mammary glands occasionally gains access to the general circulation and appears in the urine. This conclusion is confirmed by the work of Bial, Blumenthal and Tintemann, who found that certain pentosurics displayed no lessened tolerance for administered pentose. The origin of the pentose is unknown. Nucleo-protein of cell nuclei, and galactose have been suggested as possible sources. The disease has been found in different members of the same family and appears to be a harmless anomaly. The pentose found in the urine in cases of all types has sometimes been reported as optically inactive, sometimes as dextro- or levo-rotatory; l-arabinose (dextro-rotatory), d-xylose and d-xyloketose appear to have been identified.[25]

HEXOSES

Chemical Introduction.—Structural theory demands the existence of 32 isomeric hexose sugars of the formula $C_6H_{12}O_6$. The behavior of the hexoses when dissolved in very dilute alkali makes it convenient to consider them in four natural series of eight members each. Thus one series comprises the 8 hexoses whose structural formulæ appear below. This may be called the d-glucose series.

(1)	(2)	(3)	(4)	(5)	(6)	(7)	(8)
CHO	CHO	CH₂OH	CHO	CHO	CH₂OH	CH₂OH	CH₂OH
H-C-OH	HO-C-H	CO	H-C-OH	HO-C-H	CO	H-COH	HO-C-H
HO-C-H	HO-C-H	HO-C-H	H-C-OH	H-C-OH	H-C-OH	CO	CO
H-C-OH	H-C-OH	H-C-OH	H-C-OH	H-C-OH	H-C-OH	H-C-OH	H-C-OH
H-C-OH	H-C-OH	H-COH	H-C-OH	H-C-OH	H-C-OH	H-C-OH	H-C-OH
CH₂OH	CH₂OH	CH₂OH	CH₂OH	CH₂OH	CH₂OH	CH₂OH	CH₂OH
d-glucose	d-mannose	d-fructose	d-allose	d-latose	d-pseudo fructose	α-d-glutose	β-d-glutose

[24] See Garrod, "Inborn Errors of Metabolism," Oxford Med. Publ., 1909; Lancet, July, 1909.

[25] For literature see Hiller, Jour. Biol. Chem., 1917 (30). 129.

42

There is also an l-glucose series in which the members are the mirror images of the above. There is a third series comprising d-galactose, d-talose, d-tagatose, l-sorbose, l-idose, l-gulose and alpha and beta d-galtose; and a fourth series whose relationship to the d-galactose series is the same as that of the l-glucose to the d-glucose series. Consideration of the d-glucose series will bring out the principles common to all. Examination of the 8 formulæ shows that numbers 1, 2, 4 and 5 have aldehyde groups (H—C =O) at the end of the chain and are hence aldohexoses. Members 3 and 6 have ketone (C =O) groups, at the second carbon atom, and are therefore 2-keto-hexoses, while numbers 7 and 8 having ketone groups at the third carbon atom are 3-keto-hexoses. Since each series of 8 sugars has a like number of the different types there are in all 16 aldohexoses, eight 2-keto- and eight 3-keto-hexoses.

It had long been known that if a solution of any optically active sugar, such as d-glucose, was alkalinized the solution gradually lost its optical activity. It was later shown by Lobry de Bruyn and van Ekenstein that a solution of d-glucose in very dilute alkali comes to contain a group of 4 hexoses in dynamic chemical equilibrium.[26] Nef[27] held that in such solutions there is an equilibrium of at least eight hexoses as above depicted. Any one of these sugars when placed in alkali reproduces the other seven, since the members of the series are reciprocally convertible one into another. The same holds good for the members of the d-galactose series and for the l-galactose and l-glucose series. But the reciprocal transformation of the members of one series, such as d-glucose, into a hexose of another series, such as d-galactose, occurs, if at all, only to a minute degree, because such transformation involves the breaking of the hexose chain into 2, 3 and 4 carbon fragments with subsequent recombinations, and when this occurs irreversible reactions are prone to intervene. The formation of lactic acid and the saccharines are representative of these irreversible reactions. (In the body, however, glucose may be converted into lactic acid in the muscles and elsewhere, whereas in diabetes lactic acid can be converted easily back into glucose; in diabetes galatose is convertible into glucose, etc., so that in the body the transformation of hexoses of different groups one into another offers no difficulty.)

In order to explain the effects of dilute alkali on hexoses just described, some conception of labile intermediate products is a logical necessity, for when levulose changes into glucose there is necessarily some intermediate phase. The nature of these phases has been the subject of study by many chemists, and this study involves always the question of *sugar dissociation.*

Sugars are weak acids. They form salts with metals, and Cohen[28] and later Michaelis and Rona[29] have determined by physico-chemical methods the ionization constants for glucose and other sugars. Sugars are also polyatomic alcohols, and either aldehydes or ketones. Sugar chemistry reverts to the chemistry of these three classes of compounds.

A. P. Mathews[30] and Michaelis have suggested that the effect of alkali on a sugar such as glucose is to increase enormously the concentration of the glucose anion, i. e., KOH leads to the formation of K-glucosate (see Fig. 3, p. 21), which, being the combination of a powerful base with a very weak acid, has a high electrolytic dissociation constant. These anions according to this view are subject to cleavages and intramolecular rearrangements. Nef also holds that the first effect of the alkali (e. g., KOH) is to form a salt, but his far more detailed conception of the subsequent changes which lead to reciprocal transformations of hexose sugars one into another, involves other principles which represent the outgrowth of his earlier work on the properties of simpler aldehydes and ketones.

These reciprocal transformations are dependent, according to Nef, upon the aldehydic or ketonic character of the sugar, whereas the oxidative phenomena and the saccharinic acid formation to be described presently, depend upon the alcohol groups. The principles involved can best be understood if we first consider the behavior of a simple aldehyde (acetaldehyde) and a simple ketone (acetone).

[26] Rec. trav. chim. de Pays Bas (14), 158 and 203; (15), 92; (16), 257; (19), 1 and 10.
[27] Liebig's Annalen, 1907 (357), 294; 1910 (376), 1.
[28] Zeit. f. physikal. Chem., 1901 (36), 69.
[29] Biochem. Zeit., 1912 (47), 447.
[30] Jour. Biol. Chem., 1909 (6), 1.

Acetaldehyde in the presence of water forms a hydrate (comparable to chloral hydrate).

$$CH_3-C=O + HOH \rightleftarrows \overset{H}{CH}-\overset{H}{C}\ OH$$
$$OH$$

This hydrate possesses ionizable hydrogen in its OH groups, and in the presence of a metallic hydroxide, MOH, can accordingly form a salt (comparable to an

alcoholate); thus: $CH_3-\overset{H}{C}-OH$,

$$OM$$

and this salt being highly dissociable *falls apart into MOH and a "methylene enol"* (in this case hydroxyethylidene):

$$CH_3-\overset{\overset{H}{|}}{C}-OH \rightleftarrows CH_3-C-OH + MOH$$
$$OM$$

(Herein lies the point of departure of Nef's view from the foregoing.) This methylene enol then rearranges to form the "olefine dienol" $CH_2 = CHOH$ (in this case vinyl alcohol). Ketones, on the other hand, form the olefine dienol directly without forming the methylene enol. In the case of KOH and acetone (dimethyl ketone) there is the same formation of the hydrate followed by salt formation and the loss of KOH, but the latter does not all come from one C atom as it does when split out of aldehydes, thus:

$$OH \qquad\qquad OK$$
$$CH_3-C-CH_3 + KOH \rightleftarrows CH_3-C-CH_3 + H_2O \rightleftarrows CH_3-C-CH_2$$
$$OH \qquad\qquad OH \qquad\qquad OH$$
(hydrate of acetone)

In a manner entirely analogous to what occurs in the simple aldehydes and ketones, the two aldohexoses, glucose and mannose, and the ketohexose levulose, can form one and the same enol molecule. And vice versa this enol molecule may open its double bond in two ways as shown below ((a), (b) and (c)) and the dissociated molecules.

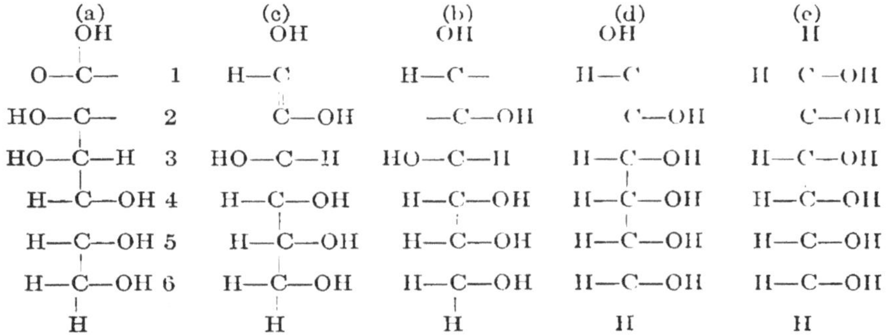

	(a)		(c)		(b)	(d)	(e)
	OH		OH		OH	OH	H
	O—C—	1	H—C		H—C—	H—C	H C—OH
	HO—C—	2	C—OH		—C—OH	C—OH	C—OH
	HO—C—H	3	HO—C—H		HO—C—H	H—C—OH	H—C—OH
	H—C—OH	4	H—C—OH		H—C—OH	H—C—OH	H—C—OH
	H—C—OH	5	H—C—OH		H—C—OH	H—C—OH	H—C—OH
	H—C—OH	6	H—C—OH		H—C—OH	H—C—OH	H—C—OH
	H		H		H	H	H

Enol molecule
(a, 1, 2 d-glucose olefine dienol)

(a) and (b) will be in dynamic equilibrium with the enol (c). Now if H and OH are again taken on by (a) and (b) this assumption of the elements of water can take place in three different ways, to regenerate d-levulose, d-mannose and d-glucose. Thus if in the case of (a), OH is added to carbon atom number one

$$H\text{—}\overset{\displaystyle OH}{\underset{\displaystyle |}{\overset{|}{C}}}\text{—}OH$$

this will form the group H—C—OH which represents a hydrated aldehyde group and will lose water to become CHO. Then H going to the second C atom completes the formula of d-mannose. In a similar way (b) can form d-glucose. But if the OH went to the second carbon atom this group would thereby become

a hydrated ketone similar to the hydrate of acetone and lose water to form $\overset{\displaystyle |}{\underset{\displaystyle |}{C}} = O$,

while H going to the end carbon atom would complete the formula of d-levulose. In a manner entirely analogous there is an enol molecule which is common to d-allose, d-lactose and d-pseudo fructose (see (d) above).

It will be noticed that each of these enols is in equilibrium with a 2-keto-hexose and two aldo-hexoses. Now these 2-keto-hexoses, d-fructose and d-pseudo fructose, in accordance with general ketone behavior, are capable of yielding another common enol (with the double bond between the second and third carbon atoms) as represented at (e) and this 2-3 enol (by a process like that just detailed for the 1–2 enols) can account for the formation of the two 3-keto-hexoses whose formulæ are given above. The same general principles hold for each of the series of hexoses (For further elaboration of the theory see Nef's original papers.) A similar use of enol molecules in this connection is made by Neuberg.

It remains now to point out that if to a simple aqueous solution of sugar, oxygen be supplied in the form of air or H_2O_2, no oxidation occurs. But if the solution be alkalinized then the sugar is readily burned. In the absence of oxygen and the presence of alkali somewhat stronger than that found most favorable for the reciprocal transformation above detailed, there occur certain irreversible reactions such as the formation of lactic acid and the so-called saccharines. When an alkaline sugar solution is treated with oxygen it yields CO_2, H_2O, and formic, glycollic, glyceric and certain trihydroxy-butyric and hexonic acids, depending on the sugar used. Without oxygen, or with too little oxygen, lactic acid and the saccharinic acids make their appearance (cf. the formation of lactic acid). The explanation of these phenomena rests in the conception that alkali increases the dissociation of sugar, and that the dissociated fragments burn or rearrange depending upon the conditions of the experiment.

In this connection, according to Nef, we are dealing with the alcohol groups of the sugars and may advantageously turn for a moment to the properties of methyl alcohol. This substance consists under ordinary circumstances of a great

Glucose (1)	Glucose ion (2) (—)	K-glucosate (3)	Methylene particle (4)
$\overset{\displaystyle O}{\underset{\displaystyle \|}{C}}$—H	$\overset{\displaystyle O}{\underset{\displaystyle \|}{C}}$—H	$\overset{\displaystyle O}{\underset{\displaystyle \|}{C}}$—H	$\overset{\displaystyle O}{\underset{\displaystyle \|}{C}}$—H
H—C—OH	H—C—O— —$\overset{+}{H}$	H—C—OK	—C—
OH—C—H	OH—C—H	OH—C—H	HO—C—H+KOH
H—C—OH	H—C—OH	H—C—OH	H—C—OH
H—C—OH	H—C—OH	H—C—OH	H—C—OH
H—C—OH	H—C—OH	H—C—OH	H—C—OH
H	H	H	H

preponderance of undissociated molecules in dynamic equilibrium, with a very minute quantity of dissociated methylene $CH_3OH \rightleftarrows CH_2 + H_2O$. The primary effect of alkali (KOH) is to form a salt, $CH_3—OK$ (or K-methylate), which being highly dissociable breaks down to give CH_2 and KOH. The proportion of free methylene is thereby enormously increased. What then befalls the methylene will depend on the amount of oxygen present and on the various other factors which enter into the conditions of the experiment. These general principles are applicable directly to the polyatomic alcohols—the hexoses and other sugars as shown on preceding page.

In the presence of sufficient oxygen the methylene particle takes on oxygen to form first an osone. In the absence of oxygen it undergoes intramolecular rearrangements, the details of which need not here be entered into. It is these which gives rise to the 6-carbon acids known as the saccharines or saccharinic acids.

GALACTOSE

A normal individual weighing 75 kilos may eat about 50 grams of galactose and show but a trace of melituria. More than this is likely to cause the presence of measurable amounts of galactose in the urine, the alimentary tolerance limit for this sugar being therefore about 0.6 to 0.8 grams per kilogram of body weight. We have no direct data concerning the time within which 50 grams of galactose are absorbed by a man of average weight. When given intravenously at uniform rates, unchanged galactose appears in the urine of dogs receiving slightly more than 0.1 per kilo per hour. The tolerance for galactose appears to be lessened in phosphorus poisoning and in many other conditions which cause apparent parenchymatous changes in the liver, so that after administration of 50 grams of galactose by mouth, as much as 10 to 12 grams may be excreted in the urine (Bauer). On the other hand, ligation of the common duct does not lessen the tolerance for galactose in rabbits (Reiss and Jehn, Hierose) so that the lowered tolerance following phosphorus administration appears to be independent of the disturbed biliary function. Infants suffering from gastro-enteritis may show alimentary lactosuria, and along with the lactose some of its constituent galactose may appear in the urine. The question thus naturally arises as to whether the lowered tolerance for galactose in phosphorus poisoning and other liver diseases may not be due to an increased permeability of the intestinal wall, or to changes elsewhere in the body besides the liver. Wörner found that galactose injected directly into the portal vein was handled by healthy and phosphorized rabbits in the same relative proportions as when given to these animals by mouth, thus apparently excluding the bowel as a contributer to the decreased tolerance. It is unlikely also that the kidneys in phosphorized animals were rendered abnormally permeable for galactose, since when the kidneys alone are phosphorized without affecting the liver, the excretion of galactose after administration by mouth or into a vein has been retarded rather than hastened. These principles have become incorporated in a clinical test for disease of the hepatic parenchyma. When galactose is administered to a fully diabetic animal it is capable of being converted quantitatively into glucose. Existing data indicate that galactose, like diose and glyceric aldehyde, is chiefly converted into glucose before further utilization, and that this process is carried out mainly in the liver and bowel wall. The literature of the subject is given below.[31]

LEVULOSE (FRUCTOSE)

The group of eight sugars formed by levulose in the presence of alkali includes glucose, and any member of this group will produce all the others. Then, in cases of glycosuria with alkaline urine (whether physiological or due to medication or to bacterial decomposition), levulose might be expected to occur along with glucose. May and Koenigsfeld have reported instances of this "urinogenous levulosuria." Magnus-Levy doubts the correctness of these observations.

Alimentary Levulosuria.—The tolerance of a normal body for levulose given per os is variable. Doses of 50 to 70 gm. in man cause as a rule no levulosuria, but more is likely to do so. Animals in which the liver parenchyma has been damaged by phosphorus are said to have a lower tolerance. In many other diseases of the liver the same holds true, and H. Strauss believed this fact could be made the basis of a clinical test for liver function. Naunyn, however, emphasizes the fact that in certain cases of cirrhosis of the liver with collateral anastomoses between the portal vein and vena cava, there is also a lessened tolerance for levulose given by mouth, owing to the fact that levulose then enters the general circulation without having entered the liver. As far back as 1871 Eichhorst showed that levulose introduced per rectum, *i. e.*, where it will presumably enter an hemorrhoidal vein after resorption, is more likely to cause alimentary levulosuria than when swallowed, because of the extra-hepatic anastomoses between the hemorrhoidal veins and the vena cava. As in the case of diose, glyceric aldehyde and galactose, intravenous injection of levulose produces levulosuria in dogs when the rate of injection is between 0.1 and 0.2 gram per kilo per hour. These facts support the belief that the liver plays the same important part in "assimilating" levulose as with other sugars.

Spontaneous Alimentary Levulosuria, i. e., the appearance of levulose in the urine from such small quantities of levulose as occur naturally in the food, has been demonstrated in eight cases. In five of these levulose appears to have been the only sugar present. These persons showed a decreased tolerance for ingested levulose and ceased passing the sugar when the diet was carbohydrate-free. The tendency of thought would be to look for the cause of such phenomena in a disturbed hepatic function.

[31] Bauer, Deut. med. Woch., 1908 (35), 1505; Reiss u. Jehn. Deut. Arch. f. klin. Med., 1912 (108), 187; Roubitscheck, Deut. Arch. f. klin. Med., 1912 (108), 225; Naunyn, "Beiträge zur Lehre von Ikterus, etc.," Reichert-Dubrissches Archiv. für Anatomie, 1869, p. 579; Schöpffer, Arch. f. exp. Path. u. Phamo., 1873 (1), 73.

It is interesting to note that of the above-mentioned five cases of pure levulosuria, two showed a lessened tolerance for glucose, and one symptoms of dispituitarism, one developed during the puerperium, and one had an endocarditis; *i. e.*, four out of five had evidence of derangements of the endocrinous glands. The literature has been reviewed and a case reported by Strouse and Friedman.[32]

Mixed Levulosuria, or the occurrence of levulose along with glucose in severe cases of diabetes, is said by some to be a common event. In view of the great frequency of combined liver and pancreatic changes found at autopsy in diabetic cases, and in view also of the frequent occurrence in diabetes of signs which point to disturbances of other glands with internal secretion besides the pancreas, this would harmonize well with the view just given.

Spontaneous or Idiopathic Levulosuria, having a character similar to chronic pentosuria, and running a steady course uninfluenced by diet, has been reported in one case by Rosin. In this instance the tolerance for glucose was also diminished.

POLYSACCHARIDES

Closely related to these meliturias are the forms in which the polysaccharides,—lactose, maltose and saccharose,—are the sugars concerned.

Lactosuria:—When 2 to 3 grams of lactose per kilogram of body weight are given in pure form by mouth to a healthy adult dog or man—*alimentary lactosuria* generally occurs. Another form of lactosuria is that seen in *lactating women*. In these cases the lactose gains access to the general circulation from milk stasis in the breast. Yet another form, the *lactosuria in children*, having gastro-intestinal diseases, has its origin in the lactose of the milk or artificial food. In these cases lactosuria may develop after the ingestion of lactose, in quantity and form[33] incapable of causing it in a healthy child. The tolerance for lactose is most strikingly decreased in so-called "*intoxication*" (Finkelstein) in which lactosuria may follow ingestion of 0.4–0.5 g. per kilo of body weight. (Grósz places the assimilation limit for healthy sucklings at 8.6 g. per kilo.) This might be explained in two or more ways. The lactase in the bowel might be deficient and permit unhydrolyzed sugar of milk to accumulate in abnormal concentration in the lower bowel, and then be absorbed unsplit; or, as seems more probable, the bowel wall—because of ulcers or simple inflammatory changes—might become abnormally permeable. The intravenous tolerance limit for lactose approaches zero. During prolonged intravenous injections of lactose into dogs at the rate of 2 gm.

[32] Arch. Int. Med., 1912 (9), 99.
[33] Pure aqueous solutions of sugar differ in the rate of absorption from those in which the sugar is incorporated in heterogeneous mixtures.

per kilo per hour, lactose was excreted at the rate of injection during the fourth hour and the following four hours.[34]

Leopold and Reuss reported that when 1 gram of lactose was injected subcutaneously into a dog or infant, exactly 1 gram reappeared in the urine; but that if the injections were made daily, the quantity excreted fell little by little and finally became zero. Helmholz and Woodyatt have repeated this experiment in dogs, and found that at first the gram injected might reappear in the urine as stated. Sometimes, however, the occurrence of an increase in the reducing power of the urine above the figure representing 1 gram of lactose was noted. This suggested a splitting of the lactose into glucose and galactose. Nor could they obtain more than a temporary disappearance of the sugar following subsequent injections, even when carried on for weeks—such as Leopold and Reusse reported. The point of chief interest in these experiments is that the apparently increased hydrolysis of lactose developing with successive doses resembles a reaction of immunity, with a substance of known chemical composition as the antigen. But it is possible that the successive injections simply result in a lessened excretion of the lactose by the kidneys. Abderhalden and his co-workers reported that the serum of animals similarly treated develops an increased power to split the disaccharide employed, as determined by means of the polariscope. These experiments were paralleled with cane sugar (saccharose) and with di-, tri-, and higher peptids. Other observers have failed to corroborate these findings.

Saccharosuria (cane sugar in the urine) occurs under conditions quite similar to those mentioned for lactose, except that there is no saccharosuria corresponding to the lactosuria of women.

Maltosuria has often been reported, but the chemical detection of this sugar is uncertain.

Other polysaccharoses, such as isomaltose, glycogen, etc., have been thought by some writers, to occur in the urine.

GLYCOSURIAS

Glucose is the sugar which enters into the normal glycogen and forms the bulk of the body sugar. Glycosurias are naturally the most important of the meliturias.

(1) *Alimentary glycosuria, e saccharo.* Not infrequently it is impossible to make a healthy man eat and retain sufficient glucose to cause glycosuria, and it would be hard to define an increased glucose tolerance. This statement is corroborated by the studies of Taylor and Hulton[35] on man. As indicated before, an increased supply of glucose to the body may increase the urinary sugar and as Benedict *et al.* have stated, there may be no sharp line of division between these

[34] Unpublished experiments by W. D. Sansum.
[35] Jour. Biol. Chem., 1916 (25), 173.

changes and a gross glycosuria. In dogs weighing 10 kilos the maximum rate of glucose absorption is apparently reached with doses of 50 grams and perhaps less. Larger doses do not further increase the rate of absorption. This rate may be 1.8 gram per kilo per hour. If with this rate of absorption the rate of utilization in the bowel wall and liver is 0.9 gram per kilo per hour, or less, glucose will enter the systemic blood at the rate of 0.9 gm. per kilo per hour, or more, and this will normally cause a gross glycosuria. The physiological state of the liver and the rate of sugar absorption are factors of importance in determining alimentary glycosuria. Glycosuria following the ingestion of starch alone—*alimentary glycosuria ex amylo* was said not to occur in healthy individuals, but the feeding of large quantities of starch increases the urinary sugar and if the tests used for its detection are of sufficient delicacy the increase is measurable. With a sufficiently small urinary volume ordinary tests may detect the extra sugar.

(2) Glycosurias which depend upon the discharge of sugar from stored glycogen. These may be due to the action of (a) nerves, (b) drugs, (c) the so-called internal secretions.

(a) Claude Bernard's piqûre, or puncture of the floor of the fourth ventricle between the points of origin of the eighth and tenth pairs of nerves, causes a glycosuria which ceases when the glycogen of the liver is reduced to a low percentage. Following this operation the blood is found to contain an excess of sugar (hyperglycemia) to which the glycosuria is immediately due. If the vagus nerve is cut stimulation of the central end has a similar effect, so that the vagus is said to carry the afferent impulse to the center in the *calamus scriptorius*. By severing different portions of the nervous system and stimulating the cut surfaces, the path of the efferent impulse has been traced from the glycogenic center through the cord to the upper thoracic spinal roots, by the *rami communicantes* to the inferior cervical and superior thoracic ganglion, thence via the splanchnic nerves to the liver. This center and nervous arc form probably an important link in the mechanism for regulating the quantity of sugar in the blood. Nervous glycosurias having the same mechanism as "la piqûre" occur in a great variety of conditions associated with insult to the nervous system, *c. g.*, commotio cerebri, brain tumor, tabes, meningitis, severe mental shock, etc. How a splanchnic impulse operates to cause increased hydrolysis of glycogen is unsettled. Glycogen hydrolyzes outside the body under the influence of acids, *i. e.*, of H ions or plus charges of electricity, and a nerve impulse might theoretically operate directly, or, as McLeod has suggested, through an increase of glycogenase in the liver; or as held by the von Noorden school, by causing an increased section of epinephrine—since piqûre glycosuria is said not to occur in animals deprived of the adrenals (Mayer, Kahn, Nishi) or after section of the left splanchnic nerve, which supplies both adrenals. (b) Similar phenomena occur in asphyxia (carbonic and lactic acid accumulation), and when acids are directly administered; also after the administration of certain drugs whose effects, including lactic and carbonic acid accumulation in the body fluids, closely parallel those of a deficient oxygen supply (phosphorus, carbon monoxide, chloroform, hydrazine, arsenic, etc.). Certain other drugs, such as curare, strychnia, etc., may interfere with respiratory movements and so cause glycosuria by secondary asphyxia; although other drugs, of which there are many, may operate to cause glycosuria in any of the ways by which glycosuria can be produced.[36]

(c) The ductless gland extracts which produce glycosuria include those of the adrenal, thyroid and hypophysis. Epinephrine has been discussed in another place, and the reasons are there developed for the belief that the glycosuria it causes is due to a mobilization of sugar from glycogen, which leads to hyperglycemia. Ringer[37] showed that when an animal is fully phlorhizinized the subcutaneous injection of epinephrine causes no additional output of sugar nor alteration of the G : N ratio, a fact which has been confirmed by Sansum and Woodyatt—thus proving that epinephrine has no power to intensify a diabetes which is already at the point which is called complete. Lusk[38] also showed by respiration experiments the correctness of this interpretation. Eppinger, Falta and Rudinger[39] stated that epinephrine intensifies pancreas diabetes, and used this observation in support of their idea that epinephrine, like thyroid extract, exerts in the liver a sugar-mobilizing and sugar-building effect, antagonistic to the action of the pancreas, which, according to the doctrine of the von Noorden school, checks the formation of sugar from glycogen and also from protein and fat. But in their work there has been no adequate proof that before giving the epinephrine the pancreas diabetes was as complete as a pancreas diabetes can be, or that the increased intensity of the diabetes was any greater than could have been explained by a discharge of sugar from glycogen. The power of pituitary extracts to produce glycosuria is likewise ascribable to their effects on glycogen.

PHLORHIZIN DIABETES[40]

Phlorhizin was obtained by alcoholic extraction of the bark and roots of apple, pear, plum and cherry trees by L. de Koninck in 1835. Its glucosidic character was established by Stas, who found that it

---

[36] The production of glycosuria by a given drug should not be confused with excretion of paired glycuronic acid compounds, such as occurs after the administration of many aldehydes, ketones, alcohols and phenols. The reducing power in these cases is not due to glucose but to its oxidation product, $COOH—(CHOH)_4—COH$.

[37] Jour. Exper. Med., 1910 (12), 105.

[38] Arch. Int. Med., 1914 (13), 673.

[39] Zeit. f. klin. Med., 1908 (66), 1; 1909 (67), 380.

[40] For a treatise of the whole subject of phlorhizin glycosuria, with bibliography, see the monograph by Lusk (Phlorhizin Glykosurie, Ergeb. der Physiol., 1912 (13), 315), free use of which has been made in the following.

could be split into glucose ("phlorose") and a substance (phloretin) which by acid hydrolysis yielded phloroglucin and an acid (phloretinic acid). It was not until 1886 that von Mering published his first experiments upon its physiologic action.

While phlorhizin causes glycosuria when taken by mouth, its greatest effect is obtained by subcutaneous injection. One gram of phlorhizin triturated in 5 to 15 c.c. of olive oil, or in 20 per cent. alcohol, and injected subcutaneously once every 24 hours, will maintain the maximum glycosuria which can be produced in a dog of 10 kilogrammes. Phlorhizin is mostly (80–90 per cent.) excreted in the urine. It is soluble in ether, optically active, and gives a garnet coloration with ferric chloride, so that it interferes with the polariscopic tests for β-hydroxybutyric acid in the urine, and masks the Gerhardt reaction for aceto-acetic acid.

Phlorhizin causes glycosuria in frogs and other cold-blooded animals, as well as in warm-blooded forms in general, including birds. That geese show glycosuria with phlorhizin (von Mering, Thiel) is important, because birds do not pass sugar in the urine when operations are performed upon them which do cause a definite excess of blood sugar (pancreatectomy, Minkowski). *Phlorhizin causes glycosuria in birds—hyperglycemia does not. Hence phlorhizin does not cause glycosuria by producing hyperglycemia.* In harmony with this syllogism are the data obtained by Minkowski, Levene, von Czylharz and Schlesinger, Lewandowsky, Lépine, Porcher, Junkersdorf, Erlandsen, Frank and Isaac—all of whom have found the blood sugar concentration in phlorhizinized animals low (0.065 per cent.; 0.072 per cent.; 0.012 per cent., etc.). Conflicting results have also been published, but the methods employed in these instances have not usually been beyond criticism (Pavy, Biedle and Kolisch). Even after ligation of the renal vessels or bilateral nephrectomy, no hyperglycemia has been demonstrated in phlorizinized animals, whereas if phlorhizin acted by liberating sugar from glycogen reserves in the liver and elsewhere, or from any source distant from the kidneys, hyperglycemia might be expected. In view of these facts von Mering himself interpreted the action of phlorhizin as a *kidney* diabetes.

Zuntz injected phlorhizin directly into one renal artery and collected the urine from each kidney separately. The kidney on the injected side almost at once secreted saccharine urine, and the other kidney secreted sugar only after the lapse of minutes. This experiment has been successfully repeated by others, and seems to prove that phlorhizin can cause glycosuria by acting directly on the kidneys. The many experiments which have been made to determine the relative blood sugar content of the renal artery and vein during phlorhizin glycosuria, add little to this subject.

The questions arise: *Are the kidney cells the only structures which are directly affected by phlorhizin?* and, *What is the exact nature of the phlorhizin effect?*

Levene collected the bile of phlorhizinized dogs and found that it exhibited reducing power after the phlorhizin injection, but not before. Ray, McDermott and Lusk failed to find similar properties in vomited bile from phlorhizinized dogs. Brauer repeated Levene's work—using a different method in that he cleared the bile with lead acetate prior to making the sugar tests, and then found no reducing substance. Woodyatt obtained results like Levene's but found later no reaction for sugar when the bile was cleared in the way Brauer recommended. Still, in the native state it yields characteristic crystals of an osazon, and ferments with yeast after, but not before phlorhizinization. Karl Grube perfused tortoise livers with salt solution containing phlorhizin and was able to cause more rapid deglycogenation than when the same salt solution minus phlorhizin was used in control experiments. Now Ray, McDermott and Lusk, in working with bile which had been in the alimentary tract, used material that had had time to lose its sugar by resorption. Brauer's clearing method may take out a trace of sugar even if present originally, and it must be said that there is some evidence favoring the idea that phlorhizin acts in the liver, although much less strongly than in the kidneys. Attempts have also been made to demonstrate a direct action of phlorhizin on the mammary (Cornevins) and sweat glands (Delmare). Cornevins' positive findings were not confirmed by Cremer and Porcher, whereas Delmare's work has not been repeated. But R. Pearce, working with a blood-sugar method, found an increase of sugar in the pancreatic juice, and Underhill has brought further evidence in support of a general action. M. H. Fischer had some nephrectomized frogs, which are able to live indefinitely in water because they excrete through the skin. With the writer some of these frogs were injected with phlorhizin into the dorsal lymph sac, and sugar was found next day in the water in which the frogs were, but not in the water occupied by control frogs. The possible origin of this sugar in the slime makes it desirable to repeat this crucial experiment. Although the view most commonly held is that phlorhizin acts specifically and exclusively on the kidney cells this has never been proved, and there is much to suggest a general cell effect exhibited most strikingly in the kidney.

Regarding the fundamental nature of the action of phlorhizin, nothing satisfactory has been evolved. Minkowski suggested that phloretin and sugar are split apart in the kidney epithelium, and that the sugar is then excreted while the phloretin is retained in the body. The retained phloretin then takes up a new molecule of glucose from the blood to reform phlorhizin,—which in the kidney is again split, etc. (vehicle theory). Zuntz has determined with a given minute dose of phlorhizin how much sugar can be eliminated in a given time by one kidney; then, figuring what weight of phlorhizin is in the kidney, and how much sugar comes out of the kidney, he reckons how frequently the synthesis and hydrolysis of phlorhizin would have to occur. He makes it 26 times per minute, which he deems too fast to be probable, but in view of the work which can be accomplished by traces of organic and inorganic carriers (catalyzers, enzymes), this criticism is not convincing.

Whatever the action of phlorhizin may prove ultimately to be, this action finds its chief or final expression in the cells of the kidney, and there leads to a disturbance of equilibrium, whereby the relative blood sugar and urinary sugar concentrations are altered in favor of the urine. The blood sugar must be in equilibrium with the sugar content of the various cells, and this with the sources (glycogen and protein) from which the sugar comes. The sugar of the entire body may be conceived of as a gas exerting its partial pressure in every cell and body fluid,— here more dense, there less so, depending upon local physico-chemical conditions, but nevertheless everywhere in communication. Phlorhizin acting in the kidneys, and regardless of a possible action elsewhere, creates a void into which the blood sugar flows, and into which secondarily, as into a vortex, sugar flows from all the sources of the body.

Metabolic Phenomena.—When a fasting dog is kept continuously under the maximum effects of phlorhizin, there is at first a very great glycosuria while the urinary nitrogen remains low. The ratio of the urinary glucose to the urinary nitrogen (G : N ratio) may be as high as 10 or 15 to 1, or higher. If such a dog is killed the liver is found to have a normal appearance and to contain glycogen. As time goes on the rate of glucose excretion falls and the nitrogen tends to increase, until after two or three days the G : N ratio is about 3.65 to 1, as shown by Lusk. Then for 12 to 24 hours it may remain constant. It sometimes happens that the ratio falls to 2.8 or some point between 3.65 and 2.8 before constancy is established. It then proceeds at this lower level instead of 3.65. If a dog is killed at about the time constancy is attained, or somewhat sooner, the liver may be found in a state of fatty infiltration with the glycogen low but not absent. In later stages the excessive fat in the liver again disappears. There is then first a rapid loss of glucose and a simultaneous melting away of glycogen. To compensate for the falling out of the carbohydrate from the metabolism there is an increased breakdown of protein and a rapid mobilization of fat, finding temporary expression in a fatty infiltration of the liver. But as the fat reserves run low the fat deposited in the liver is utilized. Coincident with the partial exhaustion of the carbohydrate reserves of the body and the increased fat and protein metabolism, acetoacetic and β-hydroxy butyric acids begin to appear in the urine, and since they are excreted partly in the form of the ammonium salts the urinary ammonia is also increased. These acids arise from lower fatty acids having an even number of carbon atoms in the chain, and from certain amino-acids, whenever the mixture of fatty acids and glucose actually metabolizing is too rich in the former in comparison with the latter.

However, such animals are not free of glycogen. If they are subjected to some treatment which has a strong glycogen mobilizing effect the glycosuria may be made to rise temporarily, just as though the dog had been given a dose of sugar. Thus, exposure to cold sufficient to cause shivering, the administration of epinephrine, or an ether or nitrous oxide narcosis, injection of acid (and various other toxic substances capable of producing tissue asphyxia and acidosis), all may increase the urinary glucose without increasing the nitrogen, and thus cause an increased G : N ratio. But if the exposure to cold is long and intense enough a time comes when it ceases to have this effect, and if epinephrine is given subcutaneously in the dosage of about 0.4 mg. per kg. of body weight once every three hours there is for a time a heavy increase of the glucose output, but this becomes less and less until after 6 or 8 doses the ratio becomes constant again, regardless of whether epinephrine is given or not. In such dogs neither cold nor narcosis nor other toxic effects will increase the output of glucose, and analyses of the liver and muscles reveal no glycogen. In a long series of dogs so treated Sansum and the writer have not encountered ratios above 3.2 to 1, and the 2.8 ratio recurs frequently.

Since the glycogen is gone and the dog is fasting, the sugar which continues to appear in the urine must have its origin in body fat or protein, or both.

Sugar from Fat.—If such a dog be given large quantities of fat in the diet no change occurs in the G : N ratio, nor any increase in the glycosuria, except such as may be ascribed to the glycerol of the fat (Lusk). On the other hand, propionic acid, according to Ringer, may cause a rise in the sugar excretion and a corresponding rise in the G : N ratio.[41] From this it is concluded that the fats of the food do not as a rule form sugar in the body, although sugar formation from at least one lower fatty acid is possible in view of Ringer's experiment.

Von Noorden and Falta and their associates have regarded sugar formation from fat as a regular normal phenomenon, because in diabetes melitus they believe that high ratios occur which make this view necessary.

Sugar from Protein.—If instead of fat, protein be given to the dog above mentioned, there occurs an absolute rise in the sugar of the urine and a corresponding rise in the nitrogen, *but the G : N ratio remains constant*. Following a meat feeding there may be fluctuations of the ratio during short periods, but this statement generally holds if the time of observation is 12 to 24 hours. These facts have led Lusk to the conclusion that when in a fasting, fully phlorhizinized animal, or one fed on meat and fat alone, a constant G : N ratio of 3.65 : 1 is seen; this means that the glucose and the nitrogen are coming from one and the same source, viz., protein. A gram of nitrogen corresponds

---

[41] The dogs used by Ringer were not free of glycogen and possibly the extra sugar did not arise from the acid given.

to 6.25 grams protein, and if for each 6.25 grams protein metabolized as indicated by the N in the urine, 3.65 grams glucose are excreted, then 58 per cent. of the protein metabolized is converted into glucose and so excreted. In like manner the 2.8 : 1 ratio would indicate a 45 per cent. conversion. A percentage above 58 has not been satisfactorily proved to occur. If to the fully phlorhizinized dog a definite quantity of glucose, galactose, starch or other assimilable form of carbohydrate is given, this may under favorable circumstances be excreted quantitatively in the urine as glucose, and the ratio of G : N will rise. The sugar which appears in the urine under such circumstances over and above that represented by N × G : N has been called "extra sugar" by Lusk.

If all the carbon contained in protein were converted into glucose, and all this excreted together with the nitrogen, the G : N ratio would be 8.25 : 1. A higher ratio than this would necessarily mean that sugar was coming from some source other than protein, or that all of the N was not appearing in the urine, some being retained in the body. If the liver were free from glycogen and no carbohydrate were eaten, such a high ratio would speak in favor of sugar formation from fat. Falta reports having seen cases of diabetes in which this occurred, but in human cases it is difficult to be sure of the absence of glycogen and food carbohydrate; moreover, such high ratios, unless too long continued, might imply retention of nitrogen.

Sugar from other Substances.—A large number of other substances when administered to phlorhizinized dogs are capable of increasing the output of sugar. Of importance in this connection are certain of the amino acids, viz; glycine, alanine, aspartic and glutamic acids, and arginine. Others, such as leucine, tyrosine and phenyl alanine do not form sugar in the body but increase the output of the acetone substances. The sugar-forming power of protein is doubtless due to its content of the former group of amino acids.[42] Lactic acid and glycerol are also among the sugar formers.

The chief interest in phlorhizin diabetes lies in the opportunities it offers of studying the character of the intermediate metabolism minus that of sugar, and so of studying sugar metabolism. Another interest might be found were the physiologic effects of this glucoside in animals interpreted with relationship to its normal rôle in plant physiology.

PANCREAS, DIABETES AND DIABETES MELITUS

Historical.—In 1788 Cawley reported atrophy and stone of the pancreas in a case of diabetes. The coincidence of diabetic symptoms and lesions of the pancreas was further studied by Bright, Lloyd and Elliotson (1833). It was Bouchardat[43] who first definitely for-

[42] See Dakin, Jour. Biol. Chem., 1913 (14), 155.
[43] "De la Glycosurie, etc.," II edit., Paris, 1883. Cited from Naunyn.

mulated the belief that pancreatic disease was the cause of diabetes melitus, but his views were uncongenial to the clinicians of his time and it remained for von Mering and Minkowski[44] (1889) to prove that *complete* pancreatectomy leads invariably to the development of a severe diabetes. This applies not only to dogs but to cats, rabbits, pigs (Minkowski), tortoises,[45] frogs;[45] eels,[46] and other animals.

Effects of Pancreas Extirpation.—The glycosuria begins soon after the operation and increases in intensity. It persists in spite of a non-carbohydrate diet long after the glycogen reservoirs in the liver and muscles have become greatly impoverished (to 0.1–0.2 per cent. in the liver), but like the human disease, it usually ceases during a fast or may disappear just before death.[47] The glycosuria may be accompanied by an excretion of the acetone bodies,—acetone, aceto-acetic and β-hydroxybutyric acids. In fact, the metabolic changes secondary to this operation closely parallel those found in the human disease, with certain differences which perhaps are ascribable to species or to the fact that in the experimental diabetes digestion is altered by absence of the pancreatic juice, etc. Although Minkowski's work was assailed from many quarters, the following points have become firmly established by frequent repetition. (1) *Complete* removal of the pancreas causes a true diabetes (as above); (2) Ligation or oblitera-tion of the duct (or ducts) of Wirsung, no matter how scrupulously carried out, has no such effect; (3) If about one-fifth of the pancreas with its arterial supply be separated from the rest of the gland, this fifth may be implanted extraperitoneally at a distance from the origi-nal site. No diabetes results from this operation, or at most only a transient glycosuria. Now if the main body of the pancreas be fully extirpated with ducts, nerves and bloodvessels, still only a transient glycosuria or none at all develops. At this stage all possible damage to nerves and external secretion has been inflicted and proved incapable of causing diabetes. (4) In the course of weeks the graft atrophies (Sandmeyer's experiment), and then a persistent glycosuria supervenes; or the encapsulated fragment which has been placed in an accessible place under the skin may be extirpated, in which case within a few hours a severe diabetes ensues. (5) There is no other organ in the body extirpation of which has any similar effect, nor (except for phlor-hizinization), is there any known means of experimentally producing a *true* diabetes without injury to the pancreas. (6) No toxic sub-stance derived from the body of diabetic individuals, man or animal, has been found which is capable of causing diabetes in a second animal. *These facts lead to the conclusion (reached by Minkowski) that pancreatic*

[44] Arch. für exp. Path. u. Pharm., 1889 (26), 371; 1893 (31), 85.
[45] Aldehoff, G. Zeit. f. Biol., 1891–2 (28), 293; Velich, Wien. Med. Zeitung. 1895 (40), 502; Marcuse W., Zeit. f. klin. Med., 1894 (26), 225.
[46] Capparelli, Biol. Zentralbl., 1893 (13), 495.
[47] This statement, based on experimental work, appears in the 2d (1914) edition of this book.

tissue provides "a something," separate from the pancreatic juice, (internal secretion of the pancreas), the lack of which is responsible for the symptoms of diabetes.

Islet Theory: Morphologically the pancreas may be regarded as stroma, ducts, acini and islands of Langerhans. It has been proposed, notably by Opie[48] in this country, that the antidiabetic internal secretion of the pancreas is elaborated by islet cells. This view finds support in the following facts: (1) In diabetes melitus the islets are frequently found in a state of hydropic or hyaline degeneration, while the remaining organ may appear normal.[49] (2) Cancer, pancreatitis and the experimental injection of caustics into the ducts very frequently spare the islets and fail to cause diabetes. (3) It is claimed that in pancreatic grafts, such as described above, islet cells predominate, while acinus cells and ducts disappear.

Grafts of this kind consist of much connective tissue, generally more or less infiltrated with round cells, and collections of epithelium. Concerning the latter, remains of ducts and acini are usually present in some proportion, and there are also epithelial cell masses regarded as islets on morphological grounds. Differences of opinion still exist as to the relative proportion of the different epithelial elements. Lombroso,[50] whose exhaustive monograph reviews the literature to 1910, concludes that the internal function of the pancreas is not monopolized by islet cells. Bensley[51] developed intra-vital staining methods which, for the first time, made possible the sure differentiation of islet cells from duct or acinus epithelium without reference to form or arrangement, and appears to have proved that these cells are regenerated from duct epithelium. He also showed the great normal variations in size and number of islets in different individuals (guinea-pigs). His study explains certain of the discrepancies which occur in the literature, especially in the estimation of the quantity of islet tissue in pancreatic rests, grafts, etc. Allen[52] has reported that when proper sized fragments of pancreas, in connection with the ducts, are left *in situ,* and the remainder of the gland is removed, the subsequent development of severe diabetes may be coincident with disappearance of islet tissue while acinus cells and ducts are unaffected. This operation, according to Allen, is eminently satisfactory for producing experimental diabetes without infection and without loss of the external secretions.

The Nature of the Internal Secretion of the Pancreas.—

Direct evidence on this subject is lacking. Such a secretion has never been isolated. Even the experiments made with the feeding of fresh pancreas and with extracts of the gland have led to no solid advance. Reports of improvements following the administration of any substance in diabetes are worthless unless accompanied by proof of the constancy of the diet, of the amount of work perfomed, and of other factors which are known to influence the course of diabetes. Some glimmer of success appeared to have attended the intravenous use of an extract made by Zuelzer,[53] although deleterious by effects occured, and the apparent improvement could have been due wholly to retention. According to Hedon and Drennan, amelioration of the severity of pancreas diabetes as evidenced by a diminution of glycosuria has followed the transfusion of blood from a healthy animal or the injection of fresh defibrinated blood, and Forschbach, working with a parabiosis (or

---

[48] "Diseases of the Pancreas," Lippincott & Co., 1910.
[49] See Homans. Jour. Med. Res., 1914 (30), 49.
[50] Ergeb. der Physiol., 1910 (10), 1.
[51] Am. Jour. of Anat., 1911 (12), 297.
[52] Glycosuria and Diabetes, Boston, 1913.
[53] Zeit. f. exp. Path., 1908-9 (5), 307.

two animals so joined by operative means that permanent inter-
mingling of their blood occurs) performed pancreatectomy in one of
the animals without producing diabetes in either; from which it might
seem that the internal secretion was carried by the blood. In harmony
with these results were the investigations of Knowlton and Starling,[54]
who found that an isolated beating heart taken from a depancreatized
animal (cat) was capable of removing less sugar from the blood used
as a perfusion medium than are hearts of normal animals, but these
latter experiments have not been confirmed and are subject to criticism.
In most of the transfusion experiments reported the standardization
of the metabolism prior to giving the fresh blood has not been such
as to make the results certain. Carlson and Drennan found that
pancreatectomy in a pregnant animal near term might fail to cause
diabetes, but that diabetes developed at once following delivery. This
could be explained on the basis that an internal secretion passed from
fetus to mother, or that sugar failing of utilization in the mother was
utilized by the fetuses. Kramer and Murlin failed to note any increase
of the respiratory quotient in depancreatized dogs following blood
transfusion, and Sansum and Woodyatt saw no improvement following
transfusion in a human case.[55] Recently Kleiner[55a] has reported a diminution of the total blood sugar in dogs following infusion of pancreas emulsion, and this work revives the interest in a problem of great
importance.

Symptoms.—In the absence of extracts which contain the active
principle in measurable quantity, the attention must be turned to a
more detailed study of the effects which follow its lack. Now it is
well known that in diabetes melitus there are all grades of severity.
*What follows has reference only to the severest cases—those which may
be called "complete diabetes."* In the severest cases of diabetes, glycosuria persists even when the individual subsists on a fat-protein
diet, and after the glycogen in the body has been reduced to a mere trace.
When this stage has been reached, and provided no carbohydrate food
is eaten, it is found that the total glucose in the urine bears from day
to day a constant ratio to the total nitrogen in the urine as already
described for phlorhizin diabetes. This "G : N ratio" is not always
the same. In depancreatized dogs nourished solely on fat and protein, it is often found, as Minkowski first recognized, at 2.8 : 1, and
in human diabetes the same value for G : N is sometimes seen. But,
as in phlorhizinized dogs, higher ratios may occur in the human disease.

If to such a case of diabetes as this we give by mouth 40 grams of
glucose there may appear in the urine close to 40 grams of extra sugar.
Plainly such extra sugar has escaped utilization of any kind. It cannot have been oxidized or converted into fat, since these processes are

[54] Jour. of Physiol., 1913 (45), 146.
[55] Jour. Amer. Med. Assoc., 1914 (62), 996 for lit. references.
[55a] Jour. Biol. Chem., 1919 (40), 153.

irreversible, although it might have existed momentarily in the body as glycogen or other isomer of glucose. What phase in the utilization of this glucose is primarily disturbed is another question. To say that 40 grams of ingested glucose causes the appearance of 40 grams of extra sugar in the urine does not prove that the diabetic body is inherently incapable of using any sugar or every carbohydrate. It might still be capable of using a two, three, or four carbon atom sugar, some other member of the group of 32 hexoses, or, as some have it (von Noorden), sugar which has first been built up into glycogen, etc., provided these substances could be kept from undergoing transformations into the non-utilizable glucose. As a rule, however, when other sugars are fed to complete diabetics, they are transformed into glucose and appear as such in the urine. This phenomenon has much of significance for the general theory of sugar metabolism and is an indication of the nature of the primary disturbance in diabetes, as will now be shown.

Theory of Diabetes.—What sort of a chemical process is involved when levulose, for example, is converted in the body into glucose? As already stated in the chemical introduction, the reciprocal transformations of hexoses one into another in the alkaline solution *in vitro* depend upon a preliminary ionization of the sugars followed by salt formation, the salts then undergoing dissociation which, according to Mathews and Michaelis, is still purely electrolytic with rearrangements of the anion; but which, according to Nef, is a non-electrolytic dissociation of the type which he calls methylene dissociation. *Some form of dissociation must be a prelude also to these transformations in the body.* This view is logically just as necessary as it has been found to be for the organic chemist, and, it may be added, that for the oxidation of sugars as well as for their polymerization a preliminary dissociation is essential. Now since the diabetic body can transpose other sugars into glucose, it must be able at least to dissociate the former sugars deeply enough for this process. These transpositions are accomplished chiefly in the portal system and perhaps in other places too, but certainly levulose and many other substances can be made in the liver into glycogen, whose hydrolysis then yields glucose.

The degree or character of the dissociation necessary for reciprocal transformations differs from that which is a necessary prelude to destructive reactions such as oxidation. A very weak alkali suffices *in vitro* for the former, while for the latter it is necessary to use a somewhat stronger alkali concentration.[56] The diabetic body therefore behaves as though it were weakened with respect to the alkali concentrations which it can bring to bear on sugars.

As far back as 1871, Schultzen suggested that the error in diabetes might be found in the disability of the body to dissociate the glucose

[56] See Woodyatt, Jour. Biol. Chem., 1915 (20), 129.

molecule into two 3-carbon substances.[57]   Baumgarten[58] also supported the idea of a "fermentative splitting" which precedes oxida-
dation, because he found a greater percentage utilization of certain
substances closely allied to glucose (such as gluconic acid, saccharic
acid, mucic acid, etc.), than of glucose itself; whereas gluconic acid
and glucose, for example, differ only in that the sugar has an aldehyde
group where the acid has carboxyl.   Similar general ideas have been
expressed from time to time by others.   The present writer has urged
in place of the vaguer terms, the adoption of chemical "dissociation"
in the sense which is rapidly finding favor in the field of pure organic
chemistry, notably for the explanation of the behavior of aldehydes,
ketones and alcohols.[59]   There can be no doubt that the dissociation
of glucose in the body is a normal occurrence.   This is directly and
conclusively shown whenever muscles make lactic acid ($C_3H_6O_3$)
out of glucose ($C_6H_{12}O_6$), since in this process no chemical phenomenon
is involved save cleavage of the hexose and intramolecular rearrangement.   The polymerization of sugar into glycogen might be similarly
interpreted.   Direct proof of a failure of glucose dissociation in diabetes has not yet been brought, although its absence would explain
all the metabolic phenomena more directly and simply than any other
single physiologic error which has been hypothecated.   It is, moreover,
a tangible chemical conception, whereas to say that the body loses its
power to oxidize sugar or to "fix" it as glycogen is merely to name
effects in physiologic terms.   (Cf. Naunyn's diszoamylie.)

It might be assumed that all sugars upon entering certain phases of
the cells (phases especially well represented in liver cells), meet conditions which are equivalent to those met in a weakly alkaline solution,
favoring reciprocal transformations, and, as A. P. Mathews points
out, polymerization; but not conditions conducive to the deeper destructive reactions.   That is, especially in the liver, there may be *the
equivalent* of dilute alkali for all sugars.   Glucose, being the least
dissociable, represents the form into which all other sugars tend to
accumulate.   But in the normal body a special glucolytic enzyme
(alkali carrier or intensifier?) destroys glucose selectively.   All
other sugars must become glucose before destruction.   In diabetes
the enzyme necessary for the deep dissociation of glucose is lacking or
inactive.   The recent studies of Murlin, Kramer, Sweet and Karver,
show that alkali administration (Na_2CO_3) may increase glucose utilization, especially when introduced into the duodenum where it may
neutralize acid entering the bowel from the stomach and thus spare
the liver and pancreas from the effects of absorbed acid.   Underhill's
experiments[60] with bicarbonate feeding in diabetes confirm these
observations.

[57] Glyceric aldehyde and glycerol, according to Schultzen.
[58] Zeit. f. exp. Path. u. Pharm., 1905 (2), 53.
[59] Cf. Nef, *loc. cit.*, and Stieglitz, Qualitative Chemical Analysis, New York,
1912, 1, pp. 289-292.
[60] Jour. Amer. Med. Assoc., 1917 (68), 497.

One difference between diabetes melitus and phlorhizin diabetes is that in the former the glycosuria is due to hyperglycemia, the sugar loss being an overflow like water escaping from an overfilled tank; whereas in phlorhizin poisoning there is apparently an hypoglycemia —the loss resulting in this case, to carry out the simile, from a leak in the bottom of the tank which keeps the water at a lower level. But the results are the same. Moreover, if in diabetes melitus we could measure only the chemically active or dissociated blood sugar, it is possible we should again find for this kind of sugar an hypoglycemia comparable to that of phlorhizin diabetes. This conception coincides with the doctrine that in diabetes melitus there is *a primary underconsumption of sugar* as opposed to the idea of *a primary overproduction*.

Overproduction vs. Underconsumption. The chief exponents of overproduction have been the followers of Kraus, and of von Noorden in whose books "Die Zuckerkrankheit" and "New Aspects of Diabetes" will be found the arguments favoring this idea. A translation of Minkowski's criticism of the latter has been made by Lusk.[61] In this place it may be briefly recalled that the chief arguments favoring underconsumption in addition to what has already been said are the followng: (1) The respiratory quotient in diabetes is frequently found to be low, and when carbohydrate food is administered this quotient rises but little, whereas in health the administration of carbohydrate food results in a greater rise.[62] (2) The acetone bodies (acetone, aceto-acetic acid and beta-hydroxybutyric acid) appear in the urine when for any reason the quantity of sugar burning in the body falls below a certain minimum, as in starvation, or when a person accustomed to a mixed diet is suddenly switched to a full calory diet composed exclusively of fat, or of fat and carbohydrates, with the carbohydrate calories representing less than 10 per cent. and the fat calories more than 90 per cent. of the total (Zeller[63]). In these cases the restoration of sugar to the diet abruptly and permanently stops the output of acetone bodies. But in severe diabetes the excretion of acetone bodies is less affected by the giving of sugar. Following single large doses there may indeed be a temporary fall in the acidosis, but this is never permanently attainable. One interpretation made of these facts is as follows. In diabetes there is an acetone body output because sugar, although brought to the cells, fails to take part in certain chemical reactions which normally occur between sugars and certain of the breakdown products of butyric acid and which normally prevent the diabetic acidosis. Hence the bringing of more sugar has little effect. And here again one might suggest that

[61] Medical Record, Feb. 1, 1913.
[62] For the literature of respiration studies in diabetes see Joslin, Treatment of Diabetes Melitus, New York, 1916; Du Bois, Harvey Society Lectures, 1916; and "Studies from the Department of Physiology of Cornell University, 1915 *et seq.*; published in the Archives of Internal Medicine and reprinted as Bulletins.
[63] Arch. f. Physiol., 1914, p. 213.

in diabetes glucose fails to interact with the products mentioned because the glucose is not sufficiently dissociated. Another interpretation has been to the effect that the sugar simply causes a compensatory decrease of the fat metabolism, *i. e.*, spare fat, thereby decreasing the formation of the acidosis bodies. The mechanism of the process is in any case still a theme for research.

There are numerous other theories of diabetes, for the presentation of which the reader is referred to the larger works. Lépine has long stood for the view that the pancreas secretes a glycolytic oxidizing ferment. Naunyn's theory pays particular regard to the ability of the body to "fix" glycogen, while glycogen formation is held to be a necessary preliminary step in the utilization of sugar. The failure to fix glycogen he calls *"diszoamylie,"* and the other metabolic disturbances he regards as sequences. The complex development of this same general idea by von Noorden, with the added element of primary sugar overproduction, has already been alluded to. Pavy saw in the diabetic a failure to *assimilate sugar;* that is, a failure of the body to incorporate sugar in a colloidal combination which would at once permit of its transportation to the points of utilization, and prevent its premature excretion. The assimilation he held occurred in the villi of the intestines, and the lymphocytes he regarded as the morphologic elements which carry the sugar. Cohnheim's theory that the muscle formed glycolytic enzymes, for which the pancreas supplies an essential activator, is without any substantial experimental support at the present writing. Allen proposed that the pancreas supplies an "amboceptor" which is essential for the proper colloidal blood sugar combination. For a thorough discussion of the basal metabolism in diabetes melitus and its variations during changes of diet, etc., the reader is referred to the studies of Benedict, Lusk, DuBois, Allen and others, references to which are given in Allen's monograph.

Bronzed diabetes, the name given to that form of hemochromatosis in which, along with the hepatic cirrhosis, there is an associated fibrosis of the pancreas, and, as a result of this, the symptoms of pancreatic diabetes, will be found discussed under the heading "hemochromatosis," chapter xviii.

Diabetic coma is discussed under "acid intoxication," chapter xx.

Lipemia, which is observed frequently and most severely in diabetes, is discussed in chapter xvi.

Glycogen in pathological processes is discussed in chapter xvi.

INDEX

Blood, bactericidal power of, 314
coagulation of, 146, 201, 299, 493
composition of, **290–293**
effect of carbon dioxide on, 314
laking of, 211
menstrual, 321
pigments, 273, **481–488**
plasma, 291
platelets, 300
pressure, 341
reaction of, 292. See also *Acidosis*.
regeneration of, 302
sugar in, **649–652**
viscosity of, **293**, 315
Bone-marrow, 85, 185
Bordet-Gengou reaction, 229
Bothriocephalus, 307
anemia, 133
Botulinus toxin, 122
β-oxybutyric acid, **558–563**, 569
Brilliant green, 215
Bromin, 600, 601
Bronchiectasis, 273
fetal, 363
Bronchitis, 273
Bronzed diabetes, 488. See also *Hemochromatosis*.
Brown atrophy, 396, 478, 487
Bruck's reaction, 232
Bufagin, 155
Bufo agua, 155
Bufonin, 154
Bufotalin, 154
Burns, 362, 377
poisons of, **571–573**
Buthus, 150
Butter cysts, 522
Butyrase, 71, 72
Butyric acid, 134, 559, 565, 592

CACHEXIA, 60, 65, 73, 273, 302, 356, 567, 568
in cancer, **510–513**
Cadaverine, 118, 589, 591
Caffeine, 241, 627, 635
Calcification, 385, **439–447**
iron in, **440**
metastatic, **442**, 525
phosphoric acid in, 446
Calcium, 189, 197, 244, 256, 292, 299, 322, 360, 364, 381, 387, 394, 492, 504, 512, 545, 613
carbonate calculi, 462
gout, 443
in blood clotting, 318
metabolism. See *Osteomalacia* and *Rickets*.
oxalate, 454, 466
calculi, **461**
soaps, 445, 518
Clacospherites, 441
Calculus, Bezoar, 467
biliary, **453–458**

Calculus, calcium carbonate, 462
oxalate, **461**
cholesterol, 463
cystine, **463**
fibrin, 463
fusible, 462
indigo, 463
lung, 468
pancreatic, **465**
phosphate, **462**
salivary, **466**
urate, **461**
uric acid, **460**
urinary, **459–464**
urostealith, 463
xanthine, **463**
Cammidge reaction, 390
Cancer, 60, 65, 73, 89, 99, 190, 227, 356, 441, 525, 577
cachexia in, **510–513**
colloid, 523
gastric, 57
hemolysis in, **509**
immunity reactions in, **514–516**
metabolism in, 510
sulphur metabolism in, 511
thyroid, 508
Cantharidin, 164
Capillaries, permeability of, 333
walls, permeability of, **342**
Carbamate ammonium, 533
Carbohydrate metabolism, **642–678**
Carbohydrates, 23
bacterial, 105
fermentation of, 592
Carbolic acid, 367
gangrene, 380
Carbon dioxide, 208
effect on blood, 314
Carcinoma. See *Cancer*.
Cardiac disease, 65
edema, 348
Carotid gland, 625
Carotin, 479
Carotinemia, 479
Caseation, 94, **384–386**
Casein, 160, 161, 166, 169, 192, 197, 280, 423
Castration granulomas, 278, 519
Catalase, 54, 61, **63–65**, 68, 71, 112, 272, 283, 506, 554, 603
Catalysis, 51
Cataphoresis, 35
Cataract, 375
Cell, chemistry and physics of, **17–47**
chromophile, 480
death, physico-chemical changes, 370
division, 277
giant, 69
inorganic substances of, 24
life, 30
lymphoid, 71
mast, 42, 45, 310
mechanical injury of, 381

44

Polyneuritis gallinarum, 281
Polypeptid, 19, 125, 160, 192, 511, 57
Polyphenoloxidases, 66
Porges-Hermann-Perutz reaction, 233
Porphyrins, **484**
Portuguese-man-o'-war, 158
Postmortem changes, 65
  autolysis in, **96–97**
  hemolysis, 219
Potassium, 24, 306, 336, 360, 504, 532, 535, 542
  chlorate, 226, 325
  salts, 278
Potato, 222
Potocytosis, 333
P-oxyphenyl-ethylamine, 308
P-oxyphenyl-lactic acid, 551
Precipitation of colloids, 36
Precipitinogen, 184
Precipitins, 150, **184–188**, 202, 358
Precipitinoid, 186
Precocity, sexual, 615
Pregnancy, 60, 71, 80, 204, 276, 457
  acetonuria in, 568
  pernicious vomiting of, **546**
  toxemias of, **540–547**
Preputial concretions, 467
Pressor bases, **584–586**
Proliferation, **276–280**
Propionic acid, 579
Prostatic concretions, 457
Protamin, 20, 52, 126, 160, 161, 236, 278, 390
Proteases, 75–100, 113, 200, 292
Proteic acid, 307
Protein, 94
  Bence-Jones, **525–529**
  blood, 295
  chemistry of, **19–22**
  compound, 20
  egg, 166
  insoluble, 22
  iodized, 601
  lens, 166
  loss in sputum, 273
  of effusions, **356**
  of sputum, 273
  of tumors, **499–501**
  poisonous bacterial, **125–126**
  pyogenic, 268
  racemized, 160, 165
  serum, 176, 315
  simple, 20
  sugar from, 670
Proteolysis, 165, 198, 201, 204, 217
Proteolytic enzymes, **75–100**, 111, 129
  of leucocytes, **89–90**
Proteoses, 88, 115, 135, 143, 160, 192, 201, 218, 274, 310, 319, 320, 327, 357, 391, 427, 591, 551, **575–578**, 596
Prothrombin, 295, 298, 300, 303, 316
Protoplasm, 18, 21, 35
  structure of, **37–39**
Protoplasmic poison, 380

Protozoa, chemistry of, **129–131**
Pseudochylous effusions, 364
Pseudo-globulin, 176
Pseudoleukemia, 312
Pseudomelanosis, **485**
Pseudomucin, 430, 431
Pseudo-myxoma peritonei, 521
Ptomaïns, **116–120**, 123, 391, 509
Puerperal eclampsia, 72, 96
  sepsis, 486
Pulmonary gangrene, 273
Purine, 91, 369, 385, 499, **626–641**
  bases, 79, 94, 310
  bodies, 272
  enzymes, **502**
  metabolism, enzymes of, **630–633**
  of tumors, **502**
Purpura hemorrhagica, 234, 298, 317
  neonatorum, 322
Purpuric diseases, 298
Pus, 66, 68, 72, 74, 88, 94, 97, **267–273**
  composition of, **269–273**
Putrefaction, 111, 117, 177, 185, 209, 391, 578, 581, 591
Putrescine, 118, 589, 591
Pycnosis, 92, 328, 369
Pyin, 271, 426
Pyocyanase, 115
Pyocyaneus, 214
Pyocyanolysin, 219
Pyogenic proteins, 268
Pyopneumothorax, 365
Pyridine, 241, 244, 282, 498, 528
Pyrimidine, 282, 627
Pyrocatechin, 583, 588, 619

Quillaja, 221
Quillajic acid, 143
Quinine, 226, 251, 256, 393

Racemized protein, 160, 165
Radium, 81, 143, 99, 378, 311, 506
Ragweed, 203
Rana esculenta, 155
Rays, serum of, 158
Reaction of blood, 292. See also *Acidosis.*
  of degeneration, 395
Receptors, 124, 172, 215
Reducing enzymes, 67
Reduction as defense mechanism, 241
Regeneration, **276–280**
  of blood, 302
Renal edema, 349
Rennin, 55, 57, 61, 110, 113, 272, 292, 507
Repair, **276–280**
Resistance to hemolysis, 227
Resonance theory, 170
Retention of chlorides, 350
Rhamnose, 656
Rhinoliths, 468
Rhumbler's artificial amebæ, 262

Rhus diversiloba, 141
 toxicodendron, 111, 161
Ricin, 69, 72, 161, **138 140**, 221, 325
Ricinus communis, 138
Rickets, **449–452**
 as deficiency disease, 288
Rigor mortis, **392**
Robin, 138
Robinia pseudoacacia, 138
Roentgen rays, 185. See also *X-rays*.
Rovida's hyalin substance, 271
Russell's viper, 148

SACCHAROSURIA, 664
Salamanders, 155
Salicylic aldehyde, 106
Salivary calculi, **466**
Salmon, 278, 396
Salts, ammonium, 212
 bile, 214, 319, 322, 389, 453, **492–498**
Samandarin, 155
Sand, intestinal, 467
Saponin, 143, 211, 212, **221–223**, 227, 239
Saponins, hemolysis by, **221–223**
Sapotoxin, 222
Sapremia, 392
Sarcocystin, 130
Sarcolactic acid, 542, 551, **564**, 569
Sarcoma, 69, 99, 504, 506, 525, 583
Sarcosporidia, 128, 130
Sclerema neonatorum, 415
Sclerosis, multiple, 418.
Sclerostoma, 136
 equinum, 128
Scolopendra heros, 153
Scorpion poison, **150**
Scorpæna scorpha, 156
Scurvy, **286**, 298
Sea-snake, 148
Sea-urchin eggs, 64
Secondary anemia, **301–303**
Selenium, 81, 109, 241
Semipermeable membranes, 27
Sepsis, puerperal, 486
Septicemia, 96, 219, 547
Serosamucin, 357
Serous atrophy of fat, 342, 395
Serozyme, 316
Serum albumin, 20
 anthracidal, 209
 antiplatelet, 234, 300
 antithyroid, 612
 eel, 158, 224
 endotheliolytic, 235
 foreign, toxicity of, 196
 Lamprey, 158
 leucocytolytic, 234
 lymphatolytic, 235
 myelotoxic, 235
 nephrolytic, 235
 neurolytic, 235
 proteins, 176, 315
 snake, 149

Serum, thymotoxic, 236
 thyrolytic, 235
Sexual precocity, 615
Shock, 65, 87, 200, 566
 electric, 379
Sialolithiasis, 466
Side-chain theory, 124
Siderosis, 169
Silicates, 375, 111, 169
Silicic acid, 208, 218
Silver, 80
Sistrurus, 142
Skatole, 242, 198, 500, 569, 580, 583
 acetic acid, 579
Skatoxyl, 242, 580
Skepto-phylaxis, 197
Snake serum, 149
 venoms, **141 150**, 218
Soap-bark, 221
Soaps, 94, 97, 162, 213, 217, 223, 226, 274, 275, 386, 387, 390, 403, 413, 467
 calcium, 364, 415, 518
 cysts, 522
Soapstone, 169
Soda dropsy, 351
Solanaceæ, 218
Solanidin, 222
Solanin, 222
Specificity of immune reactions, **165–172**
Spermatocele fluid, **359**
Spermatotoxin, 236
Spermatozoa, 40, 162, 167, 216, 218, 249, 278
Spermin, 272, 312
Spheroides testudineus, 157
Spiders, 221
 poison, **152**
Spina bifida, 360
Spirochetes, 232
Spleen, 83, 90, 95, 179, 185, 209, 226, 369
Splenectomy, 224
Spongin, 691
Spores, 107, 109
Sputum, 88, 91, **273–275**
 loss of protein in, 273
 proteins of, 273
Squid, 67
Staining, Gram, 106, **108**
Stains, fat, 493
 vital, 45
Staphylococcus, 86, 89, 112, 127, 219, 479
 aureus, 107, 320
 pyogenes aureus, 110
Staphylolysin, 219
Starch, 105, 110
Starvation, 65, 82, 396, 567
 acidosis, 285
Stone. See *Calculus*.
Streptococcus, 86, 89, 110, 112, 486
 viridans, 220

THIS BOOK IS DUE ON THE LAST DATE
STAMPED BELOW

AN INITIAL FINE OF 25 CENTS

WILL BE ASSESSED FOR FAILURE TO RETURN
THIS BOOK ON THE DATE DUE. THE PENALTY
WILL INCREASE TO 50 CENTS ON THE FOURTH
DAY AND TO $1.00 ON THE SEVENTH DAY
OVERDUE.

ImTheStory.com

Lightning Source UK Ltd.
Milton Keynes UK
UKOW06f1111290616

277320UK00019B/651/P